MAIN CITIES OF EUROPE

DEAR READER

We are delighted to present the 2020 edition of the Michelin Main Cities of Europe Guide. This year we are excited to add Slovenia's capital, Ljubljana, to our selection.

- ***The guide caters for every type of visitor, from business traveller to families on holiday, and lists the best establishments across all categories of comfort and price. So whether you're visiting for work or pleasure, you'll find something that's right for you, whether that's a cosy little bistro or a luxurious restaurant.***

- ***All of the establishments in the guide have been selected by our famous Michelin inspectors, who are the eyes and ears of our readers. They always pay their own bills and their anonymity is key to ensuring that they receive the same treatment as any other guest.***

- ***Each year, they search for new establishments to add to the guide – and only the best make it through. Once the annual selection has been made, the 'best of the best' are then recognised with awards: our famous One ✿, Two ✿✿ and Three ✿✿✿ Stars and our value-for-money Bib Gourmands ☺.***

- ***Within the guide, restaurants are ordered according to the quality of their food, with Michelin Stars at the top, followed by Bib Gourmands and then Michelin Plates 🍽. Being chosen by the Michelin Inspectors for inclusion in the guide is a guarantee of quality in itself and the Plate symbol points out restaurants where you will have a good meal.***

CONTENTS

Introduction

Selection by country 12

BirdofPrey/iStock

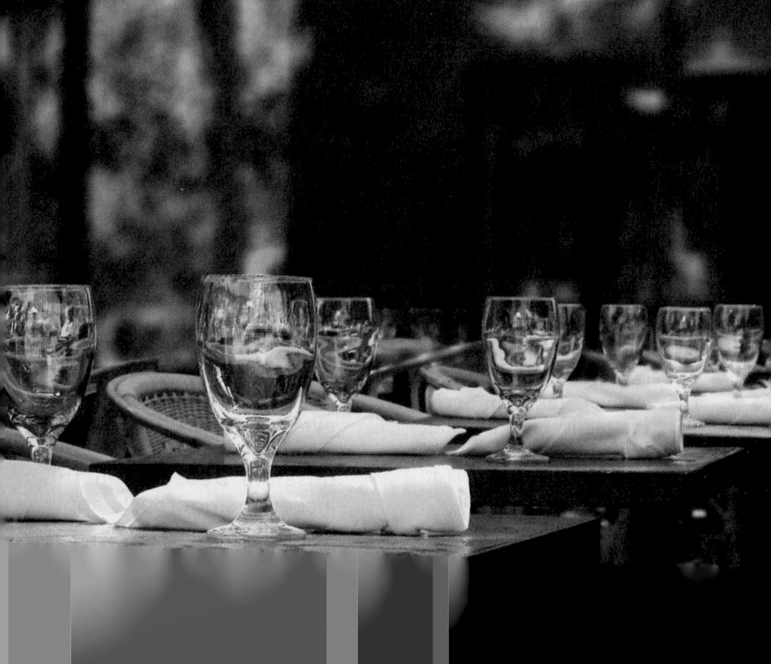

THE MICHELIN GUIDE'S COMMITMENTS

EXPERIENCED IN QUALITY!

Whether they are in Japan, the USA, China or Europe, our inspectors apply the same criteria to judge the quality of each and every hotel and restaurant that they visit. The Michelin guide commands a worldwide reputation thanks to the commitments we make to our readers – and we reiterate these below:

Anonymous inspections

Our inspectors make regular and anonymous visits to hotels and restaurants to gauge the quality of products and services offered to an ordinary customer. They settle their own bill and may then introduce themselves and ask for more information about the establishment. Our readers' comments are also a valuable source of information, which we can follow up with a visit of our own.

Independence

To remain totally objective for our readers, the selection is made with complete independence. Entry into the guide is free. All decisions are discussed with the Editor and our highest awards are considered at a European level.

Our famous One ✿, Two ✿✿ and Three ✿✿✿ Stars identify establishments serving the highest quality cuisine – taking into account the quality of ingredients, the mastery of techniques and flavours, the levels of creativity and, of course, consistency.

Selection and choice

The guide offers a selection of the best restaurants in every category of comfort and price. This is only possible because all the inspectors rigorously apply the same methods.

✿✿✿ THREE MICHELIN STARS

Exceptional cuisine, worth a special journey!

Our highest award is given for the superlative cooking of chefs at the peak of their profession. The ingredients are exemplary, the cooking is elevated to an art form and their dishes are often destined to become classics.

✿✿ TWO MICHELIN STARS

Excellent cooking, worth a detour!

The personality and talent of the chef and their team is evident in the expertly crafted dishes, which are refined, inspired and sometimes original.

✿ ONE MICHELIN STAR

High quality cooking, worth a stop!

Using top quality ingredients, dishes with distinct flavours are carefully prepared to a consistently high standard.

BIB GOURMAND

Good quality, good value cooking.

'Bibs' are awarded for simple yet skilful cooking.

THE MICHELIN PLATE

Good cooking

Fresh ingredients, carefully prepared: simply a good meal.

Annual updates

All the practical information, classifications and awards are revised and updated every year to give the most reliable information possible.

Consistency

The criteria for the classifications are the same in every country covered by the MICHELIN guide.

The sole intention of Michelin is to make your travels safe and enjoyable.

SEEK AND SELECT...

HOW TO USE THIS GUIDE

RESTAURANTS

Restaurants are listed by distinction. Within each distinction, they are then ordered alphabetically.

Distinctions:

- ✿✿✿ **Three Stars:** Exceptional cuisine, worth a special journey!
- ✿✿ **Two Stars:** Excellent cooking, worth a detour!
- ✿ **One Star:** High quality cooking, worth a stop!
- ☺ **Bib Gourmand:** Good quality, good value cooking.
- 🍴 **The Michelin Plate:** Good cooking.

Keywords

Each entry comes with two keywords, making it quick and easy to identify the type of establishment and/or the food that it serves.

Locating the establishment

Location and coordinates on the city plan, with main sights.

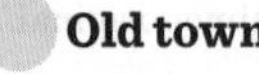

Old town

✿✿ **Number Two**

MODERN CUISINE · FRIENDLY
cocktail bar, set in the basement c
and red lacquered walls give it a pl
cate and prime Scottish ingredien
sonality.
Specialities: Roast langoustines
Wagyu beef, beetroot, smoked bone
with coconut and liquorice root.
Menu £90/105
PLAN: 3-G2 – *Balmoral Hotel, 1 Prir*
www.numbertwo.com – Closed 2-1

☺ **Fox & Hounds**

SCOTTISH · PUB A smart, village
more casual ventures. It has a woo
rustic and contemporary décor. Ex
phy and focus on the classical and
Specialities: Chicken liver parfait
chips. Vanilla cheesecake with poac
Menu £19 (lunch) – Carte £28/
PLAN: 3-E1 – *1 Comely Bank Road,*
www.foxandhounds.com

🍴 **The Montpensier**

FRENCH · ELEGANT A grand ho
modelled on a French salon. Classi
techniques introduced by Escoffier
Menu £55/70– Carte £45/85
PLAN: 3-f2 – *Waldorf Astoria Edin*
Street – ✆ 0131 222 8975 – www.the
Tuesday, Wednesday - Saturday lur

Locating a city

Different colours identify each country. Within each city, restaurants are organised by neighbourhoods, starting from the centre and moving out towards the suburbs.

Facilities & services

- Great view
- Garden or park
- Outside dining available
- Private dining room
- Restaurant offering lower priced theatre menus
- Restaurant offering vegetarian menus (United Kingdom)
- Wheelchair accessible
- Valet
- Air conditioning
- Car park
- Credit cards not accepted
- Bookings not accepted
- Nearest subway station

Other special features

- Interesting wine list
- Notable cocktail list
- Interesting sake list

Prices

Prices are given in the currency of each country.

Menu 13/28	Fixed price menu. Lowest/highest price.
Carte 20/35	À la carte menu. Lowest/highest price.

CITY PLAN KEY

- Restaurants

Sights

Place of interest	Interesting place of worship

Roads

Motorway	Junctions: complete
Dual carriageway	Junctions: limited
Pedestrian street	Station and railway

Various Signs

	Tourist Information Centre		Airport
	Mosque		Hospital
	Synagogue		Covered market
	Ruins		Public buildings:
	Garden, Park, Wood	H	Town Hall
	Coach station	R	Town Hall (Germany)
M	Metro / Underground Station	M	Museum
		U	University

Selection by country

B. Gardel/hemis.fr

AUSTRIA

ÖSTERREICH

VIENNA
WIEN

bluejayphoto/iStock

VIENNA IN...

- **ONE DAY**
  A tram ride round the Ringstrasse, St Stephen's Cathedral, a section of the Hofburg Palace, cakes in a café.
- **TWO DAYS**
  MuseumsQuartier, Spittelberg, Hundert-wasserhaus, Prater.
- **THREE DAYS**
  A day at the Belvedere, a night at the opera.

Beethoven, Brahms, Mozart, Haydn, Strauss...not a bad list of former residents, by any stretch of the imagination. One and all, they succumbed to the opulent aura of Vienna, a city where an appreciation of the arts is as conspicuous as its famed cakes. Sumptuous architecture and a refined air reflect the city's historic position as the seat of the powerful Habsburg dynasty and former epicentre of the Austro-Hungarian Empire.

Despite its grand image, Vienna has propelled itself into the 21C with a handful of innovative hotspots, most notably the MuseumsQuartier cultural complex, a stone's throw from

the mighty Hofburg Imperial Palace. This is not a big city, although its vivid image gives that impression. The compact centre teems with elegant shops, fashionable coffee-houses and grand avenues, and the empire's awesome 19C remnants keep visitors' eyes fixed forever upwards.

Many towns and cities are defined by their ring roads, but Vienna can boast a truly upmarket version: the Ringstrasse, a showpiece boulevard that cradles the inner city and the riches that lie therein. Just outside, to the southwest are the districts of Neubau and Spittelberg, both of which have taken on a quirky, modernistic feel. To the east lies Prater, the green lung of Vienna and further out lies the suburban area enhanced by the grandeur of the Schönbrunn palace.

EATING OUT

Vienna is the spiritual home of the café and Austrians drink nearly twice as much coffee as beer. It is also a city with a sweet tooth: cream cakes enhance the window displays of most eateries and is there a visitor to Vienna who hasn't succumbed to the sponge of the Sachertorte? Viennese food is essentially the food of Bohemia, which means that meat has a strong presence on the plate. Expect beef, veal and pork, alongside potatoes, dumplings or cabbage - be sure to try traditional boiled beef and the ubiquitous Wiener Schnitzel (deep-fried breaded veal). Also worth experiencing are the Heurigen, traditional Austrian wine taverns which are found in Grinzing, Heiligenstadt, Neustift and Nussdorf. You'll find plenty of snug cafés and bars too. If you want to snack, the place to go is Naschmarkt, Vienna's best market, where the stalls spill over into the vibrant little restaurants. When it comes to tipping, if you're in the more relaxed, local pubs and wine taverns, just round up the bill, otherwise add on ten per cent.

Historical centre

✿✿ Konstantin Filippou

MODERN CUISINE • MINIMALIST The elegant minimalist-style interior and view of the kitchen – there's even a cooking station in the restaurant itself – set the tone here at Konstantin Filippou. The food is creative and modern and comes with well-chosen wine recommendations.

Specialities: Salmon trout, shiso, saffron, kohlrabi. Croatian langostino, veal tongue, cochayuyo, citrus. Cherry, apple, ginger, chocolate.

Menu 47 € (lunch), 165/185 €

PLAN: 2-E2 – *Dominikanerbastei 17* – *Stubentor* – *01 5122229* – *www.konstantinfilippou.com* – *Closed Saturday, Sunday*

O boufés – See restaurant listing

✿✿ Silvio Nickol Gourmet Restaurant

MODERN CUISINE • ELEGANT The culinary creations served at Silvio Nickol are modern, highly elaborate, considered right down to the smallest detail, and made from nothing but the finest produce and ingredients. Whatever you do, don't forget to take a good look at the wine list as it contains some genuine rarities.

Specialities: Duck liver, mushroom, chocolate, spruce. Nuart lamb, cherry, ginger, parsley. Quince, Alpine milk, verbena, whey.

Menu 135/195 € – Carte 128/158 €

PLAN: 2-E2 – *Coburgbastei 4* – *Stubentor* – *01 51818130* – *www.palais-coburg.com* – *Closed 1-22 January, 2-26 August, Monday, Sunday, lunch Tuesday-Saturday*

✿✿ Steirereck im Stadtpark (Heinz Reitbauer)

CREATIVE • DESIGN This elegant, bright and minimalist-style restaurant serves top-of-the-range Austrian cuisine. Made using only the finest ingredients, it is modern, elaborate and full of sophistication, harmonious yet full of surprises. The experience is rounded off by the professional, friendly and discreet service.

Specialities: Char with beeswax, yellow carrot, pollen and sour cream. Catfish with Schönbrunn calamansi, medlars and kamut. Sharon fruit with hazelnuts, black trumpet mushrooms and salty fudge.

Menu 105 € (lunch), 149/165 € – Carte 110/130 €

PLAN: 2-F2 – *Am Heumarkt 2a* – *Stadtpark* – *01 7133168* – *www.steirereck.at* – *Closed Saturday, Sunday*

Meierei im Stadtpark – See restaurant listing

✿ [aend] (Fabian Günzel)

MODERN CUISINE • MINIMALIST This restaurant in a residential district in the west of the city offers clean-cut design and a fashionable feel to match the modern creative cuisine prepared in the open kitchen. The result is a range of punchy, pared-down dishes made using only the best, seasonal ingredients.

Specialities: Char and juniper. Duck and Brussels sprouts. Apple and grape.

Menu 44 € (lunch), 111/133 €

PLAN: 1-A3 – *Mollardgasse 76* – *Margaretengürtel* – *01 5953416* – *www.aend.at* – *Closed 27 January-7 February, Saturday, Sunday*

✿ APRON

CREATIVE • CLASSIC DÉCOR You will find this classic yet modern restaurant not far from the Stadtpark, adjoining the Sofitel Hotel. The impressive-looking open kitchen turns out a creative, seasonally influenced menu. The dishes are prepared from top-notch ingredients, beautifully handcrafted to draw out their rich flavours. You can also have lunch in the bistro.

Specialities: Trout, pineapple, kohlrabi, dill. Lamb, sheep's milk yoghurt, carrot, curry. Apricot, cacao fruit, sourdough, verjus.

Menu 81/124 € – Carte 56/68 €

PLAN: 2-E3 – *Am Heumarkt 35* – *Stadtpark* – *01 9074747* – *www.restaurant-apron.at* – *Closed 13 July-16 August, lunch Monday-Sunday*

Le Ciel by Toni Mörwald

CLASSIC CUISINE • ELEGANT The atmosphere up on the seventh floor is classically elegant and, quite naturally, the best tables are those on the roof terrace. The kitchens serve distinctive and creative food made using the best quality produce. Attentive service.

Specialities: Artichoke with shrimp, horseradish and lardo. Cod with cockle, pumpkin and buckwheat. Cape gooseberries with dulse, sea buckthorn and ras el hanout.

Menu 48 € (lunch), 101/156 € - Carte 74/100 €

PLAN: 2-E3 - *Kärntner Ring 9 - Ⓜ Karlsplatz - ✆ 01 515800 - www.leciel.at - Closed 2-10 February, 2-31 August, Monday, Sunday*

Edvard

MODERN CUISINE • ELEGANT This elegant gourmet restaurant offers a successful marriage of the modern and classic, including in its sophisticated flavoursome cuisine. A nice touch: at the start, at your table the attentive and professional waitstaff give you a rundown of the ingredients used. The competent wine advice and good wines by the glass also deserve a mention.

Specialities: Alpine caviar, Pinzgauer beef, Gillardeau oyster. Sole, Chioggia beet, Amalfi. Pumpkin, Opalys, turmeric.

Menu 39 € (lunch), 99/158 € - Carte 70/73 €

PLAN: 2-D1 - *Schottenring 24 - Ⓜ Schottenring - ✆ 01 2361000 - www.kempinski.com/vienna - Closed 6-13 January, 3-31 August, Monday, Sunday*

SHIKI

JAPANESE • TRENDY SHIKI offers fine dining Japanese-style in the heart of Vienna, close to the Opera. The elegant restaurant decorated in dark tones offers a perfect marriage of tradition and modernity. It serves ambitious, seasonal cuisine ('Shiki' means the four seasons).

Specialities: Variation of octopus. Miso-marinated duck breast. Pumpkin tart with a plum sabayon and pumpkin seed ice cream.

Menu 78/125 €

PLAN: 2-E3 - *Krugerstraße 3 - Ⓜ Karlsplatz - ✆ 01 5127397 - www.shiki.at - Closed 3-9 February, 10-23 August, Monday, Sunday*

SHIKI Brasserie & Bar - See restaurant listing

Tian

VEGETARIAN • ELEGANT The depth of flavour that you'll find in the exclusively vegan and vegetarian dishes on offer here is remarkable! And how about a bottle from the ever-growing selection of organic wines - or perhaps one of the restaurant's home-made alcohol-free drinks - to wash down the sophisticated, flavoursome fare? Friendly, professional front-of-house team.

Specialities: Red meat, Red Emmalie, radicchio. Truffle pasta. Indian Summer, apple, caramel, tonka bean.

Menu 79 € (lunch), 121/137 €

PLAN: 2-E2 - *Himmelpfortgasse 23 - Ⓜ Stephansplatz - ✆ 01 8904665 - www.tian-restaurant.com - Closed Monday, Sunday, lunch Tuesday*

Walter Bauer

CLASSIC CUISINE • COSY This listed building in the centre of the old town has oodles of Viennese charm, as well as a wonderful vaulted ceiling in the restaurant. The owners place great importance on providing attentive and personal service, as well as classic cuisine without frills. There is also an excellent wine list.

Specialities: Goose liver terrine with brioche. Pink-roasted saddle of lamb with vegetables. Kaiserschmarrn sugared pancake with stewed plum.

Menu 59/69 € - Carte 52/78 €

PLAN: 2-E2 - *Sonnenfelsgasse 17 - Ⓜ Stubentor - ✆ 01 5129871 - Closed Saturday, Sunday, lunch Monday*

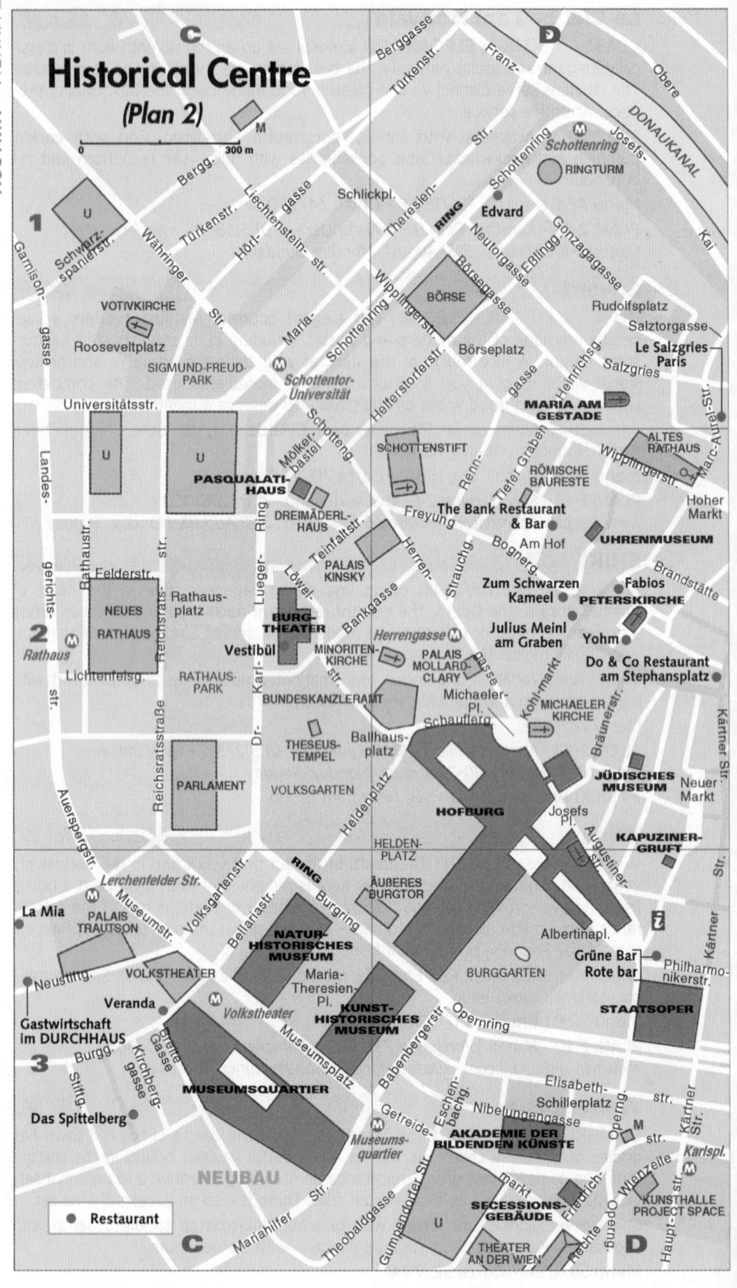

Historical Centre
(Plan 2)
0
300 m
Restaurant
VOTIVKIRCHE
Rooseveltplatz
SIGMUND-FREUD-PARK
Schottentor-Universität
Universitätsstr.
BÖRSE
Börseplatz
RINGTURM
Schottenring
Edvard
Rudolfsplatz
Salztorgasse
Le Salzgries Paris
Salzgries
MARIA AM GESTADE
SCHOTTENSTIFT
ALTES RATHAUS
RÖMISCHE BAURESTE
Hoher Markt
PASQUALATI-HAUS
DREIMÄDERL-HAUS
The Bank Restaurant & Bar
Am Hof
UHRENMUSEUM
PALAIS KINSKY
Zum Schwarzen Kameel
Fabios
PETERSKIRCHE
NEUES RATHAUS
Rathausplatz
BURG-THEATER
Vestibül
Herrengasse
MINORITEN-KIRCHE
PALAIS MOLLARD-CLARY
Julius Meinl am Graben
Yohm
Do & Co Restaurant am Stephansplatz
Rathaus
RATHAUS-PARK
BUNDESKANZLERAMT
Michaeler-Pl.
MICHAELER KIRCHE
THESEUS-TEMPEL
Ballhaus-platz
PARLAMENT
VOLKSGARTEN
HOFBURG
JÜDISCHES MUSEUM
Neuer Markt
Josefs Pl.
KAPUZINER-GRUFT
HELDEN-PLATZ
ÄUßERES BURGTOR
Lerchenfelder Str.
La Mia
PALAIS TRAUTSON
NATUR-HISTORISCHES MUSEUM
Albertinapl.
Grüne Bar
Rote bar
BURGGARTEN
VOLKSTHEATER
Maria-Theresien-Pl.
KUNST-HISTORISCHES MUSEUM
STAATSOPER
Veranda
Volkstheater
Gastwirtschaft im DURCHHAUS
MUSEUMSQUARTIER
Opernring
Schillerplatz
Das Spittelberg
AKADEMIE DER BILDENDEN KÜNSTE
Museums-quartier
Karlspl.
NEUBAU
SECESSIONS-GEBÄUDE
KUNSTHALLE PROJECT SPACE
THEATER AN DER WIEN
Mariahilfer Str.

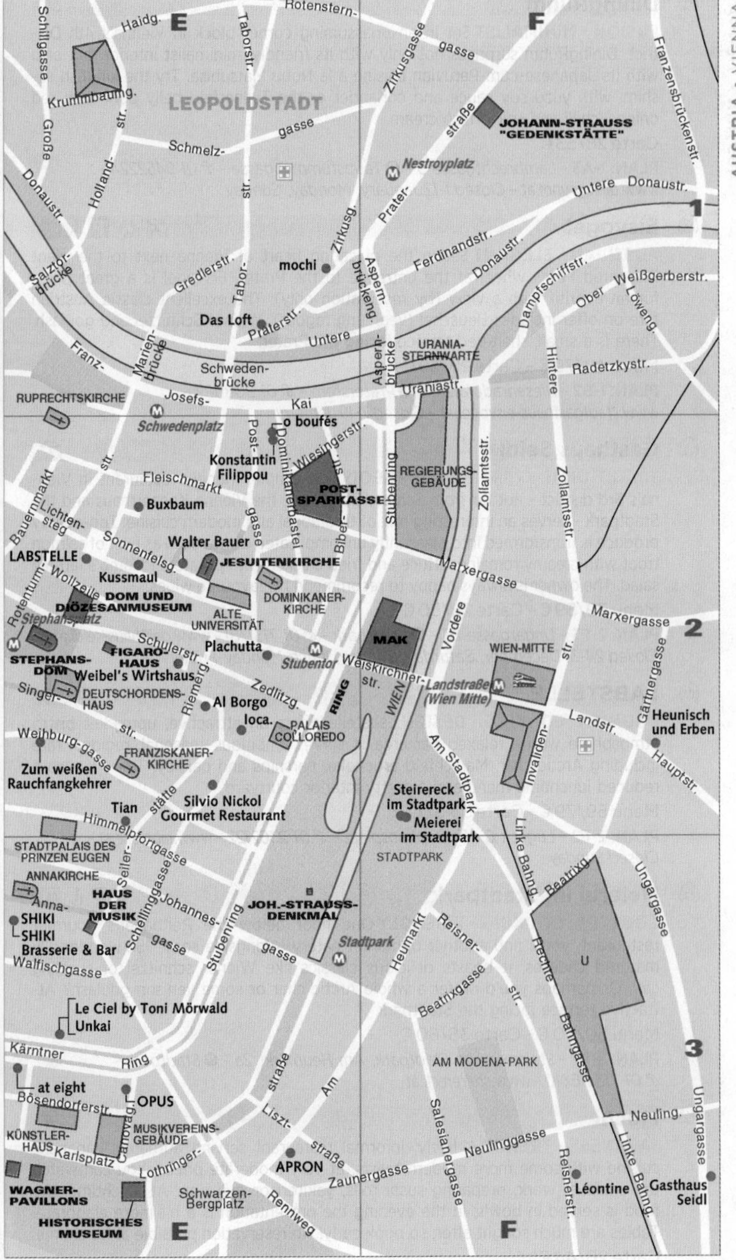
E
F
LEOPOLDSTADT
JOHANN-STRAUSS "GEDENKSTÄTTE"
Nestroyplatz
mochi
Das Loft
URANIA-STERNWARTE
RUPRECHTSKIRCHE
Schwedenplatz
o boufés
Konstantin Filippou
POST-SPARKASSE
REGIERUNGS-GEBÄUDE
Buxbaum
Walter Bauer
LABSTELLE
JESUITENKIRCHE
Kussmaul
DOM UND DIÖZESANMUSEUM
ALTE UNIVERSITÄT
DOMINIKANER-KIRCHE
MAK
Stephansplatz
STEPHANSDOM
FIGARO-HAUS
Weibel's Wirtshaus
Plachutta
Stubentor
WIEN-MITTE
Landstraße (Wien Mitte)
DEUTSCHORDENS-HAUS
Al Borgo
loca.
PALAIS COLLOREDO
RING
WIEN
Heunisch und Erben
Zum weißen Rauchfangkehrer
FRANZISKANER-KIRCHE
Silvio Nickol Gourmet Restaurant
Tian
Steirereck im Stadtpark
Meierei im Stadtpark
STADTPALAIS DES PRINZEN EUGEN
STADTPARK
ANNAKIRCHE
HAUS DER MUSIK
JOH.-STRAUSS-DENKMAL
SHIKI
SHIKI Brasserie & Bar
Stadtpark
U
Le Ciel by Toni Mörwald
Unkai
AM MODENA-PARK
at eight
OPUS
KÜNSTLER-HAUS
MUSIKVEREINS-GEBÄUDE
APRON
Léontine
Gasthaus Seidl
WAGNER-PAVILLONS
HISTORISCHES MUSEUM
1
2
3
Rotenstern-gasse
Haidg.
Taborstr.
Zirkusgasse
Schillgasse
Krummbaumg.
Große
Holland-str.
Schmelz-gasse
Praterstraße
Franzensbrückenstr.
Untere Donaustr.
Donaustr.
Salztorbrücke
Gredlerstr.
Tabor-str.
Zirkusg.
Prater-
Asperbrückeng.
Ferdinandstr.
Donaustr.
Dampfschiffstr.
Ober Weißgerberstr.
Löweng.
Praterstr.
Untere
Marienbrücke
Franz-Josefs-Kai
Schwedenbrücke
Aspernbrücke
Uraniastr.
Radetzkystr.
Hintere
Post-
Dominikanerbastei
Wiesingerstr.
Fleischmarkt
str.
Stubenring
Zollamtsstr.
Zollamtsstr.
Bauernmarkt
Lichtensteg
Sonnenfelsg.
gasse
Biber-str.
Marxergasse
Marxergasse
Rotenturm-
Wollzeile
Schulerstr.
Weiskirchner-str.
Vordere
str.
Gärtnergasse
Singer-str.
Riemerg.
Zedlitzg.
Landstr.
Hauptstr.
Weihburg-gasse
Am Stadtpark
Invaliden-
Linke Bahng.
Himmelpfortgasse
Seiler-
stätte
Beatrixg.
Ungargasse
Anna-
Johannes-gasse
Schellinggasse
Stubenring
Heumarkt
Reisner-str.
Walfischgasse
Rechte Bahngasse
Beatrixgasse
Kärntner Ring
straße
Am
Salesianergasse
Neuling.
Bösendorferstr.
Canovag.
Lisztstraße
Neulinggasse
Karlsplatz
Lothringer-
Zaunergasse
Reisnerstr.
Linke Bahng.
Ungargasse
Schwarzen-Bergplatz
Rennweg

DiningRuhm

FUSION · MINIMALIST Set in an unassuming corner block in Vienna's 4th District, DiningRuhm surprises not only with its friendly, minimalist interior, but also with its Japanese-cum-Peruvian cuisine à la Nobu Matsuhisa. Try the kingfish sashimi with yuzu soy sauce and coriander or the Tullnerfeld belly pork with red onions, chilli and spicy miso cream.

Carte 28/53€

PLAN: 1-A3 - *Lambrechtgasse 9 - Ⓜ Taubstummengasse - ✆ 01 9452224 - www.diningruhm.at - Closed 1-12 January, Monday, Sunday*

Eisvogel

AUSTRIAN · ELEGANT Set in the pulsating heart of Vienna next to the giant Riesenrad Ferris wheel at the entrance to the Prater, Eisvogel is a great place for an aperitif with a view (by reservation only). The excellent classic Austrian fare on offer includes Beuschel (veal lung ragout), Wiener Schnitzel and goulash. There is a small, sheltered terrace facing the Prater.

Menu 49/79€ - Carte 28/59€

PLAN: 1-B2 - *Riesenradplatz 5 - Ⓜ Praterstern - ✆ 01 9081187 - www.stadtgasthaus-eisvogel.at - Closed 7-19 January*

Gasthaus Seidl

TRADITIONAL CUISINE · BOURGEOIS This simple, friendly restaurant in Vienna's 3rd district - not far from Schloss Belvedere, the Vienna Konzerthaus and the Stadtpark - serves an interesting mix of traditional and modern cuisine. Top-quality produce is transformed into pleasantly uncomplicated dishes such as fillet of salmon trout with creamy romaine lettuce and fried chicken with potato and lamb's lettuce salad. The owner is always happy to recommend his favourite wines.

Menu 39/59€ - Carte 28/50€

PLAN: 2-F3 - *Ungargasse 63 - Ⓜ Stadtpark - ✆ 01 7131781 - www.gasthaus-seidl.at - Closed 24-31 December, Saturday, Sunday, lunch Monday-Friday*

LABSTELLE

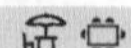

COUNTRY COOKING · DESIGN Labstelle offers an attractive, upmarket bistro atmosphere with a relaxed bar area. It serves ambitious seasonal, regional fare including Arctic char, Marschfeld artichoke, parsnips and parsley. There is also a reduced lunchtime menu and a pretty interior courtyard.

Menu 59/79€ - Carte 31/57€

PLAN: 2-E2 - *Lugeck 6 - Ⓜ Stephansplatz - ✆ 01 2362122 - www.labstelle.at - Closed Sunday*

Meierei im Stadtpark

COUNTRY COOKING · FRIENDLY One floor below the Reitbauer's gourmet restaurant, you'll find another upmarket eatery. Alongside some 150 wonderfully matured cheeses, it boasts delicious classics like Wiener schnitzel of suckling calf. Or perhaps you'd prefer a whole Arctic char or some venison goulash? Attractive terrace facing the Stadtpark.

Menu 50/70€ - Carte 35/60€

PLAN: 2-F2 - *Steirereck im Stadtpark, Am Heumarkt 2a - Ⓜ Stadtpark - ✆ 01 713316810 - www.steirereck.at*

Mochi

JAPANESE · TRENDY A lively, informal restaurant serving authentic Japanese cuisine with some more modern twists, at very moderate prices. You can watch the chefs at work, preparing sushi rolls, yakitori or gyu don. At lunchtime, the food is served in bowls; in the evening the presentation is a bit more elaborate. Tables are much sought after, so book early! No reservation possible at lunchtime.

Carte 26/44€

PLAN: 2-E1 - *Praterstraße 15 - Ⓜ Nestroyplatz - ✆ 01 9251380 - www.mochi.at - Closed Sunday*

Vestibül

INTERNATIONAL • CLASSIC DÉCOR Though the chef sets great store by using high quality Austrian ingredients, there is nothing that quite matches the lobster in Vestibül's highly prized Szegediner lobster with cabbage. The unusual location – in the famous and charming Burgtheater – is another selling point. Don't miss the excellent wines, some of which are available as magnums.

Menu 33 € (lunch), 65/72 € – Carte 37/87 €

PLAN: 2-C2 – *Universitätsring 2 – Ⓜ Herrengasse – ✆ 01 5324999 – www.vestibuel.at – Closed 1-6 January, 26 July-17 August, Monday, Sunday, lunch Saturday*

ARTNER auf der Wieden

INTERNATIONAL • TRENDY Regional and modern, the flavoursome fare on offer includes Wiener Schnitzel with parsley potatoes and Mühlbachtaler salmon trout with pan-fried citrus peel and crispy polenta, not to mention a range of grilled dishes. The interior is attractive and minimalist in style and the service is relaxed. Good value lunchtime menu.

Menu 59/79 € – Carte 33/61 €

PLAN: 1-B3 – *Floragasse 6 – Ⓜ Taubstummengasse – ✆ 01 5035033 – www.artner.co.at – Closed lunch Saturday, Sunday*

at eight

MARKET CUISINE • CONTEMPORARY DÉCOR In this restaurant with a smart, modern design, close to the opera, the atmosphere is pleasantly relaxed and the large windows give onto the busy street. Modern and seasonal cooking with Mediterranean influences. The service is friendly.

Menu 46/72 € – Carte 58/70 €

PLAN: 2-E3 – *Kärntner Ring 8 – Ⓜ Karlsplatz – ✆ 0676 31 02 356 – www.ateight-restaurant.com*

The Bank Brasserie & Bar

INTERNATIONAL • CLASSIC DÉCOR If you are looking to eat out in an unusual setting, try the period lobby in this former bank with its imposing high ceilings and marble columns. The menu offers French brasserie-style dishes that are prepared in the open show kitchen. The Am Hof café is also popular.

Carte 38/127 €

PLAN: 2-D2 – *Bognergasse 4 – Ⓜ Herrengasse – ✆ 01 227401236 – www.restaurant-thebank.com*

Al Borgo

ITALIAN • FRIENDLY Al Borgo enjoys a very central and yet secluded location in the heart of Vienna's 1st district. It serves classic Italian cuisine and a range of excellent seasonal dishes. Regular themed weeks.

Carte 30/50 €

PLAN: 2-E2 – *An der Hülben 1 – Ⓜ Stubentor – ✆ 01 5128559 – www.alborgo.at – Closed Sunday, lunch Saturday*

Buxbaum

MARKET CUISINE • COSY This comfortable, stylishly rustic restaurant lies a little out of the way in the Heiligenkreuzerhof. At midday it serves a quick business lunch; in the evenings, international and regional set menus sit alongside the à la carte offerings. Attractive terrace.

Menu 50/66 € – Carte 42/69 €

PLAN: 2-E2 – *Grashofgasse 3 – Ⓜ Schwedenplatz – ✆ 01 2768226 – www.buxbaum.restaurant – Closed Sunday*

Do & Co Restaurant am Stephansplatz

ASIAN • TRENDY An ultra-modern restaurant on the seventh floor, with a great terrace and a view of St Stephen's Cathedral. Southeast Asian dishes, including chicken kaow soy and Sushi, feature alongside Austrian classics such as braised calves' cheeks and goose liver.

Carte 50/71€

PLAN: 2-D2 – *Stephansplatz 12 – Ⓜ Stephansplatz – ✆ 01 5353969 – www.doco.com*

Fabios

ITALIAN • TRENDY A veritable Who's Who of Vienna! The Italian cuisine served in this fashionable city restaurant is just as modern and minimalist as the interior design – two equally good reasons to give it a try! The bar also serves a range of snacks.

Carte 43/78€

PLAN: 2-D2 – *Tuchlauben 6 – Ⓜ Stephansplatz – ✆ 01 5322222 – www.fabios.at – Closed Sunday*

Gastwirtschaft im DURCHHAUS

COUNTRY COOKING • COSY The former Kristian's Monastiri is a really cosy tavern with modern, jazzed-up Viennese cuisine, from fried chicken salad, beef goulash and schnitzel to apple strudel... Or perhaps you prefer something seasonal like a game dish?

Carte 24/49€

PLAN: 2-C3 – *Neustiftgasse 16 – Ⓜ Volkstheater – ✆ 01 5269448 – www.durchhaus.at – Closed 6-19 January, 24-26 December, Monday, Sunday, lunch Tuesday-Saturday*

Grüne Bar

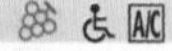

CLASSIC CUISINE • LUXURY The Hotel Sacher's fine dining restaurant with its upmarket green and wood interior features a number of original paintings by Viennese impressionist Anton Faistauer. The ambitious re-interpreted classics on offer have a strong Viennese flavour, as evidenced by the Mangalitza pigs' cheeks with calf's heart und turnips.

Menu 79/118€ – Carte 64/79€

PLAN: 2-D3 – *Philharmonikerstraße 4 – Ⓜ Karlsplatz – ✆ 01 514560 – www.sacher.com – Closed lunch Monday-Sunday*

Heunisch und Erben

COUNTRY COOKING • TRENDY In an interesting mix of modern wine bar and restaurant, Heunisch und Erben offers some 100 different wines to accompany its ambitious, market-fresh food. Menu options range from mountain trout with pumpkin, salt-baked beetroot and Uhudler wine to creamy veal goulash.

Menu 52/92€ – Carte 37/53€

PLAN: 2-F2 – *Landstrasser Hauptstraße 17 / Seidlgasse 36 – Ⓜ Landstraße (Wien-Mitte) – ✆ 01 2868563 – www.heunisch.at – Closed Sunday*

Julius Meinl am Graben

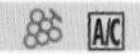

CLASSIC CUISINE • CHIC This restaurant and its sister delicatessen (housed in the same building) come to life early in the morning. Ambitious food is served using the finest quality ingredients from breakfast through to dinner (make sure you try the stuffed quail with greengages), complete with a view over Vienna's pedestrian zone.

Menu 39/98€ – Carte 58/79€

PLAN: 2-D2 – *Graben 19 – Ⓜ Stephansplatz – ✆ 01 53233346000 – www.meinlamgraben.at – Closed 3-23 August, Sunday*

Kussmaul

INTERNATIONAL • CHIC Where a slaughterhouse once stood, a long time ago, today you can dine on one of the two levels in a stylish interior and enjoy modern international, Mediterranean-influenced cuisine, e.g. confit sea bass with tomato coriander sauce, orange and potato cream. Lovely historical setting with cross vault, and a pleasant, casual atmosphere.

Carte 33/63 €

PLAN: 2-E2 – *Bäckerstraße 5 – Ⓜ Stephansplatz – ✆ 01 2861117 – www.kussmaul-vienna.com*

Léontine

MODERN FRENCH • BISTRO If you enjoy a bistro atmosphere, you will love this charming restaurant set in a quiet residential district close to the Stadtpark. It serves modern French cuisine with menu options including turbot with carrots, olives and macadamia nuts.

Menu 20 € (lunch)/58 € – Carte 54/58 €

PLAN: 2-F3 – *Reisnerstraße 39 – Ⓜ Stadtspark – ✆ 01 7125430 – www.leontine.at – Closed Monday, Sunday, dinner Tuesday-Wednesday*

loca.

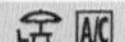

COUNTRY COOKING • COSY Better eat better is the slogan of this nice friendly little restaurant close to the Stadtpark. The decor is pared down and modern, and the food is served in the form of a surprise menu, cooked in the open kitchen – for example, trout with spinach and peas.

Menu 38/48 €

PLAN: 2-E2 – *Stubenbastei 10 – Ⓜ Stubentor – ✆ 01 5121172 – www.bettereatbetter.com – Closed lunch Monday-Sunday*

Das Loft

MODERN CUISINE • DESIGN The location on the 18th floor of the lifestyle hotel SO/Vienna is undoubtedly spectacular – the view of Vienna is phenomenal! Add to that attentive, laid-back service and modern-inspired cuisine, such as guinea fowl with barley, chestnuts, grapes and morel sauce. Great wine selection.

Menu 59 € (lunch)/99 € – Carte 70/100 €

PLAN: 2-E1 – *Praterstraße 1 – Ⓜ Schwedenplatz – ✆ 01 906168110 – www.dasloftwien.at*

Ludwig van

COUNTRY COOKING • RUSTIC The ground floor of this house where Beethoven once lived is now home to a warm and welcoming, rustic dining room with a charming front-of-house team serving contemporary takes on regional fare. Made using top-quality ingredients, the food is pleasingly simple, refined and rich in flavour.

Menu 37/71 € – Carte 40/60 €

PLAN: 1-A3 – *Laimgrubengasse 22 – Ⓜ Museumsquartier – ✆ 01 5871320 – www.ludwigvan.wien – Closed Saturday, Sunday, dinner Monday*

La Mia

ITALIAN • BISTRO This lively, friendly bistro with its covered interior courtyard serves pizzas and pasta dishes – try the excellent spaghetti frutti di mare – alongside grilled specialities including gamberoni alla diavola and tagliata di manzo. Just around the corner the same team offers traditional Viennese cuisine.

Carte 23/44 €

PLAN: 2-C3 – *Lerchenfelder Straße 13 – Ⓜ Volkstheater – ✆ 01 5224221 – www.lamia.at*

O boufés

MEDITERRANEAN CUISINE • BISTRO Located just next door to its gourmet counterpart, this relaxed restaurant with its bare walls, high ceilings and minimalist decor, serves a varied menu. It ranges from a charcuterie plate to keftedes (meatballs) with hilopites (small green pasta squares), as well as black pudding ravioli with cuttlefish, shellfish and peas. The food is accompanied by a choice of natural wines.

Carte 36/54€

PLAN: 2-E2 – *Konstantin Filippou, Dominikanerbastei 17* – *Stubentor* – *01 512222910* – *www.konstantinfilippou.com* – *Closed Sunday, lunch Monday-Saturday*

OPUS

MODERN CUISINE • ELEGANT Located in an attractive, classical building, OPUS is decorated in the style of a 1930s Viennese workshop, in elegant grey tones, with chandeliers and art on the walls. The ambitious cuisine is creative and regionally inspired.

Menu 106/140€ – Carte 70/107€

PLAN: 2-E3 – *Kärntner Ring 16* – *Karlsplatz* – *01 50110* – *www.restaurant-opus.at* – *Closed 3-10 February, 12 July-10 August, Monday, lunch Tuesday-Sunday*

Plachutta

AUSTRIAN • TRADITIONAL For years, the Plachutta family has been committed to Viennese tradition. They serve beef in many forms in the green panelled dining room or on the large terrace.

Carte 31/52€

PLAN: 2-E2 – *Wollzeile 38* – *Stubentor* – *01 5121577* – *www.plachutta.at*

Rote Bar

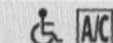

AUSTRIAN • ELEGANT A mainstay of the Hotel Sacher, which epitomises the charm of this great Viennese establishment, Rote Bar is also a champion of Austrian cuisine. Treat yourself to a Wiener schnitzel or traditional rump of beef and soak up the atmosphere!

Menu 79/118€ – Carte 42/92€

PLAN: 2-D3 – *Philharmonikerstraße 4* – *Karlsplatz* – *01 514560* – *www.sacher.com*

Le Salzgries Paris

CLASSIC FRENCH • BRASSERIE This exuberant, lively bistro is cosy, done out in fresh colours and has an eye-catching bar. The cuisine is French, from sole meunière to entrecote with French fries and béarnaise sauce, not forgetting the classic beef tartare.

Menu 20€ (lunch), 52/78€ – Carte 42/62€

PLAN: 2-D1 – *Marc-Aurel-Straße 6* – *Schwedenplatz* – *01 5334030* – *www.le-salzgries.at* – *Closed 1-8 January, Monday, Sunday*

Servitenwirt

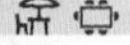

AUSTRIAN • FRIENDLY A cosy restaurant in a quiet area near the church – in summer, places on the terrace are hotly contested! The food comprises both international dishes, such as gilthead sea bream ceviche or *gazpacho andaluz*, and Viennese classics like *Riesling-Kalbsbeuschel* (veal), *gekochtes Schulterscherzel* (shoulder of beef) or *Palatschinken* (pancakes).

Menu 55/85€ – Carte 28/58€

PLAN: 1-A2 – *Servitengasse 7* – *Roßauer Lände* – *01 3152387* – *www.servitenwirt.at*

SHIKI Brasserie & Bar

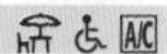

JAPANESE • BRASSERIE This minimalist-style brasserie with its large terrace is SHIKI's less formal eatery. It offers a wider range of dishes from miso soup to tempura and sushi – the latter prepared before you as you sit at the sushi bar.

Menu 62/125€ – Carte 54/154€

PLAN: 2-E3 – *SHIKI, Krugerstraße 3* – *Karlsplatz* – *01 5127397* – *www.shiki.at* – *Closed 3-9 February, 10-23 August, Monday, Sunday*

Skopik & Lohn

AUSTRIAN • FRIENDLY The first thing you'll notice here is the wonderful painted ceiling, the work of artist Otto Zitko. The service is friendly and attentive, the food flavoursome and the Austrian classics on the menu include Wiener schnitzel with cucumber, potato and sour cream salad and, for dessert, perhaps an île flottante?

Carte 31/52 €

PLAN: 1-B2 – *Leopoldsgasse 17* – Ⓜ *Taborstrasse* – ✆ *01 2198977* – *www.skopikundlohn.at – Closed Monday, Sunday, lunch Tuesday-Saturday*

Das Spittelberg

AUSTRIAN • BRASSERIE This friendly and welcoming restaurant located in the charming Spittelberg district revolves around the rotisserie grill in the open kitchen, where the matured Simmentaler beef is a speciality. The Austrian fare is accompanied by a range of good Austrian wines, including some magnums.

Menu 49/79 € – Carte 44/67 €

PLAN: 2-C3 – *Spittelbergstraße 12* – Ⓜ *Volkstheater* – ✆ *01 5877628* – *www.das-spittelberg.at – Closed Monday, Sunday, lunch Tuesday-Saturday*

Unkai

JAPANESE • MINIMALIST A pleasantly light and modern restaurant where you can eat either at authentic teppanyaki grill tables or more conventionally. You will also find the Unkai sushi bar on the ground floor serving a sushi brunch on Saturdays, Sundays and public holidays.

Menu 35/85 € – Carte 28/70 €

PLAN: 2-E3 – *Kärntner Ring 9* – Ⓜ *Karlsplatz* – ✆ *01 515809110* – *www.grandhotelwien.com – Closed Monday*

Veranda

INTERNATIONAL • TRENDY The smart, fashionable and friendly restaurant at the Hotel Sans Souci serves modern Austrian fare with the occasional sally into international cuisine. Try the creamy Jerusalem artichoke soup or the Lake Neusiedl pike with parsnip, apple, spring onion and lemon. Good wine list.

Menu 55/65 € – Carte 39/63 €

PLAN: 2-C3 – *Burggasse 2* – Ⓜ *Volkstheater* – ✆ *01 5222520194* – *www.sanssouci-wien.com*

Weibel's Wirtshaus

AUSTRIAN • FRIENDLY Just a few minutes' walk from St Stephen's Cathedral, Weibel's Wirtshaus is the archetypal Viennese restaurant – warm and friendly, rustic and snug! It also has a charming garden in the small alleyway. The food is traditional and Viennese.

Menu 35/36 € – Carte 27/51 €

PLAN: 2-E2 – *Kumpfgasse 2* – Ⓜ *Stubentor* – ✆ *01 5123986* – *www.weibel.at*

Yohm

ASIAN • TRENDY A pleasant modern restaurant with striking orange decor, occupying two floors. The open kitchen serves up contemporary twists on Southeast Asian cuisine that borrows liberally from around the globe. Good wine selection.

Menu 39/69 € – Carte 33/53 €

PLAN: 2-D2 – *Petersplatz 3* – Ⓜ *Stephansplatz* – ✆ *01 5332900* – *www.yohm.at*

Zum weissen Rauchfangkehrer

AUSTRIAN • TRADITIONAL Here, Austrian cuisine is served throughout the day in really cosy traditional dining rooms. The menu lists, for example, herb-filled breast of Styrian corn-fed chicken or grilled lake char from Gut Dornau, alongside classics such as "Rauchfangkehrer's Wiener Schnitzel". The wine and digestif selection is remarkable!

Menu 34/50 € – Carte 35/62 €

PLAN: 2-E2 – *Weihburggasse 4* – Ⓜ *Stephansplatz* – ✆ *01 5123471* – *www.weisser-rauchfangkehrer.at*

Outer districts

✿✿✿ Amador

CREATIVE • CHIC The food on offer here is pure Juan Amador: pared down, creative, intense and full of contrasts; sophisticated, multi-layered and made using nothing but the best ingredients. The surroundings are stylish, modern and upmarket. The restaurant is located in a vaulted cellar at the Hajszan winery, a spin-off of Fritz Wieninger's wine empire.

Specialities: Oxheart tomato, langoustine, mascarpone, sweetbread. Pigeon, mango, coconut, purple curry. Beetroot, raspberry, tonka bean.

Menu 95€ (lunch)/255€

PLAN: 1-A1 – *Grinzinger Straße 86 – Ⓜ Heiligenstadt – ✆ 0660 9070500 – www.restaurant-amador.com – Closed Monday, Tuesday, Sunday*

✿✿ Mraz & Sohn

CREATIVE • TRENDY Out here in the 20th district, one of the city's most creative kitchens awaits you! In a modern space you are served a surprise menu comprised of a variety of contrasting and expressive dishes with a distinct personality. And what better way to round off this gastronomic experience than with top-notch service and first-class wine advice?

Specialities: Scallop in a marinade. Steamed Chinese leaves. Carrot and yoghurt.

Menu 145€

PLAN: 1-A2 – *Wallensteinstraße 59 – Ⓜ Friedensbrücke – ✆ 01 3304594 – www.mrazundsohn.at – Closed 4-12 April, 8-30 August, 24-31 December, Saturday, Sunday, lunch Monday-Friday*

✿ Pramerl & the Wolf (Wolfgang Zankl-Sertl)

CREATIVE • BISTRO This former bar in Vienna's 9th district is simple and pleasantly unpretentious, its surprise menu promising inexpensive yet sophisticated fare that is full of contrast. No unnecessary frills here, just excellent produce and great value for money! The best way to reach it is on the U4 underground line.

Specialities: Scallop, celery, green apple, smoked goose liver. Saddle of venison, beetroot, fermented red cabbage. Dark chocolate, peanut.

Menu 95/110€

PLAN: 1-A2 – *Pramergasse 21 – Ⓜ Roßauer Lände – ✆ 01 9464139 – www.pramerlandthewolf.com – Closed 6-29 January, 20 July-19 August, Monday, Tuesday, Sunday, lunch Wednesday-Saturday*

Freyenstein

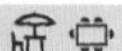

MARKET CUISINE • FAMILY This restaurant promises a warm and friendly, family ambience and attentive, pleasantly informal service. However, attention focuses on the set menu, which offers two small dishes per course, and all are flavoursome and aromatic. Demand for tables here is correspondingly high!

Menu 56/64€

Off plan – *Thimiggasse 11 – ✆ 0664 4390837 – www.freyenstein.at – Closed Monday, Sunday, lunch Tuesday-Saturday*

MAST Weinbistro

AUSTRIAN • WINSTUB No wonder MAST is so popular – the atmosphere is friendly, the decor rustic yet modern and the excellent food offers great value for money! Try the braised Jerusalem artichokes, marinated fillet steak of venison and porcini.

Menu 65€ – Carte 29/43€

PLAN: 1-A2 – *Porzellangasse 53 – Ⓜ Friedensbrücke – ✆ 01 9226679 – www.mast.wine – Closed 27 January-11 February, 3-19 August, Monday, Tuesday, lunch Saturday-Sunday*

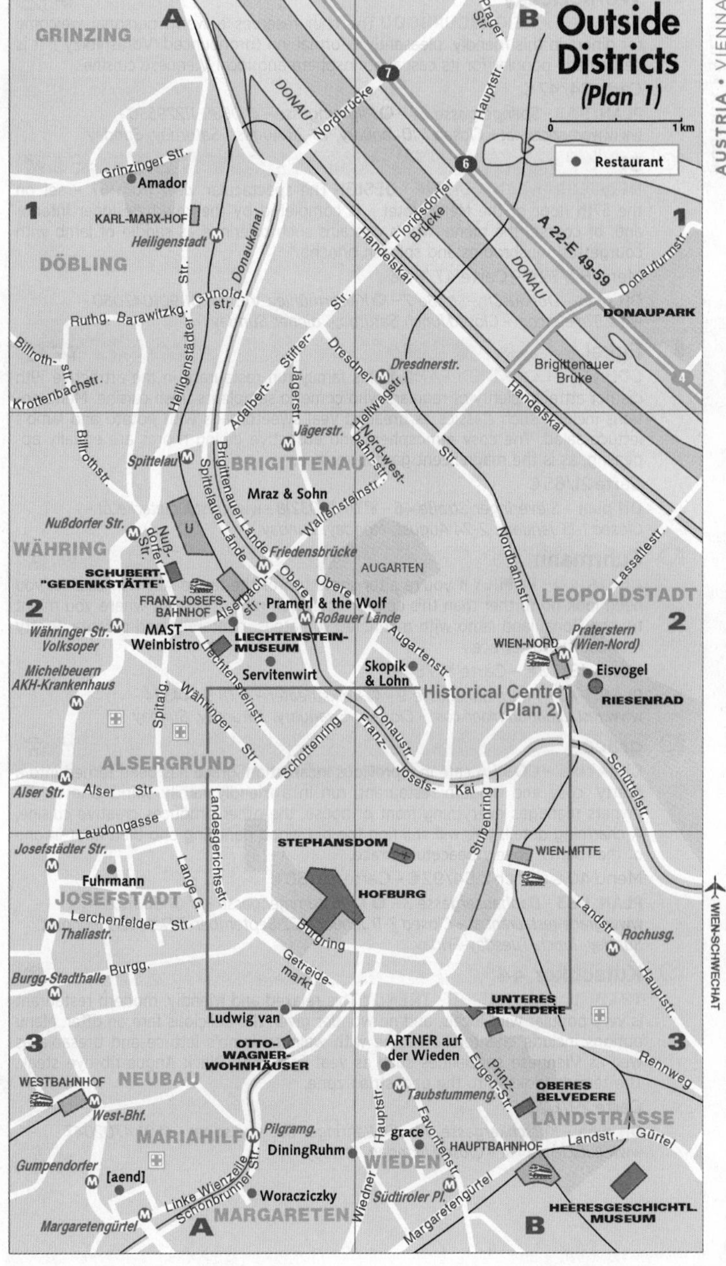
Outside Districts
(Plan 1)
0
1 km
Restaurant
A
B
1
2
3
GRINZING
DÖBLING
WÄHRING
ALSERGRUND
JOSEFSTADT
NEUBAU
MARIAHILF
MARGARETEN
WIEDEN
LANDSTRASSE
LEOPOLDSTADT
BRIGITTENAU
DONAUPARK
DONAU
Donaukanal
Nordbrücke
Floridsdorfer Brücke
Brigittenauer Brüke
A 22-E 49-59
Prager Str.
Hauptstr.
Donauturmstr.
Handelskai
Grinzinger Str.
Amador
KARL-MARX-HOF
Heiligenstadt
Heiligenstädter Str.
Gunoldstr.
Ruthg.
Barawitzkg.
Billrothstr.
Krottenbachstr.
Adalbert-Stifter-Str.
Dresdner Str.
Dresdnerstr.
Jägerstr.
Hellwagstr.
Nord-west-bahn-str.
Spittelau
Spittelauer Lände
Brigittenauer Lände
Mraz & Sohn
Wallensteinstr.
Nußdorfer Str.
Nußdorfer Str.
Friedensbrücke
AUGARTEN
Nordbahnstr.
Lassallestr.
SCHUBERT-"GEDENKSTÄTTE"
FRANZ-JOSEFS-BAHNHOF
Alserbachstr.
Obere
Pramerl & the Wolf
Roßauer Lände
Währinger Str.
Volksoper
MAST Weinbistro
LIECHTENSTEIN-MUSEUM
Augartenstr.
WIEN-NORD
Praterstern (Wien-Nord)
Eisvogel
RIESENRAD
Michelbeuern AKH-Krankenhaus
Servitenwirt
Skopik & Lohn
Historical Centre (Plan 2)
Spitalg.
Währinger Str.
Liechtensteinstr.
Schottenring
Franz-Josefs-Kai
Donaustr.
Schüttelstr.
Alser Str.
Laudongasse
Landesgerichtsstr.
Stubenring
Josefstädter Str.
Fuhrmann
STEPHANSDOM
WIEN-MITTE
Lange G.
HOFBURG
Lerchenfelder Str.
Thaliastr.
Burgring
Landstr.
Rochusg.
WIEN-SCHWECHAT
Burgg.
Burgg-Stadthalle
Getreidemarkt
Hauptstr.
UNTERES BELVEDERE
Ludwig van
OTTO-WAGNER-WOHNHÄUSER
ARTNER auf der Wieden
Rennweg
WESTBAHNHOF
West-Bhf.
Taubstummeng.
Prinz-Eugen-Str.
OBERES BELVEDERE
Pilgramg.
grace
Favoritenstr.
HAUPTBAHNHOF
Landstr.
Gürtel
DiningRuhm
Wiedner Hauptstr.
Gumpendorfer
[aend]
Linke Wienzeile
Schönbrunner Str.
Woracziczky
Südtiroler Pl.
Margaretengürtel
HEERESGESCHICHTL. MUSEUM

Woracziczky

AUSTRIAN • NEIGHBOURHOOD The chef reserves a warm personal welcome for diners in this friendly, pleasantly informal inn (pronounced 'Vorashitkzy'). It is particularly popular for its casual atmosphere and local Viennese cuisine.

Carte 24/47€

PLAN: 1-A3 - *Spengergasse 52 - Ⓜ Pilgramgasse - ✆ 0699 11229530 - www.woracziczky.at - Closed 1-10 January, 10-28 August, Saturday, Sunday*

57

MEDITERRANEAN CUISINE • DESIGN The spectacular view from 57 - set on the 57th floor of the Meliá Hotel - is completed by the smart designer interior and, of course, the menu, which contains such offerings as saddle of lamb with courgettes, mushrooms and spinach brioche.

Menu 62/72€ - Carte 47/67€

Off plan - *Donau-City-Straße 7 - Ⓜ Kaisermühlen VIC - ✆ 01 901042080 - www.57melia.com - Closed lunch Saturday, dinner Sunday*

Eckel

COUNTRY COOKING • FAMILY This family-run restaurant in the attractive 19th district attracts plenty of regulars who come to sample its fresh cuisine. Menu options include such classics as breaded veal sweetbreads with potato and lamb's lettuce salad. The cosy atmosphere and attractive dining rooms are equally appealing, as is the magnificent garden terrace.

Carte 21/65€

Off plan - *Sieveringer Straße 46 - ✆ 01 3203218 - www.restauranteckel.at - Closed 1-13 January, 2-24 August, Monday, Sunday*

Fuhrmann

AUSTRIAN • FAMILY If you're after some top-of-the-range Austrian cuisine, you need look no further than this comfortable, well-run restaurant, where you might try the Donauland lamb with marinated tomatoes, puntarelle and polenta. Pretty rear courtyard terrace.

Menu 48/73€ - Carte 37/54€

PLAN: 1-A3 - *Fuhrmannsgasse 9 - Ⓜ Volkstheater - ✆ 01 9444324 - www.restaurantfuhrmann.com - Closed 1-5 January, Saturday, Sunday*

grace

CREATIVE • COSY A café in a previous incarnation, grace has been turned into a pretty, cosy and modern restaurant, run in a friendly family spirit. One of the owners manages everything front of house, the other produces creative cuisine. A charming detail: you will still find the old wood panelling and tiled floor in one of the rooms. Lovely peaceful terrace.

Menu 40€ (lunch), 54/92€ - Carte 45/60€

PLAN: 1-B3 - *Danhausergasse 3 - Ⓜ Taubstummengasse - ✆ 01 5031022 - www.grace-restaurant.at - Closed 7-11 January, 22 September-3 October, Monday, Sunday, lunch Tuesday-Friday*

Kutschker 44

TRADITIONAL CUISINE • TRENDY This relaxed and friendly, modern restaurant is very popular with locals, and no wonder given the delicious fare on offer. Menu options include chanterelle terrine with walnuts, lamb's lettuce and bresaola as well as Viennese specialities such as veal lights and Black Angus rib-eye steak. The terrace looks onto the pedestrian zone.

Carte 29/62€

Off plan - *Kutschkergasse 44 - Ⓜ Währinger Str. Volksoper - ✆ 01 4702047 - www.kutschker44.at - Closed Monday, Sunday*

PleskyRoman/iStock

SALZBURG
SALZBURG

oriredmouse/iStock

SALZBURG IN...

→ **ONE DAY**
Festung Hohensalzburg, Museum der Moderne, Cathedral, Residenzplatz.

→ **TWO DAYS**
Mozart's birthplace, Nonntal, Kapuzinerberg, Mirabell Gardens, concert at Mozarteum.

→ **THREE DAYS**
Mozart's residence, Hangar 7, Hellbrunn Palace, concert at Landestheater.

Small but perfectly formed, Salzburg is a chocolate-box treasure, gift-wrapped in stunning Alpine surroundings. It's immortalised as the birthplace and inspiration of one of classical music's greatest stars, and shows itself off as northern Europe's grandest exhibitor of baroque style. Little wonder that in summer its population rockets, as the sound of music wafts from hotel rooms and festival hall windows during rehearsals for the Festspiele. In quieter times of the year, Salzburgers enjoy a leisurely and relaxed pace of life. Their love of music and the arts is renowned; and they

enjoy the outdoors, too, making the most of the mountains and lakes, and the paths which run along the river Salzach and zigzag through the woods and the grounds of Hellbrunn. The dramatic natural setting of Salzburg means you're never likely to get lost. Rising above the left bank (the Old Town) is the Mönchsberg Mountain and its fortress, the Festung Hohensalzburg, while the right bank (the New Town, this being a relative term) is guarded by the even taller Kapuzinerberg. In the New Town stands the Mozart family home, while the graceful gardens of the Schloss Mirabell draw the right bank crowds. The Altstadt (Old Town) is a UNESCO World Heritage Site and its star turn is its Cathedral. To the east is the quiet Nonntal area overlooked by the Nuns' Mountain.

EATING OUT

Salzburg's cuisine takes much of its influence from the days of the Austro-Hungarian Empire, with Bavarian elements added to the mix. Over the centuries it was characterised by substantial pastry and egg dishes to fill the stomachs of local salt mine workers; it's still hearty and meaty and is typified by dumplings and broths. In the city's top restaurants, a regional emphasis is still very important but the cooking has a lighter, more modern touch. Beyond the city are picturesque inns and tranquil beer gardens, many idyllically set by lakes. Do try the dumplings: Pinzgauer Nocken are made of potato pastry and filled with minced pork; another favourite is Gröstl, a filling meal of 'leftovers', including potatoes, dumplings, sausages and smoked meat roasted in a pan. If you want a snack, then Jausen is for you – cold meals with bread and sausage, cheese, dumplings, bacon etc, followed by an Obstler, made from distilled fruit. Salzburg's sweet tooth is evident in the Salzburger Nockerl, a rich soufflé omelette made with fruit and soft meringue.

Centre

Esszimmer (Andreas Kaiblinger)

CREATIVE • TRENDY Elegant but far from stiff, the Kaiblinger's restaurant is decorated with lively colour accents and the charming front-of-house team serve punchy cuisine that is modern with classical influences, always finely balanced and anything but boring! Attractive rear courtyard terrace.

Specialities: Scallop and langoustine, tomato, cucumber. Saddle and leg of rabbit with lime and paprika. Chocolate leaves stuffed with mango and pistachios.

Menu 45 € (lunch), 78/128 € - Carte 71/92 €

PLAN: 1-A1 - *Müllner Hauptstraße 33 - ✆ 0662 870899 - www.esszimmer.com - Closed Monday, Sunday*

The Glass Garden

MODERN CUISINE • ELEGANT Schloss Mönchstein boasts a great location here: a distinctive glass dome with an elegant interior, glass art that is worth seeing and a wonderful view of the city! But the food also deserves full attention. Modern and based on very good produce, it wins you over with its flavour and finesse. Wine lovers appreciate the savvy pairings.

Specialities: Salmon trout, radish, lemon, bottarga. Salzburg chamois, trumpet mushrooms, Roscoff onion, Rouennaise sauce. Farmhouse yoghurt, lime, avocado, pistachio.

Menu 58/146 € - Carte 56/108 €

PLAN: 1-A1 - *Mönchsberg Park 26 - ✆ 0662 8485550 - www.monchstein.at - Closed 4 February-18 March, 1-20 November, lunch Tuesday*

Brunnauer

FRENCH • ELEGANT Your hosts here have created a stylish restaurant in a lovely, old Ceconi-built villa. Its high ceilings, wooden floors and well-chosen furnishings provide the atmosphere, while the upmarket menu reveals French, regional and international influences. The terrace offers a wonderful view of the fortifications.

Menu 71 € - Carte 50/77 €

PLAN: 1-B2 - *Fürstenallee 5 - ✆ 0662 251010 - www.restaurant-brunnauer.at - Closed 5-19 January, Saturday, Sunday*

Goldener Hirsch

AUSTRIAN • COSY The restaurant in the hotel of the same name in the old town was once a blacksmith's shop. A striking white vaulted ceiling, lovely parquet flooring and charming Austrian furnishing details contribute to the atmosphere. The menu features modern, traditional dishes from Austria such as lightly marinated catfish, pickled chanterelles, pearl onions and watercress.

Menu 62/84 € - Carte 37/68 €

PLAN: 2-C1 - *Getreidegasse 37 - ✆ 662 80840 - www.restaurantgoldenerhirsch.at*

Goldgasse

TRADITIONAL CUISINE • COSY The speciality here is new interpretations of old Salzburg recipes taken from a cookbook published in 1719! The food is a perfect match for the period setting with modern touches and the lively atmosphere - the charming service is the icing on the cake! Try the fried breaded chicken with potato and cucumber salad and cranberries and the apple strudel with vanilla sauce.

Carte 30/83 €

PLAN: 2-D1 - *Goldgasse 10 - ✆ 0662 845622 - www.hotelgoldgasse.at*

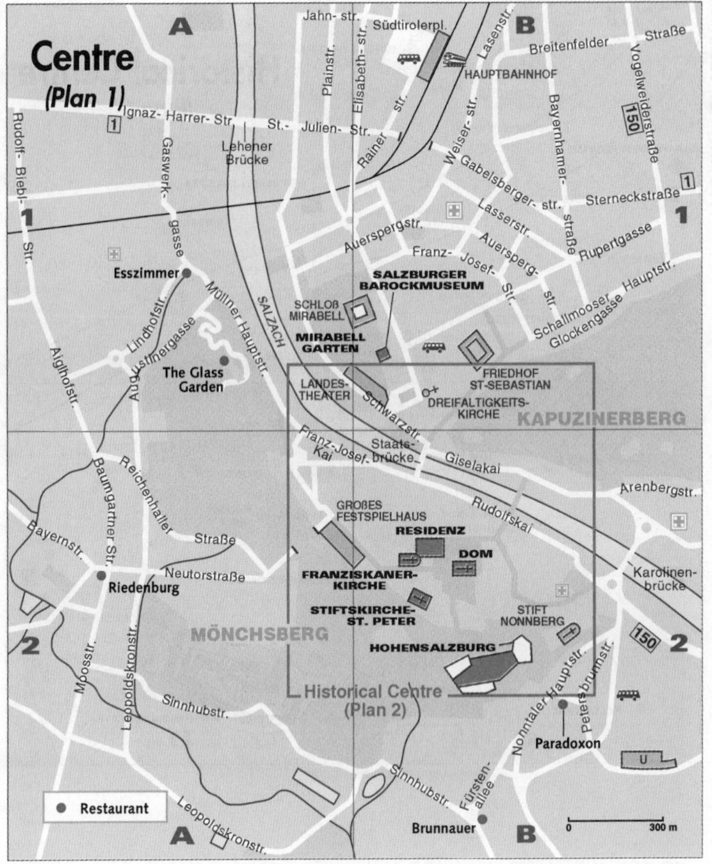

🍴 Pan e Vin

MEDITERRANEAN CUISINE • COSY Pan e Vin is set in a 600 year-old building with an interior decorated in warm tones. It serves food with a distinctly Mediterranean feel alongside a well-stocked international wine list. The Azzuro on the ground floor is also a good option.

Menu 38/89 € – Carte 33/96 €

PLAN: 2-C1 – *Gstättengasse 1 – ✆ 0662 844666 – www.panevin.at – Closed 1-11 September, Sunday*

🍴 Paradoxon

MODERN CUISINE • TRENDY Those who like a restaurant with a difference will find both the interior and the cuisine here unpretentious, unconventional and anything but staid. The one thing you can always be sure of is the quality of the food.

Carte 33/62 €

PLAN: 1-B2 – *Zugallistraße 7 – ✆ 0664 1616191 – www.restaurant-paradoxon.com – Closed 31 May-30 June, Monday, Tuesday, lunch Wednesday-Friday, dinner Sunday*

Historical Centre
(Plan 2)

● Restaurant

Riedenburg 

CLASSIC CUISINE • COSY Nicole and Helmut Schinwald offer classic Austrian cuisine. Wiener schnitzel, Tauern lamb and sea bass are served in comfortable yet elegant dining rooms with light wood, warm colours and modern pictures. Wonderful garden with chestnut trees.

Menu 52/75€ – Carte 30/67€

PLAN: 1-A2 – *Neutorstraße 31 – ✆ 0662 830815 – www.riedenburg.at – Closed 1-8 September, Monday, Sunday*

St. Peter Stiftskulinarium 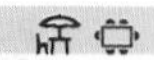

AUSTRIAN • TRADITIONAL Dating back to 803, this is one of the oldest restaurants in Europe! Diners sit comfortably in its lovely old interior to enjoy ambitious cuisine in the form of "connoisseur" dishes including braised Fassona beef with polenta, black salsify and truffle or traditional Austrian fare such as Wiener schnitzel. The wine list numbers some 600 different bottles and there is a lovely Baroque function room on the first floor.

Menu 60/100€ – Carte 37/79€

PLAN: 2-C2 – *St. Peter Bezirk 1/4 – ✆ 0662 8412680 – www.stpeter.at*

Zirbelzimmer

MARKET CUISINE • ELEGANT Sacher's culinary flagship offers a wide and varied menu ranging from poached langoustine to Styrian fried chicken, all served in a warm, friendly and typically Austrian setting. There is also an attractive balcony overlooking the River Salzach.

Menu 69/89€ – Carte 48/72€

PLAN: 2-C1 – *Schwarzstraße 5 – ☎ 0662 889770 – www.sacher.com – Closed lunch Monday-Sunday*

Environs of Salzburg

Ikarus

CREATIVE • TRENDY An unusual concept, the architecturally impressive Hangar-7 is both a Red Bull exhibition space and an ultra-modern luxury restaurant serving top quality creative cuisine. Choose from a menu devised by the international guest chef of the month or the restaurant's own Ikarus selection.

Specialities: Mussels, tomato, artichoke. Rock bass, onion, bacon, oregano. Pickled strawberries, dairy ice cream, fig leaf oil.

Menu 110/195€

Wilhelm-Spazier-Straße 7a – ☎ 0662 21970 – www.hangar-7.com – Closed 1-8 January, lunch Monday-Thursday

SENNS.Restaurant

CREATIVE • TRENDY There's plenty to look at in this former foundry with its stylish urban look and industrial charm, but as soon as the friendly yet discreet front-of-house team has served the first course, you'll find that Andreas Senn and Christian Geisler's creative, fully flavoured modern cuisine - made using the very best ingredients - demands your full attention.

Specialities: Scallop, tomato, yuzu, olive oil. Saddle of venison, carrot, sea buckthorn, sweetheart cabbage. Jerusalem artichoke, poppy seed, blackberry.

Menu 85/189€

Söllheimerstrasse 16 – ☎ 0664 4540232 – www.senns.restaurant – Closed Monday, Sunday, lunch Tuesday-Saturday

Brandstätter

COUNTRY COOKING • COSY Try the creamy veal goulash and the local venison, and don't miss the Mohr im Hemd (chocolate hazelnut pudding with an exquisite chocolate sauce). Pretty cosy dining rooms – the Swiss pine room with its tiled oven has its own charm.

Carte 32/68€

Münchner Bundesstraße 69 – ☎ 0662 434535 – www.hotel-brandstaetter.com – Closed Sunday

Gasthof Auerhahn

COUNTRY COOKING • FRIENDLY Try Topfenknödel (curd cheese dumplings) and classic dishes such as boiled beef with apple and horseradish sauce or medallions of venison with port sauce. If you like the warm and friendly dining rooms, you will love the guestrooms, which although not huge, are pretty and well kept.

Menu 48/62€ – Carte 33/52€

Bahnhofstraße 15 – ☎ 0662 451052 – www.auerhahn-salzburg.at – Closed Monday, Tuesday, dinner Sunday

Gasthof Schloss Aigen

AUSTRIAN • INN Dating back to 1402, Schloss Aigen serves traditional Austrian cuisine with modern influences. Try the boiled beef, which comes in a range of different preparations. There is also a charming interior courtyard terrace set beneath sweet chestnut trees.

Menu 64 € – Carte 24/75 €

Schwarzenbergpromenade 37 – ✆ 0662 621284 – www.schloss-aigen.at – Closed 7-16 January, 23 March-1 April, Monday, Tuesday, Wednesday

Huber's im Fischerwirt

AUSTRIAN • COSY The Hubers serve regional classics and international fare in their charming restaurant. Dishes include Viennese fried chicken with lamb's lettuce and potato salad, and game stew with bread dumplings. There is also a small shop selling jams, chocolate and caviar.

Menu 59/95 € – Carte 32/87 €

Peter-Pfenninger-Straße 8 – ✆ 0662 424059 – www.fischerwirt-liefering.at – Closed 1 February-30 March, Tuesday, Wednesday

Zum Buberl Gut

TRADITIONAL CUISINE • COSY This pretty 17C manor house offers more than just an attractive setting. The food served in the splendid, elegant dining rooms and lovely garden is delicious. It includes dishes such as tuna fish tartare with avocado and mango and paprika chutney, as well as ossobuco with creamed Jerusalem artichokes and gremolata.

Menu 28 € (lunch) – Carte 56/74 €

Gneiser Straße 31 – ✆ 0662 826866 – www.buberlgut.at – Closed Tuesday

Hallwang North-East: 6 km by Sterneckstraße B1

Pfefferschiff (Jürgen Vigné)

CLASSIC CUISINE • ELEGANT Standing at the gates of Salzburg, this top gourmet restaurant is located in a lovely 17C former parish house. The owner Jürgen Vigné's flavoursome and distinctive cuisine is matched by the charming front-of-house team managed by his wife. The dining rooms are delightful and the terrace is wonderful.

Specialities: Char, peach, verbena, buttermilk. Saddle of venison, plum, Jerusalem artichoke, coffee. Walnut, savarin and ice cream, grape, acacia, parsnip.

Menu 85/115 € – Carte 66/116 €

Söllheim 3 – ✆ 0662 661242 – www.pfefferschiff.at – Closed Monday, Sunday, lunch Tuesday-Friday

Hof bei Salzburg North-East: 18 km by Wolfgangsee Straße B1

Schloss Restaurant

CLASSIC CUISINE • ROMANTIC Where else could you enjoy ambitious cuisine with such a lovely lake view? In the Schloss Fuschl hotel restaurant the food has classical and regional influences, for example medallions of venison fillet with a pepper crust, celery and truffles. The fish comes from the restaurant's own farm. Good wine list. N.B. only open to hotel guests in peak season.

Menu 58 € (lunch)/130 € – Carte 64/114 €

Schloßstraße 19 – ✆ 06229 22530 – www.schlossfuschlsalzburg.com

Spectral-Design/iStock

MarioGuti/iStock

BELGIUM

BELGIË - BELGIQUE

BRUSSELS
BRUXELLES/BRUSSEL

sedmak/iStock

BRUSSELS IN...

→ **ONE DAY**
Grand Place, Musées Royaux des Beaux-Arts, Place Ste-Catherine.

→ **TWO DAYS**
Marolles, Place du Grand Sablon, Musical Instrument Museum, concert at Palais des Beaux-Arts.

→ **THREE DAYS**
Parc du Cinquantenaire, Horta's house, tour St Gilles and Ixelles.

There aren't many cities where you can use a 16C century map and accurately navigate your way around; or where there are enough restaurants to dine somewhere different every day for five years; or where you'll find a museum dedicated to the comic strip – but then every city isn't Brussels. It was tagged a 'grey' capital because of its EU associations but those who've spent time here know it to be, by contrast, a buzzing town. It's the home of art nouveau, it features a wonderful maze of medieval alleys and places to eat, and it's warm and friendly, with an outgoing, cosmopolitan feel – due in no small part to its

turbulent history, which has seen it under frequent occupation. Generally speaking, the Bruxellois believe that you shouldn't take things too seriously: they have a soft spot for puppets and Tintin, street music and majorettes; and they do their laundry in communal places like the Wash Club.

The area where all visitors wend is the Lower Town and the Grand Place but the northwest and southern quarters (Ste-Catherine and The Marolles) are also of particular interest. To the east, higher up an escarpment, lies the Upper Town – this is the traditional home of the aristocracy and encircles the landmark Parc de Bruxelles. Two suburbs of interest are St Gilles, to the southwest, and Ixelles, to the southeast, where trendy bars and art nouveau are the order of the day.

EATING OUT

As long as your appetite hasn't been sated at the chocolatiers, or with a cone of frites from a street stall, you'll relish the dining experience in Brussels. As long as you stay off the main tourist drag (i.e. Rue des Bouchers), you're guaranteed somewhere good to eat within a short strolling distance. There are lots of places to enjoy Belgian dishes such as moules frites, Ostend lobster, eels with green herbs, or waterzooi (chicken or fish stew with vegetables). Wherever you're eating, at whatever price range, food is invariably well cooked and often bursting with innovative touches. As a rule of thumb, the Lower Town has the best places, with the Ste-Catherine quarter's fish and seafood establishments the pick of the bunch; you'll also find a mini Chinatown here. Because of the city's cosmopolitan character there are dozens of international restaurants - ranging from French and Italian to more unusual Moroccan, Tunisian and Congolese destinations. Belgium beers are famous the world over and are served in specially designed glasses.

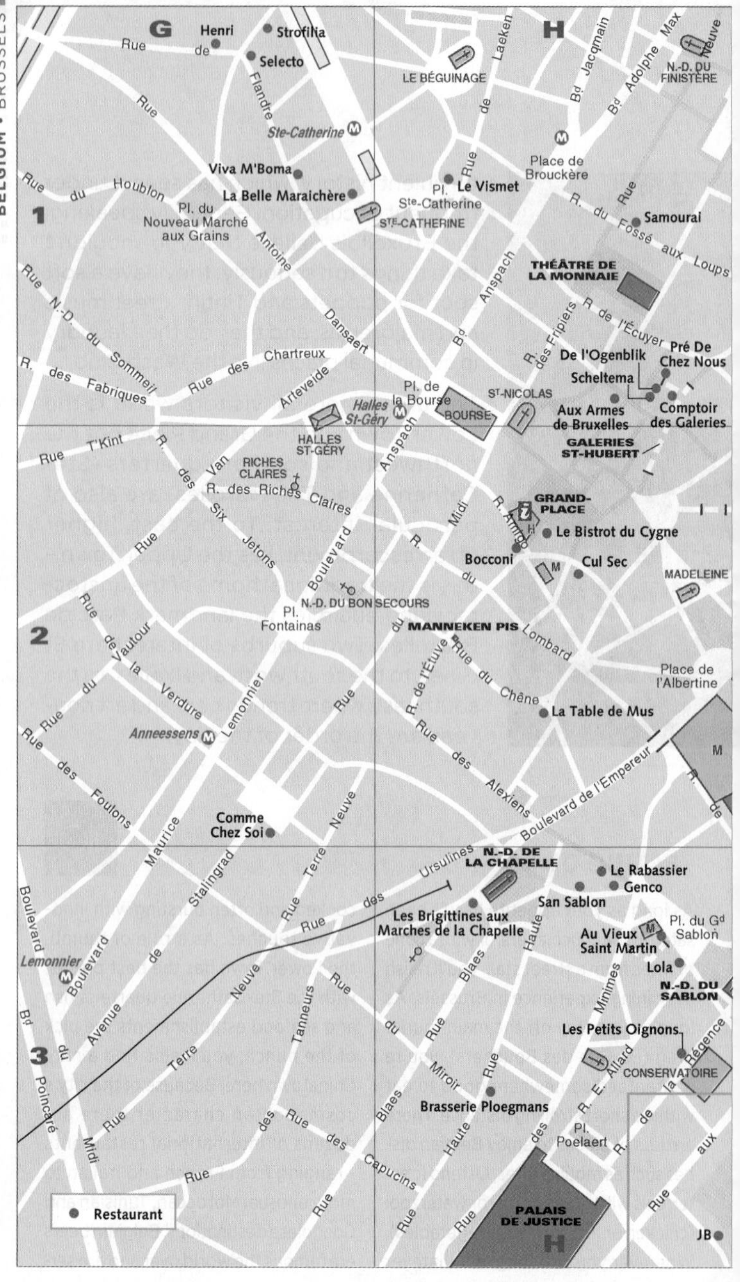

Henri
Strofilia
Selecto
Ste-Catherine
Viva M'Boma
La Belle Maraichère
Le Vismet
Samourai
THÉÂTRE DE LA MONNAIE
Pré De Chez Nous
De l'Ogenblik
Scheltema
Aux Armes de Bruxelles
Comptoir des Galeries
GALERIES ST-HUBERT
GRAND-PLACE
Le Bistrot du Cygne
Bocconi
Cul Sec
MADELEINE
MANNEKEN PIS
La Table de Mus
Place de l'Albertine
Anneessens
Comme Chez Soi
N.-D. DE LA CHAPELLE
Le Rabassier
Genco
San Sablon
Les Brigittines aux Marches de la Chapelle
Pl. du Gd Sablon
Au Vieux Saint Martin
Lola
N.-D. DU SABLON
Les Petits Oignons
CONSERVATOIRE
Brasserie Ploegmans
Pl. Poelaert
PALAIS DE JUSTICE
JB
Lemonnier
LE BÉGUINAGE
N.-D. DU FINISTÈRE
Place de Brouckère
Pl. Ste-Catherine
STE-CATHERINE
Pl. du Nouveau Marché aux Grains
Pl. de la Bourse
BOURSE
ST-NICOLAS
Halles St-Géry
HALLES ST-GÉRY
RICHES CLAIRES
N.-D. DU BON SECOURS
Pl. Fontainas
Restaurant

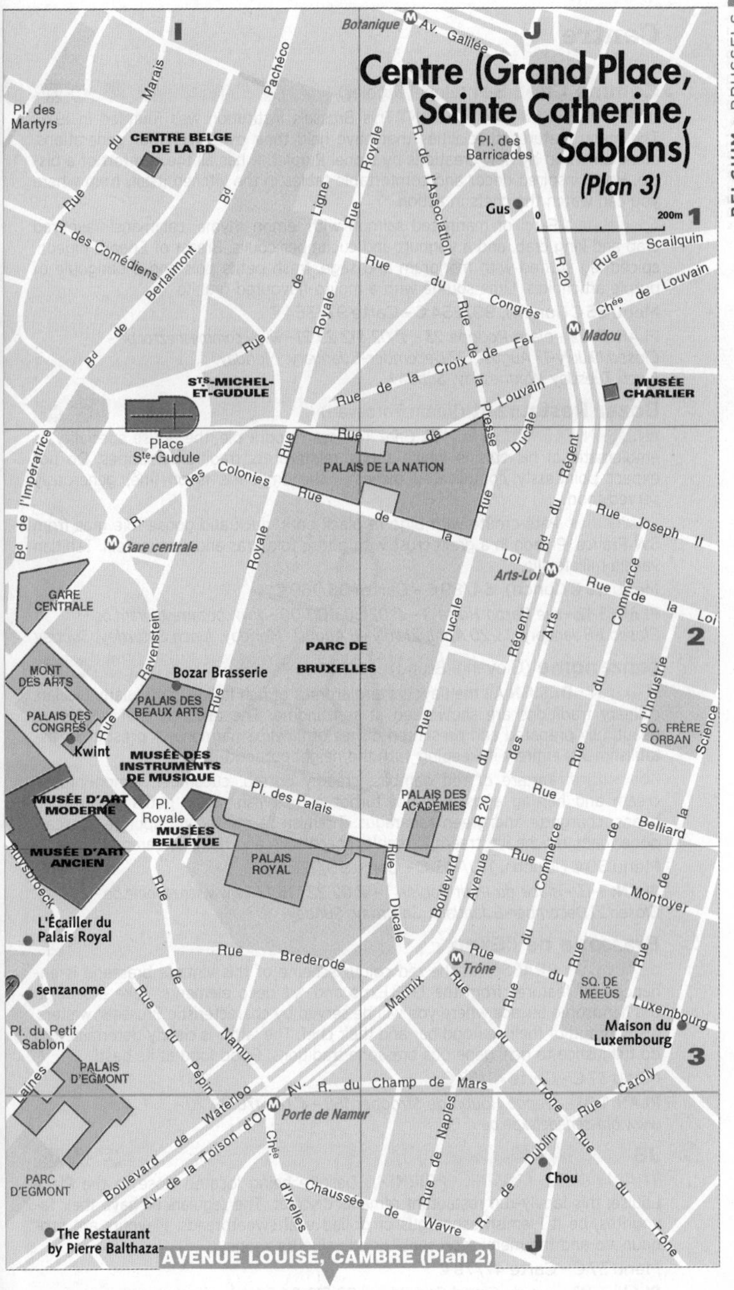

Centre (Grand Place, Sainte Catherine, Sablons)
(Plan 3)
CENTRE BELGE DE LA BD
STS-MICHEL-ET-GUDULE
PALAIS DE LA NATION
PARC DE BRUXELLES
GARE CENTRALE
MONT DES ARTS
PALAIS DES CONGRÈS
PALAIS DES BEAUX ARTS
Bozar Brasserie
Kwint
MUSÉE DES INSTRUMENTS DE MUSIQUE
MUSÉE D'ART MODERNE
MUSÉE D'ART ANCIEN
MUSÉES BELLEVUE
PALAIS ROYAL
PALAIS DES ACADÉMIES
MUSÉE CHARLIER
Gus
L'Écailler du Palais Royal
senzanome
PALAIS D'EGMONT
PARC D'EGMONT
SQ. FRÈRE ORBAN
SQ. DE MEEÛS
Maison du Luxembourg
Chou
The Restaurant by Pierre Balthazar
Botanique
Madou
Gare centrale
Arts-Loi
Trône
Porte de Namur
Pl. des Martyrs
Pl. des Barricades
Place Ste-Gudule
Pl. Royale
Pl. des Palais
Pl. du Petit Sablon
AVENUE LOUISE, CAMBRE (Plan 2)

Centre

Comme Chez Soi (Lionel Rigolet)

CREATIVE FRENCH • ELEGANT This Brussels institution was founded in 1926. The menu features specialities that have held their own over four generations, complemented by new creations by Lionel Rigolet. It has all the comfort of a bistro, Horta-inspired decor and comfortable tables in the kitchen itself, from where you can watch the chefs in action.

Specialities: Farci of marinated salmon with lemon thyme, calamansi-flavoured crab and king crab, and a yoghurt and cucumber coulis. Breast of Enéour pigeon, spiced leg stuffed with marjoram and sage, fresh petits pois and a barigoule of purple artichokes. Lime soufflé with a mojito-flavoured granita.

Menu 65€ (lunch), 99/254€ - Carte 97/354€

PLAN: 3-G2 - *place Rouppe 23 - ✆ 02 512 29 21 - www.commechezsoi.be - Closed 19 July-17 August, 22 December-6 January, Monday, lunch Tuesday-Wednesday, Sunday*

Bozar Restaurant (Karen Torosyan)

MODERN FRENCH • TRENDY Chef Torosyan's pork pie, the house speciality, is emblematic of his cuisine which subtly reinterprets traditional recipes. Do not expect pointlessly complicated dishes - the emphasis is on fine, generously served food.

Specialities: Pâté-croûte with Bigorre black pork, duck and goose foie gras from SW France. Pigeon in a grain crust with goose foie gras and smoked eel. Tahitian vanilla millefeuille.

Menu 49€ (lunch), 54/89€ - Carte 106/169€

PLAN: 3-I2 - *rue Baron Horta 3 - ✆ 02 503 00 00 - www.bozarrestaurant.be - Closed 1-8 January, 13-20 April, 21 July-18 August, Monday, lunch Saturday, Sunday*

senzanome (Giovanni Bruno)

ITALIAN • DESIGN All the flavours and aromas of rich Italian, particularly Sicilian, culinary traditions are showcased at senzanome. The talented chef rustles up beautifully prepared and presented dishes of flawless harmony. A prestigious establishment, entirely in keeping with the neighbourhood.

Specialities: Tartare of red gambas, creamy potato, cucumber, lemon-infused cream and herring eggs. Fillet of turbot with a fish stock, petits pois, broad beans, courgette and green asparagus. Tiramisu "à ma façon": sponge, mascarpone foam, mocha ice cream, crumble, cocoa tuile and ristretto caramel.

Menu 50€ (lunch), 110/135€ - Carte 90/122€

PLAN: 3-I3 - *place du Petit Sablon 1 - ✆ 02 223 16 17 - www.senzanome.be - Closed 21 December-6 January, Saturday, Sunday*

Brasserie de l'Expo

SEAFOOD • BRASSERIE The red colour scheme of this vintage brasserie is enhanced by features from the 1958 Expo and Art deco elements. Take a seat on the handsome terrace where you will be served by characteristic Brussels' waiters, justly proud of their seafood bar and their chef. The latter is clearly determined to do full justice to rich, generous brasserie traditions. Good food at its best!

Menu 37€ - Carte 41/57€

PLAN: 1-B1 - *avenue Houba de Strooper 188 - ✆ 02 476 99 70 - www.brasseriedelexpo.be*

JB

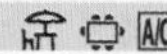

TRADITIONAL CUISINE • FRIENDLY Despite being located close to the Place Louise, this family-run restaurant remains discreet. The regulars all have their favourites, be it Flemish asparagus or grilled veal sweetbreads. Flavours are pronounced and the menu represents good value for money.

Menu 37€ - Carte 47/79€

PLAN: 3-H3 - *rue du Grand Cerf 24 - ✆ 02 512 04 84 - www.restaurantjb.com - Closed 1-31 August, 24-29 December, lunch Monday, lunch Saturday, Sunday*

Les Petits Oignons

CLASSIC CUISINE • BRASSERIE The visitor is of course charmed by the timeless decor and the lively atmosphere in this restaurant, but the delicious brasserie dishes are the real hit! Good quality produce, carefully prepared and simply presented dishes and an excellent wine list – you are in for VIP treatment!

Menu 37€ – Carte 39/63€

PLAN: 3-H3 – *rue de la Régence 25 – ✆ 02 511 76 15 – www.lespetitsoignons.be – Closed 24-25 December*

Pré De Chez Nous

ORGANIC • SIMPLE Organic local produce takes the limelight in this urban restaurant. Vegetables are pampered by the chef and the menu always features a vegetarian dish. The chef is also a "slow food" acolyte and cannot be faulted for his generous portions. The food is appetising and the selection of local beers is to die for!

Menu 21€ (lunch), 36/54€

PLAN: 3-H1 – *rue des Dominicains 19 – ✆ 02 833 37 37 – www.predecheznous.be – Closed Monday, Sunday*

Aux Armes de Bruxelles

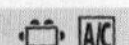

BELGIAN • BRASSERIE This institution in the heart of historic Brussels takes you on a trip back to yesteryear with its delightful traditional brasserie décor full of character and table service in period costume. The varied menu is rich in traditional Belgian favourites: tomatoes and shrimps, vol-au-vent, stoemp, mussels and chips – scrumptious!

Menu 24€ (lunch), 37/48€ – Carte 31/84€

PLAN: 3-H1 – *rue des Bouchers 13 – ✆ 02 511 55 50 – www.auxarmesdebruxelles.com*

La Belle Maraîchère

SEAFOOD • FRIENDLY This welcoming, family-run restaurant is a popular choice for locals, with its charmingly nostalgic decor. Enticing, traditional cuisine includes fish, shellfish and game depending on the season, as well as high quality sauces. Appealing set menus.

Menu 45/70€ – Carte 60/100€

PLAN: 3-G1 – *place Sainte-Catherine 11 – ✆ 02 512 97 59 – www.labellemaraichere.com – Closed dinner Tuesday, Wednesday, Thursday*

Le Bistrot du Cygne

BELGIAN • ELEGANT Welcome to one of the most beautiful restaurants of Brussels. Steeped in its own inimitable charm, it boasts wood panelling, large mirrors and classical works of art inside and a terrace overlooking the Grand Place. Superb! The menu features finely crafted Belgian staples – tradition meets the 21C.

Menu 37€ (lunch), 55/110€ – Carte 67/120€

PLAN: 3-H2 – *Grand Place 9 – ✆ 02 511 82 44 – www.lamaisonducygne.com*

Bocconi

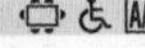

ITALIAN • ELEGANT This elegant Italian restaurant has taken up abode in the luxury Amigo Hotel, next-door to the Grand-Place and Manneken Pis. Appetising Italian fare (scrumptious risotto).

Menu 26€ (lunch), 70/80€ – Carte 64/88€

PLAN: 3-H2 – *Hôtel Amigo, rue de l'Amigo 1 – ✆ 02 547 47 15 – www.roccofortehotels.com*

Brasserie Ploegmans

BELGIAN • TRADITIONAL As you enter this former café, you will find yourself immersed in the working class ambience of the Marolles district. Everything from the decor to the menu is steeped in local traditions. Cheese croquettes, steak and chips or vol-au-vent – scrumptious!

Menu 23/28€ – Carte 34/55€

PLAN: 3-H3 – *rue Haute 148 – ✆ 02 503 21 24 – www.ploegmans.be – Closed 1 January-1 February, 29 June-15 July, Monday, dinner Sunday*

Les Brigittines Aux Marches de la Chapelle

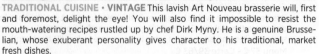

TRADITIONAL CUISINE • VINTAGE This lavish Art Nouveau brasserie will, first and foremost, delight the eye! You will also find it impossible to resist the mouth-watering recipes rustled up by chef Dirk Myny. He is a genuine Brusselian, whose exuberant personality gives character to his traditional, market fresh dishes.

Menu 35€ (lunch), 55/75€ - Carte 41/72€

PLAN: 3-H3 - *place de la Chapelle 5 -*
☎ 02 512 68 91 - www.lesbrigittines.com - Closed 21 July-15 August, lunch Saturday, Sunday

Comptoir des Galeries

CLASSIC FRENCH • BRASSERIE Vintage accents add character to this contemporary brasserie, in the heart of which stands a somewhat incongruous medal press! Pleasant establishment, ideal to savour brasserie classics made with good quality ingredients, or just for a glass of good wine.

Menu 31€ (lunch) - Carte 44/69€

PLAN: 3-H1 - *Hôtel des Galeries, Galerie du Roi 6 -*
☎ 02 213 74 74 - www.comptoirdesgaleries.be - Closed Monday, lunch Saturday, Sunday

Cul Sec

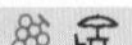

FRENCH • BISTRO While you may be tempted to knock back your wine in one go (meaning of 'cul sec'), take your time and savour the excellent French (and predominantly natural) wines served here, all the more so as this modern bistro's cuisine is a perfect pair to these fine vintages. Make a beeline for this wine bar near the Grand Place!

Menu 22€ (lunch) - Carte 37/62€

PLAN: 3-H2 - *rue des Chapeliers 16 -*
☎ 02 511 06 20 - Closed Monday, lunch Tuesday-Wednesday, lunch Saturday, Sunday

L'Écailler du Palais Royal

SEAFOOD • TRADITIONAL Since 1967, this luxurious institution has been pampering its discerning clientele. The house specialty - seafood - is remarkable. The chef assembles premium produce into generous dishes that reveal the full depth and flavour of each ingredient. A classic!

Menu 55/115€ - Carte 82/154€

PLAN: 3-I3 - *rue Bodenbroek 18 -*
☎ 02 512 87 51 - www.lecaillerdupalaisroyal.be - Closed 25 December-2 January

Genco

ITALIAN • TRADITIONAL You will be welcomed into this Italian restaurant like a long-lost friend. Sit and sample the chef's concoctions, whose generosity is equalled only by their flawless classicism. It is not difficult to understand why Genco has such a faithful clientele!

Carte 31/67€

PLAN: 3-H3 - *rue Joseph Stevens 28 - ☎ 02 511 34 44 - Closed Monday, dinner Sunday*

Gus

SEASONAL CUISINE • BRASSERIE This cosy Brussels brewery-bistro is ideal to discover the "brassonomie" concept. Aurélien brews seasonal beers, which Pierre and Jonathan skilfully incorporate into their Franco-Belgian repertory. The talented team is devoted to creating dishes that are both appetising and unexpected.

Menu 25€ (lunch), 42/50€ - Carte 48/65€

PLAN: 3-J1 - *rue des Cultes 36 -*
☎ 02 265 79 61 - www.gus-brussels.be - Closed 13-19 April, 21 July-12 August, 23 December-2 January, Monday, Sunday

Henri

MODERN FRENCH • FRIENDLY The tables are packed elbow to elbow in this simple, friendly setting with relaxed table service. Welcome to Henri's, the quintessential laid-back bistro. The dishes are equally free of frills, all the more to allow the ingredients to take front of stage. A consummate example of modern bistro art.

Carte 40/69€

PLAN: 3-G1 - *rue de Flandre 113 - ✆ 02 218 00 08 - www.restohenri.be - Closed 20 December-1 January, Saturday, Sunday*

Kwint

CLASSIC CUISINE • BRASSERIE An amazing sculpture by artist Arne Quinze adds cachet to this elegant brasserie. It serves a tasty up-to-the-minute menu in which fine quality produce takes pride of place. The view of the city from the Mont des Arts is breathtaking. A great way to see another side of Brussels.

Menu 46€ - Carte 36/62€

PLAN: 3-I2 - *Mont des Arts 1 - ✆ 02 505 95 95 - www.kwintbrussels.com*

Les Larmes du Tigre

THAI • EXOTIC DÉCOR A real voyage for the taste buds! They have been serving authentic Thai food here for over 30 years, and the enjoyment for money ratio is excellent. Buffet at lunch and Sunday evenings.

Menu 17€ (lunch), 35/45€ - Carte 37/48€

PLAN: 1-B2 - *rue de Wynants 21 - ✆ 02 512 18 77 - www.leslarmesdutigre.be - Closed Monday, Tuesday*

Lola

MODERN CUISINE • BRASSERIE Established in the swanky Sablon district since 1994, this friendly brasserie is ideal for a quick lunch at the bar-counter. Fantastic selection of traditional brasserie fare ranging from the classic vol-au-vent to Asian-influenced spring rolls, all of which are coupled with a modern twist. A blue-chip value every time.

Carte 39/72€

PLAN: 3-H3 - *place du Grand Sablon 33 - ✆ 02 514 24 60 - www.lola-restaurant.be*

De l'Ogenblik

CLASSIC CUISINE • BISTRO A loyal band of regulars add a warm, friendly vibe to this former café, which has lost none of its authentic charm since it first opened its doors back in 1969. Classical repertory, bistro dishes and a fine selection of seasonal suggestions.

Menu 48/60€ - Carte 48/75€

PLAN: 3-H1 - *Galerie des Princes 1 - ✆ 02 511 61 51 - www.ogenblik.be - Closed 27 July-16 August, Sunday*

Le Rabassier

CLASSIC CUISINE • ELEGANT Whether black or white, from January to December the truffle is the star of this pocket-handkerchief restaurant. The chef is a past master in the art of extracting the full flavour of this noble ingredient. Fine French wines, attractive menus and delightful manageress.

Menu 78/155€

PLAN: 3-H3 - *rue de Rollebeek 23 - ✆ 02 502 04 00 - www.lerabassier.be - Closed 1-21 July, lunch Monday-Saturday, Sunday*

The Restaurant by Pierre Balthazar

MODERN CUISINE • CHIC Trendy bar food, made-to-measure cocktails, an inventive menu concept and a sexy lounge ambience depict The Restaurant. Chef Balthazar changes the menu weekly to allow free rein to his inspiration. The result is an enticing range of dishes with ingredients and recipes from all over the world.

Menu 35€ (lunch), 59/69€ - Carte 55/75€

PLAN: 3-I3 - *The Hotel, boulevard de Waterloo 38 - ✆ 02 504 13 33 - www.therestaurant.be - Closed 15 July-15 August, lunch Monday, lunch Saturday, Sunday*

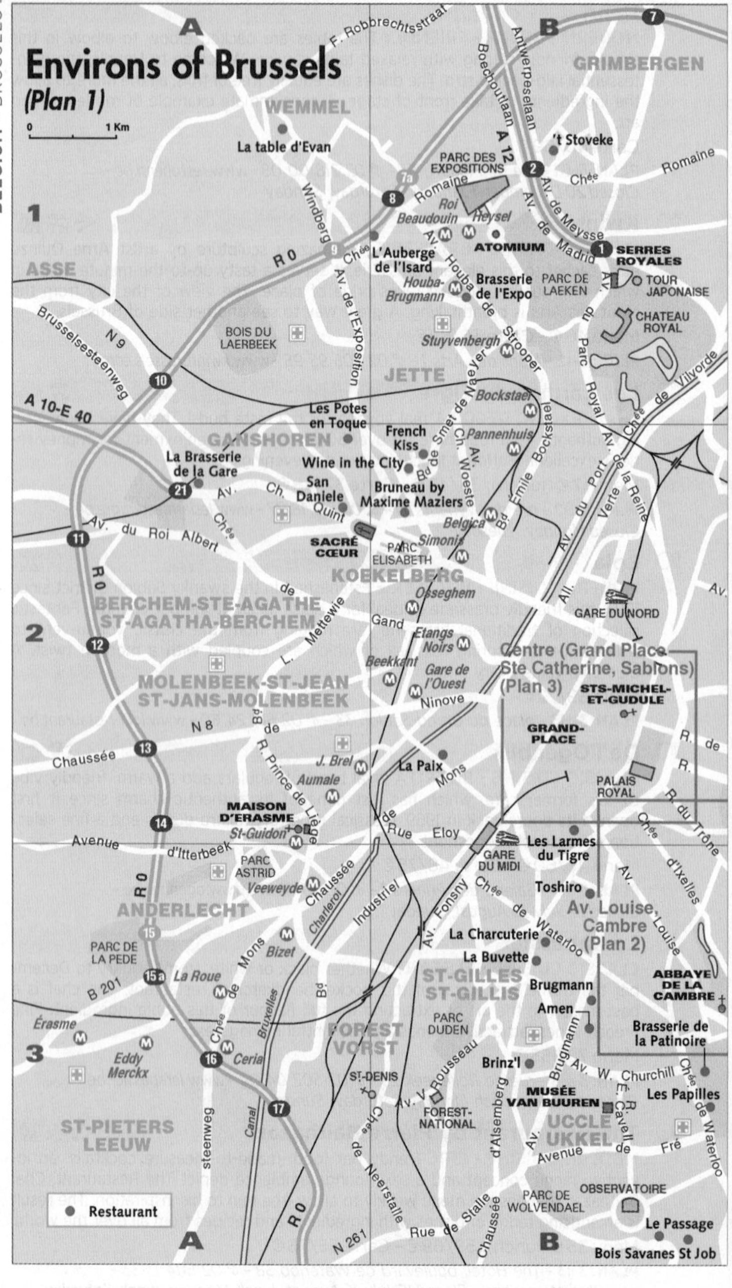
Environs of Brussels
(Plan 1)
0
1 Km
A
B
1
2
3
WEMMEL
GRIMBERGEN
ASSE
JETTE
GANSHOREN
KOEKELBERG
BERCHEM-STE-AGATHE
ST-AGATHA-BERCHEM
MOLENBEEK-ST-JEAN
ST-JANS-MOLENBEEK
ANDERLECHT
ST-GILLES
ST-GILLIS
FOREST
VORST
UCCLE
UKKEL
ST-PIETERS
LEEUW
La table d'Evan
't Stoveke
PARC DES EXPOSITIONS
L'Auberge de l'Isard
ATOMIUM
SERRES ROYALES
TOUR JAPONAISE
Brasserie de l'Expo
PARC DE LAEKEN
CHATEAU ROYAL
BOIS DU LAERBEEK
Les Potes en Toque
French Kiss
La Brasserie de la Gare
Wine in the City
San Daniele
Bruneau by Maxime Maziers
SACRÉ CŒUR
PARC ELISABETH
GARE DU NORD
Centre (Grand Place Ste Catherine, Sablons) (Plan 3)
STS-MICHEL-ET-GUDULE
GRAND-PLACE
PALAIS ROYAL
La Paix
MAISON D'ERASME
Les Larmes du Tigre
GARE DU MIDI
PARC ASTRID
Toshiro
Av. Louise, Cambre (Plan 2)
La Charcuterie
La Buvette
PARC DE LA PEDE
Brugmann
Amen
ABBAYE DE LA CAMBRE
PARC DUDEN
Brasserie de la Patinoire
Brinz'l
ST-DENIS
MUSÉE VAN BUUREN
Les Papilles
FOREST-NATIONAL
PARC DE WOLVENDAEL
OBSERVATOIRE
Le Passage
Bois Savanes St Job
Restaurant
Roi Beaudouin
Heysel
Houba-Brugmann
Stuyvenbergh
Bockstael
Pannenhuis
Belgica
Simonis
Osseghem
Etangs Noirs
Beekkant
Gare de l'Ouest
J. Brel
Aumale
St-Guidon
Veeweyde
Bizet
La Roue
Érasme
Eddy Merckx
Ceria
F. Robbrechtsstraat
Boechoutlaan
Antwerpeselaan
A 12
Romaine
Chée Romaine
Av. de Meysse
Av. de Madrid
Windberg
R0
Av. de l'Exposition
Av. Houba de Strooper
Av. du Parc Royal
Chée de Vilvorde
Brusselsesteenweg
N 9
A 10-E 40
Bd de Smet de Naeyer
Av. Ch. Woeste
Bd Emile Bockstael
Av. du Port
Av. de la Reine
All. Verte
Av. Ch. Quint
Av. du Roi Albert
Chée de Gand
Bd L. Mettewie
Chée de Ninove
N 8
Chaussée de Mons
Bd R. Prince de Liège
Rue Eloy
Avenue d'Itterbeek
Chaussée de Charleroi
Bd Industriel
Av. Fonsny
Chée de Waterloo
R. de la Loi
R. du Trône
Chée d'Ixelles
Av. Louise
B 201
Chée de Mons
Bd de Bruxelles
Canal
steenweg
Av. V. Rousseau
Chée de Neerstalle
Av. Brugmann
Av. d'Alsemberg
Av. W. Churchill
Av. E. Cavell
Avenue de Fré
Chée de Waterloo
Rue de Stalle
Chaussée
N 261

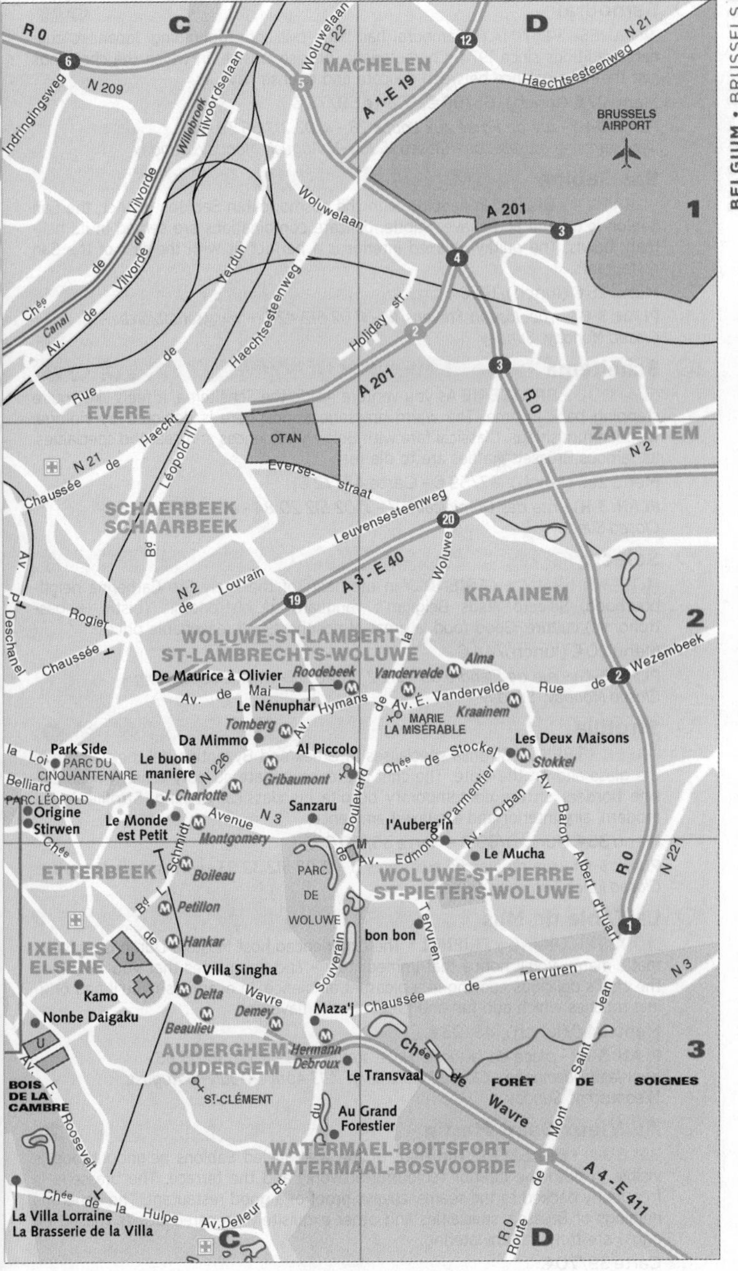
MACHELEN
BRUSSELS AIRPORT
EVERE
OTAN
ZAVENTEM
SCHAERBEEK
SCHAARBEEK
KRAAINEM
WOLUWE-ST-LAMBERT
ST-LAMBRECHTS-WOLUWE
De Maurice à Olivier
Le Nénuphar
Da Mimmo
Park Side
Le buone maniere
Al Piccolo
Les Deux Maisons
Sanzaru
Origine
Stirwen
Le Monde est Petit
l'Auberg'in
Le Mucha
ETTERBEEK
PARC DE WOLUWE
WOLUWE-ST-PIERRE
ST-PIETERS-WOLUWE
bon bon
IXELLES
ELSENE
Villa Singha
Kamo
Nonbe Daigaku
Maza'j
AUDERGHEM
OUDERGEM
Le Transvaal
FORÊT DE SOIGNES
BOIS DE LA CAMBRE
Au Grand Forestier
WATERMAEL-BOITSFORT
WATERMAEL-BOSVOORDE
La Villa Lorraine
La Brasserie de la Villa

Samouraï

JAPANESE • INTIMATE Samouraï has been brilliantly upholding Japanese culinary traditions since 1974. Characteristic, precise cuisine, in which the chef finds just the right balance between delicate and intense flavours.

Menu 27 € (lunch), 65/99 € - Carte 59/75 €

PLAN: 3-H1 - *rue du Fossé aux Loups 28 - ✆ 02 217 56 39 - www.samourai-bruxelles.be - Closed 15 July-17 August, Monday, Sunday*

San Sablon

CREATIVE • BISTRO In keeping with the cosmopolitan Sablons district, the San Sablon is urbane and suave. Subtle, delicate combinations are served in its hallmark bowls. The quirky, relaxed interior is a perfect fit with the rest of the San restaurants.

Menu 25 € (lunch)/65 €

PLAN: 3-H3 - *rue Joseph Stevens 12 - ✆ 02 512 42 12 - www.sansablon.be - Closed Monday, Sunday*

Scheltema

SEAFOOD • BRASSERIE As you venture inside the Scheltema, it feels like you're stepping back in time. The warm brasserie atmosphere is depicted by vintage, wooden furnishings. Classical fare with Belgian influences and seafood specialties. Its famous Brussels waffles are to die for!

Menu 21 € (lunch), 37/59 € - Carte 43/72 €

PLAN: 3-H1 - *rue des Dominicains 7 - ✆ 02 512 20 84 - www.scheltema.be - Closed Sunday*

Selecto

MODERN FRENCH • FRIENDLY In the heart of the lively Ste Catherine neighbourhood, Selecto leads Belgium's vanguard of bistronomic (bistro + gastronomic) culture. Good food, a great atmosphere and reasonable prices!

Menu 20 € (lunch)/44 €

PLAN: 3-G1 - *rue de Flandre 95 - ✆ 02 511 40 95 - www.le-selecto.com - Closed Monday, Sunday*

Strofilia

GREEK • TRENDY Strofilia specialises in Greek and Byzantine delicacies, both in the glass and on the plate. The chef is a consummate culinary artist, whose cuisine borders on the contemporary despite his classical training. Strofilia has a modern, airy interior and a relaxed ambience.

Menu 35 € (lunch)/39 € - Carte 35/50 €

PLAN: 3-G1 - *rue du Marché aux Porcs 11 - ✆ 02 512 32 93 - www.strofilia.brussels - Closed lunch Saturday, Sunday*

La Table de Mus

MODERN CUISINE • FRIENDLY The experienced host Mustafa Duran is a charismatic man - you'll notice that immediately - and he ensures that you will enjoy the chef's delicious cooking in a pleasant ambience. In every dish you'll find original touches which add fun and punch to the flavours.

Menu 34 € (lunch), 48/93 €

PLAN: 3-H2 - *place de la Vieille Halle aux Blés 31 - ✆ 02 511 05 86 - www.latabledemus.be - Closed 1-8 January, 7-13 April, 20 July-15 August, Wednesday, Sunday*

Au Vieux Saint Martin

BELGIAN • BRASSERIE The spirit of the well-heeled Sablons neighbourhood is visible in both the interior (colourful artwork) and the terrace. The brasserie is frequently packed to the seams, always proof of a good restaurant. The generous helpings of Brussels specialties and other exquisitely prepared dishes (based on eggs) are truly mouthwatering.

Carte 39/70 €

PLAN: 3-H3 - *place du Grand Sablon 38 - ✆ 02 512 64 76 - www.auvieuxsaintmartin.be*

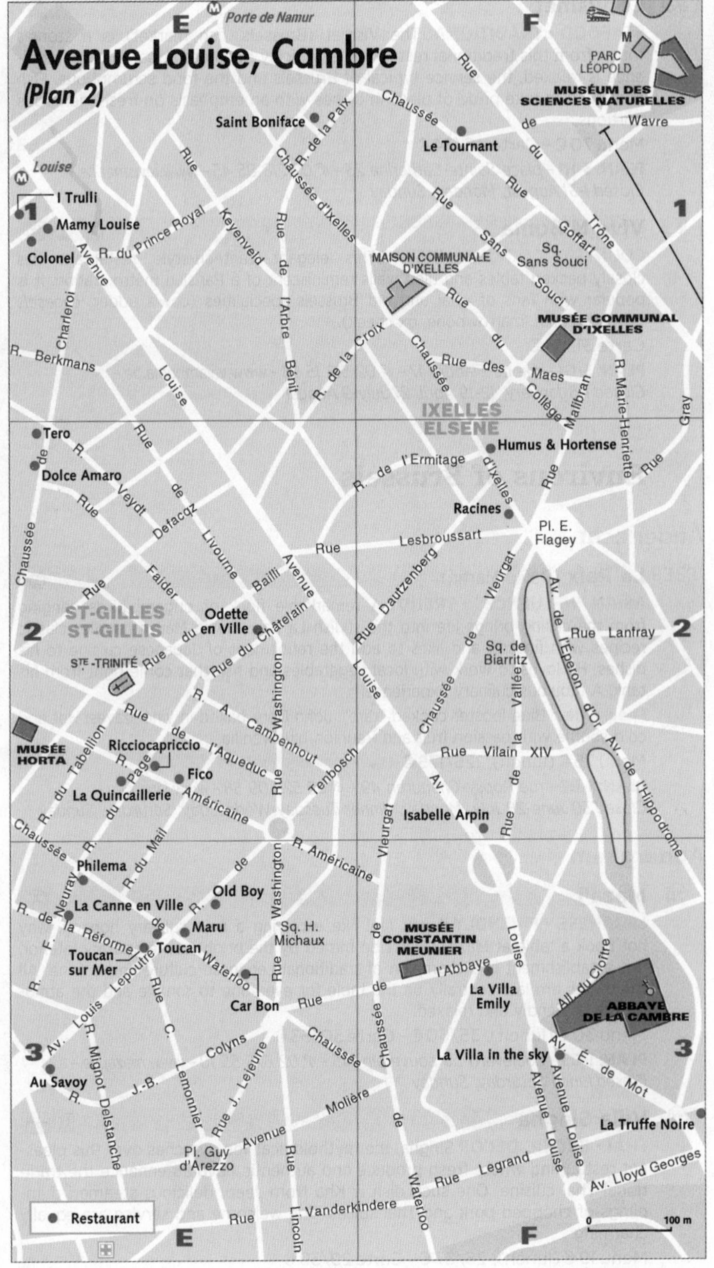
Avenue Louise, Cambre
(Plan 2)
Porte de Namur
Louise
I Trulli
Mamy Louise
Colonel
Saint Boniface
Le Tournant
PARC LÉOPOLD
MUSÉUM DES SCIENCES NATURELLES
MAISON COMMUNALE D'IXELLES
Sq. Sans Souci
MUSÉE COMMUNAL D'IXELLES
IXELLES ELSENE
Humus & Hortense
Racines
Pl. E. Flagey
Tero
Dolce Amaro
ST-GILLES ST-GILLIS
STE-TRINITÉ
Odette en Ville
Sq. de Biarritz
MUSÉE HORTA
Ricciocapriccio
Fico
La Quincaillerie
Isabelle Arpin
Philema
Old Boy
La Canne en Ville
Maru
Toucan
Toucan sur Mer
Sq. H. Michaux
MUSÉE CONSTANTIN MEUNIER
La Villa Emily
ABBAYE DE LA CAMBRE
Car Bon
La Villa in the sky
Au Savoy
La Truffe Noire
Pl. Guy d'Arezzo
Restaurant
0 100 m

Le Vismet

SEAFOOD • TRADITIONAL The Vismet (Brussels' fish market) is a stone's throw from this traditional restaurant, as quickly becomes apparent. The ambience is relaxed, the service typical of Brussels and the food scrumptious. Fish and shellfish take pride of place in dishes with an emphasis on fresh, generous portions.

Menu 70€ - Carte 46/74€

PLAN: 3-H1 - *place Sainte-Catherine 23 - ✆ 02 218 85 45 - www.levismet.be - Closed 1-31 August, Monday, Sunday*

Viva M'Boma

COUNTRY COOKING • BISTRO This elegant canteen-style restaurant has closely packed tables and tiled walls reminiscent of a Parisian métro station. It is popular with fans of offal and old Brussels specialities (cow's udder, *choesels* (sweetbreads), marrowbone, ox cheek).

Carte 31/64€

PLAN: 3-G1 - *rue de Flandre 17 - ✆ 02 512 15 93 - www.vivamboma.be - Closed 1-5 January, 12-19 April, 27 July-9 August*

Environs of Brussels

Anderlecht

La Paix (David Martin)

ASIAN INFLUENCES • TRENDY A remarkable flock of origami birds hanging from the ceiling brings life into the stylish La Paix. David Martin handles classic recipes with finesse, and likes to add the refinement of Japanese cuisine to his dishes. He loves to work with local vegetables and fish that come right from his tank. A fabulous culinary experience!

Specialities: Blue lobster cooked "rare". John Dory baked in vine leaves. Hot and cold soufflé with passion fruit and Réunion blue vanilla.

Menu 75€ (lunch), 125/175€

PLAN: 1-B2 - *rue Ropsy-Chaudron 49 - ✆ 02 523 09 58 - www.lapaix.eu - Closed 30 June-28 July, Monday, dinner Tuesday-Wednesday, Saturday, Sunday*

Auderghem

Maza'j

LEBANESE • FRIENDLY If you feel like exploring a new culinary horizon, why not book a table at Maza'j? Don't be misled by the bright contemporary interior, this establishment is a champion of traditional Lebanese culture and cuisine. All the dishes are laid centrally on the table for everyone to sample and the atmosphere is friendly and relaxed.

Menu 30€ (lunch), 35/60€ - Carte 30/53€

PLAN: 1-C3 - *boulevard du Souverain 145 - ✆ 02 675 55 10 - www.mazaj.be - Closed lunch Saturday, Sunday*

Villa Singha

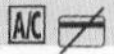

THAI • EXOTIC DÉCOR Singha, the mythological lion, watches over this pleasant restaurant, where fresh produce and authentic flavours enhance the traditional Thai cuisine. One such dish is Kha Nom Jeep, delicious steamed dumplings of chopped pork and Thai spices. The welcome and service are equally charming.

Menu 19€ (lunch), 26/37€ - Carte 29/39€

PLAN: 1-C3 - *rue des Trois Ponts 22 - ✆ 02 675 67 34 - www.singha.be - Closed 6 July-3 August, Monday, lunch Saturday, Sunday*

Le Transvaal

MARKET CUISINE • BISTRO This former butcher's shop has revived the local neighbourhood bistro concept. The talented chef has no qualms about adding a sprinkling of originality to his concoctions (in particular the starters). Deliciously reasonable prices.

Carte 43/55€

PLAN: 1-C3 – *avenue Joseph Chaudron 40 – ✆ 02 660 95 76 – www.letransvaal.be – Closed dinner Monday-Tuesday, Saturday, Sunday*

Berchem-Sainte-Agathe

La Brasserie de la Gare

BELGIAN • BRASSERIE For a typical Brussels experience, come and discover this old café, which has retained all of its retro charm. The chef's cooking honours tradition by having a pleasing simplicity and you can enjoy succulent boar in season or a timeless steak tartare and chips. This is one of life's certainties!

Menu 37€ – Carte 38/55€

PLAN: 1-A2 – *chaussée de Gand 1430 – ✆ 02 469 10 09 – www.brasseriedelagare.be – Closed lunch Saturday, Sunday*

Etterbeek et Quartier de l'Europe

Park Side

MODERN CUISINE • TRENDY Park Side sits in a great location besides the Jubilee Park (parc du Cinquantenaire). Inside it's equally appealing, with chic decor and ultra-modern design features – the main light in particular is a talking point! Modern brasserie specialities feature on the à la carte menu.

Menu 37/59€ – Carte 33/55€

PLAN: 1-C2 – *avenue de la Joyeuse Entrée 24 – ✆ 02 238 08 08 – www.restoparkside.be – Closed 27 July-18 August, 20 December-5 January, Saturday, Sunday*

Le Buone Maniere

ITALIAN • TRADITIONAL Maurizio Zizza's manners are certainly impeccable! He enjoys explaining his authentic dishes in this stylish townhouse, which boasts a terrace. Simple, tasty dishes, which sometimes surprise, transport the diner to the Mediterranean.

Menu 45€ (lunch), 60/95€ – Carte 65/93€

PLAN: 1-C2 – *avenue de Tervueren 59 – ✆ 02 762 61 05 – www.buonemaniere.be – Closed lunch Saturday, Sunday*

Le Monde est Petit

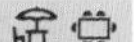

CREATIVE FRENCH • FRIENDLY In this pleasant establishment, nicely situated between Montgomery and the Parc du Cinquantenaire, the market decides what will be served. The chef uses all this quality produce in well-thought-out preparations that are as international as the guests who like to eat here.

Carte 55/75€

PLAN: 1-C2 – *rue des Bataves 65 – ✆ 02 732 44 34 – www.lemondeestpetit.be – Closed 24-28 February, 23 December-3 January, Saturday, Sunday*

Origine

MODERN FRENCH • BISTRO The whimsical décor of the Origine is depicted by colourful creatures and plants, setting the scene for a modern restaurant run by Xavier Lizen, who demonstrates great maturity despite his youth. The menu is renewed each month and illustrates the chef's international and original approach, in which each flavour lives up to expectations.

Menu 38€

PLAN: 1-C2 – *rue Général Leman 36 – ✆ 02 256 68 93 – www.origine-restaurant.be – Closed 15 July-15 August, 28 October-3 November, Monday, lunch Saturday, Sunday*

Stirwen

MODERN FRENCH • BOURGEOIS Elegance and comfort depict this restaurant, a long-standing institution in the European district. François-Xavier Lambory takes a new look at textbook Gallic cuisine. He painstakingly sources his ingredients, assembling them into highly inspired, unusual recipes.

Menu 49€ (lunch), 65/90€ - Carte 65/110€

PLAN: 1-C2 - *chaussée Saint-Pierre 15 - ✆ 02 640 85 41 - www.stirwen.be - Closed 2-5 January, 13-19 April, 20 July-23 August, Saturday, Sunday*

Forest

Brugmann

MODERN CUISINE • ELEGANT Brugmann is a picture of elegance. The interior is adorned with fine modern art and the rear terrace is attractive. What is more the chef's cuisine is equally stylish, combining ingredients and techniques in dishes that are as modern as the decor. A first-class establishment.

Menu 26€ (lunch), 55/95€ - Carte 72/88€

PLAN: 1-B3 - *avenue Brugmann 52 - ✆ 02 880 55 54 - www.brugmann.com - Closed 1-14 January, Monday, lunch Saturday*

Ganshoren

San Daniele (Franco Spinelli)

ITALIAN • INTIMATE Welcome to the Spinelli family's fiefdom – they have made the San Daniele a blue-chip culinary establishment since 1983. The revamped interior is stylish and the food fervently upholds Italian tradition. Seabass in a salt crust is filleted at the table. Depth of taste is the house signature.

Specialities: Scialatelli pasta with red mullet, basil, artichokes and clams. Medley of lamb with citrus fruit, fennel and celery confit. Pineapple ravioli, crème brûlée, blood orange sorbet and mascarpone.

Menu 50€ (lunch), 110/130€ - Carte 75/130€

PLAN: 1-A2 - *avenue Charles-Quint 6 - ✆ 02 426 79 23 - www.san-daniele.be - Closed 15 July-15 August, Monday, Sunday*

Les Potes en Toque

CLASSIC CUISINE • RUSTIC This renovated farm cottage in the heart of a residential neighbourhood is depicted by a characteristic Belgian blend of rural chic. The menu majors in flawlessly prepared brasserie favourites, served generously.

Menu 17€ (lunch)/37€ - Carte 25/57€

PLAN: 1-A2 - *drève du Château 71 - ✆ 02 428 37 37 - www.lespotesentoque.be - Closed 24 December, 31 December*

Bruneau by Maxime Maziers

MODERN FRENCH • ELEGANT Maxime Maziers has given this venerable establishment near the basilica a new lease of life. His mentor's hallmark dishes have made way for his own creations. He demonstrates his respect for tradition with excellent sauces and premium produce, adding his personal flair and modernity.

Menu 48€ (lunch)/95€ - Carte 95/164€

PLAN: 1-B2 - *avenue Broustin 73 - ✆ 02 421 70 70 - www.bruneau.be - Closed 18 August-2 September, Tuesday, Wednesday*

Ixelles et Quartier Louise

La Canne en Ville (Kevin Lejeune)

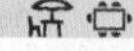

MARKET CUISINE • FAMILY La Canne en Ville sports an urban charm, where souvenirs of the former butcher's shop elegantly underscore a contemporary vibe. Inviting pavement terrace. Talented Kevin Lejeune whisks up tempting dishes that delve freely into his classical training. He enjoys adding a personal, inventive stamp to familiar family favourites. Subtle yet comforting.

Specialities: Langoustines cooked with rosemary, stuffed veal trotter and garden vegetables. Red-label salmon with peas, nasturtiums and a roasted potato bouillon. Brioche "pain perdu" with Réunion blue vanilla ice cream.

Menu 42 € (lunch), 67/83 € – Carte 64/84 €

PLAN: 2-E3 – *rue de la Réforme 22 – ✆ 02 347 29 26 – www.lacanneenville.be – Closed 5-12 April, 17-30 August, 2-8 November, 23 December-9 January, Monday, lunch Tuesday, lunch Saturday, Sunday*

✿ **Kamo** (Tomoyasu Kamo)

JAPANESE • TRENDY A slice of Tokyo in Ixelles: the classics of Japanese cuisine and remarkable combinations with bold flavours are served in a pared-down setting with a trendy atmosphere. Sit at the counter to admire the skills of the chefs at work. Good lunch bento.

Specialities: Taro and eel croquette. Lobster tempura with a sweet-and-sour sauce. Black sesame mousse.

Menu 25 € (lunch), 75/120 € – Carte 68/92 €

PLAN: 1-C3 – *chaussée de Waterloo 550a – ✆ 02 648 78 48 – www.restaurant-kamo.be – Closed lunch Wednesday, Saturday, Sunday*

✿ **La Truffe Noire**

ITALIAN • ELEGANT The purple colour scheme of this restaurant, rich in nostalgic appeal and decorated with art work, provides the setting for the charismatic chef to prepare beef carpaccio in front of diners. This show takes place every day, as the chef demonstrates his love of classical cuisine. Truffles, naturally, take pride of place in his mouth-watering menu.

Specialities: Carpaccio de Luigi with truffles. John Dory stuffed with truffles and truffle nectar. Hot soufflé with grilled hazelnuts.

Menu 50/225 € – Carte 85/195 €

PLAN: 2-F3 – *boulevard de la Cambre 12 – ✆ 02 640 44 22 – www.truffenoire.com – Closed 6-13 April, 3-16 August, 23 December-1 January, lunch Monday, lunch Saturday, Sunday*

✿ **La Villa Emily**

MEDITERRANEAN CUISINE • ELEGANT This little jewel combines the elegant atmosphere of a boudoir with subtle designer elements and a huge chandelier. This impressive balance of styles is equally visible in the food. Main courses are accompanied by sophisticated sauces and impeccable side dishes. It's splendidly classical.

Specialities: Confit onions, Jerusalem artichoke and a truffle jus. Crispy sweetbreads, parsley root and salted praline. Marron glacé flakes, chiboust cream, blueberry sorbet.

Menu 125 € – Carte 86/114 €

PLAN: 2-F3 – *rue de l'Abbaye 4 – ✆ 02 318 18 58 – www.lavillaemily.be – Closed Monday, lunch Saturday, Sunday*

✿ **La Villa in the Sky** (Alexandre Dionisio)

CREATIVE • DESIGN Taking a seat in this glass box, a full 120m/393ft high, commanding a breathtaking view of Brussels, is a once in a lifetime experience. Not only for the unusual location, but for Alexandre Dionisio's whimsical menu. His matchless culinary craftsmanship is carefully creative and premium quality ingredients are combined into an unforgettable feast of flavours.

Specialities: Langoustine tartare, shallot and chive cream, fish head espuma and quinoa soufflé. Fillet of mature Castilian beef, green asparagus, Ossetra caviar and "siphon" purée potatoes. Medley of red beetroot, beetroot and white chocolate ganache and Greek yoghurt ice cream.

Menu 90 € (lunch), 165/210 €

PLAN: 2-F3 – *avenue Louise 480 – ✆ 02 644 69 14 – www.lavillainthesky.be – Closed 4-13 April, 8-31 August, 7-12 November, Monday, lunch Saturday, Sunday*

Brasserie de la Patinoire

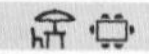

CLASSIC FRENCH • BRASSERIE This establishment cannot be faulted for its stylish, classy allure. Book a table and enjoy this luxury brasserie with a hint of British charm and an ambience that is both friendly yet elegant. Terrace overlooking the Cambre wood. The enthusiastic, generous chef takes a new look at brasserie classics.

Menu 18 € (lunch)/37 € – Carte 36/59 €

PLAN: 1-B3 – *chemin du Gymnase 1* – *✆ 02 649 70 02* – *www.brasseriedelapatinoire.be*

Car Bon

CHINESE • SIMPLE Far more than the cliché of a little neighbourhood eatery with an extensive menu and mainly Chinese clientele, Car Bon offers a host of other appeals. The food is authentic, with a focus on the Sichuan region, known for its light, subtle and assertive cuisine. A fascinating culinary journey.

Menu 15/40 € – Carte 25/40 €

PLAN: 2-E3 – *chaussée de Waterloo 552* – *✆ 02 346 64 60* – *www.restaurantcarbon.be* – *Closed Thursday*

Maison du Luxembourg

REGIONAL CUISINE • FRIENDLY Country cooking from Luxembourg moves to Brussels. This contemporary restaurant offers well-presented classical fare, highlighting produce sourced from the French-speaking province of Luxembourg. The ingredients are superlatively fresh and the vegetable side dishes are delicious. A great advertisement for the region.

Menu 33 € (lunch)/37 € – Carte 39/55 €

PLAN: 3-J3 – *rue du Luxembourg 37* – *✆ 02 511 99 95* – *www.maisonduluxembourg.be* – *Closed 3-24 August, 23 December-4 January, dinner Friday, Saturday, Sunday*

Maru

KOREAN • MINIMALIST If your mouth is already watering at the prospect of crunchy deep-fried pancakes or sweet and sour tangsuyuk, head straight for this 'urban-style' Korean restaurant whose fresh ingredients are equalled by the authentic cooking methods. Even better, the wine list is full of pleasant surprises.

Menu 25 € (lunch), 45/85 € – Carte 34/85 €

PLAN: 2-E3 – *chaussée de Waterloo 510* – *✆ 02 346 11 11* – *Closed 15 July-18 August, 23 December-2 January, Monday*

Saint Boniface

CUISINE FROM SOUTH WEST FRANCE • BISTRO Tightly packed tables, posters on the walls and a collection of biscuit tins characterise this extremely welcoming bistro. The locals flock here to sample its Basque, Lyonnaise and South-western French specialities. Cooking is generous and delicious!

Menu 25 € (lunch), 45/50 € – Carte 25/55 €

PLAN: 2-E1 – *rue Saint-Boniface 9* – *✆ 02 511 53 66* – *www.saintboniface.be* – *Closed Monday, lunch Saturday, Sunday*

Toucan

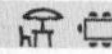

MODERN CUISINE • BISTRO The plumage of this toucan adds the finishing touch to a lovely classical brasserie, embellished with the occasional modern design twist. The ambience is one of the highlights of the establishment, as is the seamless service. The chef uses only the best quality produce and has no qualms about piling the plates high with tasty fare.

Menu 37 € – Carte 41/67 €

PLAN: 2-E3 – *avenue Louis Lepoutre 1* – *✆ 02 345 30 17* – *www.toucanbrasserie.com*

Amen

MARKET CUISINE • FRIENDLY Two-star chef Pascal Devalkeneer (Le Chalet de la Forêt) has a knack for picking the best produce. From the contemporary dishes and intense flavours to the range of textures, his dishes are masterpieces of culinary art. Amen!

Menu 23€ (lunch)/54€ – Carte 50/79€

PLAN: 1-B3 – *rue Franz Merjay 165 – ✆ 02 217 10 19 – www.amen.restaurant – Closed Monday, Sunday*

Au Savoy

TRADITIONAL CUISINE • CONTEMPORARY DÉCOR The Niels family of veteran hoteliers has set up shop at Au Savoy. The upscale restaurant sports a handsome terrace. Quintessential Belgian classics are flawlessly executed: crunchy cheese croquettes, pink veal's kidneys... excellent from breakfast to dinner!

Menu 50€ (lunch), 60/80€ – Carte 55/75€

PLAN: 2-E3 – *place Georges Brugmann 35 – ✆ 02 344 32 10 – www.ausavoy.be – Closed 31 December-1 February*

Chou

MARKET CUISINE • INTIMATE Close to the European district, chef Akandar prepares tasty, balanced dishes which are in tune with the times. It's no wonder many institution officials have made it their local!

Menu 23€ (lunch)/45€ – Carte 43/53€

PLAN: 3-J3 – *place de Londres 4 – ✆ 02 502 22 32 – www.restaurantchou.eu – Closed Saturday, Sunday*

Fico

ITALIAN • FRIENDLY Nadia Bruno, sister of stellar Giovanni (senzanome), pays homage to her Sicilian mother at Fico. Her specialty is appetising dishes from antipasti to pasta, all of which remain true to the tradition of fresh Italian produce. The colourful interior, dotted with vintage memorabilia, further adds to this moving testimonial.

Menu 26€ (lunch), 45/55€

PLAN: 2-E2 – *rue Américaine 118 – ✆ 02 241 41 41 – www.ficosteria.be – Closed Monday, Sunday*

Humus x Hortense

CREATIVE • VINTAGE The encounter between vegetables and an inspired and inventive chef could not fail to produce something special, which is light years from culinary tradition! Get ready to enjoy surprising, attractively presented dishes with contrasting flavours, washed down with equally intriguing cocktails – under the watchful eyes of the angels on the ceiling.

Menu 39€ (lunch), 37/66€

PLAN: 2-F2 – *rue de Vergnies 2 – ✆ 0474 65 37 06 – www.humushortense.be – Closed 3-10 February, 11-18 May, 1-22 September, Monday, lunch Tuesday-Thursday, Sunday*

Isabelle Arpin

MODERN CUISINE • CONTEMPORARY DÉCOR Talented Isabelle Arpin is renowned for her colourful, painstaking creations. Her elegant combinations of sweet, savoury and spicy flavours are equally acclaimed, leading to an international menu with a focus on texture. The contemporary, minimalist interior of her spacious Brussels establishment further enhances the quality of the food.

Menu 32€ (lunch), 55/110€ – Carte 32/110€

PLAN: 2-F2 – *avenue Louise 362 – ✆ 0492 97 19 27 – www.isabellearpin.com – Closed 21 July-20 August, Monday, lunch Saturday, Sunday*

Nonbe Daigaku

JAPANESE • MINIMALIST If you like eating Japanese, you shouldn't miss this modest venue. The very experienced chef has mastered the subtlety and nuances that are typical of the cuisine of his home country. You can see him at work behind the sushi bar, driven and precise, creating a delicious variety of flavours and textures.

Menu 20€ (lunch)/35€ - Carte 45/123€

PLAN: 1-C3 - *avenue Adolphe Buyl 31 - ✆ 02 649 21 49 - Closed Monday, Sunday*

Odette en Ville

CREATIVE FRENCH • TRENDY Odette is depicted by an ultra-trendy interior set in a handsome townhouse. Add to this a contemporary restaurant and luxurious guestrooms. The establishment is in the heart of a fashionable district, which has rubbed off onto the menu of tasty, international dishes.

Menu 35€ (lunch) - Carte 40/78€

PLAN: 2-E2 - *rue du Châtelain 25 - ✆ 02 640 26 26 - www.odetteenville.be - Closed 24-25 December, 29 December-6 January, lunch Saturday-Sunday*

Old Boy

ASIAN • BISTRO 'Fusion' cuisine poised between Belgian ingredients, Thai spices and Chinese intensity, combined with panache and flair. For example, the excellent bao of slightly spicy braised pork. A word of advice: turn up early as the restaurant does not accept bookings.

Menu 14€ (lunch) - Carte 20/45€

PLAN: 2-E3 - *rue de Tenbosch 110 - ✆ 02 544 15 55 - www.oldboyrestaurant.be - Closed lunch Monday, Sunday*

Philema 

GREEK • FRIENDLY In this charming sunny bistro, sample genuine Greek fare, light years from the usual hackneyed clichés. You can expect fresh Mediterranean dishes thanks to top-notch ingredients (that you can also purchase from the shop). For example, the delicious cream vinaigrette, both delicate and powerful!

Carte 35/60€

PLAN: 2-E3 - *chaussée de Waterloo 437 - ✆ 02 344 58 76 - www.philemabrussels.be - Closed 11-31 August, 23 December-2 January, Monday, dinner Sunday*

La Quincaillerie 

CLASSIC CUISINE • BRASSERIE This brasserie and oyster bar is an institution in the town. Housed in a former hardware store (1903), its Art nouveau décor is worth a visit in its own right. The interior, dotted with period chests of drawers and shelves, is ideal to sample delicious Franco-Belgian classics.

Menu 20€ (lunch)/58€ - Carte 40/85€

PLAN: 2-E2 - *rue du Page 45 - ✆ 02 533 98 33 - www.quincaillerie.be - Closed lunch Saturday-Sunday*

Racines 

ITALIAN • TRATTORIA Francesco and Ugo are proud of their Italian heritage. One of them pulls up a chair to walk you through the menu, rich in delicious specialties from their homeland, prepared creatively and masterfully. Organic and biodynamic wines figure prominently on the wine list, which is definitely worth a close look.

Menu 36€ (lunch), 60/84€ - Carte 46/80€

PLAN: 2-F2 - *chaussée d'Ixelles 353 - ✆ 02 642 95 90 - www.racinesbruxelles.com - Closed 25 July-16 August, lunch Saturday, Sunday*

Ricciocapriccio 

ITALIAN • BISTRO A delightful Italian-inspired ristorante tucked away in the Châtelain district. The slate menu features an enticing array of Italian delicacies, subtly reworked by the chef. The house speciality is seafood (including sea urchins and squid), rich in enticing Mediterranean flavours.

Menu 75€ - Carte 42/64€

PLAN: 2-E2 - *rue Américaine 90 - ✆ 02 852 39 69 - www.ricciocapriccio.be - Closed lunch Saturday*

Toucan sur Mer

SEAFOOD • BISTRO The impeccable quality and freshness of the fish and shellfish of the Toucan sur Mer are more than comparable with seafood restaurants on the coast. This pleasant bistro will certainly appeal to seafood lovers.

Carte 46/62 €

PLAN: 2-E3 – *avenue Louis Lepoutre 17 – ✆ 02 340 07 40 – www.toucanbrasserie.com*

Le Tournant

MARKET CUISINE • BISTRO The chef of this neighbourhood restaurant was a movie producer in a former life and his cinematographic flair is clearly visible in the restaurant's friendly interior. The stage is set for a varied wine list and authentic bistro fare that will suit all tastes. The slow cooked meat dishes are, however, what top the bill.

Menu 24 € (lunch), 35/39 € – Carte 39/55 €

PLAN: 2-F1 – *chaussée de Wavre 168 – ✆ 02 502 61 65 – www.restaurantletournant.com – Closed 22 June-9 August, Monday, lunch Tuesday-Wednesday, lunch Saturday, Sunday*

Jette

Wine in the City (Eddy Münster)

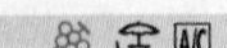

CREATIVE • WINE BAR Wine in the City is more than a wine merchant, it is also a fine restaurant and a tapas bar (only on Sunday) with a relaxed terrace on the Place du Miroir. Chef Eddy Münster lets his creativity run free, concocting dishes whose flavours take you from West to East on a whirlwind of inventive, intense pairings. It is even possible to take a bottle of the delicious wines available home with you.

Specialities: Scampi and chorizo ravioli, crab consommé and marinated spring onion. Century egg "inspiration" with a truffle mousseline. Cocoa biscuit with white and black ganache, blood orange cream and cocoa sorbet.

Menu 45 € (lunch), 80/100 €

PLAN: 1-B2 – *place Reine Astrid 34 – ✆ 02 420 09 20 – www.wineinthecity.be – Closed 1-5 January, Monday, Tuesday, dinner Wednesday-Thursday, lunch Saturday, Sunday*

French Kiss

MEATS AND GRILLS • FRIENDLY A pleasant restaurant renowned for its excellent grilled dishes and impressive wine list. Dining area with a low ceiling and bright paintings adding colour to the brick walls.

Menu 29 € (lunch)/37 € – Carte 38/56 €

PLAN: 1-B2 – *rue Léopold I 470 – ✆ 02 425 22 93 – www.restaurantfrenchkiss.com – Closed 27 July-6 August, 24 December-2 January, Monday*

Saint-Gilles

La Charcuterie

SHARING • BISTRO The vintage charm of this former butcher's with its tiles and wood panelling is enhanced by a friendly vibe. Walk past the delicatessen counter to the tiny bistro. Premium produce, with a special focus on charcuterie. Authentic fare, washed down with fine wines.

Carte 30/50 €

PLAN: 1-B3 – *avenue Paul Dejaer 16 – ✆ 02 850 88 12 – www.lacharcuterie.be – Closed Tuesday, Sunday*

Tero

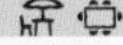

ORGANIC • FRIENDLY Sustainability and respect for the product come first at Tero. The vegetables, aromatic herbs and even the pigs and cows come from their farm. The chefs delicately craft clean, light, veg-centric cuisine, whose generous flavours hit the spot every time. All in a pleasing natural setting.

Menu 16 € (lunch)/45 € – Carte 30/65 €

PLAN: 2-E2 – *rue Saint Bernard 1 – ✆ 02 347 79 46 – www.tero-restaurant.com – Closed 22 December-2 January, Sunday*

La Buvette

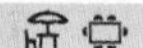

MODERN CUISINE • BISTRO This simply appointed restaurant, formerly a butcher's shop, has foregone starched tablecloths and plush armchairs for vintage formica furniture. Who cares though – what counts is what is on the plate! Good food lovers will appreciate the flavoursome cuisine in touch with contemporary tastes in this modern-day 'watering hole'.

Menu 44/64€

PLAN: 1-B3 – *chaussée d'Alsemberg 108* – *✆ 02 534 13 03* – *www.la-buvette.be* – *Closed Monday, lunch Tuesday-Saturday, Sunday*

Colonel

MEATS AND GRILLS • BRASSERIE Generous cuts of meat greet you as you enter this brasserie, making the house speciality blatantly clear. The quality of the charcuterie, perfectly cooked red meat, french fries and delicious sauces are quite stunning. A paradise for carnivores!

Carte 48/75€

PLAN: 2-E1 – *rue Jean Stas 24* – *✆ 02 538 57 36* – *www.colonelbrussels.com* – *Closed 1-24 August, Monday, Sunday*

Dolce Amaro

ITALIAN • TRENDY In only a few years, the enterprising Dolce Amaro has become a blue-chip value. This is hardly surprising when you taste the characterful Italian cuisine, rich in authentic flavour. If only we could eat here every day!

Menu 17€ (lunch) – Carte 49/58€

PLAN: 2-E2 – *chaussée de Charleroi 115* – *✆ 02 538 17 00* – *www.dolceamaro.be* – *Closed lunch Saturday, Sunday*

I Trulli

ITALIAN • FRIENDLY This handsome, revamped restaurant, reminiscent of southern Italy, has stood in the heart of Saint Gilles since 1986! A blue-chip value on the culinary scene, it is depicted by fine ingredients, flawless know-how and a fantastic wine list. The antipasti buffet is irresistible.

Carte 48/81€

PLAN: 2-E1 – *rue Jourdan 18* – *✆ 02 537 79 30* – *Closed Monday, Sunday*

Mamy Louise

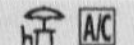

CLASSIC CUISINE • BRASSERIE In a pedestrian street, this pleasant tavern style restaurant provides a varied menu, including traditional bistro style meals, salads, sandwiches and daily specials. In the afternoon, Mamy Louise is a tea-room.

Carte 42/59€

PLAN: 2-E1 – *rue Jean Stas 12* – *✆ 02 534 25 02* – *www.mamylouise.be* – *Closed dinner Monday-Saturday, Sunday*

Toshiro

ASIAN • MINIMALIST Toshiro is an ode to purity, be it in the tasteful interior or in chef Fujii's cuisine. After many years as Sang-Hoon Degeimbre's right-hand man, the chef is now nurturing his own Japanese roots, subtly and precisely combining his sensitivity with French influences. The result is delicate and creative, light yet rich in flavour.

Menu 35€ (lunch), 70/90€

PLAN: 1-B3 – *rue de la Source 73* – *✆ 02 245 09 55* – *www.toshiro.be* – *Closed Monday, Sunday*

Strombeek-Bever

't Stoveke (Daniel Antuna)

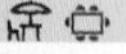

MODERN CUISINE • COSY The chef of 't Stoveke follows in the footsteps of some of the best-known chefs in the world, but has added his own personal touch. This has ensured that his cuisine remains resolutely up to date. The dishes reveal an explosion of flavours that are as much a delight to the eye as to the palate.

Specialities: A blend of North Sea crab and langoustine with kohlrabi and a dashi and soy jus. Turbot with pointed cabbage, leek marinade and mousseline sauce. Chocolate and pear with linden and acacia ice cream.

Menu 36 € (lunch), 67/85 € – Carte 80/130 €

PLAN: 1-B1 – *Jetsestraat 52 – ✆ 02 267 67 25 – www.tstoveke.be – Closed 27 July-15 August, 23 December-4 January, Tuesday, Wednesday, lunch Saturday, dinner Sunday*

Uccle

✿✿ Le Chalet de la Forêt (Pascal Devalkeneer)

CREATIVE • ELEGANT This chalet with its lovely terrace, set on the edge of the Sonian Forest, combines elegance and sophistication. The food has a certain cachet, with its consummate combinations of classicism and creativity, finesse and generosity. Intense sensations are guaranteed.

Specialities: "Regis Borde" oyster tartare with Ossetra caviar and broccoli flower parmentier. Ardennes venison finished over a wood fire, autumn fruits and vegetables, juniper and lemon. Honey from our own hives, farm yoghurt and a lemon-honey gel.

Menu 78 € (lunch), 175/235 € – Carte 148/198 €

Off plan – *drêve de Lorraine 43 – ✆ 02 374 54 16 – www.lechaletdelaforet.be – Closed 21 December-6 January, Saturday, Sunday*

✿ Le Pigeon Noir (Henri De Mol)

COUNTRY COOKING • BISTRO The house has a modest appearance, along the lines of a small local bar, but you can expect to find well-prepared traditional cuisine at reasonable prices! Pavement terrace.

Specialities: "Chef Basso's" langoustine ravioli. Young pigeon salmis with sage. Crémèt de Beersel.

Menu 32 € (lunch) – Carte 42/76 €

Off plan – *rue Geleytsbeek 2 – ✆ 02 375 23 74 – www.lepigeonnoir.be – Closed 1-5 January, 20 July-9 August, Saturday, Sunday*

✿ La Villa Lorraine

CREATIVE • ELEGANT Since 1953, this grande dame of the Brussels gastronomic scene has been a popular meeting place for gourmets. The grand, luxurious interior commands respect, as does the cooking. Classical dishes come with modern touches and are packed with flavour. There's also a charming terrace for warmer days.

Specialities: Crab with broccoli, wakame and green apples. Turbot with white asparagus, morel mushrooms and a truffle sabayon. Chocolate praline, vanilla and roasted pecan nuts.

Menu 56 € (lunch), 85/165 € – Carte 99/155 €

PLAN: 1-C3 – *avenue du Vivier d'Oie 75 – ✆ 02 374 31 63 – www.villalorraine.be – Closed 1-6 January, Monday, Sunday*

La Brasserie de la Villa – See restaurant listing

La Branche d'Olivier

CLASSIC CUISINE • BISTRO Typical old bistro given a new lease of life in 2004 (old tiling, beams, patinated wood) in a residential area. Friendly atmosphere, market-fresh cuisine, pavement terrace.

Menu 17 € (lunch)/36 € – Carte 38/71 €

Off plan – *rue Engeland 172 – ✆ 02 374 47 05 – www.labranchedolivier.be – Closed lunch Saturday, Sunday*

La Brasserie de la Villa

CLASSIC CUISINE • ELEGANT The little sister of the Villa Lorraine where you can soak up the atmosphere of that prestigious establishment at more affordable prices. Classic brasserie dishes and appetising light meals.

Menu 37 € – Carte 44/74 €

PLAN: 1-C3 – *La Villa Lorraine, avenue du Vivier d'Oie 75 – ✆ 02 374 31 63 – www.villalorraine.be – Closed 1-6 January, Sunday*

Bois Savanes Saint Job

THAI • TRENDY The smart, designer inspired Bois Savanes has been popular since 1984. The move to the up-and-coming Saint Job district has breathed a new lease of life into the business. The first generation has passed their chef's hat and distinctive Thai recipes down to their children, who add a contemporary spin to their heritage.

Menu 13€ (lunch)/30€ - Carte 30/38€

PLAN: 1-B3 - *place de Saint-Job 24 - ✆ 02 358 37 78 - www.boissavanes.be - Closed 21 July-20 August, 31 December-5 January, Monday, lunch Saturday*

Brinz'l

MODERN FRENCH • CONTEMPORARY DÉCOR While Brinzelle (Creole for aubergine) may evoke the chef's Mauritian roots, her cuisine is nonetheless firmly French! After learning her trade in several Starred restaurants, she now excels in flavoursome, carefully assembled meals that, above all, seek to enhance the quality of the ingredients.

Menu 65/95€ - Carte 49/95€

PLAN: 1-B3 - *rue des Carmélites 93 - ✆ 02 218 23 32 - www.brinzl.be - Closed 30 December-2 January, Monday, lunch Tuesday-Wednesday, lunch Saturday-Sunday*

Les Papilles

TRADITIONAL CUISINE • WINE BAR Your taste buds will definitely start tingling when you enter this delightful establishment with a terrace to the rear. It specialises in generous French classics, using quality produce. Before sitting down for your meal, pick yourself a bottle of wine directly from the shelves. Friendly and relaxed.

Menu 22€ (lunch)/39€ - Carte 41/62€

PLAN: 1-B3 - *chaussée de Waterloo 782 - ✆ 02 374 69 66 - www.lespapilles.mobi - Closed 1-2 January, 1-2 May, 15-16 July, 24-25 December, Monday, Sunday*

Le Passage

CLASSIC CUISINE • COSY This establishment and its lunchtime set menu are a favourite with the locals, such is chef Rocky Renaud's reputation for creativity and flair, mingling tradition with modernity. Distinctive food with bold international accents!

Menu 35€ (lunch), 55/75€ - Carte 35/80€

PLAN: 1-B3 - *avenue Jean et Pierre Carsoel 17 - ✆ 02 374 66 94 - www.lepassage.be - Closed 18 July-1 August, Monday, lunch Saturday, Sunday*

Watermael-Boitsfort

Au Grand Forestier

BELGIAN • CONTEMPORARY DÉCOR Pure luxury is essentially a question of detail, as this delightful brasserie so admirably illustrates! A flawless welcome and personalised service set the scene to make you feel at home. The same attention to detail can be tasted in the immaculately cooked meat, served with delicious sauces - a princely treat for your taste buds!

Carte 42/60€

PLAN: 1-C3 - *avenue du Grand Forestier 2 - ✆ 02 672 57 79 - www.augrandforestier.be*

Wemmel

L'Auberge de l'Isard

CLASSIC FRENCH • FRIENDLY To escape the bustle of Heysel and Brussels' ring road, head for the elegant villa of Roland Taildeman, who opened his restaurant in 1989. Guests are particularly taken with the extensive set menu. There is a wide and varied choice with one constant byword - taste.

Menu 30€ (lunch), 37/60€ - Carte 46/65€

PLAN: 1-B1 - *Romeinsesteenweg 964 - ✆ 02 479 85 64 - www.isard.be - Closed Monday, Tuesday, dinner Sunday*

La table d'Evan

MEDITERRANEAN CUISINE • BRASSERIE Chef Evan's restaurant is modern, comfortable and free of unnecessary frills. On a constant quest for fine produce, he deploys his talent and experience to create delicious dishes. 'Quality before all else' is his motto – much to the delight of our taste buds!

Menu 35€ (lunch), 55/110€ – Carte 70/100€

PLAN: 1-A1 – *Brusselsesteenweg 21 – ✆ 02 460 52 39 – www.evanrestaurants.be – Closed 13-19 April, 18 July-3 August, 21 December-6 January, Saturday, Sunday*

Woluwe-Saint-Lambert

Da Mimmo

ITALIAN • COSY As soon as you venture over the threshold of this elegant restaurant and meet the charismatic chef, you know you are in good hands! The chef subtly combines top-notch ingredients into dishes rich in southern aromas. Delicate, yet unsophisticated Italian dishes, steeped in authenticity and flanked by an excellent wine list!

Specialities: Octopus cooked two ways with petits pois, burrata, mint and basil. Tagliolini with black truffle. Arabica mousse, caramel ice cream, muscovado and a whisky sauce.

Menu 52€ (lunch), 85/115€ – Carte 58/108€

PLAN: 1-C2 – *avenue du Roi Chevalier 24 – ✆ 02 771 58 60 – www.da-mimmo.be – Closed 5-13 April, 2-17 August, 1-9 November, 29 December-6 January, Monday, Sunday*

De Maurice à Olivier

CLASSIC CUISINE • VINTAGE Maurice, the father, has passed the business onto his son Olivier. He has also bequeathed a rich culinary heritage of French cuisine enriched in Mediterranean influences; the dishes are beautifully presented. Amusingly, the restaurant is also a newsagents.

Menu 55€ – Carte 40/62€

PLAN: 1-C2 – *chaussée de Roodebeek 246 – ✆ 02 771 33 98 – www.demauriceaolivier.be – Closed 8-24 April, 22 July-22 August, dinner Monday, Sunday*

Al Piccolo

ITALIAN • FRIENDLY A couple have harnessed their years of experience into creating this inviting restaurant. The care with which they rustle up authentic Italian dishes can be tasted in each morsel. Never over-the-top, they seek to enhance generous traditional flavours. Excellent wine list.

Menu 45/65€ – Carte 40/100€

PLAN: 1-C2 – *rue Voot 20 – ✆ 02 770 05 55 – www.alpiccolo.net – Closed Monday, lunch Saturday, Sunday*

Le Nénuphar

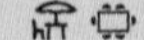

VIETNAMESE • NEIGHBOURHOOD A tastefully decorated, neighbourhood Vietnamese restaurant, in which culinary techniques are passed down from father to son. Updated, traditional dishes, with fish taking pride of place. Ideal to dig into yummy Asian cuisine.

Menu 16€ (lunch), 30/36€ – Carte 38/49€

PLAN: 1-C2 – *chaussée de Roodebeek 76 – ✆ 02 770 08 88 – www.lenenuphar.be – Closed 15 August-15 September, 24 December-1 January, Monday, lunch Saturday, dinner Sunday*

Woluwe-Saint-Pierre

bon bon (Christophe Hardiquest)

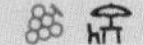

CREATIVE • ELEGANT Christophe Hardiquest invites you on an adventure. A quest for culinary harmony, first-class ingredients, inventive recipes and rich flavours... this is a chef who combines flair with subtlety. Take a seat in the elegant, contemporary interior and order with complete confidence.

Specialities: Langoustine with a tea and lemon emulsion. Pigeon "à la liégeoise". "Chez Humberto" iced soufflé with citrus fruit.

Menu 75€ (lunch), 185/245€ - Carte 140/245€

PLAN: 1-D3 - *av. de Tervueren 453 - ✆ 02 346 66 15 - www.restaurant-bon-bon.be - Closed 6-20 April, 20 July-10 August, 23 December-6 January, Monday, Saturday, Sunday*

Les Deux Maisons

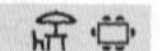

CLASSIC FRENCH • CLASSIC DÉCOR Two houses have merged to create this elegant restaurant, where a classically trained chef rustles up tempting dishes using excellent ingredients. The 'Tradition' menu with its luscious selection of desserts is highly recommended. There's also a fine wine cellar.

Menu 21€ (lunch), 37/65€ - Carte 53/84€

PLAN: 1-D2 - *Val des Seigneurs 81 - ✆ 02 771 14 47 - www.deuxmaisons.be - Closed 5-13 April, 2-25 August, 22 December-2 January, Monday, Sunday*

Le Mucha

CLASSIC CUISINE • NEIGHBOURHOOD The interior of Le Mucha is reminiscent of Parisian brasseries in the 1900s. It's an ideal place to sample traditional French cuisine from a fine choice of classical dishes, without forgetting a few Italian favourites.

Menu 19€ (lunch), 37/50€ - Carte 40/65€

PLAN: 1-D3 - *avenue Jules Du Jardin 23 - ✆ 02 770 24 14 - www.lemucha.be - Closed 2-6 January, 24 August-7 September, Monday, dinner Sunday*

l'Auberg'in

MEATS AND GRILLS • RUSTIC You may be surprised to see this little farmhouse right in the centre of town! In the friendly, rustic interior, the chef grills the meat over the open fire. Traditional fare full of flavour, as warming and wholesome as the atmosphere.

Menu 44€ - Carte 49/55€

PLAN: 1-D2 - *rue au Bois 198 - ✆ 02 770 68 85 - www.laubergin.be - Closed lunch Saturday, Sunday*

Sanzaru

PERUVIAN • TRENDY Behind the Art nouveau façade, you will discover an engaging restaurant adorned with colourful murals, waiting to whisk you off on a journey of discovery. Japanese and Peruvian cooking, better known under the name of Nikkei cuisine. A whirlwind of fascinating flavours not to be missed, like the cocktail bar upstairs.

Menu 25€ (lunch)/55€ - Carte 50/75€

PLAN: 1-C2 - *avenue de Tervueren 292 - ✆ 02 773 00 80 - www.sanzaru.be - Closed 23 December-1 January, Monday, lunch Saturday, Sunday*

littleclie/iStock

ANTWERP
ANTWERPEN

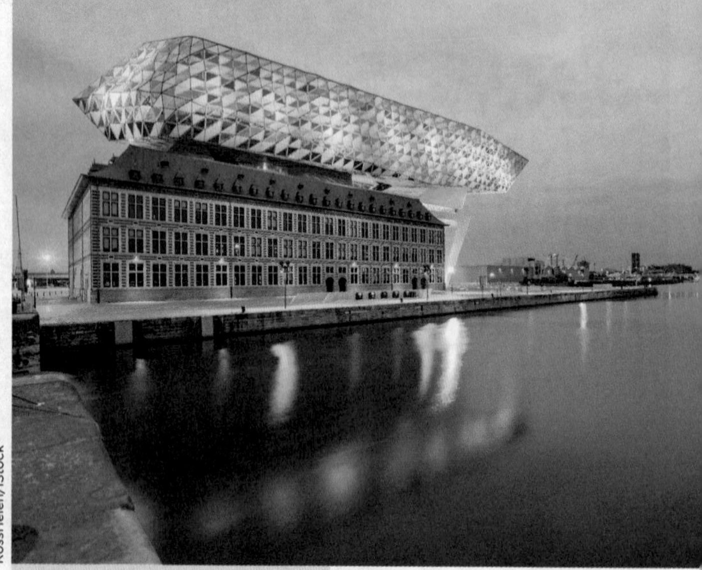

RossHelen/iStock

ANTWERP IN...

→ **ONE DAY**
Grote Markt, Our Lady's Cathedral, MoMu, Het Zuid.

→ **TWO DAYS**
Rubens' House, Royal Museum of Fine Arts, a stroll to the Left Bank via the Sint-Anna tunnel.

→ **THREE DAYS**
Het Eilandje and MAS, a river trip, Kloosterstraat, Nationalestraat.

Antwerp calls itself the pocketsize metropolis, and with good reason. Although it's Europe's second largest port, it still retains a compact intimacy, defined by bustling squares and narrow streets. It's a place with many facets, not least its marked link to Rubens, the diamond trade and, in later years, the fashion collective The Antwerp Six. The city's centre teems with ornate gabled guildhouses, and in summer, open-air cafés line the area beneath the towering cathedral, giving the place a festive, almost bohemian air. It's a fantastic place to shop: besides clothing boutiques, there are antiques emporiums and diamond stores – to say

nothing of the chocolate shops with their appealing window displays. Bold regeneration projects have transformed the skyline and the waterfront's decrepit warehouses have started new lives as ritzy storerooms of 21C commerce. The nightlife here is the best in Belgium, while the beer is savoured the way others might treat a vintage wine. The Old Town is defined by Grote Markt, Groenplaats and The Meir shopping street – these are a kind of dividing line between Antwerp's north and south. North of the centre is Het Eilandje, the hip former warehouse area; to the east is the Diamond District. Antique and bric-a-brac shops are in abundance in the 'designer heart' Het Zuid, south of the centre, which is also home to the best museums and art galleries.

EATING OUT

The menus of Flanders are heavily influenced by the lush meadows, the canals swarming with eels and the proximity of the North Sea – but the eating culture in Antwerp offers more than just seafood. With its centuries old connection to more exotic climes, there's no shortage of fragrant spices such as cinnamon in their dishes, especially in the rich stews so beloved by the locals. If you want to eat with the chic, hang around the Het Eilandje dockside or the rejuvenated ancient warehouses south of Grote Markt. For early risers, the grand cafés are a popular port of call, ideal for a slow coffee and a trawl through the papers. Overall the city boasts the same tempting Belgian specialities as Brussels (stewed eel in chervil sauce; mussels; dishes containing rabbit; beef stew and chicory), but also with a focus on more contemporary cuisine. Don't miss out on the local chocolate (shaped like a hand in keeping with the legend which gave Antwerp its name), and be sure to try their De Koninck beer, served in a glass designed like an open bowl.

✿✿ The Jane (Nick Bril)

CREATIVE • TRENDY This striking chapel, now a trend-setting temple, is unique in Belgium! Chef Nick Bril can be relied upon to introduce diners to mind-blowing flavours. His food is both sophisticated and simple, steeped in powerful flavours and yet amazingly harmonious. The Upper Room Bar serves cocktails.

Specialities: Carabiñero with quinoa, tomato and vadouvan. Turbot and lobster with spinach, buttermilk and a foamy bisque. Burrata with strawberries, cellina di nardò olives.

Menu 170€

PLAN: 3-H1 – *Paradeplein 1 – ✆ 03 808 44 65 – www.thejaneantwerp.com – Closed Monday, lunch Tuesday-Thursday, Sunday*

✿✿ 't Zilte (Viki Geunes)

CREATIVE • DESIGN Savour the view of Antwerp at your feet while you sample sophisticated dishes, as 't Zilte is wonderfully located on the top floor of the Museum Aan de Stroom. Viki Geunes' joyful cooking is depicted by diverse textures and flavours, a whirlwind of international ingredients and desserts of which the chef is particularly proud.

Specialities: Eastern Scheldt lobster with celeriac, kumquat, miso and hazelnut. Carré of lamb with artichoke, courgette tempura and home-made dumpling. Goat's yoghurt with sorrel, pineapple and a cedrat sorbet.

Menu 68€ (lunch), 135/185€ – Carte 138/191€

PLAN: 1-B1 – *Hanzestedenplaats 5 – ✆ 03 283 40 40 – www.tzilte.be – Closed 13-19 April, 2-8 November, 21 December-3 January, Saturday, Sunday*

✿ Bij Lam & Yin (Lap Yee Lam)

CHINESE • MINIMALIST Bij Lam & Yin is definitely not a run-of-the-mill Asian restaurant. Don't expect paper lanterns or a menu as long as the Great Wall of China! This is the place for delicate, subtle Cantonese cuisine, depicted by fresh, original flavours and a quest for authenticity before all else. Genuine saké is served in the Gang Bei.

Specialities: Dim sum served in a steamer basket. Steamed sea bass with ginger and spring onion. Baked lamb with Szechuan pepper.

Carte 55/77€

PLAN: 2-D2 – *Reynderstraat 17 – ✆ 03 232 88 38 – www.lam-en-yin.be – Closed 30 March-15 April, Monday, Tuesday, Wednesday, lunch Thursday-Sunday*

✿ Bistrot du Nord (Michaël Rewers)

TRADITIONAL CUISINE • BOURGEOIS A lesson in tradition! The chef, an authentic craftsman, knows how to get the best out of fine produce. He admits to a weakness for tripe, but diners need have no fears - whatever your choice, your taste buds will be delighted.

Specialities: Croquettes of hand-peeled Ostend shrimps. Baked sweetbread and grilled veal kidney with salsify and truffle. Glazed rhubarb with almond crumble and vanilla ice cream.

Carte 51/145€

PLAN: 1-B1 – *Lange Dijkstraat 36 – ✆ 03 233 45 49 – www.bistrotdunord.be – Closed 1-5 January, 18 July-16 August, Wednesday, Saturday, Sunday*

✿ The Butcher's son (Bert Jan Michielsen)

TRADITIONAL CUISINE • TRENDY The former De Koninck brewery is the perfect blend of smart, urban design. Red meat showcased like artwork in display cabinets reminds the visitor that meat is the star of the show here; it is traditionally prepared by the chef and served with delicious side dishes. Balanced flavours come above all else at The Butcher's son.

Specialities: Calf's head served warm with tartare sauce and brain. Filet pur à la villette with an oxtail jus. Carré confiture with fig, blackberries and sour cream.

Carte 54/84€

PLAN: 3-H1 – *Boomgaardstraat 1 – ✆ 03 230 16 38 – www.thebutchersson.be – Closed 18-26 July, 21 December-2 January, Saturday, Sunday*

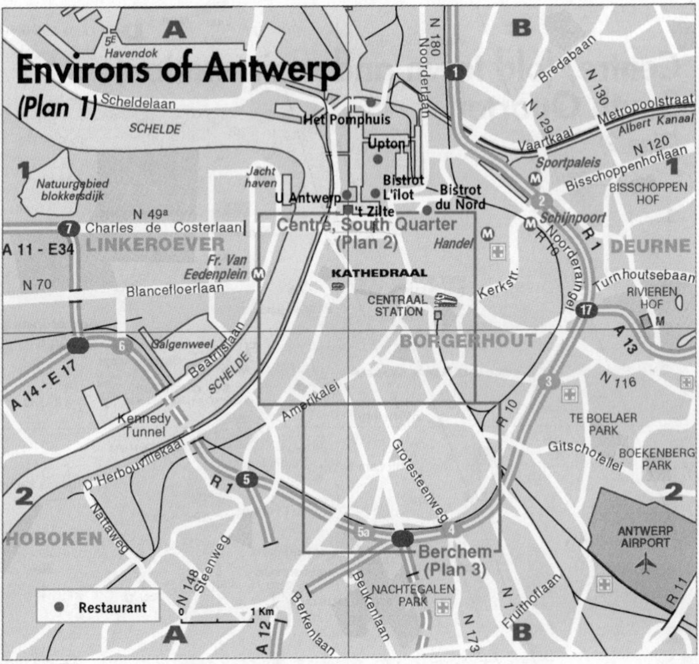

Environs of Antwerp (Plan 1)

✿ Dôme (Frédéric Chabbert)

CLASSIC FRENCH • **ELEGANT** The memory of a meal beneath the dome of this elegant restaurant will linger long after the last bite! The experienced chef, Frédéric Chabbert (who learned the trade in Hong Kong among others), will treat you to fine, classical fare using techniques that have fallen by the wayside. Top quality produce and rich flavours define the Dôme.

Specialities: Millefeuille of beetroot, marinated and fermented strawberry and smoked eel. Binchotan charcoal-grilled turbot with a blanquette of green vegetables and algae. Chocolate cake with hazelnut praline and sea salt.

Menu 45€ (lunch), 88/100€ – Carte 90/105€

PLAN: 2-F3 – *Grote Hondstraat 2 – ✆ 03 239 90 03 – www.domeantwerp.be – Closed 5-13 April, 30 August-14 September, 22 December-6 January, Monday, Sunday*

✿ ’t Fornuis (Johan Segers)

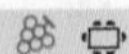

CLASSIC CUISINE • **ROMANTIC** ’t Fornuis is a restaurant that has become rare nowadays. The interior of this pretty townhouse is rustic and authentic; the service is as in the old days. In the kitchen stands a craftsman that has held a Michelin star since 1986: Johan Segers. He returns to the roots of Belgian gastronomy and gives his guests a deliciously nostalgic feel.

Specialities: Cassoulet of lobster, pig’s trotter and white beans. Wild duck with braised endive, Brussels sprouts and potato mousseline. Café frappé maison.

Carte 75/125€

PLAN: 2-D2 – *Reyndersstraat 24 – ✆ 03 233 62 70 – Closed 13-19 April, 13 July-16 August, 23 December-5 January, Saturday, Sunday*

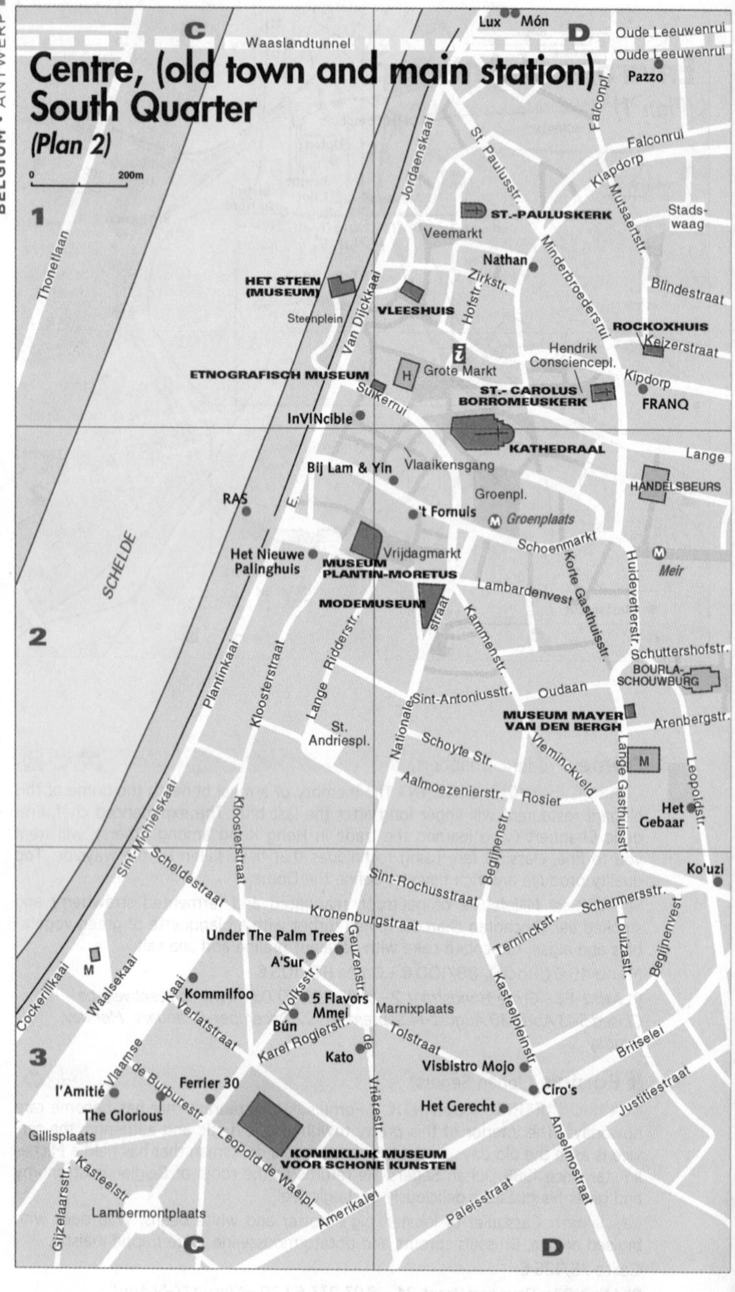
Centre, (old town and main station) South Quarter
(Plan 2)
0
200m
C
D
1
2
3
Waaslandtunnel
Lux
Món
Oude Leeuwenrui
Pazzo
Falconpl.
Falconrui
Klapdorp
Mutsaertstr.
Stads-waag
St. Paulusstr.
Jordaenskaai
ST.-PAULUSKERK
Veemarkt
Nathan
Minderbroedersrui
Blindestraat
Zirkstr.
Hofstr.
HET STEEN (MUSEUM)
VLEESHUIS
Steenplein
Van Dijckkaai
Thonetlaan
ROCKOXHUIS
Keizerstraat
Hendrik Consciencepl.
Grote Markt
ETNOGRAFISCH MUSEUM
Suikerrui
Kipdorp
ST.- CAROLUS BORROMEUSKERK
FRANQ
InVINcible
KATHEDRAAL
Lange
Bij Lam & Yin
Vlaaikensgang
HANDELSBEURS
Groenpl.
RAS
't Fornuis
Groenplaats
Schoenmarkt
Het Nieuwe Palinghuis
Vrijdagmarkt
MUSEUM PLANTIN-MORETUS
Meir
Huidevettersstr.
Korte Gasthuisstr.
Lambardenvest
SCHELDE
MODEMUSEUM
straat
Kammenstr.
Lange Riddersstr.
Kloosterstraat
Plantinkaai
Schuttershofstr.
BOURLA-SCHOUWBURG
Sint-Antoniusstr.
Oudaan
MUSEUM MAYER VAN DEN BERGH
Arenbergstr.
St. Andriespl.
Nationale
Schoyte Str.
Vleminckveld
Lange Gasthuisstr.
M
Leopoldstr.
Aalmoezenierstr.
Rosier
Het Gebaar
Sint-Michielskaai
Kloosterstraat
Begijnenstr.
Scheldestraat
Ko'uzi
Sint-Rochusstraat
Schermersstr.
Kronenburgstraat
Terninckstr.
Louizastr.
Begijnenvest
Under The Palm Trees
Geuzenstr.
A'Sur
M
Cockerillkaai
Waalsekaai
Kaai
Kommilfoo
Verlatstraat
Volksstr.
5 Flavors
Mmei
Marnixplaats
Bún
Karel Rogierstr.
Tolstraat
Kasteelpleinstr.
Britselei
Kato
de Vriêrestr.
Visbistro Mojo
Vlaamse
de Burburestr.
Ferrier 30
Ciro's
Justitiestraat
l'Amitié
The Glorious
Het Gerecht
Gillisplaats
Leopold de Waelpl.
KONINKLIJK MUSEUM VOOR SCHONE KUNSTEN
Anselmostraat
Kasteelstr.
Gijzelaarsstr.
Lambermontplaats
Amerikalei
Paleisstraat

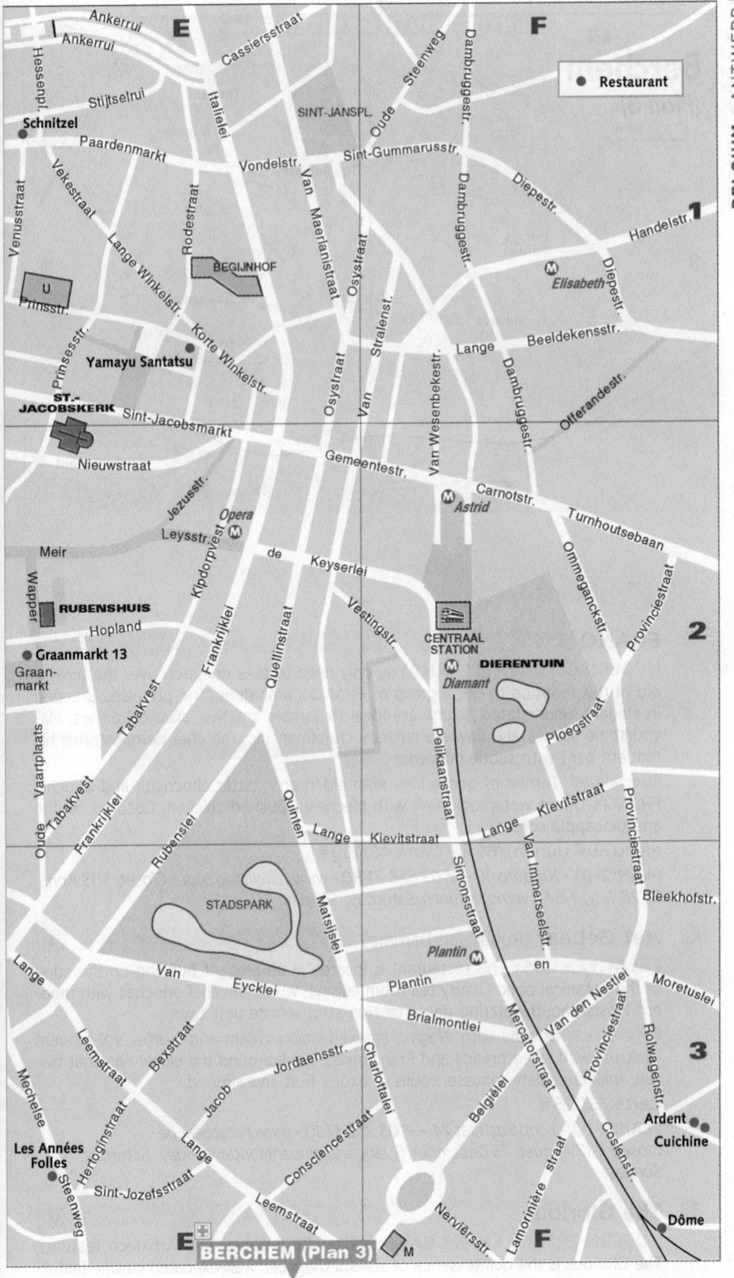
E
F
1
2
3
Restaurant
Ankerrui
Cassiersstraat
Hessenpl.
Stijfselrui
Italielei
SINT-JANSPL.
Oude
Steenweg
Dambruggestr.
Schnitzel
Paardenmarkt
Vondelstr.
Sint-Gummarusstr.
Diepestr.
Handelstr.
Vekestraat
Venusstraat
Rodestraat
Van
Maerlanistraat
Osystraat
BEGIJNHOF
Lange Winkelstr.
Elisabeth
U
Prinsstr.
Stralenst.
Lange
Beeldekensstr.
Korte Winkelstr.
Yamayu Santatsu
Prinsesstr.
Van Wesenbekestr.
Offerandestr.
ST.-
JACOBSKERK
Sint-Jacobsmarkt
Nieuwstraat
Gemeentestr.
Carnotstr.
Astrid
Turnhoutsebaan
Jezusstr.
Opera
Leysstr.
Meir
de
Keyserlei
Kipdorpvest
Ommeganckstr.
Provinciestraat
Wapper
RUBENSHUIS
Vestingstr.
Hopland
Frankrijklei
Quellinstraat
CENTRAAL
STATION
Graanmarkt 13
Graan-
markt
DIERENTUIN
Diamant
Tabakvest
Pelikaanstraat
Ploegstraat
Vaartplaats
Oude
Tabakvest
Quinten
Matsijslei
Lange
Kievitstraat
Rubenslei
Simonsstraat
Van Immerseelstr.
Bleekhofstr.
STADSPARK
Plantin
en
Moretuslei
Van
Eycklei
Van den Nestlei
Brialmontlei
Mercatorstraat
Rolwagenstr.
Leemstraat
Bexstraat
Jordaensstr.
Charlottalei
Mechelse
Jacob
Belgiëlei
Ardent
Cuichine
Hertoginstraat
Consciencestraat
Coslenstr.
Les Années
Folles
Steenweg
Sint-Jozefsstraat
Leemstraat
Nerviërsstr.
Lamorinière
straat
Dôme
BERCHEM (Plan 3)
M

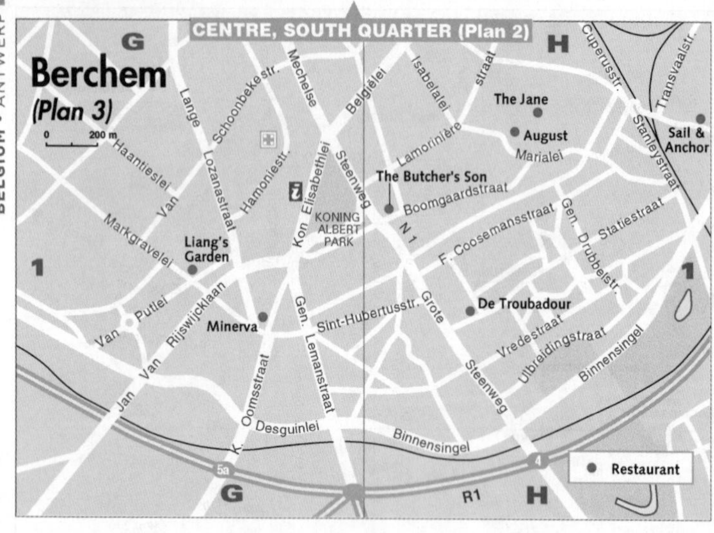

FRANQ

MODERN CUISINE • ELEGANT You only need to take one step over the threshold of this mansion to get a grasp of FRANQ's ambitions. The premises, steeped in elegant, understated luxury, are ideal to sample creative, classical dishes. Flavoursome sauces and flawless culinary craftsmanship; the chef demonstrates his modern bent with subtle nuances.

Specialities: Terrine of goose liver with elderberry, bitter chocolate and brioche. FRANQ's Ghent waterzooi stew with Mechelen Cuckoo chicken. Coconut soufflé and pineapple sorbet.

Menu 39 € (lunch)/69 € - Carte 48/169 €

PLAN: 2-D1 - *Kipdorp 10 - ☏ 03 555 31 80 - www.hotelfranq.com - Closed 5-13 April, 12-26 July, 1-8 November, lunch Saturday, Sunday*

Het Gebaar (Roger van Damme)

CREATIVE • COSY This restaurant is located in an elegant building on the edge of the botanical park. Luxury tea room cuisine, which the chef enriches with modern twists; mouthwatering desserts! Non-stop service until 6pm.

Specialities: Brioche with Wagyu, smoked onion cream and truffle. Vol-au-vent "deluxe" with sweetbreads and French fries. Rock around the clock: hazelnut biscuit, milk chocolate mousse, coulis of exotic fruit and almond.

Carte 75/125 €

PLAN: 2-D2 - *Leopoldstraat 24 - ☏ 03 232 37 10 - www.hetgebaar.be - Closed 3-17 August, 23 December-6 January, dinner Monday-Friday, Saturday, Sunday*

The Glorious

MODERN FRENCH • WINE BAR Eclectic, with baroque and Art deco features, The Glorious is the quintessence of stylish! Classical, well-executed cuisine featuring favourite recipes whose enthusiastic interpretation can astound. Fine selection of wines and cocktails. The guestrooms sport the same distinctive interior décor.

Specialities: Millefeuille with langoustines, brunoise of yellow and green courgette and Nantua sauce. Young Anjou pigeon with peas à la Clamart, chanterelle and a jus of crushed juniper berry. Riz condé with candied apricot, gooseberries, peach jelly and mint cream.

Menu 43 € (lunch), 69/95 € - Carte 81/115 €

PLAN: 2-C3 - *De Burburestraat 4a - ✆ 03 237 06 13 - www.theglorious.be - Closed 12-22 April, 12-28 July, Monday, Sunday*

Kommilfoo (Olivier de Vinck de Winnezeele)

CREATIVE • COSY Smart yet casual, Kommilfoo will acquaint you with the creative and inventive talent of a dedicated chef. The dishes are both amusing and imaginative, with a clear desire to render contrasting tastes harmonious. Pyrenean goat, the house speciality, is on the menu all year long.

Specialities: Baked Icelandic langoustines with carrot and flavours of Marrakech. Pyrenean suckling goat in 5 preparations. Apricot and basil creation.

Menu 40 € (lunch), 70/85 € - Carte 82/110 €

PLAN: 2-C3 - *Vlaamse Kaai 17 - ✆ 03 237 30 00 - www.restaurantkommilfoo.be - Closed 1 January, 1-21 July, 24-25 December, Monday, lunch Saturday, Sunday*

Nathan (Nathan Van Echelpoel)

MODERN FRENCH • TRENDY Nathan Van Echelpoel skilfully balances classicism and modernity. In his pared-down, Scandinavian-inspired restaurant, he demonstrates his know-how of classical values: first-class produce, generous helpings and flawless preparation down to the tiniest detail. A classical foundation to which he freely adds his own original plating ideas and bold combinations.

Specialities: Crunchy langoustines with mango chutney and a foam bisque. Roasted pigeon with pointed cabbage and pulses. Kiwi with chocolate crémeux, textures of hazelnut and vanilla ice cream.

Menu 30 € (lunch), 55/82 € - Carte 72/116 €

PLAN: 2-D1 - *Lange Koepoortstraat 13 - ✆ 03 284 28 13 - www.restaurant-nathan.be - Closed 7-14 April, 24 December-7 January, Monday, lunch Tuesday, lunch Saturday, Sunday*

l'Amitié

MODERN CUISINE • TRENDY When you arrive in this fully renovated bistro, it won't be friendship, but something more akin to love that you will feel. Fish takes pride of place and the first class ingredients are prepared according to modern techniques and served in small dishes. Scrumptious!

Carte 30/50 €

PLAN: 2-C3 - *Vlaamse Kaai 43 - ✆ 03 257 50 05 - www.lamitie.net - Closed 24-25 December, 28 December-5 January, Saturday, Sunday*

Bún

VIETNAMESE • FRIENDLY Bún is hip and casual, which suits its trendy crowd of regulars. The refined Vietnamese fare is enticing, stylish and packed with flavour. The chef works with local produce, seeks to satisfy current tastes and regular renews his appetising menu. Its sibling, Little Bún (Jorispoort 22), offers delicious Vietnamese street food.

Menu 24 € (lunch), 37/57 € - Carte 35/48 €

PLAN: 2-C3 - *Volkstraat 43 - ✆ 03 235 85 89 - www.bunantwerp.be - Closed Monday, Sunday*

Ciro's

BELGIAN • NEIGHBOURHOOD The nostalgic interior, working class atmosphere and traditional Belgian fare will provide the opportunity to turn a meal at Ciro's into a taste of Antwerp's past. Steak and chips with six sauces and vol-au-vent deluxe are the stars of the show. Book ahead – you won't be disappointed!

Menu 37 € - Carte 46/68 €

PLAN: 2-D3 - *Amerikalei 6 - ✆ 03 238 11 47 - www.ciros.be - Closed 1-31 July, Monday, lunch Saturday*

5 Flavors Mmei

CHINESE • SIMPLE The most well-known and the most obvious can sometimes surprise – and this restaurant is a perfect example. The chef pays homage to Chinese tradition with fresh and sometimes surprising preparations, which put paid to many prejudices regarding the cuisine of his place of birth. The dim sum are to die for!

Menu 17€ (lunch), 30/80€ – Carte 25/52€

PLAN: 2-C3 – *Volkstraat 37 – ✆ 03 281 30 37 – www.5flavors-mmei.be – Closed 1-31 July, Monday, Tuesday*

InVINcible

MODERN CUISINE • TRENDY A glass of wine from the impressive selection, accompanied by a flawlessly cooked French dish... talk about an invincible combination! The menu is brief, but the choice is not easy because the chef beautifully interweaves flavours and really makes each dish his own. Tip: a seat at the counter will complete this authentic experience.

Menu 25€ (lunch)/37€ – Carte 37/60€

PLAN: 2-C1 – *Haarstraat 9 – ✆ 03 231 32 07 – www.invincible.be – Closed Saturday, Sunday*

Schnitzel

CLASSIC CUISINE • NEIGHBOURHOOD Simple but good is the motto of this establishment. The experienced chef deploys his talents to prepare delicious cooked meats and *beuling*, a sort of black pudding. He rustles up these ingredients into dishes designed to be shared. Refreshingly down to earth and wholesome!

Menu 35/45€ – Carte 25/40€

PLAN: 2-E1 – *Paardenmarkt 53 – ✆ 03 256 63 86 – www.schnitzelantwerpen.be – Closed lunch Monday-Friday, Saturday, Sunday*

De Troubadour

MODERN CUISINE • TRENDY Out-going, sociable John Verbeeck welcomes diners with his inimitable style and fun-loving personality. Popular with gourmets since 1990, the establishment is depicted by a trendy vintage style. The menu and dishes seek to enhance and exalt the excellent seasonal ingredients and produce.

Menu 28€ (lunch), 37/49€ – Carte 28/64€

PLAN: 3-H1 – *Driekoningenstraat 72 – ✆ 03 239 39 16 – www.detroubadour.be – Closed Monday, Sunday*

A'Sur

LATIN AMERICAN • FRIENDLY Make a beeline to south Antwerp for a trip to South America! Chef Moisés blends his Venezuelan roots with his experience in top French and Belgian establishments. The "terroir" menu errs towards popular Belgian classics, while the "roots" menu is more exotic and spicier. Fine selection of rums.

Menu 27€ (lunch), 45/55€

PLAN: 2-C3 – *Volkstraat 32 – ✆ 03 434 65 34 – www.asur-restaurant.be – Closed 16 August-1 September, 30 December-7 January, Monday, Tuesday, lunch Wednesday, lunch Saturday, Sunday*

Les Années Folles

MODERN CUISINE • VINTAGE The attractive vintage interior of Les Années Folles, enhanced by subtle gilt work, is clearly inspired by the 1920's. Chef Gino's cuisine, however, is firmly anchored in the 21C and he frequently pops out to explain his dishes in person. Countless in-house preparations and exquisitely balanced flavours. The guarantee of a good meal.

Menu 29€ (lunch), 49/67€

PLAN: 2-E3 – *Mechelsesteenweg 112 – ✆ 03 216 33 03 – www.lesanneesfolles.be – Closed 6-19 April, 20 July-2 August, 23 December-5 January, Wednesday, lunch Saturday, Sunday*

Ardent

MODERN CUISINE • MINIMALIST Passion is often said to be the distinctive character trait of great chefs. Wouter Van Steenwinkel is no exception to this rule and his tasteful restaurant will give you an insight into his many talents. You can expect well-thought out and balanced meals with perfectly blended flavours.

Menu 29€ (lunch), 49/79€

PLAN: 2-F3 – *Dageraadplaats 3 – ✆ 03 336 32 99 – www.resto-ardent.be – Closed 1-7 January, Monday, Tuesday, lunch Saturday*

August

SEASONAL CUISINE • CONTEMPORARY DÉCOR As you venture into this former Augustinian convent, tastefully restored in a contemporary vein, you can expect a unique experience. Nick Bril of The Jane has devised the enticing menu, anchored in tradition, yet coupled with a sprinkling of international influences and oodles of enthusiasm.

Carte 55/75€

PLAN: 3-H1 – *Jules Bordetstraat 5 – ✆ 03 500 80 80 – www.august-antwerpen.com – Closed Monday, Sunday*

Bistrot L'îlot

MARKET CUISINE • BISTRO A Parisian vibe mixed with industrial and minimalist details sets the welcoming scene. The bistro's theme revolves around a selection of pure, varied and delicious dishes to be shared. "What you see is what you get" is their motto! The 40€ menu is great value-for-money.

Menu 27€ (lunch)/40€ – Carte 30/45€

PLAN: 1-B1 – *Kribbestraat 15 – ✆ 03 434 41 33 – www.bistrotlilot.be – Closed 26 May-9 June, 31 December-7 January, Monday, Sunday*

Cuichine

CHINESE • FRIENDLY Two childhood friends, both sons of restaurant owners, created Cuichine with the idea of serving dishes they used to eat at home. Their Cantonese recipes are well prepared from fresh produce and without fussy frills. Even better, the à la carte menu is well priced and the lunch menu unbeatable.

Menu 24€ (lunch), 43/50€ – Carte 50/67€

PLAN: 2-F3 – *Draakstraat 13 – ✆ 03 289 92 45 – www.cuichine.be – Closed 1-15 September, 24-25 December, 31 December, Monday, lunch Saturday, Sunday*

Ferrier 30

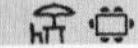

ITALIAN • DESIGN The best Italian restaurant in the area is doubtless Ferrier 30. The meat, fish and pasta dishes (lasagne al ragu, taglioni con prosciutto) are all steeped in authentic Italian flavours and are further enhanced by wines brought back by the owner in person.

Carte 45/75€

PLAN: 2-C3 – *Leopold de Waelplaats 30 – ✆ 03 216 50 62 – www.ferrier-30.be – Closed Wednesday*

Het Gerecht

MARKET CUISINE • COSY This restaurant is full of character. Peggy pampers her customers while Wim treats their taste buds to his talented creations. The photos adorning the walls are Wim's handiwork, as is the French inspired cuisine, which follows the seasons. The lunch menu is great.

Menu 34€ (lunch), 45/81€ – Carte 45/68€

PLAN: 2-D3 – *Amerikalei 20 – ✆ 03 248 79 28 – www.hetgerecht.be – Closed 6-20 April, 12 July-3 August, 24 December-5 January, Monday, dinner Wednesday, lunch Saturday, Sunday*

Graanmarkt 13

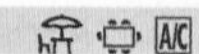

ORGANIC • MINIMALIST The days are long past when vegetables were little more than bland anonymous extras on the plate. Seppe Nobels proves that they are fully capable of taking the star role and he brilliantly and skilfully incorporates them into contemporary recipes rich in powerful flavours. Each dish is a new discovery!

Menu 35 € (lunch)/45 €

PLAN: 2-E2 - *Graanmarkt 13 - ✆ 03 337 79 91 - www.graanmarkt13.com - Closed Sunday*

Kato

JAPANESE • SIMPLE Behind Kato's seemingly nondescript facade lies a fascinating universe. The seasoned chef loves to acquaint diners with the delicacy of Japanese food. His culinary precision, flair for sourcing first-class fish and hand-prepared sushi makes every mouthful a moment of pure bliss. Not to be missed in the heart of Antwerp.

Carte 32/75 €

PLAN: 2-C3 - *De Vrièrestraat 4 - ✆ 03 344 75 58 - www.restaurant-kato.be - Closed 20 July-6 August, Monday, lunch Tuesday, lunch Sunday*

Ko'uzi

JAPANESE • MINIMALIST The interior design is as hip and minimalist as the food. Sushi and sashimi classics rub shoulders with other more inventive recipes. Enjoy delicious fare and the chance to buy different teas. Chef Kawada also organises sushi classes, which are all the rage.

Carte 25/62 €

PLAN: 2-D3 - *Leopoldplaats 12 - ✆ 03 232 24 88 - www.kouzi.be - Closed Monday, Sunday*

Liang's Garden

CHINESE • TRADITIONAL A stalwart of Chinese cuisine in the city! A spacious restaurant where the authentic menu covers specialities from Canton (dim sum), Peking (duck) and Szechuan (fondue).

Menu 28 € (lunch)/72 € - Carte 29/85 €

PLAN: 3-G1 - *Generaal Lemanstraat 54 - ✆ 03 237 22 22 - www.liangsgardenantwerp.be - Closed 6 July-2 August, Sunday*

Lux

MODERN FRENCH • CHIC This restaurant occupies the house of a former ship owner, and has a terrace that overlooks the port. There is a profusion of marble (columns, fireplaces), a wine and cocktail bar, à la carte options, plus an attractive lunch menu.

Menu 35 € (lunch), 60/80 € - Carte 82/100 €

PLAN: 2-D1 - *Adriaan Brouwerstraat 13 - ✆ 03 233 30 30 - www.luxantwerp.com - Closed Monday, lunch Saturday, Sunday*

Minerva

CLASSIC CUISINE • ELEGANT Minerva was also the name of the legendary Belgian luxury car, the repair workshops of which were located here. The site is now that of a well-oiled restaurant, serving good quality, traditional fare. You might be interested to know that all the meat is sliced in front of you!

Menu 39 € (lunch)/68 € - Carte 52/113 €

PLAN: 3-G1 - *Hotel Firean, Karel Oomsstraat 36 - ✆ 03 216 00 55 - www.restaurantminerva.be - Closed 20 July-21 August, 20 December-6 January, Saturday, Sunday*

Món

MEATS AND GRILLS • BRASSERIE The sculpture of a bull's head immediately gives you a foretaste of the menu, in which red meat takes pride of place. In fact, not just any meat but home raised Limousine beef prepared in a Josper charcoal fire. The cooking and accompaniments are a treat for your taste buds.

Carte 37/63€

PLAN: 2-D1 – *Sint-Aldegondiskaai 30 – ☎ 03 345 67 89 – www.monantwerp.com*

Het Nieuwe Palinghuis

SEAFOOD • FRIENDLY Eel is king at this seafood restaurant, only dethroned by Escaut lobster in season. The dining room and veranda are decorated with seascapes and old photographs of Antwerp. The perfect place to enjoy the pleasures of the North Sea.

Menu 40€ (lunch), 60/120€ – Carte 40/120€

PLAN: 2-C2 – *Sint-Jansvliet 14 – ☎ 03 231 74 45 – www.hetnieuwepalinghuis.be – Closed 10-31 January, 20 May-18 June, 8-30 September, Monday, Tuesday, Friday*

Pazzo

MODERN CUISINE • FRIENDLY This trendy brasserie with a lively atmosphere occupies a former warehouse near the docks. Enjoy Mediterranean - and Asian - inspired bistro cuisine and excellent wines.

Menu 24€ (lunch) – Carte 45/84€

PLAN: 2-D1 – *Oude Leeuwenrui 12 – ☎ 03 232 86 82 – www.pazzo.be – Closed 23 December-3 January, Saturday, Sunday*

Het Pomphuis

MODERN CUISINE • VINTAGE This immense former pumping station was magnificently transformed into a luxury brasserie with a terrace overlooking the port in 2002. The site's architectural interest is ideally paired to the establishment's up-to-the-minute, subtle menu.

Menu 35€ (lunch)/54€ – Carte 50/84€

PLAN: 1-B1 – *Siberiastraat – ☎ 03 770 86 25 – www.hetpomphuis.be – Closed lunch Monday-Saturday, Sunday*

RAS

MODERN CUISINE • ELEGANT The Restaurant aan de Stroom ("riverside restaurant") sports bay windows that command fine views of the Schelde River. Charcoal sketches by Rinus Van de Velde add an arty touch to the interior. The plates are graphically modern and reveal a subtle blend of pure, traditional flavours.

Carte 47/85€

PLAN: 2-C2 – *Ernest Van Dijckkaai 37 – ☎ 03 234 12 75 – www.ras.today*

Sail & Anchor

MODERN BRITISH • VINTAGE Michael Yates wavers between modern and traditional British cuisine. This English-born chef enjoys tweaking top-quality Belgian ingredients with his inimitable creativity. Amusing, refreshing, intriguing, but always a delight. Gracious Marijke is in her element to welcome you to this urban eatery.

Menu 70/86€ – Carte 25/100€

PLAN: 3-H1 – *Guldenvliesstraat 60 – ☎ 03 430 40 04 – www.sailandanchor.be – Closed Monday, Tuesday, lunch Wednesday-Saturday, dinner Sunday*

U Antwerp

MODERN CUISINE • TRENDY Arrange to meet in this delightful establishment in the Eilandje district and get ready to enjoy contemporary dishes from a modern, attractive menu concocted by Viki Geunes of 't Zilte (two stars). Finally, set your mind and body at rest and stay overnight in one of the comfortable rooms. Sheer bliss!

Menu 32/60€ – Carte 48/80€

PLAN: 1-B1 – *Nassaustraat 42 – ☎ 03 201 90 70 – www.u-eatsleep.be*

Under The Palm Trees

SEASONAL CUISINE • TRENDY A funky, jungle-inspired theme reigns in this trendy eatery, aptly adorned in climbing plants. The purity of the cuisine is the work of chef Broeckx who scours the Flemish countryside for his ingredients. The food is unpretentious and demonstrates a subtle balance between spices and acidity. Fine wine list.

Menu 28€ (lunch), 52/95€

PLAN: 2-C3 – *Volkstraat 13 – ☎ 03 238 05 71 – www.underthepalmtrees.be – Closed Monday, Tuesday, lunch Wednesday-Thursday, Sunday*

Upton

ITALIAN • NEIGHBOURHOOD Upton is a trendy establishment in an up-and-coming neighbourhood. Experienced chef, Gianfranco Van de Maele, learned how to make succulent fresh pasta with his "nonna". He has added his globe-trotting outlook, combining Italian authenticity with Asian influences gleaned from his travels. A fascinating modern culinary melting pot.

Menu 30€ (lunch)/55€ – Carte 56/76€

PLAN: 1-B1 – *Napelsstraat 42 – ☎ 03 292 57 10 – www.upton.be – Closed Monday, lunch Saturday, Sunday*

Visbistro Mojo

SEAFOOD • BISTRO Fresh fish and shellfish are attractively displayed on the counter, bringing the promise of succulent fare. Chef Johan and his sister Nuria are determined to provide diners with excellent quality produce at reasonable prices. No frills, good wholesome food!

Menu 21€ (lunch)/33€ – Carte 38/55€

PLAN: 2-D3 – *Kasteelpleinstraat 56 – ☎ 03 237 49 00 – www.visbistro-mojo.be – Closed Monday, lunch Saturday, Sunday*

Yamayu Santatsu

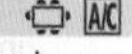

JAPANESE • SIMPLE A lively and authentic Japanese restaurant that only uses the best hand picked ingredients, and prepares sushi in full view of diners. Assorted à la carte options with four different menus for two people.

Menu 45€ – Carte 29/55€

PLAN: 2-E1 – *Ossenmarkt 19 – ☎ 03 234 09 49 – www.santatsu.be – Closed Monday, lunch Sunday*

Rogger Blogger/Shutterstock.com

phant/iStock

CROATIA

HRVATSKA

ZAGREB
ZAGREB

RudyBalasko/iStock

ZAGREB IN...

→ **ONE DAY**
Funicular, Upper Town (Gornji Grad).

→ **TWO DAYS**
Lower Town (Donji Grad), Upper Town (Gornji Grad).

→ **THREE DAYS**
Stone Gate, National Museum of Naïve Art, Church of St Mark, City Museum, Meštrović Gallery.

As both the capital and the largest city in the country, Zagreb is the cultural, scientific, religious, political and administrative centre of the Republic of Croatia, offering a melting-pot of Middle European and Mediterranean cultures.

It extends between Mt Medvednica (which protects it from the cold winter winds) to the north, and the River Sava, with its vast plain, to the south. Zagreb is home to almost a quarter of Croatia's population and over the centuries has been inhabited by people from all over Europe. This has given the city a rich and

varied cultural life as well as an exciting and tumultuous history, which is reflected in the city's architecture (its streets, squares and palatial façades) and unique atmosphere. A large yet manageable city, Zagreb has two distinct characters: the Baroque district, with its narrow alleyways, flights of steps and old buildings in the upper town offering a striking contrast to the large open areas and Art Nouveau-style palaces of the lower town.

With its lively streets for strolling around and its outdoor cafés for soaking up the sun, Zagreb is, above all, a carefree city – and one that will undoubtedly enchant visitors with its magical and timeless ambience.

EATING OUT

Year after year, the appeal of Croatia's capital as a tourist destination continues to grow. Its many restaurants and outdoor cafes, combined with its welcoming ambience, provide the backdrop for cuisine which is influenced more by the coast than inland, and by Istria, Dalmatia and neighbouring Italy rather than Austria, although the latter has also left a significant mark on the country thanks to its inclusion in the Austro-Hungarian Empire. The result is a cuisine with a strong Mediterranean influence, which includes vegetables, olive oil, fresh pasta, risottos and an equal balance of meat and fish on most menus, plus a focus on grilled dishes, while, in season, the best restaurants will include the renowned truffle in many of their dishes. A more distinctive culinary experience awaits in a small number of trendy restaurants which are gaining a reputation for their creative cuisine, although regional fare continues to hold its own in most places. Almost all restaurants are proud to offer a surprisingly good selection of local wines alongside options from outside the country.

Noel Zagreb (Goran Kočiš)

MODERN CUISINE • TRENDY A fashionable restaurant with soft lighting and trendy, internationally inspired furnishings, where guests can enjoy exciting, colourful cuisine prepared by the owner-chef. The delicious modern and creative dishes served here are accompanied by a selection of Croatian, French and Italian wines carefully chosen by the sommelier-partner.

Specialities: Almond risotto, seaweed, lobster, lobster butter. Adriatic fish, baked celery, black garlic, bone marrow. Peach, white chocolate, laurel, goat's cheese.

Menu 240 HRK (lunch), 490/770 HRK - Carte 570 HRK

PLAN: D2 - *Ulica Popa Dukljanina 1 - ✆ 01 4844 297 - www.noel.hr - Closed 1 January, 12-13 April, 24-25 December, Sunday*

Agava

INTERNATIONAL • BISTRO Climb the many steps up to this homely restaurant, unusually set into the side of a hill, and you will be rewarded with views out over historic pedestrianised Tkalčićeva Street. The extensive, internationally influenced menu offers plenty of rustic Italian dishes as well as a selection of Croatian favourites.

Menu 450/600 HRK - Carte 200/500 HRK

PLAN: B1 - *Ul. Ivana Tkalčića 39 - ✆ 01 4829 826 - www.restaurant-agava.hr - Closed 24-25 December*

Tač

TRADITIONAL CUISINE • FAMILY Despite its location in a residential district outside the city centre, this restaurant is a sound choice for its unfussy cuisine which pays little attention to passing trends. Instead, the couple in charge here focus on a Mediterranean-influenced menu offering fresh, simple dishes, many of which come from the female owner's native Istria. Announced at your table, daily specials can include ingredients such as fish, truffles, asparagus and artichokes, depending on the season and market availability.

Carte 200/500 HRK

Off plan - *Vrhovec 140 - ✆ 01 3776 757 - www.restac.hr - Closed 1 January, 12-13 April, 25 December, Monday*

Apetit

MEDITERRANEAN CUISINE • COSY Wine bar meets contemporary restaurant at this fashionable destination, tucked away off a city street. The menu travels the globe, with regular sojourns to Italy and the Med and dishes are skilfully prepared, brightly coloured and full of flavour. Wine is taken seriously and the homemade pasta is a highlight.

Carte 205/358 HRK

PLAN: B2 - *Masarykova ul. 18 - ✆ 01 4811 077 - www.apetit.hr - Closed 13 April, 25-26 December*

Beštija

MARKET CUISINE • BISTRO Situated in the town centre, just beyond an arcade, this pleasant, simply decorated bistro with a mix of old and new is run by a young and dynamic team. The dishes focus on market-fresh produce and regional recipes, all featured on a small menu which changes frequently. Equal care is taken here with the cooking process and the presentation.

Menu 30/165 HRK - Carte 140/305 HRK

PLAN: B2 - *Masarykova Ulica 11/1 - ✆ 91 324 0120 - Closed 12 April, 8 October, 25 December, Sunday*

Bistro Apetit by Marin Rendić

MEDITERRANEAN CUISINE • NEIGHBOURHOOD A delightful neighbourhood restaurant with a stylish modern look; floor to ceiling windows let in lots of light and open out onto a pretty, foliage-filled terrace. The seasonal, Italian-influenced menu is pleasingly concise, and the unfussy, vibrantly coloured dishes are fresh, flavoursome and fairly priced.

Menu 445/595 HRK - Carte 340/415 HRK

Off plan - *Jurjevska Ulica 65 - ✆ 01 4677 335 - www.bistroapetit.com - Closed 1 January, Monday*

Le Bistro Esplanade

FRENCH • TRENDY One of the capital's most popular places for meeting and eating is this smartly dressed yet informal all-day bistro, set in the city's top hotel. The classic French bistro menu offers soups and salads, steaks and schnitzel; try their signature dish, Esplanade Strukli, which has been served here since 1951.

Menu 160 HRK – Carte 235/575 HRK

PLAN: B2 – *Mihanoviceva Ulica 1 – ✆ 01 4566 611 – www.lebistro.hr*

Boban

TRADITIONAL CUISINE • COSY An unpretentious city centre spot owned by Croatian footballer Zvonimir Boban. The ground floor café-bar serves sandwiches and snacks, but head instead to the red-brick, barrel-ceilinged basement restaurant to enjoy classic Italian dishes. Cooking is fresh and hearty; homemade pastas are the highlight.

Carte 119/344 HRK

PLAN: B2 – *Gajeva 9 – ✆ 01 4811 549 – www.boban.hr – Closed 1 January, 12 April, 25 December*

Dubravkin Put

MEDITERRANEAN CUISINE • ROMANTIC This peaceful hideaway, surrounded by greenery, is located a short walk north of the city, and features a delightful terrace, perfect for an alfresco meal. Inside, it's spacious and contemporary, with a separate wine bar. International menus give a nod to Italy; home-grown wines dominate the wine list.

Carte 235/380 HRK

PLAN: B1 – *Dubravkin Put 2 – ✆ 01 4834 975 – www.dubravkin-put.com – Closed 12 April, 25 December, 31 December, Sunday*

ManO

STEAKHOUSE • TRENDY Exposed brick and high ceilings give a clue to this destination restaurant's previous life as a leather factory; nowadays it boasts an exclusive, clubby atmosphere and features soft, moody lighting and a bright open kitchen. Dishes range from the traditional to the more contemporary; go for one of the steaks.

Carte 265/525 HRK

PLAN: B1 – *Medvedgradska ul. 2 – ✆ 01 4669 432 – www.mano.hr – Closed 1-31 August, 25-26 December, Sunday*

Pod Zidom

MARKET CUISINE • COSY A modern-style bistro with a wine bar and attractive outdoor area in the city centre, just behind the main square. The chef, who describes his cuisine as "market-fresh", makes daily visits to the nearby Dolac market for his ingredients, which include seasonal vegetables, Dalmatian charcuterie and meat reared on local farms. Fresh and seasonal are the buzzwords here!

Menu 150 HRK (lunch)/380 HRK – Carte 178/323 HRK

PLAN: B1 – *Pod zidom 5 – ✆ 099 325 3600 – www.pod-zidom-bistro-wine-bar.business.site – Closed 12 April, 25 December, 31 December-1 January, Monday*

Takenoko

JAPANESE • MINIMALIST Japanese fusion is the name of the game at this trendy restaurant, simply decorated in black and cream. The wide-ranging menu offers a vast array of dishes, from sushi and sashimi to tempura and teriyaki, with wok dishes and western choices also included; portions are generous and cocktails add to the fun.

Carte 180/563 HRK

PLAN: B2 – *Masarykova Ulica 22 – ✆ 01 6463 385 – www.takenoko.hr – Closed 12 April, 25 December*

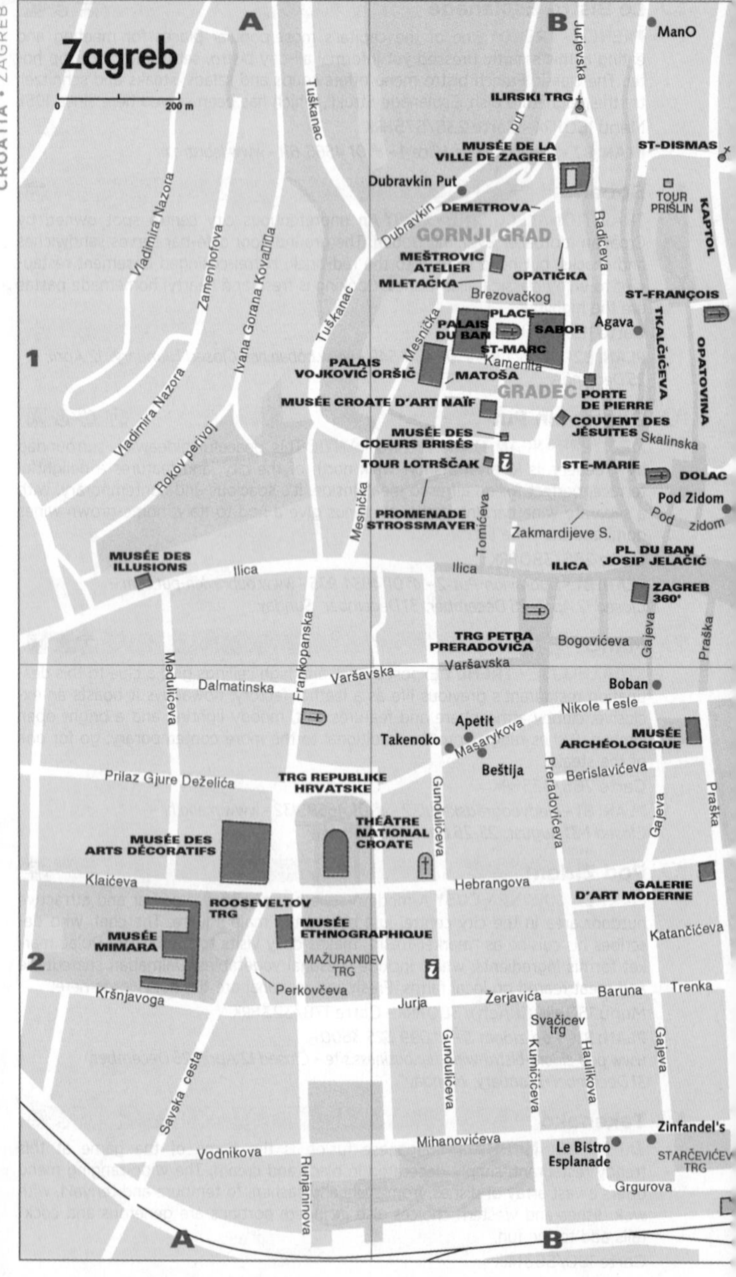
Zagreb
0
200 m
A
B
1
2
ILIRSKI TRG
ManO
MUSÉE DE LA VILLE DE ZAGREB
ST-DISMAS
Dubravkin Put
TOUR PRISLIN
KAPTOL
DEMETROVA
GORNJI GRAD
MEŠTROVIC ATELIER
MLETAČKA
OPATIČKA
ST-FRANÇOIS
Brezovačkog
PLACE
PALAIS DU BAN
SABOR
Agava
ST-MARC
PALAIS VOJKOVIĆ ORŠIĆ
MATOŠA
GRADEC
PORTE DE PIERRE
MUSÉE CROATE D'ART NAÏF
COUVENT DES JÉSUITES
Skalinska
MUSÉE DES COEURS BRISÉS
TOUR LOTRŠČAK
STE-MARIE
DOLAC
Pod Zidom
PROMENADE STROSSMAYER
Zakmardijeve S.
MUSÉE DES ILLUSIONS
Ilica
ILICA
PL. DU BAN JOSIP JELAČIĆ
ZAGREB 360°
TRG PETRA PREFADOVIĆA
Bogovićeva
Varšavska
Dalmatinska
Boban
Nikole Tesle
Apetit
Takenoko
Masarykova
Beštija
MUSÉE ARCHÉOLOGIQUE
Berislavićeva
Prilaz Gjure Deželića
TRG REPUBLIKE HRVATSKE
MUSÉE DES ARTS DÉCORATIFS
THÉÂTRE NATIONAL CROATE
Klaićeva
Hebrangova
GALERIE D'ART MODERNE
ROOSEVELTOV TRG
MUSÉE MIMARA
MUSÉE ETHNOGRAPHIQUE
MAŽURANIĆEV TRG
Katančićeva
Perkovčeva
Kršnjavoga
Jurja
Žerjavića
Baruna
Trenka
Svačićev trg
Savska cesta
Vodnikova
Mihanovićeva
Le Bistro Esplanade
Zinfandel's
STARČEVIĆEV TRG
Grgurova
Jurjevska
Radićeva
Tkalčićeva
Opatovina
Tuškanac
Vladimira Nazora
Zamenhofova
Ivana Gorana Kovačića
Mesnička
Rokov perivoj
Tomićeva
Gajeva
Praška
Frankopanska
Medulićeva
Gundulićeva
Preradovićeva
Kumičićeva
Hatulikova
Runjaninova

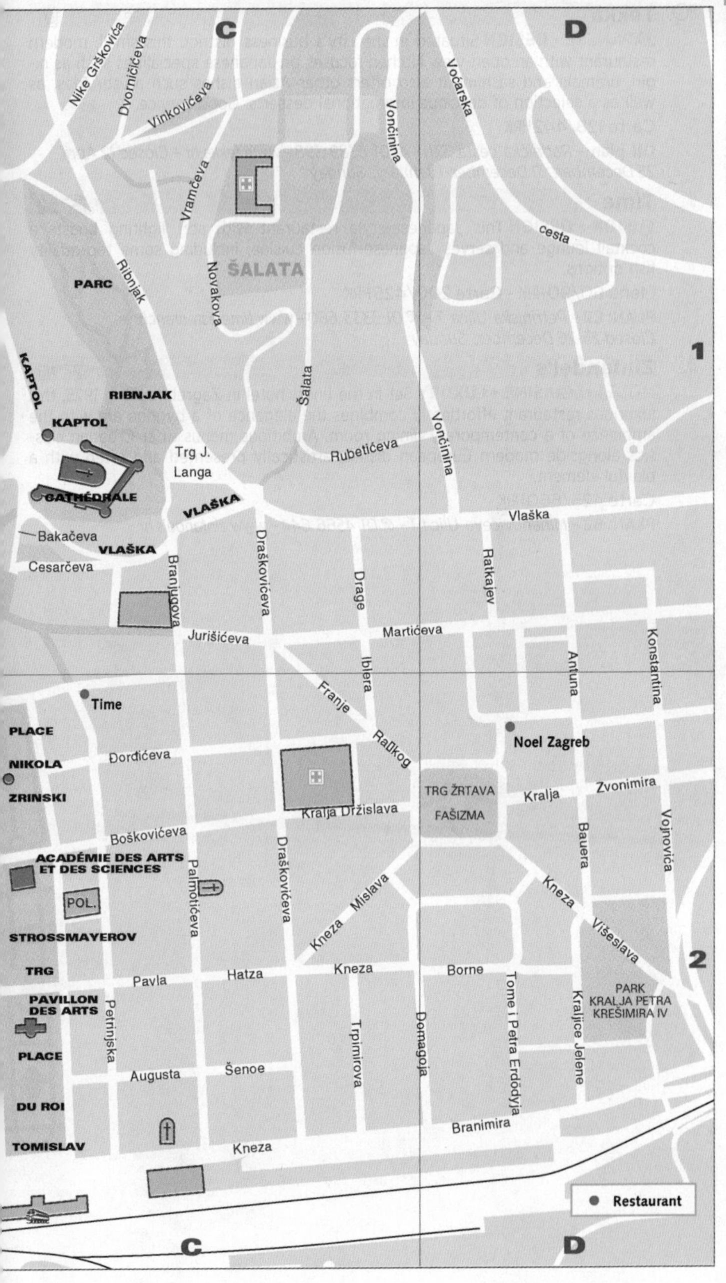

C
D
Nike Grškovića
Dvorničićeva
Vinkovićeva
Vramčeva
Vončinina
Voćarska
cesta
ŠALATA
PARC
Ribnjak
Novakova
1
KAPTOL
RIBNJAK
Šalata
KAPTOL
Vončinina
Rubetićeva
Trg J. Langa
CATHÉDRALE
VLAŠKA
Vlaška
Bakačeva
VLAŠKA
Cesarčeva
Draškovićeva
Branjugova
Drage
Ratkajev
Jurišićeva
Martićeva
Konstantina
Antuna
Iblera
Franje
Račkog
Time
PLACE
NIKOLA
ZRINSKI
Đorđićeva
Noel Zagreb
TRG ŽRTAVA FAŠIZMA
Kralja
Zvonimira
Kralja Držislava
Boškovićeva
ACADÉMIE DES ARTS ET DES SCIENCES
POL.
Palmotićeva
Draškovićeva
Bauera
Vojnovića
Kneza
Mislava
Kneza
Višeslava
STROSSMAYEROV
TRG
Pavla
Hatza
Kneza
Borne
2
PAVILLON DES ARTS
Petrinjska
Trpimirova
Domagoja
Tome i Petra Erdödyja
Kraljice Jelene
PARK KRALJA PETRA KREŠIMIRA IV
PLACE
Augusta
Šenoe
DU ROI
TOMISLAV
Branimira
Kneza
Restaurant
C
D

Tekka

JAPANESE • DESIGN Situated in the city's business district, this small, modern restaurant with an open-view kitchen focuses on Japanese specialities such as nigiri, uramaki and sashimi. It also offers other Asian dishes such as stir fries, as well as a selection of delicious international desserts. Good service.

Carte 128/442 HRK

Off plan – *Radnička cesta 37b – ✆ 01 6389 398 – www.tekka.hr – Closed 12 April, 25 December, 31 December-1 January, Sunday*

Time

FUSION • DESIGN This Japanese-style restaurant with soft lighting boasts a cocktail lounge and serves Japanese-fusion cuisine, including some top-quality fish options.

Menu 60/90 HRK – Carte 200/425 HRK

PLAN: C2 – *Petrinjska Ulica 7 – ✆ 01 3333 660 – www.timerestaurant.hr – Closed 25-26 December, Sunday*

Zinfandel's

MODERN CUISINE • LUXURY Set in the finest hotel in Zagreb, built in 1925, this luxurious restaurant effortlessly combines the elegance of a bygone era with the ambience of a contemporary dining room. Ambitious menus offer Croatian classics alongside modern European dishes; artistically presented and often with a playful element.

Carte 425/660 HRK

PLAN: B2 – *Mihanovićeva Ulica 1 – ✆ 01 4566 644 – www.zinfandels.hr*

Zdravko T/Shutterstock.com

DUBROVNIK
DUBROVNIK

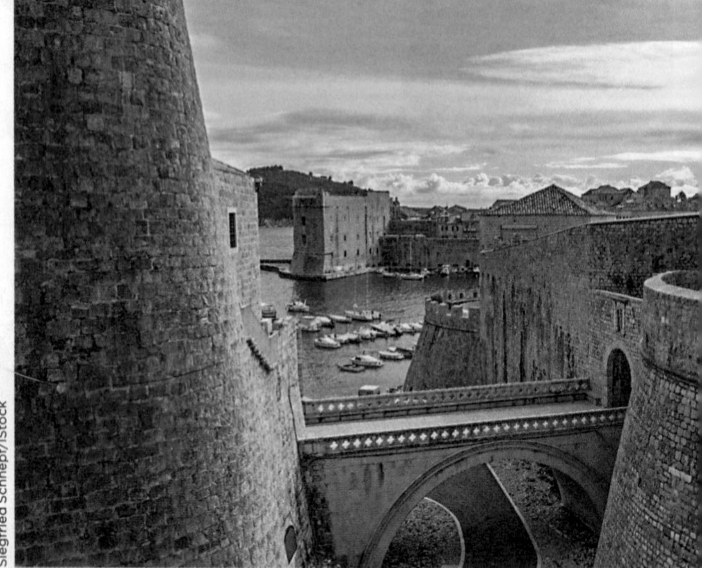
Siegfried Schnepf/iStock

DUBROVNIK IN...

→ **ONE DAY**
Walk along the city walls and visit the Old Port.

→ **TWO DAYS**
Luza Square, Rector's Palace, Dubrovnik Cathedral, Sponza Palace, Bell Tower, Church of St Blaise.

→ **THREE DAYS**
A boat trip to Lokrum Island, cable car to Mt Srd, Franciscan Monastery.

Perched on a rock and surrounded by high ramparts lapped by the sea, the former Ragusa in the historic region of Dalmatia is a real architectural gem. Nicknamed the 'pearl of the Adriatic' by the poet Lord Byron, the old town of Dubrovnik was declared a UNESCO World Heritage Site in 1979.

Although badly damaged during the Second World War and then again in the 1990s when it was heavily bombed by Serbian artillery during the civil war which followed the break-up of the former Yugoslavia, Dubrovnik has since regained

its former glory, attracting increasing numbers of tourists who are drawn here by its evocative atmosphere – the town now receives over one million visitors a year! Beautiful, romantic, distinctive – no adjective quite sums up the ambience of this extraordinary town. Its success is based on cultural and geographical factors which make it unique: the influence of Venetian, Gothic and Baroque architecture and the town's old walls combined with the crystal-clear Mediterranean and stunning features such as Lokrum Island and Srd mountain, which protects the town from the Scirocco and Bora winds.

EATING OUT

Although the narrow streets of the walled city are crowded with tourists from all around the world, Dubrovnik's cuisine remains firmly anchored in local traditions with a particular focus on simple, authentic fish and seafood dishes which are carefully cooked to preserve their fragrance and flavour. From vegetables and herbs to olive oil, the ingredients used are fresh and typical of the healthy Mediterranean diet. Visitors who love pasta will have no problem finding it here, where it is served with a wide variety of sauces, while other popular choices include risottos and an excellent selection of meat dishes. Alongside these international staples there is also evidence of a more elaborate and creative cuisine, which can be technically sophisticated and is often elegantly and beautifully presented. Finally, if you want to add a touch of romance to your dinner, it's worth knowing that some of the city's restaurants boast superb views of the Old Town or Port, while wine enthusiasts will be pleased to hear that they are also well catered for – the quality of Croatian wine will definitely surprise you!

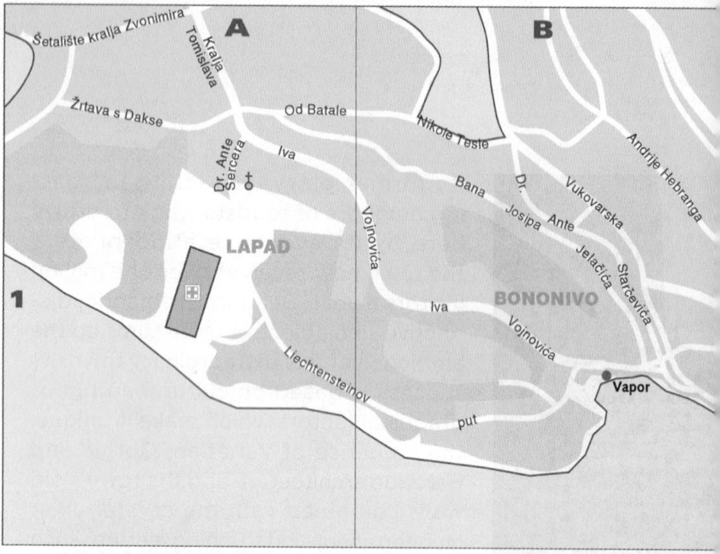

A
B
Šetalište kralja Zvonimira
Kralja Tomislava
Žrtava s Dakse
Od Batale
Nikole Tesle
Andrije Hebranga
Dr. Ante Šercera
Iva
Bana
Dr.
Vukovarska
Josipa
Ante
Vojnovića
LAPAD
Jelačića
Starčevića
1
BONONIVO
Iva
Vojnovića
Liechtensteinov
Vapor
put

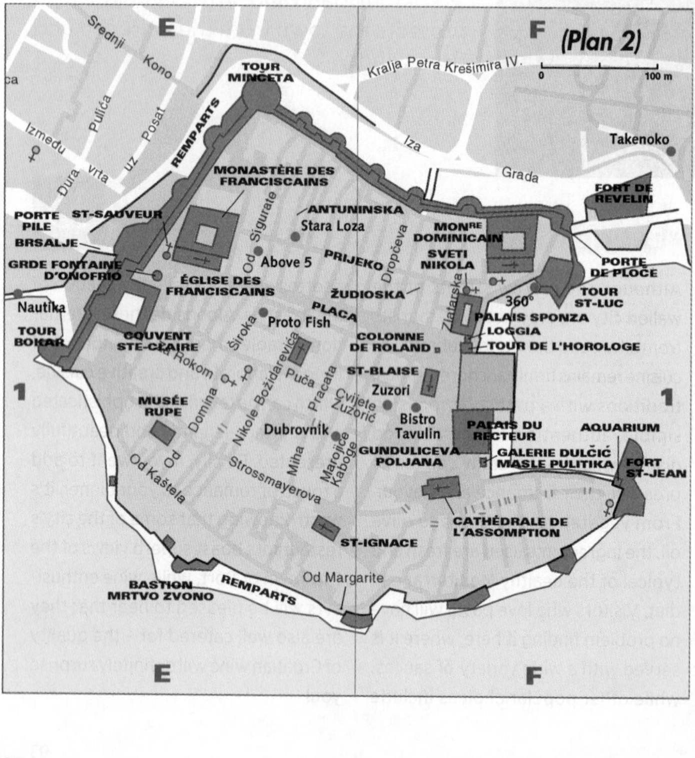

E
F
(Plan 2)
0
100 m
Srednji
Kono
TOUR MINČETA
Kralja Petra Krešimira IV.
Između
Pulića
Posat
REMPARTS
Iza
Takenoko
Dura
vrta
uz
Grada
MONASTÈRE DES FRANCISCAINS
FORT DE REVELIN
PORTE PILE
ST-SAUVEUR
ANTUNINSKA
Stara Loza
MONRE DOMINICAIN
BRSALJE
Od Sigurate
Dropčeva
GRDE FONTAINE D'ONOFRIO
Above 5
PRIJEKO
SVETI NIKOLA
PORTE DE PLOCE
ÉGLISE DES FRANCISCAINS
ŽUDIOSKA
360°
TOUR ST-LUC
Nautika
PLACA
Zlatarska
PALAIS SPONZA
Proto Fish
LOGGIA
TOUR BOKAR
COUVENT STE-CLAIRE
Široka
COLONNE DE ROLAND
TOUR DE L'HOROLOGE
Rokom
Božidarevića
Puča
ST-BLAISE
1
1
MUSÉE RUPE
Domina
Pracata
Zuzori
Cvijete Zuzorić
Bistro Tavulin
Nikole
Dubrovnik
PALAIS DU RECTEUR
AQUARIUM
Od
Miha
Marojice Kaboge
GUNDULICEVA POLJANA
GALERIE DULČIĆ MASLE PULITIKA
FORT ST-JEAN
Od Kaštela
Strossmayerova
CATHÉDRALE DE L'ASSOMPTION
ST-IGNACE
Od Margarite
BASTION MRTVO ZVONO
REMPARTS
E
F

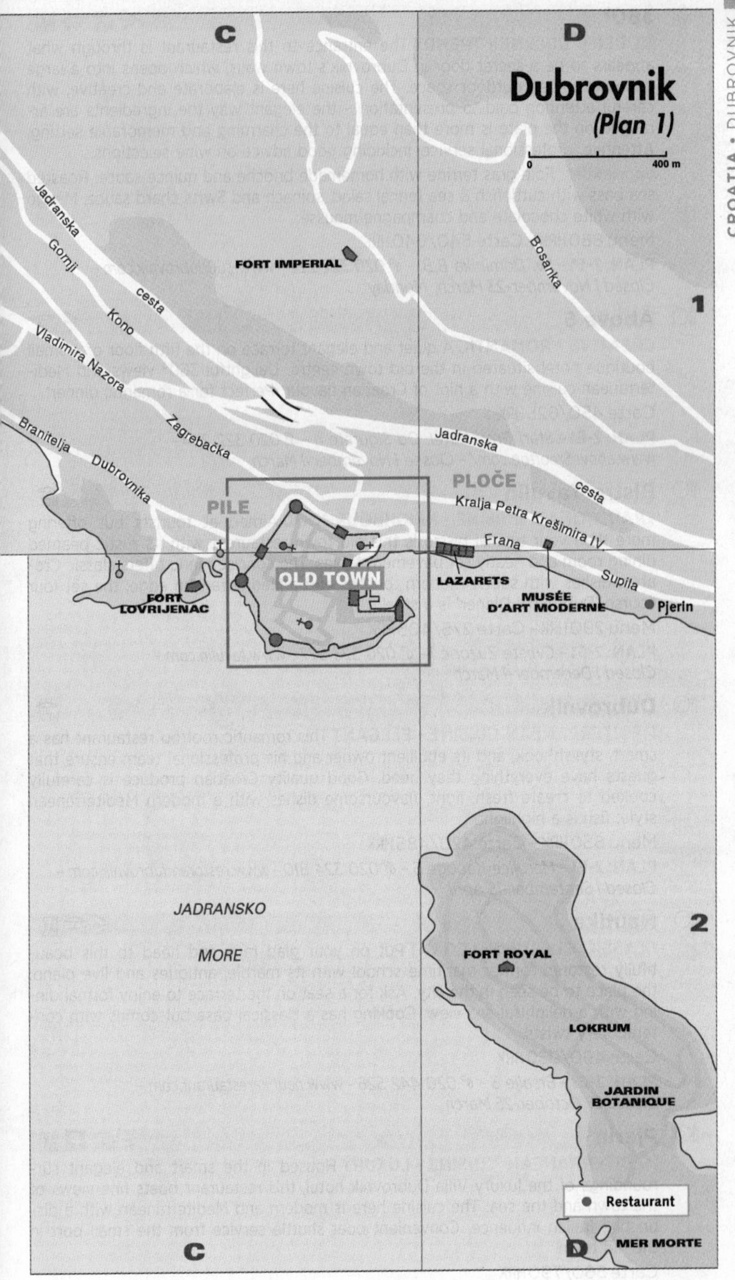
C
D
Dubrovnik
(Plan 1)
0
400 m
FORT IMPERIAL
Bosanka
1
Jadranska
Gornji
cesta
Kono
Vladimira Nazora
Zagrebačka
Branitelja
Dubrovnika
Jadranska
cesta
PLOČE
PILE
Kralja Petra Krešimira IV
Frana
Supila
OLD TOWN
LAZARETS
MUSÉE
D'ART MODERNE
Pjerin
FORT
LOVRIJENAC
JADRANSKO
MORE
2
FORT ROYAL
LOKRUM
JARDIN
BOTANIQUE
Restaurant
MER MORTE
C
D

360º

MODERN CUISINE • **TRENDY** The entrance to this restaurant is through what appears to be a secret door in Dubrovnik's town walls, which opens into a large and unexpected outdoor space. The cuisine here is elaborate and creative, with careful attention paid to presentation – the elegant way the ingredients are arranged on the plate is more than equal to the charming and memorable setting. Attentive, professional service, including good advice on wine selections.

Specialities: Foie gras terrine with homemade brioche and quince sauce. Roasted sea bass with cuttlefish & sea fennel salad, spinach and Swiss chard sauce. Mango with white chocolate and champagne mousse.

Menu 880 HRK – Carte 540/640 HRK

PLAN: 2-F1 – *Sv. Dominika B.B. – ✆ 020 322 222 – www.360dubrovnik.com – Closed 1 November-23 March, Monday*

Above 5

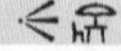

CREATIVE • **ROMANTIC** A quiet and elegant terrace on the fifth floor of a small boutique hotel situated in the old town centre. Delightful 360° views and Mediterranean cuisine with a hint of Croatian flavour. Perfect for a romantic dinner!

Carte 450/625 HRK

PLAN: 2-E1 – *Stari Grad Hotel, Od Sigurate 4 – ✆ 020 322 244 – www.above5rooftop.com/ – Closed 1 November-1 March*

Bistro Tavulin

TRADITIONAL CUISINE • **NEIGHBOURHOOD** Aimed at tourists but offering more than your typical bistro is this old town restaurant with its rustic beamed dining room and neatly set pavement tables. The concise menu offers classic Croatian dishes with subtle modern touches and a Mediterranean edge; the set four course 'Dubrovnik Dinner' is a steal.

Menu 290 HRK – Carte 275/405 HRK

PLAN: 2-F1 – *Cvijete Zuzorić 1 – ✆ 020 323 977 – www.tavulin.com – Closed 1 December-1 March*

Dubrovnik

MEDITERRANEAN CUISINE • **ELEGANT** This romantic rooftop restaurant has a smart, stylish look, and its ebullient owner and his professional team ensure that guests have everything they need. Good quality Croatian produce is carefully cooked to create fresh, light, flavoursome dishes with a modern Mediterranean style; fish is a highlight.

Menu 650 HRK – Carte 420/485 HRK

PLAN: 2-E1 – *Marojice Kaboge 5 – ✆ 020 324 810 – www.restorandubrovnik.com – Closed 1 September-15 April*

Nautika

CLASSIC CUISINE • **ELEGANT** Put on your glad rags and head to this beautifully restored former maritime school with its marble, antiques and live piano: the place to be seen in the city. Ask for a seat on the terrace to enjoy formal dining with a delightful sea view. Cooking has a classical base but comes with contemporary twists.

Carte 490/950 HRK

PLAN: 2-E1 – *Brsalje 3 – ✆ 020 442 526 – www.nautikarestaurant.com – Closed 27 October-25 March*

Pjerin

MEDITERRANEAN CUISINE • **LUXURY** Housed in the smart and elegant surroundings of the luxury Villa Dubrovnik hotel, this restaurant boats fine views of the town and the sea. The cuisine here is modern and Mediterranean with a distinctive Italian influence. Convenient boat shuttle service from the small port in the old town.

Carte 560/790 HRK

PLAN: 1-D2 – *Vlaha Bukovca 6 – ✆ 020 500 300 – www.villa-dubrovnik.hr – Closed 1 November-27 March, 3 November-27 March*

Proto Fish

SEAFOOD • MEDITERRANEAN This long-standing, family-owned fish and seafood restaurant in the heart of the old town has a loyal local following and attracts many well-heeled tourists too. Those in the know head to the lovely hidden roof terrace to enjoy the carefully prepared seasonal Mediterranean dishes; go for the catch of the day.

Menu 720 HRK – Carte 391/868 HRK

PLAN: 2-E1 – *Široka ul 1 – ✆ 020 323 234 – www.esculaprestaurants.com – Closed 1 January-29 February, 25-26 December*

Stara Loza

MEDITERRANEAN CUISINE • ELEGANT Bypass the ground floor of this elegant restaurant - set in a beautiful 15C townhouse hotel - and head instead to the wonderful rooftop room and terrace which look over the old town and out to sea. Cooking mixes Croatian, Italian and Asian influences, with visually appealing dishes prepared by a skilled team.

Carte 320/700 HRK

PLAN: 2-E1 – *Prijeko Palace Hotel, Prijeko 22 – ✆ 020 321 145 – www.prijekopalace.com – Closed 1 December-29 February*

Takenoko

JAPANESE • MINIMALIST In fine weather, take a seat on the terrace - which faces Dubrovnik's imposing walls and also has views of the port - to enjoy Takenoko's familiar Japanese classics (if the weather's not great, then try the dining room instead!). Highlights here include tuna from the Adriatic and the famous and hugely popular Wagyu beef, while our inspectors were particularly impressed by the more exotic black cod served with an orange sauce.

Carte 253/1000 HRK

PLAN: 2-F1 – *Hvarska 2 – ✆ 020 694 609 – www.takenoko.hr – Closed 16 October-14 April, lunch Monday-Sunday*

Vapor

MODERN CUISINE • TRENDY Floor to ceiling windows mean it's not only those on the terrace who can enjoy fantastic views of the Adriatic at this elegant restaurant, which is set in a luxury hotel built into the cliffside. Croatian produce is showcased in modern, eye-catching, boldly flavoured dishes with influences from the Med.

Menu 415 HRK (lunch)/620 HRK – Carte 390/650 HRK

PLAN: 1-B1 – *Bellevue Hotel, Pera Čingrije 7 – ✆ 020 330 000 – www.adriaticluxuryhotels.com – Closed 25 November-1 March*

Zuzori

MEDITERRANEAN CUISINE • BISTRO A bistro serving imaginative, out-of-the-ordinary cuisine with Mediterranean-style options as well as some interesting traditional local dishes. Attractive classic outdoor dining area in an alleyway in the town centre. Friendly service.

Menu 350/440 HRK – Carte 403/549 HRK

PLAN: 2-F1 – *Cvijete Zuzoric 2 – ✆ 020 324 076 – www.zuzori.com – Closed 8 January-15 March, 24-25 December*

MarekKijevsky/iStock

CZECH REPUBLIC

ČESKÁ REPUBLIKA

PRAGUE
PRAHA

satariel/iStock

PRAGUE IN...

→ **ONE DAY**
Old Town Square, the astronomical clock, Charles Bridge, Prague Castle, Petřín Hill.

→ **TWO DAYS**
Josefov, the National Theatre, Golden Lane.

→ **THREE DAYS**
Wenceslas Square, the National Museum, cross the bridge to look round Malá Strana.

Prague's history stretches back to the Dark Ages. In the ninth century a princely seat comprising a simple walled-in compound was built where the castle now stands; in the tenth century the first bridge over the Vltava arrived; and by the 13C the enchanting cobbled alleyways below the castle were complete. But Prague has come of age and Europe's most perfectly preserved capital now proffers consumer choice as well as medieval marvels. Its state-of-the-art shopping malls and pulsing nightlife bear testament to its popularity with tourists – the iron glove of communism long since having given way to western consumerism.

These days there are practically two versions of Prague: the lively, youthful, 'stag party capital', and the sedate, enchanting 'city of a hundred spires'.

The four main zones of Prague were originally independent towns in their own right. The river Vltava winds its way through their heart and is spanned by the iconic Charles Bridge. On the west side lie Hradcany – the castle quarter, built on a rock spur – and Malá Strana, Prague's most perfectly preserved district, located at the bottom of the castle hill. Over the river are Staré Město, the old town with its vibrant medieval square and outer boulevards, and Nové Město, the new town, which is the city's commercial heart and where you'll find Wenceslas Square and Prague's young partygoers.

EATING OUT

Since the late 1980s, Prague has undergone a bit of a foodie revolution. Global menus have become common currency and the heavy, traditional Czech cuisine is now often served – in the better establishments – with a creative flair and an international touch. Lunch is the main meal of the Czech day and many restaurants close well before midnight. Prague was and still is, to an extent, famous for its infinite variety of dumplings – these were the glutinous staple that saw locals through the long years of stark Communist rule. The favoured local dish is still pork, pickled cabbage and dumplings, and those on a budget can also mix the likes of schnitzel, beer and ginger cake for a ridiculously cheap outlay. Some restaurants include a tip in your final bill, so check closely to make sure you don't tip twice. Czechs consume more beer than anyone else in the world and there are some excellent microbrewery tipples to be had.

On the left bank

Na Kopci

TRADITIONAL CUISINE • BISTRO Leave the city behind and escape to this buzzy bistro, whose name means 'on the hill'. The wallpaper is a montage of pictures of the owner's family and the atmosphere is warm and welcoming. Classic Czech and French dishes are packed with flavour and the local beers make a great accompaniment.

Menu 790/990 Kč – Carte 565/900 Kč

Off plan – *K Závěrce 2774/20 – Ⓜ Smíchovské Nádraží – ✆ 251 553 102 – www.nakopci.com – Closed 5-19 July*

Café Savoy

TRADITIONAL CUISINE • ELEGANT This atmospheric grand café with its superb neo-renaissance ceiling has been open since 1893. Arrive early for breakfast; pop in for coffee and a cake from their patisserie; enjoy the daily lunch special accompanied by a beer; or come for generously sized Czech and French classics at dinner.

Carte 263/575 Kč

PLAN: B2 – *Vitězná 5 – Ⓜ Anděl – ✆ 731 136 144 – www.cafesavoy.ambi.cz*

Kampa Park

MODERN CUISINE • TRENDY Kampa Park is stunningly located by the water's edge, next to Charles Bridge. Choose from several dining areas: the best spots are the Winter Garden and the riverside terrace. The décor is contemporary, as is the interesting menu.

Carte 945/1915 Kč

PLAN: B2 – *Na Kampe 8b, Malá Strana – Ⓜ Malostranská – ✆ 257 532 685 – www.kampapark.com*

On the right bank

La Degustation Bohême Bourgeoise (Oldřich Sahajdák)

MODERN CUISINE • INTIMATE It might be set in a historic building at the end of a narrow lane, but this restaurant is surprisingly stylish, with bespoke chandeliers hung above tables inlaid with slices of oak. Marie B Svobodová's 19C cookery school provides the inspiration for creative modern dishes which stimulate the taste buds.

Specialities: Beef tartare with bread chips. Dumpling with white cabbage and rabbit. Brioche with honey and cinnamon.

Menu 3450 Kč

PLAN: C1 – *Haštalská 18 – Ⓜ Náměsti Republiky – ✆ 222 311 234 – www.ladegustation.cz – Closed Monday, lunch Tuesday-Sunday*

Field (Radek Kašpárek)

MODERN CUISINE • DESIGN Two friends run this stylishly understated restaurant, which has a warm, intimate feel. An eye-catching mural is projected overhead and the light, well-balanced Scandinavian cooking is equally stimulating. Alongside the wine pairings are non-alcoholic drink matches, such as tomato, cucumber and chilli juice.

Specialities: Goose liver, wine spirit, cherry and pistachio. Pike perch with kohlrabi, horseradish and quinoa. Sea buckthorn, juniper, bergamot and beze.

Menu 1300 Kč (lunch)/3600 Kč – Carte 1240/1460 Kč

PLAN: C1 – *U Milosrdných 12 – Ⓜ Staroměstská – ✆ 222 316 999 – www.fieldrestaurant.cz*

Divinis

ITALIAN • FRIENDLY You'll find this intimate, homely restaurant tucked away on a side street; it's run with great passion and has a friendly feel. Rustic, seasonal Italian dishes have original touches and are cooked with flair. The perfect accompaniment comes in the form of a large collection of wines from Italian growers.

Carte 920/1195 Kč

PLAN: C1 – *Týnská 21 – Náměsti Republiky – 222 325 440 – www.divinis.cz – Closed 17 August-3 September, lunch Saturday, Sunday*

Eska

TRADITIONAL CUISINE • DESIGN A café, bakery and restaurant in a converted fabric factory. The dining room has a stark, industrial feel with exposed bricks, pipework and girders, and the open kitchen adds to the buzz. Old family favourites are given modern makeovers; much use is made of traditional techniques like marinating and fermenting.

Carte 475/1055 Kč

Off plan – *Pernerova 49, Karlín – Křižíkova – 731 140 884 – www.eska.ambi.cz*

Sansho

ASIAN • NEIGHBOURHOOD A fun neighbourhood eatery that uses organic and free range ingredients from the owner's butcher's shop. Dishes have an Asian base and could include the likes of soft shell crab sliders or dry sweet pork with coconut rice and papaya; at dinner, they serve a 6 course tasting menu. Some tables are for sharing.

Menu 1100 Kč – Carte 460/600 Kč

PLAN: D1 – *Petrská 25 – Florenc – 222 317 425 – www.sansho.cz – Closed 22 December-2 January, Sunday*

Alcron

MODERN CUISINE • INTIMATE An intimate, semi-circular restaurant dominated by an art deco mural of dancing couples by Tamara de Lempicka. Choose 'hot' or 'cold' dishes from an elaborate international menu. There's a good choice of wines and staff are attentive.

Menu 1800/2600 Kč – Carte 2000/2400 Kč

PLAN: D2 – *Alcron Hotel Prague, Stepanska 40 – Muzeum – 222 820 000 – www.alcron.cz – Closed Monday, lunch Tuesday-Thursday, Sunday*

Aromi

ITALIAN • BRASSERIE A friendly team welcomes you to this bright, contemporary restaurant. Simply prepared, classically based Italian dishes are given modern touches; the fresh fish display demonstrates the owners' commitment to sourcing good quality produce.

Carte 755/1315 Kč

PLAN: D3 – *Náměstí Míru 6 – Náměstí Míru – 222 713 222 – www.aromi.lacollezione.cz*

Bellevue

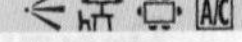

MODERN CUISINE • CHIC Sit on the pleasant terrace or in the contemporary, pastel-hued dining room of this elegant 19C townhouse and take in the view over Charles Bridge and the river. Ambitious, original modern dishes consist of many different elements.

Menu 890 Kč (lunch) – Carte 1150/1815 Kč

PLAN: C2 – *Smetanovo Nábreží 18 – Staroměstská – 222 221 443 – www.bellevuerestaurant.cz*

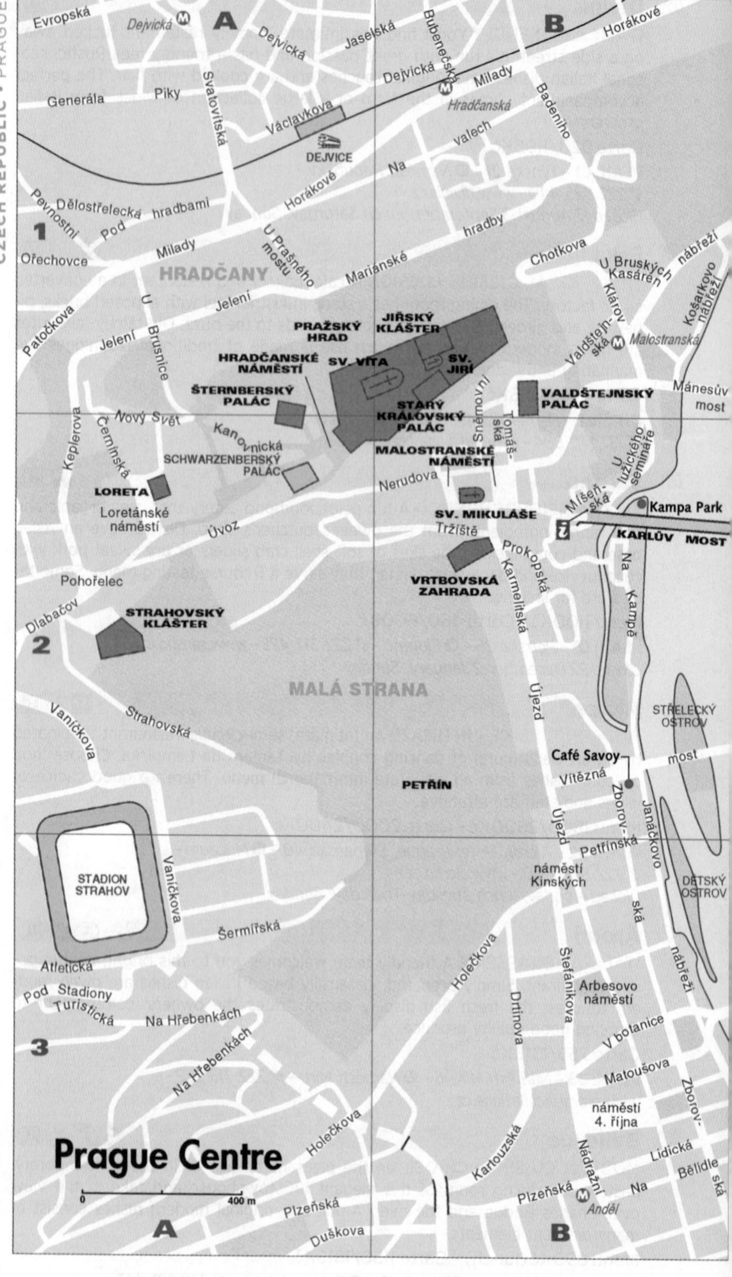
Prague Centre
0
400 m
A
B
1
2
3
Evropská
Dejvická
Dejvická
Jaselská
Bubenečská
Dejvická
Horákové
Milady
Hradčanská
Generála
Piky
Svatovítská
Václavkova
DEJVICE
Badeniho
valech
Na
Horákové
Pevnostní
Dělostřelecká
Pod
hradbami
U Prašného mostu
Ořechovce
Milady
HRADČANY
Mariánské
hradby
Chotkova
U Bruských Kasáren
nábřeží
Kosárkovo nábřeží
Klárov
Patočkova
Jelení
U Brusnice
Jelení
PRAŽSKÝ HRAD
JIŘSKÝ KLÁŠTER
Valdštejnská
Malostranská
HRADČANSKÉ NÁMĚSTÍ
SV. VÍTA
SV. JIŘÍ
ŠTERNBERSKÝ PALÁC
STARÝ KRÁLOVSKÝ PALÁC
Sněmovní
VALDŠTEJNSKÝ PALÁC
Mánesův most
Nový Svět
Keplerova
Černínská
Kanovnická
SCHWARZENBERSKÝ PALÁC
MALOSTRANSKÉ NÁMĚSTÍ
Tomášská
U lužického semináře
Nerudova
LORETA
Loretánské náměstí
Úvoz
SV. MIKULÁŠE
Mišeňská
Kampa Park
Tržiště
KARLŮV MOST
Prokopská
Pohořelec
Karmelitská
Na Kampě
VRTBOVSKÁ ZAHRADA
Dlabačov
STRAHOVSKÝ KLÁŠTER
MALÁ STRANA
Vaníčkova
Strahovská
Újezd
STŘELECKÝ OSTROV
Café Savoy
most
Vítězná
PETŘÍN
Zborovská
Janáčkovo
Újezd
Petřínská
náměstí Kinských
STADION STRAHOV
Vaníčkova
DĚTSKÝ OSTROV
Šermířská
ská
Holečkova
Štefánikova
nábřeží
Atletická
Pod Stadiony
Turistická
Na Hřebenkách
Arbesovo náměstí
Drtinova
V botanice
Na Hřebenkách
Matoušova
Zborov-
náměstí 4. října
Holečkova
Kartouzská
Nádražní
Lidická
Bělidle
ská
Plzeňská
Na
Anděl
Plzeňská
Duškova

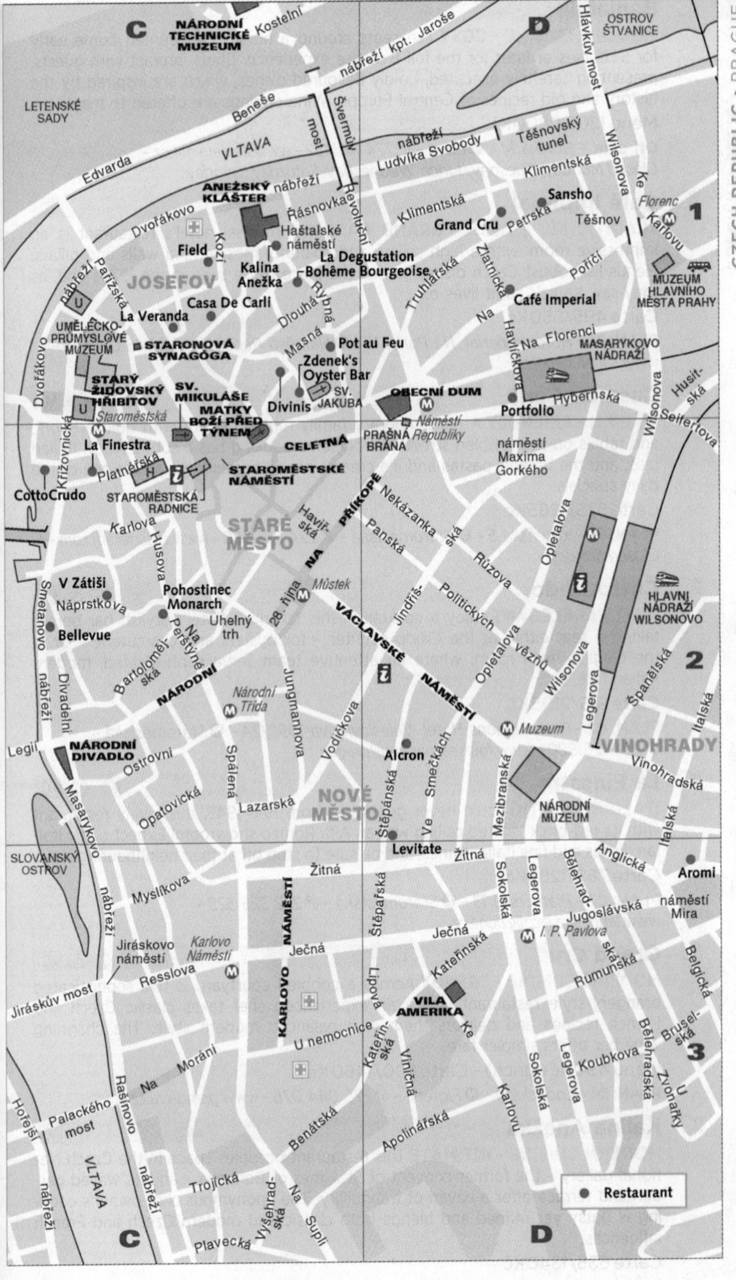
C
D
NÁRODNÍ TECHNICKÉ MUZEUM
Kostelní
nábřeží kpt. Jaroše
OSTROV ŠTVANICE
Hlávkův most
LETENSKÉ SADY
Edvarda Beneše
Švermův most
VLTAVA
nábřeží Ludvíka Svobody
Těšnovský tunel
Klimentská
Wilsonova
Ke Karlovu
Florenc
1
ANEŽSKÝ KLÁŠTER
nábřeží
Řásnovka
Revoluční
Haštalské náměstí
Klimentská
Grand Cru
Sansho
Petrská
Těšnov
Dvořákovo
Field
Kozí
Kalina
Anežka
La Degustation Bohême Bourgeoise
Truhlářská
Zlatnická
Poříčí
MUZEUM HLAVNÍHO MĚSTA PRAHY
nábřeží
Pařížská
JOSEFOV
Casa De Carli
Dlouhá
Rybná
Café Imperial
Na Florenci
U
La Veranda
UMĚLECKO-PRŮMYSLOVÉ MUZEUM
STARONOVÁ SYNAGÓGA
Masná
Pot au Feu
Havlíčkova
MASARYKOVO NÁDRAŽÍ
Dvořákovo
STARÝ ŽIDOVSKÝ HŘBITOV
SV. MIKULÁŠE
Zdenek's Oyster Bar
SV. JAKUBA
OBECNÍ DUM
Hybernská
Husitská
U
Staroměstská
MATKY BOŽÍ PŘED TÝNEM
Divinis
Portfolio
Wilsonova
Seifertova
Náměstí Republiky
Křižovnická
La Finestra
CELETNÁ
PRAŠNÁ BRÁNA
náměstí Maxima Gorkého
Platnéřská
H
STAROMĚSTSKÉ NÁMĚSTÍ
CottoCrudo
STAROMĚSTSKÁ RADNICE
NA PŘÍKOPĚ
Nekázanka
Karlova
STARÉ MĚSTO
Havířská
Panská
Růžova
Opletalova
Husova
V Zátiší
Náprstkova
Smetanovo nábřeží
Pohostinec Monarch
28. října
Můstek
Jindřišská
Politických vězňů
HLAVNÍ NÁDRAŽÍ WILSONOVO
Bellevue
Uhelný trh
Na Perštýně
VÁCLAVSKÉ NÁMĚSTÍ
Opletalova
Wilsonova
Bartolomějská
Jungmannova
2
Divadelní
Španělská
NÁRODNÍ
Národní Třída
Legerova
Italská
Legií
NÁRODNÍ DIVADLO
Vodičkova
Muzeum
VINOHRADY
Ostrovní
Alcron
Spálená
Smečkách
Vinohradská
Masarykovo
Štěpánská
Mezibranská
Opatovická
NOVÉ MĚSTO
Lazarská
NÁRODNÍ MUZEUM
Ve
Italská
Levitate
Žitná
SLOVANSKÝ OSTROV
Anglická
Aromi
Žitná
Sokolská
Legerova
Bělehradská
Myslíkova
KARLOVO NÁMĚSTÍ
Štěpařská
náměstí Míra
nábřeží
Jugoslávská
Ječná
I. P. Pavlova
Jiráskovo náměstí
Karlovo Náměstí
Ječná
Kateřinská
Rumunská
Belgická
Resslova
Jiráskův most
Lipová
VILA AMERIKA
Ke
U nemocnice
Bruselská
3
Kateřinská
Viničná
Sokolská
Legerova
Koubkova
Bělehradská
Zvonařky
Moráni
Na
Karlovu
Rašínovo
Hořejší
Palackého most
Benátská
Apolinářská
VLTAVA
nábřeží
nábřeží
Trojická
Vyšehradská
Na Slupi
Restaurant
Plavecká
C
D

Benjamin

MODERN CUISINE • COSY Ten seats around a horseshoe counter; come early for 5 courses or later for the full 8 course experience. Chefs interact with guests, presenting carefully executed, boldly flavoured dishes, which are inspired by the history and old recipes of Central Europe. Wine pairings are offered to match.

Menu 1200/1800 Kč

Off plan - *Norská 14 - Ⓜ Flora - ✆ 774 141 432 - www.benjamin14.cz - Closed Monday, Tuesday, lunch Wednesday-Saturday, Sunday*

Café Imperial

TRADITIONAL CUISINE • GRAND CAFÉ The Imperial hotel's restaurant is an impressive room, with a high ceiling and colourful mosaic-tiled walls and pillars. Menus list robust Czech dishes. It was the place to be seen in the 1920s and, as they say, Kafka's spirit lives on...

Carte 495/850 Kč

PLAN: D1 - *Hotel Imperial, Na Poricí 15 - Ⓜ Náměsti Republiky - ✆ 246 011 440 - www.cafeimperial.cz*

Casa De Carli

ITALIAN • FRIENDLY A contemporary family-run restaurant with bold artwork, and tables on the cobbled street. Flavoursome cooking has a subtle North Italian bias, and the breads, pastas and ice creams are all homemade; go for one of the daily specials.

Carte 575/1265 Kč

PLAN: C1 - *Vězeňská 5 - Ⓜ Staromestská - ✆ 224 816 688 - www.casadecarli.com - Closed Sunday*

CottoCrudo

ITALIAN • ELEGANT Enjoy a cocktail in this luxurious hotel's stylish bar before taking a seat either at the Crudo counter – for oysters and charcuterie – or in the elegant main room, where an attentive team serve sophisticated, modern Italian fare.

Carte 915/2105 Kč

PLAN: C2 - *Four Seasons Hotel, Veleslavínova 1098/2A - Ⓜ Staroměstská - ✆ 221 426 880 - www.fourseasons.com/prague*

La Finestra

ITALIAN • RUSTIC You'd never guess but from 1918-1945, this lovely restaurant with its red-brick vaulted ceiling was an Alfa Romeo showroom! Expect rustic Italian dishes and fine Italian wines, and be sure to stop off at their neighbouring shop.

Carte 765/1285 Kč

PLAN: C2 - *Platnérská 13 - Ⓜ Staroměstská - ✆ 222 325 325 - www.lafinestra.lacollezione.cz*

Grand Cru

MODERN CUISINE • TRENDY Across a cobbled courtyard is this sophisticated orangery-style restaurant where an experienced chef takes classic Czech and French recipes and delivers them in a balanced modern style. The charming wine bar offers simpler fare.

Menu 490 Kč (lunch) - Carte 620/1460 Kč

PLAN: D1 - *Lodecká 4 - Ⓜ Florenc - ✆ 775 044 076 - www.grand-cru.cz*

Kalina Anežka

MODERN CUISINE • INTIMATE This restaurant occupies space in the Czech National gallery – the former convent of St Agnes of Bohemia – and its walled garden and terrace offer a haven of tranquillity. The eponymous chef-owner's cooking is gutsy yet refined and blends both classic and modern Czech and French influences.

Carte 635/1340 Kč

PLAN: C1 - *Anežská 811/12 - Ⓜ Staromestská - ✆ 222 317 715 - www.kalinarestaurant.cz*

Levitate

CREATIVE • DESIGN Living plant walls and a nature soundtrack feature at this 22-seater basement restaurant. The young Vietnamese chef fuses regional ingredients with Czech, Nordic and Asian cuisine to create a unique set menu themed around 'Flora, Fauna & Aqua'. Choose between Czech and International wine pairings.

Menu 2800 Kč

PLAN: D2 – *Štěpánská 14 – ✆ 724 516 996 – www.levitaterestaurant.cz – Closed Monday, lunch Tuesday-Sunday*

Pohostinec Monarch

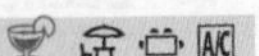

TRADITIONAL CUISINE • PUB The baby sister of Grand Cru has a relaxed, pub-like atmosphere, a large bar and liberal use of black in its decoration. The kitchen, visible through a large hatch, focuses on traditional Czech cooking, with steaks a speciality.

Carte 370/1800 Kč

PLAN: C2 – *Na Perštýně 15 – Ⓜ Můstek – ✆ 703 182 801 – www.monarch.pohostinec.cz*

Portfolio

MODERN CUISINE • CONTEMPORARY DÉCOR A keenly run restaurant with an appealingly relaxed atmosphere, set over two floors and decorated in a contemporary style. The cooking has its roots in French and Italian cuisine and the ambitious dishes are elaborate in their construction.

Carte 535/1285 Kč

PLAN: D1 – *Lannův Palác, Havlíčkova 1030/1 – Ⓜ Náměsti Republiky – ✆ 224 267 579 – www.portfolio-restaurant.cz – Closed 24-25 December, lunch Saturday, Sunday*

Pot au Feu

FRENCH • INTIMATE The chef-owner's cooking is inspired by the French classics but also by his travels. The intimate interior comes with striking artwork and shelves packed with directly sourced French wines. Service is relaxed yet clued-up.

Menu 855/1035 Kč – Carte 665/1355 Kč

PLAN: C1 – *Rybná 13 – Ⓜ Náměsti Republiky – ✆ 739 654 884 – www.potaufeu.cz – Closed Monday, lunch Saturday, Sunday*

Salabka

MODERN CUISINE • TRENDY Set in a boutique winery on the outskirts of the city; vines have been grown on the hillside here since the 13C. Imaginative modern cooking focuses on local ingredients, with each plate containing many textures and flavours. The best tables are on the first floor overlooking the vines. Six spacious and stylish apartments.

Menu 1350 Kč (lunch), 2150/2650 Kč

Off plan – *K Bohnicím 2 – ✆ 778 019 002 – www.salabka.cz – Closed 28 June-14 July, 20 December-19 January, Monday, Tuesday, Sunday*

La Veranda

MEDITERRANEAN CUISINE • COSY Sit surrounded by books in the colourfully decorated main room or head down to the intimate basement. Cooking takes its inspiration from the Med, with Italy playing a big part. Staff are friendly and welcoming.

Menu 1560 Kč – Carte 775/1235 Kč

PLAN: C1 – *Elišky Krásnohorské 2 – Ⓜ Staroměstská – ✆ 224 814 733 – www.laveranda.cz*

V Zátiši

MODERN CUISINE • COSY This modern city centre restaurant is a popular spot. Its name means 'timeless' and with its clever blend of modern Czech and Indian dishes, well-judged spicing and attractive presentation, it looks set to stand up to its name.

Menu 590 Kč (lunch)/1490 Kč – Carte 985/1435 Kč

PLAN: C2 – *Liliová 1, Betlémské Nám. – Ⓜ Můstek – ✆ 222 221 155 – www.vzatisi.cz*

Yamato

JAPANESE • ELEGANT The chef is a local but he trained in Japan, so alongside an array of authentic dishes you'll find some original creations. A selection of Japanese beers and whiskies complement the cooking, and the place is run with real passion.

Menu 380 Kč (lunch)/680 Kč – Carte 650/5500 Kč

Off plan – *U Kanálky 14 – Ⓜ Jiřího z Poděbrad – ✆ 222 212 617 – www.yamato.cz – Closed 6-19 July, lunch Saturday, Sunday*

Zdenek's Oyster Bar

SEAFOOD • BISTRO Deep in the heart of the city is this atmospheric, dimly lit restaurant with a pretty pavement terrace. Menus include tapas, caviar, elaborate seafood platters, dishes from the Josper grill and, of course, 8 different types of oyster.

Carte 900/2430 Kč

PLAN: C1 – *Malá Štupartská 5 – Ⓜ Náměsti Republiky – ✆ 725 946 250 – www.oysterbar.cz*

Yingko/iStock

Westersoe/iStock

DENMARK

DANMARK

COPENHAGEN
KØBENHAVN

AleksandarGeorgiev/iStock

COPENHAGEN IN...

→ **ONE DAY**
Walk along Strøget, National Museum, Ny Carlsberg Glyptotek, Black Diamond, boat watching at Nyhavn.

→ **TWO DAYS**
Tivoli Gardens, Vesterbro, Opera House, Christiania.

→ **THREE DAYS**
Royal palaces at Frederiksstaden, train ride along the coast.

Some cities overwhelm you, and give the impression that there's too much of them to take in. Not Copenhagen. Most of its key sights are neatly compressed within its central Slotsholmen 'island', an area that enjoyed its first golden age in the early seventeenth century in the reign of Christian IV, when it became a harbour of great consequence. It has canals on three sides and opposite the harbour is the area of Christianshavn, home of the legendary freewheeling 'free-town' community of Christiania. Further up from the centre are Nyhavn, the much-photographed canalside with brightly coloured buildings where the sightseeing cruises leave from, and

the elegant Frederiksstaden, whose wide streets contain palaces and museums. West of the centre is where Copenhageners love to hang out: the Tivoli Gardens, a kind of magical fairyland. Slightly more down-to-earth are the western suburbs of Vesterbro and Nørrebro, which were run-down areas given a street credible spit and polish for the 21C, and are now two of the trendiest districts.

Once you've idled away some time in the Danish capital, you'll wonder why anyone might ever want to leave. With its waterfronts, quirky shops and cafés, the city presents a modern, user-friendly ambience – but it also boasts world class art collections, museums, and impressive parks, gardens and lakes, all of which bear the mark of an earlier time.

EATING OUT

Fresh regional ingredients have revolutionized the menus of Copenhagen's hip restaurants and its reputation for food just keeps getting bigger. The city's dining establishments manage to marry Danish dining traditions such as herring or frikkadeller meatballs with global influences to impressive effect. So impressive that in recent times the city has earned itself more Michelin stars, for its crisp and precise cooking, than any other in Scandinavia. Many good restaurants blend French methods and dishes with regional ingredients and innovative touches and there is a trend towards fixed price, no choice menus involving several courses, which means that dinner can be a pleasingly drawn-out affair, stretching over three or four hours. There's no need to tip, as it should be included in the cost of the meal. Danes, though, have a very good reputation as cheerful, helpful waiting staff, so you might feel like adding a bit extra. But be warned, many restaurants – and even hotels – charge between 2.5% and 5% for using a foreign credit card.

Centre

✿✿✿ Geranium (Rasmus Kofoed)

CREATIVE • DESIGN This luxurious restaurant is unusually located on the 8th floor of the National Football Stadium and its full-length windows afford panoramic park views. The surprise tasting menu sees many small, detailed dishes brought to the table in succession; each showcasing the finest organic and biodynamic ingredients using modern techniques.

Specialities: Crispy leaves of Jerusalem artichoke with pickled walnut. Lamb with aromatic herbs, truffle and pickled pine. Caramel with roasted grains and frozen chamomile tea.

Menu 2600 DKK

Off plan – *Per Henrik Lings Allé, Parken National Stadium – Ⓜ Vibenshus Runddel – ✆ 69 96 00 20 – www.geranium.dk – Closed 6-27 July, 21 December-4 January, Monday, Tuesday, Sunday*

✿✿ Alchemist (Rasmus Munk)

INNOVATIVE • DESIGN An immersive and perfectly choreographed dining experience. The 50-course dinner is divided into 5 acts, served at various locations, including a spectacular planetarium-like dome. Dishes are technically complex and highly creative with dramatic contrasts; some make a statement about issues such as plastic pollution in the oceans or overcrowding in chicken farms.

Specialities: "The Toast". "Plastic Fantastic". "Andy Warhol".

Menu 2500 DKK

Off plan – *Refshalevej 173C – Ⓜ Christianshavn – ✆ 31 71 61 61 – www.alchemist.dk – Closed 14 July-1 August, 24 December-6 January, Monday, Tuesday, lunch Wednesday-Saturday, Sunday*

✿✿ a|o|c (Søren Selin)

MODERN CUISINE • ELEGANT A spacious, simply decorated restaurant in the vaults of an eye-catching 17C building close to Nyhavn harbour; owned and run by a chef and an experienced sommelier. Skilful, well-judged and, at times, playful cooking has a Danish heart and shows great originality, as well as a keen eye for detail, flavour and texture.

Specialities: Grilled langoustine with fermented cherries. Dry-aged lamb with pickled greens and lettuce sauce. Rhubarb with strawberries and roses.

Menu 2000 DKK

PLAN: D2 – *Dronningens Tværgade 2 – Ⓜ Kongens Nytorv – ✆ 33 11 11 45 – www.aoc.dk – Closed 8-22 February, 6-30 July, 22 December-3 January, Monday, lunch Tuesday-Saturday, Sunday*

✿✿ Kadeau Copenhagen (Nicolai Nørregaard)

MODERN CUISINE • DESIGN You'll receive a warm welcome at this delightful restaurant, where the open kitchen adds a sense of occasion to the sophisticated room. The chefs have an innate understanding of how best to match fresh and aged produce, and use their experience in preserving and fermenting to add many elements to each dish.

Specialities: Oysters with white asparagus, blackcurrant wood & leaf oil. Cold and hot smoked salmon with fermented tomato water and figs. Sour cream with raspberries and gooseberry juice.

Menu 2150 DKK

PLAN: D3 – *Wildersgade 10B – Ⓜ Christianshavn – ✆ 33 25 22 23 – www.kadeau.dk – Closed Monday, lunch Tuesday-Friday, Sunday*

✿✿ noma (René Redzepi)

CREATIVE • CONTEMPORARY DÉCOR An urban oasis set on former Navy land, this waterside restaurant has a strong connection to nature. Ingredients are organic and they have their own composting machine. Their considered and holistic approach sees unusual seasonal ingredients showcased in creative, complex dishes with vivid natural flavours. The test kitchen is one of the most advanced in the world.

Specialities: Asparagus with wild herbs and barley. Barbecued cod with condiments. Woodruff ice cream with birch sap and pine cones.

Menu 2500 DKK

Off plan – *Refshalevej 96 – Ⓜ Christianshavn – ✆ 32 96 32 97 – www.noma.dk – Closed 6-20 June, 26 September-12 October, 20 December-4 January, Monday, lunch Tuesday-Friday, dinner Saturday, Sunday*

✿ **Alouette** (Nick Curtin)

MODERN CUISINE • TRENDY Graffiti-covered corridors and a freight lift lead to this light, modern restaurant in a former pencil factory. "Delicious First" is how the chef describes his philosophy; he works closely with farmers to see which ingredients are at their peak and then uses them in pared-back, sublimely flavoured dishes. The open fire is used to great effect.

Specialities: Beef tartare with caviar, samphire and tomato vine vinegar. Turbot with roasted bone sauce and smoked lemon skin oil. Berries of the moment with rose petal oil.

Menu 795 DKK

Off plan – *Sturlasgade 14 – Ⓜ Islands Brygge – ✆ 31 67 66 06 – www.restaurantalouette.dk – Closed 13-26 July, 21 December-3 January, Monday, Tuesday, Wednesday, lunch Thursday-Saturday, Sunday*

✿ **Clou** (Jonathan Berntsen)

MODERN CUISINE • INTIMATE This intimate, suburban restaurant puts wine at the heart of everything it does: unusually, the tasting menu is designed to match 6 or 7 carefully chosen wines rather than vice versa. Creative dishes stimulate the senses with their intense natural flavours and well-balanced contrasts in texture and taste.

Specialities: Hand-dived scallops with fermented honey, lime and roasted pepper. Foie gras with lemon sorbet and baked lemon curd. Banana with liquorice, olive oil and ice cream.

Menu 1700 DKK

PLAN: C1 – *Øster Farimagsgade 8 – Ⓜ Nørreport – ✆ 91 92 72 30 – www.restaurant-clou.dk – Closed Monday, Tuesday, lunch Wednesday-Saturday, Sunday*

✿ **formel B** (Kristian Arpe-Møller)

MODERN CUISINE • TRENDY The friendly team create a relaxed environment at this appealing modern restaurant. Menus provide flexibility and the complex small plates are crafted with an assured touch; try at least one of their signature dishes. The wine list offers plenty of Burgundy and Claret, along with some modern producers.

Specialities: Langoustine with sauce nage, carrot purée and vegetables. Roasted turbot with braised ox cheek, parsley & garlic sauce. Sea buckthorn 'en surprise'.

Menu 995 DKK – Carte 450/600 DKK

Off plan – *Vesterbrogade 182-184, Frederiksberg – Ⓜ Enghave Plads – ✆ 33 25 10 66 – www.formelb.dk – Closed lunch Monday-Saturday, Sunday*

✿ **Kiin Kiin**

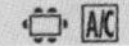

THAI • EXOTIC DÉCOR A charming restaurant, whose name means 'come and eat'. Start with refined versions of street food in the moody lounge, then head for the tasteful dining room decorated with golden Buddhas and fresh flowers. Menus offer modern, personal interpretations of Thai dishes, which have vibrant flavour combinations.

Specialities: Frozen red curry with lobster. Quail with lemongrass and chanterelles. Steamed banana cake with salted coconut ice cream.

Menu 495/975 DKK

PLAN: A1 – *Guldbergsgade 21 – Ⓜ Nørrebros Runddel – ✆ 35 35 75 55 – www.kiin.dk – Closed lunch Monday-Saturday, Sunday*

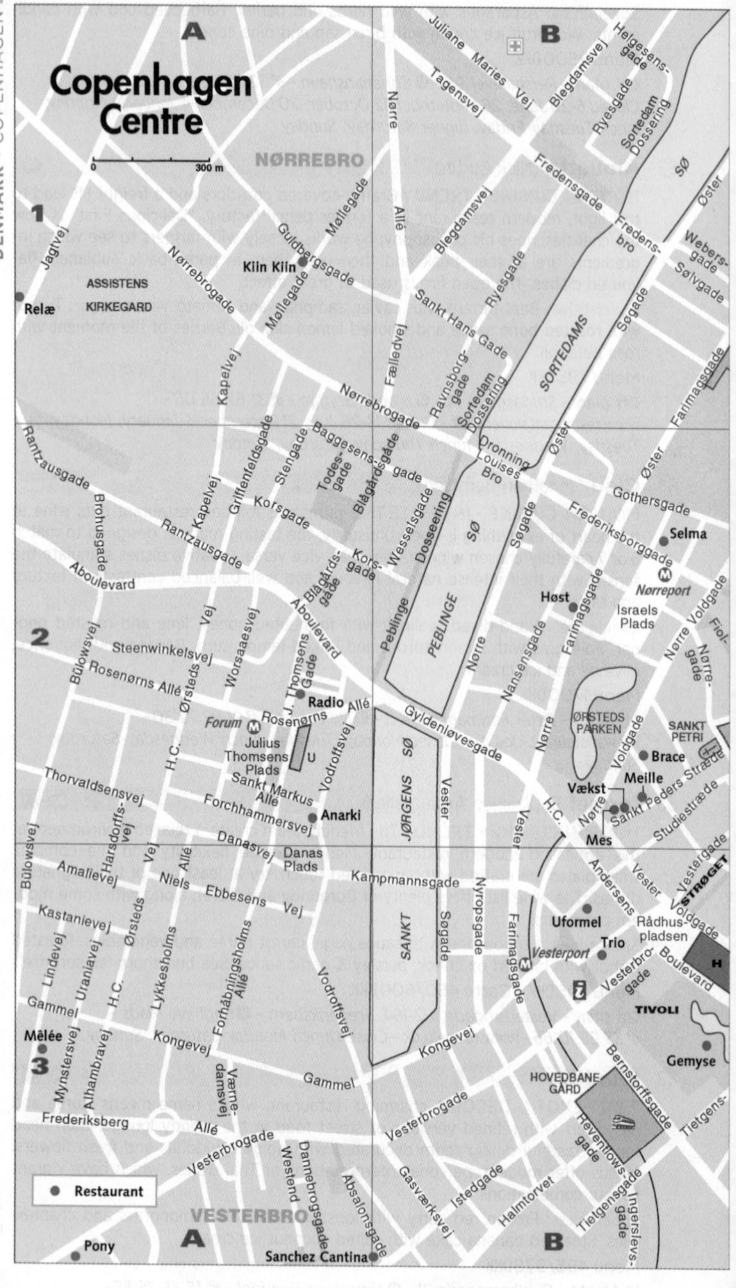
Copenhagen Centre
0
300 m
A
B
1
2
3
NØRREBRO
ASSISTENS KIRKEGARD
Relæ
Kiin Kiin
Selma
Nørreport
Høst
Israels Plads
Radio
Forum
Julius Thomsens Plads
Anarki
ØRSTEDS PARKEN
SANKT PETRI
Brace
Meille
Vækst
Mes
Uformel
Trio
Rådhuspladsen
Vesterport
TIVOLI
Gemyse
HOVEDBANE GARD
Mêlée
Pony
Sanchez Cantina
VESTERBRO
STRØGET
PEBLINGE SØ
SORTEDAMS SØ
SANKT JØRGENS SØ
Restaurant
Jagtvej
Nørrebrogade
Guldbergsgade
Møllegade
Fælledvej
Blegdamsvej
Ryesgade
Sankt Hans Gade
Fredensgade
Fredensbro
Tagensvej
Juliane Maries Vej
Helgesensgade
Sortedam Dossering
Øster Søgade
Webersgade
Sølvgade
Øster Farimagsgade
Rantzausgade
Kapelvej
Griffenfeldsgade
Stengade
Todesgade
Baggesensgade
Blågårdsgade
Korsgade
Wesselsgade
Peblinge Dossering
Oronning Louises Bro
Gothersgade
Frederiksborggade
Nørre Søgade
Nansensgade
Nørre Farimagsgade
Nørre Voldgade
Fiolgade
Nørregade
Brohusgade
Åboulevard
Steenwinkelsvej
Rosenørns Allé
Bülowsvej
Ørsteds Vej
Worsaaesvej
J. Thomsens Gade
Vodroffsvej
Gyldenløvesgade
Sankt Markus Allé
Forchhammersvej
Thorvaldsensvej
Harsdorffsvej
H.C. Ørsteds Vej
H.C. Andersens Boulevard
Sankt Peders Stræde
Studiestræde
Vestergade
Vester Voldgade
Danasvej
Danas Plads
Kampmannsgade
Amalievej
Niels Ebbesens Vej
Kastanievej
Lindevej
Uranievej
Lykkesholms Allé
Forhåbningsholms Allé
Vester Søgade
Nyropsgade
Vester Farimagsgade
Vesterbrogade
Gammel Kongevej
Kongevej
Mynstersvej
Alhambravej
Værnedamsvej
Frederiksberg Allé
Westend
Dannebrogsgade
Absalonsgade
Gasværksvej
Istedgade
Halmtorvet
Bernstorffsgade
Reventlowsgade
Tietgensgade
Ingerslevsgade

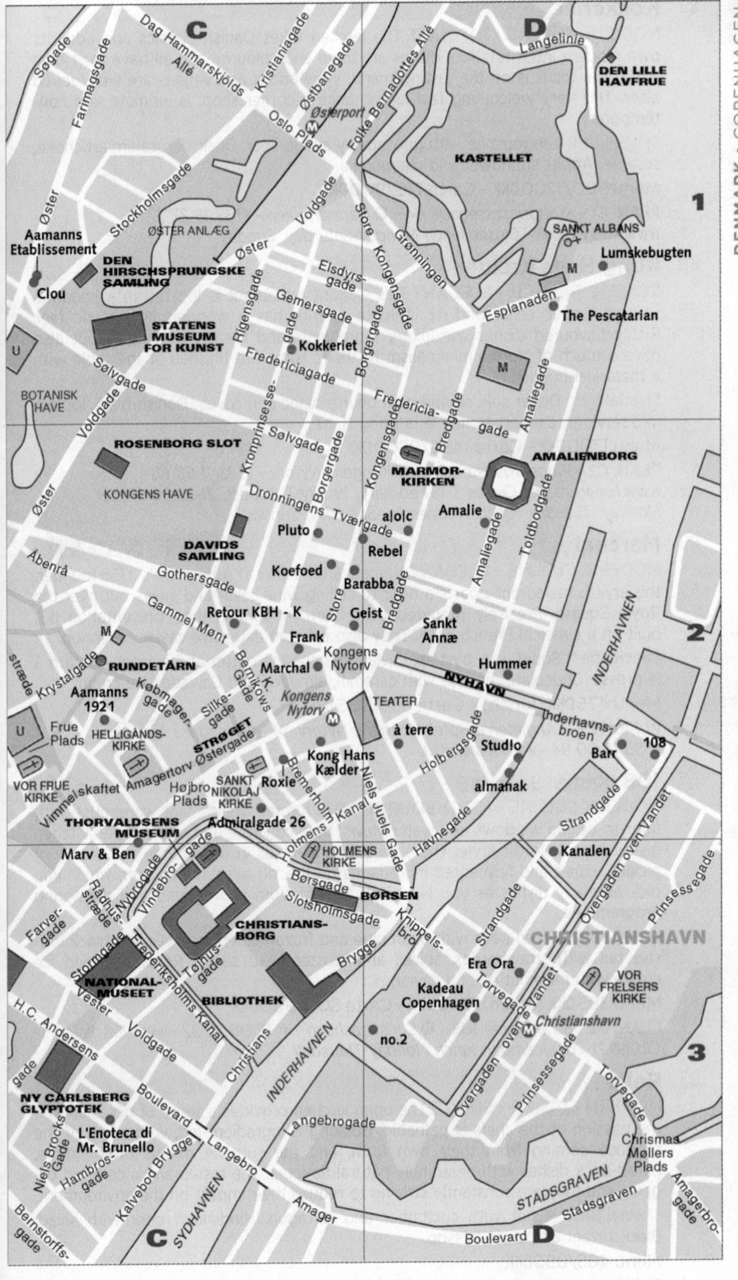
C
D
1
2
3
Søgade
Farimagsgade
Dag Hammarskjölds Allé
Kristianiagade
Østbanegade
Østerport
Oslo Plads
Folke Bernadottes Allé
Langelinie
DEN LILLE HAVFRUE
KASTELLET
Stockholmsgade
Øster Voldgade
ØSTER ANLÆG
Aamanns Etablissement
Clou
DEN HIRSCHSPRUNGSKE SAMLING
STATENS MUSEUM FOR KUNST
Store Kongensgade
Grønningen
SANKT ALBANS
Lumskebugten
M
Esplanaden
The Pescatarian
Elsdyrsgade
Gemersgade
Rigensgade
Kokkeriet
Fredericiagade
Borgergade
Sølvgade
U
BOTANISK HAVE
Voldgade
Kronprinsessegade
Fredericia-gade
Bredgade
Amaliegade
ROSENBORG SLOT
KONGENS HAVE
MARMOR-KIRKEN
AMALIENBORG
Toldbodgade
Øster
Dronningens Tværgade
a|o|c
Amalie
Pluto
Rebel
DAVIDS SAMLING
Abenrå
Gothersgade
Koefoed
Barabba
Gammel Mønt
Retour KBH - K
Geist
Sankt Annæ
Frank
Kongens Nytorv
INDERHAVNEN
stræde
Krystalgade
RUNDETÅRN
Bernikows Gade
K.
Marchal
Hummer
NYHAVN
Aamanns 1921
Købmagergade
Silkegade
Kongens Nytorv
TEATER
Frue Plads
HELLIGÅNDS-KIRKE
STRØGET
Østergade
à terre
Holbergsgade
Studio
Inderhavnsbroen
Barr
108
VOR FRUE KIRKE
Vimmelskaftet
Amagertorv
Højbro Plads
SANKT NIKOLAJ KIRKE
Roxie
Kong Hans Kælder
Bremerholm
Niels Juels Gade
almanak
THORVALDSENS MUSEUM
Admiralgade 26
Holmens Kanal
Havnegade
Strandgade
Marv & Ben
Vindebrogade
HOLMENS KIRKE
Kanalen
Overgaden oven Vandet
Prinsessegade
Rådhusstræde
Nybrogade
Børsgade
BØRSEN
Slotsholmsgade
Knippelsbro
Farvergade
CHRISTIANSBORG
CHRISTIANSHAVN
Stormgade
Frederiksholms Kanal
Tøjhusgade
Brygge
Era Ora
NATIONAL-MUSEET
Torvegade
VOR FRELSERS KIRKE
BIBLIOTHEK
Kadeau Copenhagen
Vester Voldgade
Christianshavn
H.C. Andersens Boulevard
Christians
INDERHAVNEN
no.2
Overgaden oven Vandet
Prinsessegade
Torvegade
gade
NY CARLSBERG GLYPTOTEK
Langebrogade
L'Enoteca di Mr. Brunello
Niels Brocks Gade
Hambrosgade
Kalvebod Brygge
Langebro
Chrismas Møllers Plads
STADSGRAVEN
Stadsgraven
Amagerbrogade
Bernstorffsgade
SYDHAVNEN
Amager Boulevard

Kokkeriet

MODERN CUISINE • INTIMATE The kitchen takes Danish classics and adds its own modern interpretation; dishes are fresh and colourful and all have their own story. The focus is on the tasting menu; vegetarians and vegans are well looked after. This very welcoming restaurant, once a corner shop, is intimate and contemporary.

Specialities: Langoustine with gooseberry and juniper. Duck, Jerusalem artichoke, sesame. Apple, sunflower and chamomile.

Menu 900/1200 DKK – Carte 710/900 DKK

PLAN: C1 – *Kronprinsessegade 64 – Ⓜ Marmorkirken – ✆ 33 15 27 77 – www.kokkeriet.dk – Closed lunch Monday-Saturday, Sunday*

Kong Hans Kælder

CLASSIC FRENCH • ELEGANT This elegant restaurant is located in a beautiful vaulted Gothic cellar and its intimate interior has a wonderfully historic feel. Richly flavoured dishes use luxury ingredients and French techniques but also have a touch of Nordic minimalism to them; some are finished at the table with a theatrical flourish.

Specialities: Dover sole soufflé with beurre blanc and caviar. Danish black lobster in 3 servings. Dessert trolley 'à la Kong Hans'.

Menu 1700 DKK – Carte 1450/2500 DKK

PLAN: C2 – *Vingaardsstræde 6 – Ⓜ Kongens Nytorv – ✆ 33 11 68 68 – www.konghans.dk – Closed 3-18 February, 19 July-11 August, 21-29 December, Monday, Tuesday, lunch Wednesday-Saturday, Sunday*

Marchal

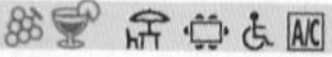

MODERN CUISINE • ELEGANT Named after Hotel D'Angleterre's 1755 founder, this stylish restaurant boasts a floor to ceiling wine cellar and views out over the Royal Square. Precisely prepared dishes are modern in their presentation but built on a classical French base. They also offer an extensive caviar collection.

Specialities: Squid with oysters, caviar, champagne butter and spinach. Canard à la presse. Chocolate mousse with caramel, almonds and Calvados ice cream.

Menu 475 DKK (lunch) – Carte 630/985 DKK

PLAN: C2 – *D'Angleterre Hotel, Kongens Nytorv 34 – Ⓜ Kongens Nytorv – ✆ 33 12 00 94 – www.marchal.dk*

108 (Kristian Baumann)

MODERN CUISINE • NEIGHBOURHOOD A former whale meat warehouse with floor-to-ceiling windows and water views; bare concrete and a semi-open kitchen give it a cool Nordic style. There's a Noma alumnus in the kitchen and plenty of pickled, cured and fermented ingredients on the 'no rules' menu, from which you pick as many dishes as you like. Staff benefit from sponsorship and mentoring programmes.

Specialities: Green peas with fresh pine and frozen elderflower. Grilled black lobster tail with strawberries, spices and lobster head sauce. Roast seaweed ice cream with hazelnut oil and caviar.

Menu 395 DKK (lunch)/1195 DKK – Carte 500/900 DKK

PLAN: D2 – *Strandgade 108 – Ⓜ Christianshavn – ✆ 32 96 32 92 – www.108.dk – Closed 21-26 December, lunch Monday-Thursday*

Relæ

MODERN CUISINE • SIMPLE The open kitchen provides a sense of occasion and the passion of the chefs is palpable. Cooking is ingredient-led, with much of the produce coming from their own farm, and the surprise menus offer simple, pared-back dishes with beautifully natural flavours. The restaurant is certified organic and they are constantly striving to reduce their impact on the environment.

Specialities: Mullet with cucumber and tarragon. Hindsholm pork with salad. Blackcurrant and anise hyssop.

Menu 485/895 DKK

PLAN: A1 – *Jægersborggade 41 – Ⓜ Nuuks Plads – ✆ 36 96 66 09 – www.restaurant-relae.dk – Closed Monday, lunch Tuesday-Thursday, Sunday*

Anarki

TRADITIONAL CUISINE • NEIGHBOURHOOD An unassuming and proudly run neighbourhood bistro, set just over the water in Frederiksberg. The interesting menu of gutsy, flavourful dishes draws inspiration from across the world, so expect to see words like ceviche, paella and burrata as well as bakskuld, along with plenty of offal and some great wines.

Menu 395 DKK – Carte 285/450 DKK

PLAN: A2 – *Vodroffsvej 47 – Ⓜ Forum – ✆ 22 13 11 34 – www.restaurant-anarki.dk – Closed 13 July-9 August, Monday, lunch Tuesday-Sunday*

Barabba

ITALIAN CONTEMPORARY • FRIENDLY Two young Italians run this shabby-chic restaurant hung with specially commissioned mint green chandeliers. Choose authentic flavours on the 'Traditional' menu or enjoy modern twists, such as seaweed tiramisu, on the 'Attitude' menu. Unusually for the city, it's open until late.

Menu 400/600 DKK – Carte 350/480 DKK

PLAN: C2 – *Store Kongensgade 34 – Ⓜ Kongens Nytorv – ✆ 33 10 10 40 – www.barabba.dk – Closed 1-31 July, Monday, Tuesday, lunch Wednesday-Sunday*

Enomania

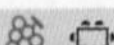

ITALIAN • WINE BAR A simple, bistro-style restaurant near Frederiksberg Park – its name means 'Wine Mania'. The wine cellar comes with a table for tasting and there's an excellent list of over 600 bins, mostly from Piedmont and Burgundy. These are complemented by straightforward, tasty Italian dishes from a weekly 4 course menu.

Menu 390 DKK – Carte 260/390 DKK

Off plan – *Vesterbrogade 187 – Ⓜ Frederiksberg Allé – ✆ 33 23 60 80 – www.enomania.dk – Closed 13-22 February, 4 July-3 August, 10-19 October, 19 December-4 January, Monday, lunch Tuesday-Wednesday, Saturday, Sunday*

Kødbyens Fiskebar

SEAFOOD • SIMPLE This buzzy, industrial-style restaurant is set – somewhat incongruously – in a former butcher's shop in a commercial meat market. Menus feature freshly prepared 'hot' and 'cold' seafood dishes which are based around the latest catch, and oysters are a speciality. The terrace is a popular spot come summer.

Menu 300 DKK (lunch) – Carte 295/560 DKK

Off plan – *Flæsketorvet 100 – Ⓜ København H – ✆ 32 15 56 56 – www.fiskebaren.dk*

Marv & Ben

MODERN CUISINE • BISTRO The young owners bring plenty of enthusiasm to this little restaurant, where dining is split over two dimly lit floors. Organic produce features in seasonal cooking which displays purity and depth of flavour. They produce 6 dishes each evening, which are priced individually or as 4 or 6 courses.

Menu 400/600 DKK – Carte 405/455 DKK

PLAN: C2-3 – *Snaregade 4 – Ⓜ Kongens Nytorv – ✆ 23 81 02 91 – www.marvogben.dk – Closed lunch Monday-Sunday*

Mêlée

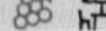

FRENCH • FRIENDLY A bustling neighbourhood bistro with a friendly, laid-back atmosphere. Concise menus change monthly: the modern, country-style cooking is French-based but has Danish influences; portions are generous and flavours are bold. The excellent wine list offers an impressive array of vintages.

Menu 325/525 DKK

PLAN: A3 – *Martensens Allé 16 – Ⓜ Frederiksberg – ✆ 35 13 11 34 – www.melee.dk – Closed lunch Monday-Saturday, Sunday*

Pluto

CLASSIC CUISINE • BISTRO An appealing restaurant with concrete pillars and an intentionally 'unfinished' feel; sit at wooden tables, at the long metal bar or at communal marble-topped tables. The enticing menu is made up of an extensive selection of small plates: cooking is rustic, unfussy and flavoursome.

Menu 475 DKK – Carte 305/430 DKK

PLAN: C2 – *Borgergade 16 – Ⓜ Kongens Nytorv – ✆ 33 16 00 16 – www.restaurantpluto.dk – Closed lunch Monday-Sunday*

Selma

SMØRREBRØD • SIMPLE A sweet, homely place, named after the chef-owner's daughter and run by a friendly young team. Lunchtime smørrebrød are modern in style yet still respect tradition; dinner dispenses with the homemade rye and sourdough bases to create dishes ideal for sharing. There's also an excellent selection of craft beers.

Menu 350/480 DKK – Carte 300/450 DKK

PLAN: B2 – *Rømersgade 20 – Ⓜ Nørreport – ✆ 93 10 72 03 – www.selmacopenhagen.dk – Closed dinner Monday-Tuesday, dinner Sunday*

Aamanns Etablissement

DANISH • BISTRO This cosy, contemporary restaurant is the perfect setting for classic smørrebrød. Choose one of their fixed selections which feature their signature herrings and fried plaice – and order their homemade snaps, flavoured with handpicked herbs, to accompany.

Menu 315 DKK (lunch) – Carte 310/385 DKK

PLAN: C1 – *Øster Farimagsgade 12 – Ⓜ Nørreport – ✆ 20 80 52 02 – www.aamanns.dk/etablissement – Closed dinner Monday-Sunday*

Aamanns 1921

MODERN CUISINE • BRASSERIE An appealing restaurant with original stone arches. Lunch sees traditional smørrebrød offered, while dinner focuses on modern dishes. They grind and mill their own flours, marinate their herring for 6-12 months and gather the herbs for their snaps.

Menu 410 DKK (lunch)/590 DKK – Carte 270/430 DKK

PLAN: C2 – *Niels Hemmingsens Gade 19-21 – Ⓜ Kongens Nytorv – ✆ 20 80 52 04 – www.aamanns.dk/aamanns-1921 – Closed dinner Monday, dinner Sunday*

Admiralgade 26

MODERN CUISINE • INTIMATE This historic house dates from 1796 and sits in one of the oldest parts of the city. It's a relaxed place – a mix of wine bar, café and bistro – and, alongside an appealing modern menu, offers around 4,000 frequently changing wines.

Menu 395 DKK – Carte 395/425 DKK

PLAN: C2 – *Admiralgade 26 – Ⓜ Kongens Nytorv – ✆ 33 33 79 73 – www.admiralgade26.dk – Closed 1-31 July, Sunday*

almanak

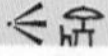

MODERN CUISINE • CONTEMPORARY DÉCOR A chic restaurant on the ground floor of an impressive art deco customs building on the waterfront. At lunch, it's all about smørrebrød, while dinner sees a concise menu of updated Danish classics. An open kitchen adds to the theatre.

Menu 375 DKK (lunch)/650 DKK – Carte 265/600 DKK

PLAN: D2 – *The Standard, Havnegade 44 – Ⓜ Kongens Nytorv – ✆ 72 14 88 08 – www.almanakcph.dk – Closed 1-31 January, Monday*

Stud!o – See restaurant listing

Amalie

SMØRREBRØD • INTIMATE A charming 18C townhouse by Amalienborg Palace, with two tiny, cosy rooms filled with old paintings and elegant porcelain. The Danish menu offers a large choice of smørrebrød, herring, salmon and salads. Service is warm and welcoming.

Carte 250/385 DKK

PLAN: D2 – *Amaliegade 11* – Ⓜ *Kongens Nytorv* – ☎ *33 12 88 10* – *www.restaurantamalie.dk* – *Closed dinner Monday-Saturday, Sunday*

Amass

DANISH • MINIMALIST Sustainability is more than just a byword for this large restaurant: its credentials are evident in everything from the way it recycles to its insistence on only using meats from farms that practise ethical animal husbandry. It has an urban, industrial feel courtesy of graffitied concrete walls and huge windows overlooking the old docks.

Menu 495 DKK (lunch), 695/1095 DKK

Off plan – *Refshalevej 153* – Ⓜ *Christianshavn* – ☎ *43 58 43 30* – *www.amassrestaurant.com* – *Closed 1-29 February, Monday, lunch Tuesday-Thursday, Sunday*

à terre

FRENCH • CONTEMPORARY DÉCOR The experienced chef-owner of this cosy, contemporary bistro, tucked away behind the Royal Danish Theatre, has strong links to France and it is this that forms the basis of most of his menu. Good quality ingredients are carefully cooked to produce pared-back, boldly flavoured dishes.

Menu 350 DKK – Carte 395/685 DKK

PLAN: D2 – *Tordenskjoldsgade 11* – Ⓜ *Kongens Nytorv* – ☎ *71 99 56 99* – *www.aterre.dk* – *Closed 12 July-3 August, Monday, lunch Tuesday-Saturday, Sunday*

Barr

MODERN CUISINE • TRENDY A laid-back quayside restaurant with wood-clad walls. Its name means 'Barley' and it has an amazing array of cask and bottled beers (some custom-brewed), along with beer pairings to match the food. Intensely flavoured, rustic dishes have classic Nordic roots but are taken to new heights; the sweet cake is a must.

Menu 600 DKK – Carte 550/700 DKK

PLAN: D2 – *Strandgade 93* – Ⓜ *Christianshavn* – ☎ *32 96 32 93* – *www.restaurantbarr.com* – *Closed lunch Monday-Thursday*

Brace

ITALIAN • ELEGANT The name of this stylish restaurant refers both to its external structure and to the solidarity of the tightly-knit team. The brightly painted building is set in the heart of the city yet has a tranquil country feel. Refined, eye-catching dishes take on a modern Italian style.

Menu 365 DKK (lunch)/495 DKK – Carte 290/430 DKK

PLAN: B2 – *Teglgårdstræde 8a* – Ⓜ *Nørreport* – ☎ *28 88 20 01* – *www.restaurantbrace.dk* – *Closed 3-10 January, 3-10 May, 19 July-2 August, 20-27 December, lunch Monday-Thursday, Sunday*

L' Enoteca di Mr. Brunello

ITALIAN • ELEGANT Tucked away near the Tivoli Gardens is this restaurant and wine shop run by passionate, experienced owners. Refined, classic Italian cooking uses good quality produce imported from Italy. As you'd hope, the good value Italian wine list offers over 150 different Brunello di Montalcinos.

Menu 495/695 DKK – Carte 570/590 DKK

PLAN: C3 – *Rysensteensgade 16* – Ⓜ *København Hovedbane Gård* – ☎ *33 11 47 20* – *www.lenoteca.dk* – *Closed 5 July-11 August, 22 December-5 January, Monday, lunch Tuesday-Saturday, Sunday*

Era Ora

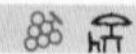

ITALIAN • ELEGANT This long-standing restaurant with an enclosed rear terrace and a formal air sits on a quaint cobbled street by the canal. Modern dishes have an Italian slant and feature lots of different ingredients – many of which are imported from Italy. The wine cellar boasts an impressive 90,000+ bottles.

Menu 500 DKK (lunch), 980/1280 DKK

PLAN: D3 – *Overgaden Neden Vandet 33B* – Ⓜ *Christianshavn* – ✆ *32 54 06 93* – *www.era-ora.dk* – *Closed lunch Monday, Sunday*

Frank

MODERN CUISINE • CHIC Soft lighting, flickering candles and a mix of comfy sofas and designer wooden furnishings give Frank a relaxed air. Choose between an à la carte and a tasting menu – both of which offer flavour-packed modern dishes with a French slant.

Menu 545 DKK – Carte 380/580 DKK

PLAN: C2 – *Ny Adelgade 3* – Ⓜ *Kongens Nytorv* – ✆ *38 41 41 37* – *www.restaurantfrank.dk* – *Closed lunch Monday-Saturday, Sunday*

Frederiks Have

DANISH • NEIGHBOURHOOD A sweet two-roomed neighbourhood restaurant hidden just off the main street in a residential area. Sit inside – surrounded by flowers and vivid local art – or outside on the terrace. Good value menus offer a mix of traditional Danish and French dishes.

Menu 295 DKK (lunch)/400 DKK – Carte 510/550 DKK

Off plan – *Smallegade 41* – Ⓜ *Fasanvej St.* – ✆ *38 88 33 35* – *www.frederikshave.dk* – *Closed Sunday*

Geist

MODERN CUISINE • DESIGN When the weather's right, find a seat on the terrace of this lively restaurant; when it's not, take in the view of the square through the floor to ceiling windows. There's a large counter to the front and a more intimate room to the rear. Cleverly crafted dishes display a lightness of touch; 4 should suffice.

Carte 400/500 DKK

PLAN: C2 – *Kongens Nytorv 8* – Ⓜ *Kongens Nytorv* – ✆ *33 13 37 13* – *www.restaurantgeist.dk*

Gemyse

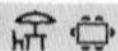

VEGETARIAN • RUSTIC Gemyse sits in the heart of the Tivoli Gardens; it only opens when they do and admission must be paid, so arrive early to wander around. Garden tools decorate the walls and it has its own greenhouse and raised beds. The attractively presented, creative small plates are vegetable-orientated and 100% organic.

Menu 550 DKK – Carte 340/450 DKK

PLAN: B3 – *Tivoli Gardens, Bernstoffsgade 5* – Ⓜ *København H* – ✆ *88 70 00 00* – *www.nimb.dk* – *Closed 6 January-4 April, 23 September-11 October, 4-16 November*

Høst

MODERN CUISINE • FRIENDLY A busy neighbourhood bistro with fun staff and a lively atmosphere; sit in the shabby-chic Garden Room. The good value set menu comprises 3 or 5 courses but comes with lots of extra 'surprises'. Modern, boldly flavoured, visually impressive dishes focus on Nordic fish and shellfish.

Menu 350/450 DKK

PLAN: B2 – *Nørre Farimagsgade 41* – Ⓜ *Nørreport* – ✆ *89 93 84 09* – *www.cofoco.dk/restauranter/hoest* – *Closed lunch Monday-Sunday*

Hummer

SEAFOOD • FRIENDLY Lobster is the mainstay of the menu at this seafood-orientated restaurant, situated among the brightly coloured buildings on the famous Nyhavn strip. Enjoy a meal on the sunny terrace or in the modish, nautically styled dining room.

Menu 350/475 DKK – Carte 330/655 DKK

PLAN: D2 – *Nyhavn 63a – Ⓜ Kongens Nytorv – ✆ 33 33 03 39 – www.restauranthummer.dk*

Kanalen

DANISH • BISTRO Find a spot on the delightful canalside terrace of this quaint, shack-like building – formerly the Harbour Police office – and watch the boats bobbing up and down as you eat. Modern-looking dishes follow the seasons; some honour Danish traditions, while others bring Mediterranean ingredients into play.

Menu 360 DKK (lunch), 480/700 DKK – Carte 380/700 DKK

PLAN: D3 – *Wilders Plads 2 – Ⓜ Christianshavn – ✆ 32 95 13 30 – www.restaurant-kanalen.dk – Closed Sunday*

Kiin Kiin VeVe

VEGETARIAN • DESIGN A former bread factory houses this chic restaurant which serves sophisticated vegetarian cuisine. The 6 course tasting menu revolves around the seasons and offers some imaginative combinations. Wine and juice pairings accompany.

Menu 750 DKK

Off plan – *Dampfærgevej 7 – Ⓜ Østerport – ✆ 51 22 59 55 – www.veve.dk – Closed Monday, Tuesday, lunch Wednesday-Saturday, Sunday*

Koefoed

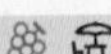

MODERN CUISINE • INTIMATE An intimate collection of rooms in an old coal cellar, where everything from the produce to the glassware celebrates Bornholm island. Modern cooking is accompanied by an impressive range of bordeaux wines. Lunch sees reinvented smørrebrød.

Menu 290 DKK (lunch)/495 DKK – Carte 300/500 DKK

PLAN: C2 – *Landgreven 3 – Ⓜ Kongens Nytorv – ✆ 56 48 22 24 – www.restaurant-koefoed.dk – Closed Monday, Sunday*

Lumskebugten

TRADITIONAL CUISINE • COSY A traditional quayside restaurant with period décor, charming staff and a warm ambience. Lunch sees plenty of herring and smørrebrød, while dinner offers traditional dishes like fried fish on the bone or Danish rib-eye steaks.

Menu 375 DKK (lunch), 485/685 DKK – Carte 375/800 DKK

PLAN: D1 – *Esplanaden 21 – Ⓜ Marmorkirken – ✆ 33 15 60 29 – www.lumskebugten.dk – Closed 13 July-2 August, 23 December-3 January, dinner Monday-Tuesday, Sunday*

Meille

MODERN CUISINE • BISTRO Sister to Mes round the corner, 'Us' is a busy bistro with shelves full of cookbooks, wine bottles and jars of preserved, fermented and marinated produce. Lunch offers a classic smørrebrød selection; dinner sees a 3 or 5 course set menu of creative modern Nordic dishes with a rustic edge.

Menu 195 DKK (lunch), 300/350 DKK – Carte 285/305 DKK

PLAN: B2 – *Sankt Peders Stræde 24a – Ⓜ Nørreport – ✆ 53 65 14 53 – www.restaurant-meille.dk – Closed 23 December-5 January, Monday, lunch Tuesday-Wednesday*

Mes

DANISH • INTIMATE A sweet little restaurant run by a tight-knit team. The frequently changing set menu lists classic dishes – some of which are pepped up with modern techniques. A 120 year old German cooling cabinet plays host to the wines.

Menu 350 DKK

PLAN: B2 – *Jarmers Plads 1 – Ⓜ Nørreport – ✆ 25 36 51 81 – www.restaurant-mes.dk – Closed 23 December-4 January, lunch Monday-Saturday, Sunday*

Mielcke & Hurtigkarl

CREATIVE • ELEGANT Set in a delightful spot in Frederiksberg Gardens, its walls painted with garden scenes, is this charming 1744 orangery with a fire-lit terrace. Dishes come from around the globe, with Asian influences to the fore – and an amazing array of herbs from the gardens.

Menu 800/1100 DKK

Off plan – *Runddel 1 – Ⓜ Frederiksberg Allé – ✆ 38 34 84 36 – www.mhcph.com – Closed 19 December-15 January, Monday, lunch Tuesday-Saturday, Sunday*

no.2

MODERN CUISINE • DESIGN Set among smart offices and apartments on the edge of the dock is this elegant restaurant; a sister to a|o|c. Fresh, flavoursome dishes focus on quality Danish ingredients – highlights include the cured hams, cheeses and ice creams.

Menu 325 DKK (lunch)/475 DKK – Carte 300/395 DKK

PLAN: D3 – *Nicolai Eigtveds Gade 32 – Ⓜ Christianshaven – ✆ 33 11 11 68 – www.nummer2.dk – Closed 6-14 April, 13 July-4 August, lunch Saturday, Sunday*

Pony

DANISH • BISTRO A buzzy restaurant with friendly, chatty service; sit on high stools by the kitchen or in the retro dining room. Modern menus are defined by the seasons and are 100% produce-led, with natural flavours leading the way. Choose from the concise à la carte or try the more adventurous 4 course 'Pony Kick'.

Menu 445/495 DKK

PLAN: A3 – *Vesterbrogade 135 – Ⓜ Frederiksberg Allé – ✆ 33 22 10 00 – www.ponykbh.dk – Closed 29 June-11 August, 21-28 December, Monday, lunch Tuesday-Sunday*

Radio

MODERN CUISINE • MINIMALIST An informal restaurant with an unfussy urban style, wood-clad walls and cool anglepoise lighting. Oft-changing menus feature full-flavoured, good value dishes and use organic ingredients grown in the restaurant's nearby fields. Pick 3 or 5 dishes from the five understated choices.

Menu 350/435 DKK

PLAN: A2 – *Julius Thomsens Gade 12 – Ⓜ Forum – ✆ 25 10 27 33 – www.restaurantradio.dk – Closed 20 July-2 August, Monday, lunch Tuesday-Thursday, Sunday*

Rebel

MODERN CUISINE • BISTRO Located in a busy part of the city; a simply decorated restaurant with closely set tables and a buzzy vibe. Choose 4 dishes from the list of small plates or go for the tasting menu; cooking is modern and refined, and relies largely on Danish produce. The atmospheric lower floor is often used for parties.

Menu 525 DKK – Carte 520/600 DKK

PLAN: C-D2 – *Store Kongensgade 52 – Ⓜ Kongens Nytorv – ✆ 33 32 32 09 – www.restaurantrebel.dk – Closed 27 July-10 August, 21 December-4 January, Monday, lunch Tuesday-Saturday, Sunday*

Retour KBH - K

STEAKHOUSE • BISTRO A relaxed, informal restaurant with a stark white interior and contrasting black furnishings. A small menu offers simply prepared grills, good quality American rib-eye steaks and an affordable selection of wines.

Carte 240/625 DKK

PLAN: C2 – *Ny Østergade 21* – Ⓜ *Kongens Nytorv* – ✆ *33 16 17 19* – *www.retoursteak.dk*

Roxie

MODERN CUISINE • DESIGN Little sister to Kadeau is this chic, industrial-style restaurant set over three floors of a boutique hotel. The modern bistro dishes use lots of pickled, fermented and preserved produce and are full of interesting textures and flavours. Relaxed but professional service comes from a knowledgeable team.

Menu 550/800 DKK – Carte 520/710 DKK

PLAN: C2 – *Herman K Hotel, Bremerholm 6* – Ⓜ *Kongens Nytorv* – ✆ *53 89 10 69* – *www.roxie.dk* – *Closed lunch Monday-Sunday*

Sanchez Cantina

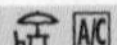

MEXICAN • NEIGHBOURHOOD A neighbourhood cantina offering Mexican small plates, powerful flavours and a lot of fun; grab a seat at the counter, order a mezcal and watch the chefs at work. The best choice is the 'favourite servings', which is five dishes selected by the kitchen. Come for brunch at the weekend.

Menu 400 DKK – Carte 265/400 DKK

PLAN: A-B3 – *Istedgade 60* – Ⓜ *København Hovedbane Gård* – ✆ *31 11 66 40* – *www.lovesanchez.com* – *Closed 1-15 February, lunch Monday-Friday*

Sankt Annæ

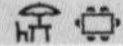

SMØRREBRØD • COSY An attractive terraced building with a traditional, rather quaint interior. There's a seasonal à la carte and a daily blackboard menu: prices can vary so check before ordering. The lobster and shrimp – fresh from local fjords – are a hit.

Carte 210/300 DKK

PLAN: D2 – *Sankt Annæ Plads 12* – Ⓜ *Kongens Nytorv* – ✆ *33 12 54 97* – *www.restaurantsanktannae.dk* – *Closed 13 July-3 August, dinner Monday-Saturday, Sunday*

Stud!o

MODERN CUISINE • DESIGN The open kitchen is the focal point of this stylishly understated restaurant on the top floor of a former Customs House; sit at the marble-topped counter or at one of the eight or so tables. Set menus offer light, modern dishes which use local ingredients and some classic French techniques.

Menu 700 DKK (lunch)/1500 DKK

PLAN: D2 – *The Standard, Havnegade 44* – Ⓜ *Kongens Nytorv* – ✆ *72 14 88 08* – *www.thestandardcph.dk* – *Closed 1-31 January, 2-20 August, Monday, Tuesday, lunch Wednesday, Sunday*

Sushi Anaba

JAPANESE • CONTEMPORARY DÉCOR The young Danish chef-owner of this compact quayside restaurant trained in Tokyo, so you can be sure of an authentic experience. It seats just 8 diners at the counter – or there's a small tatami room for groups. Top quality Nordic ingredients underpin the classic Edomae sushi; go for the sake pairings.

Menu 1400 DKK

Off plan – *Sandkaj 39* – Ⓜ *Nordhavn* – ✆ *61 61 51 86* – *www.sushianaba.com* – *Closed Monday, Tuesday, lunch Wednesday-Saturday, Sunday*

The Pescatarian

CREATIVE • CONTEMPORARY DÉCOR Dine in one of three rooms at this buzzing, minimalist restaurant in the north of the city. Choose a seafood or a vegetarian tasting menu of either 4 or 8 courses. The chef prepares modern dishes with all the typical Danish hallmarks, including preservation techniques and a lightness of touch.

Menu 400/600 DKK

PLAN: D1 – *Amaliegade 49 – Ⓜ Marmorkirken – ☎ 30 63 83 22 – www.thepescatarian.dk – Closed lunch Monday-Sunday*

Trio

MODERN CUISINE • DESIGN The highest restaurant in the city is located on floors 9 and 10 of the striking Axel Towers building; enjoy a cocktail while taking in the view. Accomplished dishes take their influences from both classic French and modern Nordic cuisine.

Menu 400 DKK (lunch)/725 DKK – Carte 380/495 DKK

PLAN: B3 – *Axel Towers, Jernbanegade 11 – Ⓜ København Hovedbane Gård – ☎ 44 22 74 74 – www.restauranttrio.dk – Closed 6-14 April, 13 July-4 August, 23 December-4 January, Sunday*

Uformel

MODERN CUISINE • TRENDY In the heart of the city, you'll find this informal sister to Formel B, with its black and gold décor, smart open kitchen and lively cocktail bar. Dishes blend traditional flavours with more unusual combinations; all are uniformly priced tasting plates, and 3-5 per person is about right.

Carte 375/435 DKK

PLAN: B3 – *Studiestraede 69 – Ⓜ Vesterport – ☎ 70 99 91 11 – www.uformel.dk – Closed lunch Monday-Sunday*

Vækst

MODERN CUISINE • RUSTIC Dining outside 'inside' is the theme here, and you'll find plants, garden furniture and a full-sized greenhouse at the centre of the room. Interesting Danish cooking follows the seasons and is light, stimulating and full of flavour.

Menu 325 DKK – Carte 375/564 DKK

PLAN: B2 – *Sankt Peders Stræde 34 – Ⓜ Nørreport – ☎ 38 41 27 27 – www.cofoco.dk/en/restaurants/vaekst/ – Closed lunch Sunday*

Environs of Copenhagen

at Gentofte North : 8 km by Ostbanegade and Road 2

✿✿ Jordnær (Eric Kragh Vildgaard)

DANISH • ROMANTIC At the passionately run 'Down to Earth', many of the ingredients are foraged by the talented chef, Eric Kragh Vildgaard, whose beautifully crafted, minimalistic plates of food have subtle, harmonious flavours. The enthusiastic chefs deliver dishes and are happy to chat. It's worth opting for the wine pairings.

Specialities: Caviar, cauliflower and salted cream. Turbot with truffle and yuzu kosho beurre blanc. Pineapple weed with raw milk and green rhubarb.

Menu 850/1650 DKK

Off plan – *Gentofte Hotel,, Gentoftegade 29 – ☎ 22 40 80 20 – www.restaurantjordnaer.dk – Closed 10-16 February, 6-26 July, 12-18 October, 21 December-3 January, Monday, Tuesday, lunch Wednesday, Sunday*

at Klampenborg North : 12 km by Folke Bernadottes Allé and Road 2

Den Røde Cottage

MODERN CUISINE • COSY Run with real enthusiasm by a young team of friends, this cosy 'Red Cottage' sits in a charming spot in a wooded park close to the sea. Dishes reflect the changing seasons and the modern, well-balanced cooking respects the classics whilst also having its own original style.

Menu 450 DKK (lunch), 575/825 DKK

Off plan – *Strandvejen 550 – ✆ 31 90 46 14 – www.denroedecottage.dk – Closed 10-16 February, 12-18 October, Monday, Tuesday, lunch Wednesday-Thursday*

at Søllerød North : 20 km by Tagensvej (take the train to Holte then taxi) - F 2840 Holte

Søllerød Kro

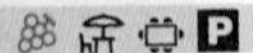

MODERN CUISINE • INN A characterful 17C thatched inn by a pond in a picturesque village, with a delightful courtyard terrace and three elegant, intimate rooms. In keeping with the surroundings, cooking has a classical heart but is presented in a modern style. Dishes have deceptive depth and the wine list is a tome of beauty.

Specialities: Oscietra caviar 'en surprise'. Turbot with snails, broad beans, olives and ramsons. Matcha with white chocolate, woodruff and almond milk.

Menu 495 DKK (lunch), 1195/1795 DKK – Carte 960/1200 DKK

Off plan – *Søllerødvej 35 – ✆ 45 80 25 05 – www.soelleroed-kro.dk – Closed 11-19 February, 6-14 April, 13 July-4 August, Monday, Tuesday, dinner Sunday*

AARHUS

AARHUS

Urilux/iStock

AARHUS IN...

→ **ONE DAY**
AROS Art Museum, the Viking Museum, Aarhus Cathedral, stroll around the Latin Quarter.

→ **TWO DAYS**
Den Gamle By (open air 'living' museum), hire a bike and ride into the country.

→ **THREE DAYS**
Marselisborg Palace (summer residence of the Royal family), Moesgaard Museum.

Known as the world's smallest big city, Denmark's second city is a vibrant, versatile place, yet has the charm of a small town. It was originally founded by the Vikings in the 8th century and has been an important trading centre ever since. It's set on the Eastern edge of Jutland and is the country's main port; lush forests surround it, and there are beautiful beaches to the north and south. It's easy to enjoy the great outdoors, while also benefiting from the advantages of urban life.

There's plenty to see and do, and most of it is within walking distance: the city centre is awash with shops – from

big chains to quirky boutiques – as well as museums, bars and restaurants, and the student population contributes to its youthful feel. The most buzzing area is Aboulevarden; a pedestrianized street which runs alongside the river, lined with clubs and cafés. Cultural activities are also high on the agenda of the European Capital of Culture 2017: visit the 12th century Cathedral and the ARoS Art Museum with its colourful rooftop panorama; witness the 2000 year old Grauballe man on display at the Moesgaard prehistoric museum; or step back in time at Den Gamle By. This is not a place that stands still and bold redevelopment projects are reshaping the cityscape, with shiny new apartment and office blocks springing up around the harbour.

EATING OUT

Being a student city, Aarhus hums with café culture all year round; you'll find cosy coffee shops on almost every street, offering breakfasts, cakes, sandwiches and light lunches – some are also popular places to enjoy an evening drink, especially in the lively Aboulevarden area. Eating out is something the Danes excel at and restaurants range from friendly bistros to elegant fine dining establishments; most offer food with a Danish heart but influences come from around the globe. Local produce includes freshly caught fish landed at the harbour and vegetables from the island of Samso; restaurants tend to offer set menus of between 3 and 7 courses and these are great way to sample a varied selection of dishes. They tend to open early – at around 6pm – while the bars and clubs stay open late, and often offer live music. Not to be overlooked are the city's classic Danish smørrebørd restaurants, where satisfying and wonderfully tasty open sandwiches are served, often along with a tempting selection of cakes and pastries. Tipping is not expected, but obviously greatly appreciated.

✿ Domestic (Morten Rastad and Christoffer Norton) 

MODERN CUISINE • **TRENDY** This restaurant sets itself the challenge of using only Danish ingredients - hence the name - so expect lots of different techniques, creativity and imagination in their 4 and 8 course menus. It's housed in a period property that's been everything from a school to a dairy; the burnt oak dining tables are lovely.

Specialities: Turbot, grilled cucumber, herbs and angelica. Aged pork, roasted onions and fermented unripe plums. Sweet taco, barley, koji and rose.

Menu 600/1000 DKK

PLAN: B2 – *Mejlgade 35B – ✆ 61 43 70 10 – www.restaurantdomestic.dk – Closed Monday, lunch Tuesday-Saturday, Sunday*

✿ Frederikshøj (Wassim Hallal) 

CREATIVE • **ELEGANT** Set in the former staff lodge to the Royal Palace, this restaurant is smart, luxurious and contemporary. Ask for a table by the floor to ceiling windows for a view over the gardens and out to sea. The elaborate, creative, modern dishes have French influences and service is professional and knowledgeable.

Specialities: Norwegian lobster with new potatoes from Samsø. Forest chicken with morels. Cherries 'à la WH'.

Menu 1200/1800 DKK

Off plan – *Oddervej 19-21 – ✆ 86 14 22 80 – www.frederikshoj.com – Closed 13 July-9 August, 12-18 October, 14-27 December, Monday, Tuesday, lunch Wednesday-Saturday, Sunday*

✿ Gastromé (William Jørgensen) 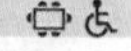

MODERN CUISINE • **TRENDY** This intimate, keenly run Latin Quarter restaurant features a semi open plan kitchen and stark white walls punctuated with contemporary art. Various menus are available, with added 'snacks' – and wines to match if desired. Refined, complex cooking showcases top-notch seasonal produce and modern techniques.

Specialities: Halibut with lemon confit and watercress. Beef, cherries and chanterelles. Strawberries with rice, elderflower and spruce.

Menu 800/1700 DKK

PLAN: B2 – *Rosensgade 28 – ✆ 28 78 16 17 – www.gastrome.dk – Closed Monday, lunch Tuesday-Friday, Sunday*

Hærværk 

DANISH • **INTIMATE** Run by a group of friends, this restaurant's ersatz industrial feel comes from a concrete floor, stark white décor and a glass-fronted fridge of hanging meats. The menu focuses on organic produce in dishes that are earthy and natural. Their ingredient options initially made them think more about sustainability, which now underpins all their actions.

Menu 455 DKK

PLAN: A2 – *Frederiks Allé 105 – ✆ 50 51 26 51 – www.restaurant-haervaerk.dk – Closed Monday, Tuesday, lunch Wednesday-Saturday, Sunday*

Pondus 

MODERN CUISINE • **BISTRO** Set by the narrow city centre canal, the little sister to Substans is a small, rustic bistro with a friendly vibe and a stripped-back style. The blackboard menu offers flavoursome cooking which uses organic Danish produce. Dishes are bright and colourful and represent great value.

Menu 350 DKK – Carte 285/480 DKK

PLAN: B2 – *Åboulevarden 51 – ✆ 28 77 18 50 – www.restaurantpondus.dk – Closed lunch Monday-Sunday*

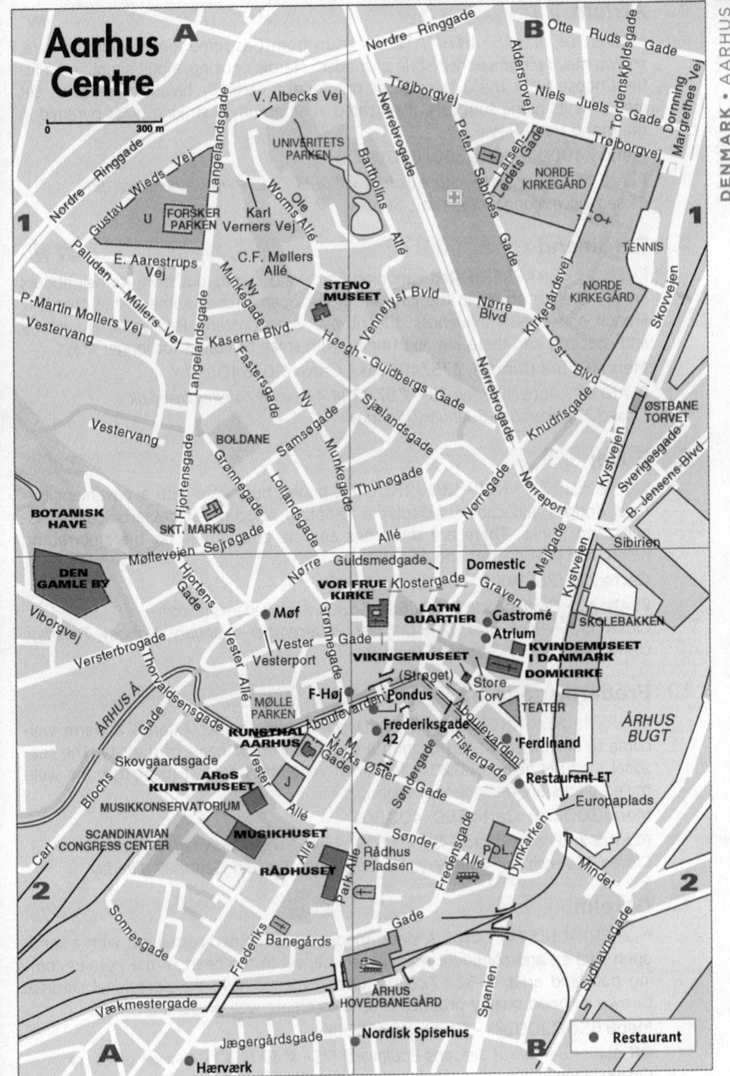
Aarhus Centre
300 m
A
B
1
2
Nordre Ringgade
Otte Ruds Gade
Alderstovej
Tordenskjoldsgade
Niels Juels Gade
Dorning Margrethes Vej
Trøjborgvej
V. Albecks Vej
Langelandsgade
UNIVERITETS PARKEN
Nørrebrogade
Peter Sabroes Gade
Larsen-Ledets Gade
NORDE KIRKEGÅRD
Bartholins Allé
Ole Worms Allé
Karl Verners Vej
Gustav Wieds Vej
FORSKER PARKEN
U
TENNIS
E. Aarestrups Vej
C.F. Møllers Allé
Paludan-Müllers Vej
STENO MUSEET
Vennelyst Bvld
Nørre Blvd
Kirkegårdsvej
Skovvejen
P-Martin Mollers Vej
Vestervang
Ny Munkegade
Kaserne Blvd.
Høegh-Guidbergs Gade
Øst Blvd
Fastersgade
Langelandsgade
Knudrisgade
ØSTBANE TORVET
Sjælandsgade
Samsøgade
BOLDANE
Grønnegade
Kystvejen
Sverigesgade
B. Jensens Blvd
Lollandsgade
Thunøgade
Nørregade
Nørreport
Hjortensgade
BOTANISK HAVE
SKT. MARKUS
Sejrøgade
Allé
Sibirien
Møllevejen
DEN GAMLE BY
Nørre
Guldsmedgade
Domestic
Mejlgade
Hjortens Gade
VOR FRUE KIRKE
Klostergade
Graven
Viborgvej
Møf
LATIN QUARTIER
Gastromé
SKOLEBAKKEN
Vester
Gade
Atrium
Vesterport
KVINDEMUSEET I DANMARK
Versterbrogade
VIKINGEMUSEET
DOMKIRKE
Vester Allé
(Strøget)
Store Torv
Thorvaldsensgade
F-Høj
Pondus
TEATER
ÅRHUS Å
MØLLE PARKEN
Aboulevarden
ÅRHUS BUGT
Frederiksgade 42
KUNSTHAL AARHUS
J. M. Mørks Gade
Fiskergade
'Ferdinand
Skovgaardsgade
ARoS KUNSTMUSEET
Vester Allé
Øster Gade
Søndergade
Restaurant ET
Blochs
J
Europaplads
MUSIKKONSERVATORIUM
Sønder Allé
Fredensgade
Dynkarken
SCANDINAVIAN CONGRESS CENTER
MUSIKHUSET
Rådhus Pladsen
POL.
Carl
RÅDHUSET
Park Allé
Minder
Sonnesgade
Frederiks
Banegårds Gade
Sydhavnsgade
ÅRHUS HOVEDBANEGÅRD
Spanien
Vækmestergade
Jægergårdsgade
Nordisk Spisehus
Hærværk
Restaurant

Atrium

MODERN CUISINE • INTIMATE The team from Gastromé are consultants here, so you may recognise their style of modern Nordic cooking, albeit simplified a little. Choose from the à la carte or opt for the carefully balanced seasonal set menu. As its name suggests, it's located in an atrium: a striking glass pyramid in the grand Hotel Royal.

Menu 749 DKK – Carte 360/630 DKK

PLAN: B2 – *Royal Hotel, Store Torv 4 – ✆ 31 13 77 22 – www.atriumroyal.dk – Closed lunch Monday-Saturday, Sunday*

Ferdinand

FRENCH • BRASSERIE Red-canopied Ferdinand stands out from its neighbours on the liveliest street in the city. From the open kitchen come dishes that mix French and Danish influences; the rib-eye is a constant. Bedrooms are comfy and spacious and there are apartments with small balconies for longer stays.

Menu 165 DKK (lunch), 375/495 DKK – Carte 310/640 DKK

PLAN: B2 – *Åboulevarden 28 – ✆ 87 32 14 44 – www.hotelferdinand.dk – Closed 22 December-6 January, Sunday*

F-Høj

SMØRREBRØD • NEIGHBOURHOOD A bright, busy café with a pavement terrace. Fridges and cabinets display a tempting selection of desserts, cakes, biscuits and drinks. There are three hot and six cold dishes on the smørrebrød menu; two plus dessert should suffice.

Carte 225/285 DKK

PLAN: A2 – *Grønnegade 2 – ✆ 86 14 22 80 – www.frederikshoj.com – Closed 13 July-10 August, 12-18 October, 21 December-4 January, Monday, Tuesday, dinner Wednesday-Saturday, Sunday*

Frederiksgade 42

DANISH • NEIGHBOURHOOD The larger-than-life owner extends a warm welcome to customers at this delightful restaurant in the heart of the city. The seasonal menu is geared 80:20 in favour of vegetables against meat/fish; the well-priced plates are designed for sharing.

Menu 300 DKK – Carte 360/400 DKK

PLAN: B2 – *Frederiksgade 42 – ✆ 60 68 96 06 – www.frederiksgade42.dk – Closed 23 December-4 January, Monday, lunch Tuesday-Saturday, Sunday*

Ghrelin

MODERN CUISINE • CHIC A sleek, modern two-roomed restaurant with a semi-open kitchen and confident friendly service, set in the heart of the up-and-coming dockland area. 3, 5 or 7 course tasting menus have the occasional surprise thrown in; good quality produce is used to create well-presented dishes.

Menu 650/1200 DKK – Carte 410/560 DKK

Off plan – *Bernhardt Jensens Boulevard 125 – ✆ 30 13 30 04 – www.ghrelin.dk – Closed Monday, Tuesday, Wednesday, lunch Thursday, Sunday*

Mejeriet

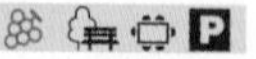

MODERN CUISINE • DESIGN A converted stable block next to a 19C manor house hosts this enthusiastically run, characterful restaurant. The kitchen makes good use of classic combinations to produce flavoursome and satisfying dishes. Some of the ingredients are supplied by the owner himself, who is a keen hunter.

Menu 495 DKK

Off plan – *Vilhelmsborg, Bedervej 101, Mårslet – ✆ 86 93 71 95 – www.restaurant-mejeriet.dk – Closed 13-26 July, 23-30 December, Monday, Tuesday, Wednesday, lunch Thursday-Saturday, dinner Sunday*

Møf

DANISH • NEIGHBOURHOOD Ask for a seat at the counter to watch the young chef-owners cook in the open kitchen. The three different menus presented at dinner allow for some flexibility; dishes are Danish at heart and made with local produce.

Menu 349 DKK – Carte 400 DKK

PLAN: A2 – *Vesterport 10 – ✆ 61 73 33 33 – www.restaurantmoef.com – Closed lunch Monday, Tuesday, Wednesday, lunch Thursday-Friday, lunch Sunday*

Nordisk Spisehus

MODERN CUISINE • NEIGHBOURHOOD You'll find this intimate restaurant behind the station; ask for a table at the back to avoid the bustle. Flavourful modern dishes are based on Danish recipes but also exhibit influences from around the globe, particularly France. Choose between 3 set menus and an 8 course menu dedicated entirely to caviar.

Menu 267 DKK (lunch), 499/899 DKK

PLAN: A-B2 – *M.P.Bruuns Gade 31 – ✆ 86 17 70 99 – www.nordiskspisehus.dk – Closed Sunday*

Restaurant ET

FRENCH • DESIGN A bright, contemporary and smoothly run brasserie split between a number of floors, including the cellar which doubles as the private dining room. The familiar Gallic dishes are generous in size and robust in flavour and come accompanied by an extensive, exclusively French wine list.

Menu 369 DKK – Carte 300/500 DKK

PLAN: B2 – *Åboulevarden 7 – ✆ 86 13 88 00 – www.restaurant-et.dk – Closed 22 December-5 January, Sunday*

scanrail/iStock

FINLAND

SUOMI

HELSINKI
HELSINGFORS

petriartturiasikainen/iStock

HELSINKI IN...

→ **ONE DAY**
Harbour market place, Uspensky Cathedral, Lutheran Cathedral, Katajanokka, Mannerheimintie.

→ **TWO DAYS**
A ferry to Suomenlinna, Church in the Rock, the nightlife of Fredrikinkatu.

→ **THREE DAYS**
Central Park, the Sibelius monument, Esplanadi.

Cool, clean and chic, the 'Daughter of the Baltic' sits prettily on a peninsula, jutting out between the landmasses of its historical overlords, Sweden and Russia. Surrounded on three sides by water, Helsinki is a busy port, but that only tells a small part of the story: forests grow in abundance around here and trees reach down to the lapping shores. This is a striking city to look at: it was rebuilt in the 19C after a fire, and many of the buildings have a handsome neoclassical or art nouveau façade. Shoppers can browse the picturesque outdoor food and tourist markets

stretching along the main harbour, where island-hopping ferries ply their trade.

In a country with over 200,000 lakes it would be pretty hard to escape a green sensibility, and the Finnish capital has made sure that concrete and stone have never taken priority over its distinctive features of trees, water and open space. There are bridges at every turn connecting the city's varied array of small islands, and a ten kilometre strip of parkland acts as a spine running vertically up from the centre. Renowned as a city of cool, it's somewhere that also revels in a hot nightlife and even hotter saunas – this is where they were invented. And if your blast of dry heat has left you wanting a refreshing dip, there's always a freezing lake close at hand.

EATING OUT

Local - and we mean local - ingredients are very much to the fore in the kitchens of Helsinki's restaurants. Produce is sourced from the country's abundant lakes, forests and seas, so your menu will assuredly be laden with the likes of smoked reindeer, reindeer's tongue, elk in aspic, lampreys, Arctic char, Baltic herring, snow grouse and cloudberries. Generally speaking, complicated, fussy preparations are overlooked for those that let the natural flavours shine through. In the autumn, markets are piled high with woodland mushrooms, often from Lapland, and chefs make the most of this bounty. Local alcoholic drinks include schnapps, vodka and liqueurs made from local berries: lakka (made from cloudberries) and mesimarja (brambleberries) are definitely worth discovering – you may not find them in any other European city. You'd find coffee anywhere in Europe, but not to the same extent as here: Finns are among the world's biggest coffee drinkers. In the gastronomic restaurants, lunch is a simpler affair, often with limited choice.

❀ **Demo** (Tommi Tuominen)

MODERN CUISINE • INTIMATE An unassuming-looking building hides this intimate room with oversized cotton pendant lights, striking red chairs, and candlelit tables. Choose 4-7 courses from the surprise menu. Finnish and European ingredients feature in modern dishes with a classic heart and a creative blend of textures and flavours.

Specialities: King crab with peach and liquorice. 21-day aged beef and braised short rib with red wine sauce. Fermented cloudberry mousse with brown butter ice cream.

Menu 65/105€

PLAN: C2 – *Uudenmaankatu 9-11* – Ⓜ *Rautatientori* –
☎ 09 22890840 – *www.restaurantdemo.fi* –
Closed 10-13 April, 27 July-9 August, 21 December-4 January, Monday, lunch Tuesday-Saturday, Sunday

❀ **Grön** (Toni Kostian)

MODERN CUISINE • NEIGHBOURHOOD A warmly run restaurant where the open kitchen is the focal point and the chefs bring the dishes to the table to explain them. Cooking has a satisfying earthiness and clever use is made of both fresh and fermented ingredients, with vegetables given equal billing as meat and fish. Natural wines are well-chosen.

Specialities: Scallop with redcurrants, herbs and vegetables. Duck fat potatoes with chanterelles, creamed corn and pike roe. Roasted apple with pine cone caramel and almond meringue.

Menu 64€

PLAN: B2 – *Albertinkatu 36* – Ⓜ *Kammpi* –
☎ 050 3289181 – *www.restaurantgron.com* –
Closed 20 December-6 January, Monday, lunch Tuesday-Saturday, Sunday

❀ **Inari** (Kim Mikkola)

CREATIVE • SIMPLE A relaxed, stripped-back restaurant, owned and run by a talented Noma alumnus and his wife. Cooking has a Nordic backbone but uses Asian flavours and techniques, and combinations are well-judged. Set menus brim with seasonal simplicity and many of the well-presented and highly original dishes are plant-based.

Specialities: Summer peas with grapes and red endive in shiso oil. Beef brisket with braised leeks, wild garlic and coriander. Strawberries with five spice and ginger.

Menu 70/120€

PLAN: B3 – *Albertinkatu 19a* – Ⓜ *Kamppi* –
☎ 050 5148155 – *www.ravintolainari.fi* –
Closed 15-29 February, 15-30 July, Monday, lunch Tuesday-Saturday, Sunday

❀ **Olo** (Jari Vesivalo)

MODERN CUISINE • DESIGN An attractive harbourside townhouse plays host to this cool, minimalist restaurant, whose four rooms have a delightfully understated feel. Local meats such as moose and elk feature in exciting, innovative dishes which are packed with flavour; these are often proudly delivered and explained by the passionate chefs.

Specialities: Reindeer liver crème with rhubarb, strawberry and kohlrabi. Crab and aromatic chicken broth. Spruce ice cream with bilberry marmalade and roasted white chocolate.

Menu 133€

PLAN: C2 – *Pohjoisesplanadi 5* – Ⓜ *Helsingin yliopisto* –
☎ 010 3206250 – *www.olo-ravintola.fi* –
Closed 20-28 February, 10-13 April, 23-26 December, Monday, lunch Tuesday-Saturday, Sunday

Ora (Sasu Laukkonen)

MODERN CUISINE • CHIC Chef-owner Sasu Laukkonen's enthusiasm for his intimate restaurant is infectious; choose a counter table for a view into his kitchen. The well-balanced set menu changes every 6 weeks according to available local produce – including some from their garden – and dishes use modern techniques to enhance classic Finnish flavours. Equal thought goes into the wine pairings.

Specialities: Perch with fennel, cucumber and tagetes. Pork with cabbage, herbs and mushrooms. Rose hip with raspberries and anise hyssop.

Menu 94€

PLAN: C3 – *Huvilakatu 28A – Ⓜ Kamppi –*
✆ 040 0959440 – www.orarestaurant.fi – Closed 15-21 February, 29 June-31 July, 20 December-1 January, Monday, Tuesday, lunch Wednesday-Saturday, Sunday

Palace

MODERN CUISINE • ELEGANT On the 10th floor of a modernist building constructed in 1952 for the Olympic Games, is this sleek restaurant with harbour views. Sophisticated, well-balanced, beautifully presented dishes come from a highly experienced chef, with luxurious ingredients presented in harmonious combinations of texture and flavour.

Specialities: Braised celeriac with Australian black truffle. Dover sole with Jerusalem artichokes and forest mushrooms. Bilberries with spruce and meringue.

Menu 145/180€

PLAN: C2 – *Eteläranta 10 – Ⓜ Helsingin yliopisto –*
✆ 050 5020718 – www.palacerestaurant.fi – Closed 1-31 July, Monday, lunch Tuesday-Saturday, Sunday

Boulevard Social

MEDITERRANEAN CUISINE • TRENDY Owned by the same people as next door Gaijin, this lively, informal restaurant offers an accessible range of authentic North African, Turkish and Eastern Mediterranean dishes; try the set or tasting menus to experience a cross-section of them all. If they're fully booked, ask for a seat at the counter.

Menu 29€ (lunch), 49/68€ – Carte 30/55€

PLAN: C2 – *Bulevardi 6 – Ⓜ Rautatientori –*
✆ 010 3229382 – www.boulevardsocial.fi – Closed Sunday

Gaijin

ASIAN • TRENDY Gaijin comes with dark, contemporary décor, a buzzing atmosphere, attentive service and an emphasis on sharing. Its experienced owners offer boldly flavoured, skilfully presented modern takes on Japanese, Korean and Northern Chinese recipes. The tasting menus are a great way to sample the different cuisines.

Menu 32€ (lunch), 58/62€ – Carte 32/70€

PLAN: C2 – *Bulevardi 6 – Ⓜ Rautatientori –*
✆ 010 3229386 – www.gaijin.fi – Closed lunch Monday, lunch Saturday-Sunday

Nolla

MODERN CUISINE • NEIGHBOURHOOD Nolla means 'Zero' and this incredibly friendly neighbourhood restaurant is all about zero waste. They don't accept packaging from their suppliers; their uniforms are made from discarded bed linen; and they have their own composter and microbrewery. Original dishes showcase local ingredients and give a nod to Spain.

Menu 48/59€

PLAN: C3 – *Fredrikinkatu 22 – Ⓜ Kamppi –*
✆ 040 1639313 – www.restaurantnolla.com – Closed Monday, lunch Tuesday-Saturday, Sunday

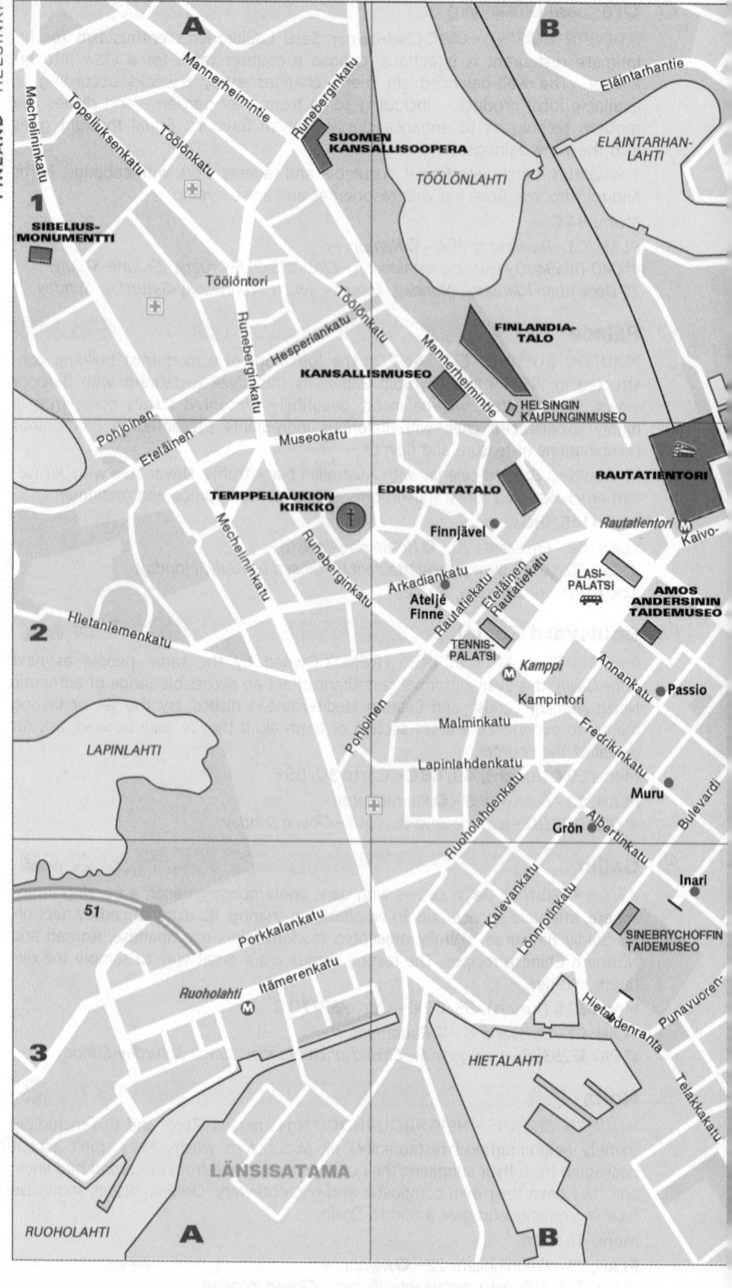
A
B
1
2
3
Mannerheimintie
Runeberginkatu
Eläintarhantie
Mechelininkatu
Topeliuksenkatu
Töölönkatu
SUOMEN KANSALLISOOPERA
ELAINTARHAN-LAHTI
TÖÖLÖNLAHTI
SIBELIUS-MONUMENTTI
Töölöntori
Hesperiankatu
FINLANDIA-TALO
KANSALLISMUSEO
HELSINGIN KAUPUNGINMUSEO
Pohjoinen
Eteläinen
Museokatu
RAUTATIENTORI
EDUSKUNTATALO
TEMPPELIAUKION KIRKKO
Finnjävel
Rautatientori
Kaivo-
Arkadiankatu
LASI-PALATSI
AMOS ANDERSININ TAIDEMUSEO
Ateljé Finne
Rautatiekatu
Eteläinen Rautatiekatu
Hietaniemenkatu
TENNIS-PALATSI
Kamppi
Annankatu
Passio
Kampintori
Malminkatu
Fredrikinkatu
LAPINLAHTI
Lapinlahdenkatu
Muru
Bulevardi
Ruoholahdenkatu
Grön
Albertinkatu
Inari
51
Porkkalankatu
Kalevankatu
Lönnrotinkatu
SINEBRYCHOFFIN TAIDEMUSEO
Ruoholahti
Itämerenkatu
Hietalahdenranta
Punavuoren-
HIETALAHTI
Telakkakatu
LÄNSISATAMA
RUOHOLAHTI

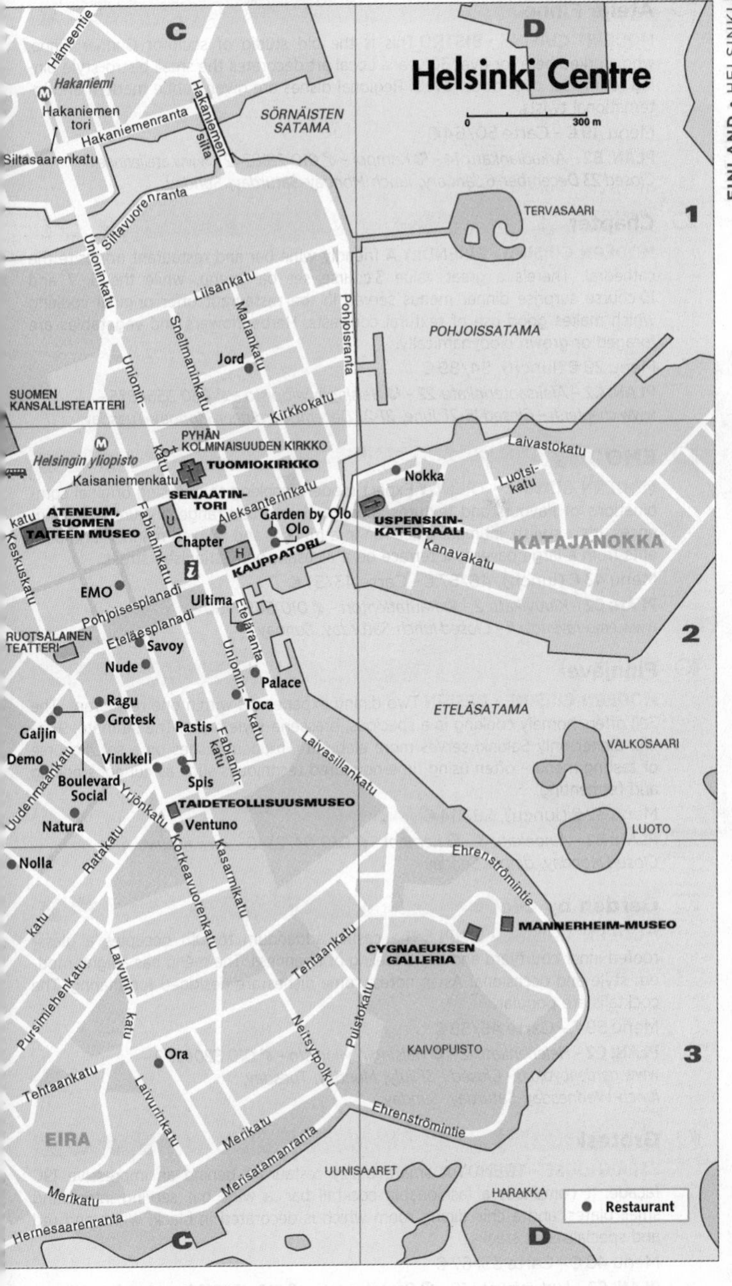
Helsinki Centre
0
300 m
C
D
1
2
3
Hämeentie
Hakaniemi
Hakaniemen tori
Siltasaarenkatu
Hakaniemenranta
Hakaniemen silta
SÖRNÄISTEN SATAMA
Siltavuorenranta
TERVASAARI
Unioninkatu
Liisankatu
Snellmaninkatu
Mariankatu
Pohjoisranta
POHJOISSATAMA
Jord
Kirkkokatu
SUOMEN KANSALLISTEATTERI
PYHÄN KOLMINAISUUDEN KIRKKO
Helsingin yliopisto
TUOMIOKIRKKO
Kaisaniemenkatu
SENAATIN-TORI
Aleksanterinkatu
Laivastokatu
Luotsikatu
Nokka
Garden by Olo
Olo
USPENSKIN-KATEDRAALI
ATENEUM, SUOMEN TAITEEN MUSEO
Keskuskatu
Fabianinkatu
Chapter
KAUPPATORI
Kanavakatu
KATAJANOKKA
EMO
Pohjoisesplanadi
Ultima
Eteläesplanadi
Eteläranta
RUOTSALAINEN TEATTERI
Savoy
Nude
Palace
Toca
ETELÄSATAMA
Ragu
Grotesk
Gaijin
Demo
Uudenmaankatu
Pastis
Vinkkeli
Spis
Boulevard Social
Yrjönkatu
Laivasillankatu
VALKOSAARI
TAIDETEOLLISUUSMUSEO
Ventuno
Natura
LUOTO
Ratakatu
Nolla
Korkeavuorenkatu
Kasarmikatu
Ehrenströmintie
MANNERHEIM-MUSEO
CYGNAEUKSEN GALLERIA
Tehtaankatu
Laivurinkatu
Pursimiehenkatu
Neitsytpolku
Puistokatu
KAIVOPUISTO
Ora
Tehtaankatu
Laivurinkatu
EIRA
Merikatu
Merisatamanranta
UUNISAARET
HARAKKA
Restaurant
Hernesaarenranta

Ateljé Finne

MODERN CUISINE • BISTRO This is the old studio of sculptor Gunnar Finne, who worked here for over 30 years. Local art decorates the small bistro-style dining rooms set over three levels. Regional dishes are given subtle modern and international twists.

Menu 49 € - Carte 50/64 €

PLAN: B2 – *Arkadiankatu 14 – Ⓜ Kamppi – ✆ 010 2818242 – www.ateljefinne.fi – Closed 23 December-6 January, lunch Monday-Saturday, Sunday*

Chapter

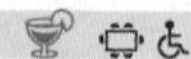

MODERN CUISINE • FRIENDLY A friendly wine bar and restaurant opposite the cathedral. There's a great value 3 course set bar menu, while the 5, 7 and 10 course surprise dinner menus served in the restaurant offer original cooking which makes good use of textural contrasts. Herbs, flowers and vegetables are foraged or grown biodynamically.

Menu 29 € (lunch), 54/89 €

PLAN: C2 – *Aleksanterinkatu 22 – Ⓜ Helsingin yliopisto – ✆ 050 3564875 – www.chapter.fi – Closed 15-21 June, 21-27 December, dinner Monday-Tuesday*

EMO

MODERN CUISINE • TRENDY Expect modern cooking showcasing original combinations of flavours and textures, along with a broad range of European influences. It's a stylish, intimate place run in a friendly and relaxed manner, and benefits from a large pavement terrace on a pleasant pedestrianised street.

Menu 43 € (lunch), 46/57 € - Carte 43/57 €

PLAN: C2 – *Kluuvikatu 2 – Ⓜ Rautatientori – ✆ 010 5050900 – www.emo-ravintola.fi – Closed lunch Saturday, Sunday*

Finnjävel

MODERN CUISINE • DESIGN Two dining experiences within one restaurant. The Sali offers homely cooking in a spacious, brasserie-style room. The intimate, 9-table, dinner-only Salonki serves more elaborate, modern dishes on a set 4 course or tasting menu – often using time-honoured techniques such as curing, smoking and fermenting.

Menu 32 € (lunch), 58/114 €

PLAN: B2 – *Ainonkatu 3 – Ⓜ Kamppi – ✆ 030 0472340 – www.finnjavel.fi – Closed Monday, dinner Sunday*

Garden by Olo

MODERN CUISINE • SIMPLE The casual addendum to Olo occupies a glass-roofed inner courtyard and has a feeling of openness. The menu has a light, modern style and occasional Asian notes; some dishes are designed for sharing. The cocktails are popular.

Menu 59 € - Carte 45/58 €

PLAN: C2 – *Helenankatu 2 – Ⓜ Helsingin yliopisto – ✆ 010 3206250 – www.gardenbyolo.fi – Closed 1-31 July, Monday, Tuesday, lunch Wednesday-Saturday, Sunday*

Grotesk

STEAKHOUSE • TRENDY A smart, buzzy restaurant behind an impressive 19C façade. It comprises a fashionable cocktail bar, a wine bar serving interesting small plates, and a chic dining room which is decorated in black, white and red and specialises in steaks.

Menu 48 € - Carte 35/67 €

PLAN: C2 – *Ludviginkatu 10 – Ⓜ Rautatientori – ✆ 010 4702100 – www.grotesk.fi – Closed Monday, lunch Tuesday-Saturday, Sunday*

Jord

FINNISH • BISTRO Its move from a shopping centre food court has seen Jord reborn as a relaxed and friendly neighbourhood bistro. Its name means 'earth' in Finnish so it comes as no surprise that they serve tasty down-to-earth dishes of organic, biodynamic and wild produce. The crockery and glassware are made locally and even the uniforms come from recycled materials.

Menu 30 € (lunch)/52 € – Carte 44/50 €

PLAN: C1 – *Vironkatu 8* – Ⓜ *Helsingin yliopisto* – ✆ *040 5828100* – *www.restaurantjord.fi* – *Closed dinner Monday, lunch Saturday, Sunday*

Muru

MODERN CUISINE • NEIGHBOURHOOD The charming team really enhance your experience at this cosy little bistro. It's a quirky place, with a wine bottle chandelier, a bar made from old wine boxes and a raised wine 'cellar'. A blackboard lists snacks and around 7 main dishes but most diners choose the 4 course daily menu with a Gallic base.

Menu 52 €

PLAN: B2 – *Fredrikinkatu 41* – Ⓜ *Kamppi* – ✆ *030 0472335* – *www.murudining.fi* – *Closed 13-26 July, 22 December-6 January, Monday, lunch Tuesday-Saturday, Sunday*

Natura

FINNISH • NEIGHBOURHOOD Carefully chosen ingredients are bound together in appealing seasonal small plates at this intimate restaurant. Techniques mix the old and the new and dishes are full of colour. Go for the 'Classic' menu, accompanied by a pure wine.

Menu 39/89 € – Carte 31/45 €

PLAN: C2 – *Iso Roobertinkatu 11* – Ⓜ *Kamppi* – ✆ *040 6891111* – *www.restaurantnatura.com* – *Closed 1-31 July, 21-27 December, Monday, Tuesday, lunch Wednesday-Sunday*

Nokka

MODERN CUISINE • ROMANTIC A huge anchor and propeller mark out this harbourside warehouse and inside, three high-ceilinged rooms juxtapose brick with varnished wood. A glass wall allows you to watch farm ingredients being prepared in a modern Finnish style.

Menu 64/72 € – Carte 44/74 €

PLAN: D2 – *Kanavaranta 7F* – Ⓜ *Helsingin yliopisto* – ✆ *09 61285600* – *www.ravintolanokka.fi* – *Closed lunch Saturday, Sunday*

Nude

MODERN CUISINE • CONTEMPORARY DÉCOR A smart, contemporary bistro where the wine is as important as the food. Choose from the concise à la carte, two surprise tasting menus or the good value 4 course set menu. Dishes are precisely cooked and full of flavour; each course has a suggested wine pairing – a bottle of which you can then order online.

Menu 55/82 € – Carte 28/50 €

PLAN: C2 – *Kasarmikatu 44* – Ⓜ *Rautatientori* – ✆ *010 4117830* – *www.nude-ravintola.fi* – *Closed Monday, lunch Tuesday-Saturday, Sunday*

Passio

MODERN CUISINE • FRIENDLY Exposed ducts, dimly lit lamps and leather-topped tables give Passio a faux industrial feel. Modern cooking showcases regional ingredients and flavours are well-defined. It's run by a local brewer, so be sure to try the artisan beers.

Menu 27 € (lunch), 52/74 €

PLAN: B2 – *Kalevankatu 13* – Ⓜ *Kamppi* – ✆ *020 7352040* – *www.passiodining.fi* – *Closed lunch Monday-Tuesday, lunch Saturday-Sunday*

Pastis

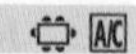

CLASSIC FRENCH • BISTRO The clue is in the name: they serve classic French dishes here, alongside several different brands of pastis. It's a popular place, so there's always a lively atmosphere. Come for Saturday brunch or, for a special occasion, book a private meal in Petit Pastis.

Menu 31€ (lunch)/57€ – Carte 49/56€

PLAN: C2 – *Pieni Roobertinkatu 2 – Ⓜ Rautatientori – ✆ 030 0472336 – www.pastis.fi – Closed 21 December-5 January, lunch Monday, Sunday*

Ragu

MODERN CUISINE • DESIGN Finland's famed seasonal ingredients are used in unfussy Italian recipes and the welcoming service and lively atmosphere also have something of an Italian feel. Choose the weekly 'Chef's Menu' to sample the latest produce. Vegetarian/vegan options are also available.

Menu 45/57€ – Carte 48/57€

PLAN: C2 – *Ludviginkatu 3-5 – Ⓜ Rautatientori – ✆ 09 596659 – www.ragu.fi – Closed lunch Monday-Saturday, Sunday*

Savoy

MODERN CUISINE • ELEGANT Opened in 1937, this local institution retains much of its original charm; it also offers impressive city rooftop views from its 8th floor setting, so ask for a window table. Updated classics are prepared in an assured, modern style using a blend of influences. Dinner is an intimate affair and the enclosed terrace is always popular.

Menu 67€ (lunch) – Carte 78/92€

PLAN: C2 – *Eteläesplanadi 14 – Ⓜ Rautatientori – ✆ 09 61285300 – www.savoyhelsinki.fi – Closed 23 December-6 January, Sunday*

Spis

MODERN CUISINE • NEIGHBOURHOOD An intimate restaurant seating just 18; the décor is 'faux derelict', with exposed brickwork and plaster walls. Creative cooking features Nordic flavours in attractive, imaginative combinations. Most of the dishes are vegetable-based.

Menu 57/77€

PLAN: C2 – *Kasarmikatu 26 – Ⓜ Rautatientori – ✆ 045 3051211 – www.spis.fi – Closed Monday, lunch Tuesday-Saturday, Sunday*

Toca

MODERN CUISINE • TRENDY A passionately run, popular little bistro with a modest, unfinished look. The 3 and 5 course set menus change daily depending on the seasonal produce available; cooking is an original mix of Italian simplicity and Finnish modernity.

Menu 45/65€

PLAN: C2 – *Unioninkatu 18 – Ⓜ Helsingin yliopisto – ✆ 044 2379922 – www.toca.fi – Closed 1-31 July, 22 December-7 January, Monday, lunch Tuesday-Saturday, Sunday*

Ultima

FINNISH • DESIGN Two of the city's most respected chefs have created an über-trendy, no-expense-spared, 'hyper-local' restaurant, which uses the latest technology to grow ingredients within the restaurant itself, such as herbs on a hydroponic wall and oyster mushrooms in coffee grounds. Two menus offer modern Finnish dishes.

Menu 74/96€

PLAN: C2 – *Eteläranta 16 – Ⓜ Helsingin yliopisto – ✆ 030 0472341 – www.restaurant-ultima.fi – Closed Monday, lunch Tuesday-Saturday, Sunday*

Ventuno

ITALIAN • **NEIGHBOURHOOD** A buzzy, modern day osteria, open from early morning for coffee and pastries. Authentic Italian dishes cover all the regions of Italy and are unfussy, full-flavoured and perfect for sharing. The all-Italian wine list is a labour of love; sit in the area next to the glass-fronted wine cabinet.

Menu 32€ (lunch) – Carte 40/70€

PLAN: C2 – *Korkeavuorenkatu 21 – Ⓜ Rautatientori –*
✆ 010 3229395 – www.ventuno.fi – Closed lunch Saturday-Sunday

Vinkkeli

CLASSIC CUISINE • **ELEGANT** A genuinely charming restaurant. The elegant, high-ceilinged room is smartly laid out and run by a delightful team, whose attentive and personable service will make you want to become a regular. The well-judged cooking is a pleasing mix of the modern and the traditional.

Menu 32€ (lunch)/56€ – Carte 47/57€

PLAN: C2 – *Pieni Roobertinkatu 8 – Ⓜ Rautatientori –*
✆ 029 1800222 – www.ravintolavinkkeli.fi – Closed 19-22 June,
23 December-7 January, dinner Monday, lunch Saturday, Sunday

Jerome_Correia/iStock

FRANCE

FRANCE

PARIS
PARIS

MaxOzerov/iStock

PARIS IN...

→ **ONE DAY**
Eiffel Tower, a café on Boulevard St Germain, Musée d'Orsay, Montmartre.

→ **TWO DAYS**
The Louvre, Musée du Quai Branly.

→ **THREE DAYS**
Canal Saint-Martin, Centre Pompidou, Picasso Museum and the Marais.

The French capital is one of the truly great cities of the world, a metropolis that eternally satisfies the desires of its beguiled visitors. With its harmonious layout, typified by the grand geometric boulevards radiating from the Arc de Triomphe like the spokes of a wheel, Paris is designed to enrapture. Despite its ever-widening tentacles, most of the things worth seeing are contained within the city's ring road. Paris wouldn't be Paris sans its Left and Right Banks: the Right Bank comprises the north and west; the Left Bank takes in the city south of the Seine. A stroll along the Left Bank conjures images of Doisneau's magical monochrome

photographs, while the narrow, cobbled streets of Montmartre vividly call up the colourful cool of Toulouse-Lautrec.

The Ile de la Cité is the nucleus around which the city grew and the oldest quarters around this site are the 1st, 2nd, 3rd, 4th arrondissements on the Right Bank and 5th and 6th on the Left Bank. Landmarks are universally known: the Eiffel Tower and the Arc de Triomphe to the west, the Sacré-Coeur to the north, Montparnasse Tower to the south, and, of course, Notre-Dame Cathedral in the middle. But Paris is not resting on its laurels. New buildings and new cultural sensations are never far away: Les Grands Travaux are forever in the wings, waiting to inspire.

EATING OUT

Food plays such an important role in Gallic life that eating well is deemed a citizen's birth-right. Parisians are intensely knowledgeable about their food and wine - simply stroll around any part of the capital and you'll come across lavish looking shops offering perfectly presented treats. Restaurants, bistros and brasseries too can call on the best available bounty around: there are close to a hundred city-wide markets teeming with fresh produce. As Charles De Gaulle said: "How can you govern a country which has 246 varieties of cheese?" Whether you want to linger in a legendary café or dine in a grand salon, you'll find the choice is endless. The city's respect for its proud culinary heritage is palpable but it is not resting on its laurels. Just as other European cities with vibrant restaurant scenes started to play catch-up, so young chefs here took up the cudgels. By breaking away from formulaic regimes and adopting more contemporary styles of cooking, they have ensured that the reputation of the city remains undimmed.

RESTAURANTS FORM A TO Z

A

B

C

D

E

deepblue4you/iStock

Champs-Élysées – Étoile – Palais des Congrès

✿✿✿ Alain Ducasse au Plaza Athénée

CREATIVE • LUXURY Alain Ducasse has rethought his entire restaurant along the lines of 'naturality' – his culinary Holy Grail is to uncover the truth of each ingredient. Based on the trilogy fish - vegetables - cereals (here too, a respect for nature prevails), some of the dishes are really outstanding, and the setting is magnificent!

Specialities: Hautes-Alpes chickpeas, golden caviar. Normandie lobster, radish and watercress, crushed herbs. Lemon from Nice, kombu seaweed with tarragon.

Menu 210 € (lunch)/395 € – Carte 250/395 €

PLAN: 2-G3 – *Hôtel Plaza Athénée, 25 avenue Montaigne (8th) – Ⓜ Alma Marceau – ✆ 01 53 67 65 00 – www.alain-ducasse.com – Closed 24 July-30 August, 19-30 December, lunch Monday-Wednesday, Saturday, Sunday*

✿✿✿ Alléno Paris au Pavillon Ledoyen (Yannick Alléno)

MODERN CUISINE • LUXURY This Parisian institution – in an elegant pavilion in the Champs - Élysées gardens – has been taken over by Yannick Alléno, who has set about writing a new chapter in its story. The chef creates a tour de force, immediately stamping his hallmark. He masterfully puts a new spin on haute cuisine, magnifying, for example, jus and sauces through clever extractions.

Specialities: Langoustine tart with grains of caviar. Millefeuille-layered Wagyu beef with Gros Paris pumpkin. Pine extract in iced jelly with coffee and spicy crystalline flakes.

Menu 380/450 € – Carte 210/350 €

PLAN: 2-H3 – *8 avenue Dutuit (8th) – Ⓜ Champs-Élysées Clemenceau – ✆ 01 53 05 10 00 – www.yannick-alleno.com – Closed lunch Monday, Tuesday, Wednesday, lunch Saturday-Sunday*

✿✿ **L'Abysse au Pavillon Ledoyen** • ✿ **Pavyllon** – See restaurant listing

✿✿✿ Le Cinq

MODERN CUISINE • LUXURY After the fabulous years at Ledoyen, Christian Le Squer is now at the helm of this renowned establishment. The majesty of the Grand Trianon inspired decor remains intact, waiters in uniform still perform their dizzying ballet, and the expertise of the chef does the rest, keeping the finest tradition alive!

Specialities: Brittany langoustines, warm mayonnaise and crispy buckwheat pancakes. Line-caught sea bass, caviar and buttermilk "from my childhood". Dairy ice with yeast flavouring.

Menu 150 € (lunch)/390 € – Carte 210/365 €

PLAN: 2-G3 – *Hôtel Four Seasons George V, 31 avenue George-V (8th) – Ⓜ George V – ✆ 01 49 52 71 54 – www.restaurant-lecinq.com – Closed Monday, Sunday*

✿✿✿ Épicure

MODERN CUISINE • LUXURY A meal at Le Bristol is an exceptional culinary moment. Overlooking the garden, a bright dining space, all demure and distinguished elegance, where French style and Éric Frechon's fresh, classic cooking work their magic. This technical virtuoso demonstrates an exacting freedom with regard to tradition, and the flavours are all the more exquisite for it.

Specialities: Stuffed macaroni, black truffle, artichoke and foie gras, and a mature parmesan gratin. Line-caught whiting in an almond "pain de mie" crust, New Zealand spinach with curry oil. Menton lemon frosted with limoncello and confit lemon flavoured with white peach and verbena.

Menu 155 € (lunch)/380 € – Carte 165/330 €

PLAN: 2-H2 – *Hôtel Le Bristol, 112 rue du Faubourg-Saint-Honoré (8th) – Ⓜ Miromesnil – ✆ 01 53 43 43 40 – www.oetkercollection.com/fr/hotels/le-bristol-paris/*

✿✿✿ Pierre Gagnaire

CREATIVE • ELEGANT The restaurant's chic and restrained contemporary decor is in complete contrast to the renowned inventiveness of this famous chef.

Specialities: "Parfums de terre". Duck with chocolate. Grand Dessert.

Menu 98€ (lunch)/325€ – Carte 360/420€

PLAN: 2-G2 – *6 rue Balzac (8th) – Ⓜ George V – ✆ 01 58 36 12 50 – www.pierregagnaire.com – Closed 1-13 January, 1-24 May, 8 August-1 September, Saturday, Sunday*

✿✿ L'Abeille

MODERN CUISINE • LUXURY The Shangri - La Hotel's 'French restaurant' has a name that gives a nod to the Napoleonic emblem of the bee. As you might expect, France's grand culinary tradition is honoured here under the auspices of a team that has inherited the best expertise. The menu promotes fine classicism and noble ingredients.

Specialities: Sea urchin and caviar royale. Cocotte of lobster. Frosted Corsican honey perfumed with lemon and eucalyptus.

Menu 230/295€ – Carte 170/240€

PLAN: 2-F3 – *Hôtel Shangri-La, 10 avenue d'Iéna (16th) – Ⓜ Iéna – ✆ 01 53 67 19 90 – www.shangri-la.com/fr/paris/shangrila/ – Closed Monday, Sunday and lunch*

✿✿ L'Abysse au Pavillon Ledoyen

JAPANESE • DESIGN A great Japanese sushi master, ingredients of stunning quality (ikejime fish from the Atlantic) and the creative touch of Yannick Alléno: L'Abysse takes us to the heady summits of Japanese gastronomy. Not to mention the tip - top service of a grand establishment and a sumptuous wine list, rich in sought - after sakés. N. B. the 12 seats at the counter are quickly snapped up.

Specialities: Collection of nigiri sushis. Fish bara chirashi with condiments and mineralised broth. Shiso modern tempura and celery root pearls.

Menu 98€ (lunch), 150/280€

PLAN: 2-H3 – *Alléno Paris au Pavillon Ledoyen, 8 avenue Dutuit (8th) – Ⓜ Champs-Élysées-Clemenceau – ✆ 01 53 05 10 00 – www.yannick-alleno.com – Closed Saturday, Sunday*

✿✿ L'Atelier de Joël Robuchon - Étoile

CREATIVE • DESIGN Paris, London, Las Vegas, Tokyo, Taipei, Hong Kong, Singapore and back to Paris... A French and international destiny for these Ateliers with their finger on the pulse. The great chef, who passed away in 2018, devised a bold concept: a long counter with bar stools, red and black colour scheme... and precisely cooked dishes drawing on France, Spain and Asia.

Specialities: Truffled langoustine ravioli with braised green cabbage. Milk-fed lamb chops with thyme flowers. Chocolate "tendance", Araguani chocolate cream, cocoa sorbet, Oreo biscuit.

Menu 49€ (lunch), 99/225€ – Carte 100/210€

PLAN: 2-F2 – *133 avenue des Champs-Élysées (8th) – Ⓜ Charles de Gaulle-Étoile – ✆ 01 47 23 75 75 – www.joel-robuchon.com*

✿✿ Le Clarence

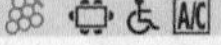

MODERN CUISINE • LUXURY This superb 1884 mansion close to the Champs-Elysées is home to the rare creative talent that is Christophe Pelé (formerly chef at La Bigarrade, in Paris), who turns the association of land and sea into an art form. The "surprise" tasting menu, composed according to the market and the chef's inspiration, is a highlight. Sumptuous wine list.

Specialities: Market-inspired cuisine.

Menu 90€ (lunch), 130/320€

PLAN: 2-H3 – *31 avenue Franklin-D.-Roosevelt (8th) – Ⓜ Franklin-D.-Roosevelt – ✆ 01 82 82 10 10 – www.le-clarence.paris – Closed 2-25 August, 30 December-7 January, Monday, lunch Tuesday, Sunday*

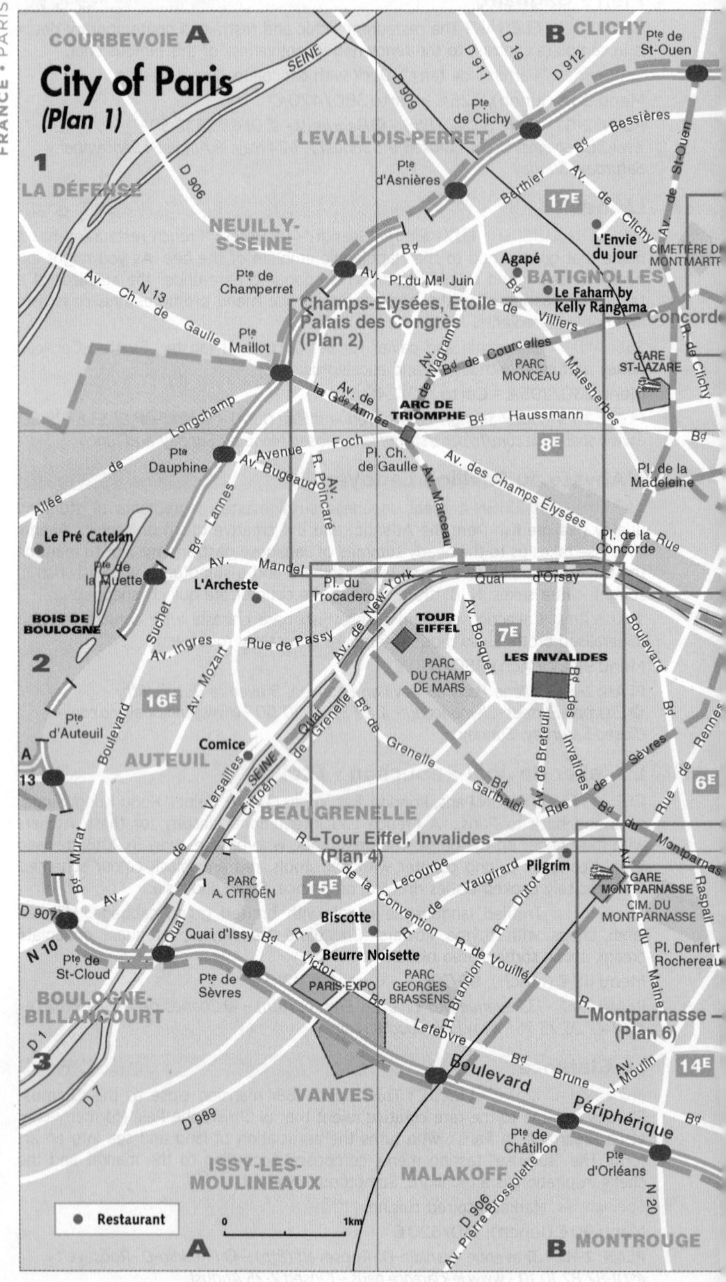

City of Paris
(Plan 1)
COURBEVOIE
A
B
CLICHY
Pte de St-Ouen
SEINE
D 19
D 911
D 912
D 909
Pte de Clichy
LEVALLOIS-PERRET
Bessières
Bd
Av. de St-Ouen
1
LA DÉFENSE
D 906
Pte d'Asnières
Berthier
Av. de Clichy
17E
NEUILLY-S-SEINE
L'Envie du jour
CIMETIÈRE DE MONTMARTRE
Agapé
BATIGNOLLES
Le Faham by Kelly Rangama
Pte de Champerret
Pl. du Mal Juin
Av. Ch. de Gaulle
N 13
Champs-Elysées, Etoile Palais des Congrès (Plan 2)
de Villiers
Concorde
Pte Maillot
Av. de Wagram
Bd de Courcelles
PARC MONCEAU
Malesherbes
GARE ST-LAZARE
R. de Clichy
Av. de la Gde Armée
ARC DE TRIOMPHE
Bd Haussmann
Allée de Longchamp
Pte Dauphine
Avenue Foch
Av. Bugeaud
Pl. Ch. de Gaulle
8E
Pl. de la Madeleine
Av. R. Poincaré
Av. Marceau
Av. des Champs Élysées
Bd Lannes
Le Pré Catelan
Pl. de la Concorde
Rue
Pte de la Muette
Av. Mandel
L'Archeste
Pl. du Trocadero
Av. de New-York
Quai d'Orsay
BOIS DE BOULOGNE
Suchet
TOUR EIFFEL
Av. Bosquet
7E
Boulevard
Av. Ingres
Rue de Passy
LES INVALIDES
2
Av. Mozart
PARC DU CHAMP DE MARS
Bd des Invalides
16E
Pte d'Auteuil
Boulevard
Quai de Grenelle
Bd de Grenelle
Av. de Breteuil
Bd
Rue de Rennes
Comice
AUTEUIL
SEINE
Bd Garibaldi
Rue de Sèvres
6E
A 13
Versailles
Citroën
Rue
Bd du Montparnasse
Rue
BEAUGRENELLE
Tour Eiffel, Invalides (Plan 4)
Bd Murat
R. de la Convention
Lecourbe
Vaugirard
Dutot
Pilgrim
GARE MONTPARNASSE
Raspail
PARC A. CITROËN
15E
CIM. DU MONTPARNASSE
D 907
Av.
Biscotte
R. de
Quai d'Issy
Bd Victor
Beurre Noisette
R. de Vouillé
R. Brancion
Pl. Denfert Rochereau
du Maine
N 10
Pte de St-Cloud
Pte de Sèvres
PARIS-EXPO
PARC GEORGES BRASSENS
Bd Lefebvre
BOULOGNE-BILLANCOURT
Montparnasse (Plan 6)
D 1
3
Boulevard
Bd Brune
Av. J. Moulin
14E
D 7
VANVES
Périphérique
D 989
Pte de Châtillon
Pte d'Orléans
ISSY-LES-MOULINEAUX
MALAKOFF
N 20
D 906
Av. Pierre Brossolette
Restaurant
0
1km
MONTROUGE

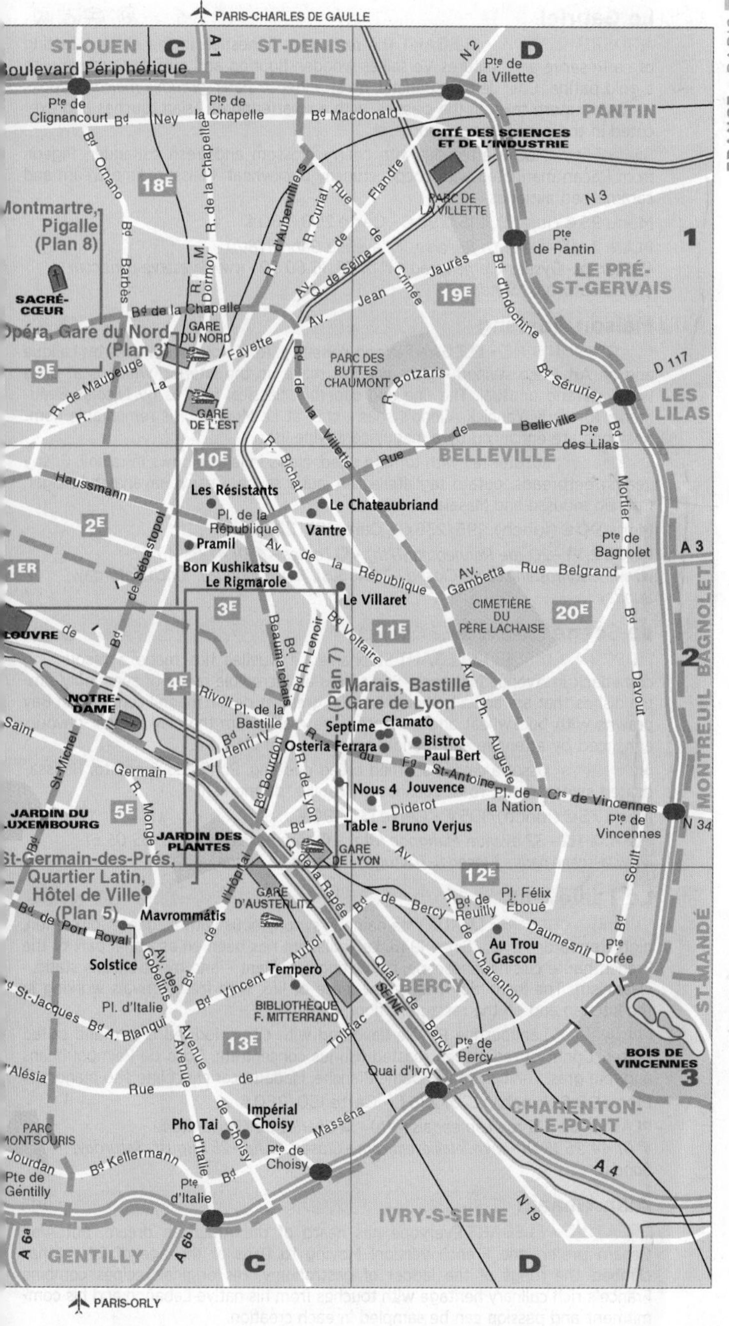
PARIS-CHARLES DE GAULLE
ST-OUEN
C
A 1
ST-DENIS
N 2
D
Pte de la Villette
Boulevard Périphérique
Pte de Clignancourt
Bd Ney
Pte de la Chapelle
Bd Macdonald
PANTIN
CITÉ DES SCIENCES ET DE L'INDUSTRIE
Bd Ornano
18E
R. de la Chapelle
R. d'Aubervilliers
R. Curial
Rue de Flandre
PARC DE LA VILLETTE
N 3
Montmartre, Pigalle (Plan 8)
Bd Barbès
R. M. Dormoy
Av. de Seine
Q. de Seine
Rue de Crimée
Av. Jean Jaurès
Pte de Pantin
1
LE PRÉ-ST-GERVAIS
SACRÉ-CŒUR
Bd de la Chapelle
19E
Bd d'Indochine
Opéra, Gare du Nord (Plan 3)
GARE DU NORD
R. La Fayette
Bd de la Villette
PARC DES BUTTES CHAUMONT
R. Botzaris
Bd Sérurier
D 117
9E
R. de Maubeuge
GARE DE L'EST
LES LILAS
Rue de Belleville
Pte des Lilas
10E
R. Bichat
BELLEVILLE
Haussmann
Les Résistants
Le Chateaubriand
Bd Mortier
2E
Pl. de la République
Vantre
Pramil
Pte de Bagnolet
A 3
1ER
Av. de la République
Bon Kushikatsu
Le Rigmarole
Av. Gambetta
Rue Belgrand
Bd de Sébastopol
3E
Le Villaret
CIMETIÈRE DU PÈRE LACHAISE
20E
LOUVRE
Bd Beaumarchais
Bd R. Lenoir
Bd Voltaire
11E
BAGNOLET
2
NOTRE-DAME
4E
Rivoli
Marais, Bastille Gare de Lyon (Plan 7)
Bd Davout
Saint
Pl. de la Bastille
Av. Ph. Auguste
MONTREUIL
Bd Henri IV
Septime
Clamato
Osteria Ferrara
Bistrot Paul Bert
R. du Fg St-Antoine
Bd St-Michel
Germain
Bd Bourdon
R. de Lyon
Nous 4
Jouvence
Pl. de la Nation
Crs de Vincennes
JARDIN DU LUXEMBOURG
5E
R. Monge
Diderot
Pte de Vincennes
N 34
JARDIN DES PLANTES
Table - Bruno Verjus
St-Germain-des-Prés, Quartier Latin, Hôtel de Ville (Plan 5)
Bd de l'Hôpital
Q. de la Rapée
GARE DE LYON
Av.
12E
Bd Soult
GARE D'AUSTERLITZ
Bd de Bercy
R. de Reuilly
Pl. Félix Éboué
Mavrommátis
Bd de Port Royal
Daumesnil
R. de Charenton
Au Trou Gascon
Pte Dorée
ST-MANDÉ
Solstice
Av. des Gobelins
Bd Auriol
Tempero
Quai de Bercy
BERCY
SEINE
Bd St-Jacques
Pl. d'Italie
Bd Vincent
BIBLIOTHÈQUE F. MITTERRAND
Bd A. Blanqui
Tolbiac
13E
Avenue d'Italie
Pte de Bercy
Alésia
Rue de Tolbiac
Quai d'Ivry
BOIS DE VINCENNES
3
CHARENTON-LE-PONT
PARC MONTSOURIS
Pho Tai
Impérial Choisy
Av. de Choisy
Bd Masséna
Pte de Choisy
Jourdan
Bd Kellermann
A 4
Pte de Gentilly
Pte d'Italie
N 19
IVRY-S-SEINE
A 6a
GENTILLY
A 6b
C
D
PARIS-ORLY

✿✿ Le Gabriel

MODERN CUISINE • ELEGANT The restaurant is nestled in the elegant setting of La Réserve and features Versailles wooden flooring and *cuir de Cordoue* with a gold patina. Chef Jérôme Banctel, no stranger to Paris' *grandes maisons*, cooks his own superb take on the classics, with a smattering of Asian touches and executed in the proper way. A success!

Specialities: Macau artichoke with cherry blossom and fresh coriander. Pigeon from Racan marinated with cocoa, crunchy buckwheat. Calisson, lime cream and caramelised almonds.

Menu 95€ (lunch), 215/295€ - Carte 208/280€

PLAN: 2-H3 - *Hôtel La Réserve, 42 avenue Gabriel (8th) - Ⓜ Champs-Élysées Clemenceau - ✆ 01 58 36 60 50 - www.lareserve-paris.com - Closed Saturday, Sunday*

✿✿ Maison Rostang

CLASSIC CUISINE • ELEGANT Wood panelling, Robj figurines, works by Lalique and an Art Deco stained - glass window make up the interior, which is at once luxurious and unusual. The fine and superbly classical food is by Nicolas Beaumann, formerly Yannick Alleno's sous - chef at Le Meurice. His remarkable compositions are enhanced by a magnificent wine list.

Specialities: Lobster tail with tomato salad, claws in jelly, elbows in ravioli. Crispy veal sweetbreads, potato tagliatelle, vin jaune sauce. Crispy Havana-style cigar, Cognac mousse and Masala ice cream.

Menu 90€ (lunch), 195/235€ - Carte 153/223€

PLAN: 2-F1 - *20 rue Rennequin (17th) - Ⓜ Ternes - ✆ 01 47 63 40 77 - www.maisonrostang.com - Closed 1-24 August, lunch Monday, lunch Saturday, Sunday*

✿✿ La Scène (Stéphanie Le Quellec)

MODERN CUISINE • ELEGANT Stéphanie Le Quellec has made a resounding comeback in Avenue Matignon. She serves an incredible range of seemingly simple dishes that are actually thought out in greatest detail: magnificent Dublin Bay prawns with buckwheat and a blancmange made from the claws. Clear flavours enhanced by attentive and friendly service. A real pleasure.

Specialities: Ossetra caviar, souffléd bread pudding, Pompadour potato. Harissa-coated sweetbreads, roast cauliflower. Vanilla "du moment".

Menu 75€ (lunch)/195€ - Carte 135/190€

PLAN: 2-H2 - *32 avenue Matignon (8th) - Ⓜ Miromesnil - ✆ 01 42 65 05 61 - www.la-scene.paris - Closed 8-30 August, Saturday, Sunday*

✿✿ Le Taillevent

CLASSIC CUISINE • LUXURY Its name is synonymous with elegance, discretion, high standards, style... Since 1946, Le Taillevent has been an essential part of the French haute cuisine landscape, cultivating a brilliant - and by no means static - classicism. The institution has a new lease of life, with fresh arrivals working in the kitchen and on the restaurant floor.

Specialities: Langoustine Royale flavoured with citrus, iodised cream and salted butter. Confit of red mullet, roasted fish jus concentrate, Coco de Paimpol beans and foie gras. Tahitian vanilla Dame Blanche, Madagascar chocolate and marjoram.

Menu 90€ (lunch), 220/275€ - Carte 150/260€

PLAN: 2-G2 - *15 rue Lamennais (8th) - Ⓜ Charles de Gaulle-Étoile - ✆ 01 44 95 15 01 - www.letaillevent.com - Closed 25 July-25 August, Saturday, Sunday*

✿ Alan Geaam

CREATIVE • ELEGANT Everyone has heard of the American dream, but Alan Geaam prefers the French version! Moving to Paris at the age of 24, he has climbed the rungs of the ladder of gastronomy. His original recipes combine France's rich culinary heritage with touches from his native Lebanon and his commitment and passion can be sampled in each creation.

Specialities: Green asparagus, sujuk and quail's egg. Pigeon in two textures with pomegranate molasses. Milk with honey "from my childhood".

Menu 48 € (lunch), 80/100 €

PLAN: 2-F2 – *19 rue Lauriston (16th) – Ⓜ Charles de Gaulle-Etoile – ✆ 01 45 01 72 97 – www.alangeaam.fr – Closed Monday, Sunday*

✿ Antoine

MODERN CUISINE • ELEGANT Under the aegis of chef Thibault Sombardier, this is one of Paris's top seafood restaurants (also serving other dishes). The menu changes daily to offer the best fresh fish and seafood, sourced directly from ports in Brittany, the Basque Country or Mediterranean; everything is made with savoir faire and inspiration. The contemporary decor is elegant. In short: don't miss this place.

Specialities: Finely sliced mushroom petals, marinated mullet and acidic cucumber, caviar-smoked milk. Grilled sole with chanterelle mushrooms, vin jaune and fish head jus. Chocolate soufflé, ice cream with buckwheat.

Menu 49 € (lunch), 120/160 € – Carte 120/175 €

PLAN: 2-F3 – *10 avenue de New-York (16th) – Ⓜ Alma Marceau – ✆ 01 40 70 19 28 – www.antoine-paris.fr – Closed 8-25 August, 21-28 December, Monday, Sunday*

✿ Apicius (Mathieu Pacaud)

MODERN CUISINE • ELEGANT Apicius is located in a sumptuous 18C private mansion that calls to mind a small palace. Created by Jean - Pierre Vigato, a champion of fine dining, it is now linked to the destiny (and talent) of Mathieu Pacaud, who creates a symbiosis of tradition and creativity. Time passes, Apicius changes... but remains!

Specialities: Vegetable Grand Arlequin. Supreme of Bresse chicken cooked in lemon leaf, chicken leg tagine with green olives. Chocolate soufflé, Bourbon vanilla ice cream and a rich cream.

Menu 95 € (lunch), 180/280 € – Carte 175/280 €

PLAN: 2-G2 – *20 rue d'Artois (8th) – Ⓜ St-Philippe du Roule – ✆ 01 43 80 19 66 – www.restaurant-apicius.com – Closed Sunday*

✿ L'Arôme

MODERN CUISINE • CHIC Sniffing an aroma, a scent, a bouquet: such is the enticing programme of this swanky establishment near the Champs-Élysées. True to its name, the restaurant boasts a wine cellar sourced from some 300 estates. Chef Thomas Boullault rustles up suave and inspired Gallic fare, in which seasonal ingredients play the star role.

Specialities: Pressé of Breton crab, avocado, koshihikari rice and tomato water. Fillet of veal, celery cake with ricotta and confit citron pulp. Hot soufflé with almonds, marmalade and apricot sorbet.

Menu 59 € (lunch), 109/159 €

PLAN: 2-G-H2 – *3 rue Saint-Philippe-du-Roule (8th) – Ⓜ St-Philippe-du-Roule – ✆ 01 42 25 55 98 – www.larome.fr – Closed 3-24 August, 23-30 December, Saturday, Sunday*

✿ 114, Faubourg

MODERN CUISINE • ELEGANT This chic brasserie within the premises of Le Bristol has a lavish interior with gilded columns, floral motifs and a grand staircase. Savour dishes from the menu of fine brasserie classics cooked with care and lots of taste.

Specialities: King crab eggs, ginger and lemon mayonnaise. Sole, spinach shoots, virgin olive oil with capers. Bourbon vanilla millefeuille with salted butter caramel.

Menu 130 € – Carte 82/150 €

PLAN: 2-H2 – *Hôtel Le Bristol, 114 rue du Faubourg-Saint-Honoré (8th) – Ⓜ Miromesnil – ✆ 01 53 43 44 44 – www.lebristolparis.com – Closed lunch Saturday-Sunday*

✿ Le Chiberta 

CREATIVE • MINIMALIST Soft lighting and a simple, understated interior by J M Wilmotte (dark colours and unusual wine bottle walls) set the scene for inventive cuisine overseen by Guy Savoy. Market - fresh, weekly changed menu. It is a pleasure to watch the chefs at work behind the counter.

Specialities: Crab remoulade with pomelo and avocado-cucumber-coriander. Sweetbreads with chanterelle mushrooms, fresh almonds and vitello tonnato-style fillet of veal with capers. Mara des Bois strawberries, pistachios and wild strawberry sorbet.

Menu 49€ (lunch)/110€ - Carte 90/120€

PLAN: 2-F2 - *3 rue Arsène-Houssaye (8th) - Ⓜ Charles de Gaulle-Étoile - ✆ 01 53 53 42 00 - www.lechiberta.com - Closed 3-24 August, lunch Saturday, Sunday*

✿ Copenhague 

DANISH • CONTEMPORARY DÉCOR The Maison du Danemark on the Champs Élysées has long been a culinary ambassador of the food of the Great North. A tasteful, low - key interior ideally showcases its gourmet ambitions. Cod in a frothy sauce of grey shrimp and smoked reindeer are some of the iconic dishes of Scandinavia served here.

Specialities: Market-inspired cuisine.

Menu 55€ (lunch), 75/115€ - Carte 60/80€

PLAN: 2-F2 - *142 avenue des Champs-Élysées (8th) - Ⓜ George V - ✆ 01 44 13 86 26 - www.restaurant-copenhague-paris.fr - Closed 3-30 August, 23-30 December, Saturday, Sunday*

✿ Dominique Bouchet

CLASSIC CUISINE • ELEGANT This is the sort of place you want to recommend to your friends: a contemporary interior that is at once chic and intimate, alert service, tasty and well put - together classic cuisine.

Specialities: Trout marinated with sansho, avocado purée, mango and pink radish. Roasted coffee- and jus-coated sweetbreads, truffle and parmesan macaroni. Revisited Norwegian omelette, pineapple coulis.

Menu 58€ (lunch)/128€ - Carte 95/120€

PLAN: 2-H2 - *11 rue Treilhard (8th) - Ⓜ Miromesnil - ✆ 01 45 61 09 46 - www.dominique-bouchet.com - Closed 10-16 February, 3-16 August, Saturday, Sunday*

✿ Étude (Keisuke Yamagishi)

MODERN CUISINE • ELEGANT Inspired by his meetings with small-scale producers and by the discovery of ingredients from afar - pepper from Taiwan with citrus notes, Iranian berries - the chef, Keisuke Yamagishi, cooks here like a tightrope walker, offering set menus named "Symphonie", "Ballade", "Prélude" in homage to Chopin. Each dish is a masterclass in harmony.

Specialities: Imperial caviar croquettes. Challans duck. Medley of grand cru chocolate.

Menu 45€ (lunch), 80/130€

PLAN: 2-F3 - *14 rue du Bouquet-de-Longchamp (16th) - Ⓜ Boissière - ✆ 01 45 05 11 41 - www.restaurant-etude.fr - Closed 1-6 January, 16 February-9 March, 2-24 August, Monday, lunch Saturday, Sunday*

✿ Frédéric Simonin

MODERN CUISINE • COSY Black - and - white decor forms the backdrop to this chic restaurant close to Place des Ternes. Fine, delicate cuisine from a chef with quite a career behind him already.

Specialities: Open langoustine ravioli with a coconut- and lemongrass-infused broth. Cocotte of Normandy veal, mushrooms and black garlic seasoning. Guanaja chocolate parfait, crushed cocoa biscuit and crunchy chocolate caramel.

Menu 55€ (lunch)/148€ - Carte 120/150€

PLAN: 2-F1 - *25 rue Bayen (17th) - Ⓜ Ternes - ✆ 01 45 74 74 74 - www.fredericsimonin.com - Closed 3-25 August, Monday, Sunday*

✿ Le George

ITALIAN • ELEGANT In the kitchens of the George since September 2016, Simone Zanoni has made an impression with his light, Italian - inspired cooking, often served in tasting - size portions. Superb dining room or conservatory in the courtyard.

Specialities: Saffron arancini and tuna tartare. Ricotta tortelli, lemon and fresh mint. Caramelised torta di mele.

Menu 65€ (lunch), 95/129€ – Carte 70/120€

PLAN: 2-G3 – *Hôtel Four Seasons George V, 31 avenue George-V (8th) – Ⓜ George V – ✆ 01 49 52 72 09 – www.legeorge.com*

✿ Helen

SEAFOOD • ELEGANT Founded in 2012, Helen has already made its mark among the fish restaurants of Paris' chic neighbourhoods. If you love fish, you will be bowled over: from the quality of the ingredients (only wild fish sourced from fishermen who bring in the catch of the day on small boats) to the care taken over the recipes. Sober and elegant decor.

Specialities: Sea bream carpaccio with citron caviar. Baked John Dory with confit shallots. "Two-lemon" meringue tart.

Menu 48€ (lunch)/138€ – Carte 80/170€

PLAN: 2-G2 – *3 rue Berryer (8th) – Ⓜ George V – ✆ 01 40 76 01 40 – www.helenrestaurant.com – Closed 1-24 August, 23 December-5 January, Monday, lunch Saturday, Sunday*

✿ Jacques Faussat

TRADITIONAL CUISINE • CONTEMPORARY DÉCOR In a quiet neighbourhood, this inviting and comfortable restaurant has recently been refurbished in a contemporary style. It proposes a menu that changes with the market's offerings and the chef's inspiration. A likeable man who hails from the Gers, he brings together traditional expertise and up - to - the - minute style. Diners passing through as well as regulars come away happy. Good value for money.

Specialities: Compression of potatoes, duck foie gras, truffle jus and truffle. Pigeon flambéed "au capucin". Seasonal fruit soufflé.

Menu 42€ (lunch), 48/90€ – Carte 55/85€

PLAN: 2-G1 – *54 rue Cardinet (17th) – Ⓜ Malesherbes – ✆ 01 47 63 40 37 – www.jacquesfaussat.com – Closed 3-21 August, 23-27 December, Saturday, Sunday*

✿ Lasserre

CLASSIC CUISINE • LUXURY An emblematic temple of Parisian gastronomy. The upper-crust interior (with its famous sliding roof), the tableware and the quality of the service all sing the praises of haute cuisine! The menu signed by chef Jean-Louis Nomicos is fully in tune with this prestigious heritage.

Specialities: Stuffed macaroni, black truffles, celeriac and duck foie gras. Duck à l'orange. Crêpes Suzette.

Carte 177/275€

PLAN: 2-H3 – *17 avenue Franklin-D.-Roosevelt (8th) – Ⓜ Franklin-D.-Roosevelt – ✆ 01 43 59 02 13 – www.restaurant-lasserre.com – Closed 1-13 January, 1-31 August, Monday, lunch Tuesday-Saturday, Sunday*

✿ Nomicos (Jean-Louis Nomicos)

MODERN CUISINE • ELEGANT After working at Lasserre, one of the temples of classical French cuisine, Jean-Louis Nomicos created this restaurant that bears his name. In an updated interior perfectly suited to his work, he creates subtle dishes, whose Mediterranean accents bear witness to his Provençal roots and meticulous craftsmanship.

Specialities: Macaroni with black truffles and duck foie gras. John Dory with sea urchin cream, fish roe, fregola sarda pasta and confit lemon. Absinthe granita, tomato confit with vanilla, and fennel ice cream.

Menu 49€ (lunch), 75/145€ – Carte 118/170€

PLAN: 2-E3 – *16 avenue Bugeaud (16th) – Ⓜ Victor Hugo – ✆ 01 56 28 16 16 – www.nomicos.fr – Closed Monday, Sunday*

✿ L'Oiseau Blanc

MODERN CUISINE • DESIGN The restaurant of the famous Peninsula, the luxurious hotel located near the Arc de Triomphe. L'Oiseau Blanc (named after the plane in which Nungesser and Coli attempted to cross the Atlantic in 1927) hosts a skilled chef in its kitchens: his dishes are characterised by flawless technique and meticulous visuals... Prepare for takeoff.

Specialities: French gambas, fish roe and fresh turmeric. Brittany turbot and white Vaucluse asparagus. "Cloud" of pink grapefruit and roasted almonds.

Menu 75€ (lunch), 128/150€

PLAN: 2-F2 – *Hôtel The Peninsula, 19 avenue Kléber (16th) – Ⓜ Kléber – ☎ 01 58 12 67 30 – www.peninsula.com*

✿ L'Orangerie

MODERN CUISINE • ELEGANT Whilst preserving the DNA of this pocket handkerchief restaurant, Alain Taudon has reworked the menu along a "light, healthy" theme, low on fat and with a preference for vegetables and seafood. The food is flavoursome, while the mind-blowing wine list is that of the George V.

Specialities: Langoustine with sushi rice. Roasted mango in a milk crust, dehydrated olives and bitter cocoa. Vacherin flower, raspberry and peppermint.

Menu 75€ (lunch), 95/125€ – Carte 103/146€

PLAN: 2-G3 – *Hôtel Four Seasons George V, 31 avenue George-V (8th) – Ⓜ George V – ☎ 01 49 52 72 24 – www.lorangerieparis.com*

✿ Pages (Ryuji Teshima)

CREATIVE • MINIMALIST Ryuji Teshima, aka Teshi, knocked about in some top establishments, before deciding to deploy his own contemporary and personal vision of French food. His "surprise" menus create incredible associations of flavours that seem most unlikely on paper but that taste somehow undisputable when in the mouth. You can even put your head into the kitchen for a closer look!

Specialities: Ozaki beef carpaccio. Grilled pullet and egg yolk. Hojicha and chocolate.

Menu 55€ (lunch), 105/175€

PLAN: 2-F2 – *4 rue Auguste-Vacquerie (16th) – Ⓜ Charles de Gaulle-Etoile – ☎ 01 47 20 74 94 – www.restaurantpages.fr – Closed 5-26 August, Monday, Sunday*

✿ Pavyllon

MODERN CUISINE • CONTEMPORARY DÉCOR Yannick Alléno's latest venture is a hit with diners. Thirty place settings along the counter, fine and delicate dishes that take classic culinary foundations as their starting point, blended with interesting flavours and the odd touch from overseas. A smart yet relaxed setting in which to enjoy an excellent meal.

Specialities: Pike mousse, brioche, celeriac extraction. Steamed brill millefeuille, fermented milk, condiments. Hot chocolate "crémeux", buckwheat tuile.

Menu 68€ (lunch), 145/235€ – Carte 100/200€

PLAN: 2-H3 – *Alléno Paris au Pavillon Ledoyen, 8 avenue Dutuit (8th) – Ⓜ Champs-Élysées Clemenceau – ☎ 01 53 05 10 10 – www.yannick-alleno.com*

✿ Penati al Baretto (Alberico Penati)

ITALIAN • CLASSIC DÉCOR Alberico Penati's Italian restaurant, opened mid - 2014, has right away imposed itself as one of the best in the city! In accordance with the finest Italian tradition, generosity and refinement distinguish each recipe. The dishes are brimming with flavour as they explore all the regions of the peninsula. A succulent voyage.

Specialities: Market-inspired cuisine.

Menu 39€ (lunch)/55€ – Carte 80/110€

PLAN: 2-G2 – *9 rue Balzac (8th) – Ⓜ George V – ☎ 01 42 99 80 00 – www.penatialbaretto.eu – Closed lunch Saturday, Sunday*

La Scène Thélème

MODERN CUISINE • CONTEMPORARY DÉCOR An unusual restaurant, where theatre and gastronomy come together. On some evenings you can see a theatre performance before your meal. Japanese chef, Yoshitaka Takayanagi, creates subtle, refined dishes, steeped in personality and using first-class ingredients. The stage is set for a memorable culinary intermission.

Specialities: Lobster and sweetbread, guacamole and chive sabayon. Red mullet cooked on its scales, saffron potato. Red fruit pavlova, vanilla cream and crunchy meringue.

Menu 43€ (lunch), 69/109€

PLAN: 2-F2 – *18 rue Troyon (17th) – Ⓜ Charles de Gaulle - Étoile – ✆ 01 77 37 60 99 – www.lascenetheleme.fr – Closed 4-19 August, Monday, lunch Saturday, Sunday*

Shang Palace

CHINESE • EXOTIC DÉCOR The Shang Palace occupies one of the lower floors of the Shangri - La hotel. It gracefully recreates the decor of a luxury Chinese restaurant with its jade columns, sculpted screens and crystal chandeliers. The menu pays homage to the full flavours and authenticity of Cantonese gastronomy.

Specialities: Lo Hei salmon. Roasted Peking duck. Mango cream, pomelo and sago pearls.

Menu 78€ (lunch)/138€ – Carte 60/150€

PLAN: 2-F3 – *Hôtel Shangri-La, 10 avenue d'Iéna (16th) – Ⓜ Iéna – ✆ 01 53 67 19 92 – www.shangri-la.com/fr/paris/shangrila – Closed Tuesday, Wednesday*

Kisin

JAPANESE • SIMPLE When a bib gourmand chef from Tokyo arrives in Paris, the first thing he does is open a restaurant, tantalising and bewitching our senses. Diners will sample Japanese produce and genuine udon, made in front of the diner. Natural, additive-free ingredients, most of which are imported direct from the land of the rising sun. Healthy, wholesome and succulent.

Menu 30/45€ – Carte 28/42€

PLAN: 2-H3 – *9 rue de Ponthieu (8th) – Ⓜ Franklin-D.-Roosevelt – ✆ 01 71 26 77 28 – www.udon-kisin.fr – Closed 1-15 August, Sunday*

Le Mermoz

MARKET CUISINE • BISTRO Manon Fleury, a former fencer who initially studied literature, trained under some of the best (Pascal Barbot, Alexandre Couillon). Her lunches are like bouquets of delicacies – veal tartar, soft apricot and oregano –, seasonal and reasonably priced. For dinner, tapas - style plates are served up in a wine bar atmosphere.

Carte 33/48€

PLAN: 2-H2 – *16 rue Jean-Mermoz (8th) – Ⓜ Champs-Élysées – ✆ 01 45 63 65 26 – Closed Saturday, Sunday*

Pomze

MODERN CUISINE • MINIMALIST The unusual concept behind Pomze is to take the humble apple as a starting point for a culinary voyage! From the food shop (where you will find cider and calvados) to the restaurant, this 'forbidden fruit' provides the central theme. Creative and intrepid dishes offer excellent value for money.

Menu 37€ – Carte 48/64€

PLAN: 2-H2 – *109 boulevard Haussmann (8th) – Ⓜ St-Augustin – ✆ 01 42 65 65 83 – www.pomze.com – Closed 22 December-2 January, dinner Saturday, Sunday*

Caïus

CREATIVE • FRIENDLY This establishment, hidden behind a demure wooden façade, turns out to be something of a surprise: lovely banquettes and chairs upholstered in black leather. Chef Notelet exhumes forgotten spices and ingredients as he reinvents everyday recipes. The cheery atmosphere adds the final cherry on the cake. Good value-for-money.

Menu 45€

PLAN: 2-F1 – *6 rue d'Armaillé (17th) – Ⓜ Charles de Gaulle-Étoile – ✆ 01 42 27 19 20 – www.caius-restaurant.fr – Closed 3-23 August, Saturday, Sunday*

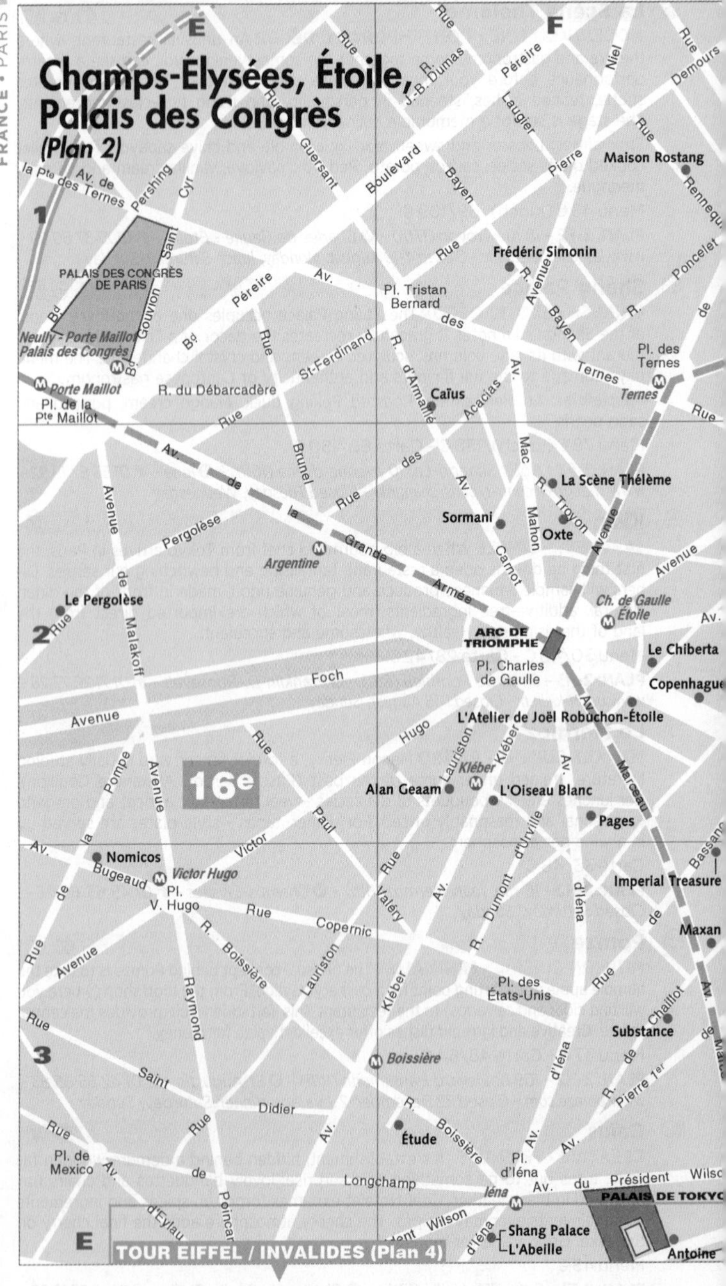
Champs-Élysées, Étoile, Palais des Congrès
(Plan 2)
PALAIS DES CONGRÈS DE PARIS
Neuilly - Porte Maillot Palais des Congrès
Porte Maillot
Pl. de la Pte Maillot
R. du Débarcadère
Pl. Tristan Bernard
Frédéric Simonin
Maison Rostang
Pl. des Ternes
Ternes
Caïus
La Scène Thélème
Sormani
Oxte
Argentine
Ch. de Gaulle Étoile
ARC DE TRIOMPHE
Pl. Charles de Gaulle
Le Chiberta
Copenhague
L'Atelier de Joël Robuchon-Étoile
Le Pergolèse
Kléber
Alan Geaam
L'Oiseau Blanc
Pages
16e
Nomicos
Victor Hugo
Pl. V. Hugo
Imperial Treasure
Maxan
Pl. des États-Unis
Substance
Boissière
Étude
Pl. de Mexico
Pl. d'Iéna
Iéna
PALAIS DE TOKYO
Shang Palace
L'Abeille
Antoine
TOUR EIFFEL / INVALIDES (Plan 4)

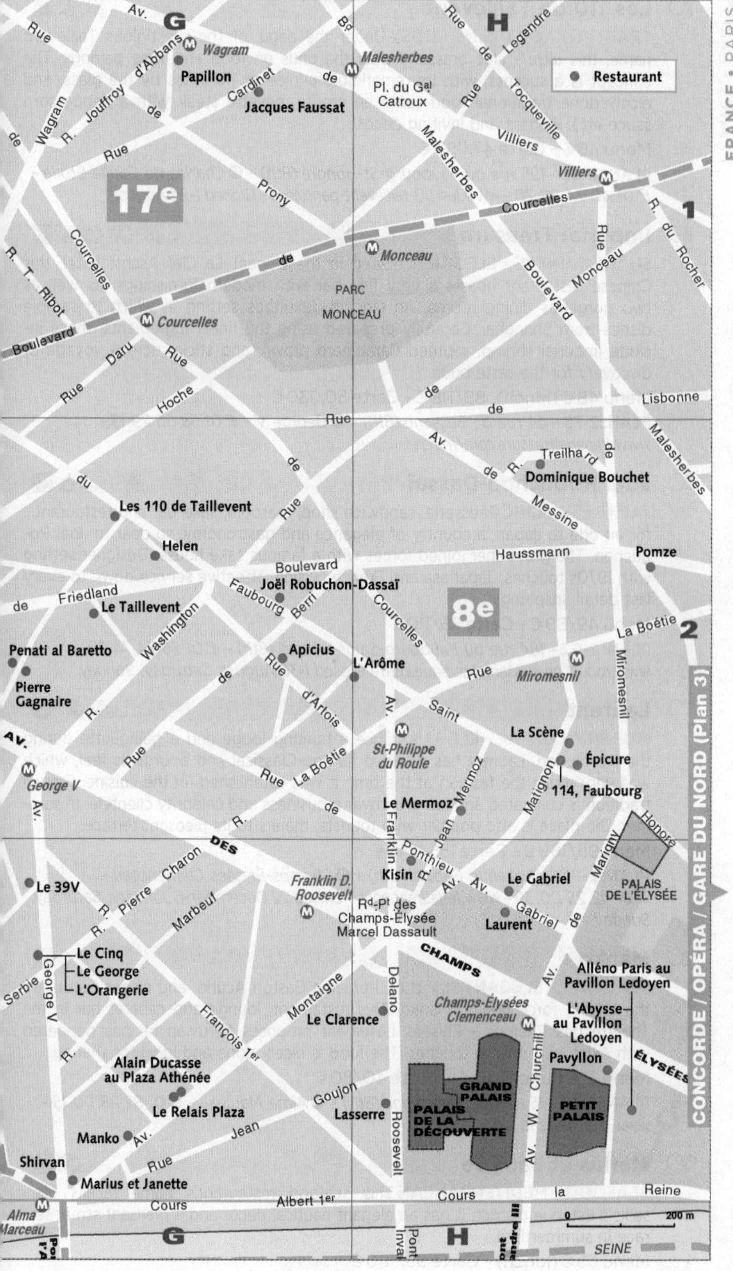
Restaurant
17e
8e
Papillon
Jacques Faussat
Dominique Bouchet
Les 110 de Taillevent
Helen
Pomze
Joël Robuchon-Dassaï
Le Taillevent
Penati al Baretto
Pierre Gagnaire
Apicius
L'Arôme
La Scène
Épicure
114, Faubourg
Le Mermoz
Kisin
Le Gabriel
Laurent
Le 39V
Le Cinq
Le George
L'Orangerie
Le Clarence
Alléno Paris au Pavillon Ledoyen
L'Abysse au Pavillon Ledoyen
Pavyllon
Alain Ducasse au Plaza Athénée
Le Relais Plaza
Lasserre
Manko
Shirvan
Marius et Janette
Wagram
Malesherbes
Villiers
Monceau
Courcelles
Miromesnil
St-Philippe du Roule
George V
Franklin D. Roosevelt
Champs-Élysées Clemenceau
Alma Marceau
PARC MONCEAU
Pl. du Gal Catroux
Rd-Pt des Champs-Élysée Marcel Dassault
PALAIS DE L'ÉLYSÉE
GRAND PALAIS
PALAIS DE LA DÉCOUVERTE
PETIT PALAIS
SEINE
CONCORDE / OPÉRA / GARE DU NORD (Plan 3)
0
200 m

Les 110 de Taillevent

TRADITIONAL CUISINE • COSY Under the aegis of the prestigious Taillevent name, this ultra - chic brasserie puts the onus on food and wine pairings. The concept is a success, with its remarkable choice of 110 wines by the glass, and nicely done traditional food (pâté en croûte, bavette steak with a peppercorn sauce etc). Elegant and inviting decor.

Menu 46 € - Carte 47/150 €

PLAN: 2-G2 – *195 rue du Faubourg-St-Honoré (8th) – Ⓜ Charles de Gaulle-Étoile – ✆ 01 40 74 20 20 – www.les-110-taillevent-paris.com – Closed 1-24 August*

Imperial Treasure

SHANGHAINESE • ELEGANT Located in the elegant La Clef Ascott hotel, this Chinese restaurant boasts a very fine bar with modern furnishings, as well as two gorgeous dining rooms. An elegant, luxurious setting in which to sample dishes from Shanghai. Carefully prepared using the finest ingredients, these include imperial shrimp, sautéed Carabinero prawn, and sticky rice. A voyage of discovery for the taste buds.

Menu 48 € (lunch), 88/118 € - Carte 50/130 €

PLAN: 2-F3 – *44 rue de Bassano (8th) – Ⓜ George V – ✆ 01 58 56 29 13 – www.imperialtreasure.com/france/*

Joël Robuchon-Dassaï

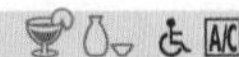

JAPANESE • CHIC Pâtisserie, sandwich shop, tearoom, sake bar and restaurant... for an ode to Japan, a country of elegance and gastronomy, so dear to Joël Robuchon. The great chef joined forces with a famous sake house. Designer setting with 1970s touches, Japanese and French cuisine, attentive service down to every last detail. Inspiring.

Menu 49/89 € - Carte 85/110 €

PLAN: 2-G2 – *184 rue du Faubourg-Saint-Honoré (8th) – ✆ 01 76 74 74 70 – www.robuchon-dassai-laboutique.com – Closed 1-30 August, Saturday, Sunday*

Laurent

MODERN CUISINE • ELEGANT Once a hunting lodge and a guinguette during the Revolution, Laurent has retained its neo-Classical and bourgeois feel, which was very much the fashion at the time it was established. In the cuisine, French tradition is cultivated and has won over a business and celebrity clientele. In summer, the place is also popular with tourists, thanks to its pleasant terrace.

Menu 95/169 € - Carte 155/245 €

PLAN: 2-H3 – *41 avenue Gabriel (8th) – Ⓜ Champs-Élysées Clemenceau – ✆ 01 42 25 00 39 – www.le-laurent.com – Closed 22 December-6 January, Saturday, Sunday*

Manko

PERUVIAN • ELEGANT Star chef, Peruvian Gaston Acurio, and singer Garou are the driving force behind Manko. This restaurant, lounge and cabaret bar in the Théâtre des Champs - Elysées basement proposes Peruvian recipes peppered with Asian and African touches. The food is nicely done and ideal for sharing.

Menu 31 € (lunch)/65 € - Carte 40/80 €

PLAN: 2-G3 – *15 avenue Montaigne (8th) – Ⓜ Alma Marceau – ✆ 01 82 28 00 15 – www.manko-paris.com*

Marius et Janette

SEAFOOD • MEDITERRANEAN This seafood restaurant's name recalls Marseille's Estaque district. It has an elegant nautical decor and a pleasant street terrace in summertime.

Menu 65 € (lunch) - Carte 95/180 €

PLAN: 2-G3 – *4 avenue George-V (8th) – Ⓜ Alma Marceau – ✆ 01 47 23 41 88 – www.mariusjanette.com*

Maxan

MODERN CUISINE • ELEGANT So this is the spot, a stone's throw from Avenue George V, where Maxan is to be found. The decor, in a palette of greys, is elegant and discreet, and it is not without pleasure that we reacquaint ourselves with the flavoursome market - based cuisine: button mushrooms, Scotch bonnet and poached egg...

Menu 40€ - Carte 48/82€

PLAN: 2-F3 – *3 rue Quentin-Bauchart (8th) – Ⓜ George V – ✆ 01 40 70 04 78 – www.rest-maxan.com – Closed 1-26 August, lunch Saturday, Sunday*

Oxte

MEXICAN • TRENDY Opened in early 2018 in the Étoile neighbourhood, near the Arc de Triomphe, this trendy restaurant proposes delicious contemporary cuisine with Mexican influences. French ingredients are infused with condiments, herbs and spices by a talented and passionate Mexican chef. A success.

Menu 45/80€

PLAN: 2-F2 – *5 rue Troyon (17th) – Ⓜ Ternes – ✆ 01 45 75 15 15 – www.restaurant-oxte.com – Closed 2-25 August, Monday, Sunday*

Papillon

MODERN CUISINE • BISTRO Christophe Saintagne has accomplished his metamorphosis, opening his own place after running the kitchens at the Plaza Athénée then at Le Meurice. Blossoming in his elegant neo - bistro, he creates classic, noble cuisine with the emphasis firmly on taste and balance. A word of advice, be sure to book!

Menu 38€ (lunch)/75€ - Carte 50/75€

PLAN: 2-G1 – *8 rue Meissonier (17th) – Ⓜ Wagram – ✆ 01 56 79 81 88 – www.papillonparis.fr – Closed 25 July-24 August, Saturday, Sunday*

Le Pergolèse

TRADITIONAL CUISINE • ELEGANT Sun - drenched cuisine given a nice new spin by a *Meilleur Ouvrier de France* chef, and served in a pared - down and elegant decor.

Menu 58€ (lunch), 125/140€ - Carte 90/140€

PLAN: 2-E2 – *40 rue Pergolèse (16th) – Ⓜ Porte Maillot – ✆ 01 45 00 21 40 – www.lepergolese.com – Closed 1-23 August, Saturday, Sunday*

Le Relais Plaza

CLASSIC CUISINE • ELEGANT Within the Plaza Athénée is this chic and exclusive brasserie, popular with regulars from the fashion houses nearby. It is impossible to resist the charm of the lovely 1930s decor inspired by the liner SS Normandie. A unique atmosphere for food that has a pronounced sense of tradition. As Parisian as it gets.

Menu 68€ - Carte 80/135€

PLAN: 2-G3 – *Hôtel Plaza Athénée, 25 avenue Montaigne (8th) – Ⓜ Alma Marceau – ✆ 01 53 67 64 00 – www.dorchestercollection.com/paris/hotel-plaza-athenee*

Shirvan

MODERN CUISINE • CONTEMPORARY DÉCOR This restaurant near the Alma Bridge is the brainchild of Akrame Benallal. Starched white linen has made way for designer cutlery, earthenware goblets and a menu inspired by the Silk Road from Morocco to India, via Azerbaijan. A delicious melting pot of culinary flavours. Professional service, open almost all - day long.

Menu 40€ (lunch) - Carte 40/100€

PLAN: 2-G3 – *5 place de l'Alma (8th) – Ⓜ Alma Marceau – ✆ 01 47 23 09 48 – www.shirvancafemetisse.fr*

Sormani 

ITALIAN • ROMANTIC Fabric wallpaper, Murano glass chandeliers, mouldings and mirrors: all the elegance of Italy comes to the fore in this chic and hushed restaurant. The cuisine pays a subtle tribute to Italian cuisine, with a particular appetite for truffles when in season.

Carte 70/140 €

PLAN: 2-F2 - *4 rue du Général-Lanrezac (17th) - Ⓜ Charles de Gaulle-Étoile - ✆ 01 43 80 13 91 - www.restaurantsormani.fr - Closed 3-23 August, Saturday, Sunday*

Substance 

MODERN CUISINE • CONTEMPORARY DÉCOR The chef, who has honed his skills in a series of prestigious establishments (Le Meurice, Portos, Lasserre, Louis XV) proposes a short and uncomplicated menu that favours short food supply chains and fine ingredients (turbot, bonito). It evolves in tune with the seasons and enjoys the odd foray into his native Jura region. The excellent wine list features 1 000 different bottles (200 of which are champagnes), most of which are organic or natural wines. A cut above.

Menu 39 € (lunch)/79 € - Carte 50/75 €

PLAN: 2-F3 - *18 rue de Chaillot (16th) - Ⓜ Alma-Marceau - ✆ 01 47 20 08 90 - www.substance.paris - Closed Saturday, Sunday*

Le 39V 

MODERN CUISINE • DESIGN International customers are flocking to the sixth floor of 39 Avenue George V... and for good reason! Overlooking the rooftops of Paris, in a refined interior, you can enjoy nicely crafted cuisine, with solid classical foundations.

Menu 40 € (lunch), 95/135 € - Carte 81/149 €

PLAN: 2-G3 - *39 avenue George-V (8th) - Ⓜ George V - ✆ 01 56 62 39 05 - www.le39v.com - Closed 3-23 August, Saturday, Sunday*

Concorde – Opéra – Bourse – Gare du Nord

✿✿✿ Kei (Kei Kobayashi)

MODERN CUISINE • ELEGANT Japanese - born Kei Kobayashi's discovery of French gastronomy on TV was a revelation to him. So much so that as soon as he was old enough he headed to France to train in some of the country's best restaurants. His career now sees him branching out on his own. He offers fine cuisine that reflects his twin influences and the passion for his work.

Specialities: Jardin of crunchy vegetables, smoked salmon, rocket mousse, lemon emulsion, tomato vinaigrette and black olive crumble. Line-caught bass roasted on crispy scales. Exotic fruit smoothie and souffléd sugar.

Menu 58 € (lunch), 110/280 €

PLAN: 3-L3 - *5 rue du Coq-Heron (1st) - Ⓜ Louvre Rivoli - ✆ 01 42 33 14 74 - www.restaurant-kei.fr - Closed 12-20 April, 2-25 August, 21 December-4 January, Monday, lunch Thursday, Sunday*

✿✿ Le Grand Restaurant - Jean-François Piège 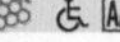

MODERN CUISINE • ELEGANT Jean - François Piège has found the perfect setting to showcase the great laboratory kitchen he had been dreaming of for so long. The lucky few to get a seat (25 maximum) can sample delicate, light dishes whose emotion can be both tasted and experienced. The quintessence of talent!

Specialities: Matured caviar, sea beetroot leaves, chicken broth. Sweetbreads grilled on walnut shells, truffle reduction macerated in walnut wine. Grand Dessert.

Menu 116 € (lunch), 306/706 € - Carte 205/276 €

PLAN: 3-J2 - *7 rue d'Aguesseau (8th) - Ⓜ Madeleine - ✆ 01 53 05 00 00 - www.jeanfrancoispiege.com - Closed 10-24 August, Saturday, Sunday*

✿✿ Le Grand Véfour (Guy Martin)

MODERN CUISINE • CLASSIC DÉCOR Bonaparte and Joséphine, Lamartine, Hugo, Sartre... For more than two centuries, the former Café de Chartres has been cultivating the legend. Nowadays it is Guy Martin who maintains the aura. Influenced by travel and painting – colours, shapes, textures – the chef 'sketches' his dishes like an artist... between invention and history.

Specialities: Foie gras ravioli, truffle emulsion cream. Oxtail parmentier with truffles. Hazelnut and grand cru chocolate pastry with caramel ice cream and Guérande sea salt.

Menu 115€ (lunch)/315€ – Carte 220/290€

PLAN: 3-L3 – *17 rue de Beaujolais (1st) – Ⓜ Palais Royal – ✆ 01 42 96 56 27 – www.grand-vefour.com – Closed 1-24 August, Saturday, Sunday*

✿✿ Le Meurice Alain Ducasse

MODERN CUISINE • LUXURY In the heart of the iconic luxury hotel, this is the epitome of a great French restaurant. Its lavish interior, inspired by the royal apartments of Versailles Palace, has been tastefully updated by Philippe Starck. Under the watchful eye of Alain Ducasse, executive chef Jocelyn Herland signs a menu that celebrates top quality produce. Stylish flair.

Specialities: Scottish langoustines and fennel-lemon. Farm chicken, chanterelles and celeriac. Baba with your choice of rum, lightly whipped cream.

Menu 110€ (lunch)/380€ – Carte 250/380€

PLAN: 3-K3 – *Hôtel Meurice, 228 rue de Rivoli (1st) – Ⓜ Tuileries – ✆ 01 44 58 10 55 – www.alainducasse-meurice.com/fr – Closed 15 February-2 March, 1-31 August, Saturday, Sunday*

✿✿ Sur Mesure par Thierry Marx

CREATIVE • DESIGN Precise 'tailor - made' (sur mesure) cuisine is the hallmark of Thierry Marx, who confirms his talent as a master culinary craftsman at the Mandarin Oriental's showcase restaurant. Every dish reveals his tireless scientific approach, which is sometimes teasing but always exacting. An experience in itself, aided by the stunning, immaculate and ethereal decor.

Specialities: Soya risotto, poached oyster. Charcoal-grilled Wagyu beef. Sweet bento.

Menu 85€ (lunch)/195€

PLAN: 3-J3 – *Hôtel Mandarin Oriental, 251 rue St-Honoré (1st) – Ⓜ Concorde – ✆ 01 70 98 73 00 – www.mandarinoriental.fr/paris – Closed 1-8 January, 12-20 April, 25 July-24 August, Monday, Sunday*

✿✿ La Table de l'Espadon

MODERN CUISINE • ELEGANT The interior, submerged in golds and drapes, is stunning. In this magical setting, the precise cuisine of young Nicolas Sale shines. Choose the bait, then the line, and finally the bite: the announcement of the meals is packed with nods to fishing and swordfish. Taste, personality, intensity: a wind of modernity is blowing over the Ritz. Superb!

Specialities: Raw langoustine, caviar, fresh lemon cream. Confit shoulder of rabbit with mustard, sage squares and house-style linguine. Chestnut honey, pear and crunchy almonds.

Menu 195/350€ – Carte 186/396€

PLAN: 3-K3 – *Hôtel Ritz, 15 place Vendôme (1st) – Ⓜ Opéra – ✆ 01 43 16 33 74 – www.ritzparis.com – Closed 27 January-11 February, 20 July-11 August, Monday, Tuesday and lunch*

✿ Accents Table Bourse (Ayumi Sugiyama)

MODERN CUISINE • DESIGN This pleasant place close to Bourse, run by a Japanese pastry chef, combines classic recipes and more cutting - edge creations. The flavours are pleasant, the preparations are precise, and the lièvre à la royale (hare – in season) is excellent. A delicious white chocolate cream flavoured with green tea is the icing on the cake of this impeccable experience. Very friendly, professional service.

Concorde, Opéra, Bourse, Gare du Nord
(Plan 3)

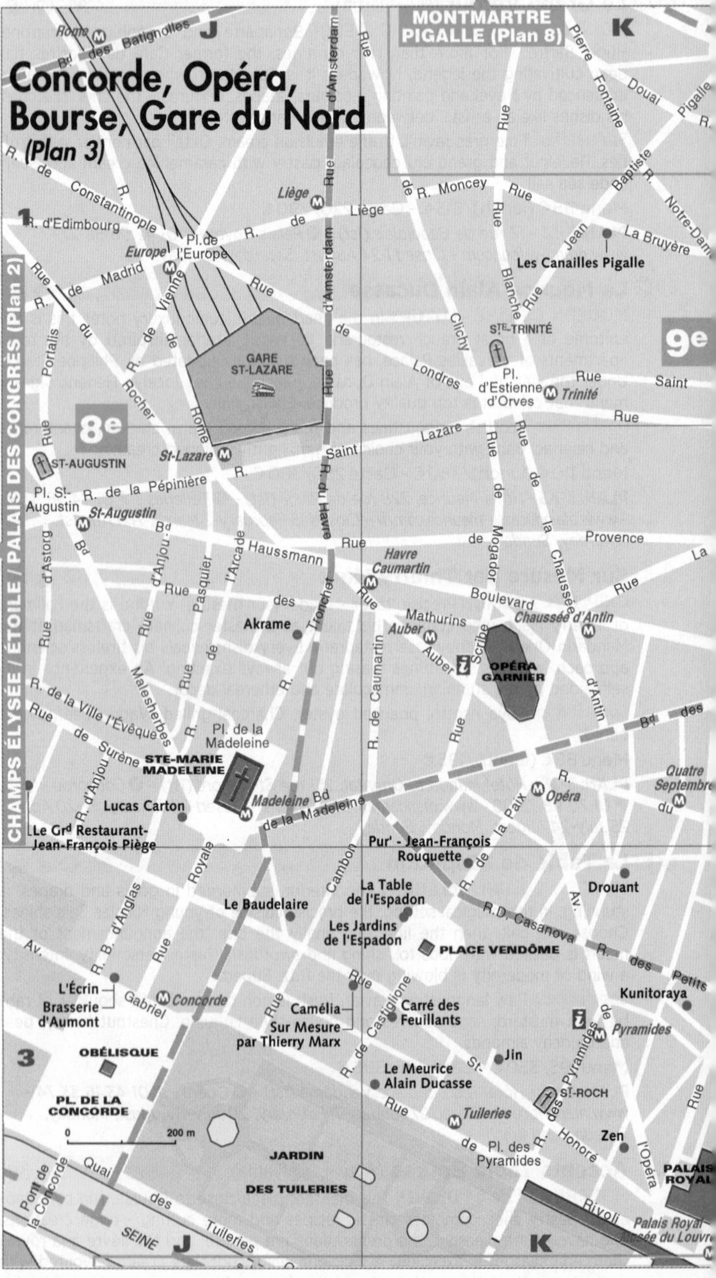

MONTMARTRE PIGALLE (Plan 8)

CHAMPS ÉLYSÉE / ÉTOILE / PALAIS DES CONGRÈS (Plan 2)

J
K
1
3
8e
9e

Rome
Bd des Batignolles
R. de Constantinople
R. d'Edimbourg
Pl. de l'Europe
Europe
R. de Madrid
R. de Vienne
R. de Rome
R. du Rocher
R. de Liège
Liège
Rue d'Amsterdam
Rue de Londres
GARE ST-LAZARE
St-Lazare
Rue Saint-Lazare
R. du Havre
ST-AUGUSTIN
Pl. St-Augustin
St-Augustin
R. de la Pépinière
Rue Portalis
Rue d'Astorg
Bd Haussmann
Bd Malesherbes
Rue d'Anjou
Rue Pasquier
Rue de l'Arcade
Rue des Mathurins
Rue Tronchet
Havre Caumartin
R. de Caumartin
Auber
Rue Auber
Rue Scribe
OPÉRA GARNIER
Chaussée d'Antin
Rue de la Chaussée d'Antin
Rue de Mogador
Rue de Provence
Rue de Clichy
Rue Blanche
STE-TRINITÉ
Pl. d'Estienne d'Orves
Trinité
Rue Saint-Lazare
R. Moncey
Rue Jean-Baptiste Pigalle
Rue La Bruyère
R. Notre-Dame
Les Canailles Pigalle
Rue Pierre Fontaine
Rue de Douai
Akrame
R. de la Ville l'Évêque
Rue de Surène
Pl. de la Madeleine
STE-MARIE MADELEINE
Madeleine
Bd de la Madeleine
Bd des Capucines
Lucas Carton
Le Grd Restaurant-Jean-François Piège
Rue Royale
Rue Boissy d'Anglas
Rue Cambon
Pur' - Jean-François Rouquette
R. de la Paix
Opéra
Quatre Septembre
R. du Quatre Septembre
Drouant
Av. de l'Opéra
R.D. Casanova
R. des Petits Champs
La Table de l'Espadon
Les Jardins de l'Espadon
Le Baudelaire
PLACE VENDÔME
Av. Gabriel
L'Écrin
Brasserie d'Aumont
Concorde
Camélia
Sur Mesure par Thierry Marx
Rue de Castiglione
Carré des Feuillants
Kunitoraya
Pyramides
Rue des Pyramides
Jin
Le Meurice Alain Ducasse
Rue St-Honoré
ST-ROCH
Tuileries
Pl. des Pyramides
Zen
PALAIS ROYAL
Palais Royal Musée du Louvre
Rue de Rivoli
OBÉLISQUE
PL. DE LA CONCORDE
0 200 m
JARDIN DES TUILERIES
Pont de la Concorde
Quai des Tuileries
SEINE

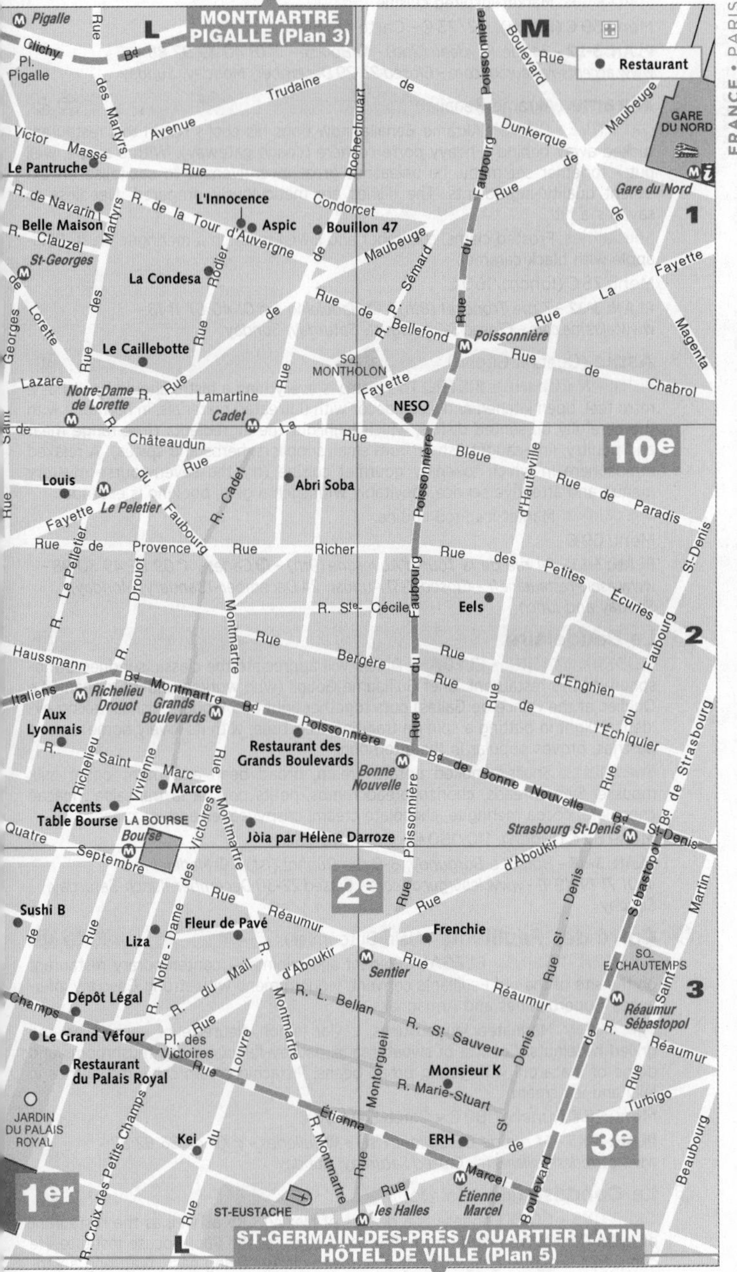
MONTMARTRE PIGALLE (Plan 3)
L
M
Restaurant
GARE DU NORD
Gare du Nord
Pigalle
Pl. Pigalle
Bd Clichy
Rue des Martyrs
Avenue Trudaine
Victor Massé
Le Pantruche
Rue Condorcet
Rue de Dunkerque
Rue de Maubeuge
Boulevard de Magenta
Rue du Faubourg Poissonnière
Rue de Rochechouart
R. de Navarin
Belle Maison
R. Clauzel
St-Georges
R. de la Tour d'Auvergne
L'Innocence
Aspic
Bouillon 47
La Condesa
Rue Rodier
Rue de Lorette
Le Caillebotte
Rue de Bellefond
R. P. Sémard
Poissonnière
Rue La Fayette
Rue de Chabrol
SQ. MONTHOLON
Rue Lazare
Notre-Dame de Lorette
R. Lamartine
Cadet
NESO
Rue de Châteaudun
Rue Bleue
Rue de Paradis
Rue d'Hauteville
10e
Louis
Le Peletier
Abri Soba
R. Cadet
Rue du Faubourg Montmartre
Rue de Provence
Rue Richer
Rue des Petites Écuries
Rue du Faubourg St-Denis
R. Le Peletier
Rue Drouot
R. Ste-Cécile
Eels
Rue Bergère
Rue d'Enghien
Rue de l'Échiquier
Haussmann
Italiens
Richelieu Drouot
Grands Boulevards
Bd Montmartre
Bd Poissonnière
Restaurant des Grands Boulevards
Aux Lyonnais
R. Saint Marc
Rue Vivienne
Rue Richelieu
Marcore
Bonne Nouvelle
Bd de Bonne Nouvelle
Accents Table Bourse
LA BOURSE
Bourse
Jòia par Hélène Darroze
Strasbourg St-Denis
Bd St-Denis
Bd de Strasbourg
Quatre Septembre
Rue des Victoires
Rue d'Aboukir
2e
Rue Réaumur
Rue St-Denis
Bd de Sébastopol
Rue St-Martin
Sushi B
Liza
Fleur de Pavé
R. Notre-Dame
Frenchie
Sentier
R. du Mail
SQ. E. CHAUTEMPS
Réaumur Sébastopol
3
Dépôt Légal
R. L. Bellan
R. St Sauveur
Champs
Le Grand Véfour
Pl. des Victoires
Restaurant du Palais Royal
Rue du Louvre
Rue Montorgueil
Monsieur K
R. Marie-Stuart
Rue Turbigo
JARDIN DU PALAIS ROYAL
Rue Étienne Marcel
R. Montmartre
ERH
3e
Rue Beaubourg
Kei
R. Croix des Petits Champs
1er
Étienne Marcel
les Halles
ST-EUSTACHE
1
2
ST-GERMAIN-DES-PRÉS / QUARTIER LATIN HÔTEL DE VILLE (Plan 5)

Specialities: Market-inspired cuisine.

Menu 39€ (lunch), 62/73€ - Carte 45/50€

PLAN: 3-L2 - *24 rue Feydeau (2nd) - Ⓜ Bourse - ✆ 01 40 39 92 88 - www.accents-restaurant.com - Closed 23-29 December, Monday, Sunday*

✿ Akrame (Akrame Benallal)

CREATIVE • DESIGN Akrame Benallal now dons his chef's hat in this restaurant tucked away behind a heavy *porte cochère* (coach gateway). With a single, well put - together set menu, he unleashes great inventiveness to capitalise on excellent quality ingredients. The dishes are meticulously prepared. Needless to say, it's a hit!

Specialities: Frosted clams, cucumber and kiwi. Pigeon in a meringue crust. Pineapple with black caramel.

Menu 75€ (lunch)/160€

PLAN: 3-J2 - *7 rue Tronchet (8th) - Ⓜ Madeleine - ✆ 01 40 67 11 16 - www.akrame.com - Closed 3-23 August, Saturday, Sunday*

✿ Aspic (Quentin Giroud)

MODERN CUISINE • BISTRO This bistro is everything a bistro should be. It has a retro feel, open kitchen and sleek decor with untreated materials, in harmony with the carefully presented dishes, which highlight the ingredients (free-range meat and poultry, line-caught fish or from small suppliers, herbs and spices). A relaxed atmosphere in which to enjoy gourmet cuisine (try the seven-course mystery menu), and attentive service. Inevitably with such a gem, booking is essential.

Specialities: Market-inspired cuisine.

Menu 69€

PLAN: 3-L1 - *24 rue de la Tour-d'Auvergne (9th) - Ⓜ Cadet - ✆ 09 82 49 30 98 - www.aspic-restaurant.fr - Closed 2-31 August, 24 December-1 January, Monday, Sunday and lunch*

✿ Le Baudelaire

MODERN CUISINE • ELEGANT Diners will appreciate the classic subdued atmosphere of this restaurant. Chef Guillaume Goupil (who worked under Stéphanie Le Quellec at the Prince de Galles) puts together light and modern dishes, taking evident delight in putting a spin on tradition. Tea Time, with its lovely home - made pastries, proves popular in the afternoon.

Specialities: Snails, smoked potato cream, broad bean and burnt onion milk mousse. Sweetbreads, chorizo breadcrumbs, petits pois "à la française". Macaé chocolate, cocoa meringue, chocolate cream, crispy leaves and ice cream.

Menu 62€ (lunch), 110/150€ - Carte 110/130€

PLAN: 3-J3 - *Hôtel Le Burgundy, 6-8 rue Duphot (1st) - Ⓜ Madeleine - ✆ 01 71 19 49 11 - www.leburgundy.com - Closed 22-30 December, lunch Saturday, Sunday*

✿ Carré des Feuillants (Alain Dutournier)

MODERN CUISINE • ELEGANT Elegant and minimalist contemporary restaurant on the site of the old Feuillants convent. Modern menu with strong Gascony influences. Superb wines and Armagnacs.

Specialities: Marinated langoustines, caviar lemon, fleurette of vegetables and grilled hazelnuts. Cocotte of sweetbreads, parsley-flavoured cep mushrooms and dome of macaroni with young broad beans. Pistachio cream cake, red berries in jelly and ice cream.

Menu 58€ (lunch)/180€ - Carte 120/160€

PLAN: 3-K3 - *14 rue de Castiglione (1st) - Ⓜ Tuileries - ✆ 01 42 86 82 82 - www.carredesfeuillants.fr - Closed Saturday, Sunday*

✿ La Condesa (Indra Carrillo)

CREATIVE • COSY Condesa is a district of Mexico City as well as the restaurant of Indra Carillo, who came from Mexico to study at the Paul Bocuse institute. He composes a high - flying culinary score with disconcerting ease, featuring a variety of cultures and influences. An excellent restaurant, further enhanced by the professional attentive personnel.

Specialities: Market-inspired cuisine.

Menu 45 € (lunch), 75/95 €

PLAN: 3-L1 – *17 rue Rodier (9th) – Ⓜ Notre-Dame de Lorette – ☎ 01 53 20 94 90 – www.lacondesa-paris.com – Closed Monday, lunch Tuesday-Thursday, lunch Saturday, Sunday*

✿ L'Écrin

MODERN CUISINE • ELEGANT The emblematic, 18C Hôtel de Crillon ushers diners into an exclusive, almost secretive and timeless dining room, in which every tiny detail has been puzzled over and preened to make perfect. The cuisine of Boris Campanella (formerly of the Cheval Blanc in Courchevel) aims at legibility, seasonality and flavour in a menu that is a picture of harmony and elegance.

Specialities: Vegetable plin with black truffle and sage. Roast turbot, squid stew "terre et mer", parsley-infused fromage blanc. Rhubarb with dill-infused milk.

Menu 195/270 € – Carte 185/250 €

PLAN: 3-J3 – *Hôtel Crillon, 10 place de la Concorde (8th) – Ⓜ Concorde – ☎ 01 44 71 15 30 – www.rosewoodhotels.com/fr/hotel-de-crillon – Closed 26 July-25 August, Monday, lunch Tuesday-Saturday, Sunday*

✿ ERH

MODERN CUISINE • ELEGANT The initials E, R and H stand for water, rice and man in French: a mysterious name for this unusual place on the same premises as a sake shop and a whisky bar. Japanese chef Keita Kitamura creates market - fresh French cuisine with a predilection for vegetables and fish. Character, flavours: an abundance of talent.

Specialities: Market-inspired cuisine.

Menu 45 € (lunch), 95/130 €

PLAN: 3-M3 – *11 rue Tiquetonne (2nd) – Ⓜ Étienne Marcel – ☎ 01 45 08 49 37 – www.restaurant-erh.com – Closed 1-7 January, Monday, Sunday*

✿ Fleur de Pavé (Sylvain Sendra)

CREATIVE • TRENDY If you liked Itinéraires you will love Fleur de Pavé, where Sylvain Sendra pursues his culinary explorations with great panache. He cooks up modern dishes that draw inspiration from all over the world. The emphasis is laid squarely on flavour, thanks to the use of top-notch ingredients – such as the highly exclusive vegetables of Asafumi Yamashita.

Specialities: Confit vegetables from our own producers, sweet pepper and tom yum sauce. Slow-cooked cod, daikon radish and coriander pesto, apple-ginger jus. Ashta-style "milk cream", gariguette strawberries and tonka beans, pistachio ice cream.

Menu 45 € (lunch), 65/95 €

PLAN: 3-L3 – *5 rue Paul-Lelong (2nd) – Ⓜ Sentier – ☎ 01 40 26 38 87 – www.fleurdepave.com – Closed Saturday, Sunday*

✿ Frenchie (Grégory Marchand)

MODERN CUISINE • FRIENDLY Young chef Grégory Marchand earned his stripes at several great restaurants in the UK and US, before setting up shop in the Sentier neighbourhood. His small restaurant is always packed, but he has his delicious contemporary cooking to "blame" for that!

Specialities: Market-inspired cuisine.

Menu 50 € (lunch)/84 €

PLAN: 3-M3 – *5 rue du Nil (2nd) – Ⓜ Sentier – ☎ 01 40 39 96 19 – www.frenchie-restaurant.com – Closed 1-16 August, 23 December-4 January, lunch Monday-Wednesday, Saturday, Sunday*

✿ L'Innocence (Anne Legrand et Clio Modafarri)

MODERN CUISINE • MINIMALIST From their kitchen opening onto the dining room, two gifted women chefs, Anne and Clio celebrate seasonal market produce in a single six-course (three at lunchtime) menu. Painstakingly selected ingredients, punchy flavours and elegant textures. The meal is a delight from start to finish of the duo's colourful dishes, which combine vegetables, meat and fish. Remember to book.

Specialities: Red mullet, courgette, haricots verts and fish head sauce. Rabbit with liver, Colonnata lard, sage, wild spinach and broad beans. Cherries, fennel seed crunch and almond mousse.

Menu 32€ (lunch)/69€

PLAN: 3-L1 – *28 rue de la Tour-d'Auvergne (9th) – Ⓜ Cadet – ✆ 01 45 23 99 13 – www.linnocence.fr – Closed 9-31 August, 30 December-6 January, Monday, lunch Tuesday-Thursday, Sunday*

✿ Les Jardins de l'Espadon

MODERN CUISINE • ROMANTIC The Ritz's restaurant for gourmet lunchtimes. In this retractable conservatory that is lined with greenery and entered via a flower - decked, gilt - edged gallery, you can sample Nicolas Sale's appealing dishes: concise menu, inventive cuisine aligned with seasonal produce, flawless service... A success.

Specialities: Langoustine cannelloni, pointed cabbage, Meursault wine sauce. Line-caught whiting, charlotte cream "à la grenobloise". Madagascar chocolate, meringue textures and chocolate sauce.

Menu 115/150€ – Carte 125/200€

PLAN: 3-K3 – *Hôtel Ritz, 15 place Vendôme (1st) – Ⓜ Opéra – ✆ 01 43 16 33 74 – www.ritzparis.com – Closed 27 January-11 February, Monday, Tuesday, Sunday and lunch*

✿ Jin 

JAPANESE • ELEGANT A new showcase for Japanese cuisine, right in the heart of Paris! Jin is first and foremost about the know - how of Takuya Watanabe, the chef, who comes from Sapporo. Before your eyes, he creates delicious sushi and sashimi, using fish sourced from Brittany, Oléron and Spain. The whole menu is a treat.

Specialities: Sashimi. Sushi. Japanese cake.

Menu 135€ (lunch), 145/255€

PLAN: 3-K3 – *6 rue de la Sourdière (1st) – Ⓜ Tuileries – ✆ 01 42 61 60 71 – Closed 1-6 January, 2-24 August, Monday, Sunday*

✿ Louis (Stéphane Pitré)

MODERN CUISINE • INTIMATE A cosy restaurant, with an open kitchen and a wine tasting bar in the basement. The Brittany chef crafts dishes that are steeped in flavour and taste, such as fillet of cod with Romanesco broccoli, Piedmont hazelnuts and Savagnin grapes. Simpler fare at the nearby Le Cellier.

Specialities: Market-inspired cuisine.

Menu 42€ (lunch), 71/91€

PLAN: 3-L2 – *23 rue de la Victoire (9th) – Ⓜ Le Peletier – ✆ 01 55 07 86 52 – www.louis.paris – Closed 7 July-18 August, Saturday, Sunday*

✿ Lucas Carton 

MODERN CUISINE • HISTORIC The story of the Lucas Carton, the iconic name on Place de la Madeleine, continues. Youthful chef, Julien Dumas, has no equal for bringing out the best of fine produce. The vegetables from small producers and his marriage of acidic and bitter flavours are particularly noteworthy. Well - balanced dishes, rich in Mediterranean scents.

Specialities: Crispy cauliflower. Buckwheat and crispy line-caught pollock. Chocolate and toasted barley.

Menu 89/189€ – Carte 144/240€

PLAN: 3-J2 – *9 place de la Madeleine (8th) – Ⓜ Madeleine – ✆ 01 42 65 22 90 – www.lucascarton.com – Closed 1-25 August, Sunday*

✿ Marcore (Marc Favier) 

MODERN CUISINE • CHIC After regaling Pigalle with their Bouillon, Marc Favier and Aurélie Alary have made the former Versance into a two-fold establishment: bistronomic bar downstairs, gourmet fare upstairs. Chef Favier whisks up signature dishes in which wholesome, simple flavours dominate to the delight of sated diners!

Specialities: Poached duck foie gras from Les Landes and a lemon balm-cherry broth. Line-caught sea bass confit in olive oil, beetroot-redcurrant pickles and herbed condiments. New Guinea vanilla-flavoured soft-crispy biscuit, white chocolate sauce and coffee ice cream.

Menu 36€ (lunch)/80€ - Carte 75/85€

PLAN: 3-L2 – *1 rue des Panoramas (2nd) – Ⓜ Bourse – ✆ 01 45 08 00 08 – www.marcore-paris.com – Closed lunch Saturday, Sunday*

✿ NESO (Guillaume Sanchez)

CREATIVE • CONTEMPORARY DÉCOR Nomos is dead: long live the NESO! The endearing Guillaume Sanchez (Top Chef 2017 and Pastry chef competitions) reveals his own imaginative and talented culinary score: cold - steamed extractions, fermented vegetables... Original, often on the ball and occasionally disconcerting: a culinary experience unlike any other.

Specialities: Market-inspired cuisine.

Menu 55€ (lunch), 90/120€

PLAN: 3-M1 – *6 rue Papillon (9th) – Ⓜ Poissonnière – ✆ 01 48 24 04 13 – www.neso.paris – Closed 23 December-2 January, lunch Monday, Saturday, Sunday*

✿ Pur' - Jean-François Rouquette

CREATIVE • ELEGANT Enjoy a sense of pure enjoyment as you dine in this restaurant. The highly elegant contemporary decor and creative dishes are carefully conjured by the chef using the finest ingredients. Attractive, delicious and refined.

Specialities: Abalone with seaweed butter, baby artichokes, vadouvan and tobiko. Gently steamed turbot, buttered mussel jus, flower oil. "Crunchy" chocolate leaf, iced rice parfait, cocoa sauce with sakura vinegar.

Menu 165/205€ - Carte 160/255€

PLAN: 3-K3 – *Hôtel Park Hyatt Paris-Vendôme, 5 rue de la Paix (2nd) – Ⓜ Opéra – ✆ 01 58 71 10 60 – www.paris-restaurant-pur.fr – Closed 3-30 August, lunch*

✿ Restaurant du Palais Royal

CREATIVE • ELEGANT Magnificently located beneath the arcades of the Palais Royal, this elegant restaurant is now the playground of young chef Philip Chronopoulos, formerly of the Atelier Etoile de Joël Robuchon. Philip concocts creative, striking meals, such as flash - fried scampi with girolle mushrooms and fresh almonds.

Specialities: Fresh nuts, chanterelles and candied chestnuts in Château-Chalon wine. Cod confit in argan oil, roasted lemon and spinach. Raspberries, rhubarb, hibiscus syrup and iced vanilla yoghurt.

Menu 57€ (lunch)/162€ - Carte 108/174€

PLAN: 3-L3 – *Galerie de Valois (1st) – Ⓜ Palais Royal – ✆ 01 40 20 00 27 – www.restaurantdupalaisroyal.com – Closed 16 February-2 March, 9-24 August, Monday, Sunday*

✿ Sushi B

JAPANESE • MINIMALIST It is enjoyable to linger in this tiny restaurant (with just seven places) on the edge of the pleasant Square Louvois for its sleek, soothing interior, of course... but particularly to witness for oneself the chef's great talent. Like an excellent artisan, he uses only the freshest top - notch ingredients, which he handles with surgical precision.

Specialities: Market-inspired cuisine.

Menu 68€ (lunch), 140/210€

PLAN: 3-L3 – *5 rue Rameau (2nd) – Ⓜ Bourse – ✆ 01 40 26 52 87 – Closed 1-7 January, 27 April-8 May, 1-18 August, Monday, Tuesday*

Abri Soba

JAPANESE • BISTRO You may have heard of soba, Japanese pasta made with buckwheat, the reputation of which is currently snowballing around the planet. The chef of this restaurant has made soba his house speciality and serves it lunch and evening in an amazing variety of preparations: hot, cold, in stock or with finely sliced duck. Simply flavoursome – get out your chopsticks!

Menu 38€ – Carte 25/40€

PLAN: 3-L2 – *10 rue Saulnier (9th) – Ⓜ Cadet – ✆ 01 45 23 51 68 – Closed 12 August-1 September, Monday, lunch Sunday*

Le Caillebotte

MODERN CUISINE • FRIENDLY Chef Franck Baranger composes the fresh and thoroughly modern dishes, the secret of which only he holds. Langoustines served raw on cucumber lasagne, albacore tuna from St Gilles and minty pea coulis... It is delicious, colourful and goes perfectly with the friendly atmosphere of the place.

Menu 38/49€

PLAN: 3-L1 – *8 rue Hippolyte-Lebas (9th) – Ⓜ Notre-Dame de Lorette – ✆ 01 53 20 88 70 – Closed 12-31 August, Saturday, Sunday*

Les Canailles Pigalle

A/C

MODERN CUISINE • BISTRO This pleasant restaurant was created in 2012 by two Bretons with impressive culinary backgrounds. They slip into the *bistronomy* (gastro bistro), serving bistro and seasonal dishes. Specialities: ox tongue carpaccio and sauce ravigote, and rum baba with vanilla whipped cream... Tuck in!

Menu 37€ – Carte 49/55€

PLAN: 3-K1 – *25 rue La Bruyère (9th) – Ⓜ St-Georges – ✆ 01 48 74 10 48 – www.restaurantlescanailles.fr – Closed 8-30 August, Saturday, Sunday*

Dépôt Légal

A/C

MODERN CUISINE • TRENDY This atypical restaurant, run by Christophe Adam, a high - profile pastry chef with an impeccable CV (Le Gavroche in London, Hôtel de Crillon and Fauchon in Paris), proposes sweets and plates to share, from breakfast to dinner. At the entrance, a large glass counter presents the pastries, including numerous éclairs (try the salted butter caramel one!). No lunch bookings taken, brunch on Sundays.

Carte 30/45€

PLAN: 3-L3 – *6 rue des Petits-Champs (2nd) – Ⓜ Bourse – ✆ 01 42 61 67 07 – www.depotlegalparis.com*

Le Pantruche

MODERN CUISINE • BISTRO 'Pantruche' is slang for Paris... an apt name for this bistro with its chic retro decor, which happily cultivates a 1940s - 1950s atmosphere. As for the food, the chef and his small team put together lovely seasonal dishes in keeping with current culinary trends.

Menu 38€

PLAN: 3-L1 – *3 rue Victor-Massé (9th) – Ⓜ Pigalle – ✆ 01 48 78 55 60 – Closed 12-31 August, Saturday, Sunday*

Zen

A/C

JAPANESE • MINIMALIST This enticing restaurant combines a refreshing contemporary interior design and authentic Japanese cooking. The menu is well - rounded and faithful to the classic sushi, grilled dishes and tempura, with house specialities of gyoza and chirashi. Ideal for a quick lunch or a relaxing 'zen' dinner.

Menu 21€ (lunch), 35/60€ – Carte 25/60€

PLAN: 3-K3 – *8 rue de l'Échelle (1st) – Ⓜ Palais Royal – ✆ 01 42 61 93 99 – www.restaurantzenparis.fr – Closed 3-25 August*

Aux Lyonnais

LYONNAISE • BISTRO This bistro founded in 1890 has a delightfully retro decor, and serves delicious cuisine that explores the city's gastronomy: tablier de sapeur (crumbed tripe), pike quenelles with sauce Nantua, veal liver with persillade, and floating islands with pink pralines.

Menu 24 € (lunch)/35 € – Carte 44/56 €

PLAN: 3-L2 – *32 rue St-Marc (2nd) – Ⓜ Richelieu Drouot – ✆ 01 42 96 65 04 – www.auxlyonnais.com – Closed 1-29 August, 21 December-2 January, Monday, lunch Saturday, Sunday*

Belle Maison

SEAFOOD • BISTRO The three associates of Pantruche and Caillebotte are back behind the wheel in this Belle Maison, named after a beach on the Island of Yeu where they used to spend their holidays. The chef rustles up seafood - inspired dishes with disconcerting expertise: crab ravioles and gazpacho; line caught croaker, peas and girolles – a tantalising experience awaits!

Carte 41/58 €

PLAN: 3-L1 – *4 rue de Navarin (9th) – Ⓜ Saint-Georges – ✆ 01 42 81 11 00 – www.restaurant-bellemaison.com – Closed Monday, Sunday*

Bouillon 47

MODERN CUISINE • FRIENDLY This is the first venture of the chef who honed his skills as assistant chef to Bruno Doucet at La Régalade St-Honoré for 3 years. The accent is on honest, bistronomic fare, with inspired associations of seasonal, high-quality ingredients. In the finest Parisian bistro tradition, the focus is on taste above all!

Menu 28 € (lunch), 42/80 €

PLAN: 3-L1 – *47 rue de Rochechouart (9th) – Ⓜ Poissonnière – ✆ 09 51 18 66 59 – www.bouillonparis.fr – Closed 1-6 January, 1-11 May, 2-24 August, Monday, Sunday*

Brasserie d'Aumont

MODERN CUISINE • BRASSERIE The Brasserie d'Aumont sports a handsome Art deco interior, whose two connecting dining rooms are flanked by a shellfish counter with bar seats. Simply - laid tables and top - quality brasserie classics with a modern touch. Concise wine list and fine choice by the glass. Pleasant terrace. Smart and succulent.

Carte 65/120 €

PLAN: 3-J3 – *Hôtel Crillon, 10 place de la Concorde (8th) – Ⓜ Concorde – ✆ 01 44 71 15 15 – www.rosewoodhotels.com/fr/hotel-de-crillon*

Camélia

MODERN CUISINE • ELEGANT Keep it simple, concentrate on the flavour of the top - notch ingredients, draw inspiration from France's gastronomical classics and enhance them with Asian touches. This is the approach of Thierry Marx at Camélia; an elegant, soothing, zen place. An unequivocal success.

Menu 63 € (lunch)/98 € – Carte 68/115 €

PLAN: 3-J3 – *Hôtel Mandarin Oriental, 251 rue St-Honoré (1st) – Ⓜ Concorde – ✆ 01 70 98 74 00 – www.mandarinoriental.fr/paris*

Drouant

TRADITIONAL CUISINE • ELEGANT The Goncourt Prize has been awarded here since 1914. Under the Gardinier family, who recently took over the establishment, traditional dishes are getting a modern reboot. New menu, new chef: this mythical place is alive and well.

Menu 45 € (lunch) – Carte 52/86 €

PLAN: 3-K3 – *16 place Gaillon (2nd) – Ⓜ Quatre Septembre – ✆ 01 42 65 15 16 – www.drouant.com*

Eels

MODERN CUISINE • TRENDY At Eels, the dishes flirt with "bistronomie", and some of them focus on eel (the clue is in the name). The young chef, Adrien Ferrand, already has considerable experience under his belt (six years for William Ledeuil, first at Ze Kitchen Galerie, then KGB). And now he has a place of his own. A success!

Menu 32€ (lunch), 48/60€ - Carte 50/60€

PLAN: 3-M2 - *27 rue d'Hauteville (10th) - Ⓜ Bonne Nouvelle - ✆ 01 42 28 80 20 - www.restaurant-eels.com - Closed 4-27 August, 21 December-2 January, Monday, Sunday*

Jòia par Hélène Darroze

CUISINE FROM SOUTH WEST FRANCE • CONTEMPORARY DÉCOR Hélène Darroze's brand new venture is all about conviviality centred on dishes drawn from her memory of her native South - West France, with nods to the culinary traditions of the Basque Country, Landes and Béarn. Bold flavours, quality ingredients: a pleasant tribute to the family cuisine of the Darroze home, which her father concocted in Villeneuve de Marsan. The power of nostalgia!

Menu 29€ (lunch) - Carte 55/75€

PLAN: 3-L2 - *39 rue des Jeûneurs (2nd) - Ⓜ Grands Boulevards - ✆ 01 40 20 06 06 - www.joiahelenedarroze.com*

Kunitoraya

JAPANESE • VINTAGE With its old zinc counter, mirrors and Métro - style tiling, Kunitoraya has the feel of a late - night Parisian restaurant from the early 1900s. Refined Japanese cuisine is based around “udon”, a thick homemade noodle prepared with wholemeal flour imported from Japan.

Menu 32€ (lunch)/100€ - Carte 50/100€

PLAN: 3-K3 - *5 rue Villedo (1st) - Ⓜ Pyramides - ✆ 01 47 03 07 74 - www.kunitoraya.com - Closed 5-19 August, 23 December-2 January, Monday, dinner Sunday*

Liza

A/C

LEBANESE • TRENDY Originally from Beirut, Liza Asseily gives pride of place to her country's cuisine. In a contemporary interior dotted with Middle Eastern touches, opt for the shish taouk or mechoui kafta (lamb, hummus and tomato preserves). Dishes are meticulously prepared using fresh ingredients. A real treat!

Menu 27€ (lunch), 38/48€ - Carte 42/50€

PLAN: 3-L3 - *14 rue de la Banque (2nd) - Ⓜ Bourse - ✆ 01 55 35 00 66 - www.restaurant-liza.com - Closed 10-16 August, dinner Sunday*

Monsieur K

THAI • FRIENDLY The chef is a true Asia enthusiast. He has travelled the length and breadth of Thailand to sample its many cuisines and to reproduce a replica of the best dishes. He is a perfectionist fighting for the good cause, and makes a mean Pad Thai.

Menu 27€ (lunch)/39€ - Carte 40/50€

PLAN: 3-M3 - *10 rue Marie-Stuart (2nd) - Ⓜ Sentier - ✆ 01 42 36 01 09 - www.kapunkaparis.com - Closed Sunday*

Restaurant des Grands Boulevards

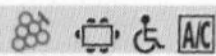

ITALIAN • CONTEMPORARY DÉCOR Beneath the hotel's central glass roof, the decoration is modern and trendy, with a "summer on the Riviera" feel... and Italian flavours, under the direction of chef Giovanni Passerini. Just one example, his interpretation of a popular Tuscan dish - *gnudi* with herbs and parmesan - is a lesson in simplicity and delicacy. Efficient and friendly service.

Menu 28€ (lunch) - Carte 45/60€

PLAN: 3-L2 - *Hôtel des Grands Boulevards, 17 boulevard Poissonnière (2nd) - Ⓜ Grands Boulevards - ✆ 01 85 73 33 32 - www.grandsboulevardshotel.com*

Tour Eiffel - Invalides

✿✿✿ Arpège (Alain Passard)

CREATIVE • ELEGANT Precious woods and a Lalique crystal decor provide the backdrop for the dazzling, vegetable - inspired cuisine of this culinary genius. He creates his astonishing dishes from organic produce grown in his three vegetable gardens!

Specialities: "Hot-Cold" egg with maple syrup, sherry vinegar and four spices. Harlequin "jardinière" and vegetable merguez. Rose-infused apple tart and milky caramel.

Menu 175€ (lunch), 340/420€ - Carte 240/350€

PLAN: 4-Q2 - *84 rue de Varenne (7th) - Ⓜ Varenne - ✆ 01 47 05 09 06 - www.alain-passard.com - Closed Saturday, Sunday*

✿✿ Astrance (Pascal Barbot)

CREATIVE • MINIMALIST As Parisians know, booking a table at Astrance can be a real challenge! Here, the cuisine is reinvented every day: the surprise "menu découverte" is thought out every morning according to the market and Pascal Barbot's mood. The wine list, composed with great care, as well as the discreet service, seal the deal.

Specialities: Mussel ceviche, coconut milk and celery branch jus. Steamed red mullet, beurre blanc, soy sauce and Koshihikari rice. Rhubarb and strawberry-raspberry tartlet with jasmine mousse.

Menu 95€ (lunch)/250€

PLAN: 4-N1 - *4 rue Beethoven (16th) - Ⓜ Passy - ✆ 01 40 50 84 40 - www.astrancerestaurant.com - Closed 26 July-24 August, 21 December-4 January, Monday, Saturday, Sunday*

✿✿ David Toutain

CREATIVE • CONTEMPORARY DÉCOR Having made a name for himself at some renowned establishments (L'Arpège, Agapé Substance), David Toutain has opened his own restaurant. All this experience is channelled into his cooking. While riding the wave of culinary trends, its finesse, creativity and palette of expressions reveal insight and singularity - a great balance!

Specialities: Egg, sweetcorn and cumin. Smoked eel and black sesame. Cauliflower, coconut and white chocolate.

Menu 70€ (lunch), 170/250€

PLAN: 4-P1 - *29 rue Surcouf (7th) - Ⓜ Invalides - ✆ 01 45 50 11 10 - www.davidtoutain.com - Closed 3-21 August, Saturday, Sunday*

✿✿ Sylvestre

MODERN CUISINE • ELEGANT Sylvestre Wahid arrived at Thoumieux, right near Les Invalides, in 2015 and soon won the hearts of the French capital's foodies. The dining space serves as a cosy setting for this authentic artist: throughout a delicate gourmet symphony, he transports diners to delicious lands. Magical.

Specialities: Crab, avocado and golden caviar. Les Costières pigeon, burlat cherry and red lentils. Lemon, sea lettuce and tarragon.

Menu 175/250€ - Carte 170/280€

PLAN: 4-P1 - *79 rue St-Dominique (7th) - Ⓜ La Tour Maubourg - ✆ 01 47 05 79 00 - www.thoumieux.fr - Closed 1-31 August, Monday, Sunday and lunch*

✿ Aida (Koji Aida)

JAPANESE • ELEGANT Be transported to the Land of the Rising Sun in this restaurant. It breathes authenticity and purity through its delicious Japanese cuisine full of finesse. The fish, presented alive and then prepared in front of you, couldn't be fresher. The art of simplicity and transparency at its best!

Specialities: Sashimi. Teppanyaki. Wagashi.

Menu 280€

PLAN: 4-Q3 - *1 rue Pierre-Leroux (7th) - Ⓜ Vaneau - ✆ 01 43 06 14 18 - www.aida-paris.net - Closed Monday and lunch*

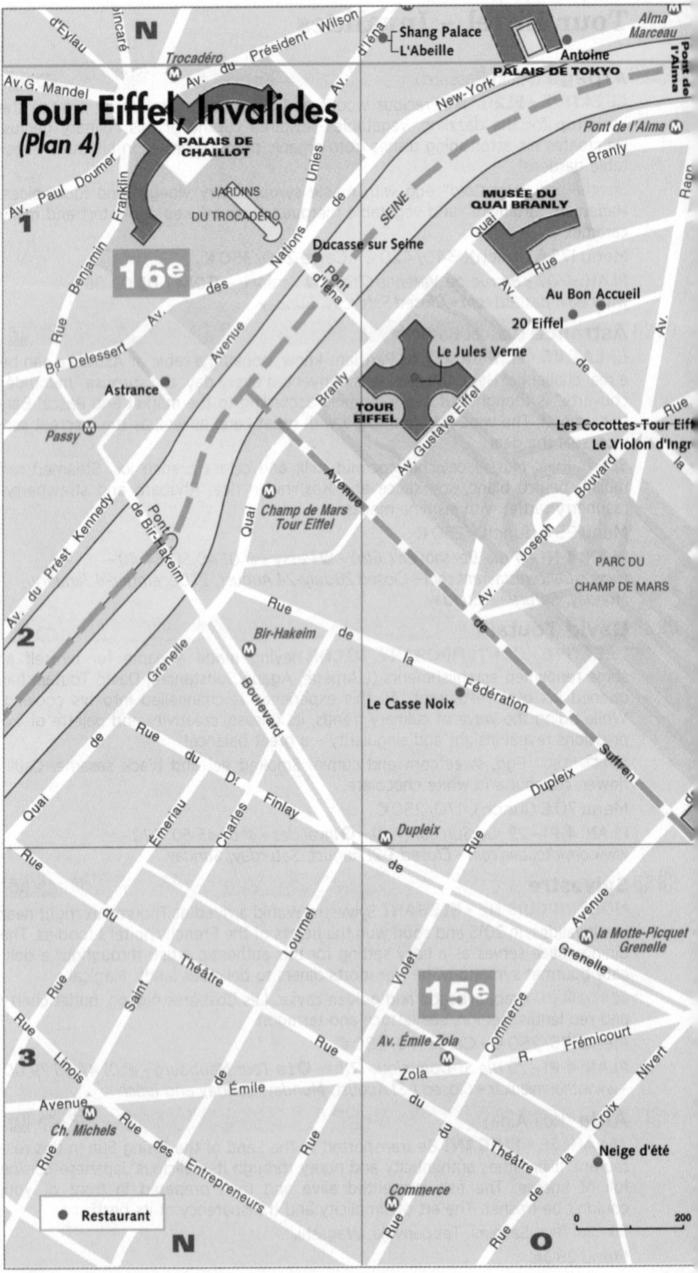

Tour Eiffel, Invalides
(Plan 4)

N
1
16e
PALAIS DE CHAILLOT
JARDINS DU TROCADÉRO
Trocadéro
Av. du Président Wilson
Av. G. Mandel
Av. Paul Doumer
Rue Benjamin Franklin
Av. des Nations Unies
Bd Delessert
Astrance
Passy
Shang Palace
L'Abeille
PALAIS DE TOKYO
Antoine
Alma Marceau
Pont de l'Alma
Av. de New-York
SEINE
Pont de l'Alma
Quai Branly
MUSÉE DU QUAI BRANLY
Ducasse sur Seine
Pont d'Iéna
Au Bon Accueil
20 Eiffel
Le Jules Verne
TOUR EIFFEL
Av. Gustave Eiffel
Les Cocottes-Tour Eiffel
Le Violon d'Ingres
Av. Rapp
Rue de la
Champ de Mars Tour Eiffel
Quai Branly
Av. du Prést Kennedy
Pont de Bir-Hakeim
Av. Joseph Bouvard
PARC DU CHAMP DE MARS
Avenue de Suffren
2
Bir-Hakeim
Rue de la Fédération
Le Casse Noix
Boulevard de Grenelle
Quai de Grenelle
Rue du Dr Finlay
Rue Émeriau
Rue Charles
Dupleix
Rue Dupleix
Rue de Lourmel
Avenue de la Motte-Picquet
la Motte-Picquet Grenelle
Rue du Théâtre
Rue Saint
Rue Violet
15e
Rue du Commerce
Av. Émile Zola
R. Frémicourt
Rue Nivert
3
Rue Linois
Avenue Émile Zola
Ch. Michels
Rue des Entrepreneurs
Rue du Théâtre
Rue de la Croix
Neige d'été
Commerce
Rue du Commerce
O
0 200

● Restaurant

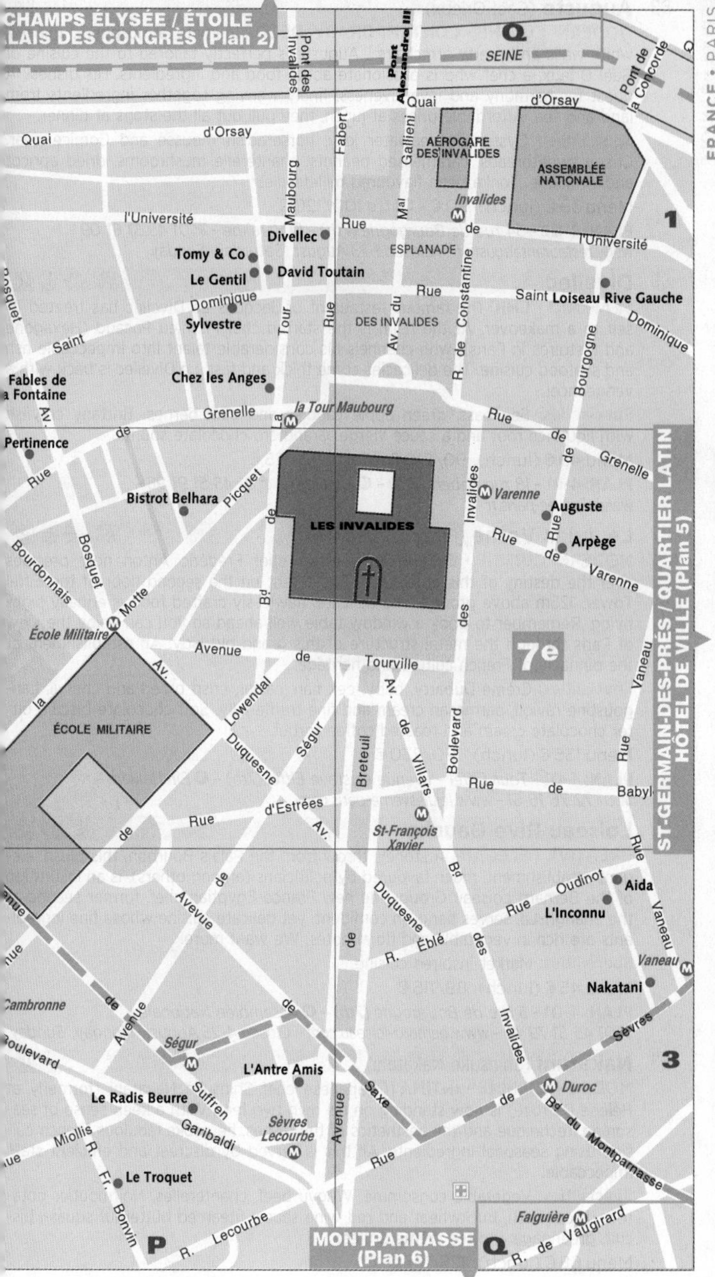
CHAMPS ÉLYSÉE / ÉTOILE
PALAIS DES CONGRÈS (Plan 2)
SEINE
Pont des Invalides
Pont Alexandre III
Pont de la Concorde
Quai d'Orsay
AÉROGARE DES INVALIDES
ASSEMBLÉE NATIONALE
Invalides
Rue de l'Université
ESPLANADE DES INVALIDES
Divellec
Tomy & Co
Le Gentil
David Toutain
Loiseau Rive Gauche
Rue Saint Dominique
Sylvestre
Fables de la Fontaine
Chez les Anges
Rue de Grenelle
la Tour Maubourg
Pertinence
Bistrot Belhara
Varenne
Auguste
Arpège
Rue de Varenne
LES INVALIDES
École Militaire
ÉCOLE MILITAIRE
Avenue de Tourville
7e
ST-GERMAIN-DES-PRÉS / QUARTIER LATIN
HÔTEL DE VILLE (Plan 5)
Rue de Babylone
St-François Xavier
Aida
L'Inconnu
Vaneau
Nakatani
Cambronne
Ségur
Duroc
L'Antre Amis
Le Radis Beurre
Sèvres Lecourbe
Le Troquet
Falguière
MONTPARNASSE (Plan 6)
R. de Vaugirard
R. Lecourbe
1
3
P
Q

✿ Auguste (Gaël Orieux)

MODERN CUISINE • CONTEMPORARY DÉCOR Intimate atmosphere, mirrors, white walls and pretty armchairs... Auguste is perfectly tailored to the cuisine of Gaël Orieux, a chef who is passionate about food and ingredients. His dishes? A quest for harmony and inventiveness, finely weaving together ingredients from land and sea. Affordable prices at lunch; they pull out all the stops at dinner.

Specialities: Oysters in seawater jelly, horseradish mousse and Comice pear. Crispy sweetbreads, caramelised peanuts, chanterelle mushrooms, dried apricot and vin jaune. Tonka bean-flavoured millefeuille.

Menu 39€ (lunch)/90€ - Carte 100/120€

PLAN: 4-Q2 - *54 rue de Bourgogne (7th) - Ⓜ Varenne - ✆ 01 45 51 61 09 - www.restaurantauguste.fr - Closed 1-23 August, Saturday, Sunday*

✿ Divellec

SEAFOOD • CHIC The famous restaurant of Jacques Le Divellec has treated itself to a makeover. At the helm is the starred chef Mathieu Pacaud (Hexagone and Histoires in Paris), who channels his considerable talent into impeccable fish and seafood cuisine. The delicacies come thick and fast. Le Divellec is back with a vengeance!

Specialities: Sea bass, green apple candies and pink berries. Brittany crayfish with liquorice root and a sauce vierge. Grand cru chocolate soufflé.

Menu 49€ (lunch), 90/210€ - Carte 92/175€

PLAN: 4-P1 - *18 rue Fabert (7th) - Ⓜ Invalides - ✆ 01 45 51 91 96 - www.divellec-paris.fr*

✿ Le Jules Verne (Frédéric Anton)

MODERN CUISINE • ELEGANT Three-star chef Frédéric Anton now presides over the destiny of this emblematic restaurant on the second floor of the Eiffel Tower, 125m above ground. The delicate, flawlessly crafted food is equally high-flying. Remember to book a window table well ahead so you can enjoy the view of Paris through the metal structure of this grand old lady. An establishment at the pinnacle of French culture and heritage.

Specialities: Crème Dubarry, baby leek flan, caviar, crisp bread and chervil. Langoustine ravioli, parmesan cream and fine truffle jelly. Soft chocolate biscuit, bitter chocolate cream and roasted coffee sorbet.

Menu 135€ (lunch), 190/230€

PLAN: 4-O1 - *Tour Eiffel - avenue Gustave Eiffel (7th) - Ⓜ Bir-Hakeim - ✆ 01 72 76 16 61 - www.lejulesverne-paris.com*

✿ Loiseau Rive Gauche

CREATIVE • ELEGANT A stone's throw from the Palais Bourbon, this plush, elegant establishment, much favoured by politicians (among others), is an institution of the Bernard Loiseau Group. The new Franco-Egyptian chef, former second at the Shangri-La, serves bang-on confident, yet delicate cuisine whose fine ingredients are rich in vegetable and floral notes. We want more!

Specialities: Market-inspired cuisine.

Menu 45€ (lunch), 89/115€

PLAN: 4-Q1 - *5 rue de Bourgogne (7th) - Ⓜ Assemblée Nationale - ✆ 01 45 51 79 42 - www.bernard-loiseau.com - Closed 4-25 August, Monday, Sunday*

✿ Nakatani (Shinsuke Nakatani)

MODERN CUISINE • INTIMATE Japanese chef Shinsuke Nakatani (formerly at Hélène Darroze) is now standing on his own two feet. With a keen sense of seasoning, technique and the aesthetics of the dishes, he cooks fabulous French cuisine using seasonal ingredients. All this is served by discreet and efficient staff. Impeccable!

Specialities: Vegetable consommé. Wagyu beef, chanterelles, Noirmoutier potatoes, broccoletti, buckwheat and red wine sauce. Steamed butternut squash biscuit, greengage and tea crème brûlée.

Menu 68€ (lunch), 125/165€

PLAN: 4-Q3 - *27 rue Pierre-Leroux (7th) - Ⓜ Vaneau - ✆ 01 47 34 94 14 - www.restaurant-nakatani.com - Closed 1-12 August, Monday, Sunday*

Neige d'Été (Hideki Nishi)

MODERN CUISINE • MINIMALIST The name (meaning 'Summer Snow') is poetically Japanese, and that is no coincidence. This restaurant was opened in mid - 2014 by a young Japanese chef, Hideki Nishi, who used to be at the George V. It also hints at the contrasts and minimalism that are the hallmarks of his work, which is always spot - on and full of counterpoints.

Specialities: Tuna beignet and tartare. Iberian pork cooked on a Japanese charcoal grill. Apricot parfait with cardamom.

Menu 55 € (lunch), 100/185 €

PLAN: 4-O3 – *12 rue de l'Amiral-Roussin (15th) – Ⓜ Avenue Émile Zola – ✆ 01 42 73 66 66 – www.neigedete.fr – Closed 15-31 August, Monday, Sunday*

Pertinence (Kwen Liew et Ryunosuke Naito)

MODERN CUISINE • DESIGN This minimalist interior, depicted by light wood Knoll chairs, near the Champs Elysees is the fief of Japanese Ryu and Malaysian Kwen. Ryu carefully and expertly nurtures and coaxes market - fresh ingredients into succulent classical French dishes, brushing off the cobwebs of tradition on the way. We expect to hear much more from this quarter!

Specialities: Market-inspired cuisine.

Menu 45 € (lunch), 105/165 € – Carte 115/180 €

PLAN: 4-P2 – *29 rue de l'Exposition (7th) – Ⓜ École Militaire – ✆ 01 45 55 20 96 – www.restaurantpertinence.com – Closed 2 August-4 September, Monday, lunch Tuesday, Sunday*

Tomy & Co (Tomy Gousset)

MODERN CUISINE • FRIENDLY This establishment bears the hallmark of the unabashed talent of Tomy Gousset (ex - Meurice and Taillevent). Tomy plays a gourmet - bistro score whose modern notes reveal a deceptively simple melody. The establishment is determined to consume locally (organic veggies from Essonne). Booking would be a good idea!

Specialities: Tartlet of ox tongue, pickled turnips and gribiche sauce. Apicius duckling fillet, chard and roasted fig, Dauphine potatoes. Ossau-Iraty cheese, black cherry and smoked chilli jam.

Menu 50/75 €

PLAN: 4-P1 – *22 rue Surcouf (7th) – Ⓜ Invalides – ✆ 01 45 51 46 93 – www.tomygousset.com – Closed 1-30 August, Saturday, Sunday*

Le Violon d'Ingres

TRADITIONAL CUISINE • CONTEMPORARY DÉCOR Christian Constant sold Le Violon d'Ingres to Bertrand Bluy, who also hails from France's South-West and is the owner of Les Papilles (in Paris's 5th *arrondissement*). Fans can rest assured: the spirit of the place - in a luxurious neo-brasserie style - and the cuisine remain unchanged. You can enjoy tasty traditional dishes with a modern twist that show a good technical mastery. Remember to book, as tables get snapped up fast.

Specialities: Spider crab jelly, herb-infused crab cream. Crispy sea bass supreme with almonds, acidulated caper and lemon jus. Hot Grand Marnier soufflé.

Menu 55 € (lunch)/140 € – Carte 90/105 €

PLAN: 4-O1 – *135 rue St-Dominique (7th) – Ⓜ École Militaire – ✆ 01 45 55 15 05 – www.maisonconstant.com*

L'Antre Amis

MODERN CUISINE • CONTEMPORARY DÉCOR The chef - patron at L'Antre Amis brings passion to his cooking. Using excellent produce sourced from Rungis Market (meat, fish, shellfish etc), he composes scrupulous dishes, precisely made and organised into a very short menu. To be accompanied by your choice from a fine wine list - around 150 bins.

Menu 38/54 € – Carte 50/65 €

PLAN: 4-P3 – *9 rue Bouchut (15th) – Ⓜ Ségur – ✆ 01 45 67 15 65 – www.lantreamis.com – Closed 1-10 January, 1-31 August, Saturday, Sunday*

Au Bon Accueil

MODERN CUISINE • BISTRO In the shadow of the Eiffel Tower in a quiet street, this discreet, but smart bistro serves appetising, market-fresh cuisine that mirrors the seasons. Grilled squid, crushed potatoes and aioli; roast saddle and confit shoulder of lamb...

Menu 37/58 € - Carte 65/85 €

PLAN: 4-O1 - *14 rue de Monttessuy (7th) - Ⓜ Alma Marceau - ✆ 01 47 05 46 11 - www.aubonaccueilparis.com - Closed 1-23 August, Saturday, Sunday*

Le Casse Noix

TRADITIONAL CUISINE • BISTRO Old signs, clocks and vintage furniture: the scene is set. As for the food, authenticity is the order of the day: delicious down - to - earth *canaille* cuisine, good wines and an amusing collection of nutcrackers picked up here and there by the owner's mum. Tasty.

Menu 35 €

PLAN: 4-O2 - *56 rue de la Fédération (15th) - Ⓜ Bir-Hakeim - ✆ 01 45 66 09 01 - www.le-cassenoix.fr - Closed 1-24 August, 24 December-3 January, Saturday, Sunday*

Chez les Anges

CLASSIC CUISINE • ELEGANT An elegant dining area for tasty, sincere cuisine that draws on both traditional and modern: langoustines, angel's hair and celeriac remoulade, or sole meunière and Bresse chicken. Accompanied by a fine wine and whisky list.

Menu 37/58 € - Carte 60/85 €

PLAN: 4-P1 - *54 boulevard de la Tour-Maubourg (7th) - Ⓜ La Tour Maubourg - ✆ 01 47 05 89 86 - www.chezlesanges.com - Closed 12-31 August, Saturday, Sunday*

Les Cocottes - Tour Eiffel

TRADITIONAL CUISINE • FRIENDLY The concept in this friendly eatery is based around bistro cuisine with a modern touch cooked in cast - iron casserole pots (cocottes), and includes popular dishes such as country paté, roast veal etc. No advance booking.

Menu 30 € (lunch)/37 € - Carte 36/60 €

PLAN: 4-O1 - *135 rue St-Dominique (7th) - Ⓜ École Militaire - ✆ 01 45 50 10 28 - www.lescocottes.paris*

Le Radis Beurre

TRADITIONAL CUISINE • BISTRO It was in 2015 on Boulevard Garibaldi in Paris that chef Jérôme Bonnet found the perfect site for his restaurant. He prepares tasty, carefully created food that bears the hallmark of his southern upbringing. An example? Pig's trotters with duck foie gras and meat juices. You may even get to nibble on a few radishes with butter while you wait.

Menu 37 € - Carte 37/45 €

PLAN: 4-P3 - *51 boulevard Garibaldi (15th) - Ⓜ Sèvres Lecourbe - ✆ 01 40 33 99 26 - www.restaurantleradisbeurre.com - Closed 24 July-17 August, 23 December-1 January, Saturday, Sunday*

20 Eiffel

TRADITIONAL CUISINE • CLASSIC DÉCOR In a quiet street a stone's throw from the Eiffel Tower, this restaurant offers a understated interior full of light. On the menu, you can choose from a range of updated dishes, prepared by two chefs, all of which place the focus on flavour and taste. For example, a delicious fillet of wild Pollack with squash.

Menu 34 € - Carte 50/65 €

PLAN: 4-O1 - *20 rue de Monttessuy (7th) - Ⓜ Alma Marceau - ✆ 01 47 05 14 20 - www.restaurant20eiffel.fr - Closed 2-13 January, 10-18 May, 22 August-8 September, Monday, Sunday*

Bistrot Belhara

TRADITIONAL CUISINE • BISTRO Belhara is a site that is famous for its superb waves on the Basque coast - and this is the chef's nod to his origins. It is a tough call to summarise his impressive career path (Guérard, Loiseau, Ducasse etc). A convert to the bistro mode, Thierry Dufroux works wonders as he revisits the classics – the chef is definitely on the crest of the wave!

Menu 34€ (lunch), 41/60€

PLAN: 4-P2 – *23 rue Duvivier (7th) – Ⓜ École Militaire – ✆ 01 45 51 41 77 – www.bistrotbelhara.com – Closed 13-27 August, Monday, Sunday*

Ducasse sur Seine

MODERN CUISINE • DESIGN Well, no one can say that Alain Ducasse lacks for boldness or ideas, as the Ducasse sur Seine once again proves. An electric boat, moored on the quayside of Port Debilly in the swanky 16th arrondissement, offers a gastronomic cruise that is both ecological and silent. At the same time as you discover Parisian monuments, you will taste up - to - the - minute cuisine, masterfully crafted by a kitchen team worthy of the best restaurants. Well done, mon capitaine!

Menu 100€ (lunch), 150/190€

PLAN: 4-N1 – *Port Debilly (16th) – Ⓜ Trocadéro – ✆ 01 58 00 22 08 – www.ducasse-seine.com – Closed 27 January-7 February*

Les Fables de La Fontaine

MODERN CUISINE • BISTRO The former sous - chef of Les Fables has slipped effortlessly into the role of chef. He composes modern cuisine that is fragrant and bursting with colours, demonstrating an impressive maturity and undeniable talent. Relish your meal in a sleek, light and elegant bistro decor.

Carte 56/75€

PLAN: 4-P1 – *131 rue St-Dominique (7th) – Ⓜ École Militaire – ✆ 01 44 18 37 55 – www.lesfablesdelafontaine.net*

Le Gentil

MODERN CUISINE • SIMPLE This newcomer on Rue Surcouf, strewn with eateries, is the work of Japanese chef Fumitoshi Kumagai, seconded by his wife in the dining room. The updated Gallic menu is dotted with the occasional Asian influence: pig's trotters stuffed with pak choi, beef faux-filet with a Japanese sauce... High quality ingredients assembled precisely and subtly.

Menu 23€ (lunch) – Carte 43/53€

PLAN: 4-P1 – *26 rue Surcouf (7th) – Ⓜ Invalides – ✆ 09 52 27 01 36 – Closed Saturday, Sunday*

L'Inconnu

MODERN CUISINE • COSY The chef, who for a long time was second-in-command at Passage 53, concocts Italian-inspired cuisine with influences from France, as well as his native Japan. He only works with the finest ingredients, using them to produce original and creative dishes, such as Breton langoustine tails topped with a cider and confit lemon emulsion.

Menu 30€ (lunch)/85€

PLAN: 4-Q3 – *4 rue Pierre-Leroux (7th) – Ⓜ Vanneau – ✆ 01 53 69 06 03 – www.restaurant-linconnu.fr*

Le Troquet

TRADITIONAL CUISINE • BISTRO A traditional bistro in all its splendour: authentic decor, moleskin banquettes, blackboard menus, mirrors, small tables that set a convivial mood. As for the food, you'll find a menu with lots of variety, including pork terrine, scallop tartar, fresh tagliatelle with black truffles.

Menu 34€ (lunch), 35/42€

PLAN: 4-P3 – *21 rue François-Bonvin (15th) – Ⓜ Cambronne – ✆ 01 45 66 89 00 – www.restaurantletroquet.fr – Closed 3-23 August, Monday, Sunday*

Saint-Germain des Prés – Quartier Latin – Hôtel de Ville

✿✿✿ Guy Savoy

CREATIVE • LUXURY Guy Savoy, act II, in the Hôtel de la Monnaie, on the bank of the Seine. The setting is sumptuous – six rooms adorned with contemporary works lent by François Pinault –, and the host, true to himself: sincere and passionate, inventive without excess, unfailing generosity. Irresistible!

Specialities: Artichoke soup with a layered mushroom and black truffle brioche. Duckling matured in spices with a bay leaf-flavoured gratin. Open millefeuille with Tahitian vanilla.

Menu 250 € (lunch)/478 € – Carte 250/290 €

PLAN: 5-S1 – *11 quai de Conti (6th) – Ⓜ St-Michel – ✆ 01 43 80 40 61 – www.guysavoy.com – Closed 2-24 August, Monday, lunch Saturday, Sunday*

✿✿ L'Atelier de Joël Robuchon - St-Germain

CREATIVE • DESIGN A long counter flanked by bar stools, a small, intimate dining area, red and black colour scheme, a carefully designed half - light and stunning food (over 80 different dishes), prepared with a watchmaker's precision. A must in its genre, invented by the great chef, who died in 2018.

Specialities: Caviar on a soft poached egg with crispy batter and smoked salmon. Milk-fed lamb chops with thyme flowers. Araguani chocolate ganache, ground cocoa ice cream, Oreo biscuit.

Menu 185 € – Carte 90/175 €

PLAN: 5-R1 – *5 rue de Montalembert (7th) – Ⓜ Rue du Bac – ✆ 01 42 22 56 56 – www.joel-robuchon.net*

✿ Alliance (Toshitaka Omiya)

MODERN CUISINE • CONTEMPORARY DÉCOR Alliance brings together two alumni of the restaurant Agapé Substance as partners in this new adventure. A starter of oyster, onion and lemon; foie gras, vegetable pot - au - feu and Corsican broth... The chef's dishes are flashes of simplicity, at once subtle and well executed. We will be going back for more.

Specialities: Artichoke, abalone and coriander. Patte Noire chicken and lobster roe. Rhubarb, olive oil and white tea.

Menu 55 € (lunch), 120/185 €

PLAN: 5-U2 – *5 rue de Poissy (5th) – Ⓜ Maubert Mutualité – ✆ 01 75 51 57 54 – www.restaurant-alliance.fr – Closed 1-23 August, Saturday, Sunday*

✿ Benoit

CLASSIC CUISINE • BISTRO Alain Ducasse supervises this chic and lively bistro, one of the oldest in Paris: Benoit celebrated its 100th anniversary in 2012! The classic food is prepared in time - honoured tradition, and respects the soul of this authentic and fine establishment.

Specialities: Lucullus ox tongue, heart of Romaine lettuce with a mustard cream. Sautéed sweetbreads, cockerel kidneys and comb, foie gras and a truffle jus. Benoit profiteroles, hot chocolate sauce.

Menu 39 € (lunch) – Carte 70/100 €

PLAN: 5-U1 – *20 rue St-Martin (4th) – Ⓜ Châtelet-Les Halles – ✆ 01 42 72 25 76 – www.benoit-paris.com – Closed 26 July-23 August*

✿ Les Climats

MODERN CUISINE • CHIC Mosaic floors, brass light fittings, vert d'Estours marbles: the Maison des Dames des Postes building (postal and telecommunications service operators from 1905) has heaps of character. As for the food, fine ingredients and creative combinations reconnect all the senses. The list of Burgundy wines is remarkable, with nearly 2 000 bins.

Specialities: Langoustines pan-fried in butter, stew of petit pois with marigold and grapefruit. Sweetbreads braised with confit lemon, cucumber with new garlic and almond flakes. Imperial Mandarin soufflé, mandarin with olive oil and mandarin sorbet.

Menu 49€ (lunch), 130/240€ - Carte 108/130€

PLAN: 5-R1 - *41 rue de Lille (7th) - Ⓜ Rue du Bac - ✆ 01 58 62 10 08 - www.lesclimats.fr - Closed 1-13 January, 2-25 August, Monday, Sunday*

✿ La Dame de Pic

CREATIVE • DESIGN Anne - Sophie Pic's Parisian restaurant stands a stone's throw from the Louvre. A fine understanding of flavours, a precise touch and the ability to bring together unexpected ingredients are the hallmarks of the Valence - born chef: *berlingots à la fondue fribourgeoise* in a foamy Sansho pepper broth, and *tourteau de casier* (crab) served on a delicate mandarin jelly.

Specialities: Berlingots with smoked Brillat-Savarin cheese, wild mushrooms and Tonka beans. Sea bream with a dashi bouillon. Citrus millefeuille.

Menu 69€ (lunch), 119/149€

PLAN: 5-T1 - *20 rue du Louvre (1st) - Ⓜ Louvre Rivoli - ✆ 01 42 60 40 40 - www.anne-sophie-pic.com - Closed 10-16 August*

✿ Emporio Armani Caffè Ristorante (Massimo Tringali)

ITALIAN • CONTEMPORARY DÉCOR On the first storey of the boutique located in the heart of this chic Left Bank neighbourhood, this *ristorante* turns out to be an excellent surprise. The chef, former second - in - command at Porto - Vecchio's Casadelmar, creates elegant and refined Italian cuisine, replete with noble products. It's fresh, tasty, brilliantly handled: a fine work of art.

Specialities: Violet artichoke mangetout, baby vegetables, crunchy and soft fruits. Burrata and smoked aubergine ravioli. Baba flambéed with Strega liqueur.

Menu 49€ (lunch), 90/120€ - Carte 86/151€

PLAN: 5-S2 - *149 boulevard St-Germain (6th) - Ⓜ St-Germain des Prés - ✆ 01 45 48 62 15 - www.mori.paris - Closed 5-19 August, Sunday*

✿ ES (Takayuki Honjo)

MODERN CUISINE • MINIMALIST A restaurant run by Takayuki Honjo, a young Japanese chef who is a fan of French cuisine. From the first mouthful, his talent jumps out at you. Foie gras and sea urchins, pigeon and cacao: all the pairings work, with never a wrong note; he masters the flavours and always has in mind the bigger picture. Clarity and harmony.

Specialities: Market-inspired cuisine.

Menu 55€ (lunch)/105€

PLAN: 5-R1 - *91 rue de Grenelle (7th) - Ⓜ Solférino - ✆ 01 45 51 25 74 - www.es-restaurant.fr - Closed 5-26 August, Monday, lunch Tuesday-Thursday, Sunday*

✿ Marsan par Hélène Darroze

MODERN CUISINE • CONTEMPORARY DÉCOR Hélène Darroze has reopened her restaurant in 2019 after several months of refurbishment. Elegant, cosy décor, subtle, delicate cuisine in a single, seasonal menu that has not forgotten south-west France, so dear to her heart... The lucky few may even be able to eat at the table (6 - 8 seats) right in the kitchen to get even closer to the action!

Specialities: "White pearl" oyster, iced haricot velouté, Ossetra caviar. Tandoori lobster, carrot mousse with citrus fruit. Raspberries, sorrel and olive oil.

Menu 75€ (lunch), 175/225€

PLAN: 5-R2 - *4 rue d'Assas (6th) - Ⓜ Sèvres Babylone - ✆ 01 42 22 00 11 - www.helenedarroze.com - Closed Saturday, Sunday*

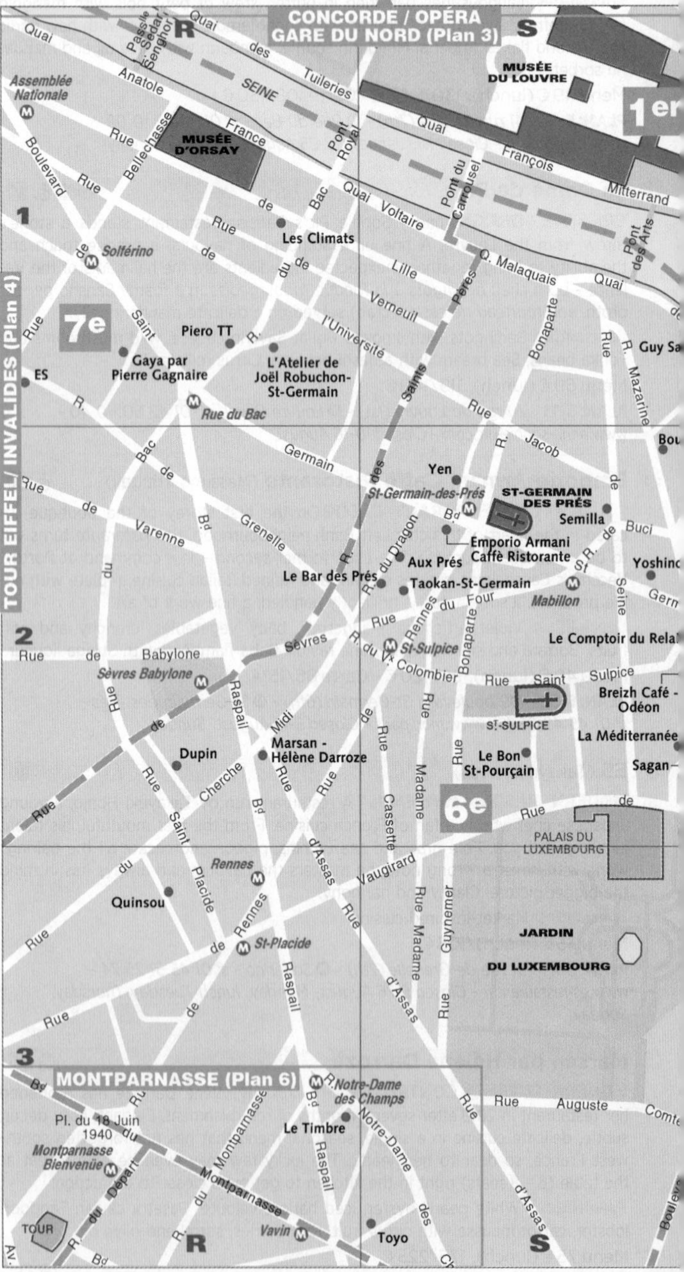

CONCORDE / OPÉRA
GARE DU NORD (Plan 3)

TOUR EIFFEL/ INVALIDES (Plan 4)

MONTPARNASSE (Plan 6)

1
2
3
R
S
1er
7e
6e

SEINE
Quai Anatole France
Quai des Tuileries
Quai François Mitterrand
Quai Voltaire
Q. Malaquais
Quai
Passle Sédar Senghor
Pont Royal
Pont du Carrousel
Pont des Arts
MUSÉE DU LOUVRE
MUSÉE D'ORSAY
Assemblée Nationale
Solférino
Rue du Bac
St-Germain-des-Prés
Mabillon
St-Sulpice
Sèvres Babylone
Rennes
St-Placide
Notre-Dame des Champs
Montparnasse Bienvenüe
Vavin
Boulevard Saint Germain
Rue de Bellechasse
Rue de Lille
Rue de Verneuil
Rue de l'Université
R. du Bac
Rue Jacob
Rue des Saints Pères
R. Bonaparte
Rue de Seine
R. Mazarine
Rue de Buci
Rue de Varenne
Rue de Grenelle
Bd Raspail
R. du Dragon
Rue du Four
Rue de Sèvres
Rue de Babylone
R. du Vx Colombier
Rue Saint Sulpice
Rue de Rennes
Rue du Cherche Midi
Rue de Cassette
Rue Madame
Rue Guynemer
Rue de Vaugirard
Rue d'Assas
Rue Saint Placide
Rue Auguste Comte
Bd du Montparnasse
Bd Raspail
R. Notre-Dame des Champs
R. du Départ
Pl. du 18 Juin 1940
TOUR
ST-GERMAIN DES PRÉS
ST-SULPICE
PALAIS DU LUXEMBOURG
JARDIN DU LUXEMBOURG

Les Climats
Piero TT
Gaya par Pierre Gagnaire
L'Atelier de Joël Robuchon-St-Germain
ES
Yen
Semilla
Emporio Armani Caffè Ristorante
Aux Prés
Le Bar des Prés
Taokan-St-Germain
Guy Sa
Bou
Yoshino
Le Comptoir du Rela
Breizh Café - Odéon
La Méditerranée
Sagan
Le Bon St-Pourçain
Dupin
Marsan - Hélène Darroze
Quinsou
Le Timbre
Toyo

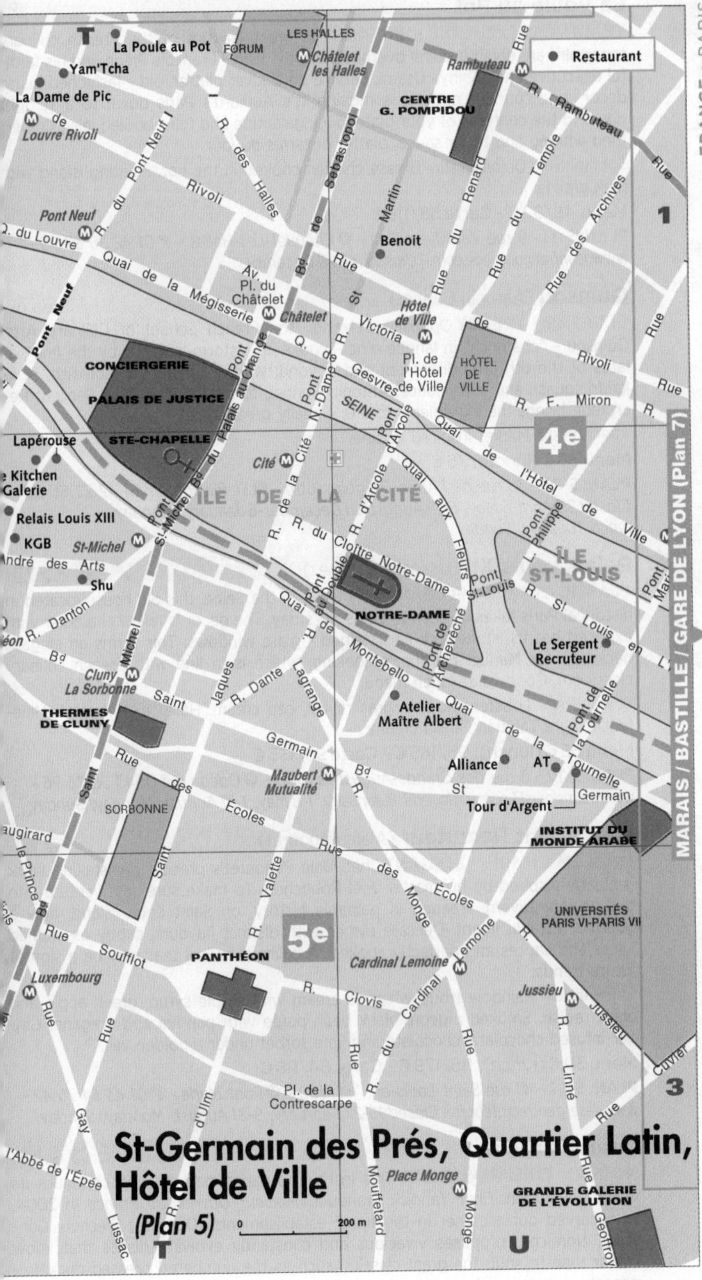

St-Germain des Prés, Quartier Latin, Hôtel de Ville

(Plan 5)

0 — 200 m

● Restaurant

T
U
1
3
4e
5e

La Poule au Pot
Yam'Tcha
La Dame de Pic
Benoit
Lapérouse
Kitchen Galerie
Relais Louis XIII
KGB
Shu
Le Sergent Recruteur
Atelier Maître Albert
Alliance
AT
Tour d'Argent

LES HALLES
FORUM
Châtelet les Halles
Rambuteau
CENTRE G. POMPIDOU
Louvre Rivoli
Pont Neuf
Châtelet
Hôtel de Ville
HÔTEL DE VILLE
Pl. de l'Hôtel de Ville
Pl. du Châtelet
CONCIERGERIE
PALAIS DE JUSTICE
STE-CHAPELLE
Cité
ÎLE DE LA CITÉ
ÎLE ST-LOUIS
NOTRE-DAME
SEINE
St-Michel
Cluny La Sorbonne
THERMES DE CLUNY
SORBONNE
Maubert Mutualité
INSTITUT DU MONDE ARABE
UNIVERSITÉS PARIS VI-PARIS VII
PANTHÉON
Cardinal Lemoine
Jussieu
Luxembourg
Pl. de la Contrescarpe
Place Monge
GRANDE GALERIE DE L'ÉVOLUTION

R. de Rivoli
R. des Halles
R. du Pont Neuf
Q. du Louvre
Quai de la Mégisserie
Av. Victoria
Bd. de Sébastopol
Rue St Martin
Rue du Renard
Rue du Temple
Rue des Archives
R. Rambuteau
Rue de Rivoli
R. F. Miron
Q. de Gesvres
Quai de l'Hôtel de Ville
Pont Neuf
Pont au Change
Bd. du Palais
Pont N.-Dame
R. de la Cité
Pont d'Arcole
R. d'Arcole
Quai aux Fleurs
R. du Cloître Notre-Dame
Pont St-Louis
Pont L. Philippe
Pont Marie
R. St Louis en L'Île
Pont St-Michel
André des Arts
R. Danton
Bd Saint Michel
Bd Saint Germain
R. St Jacques
R. Dante
R. Lagrange
Pont au Double
Quai de Montebello
Pont de l'Archevêché
Quai de la Tournelle
Pont de la Tournelle
Bd St Germain
Rue des Écoles
R. Saint Jacques
R. Valette
Rue Monge
R. Lemoine
R. Jussieu
Rue Cuvier
Rue Soufflot
R. Clovis
R. du Cardinal
Rue Mouffetard
Rue Monge
R. Linné
Rue Geoffroy
Rue Gay Lussac
R. d'Ulm
R. de l'Abbé de l'Épée
Vaugirard
Bd St Michel
Rue le Prince

MARAIS / BASTILLE / GARE DE LYON (Plan 7)

La Poule au Pot

TRADITIONAL CUISINE • **VINTAGE** The great classics of the French culinary repertoire are given a skilful overhaul here by Jean - François Piège and his faithful executive chef, Shinya Usami. Service on a silver platter, old - fashioned bistro decor, zinc counter: nothing is missing. It's Audiard's Paris down to a T, right down to the contents of your plate: duck galantine and full - bodied jelly, Colbert fried whiting and tartar sauce, platter of *tartes du jour*.

Specialities: Onion gratin. Bresse chicken cooked in the pot. Floating island with pink praline.

Menu 48/82€ - Carte 58/116€

PLAN: 5-T1 – *9 rue Vauvilliers (1st) – Ⓜ Châtelet-Les-Halles – ✆ 01 42 36 32 96 – www.jeanfrancoispiege.com – Closed 24-26 December*

Quinsou (Antonin Bonnet)

CREATIVE • **TRENDY** Opposite Ferrandi, the French School of Culinary Arts, Quinsou – "chaffinch" in langue d'oc – cooks up a storm, relished by the fine palates of the 6th arrondissement and beyond, with, for instance, monkfish, Hokkaido squash and curry sauce: Antonin Bonnet, former chef from Le Sergent Recruteur, brings the ingredients to life. A really great place.

Specialities: Market-inspired cuisine.

Menu 38€ (lunch)/75€

PLAN: 5-R3 – *33 rue de l'Abbé-Grégoire (6th) – Ⓜ St-Placide – ✆ 01 42 22 66 09 – Closed 29 April-6 May, 5-19 August, 21 December-6 January, Monday, lunch Tuesday, Sunday*

Relais Louis XIII (Manuel Martinez)

CLASSIC CUISINE • **ELEGANT** Very close to the Seine, this old house located in historical Paris takes us back to Louis XIII's day. The decor is full of character with exposed beams, stonework and stained - glass windows. This forms an elegant backdrop for Manuel Martinez's cooking, which is in line with French culinary classicism. Good value lunch menu.

Specialities: Lobster and foie gras ravioli, cep cream. Hare "à la royale". Millefeuille, light Tahitian vanilla cream.

Menu 65€ (lunch), 95/145€ - Carte 95/135€

PLAN: 5-T2 – *8 rue des Grands-Augustins (6th) – Ⓜ Odéon – ✆ 01 43 26 75 96 – www.relaislouis13.com – Closed 1-8 January, 1-8 May, 1-31 August, Monday, Sunday*

Le Sergent Recruteur (Alain Pégouret)

MODERN CUISINE • **ELEGANT** Chef Alain Pégouret's precise, painstaking work is clearly inspired by his master Joël Robuchon. To make sure, just venture into this ancient tavern, steeped in palpable history, on Saint Louis Island, now a gourmet establishment. Delicate dishes with distinct flavours, subtly assembled juices and sauces and perfectly cooked. A culinary revival that may be a sign of future trends.

Specialities: Rainbow trout, whipped cream with maple syrup, green apple and black radish. Smoked pigeon, black bean purée with paprika and oregano. Ginger-infused chocolate, chocolate and lime sorbet under a golden veil.

Menu 39€ (lunch), 85/179€ - Carte 84/118€

PLAN: 5-U2 – *41 rue Saint-Louis-en-l'Île (4th) – Ⓜ Pont Marie – ✆ 01 43 54 75 42 – www.lesergentrecruteur.fr – Closed 16-27 February, 9-31 August, Monday, Sunday*

Tour d'Argent

MODERN CUISINE • **LUXURY** This institution dating back to 1582 continues its velvet revolution. Chef Yannick Franques, *Meilleur Ouvrier de France* in 2004 who carved out a career in the finest establishments (Ducasse, Frechon, Constant, Nomicos) proposes vivacious and constantly evolving dishes that know better than to snub the great classics, such as the numbered pressed duck. Impeccable service and an exceptional wine cellar boasting some 320 000 bottles. Tradition hand in hand with modernity.

Specialities: Chicory, black truffles cooked "en vessie", winter vegetables and swede mousseline. Frédéric Delair duckling. Crêpes "mademoiselle" with raw milk curd sorbet.

Menu 105 € (lunch), 360/380 € - Carte 200/350 €

PLAN: 5-U2 - *15 quai de la Tournelle (5th) - Ⓜ Maubert Mutualité - ✆ 01 43 54 23 31 - www.tourdargent.com - Closed 3-24 August, Monday, Sunday*

✿ Yam'Tcha (Adeline Grattard)

CREATIVE • ELEGANT No pretension here; just superb flavour combinations: in rue St Honoré, Adeline Grattard works wonders. With a remarkable feel for her ingredients, she turns out simple and striking culinary pairings - with influences from France and Asia - designed in accordance with a selection of excellent teas. An energetic, spontaneous, moving accomplishment: this is great art.

Specialities: Marinated raw tuna, foie gras coulis and mushrooms. Milk-fed veal and Sichuan-style aubergines. Black sesame soup and vanilla ice cream.

Menu 150 €

PLAN: 5-T1 - *121 rue Saint-Honoré (1st) - Ⓜ Louvre Rivoli - ✆ 01 40 26 08 07 - www.yamtcha.com - Closed 2 August-9 September, 22 December-8 January, Monday, Tuesday, Sunday*

✿ Yoshinori (Yoshinori Morié)

MODERN CUISINE • INTIMATE Yoshinori Morié's latest born is already sparkling in the culinary firmament. The Japanese chef regales us with his refined, vegetable - based, aesthetic cuisine, presented as a seasonal menu. For instance, tartare of milk - fed Corrèze veal with cauliflower, or monkfish with lotus blossom and mushrooms. So many unabashed odes to elegance and taste. Excellent set lunch menu. A real winner.

Specialities: Market-inspired cuisine.

Menu 45 € (lunch), 70/150 €

PLAN: 5-S2 - *18 rue Grégoire-de-Tours (6th) - Ⓜ Odéon - ✆ 09 84 19 76 05 - www.yoshinori-paris.com - Closed 3-31 August, 24 December-4 January, Monday, Sunday*

✿ Ze Kitchen Galerie (William Ledeuil) A/C

CREATIVE • CONTEMPORARY DÉCOR William Ledeuil has breathed his love of Southeast Asian flavours (Thailand, Vietnam and Japan) that inspire his creations into this establishment. Galanga, ka - chaï, curcuma, wasabi and ginger - herbs, roots, spices and condiments from all over the world at the service of French classics.

Specialities: Market-inspired cuisine.

Menu 48 € (lunch), 85/98 €

PLAN: 5-T2 - *4 rue des Grands-Augustins (6th) - Ⓜ St-Michel - ✆ 01 44 32 00 32 - www.zekitchengalerie.fr - Closed 27 July-21 August, Saturday, Sunday*

La Méditerranée A/C

SEAFOOD • MEDITERRANEAN The frescoes evoke the Mediterranean in this restaurant opposite the Théâtre de l'Odéon. The maritime inspired cuisine, in which particular attention is paid to the best ingredients, is influenced by the accents of the south. In summer dine beneath the azure blue awning.

Menu 37 € - Carte 55/80 €

PLAN: 5-S2 - *2 place de l'Odéon (6th) - Ⓜ Odéon - ✆ 01 43 26 02 30 - www.la-mediterranee.com*

AT A/C

CREATIVE • DESIGN A stone's throw from the banks of the Seine and the Tour d'Argent, the minimalist interior of this small restaurant embodies the quintessence of Japan. Chef Tanaka, formerly with Pierre Gagnaire, loves fresh ingredients and precise cooking and is forever surprising us with his creative recipes. Vaulted basement.

Menu 55 € (lunch)/115 €

PLAN: 5-U2 - *4 rue du Cardinal-Lemoine (5th) - Ⓜ Cardinal Lemoine - ✆ 01 56 81 94 08 - www.atsushitanaka.com - Closed 7-31 August, lunch Monday, Sunday*

Atelier Maître Albert

TRADITIONAL CUISINE • FRIENDLY An attractive medieval fireplace and roast ing spits take pride of place in this handsome interior designed by Jean - Miche Wilmotte. Guy Savoy is responsible for the mouthwatering menu.

Menu 36 € (lunch)/39 € – Carte 35/45 €

PLAN: 5-U2 – *1 rue Maître-Albert (5th) – Ⓜ Maubert Mutualité – ✆ 01 56 81 30 01 – www.ateliermaitrealbert.com – Closed 1 January, 9-25 August, lunch Saturday-Sunda*

Aux Prés

MODERN CUISINE • BISTRO An openly vintage bistro (red banquette seating smoked - glass mirrors, floral wallpaper) in St Germain and international cuisin by Cyril Lignac, whose creativity never strays entirely from its French countr roots.

Carte 50/90 €

PLAN: 5-S2 – *27 rue du Dragon (6th) – Ⓜ St-Germain des Prés – ✆ 01 45 48 29 68 – www.restaurantauxpres.com*

Le Bar des Prés

MODERN CUISINE • DESIGN Cyril Lignac has placed a Japanese chef with strong track record in the kitchens of Le Bar des Prés, next door to his restaurar Aux Prés. On the menu, extremely fresh sushi and sashimi, but also a few con temporary dishes: tartare of sea bream and petits pois with menthol; *galette cra quante* and crab with Madras curry. Cocktails courtesy of a mixologist.

Carte 50/75 €

PLAN: 5-S2 – *25 rue du Dragon (6th) – Ⓜ St-Germain des Prés – ✆ 01 43 25 87 67 – www.lebardespres.com*

Le Bon Saint-Pourçain

MODERN CUISINE • BISTRO Tucked away behind St Sulpice church in the hear of the high - brow Saint Germain des Prés district, this former 'bougnat' restaurar reopened in the spring of 2015. Bistro traditions with a modern twist depict the de licious food – doubtless due to the high quality fresh produce. Booking advisable

Carte 47/67 €

PLAN: 5-S2 – *10 bis rue Servandoni (6th) – Ⓜ Mabillon – ✆ 01 42 01 78 24 – Closed 4-24 August, 24-4 December, Monday, Sunday*

Boutary

MODERN CUISINE • CHIC In the middle of rue Mazarine, this old building host a Japanese - Korean chef with a fine track record. Armed with magnificent ingre dients, he proposes fine and tasty recipes that pop with colours and brim wit ideas. Taste has come home to roost here: a pleasant dining experience, not leas as the bill won't break the bank.

Menu 36 € (lunch)/89 € – Carte 36/78 €

PLAN: 5-S2 – *25 rue Mazarine (6th) – Ⓜ Odéon – ✆ 01 43 43 69 10 – Closed 10-23 August, Monday, lunch Saturday, Sunday*

Breizh Café - Odéon

BRETON • CONTEMPORARY DÉCOR The location, for a start, couldn't be bet ter: a freestone building right on the Carrefour de l'Odéon is home to the youn gest of Bertrand Larcher's crêperies. This Brittany - born chef spent time in Japa before settling down in France. Tuck into savoury *galettes* and sweet *crêpes* made with organic flour and artisanal ingredients and accompanied by quality ci ders and sakes.

Carte 26/52 €

PLAN: 5-S2 – *1 rue de l'Odéon (6th) – Ⓜ Odéon – ✆ 01 42 49 34 73*

Le Comptoir du Relais

TRADITIONAL CUISINE • BISTRO In this pleasant, tiny 1930s bistro, Yves Camdeborde works with two formats: on weekday evenings, he creates a single ambitious set menu, renewed every day (reservation mandatory); at lunchtime and on weekends, he cooks up good brasserie dishes (no reservation required). Heated terrace overlooking Odéon.

Menu 60 € – Carte 29/65 €

PLAN: 5-S2 – *Hôtel Relais St-Germain, 5 carrefour de l'Odéon (6th) – Ⓜ Odéon – ✆ 01 44 27 07 50 – www.hotel-paris-relais-saint-germain.com*

Dupin

MODERN CUISINE • FRIENDLY L'Épi Dupin has become the Dupin and François Pasteau has handed over the reins to Nathan Helo (from Rostang), but the establishment's founding ecological and locavore philosophy has not changed: locally sourced fruit and vegetables, recycling of organic waste and drinking water filtered on site, etc. A sustainable ethos in tune with nature and well-being.

Menu 42/56 €

PLAN: 5-R2 – *11 rue Dupin (6th) – Ⓜ Sèvres Babylone – ✆ 01 42 22 64 56 – www.epidupin.com – Closed 2-24 August, Monday, Saturday, Sunday*

Gaya par Pierre Gagnaire 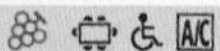

MODERN CUISINE • CHIC In place of the former Ferme Saint-Simon (an institution dating back to 1933), Gaya by Pierre Gagnaire is depicted by up-to-date cuisine with a preference for fish (tartare of red tuna, beef and smoked eels, skate wings à la meunière), but that is not all. The décor is emblematic of a smart brasserie.

Menu 49 € (lunch)/80 € – Carte 65/125 €

PLAN: 5-R1 – *6 rue de Saint-Simon (7th) – Ⓜ Rue du Bac – ✆ 01 45 44 73 73 – www.pierre-gagnaire.com – Closed 2-25 August, Monday, Sunday*

KGB

MODERN CUISINE • CONTEMPORARY DÉCOR KGB stands for Kitchen Gallery Bis, 'bis' referring to the fact that is the second KGB restaurant in Paris. A cross between an art gallery and a less than conventional restaurant, it has the same feel as its elder sibling. The original cuisine explores sweet and sour associations, flavoured with the spices of Asia.

Menu 36 € (lunch), 55/66 €

PLAN: 5-T2 – *25 rue des Grands-Augustins (6th) – Ⓜ St-Michel – ✆ 01 46 33 00 85 – www.zekitchengalerie.fr – Closed 4-12 January, 1-23 August, Monday, Sunday*

Lapérouse 

CLASSIC CUISINE • HISTORIC A mythical meeting place of Parisian high society in the late 19C, the Lapérouse has been treated to a masterful makeover without forgoing its soul. Rare wood, gilt work and fabrics – the cobalt blue façade and private rooms have lost none of their charm. Ten out of ten!

Menu 75 € (lunch)/200 € – Carte 90/180 €

PLAN: 5-T2 – *51 quai des Grands-Augustins (6th) – Ⓜ Saint-Michel – ✆ 01 43 26 68 04 – www.laperouse.com – Closed Monday, lunch Saturday, Sunday*

Piero TT

ITALIAN • TRATTORIA Welcome to Pierre Gagnaire's Italian trattoria. Building on the success of Les Airelles (Courchevel) with the same formula, the great chef proposes Italian cuisine, executed by young chef Ivan Ferrara (who has worked in his three-star restaurant in rue Balzac, as well as the three-star L'Enoteca Pinchiorri, in Florence). Front of house, Michele and Gianluca propose pasta and rigorously selected produce in a smart and relaxed setting. Be sure to reserve.

Carte 35/90 €

PLAN: 5-R1 – *44 rue du Bac (7th) – Ⓜ Rue du Bac – ✆ 01 43 20 00 40 – www.restaurantpiero.com – Closed Monday, Sunday*

Sagan

JAPANESE • MINIMALIST Near to Odéon, a tiny restaurant (15 covers) from the owner of Lengué in the 5th *arrondissement*. In an unadorned, hushed and intimate interior, diners sample inventive and often surprising Japanese food, such as Japanese - style ratatouille, tuna tataki, horsemeat sashimi and squab with Japanese pepper. Fine wine list.

Carte 35/60€

PLAN: 5-S2 – *8 rue Casimir-Delavigne (6th) – Ⓜ Odéon – ✆ 06 69 37 82 19 – Closed 4-28 August, 23 December-7 January, Monday, lunch Tuesday-Saturday, Sunday*

Semilla

MODERN CUISINE • TRENDY This bistro – a good "seed" (*semilla* in Spanish) – was founded in 2012 on the initiative of the owners of Fish La Boissonnerie, which is just opposite. Find a convivial atmosphere, trendy decor and, in the kitchens, a young and passionate team, who work exclusively with hand - picked suppliers. Delicious and well done!

Menu 40€ (lunch) – Carte 50/75€

PLAN: 5-S2 – *54 rue de Seine (6th) – Ⓜ Odéon – ✆ 01 43 54 34 50 – www.semillaparis.com – Closed 5-19 August, 23 December-3 January*

Shu

JAPANESE • MINIMALIST You have to stoop to get through the doorway that leads to this 17C cellar. In a minimalist decor, discover authentic and finely executed Japanese cuisine, in which the freshness of the ingredients works its magic in kushiage, sushi and sashimi.

Menu 42/52€

PLAN: 5-T2 – *8 rue Suger (6th) – Ⓜ St-Michel – ✆ 01 46 34 25 88 – www.restaurant-shu.com – Closed 5-13 April, 19 July-3 August, lunch Monday-Saturday, Sunday*

Taokan - St-Germain

CHINESE • TRENDY Come inside this pretty restaurant in the heart of St-Germain-des-Prés to enjoy light and fragrant Cantonese cuisine, with a few detours to the territory of Southeast Asia: the obligatory dim sum, steamed fish, spicy beef or lok lak. Lovely presentation and good ingredients: a real ambassador for Chinese food.

Menu 24€ (lunch)/70€ – Carte 42/65€

PLAN: 5-S2 – *8 rue du Sabot (6th) – Ⓜ St-Germain des Prés – ✆ 01 42 84 18 36 – www.taokan.fr – Closed 2-23 August, lunch Sunday*

Yen

JAPANESE • MINIMALIST The highly refined Japanese decor in this restaurant will appeal to fans of the minimalist look. The menu showcases the chef's speciality, soba – buckwheat noodles served hot or cold and prepared in front of you.

Menu 49€ (lunch), 60/120€ – Carte 40/90€

PLAN: 5-S2 – *22 rue St-Benoît (6th) – Ⓜ St-Germain-des-Prés – ✆ 01 45 44 11 18 – www.yen-paris.fr – Closed 2-17 August, Sunday*

Montparnasse – Denfert

Cobéa (Philippe Bélissent)

MODERN CUISINE • ELEGANT Co, as in Jérôme Cobou, in the restaurant, Bé, as in Philippe Bélissent, in the kitchens, and A for Associates. Cobéa is the venture of two passionate young professionals, who have created a place in their image that is, guided by the taste for good things! A feel for ingredients, harmony and strength of flavours and finesse. A delicious restaurant.

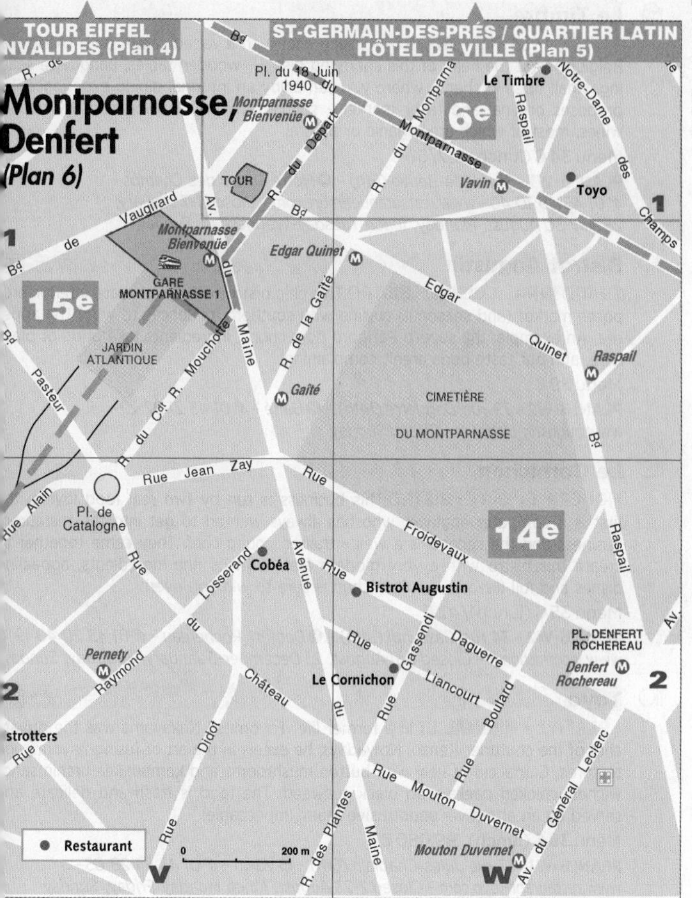

Specialities: Courgette "chez Bruno Cayron". Chicken, black truffle and parmesan gnocchi. Baked apricots, almond milk ice cream and homemade gingerbread.

Menu 55 € (lunch), 90/125 €

PLAN: 6-V2 – *11 rue Raymond-Losserand (14th)* – *Gaîté* – *01 43 20 21 39* – *www.cobea.fr* – *Closed 27 July-24 August, 21-28 December, Monday, Sunday*

Bistrotters

MODERN CUISINE • BISTRO A lovely place in the southern reaches of the 14th *arrondissement* near Métro Plaisance. The Spanish chef carefully selects his ingredients, with a preference for small-scale producers in the Paris region, and instils them with various influences (Asian, Mediterranean etc). Laid-back service.

Menu 23 € (lunch)/37 €

PLAN: 6-V2 – *9 rue Decrès (14th)* – *Plaisance* – *01 45 45 58 59* – *www.bistrotters.com* – *Closed 24-31 December*

Le Timbre

MODERN CUISINE • BISTRO A young chef with a varied career path (Australia, Belgium) is at the helm of this charming bistro - wooden tables, banquette seating, small open kitchen - where you can enjoy an informal dining experience. He proposes original and tasty market - sourced cuisine, accompanied by decent wines, most of which are organic or natural.

Menu 34€ (lunch), 37/59€

PLAN: 6-W1 - *3 rue Ste-Beuve (6th) - Ⓜ Notre-Dame des Champs - ✆ 01 45 49 10 40 - www.restaurantletimbre.com - Closed 1-7 January, 28 July-30 August, Monday, lunch Tuesday-Wednesday, Sunday*

Bistrot Augustin

TRADITIONAL CUISINE • BISTRO This chic bistro with an intimate interior proposes market (and seasonal) cuisine with southern influences to whet the appetite. An example: the superb Périgord pork chop... Ingredients take pride of place here, and our taste buds aren't complaining!

Menu 39€

PLAN: 6-W2 - *79 rue Daguerre (14th) - Ⓜ Gaîté - ✆ 01 43 21 92 29 - www.augustin-bistrot.fr - Closed Sunday*

Le Cornichon

MODERN CUISINE • BISTRO This business is run by two real food lovers: the first is a computer engineer who has always wanted to get into the restaurant business and the second is a well - trained young chef. They came together to create this bistro with a very modern feel. With its fine ingredients, appealing dishes and full flavours, Le Cornichon is sure to win you over!

Menu 35€ (lunch)/42€

PLAN: 6-W2 - *34 rue Gassendi (14th) - Ⓜ Denfert Rochereau - ✆ 01 43 20 40 19 - www.lecornichon.fr - Closed 1-31 August, 23 December-5 January, Saturday, Sunday*

Toyo

CREATIVE • MINIMALIST In a former life, Toyomitsu Nakayama was the private chef of the couturier Kenzo. Nowadays, he excels in the art of fusing flavours and textures. Carpaccio of veal with button mushrooms and kombu; sea urchin sandwiches; chicken paella with black seaweed...The food is fresh and delicate and served by an attentive, unobtrusive team. Impeccable!

Menu 39€ (lunch), 99/150€

PLAN: 6-W1 - *17 rue Jules-Chaplain (6th) - Ⓜ Vavin - ✆ 01 43 54 28 03 - www.restaurant-toyo.com - Closed 2-23 August, lunch Monday-Friday, Sunday*

Marais - Bastille - Gare de Lyon

L'Ambroisie (Bernard Pacaud)

CLASSIC CUISINE • LUXURY Ambrosia was the food of the gods on Mount Olympus. Without question, the cuisine of Bernard Pacaud reaches similar heights, with its explosion of flavours, its scientific approach and its perfect execution. Incomparable classicism and an immortal feast for the senses in the regal setting of a townhouse on Place des Vosges.

Specialities: Langoustine feuillantines with sesame seeds and a curry sauce. Escalopes of sea bass with artichoke hearts and golden caviar. Delicate bitter chocolate tart with Bourbon vanilla ice cream.

Carte 220/330€

PLAN: 7-X2 - *9 place des Vosges (4th) - Ⓜ St-Paul - ✆ 01 42 78 51 45 - www.ambroisie-paris.com - Closed 9-24 February, 26 April-4 May, 2-24 August, Monday, Sunday*

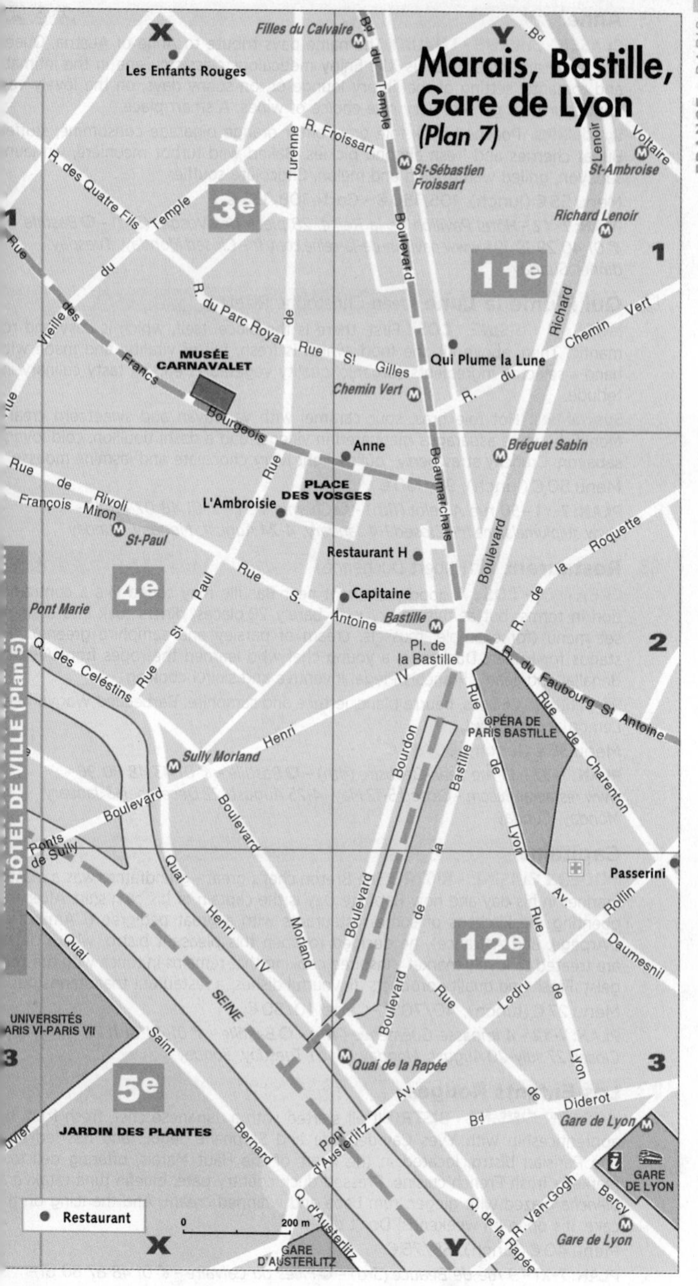
Marais, Bastille, Gare de Lyon
(Plan 7)
Les Enfants Rouges
Filles du Calvaire
St-Sébastien Froissart
St-Ambroise
Richard Lenoir
Musée Carnavalet
Qui Plume la Lune
Chemin Vert
Anne
Bréguet Sabin
Place des Vosges
L'Ambroisie
St-Paul
Restaurant H
Capitaine
Bastille
Pl. de la Bastille
Pont Marie
Opéra de Paris Bastille
Sully Morland
Passerini
Seine
Universités Paris VI-Paris VII
Quai de la Rapée
Jardin des Plantes
Gare de Lyon
Gare d'Austerlitz
3e
4e
5e
11e
12e
Restaurant
200 m
Hôtel de Ville (Plan 5)

✿ Anne

CLASSIC CUISINE • LUXURY The name pays tribute to Anne of Austria, Quee of France and wife of Louis XIII. Enjoy meticulous classic cuisine in the intimat and romantic setting of the library lounge or, on sunny days, on the lovely ver dant courtyard garden. Very nice choice of wines. A smart place.

Specialities: Poached duck foie gras, bitter orange bigarade consommé, stuffe Burlat cherries and fresh almond pickles. Baked wild turbot meunière, vin jaun sabayon, grilled watermelon and melon. Chocolate soufflé.

Menu 55€ (lunch), 105/150€ - Carte 108/138€

PLAN: 7-Y2 - *Hôtel Pavillon de la Reine, 28 place des Vosges (3rd) - Ⓜ Bastille - ✆ 01 40 29 19 19 - www.pavillon-de-la-reine.com/fr - Closed Monday, Tuesday, dinner Sunday*

✿ Qui Plume la Lune (Jean-Christophe Rizet)

MODERN CUISINE • COSY First, there is the place itself, which is cosy and ro mantic. Then, above all, the food, which is fresh, full of vitality, and made wit hand - selected ingredients (organic, quality vegetables etc). A tasty culinary in terlude.

Specialities: Hot foie gras, sour caramel with vadouvan and sweetcorn crear Monkfish, white asparagus marinated in vinegar and a dashi bouillon, cold lovag sabayon. Crunchy strawberry "bulle", light ivory chocolate and jasmine mousse.

Menu 50€ (lunch), 90/130€

PLAN: 7-Y1 - *50 rue Amelot (11th) - Ⓜ Chemin Vert - ✆ 01 48 07 45 48 - www.quiplumelalune.fr - Closed 1-4 January, 4-24 August, Monday, Sunday*

✿ Restaurant H (Hubert Duchenne)

CREATIVE • COSY A good restaurant near Bastille may sound like a contradic tion in terms, but at this eatery with barely 20 places, diners tuck into a singl set menu (for example: mussels, cream of parsley and samphire greens). "H stands for Hubert Duchenne, a young chef who learned the ropes from Akram Benallal and Jean - François Piège. Inventive and skilful cooking.

Specialities: Cockles, beurre blanc, lettuce and samphire. Barbecued Wagyu bee Lemon and hazelnut.

Menu 35€ (lunch), 60/80€

PLAN: 7-Y2 - *13 rue Jean-Beausire (4th) - Ⓜ Bastille - ✆ 01 43 48 80 96 - www.restauranth.com - Closed 5-12 May, 4-25 August, 22 December-3 January, Monday, Sunday*

Capitaine

MODERN CUISINE • BISTRO The Breton chef's great - grandfather was a maste mariner in his day and now Baptiste Day is the captain of his own ship. After fre quenting the kitchens of some restaurants with a great pedigree (L'Ambroisi L'Arpège, and Astrance), he decided to open this pleasant bistro, where diner are treated to lovely market - inspired cooking that remains in touch with the zeit geist. Fresh and quality products, flavourful dishes: a restaurant that stands out.

Menu 27€ (lunch), 40/70€ - Carte 40/50€

PLAN: 7-Y2 - *4 impasse Guéménée (4th) - Ⓜ Bastille - ✆ 01 44 61 11 76 - Closed 27 July-20 August, Monday, lunch Tuesday, Sunday*

Les Enfants Rouges

MODERN CUISINE • BISTRO It all started with a Japanese chef, fresh from hi apprenticeship with Yves Camdeborde and Stéphane Jégo... and has led to fine Parisian bistro, located in the heart of the Haut Marais, offering deliciou market - fresh French cuisine. Pressed duck country pâté, bluefin tuna tataki *a plancha* glazed with ginger, rum baba and whipped cream. And the icing on th cake: it's open on weekends! Don't delay.

Menu 40€ (lunch), 55/75€

PLAN: 7-X1 - *9 rue de Beauce (3rd) - Ⓜ Filles du Calvaire - ✆ 01 48 87 80 61 - www.les-enfants-rouges.fr - Closed 4-24 August, Tuesday, Wednesday, lunch Thursday*

Passerini

ITALIAN • CONTEMPORARY DÉCOR Giovanni Passerini has a keen eye, a ton of talent and the ambition to go with it. Here, we tuck into Italian food, for instance, tripe "cacio e ova", artichokes and white truffle, a rarity in Paris. The spotlight remains firmly on the ingredients. The house "specialty" remains the sharing dishes, such as the two - course lobster. Not to mention the Saturday evening set menu, centred on small plates. It's tasty and meticulous. A real pleasure.

Menu 27€ (lunch)/48€ - Carte 50/80€

PLAN: 7-Y3 - *65 rue Traversière (12th) - Ⓜ Ledru Rollin - ✆ 01 43 42 27 56 - www.passerini.paris - Closed 9-31 August, 23 December-2 January, Monday, lunch Tuesday, Sunday*

Montmartre – Pigalle

L'Arcane (Laurent Magnin)

MODERN CUISINE • ELEGANT Established on the premises of the former Chamarré Montmartre, Laurent Magnin continues to woo us with his immense talent. Culinary technique and flavours are combined to produce a surprise menu (5-7 courses in the evening) or an à la carte menu. The splendid wine list does not hesitate to push new boundaries.

Specialities: Market-inspired cuisine.

Menu 55€ (lunch), 120/150€ - Carte 80/110€

PLAN: 8-AA1 - *52 rue Lamarck (18th) - Ⓜ Lamarck Caulaincourt - ✆ 01 46 06 86 00 - www.restaurantlarcane.com - Closed 2-31 August, 20-28 December, Monday, lunch Tuesday, Sunday*

Ken Kawasaki

CREATIVE • MINIMALIST Ken Kawasaki's son is now at the head of the kitchen of this restaurant. He concocts French dishes, sprinkled with Japanese influences, served in the form of small, exquisitely graphic dishes. Everything is prepared in front of the diner in pure Japanese tradition. Excellent value-for-money, particularly at lunchtime.

Specialities: Market-inspired cuisine.

Menu 45€ (lunch)/90€

PLAN: 8-Z1 - *15 rue Caulaincourt (18th) - Ⓜ Blanche - ✆ 09 70 95 98 32 - www.restaurantkenkawasaki.fr - Closed Monday, Sunday*

La Table d'Eugène (Geoffroy Maillard)

MODERN CUISINE • ELEGANT Without any difficulty, Geoffroy Maillard - whose CV includes Frechon - will have raised his charming place to the ranks of the best. Good news for the 18th *arrondissement* and all foodies! He creates very fresh cuisine, full of colours and aromas. Let the "carte blanche" menu transport you, with marriages of dishes and wines. Strength and finesse.

Specialities: Market-inspired cuisine.

Menu 45€ (lunch), 99/130€

PLAN: 8-AA1 - *18 rue Eugène-Süe (18th) - Ⓜ Jules Joffrin - ✆ 01 42 55 61 64 - www.latabledeugene.com - Closed 21-29 April, 4-26 August, 24 December-8 January, Monday, Sunday*

Etsi

GREEK • FRIENDLY Mikaela, a young chef of Greek origin, has turned her focus to the cuisine of her childhood, after cutting her teeth in some prestigious establishments. Here, she proposes strikingly fresh mezze with bold touches. The feta, olives, capers, charcuterie, cheeses and olive oil have all come straight from Greece. Enjoy in the exceedingly warm and friendly setting.

Menu 35€ - Carte 30/35€

PLAN: 8-Z1 - *23 rue Eugène-Carrière (18th) - Ⓜ Place de Clichy - ✆ 01 71 50 00 80 - www.etsi-paris.fr - Closed 3-23 August, 24 December-1 January, Monday, lunch Tuesday-Friday, dinner Sunday*

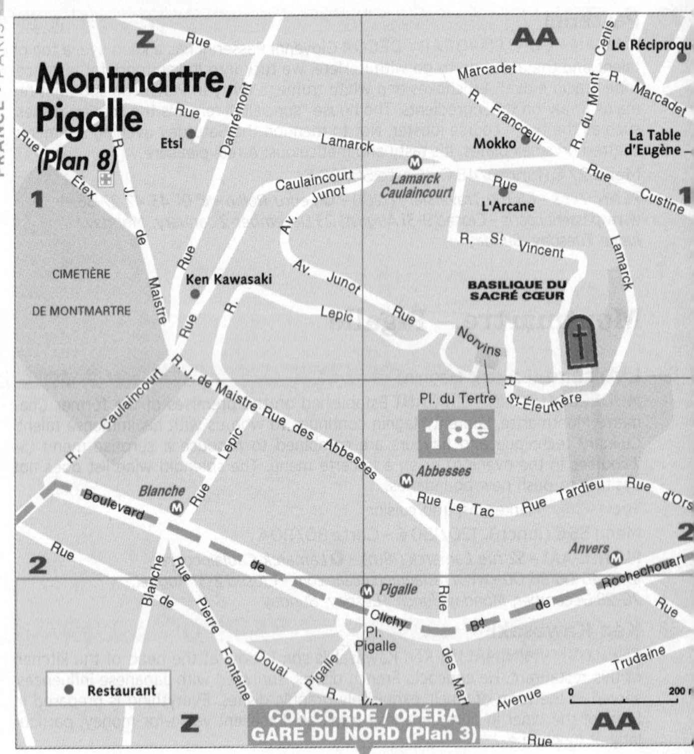

Mokko

MARKET CUISINE • CONTEMPORARY DÉCOR Arthur Hantz, who came to th business late in his career, has no complexes and his restaurant at the foot c Montmartre gets right down to brass tacks. He applies a devilishly effectiv method which involves no more than three or four ingredients per dish, addin interesting twists with textures and flavours. The result is colourful and vivaciou

Menu 24 € (lunch), 36/45 € – Carte 32/44 €

PLAN: 8-AA1 – *3 rue Francoeur (18th)* – *Métro Lamarck-Caulaincourt* – *09 80 96 93 60 – Closed Monday, lunch Tuesday-Wednesday, dinner Sunday*

Le Réciproque

TRADITIONAL CUISINE • CONTEMPORARY DÉCOR Tucked away in a sma side street behind the 18th town hall, this restaurant is the work of two youthf partners, each of whom boasts an impressive résumé. One is in the kitchen wher he excels at cooking traditional, flavoursome recipes, while the other is in charg of the friendly, courteous service. Reasonable prices to boot!

Menu 25 € (lunch), 38/45 €

PLAN: 8-AA1 – *14 rue Ferdinand-Flocon (18th)* – *Jules Joffrin* – *09 86 37 80 7 – www.lereciproque.com – Closed 26 July-17 August, 20 December-4 January, Monday, Sunday*

Outside Central Area

✿✿ Le Pré Catelan

CREATIVE • LUXURY Set within the Bois de Boulogne, the superb Napoleon - III pavilion installed here since 1905 is easily recognisable. In this dream location, Frédéric Anton works wonders: the precision and rigour passed on by his mentors (who include Robuchon) are his signature, along with his taste for original pairings. Topped off by a prestigious wine cellar and perfect service.

Specialities: Langoustine prepared in ravioli with foie gras and delicate goldleaf jelly. Cherry wood-smoked salmon, wasabi cream, biscuit, courgette flower. Crunchy souffléed apple, caramel ice cream, cider and sparkling sugar.

Menu 140 € (lunch), 230/290 € - Carte 260/320 €

PLAN: 1-A2 – *Route de Suresnes - Bois de Boulogne (16th) – ✆ 01 44 14 41 14 – www.precatelanparis.com – Closed 9-24 February, 2-24 August, 25 October-2 November, Monday, Sunday*

✿ Agapé

MODERN CUISINE • ELEGANT Soft hues, a sculpture by Nathalie Decoster, and paintings by contemporary artists: the Agapé dining area is wonderfully hushed and intimate. As for the food, the chef celebrates the seasons and the ingredients with undeniable talent. Subtle flavours, perfect seasoning, precision cooking – a sure-fire winner.

Specialities: Cushion of veal tartare with gambero rosso shrimps and caviar. Lobster, cavatelli and lemon basil. Ethiopian mocha and wild fennel.

Menu 52 € (lunch), 109/149 € - Carte 140/180 €

PLAN: 1-B1 – *51 rue Jouffroy-D'Abbans (17th) – Ⓜ Wagram – ✆ 01 42 27 20 18 – www.agape-paris.fr – Closed 3-24 August, Saturday, Sunday*

✿ L'Archeste (Yoshiaki Ito)

CREATIVE • MINIMALIST Yoshiaki Ito, former chef at Hiramatsu, astounds in this restaurant with a pared - down interior... in keeping with his work. The set menus (three or five courses at lunch, seven at dinner) are models of creativity and precision, espousing the seasons and always giving the best of excellent ingredients. Fine recipes from a repertoire of contemporary French cuisine, which have already garnered quite a following.

Specialities: Normandy oysters and veal tartare. Roast pigeon, cocoa sauce. Strawberry vacherin.

Menu 52 € (lunch), 110/180 €

PLAN: 1-A2 – *79 rue de la Tour (16th) – Ⓜ Rue de la Pompe – ✆ 01 40 71 69 68 – www.archeste.com – Closed 16-24 February, 2-31 August, Monday, lunch Saturday, Sunday*

✿ Le Chateaubriand

MODERN CUISINE • BISTRO The high profile chef at this in vogue restaurant offers a unique menu that changes with his inspiration and the seasons. Well worth a visit for the presentation alone!

Specialities: Market-inspired cuisine.

Menu 75/140 €

PLAN: 1-C2 – *129 avenue Parmentier (11th) – Ⓜ Goncourt – ✆ 01 43 57 45 95 – www.lechateaubriand.net – Closed Monday, Sunday and lunch*

✿ Comice (Noam Gedalof)

MODERN CUISINE • ELEGANT A Canadian couple had the excellent idea to open their first restaurant in Paris: the chef, Noam, draws inspiration from the foundations of French cuisine, which he gives a modern tweak. Etheliya manages the service and wine. From their complicity a vibrant array of flavours is born; for you to sample in an elegant, intimate interior. A success!

Specialities: Carpaccio of scallops, Buddha's hand, citron confit, radish and fen nel. Corsican veal, artichokes, haricot beans and veal jus. Chocolate soufflé an vanilla ice cream.

Menu 140 € – Carte 92/144 €

PLAN: 1-A2 – *31 avenue de Versailles (16th) – Ⓜ Mirabeau – ✆ 01 42 15 55 70 – www.comice.paris – Closed 5-20 April, 26 July-17 August, 20 December-4 January, Monday, Sunday and lunch*

✿ Le Faham by Kelly Rangama

MODERN CUISINE • CHIC Kelly Rangama (a *Top Chef* contestant in 2017) chos a flower native to Réunion that is locally known as *faham* to symbolise her unio with pastry chef Jérôme Devreese and their creation: this sleek and elegant res taurant. Here the chef proposes a cuisine that abounds with vibrancy and finesse with a touch of exoticism that makes all the difference. A real delight.

Specialities: Wild shrimp, celeriac textures with massala, iced bisque. Pavé o toothfish, sweet and sour carrot-ginger, tomato paste, crunchy rice. Sweet potat gâteau, sweet potato tatin and sorbet, cinnamon berry emulsion.

Menu 32 € (lunch)/69 € – Carte 59/70 €

PLAN: 1-B1 – *108 rue Cardinet (17th) – Ⓜ Malesherbes – ✆ 01 53 81 48 18 – www.lefaham.com – Closed 3-24 August, Monday, Sunday*

✿ La Grande Cascade

MODERN CUISINE • CLASSIC DÉCOR A charming pavilion (1850) just a stone' throw from the large waterfall (Grande Cascade) in the Bois de Boulogne. To sa vour the refined cuisine here beneath the majestic rotunda or on the delightfu terrace is a rare and elegant treat.

Specialities: Macaroni, black truffle, celeriac, parmesan gratin. Crunchy sweet breads with "tortue" herbs, carrots and ginger-orange. Waffle millefeuille with light Tahitian vanilla cream.

Menu 89/192 € – Carte 172/216 €

Off plan – *Bois de Boulogne (16th) – ✆ 01 45 27 33 51 – www.restaurantsparisiens.com – Closed 21 December-12 January*

✿ Mavrommatis

GREEK • ELEGANT A heroic wind worthy of Odysseus is blowing over Cypric chef Andrés Mavrommatis' establishment. You will be treated to generous, wel crafted text-book Gallic food, combined with first-class Mediterranean ingred ents. Revamped by architect Régis Botta, the modern, stripped-down interior i the perfect foil to a succulent gourmet adventure.

Specialities: Aubergine confit with thyme, raw and cooked vegetables, prawr and Colonnata lard. Stuffed squid, grilled prawns, fennel confit and turmeri rouille. Chocolate ganache with olives, chocolate-basil cream and orange blosso ice cream.

Menu 45 € (lunch), 85/115 € – Carte 78/110 €

PLAN: 1-C3 – *42 rue Daubenton (5th) – Ⓜ Censier Daubenton – ✆ 01 43 31 17 17 – www.mavrommatis.com – Closed 9-31 August, Monday, lunch Tuesday-Thursday, Sunday*

✿ Pilgrim

MODERN CUISINE • CONTEMPORARY DÉCOR Hideki Nishi (owner of Neig d'Été in Paris) put Terumitsu Saito behind the stove at this restaurant near Mor tparnasse. In a central and slightly raised kitchen, the chef fashions his refine and delicate dishes, like so many masterpieces drawing on France and Japan. is a pure delight and could well be a future place of pilgrimage.

Specialities: Crab meat with sashi jelly. Iberian pork with a carrot medley. Ric pudding with saké.

Menu 45 € (lunch), 100/150 €

PLAN: 1-B2-3 – *8 rue Nicolas-Charlet (15th) – Ⓜ Pasteur – ✆ 01 40 29 09 71 – www.pilgrimparis.com – Closed 1-15 August, Saturday, Sunday*

✿ Le Rigmarole (Jessica Yang et Robert Compagnon) A/C

MODERN CUISINE • CONTEMPORARY DÉCOR Brainchild of Jessica Yang and Robert Compagnon, the concept is inspired by Japanese yakitori and robatayaki restaurants, as well as Italian and French (to name but a few) gourmet traditions. Flawlessly fresh ingredients, competently grilled over charcoal and served with splendid side dishes.

Specialities: Market-inspired cuisine.

Menu 35/69€

PLAN: 1-C2 – *10 rue du Grand-Prieuré (11th) – Ⓜ Oberkampf – ✆ 01 71 24 58 44 – www.lerigmarole.com – Closed Monday, Tuesday and lunch*

✿ Septime (Bertrand Grébaut)

MODERN CUISINE • CONTEMPORARY DÉCOR A hotchpotch of good ideas, freshness and ease, passion and even a little mischief, but unfailingly precise and spot on: led by the young Bertrand Grébaut, Septime is the joy of Parisian palates! Such is its popularity that you will have to book three weeks in advance for a chance to enjoy it for yourself.

Specialities: Market-inspired cuisine.

Menu 60€ (lunch)/95€

PLAN: 1-D2 – *80 rue de Charonne (11th) – Ⓜ Charonne – ✆ 01 43 67 38 29 – www.septime-charonne.fr – Closed 3-26 August, lunch Monday, Saturday, Sunday*

✿ Solstice (Eric Trochon) A/C

CREATIVE • CONTEMPORARY DÉCOR *Meilleur Ouvrier de France*, pillar of the Ferrandi school, promoter of culinary design, restaurateur in Séoul, Éric Trochon has already achieved so much. He is now very much at home in this intimate, modern restaurant, working alongside a Korean sommelier, who also happens to be his wife. His creative, forthright cuisine plays on textures and contrasts, e. g. the *nage* (aromatic broth) of coco de Paimpol beans, pickled fennel and melon, and meadowsweet granita.

Specialities: Nage of Coco de Paimpol beans, pickled fennel and melon, meadowsweet granita. Catch of the day cooked on a Binchotan grill, celeriac, hazelnut praline and chicken jus. Green apple papillotes, yuzu ice cream and yoghurt.

Menu 35€ (lunch), 65/90€ – Carte 67/83€

PLAN: 1-C3 – *45 rue Claude-Bernard (5th) – Ⓜ Censier Daubenton – ✆ 06 52 31 83 84 – www.solsticeparis.com – Closed Monday, lunch Tuesday, Sunday*

✿ Table - Bruno Verjus

MODERN CUISINE • DESIGN Bruno Verjus talks about his supplier partners with a twinkle in his eye, which speaks volumes about his philosophy of putting produce centre stage. He crafts his ingredients (on this day scallops and sweetbreads) like so many rough diamonds, with the energy of a true devotee. Good wine list.

Specialities: Fresh pot-caught Île-d'Yeu lobster. Wild John Dory "terre-mer" mirror. Porcelana grand cru chocolate tart.

Menu 70€ (lunch), 120/300€ – Carte 70/300€

PLAN: 1-C2 – *3 rue de Prague (12th) – Ⓜ Ledru Rollin – ✆ 01 43 43 12 26 – www.table.paris – Closed 2-26 August, 22 December-5 January, lunch Monday, lunch Saturday, Sunday*

Biscotte

MODERN CUISINE • TRENDY Pauline and Maximilien, two alumni of the most prestigious establishments (Le Bristol, Lasserre, Arpège), have set up their own place near Porte de Versailles. Convivial bistro interior, large atelier windows separating the kitchen, tasty and studied dishes: all the ingredients are in place for an enjoyable experience.

Menu 38/49€

PLAN: 1-A3 – *22 rue Desnouettes (15th) – Ⓜ Convention – ✆ 01 45 33 22 22 – www.restaurant-biscotte.com – Closed 24 July-18 August, 23 December-5 January, Monday, dinner Saturday-Sunday*

Clamato

SEAFOOD • TRENDY The Septime's little sister is becoming something of a bis tronomic hit, thanks to its fashionable interior and concise menu focused o seafood and vegetables. Each ingredient is selected carefully and meals ar served in a genuinely friendly atmosphere. No bookings are taken – it's firs come, first served!

Carte 35/70 €

PLAN: 1-D2 – *80 rue de Charonne (11th) – Charonne – 01 43 72 74 53 – www.clamato-charonne.fr – Closed 5-25 August*

L'Envie du Jour

MODERN CUISINE • FRIENDLY Charlotte Gondor's dishes reveal precision, co our and flavour: cf. the hangar steak tataki or cod and salad of split peas, the pre sentation of which is so sharp it whets the appetite. A small selection of well chosen wines accompanies your choice. A real treat.

Menu 32 € (lunch), 35/46 €

PLAN: 1-B1 – *106 rue Nollet (17th) – Brochant – 01 42 26 01 02 – www.lenviedujour.com – Closed 10 August-1 September, Monday, dinner Sunday*

Impérial Choisy

CHINESE • SIMPLE A genuine Chinese restaurant frequented by many local Chi nese people who use it as their lunchtime canteen. Hardly surprising given th delicious Cantonese specials on offer!

Carte 20/50 €

PLAN: 1-C3 – *32 avenue de Choisy (13th) – Porte de Choisy – 01 45 86 42 40*

Jouvence

MODERN CUISINE • VINTAGE Situated on the corner of rue de Cîteaux, this for mer apothecary - style shop from the 1900s does not merely rest on its decora tive laurels. They serve contemporary cuisine, replete with quality ingredient such as prawn tempura, cucumber kimchi and celery juice. The young chef, for merly with Dutournier (Pinxo restaurant), certainly has talent.

Menu 24 € (lunch) – Carte 37/49 €

PLAN: 1-D2 – *172 bis rue du Faubourg-St-Antoine (12th) – Faidherbe-Chaligny – 01 56 58 04 73 – www.jouvence.paris – Closed 1-30 August, Monday, Sunday*

Pho Tai

VIETNAMESE • SIMPLE In a quiet street in the Asian quarter, this small Vietnam ese restaurant stands out from the crowd. All credit to the chef, Mr Te, who ar rived in France in 1968 and is a magnificent ambassador for Vietnamese cuisin Dumplings, crispy chicken with fresh ginger, bo bun and phô soups: everything i full of flavour.

Carte 25/35 €

PLAN: 1-C3 – *13 rue Philibert-Lucot (13th) – Maison Blanche – 01 45 85 97 36*

Les Résistants

MODERN CUISINE • FRIENDLY These résistants believe that taste and trace ability should be the backbone of all food. Indeed, the credo of owner, Flore Piard, is none other than "good food that respects natural cycles! " and he amp proves his case in this cheerful establishment. The concise menu changes daily i keeping with market availability and the prices are never outlandish. Natur wines bien sûr!

Menu 19 € (lunch) – Carte 33/40 €

PLAN: 1-C2 – *16 rue du Château-d'Eau (10th) – République – 01 77 32 77 61 – www.lesresistants.fr – Closed 9-24 August, Monday, Sunday*

Tempero

CREATIVE • BISTRO A friendly little bistro, which is rather like its chef, Alessandra Montagne. Originally from Brazil, she worked at some fine Parisian establishments before opening her own place. Here she cooks with market - fresh ingredients, creating invigorating and reasonably priced dishes that draw on French, Brazilian and Asian cooking. A lovely fusion!

Menu 26 € (lunch), 28/45 €

PLAN: 1-C3 – *5 rue Clisson (13th) – Ⓜ Chevaleret – ✆ 09 54 17 48 88 – www.tempero.fr – Closed 1-23 August, 25-31 December, dinner Monday-Wednesday, lunch Saturday-Sunday*

Le Villaret

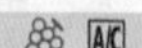

TRADITIONAL CUISINE • FRIENDLY The delicious aromas that greet you as soon as you walk in the door let you know you're in for a culinary treat! Chef - owner Olivier Gaslain is an enthusiastic cook, proposing traditional and generous cuisine made using seasonal ingredients (truffles and game, shown to best effect). Superb wine list (more than 800 bins).

Menu 28 € (lunch), 35/60 € – Carte 50/70 €

PLAN: 1-C2 – *13 rue Ternaux (11th) – Ⓜ Parmentier – ✆ 01 43 57 75 56 – Closed 3-16 August, lunch Saturday, Sunday*

Au Trou Gascon

CUISINE FROM SOUTH WEST FRANCE • ELEGANT This institution, dedicated to the cuisine of Southwest France, transports diners to the area between the River Adour and the ocean. It has earned the loyalty of many long - standing regulars with its pâté en croûte with duck foie gras, lièvre à la royale (hare), and warm and crusty tourtière - not to mention the ever - popular cassoulet.

Menu 48 € (lunch)/88 € – Carte 66/87 €

PLAN: 1-D3 – *40 rue Taine (12th) – Ⓜ Daumesnil – ✆ 01 43 44 34 26 – www.autrougascon.fr – Closed Saturday, Sunday*

Beurre Noisette

TRADITIONAL CUISINE • BISTRO A flavoursome bistro, with a following of regulars. Thierry Blanqui draws his inspiration from the market: cèpe tart; Challan duckling roasted on the bone, spinach and quince; Mont-blanc dessert and tasty, wholesome *canaille* dishes. Straddling the traditional and the new: most enjoyable. Always a good bet.

Menu 34 € (lunch), 42/60 € – Carte 38/51 €

PLAN: 1-A3 – *68 rue Vasco-de-Gama (15th) – Ⓜ Lourmel – ✆ 01 48 56 82 49 – www.restaurantbeurrenoisette.com – Closed 9-24 August, Monday, Sunday*

Bistrot Paul Bert

TRADITIONAL CUISINE • BISTRO The façade of this pleasant bistro promises "cuisine familiale". Translate this as: feuilleté of calf sweetbreads with mushrooms, and roast venison with cranberries and celeriac purée. Generous, tasty dishes are prepared without frills. You will be asking for more but be sure to save some room for the rum baba!

Menu 22 € (lunch)/41 € – Carte 50/60 €

PLAN: 1-D2 – *18 rue Paul-Bert (11th) – Ⓜ Faidherbe Chaligny – ✆ 01 43 72 24 01 – Closed Monday, Sunday*

Bon Kushikatsu

JAPANESE • INTIMATE This restaurant is an express trip to Osaka to discover the city's culinary speciality of *kushikatsu* (meat, vegetables or seafood skewers coated with breadcrumbs and deep - fried). Dish after dish reveals fine flavours, such as: beef sancho, peppered foie gras, and shiitake mushrooms. The courteous service transports you to Japan.

Menu 58 €

PLAN: 1-C2 – *24 rue Jean-Pierre-Timbaud (11th) – Ⓜ Oberkampf – ✆ 01 43 38 82 27 – www.kushikatsubon.fr – Closed 15-31 August, Sunday, Wednesday and lunch*

Nous 4

TRADITIONAL CUISINE • BISTRO Pork in a melt - in - the - mouth crust w lentils and mustard sauce; poached egg with cabbage and bacon cream... you' probably got the picture. Here you can tuck into a no - nonsense, delicious me that offers great value for money, considering how much you'll enjoy it. The op kitchen means you can also talk to the chef. A really lovely place, the like which we'd be happy to see more of in Paris.

Menu 26 € (lunch), 32/42 €

PLAN: 1-D2 – *3 rue Beccaria (12th) – Ⓜ Gare de Lyon – ✆ 06 06 70 64 92 – www.nous4restaurant.com – Closed Monday, Sunday*

Osteria Ferrara

ITALIAN • OSTERIA Gourmets come here, safe in the knowledge they ha found sanctuary in this elegant interior. The Sicilian chef whips up mouth - wate ing Italian recipes based on excellent ingredients. Loin of veal à la Milanese wi stir - fried spinach leaf. This Osteria has soul and a fine wine list to boot!

Carte 36/50 €

PLAN: 1-D2 – *7 rue du Dahomey (11th) – Ⓜ Faidherbe Chaligny – ✆ 01 43 71 67 69 www.osteriaferrara.com – Closed 8-30 August, 21 December-6 January, Saturday, Sunday*

Pramil

MODERN CUISINE • BISTRO The elegant yet restrained decor helps focus t senses on the attractive and honest seasonal cuisine conjured up by Alain Pram He is a self - taught chef passionate about food who, in another life, was a phy ics teacher!

Menu 33/43 € – Carte 38/48 €

PLAN: 1-C2 – *9 rue Vertbois (3rd) – Ⓜ Temple – ✆ 01 42 72 03 60 – www.pramil.fr Closed 17-31 August, 21-28 December, Monday, lunch Sunday*

Vantre

MODERN CUISINE • BISTRO In the Middle Ages, a vantre was a "place of enjo ment" and indeed that's what it is today, for stomach and soul. Two partners chef – formerly sous - chef at Saturne – and a wine waiter (Le Bristol, Le Tail vent), offer food featuring select ingredients. More than 2 000 wines, a frienc welcome... and well - deserved success.

Menu 21 € (lunch) – Carte 42/80 €

PLAN: 1-C2 – *19 rue de la Fontaine-au-Roi (11th) – Ⓜ Goncourt – ✆ 01 48 06 16 96 www.vantre.fr – Closed 1-25 August, Saturday, Sunday*

LYONS
LYON

matteo69/iStock

LYONS IN...

→ **ONE DAY**
Old town including funicular up Fourvière hill, Musée des Beaux-Arts.

→ **TWO DAYS**
Musée des Tissus, La Croix-Rousse, evening river trip, Opera House.

→ **THREE DAYS**
Traboule hunting (map in hand), antique shops in rue Auguste Comte.

Lyons is a city that needs a second look, because the first one may be to its disadvantage: from the outlying autoroute, drivers get a vision of the petrochemical industry. But strip away that industrial façade and look what lies within: the gastronomic epicentre of France; a wonderfully characterful old town of medieval and Renaissance buildings with a World Heritage Site stamp of approval; and the peaceful flow of two mighty rivers. Lyons largely came of age in the 16C thanks to its silk industry; many of the city's finest buildings were erected by Italian merchants who flocked

here at the time. What they left behind was the largest Renaissance quarter in France, with glorious architecture and an imposing cathedral.

Nowadays it's an energised city whose modern industries give it a 21C feel but that hasn't pervaded the three-hour lunch ethos of the older quarters. The rivers Saône and Rhône provide the liquid heart of the city. Modern Lyons in the shape of the new Villeurbanne and La Part Dieu districts are to the east of the Rhône. The medieval sector, the old town, is west of the Saône. Between the two rivers is a peninsula, the Presqu'ile, which is indeed almost an island. This area is renowned for its red-roofed 16C and 17C houses. Just north of here on a hill is the old silk-weavers' district, La Croix-Rousse.

EATING OUT

yons is a great place for food. In the ld town virtually every square metre occupied by a restaurant but if you ant a real encounter with the city, tep inside a Lyonnais bouchon. These rovide the true gastronomic heart-eat of the city - authentic little esta-lishments where the cuisine revolves round the sort of thing the silk wor-ers ate all those years ago: tripe, pigs' rotters, calf's head; fish lovers go for uenelles. For the most atmospheric xample of the bouchon, try one in a unnel-like recess inside a medieval building in the old town. Lyons also has plenty of restaurants serving dishes from every region in France and is a city that loves its wine: it's said that Lyons is kept afloat on three rivers: the Saône, the Rhône and the Beaujolais. Furthermore, the locals still enthusiastically embrace the true concept of lunch and so, unlike in many cities, you can enjoy a midday meal that continues for quite a few hours. With the reputation the city has for its restaurants, it's usually advisable to book ahead.

Old Town

Au 14 Février (Tsuyoshi Arai)

CREATIVE • ELEGANT In rue du Bœuf, in the heart of Vieux Lyon, Japane chef Tsuyoshi Arai sublimates outstanding produce (e.g. Maison Masse squa Wagyu beef) by playing on textures and bitterness. Talent, precision, imaginatic and extremely gracious service.

Specialities: Beetroot tatin with foie gras, hazelnut and lovage ice cream. Grill entrecôte of Wagyu beef, ponzu and fresh wasabi. Vacherin-style rose in a clocl with raspberry parfait.

Menu 92€

PLAN: 2-E2 - *36 rue du Bœuf (5th) - Ⓜ Vieux Lyon - ✆ 04 78 92 91 39 - www.ly-au14fevrier.com - Closed 3-17 August, 21 December-4 January, Monday, lunch Tuesday-Friday, Sunday*

Auberge de l'Île Barbe (Jean-Christophe Ansanay-Alex)

CLASSIC CUISINE • ELEGANT A country feel in the heart of the leafy île Barb an island in the Saône. The walls date from 1601 and there is a softly intimate a mosphere. The very refined cuisine has remarkable flavour associations and cre tive flights of fancy.

Specialities: Cabbage stuffed with langoustine and a Condrieu wine beurre blar Red mullet "de l'île", modern bouillabaisse. Chestnut tart.

Menu 50€ (lunch), 98/158€

PLAN: 1-B1 - *place Notre-Dame (9th) - ✆ 04 78 83 99 49 - www.aubergedelile.cor*

Jérémy Galvan

CREATIVE • COSY Cuisine based on instinct is what is promised here, with m nus labelled "Interlude", "Let go" and "Perfume" setting the tone for the dish These are original, creative and playful; deviating from well - trodden paths b always respecting the seasons and nature.

Specialities: Market-inspired cuisine.

Menu 35€ (lunch), 69/109€

PLAN: 2-E2 - *29 rue du Bœuf (5th) - Ⓜ Vieux-Lyon - ✆ 04 72 40 91 47 - www.jeremygalvanrestaurant.com - Closed 26 April-4 May, 17-27 July, 23-26 December, Monday, lunch Wednesday, lunch Saturday, Sunday*

Les Loges

MODERN CUISINE • ROMANTIC Time seems to have stood still in this encha ting and romantic setting. Find a Florentine courtyard ringed by three floors galleries and crowned by a contemporary glass ceiling. Savour the refined and ventive cuisine with flickering candlelight adding a final touch.

Specialities: Escalope of confit duck foie gras with duck bouillon. Pigeon with mushroom and spiced fruit crust. Grand cru cocoa, chuao glacé and ligh smoked ceylan.

Menu 105/145€ - Carte 95/115€

PLAN: 2-E2 - *Cour des Loges, 6 rue du Boeuf (5th) - Ⓜ Vieux Lyon - ✆ 04 72 77 44 44 - www.courdesloges.com - Closed Monday, lunch Tuesday-Sunc*

La Sommelière

MODERN CUISINE • INTIMATE A sommelier owner, a relentlessly rigorous panese chef, a single set menu served in a tiny restaurant. As for the food: ve elegant French cuisine, such as lobster and shellfish cream, or fillet of wild s bass cooked in its skin. Attentive service and excellent value for money. Reme ber to book, as competition for a table is stiff.

Specialities: Shrimp bisque with farmer's eggs. Roasted rib of Charolais be Opéra.

Menu 72€

PLAN: 2-E2 - *6 rue Mourguet (5th) - Ⓜ Vieux Lyon - ✆ 04 78 79 86 45 - www.la-sommeliere.net - Closed Monday, lunch Tuesday-Friday, Sunday*

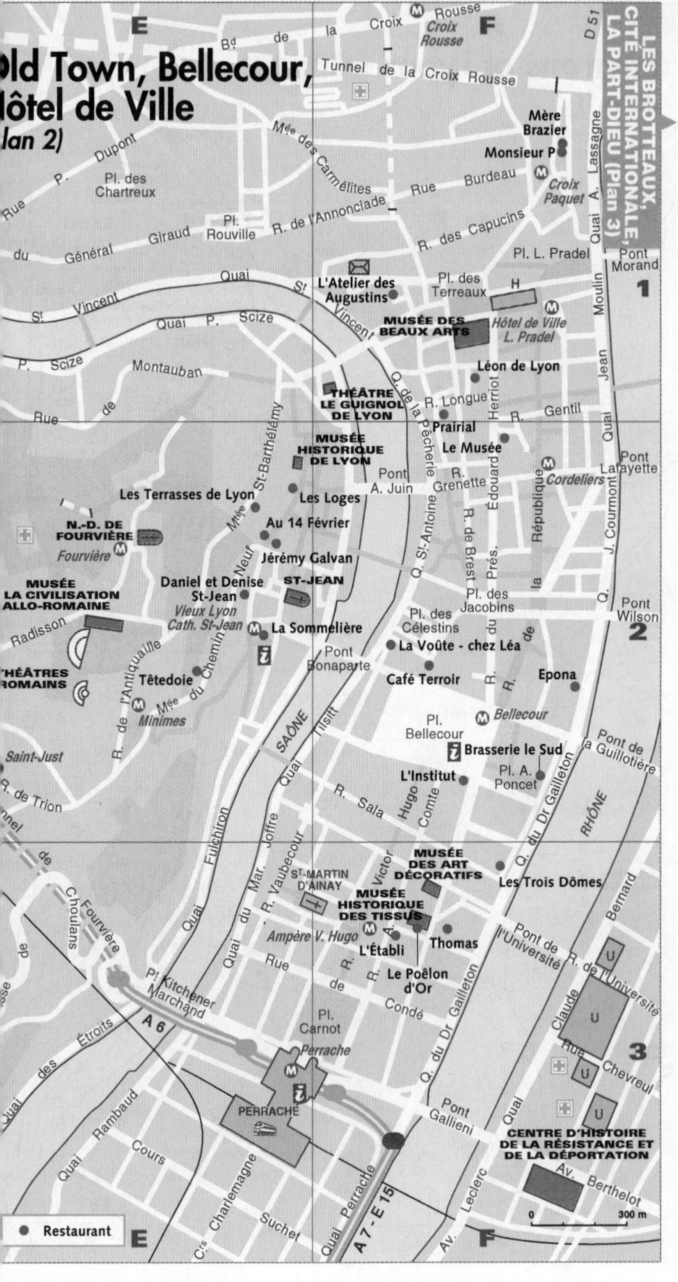
Old Town, Bellecour, Hôtel de Ville
(Plan 2)
LES BROTTEAUX, CITÉ INTERNATIONALE, LA PART-DIEU (Plan 3)
Mère Brazier
Monsieur P
L'Atelier des Augustins
MUSÉE DES BEAUX ARTS
Hôtel de Ville L. Pradel
Léon de Lyon
THÉÂTRE LE GUIGNOL DE LYON
Prairial
Le Musée
MUSÉE HISTORIQUE DE LYON
Les Terrasses de Lyon
Les Loges
N.-D. DE FOURVIÈRE
Fourvière
Au 14 Février
Jérémy Galvan
MUSÉE LA CIVILISATION ALLO-ROMAINE
Daniel et Denise St-Jean
ST-JEAN
Vieux Lyon Cath. St-Jean
La Sommelière
La Voûte - chez Léa
THÉÂTRES ROMAINS
Têtedoie
Café Terroir
Epona
Minimes
Bellecour
Saint-Just
Pl. Bellecour
Brasserie le Sud
L'Institut
Pl. A. Poncet
MUSÉE DES ART DÉCORATIFS
Les Trois Dômes
ST-MARTIN D'AINAY
MUSÉE HISTORIQUE DES TISSUS
Ampère V. Hugo
L'Établi
Thomas
Le Poêlon d'Or
Perrache
PERRACHE
CENTRE D'HISTOIRE DE LA RÉSISTANCE ET DE LA DÉPORTATION
SAÔNE
RHÔNE
Croix Rousse
Croix Paquet
Cordeliers
Pont Morand
Pont Lafayette
Pont Wilson
Pont Bonaparte
Pont de la Guillotière
Pont de l'Université
Pont Gallieni
0 300 m
Restaurant

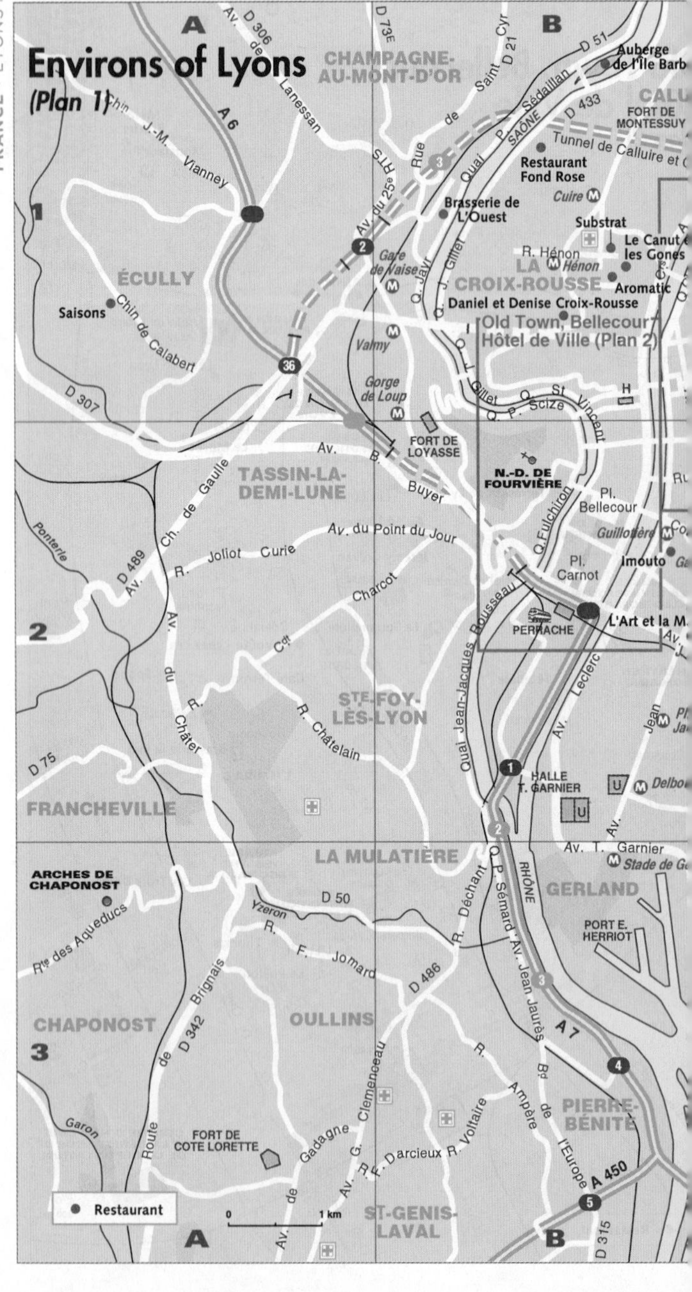
Environs of Lyons
(Plan 1)
CHAMPAGNE-AU-MONT-D'OR
ÉCULLY
Saisons
TASSIN-LA-DEMI-LUNE
ST-FOY-LÈS-LYON
FRANCHEVILLE
LA MULATIÈRE
ARCHES DE CHAPONOST
CHAPONOST
OULLINS
FORT DE COTE LORETTE
ST-GENIS-LAVAL
PIERRE-BÉNITE
GERLAND
PORT E. HERRIOT
HALLE T. GARNIER
PERRACHE
L'Art et la M
Imouto
N.-D. DE FOURVIÈRE
FORT DE LOYASSE
Pl. Bellecour
Pl. Carnot
LA CROIX-ROUSSE
Daniel et Denise Croix-Rousse
Old Town, Bellecour, Hôtel de Ville (Plan 2)
Brasserie de L'Ouest
Restaurant Fond Rose
Substrat
Le Canut et les Gones
Aromatic
Auberge de l'Île Barb
FORT DE MONTESSUY
Tunnel de Caluire et C
Gare de Vaise
Valmy
Gorge de Loup
Cuire
Hénon
Guillotière
Delbo
Stade de G
Restaurant
0
1 km
A
B
1
2
3

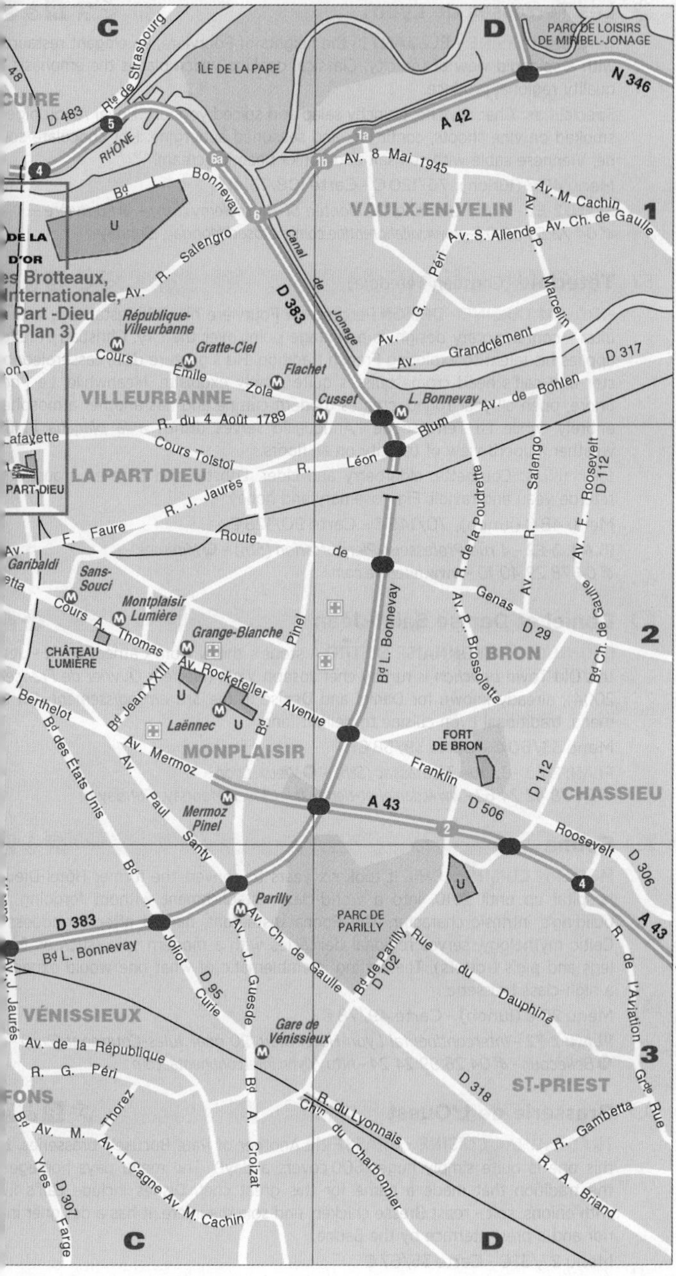

C D
PARC DE LOISIRS DE MIRIBEL-JONAGE
ÎLE DE LA PAPE
N 346
A 42
CUIRE
D 483
Rte de Strasbourg
RHÔNE
Av. 8 Mai 1945
Bd L. Bonnevay
VAULX-EN-VELIN
Av. M. Cachin
Av. Ch. de Gaulle
Av. S. Allende
Av. P. Marcelin
Av. G. Péri
Canal de Jonage
D 383
Av. R. Salengro
DE LA D'OR
les Brotteaux, Internationale, Part-Dieu (Plan 3)
République-Villeurbanne
Gratte-Ciel
Cours Émile Zola
Flachet
Cusset
L. Bonnevay
Av. Grandclément
D 317
Av. de Bohlen
VILLEURBANNE
R. du 4 Août 1789
R. Léon Blum
Cours Tolstoï
LA PART DIEU
Lafayette
PART-DIEU
R. J. Jaurès
Av. F. Faure
Route de Genas
R. de la Poudrette
Av. R. Salengo
Av. F. Roosevelt D 112
Garibaldi
Sans-Souci
Montplaisir Lumière
Cours A. Thomas
CHÂTEAU LUMIÈRE
Grange-Blanche
Pinel
Bd L. Bonnevay
D 29
BRON
Av. P. Brossolette
Bd Ch. de Gaulle
Av. Rockefeller
Bd Jean XXIII
Laënnec
Berthelot
Bd des États Unis
Av. Mermoz
MONPLAISIR
Avenue Franklin Roosevelt
FORT DE BRON
D 112
CHASSIEU
A 43
D 506
Av. Paul Santy
Mermoz Pinel
D 306
Parilly
PARC DE PARILLY
D 383
Bd L. Bonnevay
Bd J. Joliot Curie D 95
Av. J. Guesde
Av. Ch. de Gaulle
Bd de Parilly D 102
Rue du Dauphiné
R. de l'Aviation
LYON-ST EXUPÉRY
Av. J. Jaurès
VÉNISSIEUX
Gare de Vénissieux
Av. de la République
R. G. Péri
FONS
Thorez
Bd Av. M.
Bd A. Croizat
R. du Lyonnais
Chin du Charbonnier
D 318
ST-PRIEST
R. Gambetta
Grde Rue
R. A. Briand
Av. J. Cagne
Av. M. Cachin
Bd Yves Farge D 307
1 2 3

✿ Les Terrasses de Lyon

CLASSIC CUISINE • ELEGANT In the heights of Fourvière; an elegant restaura with a splendid view of the city. Classical cooking which places the emphasis quality regional produce.

Specialities: Char ceviche, crunchy salad and spiced yoghurt. Royal Anjou pige smoked on vine shoots, confit leg, and seasoned aubergine. Hot chocolate so flé, Viennese sablé with sea salt and Tonka bean ice cream.

Menu 49€ (lunch), 76/120€ - Carte 108/131€

PLAN: 2-E2 - *Villa Florentine, 25 Montée St-Barthélémy (5th) - Ⓜ Fourvière - ✆ 04 72 56 56 02 - www.villaflorentine.com - Closed Monday, Sunday*

✿ Têtedoie (Christian Têtedoie)

MODERN CUISINE • DESIGN Perched on Fourvière hill, this restaurant, with ultra - contemporary design, is a vantage point over the city. Christian Têted applies his talent to exploring French tradition. His signature dish, casseroled lc ster and calf's head cromesquis, is quite simply exquisite. Meanwhile, Le Ph phore, open all year round, creates modern cuisine and has another atmosphe entirely, while La Terrasse de l'Antiquaille serves dishes *a la plancha* in f weather. Superb view of the city on all floors.

Specialities: Courgette, elderberry and cider. Lobster and pâté en croûte-st tête de veau and ravioli. Fig, rosemary and honey.

Menu 48€ (lunch), 70/145€ - Carte 90/125€

PLAN: 2-E2 - *4 rue Professeur-Pierre-Marion (5th) - Ⓜ Minimes - ✆ 04 78 29 40 10 - www.tetedoie.com*

Daniel et Denise Saint-Jean

LYONNAISE • LYONNAISE BISTRO A stone's throw from Cathédrale St - Je this Old Town *bouchon* is run by chef Joseph Viola (*Meilleur Ouvrier de France* 2004), already known for Daniel and Denise in the 3rd *arrondissement*. On menu, traditional Lyon cuisine to delight fans.

Menu 33/60€ - Carte 39/58€

PLAN: 2-E2 - *32 rue Tramassac (5th) - Ⓜ Vieux Lyon - ✆ 04 78 42 24 62 - www.daniel-et-denise.fr - Closed Monday, Sunday*

Epona

MODERN CUISINE • CHIC It took six years to convert the former Hôtel-Dieu hospital up until 2010, into a world-class establishment without forgoing building's intrinsic character. The Epona restaurant, named after a goddess Celtic mythology, serves regional delicacies with a modern spin (such as fro legs and pig's trotters). The setting is emblematic of what one would expect a high-class brasserie.

Menu 29€ (lunch) - Carte 49/78€

PLAN: 2-F2 - *Intercontinental Lyon-Hôtel Dieu, 20 quai Jules-Courmont (2nd) - Ⓜ Bellecour - ✆ 04 26 99 24 24 - http://lyon.intercontinental.com*

Brasserie de L'Ouest

TRADITIONAL CUISINE • BRASSERIE Another of Paul Bocuse's brasseries, this one is quite simply huge (600 covers a day!). The menu pays homage the tradition that made a name for this great chef. Dishes include calf's li with onions, spit - roast Bresse chicken, and sole meunière. It has a designer in rior and a pretty terrace by the Saone.

Menu 27/31€ - Carte 35/67€

PLAN: 1-B1 - *1 quai du Commerce (9th) - Ⓜ Gare de Vaise - ✆ 04 37 64 64 64 - www.brasseries-bocuse.com*

Les Brotteaux – Cité Internationale – La Part-Dieu

Le Neuvième Art (Christophe Roure)

CREATIVE • DESIGN Good news: Christophe Roure continues to propose the best! Subtle inventiveness, precise marriages of flavours and an understanding of textures mark him out as an artist. Nor does he put a foot wrong in the fine wine list, with almost 400 bottles to choose from. A must.

Specialities: Tomato in all its guises, tonnato and raw marinated line-caught mackerel. Cévennes char cooked in beeswax with lemon butter and fried artichoke. Matefaim with apricots, almond sorbet and a cold thyme infusion.

Menu 98/163 € – Carte 123/147 €

PLAN: 3-H2 – *173 rue Cuvier (6th) – Ⓜ Brotteaux – ✆ 04 72 74 12 74 – www.leneuviemeart.com – Closed 23 February-9 March, 9 August-1 September, Monday, Sunday*

Takao Takano

CREATIVE • DESIGN It would be hard not to be won over by Japanese chef Takao Takano's sense of precision, his humility before his ingredients, his absolute respect of flavours and his subtle compositions. Exquisite. Book to avoid disappointment.

Specialities: Wild mushrooms, pig's trotter seasoning and truffle. Line-caught pollock, chard, snails, parsley and smoked hollandaise. Chocolate tartlet, milk confiture with Earl Grey tea.

Menu 50 € (lunch), 100/140 €

PLAN: 3-G2 – *33 rue Malesherbes (6th) – Ⓜ Foch – ✆ 04 82 31 43 39 – www.takaotakano.com – Closed 27 July-18 August, 23 December-7 January, Saturday, Sunday*

Les Apothicaires (Tabata et Ludovic Mey)

CREATIVE • INTIMATE Tabata, a young chef of Brazilian origin, and Ludovic Mey met in one of Paul Bocuse's Lyon brasseries. In a cheerful and comfortable "bourgeois bohemian" bistro atmosphere (library, wall seats), they propose creative cuisine with a few Scandinavian and South American touches. A treat.

Specialities: Market-inspired cuisine.

Menu 29 € (lunch)/59 €

PLAN: 3-G2 – *23 rue de Sèze (6th) – Ⓜ Foch – ✆ 04 26 02 25 09 – www.lesapothicairesrestaurant.com – Closed 1-24 August, Saturday, Sunday*

Le Gourmet de Sèze (Bernard Mariller)

CLASSIC CUISINE • ELEGANT In a contemporary interior done out in black and white tones, come and enjoy dishes that show off chef Bernard Mariller's inventiveness and attention to detail: he pays a fitting tribute to his mentors, who include the late Joël Robuchon, Jacques Lameloise and Michel Troigros. Modern and tasty cuisine.

Specialities: Erquy scallops. Line-caught bass. Grand cru chocolate "intensity".

Menu 40 € (lunch), 63/107 €

PLAN: 3-H2 – *125 rue de Sèze (6th) – Ⓜ Masséna – ✆ 04 78 24 23 42 – www.legourmetdeseze.com – Closed 25 July-20 August, Monday, Sunday*

Ani

CREATIVE • TRENDY Located between La Part - Dieu and the banks of the Rhône, the third Lyon restaurant to be opened by chef - patron Gaby Didonna is bound to win you over: open kitchen, with the option of eating at the bar, industrial loft interior and creative, well - made and flavoursome dishes that lay the emphasis squarely on seafood. A success story.

Menu 23 € (lunch)/33 € – Carte 60/80 €

PLAN: 3-G3 – *199 rue de Créqui (3rd) – Ⓜ Place Guichard – ✆ 09 67 23 51 33 – Closed 30 July-26 August, 22 December-1 January, Monday, Sunday*

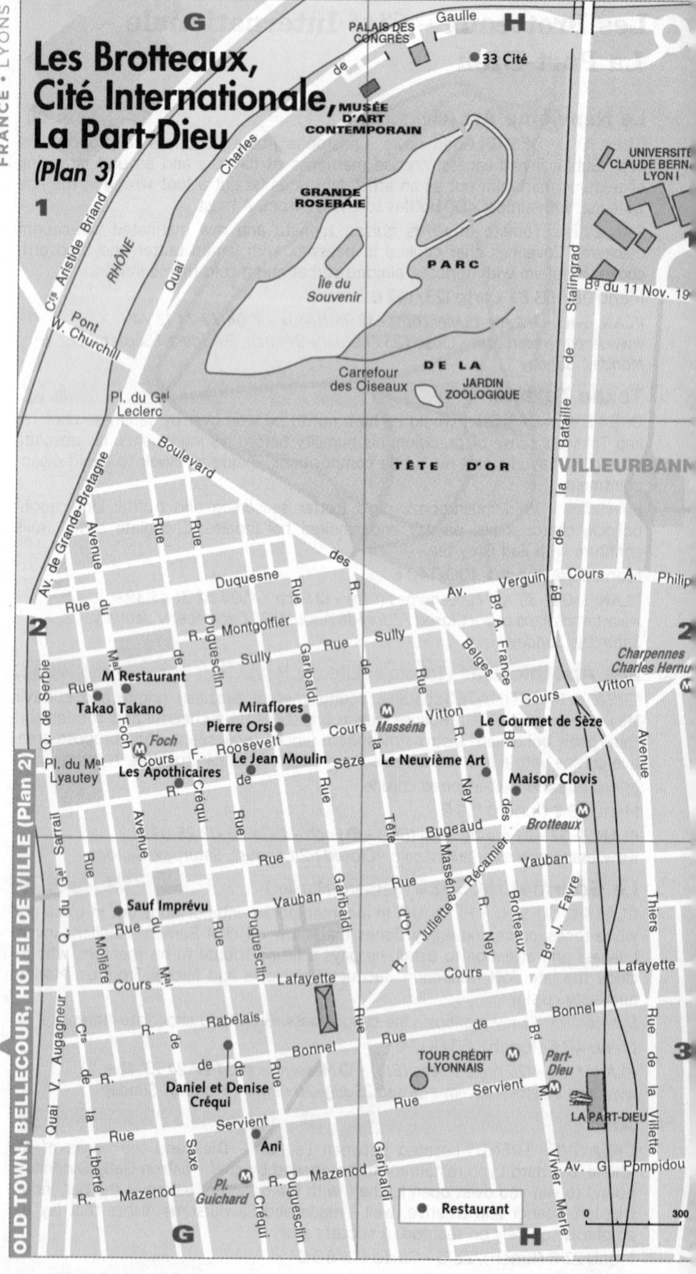
Les Brotteaux,
Cité Internationale,
La Part-Dieu
(Plan 3)
G
H
1
2
3
Gaulle
PALAIS DES CONGRÈS
33 Cité
MUSÉE D'ART CONTEMPORAIN
UNIVERSITÉ CLAUDE BERNARD LYON I
GRANDE ROSERAIE
PARC
DE LA
TÊTE D'OR
Île du Souvenir
Carrefour des Oiseaux
JARDIN ZOOLOGIQUE
RHÔNE
Quai Charles de Gaulle
Crs Aristide Briand
Pont W. Churchill
Pl. du Gal Leclerc
Boulevard des Belges
VILLEURBANNE
Bd de la Bataille de Stalingrad
Bd du 11 Nov. 19
Av. de Grande-Bretagne
Avenue du Mal Foch
Rue Duquesne
Av. Verguin
Cours A. Philip
R. Montgolfier
Rue Sully
Charpennes Charles Hernu
Cours Vitton
M Restaurant
Takao Takano
Miraflores
Pierre Orsi
Masséna
Le Gourmet de Sèze
Foch
Cours F. Roosevelt
Le Jean Moulin
Rue de Sèze
Le Neuvième Art
Pl. du Mal Lyautey
Les Apothicaires
Maison Clovis
Brotteaux
Q. de Serbie
Rue Créqui
Rue Duguesclin
Rue Garibaldi
Rue Tête d'Or
R. Ney
Bd A. France
Bd des Brotteaux
Rue Bugeaud
Rue Vauban
Rue Juliette Récamier
Rue Masséna
Avenue Thiers
Q. du Gal Sarrail
Sauf Imprévu
Rue Molière
Cours Lafayette
Bd J. Favre
Rabelais
Rue Bonnel
TOUR CRÉDIT LYONNAIS
Part-Dieu
Bd M. Vivier Merle
Daniel et Denise Créqui
Rue Servient
LA PART-DIEU
Rue de la Villette
Quai V. Augagneur
Crs de la Liberté
Ani
Rue de Saxe
Av. G. Pompidou
R. Mazenod
Pl. Guichard
Restaurant
0
300
OLD TOWN, BELLECOUR, HOTEL DE VILLE (Plan 2)

Daniel et Denise Créqui

LYONNAISE • LYONNAISE BISTRO Joseph Viola – *Meilleur Ouvrier de France* – reigns over this dyed - in - the - wool *bouchon*, with the patina of age. It serves traditional dishes perfectly made with superb ingredients, along with some seasonal suggestions. The cult dish is pâté en croûte with calf sweetbreads and foie gras.

Menu 33/60 € – Carte 31/64 €

PLAN: 3-G3 – *156 rue de Créqui (3rd) – Ⓜ Place Guichard – ✆ 04 78 60 66 53 – www.daniel-et-denise.fr – Closed Saturday, Sunday*

Le Jean Moulin

MODERN CUISINE • CONTEMPORARY DÉCOR The menu changes daily, but let's cite two dishes to give you an idea: chicken liver terrine, fondant of leeks, crayfish and Nantua sauce; slow - cooked smoked egg, cream of cauliflower, comté cheese and smoked magret of duck ... The food is fresh, perfectly cooked and served in a post - industrial, hip interior.

Menu 25 € (lunch), 34/44 €

PLAN: 3-G2 – *45 rue de Sèze (6th) – Ⓜ Masséna – ✆ 04 78 37 37 97 – www.lejeanmoulin-lyon.com – Closed Monday, Sunday*

M Restaurant

MARKET CUISINE • TRENDY The charming and fashionable M serves delicious gourmet cuisine which is full of flavour. The decor is slightly psychedelic.

Menu 29 € (lunch), 33/39 €

PLAN: 3-G2 – *47 avenue Foch (6th) – Ⓜ Foch – ✆ 04 78 89 55 19 – www.mrestaurant.fr – Closed 29 February-8 March, 26 July-17 August, Saturday, Sunday*

Sauf Imprévu

TRADITIONAL CUISINE • SIMPLE "Marguerite" terrine in homage to his great - grandmother, coco de Paimpol beans with shellfish, grilled prime rib of beef with homemade chips... With his focus firmly on tradition, Félix Gagnaire proposes delicious and copious dishes. Everything is fresh, homemade and spot on, and the prices are also fair!

Menu 26 € (lunch)/29 €

PLAN: 3-G3 – *40 rue Pierre-Corneille (6th) – Ⓜ Foch – ✆ 04 78 52 16 35 – Closed dinner Monday-Wednesday, dinner Friday, Saturday, Sunday*

33 Cité

TRADITIONAL CUISINE • BRASSERIE Three talented chefs – Mathieu Viannay (Meilleur Ouvrier de France), Christophe Marguin and Frédéric Berthod (alumnus of Bocuse) – joined forces to create this chic, tasty brasserie. It opens onto the Tête - d'Or Park. On the menu find great brasserie specialities.

Menu 28 € – Carte 35/59 €

PLAN: 3-H1 – *33 quai Charles-de-Gaulle (6th) – ✆ 04 37 45 45 45 – www.33cite.com – Closed 15-22 August, dinner Sunday*

L'Art et la Manière

TRADITIONAL CUISINE • BISTRO A bistro that champions conviviality, market - fresh cooking and lively, reasonably priced wines... and a good excuse to come and explore the Guillotière neighbourhood. The place has a loyal local following, so if you've not booked, instead try Les Bonnes Manières, their second eatery.

Menu 31/35 € – Carte 36/55 €

PLAN: 1-B2 – *102 Grande-Rue-de-la-Guillotière (7th) – Ⓜ Saxe-Gambetta – ✆ 04 37 27 05 83 – www.art-et-la-maniere.fr – Closed 3-23 August, 29 December-6 January, Saturday, Sunday*

Imouto

FUSION • DESIGN Originally from Vietnam, Gaby Didonna opened Imouto ("litt sister" in Japanese) in a working - class area of Lyon. Australian chef Guy Kend dreams up tasty recipes, a fusion of French tradition and Japanese influence Flavoursome and always impressive!

Menu 25€ (lunch), 45/100€

PLAN: 1-B2 – *21 rue Pasteur (7th) – Ⓜ Guillotière – ✆ 04 72 76 99 53 – Closed Monday, Sunday*

Maison Clovis

MODERN CUISINE • CONTEMPORARY DÉCOR Exotic wood furniture, metall grey tones: the place is stylish and elegant, without being stuffy. A fine chef, Cl vis Khoury creates seasonal creations that are truly original and at least as tast

Menu 32€ (lunch), 59/95€ – Carte 57/74€

PLAN: 3-H2 – *19 boulevard des Brotteaux (6th) – Ⓜ Brotteaux – ✆ 04 72 74 44 61 www.maisonclovis.com – Closed 1-11 May, 9-17 September, 28 December-6 January, Monday, Sunday*

Pierre Orsi

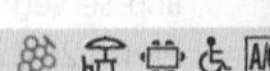

CLASSIC CUISINE • BOURGEOIS First, you come face to face with the love ochre Florentine façade, then, on entering, you discover the elegance and luxu ous comfort of an opulent bourgeois house. As for the food: the cuisine is fir and precise, of the moment, based on top - notch ingredients and accompanie by superb wines.

Menu 60€ (lunch), 130/140€ – Carte 91/173€

PLAN: 3-G2 – *3 place Kléber (6th) – Ⓜ Masséna – ✆ 04 78 89 57 68 – www.pierreorsi.com – Closed Monday, Sunday*

Town Centre

Mère Brazier (Mathieu Viannay)

CLASSIC CUISINE • ELEGANT The guardian of Lyon cuisine, Eugénie Brazi (1895 - 1977) is without doubt looking down on Mathieu Viannay – winner of t Meilleur Ouvrier de France award – with pride. An emblematic restaurant whe high - powered classics and creativity continue to be served.

Specialities: Artichoke and foie gras. Pike loaf with crayfish and a shell jus wi vin jaune. Paris-Brest.

Menu 75€ (lunch), 120/180€ – Carte 153/250€

PLAN: 2-F1 – *12 rue Royale (1st) – Ⓜ Hôtel de Ville – ✆ 04 78 23 17 20 – www.lamerebrazier.fr – Closed 29 February-8 March, 1-30 August, Saturday, Sunda*

Prairial (Gaëtan Gentil)

MODERN CUISINE • MINIMALIST Gaëtan Gentil took over this restaurant in t city's Presqu'île district in the spring of 2015. In this pleasant setting, comple with a green wall, he creates his *"gastronomy décomplexée"*: contemporary c sine, resolutely creative, with vegetables at its core.

Specialities: Tomato, marigold and grapefruit. Lake trout, carrot and spruce. paco grand cru chocolate, raspberries, sweet clover.

Menu 35€ (lunch), 59/94€

PLAN: 2-F1 – *11 rue Chavanne (1st) – Ⓜ Cordeliers – ✆ 04 78 27 86 93 – www.prairial-restaurant.com – Closed 28 January-1 February, 1-19 September, Monday, lunch Thursday, Sunday*

Les Trois Dômes

MODERN CUISINE • CONTEMPORARY DÉCOR On the top floor of the hot high - level cooking with the accent on delicious food and wine pairings. From terrine of pot au feu with foie gras to leg of Limousin lamb, the classics are sk fully reworked. Magical views of the city from the elegant and contemporary di ing room.

Specialities: Lobster salad with multicoloured tomato tartare, gazpacho and jelly. Fillet of Salers beef with summer truffles. Chocolate cigar with Baileys cream and saffron ice cream.

Menu 48 € (lunch), 83/125 € - Carte 44/87 €

PLAN: 2-F3 – *Hôtel Sofitel Lyon Bellecour, 20 quai du Docteur-Gailleton (2nd) – Ⓜ Bellecour – ✆ 04 72 41 20 97 – www.les-3-domes.com – Closed 12-19 April, 1-31 August, Monday, Sunday*

Aromatic

MODERN CUISINE • TRENDY Look out for this gem in the neighbourhood of La Croix Rousse! Partners Frédéric Taghavi and Pierre Julien Gay cook up tasty modern recipes based on ultra-fresh produce – including beautiful wild fish. Everything is mouth-watering, and the wild cod with its bouillabaisse jus was no exception... We're still licking our lips.

Menu 21€ (lunch), 33/48 €

PLAN: 1-B1 – *15 rue du Chariot-d'Or (4th) – Ⓜ Croix-Rousse – ✆ 04 78 23 73 61 – www.aromaticrestaurant.fr – Closed 15-23 March, 1-25 August, Monday, Sunday*

Le Canut et les Gones

MODERN CUISINE • BISTRO A unique atmosphere, somewhere between bistro and secondhand shop – formica bar, wooden floorboards, vintage tapestry, collection of old clocks on the walls -, modern cuisine in tune with the seasons, a wine list boasting over 300 types... In a little-frequented area of La Croix - Rousse, this is definitely one to try out.

Menu 22 € (lunch)/34 €

PLAN: 1-B1 – *29 rue Belfort (4th) – Ⓜ Croix-Rousse – ✆ 04 78 29 17 23 – www.lecanutetlesgones.com – Closed Monday, Sunday*

Substrat

MODERN CUISINE • BISTRO This restaurant that feels like a cross between a country house and an artisan's workshop promises "produce of the harvest and wines for drinking". The promise is kept: wild garlic, cranberries, ceps, boletus and bilberries accompany tasty dishes bursting with nature, accompanied by good wines. A real treat!

Menu 23 € (lunch), 33/44 €

PLAN: 1-B1 – *7 rue Pailleron (4th) – Ⓜ Hénon – ✆ 04 78 29 14 93 – www.substrat-restaurant.com – Closed 10-24 August, Sunday*

L'Atelier des Augustins

MODERN CUISINE • CONTEMPORARY DÉCOR After stints in some fine establishments, the former chef of the embassies of France in London and Bamako, Nicolas Guilloton, left the world of diplomatic missions to open this refined Atelier. Here food remains an important matter. He creates lovely recipes that are full of colour and flavour, and are nicely modern!

Menu 29 € (lunch), 48/62 € - Carte 50/70 €

PLAN: 2-F1 – *11 rue des Augustins (1st) – Ⓜ Hôtel de Ville – ✆ 04 72 00 88 01 – www.lateliersdesaugustins.com – Closed 23-31 December, Monday, lunch Saturday, Sunday*

Café Terroir

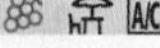

COUNTRY COOKING • FRIENDLY The philosophy of the two owners of Café Terroir, near the Théâtre des Célestins, is to source the best of the region's ingredients and turn them into gourmet dishes. The house classics: *terrine de maman*, roast pistachio sausage and red wine sauce, gâteau lyonnais. A fine selection of wines, from the Rhône and elsewhere.

Menu 22 € (lunch)/32 € - Carte 30/50 €

PLAN: 2-F2 – *14 rue d'Amboise (2nd) – Ⓜ Bellecour – ✆ 09 53 36 08 11 – www.cafeterroir.fr – Closed 23-31 December, Monday, Sunday*

Daniel et Denise Croix-Rousse

LYONNAISE • LYONNAISE BISTRO Daniel and Denise Croix - Rousse – th third in the series, after locations on rue de Créqui and in the St Jean quarter is enjoying the same success as its older siblings. Fill up on hearty Lyon cuisi in a traditional *bouchon* (tavern) setting.

Menu 28/40 € – Carte 38/55 €

PLAN: 1-B1 – *8 rue de Cuire (4th) – Ⓜ Croix-Rousse – ✆ 04 78 28 27 44 – www.daniel-et-denise.fr – Closed Monday, Sunday*

L'Établi

MODERN CUISINE • TRENDY This restaurant run by an alumnus of Christian Te tedoie is a real favourite. Unbeatable value for money, creative or unapologeti cally traditional dishes (onion soup and pot - au - feu), but always skilfully han dled: from start to finish it's a wonderful treat. Not to spoil anything, the servic is also attentive.

Menu 28 € (lunch), 54/69 €

PLAN: 2-F3 – *22 rue des Remparts-d'Ainay (2nd) – Ⓜ Ampère Victor Hugo – ✆ 04 78 37 49 83 – www.letabli-restaurant.fr – Closed 1-11 January, 1-30 August, Saturday, Sunday*

L'Institut

MODERN CUISINE • CONTEMPORARY DÉCOR On Place Bellecour, the trainin restaurant of the Paul Bocuse Institute feels nothing like a school! In a contempo rary decor designed by Pierre - Yves Rochon, with open kitchens giving onto th restaurant, the students deliver a high standard of service. The dishes are ex tremely well made and deserve a high mark.

Menu 39 € (lunch)/51 €

PLAN: 2-F2 – *Hôtel Le Royal, 20 place Bellecour (2nd) – Ⓜ Bellecour – ✆ 04 78 37 23 02 – www.linstitut-restaurant.fr – Closed 3-24 August, 23 December-7 January, Monday, Sunday*

Léon de Lyon

TRADITIONAL CUISINE • ELEGANT This Lyon institution, founded in 1904, wa taken over by a trio of partners including humorist (and bon viveur) Lauren Gerra. Nicely restored space (wallpaper, paintings), classic French cuisine with twist (farm-reared pork and foie gras terrine; soufflé with green Chartreuse wine list of 950 references. A sound choice.

Menu 55 € – Carte 69/107 €

PLAN: 2-F1 – *1 rue Pleney (1st) – Ⓜ Hôtel de Ville – ✆ 04 72 10 11 12 – www.leondelyon.com*

Le Musée

LYONNAISE • LYONNAISE BISTRO A sincere and authentic bouchon with a de cor of checked tablecloths, closely packed tables and a buzzing atmosphere. In the kitchen, the young chef creates the classics with real know - how, such as Lyonnaise pork, foie de veau persillé (calf's liver), trotters and brawn salad.

Menu 26 € (lunch)/30 €

PLAN: 2-F2 – *2 rue des Forces (2nd) – Ⓜ Cordeliers – ✆ 04 78 37 71 54 – Closed 1-31 August, 24 December-2 January, Monday, dinner Saturday, Sunday*

Le Poêlon d'or

LYONNAISE • LYONNAISE BISTRO It's hard to say whether or not the che does actually use a golden saucepan (poêlon d'or), but he must have a secret weapon – he revisits Lyon's terroir so well and creates food that is as tasty as it is perfectly put together - from the gâteau de foie de volaille (chicken liver) with tomato coulis, to the pike quenelle gratin with béchamel sauce. A must!

Menu 18 € (lunch), 27/34 € – Carte 27/51 €

PLAN: 2-F3 – *29 rue des Remparts-d'Ainay (2nd) – Ⓜ Ampère – ✆ 04 78 37 65 60 – www.lepoelondor-restaurant.fr – Closed 7-30 August, lunch Saturday, Sunday*

Restaurant Fond Rose

TRADITIONAL CUISINE • BRASSERIE A 1920s mansion transformed into a chic brasserie by the Bocuse group. With its terrace surrounded by 100 year - old trees, it is the epitome of peace and quiet. The food is tasty and generous and squarely in the tradition of the areas around the River Saône, with frogs' legs and quenelles etc.

Menu 32/35€ – Carte 40/70€

PLAN: 1-B1 – *23 chemin de Fond-Rose - à Caluire-et-Cuire* – *04 78 29 34 61* – *www.brasseries-bocuse.fr*

Brasserie le Sud

MEDITERRANEAN CUISINE • BRASSERIE There is an elegant Greek feel to the white and blue decor of this Bocuse brasserie situated a hop, skip and a jump from Place Bellecour. The name is no coincidence: here, it's the South – chicken pastilla with cinnamon and coriander; lamb shank in couscous; fresh cod with aioli – and even more so in summer, on the terrace!

Menu 27€ (lunch) – Carte 35/60€

PLAN: 2-F2 – *11 place Antonin-Poncet (2nd)* – *Bellecour* – *04 72 77 80 00* – *www.brasseries-bocuse.com*

Thomas

TRADITIONAL CUISINE • BISTRO In this contemporary bistro, chef-patron Thomas Ponson (who also owns Bistro and Bouchon, located opposite) concocts pleasant lunch menus, and a more elaborate offering in the evening, with premium ingredients (Breton mackerel, pressed Challans duck). A serious place.

Menu 23€ (lunch), 47/60€

PLAN: 2-F3 – *6 rue Laurencin (2nd)* – *Bellecour* – *04 72 56 04 76* – *www.restaurant-thomas.com – Closed Saturday, Sunday*

La Voûte - Chez Léa

LYONNAISE • LYONNAISE BISTRO One of the oldest restaurants in Lyon: in a welcoming atmosphere, tradition carries on with verve. A fine menu with tasty regional dishes and game in autumn.

Menu 21€ (lunch), 31/45€ – Carte 31/69€

PLAN: 2-F2 – *11 place Antonin-Gourju (2nd)* – *Bellecour* – *04 78 42 01 33* – *www.lavoutechezlea.com* – *Closed dinner Sunday*

Environs of Lyons

Collonges-au-Mont-d'Or

Paul Bocuse

CLASSIC CUISINE • ELEGANT Since the loss of Monsieur Paul in 2018, the team at this legendary establishment has been perpetuating the dishes created by the great chef (crayfish tail gratin; VGE soup with chicken, beef and truffles; Bresse chicken fricassee) and also offers reinvented classics. The story continues in Collonges-au-Mont-d'Or.

Specialities: Red mullet dressed in crusty potato scales. Œuf à la neige "grand-mère".

Menu 175/280€ – Carte 180/250€

Off plan – *40 quai de la Plage* – *04 72 42 90 90* – *www.bocuse.fr* – *Closed 2-23 January*

Charbonnières-les-Bains

La Rotonde (Jean-François Malle)

MODERN CUISINE • ELEGANT In this pleasantly leafy area on the outskirts o town: a fine legacy of the Art Deco period which also houses the casino Le Lyo Vert. The menu is in a classic French vein and combines timeless dishes with ne influences - not forgetting the great repertoire of Lyon cuisine.

Specialities: "2013 World Champion" pâté en croûte. Monkfish "de petit bateau with shellfish and a marinière emulsion. Finger praline with lemon, hazelnuts an Gianduja chocolate ice cream.

Menu 48€ (lunch), 78/135€

Off plan – *Hôtel Pavillon de la Rotonde, avenue du Casino – ✆ 04 78 87 00 97 – www.restaurant-rotonde.com – Closed 2-26 August, Monday, lunch Tuesday, lunch Saturday, Sunday*

Écully

Saisons

MODERN CUISINE • BOURGEOIS The seasons take pride of place in this 19 château, which houses the international hospitality school, formerly under th aegis of Paul Bocuse. Chef Davy Tissot and his team of students (of cooker pastry-making, baking, waitering, etc.) compose savoury menus, featuring exce lent produce. Flawless technique and the occasional creative twist. An enjoyab experience.

Specialities: Aiguillette of acidulated John Dory and Isigny oyster pearl. Saddle o slow-cooked Limousin lamb, roasted carrot tops and petits pois "à la française Citrus-infused biscuit, fromage blanc mousse and acidulated meringue.

Menu 45/78€

PLAN: 1-A1 – *1 A chemin de Calabert – ✆ 04 26 20 97 57 – www.saisons-restaurant.fr – Closed 8 August-1 September, 19 December-5 January, Saturday, Sunday*

bluejayphoto/iStock

GERMANY

DEUTSCHLAND

BERLIN
BERLIN

TomasSereda/iStock

BERLIN IN...

- **ONE DAY**
  Unter den Linden, Museum Island, Nikolaiviertel, coffee at TV Tower.
- **TWO DAYS**
  Potsdamer Platz, Reichstag, Regierungsviertel including the Gemäldegalerie, concert at Philharmonie.
- **THREE DAYS**
  KaDeWe, Kurfürstendamm, Charlottenburg Palace.

Berlin's parliament faces an intriguing dilemma when it comes to where to call its heart, as, although they are homogeneous in many other ways, the east and the west of the city still lay claim to separate centres after 40 years of partition. Following the tempestuous 1990s, Berlin sought to resolve its new identity, and it now stands proud as one of the most dynamic and forward thinking cities in the world. Alongside its idea of tomorrow, it's never lost sight of its bohemian past, and many parts of the city retain the arty sense of adventure that characterised downtown Berlin during the 1920s: turn any corner and you might find a

modernist art gallery, a tiny cinema or a cutting-edge club.

The eastern side of the River Spree, around Nikolaiviertel, is the historic heart of the city, dating back to the 13C. Meanwhile, way over to the west of the centre lie Kurfürstendamm and Charlottenburg; smart districts which came to the fore after World War II as the heart of West Berlin. Between the two lie imposing areas which swarm with visitors: Tiergarten is the green lung of the city, and just to its east is the great boulevard of Unter den Linden. Continuing eastward, the self-explanatory Museum Island sits snugly and securely in the tributaries of the Spree. The most southerly of Berlin's sprawling districts is Kreuzberg, renowned for its bohemian, alternative character.

EATING OUT

Many of Berlin's best restaurants are found within the grand hotels and you only have to go to Savignyplatz near Ku'damm to realise how smart dining has taken off. Dinner is the most popular meal and you can invariably eat late, as lots of places stay open until 2 or 3am. Berlin also has a reputation for simple, hearty dishes, inspired by the long, hard winter and, when temperatures drop, the city's comfort food has an irresistible allure – there's pork knuckle, Schnitzel, Bratwurst in mustard, chunky dumplings... and the real Berlin favourite, Currywurst. Bread and potatoes are ubiquitous but since reunification, many dishes have also incorporated a more global influence, so produce from the local forests, rivers and lakes may well be given an Asian or Mediterranean twist (Berlin now claims a wider range of restaurants than any other German city). Service is included in the price of your meal but it's customary to round up the bill. Be sure to try the local 'Berliner Weisse mit Schuss' – a light beer with a dash of raspberry or woodruff.

Centre

✿✿✿ Rutz

MODERN CUISINE • DESIGN Marco Müller's set Inspirations menu promise well-balanced, creative combinations of top-quality ingredients, skilfully show casing particular flavours to give each dish its own special character. Diners enjc their food in the modern interior accompanied by some expert wine suggestior drawn from a fine wine list.

Specialities: Mussels, dune greens and shoyu. Saltmarsh lamb, elder and onion barley. Blueberries and spruce, Amazake.

Menu 158/198€

PLAN: 1-C2 – *Chausseestraße 8 – Ⓜ Oranienburger Tor – ✆ 030 24628760 – www.rutz-restaurant.de – Closed 5-13 January, Monday, Sunday, lunch Tuesday-Saturda*

✿✿ FACIL

CREATIVE • CHIC FACIL is an oasis of calm amid the hustle and bustle of th Potsdamer Platz. It is pleasantly light and airy, especially in the summer, wi plenty of greenery outside even though it's on the fifth floor! The modern, cre tive food is beautifully presented.

Specialities: Scallop, celeriac, camomile and wasabi. Saddle of Fläming veniso turnips, pomegranate and Ras el-Hanout. Passion fruit, lychee, coconut and Ba hibe chocolate.

Menu 57€ (lunch), 104/210€ – Carte 57/135€

PLAN: 2-F2 – *THE MANDALA, Potsdamer Straße 3 – Ⓜ Potsdamer Platz – ✆ 030 590051234 – www.facil.de – Closed 4-19 January, 18 July-9 August, Saturday Sunday*

✿✿ Lorenz Adlon Esszimmer

CREATIVE • LUXURY The Adlon inevitably conjures up an image of stylish fin dining, with its sumptuous interior, charming professional service - including exce lent wine recommendations - and top-class creative cuisine. The food itself is co ceived with great imagination and prepared with consummate skill using only th very best ingredients. The view of the Brandenburg Gate is the icing on the cake

Specialities: Crème and parfait of goose liver, candied citrus, fig, lardo. Neustre litz saddle of venison, camomile, dried sour cherries, spring onions. Oat crean blood orange sorbet, orange-jasmine extract, herb snow.

Menu 135/205€

PLAN: 2-G1 – *Adlon Kempinski, Unter den Linden 77 – Ⓜ Brandenburger Tor – ✆ 030 22611960 – www.lorenzadlon-esszimmer.de – Closed 1-15 January, 20 July-5 August, Monday, Tuesday, Sunday, lunch Wednesday-Saturday*

✿ Bandol sur Mer (Andreas Saul)

MODERN FRENCH • NEIGHBOURHOOD This friendly, low-key little restaurar is proof that down-to-earth food can also be ambitious. The open kitchen pr duces creative, flavoursome cuisine full of contrast and rich in intensity, which also a feast for the eyes.

Specialities: Sturgeon, potato, asparagus, unripe strawberries. Havel pike perc nettle, escargot, buckwheat. Pear, Jerusalem artichoke, verbena.

Menu 119€

PLAN: 1-C2 – *Torstraße 167 – Ⓜ Rosenthaler Platz – ✆ 030 67302051 – www.bandolsurmer.de – Closed Tuesday, Wednesday, lunch Monday and Thursday-Sunday*

✿ Bieberbau (Stephan Garkisch)

MODERN CUISINE • COSY The atmosphere here is genuinely unique, not leas thanks to Richard Bieber's remarkable stuccowork! The chef cooks modern sea sonal fare, skilfully placing herbs and spices centre stage, while his partner ove sees the charming front-of-house team. Excellent value for money!

Specialities: Meagre with Waldorf salad, saffron and garden cress. Saddle of lamb with beans, purslane and mint. Melon with green tea, raspberries, oats and lemon verbena.

Menu 52/74€

PLAN: 1-B3 - *Durlacher Straße 15 - Ⓜ Bundesplatz - ✆ 030 8532390 - www.bieberbau-berlin.de - Closed Saturday, Sunday, lunch Monday-Friday*

✿ 5 - Cinco by Paco Pérez

CREATIVE • DESIGN You no longer have to make the journey to Miramar in Spain for Paco Pérez' Michelin-starred cuisine. You can now sample his upmarket creations in this modern restaurant – with 86 copper pans hanging from the centre of the ceiling – as you marvel at the intense activity in the kitchens. Choose the 'Experience Menu' or go à la carte.

Specialities: Amberjack, umami and caviar. Pigeon, sweetcorn, molé and huitlacoche. Yuzu, mango, yoghurt.

Menu 130/200€

PLAN: 3-L2 - *SO/ Berlin Das Stue, Drakestraße 1 - Ⓜ Wittenbergplatz - ✆ 030 3117220 - www.das-stue.com/en/restaurants-bar/cinco-by-paco-perez - Closed Monday, Tuesday, Sunday, lunch Wednesday-Saturday*

✿ Cookies Cream

VEGETARIAN • TRENDY Finding your way here through a maze of backyards to ring the bell at the unassuming door is an adventure in itself! Up on the first floor you'll find a vibrant restaurant decorated in an "industrial" style (it was once a fashionable night club). The vegetarian cuisine, artful and sophisticated, is served to a soundtrack of electronic music.

Specialities: Vegetarian caviar with egg yolk. Parmesan dumpling with Alba truffle. Celery ice cream with apple.

Menu 59/79€

PLAN: 2-G1 - *Behrenstraße 55 - Ⓜ Französische Straße - ✆ 030 680730448 - www.cookiescream.com - Closed Monday, Sunday, lunch Tuesday-Saturday*

✿ Cordo

CREATIVE • CHIC Highly sophisticated yet unpretentious, from the trendy ambience and the charming, laid-back service (the chef occasionally comes to the table himself) to the inventive dishes that create culinary harmony by way of contrasting flavours. What's more, dishes on the set menus are available in a snack-size version at the distinctive-looking bar.

Specialities: Matjes herring "Müllerin Art". "Caesar" corn-fed chicken. Hamburg-style red berry compote.

Menu 42/105€

PLAN: 2-H1 - *Große Hamburger Straße 32 - Ⓜ Hackescher Markt - ✆ 030 27581215 - www.cordobar.net - Closed Monday, Sunday, lunch Tuesday-Saturday*

✿ einsunternull

CREATIVE • DESIGN Berlin's culinary diversity is showcased in this restaurant, which serves modern, creative and internationally inspired dishes made from top-quality produce. Local ingredients feature on the menu, alongside influences from across the globe. An attractive wine list accompanies the menu, plus a selection of non-alcoholic options.

Specialities: Trout, cucumber, watermelon, buttermilk. Rabbit, chanterelles, vegetables. Strawberry, basil, pine nuts.

Menu 129€

PLAN: 1-C2 - *Hannoversche Straße 1 - Ⓜ Oranienburger Tor - ✆ 030 27577810 - www.einsunternull.com - Closed 14-29 January, Tuesday, Wednesday, lunch Monday and Thursday-Sunday*

✿ GOLVET

CREATIVE • DESIGN GOLVET offers an impressive view over Potsdamer Platz, a stylish interior complete with open kitchen and artful, modern, pared-down cuisine made using the very best ingredients. Then of course, there's the top-quality service and excellent wine recommendations.

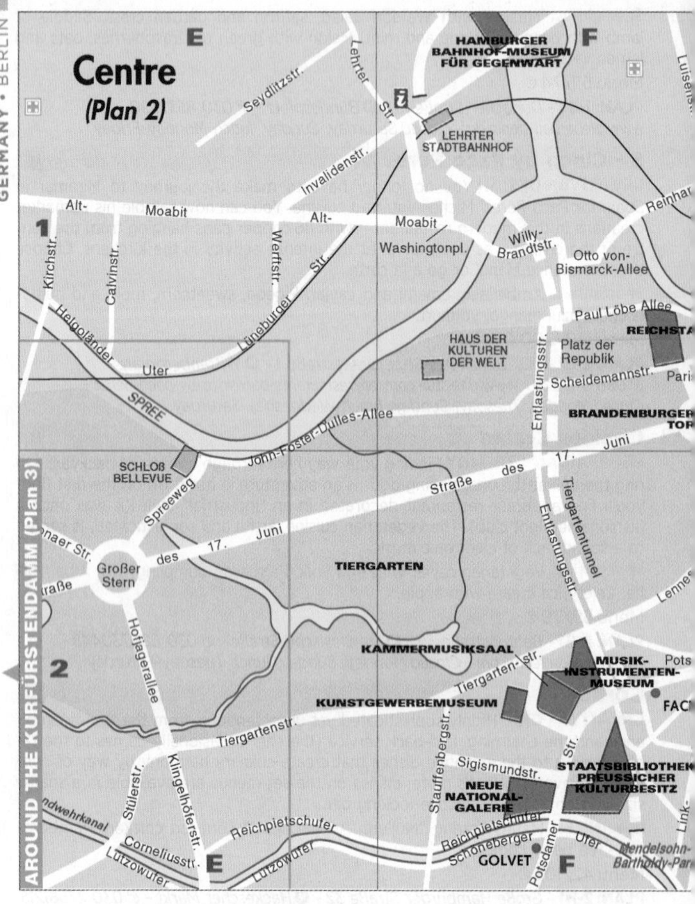

Specialities: Jerusalem artichoke ice cream with chicory, lime and crosn... Roasted piglet shoulder with nettle, blackcurrants and jalapeño sauce hollandais... Dessert of purple aubergines with passion fruit, vanilla and basil.

Menu 90/128 €

PLAN: 2-F2 – *Potsdamer Straße 58* – Ⓜ *Potsdamer Brücke* – ✆ *030 89064222* – *www.golvet.de* – *Closed 13-27 July, Monday, Sunday, lunch Tuesday-Saturday*

✿ Hugos

MODERN CUISINE • CHIC It is true that the view from the 14th floor is fantast... but this elegant, minimalist-style restaurant is known first and foremost for i... classic, modern cuisine, which is both beautifully crafted and delicious.

Specialities: Brittany langoustine, coconut, calamansi, seaweed tempura. Schor... heide venison, spruce tips, pecan nut, rowan berries. Hazelnut and Jerusalem a... tichoke, Abate Fetel pear, ice cream, tartlet, espresso.

Menu 110/165 €

PLAN: 3-L2 – *InterContinental, Budapester Straße 2* – Ⓜ *Wittenbergplatz* – ✆ *030 26021263* – *www.hugos-restaurant.de* – *Closed 1-13 January, 12-20 April, 5 July-24 August, Monday, Sunday, lunch Tuesday-Saturday*

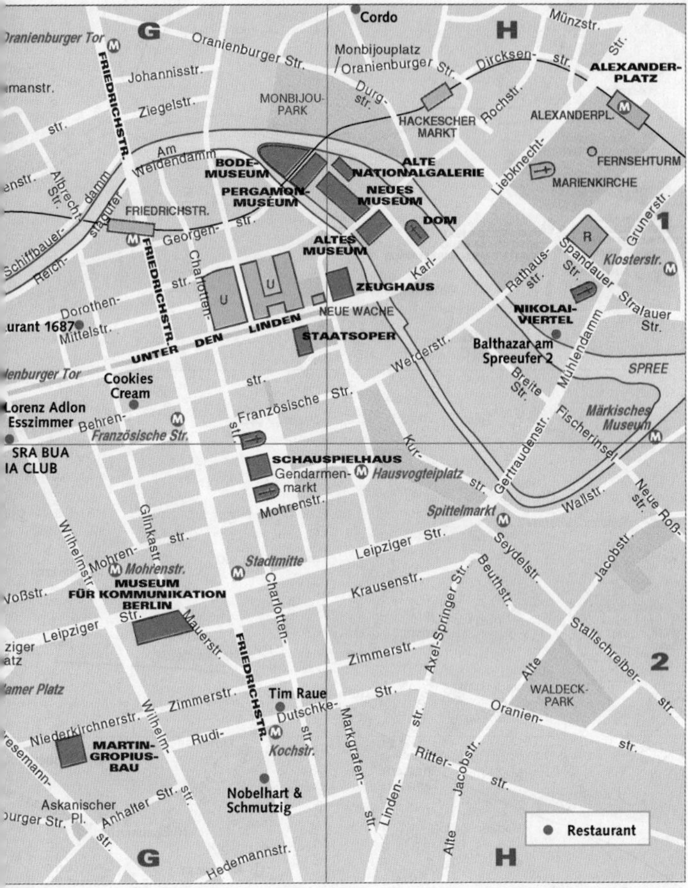

Kin Dee

THAI • DESIGN This friendly, minimalist-style restaurant more than lives up to its name, Kin Dee or "eat well". The food is authentically Thai, made using top-quality local ingredients which are combined with great skill and the real taste of Thailand. Good, attentive service.

Specialities: Cornfed chicken breast, golden beet, peanuts. Wild boar, clams "Pat Nam Prik Pao". Coconut ice cream, palm sugar, milk bread, berries.

Menu 55 €

PLAN: 1-C2 – *Lützowstraße 81 – Ⓜ Kurfürstenstraße – ✆ 030 2155294 – www.kindeeberlin.com – Closed Monday, Sunday, lunch Tuesday-Saturday*

Pauly Saal

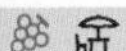

MODERN FRENCH • TRENDY If you're looking for somewhere elegant yet relaxed to eat, this is it. The high-ceilinged hall in this former Jewish girls' school boasts a striking decorative rocket above the window into the kitchen and stylish Murano glass chandeliers. Classic cuisine with modern influences, plus excellent wine recommendations from the sommelier.

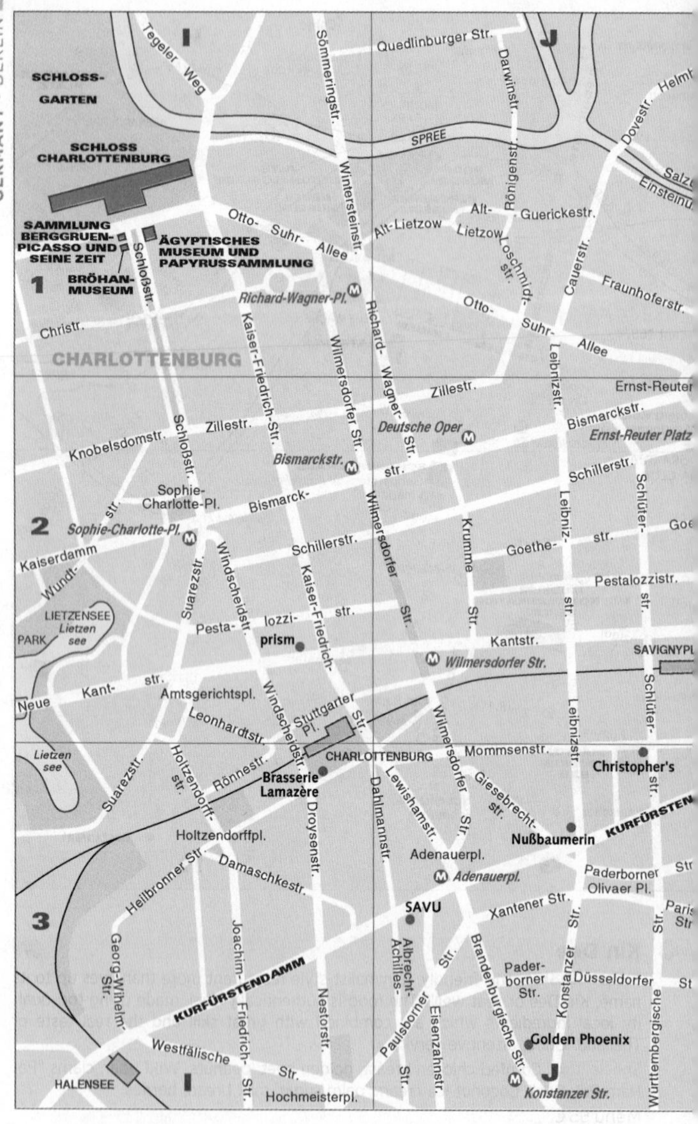

Specialities: Marbled goose liver terrine, smoked duck breast, Arabica reduction, fig brioche. Steamed turbot, algae butter, mussels in a herb stock, black rice, calamari, fennel. Jivara chocolate and raspberries, fermented milk sorbet, candied cocoa.

Menu 85/115 €

PLAN: 1-C2 – *Auguststraße 11* – Ⓜ *Weinmeisterstr.* – ✆ *030 33006070* – *www.paulysaal.com – Closed Monday, Sunday, lunch Tuesday-Saturday*

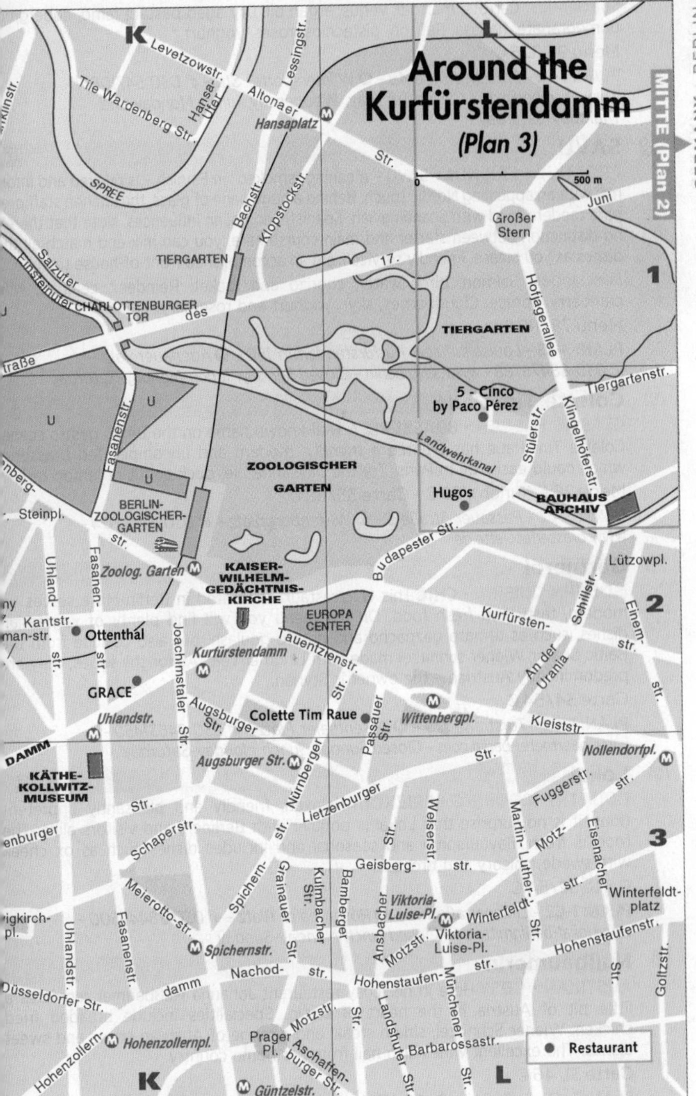

prism (Gal Ben Moshe)

ISRAELI • CHIC In a chic, minimalist ambience, chef-owner Gal Ben Moshe offers up exciting cuisine that gives a nod to his Israeli roots as well as to modern European standards. His interesting dishes, made from excellent ingredients, are replete with contrasts and varying flavours. They are accompanied by first-rate wines recommended by much-lauded sommelier, Jacqueline Lorenz.

Specialities: Carrots, maftoul, verjus, argan oil. Dry aged pasture lamb, aubergine, pomegranate, harissa. Saffron, pistachios, roses, yoghurt.

Menu 95/125 €

PLAN: 3-I2 – *Fritschestraße 48* – Ⓜ *Wilmersdorfer Str.* – *☏ 030 54710861* – *www.prismberlin.de* – *Closed Tuesday, Wednesday, lunch Monday and Thursday-Saturday*

SAVU

CREATIVE • FRIENDLY SAVU – meaning "smoked" in Finnish – is relaxed and informal with an appealing Nordic touch. Behind a huge pane of glass, the kitchen staff prepare modern food with Scandinavian, Spanish and Italian influences. Note that there no distinction between starter and main course here, you can mix and match all the dishes as you please. Friendly service from an accomplished front-of-house team.

Specialities: Salmon, birch water, chorizo and rocket. Reindeer, celeriac, wild cranberry, spruce. Cloudberries, skyr, yoghurt and rosemary.

Menu 78/118 €

PLAN: 3-J3 – *Louisa's Place, Kurfürstendamm 160* – Ⓜ *Adenauerplatz* – *☏ 030 88475788* – *www.savu.berlin* – *Closed Sunday, lunch Monday-Saturday*

Colette Tim Raue

CLASSIC FRENCH • BRASSERIE A well-known name on the Berlin gastro scene, Colette Tim Raue has created a friendly, modern and uncomplicated brasserie which could easily be in Paris. Try the paysanne pie, duck confit or lemon tart.

Menu 26 € (lunch)/59 € – Carte 35/68 €

PLAN: 3-L2 – *Passauer Straße 5* – Ⓜ *Wittenbergplatz* – *☏ 030 21992174* – *www.brasseriecolette.de*

Gärtnerei

MODERN CUISINE • CHIC This chic restaurant located in Berlin-Mitte serves up modern, tasty and fresh food. On the menu you will find plenty of vegetarian dishes, such as tomato gazpacho and potato goulash, but also ceviche from the Baltic Sea or Wiener schnitzel made with Linumer veal. As for the wines, they are predominantly Austrian – the owner is Styrian.

Carte 34/54 €

PLAN: 1-C2 – *Torstraße 179* – Ⓜ *Rosenthaler Platz* – *☏ 030 24631450* – *www.gaertnerei-berlin.com* – *Closed Sunday, lunch Monday-Saturday*

Lokal

COUNTRY COOKING • FRIENDLY Relaxed, friendly and pleasantly unpretentious, it is no surprise that Lokal is popular with Berliners and visitors alike. The food is fresh, flavoursome and seasonal and includes dishes such as ox cheek with swede, chicory and broccoli.

Carte 32/54 €

PLAN: 1-C2 – *Linienstraße 160* – Ⓜ *Rosenthaler Platz* – *☏ 030 28449500* – *www.lokal-berlinmitte.de* – *Closed lunch Monday-Sunday*

Nußbaumerin

AUSTRIAN • COSY Here in her cosy restaurant Johanna Nußbaumer recreates a little bit of Austria in the heart of Berlin. Specialities include breaded fried chicken, Wiener Schnitzel, sirloin steak, and a range of Austrian stews and sweet dishes. The excellent wines also hail from her home country.

Carte 31/46 €

PLAN: 3-J3 – *Leibnizstraße 55* – Ⓜ *Adenauerplatz* – *☏ 030 50178033* – *www.nussbaumerin.de* – *Closed 1-15 January, Monday, Sunday, lunch Tuesday-Saturday*

Brasserie Lamazère

FRENCH • BRASSERIE You might almost be in France here in the heart of Charlottenburg at Brasserie Lamazère thanks to its charming, straightforward bistro feel and authentic, constantly changing menu of fresh and tasty seasonal fare. Try the *oeufs en cocotte* with Bayonne ham or Atlantic cod with tomato and paprika mussels.

Menu 42/54 € – Carte 44/60 €

PLAN: 3-I3 – *Stuttgarter Platz 18* – Ⓜ *Wilmersdorfer Str.* – *☏ 030 31800712* – *www.lamazere.de* – *Closed Monday, lunch Tuesday-Sunday*

Christopher's

MARKET CUISINE • BISTRO A hip urban restaurant in which you can expect ambitious, seasonal cuisine, as in the pork with quince, mustard and black salsify. The fresh, youthful concept and friendly atmosphere are appreciated by diners. The question of wine is taken seriously here, but you can also opt for a stylish cocktail.

Menu 45/65€ – Carte 53/61€

PLAN: 1-J3 – *Mommsenstraße 63 – Ⓜ Adenauerplatz – ✆ 030 24356282 – www.christophers.online – Closed Sunday, lunch Monday-Saturday*

Golden Phoenix

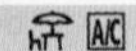

FUSION • CHIC Another restaurant belonging to multiple restaurant owner The Duc Ngo, located in the stylish Provocateur hotel. Expect a personal and informal welcome in a chic and elegant setting. Chinese cuisine with french influences features interesting Dim Sum and chicken in a yuzu and beurre blanc sauce, with a selection of drinks available from the adjoining award-winning bar.

Menu 75/115€ – Carte 44/77€

PLAN: 3-J3 – *Provocateur, Brandenburgische Straße 21 – Ⓜ Konstanzer Straße – ✆ 030 220560633 – www.goldenphoenix.berlin – Closed Monday, Sunday, lunch Tuesday-Saturday*

GRACE

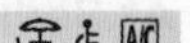

INTERNATIONAL • CHIC Combining stylish, modern design and vintage flair, Grace is a really smart place to eat. The food is modern and international and includes such delights as creamy rock shrimps with cucumber, coriander, peanuts and chilli.

Menu 69/99€ – Carte 40/111€

PLAN: 3-K2 – *Zoo Berlin, Kurfürstendamm 25 – Ⓜ Uhlandstr. – ✆ 030 88437750 – www.grace-berlin.com – Closed 13 July-10 August, Monday, Sunday, lunch Tuesday-Saturday*

INDIA CLUB

INDIAN • ELEGANT Authentic Indian food in Berlin! The self-styled 'rustic cuisine' from the north of India includes some delicious curries (try the lamb shank curry) as well as original tandoori dishes such as the 'maachi tikka'. The upmarket interior features dark wood and typically Indian colours and motifs.

Carte 39/61€

PLAN: 2-G2 – *Behrenstraße 72 – Ⓜ Brandenburger Tor – ✆ 030 20628610 – www.india-club-berlin.com – Closed lunch Monday-Sunday*

Ottenthal

AUSTRIAN • CLASSIC DÉCOR The typically Austrian tavern fare is a great success. In his friendly restaurant (named after his home town in Lower Austria) chef Arthur Schneller produces unfussy dishes including Wiener Tafelspitz (boiled rump of beef Viennese style) and apple strudel. Good wine selection.

Menu 34€ – Carte 38/66€

PLAN: 3-K2 – *Kantstraße 153 – Ⓜ Zoologischer Garten – ✆ 030 3133162 – www.ottenthal.com – Closed lunch Monday-Sunday*

Restaurant 1687

MEDITERRANEAN CUISINE • DESIGN This tasteful and stylish restaurant with a pretty terrace is set in a narrow side street just off Unter den Linden. The cuisine is predominantly Mediterranean with hints of a few other international influences. A reduced menu is served at lunchtime. You can also have breakfast here.

Menu 45/54€ – Carte 30/72€

PLAN: 2-G1 – *Mittelstraße 30 – Ⓜ Friedrichstraße – ✆ 030 20630611 – www.1687.berlin – Closed Sunday*

SRA BUA

ASIAN • ELEGANT Authentic produce and a variety of South-East Asian influences combine at SRA BUA to produce ambitious fare which includes some interesting Izakaya-style bar food. The upmarket, minimalist-style interior is at once elegant and cosy and the service attentive.

Menu 39/74€ – Carte 50/90€

PLAN: 3-G1 – *Adlon Kempinski, Behrenstraße 72 – Ⓜ Brandenburger Tor – ✆ 030 22611590 – www.srabua-berlin.de – Closed 26 January-3 February, 9 July-30 August, Monday, Sunday, lunch Tuesday-Saturday*

Environs of Berlin

At Berlin-Wedding

✿ Ernst (Dylan Watson-Brawn)

CREATIVE • MINIMALIST Somewhat unprepossessing from the outside, Ernst tells quite a different story inside. Diners ring the bell on the great stainless-steel door to enter this sober, industrial-style restaurant, where 13 counter seats face the open kitchen. "Less is more" is the order of the day here. In a set menu with up to 40 individual plates, everything revolves around the produce. A memorable three-hour gourmet experience! Book by purchasing a ticket online.

Specialities: Cucumber with salt and sorrel flowers. Veal fillet cooked in duck fat, veal jus, choux pastry. Grilled peach with lime tea.

Menu 190 €

PLAN: 1-B1 – *Gerichtstraße 54 – Ⓜ Wedding – www.ernstberlin.de – Closed Monday, Tuesday, Sunday, lunch Wednesday-Saturday*

At Berlin-Friedrichshain

Michelberger

MODERN CUISINE • BISTRO Don't be put off by the Michelberger hotel's plain façade, as the team at the eponymous restaurant takes regional organic produce and transforms it into modern, tapas-style dishes which are great for sharing. The atmosphere is appropriately hip and trendy and there's a great interior courtyard. The simpler lunchtime menu includes a "lunch tray".

Carte 15/35 €

PLAN: 1-D2 – *Warschauer Straße 39 – Ⓜ Warschauer Str. – ✆ 030 29778590 – www.michelbergerhotel.com – Closed Sunday, dinner Monday, lunch Saturday*

At Berlin-Grunewald

✿ Frühsammers Restaurant

MODERN CUISINE • FRIENDLY The menu at Frühsammers, set in its red villa in the grounds of a tennis Club, promises aromatic cuisine full of interesting textures and contrasts, and made with great care using choice produce. The setting is classically elegant, the service attentive and professional.

Specialities: Carrot medley, peanut, vanilla and herb stock. Braised pigeon, black trumpet mushrooms, green beans, pear, bay. Coffee cream, pineapple, rum, honey.

Menu 115/144 €

PLAN: 1-A3 – *Flinsberger Platz 8 – ✆ 030 89738628 – www.fruehsammers.de – Closed 1-14 January, Monday, Tuesday, Sunday, lunch Wednesday-Saturday*

Grundschlag – See restaurant listing

Grundschlag

MARKET CUISINE • COSY This is the bistro alternative to the Frühsammer's gourmet restaurant. Diners here enjoy internationally influenced cuisine and popular classics served in a snug and friendly atmosphere – don't miss the wonderful selection of sardines!

Carte 32/49 €

PLAN: 1-A3 – *Frühsammers Restaurant, Flinsberger Platz 8 – ✆ 030 89738628 – www.fruehsammers.de – Closed 1-13 January, Sonntag, mittags: Montag*

At Berlin-Kreuzberg

✿✿ Horváth (Sebastian Frank)

CREATIVE • MINIMALIST The talent and creativity of the Austrian chef Sebastian Frank are undeniable. He cooks with a very personal touch and reduces his cuisine to just a few components; the quality of the produce is excellent – totally unforgettable! The 6- or 8-course menus are paired with beautiful wines from the wine-growing regions of the former Austro-Hungarian empire. Interesting alcohol-free alternatives also available.

Specialities: Trout fillet flambé, iced chocolate cream, dill and roasted mustard seed with mustard oil. Grilled celeriac, vegetable bechamel, paprika-mint reduction, Mangalica pork cheek with tarragon and garlic foam. Creamy meringue with caraway seed, toasted black bread, iced spruce needle oil and sweet woodruff vinegar.

Menu 120/145€

PLAN: 1-D2 – *Paul-Lincke-Ufer 44a – Ⓜ Kottbusser Tor – ✆ 030 61289992 – www.restaurant-horvath.de – Closed Monday, Tuesday, lunch Wednesday-Sunday*

✿✿ Tim Raue

ASIAN • TRENDY Originality is what makes Tim Raue's cuisine so unique. He uses top-notch ingredients with great precision and successfully combines flavours, creating personal signature dishes that, as ever, feature Asian elements. There is also the option of a vegan set menu at lunch and dinner. The attentive and absolutely unpretentious service is extremely pleasant, as is the pared-down and elegant interior.

Specialities: Langoustine, wasabi, mango. Pike perch Sangohachi, sake, green radish. Quince, macadamia, nougat, passion fruit.

Menu 88€ (lunch), 188/218€

PLAN: 2-G2 – *Rudi-Dutschke-Straße 26 – Ⓜ Kochstr. – ✆ 030 25937930 – www.tim-raue.com – Closed Monday, Sunday, lunch Tuesday-Thursday*

✿ Nobelhart & Schmutzig

CREATIVE • TRENDY This 'food bar' offers its own special mix of trendy, urban chic and relaxed but professional service. The cuisine also has its own particular style, consciously eschewing any hint of luxury or chichi. The powerful and creative food is made using predominantly regional Brandenburg produce.

Specialities: Stewed cucumber, dill. Celery, egg. Blackberries, spiced fennel salad.

Menu 95/120€

PLAN: 2-G2 – *Friedrichstraße 218 – Ⓜ Kochstr. – ✆ 030 25940610 – www.nobelhartundschmutzig.com – Closed 19 July-13 August, Monday, Sunday, lunch Tuesday-Saturday*

✿ Richard

MODERN FRENCH • TRENDY Yes, this really is it, but don't be put off by the somewhat lacklustre exterior. Inside the former Köpenicker Hof, built in 1900, the fine interior boasts an ornate ceiling, designer lighting and artwork (the owner Hans Richard is also a painter). It provides the perfect setting for the excellent, artful and reasonably priced set menu.

Specialities: Braised celery with a liquorice and vegetable jus and Beurre Noisette. Pigeon with a date and nut condiment, Trevisano, beetroot and mint. Honey ice cream with macadamia nut and olive oil, rhubarb and mulberry.

Menu 68/120€

PLAN: 1-D2 – *Köpenicker Straße 174 – Ⓜ Schlesisches Tor – ✆ 030 49207242 – www.restaurant-richard.de – Closed Monday, Sunday, lunch Tuesday-Saturday*

✿ tulus lotrek (Maximilian Strohe)

MODERN CUISINE • TRENDY The USPs here are the warm and welcoming female owner and the charmingly relaxed interior with its high stuccoed ceilings, wooden floors, artwork and original wallpaper. As for the food, it's modern, sophisticated and punchy with an international bent. How about a glass of cider to wash it down?

Specialities: Scallop and sea urchin, yuzu and carrot. BBQ quail à la bergamotte. Amalfi lemon, milk and olive oil.

Menu 115/160€

PLAN: 1-D3 – *Fichtestraße 24 – Ⓜ Südstern – ✆ 030 41956687 – www.tuluslotrek.de – Closed 1-9 January, 26 June-9 July, Wednesday, Thursday, lunch Monday-Tuesday and Friday-Sunday*

Chicha

PERUVIAN • VINTAGE Bustling, loud, rustic, and just a touch "shabby"... Chicha has succeeded in creating an informal authentically South American atmosphere to complement its modern Peruvian cooking. Quality fresh products are ambitiously blended to mouthwatering effect, with dishes such as ceviche of meagre fish and Thüringer Duroc belly of pork with smoked banana featuring on the menu.

Carte 29/41€

PLAN: 3-D3 – *Friedelstraße 34 – Ⓜ Schönleinstraße – ✆ 030 62731010 – www.chicha-berlin.de – Closed Monday, Tuesday, lunch Wednesday-Sunday*

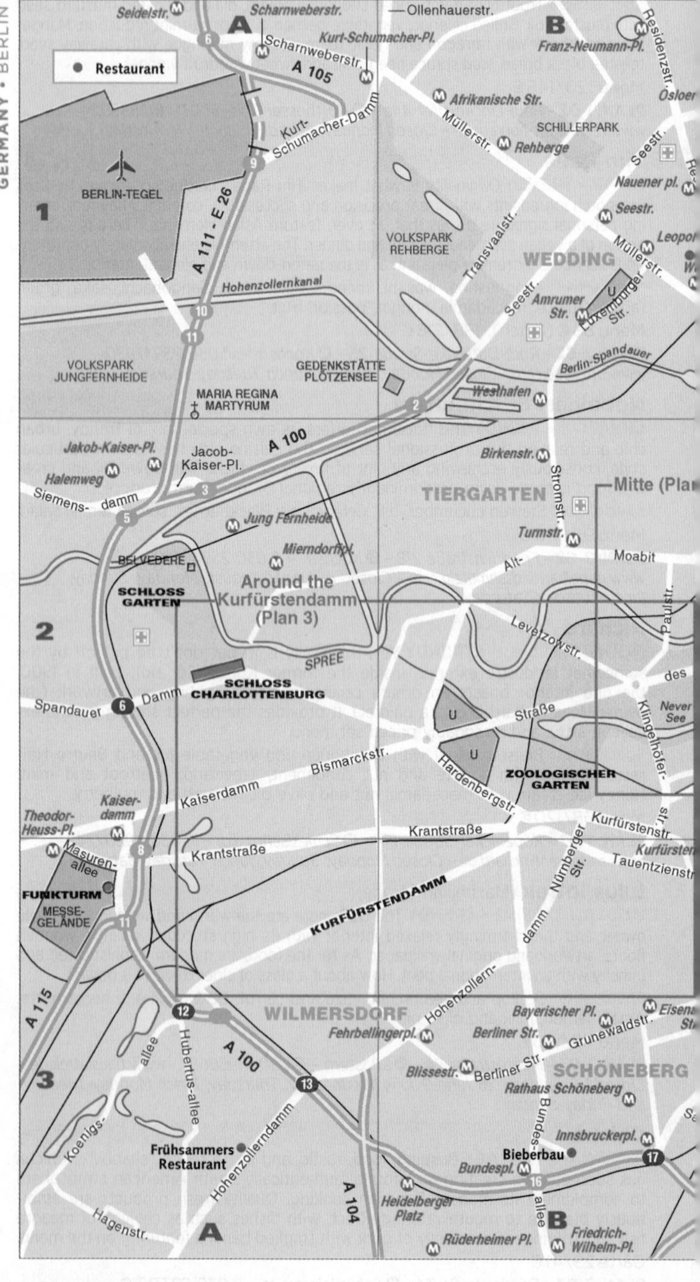

Restaurant
A
B
1
2
3
Seidelstr.
Scharnweberstr.
Ollenhauerstr.
Kurt-Schumacher-Pl.
Scharnweberstr.
A 105
Kurt-Schumacher-Damm
Franz-Neumann-Pl.
Residenzstr.
Osloer
Afrikanische Str.
Müllerstr.
Rehberge
SCHILLERPARK
Seestr.
Nauener pl.
Seestr.
Leopol
BERLIN-TEGEL
A 111 - E 26
VOLKSPARK REHBERGE
Transvaalstr.
WEDDING
Müllerstr.
Hohenzollernkanal
Seestr.
Amrumer Str.
Luxemburger Str.
U
VOLKSPARK JUNGFERNHEIDE
GEDENKSTÄTTE PLÖTZENSEE
Berlin-Spandauer
Westhafen
MARIA REGINA MARTYRUM
A 100
Jakob-Kaiser-Pl.
Jacob-Kaiser-Pl.
Birkenstr.
Halemweg
Siemens- damm
Stromstr.
TIERGARTEN
Mitte (Pla
Jung Fernheide
Turmstr.
Mierndorffpl.
BELVEDERE
Alt-
Moabit
Around the Kurfürstendamm (Plan 3)
SCHLOSS GARTEN
Levetzowstr.
Paulstr.
SPREE
SCHLOSS CHARLOTTENBURG
des
Spandauer Damm
Straße
Never See
Klingelhöfer-str.
Bismarckstr.
Hardenbergstr.
ZOOLOGISCHER GARTEN
Kaiser-damm
Kaiserdamm
Theodor-Heuss-Pl.
Krantstraße
Kurfürstenstr.
Masuren-allee
Krantstraße
Nürnberger Str.
Kurfürsten
Tauentzienstr
FUNKTURM
MESSE-GELÄNDE
KURFÜRSTENDAMM
damm
Hohenzollern-
A 115
WILMERSDORF
Bayerischer Pl.
Eisena
Fehrbellingerpl.
Berliner Str.
Grunewaldstr.
allee
Hubertus-allee
A 100
Blissestr.
Berliner Str.
SCHÖNEBERG
Rathaus Schöneberg
Koenigs-
Hohenzollerndamm
Bundes-allee
Innsbruckerpl.
Frühsammers Restaurant
Bieberbau
Bundespl.
A 104
Heidelberger Platz
Hagenstr.
Rüderheimer Pl.
Friedrich-Wilhelm-Pl.

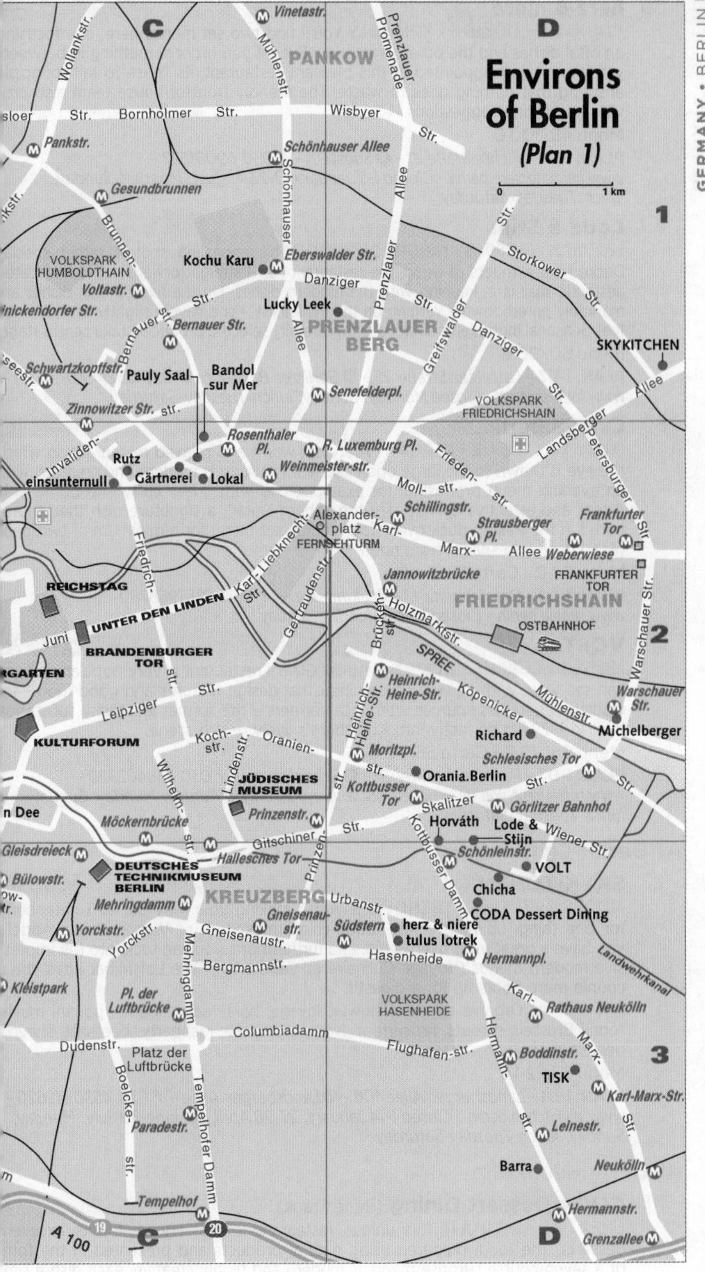
Environs of Berlin
(Plan 1)
0
1 km
C
D
1
2
3
PANKOW
PRENZLAUER BERG
FRIEDRICHSHAIN
KREUZBERG
Vinetastr.
Mühlenstr.
Prenzlauer Promenade
Wollankstr.
Bornholmer Str.
Wisbyer Str.
Pankstr.
Schönhauser Allee
Gesundbrunnen
Brunnenstr.
VOLKSPARK HUMBOLDTHAIN
Voltastr.
Kochu Karu
Eberswalder Str.
Danziger Str.
Prenzlauer Allee
Storkower Str.
Greifswalder Str.
Lucky Leek
Bernauer Str.
Schwartzkopffstr.
Pauly Saal
Bandol sur Mer
Senefelderpl.
SKYKITCHEN
Landsberger Allee
VOLKSPARK FRIEDRICHSHAIN
Zinnowitzer Str.
Invalidenstr.
Rosenthaler Pl.
R. Luxemburg Pl.
Weinmeister-str.
Rutz
Gärtnerei
Lokal
einsunternull
Friedenstr.
Petersburger Str.
Mollstr.
Schillingstr.
Strausberger Pl.
Frankfurter Tor
Alexanderplatz
FERNSEHTURM
Karl-Marx-Allee
Weberwiese
FRANKFURTER TOR
Karl-Liebknecht-Str.
Friedrichstr.
REICHSTAG
UNTER DEN LINDEN
BRANDENBURGER TOR
Gertraudenstr.
Jannowitzbrücke
Brückenstr.
Holzmarktstr.
OSTBAHNHOF
SPREE
Warschauer Str.
Leipziger Str.
Heinrich-Heine-Str.
Köpenicker Str.
Mühlenstr.
Michelberger
KULTURFORUM
Kochstr.
Oranienstr.
Lindenstr.
JÜDISCHES MUSEUM
Wilhelmstr.
Moritzpl.
Richard
Schlesisches Tor
Orania.Berlin
Kottbusser Tor
Skalitzer Str.
Görlitzer Bahnhof
Möckernbrücke
Prinzenstr.
Gitschiner Str.
Horváth
Lode & Stijn
Wiener Str.
Gleisdreieck
Hallesches Tor
Schönleinstr.
VOLT
Bülowstr.
DEUTSCHES TECHNIKMUSEUM BERLIN
Kottbusser Damm
Chicha
Mehringdamm
Urbanstr.
CODA Dessert Dining
Yorckstr.
Gneisenaustr.
Südstern
herz & niere
tulus lotrek
Bergmannstr.
Hasenheide
Hermannpl.
Landwehrkanal
Kleistpark
Pl. der Luftbrücke
VOLKSPARK HASENHEIDE
Karl-Marx-Str.
Rathaus Neukölln
Columbiadamm
Dudenstr.
Platz der Luftbrücke
Flughafen-str.
Hermannstr.
Boddinstr.
TISK
Boelckestr.
Tempelhofer Damm
Paradestr.
Leinestr.
Barra
Neukölln
Tempelhof
Hermannstr.
A 100
19
20
Grenzallee

herz & niere

COUNTRY COOKING • FRIENDLY You'll find two set menus here: one focusin on offal dishes and the other vegetarian. Even if you order something in betweer you won't be disappointed at this pleasant restaurant, its "nose to tail" principl ensuring that nothing goes to waste. The friendly front-of-house team also pro vide good wine suggestions.

Menu 48/100€

PLAN: 1-D3 – *Fichtestraße 31 – Südstern – 030 69001522 – www.herzundniere.berlin – Closed 1-9 January, 9-23 August, Monday, Sunday, lunch Tuesday-Saturday*

Lode & Stijn

MODERN CUISINE • NEIGHBOURHOOD This appealing spot is rather specia Decked out with lots of wood, the restaurant has a straightforward yet sophisticate aesthetic that is in keeping with the modern dishes. On the fixed menu, dishes ar markedly pared down – verging on the minimalist – and have a slightly Scandinavia feel. Seasonal ingredients sourced from carefully selected producers take centre stage

Menu 60/90€

PLAN: 1-D3 – *Lausitzer Straße 25 – Görlitzer Bahnhof – 030 65214507 – www.lode-stijn.de – Closed Monday, Sunday, lunch Tuesday-Saturday*

Orania.Berlin

MODERN CUISINE • ELEGANT A stylish, warm and relaxed restaurant, in whic the eye is drawn to the large open kitchen. The food is modern and creative, wit an evening menu proposing, for example, cod with green curry and burnt leel Adept and attentive service. Try the "Xberg Duck", a signature dish that is pre pared in the Peking duck oven (four-course set menu for a minimum of two peo ple). Lunch and snacks from noon.

Menu 54€ – Carte 58/64€

PLAN: 1-D2 – *Oranienplatz 17 – Moritzplatz – 030 6953968780 – www.orania.berlin – Closed lunch Monday-Sunday*

VOLT

MODERN CUISINE • DESIGN Matthias Gleiß's restaurant is very popular and yo can see why. With its well-chosen industrial design features and good food – in cluding vegetables sourced from local farmers – this former electricity substatio built in 1928 fits perfectly into Kreuzberg's lively gastro scene.

Menu 68/79€ – Carte 56/72€

PLAN: 1-D3 – *Paul-Lincke-Ufer 21 – Schönleinstr. – 030 338402320 – www.restaurant-volt.de – Closed 1-8 January, 20 July-9 August, Monday, Sunday, lunch Tuesday-Saturday*

At Berlin-Lichtenberg

SKYKITCHEN

MODERN CUISINE • TRENDY It is worth making your way out to Lichtenberg for one thing, up here in the urban-chic atmosphere of Vienna House Andel' you have a great view over Berlin, and furthermore, you can tuck into the impres sive modern menus (Voyage Culinaire or Vegetarian). The Loft14 bar lures you couple more floors up for a digestif.

Specialities: Organic egg, cauliflower, lovage, horseradish. Game, porcini mush room, Brussels sprouts, redcurrant. Ivoire chocolate, raspberry, beetroot, sheep' milk yoghurt.

Menu 67/124€

PLAN: 1-D1 – *Landsberger Allee 106 – Landsberger Allee – 030 4530532620 – www.skykitchen.berlin – Closed 1-14 January, 23-28 April, 29 June-30 July, Monday, Sunday, lunch Tuesday-Saturday*

At Berlin-Neukölln

CODA Dessert Dining (René Frank)

CREATIVE • INTIMATE This unique restaurant is best known for its exceller desserts. The food, prepared using natural products and presented in the forn of a seven-course surprise menu, is modern and highly creative, each dish a sim ple yet successful combination of contrasting flavours and aromas. There's als an extremely well-balanced selection of drinks, including sake, cocktails and wine

Specialities: Nacional cacao, chicory, hazelnut, purple carrot. Watermelon, nori alga, Taggiasca olive. Aubergine, pecan, apple balsamic vinegar, liquorice salt.

Menu 58/148 €

PLAN: 1-D3 – *Friedelstraße 47* – *Ⓜ Hermannplatz* – *✆ 030 91496396* – *www.coda-berlin.com* – *Closed 20 January-5 February, Monday, Wednesday, Sunday, lunch Tuesday and Thursday-Saturday*

Barra

CREATIVE • MINIMALIST A thoroughly straightforward, trendy concept, from the minimalist urban look to the relaxed, pleasantly neighbourly atmosphere through to the nicely pared-down and modern food served in the form of small "sharing" dishes. Sourced in the region as far as possible, the high-quality ingredients are transformed into such delights as rainbow trout with raspberry and coriander.

Carte 34/47 €

PLAN: 1-D3 – *Okerstraße 2* – *Ⓜ Leinestraße* – *✆ 030 81860757* – *www.barraberlin.com* – *Closed Tuesday, Wednesday, lunch Monday and Thursday-Sunday*

TISK

GERMAN • FRIENDLY Situated in a quiet side street of Neukölln, TISK (old German for table) calls itself a Speisekneipe (food pub) – and the description works well. It offers a young, urban ambience and modern German cuisine with pepped-up flavours. Options include set menus (e.g. with meatballs or knuckle of lamb) and roast chicken for two people.

Menu 39/59 € – Carte 35/39 €

PLAN: 1-D3 – *Neckarstraße 12* – *Ⓜ Boddiner Str.* – *✆ 030 398200000* – *www.tisk-speisekneipe.de* – *Closed Monday, Sunday, lunch Tuesday-Saturday*

At Berlin-Prenzlauer Berg

Kochu Karu

KOREAN • MINIMALIST This pretty little minimalist-style restaurant combines the best of Spain and Korea with passion to create ambitious, flavoursome tapas such as mackerel adobo with barley and apricots and chicory with buckwheat and wild orange. Main dishes include options such as beef ribs with red cabbage kimchi, ginko nuts and sherry jus.

Menu 37/59 € – Carte 28/49 €

PLAN: 1-C1 – *Eberswalder Straße 35* – *Ⓜ Eberswalder Str.* – *✆ 030 80938191* – *www.kochukaru.de* – *Closed 1-9 January, Monday, Sunday*

Lucky Leek 

VEGAN • NEIGHBOURHOOD Lucky Leek is a genuinely modern restaurant with a friendly, personal note. Josita Hartanto cooks vegan cuisine including vegetable consommé with potato and cress ravioli, pear and chilli risotto with tandoori cabbage and nori tempeh rolls.

Menu 37/59 €

PLAN: 1-D1 – *Kollwitzstraße 54* – *Ⓜ Senefelderplatz* – *✆ 030 66408710* – *www.lucky-leek.com* – *Closed Monday, Tuesday, lunch Wednesday-Sunday*

At Berlin-Wilmersdorf

Pastis Wilmersdorf 

CLASSIC FRENCH • BRASSERIE This authentic "brasserie française" is fully deserving of its popularity with diners. Here fresh, quality ingredients are used to prepare delicious dishes: be sure to try, for example, the monkfish with mussels, green asparagus and artichokes. The lively, exuberant atmosphere and friendly service (as exemplified by the charming owner) seal the deal.

Menu 36/90 € – Carte 35/65 €

Off plan – *Rüdesheimer Straße 9* – *Ⓜ Rüdesheimer Platz* – *✆ 030 81055769* – *www.restaurant-pastis.de*

HAMBURG
HAMBURG

ponomarevvb/iStock

HAMBURG IN...

→ **ONE DAY**
Boat trip from Landungsbrücken, Speicherstadt, Kunsthalle, Fishmarket (Sunday morning). Elbphilharmonie

→ **TWO DAYS**
Steamboat on the Alster, Hamburg History Museum, St Pauli by night.

→ **THREE DAYS**
Arts and Crafts Museum, canal trip, concert at Musikhalle.

With a maritime role stretching back centuries, Germany's second largest city has a lively and liberal ambience. Hamburg is often described as 'The Gateway to the World', and there's certainly a visceral feel here, particularly around the big, buzzy and bustling port area. Locals enjoy a long-held reputation for their tolerance and outward looking stance, cosmopolitan to the core. Space to breathe is seen as very important in Hamburg: the city authorities have paid much attention to green spaces, and the city can proudly claim an enviable amount of parks, lakes and tree-lined canals.

There's no cathedral here (at least not a standing one, as war-destroyed St Nikolai remains a ruin), so the Town Hall acts as the central landmark. Just north of here are the Binnenalster (inner) and Aussenalster (outer) lakes. The old walls of the city, dating back over eight hundred years, are delineated by a distinct semicircle of boulevards that curve attractively in a wide arc south of the lakes. Further south from here is the port and harbour area, defined by Landungsbrücken to the west and Speicherstadt to the east. The district to the west of the centre is St Pauli, famed for its clubs and bars, particularly along the notorious Reeperbahn, which pierces the district from east to west. The contrastingly smart Altona suburb and delightful Blankenese village are west of St Pauli.

EATING OUT

Being a city immersed in water, it's no surprise to find Hamburg is a good place for fish. Though its fishing industry isn't the powerhouse of old, the city still boasts a giant trawler's worth of seafood places to eat. Eel dishes are mainstays of the traditional restaurant's menu, as is the herring stew with vegetables called Labskaus. Also unsurprisingly, considering it's the country's gateway to the world, this is somewhere that offers a vast range of international dishes. Wherever you eat, the portions are likely to be generous. There's no problem with finding somewhere early: cafés are often open at seven, with the belief that it's never too early for coffee and cake. Bakeries also believe in an early start, and the calorie content here, too, can be pretty high. Bistros and restaurants, usually open by midday, are proud of their local ingredients, so keep your eyes open for Hamburgisch on the menu. Service charges are always included in the bill, so tipping is not compulsory, although most people will round it up and possibly add five to ten per cent.

Centre

✿✿✿ The Table Kevin Fehling

CREATIVE • DESIGN This relaxed restaurant really is one of a kind! Diners sit a a long, curved table as the chefs – a study of concentration – combine fine inter national ingredients to perfection before their eyes with the precision, subtlet and stunning presentation for which Kevin Fehling is famed. Excellent wine re commendations.

Specialities: Fjord trout marinated in Indian spices, tandoori, mango, mustar seeds and coconut stock. Saddle of venison with a walnut pepper crust, fermen ted blueberries, sherry vinegar hollandaise and rosemary jus. Hazelnut crémeux calamansi jelly, guava, banana curry ice cream, turmeric.

Menu 220€

PLAN: 1-C2 – *Shanghaiallee 15 – Ⓜ HafenCity Universität – ✆ 040 22867422 – www.the-table-hamburg.de – Closed 1-7 January, 12-20 April, 12 July-3 August, 20-31 December, Monday, Sunday, lunch Tuesday-Saturday*

✿✿ bianc (Matteo Ferrantino)

CREATIVE • DESIGN Mediterranean cuisine in a modern and creative style – thi is the approach adopted by Matteo Ferrantino whose personal signature dishe reveal both his talent and his vast experience. Located among the office building in the harbourside HafenCity district, the restaurant's piazza ambience designe by Julia Erdmann provides an elegant setting in which to enjoy superb cuisine.

Specialities: Scallop, celery, Amalfi lemon, Imperial caviar. Iberico-Secreto, blu mussel, pearl onion, Dijon mustard. Caramelia chocolate, mascarpone, fig, vanilla

Menu 125/175€

PLAN: 1-C3 – *Am Sandtorkai 50 – Ⓜ Überseequartier – ✆ 040 18119797 – www.bianc.de – Closed 7-23 January, 4-25 August, Monday, Sunday, lunch Tuesday-Saturday*

✿✿ Haerlin

CREATIVE FRENCH • LUXURY The food at Haerlin is powerful and intensely fla voured. The dishes brought to your table are creative and technically perfect, an use nothing but the very best ingredients. The culinary quality is matched by th exquisite interior where everything is of the finest quality. The view over the In ner Alster Lake adds the finishing touch.

Specialities: Turbot with celery, bergamot and spicy Chorizo vinaigrette. Limou sin lamb with zucchini, green olive sauce and braised lamb praline. Blueberry wit quark ice cream, macadamia nut, creamed chervil and Cru Virunga chocolate.

Menu 155/215€

PLAN: 2-F2 – *Fairmont Hotel Vier Jahreszeiten, Neuer Jungfernstieg 9 – Ⓜ Jungfernstieg – ✆ 040 34943310 – www.restaurant-haerlin.de – Closed 1-6 January 1-9 March, 12 July-10 August, 11-19 October, Monday, Sunday, lunch Tuesday-Saturday*

✿ SE7EN OCEANS

CLASSIC FRENCH • CHIC Ideal for escaping the crowds, this modern eatery ha a great view of the Inner Alster Lake and the Jungfernstieg promenade. It offer peace and quiet in the midst of the Europa Passage shopping centre and serve classic international cuisine. The glass front opens up in the summer.

Specialities: Markklößchen soup, lovage, roast chicken fat. Guinea fowl, Tom Kh Gai, tomato, shiitake. Peanut, caramel, salt.

Menu 56€ (lunch), 69/148€ – Carte 74/94€

PLAN: 2-G2 – *Ballindamm 40 – Ⓜ Jungfernstieg – ✆ 040 32507944 – www.se7en-oceans.de – Closed 10-23 February, 10-23 August, Monday, Sunday*

Die Gute Botschaft

REGIONAL CUISINE • TRENDY There is a lively and informal atmosphere here in the former US Consulate General. Guests have a direct view of the kitchen as it is completely open and virtually part of the restaurant. The service is quick and efficient – it is quite clear that professionals are at work here. The dishes are a mix of regional cuisine and Japanese creations. The Omakase menu is highly recommended.

Menu 63€ – Carte 28/81€

PLAN: 2-G1 – *Alsterufer 3 – Ⓜ Dammtor – ✆ 040 28410014 – www.dgb.hamburg – Closed Sunday, dinner Monday-Tuesday, lunch Saturday*

DIE BANK

INTERNATIONAL • BRASSERIE This brasserie and bar is a fashionable venue and one of the city's hotspots. A former bank, it was built in 1897, and its first floor banking hall is an impressive feature.

Menu 29€ (lunch), 65/74€ – Carte 48/72€

PLAN: 2-F2 – *Hohe Bleichen 17 – Ⓜ Gänsemarkt – ✆ 040 2380030 – www.diebank-brasserie.de – Closed Sunday*

Basil & Mars

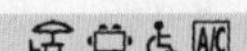

MODERN CUISINE • TRENDY The restaurant close to the Kennedy Bridge is chic and fashionable but also pleasantly relaxed. The food prepared in the open kitchens has Mediterranean and Asian influences: calamaretti from the grill; salmon fillet with sesame spinach and yakitori sauce; US Black Angus steak... Tip: the six-course "Chef's Choice" menu. A simpler lunch menu is served Mon-Fri.

Menu 18€ (lunch)/47€ – Carte 36/85€

PLAN: 2-G1 – *Alsterufer 1 – Ⓜ Dammtor – ✆ 040 41353535 – www.basilundmars.com – Closed Sunday, lunch Saturday*

Bootshaus Bar & Grill

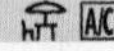

MEATS AND GRILLS • CONTEMPORARY DÉCOR The Bootshaus is situated right in the heart of Hamburg's HafenCity district. Sit in the comfortable "Boot" (boat) dining room with a view of the open-plan kitchen or, if you prefer, look out over the Grasbrookhafen marina from the light and airy bar area. The Josper meat grill is the focus here, serving "New York Strip" and "Rib Eye" just how you like it! Good choice of side-orders and delicious sauces.

Carte 33/84€

PLAN: 1-C3 – *Am Kaiserkai 19 – Ⓜ Überseequartier – ✆ 040 33473744 – www.bootshaus-hafencity.de – Closed Monday, Sunday, lunch Tuesday-Saturday*

Brook

INTERNATIONAL • BISTRO The most popular dishes at this relaxed modern restaurant include classics such as braised calves' cheeks, but fish fresh from the famous fish market just round the corner are also firm favourites, as is the very reasonable set lunchtime menu. It is worth coming here in the evenings too, when you can enjoy views of the illuminated warehouse district.

Menu 19€ (lunch), 39/43€ – Carte 16/56€

PLAN: 2-G3 – *Bei den Mühren 91 – Ⓜ Meßberg – ✆ 040 37503128 – www.restaurant-brook.de – Closed Monday, Sunday*

Butcher's american steakhouse

MEATS AND GRILLS • FAMILY At Butcher's american steakhouse you can enjoy fine Nebraska beef that the chef presents to the table personally. The cosy restaurant is dominated by dark wood and warm colours.

Carte 71/173€

PLAN: 1-C2 – *Milchstraße 19 – Ⓜ Hallerstraße – ✆ 040 446082 – www.butchers-steakhouse.de – Closed Sunday, lunch Saturday*

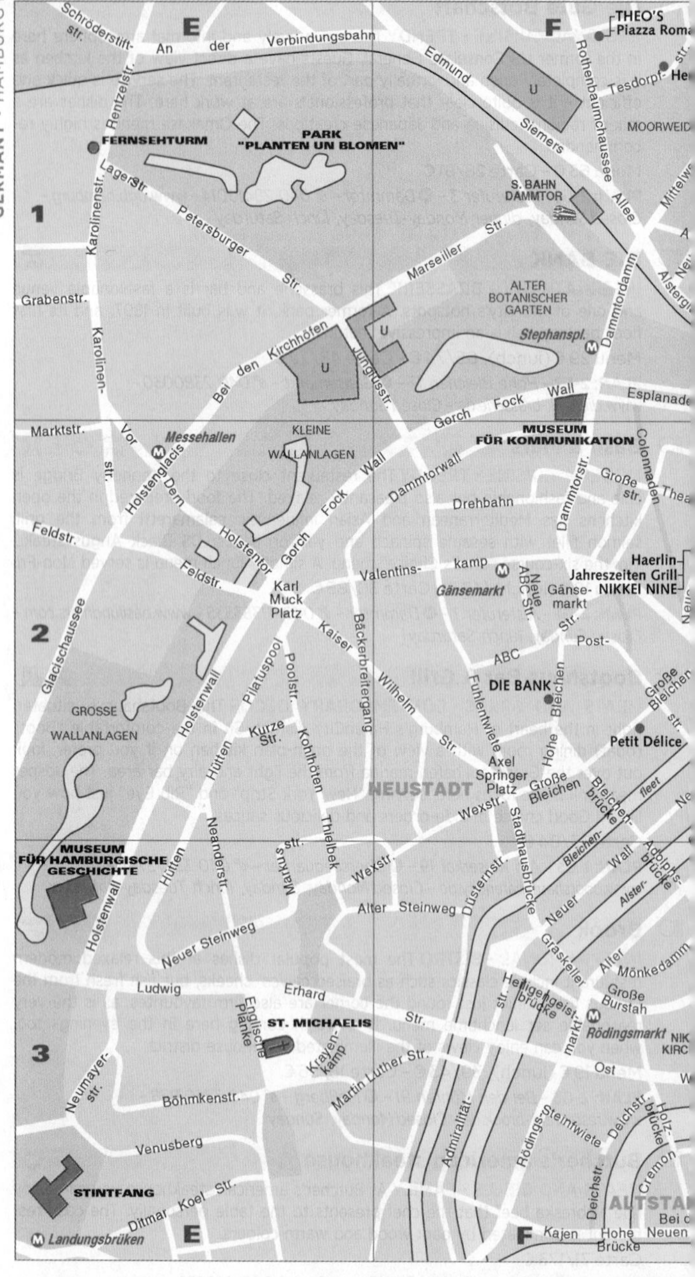
E
F
1
2
3
THEO'S
Piazza Roma
FERNSEHTURM
PARK
"PLANTEN UN BLOMEN"
S. BAHN
DAMMTOR
ALTER
BOTANISCHER
GARTEN
Stephanspl.
MOORWEIDE
Schröderstift-str.
An der Verbindungsbahn
Edmund Siemers Allee
Rothenbaumchaussee
Tesdorpf-str.
Rentzelstr.
Lagerstr.
Karolinenstr.
Petersburger Str.
Marseiller Str.
Grabenstr.
Karolinen-
Bei den Kirchhöfen
Jungiusstr.
Dammtordamm
Esplanade
Gorch Fock Wall
MUSEUM
FÜR KOMMUNIKATION
Marktstr.
Vor
Messehallen
KLEINE
WALLANLAGEN
Holstenglacis
Dammtorwall
Dammtorstr.
Große Theaterstr.
Colonnaden
Drehbahn
Feldstr.
Holstentor
Valentinskamp
Gänsemarkt
Neue ABC Str.
Haerlin
Jahreszeiten Grill
NIKKEI NINE
Karl
Muck
Platz
Kaiser Wilhelm Str.
Bäckerbreitergang
Poolstr.
Pilatuspool
Post-Str.
ABC
Glacischaussee
Holstenwall
DIE BANK
Fuhlentwiete
Bleichen
Große Bleichen
Petit Délice
GROSSE
WALLANLAGEN
Kurze Str.
Kohlhöfen
Hütten
Axel Springer Platz
NEUSTADT
Bleichenbrücke
Neanderstr.
Thielbek
Wexstr.
Stadthausbrücke
MUSEUM
FÜR HAMBURGISCHE
GESCHICHTE
Markusstr.
Düsternstr.
Neuer Wall
Alsterfleet
Adolphsbrücke
Alter Steinweg
Neuer Steinweg
Graskeller
Alter Mönkedamm
Ludwig Erhard Str.
Heiligengeistbrücke
Große Burstah
Englische Planke
ST. MICHAELIS
Rödingsmarkt
Krayenkamp
Martin Luther Str.
Ost-West-Str.
Neumayerstr.
Böhmkenstr.
Admiralität-str.
Rödingsmarkt
Steinfwiete
Deichstr.
Holzbrücke
Cremon
Venusberg
STINTFANG
Ditmar Koel Str.
ALTSTADT
Landungsbrüken
Kajen
Hohe Brücke
Bei den Neuen

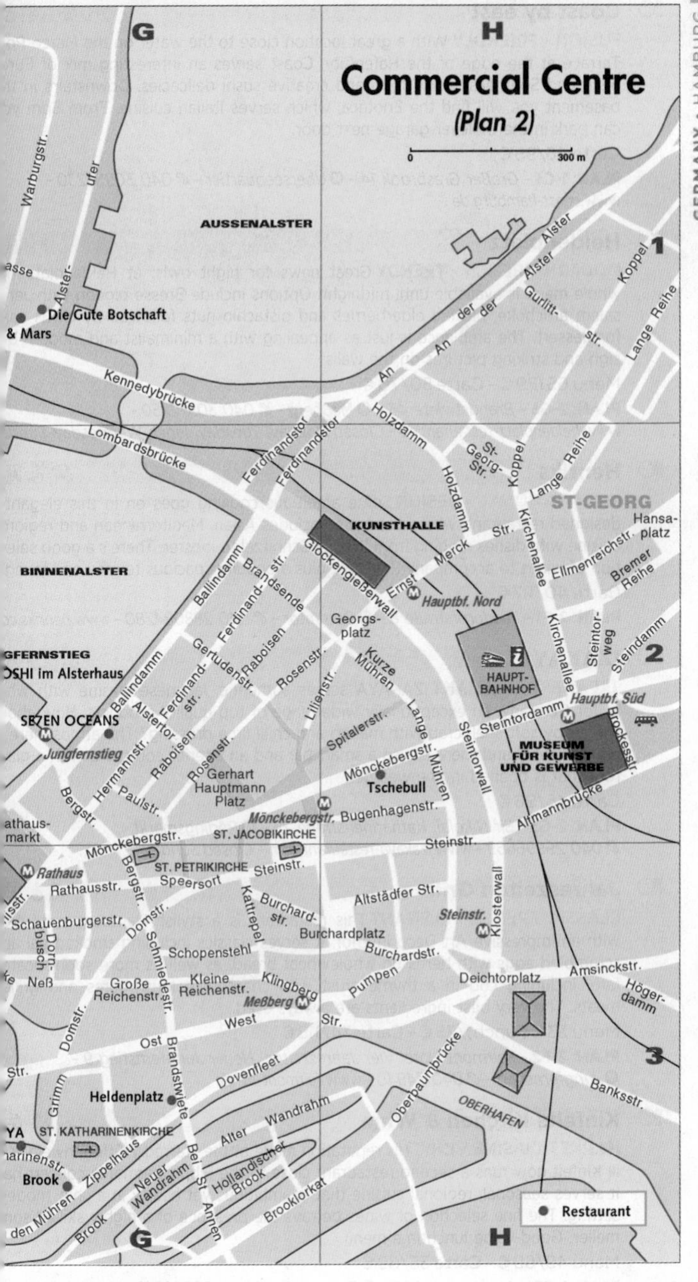
Commercial Centre
(Plan 2)
0
300 m
G
H
1
2
3
AUSSENALSTER
BINNENALSTER
KUNSTHALLE
ST-GEORG
HAUPT-
BAHNHOF
MUSEUM
FÜR KUNST
UND GEWERBE
OBERHAFEN
Die Gute Botschaft
& Mars
SEVEN OCEANS
Tschebull
Heldenplatz
Brook
Restaurant
Warburgstr.
Alster-
ufer
Kennedybrücke
Lombardsbrücke
Ferdinandstor
An der Alster
Holzdamm
St-Georg-Str.
Koppel
Lange Reihe
Gurlitt-str.
Hansa-
platz
Ellmenreichstr.
Bremer
Reihe
Kirchenallee
Steintor-
weg
Steindamm
Ernst Merck Str.
Hauptbf. Nord
Hauptbf. Süd
Steintordamm
Brockesstr.
Glockengießerwall
Ballindamm
Brandsende
Ferdinand-str.
Georgs-
platz
Gertudenstr.
Raboisen
Rosenstr.
Lilienstr.
Kurze Mühren
Lange Mühren
Spitalerstr.
Steintorwall
Alstertor
Hermannstr.
Jungfernstieg
Paulstr.
Bergstr.
Gerhart
Hauptmann
Platz
Mönckebergstr.
Bugenhagenstr.
Altmannbrücke
Steinstr.
ST. JACOBIKIRCHE
ST. PETRIKIRCHE
Rathaus
Rathausstr.
Speersort
Kattrepel
Burchard-str.
Altstädter Str.
Steinstr.
Klosterwall
Burchardplatz
Burchardstr.
Schauenburgerstr.
Domstr.
Schmiedestr.
Dorn-
busch
Schopenstehl
Neß
Große
Reichenstr.
Kleine
Reichenstr.
Klingberg
Meßberg
Pumpen
Deichtorplatz
Amsinckstr.
Höger-
damm
Ost West Str.
Brandstwiete
Dovenfleet
Oberbaumbrücke
Banksstr.
Grimm
ST. KATHARINENKIRCHE
Alter Wandrahm
Zippelhaus
Neuer Wandrahm
Holländischer Brook
Bei St. Annen
Brooklorkai
den Mühren

Coast by east

FUSION • FRIENDLY With a great location close to the water on the Marco Po Terrace at the edge of the HafenCity, Coast serves an interesting mix of Eur pean and Southeast Asian food and creative sushi delicacies. Downstairs in th basement you will find the Enoteca, which serves Italian cuisine. From 6pm yo can park in the Unilever garage next door.

Carte 46/95€

PLAN: 1-C3 – *Großer Grasbrook 14 – Ⓜ Überseequartier – ✆ 040 30993230 – www.coast-hamburg.de*

Heldenplatz

MODERN FRENCH • TRENDY Great news for night owls: at Heldenplatz th whole menu is available until midnight! Options include Bresse pigeon with Jeru salem artichoke, pickled elderberries and pistachio nuts followed by citrus cak for dessert. The ambience is just as appealing with a minimalist and modern de sign and striking pictures on the walls.

Menu 65/79€ – Carte 50/70€

PLAN: 2-G3 – *Brandstwiete 46 – Ⓜ Meßberg – ✆ 040 30372250 – www.heldenplatz-restaurant.de – Closed Monday, Tuesday, lunch Wednesday-Sunda*

Henriks

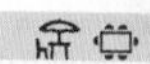

INTERNATIONAL • DESIGN Some ambitious cooking goes on in this elegantl designed restaurant, where the menu includes Asian, Mediterranean and regiona cuisine with dishes ranging from Wiener Schnitzel to lobster. There's a good selec tion of wines to accompany the food, plus a popular spacious terrace and lounge

Carte 40/117€

PLAN: 2-F1 – *Tesdorpfstraße 8 – Ⓜ Dammtor – ✆ 040 288084280 – www.henriks.cc*

IZAKAYA

JAPANESE • ELEGANT IZAKAYA serves authentic Japanese cuisine with wha is, for Germany, an exceptionally wide range of top-quality products. How abou the crispy soft-shell crab with mango and chilli lime dressing? The atmosphere i hip and lively and there is also a smart bar and an interior courtyard with a glas roof that is opened in fine weather.

Carte 45/96€

PLAN: 2-G3 – *Sir Nikolai, Katharinenstraße 29 – Ⓜ Rödingsmarkt – ✆ 040 29996669 – www.izakaya-restaurant.com – Closed Sunday*

Jahreszeiten Grill

CLASSIC FRENCH • ELEGANT This restaurant is a stylish Hamburg institutior with an impressive Art Deco interior. It serves classics including smoked eel anc scrambled eggs with herbs on wholewheat bread, as well as more sophisticatec fare, including cod in a thyme crust with chanterelle mushrooms and grillec meats. The very best ingredients are always used.

Menu 33€ (lunch)/75€ – Carte 74/118€

PLAN: 2-F2 – *Fairmont Hotel Vier Jahreszeiten, Neuer Jungfernstieg 9 – Ⓜ Jungfernstieg – ✆ 040 34940 – www.fairmont-hvj.de*

Kinfelts Kitchen & Wine

MARKET CUISINE • CHIC His reputation made at the starred Trüffelschwein, Kirill Kinfelt now runs a second restaurant close to the Elbphilharmonie concert hall. It serves seasonal, regional cuisine that is ambitious yet hearty in a chic, modern setting. The fine selection of wines betrays the presence of a highly skilled sommelier. Good-value lunchtime menu.

Menu 49/69€ – Carte 35/69€

PLAN: 1-C3 – *Am Kaiserkai 56 – Ⓜ Baumwall – ✆ 040 30068369 – www.kinfelts.de – Closed 1-5 January, Monday, lunch Tuesday-Saturday*

NIKKEI NINE

JAPANESE • CHIC This is one of the most fashionable culinary hotspots in Hamburg! The ambience is stylish yet warm and the food is Japanese with Peruvian influences. Menu options include seafood toban yaki, cold soba noodles with egg, caviar and dashi soy, wagyu steak, sushi and sashimi – all made with first-class ingredients.

Menu 32 € (lunch)/89 € – Carte 47/185 €

PLAN: 2-F2 – *Fairmont Hotel Vier Jahreszeiten, Neuer Jungfernstieg 9* – Ⓜ *Jungfernstieg* – ✆ *040 34943399* – *www.nikkei-nine.de*

Petit Délice

CLASSIC FRENCH • NEIGHBOURHOOD In the chic, centrally located Galleria shopping arcade, the Henssler brothers (whose father ran the show from the 1980s) ensure that the younger generation continues to provide attentive service and classic, no-frills cuisine, such as turbot with pea puree and champagne sauce. The terrace overlooking the canal is delightful!

Menu 60/90 € – Carte 45/81 €

PLAN: 2-F2 – *Große Bleichen 21* – Ⓜ *Jungfernstieg* – ✆ *040 343470* – *www.petit-delice-hamburg.de* – *Closed Sunday*

STRAUCHS FALCO

INTERNATIONAL • TRENDY Strauchs Falco serves a wide range of good Mediterranean dishes, steaks and classic fare. The restaurant itself is modern in style with an open kitchen and a large terrace in summer. The tapas bar on the first floor doubles up as a café during the day.

Carte 27/86 €

PLAN: 1-C3 – *Koreastraße 2* – Ⓜ *HafenCity Universität* – ✆ *040 226161511* – *www.falco-hamburg.de*

Tschebull

AUSTRIAN • CONTEMPORARY DÉCOR In the centre of this exclusive shopping arcade sits a little piece of Austria, courtesy of Carinthian chef Alexander Tschebull. As you would expect, the Austrian classics, such as Tafelspitz (Viennese-style boiled beef) and Fiaker (beef) goulash are excellent, as are the more modern dishes. These include skrei cod with potato and caper champ, radish and pearl onions.

Menu 50/60 € – Carte 42/79 €

PLAN: 2-H2 – *Mönckebergstraße 7* – ✆ *040 32964796* – *www.tschebull.de* – *Closed Sunday*

YOSHI im Alsterhaus

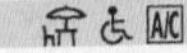

JAPANESE • FRIENDLY Christened 'Gourmet Boulevard', the fourth floor of Hamburg's upmarket Alsterhaus shopping plaza is the meeting place for enthusiasts of Japanese food and culture. The teriyaki and sushi dishes prepared by the Japanese chefs achieve a perfect marriage of the traditional and the modern. Popular roof terrace.

Menu 28 € (lunch), 48/98 € – Carte 36/113 €

PLAN: 2-G2 – *Jungfernstieg 16* – Ⓜ *Jungfernstieg* – ✆ *040 36099999* – *www.yoshi-hamburg.de* – *Closed Sunday*

Environs of Hamburg

At Hamburg-Altona

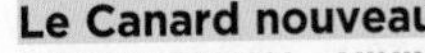

Le Canard nouveau

INTERNATIONAL • MINIMALIST A new team is at work in this restaurant, which reopened with a sleek new design after closing due to a fire. You can take in great views of the harbour (the terrace is a must!) while tucking into precise and creative dishes. The focus here is on excellent produce, successfully complemented with plenty of herbs and essences.

Environs of Hamburg

(Plan 1)

A
B
1
2
3
STELLINGEN
Kieler
Koppel-
str.
Hagenbecks Tierpark
Julius
Str.
Vosseler
Str.
Hoheluft
Gärtnerstr.
Zipa
Lutterothstr.
Müggenkampstr.
Heimatjuwel
Osterstr.
Osterstr.
Osterstr.
Im Gehölz
Bund
EIMSBÜTTEL
Schnackenburgallee
VOLKSPARK
A 7-E 45
Schnackenburgallee
Holstenkamp
BAHRENFELD
Emilienstr.
Frucht-
allee
Christskirche
Doormanns-
weg
Witwenball
Kieler
Str.
Rach & Ritchy
Leunastr.
Sternschan
Alsen-
str.
Altonaer
Bahrenfelder
Chaussee
Stresemannstr.
Stresemannstr.
Schanzen
Holstenstr.
Allee
ph
Fel
Pfitznerstr.
Daimlerstr.
Friedensallee
Barner
Str.
Julius
Leber Str.
Brauer
Nil
Budap
ST-
PAULI
Holstenstr.
HACO
Behringstr.
Hohenzollernring
Behringstr.
Max
ALTONA
Louise
Schroeder
Str.
Simon von
Utrecht St
Reeperbah
OTHMARSCHEN
Zur Flottbeker
Schmiede
NORDDEUTSCHES
LANDESMUSEUM
Ehrenberg-
str.
Königstr.
Königstr.
Clouds-Hea
Bar & Kite
Palmaille
Breite Str.
St Pauli
Fischmarkt
Elbchaussee
Elbchaussee
Harbour and
Altona (Plan 3)
ELBE
A 7-E 45
Süderelbe
0
1 km
A
B

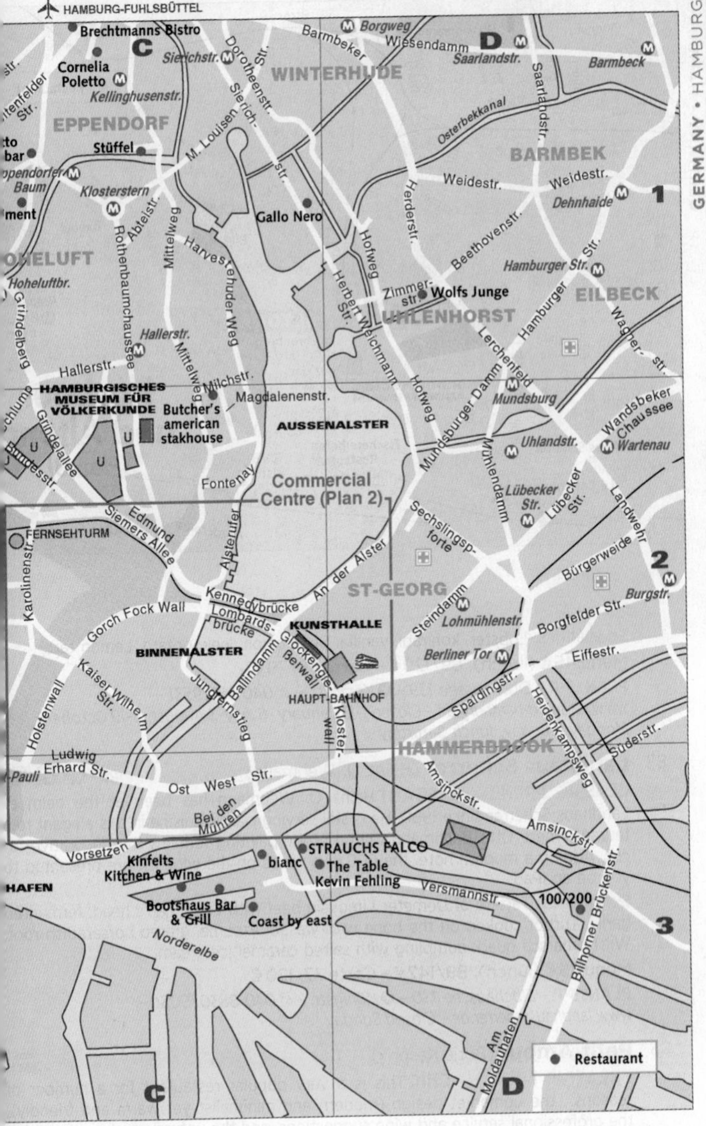
HAMBURG-FUHLSBÜTTEL
Brechtmanns Bistro
Cornelia Poletto
Stüffel
Gallo Nero
Wolfs Junge
EPPENDORF
WINTERHUDE
BARMBEK
UHLENHORST
EILBECK
HOHELUFT
HAMBURGISCHES MUSEUM FÜR VÖLKERKUNDE
Butcher's american stakhouse
AUSSENALSTER
Commercial Centre (Plan 2)
FERNSEHTURM
ST-GEORG
KUNSTHALLE
BINNENALSTER
HAUPT-BAHNHOF
HAMMERBROOK
STRAUCHS FALCO
bianc
The Table Kevin Fehling
Kinfelts Kitchen & Wine
Bootshaus Bar & Grill
Coast by east
100/200
HAFEN
Norderelbe
Restaurant

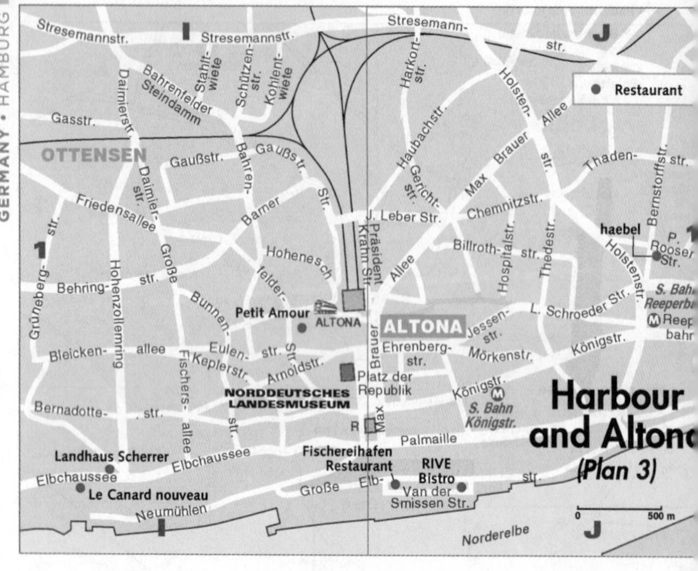

Specialities: Lobster, kohlrabi, vanilla. Beef, onion, leek, potato. Lemon tart.

Menu 45€ (lunch), 89/129€ - Carte 66/79€

PLAN: 3-I1 - *Elbchaussee 139* - *Königstr.* - *040 88129531* - *www.lecanard-hamburg.de* - *Closed 1-13 January, 6 July-3 August, 3-19 October, Monday, Sunday, lunch Saturday*

Landhaus Scherrer (Heinz O. Wehmann)

CLASSIC FRENCH • ELEGANT Heinz O. Wehmann has been at the helm Landhaus Scherrer since 1980. He is still serving classic cuisine in this elegant re taurant where Otto Bachmann's large erotic painting remains the decorative f cus. Adding a modern note, the 600 plus wines on the wine list are presented you on an iPad.

Specialities: Tartare of Demeter Limousin beef with cured calf's head, fermente garlic. Turbot cooked on the bone with wasabi espuma, grated horseradish roc Wilstermarsch quark dumpling with salted caramel ice cream.

Menu 75€ (lunch), 89/142€ - Carte 77/120€

PLAN: 3-I1 - *Elbchaussee 130* - *Königstr.* - *040 883070030* - *www.landhausscherrer.de* - *Closed Sunday*

Petit Amour (Boris Kasprik)

CREATIVE FRENCH • CHIC This is a very popular restaurant for a number reasons... the upmarket design (modern and minimalist yet warm and friendly the professional service and wine suggestions, and the unfussy, ambitious cuisi with international influences.

Specialities: Terrine of Foie Gras with dates, sea buckthorn and salted lemo Pastilla of pigeon with cherries, pine nuts and liquorice. Iced port wine fig, pist chio ganache and Fromage Blanc.

Menu 149/199€

PLAN: 3-I1 - *Spritzenplatz 11* - *Altona* - *040 30746556* - *www.petitamour-hh.com* - *Closed 13-27 January, Monday, Tuesday, Sunday, lunch Wednesday-Saturday*

Fischereihafen Restaurant

SEAFOOD • CLASSIC DÉCOR This fish restaurant overlooking the port is a veritable Hamburg institution. The service is excellent, as is the great value lunchtime menu.

Menu 25 € (lunch), 46/75 € – Carte 42/118 €

PLAN: 3-J1 – *Große Elbstraße 143 – Ⓜ Königstr. – ✆ 040 381816 – www.fischereihafenrestaurant.de*

HACO

MODERN CUISINE • COSY There is a trendy and relaxed feel to this attractive corner restaurant (the name "HACO" is derived from "HAmburg" and "COrner"). The modern Scandinavian style of the furnishings is also reflected in the produce-oriented cuisine which is also a real delight for vegetarians and vegans.

Menu 59/99 € – Carte 49/96 €

PLAN: 1-B2 – *Clemens-Schultz-Straße 18 – Ⓜ St. Pauli – ✆ 040 74203939 – www.restaurant-haco.com – Closed Monday, Sunday, lunch Tuesday-Saturday*

RIVE

SEAFOOD • BRASSERIE Sitting right on the port, this bistro is run by the same team as Tschebull. It serves good quality, flavoursome seafood and grilled meats alongside classic dishes such as Hamburger Pannfisch and Wiener Schnitzel. In summer the wonderful terrace is a must! Hot food served throughout the day.

Menu 33 € (lunch), 55/65 € – Carte 41/116 €

PLAN: 3-J1 – *Van-der-Smissen-Straße 1 – Ⓜ Königstr. – ✆ 040 3805919 – www.rive.de – Closed 2-13 January, Monday*

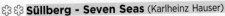

At Hamburg-Blankenese West: 16 km

Süllberg - Seven Seas (Karlheinz Hauser)

MODERN FRENCH • LUXURY Dedication, talent and creativity is required to direct operations at the luxury Süllberg restaurant and nobody can hold a candle to Karlheinz Hauser. His classic, creative cuisine is outstanding, the service exceptional and last but not least, the location is fantastic! A small number of stylish guestrooms are also available.

Specialities: Scallops with tandoori spices, mango, rice, crispy chicken skin. Black-feathered chicken, artichoke, watercress, razor clam. "Tea Time" Earl Grey, bergamot, honey.

Menu 95/195 €

Off plan – *Süllbergsterrasse 12 – ✆ 040 8662520 – www.karlheinzhauser.de – Closed 1 January-19 February, Monday, Tuesday, lunch Wednesday-Sunday*

At Hamburg-Eimsbüttel

Zipang

JAPANESE • MINIMALIST The minimalist interior at Zipang has clean lines, muted colours and a smart silver sheen. This makes a perfect match for chef Toshiharu Minami's mix of traditional and modern Japanese cooking styles. The restaurant is popular with Japanese diners – always a good sign.

Menu 26 € (lunch), 49/69 € – Carte 37/57 €

PLAN: 1-B1 – *Eppendorfer Weg 171 – Ⓜ Hoheluftbrücke – ✆ 040 43280032 – www.zipang.de – Closed Monday, Sunday*

Heimatjuwel

CREATIVE • MINIMALIST Marcel Görke, no stranger to the Hamburg culinar scene, runs this rustic, minimalist-style little restaurant with its friendly, informa atmosphere. It serves creative, fully-flavoured regional cuisine that represent great value for money. There is a very short and simple lunchtime menu. Sma pavement terrace.

Menu 22 € (lunch), 48/80 €

PLAN: 1-B1 – *Stellinger Weg 47 – Ⓜ Lutterothstraße – ✆ 040 42106989 – www.heimatjuwel.de – Closed 1-9 January, 13 July-3 August, Monday, Sunday, lunch Tuesday, Wednesday and Saturday*

Witwenball

MODERN CUISINE • BISTRO This former dancing bar is now a trendy, moder deluxe bistro with pale green chairs and azure blue bench seats, shining marbl tables, a striking white marble counter and decorative wine shelving. The theme menu changes every few weeks. There are over 300 wines to choose from a pairings to the delicious dishes – the emphasis here is on organic viticulture. Th desserts are highly recommended.

Carte 25/40 €

PLAN: 1-B2 – *Weidenallee 20 – Ⓜ Christuskirche – ✆ 040 53630085 – www.witwenball.com – Closed Monday, lunch Tuesday-Sunday*

At Hamburg-Eppendorf

Piment (Wahabi Nouri)

CREATIVE • NEIGHBOURHOOD Wahabi Nouri has an instinctive feel for a pro duct, enabling him to create original dishes in which the high quality of the ingre dients is the main focus, while his North African origins also shine throug Friendly, professional service, plus helpful advice on wine selection.

Specialities: Foie gras with tajine flavours. Braised pigeon à la Marrakech. Maroc can almond paste with argan oil ice cream.

Menu 78/115 €

PLAN: 1-C1 – *Lehmweg 29 – Ⓜ Eppendorfer Baum – ✆ 040 42937788 – www.restaurant-piment.de – Closed Wednesday, Sunday, lunch Monday-Tuesday and Thursday-Saturday*

Brechtmanns Bistro

ASIAN INFLUENCES • MINIMALIST Brechtmanns is an extremely popula friendly minimalist-style bistro serving South East Asian-inspired market-fres cuisine including crispy tuna fish tartare with cucumber, wasabi and sweet an sour pineapple, and boiled topside of beef in broth with root vegetables an apple.

Menu 39 € – Carte 28/58 €

PLAN: 1-C1 – *Erikastraße 43 – Ⓜ Kellinghusenstraße – ✆ 040 41305888 – www.brechtmann-bistro.de – Closed Sunday, lunch Saturday*

Stüffel

MARKET CUISINE • CHIC The riverside location here is every bit as appealing a the seasonal cuisine with Mediterranean and regional influences in which top quality produce combines to create dishes such as fillet of spined loach with to mato, bread and basil salad. You can eat in the stylish modern bistro or outsid on the waterfront. The wine list is well chosen and if you're lucky the owner him self will advise you on your choice.

Menu 37/58 € – Carte 25/66 €

PLAN: 1-C1 – *Isekai 1 – Ⓜ Eppendorfer Baum – ✆ 040 60902050 – www.restaurantstueffel.de – Closed 1-3 January, Monday, lunch Saturday*

Cornelia Poletto

ITALIAN • FRIENDLY Cornelia Poletto brings a piece of Italy to Hamburg in the form of a cosy modern restaurant serving ambitious cuisine. The menu is divided into "Cornelia Poletto Classico" and "Menu Degustazione". There is also a cookery school.

Menu 65/159 € – Carte 45/86 €

PLAN: 1-C1 – *Eppendorfer Landstraße 80 – Ⓜ Kellinghusenstraße – ✆ 040 4802159 – www.cornelia-poletto.de – Closed 1-7 January, Monday, Sunday*

Poletto Winebar

ITALIAN • COSY This lively wine bar is definitely one of the places to be in Eppendorf. The food is flavoursome, and Italian in style, and includes classics such as vitello tonnato and tiramisu, alongside excellent cold meats straight from the Berkel meat slicer. The adjacent wine shop has a great selection.

Menu 32 € – Carte 35/62 €

PLAN: 1-C1 – *Eppendorfer Weg 287 – Ⓜ Eppendorfer Baum – ✆ 040 38644700 – www.poletto-winebar.de*

At Hamburg-Flottbek

Zur Flottbeker Schmiede

PORTUGUESE • BISTRO Hamburg offers a taste of Portugal in this old listed forge building, where a traditional German ambience (with authentic decor and an old open fireplace) combines with a more informal southern European feel. The menu focuses on Portuguese-Mediterranean cuisine, with a selection of delicious tapas.

Carte 25/47 €

PLAN: 1-A3 – *Baron-Voght-Straße 79 – Ⓜ Klein Flottbek – ✆ 040 20918236 – www.zurflottbekerschmiede.de – Closed 1-8 January, Monday, lunch Tuesday-Sunday*

HYGGE Brasserie & Bar

COUNTRY COOKING • BRASSERIE In Danish, 'hygge' describes a feeling of warmth, cosiness and well-being - just the atmosphere conjured up in this chic, stylish and relaxed timber-framed restaurant with an open hearth at its centre. The food is seasonal and regional, and includes dishes such as cod fillet with braised cucumbers, horseradish and mash. The bar-lounge is a trendy spot.

Menu 36/48 € – Carte 38/71 €

Off plan – *Landhaus Flottbek, Baron-Voght-Straße 179 – ✆ 040 82274160 – www.hygge-hamburg.de – Closed 1-12 January, lunch Monday-Sunday*

At Hamburg-Nienstedten West: 13 km by Elbchaussee A2

✿✿ Jacob's Restaurant

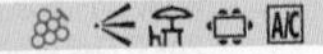

CLASSIC FRENCH • CHIC Thomas Martin's food – classic, simple, free of fancy flourishes, and placing great emphasis on top-quality ingredients – is available from an à la carte menu. The dining experience is rounded off by the accomplished service, the stylish decor and the magnificent lime tree shaded terrace overlooking the Elbe.

Specialities: Sturgeon mousse and Imperial caviar. Turbot with Beurre Blanc. Caramelised Altländer apple pie, crème Chantilly.

Menu 102/148 € – Carte 71/117 €

Off plan – *Louis C. Jacob, Elbchaussee 401 – ✆ 040 82255406 – www.hotel-jacob.de – Closed Monday, Tuesday, lunch Wednesday-Sunday*

Weinwirtschaft Kleines Jacob

CLASSIC CUISINE • WINE BAR No wonder so many people describe Kleines Ja cob as their favourite restaurant with its wine bar charm, candlelit tables and a tentive service. The dishes coming out of the open kitchens include chicken fri assee vol-au-vents and rice. All the wines come from vineyards in Germar speaking countries.

Menu 36 € – Carte 36/67 €

Off plan – *Louis C. Jacob, Elbchaussee 404 – 𝒞 040 82255510 – www.kleines-jacob.de – Closed lunch Monday-Saturday*

At Hamburg-Rothenburgsort

100/200 (Thomas Imbusch)

CREATIVE • CHIC 100/200 promises industrial chic in an urban loft-style roor with an eye-catching open kitchen that is visible from all sides and boasts smart Molteni oven. It's here at between 100° and 200°C – hence the name that the chefs produce a creative surprise menu based on the "nose to tail" prir ciple, which they then serve up themselves at stylish tree-trunk tables. Ticket type booking system.

Specialities: Offal ragout. "Pfaffenstück" with salted lemon. Brioche with green gages.

Menu 95/119 €

PLAN: 1-D3 – *Brandshofer Deich 68 – 𝒞 040 30925191 – www.100200.kitchen – Closed Saturday, Sunday, lunch Monday-Friday*

At Hamburg-St. Pauli

Nil

INTERNATIONAL • NEIGHBOURHOOD Located in Hamburg's fashionabl Schanze district, Nil is cosy, though perhaps a little cramped, and serves a rang of well-cooked dishes including young goat bratwurst with lentils, parsnips an apple mustard and pan-fried skrei with baked carrots and coriander. There is a attractive garden to the rear and cookery courses next door.

Menu 34/45 € – Carte 37/52 €

PLAN: 1-B2 – *Neuer Pferdemarkt 5 – Ⓜ Feldstraße – 𝒞 040 4397823 – www.restaurant-nil.de – Closed lunch Monday-Sunday*

philipps

INTERNATIONAL • TRENDY Hidden away in a side street, philipps is a grea place to eat. Walk down the few stairs to this friendly little restaurant with low ceilings, a relaxed atmosphere and international menu. It promises flavoursome and skilfully prepared dishes such as ox cheeks with leek champ.

Menu 40/60 € – Carte 36/58 €

PLAN: 1-B2 – *Turnerstraße 9 – Ⓜ Feldstraße – 𝒞 040 63735108 – www.philipps-restaurant.de – Closed 19 January-3 February, 10-13 April, 14-28 July, 24-31 December, Monday, Sunday, lunch Tuesday-Saturday*

Clouds - Heaven's Bar & Kitchen

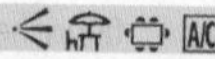

MODERN FRENCH • DESIGN Set high above the River Elbe and St Michael's church, Clouds offers a truly amazing view and good modern cuisine including a selection of meat cuts and a classic steak tartare prepared at your table. The interior is stylishly urban and from May onwards the Heaven's Nest roof terrace serves drinks and snacks.

Carte 52/130 €

PLAN: 1-B3 – *Reeperbahn 1 – Ⓜ St. Pauli – 𝒞 040 30993280 – www.clouds-hamburg.de – Closed lunch Saturday-Sunday*

East

FUSION • DESIGN This restaurant with fantastic industrial architecture and a smart, unfussy interior is a real eye-catcher. The centrepiece in this former factory hall is the sushi counter. Choose from modern dishes such as sweet and sour red snapper or steaks cooked on the Southbend grill.

Carte 42/105€

PLAN: 1-B2 – *Simon-von-Utrecht-Straße 31 – Ⓜ St. Pauli – ✆ 040 309933 – www.east-hamburg.de – Closed lunch Saturday-Sunday*

haebel

CREATIVE FRENCH • CONTEMPORARY DÉCOR This tiny, bistro-style restaurant with its open kitchen serves a Nordic/French-inspired surprise menu that showcases excellent ingredients, which are subsequently fashioned into a range of creative and pleasingly pared-down dishes.

Menu 39€ (lunch), 85/105€

PLAN: 3-J1 – *Paul-Roosen-Straße 31 – Ⓜ Reeperbahn – ✆ 01517 2423046 – www.haebel.hamburg – Closed Monday, Sunday, lunch Tuesday-Friday*

At Hamburg-Uhlenhorst

Wolfs Junge

MARKET CUISINE • FRIENDLY The accent here is on sustainable, regional cuisine, the very epitome of "nose to tail" eating. The ingredients are sourced from selected producers with some of the vegetables and herbs grown by the restaurant itself. Serves simple midday fare such as home-made bratwurst and an ambitious, creative set menu including Angeln Saddleback, kimchi and fermented onion in the evenings.

Menu 24€ (lunch)/79€

PLAN: 1-D1 – *Zimmerstraße 30 – Ⓜ Mundsburg – ✆ 040 20965157 – www.wolfs-junge.de – Closed Monday, Sunday, lunch Saturday*

At Hamburg-Winterhude

Gallo Nero

ITALIAN • MEDITERRANEAN A restaurant, wine shop and "alimentari con cucina" with three lovely terraces, this Winterhuder institution promises authentic Italian cuisine made using top-quality produce including dishes such as burrata con datterino e culatello di Zibello and calamaretti alla griglia... all washed down with a selection of good Italian reds and some lovely Rieslings.

Menu 54/69€ – Carte 39/68€

PLAN: 1-C1 – *Sierichstraße 46 – Ⓜ Sierichstraße – ✆ 040 27092229 – www.gallo-nero.net*

MUNICH
MÜNCHEN

gameover2012/iStock

MUNICH IN...

→ **ONE DAY**
The old town, Frauenkirche, English Garden, Wagner (if possible!) at the National Theatre.

→ **TWO DAYS**
Schwabing, Pinakothek, Hofbräuhaus.

→ **THREE DAYS**
Olympic Park, Schloss Nymphenburg, Deutsches Museum, an evening in a traditional Bavarian inn.

Situated in a stunning position not far north of the Alps, Munich is a cultural titan. Famously described as the 'village with a million inhabitants', its mix of German organisation and Italian lifestyle makes for a magical mix with an enviable amount of Italian restaurants to seek out and enjoy. This cultural capital of Southern Germany boasts over forty theatres and dozens of museums; temples of culture that blend charmingly with the Bavarian love of folklore and lederhosen. Perhaps in no other world location – certainly not in Western Europe – is there such an enjoyable abundance of folk festivals

and groups dedicated to playing the local music. And there's an abundance of places to see them, too: Munich is awash with Bierhallen, Bierkeller, and Biergarten.

The heart of Munich is the Old Town, with its epicentre the Marienplatz in the south, and Residenz to the north: there are many fine historic buildings around here. Running to the east is the River Isar, flanked by fine urban thoroughfares and green areas for walks. Head north for the area dissected by the Ludwigstrasse and Leopoldstrasse – Schwabing – which is full of students as it's the University district. To the east is the English Garden, a denizen of peace. West of here, the Museums district, dominated by the Pinakothek, is characterised by bookshops, antique stores and galleries.

EATING OUT

Munich is a city in which you can eat well - especially if you're a meat-eater – and in large quantities. The local specialities are meat and potatoes, with large dollops of cabbage on the side; you won't have trouble finding roast pork and dumplings or meatloaf and don't forget the local white veal sausage, weisswurst. The meat is invariably succulent, and cabbage is often adorned with the likes of juniper berries. Potatoes, meanwhile, have a tendency to evolve into soft and buttery dumplings. And sausage? Take your pick from over 1,500 recognised species. Other specialities include Schweinshaxe (knuckle of pork) and Leberkäs (meat and offal pâté). Eating out in Munich, or anywhere in Bavaria, is an experience in itself, with the distinctive background din of laughter, singing and the clinking of mugs of Bavarian Weissbier. It's famous for the Brauereigaststätten or brewery inn; be prepared for much noise, and don't be afraid to fall into conversation with fellow diners and drinkers. The many Italian restaurants in the city provide an excellent alternative.

Centre

✿✿✿ Atelier

CREATIVE FRENCH • ELEGANT With its artistic interior designed by Axel Vervoordt, this restaurant more than lives up to its name. You will find the cuisine of young and talented chef Jan Hartwig equally modern and individual in style. His tasty culinary creations are masterpieces of balance and intensity.

Specialities: Smoked eel and suckling pig pork belly, zucchini, dill, saffron dashi with pastis. Souffléed quail breast with amaranth, braised mushrooms, leek and Vin Jaune. Caramelised Felchlin "Edelweiß" with ginger and olive brittle.

Menu 185/245€

PLAN: 2-G2 – *Bayerischer Hof, Promenadeplatz 2 – Ⓜ Marienplatz – ✆ 089 21200 – www.bayerischerhof.de – Closed 1-7 January, 5-14 April, 26 July-1 September, 24-31 December, Monday, Sunday, lunch Tuesday-Saturday*

✿✿ Alois - Dallmayr Fine Dining

MODERN FRENCH • ELEGANT In both the delicatessen and the gourmet restaurant of this renowned and long-established eatery, you can be absolutely sure that the ingredients will be top-notch. The stylish dining rooms are done out in an extremely chic design, the cuisine is modern and distinctive, pleasingly pared down and well balanced. The service and the wine recommendations are equally good.

Specialities: Veal, pine nuts, grape. Brill, sea urchin, black truffle. Cironé, pistachio, cedro.

Menu 59€ (lunch), 98/198€

PLAN: 2-G2 – *Dienerstraße 14 – Ⓜ Marienplatz – ✆ 089 2135100 – www.dallmayr.com/alois – Closed 6-21 April, 31 May-9 June, 2 August-1 September, 24-31 December, Monday, Tuesday, Sunday, lunch Wednesday*

✿✿ Les Deux

MODERN FRENCH • CHIC The name "Les Deux" refers to Fabrice Kieffer and Edip Sigl - host and head chef at this popular, chic designer-style restaurant which boasts a prime city location. The cuisine is modern yet classic, the service pleasant and friendly, and there is a fine wine list.

Specialities: Ravioli of young peas, chanterelles, hazelnut, chive sauce. Brittany monkfish, Jerusalem artichoke, chervil tarragon stock. Toffifee "Les Deux".

Menu 59€ (lunch), 85/125€ – Carte 83/136€

PLAN: 2-G2 – *Maffeistraße 3a – Ⓜ Marienplatz – ✆ 089 710407373 – www.lesdeux-muc.de – Closed 3-21 August, Sunday, lunch Saturday*

✿ mural

CREATIVE • MINIMALIST This restaurant in MUCA, the Museum of Urban and Contemporary Art – which explains the design of the mural – is a museum café serving simpler dishes at lunchtime, while in the evening, the kitchen team create imaginative fare with a focus on full flavours. The ingredients are nearly all from Bavaria. Interesting selection of recommended wines.

Specialities: Char, parsley, egg yolk, mustard. Lamb, red pepper, white bean. Apricot, whey, buckwheat.

Menu 89/139€

PLAN: 2-F2 – *Hotterstraße 12 – Ⓜ Marienplatz – ✆ 089 23023186 – mural.restaurant – Closed Monday, Tuesday, Sunday, lunch Wednesday-Saturday*

Schwarzreiter

MODERN CUISINE • ELEGANT Chic and upmarket without being overly formal, Schwarzreiter is this classic Munich hotel's fine dining restaurant. The "Young Bavarian Cuisine" served here is sophisticated food of the very highest calibre, and the friendly and professional front-of-house team will be only too pleased to provide wine recommendations.

Specialities: Bavarian shrimp, butterhead lettuce, perennial rye, turnips. Pike perch, potato, cabbage, beech mushrooms, Tyrolean Speck. Rice "Trautmannsdorf", rice pudding, peach, cinnamon, macadamia.

Menu 125/165€

PLAN: 2-H2 – *Vier Jahreszeiten Kempinski, Maximilianstraße 17 – Lehel – 089 21250 – www.schwarzreiter.com – Closed 1-6 January, 5-20 April, 2-31 August, Monday, Sunday, lunch Tuesday-Saturday*

Sparkling Bistro (Jürgen Wolfsgruber)

MODERN CUISINE • BISTRO This pretty, friendly bistro is a little out of the way, but well worth searching for. It is run with dedication and a personal touch, and this approach is also reflected in the produce- and market-oriented cuisine, which is served as an ambitious "Bistro Menu" in the evening. In summer, a business lunch option is available.

Specialities: Char, sweet and sour plums, porcini mushroom, hazelnut. Venison, Foie Gras, pumpkin, rowan berry. Apple quince, Buchtel roll, sheep's milk, kernel oil.

Menu 85/150€

PLAN: 1-B2 – *Amalienstraße 79 – Universität – 089 46138267 – www.sparklingbistro.de – Closed 1-8 January, Sunday, lunch Monday-Saturday*

Tian

VEGETARIAN • TRENDY Even though this restaurant focuses exclusively on vegetarian and vegan cuisine, the resulting dishes are still full of flavour. Guests can look forward to creative plates demonstrating finesse and intensity from either the shorter lunch menu or the evening menu and it is possible to select dishes from either menu at lunchtime. Add to all this trendy design, an attractive bar, a stylish inner courtyard terrace and a prime location on the Viktualienmarkt.

Specialities: Jerusalem artichoke, black salsify, walnut, grape. Ravioli, potato, cabbage. Hazelnut nougat, plum, poppy seed.

Menu 47€ (lunch), 99/122€

PLAN: 2-G3 – *Frauenstraße 4 – Isartor – 089 885656712 – www.tian-restaurant.com – Closed 12-27 January, 27 September-5 October, Monday, Sunday, lunch Tuesday*

Colette Tim Raue

FRENCH • BRASSERIE Tim Raue really has his finger on the pulse with his new culinary concept at Colette. It is as relaxed as a French brasserie, friendly with pleasantly informal service, and offers good food at great prices. The first class ingredients speak for themselves in dishes such as *boeuf bourguignon* with speck, mushrooms and shallots.

Menu 59€ – Carte 35/68€

PLAN: 1-B3 – *Klenzestraße 72 – Frauenhoferstraße – 089 23002555 – www.brasseriecolette.de – Closed lunch Monday-Sunday*

Ménage Bar

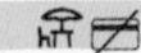

CREATIVE • TRENDY This trendy little bar in the Glockenbachviertel is urban, yet cosy. The concept: extremely unusual house-created cocktails and equally creative small plates. Very good ingredients go into making dishes such as white chocolate risotto, fish chicharrón and char caviar. The bar snacks are also interesting. Until 8.30pm there's the bargain "Early Bird Menu".

Menu 31/43€ – Carte 26/41€

PLAN: 2-H3 – *Buttermelcherstraße 9 – Frauenhoferstraße – 089 23232680 – www.menage-bar.com – Closed Sunday, lunch Monday-Saturday*

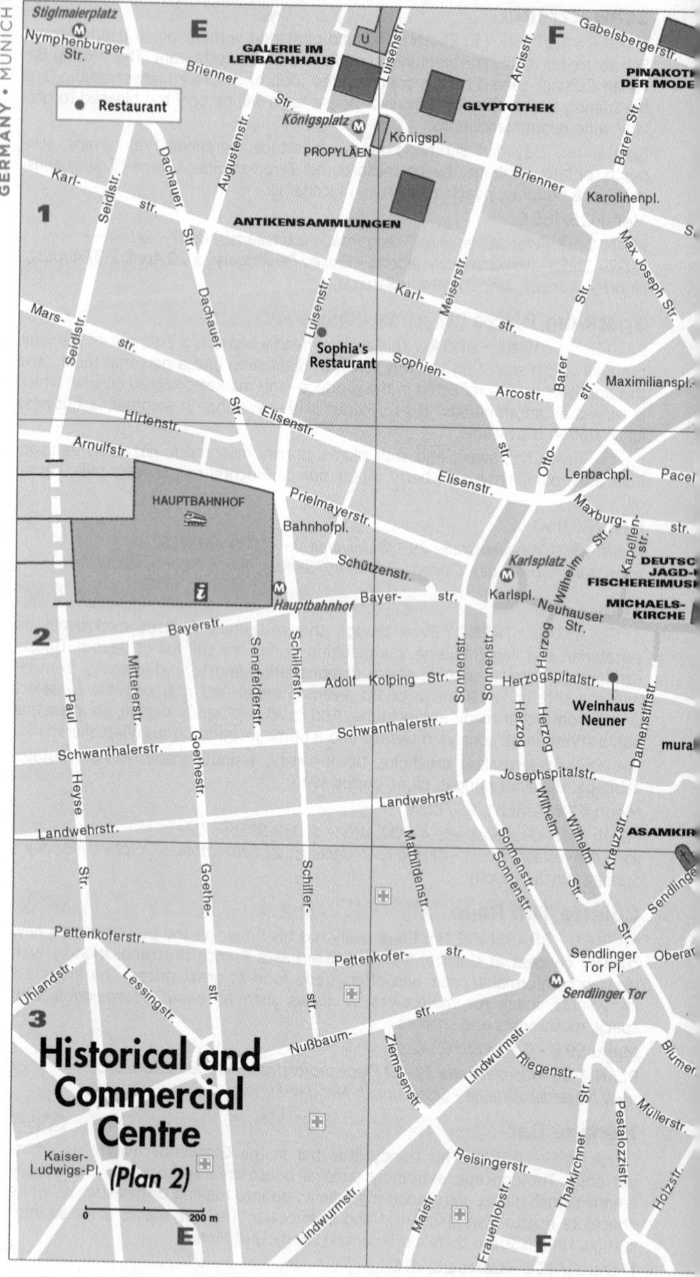

Historical and Commercial Centre *(Plan 2)*

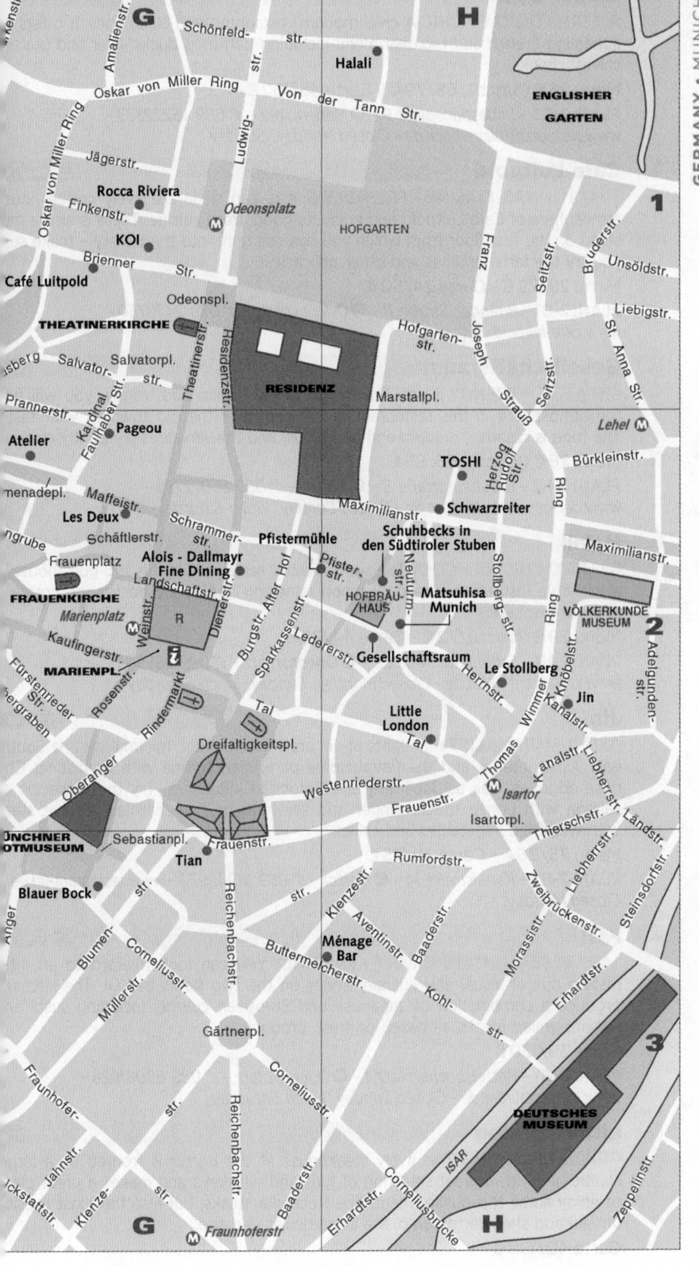

G
H
1
2
3
Schönfeld-str.
Halali
Amalienstr.
Ludwig-str.
Oskar von Miller Ring
Von der Tann Str.
ENGLISHER GARTEN
Jägerstr.
Rocca Riviera
Finkenstr.
Odeonsplatz
HOFGARTEN
KOI
Brienner Str.
Café Luitpold
Odeonspl.
THEATINERKIRCHE
Theatinerstr.
Residenzstr.
RESIDENZ
Hofgarten-str.
Franz Joseph Strauß Ring
Seitzstr.
Bruderstr.
Unsöldstr.
Liebigstr.
St. Anna Str.
Salvatorpl.
Salvator-str.
Marstallpl.
Prannerstr.
Kardinal Faulhaber Str.
Pageou
Atelier
Lehel
Bürkleinstr.
TOSHI
Herzog Rudolf Str.
Maffeistr.
Maximilianstr.
Schwarzreiter
Les Deux
Schrammer-str.
Schäftlerstr.
Pfistermühle
Schuhbecks in den Südtiroler Stuben
Maximilianstr.
Frauenplatz
Alois - Dallmayr Fine Dining
Pfister-str.
Neuturm-str.
Stollberg-str.
Landschaftstr.
Dienerstr.
FRAUENKIRCHE
Alter Hof
HOFBRÄU-HAUS
Matsuhisa Munich
VÖLKERKUNDE MUSEUM
Marienplatz
R
Weinstr.
Burgstr.
Sparkassenstr.
Ledererstr.
Adelgunden-str.
Kaufingerstr.
Gesellschaftsraum
MARIENPL.
Fürstenrieder Str.
Rosenstr.
Herrnstr.
Le Stollberg
Knöbelstr.
Jin
Rindermarkt
Tal
Little London
Thomas Wimmer Ring
Kanalstr.
Dreifaltigkeitspl.
Liebherrstr.
Oberanger
Westenriederstr.
Isartor
Frauenstr.
Isartorpl.
Thierschstr.
Ländstr.
Sebastianpl.
Frauenstr.
Tian
Rumfordstr.
Blauer Bock
Klenzestr.
Aventinstr.
Zweibrückenstr.
Steinsdorfstr.
Reichenbachstr.
Ménage Bar
Baaderstr.
Morassistr.
Blumen-str.
Corneliusstr.
Buttermelcherstr.
Kohl-str.
Erhardtstr.
Müllerstr.
Gärtnerpl.
Fraunhofer-str.
Corneliusstr.
DEUTSCHES MUSEUM
ISAR
Jahnstr.
Klenze-str.
Baaderstr.
Erhardtstr.
Corneliusbrücke
Zeppelinstr.
Fraunhoferstr

Blauer Bock

INTERNATIONAL • CHIC A chic, modern restaurant with clean lines. It offers a appealing French and regional menu including pan-fried ducks' liver and braise calves' cheeks.

Menu 26€ (lunch), 65/79€ - Carte 45/162€

PLAN: 2-G3 - *Sebastiansplatz 9 - Ⓜ Marienplatz - ✆ 089 45222333 - www.restaurant-blauerbock.de - Closed Monday, Sunday*

Cafe Luitpold

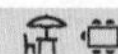

TRADITIONAL CUISINE • FRIENDLY Guests can sit in the lively coffee hous atmosphere of Cafe Luitpold and enjoy its good, fresh cuisine. There is also a mu seum on the first floor from which you can see right into the bakery - make su you try the tarts, pralines and other delicacies!

Menu 29/79€ - Carte 24/50€

PLAN: 2-G1 - *Brienner Straße 11 - Ⓜ Odeonsplatz - ✆ 089 2428750 - www.cafe-luitpold.de*

Gesellschaftsraum

CREATIVE • TRENDY If you like things casual, urban and trendy, you will fin the atmosphere in this restaurant in the centre of the old town to your tast The food is creative, modern and ambitious, and the service is pleasantly relaxe

Menu 26€ (lunch), 65/95€

PLAN: 2-H2 - *Bräuhausstraße 8 - Ⓜ Isartor - ✆ 089 55077793 - www.der-gesellschaftsraum.de - Closed Sunday, lunch Saturday*

Halali

CLASSIC CUISINE • COSY The sophisticated restaurant in this 19C guesthouse a veritable institution. The dark wood panelling and lovely decoration create cosy atmosphere.

Menu 29€ (lunch)/72€ - Carte 44/78€

PLAN: 2-H1 - *Schönfeldstraße 22 - Ⓜ Odeonsplatz - ✆ 089 285909 - www.restaurant-halali.de - Closed Monday, Sunday, lunch Saturday*

Jin

ASIAN • MINIMALIST Highlights at Jin are the upmarket, minimalist-style Sout east Asian interior and the flavoursome pan-Asian cuisine with its distinct Ch nese edge, as well as Japanese and European influences. Try the carpaccio salmon with ponzu sauce, ginger and seaweed or the Charolais rib-eye stea with wok-fried vegetables and chilli.

Menu 75/96€ - Carte 39/75€

PLAN: 2-H2 - *Kanalstraße 14 - Ⓜ Isartor - ✆ 089 21949970 - www.restaurant-jin.de Closed Monday*

KOI

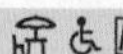

JAPANESE CONTEMPORARY • FRIENDLY You can look forward to an inte resting mix of visual and culinary styles on the two floors at KOI. The kitcher produce a combination of Japanese and European cuisine, including sushi an Robata-grilled meats, all based on fresh produce.

Carte 39/130€

PLAN: 2-G1 - *Wittelsbacherplatz 1 - Ⓜ Odeonsplatz - ✆ 089 89081926 - www.koi-restaurant.de - Closed Sunday, lunch Saturday*

Little London

GRILLS • FRIENDLY This lively steakhouse at the Isartor is fronted by a larg classic bar with a great selection of gins and whiskeys and makes a great plac to enjoy some top-quality meat. The Nebraska steaks, but also the roast topsic of veal and shoulder of lamb, are in particular demand.

Carte 40/198€

PLAN: 2-H2 - *Tal 31 - Ⓜ Marienplatz - ✆ 089 122239470 - www.little-london.de - Closed lunch Monday-Sunday*

Matsuhisa Munich

JAPANESE CONTEMPORARY • TRENDY The high quality evident throughout the luxury Mandarin Oriental is also reflected in the minimalist-style restaurant run by Nobu Matsuhisa, who runs restaurants around the world. The cuisine is modern Japanese and interesting, refined with Peruvian flavours and techniques – an exciting mix. Don't miss the sushi and sashimi or the classic Black Cod Miso dish!

Menu 39 € (lunch), 95/125 € – Carte 41/178 €

PLAN: 2-H2 – *Mandarin Oriental, Neuturmstraße 1 – Ⓜ Isartor – ✆ 089 290981875 – www.mandarinoriental.com*

Museum

SEASONAL CUISINE • CHIC A hip address in the Bavarian National Museum. The best thing is to sit outside on the cosy terrace, otherwise beneath the cross vaults and high ceilings in the chic modern brasserie ambience. Shorter, simpler menu at lunchtime, more ambitious seasonal Mediterranean cuisine in the evening. Wine list with specialities, but also wines for any time.

Menu 65/89 € – Carte 38/67 €

PLAN: 1-C2 – *Prinzregentenstraße 3 – Ⓜ Lehel – ✆ 089 45224430 – www.museum-muenchen.de – Closed Monday, dinner Sunday*

Pageou

MEDITERRANEAN CUISINE • COSY Behind the magnificent historical façade, Ali Güngörmüs (previously chef at Le Canard nouveau in Hamburg) serves Mediterranean cuisine with North African influences in a relaxed, tasteful interior. Quiet, attractive terrace in the courtyard. Business lunch menu.

Menu 54 € (lunch), 79/145 € – Carte 70/80 €

PLAN: 2-G2 – *Kardinal-Faulhaber-Straße 10 – Ⓜ Marienplatz – ✆ 089 24231310 – www.pageou.de – Closed 24-28 December, Monday, Sunday*

Pfistermühle

COUNTRY COOKING • REGIONAL A separate entrance leads into the former ducal mill (1573) where you can sample regional fare in a stylish Bavarian setting (including a lovely vaulted ceiling). Try dishes such as braised calves' cheeks with parsnip puree, creamy savoy cabbage and dried fruit sauce.

Menu 20 € (lunch), 55/95 € – Carte 50/70 €

PLAN: 2-G2 – *Platzl, Pfisterstraße 4 – Ⓜ Marienplatz – ✆ 089 23703865 – www.pfistermuehle.de – Closed Sunday*

Rocca Riviera

MEDITERRANEAN CUISINE • TRENDY Rocca Riviera is a relaxed and stylish restaurant with a pleasant atmosphere not far from the Odeonsplatz. It serves Mediterranean-French fusion cuisine on a sharing plate basis, as well as meat and fish from the charcoal grill.

Menu 59/99 € – Carte 33/82 €

PLAN: 2-G1 – *Wittelsbacherplatz 2 – Ⓜ Odeonsplatz – ✆ 089 28724421 – www.roccariviera.com – Closed Sunday, lunch saturday*

Rüen Thai

THAI • FAMILY True to his roots, Anuchit Chetha has dedicated himself to the cuisine of southern Thailand, preparing a range of dishes including gung pla and nüe san kua, as well as a finger food menu. In addition to specialising in interesting spice combinations, he is also passionate about wine – the restaurant boasts a cellar containing a number of real rarities.

Menu 56/86 € – Carte 31/57 €

PLAN: 1-A3 – *Kazmairstraße 58 – Ⓜ Schwanthalerhöhe – ✆ 089 503239 – www.rueen-thai.de – Closed 2-23 August, lunch Friday-Sunday*

Schuhbecks in den Südtiroler Stuben

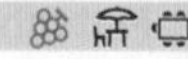

COUNTRY COOKING • RUSTIC Alfons Schuhbeck's little empire on P square was born here. After opening the gourmet restaurant Alfons around corner, it was decided to focus here on cosmopolitan Bavarian cuisine serve the usual elegant ambience, with dishes such as cod on lukewarm asparagus- til salad on the menu. Schuhbeck also sells ice cream, chocolate and spices the Platzl.

Menu 35€ (lunch), 52/84€ – Carte 35/70€

PLAN: 2-H2 – *Platzl 6 – Ⓜ Marienplatz – ✆ 089 2166900 – www.schuhbeck.de – Closed 1-5 January, Sunday*

Sophia's Restaurant

MODERN CUISINE • CHIC High, airy ceilings in a trendy, elegant bistro-style taurant decorated in calming natural tones. The decor is a nod to the adja Old Botanic Garden. Modern, seasonal cooking made from top- quality ingr ents, with dishes such as cornfed chicken breast from Gutshof Polting roasted cauliflower, chives and radishes on the menu. Attentive service. Slig more limited lunchtime menu.

Menu 27€ (lunch)/75€ – Carte 43/78€

PLAN: 2-E1 – *The Charles, Sophienstraße 28 – Ⓜ Hauptbahnhof – ✆ 089 5445551200 – www.roccofortehotels.com*

Le Stollberg

CLASSIC CUISINE • FRIENDLY This pleasant and lively small restauran managed personally by its owner and chef, Anette Huber, who offers g freshly prepared food at a fair price. The menu features French-inspired dis with tasty creations such as Onglet steak of US beef, green asparagus, olive potato spring roll. Good wine recommendations, plus light bites available in daytime bistro Le Petit Stollberg opposite.

Menu 28€ (lunch), 62/80€ – Carte 50/64€

PLAN: 2-H2 – *Stollbergstraße 2 – Ⓜ Isartor – ✆ 089 24243450 – www.lestollberg. Closed Sunday*

TOSHI

JAPANESE • MINIMALIST It is just a short hop from the ritzy Maximilianstr to this authentic Japanese restaurant. The menu – as characteristic as the m malist design – offers fresh Far Eastern dishes. These include sushi, teppan and 'pan-Pacific' cuisine.

Menu 50/140€ – Carte 40/180€

PLAN: 2-H2 – *Wurzerstraße 18 – Ⓜ Lehel – ✆ 089 25546942 – www.restaurant-toshi.de – Closed 5-15 April, 9-17 August, Monday, Sunday, lunch Saturday*

Weinhaus Neuner

TRADITIONAL CUISINE • TRADITIONAL With its cross-vaulted ceiling, herr bone parquet and wood panelling, this old restaurant has lost nothing of its ditional charm. The food is just what you would expect from an upmarket Mu restaurant – try the flaky pastry crust chicken fricassee pie.

Menu 25€ (lunch), 59/65€ – Carte 25/62€

PLAN: 2-F2 – *Herzogspitalstraße 8 – Ⓜ Karlsplatz – ✆ 089 2603954 – www.weinhaus-neuner.de*

Environs of Munich

München-Bogenhausen

Acquarello (Mario Gamba)

MEDITERRANEAN CUISINE • FRIENDLY The Latin flair of this friendly, elegant restaurant is the perfect match for the Italian/Mediterranean and French cuisine which Mario Gamba and his team have been preparing here since 1994. The food is light, sophisticated, made with the very best ingredients and accompanied by Italian wines. The service is attentive and professional.

Specialities: Fig tortelli with fried goose liver on a white wine foam. Monkfish in a crispy crust with lobster bisque. Yuzu panna cotta.

Menu 60€ (lunch)/118€ - Carte 80/100€

PLAN: 1-D2 - *Mühlbaurstraße 36 - Ⓜ Böhmerwaldplatz - ✆ 089 4704848 - www.acquarello.com - Closed 1-4 January, Monday, lunch Saturday-Sunday*

Bogenhauser Hof

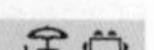

CLASSIC CUISINE • TRADITIONAL This elegant yet comfortable restaurant, housed in a building dating back to 1825, serves classic cuisine prepared using the finest ingredients, which explains why it has so many regulars. It also has a leafy garden complete with mature chestnut trees.

Menu 92€ - Carte 61/93€

PLAN: 1-C2 - *Ismaninger Straße 85 - Ⓜ Böhmerwaldplatz - ✆ 089 985586 - www.bogenhauser-hof.de - Closed 1-6 January, 24-31 December, Sunday*

Hippocampus

ITALIAN • ELEGANT Hippocampus is not just any Italian restaurant in the elegant district of Bogenhausen but an attractive, lively ristorante with classic Italian cuisine where the superb pasta dishes are just as good as the monkfish or breaded cutlet of suckling calf! The wine recommendations are also excellent.

Menu 29€ (lunch)/62€ - Carte 52/66€

PLAN: 1-C3 - *Mühlbaurstraße 5 - Ⓜ Prinzregentenplatz - ✆ 089 475855 - www.hippocampus-restaurant.de - Closed Monday, lunch Saturday*

Käfer-Schänke

SEASONAL CUISINE • COSY The name "Käfer" has become synonymous with Munich's restaurant scene. The presence of a delicatessen under the same roof as this cosy restaurant guarantees the top-class ingredients, used to make its popular classics. There are also a number of stylish function rooms for special occasions.

Menu 104€ - Carte 54/145€

PLAN: 1-C3 - *Prinzregentenstraße 73 - Ⓜ Prinzregentenplatz - ✆ 089 4168247 - www.feinkost-kaefer.de/schaenke - Closed Sunday*

München-Giesing

Gabelspiel (Florian Berger)

MODERN CUISINE • FAMILY Gabelspiel offers a genuinely pleasant and entirely unpretentious, informal atmosphere. The food is fresh, ambitious and modern. Try the prawn, ponzu and radish fusion or the pigeon, falafel and spring onion étouffée with poppadoms.

Specialities: Pumpkin, soy, tonka bean, air bread. Saddle of venison, blueberry, black salsify, coffee. Parsnip, mandarin, chocolate.

Menu 95/135€

Off plan - *Zehentbauernstraße 20 - Ⓜ Silberhornstraße - ✆ 089 12253940 - www.restaurant-gabelspiel.de - Closed 1-6 January, 24 May-9 June, Monday, Sunday, lunch Tuesday-Saturday*

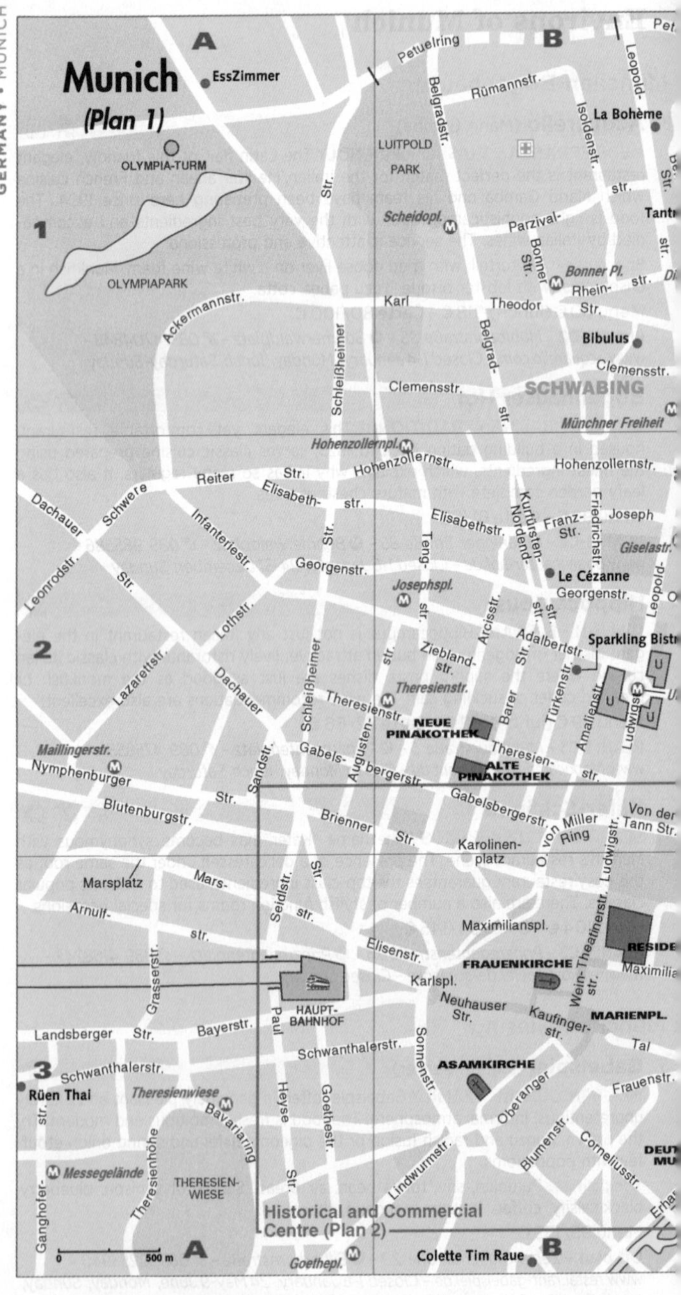
Munich
(Plan 1)
A
B
1
2
3
EssZimmer
OLYMPIA-TURM
OLYMPIAPARK
Petuelring
Rümannstr.
Belgradstr.
Leopold-
Isoldenstr.
La Bohème
LUITPOLD PARK
Scheidopl.
Parzival-
str.
Tantr
Bonner Str.
Bonner Pl.
Rhein-
str.
Ackermannstr.
Karl Theodor Str.
Belgrad-str.
Schleißheimer Str.
Bibulus
Clemensstr.
SCHWABING
Münchner Freiheit
Hohenzollernpl.
Hohenzollernstr.
Schwere Reiter Str.
Elisabeth-str.
Elisabethstr.
Dachauer Str.
Infanteriestr.
Teng-str.
Kurfürsten-str.
Nordend-str.
Franz-Joseph Str.
Friedrichstr.
Giselastr.
Leonrodstr.
Georgenstr.
Josephspl.
Le Cézanne
Lothstr.
Arcisstr.
Adalbertstr.
Sparkling Bistr
Ziebland-str.
Barer Str.
Türkenstr.
Lazarettstr.
Theresienstr.
Amalienstr.
Ludwigstr.
NEUE PINAKOTHEK
ALTE PINAKOTHEK
Augusten-str.
Gabelsbergerstr.
Maillingerstr.
Nymphenburger Str.
Sandstr.
Blutenburgstr.
Brienner Str.
Von der Tann Str.
O. von Miller Ring
Karolinen-platz
Marsplatz
Mars-str.
Seidlstr.
Arnulf-str.
Maximilianspl.
Elisenstr.
FRAUENKIRCHE
RESIDE
Maximilia
Karlspl.
Wein-Theatinerstr.
Grasserstr.
HAUPT-BAHNHOF
Neuhauser Str.
Kaufinger-str.
MARIENPL.
Landsberger Str.
Bayerstr.
Paul Heyse Str.
Sonnenstr.
Tal
Schwanthalerstr.
ASAMKIRCHE
Frauenstr.
Rüen Thai
Theresienwiese
Bavariaring
Goethestr.
Oberanger
Blumenstr.
Corneliusstr.
Messegelände
Theresienhöhe
THERESIEN-WIESE
Lindwurmstr.
Ganghofer-str.
Historical and Commercial Centre (Plan 2)
0
500 m
Goethepl.
Colette Tim Raue

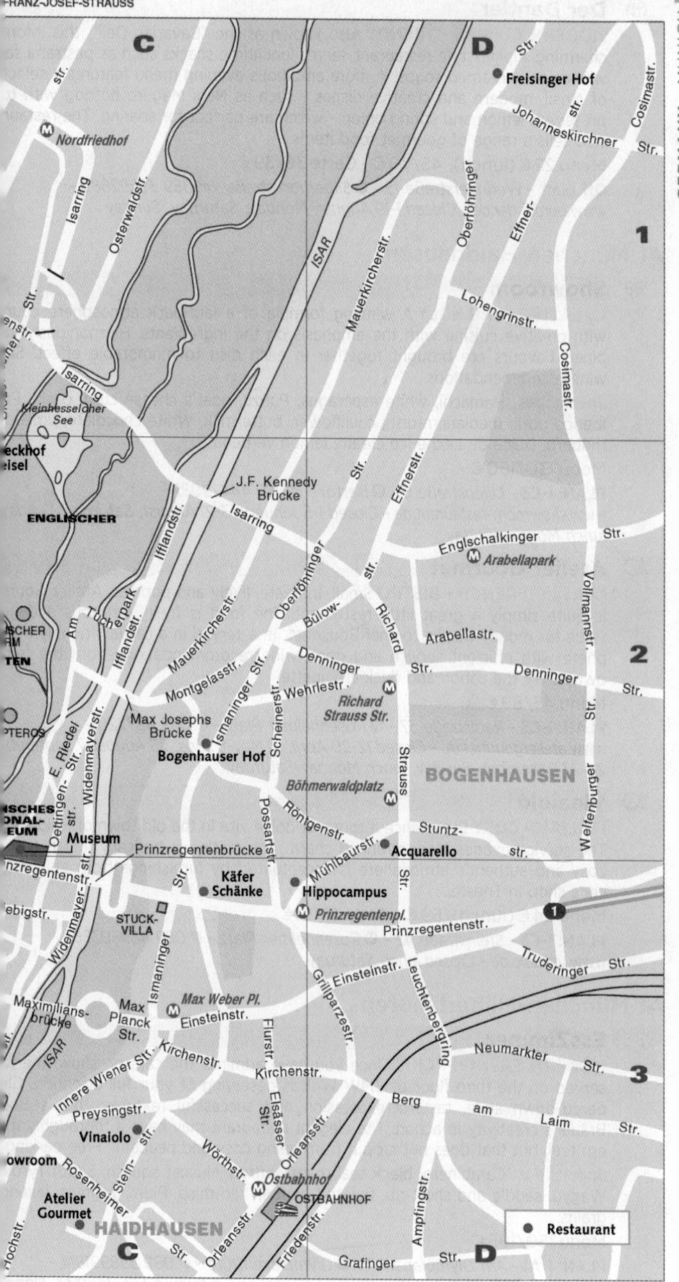
FRANZ-JOSEF-STRAUSS
C
D
1
2
3
Freisinger Hof
Nordfriedhof
ISAR
Isarring
Osterwaldstr.
Mauerkircherstr.
Oberföhringer
Effner-
Johanneskirchner Str.
Cosimastr.
Lohengrinstr.
Kleinhesselòher See
J.F. Kennedy Brücke
ENGLISCHER
Ifflandstr.
Effnerstr.
Englschalkinger Str.
Arabellapark
Vollmannstr.
Tucherpark
Bülow-
Richard
Arabellastr.
Denninger Str.
Montgelasstr.
Wehrlestr.
Richard Strauss Str.
Max Josephs Brücke
Ismaninger Str.
Bogenhauser Hof
Scheinerstr.
BOGENHAUSEN
Böhmerwaldplatz
Röntgenstr.
Stuntz- str.
Acquarello
Mühlbaurstr.
Possartstr.
Museum
Prinzregentenbrücke
Oettingen- str.
E. Riedel Str.
Widenmayerstr.
Prinzregentenstr.
Käfer Schänke
Hippocampus
Prinzregentenpl.
STUCK-VILLA
Truderinger Str.
Einsteinstr.
Leuchtenbergring
Grillparzerstr.
Max Weber Pl.
Maximiliansbrücke
Max Planck Str.
Kirchenstr.
Innere Wiener Str.
Flurstr.
Neumarkter Str.
Berg am Laim Str.
Elsässer Str.
Preysingstr.
Vinaiolo
Stein- str.
Wörthstr.
Orleansstr.
Ostbahnhof
OSTBAHNHOF
Rosenheimer Str.
Atelier Gourmet
HAIDHAUSEN
Friedenstr.
Ampfingstr.
Grafinger Str.
Restaurant

Der Dantler

MODERN CUISINE • TRENDY Also known as the "Bavarian Deli", this inforr charming Alpine-style restaurant serves lunchtime snacks such as pastrami sa wiches and creamed soups. A more ambitious evening menu features a select of small, modern and creative dishes - such as Negi Maguro hotdog with tu preserved lemon and spring onion - which are perfect for sharing. The restaur also sells a range of gourmet food items.

Menu 22€ (lunch), 45/70€ - Carte 36/39€

Off plan - *Werinherstraße 15 - Ⓜ Silberhornstraße - ✆ 089 39292689 - www.derdantler.de - Closed 1-19 August, Monday, Saturday, Sunday*

At München-Haidhausen

Showroom

CREATIVE • FRIENDLY A winning formula of a laid-back atmosphere coup with creative cuisine with the emphasis on the ingredients. Harmoniously co bined flavours are brought together in each dish to memorable effect. Sa wine recommendations.

Specialities: Hamachi, white asparagus, Ponzu, goat's cheese curd, dashi. Pr Iberico pork, medlars, radish, cauliflower, buttermilk. White chocolate, umebo rhubarb, Dulce de Leche ice cream, lemon verbena.

Menu 130/160€

PLAN: 1-C3 - *Lilienstraße 6 - Ⓜ Isartor - ✆ 089 44429082 - www.showroom-restaurant.de - Closed 1-5 January, 3-21 August, Saturday, Sunda lunch Monday-Friday*

Atelier Gourmet

CLASSIC FRENCH • BISTRO Small, intimate, lively and popular, Atelier Gour is quite simply a great little restaurant. The food is fresh, delicious and go value for money thanks to chef Bousquet. It is served in a casual, friendly atm phere with efficient service and good wine recommendations from the fem owner. Try the capon and duck crépinette.

Menu 45/89€

PLAN: 1-C3 - *Rablstraße 37 - Ⓜ Rosenheimer Platz - ✆ 089 487220 - www.ateliergourmet.de - Closed 12-20 April, 31 May-8 June, 23 August-7 Septemb 24-27 December, Sunday, lunch Monday-Saturday*

Vinaiolo

ITALIAN • COSY Experience a touch of dolce vita in the old town of Haidhaus The service exudes Mediterranean charm, the cuisine is typically Italian and cosy and authentic atmosphere is accentuated by furnishings from an old g cer's shop in Trieste.

Menu 24€ (lunch)/59€ - Carte 51/61€

PLAN: 1-C3 - *Steinstraße 42 - Ⓜ Rosenheimer Platz - ✆ 089 48950356 - www.vinaiolo.de - Closed lunch Saturday*

At München-Milbertshofen

EssZimmer

MODERN FRENCH • CHIC Once you have admired the cars on show, the f served on the third floor of BMW Welt is deserving of your full attention. Cl pared-down style, tasteful expression and successful textures: this is Bo Bräuer's creativity in action. The elegant restaurant may have a thoroughly m ern feel, but that does not stop it from being cosy and peaceful. Free parking

Specialities: Carabinero, black seabream, saffron, Muscat squash. South Tyrol Wagyu, saddle and short rib, pointed pepper, red miso. Plum, yoghurt, laven grains.

Menu 150/195€

PLAN: 1-A1 - *Am Olympiapark 1 - Ⓜ Olympiazentrum - ✆ 089 358991814 - www.esszimmer-muenchen.de - Closed 1-16 January, 4 August-1 September, Mond Sunday, lunch Tuesday-Saturday*

München-Nymphenburg

Acetaia

ITALIAN • COSY Serving Italian cuisine in a comfortable Art Nouveau setting, Acetaia takes its name from the aged balsamic vinegar you will find on sale here. Walkers will enjoy a stroll along the Nymphenburger Canal to the palace with its lovely grounds.

Menu 29€ (lunch)/70€ – Carte 50/70€

Off plan – *Nymphenburger Straße 215 – Ⓜ Rotkreuzplatz – ✆ 089 13929077 – www.acetaia.de – Closed lunch Saturday*

München-Oberföhring

Freisinger Hof

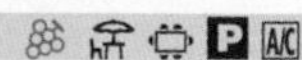

COUNTRY COOKING • INN This is just what you imagine a traditional Bavarian restaurant to be like. Dating back to 1875, it stands just outside the city gates and serves typical Bavarian and Austrian cuisine. Dishes include Krosser saddle of suckling pig, and Vienna-style beef boiled in broth.

Carte 35/70€

PLAN: 1-D1 – *Oberföhringer Straße 189 – ✆ 089 952302 – www.freisinger-hof.de*

München-Schwabing

Tantris

CLASSIC FRENCH • VINTAGE Tantris is quite simply THE place to eat with its near legendary 1970s-style and Hans Haas' sublime, product-based classic cuisine. The cult setting and fine dining are accompanied by a well-practised, friendly and professional front-of-house team, as well as good wine recommendations.

Specialities: Variation of tuna. Lamb served on a bed of artichokes with curried artichoke stock. Poppy seed soufflé with blueberry cream and sour cherry ice cream.

Menu 100€ (lunch), 200/235€ – Carte 130/175€

PLAN: 1-B1 – *Johann-Fichte-Straße 7 – Ⓜ Dietlindenstraße – ✆ 089 3619590 – www.tantris.de – Closed 1-15 January, 5-21 April, 30 August-8 September, 20-28 December, Monday, Tuesday, Sunday*

Werneckhof by Geisel

MODERN CUISINE • COSY The cuisine prepared by Tohru Nakamura is anything but 'off the peg'. The finesse and fluency with which he combines top-quality produce, classic principles and Japanese influences to create elegant, creative dishes is genuinely impressive and clearly bears his inimitable signature.

Specialities: Hamachi, crab, nasturtium and celery. Ozaki Wagyu, Kashihikari, black salsify, gobo and wasabi. Tokyo Banana, coriander, Mirin sabayon, black sesame and passion fruit.

Menu 180/215€

PLAN: 1-C2 – *Werneckstraße 11 – Ⓜ Münchner Freiheit – ✆ 089 38879568 – www.geisels-werneckhof.de – Closed 1-8 January, 5-20 April, 2 August-7 September, Monday, Sunday, lunch Tuesday-Saturday*

Le Cézanne

FRENCH • FAMILY In this friendly corner restaurant the chef cooks dishes from his French homeland. You can choose from the blackboard or the small menu of classic dishes. In summer, enjoy your meal outdoors or by the open, glass façade.

Menu 49/54€ – Carte 34/65€

PLAN: 1-B2 – *Konradstraße 1 – Ⓜ Giselastraße – ✆ 089 391805 – www.le-cezanne.de – Closed Monday*

Bibulus

ITALIAN • ELEGANT It says something when a restaurant is popular with the cals, and the people of Schwabing clearly appreciate the uncomplicated and voursome Italian food. It is especially nice outside in the little square under plane trees. Charming service.

Menu 55/84 € – Carte 44/67 €

PLAN: 1-B1 – *Siegfriedstraße 11* – Ⓜ *Münchner Freiheit* – ✆ *089 396447* – *www.bibulus-ristorante.de* – *Closed Sunday, lunch Saturday*

La Bohème

MEATS AND GRILLS • TRENDY A pleasantly convivial and relaxed place to e This trendy urban restaurant is just the ticket for fans of high-quality steak cu There are even 1000g steaks as a sharing variant. The mixed plates are also av able for sharing. The Sunday brunch is a popular event.

Menu 37/99 € – Carte 35/137 €

PLAN: 1-B1 – *Leopoldstraße 180* – Ⓜ *Dietlindenstraße* – ✆ *089 23762323* – *www.boheme-schwabing.de* – *Closed Monday, lunch Saturday*

Mlenny/iStock

GREECE

ELLÁDA

ATHENS
ATHÍNA

tanukiphoto/iStock

ATHENS IN...

→ **ONE DAY**
Acropolis (Parthenon), Agora and Temple of Hephaestus, Plaka.

→ **TWO DAYS**
Kolonaki, National Archaeological Museum, Filopappou Hill.

→ **THREE DAYS**
Monastiraki flea-market (Sunday), Benaki Museum, Technopolis, National Gardens, Lykavittos Hill.

Inventing democracy, th theatre and the Olympi Games… and planting th seeds of philosophy an Western Civilisation – Athen was central to all of these, city that became a bywor for glory and learning, a plac whose golden reputatio could inspire such awe tha centuries later just the men tion of its name was enough t turn people misty-eyed. It's magical place, built upon eight hills and plains, with a histor stretching back at least 3,000 years. Its short but highl productive golden age resulted in the architectural glory o The Acropolis, while the likes of Plato, Aristotle and Socrate were in the business of changing the mindset of society.

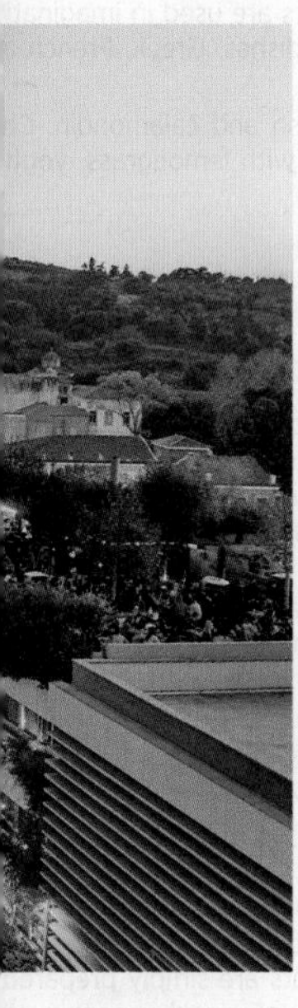

The Acropolis still dominates Athens and can be seen peeking through alleyways and turnings all over the city. Beneath it lies a teeming metropolis, part urban melting pot, part über-buzzy neighbourhood. Plaka, below the Acropolis, is the old quarter, and the most visited, a mixture of great charm and cheap gift shops. North and west, Monastiraki and Psiri have become trendy zones; to the east, Syntagma and Kolonaki are notably modern and smart, home to the Greek parliament and the famous. The most northerly districts of central Athens are Omonia and Exarcheia, distinguished by their rugged appearance and steeped in history; much of the life in these parts is centred round the polytechnic and the central marketplace.

EATING OUT

n recent times, a smart wave of res- aurants has hit the city and, with many hefs training abroad before returning ome, this is a good time to eat out n the shadow of The Acropolis. If you ant the full experience, dine with e locals rather than the tourists and ake your reservation for late eve- ing, as Greeks rarely go out for dinner efore 10pm. The trend towards a more clectic restaurant scene now means at you can find everything from clas- ical French and Italian cuisine to Asian nd Moroccan dishes, and even sushi. Modern tavernas offer good attention to detail, but this doesn't mean they're replacing the wonderfully traditional favourites. These older tavernas, along with mezedopoleia, are the backbone of Greek dining, and most visitors wouldn't think their trip was complete without eating in one; often the waiter will just tell you what's cooking that day - and you're usually very welcome to go into the kitchen and make your selection. Greece is a country where it is customary to tip good service; ten per cent is the normal rate.

Centre

Spondi

FRENCH • ROMANTIC A discreet, intimate restaurant with two delightful cou yards and two charming dining rooms – one built from reclaimed bricks in t style of a vaulted cellar. Top quality seasonal ingredients are used in imaginati deftly executed, stunningly presented modern French dishes. Greek, French a Italian wines feature on an impressive list.

Specialities: Langoustine with caviar, watermelon radish and calamondin. Ch lans duck with cherries, red shiso and beetroot. Apple with lemongrass, yogh and apple sorbet.

Menu 110/160 €

PLAN: D3 – *5 Pyrronos, Pangrati – ✆ 21 0756 4021 – www.spondi.gr – Closed lunch Monday-Sunday*

Hytra

MODERN CUISINE • DESIGN Take the express lift up to the 6th floor of t striking Onassis Cultural Centre; here you'll find a sultry restaurant looking c over Syngrou. Classic Greek recipes are executed in a refined modern manne for something a little different try the cocktail pairings. They also offer a bis menu at the bar.

Specialities: Crayfish with wild garlic cream, crab sauce and basil. Milk-fed la with vine leaves, pistachio nuts and yoghurt. Apple with cashew biscuit and ca mel ice cream.

Menu 62/80 € – Carte 71/90 €

Off plan – *107-109 Syngrou Avenue – ✆ 21 0331 6767 – www.hytra.gr – Closed 17-20 April, 30 April-3 May, lunch Monday-Sunday*

Athiri

GREEK • NEIGHBOURHOOD In winter, sit inside, surrounded by blue, white a grey hues; in summer, head out to the courtyard and well-spaced tables s rounded by lush green plants. Local, seasonal ingredients are simply prepared order to reveal their natural flavours. Dishes are good value and generous, w creative touches.

Carte 29/40 €

PLAN: A2 – *15 Plateon – Ⓜ Keramikós – ✆ 21 0346 2983 – www.athirirestaurant.gr – Closed 1-5 January, 17-23 April, 9-23 August, Monday, lunch Tuesday-Saturday, Sunday*

Nolan

FUSION • TRENDY This small, contemporary bistro stands out from the oth restaurants in this busy neighbourhood. The young chef has Greek, German a Asian roots and his cooking fuses influences from all three countries along w many other international flavours. Dishes provide plenty of appeal and are gre for sharing.

Carte 27/40 €

PLAN: C3 – *31-33 Voulis Street – Ⓜ Syntagma – ✆ 21 0324 3545 – www.nolanrestaurant.gr – Closed 9-17 August, Sunday*

Oikeîo

GREEK • RUSTIC A sweet little restaurant in a chic neighbourhood, with tab on two different levels, as well as outside. The décor is traditional and the pla has a warm, cosy feel. Menus offer great value family-style dishes made with fre ingredients and feature the likes of sardines, moussaka and octopus in vinegar.

Carte 20/25 €

PLAN: D2 – *15 Ploutarhou Street – Ⓜ Evangelismos – ✆ 21 0725 9216 – Closed 1-31 August, Sunday*

7 Food Sins 

GREEK • NEIGHBOURHOOD A vibrant, personally run restaurant in the centre of busy Plaka; its name refers to their philosophy, which is built around 7 sins of eating, including using your hands, feeding friends and being gluttonous. Appealing modern menus offer well-priced, tasty Greek and Mediterranean dishes.

Carte 36/58€

PLAN: C3 - *Square Filomousou Etaireias 1 - Ⓜ Syntagma - ✆ 21 0701 1108 - www.7foodsins.com - Closed lunch Monday-Sunday*

Alficon 

MODERN CUISINE • NEIGHBOURHOOD Alficon sits within a charming neoclassical building tucked away in a side street and comes with a pretty pavement terrace. The keen young chefs prepare a short seasonal menu of modern Greek dishes which are presented by an engaging serving team and accompanied by organic Greek wines.

Menu 50/85€ - Carte 35/55€

PLAN: D3 - *8 Ironda - Ⓜ Syntagma - ✆ 21 6900 5059 - www.alficonathens.com - Closed 13-20 April, Monday, lunch Tuesday-Saturday, Sunday*

Birdman 

JAPANESE • NEIGHBOURHOOD A bright neon sign marks out this on-trend Japanese izakaya. A great soundtrack and a serious cocktail list set the mood and the young team are full of energy. Japanese snacks and grill-based dishes have a modernised Western edge; they arrive as they're ready and you can order more as you go along.

Carte 25/45€

PLAN: C3 - *35 Voulis - Ⓜ Syntagma - ✆ 21 0321 2800 - Closed Sunday*

Cookoovaya 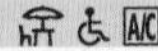

GREEK • FRIENDLY A group of the city's leading chefs came together to open this bustling restaurant, where rustic, homely cooking is the order of the day and generous dishes are designed for sharing. The homemade pies from the wood-oven are a hit.

Carte 42/68€

PLAN: D2 - *2A Chatzigianni Mexi Street - Ⓜ Evangelismos - ✆ 21 0723 5005 - www.cookoovaya.gr - Closed 10-15 April, 9-23 August*

CTC 

MODERN CUISINE • INTIMATE The ambitious chef-owner of this sleek, intimate restaurant likes to explore and push the boundaries. Choose between 3 surprise tasting menus where cooking is a modern blend of Greek and Gallic elements. Presentation is elaborate and the crockery is carefully selected to enhance each course.

Menu 38/90€

PLAN: D2 - *14 Oumplianis - Ⓜ Evangelismos - ✆ 21 0722 8812 - www.ctc-restaurant.com - Closed 25 July-25 August, Monday, lunch Tuesday-Saturday, Sunday*

Electra Roof Garden 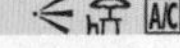

MEDITERRANEAN CUISINE • ROMANTIC Set on the top floor of the Electra Palace hotel, this superbly located restaurant offers unrivalled views of The Acropolis and downtown Athens. Well-made dishes are a mix of traditional Greek and more international flavours.

Menu 30€ (lunch), 35/60€ - Carte 35/65€

PLAN: C3 - *Electra Palace Hotel, 18-20 Nikodimou Street - Ⓜ Syntagma - ✆ 21 0337 0000 - www.electrahotels.gr*

A
B
Liosion
Paloniou
Michail
Acharnon
Pl. Egiptou
Tritis Septemvriou
Boumpoulinas
Spyridonos Trikoupi
Leoforos Konstantinoupoleos
T. Diligianni
Ioulianou
Metsovou
Maroneias
Ioulianou
Voda
28 Oktovriou
V. Irakleiou
Larissis
ETHNIKÓ ARHEOLOGIKÓ MOUSSÍO
Sidirodromon
Ipeirou
Neof. Metaxa
Tosits
1
Liosion
Acharnon
Marni
Ioanninon
H
Stournari
Akominatou
Psaron
Chiou
PELOPONISSOS
Pl. Vathis
(Patission)
POLITEHNÍOU
Tritis Septemvriou
Pl. Kaningos
Emmanouil
T. Diligianni
Favierou
Marni
Lenorman
Satovriandou
Akadimias
Karolou
Metaxourghio
Pl. Karaïskaki
Omonia
OMONOIA
Ag. Konstantinou
L. Konstantinoupoleos
Menandrou
El. Venizelou
Deligiorgi
Athinas
Sokratous
Achilleos
Alexandrou
Stadiou
Kolokynthous
H Pl. Kodzia
METAXOURGÍO
Thermopylon
Panepistimiou
2
Myllerou
Tsaldari
Sofokleous
KENDRIKÍ AGORÁ
Pl. Klafthmonos
Evripidou
Keramei kou
Pl. Eleftherias
Praxitelous
Megalou
Plataion
Panagi
Aristofanous
Aiolou
Kriezi
Sarri
Athiri
Kolokotroni
Athinas
(Peiraios)
Athinaidos
Iera Odos
KAPNIKARÉA
Keramikós
KERAMIKÓS
PL. MONASTIRÁKI
Ergon
Ermou
Mitropoleos
Voutadon
Ermou
Thissio
MIKRÍ MITRÓPOLI
Adrianou
Monastiraki
Eptachalkou
Thessalonikis
Adrianou
Peiraios
THISSÍO
MONASTIRAKI
ROMAÏKÍ AGORÁ
ARHÉA AGORÁ
PLÁKA
Nileos
Aktaiou
Nileos
Apostolou
Akamantos
M
Theorias
Kymaion
ÁRIOS PÁGOS
3
ASTEROSKOPÍO
AKRÓPOLI
LÓFOS NIMFÓN
Pavlou
Thessalonikis
Trion Ierarchon
Dimofontos
ODIOU IRÓDOU ATIKOÚ
THÉATRO DIONÍSSOU
Aeropagitou
PNÍKA
Dionysiou
Karyatidon
M
Apolloniou
Rovertou Gkalli
Parthenonos
Garivaldi
Chatzi
A
LÓFOS FILOPÁPOU
B

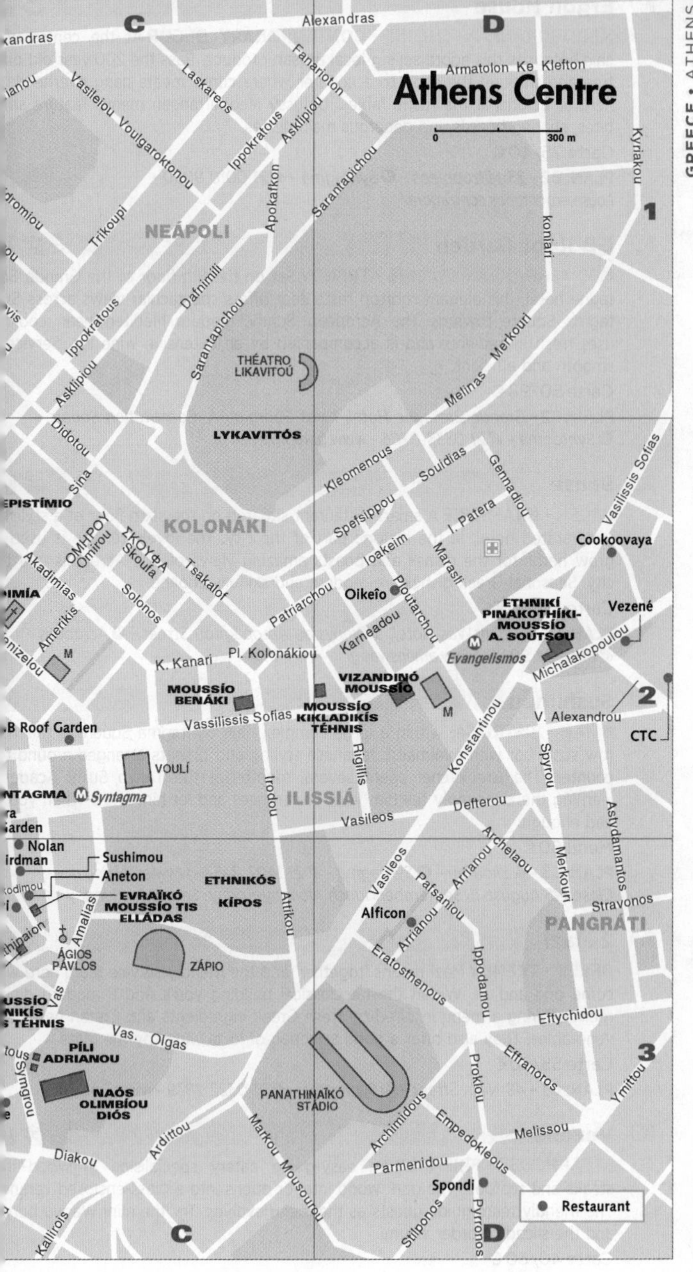
Athens Centre
0
300 m
Alexandras
Armatolon Ke Klefton
Fanarioton
Laskareos
Vasileiou Voulgaroktonou
Ippokratous
Asklipiou
Apokafkon
Sarantapichou
Kyriakou
Koniari
Trikoupi
NEÁPOLI
Dafnimili
Melinas Merkouri
THÉATRO LIKAVITOÚ
LYKAVITTÓS
Didotou
Sina
Kleomenous
Souldias
Gennadiou
Vasilissis Sofias
Spefsippou
I. Patera
KOLONÁKI
ΟΜΗΡΟΥ Omirou
ΣΚΟΥΦΑ Skoufa
Tsakalof
Akadimias
Ioakeim
Marasli
Cookoovaya
Oikeîo
Ploutarchou
Patriarchou
Solonos
Amerikis
Karneadou
ETHNIKÍ PINAKOTHÍKI-MOUSSÍO A. SOÚTSOU
Vezené
Evangelismos
Michalakopoulou
K. Kanari
Pl. Kolonákiou
VIZANDINÓ MOUSSÍO
MOUSSÍO BENÁKI
MOUSSÍO KIKLADIKÍS TÉHNIS
Vassilissis Sofias
Konstantinou
V. Alexandrou
CTC
Roof Garden
VOULÍ
Rigillis
Irodou
Spyrou
ILISSIÁ
Syntagma
Defterou
Vasileos
Astydamantos
Nolan
Sushimou
Aneton
Archelaou
Merkouri
ETHNIKÓS KÍPOS
EVRAÏKÓ MOUSSÍO TIS ELLÁDAS
Attikou
Vasileos
Pafsaniou
Arrianou
Stravonos
Alficon
PANGRÁTI
Amalias
ÁGIOS PÁVLOS
ZÁPIO
Eratosthenous
Ippodamou
Eftychidou
Vas. Olgas
PÍLI ADRIANOU
Syngrou
NAÓS OLIMBÍOU DIÓS
Efranoros
Ymittou
PANATHINAÏKÓ STÁDIO
Proklou
Archimidous
Empedokleous
Melissou
Diakou
Arditou
Markou Mousourou
Parmenidou
Spondi
Restaurant
Stilponos
Pyrronos
Kallirois
C
D
1
2
3

Ergon House

MEDITERRANEAN CUISINE • CONTEMPORARY DÉCOR At the centre of chic hotel sits this agora selling local artisan produce. Pass the 200 year old oli tree and through the shop to a counter where cured meats hang overhead; here or at one of the rustic tables. Unfussy Mediterranean menus feature sm bites, sharing boards and generous main dishes.

Carte 25/40€

PLAN: B2 – *23 Mitropoleos* – Ⓜ *Syntagma* – ✆ *21 0010 9090* – *house.ergonfoods.com/agora/*

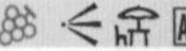

GB Roof Garden

MEDITERRANEAN CUISINE • TRENDY Set on the 8th floor of the Grande B tagne hotel, this elegant rooftop restaurant offers spectacular views across Sy tagma Square towards The Acropolis. Sunny, modern Mediterranean cooki uses fresh ingredients and is accompanied by an extensive wine list. Service smooth and efficient.

Carte 50/98€

PLAN: C2 – *Grande Bretagne Hotel, 1 Vas Georgiou A, Constitution Square* – Ⓜ *Syntagma* – ✆ *21 0333 0766* – *www.gbroofgarden.gr*

Sense

GREEK • BRASSERIE A smart restaurant situated on the sixth floor of a stylis understated hotel, in the historic part of the city. The lovely terrace is used grow herbs for the dishes and boasts amazing views of The Acropolis and t city. Seasonal Greek dishes are modern and skilfully cooked.

Carte 30/50€

PLAN: C3 – *AthensWas Hotel, 5 Dionysiou Areopagitou Street* – Ⓜ *Acropolis* – ✆ *21 0924 9954* – *www.athenswas.gr*

Sushimou

ASIAN • BISTRO Set within a large complex near Syntagma Square is this n row sushi bar with minimalist Japanese styling and 12 seats arranged around counter. The Greek chef spent several months at the Tokyo Sushi Acade learning the art; simply tell him your preferences and let him know when you had enough.

Menu 60€

PLAN: C3 – *6 Skoufou* – Ⓜ *Syntagma* – ✆ *21 1407 8457* – *www.sushimou.gr* – *Closed 15 August-15 September, lunch Monday-Friday, Saturday, Sunday*

2 Mazi

GREEK • TRENDY Mazi means 'together' and the friendly service team here w come one and all. Within the neoclassical building you'll find a modern din room offering a menu inspired by fresh Greek ingredients and Cretan herbs a vegetables. They also offer a good selection of local wines by the glass.

Carte 55/70€

PLAN: C3 – *48 Nikis Street* – Ⓜ *Syntagma* – ✆ *21 0322 2839* – *www.2mazi.gr*

Vezené

STEAKHOUSE • FRIENDLY An easy-going eatery specialising in wood-fi steaks and seafood. The dark wood interior opens into a glass-enclosed veran The friendly team guide guests as the menu evolves. Try the mini Wagyu bur and the sliced-to-order salumi.

Carte 40/60€

PLAN: D2 – *Vrasida 11* – Ⓜ *Evangelismos* – ✆ *21 0723 2002* – *www.vezene.gr* – *Closed lunch Monday-Saturday, Sunday*

Environs of Athens

at Halandri Northeast: 11 km by Vas. Sofias

✿ Botrini's (Ettore Botrini)

MEDITERRANEAN CUISINE • DESIGN A keenly run, ultra-modern restaurant away from the centre of the city; sit in the main room with its view of the chefs at work. Creative, characterful, flavour-packed dishes showcase the owner-chef's Greek-Italian heritage. He hails from Corfu and ingredients from the island are well used.

Specialities: As "Carbonara" from land and sea. "The Corfu Bourdeto that would like to become Cacciuco alla Livornese". "The Last Temptation".

Menu 70/120 € – Carte 73/122 €

Off plan – *24b Vasileos Georgiou – ✆ 21 0685 7323 – www.botrinis.com – Closed 5-25 August, Monday, lunch Tuesday-Saturday, Sunday*

at Maroussi Northeast: 12. 5 km by Vas. Sofias

Aneton

GREEK • FRIENDLY It's worth travelling into the smart city suburbs to seek out this appealing neighbourhood restaurant. Menus follow the seasons; in summer they have a Mediterranean base and some Middle Eastern spicing, while in winter, hearty stews and casseroles feature. The hands-on owner really brings the place to life.

Carte 20/60 €

PLAN: C3 – *3 Navarchou Nikodimou – Ⓜ Maroussi – ✆ 21 0806 6700 – www.aneton.gr – Closed Sunday*

at Piraeus Southwest: 8 km by Singrou

Varoulko Seaside (Lefteris Lazarou)

SEAFOOD • CLASSIC DÉCOR Varoulko sits in a great spot in Mikrolimano Marina – the chef's old neighbourhood. Watch the yachts glide by from the maritime-themed dining room which opens onto the water. Greek and Mediterranean dishes showcase organic vegetables, Cretan olive oil and the freshest seafood; squid and octopus feature highly.

Specialities: Red mullet tartare with Florina pepper, raisins and bottarga powder. Grouper with beets, broccolini, black garlic and béarnaise sauce. Cherry ganache with pistachio mousse, hibiscus and kaimaki sorbet.

Menu 60/90 € – Carte 54/58 €

Off plan – *Akti Koumoundourou, 54-56 Mikrolimano Marina – Ⓜ Piraeus – ✆ 21 0522 8400 – www.varoulko.gr*

focusstock/iStock

HUNGARY

MAGYARORSZÁG

BUDAPEST
BUDAPEST

jon chica parada/iStock

BUDAPEST IN...

→ **ONE DAY**
Royal Palace, the Parliament Building,
a trip on the Danube.

→ **TWO DAYS**
Gellert Baths, a stroll down Váci utca,
a concert at the State Opera House.

→ **THREE DAYS**
Museum of Applied Arts, Margaret Island, coffee and cake at Gerbeaud.

No one knows quite where the Hungarian language came from: it's not quite Slavic, not quite Turkic, and its closest relatives appear to be in Finland and Siberia. In much the same way, Hungary's capital is a bit of an enigma. A lot of what you see is not as old as it appears. Classical and Gothic buildings are mostly neoclassical and neo-Gothic and the fabled baroque of the city is of a more recent vintage than in other European capitals. That's because Budapest's frequent invaders and conquerors, from all compass points of the map, left little but rubble behind them when they left; the grand look of today took shape for the most part no earlier than the mid-19C.

It's still a beautiful place to look at, with hilly Buda keeping watch – via eight great bridges – over sprawling Pest on the other side of the lilting, bending Danube. These were formerly two separate towns, united in 1873 to form a capital city. It enjoyed its heyday around that time, a magnificent city that was the hub of the Austro-Hungarian Empire. Defeats in two world wars and fifty years behind the Iron Curtain put paid to the glory, but battered Budapest is used to rising from the ashes and now it's Europe's most earthily beautiful capital, particularly when winter mists rise from the river to shroud it in a thick white cloak. In summer the days can swelter, and the spas are definitely worth a visit.

EATING OUT

The city is most famous for its coffee houses so, before you start investigating restaurants, find time to tuck into a cream cake with a double espresso in, say, the Ruszwurm on Castle Hill, the city's oldest, and possibly cosiest, café. In tourist areas, it's not difficult to locate goulash on your menu, and you never have to travel far to find beans, dumplings and cabbage in profusion. Having said that, Budapest's culinary scene has moved on apace since the fall of communism, and Hungarian chefs have become much more inventive with their use of local, seasonal produce. Pest is where you'll find most choice but even in Buda there are plenty of worthy restaurants. Lots of locals like to eat sausage on the run and if you fancy the idea, buy a pocket knife. Sunday brunch is popular in Budapest, especially at the best hotels. Your restaurant bill might well include a service charge; don't feel obliged to pay it, as tipping is entirely at your own discretion – though you may find the persistence of the little folk groups that pop up in many restaurants hard to resist.

Pest

✿✿ Onyx

MODERN CUISINE • ELEGANT A listed building in the city's heart plays host t this opulent restaurant with a contemporary black and silver colour scheme an onyx adornments. Passionately prepared, precisely crafted dishes keep Hungaria flavours to the fore yet are elevated to another level with their carefully balance originality.

Specialities: Duck liver, coffee and truffle. Pigeon with carrot and golden raisin Gianduja tart with bergamot and baguette ice cream.

Menu 19900 Ft (lunch)/33900 Ft

PLAN: 2-E2 – *Vörösmarty tér 7-8 – Ⓜ Vörösmarty tér – ✆ (30) 508 0622 – www.onyxrestaurant.hu – Closed 11-26 January, 3-25 August, Monday, lunch Tuesday-Wednesday, Sunday*

✿ Babel

MODERN CUISINE • ELEGANT A stylish, intimate restaurant run with a real pas sion by the owner and his young team. Cooking is innovative and flavourfu dishes on the Babel Classic menu are informed by the chef's Transylvanian her tage and each has a story to tell, while dishes on the Tasting Menu are more am bitious, with some playful elements.

Specialities: Octopus with paprika, bacon, milk cracker and vegetables. Lam neck with homemade lavender cheese and whey. Tomato with elderflower, rh barb and yoghurt aero.

Menu 29900 Ft

PLAN: 2-E2 – *Piarista Köz 2 – Ⓜ Ferenciek ter – ✆ (70) 6000 800 – www.babel-budapest.hu – Closed 2-16 February, 4-18 August, Monday, lunch Tuesday-Saturday, Sunday*

✿ Borkonyha Winekitchen (Ákos Sárközi)

MODERN CUISINE • TRENDY A bustling wine-orientated restaurant close to th Basilica; over 200 wines are available, and around a quarter of them by the glas Skilfully executed, eye-catching dishes have subtle Hungarian influences; th kitchen keeps things simple by sourcing top-class ingredients and allowin them to shine.

Specialities: Duck liver with beetroot and cherry. Mangalica pork with soure salad and onion. Rákóczi Túrós - cottage cheese cake with meringue.

Menu 23000 Ft – Carte 8650/15950 Ft

PLAN: 2-E2 – *Sas utca 3 – Ⓜ Bajcsy-Zsilinszky út – ✆ (1) 266 0835 – www.borkonyha.hu – Closed 18-25 January, Sunday*

✿ Costes

MODERN CUISINE • DESIGN A sophisticated restaurant on a lively street. Th menu blends Hungarian classics with some Portuguese touches and is presente as a pack of playing cards: choose 4, 5, 6 or 7 of the dishes offered – or play th joker and let the kitchen surprise you. Wine and beer pairings are available to ac company your meal.

Specialities: Derelye pasta with pumpkin and sage. Mangalica with celeriac an chard. Honey, milk and chamomile.

Menu 29000/41500 Ft

PLAN: 2-F3 – *Ráday utca 4 – Ⓜ Kálvin tér – ✆ (1) 219 0696 – www.costes.hu – Closed Monday, Tuesday, lunch Wednesday-Sunday*

✿ Costes Downtown

MODERN CUISINE • TRENDY Set on the ground floor of the Prestige Hotel, th strikingly decorated restaurant brings nature inside with a living wall and ceilin ask for one of the booths or sit at the chef's table for a view of the kitchen. Me nus showcase Hungarian ingredients and flavours are gutsy and well-defined.

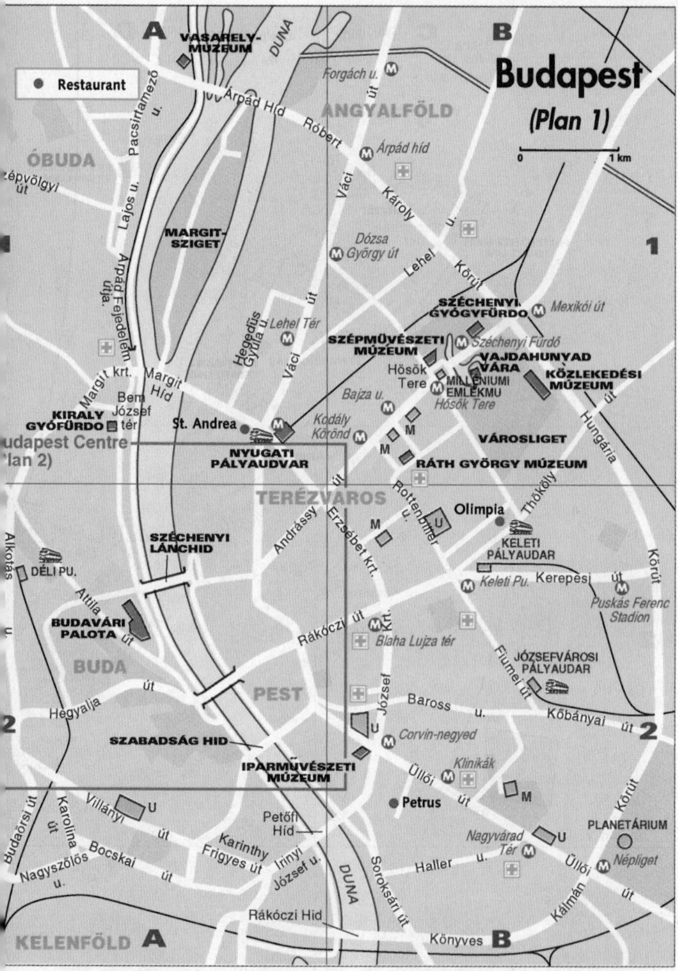

Budapest (Plan 1)

Specialities: Marinated char with plums. Mangalica chops 'Vadas' with root vegetables. Abade de Priscos pudding with wild berries.

Menu 7900 Ft (lunch), 24000/40000 Ft – Carte 8500/24200 Ft

PLAN: 2-E1 – *Prestige Hotel, Vigyázó Ferenc utca 5* – Ⓜ *Vörösmarty tér* – ✆ *(1) 920 1015* – *www.costesdowntown.hu*

✿ **Stand** (Tamás Széll and Szabina Szulló)

MODERN CUISINE • DESIGN An eye-catching modern restaurant with a glass-fronted kitchen at its hub. Cooking focuses on Hungarian gastronomy; refining classic dishes through the use of modern techniques. The wine list offers a global selection but it's well worth opting for the Hungarian recommendations.

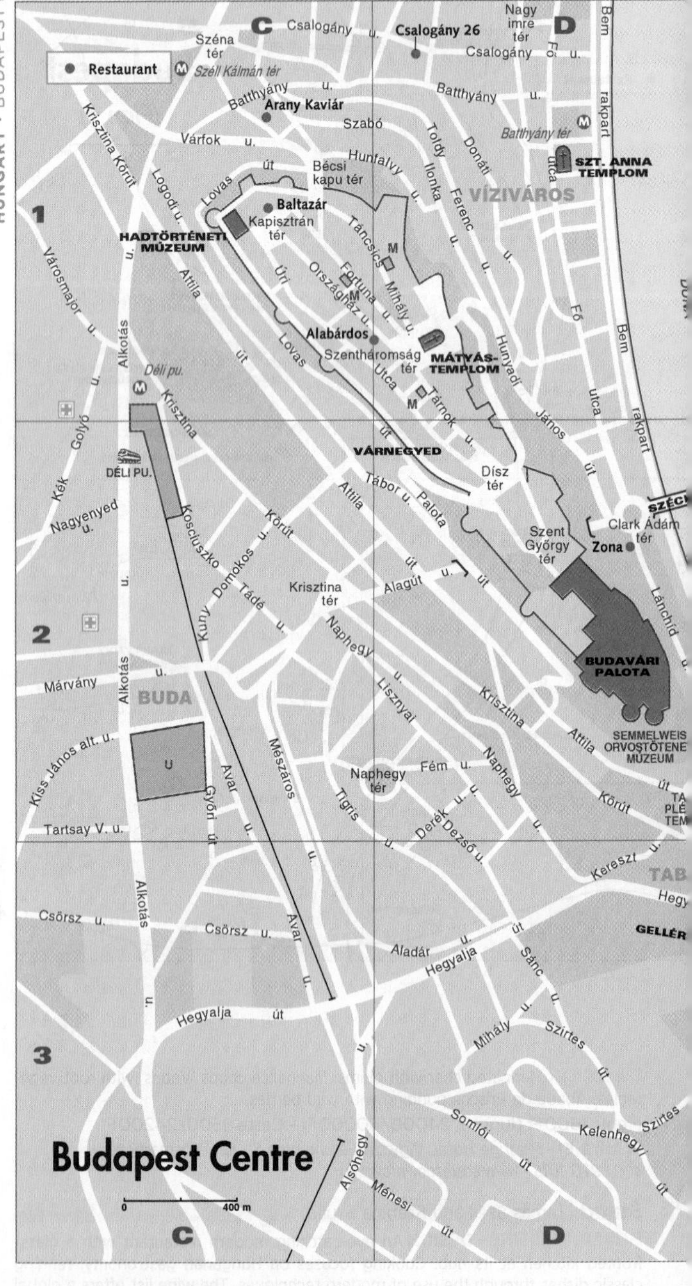
Budapest Centre
0
400 m
Restaurant
Széll Kálmán tér
Csalogány 26
Arany Kaviár
Baltazár
Alabárdos
Zona
HADTÖRTÉNETI MÚZEUM
MÁTYÁS-TEMPLOM
SZT. ANNA TEMPLOM
BUDAVÁRI PALOTA
SEMMELWEIS ORVOSTÖRTÉNETI MÚZEUM
VÁRNEGYED
VÍZIVÁROS
BUDA
GELLÉR
TAB
DÉLI PU.
Déli pu.
Batthyány tér
Széna tér
Nagy imre tér
Bécsi kapu tér
Kapisztrán tér
Szentháromság tér
Dísz tér
Szent György tér
Clark Ádám tér
Krisztina tér
Naphegy tér
Csalogány u.
Batthyány u.
Szabó
Várfok u.
Hunfalvy u.
Toldy
Ilonka
Donáti
Ferenc u.
Fő u.
Fő utca
Bem rakpart
Bem utca
Krisztina Körút
Logodi u.
Lovas út
Úri u.
Országház u.
Fortuna u.
Táncsics Mihály u.
Hunyadi János út
Tárnok u.
Tábor u.
Palota út
Attila út
Attila u.
Városmajor u.
Alkotás u.
Golyó u.
Kék
Nagyenyed u.
Kosciuszko Tádé u.
Kuny Domokos u.
Alagút u.
Naphegy u.
Lisznyai u.
Krisztina Körút
Lánchíd
Márvány u.
Kiss János alt. u.
Tartsay V. u.
Avar u.
Győri út
Mészáros u.
Tigris u.
Fém u.
Derék u.
Dezső u.
Kereszt u.
Hegy
Csörsz u.
Aladár u.
Hegyalja út
Sánc u.
Mihály u.
Szirtes út
Somlói út
Kelenhegyi út
Alsóhegy u.
Ménesi út
M
U
1
2
3
C
D

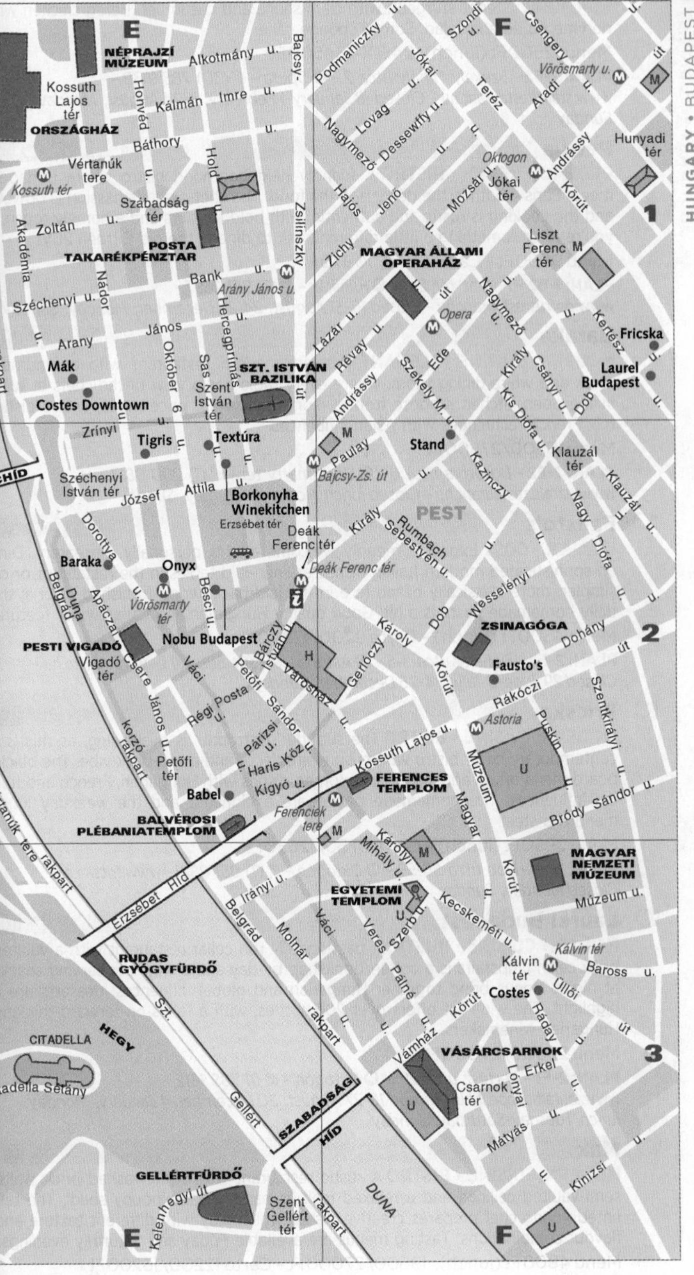

E
F
1
2
3
NÉPRAJZI MÚZEUM
Kossuth Lajos tér
ORSZÁGHÁZ
Vértanúk tere
Kossuth tér
Szabadság tér
POSTA TAKARÉKPÉNZTAR
Arany János u.
SZT. ISTVÁN BAZILIKA
Szent István tér
Mák
Costes Downtown
Tigris
Textúra
Borkonyha Winekitchen
Széchenyi István tér
Erzsébet tér
Deák Ferenc tér
Baraka
Onyx
Vörösmarty tér
PESTI VIGADÓ
Vigadó tér
Nobu Budapest
Petőfi tér
Babel
BALVÉROSI PLÉBANIATEMPLOM
Ferenciek tere
FERENCES TEMPLOM
EGYETEMI TEMPLOM
RUDAS GYÓGYFÜRDŐ
CITADELLA
GELLÉRTFÜRDŐ
Szent Gellért tér
SZABADSÁG HÍD
DUNA
VÁSÁRCSARNOK
Csarnok tér
Kálvin tér
Costes
MAGYAR NEMZETI MÚZEUM
Astoria
Fausto's
ZSINAGÓGA
PEST
Stand
Klauzál tér
Paulay
Bajcsy-Zs. út
MAGYAR ÁLLAMI OPERAHÁZ
Opera
Fricska
Laurel Budapest
Liszt Ferenc tér
Oktogon
Jókai tér
Hunyadi tér
Vörösmarty u.
Alkotmány u.
Kálmán Imre u.
Báthory u.
Honvéd u.
Hold u.
Zoltán u.
Akadémia u.
Nádor u.
Bank u.
Zsilinszky út
Bajcsy-
Széchenyi u.
Arany János u.
Október 6 u.
Hercegprímás u.
Sas u.
Zrínyi u.
József Attila u.
Dorottya u.
Apáczai Csere János u.
Duna Belgrád rakpart
Váci u.
Régi Posta u.
Petőfi Sándor u.
Bárczy István u.
Városház u.
Gerlóczy u.
Párizsi u.
Haris Köz
Kigyó u.
Kossuth Lajos u.
Károlyi Mihály u.
Irányi u.
Belgrád rakpart
Molnár u.
Veres Pálné u.
Szerb u.
Kecskeméti u.
Erzsébet Híd
Szt. Gellért rakpart
Vámház Körút
Erkel u.
Lónyai u.
Mátyás u.
Kinizsi u.
Ráday u.
Üllői út
Baross u.
Múzeum u.
Múzeum Körút
Magyar u.
Bródy Sándor u.
Puskin u.
Szentkirályi u.
Rákóczi út
Dohány u.
Wesselényi u.
Dob u.
Károly Körút
Király u.
Rumbach Sebestyén u.
Nagy Diófa u.
Klauzál u.
Kazinczy u.
Kis Diófa u.
Csányi u.
Dob u.
Kertész u.
Nagymező u.
Székely M. u.
Ede u.
Andrássy út
Révay u.
Lázár u.
Zichy Jenő u.
Hajós u.
Mozsár u.
Dessewffy u.
Nagymező u.
Lovag u.
Podmaniczky u.
Jókai u.
Szondi u.
Teréz Körút
Csengery u.
Aradi u.
Andrássy út
Citadella Sétány
Kelenhegyi út
HEGY
Vértanúk tere rakpart
korzó rakpart
HÍD

Specialities: Sterlet sturgeon with clam sauce and cucumber. Bereg chicken wi pomme purée and salad. Somlói sponge cake.

Menu 12500 Ft (lunch), 24500/34500 Ft

PLAN: 2-F2 – *Székely Mihály utca 2 – Ⓜ Opera – ✆ (30) 785 9139 – www.standrestaurant.hu – Closed 18 January-1 February, 3-24 August, Monday, Sunday*

Petrus

CLASSIC FRENCH • BISTRO A friendly neighbourhood bistro where Budape meets Paris – both in the décor and the food. The chef-owner's passion is obviou and the cooking is rustic and authentic, with bold flavours and a homely touch. you're after something a little different, ask to dine in the old Citroën 2CV!

Menu 9990 Ft – Carte 6070/10970 Ft

PLAN: 1-B2 – *Ferenc tér 2-3 – Ⓜ Klinikák – ✆ (1) 951 2597 – www.petrusrestaurant.hu – Closed 16-31 August, 24-26 December, Monday, Sunday*

Baraka

MODERN CUISINE • ELEGANT A smart modern restaurant with an intimat black and white dining room, where every table has a view of the chefs at wor in the open kitchen. Choose from a 4 or 6 course set price menu, where dishe mix French techniques with Asian influences.

Menu 19500/27500 Ft

PLAN: 2-E2 – *Dorottya utca 6 – Ⓜ Vörösmarty tér – ✆ (1) 200 0817 – www.barakarestaurant.hu – Closed lunch Monday-Saturday, Sunday*

Fausto's

ITALIAN • COSY Expect a friendly welcome at this personally run eatery. Din on sophisticated modern Italian dishes at linen-laid tables in the restaurant or o simpler, more classically based fare in the laid-back, wood-furnished osteria; th daily homemade pasta is a hit. Good quality Hungarian and Italian wines feature

Menu 4500 Ft (lunch) – Carte 8200/17200 Ft

PLAN: 2-F2 – *Dohány utca 3-5 – Ⓜ Astoria – ✆ (30) 589 1813 – www.fausto.hu – Closed 29 June-6 July, 24-26 December, Sunday*

Fricska

MODERN CUISINE • BISTRO The subtitle 'gastropub' is misleading, as this is contemporary cellar bistro with crisp white décor and a laid-back vibe. The black board menu offers appealingly unadorned dishes with Hungarian, French and Ital ian influences. The homemade pastas are a highlight and the weekday lunc menu is a steal.

Menu 2950 Ft (lunch) – Carte 8750/12650 Ft

PLAN: 2-F1 – *Dob utca 56-58 – Ⓜ Oktogon – ✆ (1) 951 8821 – www.fricska.eu – Closed Monday, Sunday*

Laurel Budapest

MODERN CUISINE • RUSTIC A passionately run cellar restaurant with a vaultec brick ceiling; upstairs is a coffee/bookshop by day and a wine bar serving snacks at night. Menus bring together Hungarian and global influences; desserts are a highlight. The wine list offers over 200 bottles, with a focus on forward-thinking Hungarian winemakers.

Menu 23000/27000 Ft

PLAN: 2-F1 – *Kertész utca 29. – Ⓜ Oktogon – ✆ 01 785 1612 – www.laurelbudapest.hu – Closed 16-27 August, 20 December-4 January, Monday, lunch Tuesday-Saturday, Sunday*

Mák

MODERN CUISINE • BISTRO A rustic restaurant with whitewashed brick walls, semi-vaulted ceilings and a relaxed feel: its name means 'poppy seed'. The talented young chef prepares creative dishes which play with different texture and flavour combinations. Tasting menus are available Friday and Saturday evenings.

Menu 4800 Ft (lunch), 19500/27000 Ft – Carte 12200/16200 Ft

PLAN: 2-E1 – *Vigyázó Ferenc utca 4 – Ⓜ Vörösmarty tér – ✆ (30) 723 9383 – www.mak.hu – Closed 16-24 August, Monday, Sunday*

Nobu Budapest

JAPANESE • MINIMALIST A minimalist restaurant set within a stylish hotel and featuring well-spaced wooden tables, Japanese lanterns, fretwork screens and an open kitchen. Numerous menus offer a huge array of Japanese-inspired dishes – with the majority of ingredients imported. Vegetarians are well catered for.

Menu 9900 Ft (lunch)/15900 Ft – Carte 6000/34000 Ft

PLAN: 2-E2 – *Kempinski Hotel Corvinus, Erzsébet tér 7-8 – Ⓜ Deák Ferenc tér – ✆ (1) 429 4242 – www.noburestaurants.com*

Olimpia

MODERN CUISINE • NEIGHBOURHOOD The local area might be uninspiring but as you step over the threshold of this bright basement restaurant, all is forgotten. Fresh, light cooking is unfussy at lunch and more complex in the evening; dinner is a surprise menu of market produce, where you choose only the number of courses.

Menu 3200 Ft (lunch), 10500/13500 Ft

PLAN: 1-B2 – *Alpár utca 5 – Ⓜ Keleti pályaudvar – ✆ (1) 321 0680 – www.olimpiavendeglo.com – Closed 2-31 August, Monday, lunch Saturday, Sunday*

St. Andrea

MODERN CUISINE • ELEGANT A stylish bar-cum-restaurant with wine-themed décor; owned by a small boutique winery. Well-presented, creative dishes are designed to match their wines – some of which aren't sold anywhere else in the world!

Menu 4800 Ft (lunch) – Carte 8000/16000 Ft

PLAN: 1-A1 – *Bajcsy-Zsilinszky út 78 – Ⓜ Nyugati pályaudvar – ✆ (1) 269 0130 – www.standreaborbar.hu – Closed Sunday*

Textúra

HUNGARIAN • DESIGN A stylish, design-led brasserie with a relaxed atmosphere, a living wall of moss and a central wooden 'tree'; set almost opposite its sister restaurant, Borkonyha Winekitchen. Seasonal, Hungarian influenced dishes are ambitious and creative.

Carte 8850/14450 Ft

PLAN: 2-E2 – *Sas utca 6 – Ⓜ Bajcsy-Zsilinszky út – ✆ (1) 617 9495 – www.texturaetterem.hu – Closed 11-17 January, Sunday*

Tigris

HUNGARIAN • TRADITIONAL A traditional bistro in a historic building designed by a Hungarian architect; it exudes a luxurious feel. Classic dishes have an appealing, earthy quality and feature foie gras specialities. The wine list champions up-and-coming producers.

Carte 11000/19000 Ft

PLAN: 2-E2 – *Mérleg utca 10 – Ⓜ Bajcsy-Zsilinszky út – ✆ (1) 317 3715 – www.tigrisrestaurant.hu – Closed 24-26 December, Sunday*

Buda

Alabárdos

HUNGARIAN • ELEGANT Set in a series of 15C buildings opposite the castle and named after the castle's guards, Alabárdos has stood here for over 50 years. It's a formal yet atmospheric place, with subtle modern touches and a delightful terrace. Cooking is rich and flavourful and features classic dishes with a modern edge.

Menu 15900/24900 Ft – Carte 11500/15600 Ft

PLAN: 2-D1 – *Orszaghaz Utca 2 – Ⓜ Széll Kármán tér – ✆ (1) 356 0851 – www.alabardos.hu – Closed lunch Monday-Friday, Sunday*

Arany Kaviár

RUSSIAN • INTIMATE Choose between an opulent, richly appointed room and larger, more modern extension which opens onto the garden. French and Russia influences guide the creative, ambitious cooking; Hungarian and Siberian caviar a speciality.

Menu 6900 Ft (lunch) – Carte 11900/30700 Ft

PLAN: 2-C1 – *Ostrom utca 19 – Ⓜ Széll Kálmán tér – ✆ (1) 201 6737 – www.aranykaviar.hu – Closed Monday*

Baltazár

MODERN CUISINE • DESIGN A hidden gem, tucked back to the north of the O Town, away from the crowds. Sit on the pretty terrace or head into the strikir bistro, where stage spotlights illuminate boldly painted concrete walls. Cookir focuses on Hungarian classics and meats from the Josper grill. Its bedrooms a also ultra-modern.

Carte 5600/18620 Ft

PLAN: 2-C1 – *Országház utca 31 – Ⓜ Széll Kálmán tér – ✆ (1) 300 7050 – www.baltazarbudapest.com*

Csalogány 26

MODERN CUISINE • BISTRO A homely neighbourhood restaurant with a simp bistro style. The passionate father and son team prepare tasty dishes in a mode manner. Choose from the main menu or from a list of daily specials chalked c the blackboard; the 3 course business lunch is good value.

Menu 3100 Ft (lunch)/15000 Ft – Carte 7800/12000 Ft

PLAN: 2-D1 – *Csalogány utca 26 – Ⓜ Batthyány tér – ✆ (1) 201 7892 – www.csalogany26.hu – Closed 26 July-10 August, Monday, dinner Tuesday-Wednesday, Sunday*

Zona

MODERN CUISINE • DESIGN A contemporary restaurant with floor to ceilir windows overlooking the river and a huge shelving unit packed with wines. Go glass balls illuminate sleek wooden tables. Modern dishes follow the seasons ar arrive smartly presented.

Menu 3950 Ft (lunch) – Carte 9000/15500 Ft

PLAN: 2-D2 – *Lánchíd utca 7-9 – ✆ (30) 422 5981 – www.zonabudapest.com*

Boyloso/iStock

ICELAND

ÍSLAND

REYKJAVIK

REYKJAVIK

dennisvdw/iStock

REYKJAVIK IN...

→ **ONE DAY**
Hallgrímskirkja Church, Harpa Concert Hall, Laugavegur: the main shopping street.

→ **TWO DAYS**
Saga Museum, the Old Harbour (Grandi).

→ **THREE DAYS**
A trip out to the Blue Lagoon or a glacier tour.

Europe's youngest landmass is a country of extremes; a dramatic wilderness where volcanic springs sit beside vast glaciers and long summer days are offset by dark winters. Its largest city, Reykjavik, lays claim to being the world's most northern capital and its settlement by a Norseman over 1100 years ago is recounted in the Icelandic Sagas. Two thirds of Icelanders live in Reykjavik, in low, colourful buildings designed to fend off the North Atlantic winds and brighten spirits through the long, dark nights. Other buildings echo nature itself: the geometric shapes of the Hallgrímskirkja Church – whose soaring tower keeps watch over the city – mirror the lava

flows, while the Harpa Concert Hall is cleverly designed to reflect both the city and nature – its cascading LEDs alluding to the incredible spectacle of the Aurora Borealis. The historic city centre, known as 101, lies between the harbour and an inland lake, and is a bustling, bohemian place filled with independent boutiques and fashionable bars. Head out further east and you can discover the secrets of the Blue Lagoon's healing thermal waters and the Golden Circle, which comprises three of Iceland's greatest natural wonders: the Þingvellir National Park (where you can walk between two tectonic plates); the Haukadalur Geothermal Field with its geysers and mud pools; and the spectacular Gullfoss Waterfall – the largest in Europe.

EATING OUT

Eating out is an important part of Icelandic life but it can be expensive, so choose wisely and avoid the tourist traps. There's a pleasing informality to most restaurants so it's easy to enjoy good cooking in relaxed surroundings, but the city is small, so reservations are recommended. Lunch is a low-key affair, with dinner being the main event, and cooking tends to be quite contemporary – the local chefs are proud of their heritage and have a great way of updating traditional recipes. Clarity of flavour leads the way and there's a pleasing reliance on the island's natural produce: seafood (particularly cod) and lamb take centre stage, and popular techniques include smoking and preserving. Rye bread is a typical accompaniment and you'll find the cultured dairy product skyr – once eaten by Vikings and farmers – in everything from starters to desserts. Icelanders love their cosy coffee shops (be sure to accompany your drink with a traditional kleina doughnut), and the Sandholt Bakery, run by the 4th generation, is worth a visit.

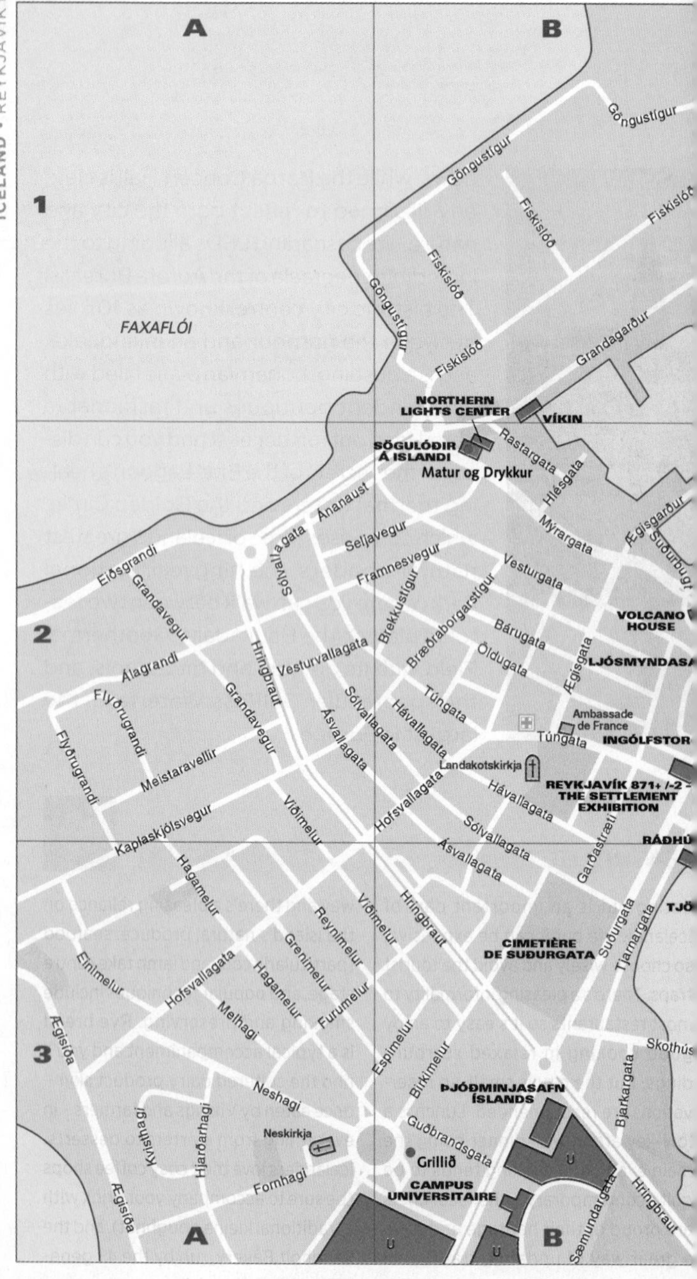
A
B
1
2
3
FAXAFLÓI
Göngustígur
Fiskislóð
Grandagarður
NORTHERN LIGHTS CENTER
VÍKIN
SÖGULÓÐIR Á ISLANDI
Matur og Drykkur
Rastargata
Hlésgata
Mýrargata
Ægisgarður
Suðurbugt
Ánanaust
Seljavegur
Sólvallagata
Eiðsgrandi
Grandavegur
Framnesvegur
Vesturgata
Brekkustígur
Bræðraborgarstígur
Bárugata
VOLCANO HOUSE
Ölduguta
Ægisgata
Hringbraut
Vesturvallagata
Álagrandi
Flyðrugrandi
Túngata
Hávallagata
Ásvallagata
Ambassade de France
INGÓLFSTOR
Landakotskirkja
REYKJAVÍK 871+ /-2 – THE SETTLEMENT EXHIBITION
Meistaravellir
Hofsvallagata
Víðimelur
Kaplaskjólsvegur
Garðastræti
Hagamelur
Reynimelur
Grenimelur
CIMETIÈRE DE SUÐURGATA
Suðurgata
Tjarnargata
Einimelur
Furumelur
Melhagi
Ægisíða
Espimelur
Birkimelur
Skothús
Neshagi
ÞJÓÐMINJASAFN ÍSLANDS
Bjarkargata
Kvisthagi
Hjarðarhagi
Neskirkja
Guðbrandsgata
Grillið
Fornhagi
CAMPUS UNIVERSITAIRE
Sæmundargata
U

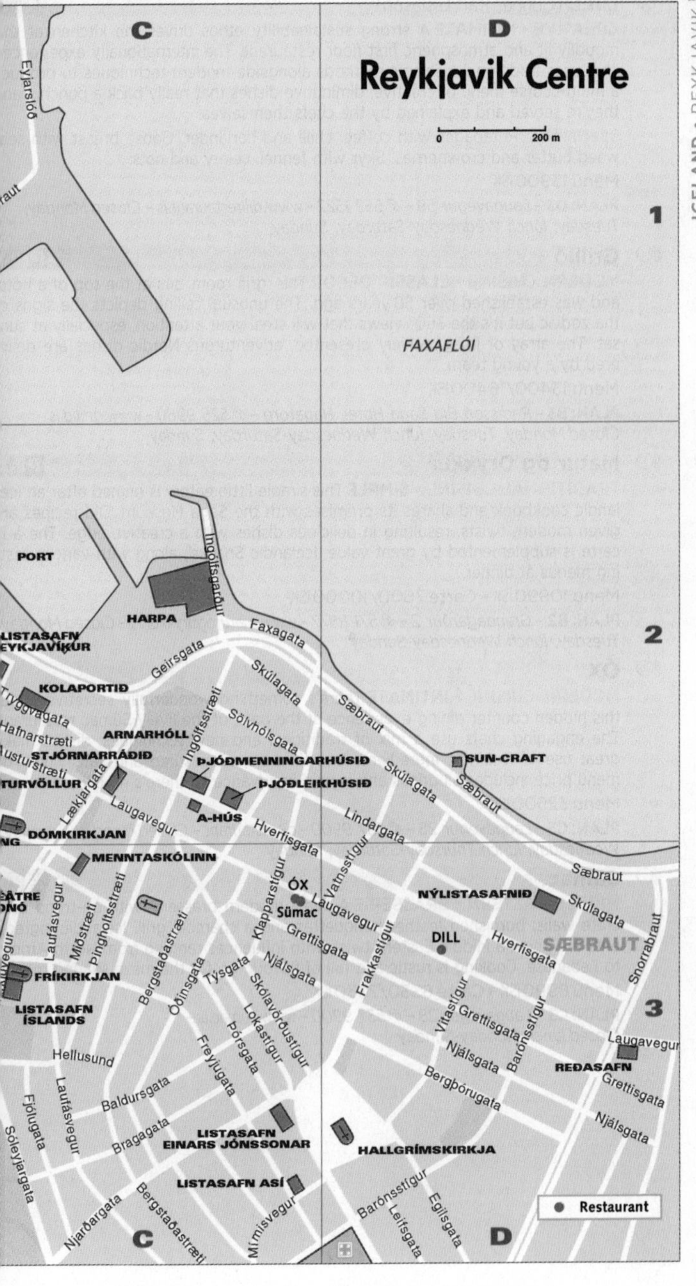
Reykjavik Centre
0
200 m
C
D
1
2
3
FAXAFLÓI
PORT
HARPA
LISTASAFN REYKJAVÍKUR
KOLAPORTIÐ
ARNARHÓLL
STJÓRNARRÁÐIÐ
ÞJÓÐMENNINGARHÚSIÐ
ÞJÓÐLEIKHÚSIÐ
A-HÚS
DÓMKIRKJAN
MENNTASKÓLINN
FRÍKIRKJAN
LISTASAFN ÍSLANDS
SUN-CRAFT
NÝLISTASAFNIÐ
SÆBRAUT
ÓX
Sümac
DILL
REÐASAFN
LISTASAFN EINARS JÓNSSONAR
HALLGRÍMSKIRKJA
LISTASAFN ASÍ
Restaurant
Eyjarslóð
Ingólfsgarður
Faxagata
Geirsgata
Skúlagata
Sæbraut
Tryggvagata
Hafnarstræti
Ingólfsstræti
Sölvhólsgata
Lækjargata
Laugavegur
Hverfisgata
Lindargata
Vatnsstígur
Klapparstígur
Grettisgata
Njálsgata
Frakkastígur
Snorrabraut
Vitastígur
Barónsstígur
Bergþórugata
Laufásvegur
Miðstræti
Pingholtsstræti
Bergstaðastræti
Óðinsgata
Týsgata
Skólavörðustígur
Lokastígur
Þórsgata
Freyjugata
Hellusund
Baldursgata
Bragagata
Fjólugata
Sóleyjargata
Njarðargata
Mímisvegur
Leifsgata
Egilsgata

DILL (Gunnar Karl Gislason)

CREATIVE • INTIMATE A strong sustainability ethos drives the kitchen at th moodily lit and atmospheric first floor restaurant. The internationally experience chef uses traditional Icelandic methods alongside modern techniques to produc a multi-course menu of creative, diminutive dishes that really pack a punch – an they're served and explained by the chefs themselves.

Specialities: Rutabagas with coffee, chilli and coriander. Goose breast with sea weed butter and crowberries. Skyr with fennel, celery and oats.

Menu 13900 ISK

PLAN: D3 – *Laugavegur 59 – ✆ 552 1522 – www.dillrestaurant.is – Closed Monday, Tuesday, lunch Wednesday-Saturday, Sunday*

Grillið

MODERN CUISINE • CLASSIC DÉCOR This 'grill room' sits at the top of a hot and was established over 50 years ago. The unusual ceiling depicts the signs c the zodiac but it's the 360° views that will steal your attention, especially at sun set. The array of imaginatively presented, adventurous Nordic dishes are deliv ered by a young team.

Menu 13400/16400 ISK

PLAN: B3 – *Radisson Blu Saga Hotel, Hagatorg – ✆ 525 9960 – www.grillid.is – Closed Monday, Tuesday, lunch Wednesday-Saturday, Sunday*

Matur og Drykkur

TRADITIONAL CUISINE • SIMPLE This simple little eatery is named after an Ice landic cookbook and shares its premises with the Saga Museum. Old recipes ar given modern twists, resulting in delicious dishes with a creative edge. The à carte is supplemented by great value 'Icelandic Snacks', along with various tast ing menus at dinner.

Menu 10990 ISK – Carte 7600/10000 ISK

PLAN: B2 – *Grandagarður 2 – ✆ 571 8877 – www.maturogdrykkur.is – Closed Monday Tuesday, lunch Wednesday-Sunday*

ÓX

MODERN CUISINE • INTIMATE There's something wonderfully secretive abou this hidden counter dining experience at the back of the lively Sümac restauran The engaging chefs use a mix of traditional and new techniques; dishes mak great use of Icelandic ingredients and flavours are assured and satisfying. Th menu price includes all drinks and is paid in advance so there's no bill at the en

Menu 32500 ISK

PLAN: C3 – *Laugavegur 28 – ✆ 537 9900 – ox.restaurant – Closed Monday, Tuesday, Wednesday, lunch Thursday-Saturday, Sunday*

Sümac

MIDDLE EASTERN • BRASSERIE A lively modern brasserie with on-trend con crete walls, burnished leather banquettes and a charcoal grill. Icelandic ingredi ents are given a Middle Eastern twist, with influences ranging from North Africa to Lebanese. Cooking is rustic and full of flavour; go for the meze sharing menus

Menu 8990 ISK – Carte 6330/7330 ISK

PLAN: C3 – *Laugavegur 28 – ✆ 537 9900 – www.sumac.is – Closed lunch Monday-Sunday*

Warchi/iStock

Republic of IRELAND

ÉIRE

DUBLIN
BAILE ÁTHA CLIATH

gianliguori/iStock

DUBLIN IN...

→ **ONE DAY**
Trinity College, Grafton Street, St Stephen's Green, Merrion Square, Temple Bar.

→ **TWO DAYS**
Christ Church Cathedral, Dublin Castle, Chester Beatty Library, the quayside.

→ **THREE DAYS**
O'Connell Street, Parnell Square, Dublin Writers' Museum, DART train to the coast.

For somewhere touted a the finest Georgian city in th British Isles, Dublin enjoys very young image. When th 'Celtic Tiger' roared to prom inence in the 1990s, Ireland' old capital took on a youthfu expression, and for the firs time revelled in the epithet 'chic' and 'trendy'. Noway it's not just the bastion o Guinness drinkers and thos here for the 'craic', but a twen ty-first century city with smart restaurants, grand ne hotels, modern architecture and impressive galleries. It handsome squares and façades took shape 250 years ago designed by the finest architects of the time. Since the

it's gone through uprising, civil war and independence from Britain, and now holds a strong fascination for foreign visitors.

The city can be pretty well divided into three. Southeast of the river is the classiest, defined by the glorious Trinity College, St Stephen's Green, and Grafton Street's smart shops. Just west of here is the second area, dominated by Dublin Castle and Christ Church Cathedral – ancient buildings abound, but it doesn't quite match the sleek aura of the city's Georgian quarter. Across the Liffey, the northern section was the last part to be developed and, although it lacks the glamour of its southern neighbours, it does boast the city's grandest ave-nue, O'Connell Street, and its most celebrated theatres.

EATING OUT

It's still possible to indulge in Irish stew but nowadays you can also dine on everything from tacos and Thai to Malaysian and Middle Eastern cuisine, particularly in the Temple Bar area. The city makes the most of its bay proximity, so seafood features highly, with smoked salmon and oysters the favourites; the latter washed down with a pint of Guinness. Meat is particularly tasty in Ireland, due to the healthy livestock and a wet climate, and Irish beef is world famous for its fulsome flavour. However, there's never been a better time to be a vegetarian in Dublin, as every type of veg from spinach to seaweed now features, and chefs insist on the best seasonal produce, cooked for just the right amount of time to savour all the taste and goodness. Dinner here is usually served until about 10pm, though many global and city centre restaurants stay open later. If you make your main meal at lunchtime, you'll pay considerably less than in the evening: the menus are often similar, but the bill in the middle of the day will probably be about half the price.

Centre

Greenhouse (Mickael Viljanen)

MODERN CUISINE • ELEGANT The Greenhouse is a chic, intimate restaura[nt] that has steadily evolved over the years. The staff are personable and the atm[o]sphere is refreshingly relaxed. Accomplished, classically based cooking has stimu[]lating flavour combinations, creative elements and plenty of personality.

Specialities: Foie gras Royale with apple, smoked eel and walnut. Lozère milk-fe[d] lamb with kombu, lemon and curry. Amedei chocolate with praline, coffee, o[r]ange and rosemary.

Menu €55 (lunch)/110

PLAN: 1-C3 – *Dawson Street – ✆ 01 676 7015 – www.thegreenhouserestaurant.ie – Closed 13-28 January, 20 July-4 August, Sunday, Monday*

Patrick Guilbaud (Guillaume Lebrun)

MODERN FRENCH • ELEGANT A truly sumptuous restaurant in an elegar[nt] Georgian house; the eponymous owner has run it for many years. Accomplishe[d] original cooking uses luxurious ingredients and mixes classical French cookin[g] with modern techniques. Dishes are well-crafted and visually stunning with a su[]perb balance of textures and flavours.

Specialities: Blue lobster ravioli with coconut scented lobster cream, toasted al[]monds and curry dressing. Lamb fillet, wet garlic and black olive oil. Opalys choc[]olate and tropical fruit "Cocoon".

Menu €62 (lunch), €130/160

PLAN: 1-D3 – *21 Upper Merrion Street – ✆ 01 676 4192 – www.restaurantpatrickguilbaud.ie – Closed 25 December-3 January, Sunday, Monday*

Chapter One (Ross Lewis)

MODERN CUISINE • INTIMATE Good old-fashioned hospitality meets with mod[]ern Irish cooking in this stylish basement restaurant beneath the Writers Museum[.] The series of interconnecting rooms have an understated elegance and strikin[g] bespoke art hangs on the walls. Boldly flavoured dishes showcase produce fro[m] local artisan producers.

Specialities: Cured organic salmon, Lambay crab, smoked cod roe and buttermil[k] pancake. Brill, cauliflower, pickled red dulse, horseradish. Flavours and textures o[f] Irish milk and honey.

Menu €42/115

PLAN: 1-C1 – *The Dublin Writers Museum, 18-19 Parnell Square – ✆ 01 873 2266 – www.chapteronerestaurant.com – Closed 24 December-7 January, Sunday, Monday, lunch Tuesday-Thursday, lunch Saturday*

L'Ecrivain (Derry Clarke)

MODERN CUISINE • CHIC A well-regarded restaurant with an attractive terrace, a glitzy bar and a private dining room which screens live kitchen action. The re[]fined, balanced menu has a classical foundation whilst also displaying touches of modernity; the ingredients used are superlative. Service is structured yet has personality.

Specialities: Kilkeel crab with mango and pickled beech mushroom. Aged Wick[]low Venison, celeriac and Savoy cabbage. Chocolate 'Snickers'.

Menu €37 (lunch), €85/115 – Carte €70/96

PLAN: 1-D3 – *109a Lower Baggot Street – ✆ 01 661 1919 – www.lecrivain.com – Closed Sunday, lunch Monday-Thursday, lunch Saturday*

Variety Jones (Keelan Higgs)

A/C

MODERN CUISINE • FRIENDLY This tiny restaurant has a long, narrow room with a funky, modern style and a cool, laid-back atmosphere. Charming chef-owner Keelan Higgs works calmly in the open kitchen, preparing highly original, refined yet unfussy dishes which burst with freshness and flavour; many are cooked over the open fire.

Specialities: Lobster with grilled baby gem and brown butter. Duck with charred broccoli, hearts and confit leg. Rhubarb and almond cake with poached rhubarb and cultured cream.

Carte €50/60

PLAN: 1-A2 – *78 Thomas Street – ✆ 01 516 2470 – www.varietyjones.ie – Closed 29 July-13 August, Sunday, Monday, lunch Tuesday-Saturday*

Clanbrassil House

MODERN CUISINE • RUSTIC Bastible's younger sister is a small place seating just 25. The concise menu focuses on the charcoal grill, with everything from home-made sausages to prime cuts. The hash brown chips are a favourite; the early evening menu is a steal; and if you're in a group you can share dishes 'family-style'.

Menu €28 – Carte €35/47

PLAN: 2-E1 – *6 Clanbrassil Street Upper – ✆ 01 453 9786 – www.clanbrassilhouse.com – Closed Sunday, Monday, lunch Tuesday-Friday*

Pichet

CLASSIC FRENCH • CHIC You can't miss the bright red signs and blue and white striped canopies of this buzzy brasserie – and its checkerboard flooring makes it equally striking inside. Have snacks at the bar or classic French dishes in the main room. A good selection of wines are available by the glass or pichet.

Menu €24/30 – Carte €36/51

PLAN: 1-C2 – *14-15 Trinity Street – ✆ 01 677 1060 – www.pichet.ie – Closed lunch Sunday*

Richmond

MODERN CUISINE • NEIGHBOURHOOD A real gem of a neighbourhood restaurant with a rustic look and a lively feel; sit upstairs for a more sedate experience. The vibrant, gutsy dishes change regularly – apart from the Dexter burger and rib-eye which are mainstays; on Tuesdays they serve a good value tasting menu where they try out new ideas.

Menu €26/30 – Carte €35/48

PLAN: 2-E1 – *43 Richmond Street South – ✆ 01 478 8783 – www.richmondrestaurant.ie – Closed Monday, lunch Tuesday-Friday*

Uno Mas

MEDITERRANEAN CUISINE • NEIGHBOURHOOD The smell of freshly baked bread lures you into this stripped-back bistro located in a historic building near the city centre. It's run by a very friendly team and offers great value menus of cleanly executed, unfussy Spanish dishes that are packed with flavour. A Spanish wine and sherry list accompanies.

Menu €24 (lunch)/28 – Carte €31/45

PLAN: 1-B2 – *6 Aungier Street – ✆ 01 4758538 – www.unomas.ie – Closed Sunday, lunch Monday*

Bang

MODERN CUISINE • BISTRO Stylish restaurant with an intimate powder blue basement, a bright mezzanine level and a small, elegant room above. There are good value pre-theatre menus, a more elaborate à la carte and tasting menus showcasing top Irish produce.

Menu €35 (lunch)/38 – Carte €34/62

PLAN: 1-C3 – *11 Merrion Row – ✆ 01 400 4229 – www.bangrestaurant.com – Closed Sunday, lunch Monday*

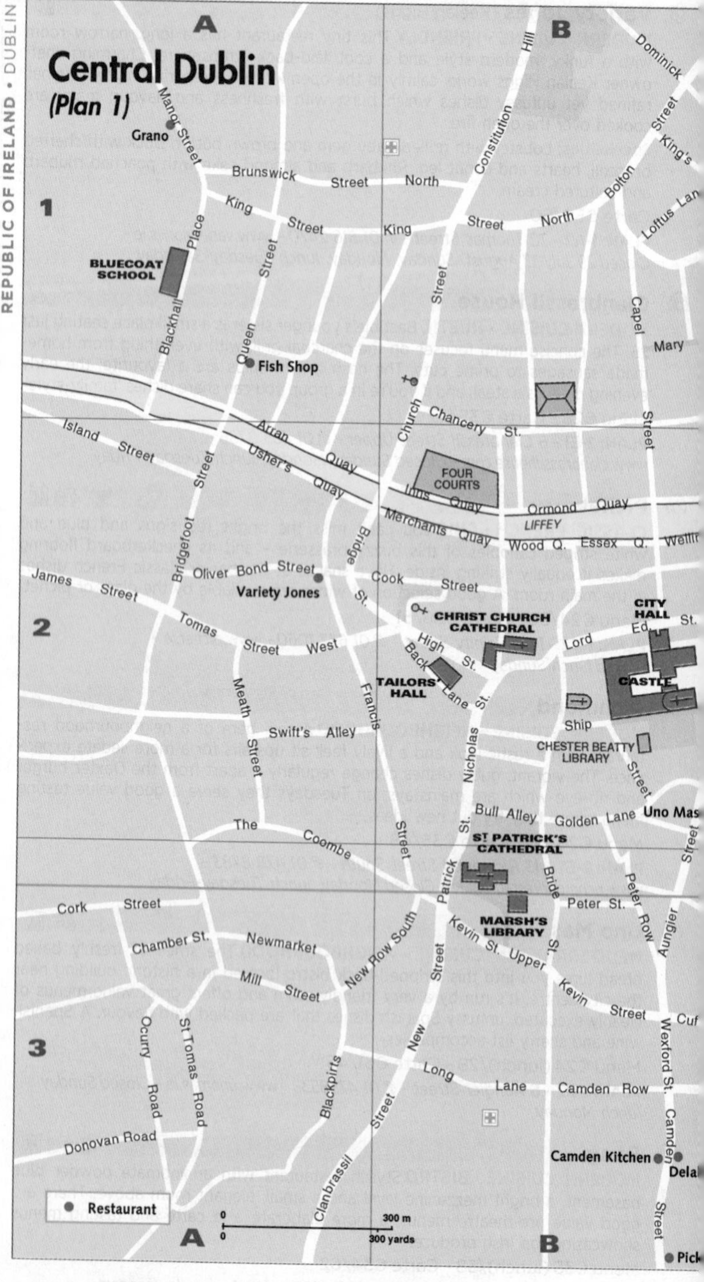
Central Dublin
(Plan 1)
A
B
1
2
3
Grano
Manor Street
Brunswick Street North
King Street North
King Street
Constitution Hill
Dominick Street
Bolton Street
King's
Loftus Lane
BLUECOAT SCHOOL
Blackhall Place
Queen Street
Fish Shop
Church Street
Capel Street
Mary
Chancery St.
Island Street
Arran Quay
Usher's Quay
FOUR COURTS
Inns Quay
Ormond Quay
LIFFEY
Merchants Quay
Wood Q.
Essex Q.
Bridgefoot Street
Bridge St.
Oliver Bond Street
Cook Street
James Street
Variety Jones
Tomas Street West
CHRIST CHURCH CATHEDRAL
CITY HALL
Lord Ed. St.
High St.
Back Lane
TAILORS' HALL
CASTLE
Meath Street
Francis Street
Nicholas St.
Swift's Alley
Ship Street
CHESTER BEATTY LIBRARY
Bull Alley
Golden Lane
Uno Mas
The Coombe
ST PATRICK'S CATHEDRAL
Patrick St.
Bride St.
Peter Row
Aungier Street
Peter St.
MARSH'S LIBRARY
Cork Street
Chamber St.
Newmarket
Mill Street
New Row South
Kevin St. Upper
Kevin Street
Cuf
Wexford St.
Ocurry Road
St Tomas Road
New Street
Blackpirts
Long Lane
Camden Row
Camden Street
Donovan Road
Clanbrassil Street
Camden Kitchen
Dela
Pick
Restaurant
0
300 m
0
300 yards

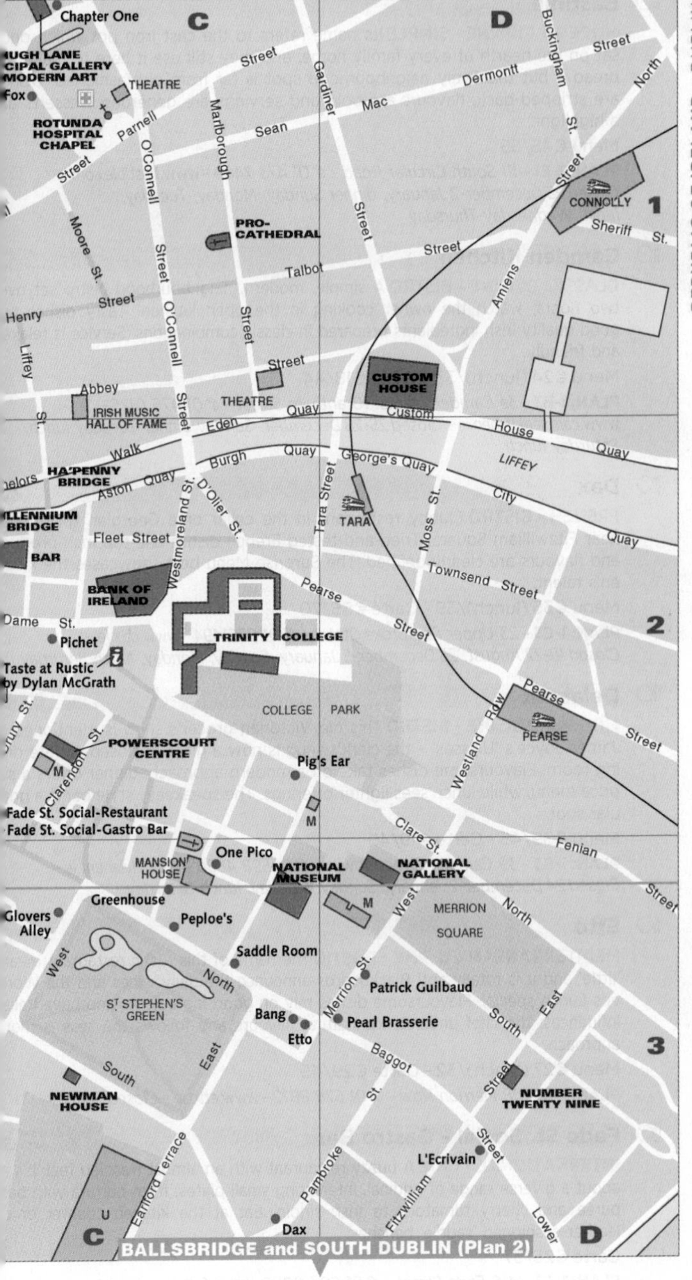

Chapter One
C
D
HUGH LANE
CIPAL GALLERY
MODERN ART
THEATRE
Fox
ROTUNDA
HOSPITAL
CHAPEL
Parnell
Street
Sean
Mac
Dermott
Street
Gardiner
Street
Buckingham
St.
North
Street
Marlborough
Street
O'Connell
Street
Moore
St.
PRO-
CATHEDRAL
CONNOLLY
Sheriff
St.
1
Talbot
Street
Amiens
Henry
Street
Liffey
St.
Abbey
Street
CUSTOM
HOUSE
THEATRE
IRISH MUSIC
HALL OF FAME
Eden
Quay
Custom
House
Quay
LIFFEY
Walk
Burgh
Quay
George's Quay
City
Quay
HA'PENNY
BRIDGE
Aston
Quay
Westmoreland St.
D'Olier St.
Tara Street
TARA
Moss
St.
LLENNIUM
BRIDGE
Fleet Street
BAR
BANK OF
IRELAND
Townsend
Street
Pearse
Street
Dame St.
Pichet
TRINITY COLLEGE
2
Taste at Rustic
by Dylan McGrath
COLLEGE PARK
Pearse
Street
PEARSE
Westland Row
Drury St.
POWERSCOURT
CENTRE
Clarendon St.
M
Pig's Ear
M
Fade St. Social-Restaurant
Fade St. Social-Gastro Bar
Clare St.
Fenian
Street
One Pico
MANSION
HOUSE
NATIONAL
MUSEUM
NATIONAL
GALLERY
Greenhouse
M
West
MERRION
SQUARE
North
Glovers
Alley
Peploe's
Saddle Room
West
North
Merrion St.
Patrick Guilbaud
ST STEPHEN'S
GREEN
Bang
Pearl Brasserie
Etto
South
East
3
Baggot
St.
South
East
Street
NUMBER
TWENTY NINE
NEWMAN
HOUSE
Earlsfort Terrace
L'Ecrivain
Street
Pembroke
Fitzwilliam
Lower
U
Dax
C
D
BALLSBRIDGE and SOUTH DUBLIN (Plan 2)

Bastible

MODERN CUISINE • SIMPLE Its name refers to the cast iron pot which on sat on the hearth of every family home, and they still use it here to make th bread – but this lively neighbourhood spot is far from old-fashioned. Dish are stripped-back, flavours are bold and servings are generous. Desserts a a highlight.

Menu €45/55

PLAN: 2-E1 – *111 South Circular Road – ✆ 01 473 7409 – www.bastible.com – Closed 25 December-2 January, dinner Sunday, Monday, Tuesday, lunch Wednesday-Thursday*

Camden Kitchen

CLASSIC CUISINE • BISTRO A simple, modern, neighbourhood bistro set ov two floors; watch the owner cooking in the open kitchen. Tasty dishes us good quality Irish ingredients prepared in classic combinations. Service is relaxe and friendly.

Menu €24 (lunch)/33 – Carte €18/44

PLAN: 1-B3 – *3a Camden Market, Grantham Street – ✆ 01 476 0125 – www.camdenkitchen.ie – Closed 25-28 December, Sunday dinner-Tuesday lunch, Saturday lunch*

Dax

A/C

FRENCH • BISTRO Clubby restaurant in the cellar of a Georgian townhous near Fitzwilliam Square. Tried-and-tested French dishes use top Irish produc and flavours are clearly defined. The Surprise Menu best showcases the kitch en's talent.

Menu €35 (lunch)/39 – Carte €55/70

PLAN: 1-C3 – *23 Upper Pembroke Street – ✆ 01 6761494 – www.dax.ie – Closed 18-22 August, 25 December-5 January, Sunday, Monday, lunch Saturday*

Delahunt

MODERN CUISINE • BISTRO This old Victorian grocer's shop is mentioned i James Joyce's 'Ulysses' – the clerk's snug is now a glass-enclosed private dir ing room. Flavoursome dishes take on a modern approach; dinner offers a se price menu, while lunch sees lighter offerings. The speakeasy style bar is a pop ular spot.

Menu €39/45 – Carte €19/45

PLAN: 1-B3 – *39 Camden Street Lower – ✆ 01 598 4880 – www.delahunt.ie – Closed 24 December-2 January, Sunday, Monday, lunch Saturday*

Etto

MEDITERRANEAN CUISINE • RUSTIC The name of this rustic restaurant mean 'little' and it is totally apt! Blackboards announce the daily wines and the Work er's Lunch special. Flavoursome dishes rely on good ingredients and have Italia influences; the chef understands natural flavours and follows the 'less is more approach.

Menu €27 (lunch)/32 – Carte €29/45

PLAN: 1-C3 – *18 Merrion Row – ✆ 01 678 8872 – www.etto.ie – Closed Sunday*

Fade St. Social - Gastro Bar

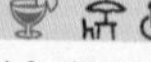

INTERNATIONAL • CHIC A buzzy restaurant with an almost frenzied feel. It's al about a diverse range of original, interesting small plates, from burrata with basi purée and cherry tomatoes to Irish sirloin. Eat at the kitchen counter or or leather-cushioned 'saddle' benches.

Carte €25/57

PLAN: 1-C2 – *4-6 Fade Street – ✆ 01 604 0066 – www.fadestreetsocial.com – Closed lunch Monday-Friday*

Fade St. Social - Restaurant

MODERN CUISINE • BRASSERIE Have cocktails on the terrace then head for the big, modern brasserie. Dishes use Irish ingredients but have a Mediterranean feel; they specialise in sharing and wood-fired dishes, and use large cuts of meat such as chateaubriand.

Menu €37 – Carte €38/70

PLAN: 1-C2 – *4-6 Fade Street – ✆ 01 604 0066 – www.fadestreetsocial.com – Closed lunch Sunday-Wednesday, lunch Saturday*

Fish Shop

SEAFOOD • RUSTIC A very informal little restaurant where they serve a daily changing seafood menu which is written up on the tiled wall. Great tasting, supremely fresh, unfussy dishes could be prepared raw or roasted in the wood-fired oven.

Menu €45

PLAN: 1-A1 – *6 Queen Street – ✆ 01 430 8594 – www.fish-shop.ie – Closed Sunday, Monday, Tuesday, lunch Wednesday-Saturday*

Glovers Alley

MODERN CUISINE • DESIGN This second floor hotel restaurant looks out over St Stephen's Green and is named in honour of the city's glove-makers who once occupied the neighbouring alleyway. Pinks, greens and floral arrangements give the room a soft touch, while dishes display contrastingly bold flavours and textures.

Menu €45 (lunch)/80

PLAN: 1-C3 – *Fitzwilliam Hotel, 127-128 St. Stephen's Green – ✆ 01 244 0733 – www.gloversalley.com – Closed 25 December-8 January, Sunday, Monday, lunch Tuesday-Wednesday*

Grano

ITALIAN • FRIENDLY To the northwest of the city you'll find this lovely little osteria specialising in homemade pasta. The owner and his chef hail from Calabria and regularly import produce from their home town. Cooking is fresh and unfussy and the all-Italian wine list features organic and biodynamic wines.

Menu €12 (lunch)/24 – Carte €25/35

PLAN: 1-A1 – *5 Norseman Court, Manor Street, Stoneybatter – ✆ 01 538 2003 – www.grano.ie – Closed Monday, lunch Tuesday*

Locks

MODERN CUISINE • BISTRO Locals love this restaurant overlooking the canal – downstairs it's buzzy, while upstairs is more intimate, and the personable team add to the feel. Natural flavours are to the fore and dishes are given subtle modern touches; for the best value menus come early in the week or before 7pm.

Menu €30/45 – Carte €30/60

PLAN: 2-E1 – *1 Windsor Terrace – ✆ 01 416 3655 – www.locksrestaurant.ie – Closed dinner Sunday, Monday, lunch Tuesday-Thursday*

Mr Fox

MODERN CUISINE • INTIMATE In the basement of a striking Georgian house you'll find this light-hearted restaurant with a lovely tiled floor and a small terrace. The charming team present tasty international dishes, some of which have a playful touch.

Menu €28 – Carte €40/51

PLAN: 1-C1 – *38 Parnell Square West – ✆ 01 874 7778 – www.mrfox.ie – Closed 1-8 January, Sunday, Monday*

One Pico

MODERN CUISINE • ELEGANT This discreet, passionately run restaurant tucke away on a side street is a well-regarded place that's a regular haunt for MPs. S on comfy banquettes or velour chairs, surrounded by muted colours. The moder Irish cooking has plenty of flavour and dishes are attractively presented.

Menu €39 (lunch)/50 – Carte €55/75

PLAN: 1-C3 – *5-6 Molesworth Place – ✆ 01 676 0300 – www.onepico.com – Closed Sunday*

Pearl Brasserie

MODERN CUISINE • BRASSERIE Formal basement restaurant with a small bar lounge and two surprisingly airy dining rooms; sit in a stylish booth in one of th old coal bunkers. Intriguing modern dishes have a classical base and Mediterra nean and Asian influences.

Menu €36 (lunch)/39 – Carte €40/70

PLAN: 1-D3 – *20 Merrion Street Upper – ✆ 01 6613572 – www.pearl-brasserie.com – Closed Sunday*

Peploe's

MEDITERRANEAN CUISINE • COSY Atmospheric cellar restaurant – formerly bank vault – named after the artist. The comfy room has a warm, clubby fee and a large mural depicts the owner. The well-drilled team present Mediterranea dishes and an Old World wine list.

Menu €38 (lunch) – Carte €46/70

PLAN: 1-C3 – *16 St Stephen's Green – ✆ 01 676 3144 – www.peploes.com – Closed 25-26 December*

Pickle

INDIAN • BISTRO It might not look much from the outside but inside the plac really comes alive. Spices are lined up on the kitchen counter and dishes are fresl and vibrant; the lamb curry with bone marrow is divine. Try a Tiffin Box for lunch

Menu €24 – Carte €28/57

PLAN: 1-B3 – *43 Lower Camden Street – ✆ 01 555 7755 – www.picklerestaurant.com – Closed Monday*

Pig's Ear

MODERN CUISINE • BISTRO Look out for the bright pink door of this three sto- rey Georgian townhouse overlooking Trinity College Gardens. The first and second floors have a homely retro feel while the third floor is a private dining room with its own kitchen and library. Irish produce features in refined yet comforting dishes.

Menu €23/28 – Carte €35/49

PLAN: 1-C2 – *4 Nassau Street – ✆ 01 670 3865 – www.thepigsear.ie – Closed 1-8 January, Sunday*

Saddle Room

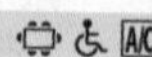

MEATS AND GRILLS • ELEGANT A renowned restaurant with a history as long as that of the grand hotel in which it stands. The warm, inviting room features intimate gold booths and a crustacea counter. Menus offer a mix of grills and classic dishes, with some finished off at the table in front of you.

Menu €30 (lunch), €37/50 – Carte €30/125

PLAN: 1-C3 – *Shelbourne Hotel, 27 St. Stephen's Green – ✆ 01 663 4500 – www.shelbournedining.ie*

Suesey Street

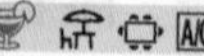

MODERN CUISINE • INTIMATE An intimate restaurant with sumptuous, eye-catching décor, set in the basement of a Georgian townhouse; sit on the superb courtyard terrace. Refined, modern cooking brings out the best in home-grown Irish ingredients.

Menu €30 – Carte €38/59

PLAN: 2-F1 – *26 Fitzwilliam Place – ✆ 01 669 4600 – www.sueseystreet.ie – Closed 25-30 December, Sunday, Monday*

Taste at Rustic by Dylan McGrath

ASIAN • RUSTIC Dylan McGrath's love of Japanese cuisine inspires dishes which explore the five tastes: sweet, salt, bitter, umami and sour. Ingredients are top-notch and flavours, bold and masculine. Personable staff are happy to recommend dishes.

Menu €45 – Carte €40/78

PLAN: 1-C2 – *17 South Great George's Street – 01 526 7701 – www.tasteatrustic.com – Closed 1-8 January, Sunday, Monday, Tuesday, lunch Wednesday-Saturday*

Environs of Dublin

at Ballsbridge

Chop House

MEATS AND GRILLS • PUB An imposing pub not far from the stadium. For warmer days there's a small terrace; in colder weather head up the steps, through the bar and into the bright conservatory. The relaxed lunchtime menu is followed by more ambitious dishes in the evening, when the kitchen really comes into its own.

Carte €33/56

PLAN: 2-G1 – *2 Shelbourne Road – 01 660 2390 – www.thechophouse.ie – Closed lunch Saturday*

Old Spot

TRADITIONAL CUISINE • PUB This grey pub is just a stone's throw from the stadium. The appealing bar has a stencilled maple-wood floor and a great selection of snacks and bottled craft beers. Downstairs, the relaxed, characterful restaurant is filled with vintage posters and serves pub classics with a modern edge.

Menu €29 – Carte €31/51

PLAN: 2-G1 – *14 Bath Avenue – 01 660 5599 – www.theoldspot.ie – Closed lunch Saturday*

Shelbourne Social

CONTEMPORARY • BRASSERIE A smart high rise plays host to this large brasserie deluxe with its profusion of glass and modish feel. Choose from a great selection of cocktails in the first floor loft-style bar, then pick from the wide-ranging menu which sees global dishes sitting alongside local steaks. Sharing is encouraged.

Menu €35 (lunch)/40 – Carte €27/68

PLAN: 2-G1 – *Number One, Shelbourne Road – 01 963 9777 – www.shelbournesocial.com – Closed dinner Sunday-Monday*

at Blackrock Southeast : 7. 5 km by R 118

Liath (Damien Grey)

MODERN CUISINE • FRIENDLY A chic restaurant in a bohemian suburban market. Lunch sees a fixed price menu where each course relates to one of the five senses, but the set multi-course dinner menu is the highlight. Intensely flavoured, well-judged dishes draw on natural flavours and are full of contrasting colours, textures and tastes.

Specialities: Langoustine, wild garlic and morels. Angus beef, kelp and sandwort. Chocolate and preserved raspberries.

Menu €58 (lunch), €78/96

Off plan – *Blackrock Market, 19a Main Street – 01 212 3676 – www.liathrestaurant.com – Closed 2-16 August, 22 December-5 January, Sunday, Monday, Tuesday, lunch Wednesday-Friday*

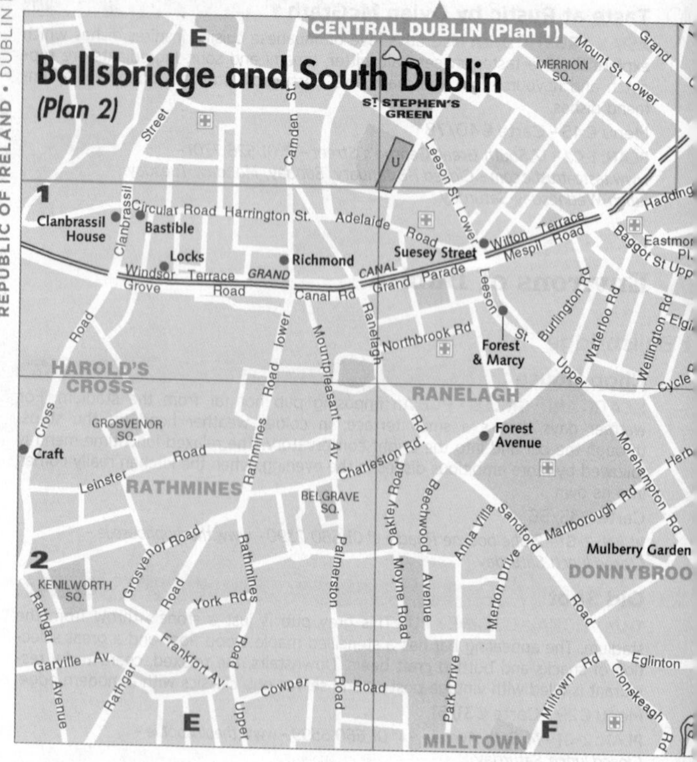

3 Leaves

INDIAN • SIMPLE This sweet little eatery sits within a bohemian market and i[s] always packed. Simple lunches follow a 'when it's gone, it's gone' approach – go for the great value 'Taster' menu. Three nights a week they offer dinner, which i[s] a more ambitious affair. They're unlicensed, so BYO.

Menu €31 – Carte €25/35

Off plan – *Unit 30, Blackrock Market, 19A Main Street – ✆ 087 769 1361 – www.3leaves.ie – Closed 17-30 August, 30 December-19 January, dinner Sunday, Monday, Tuesday, dinner Wednesday, lunch Thursday, dinner Friday*

at Clontarf Northeast : 5. 5 km by R105

Pigeon House

MODERN CUISINE • NEIGHBOURHOOD A slickly run neighbourhood bistro set just off the coast road in an up-and-coming area. It has a lovely front terrace, a lively feel and a bar counter laden with freshly baked goodies. Cooking is modern and assured and dishes are full of flavour. It's open all day and for weekend brunch too.

Menu €26/30 – Carte €26/49

Off plan – *11b Vernon Avenue – ✆ 01 805 7567 – www.pigeonhouse.ie – Closed Monday*

Fishbone 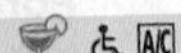

SEAFOOD • NEIGHBOURHOOD A friendly little restaurant opposite the Bull Bridge, with a cocktail bar at its centre and a glass-enclosed kitchen to the rear. Prime seafood from the plancha and charcoal grill is accompanied by tasty house sauces.

Menu €25 (lunch)/29 – Carte €25/45

Off plan – *324 Clontarf Road* – *☎ 01 536 9066* – *www.fishbone.ie* – *Closed 25-26 December*

at Donnybrook

Mulberry Garden 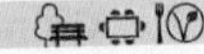

MODERN CUISINE • COSY Hidden away in the suburbs is this delightful little restaurant, with an interesting L-shaped dining room set around a small court-yard terrace. The biweekly menu offers three dishes per course and the original modern cooking relies on good quality local produce.

Menu €45 (lunch), €55/80

PLAN: 2-F2 – *Mulberry Lane* – *☎ 01 269 3300* – *www.mulberrygarden.ie* – *Closed 1-7 January, Sunday, Monday, Tuesday, lunch Wednesday-Saturday*

at Dundrum South: 7. 5 km by R 117

Ananda

INDIAN • EXOTIC DÉCOR Its name means 'bliss' and it's a welcome escap from the bustle of the shopping centre. The stylish interior encompasses a sma cocktail bar, attractive fretwork and vibrant art. Accomplished Indian cooking modern and original.

Menu €65 – Carte €42/57

Off plan – *Sandyford Road, Dundrum Town Centre – ✆ 01 296 0099 – www.anandarestaurant.ie – Closed lunch Monday-Thursday*

at Foxrock Southeast: 13 km by N 11

Bistro One

TRADITIONAL CUISINE • NEIGHBOURHOOD Long-standing neighbourhoc bistro above a parade of shops; run by a father-daughter team and a real h with the locals. Good value daily menus list a range of Irish and Italian dishe They produce their own Tuscan olive oil.

Menu €29 – Carte €29/52

Off plan – *3 Brighton Road – ✆ 01 289 7711 – www.bistro-one.ie – Closed dinner Sunday, Monday, lunch Tuesday-Thursday*

at Ranelagh

Forest & Marcy

MODERN CUISINE • CHIC There's a lively buzz to this lovely little win kitchen with high-level seating. Precisely prepared, original dishes burst wit flavour; many are prepared at the counter and the chefs themselves ofte present and explain what's on the plate. Choose between a 4 or 6 course tast ing menu.

Menu €49/58

PLAN: 2-F1 – *126 Leeson Street Upper – ✆ 01 660 2480 – www.forestandmarcy.ie – Closed 6-14 April, 17 August-2 September, 23 December-7 January, lunch Sunday, Monday, Tuesday, lunch Wednesday-Saturday*

Forest Avenue

MODERN CUISINE • NEIGHBOURHOOD This rustic neighbourhood restauran is named after a street in Queens and has a fitting 'NY' vibe. Elaborately pre sented tasting plates are full of originality and each dish combines many differ ent flavours.

Menu €35 (lunch)/68

PLAN: 2-F2 – *8 Sussex Terrace – ✆ 01 667 8337 – www.forestavenuerestaurant.ie – Closed 23 December-7 January, Sunday, Monday, Tuesday, lunch Wednesday*

at Sandyford South: 10 km by R 117 off R 825

China Sichuan

CHINESE • BRASSERIE A smart interior is well-matched by creative menus where Irish produce features in tasty Cantonese classics and some Sichuan speci- alities. It was established in 1979 and is now run by the third generation of the family.

Menu €17 (lunch)/31 – Carte €29/43

Off plan – *The Forum, Ballymoss Road – ✆ 01 293 5100 – www.china-sichuan.ie – Closed 25-27 December, Monday, lunch Saturday*

t Terenure

Circa

MODERN CUISINE · FRIENDLY Four young friends run this modern neighbourhood restaurant with a laid-back vibe. The appealing monthly menu lists around a dozen dishes – half of which are small plates. Irish produce is kept to the fore and cooking is full of flavour. You can sit in the bar, at the counter or at regular tables.

Carte €33/51

Off plan – *90 Terenure Road North – ✆ 01 534 2644 – www.restaurantcirca.com – Closed Sunday, Monday, Tuesday, lunch Wednesday-Thursday*

Craft

MODERN CUISINE · NEIGHBOURHOOD A busy southern suburb plays host to this friendly neighbourhood bistro. Concise menus evolve with seasonal availability and there's a good value early bird selection. Dishes are modern and creative with vibrant colours and fresh, natural flavours. The dripping roasted potatoes are delicious.

Menu €25/30 – Carte €25/55

PLAN: 2-E2 – *208 Harold's Cross Road – ✆ 01 497 8632 – www.craftrestaurant.ie – Closed dinner Sunday, Monday, Tuesday, lunch Wednesday-Thursday*

MasterLu/iStock

ITALY

ITALIA

ROME
ROMA

ROMAOSLO/iStock

ROME IN...

→ **ONE DAY**
Capitol, Forum, Colosseum, Pantheon, Trevi Fountain, Spanish Steps.

→ **TWO DAYS**
Via Condotti, Piazza Navona and surrounding churches, Capitoline museums.

→ **THREE DAYS**
A day on the west bank of the Tiber at Trastevere, Vatican City.

Rome wasn't built in a day and, when visiting, it's pretty hard to do it justice in less than three. The Italian capital is richly layered in Imperial, Renaissance, baroque and modern architecture, and its broad piazzas, hooting traffic and cobbled thoroughfares all lend their part to the heady fare: a theatrical stage cradled within seven famous hills. Being Eternal, Rome never ceases to feel like a lively, living city, while at the same time a scintillating monument to Renaissance power and an epic centre of antiquity. Nowhere else offers such a wealth of classical remains; set alongside palaces and churches and bathed in the soft, golden light for which it is famous

When Augustus became the first Emperor of Rome, he could hardly have imagined the impact his city's language, laws and calendar would have upon the world. The River Tiber snakes its way north to south through the heart of Rome. On its west bank lies the characterful and 'independent' neighbourhood of Trastevere, while north of here is Vatican City. Over the river the Piazza di Spagna area to the north has Rome's smartest shopping streets, while the southern boundary is marked by the Aventine and Celian hills, the latter overlooking the Colosseum. Esquiline's teeming quarter is just to the east of the city's heart; that honour goes to The Capitol, which gave its name to the concept of a 'capital' city.

EATING OUT

Despite being Italy's capital, Rome largely favours a local, traditional cuisine, typically found in an unpretentious trattoria or osteria. Although not far from the sea, the city doesn't go in much for fish, and food is often connected to the rural, pastoral life with products coming from the surrounding Lazio hills, which also produce good wines. Pasta, of course, is not to be missed, and lamb is favoured among meats for the main course. So too, the 'quinto quarto': a long-established way of indicating those parts of the beef (tail, tripe, liver, spleen, lungs, heart, kidney) left over after the best bits had gone to the richest families. For international cuisine combined with a more refined setting, head for the elegant hotels: very few other areas of Italy have such an increasing number of good quality restaurants within a hotel setting. Locals like to dine later in Rome than say, Milan, with 1pm, or 8pm the very earliest you'd dream of appearing for lunch or dinner. In the tourist hotspots, owners are, of course, only too pleased to open that bit earlier.

Centre

Centro Storico

✿✿ Il Pagliaccio (Anthony Genovese)

CREATIVE • ELEGANT The appearance of the menu – no more than a simple li of the ingredients used – hides the fact that this restaurant serves some of th most original and sophisticated dishes in Rome. The chef here has real passic for the aesthetics and ingredients of the Far East, as well as a new awareness c the vegetarian requirements of his guests, which means that many of the dish are also available as a vegetable-based version.

Specialities: "The journey": amberjack and foie gras. "Scented memories". Bab laurel and vermouth with added quinine.

Menu 85€ (lunch), 165/185€ – Carte 100/150€

PLAN: 2-E2 – *via dei Banchi Vecchi 129/a – ✆ 06 6880 9595 – www.ristoranteilpagliaccio.com – Closed 1-10 February, 10 August-1 September, Monday, lunch Tuesday, Sunday*

✿ Acquolina

SEAFOOD • MINIMALIST Located on the ground floor of the centrally locate luxury The First Roma hotel, with its elegant atmosphere and decor of origin artwork, paintings and sculptures, the chic, minimalist-style Acquolina restaura provides the setting for fish-based dishes with a Mediterranean flavour and a added twist of creativity, all accompanied by a good wine selection.

Specialities: Made in Italy – bread and tomatoes. Monkfish – sweet peppers, ba samic vinegar and almonds. Passion Cheesecake – passion fruit, white chocola and sweet marjoram.

Menu 105/135€ – Carte 76/159€

PLAN: 2-F1 – *Hotel The First Roma, via del Vantaggio 14 – Ⓜ Spagna – ✆ 06 320 0655 – www.acquolinaristorante.it – Closed lunch Monday-Saturday, Sunday*

✿ Il Convivio-Troiani

MODERN CUISINE • ELEGANT Situated in the maze of alleyways not far fro Piazza Navona, Il Convivio welcomes its guests in elegant, themed dining room – the Chiostro (cloister room), Loggia (the old entrance), Rimessa (carriag room) and the Galleria (art room). The menu features skilful reinterpretations c classic dishes from Lazio and Italy with the occasional imaginative twist, whi the wine list offers a tempting selection of over 3 600 wines, many available b the glass.

Specialities: Pan-seared octopus, fake mayonnaise, raspberry and green appl Amatriciana. Cigar, 68% dark chocolate, whisky fior di latte and tobacco.

Menu 125€ – Carte 86/142€

PLAN: 2-E2 – *vicolo dei Soldati 31 – ✆ 06 686 9432 – www.ilconviviotroiani.com – Closed lunch Monday-Saturday, Sunday*

✿ Enoteca al Parlamento Achilli

CREATIVE • ELEGANT Although little suggests from the outside that this ci centre building houses a restaurant, the elegant wine bar leads to two successiv dining rooms furnished in wood. The cuisine is highly individual, based on strikir contrasts and bold presentations, making it perfect for those looking for change from traditional fare.

Specialities: Scallop, foie gras, coffee reduction. King crab, baby spinach, parm san cheese, pear and marrow. Banana, caviar and white chocolate.

Menu 100/160€ – Carte 70/130€

PLAN: 2-F2 – *via dei Prefetti 15 – Ⓜ Spagna – ✆ 06 8676 1422 – www.enotecalparlamento.com – Closed 20 January-1 February, 14-31 August, Sunda*

Idylio by Apreda

ITALIAN CONTEMPORARY · TRENDY Originally from Campania, the chef at this modern, trendy restaurant adds spices and Asian touches to his Neapolitan-influenced cuisine. Choose from the à la carte options or – as our inspectors recommend – go for one of the three tasting menus ("Inside The Pantheon", "Seasons at the Pantheon", and "Iconic Signature at the Pantheon").

Specialities: Foie gras, dried fruit and spices. Cheese, pepper and sesame risotto. Sweet buffalo mozzarella.

Menu 120/160 € – Carte 75/110 €

PLAN: 2-F2 – *Hotel The Pantheon, via di Santa Chiara 4 – 06 8780 7080 – www.thepantheonhotel.com – Closed 6-18 January, 11-21 August, Monday, lunch Tuesday-Saturday, Sunday*

Imàgo

MODERN CUISINE · LUXURY Imàgo, the panoramic restaurant at the Hassler hotel, offers a unique sensorial experience which includes superb views of Rome and exciting gastronomy. New chef Antonini pays tribute to Italy in his cuisine, focusing on traditional, seasonal ingredients which he transforms into imaginative and contemporary-style dishes.

Specialities: Mullet, panzanella salad and lemon. Spaghetti, sea urchins and pecorino cheese. Chocolate and chilli peppers.

Menu 130/150 € – Carte 92/164 €

PLAN: 2-F1 – *Hotel Hassler, piazza Trinità dei Monti 6 – Ⓜ Spagna – 06 6993 4726 – www.imagorestaurant.com – Closed 7-23 January, lunch Monday-Sunday*

Per Me Giulio Terrinoni

CREATIVE · CONTEMPORARY DÉCOR This restaurant in Vicolo del Malpasso in the historic centre of Rome, famous for its "tappi" (tapas-style snacks), fully expresses the strong personality of its chef, as well as his striking originality. This is a place of experimentation, technical expertise and imagination, where creativity and top-quality ingredients are constant throughout. However, the food varies slightly between lunch (more informal) and dinner, when tasting menus (including the outstanding "Terra e Mare") take centre stage.

Specialities: Scampi carpaccio, marinated foie gras. Medley of monkfish, coppa ham, tripe, roast suckling pig, millefeuille. Mediterranean Maquis: pistachio, blueberries, goat's milk ice cream.

Menu 33 € (lunch), 85/140 € – Carte 80/128 €

PLAN: 2-E3 – *vicolo del Malpasso 9 – 06 687 7365 – www.giulioterrinoni.it – Closed 9-19 August*

Pipero Roma

CREATIVE · ELEGANT This establishment long-favoured by food enthusiasts in the capital has moved to new premises. Alessandro Pipero now presides over an elegant, stylish contemporary restaurant opposite the Chiesa Nuova, with a mezzanine area for guests wanting a bit more privacy. In the kitchen, the chef uses just a few ingredients to create seemingly simple dishes which are nonetheless full of character.

Specialities: Anchovies and tomato. Pipero's carbonara. La Dolce Roma, ricotta cheese, mint and hazelnuts.

Menu 60 € (lunch)/125 € – Carte 85/165 €

PLAN: 2-E2-3 – *corso Vittorio Emanuele 246 – 06 6813 9022 – www.piperoroma.it – Closed lunch Monday, lunch Saturday-Sunday*

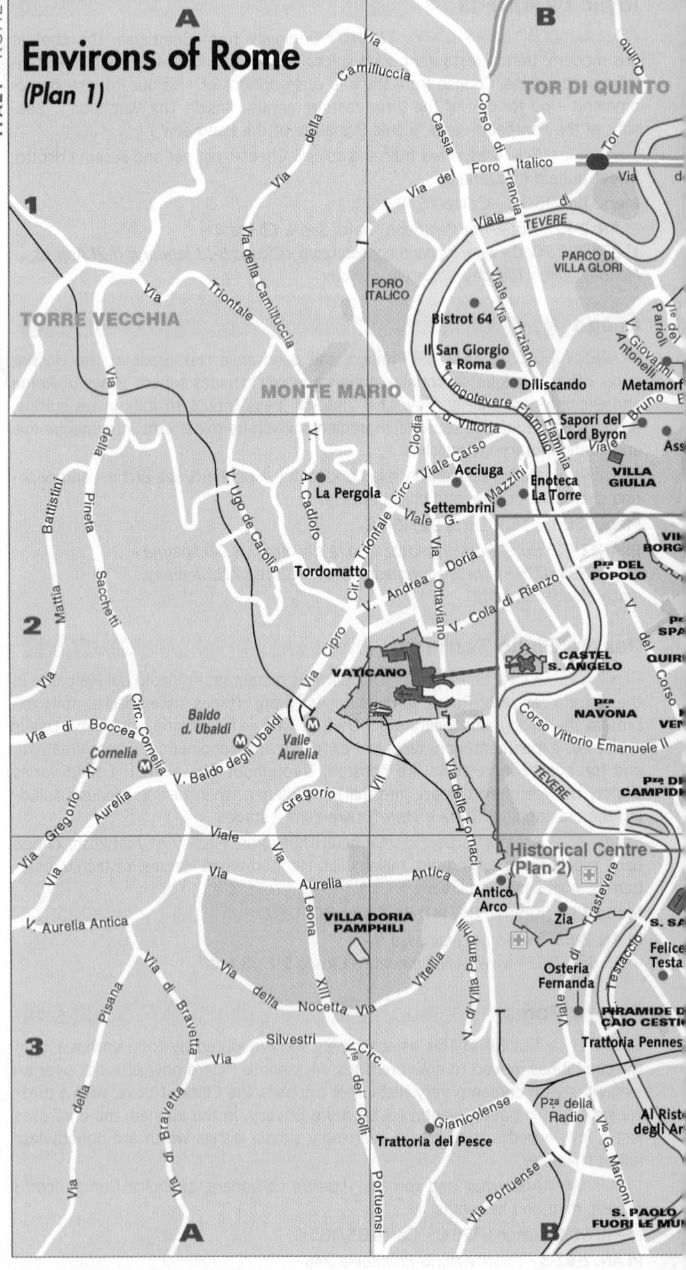
Environs of Rome
(Plan 1)
A
B
1
2
3
TOR DI QUINTO
TORRE VECCHIA
MONTE MARIO
FORO ITALICO
PARCO DI VILLA GLORI
Bistrot 64
Il San Giorgio a Roma
Diliscando
Sapori del Lord Byron
Acciuga
Enoteca La Torre
Settembrini
La Pergola
Tordomatto
VILLA GIULIA
Pza DEL POPOLO
CASTEL S. ANGELO
Pza NAVONA
VATICANO
Baldo d. Ubaldi
Cornelia
Valle Aurelia
VILLA DORIA PAMPHILI
Antico Arco
Zia
Osteria Fernanda
Felice a Testa
PIRAMIDE DI CAIO CESTIO
Trattoria Pennestri
Al Ristoro degli Ar
Trattoria del Pesce
Pza della Radio
S. PAOLO FUORI LE MURA
Historical Centre (Plan 2)
Via Foro Italico
Via Trionfale
Via della Camilluccia
Via Cassia
Corso di Francia
Viale Tiziano
Lungotevere Flaminio
Via Flaminia
Via di Boccea
V. Baldo degli Ubaldi
Circ. Cornelia
Via Aurelia
Via Gregorio XI
Viale Gregorio VII
Via delle Fornaci
Via Aurelia Antica
V. Aurelia Antica
Via Leone XIII
Via della Nocetta
Via di Bravetta
Via della Pisana
Via Silvestri
Vle dei Colli Portuensi
Circ. Gianicolense
Via Portuense
Vle G. Marconi
Viale di Trastevere
Corso Vittorio Emanuele II
V. Cola di Rienzo
V. Andrea Doria
Via Ottaviano
Viale G. Mazzini
Viale Carso
Circ. Clodia
Circ. Trionfale
V. Ugo de Carolis
V. A. Cadlolo
Via della Pineta Sacchetti
Via Mattia Battistini
V. di Villa Pamphili
Via Vitellia
TEVERE

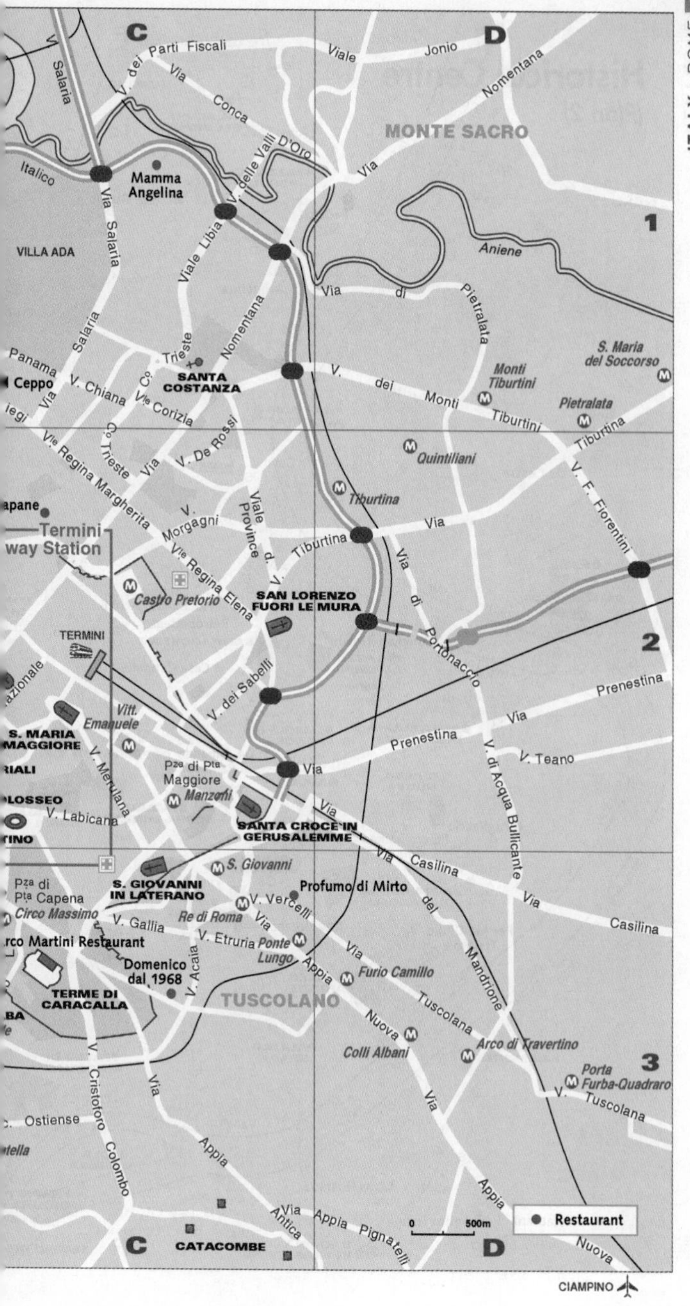
C
D
1
2
3
MONTE SACRO
V. dei Parti Fiscali
Via Conca D'Oro
Viale Jonio
Nomentana
V. delle Valli
Via Salaria
Italico
Mamma Angelina
VILLA ADA
Viale Libia
Aniene
Via di Pietralata
S. Maria del Soccorso
Monti Tiburtini
Pietralata
V. dei Monti Tiburtini
Tiburtina
Quintiliani
Tiburtina
Trieste
SANTA COSTANZA
Panama
Ceppo
V. Chiana
Vle Corizia
Co. Trieste
V. De Rossi
Vle Regina Margherita
V. Morgagni
Viale d. Province
Via Tiburtina
V. F. Fiorentini
Termini Railway Station
Castro Pretorio
Vle Regina Elena
SAN LORENZO FUORI LE MURA
Via di Portonaccio
TERMINI
V. dei Sabelli
Vitt. Emanuele
S. MARIA MAGGIORE
V. Merulana
Pza di Pta Maggiore
Manzoni
Via Prenestina
Via Prenestina
V. Teano
V. di Acqua Bulicante
V. Labicana
SANTA CROCE IN GERUSALEMME
Via Casilina
Via Casilina
S. Giovanni
S. GIOVANNI IN LATERANO
Profumo di Mirto
V. Vercelli
Via del Mandrione
Pza di Pta Capena
Circo Massimo
V. Gallia
Re di Roma
Via
V. Etruria
Ponte Lungo
Via Appia
Furio Camillo
Via Tuscolana
Marco Martini Restaurant
Domenico dal 1968
V. Acaia
TERME DI CARACALLA
TUSCOLANO
Nuova
Colli Albani
Arco di Travertino
Porta Furba-Quadraro
V. Tuscolana
V. Cristoforo Colombo
Via Appia
Ostiense
Via Appia
Via Appia Antica
Via Appia Pignatelli
Appia Nuova
CATACOMBE
0 500m
Restaurant
CIAMPINO

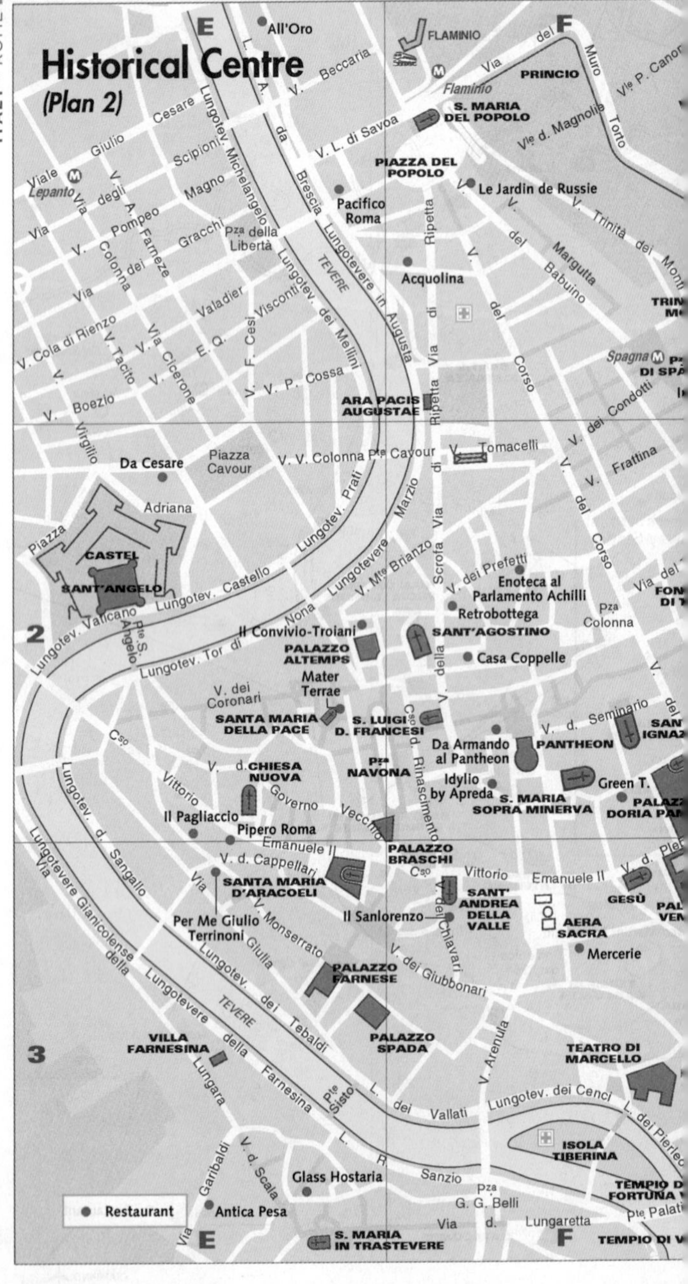
Historical Centre
(Plan 2)
All'Oro
FLAMINIO
Flaminio
PRINCIO
S. MARIA DEL POPOLO
PIAZZA DEL POPOLO
Le Jardin de Russie
Pacifico Roma
Acquolina
Lepanto
Pza della Libertà
TEVERE
ARA PACIS AUGUSTAE
Spagna
Da Cesare
Piazza Cavour
Adriana
Piazza
CASTEL SANT'ANGELO
Tomacelli
Enoteca al Parlamento Achilli
Retrobottega
Pza Colonna
Il Convivio-Troiani
PALAZZO ALTEMPS
SANT'AGOSTINO
Casa Coppelle
Mater Terrae
SANTA MARIA DELLA PACE
S. LUIGI D. FRANCESI
Da Armando al Pantheon
PANTHEON
Pza NAVONA
CHIESA NUOVA
Idylio by Apreda
S. MARIA SOPRA MINERVA
Green T.
Il Pagliaccio
Pipero Roma
PALAZZO BRASCHI
SANTA MARIA D'ARACOELI
SANT' ANDREA DELLA VALLE
AERA SACRA
GESÙ
Per Me Giulio Terrinoni
Il Sanlorenzo
Mercerie
PALAZZO FARNESE
PALAZZO SPADA
VILLA FARNESINA
TEATRO DI MARCELLO
ISOLA TIBERINA
Glass Hostaria
Antica Pesa
Pza G. G. Belli
S. MARIA IN TRASTEVERE
Restaurant
E
F
2
3

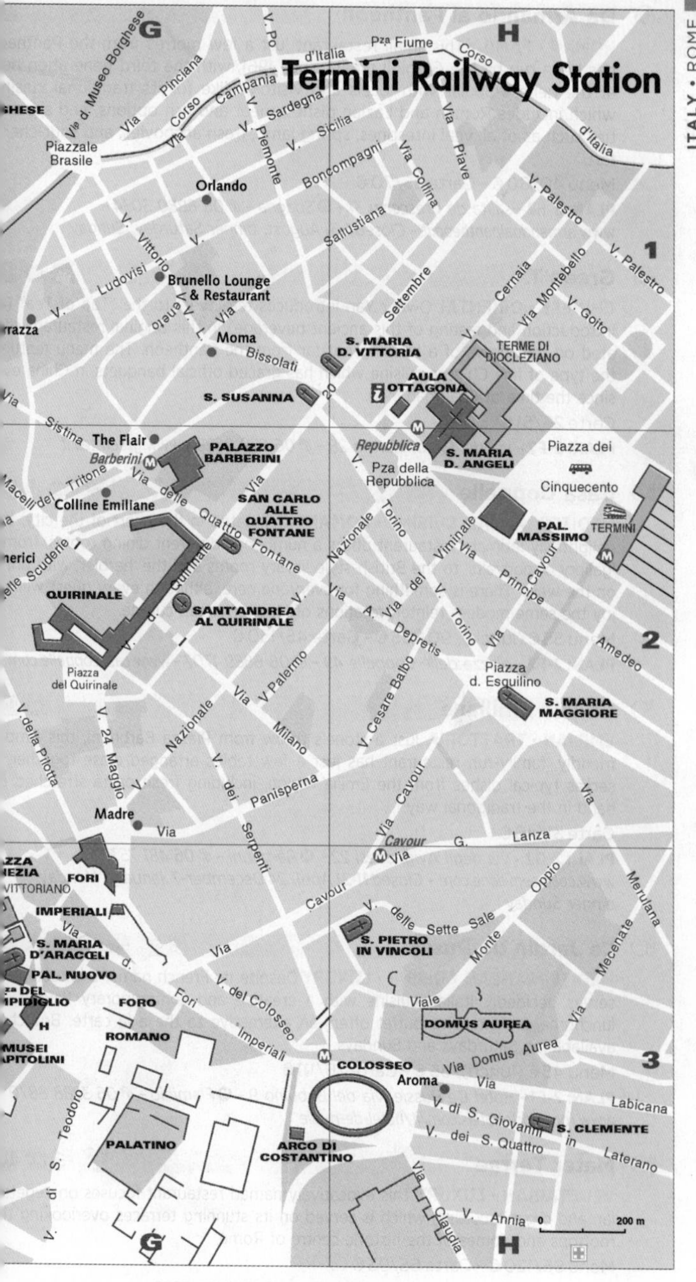
Termini Railway Station
G
H
1
2
3
Pza Fiume
d'Italia
Corso
Corso
d'Italia
Via Pinciana
Vle d. Museo Borghese
V. Po
Via Campania
V. Sardegna
V. Piemonte
V. Sicilia
Via Piave
Via Collina
V. Boncompagni
Sallustiana
Piazzale Brasile
Orlando
V. Vittorio V. Veneto
Ludovisi
Brunello Lounge & Restaurant
Moma
V. L. Bissolati
V. Palestro
V. Palestro
V. Goito
Via Montebello
Cernaia
V. XX Settembre
S. MARIA D. VITTORIA
TERME DI DIOCLEZIANO
AULA OTTAGONA
S. SUSANNA
Repubblica
S. MARIA D. ANGELI
Pza della Repubblica
Piazza dei Cinquecento
TERMINI
PAL. MASSIMO
Via Sistina
The Flair
Barberini
PALAZZO BARBERINI
Via del Tritone
Colline Emiliane
Via delle Quattro Fontane
SAN CARLO ALLE QUATTRO FONTANE
V. Nazionale
Via Torino
Via del Viminale
Via Principe Amedeo
Via Cavour
QUIRINALE
V. d. Quirinale
SANT'ANDREA AL QUIRINALE
Via A. Depretis
V. Torino
Piazza del Quirinale
Piazza d. Esquilino
S. MARIA MAGGIORE
V. della Pilotta
V. 24 Maggio
Via Nazionale
Via Milano
V. Palermo
V. Cesare Balbo
V. dei Serpenti
Panisperna
Via Cavour
Via
Madre
Via G. Lanza
Cavour
FORI IMPERIALI
VITTORIANO
Merulana
Via Cavour
V. delle Sette Sale
Via Monte Oppio
S. MARIA D'ARACOELI
PAL. NUOVO
Via d. Fori Imperiali
S. PIETRO IN VINCOLI
Via Mecenate
FORO ROMANO
V. del Colosseo
Viale DOMUS AUREA
MUSEI CAPITOLINI
COLOSSEO
Via Domus Aurea
Aroma
Via Labicana
V. di S. Giovanni in Laterano
S. CLEMENTE
V. dei S. Quattro
V. di S. Teodoro
PALATINO
ARCO DI COSTANTINO
Via Claudia
V. Annia
0 200 m

Da Armando al Pantheon

ROMAN • FAMILY This small restaurant just a few metres from the Panthe has been run by the Gargioli family since 1961, with the third generation no at the helm. Popular with locals and visitors alike for its traditional cuisin which includes Roman and Lazian dishes, meat and fish options, and specia ties such as offal, veal intestines, spring lamb, fresh anchovies, and sour-cher tart.

Menu 40/60 € - Carte 35/70 €

PLAN: 2-F2 - *salita dè Crescenzi 31 - Ⓜ Spagna - ✆ 06 6880 3034 - www.armandoalpantheon.it - Closed 1-31 August, dinner Saturday, Sunday*

Green T.

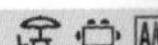

CHINESE • ORIENTAL Owner Yan introduces tea lovers to the "Tao of Tea" (introduction and tasting of this ancient beverage) in this original restaurant sit ated on four floors of a building not far from the Pantheon. The menu featur the type of fine Chinese cuisine which has graced official banquets in China ev since the time of Chairman Mao.

Carte 26/51 €

PLAN: 2-F2 - *via del Piè di Marmo 28 - ✆ 06 679 8628 - www.green-tea.it*

Casa Coppelle

MEDITERRANEAN CUISINE • ROMANTIC Situated in the heart of the city, th delightfully intimate restaurant offers a number of different dining rooms, from 'gallery of portraits' to the British-style library rooms and the 'herbier' with prir on the walls. There is something for everyone here, although every guest will e joy the same modern reinterpretations of Mediterranean cuisine.

Menu 55 € (lunch), 90/135 € - Carte 45/130 €

PLAN: 2-F2 - *piazza delle Coppelle 49 - ✆ 06 6889 1707 - www.casacoppelle.com*

Colline Emiliane

EMILIAN • TRATTORIA Just a stone's throw from Piazza Barberini, this simp friendly, family-run restaurant has just a few tables arranged close together. serves typical dishes from the Emilia region, including fresh pasta stretched hand in the traditional way.

Carte 31/46 €

PLAN: 2-G2 - *via degli Avignonesi 22 - Ⓜ Barberini - ✆ 06 481 7538 - www.collineemiliane.com - Closed 11-21 April, 24 December-7 January, Monday, dinner Sunday*

Le Jardin de Russie

MEDITERRANEAN CUISINE • LUXURY Despite its French name, this restaura serves decidedly Italian cuisine with a creative and contemporary flavour. lunchtime, an extensive buffet offers an alternative to the à la carte. Brunch available on Saturdays and Sundays.

Menu 45 € (lunch)/65 € - Carte 76/111 €

PLAN: 2-F1 - *Hotel De Russie, via del Babuino 9 - Ⓜ Flaminio - ✆ 06 3288 8870 www.roccofortehotels.com/it/hotel-de-russie*

Mater Terrae

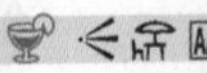

VEGETARIAN • LUXURY This evocatively named restaurant focuses on veget ian and organic cuisine, which is served on its stunning terraces overlooking t rooftops and domes of the historic centre of Rome.

Menu 95/120 € - Carte 65/93 €

PLAN: 2-E2 - *Hotel Raphaël, largo Febo 2 - ✆ 06 6828 3762 - www.raphaelhotel.com*

Mercerie

CONTEMPORARY • TRENDY High-quality street food has arrived in the capital in the form of this modern, fashionable restaurant which bears the signature of famous chef Igles Corelli. The flavours here are typically Italian, with a few Roman and Lazian favourites on the menu. Dishes are also available to take away.

Menu 12€ (lunch), 45/55€ – Carte 30/70€

PLAN: 2-F3 – *via di San Nicola de' Cesarini 4/5 – ✆ 347 971 4949 – www.mercerie.eu – Closed 1-31 August, Monday*

Pacifico Roma

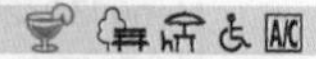

PERUVIAN • TRENDY This restaurant is almost the twin of the Pacifico Milano – an Italian brand dedicated to fusion cuisine with a particular emphasis on Peru. The mentor is Jaime Pesaque, an experienced Peruvian chef, who, while not the permanent chef here, influences and supervises the style of cuisine, adding his own imaginative touches. The menu features different types of ceviche alongside creative dishes influenced by culinary traditions from around the world. Restricted menu at lunchtime.

Carte 40/100€

PLAN: 2-E1 – *Hotel Palazzo Dama, lungotevere Arnaldo da Brescia 2 – Ⓜ Lepanto – ✆ 06 320 7042 – wearepacifico.com*

Retrobottega

CONTEMPORARY • MINIMALIST Minimalist decor and clean lines characterise this restaurant decorated in dark tones, where the two owner-chefs have both worked in various Michelin-starred restaurants (and others) over the years. Modern cuisine which showcases seasonal ingredients in regional yet refined dishes.

Menu 55€ – Carte 50/70€

PLAN: 1-F2 – *via della Stelletta 4 – ✆ 06 6813 6310 – www.retro-bottega.com – Closed 10-16 August, lunch Monday*

Il Sanlorenzo

SEAFOOD • ELEGANT A historic palazzo built over the foundations of the Teatro Pompeo is home to this atmospheric restaurant, which brings together history and contemporary art. However, the real star is the fish on the menu, most of which comes from the island of Ponza, and is served either raw or cooked very simply in a modern style.

Menu 90€ – Carte 70/115€

PLAN: 2-F3 – *via dei Chiavari 4/5 – ✆ 06 686 5097 – www.ilsanlorenzo.it – Closed 3-26 August, lunch Monday, lunch Saturday, Sunday*

Le Tamerici

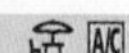

MEDITERRANEAN CUISINE • COSY Just a few metres from the Trevi Fountain, this unusual top-quality restaurant stands out among the many ordinary tourist-style options available in this district. In a quiet outdoor ambience in the alleyway, enjoy excellent modern Mediterranean cuisine created by the chef and owner.

Menu 60/90€ – Carte 45/70€

PLAN: 2-G2 – *vicolo Scavolino 79 – Ⓜ Barberini – ✆ 06 6920 0700 – www.letamerici.com – Closed 9-30 August, lunch Monday, Sunday*

tazione Termini

Moma

CREATIVE • CONTEMPORARY DÉCOR A plain, simple and contemporary-style restaurant on the first floor of a palazzo to the rear of Via Veneto, where all the attention is focused on the quality of the food. Unexpectedly elegant and creative, and occasionally based on original combinations, the dishes here showcase the personality of the talented young chef.

Specialities: Our seasonal vegetables. Chitarrini pasta "alla gricia". Ricotta and wild sour cherry dessert.

Menu 50€ (lunch), 75/95€ – Carte 52/94€

PLAN: 2-G1 – *via San Basilio 42/43 – Ⓜ Barberini – ✆ 06 4201 1798 – www.ristorantemoma.it – Closed 15-22 August, Sunday*

✿ La Terrazza

MODERN CUISINE • LUXURY Sitting in the modern, elegant dining room of Terrazza, your attention is drawn to the spectacular roof-garden restaurant ove looking the city's rooftops. Also competing for your attention is the creative a original cuisine which has a hint of local flavour, although the main influence he is the chef's imagination.

Specialities: Sea urchin cream. Veal broth ravioli and horseradish. Tiramisù with twist.

Menu 130/280€ – Carte 118/180€

PLAN: 2-G1 – *Hotel Eden, via Ludovisi 49 – Ⓜ Barberini – ✆ 06 4781 2752 – www.dorchestercollection.com – Closed 13-28 January, 10-25 August, lunch Monday Tuesday, lunch Wednesday-Sunday*

Brunello Lounge & Restaurant

MODERN CUISINE • INTIMATE This warm, elegant restaurant has a faintly Oriental feel. It provides the perfect setting to enjoy superb Mediterranean cuisine as well as international dishes that will appeal to foreign visitors to the capital.

Menu 75/85€ – Carte 60/120€

PLAN: 2-G1 – *Regina Hotel Baglioni, via Vittorio Veneto 72 – Ⓜ Barberini – ✆ 06 421111 – www.baglionihotels.com*

The Flair

CONTEMPORARY • CONTEMPORARY DÉCOR A brand-new concept on th panoramic top floor of this famous Roman hotel. Although the beautiful views the city centre are unchanged, there's now a new, young Sicilian chef at the hel in the kitchen who is consolidating his reputation with his delicious contempora Italian cuisine. Only open in the evening, while the bistro formula at lunchtime f cuses on simpler options.

Menu 35€ (lunch), 80/100€ – Carte 90/120€

PLAN: 2-G2 – *Hotel Sina Bernini Bristol, piazza Barberini 23 – Ⓜ Barberini – ✆ 06 4201 0469 – www.sinahotels.com*

Orlando

SICILIAN • REGIONAL An elegant, contemporary-style restaurant just a stone throw from Via Veneto. It serves traditional Sicilian cuisine with a modern twist

Menu 20€ (lunch)/40€ – Carte 40/80€

PLAN: 2-G1 – *via Sicilia 41 – ✆ 06 4201 6102 – www.orlandoristorante.it – Closed 9-23 August, lunch Saturday, Sunday*

Roma Antica

✿ Aroma

CREATIVE • LUXURY The brand-new open-view kitchen is the first thing guest see when they arrive at this delightful roof-garden restaurant which offers view of Ancient Rome from the Colosseum to the dome of St Peter's. The name pay tribute to both the city and the aromas provided by the creative and imaginativ Mediterranean cuisine served here. There's also now a bistro-style eatery offerin more informal dining.

Specialities: Steamed monkfish with Romanesco courgettes, pink grapefruit an sweet peppers. Marinated cod with purple carrots, Tropea onion foam and Swis chard. "Il Nido" – mango, passion fruit and fresh cream cheese.

Menu 100€ (lunch), 120/170€ – Carte 120/180€

PLAN: 2-H3 – *Hotel Palazzo Manfredi, via Labicana 125 – Ⓜ Colosseo – ✆ 06 9761 5109 – www.aromarestaurant.it*

✿ Marco Martini Restaurant

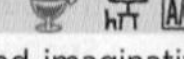

CREATIVE • TRENDY Chef Martini and his team create modern and imaginativ cuisine in this restaurant which boasts a winter garden-style dining room with contemporary feel as well as a terrace-cum-lounge for aperitifs and snacks, dom inated by a life-size marble Superman. The gourmet menu is also available a lunchtime if you book ahead.

Specialities: Sweetbreads, mozzarella, mullet roe and rhubarb. Cod, pata negra ham and bitter orange. White chocolate, extra virgin olive oil and Matcha tea.
Menu 100/135 € – Carte 70/100 €

PLAN: 1-C3 – *viale Aventino 121 – ✆ 06 4559 7350 – www.marcomartinichef.com – Closed 11-20 August, lunch Saturday, Sunday*

Madre

MEDITERRANEAN CUISINE • TRENDY A gourmet pizzeria that also serves raw fish specialities such as ceviche, in an attractive, modern setting where plants and the sound of water evoke the atmosphere of a fresh garden. Three set menus are available at lunchtime from Monday to Friday.
Menu 45/65 € – Carte 46/78 €

PLAN: 2-G2 – *largo Angelicum 1/a – ✆ 06 678 9046 – www.madreroma.com – Closed lunch Monday-Friday*

San Pietro (Città del Vaticano)

La Pergola

MODERN CUISINE • LUXURY This superb restaurant is suspended above the Eternal City in the magnificent setting of a panoramic roof garden. Mediterranean cuisine (chef Heinz Beck's constant passion), a systematic search for the best quality ingredients, and an added dose of creativity all come together in La Pergola. The restaurant's success speaks for itself.

Specialities: Duck foie gras with pear and ginger. Turbot with asparagus and codium (seaweed). Mini fruit salad with lemongrass jelly and ginger ice cream.
Menu 225/260 € – Carte 141/250 €

PLAN: 1-A2 – *Hotel Rome Cavalieri, via Cadlolo 101 – ✆ 06 3509 2152 – www.romecavalieri.com/lapergola – Closed Monday, lunch Tuesday-Saturday, Sunday*

Enoteca la Torre

MODERN CUISINE • LIBERTY STYLE This restaurant has a distinctly refined and elegant look. The antique furniture, flowers, columns and stucco all contribute to an Art Nouveau feel that would not be out of place in Paris. The chef continues to celebrate creativity with excellent results.

Specialities: Egg, buffalo Taleggio cheese, black truffle and spring vegetables. Lemon risotto, marinated squid, asparagus and buffalo yoghurt. Coffee mousse, elderflower, tobacco and liquorice.
Menu 60 € (lunch), 105/130 € – Carte 95/135 €

PLAN: 1-B2 – *Hotel Villa Laetitia, lungotevere delle Armi 22/23 – Ⓜ Lepanto – ✆ 06 4566 8304 – www.enotecalatorreroma.com – Closed 2-28 August, lunch Monday, Sunday*

Tordomatto (Adriano Baldassarre)

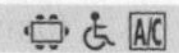

MODERN CUISINE • TRENDY Herbs in pots on the window sills add an attractive touch to this restaurant situated just a stone's throw from the Vatican Museums. According to the chef "the cuisine is traditional and yet at the same time creative, with a real focus on local traditions as we believe that dishes should always reflect their locality". His bold and intelligent dishes more than live up to this claim.

Specialities: Quail, oysters, potatoes and parsley. Spaghetti with cheese, pepper and turmeric. Tiramisù.
Menu 70/90 € – Carte 60/100 €

PLAN: 1-A-B 2 – *via Pietro Giannone 24 – ✆ 06 6935 2895 – www.tordomattoroma.com – Closed 10-20 August, 24-26 December, lunch Monday-Friday*

Acciuga

MEDITERRANEAN CUISINE • CONTEMPORARY DÉCOR A new, attractive a welcoming restaurant with limited capacity, where the young chef specialises fish dishes with a focus on sustainability, both in terms of the fish chosen a fishing methods used. Simple, carefully prepared dishes.

Menu 25€ (lunch), 45/68€ – Carte 30/50€

PLAN: 1-B2 – *via Vodice 25 – Ⓜ Lepanto – ✆ 06 372 3395 – www.acciugaroma.it – Closed 1-9 January, 12-28 August, Sunday*

Antico Arco

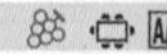

CREATIVE • CHIC The chef at this modern, bright and fashionable restaurant s lects the best Italian ingredients to create innovative dishes based on traditio specialities.

Menu 39€ (lunch), 79/120€ – Carte 59/75€

PLAN: 1-B3 – *piazzale Aurelio 7 – ✆ 06 581 5274 – www.anticoarco.it*

Da Cesare

CLASSIC CUISINE • TRATTORIA As the Florentine lily on the glass at the e trance implies, the specialities of this place are Tuscan in origin as well as se food. Friendly atmosphere, ample wine list.

Carte 22/65€

PLAN: 2-E2 – *via Crescenzio 13 – Ⓜ Lepanto – ✆ 06 686 1227 – www.ristorantecesare.com – Closed 16 August-2 September*

Parioli

Assaje

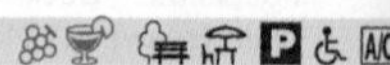

MEDITERRANEAN CUISINE • MEDITERRANEAN The new owner of this hot has completely renovated its restaurant, now named Assaje, which means "abu dance" in the Neapolitan dialect. The focus is on Mediterranean cuisine. The me offers imaginative, modern dishes alongside more traditional, classic fare with range of fish and meat options available. Professional, friendly service.

Specialities: Cold yellow tomato soup with smoked dried cod, green chillies a cuttlefish ink crisps. Candela spezzata pasta with oxtail, cocoa and Provolone d Monaco cheese. Baba baked in a glass with rum ice cream and blackberry co pote.

Carte 80/140€

PLAN: 1-B2 – *Hotel Aldrovandi Villa Borghese, via Ulisse Aldrovandi 15 – ✆ 06 322 3993 – www.aldrovandi.com – Closed 8 January-10 February, lunch Monday-Sunday*

Metamorfosi (Roy Caceres)

CREATIVE • DESIGN Situated near the Auditorium della Musica in the Parioli dis trict, this contemporary-style restaurant has a minimalist yet warm ambience. Th cuisine created by owner-chef Roy echoes his experiences, which are trans formed into innovative, creative and constantly evolving dishes with the occa sional influence from his native Colombia or Latin America in general.

Specialities: Raw tuna and herbs wrapped in chard leaves. Eel, crushed spelt an iced carpione. Yuzu, almonds and camomile.

Menu 110/150€ – Carte 80/130€

PLAN: 1-B1 – *via Giovanni Antonelli 30/32 – ✆ 06 807 6839 – www.metamorfosiroma.it – Closed lunch Saturday, Sunday*

All'Oro (Riccardo Di Giacinto)

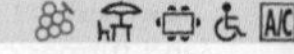

CREATIVE • DESIGN Enjoy cuisine created by Riccardo, the restaurant's owner chef, in the modern, pleasantly sophisticated New York-style dining room, or i the dining room with its vaguely English decor. The dishes are a mix of traditiona Italian flavours and recipes with the occasional influence from Lazio, all prepare with a creative flair.

Specialities: Carbonara reduction. Mascarpone raviolini with a duck ragout and red wine reduction. Tiramisù All'Oro.

Menu 88/150 € – Carte 80/104 €

PLAN: 2-E1 – *Hotel The H'All Tailor Suite, via Giuseppe Pisanelli 25 – ✆ 06 9799 6907 – www.ristorantealloro.it – Closed lunch Monday-Friday*

Al Ceppo

MEDITERRANEAN CUISINE • ELEGANT Bistro-styled wood panelling welcomes guests to this rustic yet elegant restaurant which serves Mediterranean cuisine reinterpreted with a contemporary twist. Specialities include grilled fish and meat dishes prepared in front of guests in the dining room.

Menu 25 € (lunch), 60/80 € – Carte 45/85 €

PLAN: 1-C1 – *via Panama 2 – ✆ 06 855 1379 – www.ristorantealceppo.it – Closed 7-25 August, lunch Monday*

Diliscando

SEAFOOD • BISTRO Situated in the Flaminia district, this modern bistro-style restaurant offers a friendly ambience and professional service. The menu focuses on fish dishes, serving daily specials based on market availability. Good selection of carefully chosen wines.

Carte 20/70 €

PLAN: 1-B1 – *viale del Vignola 9 – ✆ 06 8913 1376 – www.diliscando.it – Closed lunch Monday, dinner Sunday*

Il San Giorgio a Roma

CREATIVE • CONTEMPORARY DÉCOR The owner-chef at this restaurant has a creative and inventive approach, producing decidedly contemporary dishes which are always beautifully presented and which feature meat and fish – sometimes even cooked together!

Menu 45/85 € – Carte 61/81 €

PLAN: 1-B1 – *viale del Vignola 20 – ✆ 06 6452 0871 – www.ilsangiorgioaroma.it – Closed 9-16 August, Sunday*

Sapori del Lord Byron 

ITALIAN • LUXURY Mirror-covered walls, dark octagonal tables and fine marble decor all add to the delightful Art Deco style of this restaurant. The menu features delicious cuisine from across Italy, superbly prepared by a highly experienced chef.

Carte 75/95 €

PLAN: 1-B2 – *Hotel Lord Byron, via G. De Notaris 5 – ✆ 06 322 0404 – www.lordbyronhotel.com – Closed lunch Monday-Saturday, Sunday*

Trastevere - Testaccio

Glass Hostaria (Cristina Bowerman)

CREATIVE • DESIGN Situated in the heart of Trastevere, this restaurant boasts an ultra-modern design with an interesting play of light and a slightly unsettling atmosphere. The excellent cuisine also features highly modern touches.

Specialities: Veal heart, smoked potatoes and coffee. Gnocchetti, bagna cauda dip with black garlic, sea urchins and truffles. Condensed milk soup, espresso jelly, sugar-coated almonds and whisky-cream ice cream.

Menu 95/150 € – Carte 69/100 €

PLAN: 2-E3 – *vicolo del Cinque 58 – ✆ 06 5833 5903 – www.glasshostaria.it – Closed 7-13 January, 27 July-6 August, Monday, lunch Tuesday-Sunday*

Antica Pesa

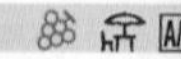

CUISINE FROM LAZIO • ELEGANT Typical Roman dishes made from carefu selected ingredients grace the menu of this restaurant, which is housed in a gra storehouse that once belonged to the neighbouring Papal State. Large paintin by contemporary artists hang on the walls and there is a small lounge with a fir place near the entrance.

Carte 57/77€

PLAN: 2-E3 – *via Garibaldi 18 – ✆ 06 580 9236 – www.anticapesa.it – Closed lunch Monday-Saturday, Sunday*

Felice a Testaccio

TRADITIONAL CUISINE • FRIENDLY The simple, family, trattoria-style atm sphere of Felice a Testaccio is so popular that it is now almost essential to boc ahead for a table. Make sure you try the legendary roast lamb with potatoes, well as the *cacio e pepe* tonnarelli pasta and the tiramisù. Without a doubt, or of the standard-bearers of Latium cuisine.

Carte 30/56€

PLAN: 1-B3 – *via Mastrogiorgio 29 – ✆ 06 574 6800 – www.feliceatestaccio.com*

Osteria Fernanda

CREATIVE • MINIMALIST In the district famous for its Porta Portese market, th restaurant run by two talented business partners is definitely worth a visit. One the partners manages the front of house, while the other shows real passion his creative cuisine made from locally sourced ingredients, as well as produc from further afield.

Menu 29€ (lunch), 49/100€ – Carte 47/72€

PLAN: 1-B3 – *via Crescenzo Del Monte 18/24 – ✆ 06 589 4333 – www.osteriafernanda.com – Closed 11-25 August, lunch Monday-Tuesday, Sunday*

Zia

MODERN CUISINE • CONTEMPORARY DÉCOR Situated in Trastevere, this res taurant makes use of top-quality ingredients from all over Italy, from Lazio to th Apennines and the Mediterranean, all served with a smile by the charming Ida.

Menu 30€ (lunch)/75€ – Carte 52/76€

PLAN: 1-B3 – *via Goffredo Mameli 45 – ✆ 0623488093 – www.ziarestaurant.com – Closed 7-19 January, 10-30 August, lunch Monday-Wednesday, Sunday*

Environs of Roma

Zona Urbana Nord

Bistrot 64 (Kotaro Noda)

MEDITERRANEAN CUISINE • BISTRO This restaurant boasts the attractive, in formal decor of a bistro combined with surprisingly creative and imaginative cui sine. Courteous and attentive service.

Specialities: Potato spaghetti with butter and anchovies. Bonito, asparagus an soya sabayon. Yellow Chantilly cream, sponge cake and passion fruit.

Menu 50/80€ – Carte 67/88€

PLAN: 1-B1 – *via Guglielmo Calderini 64 – ✆ 06 323 5531 – www.bistrot64.it – Closed 7-15 January, 10-24 August, lunch Monday-Saturday, Sunday*

Mamma Angelina

SEAFOOD • TRATTORIA After the antipasto buffet, the cuisine in this restauran follows two distinct styles – fish and seafood, or Roman specialities. The paccher pasta with seafood and fresh tomatoes sits in both camps!

Menu 35€ – Carte 27/41€

PLAN: 1-C1 – *viale Arrigo Boito 65 – ✆ 06 860 8928 – Closed 1-31 August, Wednesday*

Marzapane

ITALIAN CONTEMPORARY • CONTEMPORARY DÉCOR This young restaurant has turned the page and is the focus of renewed attention in 2019, having returned to its original roots - in other words, to the ideas that led to its opening in 2013. The menu features a choice of Italian dishes, including specialities from Lazio, which focus not so much on complicated cooking methods as on the quality and flavours of the ingredients used.

Menu 55€ - Carte 47/59€

PLAN: 1-C2 - *via Velletri 39 - 06 6478 1692 - www.marzapaneroma.com - Closed 2-8 January, 12-31 August, Monday, lunch Tuesday*

ona Urbana Sud

Domenico dal 1968

ROMAN • SIMPLE It's well worth heading off the usual tourist trail to experience this authentic Roman trattoria, where you can try specialities such as fish broth with broccoli and local tripe. The restaurant also serves a selection of fish-based dishes which vary according to market availability.

Carte 35/51€

PLAN: 1-C3 - *via Satrico 21 - 06 7049 4602 - www.domenicodal1968.it - Closed Monday, dinner Sunday*

Profumo di Mirto

SEAFOOD • FAMILY The cuisine at this restaurant pays tribute to its owners' native Sardinia, in addition to other typical Mediterranean fare. There's a focus on fish and seafood reinterpreted in delicious, home - style dishes, including specialities such as ravioli with sea bass, prawns cooked in Vernaccia di Oristano and *seadas* fritters.

Menu 25€ (lunch), 35/55€ - Carte 35/55€

PLAN: 1-C3 - *viale Amelia 8/a - 06 786206 - www.profumodimirto.it - Closed 11 August-2 September, Monday*

Al Ristoro degli Angeli

ROMAN • VINTAGE Situated in the Garbatella district, this restaurant with a bistro feel is embellished with vintage tables, chairs and lighting. The menu focuses on dishes from Lazio, such as mezze maniche pasta alla gricia (with bacon and cheese) flavoured with lemon, and sour-cherry tart. Delicious fish and vegetable options are also available.

Carte 26/43€

PLAN: 1-B3 - *via Luigi Orlando 2 - 338 875 1157 - www.ristorodegliangeli.it - Closed 1-10 January, 2 August-10 September, lunch Monday-Saturday, Sunday*

Trattoria Pennestri

REGIONAL CUISINE • VINTAGE Although both the decor and cuisine at this restaurant are fairly traditional, there's also a contemporary feel to the seasonal ingredients and the way these are cooked and simply yet carefully presented. A good, authentic restaurant which has become a firm favourite with locals in a short space of time.

Menu 28/35€ - Carte 28/35€

PLAN: 1-B3 - *via Giovanni Da Empoli 5 - Piramide - 06 574 2418 - trattoriapennestri.it - Closed 7-13 January, 8-24 August, Monday, lunch Tuesday-Thursday*

Trattoria del Pesce

SEAFOOD • BISTRO A good selection of fresh and raw fish dishes served in a welcoming, vaguely bistro-style restaurant with young and competent staff. Parking can be difficult, but your patience is definitely rewarded!

Carte 35/85€

PLAN: 1-B3 - *via Folco Portinari 27 - 349 335 2560 - www.trattoriadelpesce.it - Closed 12-19 August, lunch Monday*

MILAN
MILANO

da-kuk/iStock

MILAN IN...

- **ONE DAY**
  Duomo, Leonardo da Vinci's 'The Last Supper' (remember to book first), Brera, Navigli.
- **TWO DAYS**
  Pinacoteca Brera, Castello Sforzesco, Parco Sempione, Museo del Novecento, a night at La Scala.
- **THREE DAYS**
  Giardini Pubblici and its museums, trendy Savona district.

If it's the romantic charm c places like Venice, Florence o Rome you're looking for, the best avoid Milan. If you're han kering for a permanent pano rama of Renaissance chapels palazzi, shimmering canal and bastions of fine art, the you're in the wrong place What Milan does is relentles fashion, churned out wit oodles of attitude and style Italy's second largest city i constantly reinventing itself, and when Milan does a make over, it invariably does it with flair and panache. That's not t say that Italy's capital of fast money and fast fashion doesn have an eye for its past. The centrepiece of the whole city i

the magnificent gleaming white Duomo, which took five hundred years to complete, while up la via a little way, La Scala is quite simply the world's most famous opera house. But this is a city known primarily for its sleek andmodern towers, many housing the very latest threads from the very latest fashion gurus.

Just north of Milan's centre lies Brera, with its much prized old-world charm, and Quadrilatero d'Oro, with no little new-world glitz; the popular Giardini Pubblici are a little further north east from here. South of the centre is the Navigli quarter, home to rejuvenated Middle Age canals, while to the west are the green lungs of the Parco Sempione. For those into art or fashion, the trendy Savona district is also a must.

EATING OUT

or a taste of Italy's regional cuisines, ilan is a great place to be. The city is ften the goal of those leaving their ome regions in the south or centre f the country; many open trattoria or estaurants, with the result that Milan ffers a wide range of provincial enus. Excellent fish restaurants, spired by recipes from the south, re a big draw despite the fact that the ity is a long way from the sea. Going eyond the local borders, the emphasis n really good food continues and the uality of internationally diverse places eat is better in Milan than just about anywhere else in Italy, including Rome. You'd expect avant-garde eating destinations to be the thing in this city of fashion and style, and you'd be right: there are some top-notch cutting-edge restaurants, thanks to Milan's famous tendency to reshape and experiment as it goes. For those who want to try out the local gastronomic traditions, risotto allo zafferano is not to be missed, nor is the cotoletta alla Milanese (veal cutlet) or the casoeula (a winter special made with pork and cabbage).

Centre

Centro Storico

✿✿ Seta by Antonio Guida

CREATIVE • DESIGN A complete dining experience offering sophisticated el gance, glamour and beautifully presented cuisine which is classic and moder light and yet luxurious. Antonio Guida creates a menu which includes meat a fish dishes, combining the flavours of northern Italy with the scents of the sou with outstanding results.

Specialities: Veal sweetbread with rhubarb and maple syrup, mango, grapefr and liquorice. Herbed lamb with cuttlefish ink polenta and stuffed sweet pepp Pineapple with hazelnut, passion fruit tapioca, and pepper and ginger ice crean

Menu 70€ (lunch), 90/230€ - Carte 110/150€

PLAN: 2-G1 - *Hotel Mandarin Oriental Milano, via Monte di Pietà 18 - Ⓜ Montenapoleone - ✆ 02 8731 8897 - www.mandarinoriental.com - Closed 1-7 January, 6-26 August, Sunday*

✿✿ Vun Andrea Aprea

MODERN CUISINE • ELEGANT In this elegant and cosmopolitan restaurant de orated in neutral colours and adorned with drapery, Neapolitan chef Andre Aprea serves the best of traditional Italian cuisine and a few dishes with the in mediately recognisable character of his native city.

Specialities: Sweet and savoury Caprese. "Sub-marine" risotto. Gianduia choc late and raspberries.

Menu 160/315€ - Carte 120/150€

PLAN: 2-G2 - *Hotel Park Hyatt Milano, via Silvio Pellico 3 - Ⓜ Duomo - ✆ 02 8821 1234 - www.ristorante-vun.it - Closed 1-6 January, 4-31 August, Monday, lunch Tuesday-Saturday, Sunday*

✿ Cracco

MODERN CUISINE • ELEGANT Arranged over several floors, this restaurant, or of the most versatile in the city, is connected directly to the Galleria thanks t skilful reconstruction work. Cracco is not just a restaurant - there's also a bar, bistro serving snacks, a pastry shop and a wine boutique which is well worth visit, plus the venue is often used to host special events. The menu features cr ative dishes alongside more traditional fare.

Specialities: "L'uovo in nero": breaded soft egg, almond cream, black truffles an caviar. Quail stuffed with green asparagus and giblets, garden cress with gree pepper. Selection of iced fruit.

Menu 195€ - Carte 135/165€

PLAN: 2-G2 - *galleria Vitttorio Emauele II - Ⓜ Duomo - ✆ 02 876774 - www.ristorantecracco.it - Closed 9-29 August, 22 December-12 January, dinner Saturday, Sunday*

✿ Felix Lo Basso

CREATIVE • CONTEMPORARY DÉCOR Puglian chef Felice Lo Basso is now a new premises offering breathtaking views of the Duomo. He continues to prov his talent with his recognised trademark of light, creative and colourful cuisine which is often playful and always focuses on the use of top-quality Italian ingre dients.

Specialities: Mamma's parmigiana in a risotto. Roasted octopus in barbecu sauce, herb foam and crunchy dried sweet peppers. Chiccocremoso with mascar pone and a coffee centre, cocoa tapioca.

Menu 130/170€ - Carte 98/150€

PLAN: 2-G2 - *Hotel Townhouse Duomo, piazza Duomo 21 (5° piano) - Ⓜ Duomo - ✆ 02 4952 8914 - www.felixlobassorestaurant.it - Closed 1-10 January, 10-25 August, lunch Monday, lunch Saturday, Sunday*

IT Milano

CONTEMPORARY • ELEGANT Often concentrated on one main ingredient with just a few surprising additions, the dishes served at this restaurant have a southern Italian feel. Contrasting yet harmonious cuisine that is full of fresh and original flavours.

Specialities: Stuffed anchovies. Tuna belly and puttanesca sauce. Red berry tartlet and buffalo kefir ice cream.

Menu 41€ (lunch)/80€ - Carte 59/89€

PLAN: 2-F1 - *Via Fiori Chiari 32 - Ⓜ Lanza - ✆ 02 9997 9993 - www.itrestaurants.com - Closed 3-28 August, Sunday*

Il Ristorante Trussardi alla Scala

MODERN CUISINE • LUXURY This restaurant serves creative cuisine inspired by regional traditions. The use of seasonal ingredients is a real hallmark of his culinary philosophy.

Specialities: Gragnano spaghetti, cheese, pepper and sea urchins. Pigeon in a "Bellini" casserole. Meringue, cream and wild strawberries.

Menu 160€ - Carte 80/157€

PLAN: 2-G1 - *piazza della Scala 5 - Ⓜ Duomo - ✆ 02 8068 8201 - www.trussardiallascala.com - Closed 1-6 January, 10-23 August, 19-31 December, lunch Saturday, Sunday*

Armani

MODERN CUISINE • LUXURY Elegant and carefully prepared contemporary cuisine served on the seventh floor of a palazzo which is totally dedicated to the world of Armani. Superb views of Milan combine with a decor of black marble and backlit onyx to create an exclusive and fashionable ambience.

Menu 45€ (lunch), 110/150€ - Carte 45/170€

PLAN: 2-G1 - *Armani Hotel Milano, via Manzoni 31 - Ⓜ Montenapoleone - ✆ 02 8883 8702 - www.armanihotelmilano.com - Closed 1-7 January, 2-31 August, 27-31 December, dinner Monday, Sunday*

La Brisa

MODERN CUISINE • TRADITIONAL Opposite an archaeological site dating from Roman times, this trattoria serves modern, regional cuisine. Summer dining on the veranda overlooking the garden.

Menu 34€ (lunch)/58€ - Carte 42/83€

PLAN: 2-F2 - *via Brisa 15 - Ⓜ Cairoli Castello. - ✆ 02 8645 0521 - www.ristorantelabrisa.it - Closed 9 August-2 September, 24 December-6 January, Saturday, lunch Sunday*

Don Carlos

MODERN CUISINE • ROMANTIC The tribute paid to Verdi by the Grand Hotel is accompanied in the small Don Carlos dining rooms by a homage to Italian and Milanese cuisine. Amid a setting of sketches, pictures and paintings dedicated to the world of opera, this restaurant is a favourite with music-lovers who come here after attending a performance in La Scala opera house nearby. Also perfect for a romantic dinner.

Carte 78/119€

PLAN: 2-G1 - *Grand Hotel et de Milan, via Manzoni 29 - Ⓜ Montenapoleone - ✆ 02 7231 4640 - www.ristorantedoncarlos.it - Closed 1-31 August, lunch Monday-Sunday*

Giacomo Arengario

MEDITERRANEAN CUISINE • ELEGANT A restaurant with a view, but without compromising on quality. Housed in the Museo del Novecento, Giacomo Arengario enjoys superb views of the Duomo's spires, especially from its attractive summer terrace. The cuisine is contemporary in style, with equal focus on meat and fish dishes.

Carte 60/110€

PLAN: 2-G2 - *via Guglielmo Marconi 1 - ✆ 02 7209 3814 - www.giacomoarengario.com*

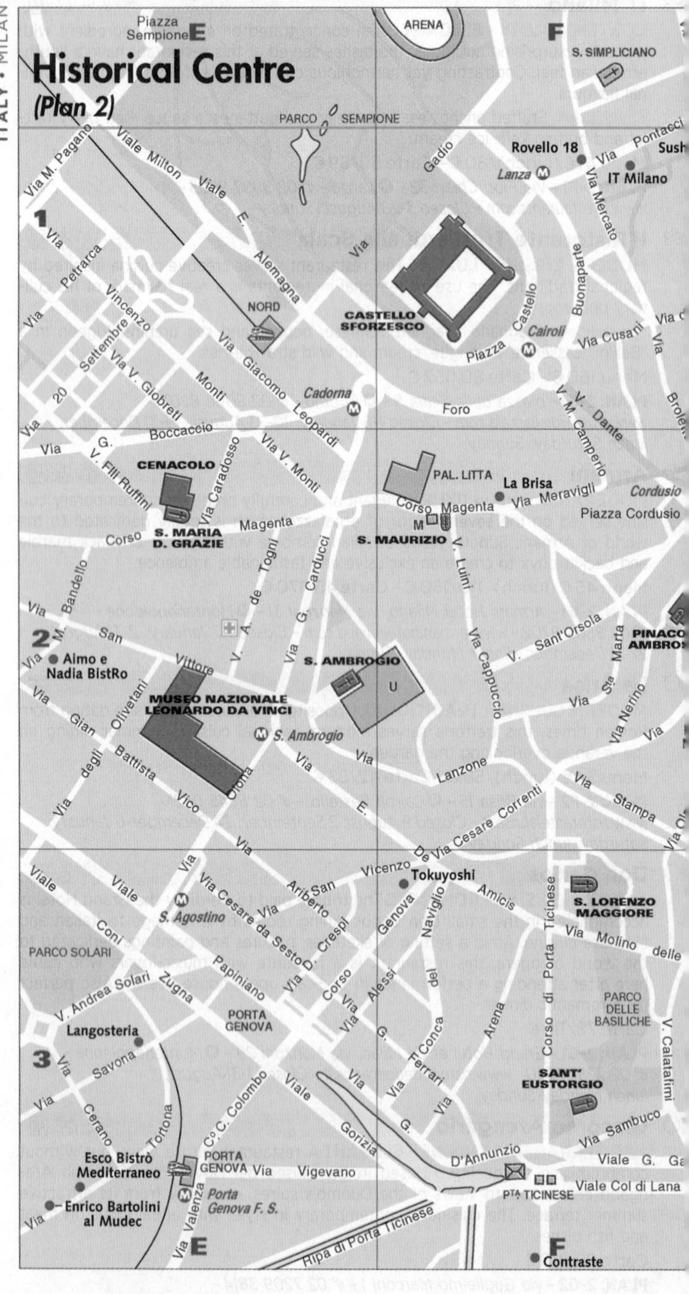
Historical Centre
(Plan 2)
Piazza Sempione
ARENA
S. SIMPLICIANO
PARCO SEMPIONE
Rovello 18
Lanza
IT Milano
CASTELLO SFORZESCO
NORD
Cairoli
Cadorna
CENACOLO
S. MARIA D. GRAZIE
PAL. LITTA
La Brisa
Cordusio
Piazza Cordusio
S. MAURIZIO
Aimo e Nadia BistRo
S. AMBROGIO
MUSEO NAZIONALE LEONARDO DA VINCI
S. Ambrogio
Tokuyoshi
S. LORENZO MAGGIORE
S. Agostino
PARCO SOLARI
PORTA GENOVA
PARCO DELLE BASILICHE
Langosteria
SANT' EUSTORGIO
Esco Bistrò Mediterraneo
Enrico Bartolini al Mudec
PORTA GENOVA
Porta Genova F. S.
PTA TICINESE
Contraste
Ripa di Porta Ticinese

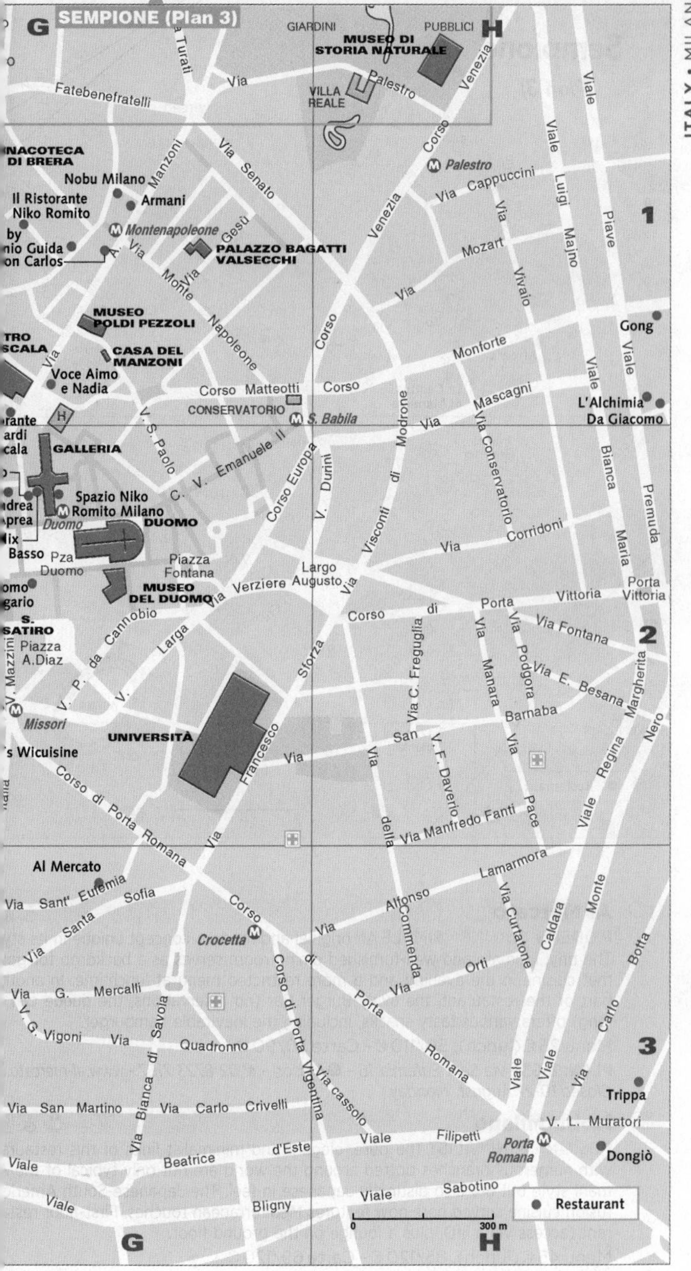

SEMPIONE (Plan 3)
G
H
1
2
3
GIARDINI PUBBLICI
MUSEO DI STORIA NATURALE
VILLA REALE
Fatebenefratelli
Via Palestro
Corso Venezia
Palestro
Via Cappuccini
Viale Piave
Viale Luigi Majno
Via Vivaio
Via Mozart
Via Senato
Via Manzoni
Nobu Milano
Armani
Il Ristorante Niko Romito
Montenapoleone
Via Gesù
PALAZZO BAGATTI VALSECCHI
Via Monte Napoleone
MUSEO POLDI PEZZOLI
CASA DEL MANZONI
Voce Aimo e Nadia
Corso Matteotti
CONSERVATORIO
S. Babila
Corso Monforte
Gong
Viale Bianca Maria
L'Alchimia
Da Giacomo
Via Mascagni
Via Conservatorio
Via Visconti di Modrone
V. Durini
Corso Europa
C. V. Emanuele II
V. S. Paolo
GALLERIA
Spazio Niko Romito Milano
Duomo
DUOMO
Pza Duomo
Piazza Fontana
MUSEO DEL DUOMO
Via Verziere
Largo Augusto
Via Corridoni
Viale Premuda
Porta Vittoria
Corso di Porta Vittoria
Via Fontana
S. SATIRO
Piazza A.Diaz
Via Cannobio
Via Larga
Via C. Freguglia
Via Manara
Via Podgora
Via E. Besana
Barnaba
Viale Regina Margherita
Nero
Missori
UNIVERSITÀ
Via Francesco Sforza
Via San
V. F. Daverio
Via della
Via Pace
Via Manfredo Fanti
Corso di Porta Romana
Al Mercato
Via Sant' Eufemia
Via Santa Sofia
Via Lamarmora
Via Alfonso
Commenda
Via Curtatone
Viale Caldara
Monte
Crocetta
Corso di Porta Vigentina
Via Orti
Via Botta
Via G. Mercalli
V. G. Vigoni
Via Quadronno
Via di Savoia
Via Bianca
Via cassolo
Viale Carlo
Trippa
Via San Martino
Via Carlo Crivelli
V. L. Muratori
Viale Filipetti
Porta Romana
Dongiò
Viale Beatrice d'Este
Viale Bligny
Viale Sabotino
0
300 m
Restaurant

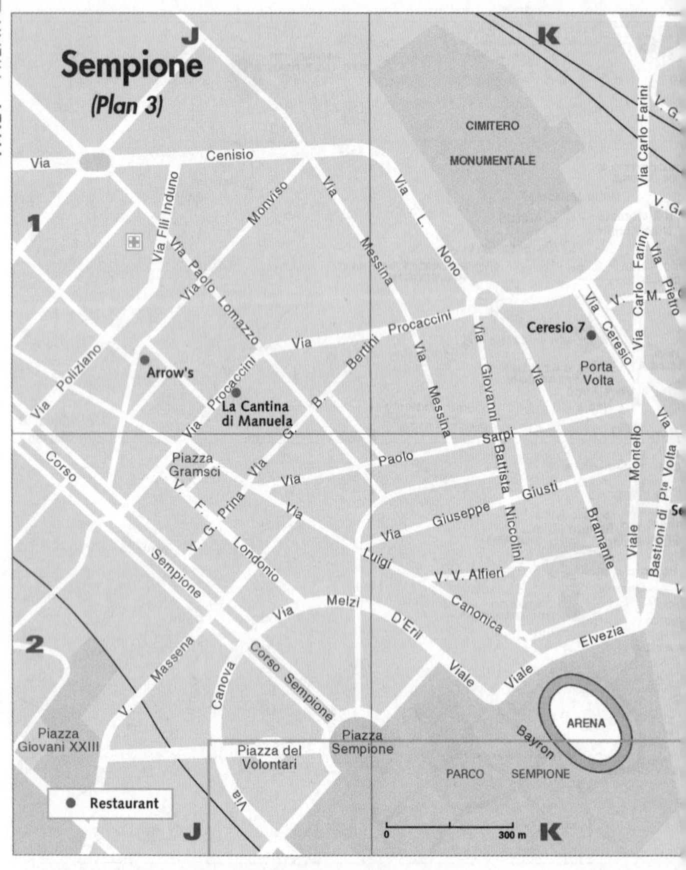

Al Mercato

MODERN CUISINE • SIMPLE An original and modern concept unique in its sty The tiny, intimate and well-furnished dining room serves as a backdrop for go met cuisine in the evening and a more restricted menu at lunchtime. In anoth part of the restaurant, the lively Burger Bar (no reservations; the queue can long) offers various tasty snacks, including the inevitable hamburger.

Menu 25€ (lunch), 50/110€ – Carte 30/90€

PLAN: 2-G3 – *via Sant'Eufemia 16* – Ⓜ *Missori* – ✆ *02 8723 7167* – *www.al-mercato.* *Closed 10-27 August, Monday*

Nobu Milano

FUSION • MINIMALIST The pure, elegant and minimalist lines of this restaura with numerous branches dotted around the world are not only typical of the mani style but are also distinctly Japanese in feel. The Japanese-South Americ fusion cuisine served here now features Mediterranean touches. First-floor resta rant (access via a lift), plus a lounge on the ground floor.

Menu 45€ (lunch), 85/120€ – Carte 69/120€

PLAN: 2-G1 – *via Pisoni 1* – Ⓜ *Montenapoleone* – ✆ *02 6231 2645* – *www.noburestaurants.com* – *Closed 9-16 August, 24-27 December, lunch Sunday*

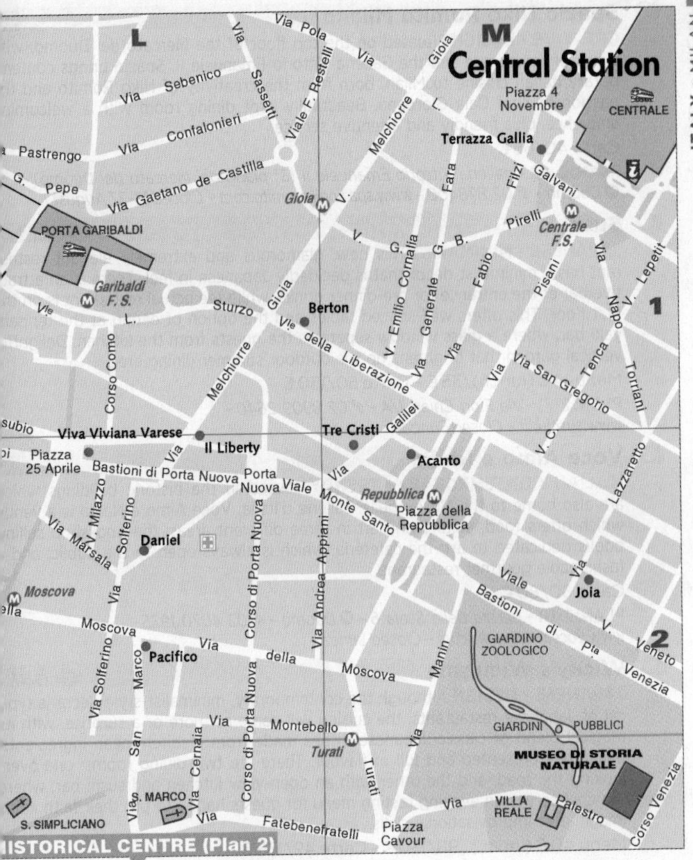

Il Ristorante Niko Romito

MODERN CUISINE • TRENDY Overlooking one of the most beautiful gardens in the city, Il Ristorante Niko Romito brings to Milan the same restaurant concept already available in Bulgari hotels around the world. Guests are taken on an extraordinary culinary journey through Italian cuisine, with classic dishes reinterpreted with a contemporary twist by the chef. From the Italian-style antipasti (including lots of small dishes to share) to the lasagne, and the Milanese veal cutlet to the tiramisù, the menu pays tribute to the hotel's elegant beauty, which is also evident in the decor and the well-stocked wine cellar.

Carte 75/140€

PLAN: 2-G1 – *Hotel Bulgari, via Privata Fratelli Gabba 7B – Ⓜ Montenapoleone – ✆ 02 805 8051 – www.bulgarihotels.com*

Rovello 18

ITALIAN • VINTAGE A simple setting for cuisine which focuses on carefully chosen ingredients presented with the minimum of fuss. Although the menu features a few specialities from Milan, most of the dishes served here are classically Italian in style.

Carte 42/100€

PLAN: 2-F1 – *via Tivoli 2, ang. corso Garibaldi – Ⓜ Lanza – ✆ 02 7209 3709 – www.rovello18.it – Closed 1-6 January, 10-27 August, 24-26 December, lunch Sunday*

Spazio Niko Romito Milano

CREATIVE • DESIGN Situated on the top floor of the Mercato del Duomo, wi views of the square and the Galleria Vittorio Emanuele II, Spazio brings conten porary Italian cuisine to Milan, born from the creativity of Niko Romito and th passion of chef Gaia Giordano. Beautifully kept dining room with a welcomir ambience, plus friendly and attentive service.

Carte 40/65€

PLAN: 2-G2 – *galleria Vittorio Emanuele II (3° piano del Mercato del Duomo) – Ⓜ Duomo – ✆ 02 878400 – www.spazionikoromito.com – Closed 13-27 August*

Sushi B

JAPANESE • MINIMALIST This new, glamorous and extremely elegant resta rant has a minimalist decor that is decidedly Japanese in feel. There is an attra tive bar at the entrance for pre-dinner drinks, while the actual restaurant is on th first floor. This offers well-spaced tables and the option of eating at the teppa yaki bar, where a glass window separates the guests from the kitchen. Delightf vertical garden that brightens up the outdoor summer dining area.

Menu 14€ (lunch)/35€ – Carte 50/130€

PLAN: 2-F1 – *via Fiori Chiari 1/A – ✆ 02 8909 2640 – www.sushi-b.it – Closed Sunday*

Voce Aimo e Nadia

ITALIAN CONTEMPORARY • TRENDY Housed in the historic buildings whi are also home to the Museo delle Gallerie d'Italia, Voce Aimo e Nadia is a ven which offers food, culture and art in three different areas: the bookshop sellir books dedicated to art; the cafeteria, which is always open to the public; and fashionable gourmet restaurant.

Carte 60/80€

PLAN: 2-G1 – *piazza della Scala 6 – Ⓜ Duomo – ✆ 02 4070 1935 – www.voceaimoenadia.com – Closed Sunday*

Wicky's Wicuisine

JAPANESE • DESIGN Although the contemporary, minimalist-style decor is typ cal of Japanese restaurants, the cuisine will come as more of a surprise, with magical blend of classic Japanese dishes made from Mediterranean ingredient beautifully presented and full of flavour. There are two dining rooms: one ove looking the road, and the other with an open-view kitchen and sushi bar, whe the chef serves an evening tasting menu for guests happy to put their faith in h imaginative improvisational skills.

Menu 40€ (lunch), 98/130€ – Carte 49/135€

PLAN: 2-G2 – *corso Italia 6 – Ⓜ Missori – ✆ 02 8909 3781 – www.wicuisine.it – Closed 9-23 August, lunch Monday, lunch Saturday, Sunday*

Isola - Porta Nuova

Berton

CREATIVE • DESIGN Light, modern and minimalist in style, the restaurant dec echoes the cuisine served here, which uses just a few ingredients to create orig nal and beautifully presented dishes.

Specialities: Raw and cooked red crayfish from Sicily, crunchy amaranth, Ta giasca olive oil and beetroot sorbet. Duo of cod, potato ravioli in a cod bro and fillet with saffron cream. Yoghurt and mango egg.

Menu 45€ (lunch), 130/140€ – Carte 45/120€

PLAN: 3-L1 – *via Mike Bongiorno 13 – Ⓜ Gioia – ✆ 02 6707 5801 – www.ristoranteberton.com – Closed 8-31 August, 26 December-8 January, lunch Monday, lunch Saturday, Sunday*

Viva Viviana Varese

CREATIVE • DESIGN The most popular tables at this restaurant on the seco floor of the Eataly complex are the large tables in fossil wood facing the ope view kitchen and the tables by the glass wall with views of the square. Create by a talented chef, the vibrant dishes are striking and original.

Specialities: "Spugna" – mussels in acidulated beurre noisette on soft almond cream and tarragon extract. "Super": fine spaghetti with smoked fish broth, squid julienne, clams, Tarallo biscuit crumbs and candied lemon. Amalfi lemon soufflé, lemon ganache and dark chocolate.

Menu 45 € (lunch), 80/150 € – Carte 87/150 €

PLAN: 3-L2 – *piazza XXV Aprile 10 – Ⓜ Porta Garibaldi FS – ✆ 02 4949 7340 – www.vivavivianavarese.it – Closed 24-27 December, dinner Sunday*

Serendib

A/C

INDIAN • ORIENTAL *Serendib*, the old name for Sri Lanka, means "to make happy" – an ambitious promise, but one which this restaurant manages to keep! True to its origins, the tempting menu focuses on Indian and Sri Lankan cuisine, including dishes such as biriyani rice and chicken curry.

Menu 20/40 € – Carte 15/25 €

PLAN: 3-K2 – *via Pontida 2 – Ⓜ Moscova – ✆ 02 659 2139 – www.serendib.it*

Barbacoa

A/C

GRILLS • INTIMATE Meat-lovers will be in their element here. For a fixed price, guests help themselves to as much as they want from the buffet (mainly salads and vegetables), while waiters move from table to table serving a selection of around fifteen meat options, all barbecued in churrasceria style over a traditional Brazilian rodizio. A unique flavour of South America in Milan.

Menu 52/80 €

PLAN: 1-C1 – *via delle Abbadesse 30 – Ⓜ Zara – ✆ 02 688 3883 – www.barbacoa.it – Closed lunch Monday-Saturday*

Casa Fontana-23 Risotti

A/C

LOMBARDIAN • TRADITIONAL A small yet comfortable restaurant which is not lacking in elegance. Risottos are the house speciality here, available in different recipes which change according to the seasons and ingredients available. The menu also features meat options and traditional dishes from Lombardy.

Carte 36/70 €

PLAN: 1-C1 – *piazza Carbonari 5 – Ⓜ Sondrio – ✆ 02 670 4710 – www.23risotti.it – Closed 1-13 January, 1-31 August, Monday*

Ceresio 7

A/C

MODERN CUISINE • TRENDY This designer-style restaurant is housed on the fourth floor of the historic ENEL palazzo, remodelled and converted into the Dsquared2 building. It combines the use of brass, marble and wood to create a successful blend of attractive colours and vintage decor. The view of Milan (even better from the long outdoor terrace with its two swimming pools) completes the picture, while the cuisine reinterprets Italian classics with a contemporary twist.

Menu 48 € (lunch)/95 € – Carte 45/100 €

PLAN: 3-K1 – *via Ceresio 7 – Ⓜ Monumentale – ✆ 02 3103 9221 – www.ceresio7.com – Closed 1-4 January*

Daniel

A/C

ITALIAN • CONTEMPORARY DÉCOR One of the first things to strike you in this restaurant is the open - view kitchen, where the young friendly chef happily interacts with diners. His menu focuses on traditional Italian classics, as well as a few more inventive offerings, all of which are prepared using the very best ingredients. Simpler fare available at lunchtime.

Menu 18 € (lunch)/30 € – Carte 58/86 €

PLAN: 3-L2 – *via Castelfidardo 7, angolo via San Marco – Ⓜ Moscova – ✆ 02 6379 3837 – www.danielcanzian.com – Closed 1-5 January, 10-16 August, lunch Saturday, Sunday*

Finger's Garden

FUSION • TRENDY Firmly aimed at the fashionable crowd, this restaurant ha subtle lighting and an Oriental feel. The owner-chef skilfully creates a range c dishes, including raw fish options and original fusion cuisine with a hint of Braz lian flavour. Gourmet diners will be happy to give full rein to the chef.

Menu 80/130 € – Carte 65/150 €

PLAN: 1-C1 – *via Keplero 2 –*
02 606544 – www.fingersrestaurants.com – Closed lunch Monday-Saturday, Sunday

Il Liberty

CREATIVE • COSY Occupying an Art Nouveau-style palazzo, this small restau rant with two rooms and a loft area has a friendly, welcoming atmosphere. Th menu includes a selection of fish and meat dishes, with a choice of simpler an more reasonably priced options at lunchtime.

Carte 65/80 €

PLAN: 3-L2 – *viale Monte Grappa 6 –*
02 2901 1439 – www.il-liberty.it – Closed 1-6 January, 9-31 August, lunch Saturday, Sunday

Pacifico

PERUVIAN • BISTRO Although its dining rooms are fairly small, this restaurant which acts as an ambassador for Peruvian cuisine with the occasional Asian influ ence, has an attractive, trendy ambience and a theatrical feel. Excellent choice o ceviche – raw fish or seafood dishes marinated in lemon and flavoured with spices such as chilli pepper and coriander – which are a typical speciality of Latir American countries along the Pacific coast.

Menu 60/120 € – Carte 34/86 €

PLAN: 3-L2 – *via Moscova 29 – Ⓜ Moscova –*
02 8724 4737 – www.wearepacifico.com – Closed 10-20 August, 20 December-2 January

Tre Cristi

MODERN CUISINE • CLASSIC DÉCOR The young chef at this restaurant has already developed a precise and original style which is based on sustainability, the full use of ingredients avoiding any waste, and an emphasis on vegetables. In a modern dining room with an open-view kitchen, his dishes certainly merit attention. Simpler, more restricted and cheaper menu available at lunchtime.

Menu 30 € (lunch), 70/90 € – Carte 30/100 €

PLAN: 3-M2 – *via Galileo Galilei 5 – Ⓜ Repubblica –*
02 2906 2923 – www.trecristimilano.com – Closed 1-25 August, 22 December-8 January, lunch Saturday, Sunday

Stazione Centrale

Joia (Pietro Leemann)

VEGETARIAN • MINIMALIST The pupil of a great master, the chef here became a vegetarian after a gradual philosophical and spiritual transformation in Asia. After many years, his focus is now on natural food, which is avant-garde, experimental, skilfully prepared and beautifully presented. Full of flavour, the menu here is 80% vegan and gluten free.

Specialities: "A titanic force for good". "Enjoyment, thinking of spring and Zen". "Five minutes".

Menu 25 € (lunch), 90/130 € – Carte 90/120 €

PLAN: 3-M2 – *via Panfilo Castaldi 18 – Ⓜ Repubblica –*
02 2952 2124 – www.joia.it – Closed 15-23 August, 22 December-6 January, Sunday

Da Giannino-L'Angolo d'Abruzzo

CUISINE FROM ABRUZZO • TRADITIONAL A warm welcome combined with a simple but lively atmosphere and typical dishes from the Abruzzo region make this a popular place to eat. Generous portions and excellent roast dishes.

Menu 25/40€ – Carte 33/43€

PLAN: 1-D2 – *via Pilo 20* – *Ⓜ Porta Venezia* – *☏ 02 2940 6526* – *www.dagianninolangolodabruzzomilano.it*

Acanto

MODERN CUISINE • LUXURY Large elegant spaces full of light characterise this modern restaurant which pampers its guests with attentive service and classic cuisine with a contemporary twist. There's an excellent brunch on Sundays, which is increasing in popularity with locals and visitors alike.

Menu 35€ (lunch), 90/120€ – Carte 81/100€

PLAN: 3-M2 – *Hotel Principe di Savoia, piazza della Repubblica 17* – *Ⓜ Repubblica* – *☏ 02 6230 2026* – *www.dorchestercollection.com*

La Cantina di Manuela

MODERN CUISINE • BISTRO The dining room in this young, dynamic restaurant is surrounded by bottles of wine. Elaborate dishes feature on the menu, with antipasti available in the evening. At lunchtime these are replaced by various salads aimed at a business clientele in a hurry. Milanese-style cutlets are the house speciality.

Carte 32/58€

PLAN: 1-C2 – *via Carlo Poerio 3* – *☏ 02 7631 8892* – *www.lacantinadimanuela.it*

La Risacca Blu

SEAFOOD • FAMILY A family restaurant run by two brothers from Calabria. The menu features fish and seafood dishes which are unfussy, authentic and full of flavour.

Carte 40/70€

PLAN: 1-C2 – *via Tunisia angolo via Tadino* – *☏ 02 2048 0964* – *www.larisaccablu.com* – *Closed 5-27 August, Monday, lunch Tuesday*

Sol Levante

JAPANESE • ORIENTAL A tiny, secluded restaurant serving traditional Japanese cuisine comprising numerous small dishes (kaiseki). In addition to the usual classics, Sol Levante also offers a few more unusual but equally exciting options.

Menu 65/100€

PLAN: 1-D2 – *via Lambro 11* – *☏ 02 4547 6502* – *Closed 10-23 August, lunch Monday-Saturday, Sunday*

Terrazza Gallia

CREATIVE • LUXURY Situated on the seventh floor with panoramic views of the city, this restaurant is an excellent choice for a light lunch, a cocktail or an informal dinner. Two young brothers from Naples are at the helm here, creating traditional Italian and Lombardian dishes with a creative and contemporary touch.

Carte 62/112€

PLAN: 3-M1 – *Excelsior Hotel Gallia, piazza Duca d'Aosta 9* – *Ⓜ Centrale FS* – *☏ 02 6785 3514* – *www.terrazzagallia.com*

Romana - Vittoria

L'Alchimia

CREATIVE • CONTEMPORARY DÉCOR The cuisine is remarkably minimalist, but this is amply counterbalanced by the careful selection of ingredients. The chic modern setting is most pleasant. L'Alchimia is located in the centre, yet has a neighbourhood atmosphere. It is the ideal spot for a business lunch, a romantic dinner or a relaxed gourmet experience. The adjacent bistro offers a quick lunch and a good aperitivo.

Specialities: False strips of beef, sweet pepper, rocket pesto and parmesa cheese. Milano-Roma risotto. Alchimia tiramisù.

Menu 60/85 € – Carte 60/90 €

PLAN: 2-H1 – *viale Premuda 34 – ✆ 02 8287 0704 – www.ristorantelalchimia.com – Closed 1-10 January*

Dongiò

A/C

CALABRIAN • FAMILY A taste of Calabria in Milan. This family-run restaurant simply furnished and always busy – a typical traditional trattoria of the type tha is more and more difficult to find. The house speciality is *spaghettoni alla tamarr* (with a sausage and tomato sauce), while the menu also features fresh pasta 'nduja sausage and the ever-present peperoncino.

Carte 20/40 €

PLAN: 2-H3 – *via Corio 3 – Ⓜ Porta Romana – ✆ 02 551 1372 – www.dongio.it – Closed 10-25 August, lunch Saturday, Sunday*

Trippa

A/C

ITALIAN • TRATTORIA Simple, informal and with a slightly retro feel, this res taurant serves a range of dishes from all over Italy, including the tripe whic gives the restaurant its name. Unfussy and uncomplicated, the cuisine prepare by the skilful young chef using top-quality ingredients makes this one of th best trattorias in Italy. House specialities include Milanese risotto with grilled mar row, *vitello tonnato* and, of course, the ever-present tripe!

Carte 32/45 €

PLAN: 2-H3 – *Via Giorgio Vasari, 3 – Ⓜ Porta Romana – ✆ 327 668 7908 – www.trippamilano.it – Closed 1-6 January, 14 August-6 September, lunch Monday-Saturday, Sunday*

Le Api Osteria

A/C

MODERN CUISINE • SIMPLE After a number of years working in Italy and else where in Europe, chef Hide Matsumoto has at last opened his own restaurant where his gently creative Mediterranean cuisine takes centre stage in the simply decorated dining room.

Menu 16 € (lunch), 53/68 € – Carte 40/63 €

PLAN: 1-D2 – *via Carlo Foldi 1 – ✆ 02 8457 5100 – www.leapiosteria.com – Closed 5-24 August, 24 December-4 January, Sunday*

Da Giacomo

A/C

SEAFOOD • FRIENDLY This old Milanese trattoria dates from the early 20C Seafood enthusiasts will be delighted by the numerous fish specialities on offer The menu also includes a few meat dishes, as well as Alba truffles, Caesar's mushrooms and cep mushrooms in season.

Carte 45/120 €

PLAN: 2-H1 – *via P. Sottocorno 6 – ✆ 02 7602 3313 – www.giacomoristorante.com*

Gong

A/C

CHINESE • MINIMALIST Italy meets the Far East in this elegant restaurant with a menu that includes Chinese specialities, internationally influenced dishes and plenty of other tempting delicacies. The imposing onyx gongs which lend their name to the restaurant are a striking feature in the dining room.

Carte 50/175 €

PLAN: 2-H1 – *corso Concordia 8 – ✆ 02 7602 3873 – www.gongmilano.it – Closed 1-31 August, lunch Monday*

Masuelli San Marco

A/C

LOMBARDIAN • VINTAGE A rustic atmosphere with a luxurious feel in a typical trattoria, with the same management since 1921; cuisine strongly linked to traditional Lombardy and Piedmont recipes.

Menu 22 € (lunch) – Carte 39/71 €

PLAN: 1-D3 – *viale Umbria 80 – Ⓜ Lodi TIBB – ✆ 02 5518 4138 – www.masuellitrattoria.it – Closed 1-7 January, 25 August-9 September, 26-30 December, lunch Monday, Sunday*

Un Posto a Milano

ORGANIC • COUNTRY HOUSE Occupying an old restored farmhouse in urban Milan, the Cascina Cuccagna is both a restaurant and a cultural centre. It is surrounded by greenery, providing a delightful oasis in the city. At lunchtime, choose from a copious and reasonably priced buffet. The evening menu is more elaborate but still offers good value for money.

Menu 15 € (lunch)/20 € – Carte 29/60 €

PLAN: 1-D3 – *via Cuccagna 2 – ✆ 02 545 7785 – www.unpostoamilano.it – Closed 24 December-6 January*

Navigli

Enrico Bartolini al Mudec

CREATIVE • CONTEMPORARY DÉCOR This elegant, contemporary-style restaurant on the third floor of the Museo delle Culture offers an original location and attentive, solicitous service. The apparent simplicity of the menu sets the tone for a concert of dishes which feature extraordinary soloists backed by choirs of ingredients and variations on the same theme, all arranged across several courses which are striking for their imaginative quality. The conductor of this culinary orchestra is young Bartolini, poised and composed on the outside yet full of passion and energy within.

Specialities: Anchovies, oyster and 2019 caviar. Spaghetto with smoked eel. Traditional sabayon, "orange tree" and Bronte pistachio ice cream.

Menu 160/300 € – Carte 115/200 €

PLAN: 2-E3 – *via Tortona 56 – Ⓜ Porta Genova – ✆ 02 8429 3701 – www.enricobartolini.net – Closed 1-31 August, lunch Monday, Sunday*

Contraste (Matias Perdomo)

MODERN CUISINE • ELEGANT Glittering red silicon chandeliers hover above diners at this restaurant, which is decorated here and there with Art Nouveau touches. The cuisine is traditional yet reinterpreted in presentation and appearance, offering contrasting flavours that leave guests impressed and delighted.

Specialities: Mussels with cheese and pepper. Rabbit kidney, eel and vinegar. Apple tarte tatin with shortcrust pastry ice cream.

Menu 120/150 €

PLAN: 2-F3 – *via Meda 2 – ✆ 02 4953 6597 – www.contrastemilano.it – Closed 1-7 January, 7-17 August, lunch Monday-Saturday, dinner Sunday*

Sadler

CREATIVE • ELEGANT One of the first chefs to pay particular attention to aesthetics of a dish, with a focus on modern, geometric and colourful presentations, Sadler prepares beautiful creations which can be compared with contemporary art, of which he is an avid fan. Dishes are listed with the year in which they were invented: starting with the famous padellata di crostacei (sautéed shellfish) of 1996, the menu features a selection of mainly fish and seafood dishes which tell the story of the gastronomic history of Milan and other areas of Italy.

Specialities: "Italian sashimi" fifth version. Lamb cutlet stuffed with black truffles and foie gras in a bread and toasted almond crust. Passion fruit mousse with a liquid salted caramel centre, praline puff and passion fruit caviar.

Menu 90/130 € – Carte 80/130 €

PLAN: 1-B3 – *via Ascanio Sforza 77 – Ⓜ Romolo – ✆ 02 5810 4451 – www.sadler.it – Closed 1-8 January, 3-23 August, lunch Monday-Saturday, Sunday*

Tokuyoshi

CREATIVE • MINIMALIST Mention creative cuisine in Milan and Yoji Tokuyoshi immediately comes to mind. With typical Japanese humility and precision, this chef has been serving imaginative cuisine in his eponymous restaurant for the past couple of years. His original dishes full of decisive flavours take diners on a culinary voyage around his native Japan and adopted home of Italy, the country that has nurtured his professional development.

Specialities: Gyotaku. Duck and eel. Cowhide cheesecake.
Menu 135€ – Carte 75/150€

PLAN: 2-F3 – *via San Calocero 3 – Ⓜ Sant'Ambrogio – ✆ 0284254626 – www.ristorantetokuyoshi.com – Closed 5-31 August, Monday, lunch Tuesday-Saturda*

Esco Bistrò Mediterraneo

MEDITERRANEAN CUISINE • TRENDY A modern restaurant which is inform and welcoming, and where your first (but not only) impression is that of findir yourself in an architect's studio, as a guest of the owner. Attractive, contempo rary-style cuisine with a hint of Piedmontese flavour.

Menu 16€ (lunch) – Carte 31/45€

PLAN: 2-E3 – *via Tortona 26 – Ⓜ Porta Genova – ✆ 02 835 8144 – www.escobistromediterraneo.it – Closed 7-28 August, 23 December-7 January, lunch Saturday, Sunday*

Langosteria

SEAFOOD • TRENDY If you are looking for fish specialities, you will find this res taurant a real revelation. Raw dishes, oysters and seafood take pride of place o the menu, alongside freshly caught fish. An excellent wine selection and a glam orous ambience complete the picture.

Carte 57/128€

PLAN: 2-E3 – *via Savona 10 – Ⓜ Porta Genova FS – ✆ 02 5811 1649 – www.langosteria.com – Closed 10-24 August, lunch Monday-Saturday, Sunday*

Al Pont de Ferr

CREATIVE • OSTERIA Excellent cuisine with a playful touch and an emphasi on Italy's fine culinary traditions, which have been given a new, contemporar twist by chef Ivan. The wine cellar continues to be enhanced by a constan search for new wines and innovative producers, with a good selection also avail able by the glass. The lunchtime business menu offers smaller portions of th same delicious cuisine.

Menu 20€ (lunch), 55/130€ – Carte 44/104€

PLAN: 1-B3 – *Ripa di Porta Ticinese 55 – Ⓜ Porta Genova FS – ✆ 02 8940 6277 – www.pontdeferr.it – Closed 6-21 January*

City Life-Sempione

Iyo

JAPANESE • DESIGN The presence of international chefs from Italy and Japan i this restaurant ensures that Iyo's distinctive culinary style is kept alive. The cui sine served here is always original, creative and inspired by Japan, while at the same time looking towards the future. The wine list is also excellent, with its se lection of around 800 wines and a good choice of sake, with different varieties to accompany different dishes.

Specialities: Kakisu – Normandy oyster and jelly, kombu, daikon granita with rice and yuzu vinegar, seaweed. Crispy tamago – soft egg, umadashi, gin and miso sauce, seasonal vegetables. Macigaeta tacos – crunchy biscuit with caramelised banana, chocolate and cinnamon foam, vermouth and wasabi granita.

Menu 110€ – Carte 70/130€

PLAN: 1-B1 – *via Piero della Francesca 74 – Ⓜ Gerusalemme – ✆ 02 4547 6898 – www.iyo.it – Closed 4-24 August, Monday, lunch Tuesday*

Aimo e Nadia BistRo

ITALIAN • CHIC This bistro with a small yet charming and original dining room is a simpler and more informal version of the famous 2-star restaurant. The focus is the same, with an emphasis on Italian ingredients used in dishes which bring out their full flavour and integrity.

Menu 30€ (lunch) – Carte 47/68€

PLAN: 2-E2 – *via Matteo Bandello 14 – Ⓜ Conciliazione – ✆ 02 4802 6205 – www.bistroaimoenadia.com – Closed 1-8 January, 10-30 August, Sunday*

Altriménti

MODERN CUISINE • CONTEMPORARY DÉCOR An informal and contemporary restaurant which is elegant and yet retains a bistro feel. The cuisine is modern with meat and fish dishes featured on the menu, as well as a good number of vegetarian options. Good wine list.

Carte 49/75€

PLAN: 1-A2 – *via Monte Bianco 2/a – Ⓜ Amendola-Fiera – ✆ 02 8277 8751 – www.altrimenti.eu – Closed 12-16 April, 12 August-3 September, 25 December-2 January, Monday, lunch Saturday*

Arrow's

SEAFOOD • FAMILY Packed, even at midday; the atmosphere becomes cosier in the evening but the seafood cuisine, prepared according to tradition, remains the same.

Menu 25€ (lunch)/60€ – Carte 35/77€

PLAN: 3-J1 – *via A. Mantegna 17/19 – Ⓜ Gerusalemme – ✆ 02 341533 – www.ristorantearrows.it – Closed lunch Monday, Sunday*

Ba

CHINESE • ORIENTAL The Liu family who run this restaurant have plenty of experience in the restaurant business - and it shows. The elegant dining room, illuminated by subtle lighting, has an international, almost fashionable appeal, while the typically Chinese cuisine is carefully prepared using top-quality ingredients with the occasional Italian influence.

Carte 60/110€

PLAN: 1-A2 – *via R. Sanzio 22, ang. via Carlo Ravizza 10 – Ⓜ De Angeli – ✆ 02 469 3206 – www.ba-restaurant.com – Closed 4-26 August, 22-28 December, Monday*

La Cantina di Manuela

MODERN CUISINE • NEIGHBOURHOOD As its name suggests ("cantina" is the Italian for cellar), this restaurant offers a good selection of wines, many of which are available by the glass and to take away. Modern cuisine with a focus on Italian recipes and meat specialities.

Carte 35/45€

PLAN: 3-J1 – *via Procaccini 41 – Ⓜ Gerusalemme – ✆ 02 345 2034 – www.lacantinadimanuela.it*

Zero Milano

JAPANESE • MINIMALIST There's absolutely zero compromise on attention and quality in this restaurant, where the cuisine is made from top-quality ingredients using all the technical expertise typical of Japanese cooking. Chef Hide is now assisted by two of his compatriots who are real sushi experts, emphasising Zero Milano's ambition to be one of the best Japanese restaurants in Milan, with its menu featuring Japanese specialities alongside dishes with a more contemporary Western flavour.

Menu 48/60€ – Carte 45/96€

PLAN: 1-B2 – *corso Magenta 87 – Ⓜ Conciliazione – ✆ 02 4547 4733 – www.zero-milano.it – Closed lunch Monday-Sunday*

Environs of Milan

Zona urbana Nord - Ovest

Innocenti Evasioni (Tommaso Arrigoni)

CREATIVE • ELEGANT Although his colleague in the kitchen has moved on, the owner-chef at this restaurant continues to prepare creative cuisine, including reinterpretations of Milanese dishes. Meat and fish specialities feature on the menu, to be enjoyed in the unexpectedly delightful garden with just a few sought-after tables.

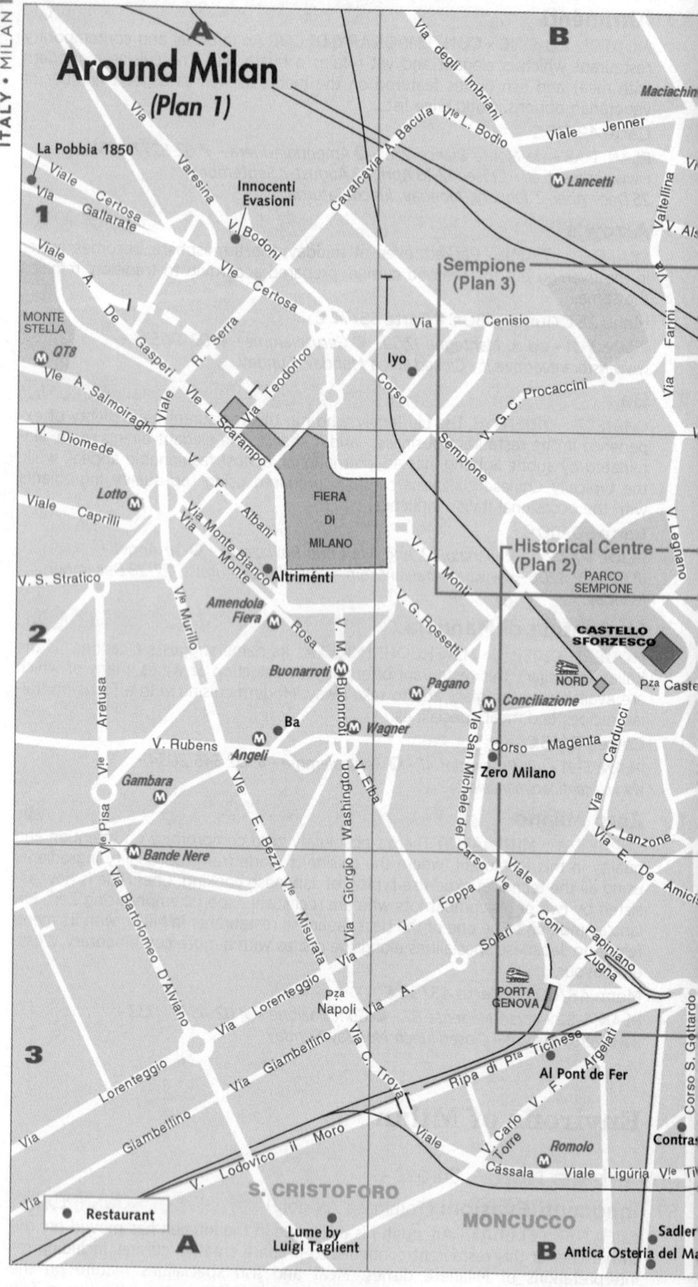
Around Milan
(Plan 1)
La Pobbia 1850
Innocenti Evasioni
Iyo
Altriménti
Ba
Zero Milano
Al Pont de Fer
Lume by Luigi Taglient
Antica Osteria del Ma
Sadler
Contras
Sempione (Plan 3)
Historical Centre (Plan 2)
FIERA DI MILANO
CASTELLO SFORZESCO
PARCO SEMPIONE
MONTE STELLA
S. CRISTOFORO
MONCUCCO
NORD
PORTA GENOVA
Restaurant

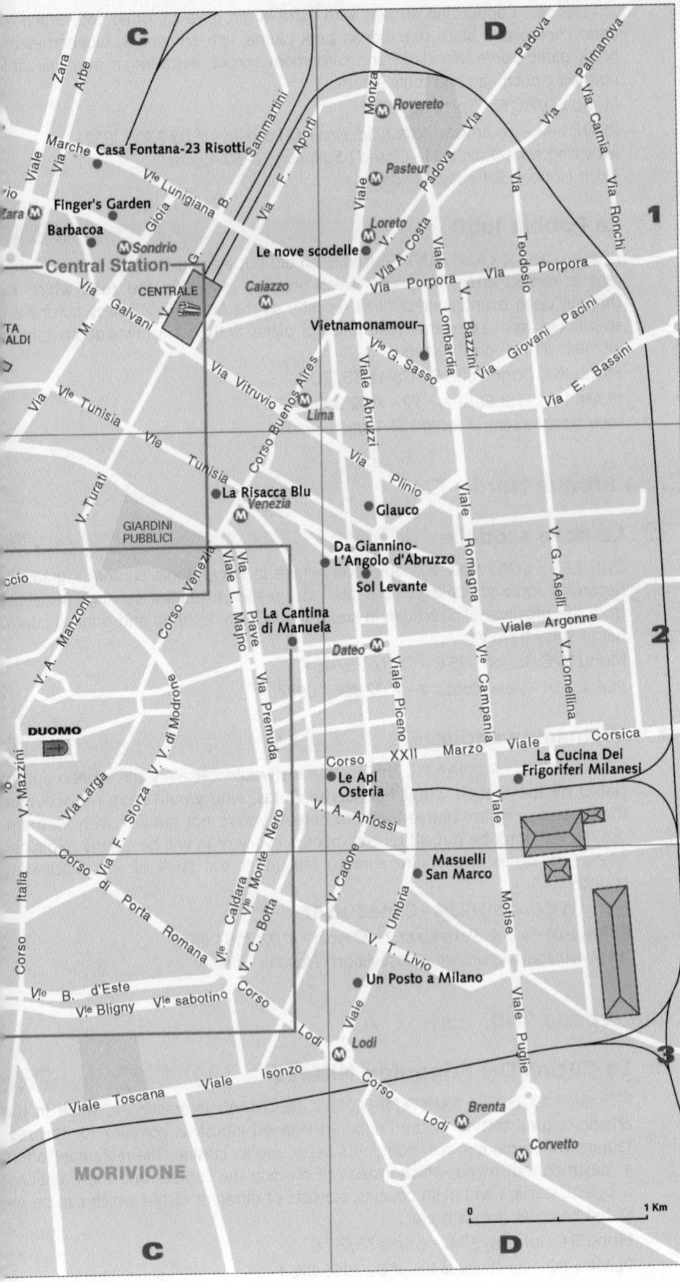
C
D
1
2
3
Casa Fontana-23 Risotti
Finger's Garden
Barbacoa
Central Station
CENTRALE
Le nove scodelle
Vietnamonamour
La Risacca Blu
Glauco
Da Giannino-
L'Angolo d'Abruzzo
Sol Levante
La Cantina
di Manuela
DUOMO
Le Api
Osteria
La Cucina Dei
Frigoriferi Milanesi
Masuelli
San Marco
Un Posto a Milano
GIARDINI
PUBBLICI
MORIVIONE
Rovereto
Pasteur
Loreto
Sondrio
Caiazzo
Lima
Venezia
Dateo
Lodi
Brenta
Corvetto
Zara
Via Padova
Via Palmanova
Via Carnia
Via Ronchi
Via Teodosio
Via Porpora
Viale Monza
Via A. Costa
Viale Lombardia
V. Bazzini
Via Giovani Pacini
Via E. Bassini
Vle G. Sasso
Viale Abruzzi
Via Plinio
Corso Buenos Aires
Via Vitruvio
Via Galvani
Via M. Gioia
Vle Lunigiana
Via B. Marcello
Via F. Aporti
Sammartini
Viale Marche
Via Arbe
Vle Tunisia
V. Turati
Corso Venezia
Viale L. Majno
Via Piave
Via Premuda
Viale Piceno
Viale Romagna
Vle Campania
Viale Argonne
V. G. Aselli
V. Lomellina
Viale Corsica
Corso XXII Marzo
V. A. Manzoni
V. V. di Modrone
Via Larga
V. Mazzini
Via F. Sforza
Corso di Porta Romana
Corso Italia
V. A. Anfossi
Viale Monte Nero
V. Cadore
Viale Umbria
V. T. Livio
Viale Molise
Viale Puglie
Vle Caldara
V. C. Botta
Vle B. d'Este
Vle Bligny
Vle sabotino
Corso Lodi
Viale Isonzo
Viale Toscana
FORLANINI DI LINATE EST
0
1 Km

Specialities: Cappuccino of peas with extra-virgin olive oil, dried cod, Grana P dano cheese and black tea. Iberian pork pluma, late artichokes, blueberries ar black garlic purée. Mandarin and cardamom sorbet, extra-virgin olive oil sabl nutmeg crunch, gin and tonic cream.

Menu 50/80 € - Carte 55/88 €

PLAN: 1-A1 - *via privata della Bindellina - Ⓜ Portello - ✆ 02 3300 1882 - www.innocentievasioni.com - Closed 1-5 January, 8-30 August, lunch Monday-Saturday, Sunday*

La Pobbia 1850

LOMBARDIAN • ELEGANT Housed in an old but elegant farmhouse, this resta rant is named after the poplar trees growing alongside the road which ra through open countryside until as recently as the late 19C. Milanese cuisine ar specialities from Lombardy take pride of place, with just a few options (almo all meat dishes) on the menu.

Menu 16 € (lunch)/18 € - Carte 35/70 €

PLAN: 1-A1 - *via Gallarate 92 - ✆ 02 3800 6641 - www.lapobbia.com - Closed 1-31 August, Sunday*

Zona urbana Nord - Est

Le nove scodelle

CHINESE • COSY Now available everywhere in Italy, ethnic cuisine is graduall becoming more specialised, as is the case in this restaurant serving specialiti from the province of Szechuan in south-west China. Exciting and original cuisi full of spicy flavours.

Menu 10 € (lunch)/15 € - Carte 25/45 €

PLAN: 1-D1 - *viale Monza 4 - ✆ 02 4967 0957*

Vietnamonamour

VIETNAMESE • ROMANTIC This restaurant would certainly have been appr ciated by the French writer Marguerite Duras, who would have rediscovere the ambience of her native Vietnam here. If you're not familiar with Vietnan ese dishes, don't be put off by the menu - everything will be clearly explaine when you order and you're sure to fall under the spell of this fascinatir country.

Menu 13 € (lunch)/25 € - Carte 30/58 €

PLAN: 1-D1 - *via A. Pestalozza 7 - Ⓜ Piola - ✆ 02 7063 4614 - www.vietnamonamour.com - Closed lunch Monday, Sunday*

Zona urbana Sud - Est

La Cucina Dei Frigoriferi Milanesi

MODERN CUISINE • CONTEMPORARY DÉCOR An interesting location in th artistic-cultural setting of the Frigoriferi Milanesi industrial complex for this re taurant with a modern feel both in its decor and its cuisine. The restaurant offe a "destructured" menu, which instead of dividing the courses into the traditior antipasti, starters and main courses, consists of different dishes which can be s lected however guests prefer.

Menu 9 € (lunch)/37 € - Carte 35/37 €

PLAN: 1-D2 - *via Piranesi 10 - ✆ 02 3966 6784 - www.lacucinadeifrigoriferimilanesi.it - Closed 1-7 January, 10-31 August, lunch Saturday, Sunday*

ona urbana Sud - Ovest

✿✿ Il Luogo di Aimo e Nadia (Alessandro Negrini e Fabio Pisani)

CREATIVE • DESIGN Although Aimo and Nadia are no longer at the helm of this restaurant, their style of cuisine is echoed by two excellent chefs. They have maintained the restaurant's tradition of creating Italian regional dishes with a modern twist. The focus has always been on top-quality ingredients (even before it was fashionable), making this restaurant in Via Montecuccoli one of the cradles of this culinary ethos. This is now kept alive through exciting, memorable cuisine created by two fine chefs.

Specialities: Dried cod in a crunchy Matera bread raviolo and turnips in apple vinegar. Gragnano pasta twists with Murge beans, sea urchin roe, anchovy and fennel sauce. "Amari": Venezuelan chocolate, bitter oranges, gentian sauce.

Menu 50 € (lunch)/200 € – Carte 107/165 €

Off plan – *via Montecuccoli 6 – Ⓜ Primaticcio – ✆ 02 416886 – www.aimoenadia.com – Closed 4-27 August, lunch Saturday, Sunday*

✿ Lume by Luigi Taglienti

MODERN CUISINE • DESIGN Offering a delightful experience for all the senses, this restaurant has recently been extended with an outdoor area, Orto di Lume, a garden blooming with plants whose fruits are used in the imaginative dishes created by chef Luigi Taglienti. The cuisine focuses on the culinary heritage of Italian flavours, combined with the liberal use of various sauces.

Specialities: Veal musetto, oyster cream, fruit mostarda, chickpeas and black truffles. Rossini-style steak with Perigueux sauce. Luigi Taglienti "grand dessert".

Menu 60 € (lunch), 130/170 € – Carte 121/205 €

PLAN: 1-A3 – *via Watt 37 – ✆ 02 8088 8624 – www.lumemilano.com – Closed 1-10 January, 3-24 August, Monday, dinner Sunday*

Antica Osteria del Mare

SEAFOOD • FAMILY This fish restaurant has an attractive display right by the entrance where diners can choose their own fish, with advice from the owner. Professionally run family restaurant with an informal and welcoming ambience.

Carte 40/60 €

PLAN: 1-B3 – *via Sforza 105 – ✆ 02 8954 6534 – www.anticaosteriadelmare.it – Closed 7-27 August, lunch Monday, Sunday*

SerrNovik/iStock

LUXEMBOURG

LËTZEBUERG

LUXEMBOURG
LËTZEBUERG

Xantana/iStock

LUXEMBOURG CITY IN...

→ **ONE DAY**
Place d'Armes, Ducal Grand Palace, National Museum of History and Art, Chemin de la Corniche.

→ **TWO DAYS**
Luxembourg City History Museum, Bock Casemates, the Grund.

→ **THREE DAYS**
Kirchberg Plateau, Museum of Modern Art, concert at Luxembourg Philharmonic Hall.

Luxembourg may be small but it's perfectly formed. Standing high above two rivers on a sandstone bluff, its commanding position over sheer gorges may be a boon to modern visitors, but down the centuries that very setting has rendered it the subject of conquest on many occasions. Its eye-catching geography makes it a city of distinctive districts, linked by spectacular bridges spanning lush green valleys.

The absolute heart of the city is the old town, its most prominent landmarks the cathedral spires and the city squares with their elegant pastel façades – an ideal backdrop to

the 'café culture' and a worthy recipient of UNESCO World Heritage Status. Winding its way deep below to the south west is the river Pétrusse, which has its confluence with the river Alzette in the south east. Follow the Chemin de la Corniche, past the old city walls and along the Alzette's narrow valley to discover the ruins of The Bock, the city's first castle, and the Casemates, a labyrinth of rocky 17C and 18C underground defences. Directly to the south of the old town is the railway station quarter, while down at river level to the east is the altogether more attractive Grund district, whose northerly neighbours are Clausen and Pfaffenthal. Up in the north east, connected by the grand sounding Pont Grand-Duchesse Charlotte, is Kirchberg Plateau, a modern hub of activity for the EU.

EATING OUT

he taste buds of Luxembourg have een very much influenced by French lassical cuisine, particularly around nd about the Old Town, an area that ecomes a smart open-air terrace in ummer. Look out for the local speciaty Judd mat Gaardebounen, smoked eck of pork with broad beans. The entre of town is an eclectic place to at as it runs the gauntlet from fasttyle pizzeria to expense account resaurants favoured by businessmen. A ood bet for atmosphere is the Grund, vhich offers a wide variety of restauants and price ranges, and is certainly the area that boasts the most popular cafés and pubs. A few trendy places have sprouted over recent times near the Casemates, and these too are proving to be pretty hot with the younger crowd. A service charge is included in your bill but if you want to tip, ten per cent is reasonable. The Grand Duchy produces its own white and sparkling wines on the borders of the Moselle. Over the last decade it has produced some interesting varieties but you'll rarely find these abroad, as they're eagerly snapped up by the locals.

Clairefontaine (Arnaud Magnier)

CREATIVE FRENCH • ELEGANT This attractive restaurant with a terra stands on an elegant square. It has traditional decor with old wooden pane ling and contemporary furnishings. Creative, modern cuisine and astute wi pairings.

Specialities: Spider crab meat, creamed cucumber, radish in honey and tarrag jelly. Bresse chicken studded with truffles and cooked "en vessie", foie gras stu ing and truffle purée. Crêpe Suzette reinterpreted by Ben and Adry.

Menu 59€ (lunch)/102€ - Carte 82/110€

PLAN: B1 – *9 place de Clairefontaine – ☎ 46 22 11 – www.restaurantclairefontaine.lu – Closed 11-19 April, 15 August-7 September, 25 December-5 January, Saturday, Sunday*

La Cristallerie

MODERN FRENCH • CLASSIC DÉCOR In terms of decor, this crystal glasswor is the epitome of stylish, classical elegance. The chef amply demonstrates ho subtle touches of creativity can enhance fine ingredients. His well-balanced cre tions feature the occasional Asian influence.

Specialities: Green asparagus and eel with green herbs. Line-caught turbot ar miso, grilled mashed potato. Domori chocolate and timut pepper.

Menu 58€ (lunch), 98/228€ - Carte 155/188€

PLAN: A1 – *Hôtel Le Place d'Armes, 18 place d'Armes – ☎ 27 47 37 42 1 – www.la-cristallerie.com – Closed 18-22 February, 14-18 April, 28 July-15 August, Monday, lunch Saturday, Sunday*

Les Jardins d'Anaïs

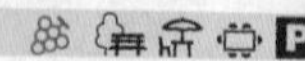

MODERN FRENCH • ELEGANT Undeniably classy. Attentive staff. An unde stated elegant interior and a delightful conservatory. The experienced chef pu sues his sophisticated culinary adventure crafting traditional recipes, in whic nothing is left to chance. Quality is the name of the game here, extending c course to the lavish, luxurious guestrooms.

Specialities: Carpaccio of langoustines and caviar, baba in a shellfish coulis an apple sorbet. Line-caught John Dory and Brittany carrots. Crunchy black choc late leaves, praline and biscuit.

Menu 39€ (lunch), 79/149€ - Carte 101/118€

Off plan – *2 place Sainte Cunégonde – ☎ 28 99 80 00 – www.jardinsdanais.lu – Closed 23 December-1 January, Saturday, Sunday*

Mosconi (Ilario Mosconi)

ITALIAN • ELEGANT Ilario and Simonetta Mosconi are an enthusiastic coupl that proudly pay homage to the gastronomic traditions of Italy. Their Italia cuisine is as full of flair as it is steeped in flavours. The secret of their succes no doubt lies in the infinite care and attention they devote to choosing thei suppliers.

Specialities: Octopus and watermelon with mint, fermented tomatoes and swee almonds. Sole with razor clams, chanterelles, grapefruit and potatoes, parsley oi Tomato stuffed with apple, pear and raspberry, vanilla ice cream.

Menu 55€ (lunch), 115/149€ - Carte 110/150€

PLAN: A1 – *13 rue Münster – ☎ 54 69 94 – www.mosconi.lu – Closed 4-15 April, 8-31 August, Monday, lunch Saturday, Sunday*

L'Atelier Windsor

CLASSIC CUISINE • FRIENDLY Escoffier, Bocuse; the sources of inspiration immediately set the scene in Jan Schneidewind's restaurant, which honours classica cuisine. The experienced chef seduces the senses with excellent produce, precise preparations and pleasing accompaniments. The décor is equally attractive courtesy of large windows, antique tiling and contemporary furniture... superb!

Menu 24€ (lunch), 36/98€ - Carte 41/75€

Off plan – *2 rue de Rollingergrund – ☎ 28 13 88 – www.atelierwindsor.lu – Closed dinner Monday, lunch Saturday, Sunday*

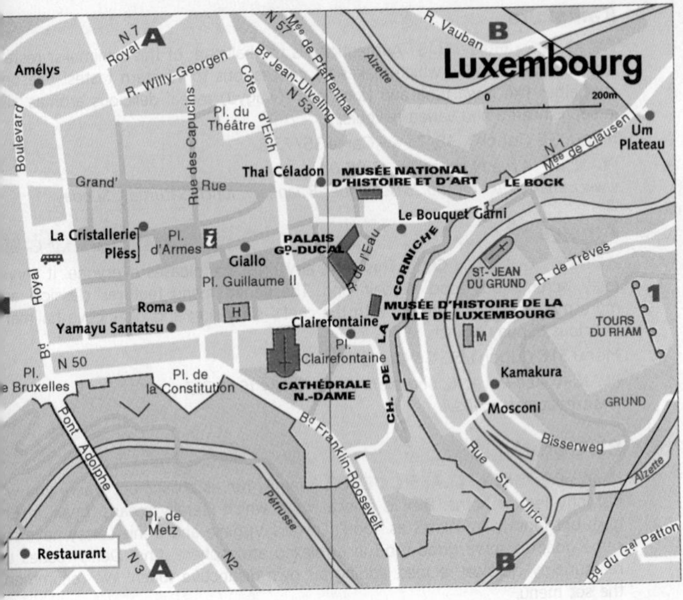

La Bergamote

MODERN CUISINE • TRENDY Have you ever actually tasted bergamot? The subtle, fresh taste of this small citrus fruit is a recurring ingredient in the sun-drenched cuisine of this restaurant. You'll find the likes of vitello tonnato, roast sea bream and shrimp polenta, without forgetting a few modern, French touches.

Menu 30€ (lunch), 37/65€ – Carte 46/66€

Off plan – *2 place de Nancy – ✆ 26 44 03 79 – www.labergamote.lu – Closed 15-31 August, 22 December-4 January, Monday, lunch Saturday, Sunday*

Brasserie des Jardins

TRADITIONAL CUISINE • BRASSERIE If only we lived next-door to this modern brasserie... Run by a highly professional team, it boasts a fine terrace. However, the star is the traditional fare, prepared with skill and attention to detail. The chef's touches of modernity are always perfectly balanced. High-quality ingredients in good hands!

Menu 37€ – Carte 43/83€

Off plan – *27b boulevard Marcel Cahen – ✆ 26 25 93 48 – www.brasseriedesjardins.lu*

La Cantine du Châtelet

MARKET CUISINE • COSY A lounge-inspired dining room and trendy vibe on the left-hand side and a more classical ambience on the right: choose your setting depending on your mood. Creative fare with varied, international influences, in which the chef draws upon his know-how of Belgian favourites with his experience of Spain. Delicious, no-frills food.

Menu 27€ (lunch)/37€ – Carte 48/68€

Off plan – *2 boulevard de la Pétrusse – ✆ 40 21 01 – www.chatelet.lu – Closed 22-31 December, dinner Monday, lunch Saturday, Sunday*

Kamakura

JAPANESE • MINIMALIST Authenticity is the hallmark of this minimalist resta rant founded in 1988, which makes no concessions to Western tastes! Seasor specialties like fresh tuna and Kobe beef (wagyu) reveal delicious aromas, ri in sophisticated and varied flavours.

Menu 15€ (lunch), 35/73€ – Carte 35/73€

PLAN: B1 – *4 rue Münster – ✆ 47 06 04 – www.kamakura.lu – Closed 25 December-8 January, lunch Saturday, Sunday*

Amélys

MODERN CUISINE • COSY This light, airy brasserie pleases everyone. It serv tasty, scrumptious food all day long. The varied menu features classical ar more modern dishes, always with the chef's surprising and distinctive hallmar Delicious Sunday brunch.

Menu 31€ (lunch)/55€ – Carte 48/79€

PLAN: A1 – *Le Royal, 12 boulevard Royal – ✆ 24 16 16 737 – www.restaurant-amelys.lu*

Bick Stuff

HOME COOKING • CLASSIC DÉCOR A family-run establishment where you w instantly feel at home. Bick is a local word which literally means 'beak' in E glish but loosely translates as 'food'. Owners Virginie and Denis Laissy have th same goal: to serve good food in a relaxed atmosphere. Chef Denis rustles u reassuringly classical recipes, adding his own distinctive touch. We recommen the set menu.

Menu 24€ (lunch), 36/46€ – Carte 50/70€

Off plan – *95 rue de Clausen – ✆ 26 09 47 31 – www.bickstuff.lu – Closed 30 May-7 June, 21 August-2 September, 22 December-5 January, Monday, dinner Thursday, lunch Saturday, dinner Sunda*

Le Bouquet Garni

CLASSIC FRENCH • ROMANTIC This 18C abode is steeped in charm, and bar stones and low ceilings set the inviting scene. The bouquet garni seeks to en hance and develop the strength of classical dishes. The chef focuses on the es sentials without unnecessary frills, offering diners an attractive repertory.

Menu 34€ (lunch)/55€

PLAN: B1 – *32 rue de l'Eau – ✆ 26 20 06 20 – www.lebouquetgarni.lu – Closed 1-6 January, Monday, lunch Sunday*

Thai Céladon

THAI • INTIMATE Lovers of Thai cuisine won't be disappointed by the fresh pro duce and authentic Asian flavours of Thai Céladon. Vegetarians will no doubt b in seventh heaven with the range that is on offer.

Menu 45/57€ – Carte 40/70€

PLAN: A1 – *1 rue du Nord – ✆ 47 49 34 – www.thai.lu – Closed lunch Saturday, Sunday*

Giallo

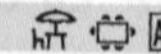

ITALIAN • DESIGN The two-storey water feature is one of the most striking ele ments of the oh so stylish Giallo's handsome modern interior. The establishmen is also rich in culinary ambition, backed up by first-class produce, which is per haps unsurprising when the aim is to serve authentic Italian cuisine.

Carte 45/63€

PLAN: A1 – *24 rue du Curé – ✆ 26 20 00 27 – www.giallo.lu – Closed dinner Sunday*

Hostellerie du Grünewald

MODERN FRENCH • TRENDY Fresh, healthy food, but also deliciously generous. This very pleasant bistro with a fine terrace provides an opportunity to sample simple ingredients devoid of unnecessary frills. Save room for the scrumptious desserts. Elegant guestrooms ensure sweet dreams.

Menu 27€ (lunch)/62€ – Carte 52/70€

Off plan – *10 route d'Echternach – ☎ 24 51 49 20 – www.hdg.lu – Closed Monday, Tuesday, lunch Saturday*

Oro e Argento

ITALIAN • INTIMATE An attractive Italian restaurant in a luxury hotel. Contemporary cuisine is served to a backdrop of plush decor with a Venetian touch. Intimate atmosphere and stylish service.

Menu 41€ (lunch), 52/80€ – Carte 63/74€

Off plan – *Hôtel Sofitel Europe, 6 rue du Fort Niedergrünewald – ☎ 43 77 68 70 – www.sofitel.com – Closed lunch Saturday*

Plëss

CLASSIC CUISINE • BRASSERIE Plëss means 'square' in Luxembourgish – an obvious reference to the Place d'Armes, which is where this lovely contemporary brasserie is located, right in the heart of town. Carvery and plancha-cooked meats features prominently. A mouth-watering "plëss-ure"!

Menu 45€ (lunch)/56€ – Carte 61/92€

PLAN: A1 – *Hôtel Le Place d'Armes, 18 place d'Armes – ☎ 27 47 37 41 1 – www.hotel-leplacedarmes.com*

Roma

ITALIAN • FRIENDLY The first Italian restaurant to be opened in Luxembourg, in 1950, the Roma continues to brilliantly uphold authentic, traditional cuisine, including homemade pasta. Themed festivals and a varied menu transform each meal into a feast.

Carte 41/61€

PLAN: A1 – *5 rue Louvigny – ☎ 22 36 92 – www.roma.lu – Closed Monday, dinner Sunday*

Schéiss

CLASSIC CUISINE • DESIGN The colourful "lounge" vibe of the Schéiss provides a perfect backdrop to its owners' very personal vision of classicism. The meat is carved before diners at the table and the menu is essentially composed of traditional dishes, to which the chef adds his own modern flourish.

Menu 34€ (lunch)/100€ – Carte 80/100€

Off plan – *142 Val Sainte-Croix – ☎ 24 61 82 – www.scheiss.lu – Closed 1-5 January, lunch Saturday, Sunday*

Thailand

THAI • EXOTIC DÉCOR In the heart of Belair, an exotic restaurant which stands out for its wide choice of Thai dishes and typical but not overdone decor. The ceiling is decorated with parasols.

Menu 50/57€ – Carte 42/72€

Off plan – *72 avenue Gaston Diderich – ☎ 44 27 66 – www.thai-belair.lu – Closed Monday, lunch Saturday*

Tomo

SUSHI • SIMPLE Don't be put off by the rather unassuming exterior: this is the place to sample fine Japanese and Chinese cuisine. Authentic flavours, sometimes surprising, but always harmonious. We recommend taking a seat at the counter to admire the chef's high-flying, culinary craftsmanship.

Menu 20€ (lunch) – Carte 23/60€

Off plan – *287 route de Longwy – ☎ 26 44 15 31 – www.tomosushibar.lu – Closed Sunday*

Um Plateau

MODERN CUISINE • CHIC Diners appreciate the smart lounge ambience an cosy interior of this restaurant. After a glass of wine in the lively bar, treat you self to a meal in which fine produce takes pride of place. Authentic flavours an painstaking preparations are the hallmarks of this establishment.

Menu 28 € (lunch) – Carte 45/95 €

PLAN: B1 – *6 Plateau Altmünster* – *☎ 26 47 82 6* – *www.umplateau.lu* – *Closed lunch Saturday, Sunday*

Yamayu Santatsu

JAPANESE • MINIMALIST Don't be misled by the low-key interior, you are the right place to taste the best sushi in the city of Luxemburg. The chef prepare it at the last minute at the sushi bar and is a stickler for super fresh fish. A blu chip value since 1989.

Menu 17 € (lunch)/35 € – Carte 28/61 €

PLAN: A1 – *26 rue Notre-Dame* – *☎ 46 12 49* – *Closed 26 July-17 August, Monday, Sunday*

AleksandarGeorgiev/iStock

NETHERLANDS

NEDERLAND

AMSTERDAM
AMSTERDAM

AndreyKrav/iStock

AMSTERDAM IN...

→ **ONE DAY**
A trip on a canal boat, Rijksmuseum, Anne Frank Museum, Van Gogh Museum.

→ **TWO DAYS**
Begijnhof, shopping in the '9 Straatjes', Vondelpark, evening in a brown café.

→ **THREE DAYS**
The Jordaan, Plantage and Entrepotdok, red light district.

Once visited, never forgotten; that's Amsterdam's grea claim to fame. Its endearin horseshoe shape – define by 17C canals cut to drai land for a growing population – allied to finely detaile gabled houses, has produce a compact city centre of aesthetically splendid symmetr and matchless consistenc Exploring the city on foot c by bike is the real joy here and visitors rarely need to jum on a tram or bus.

'The world's biggest small city' displays a host of distinc tive characteristics, ranging from the world-famous re light district to the cosy and convivial brown cafés, fror

the wonderful art galleries and museums to the quirky shops, and the medieval churches to the tree-lined waterways with their pretty bridges. There's the feel of a northern Venice, but without the hallowed and revered atmosphere. It exists on a human scale, small enough to walk from one end to the other. Those who might moan that it's just too small should stroll along to the former derelict docklands on the east side and contemplate the shiny new apartments giving the waterfront a sleek, 21C feel. Most people who come here, though, are just happy to cosy up to old Amsterdam's sleepy, relaxed vibe. No European city does snug bars better: this is the place to go for cats kipping on beat-up chairs and candles flickering on wax-encrusted tables...

EATING OUT

Amsterdam is a vibrant and multicultural city and, as such, has a wide proliferation of restaurants offering a varied choice of cuisines, where you can eat well without paying too much. Head for an eetcafe and you'll get a satisfying three course meal at a reasonable price. The Dutch consider the evening to be the time to eat your main meal, so some restaurants shut at lunchtime. Aside from the eetcafe, you can top up your middle-of-day fuel levels with simple, home-cooked meals and local beers at a bruin (brown) café, or for something lighter, a café specialising in coffee and cake. If you wish to try local specialities, number one on the hit list could be rijsttafel or 'rice table', as the Dutch have imported much from their former colonies of Indonesia. Fresh raw herring from local waters is another nutritious local favourite, as are apple pies and pancakes of the sweet persuasion; often enjoyed with a hot chocolate. Restaurants are never too big but are certainly atmospheric and busy, so it's worth making reservations.

Centre

&Moshik (Moshik Roth)

CREATIVE • DESIGN Moshik Roth invites you on an adventure. This fashionab establishment will take you from one pleasant surprise to the next. The ch knows how to combine inventiveness with refinement for a fantastic flavour e perience, extracting the best from top-quality ingredients with absolute precisio

Specialities: Jardin du marin. Pigeon with cherries. Trilogy of desserts.

Menu 65€ (lunch), 125/230€ - Carte 115/245€

PLAN: 2-H1 - *Oosterdokskade 5 - ✆ 020 260 2094 - www.moshikrestaurant.com - Closed 1-10 January, 24-31 December, Monday, Tuesday, lunch Wednesday-Thursday, lunch Saturday*

Spectrum

CREATIVE • LUXURY Extraordinarily beautiful and classy! This refined, class restaurant offers a true fine dining experience. The food is elegant, with a uniq interplay of textures and tastes that is spot on, creating a wonderful harmo where every bite surprises. Definitely worth a visit!

Specialities: Coffee-coated cuttlefish, mango and coriander, light cardamo Crispy duck with roasted aubergine, tulip bulb, pomegranate jus and black oliv Creation of brown rum and blue cheese with caramel, toasted hazelnut, raisi and chocolate.

Menu 142/180€ - Carte 96/143€

PLAN: 2-G3 - *Hotel Waldorf Astoria, Herengracht 542 - ✆ 020 718 4643 - www.restaurantspectrum.com - Closed 1-20 January, 26 July-17 August, Sunday, Monday, lunch Tuesday-Saturday*

Bord'Eau

CREATIVE • ELEGANT Bord'Eau is a delightful luxurious restaurant with a class feel which is evident throughout, from the stylish decor to the beautifully dresse plates. The chef uses ingredients from all corners of the world to create strong contrasting flavours in delicate combinations. Make sure you try the cheese - th selection is great!

Specialities: Red mullet and pomegranate. Dairy cow beef and horseradish. Apri cot and cucumber.

Menu 98/138€ - Carte 63/102€

PLAN: 2-G2 - *Hotel de l'Europe, Nieuwe Doelenstraat 2 - ✆ 020 531 1619 - www.bordeau.nl - Closed Sunday, Monday, lunch Tuesday-Saturday*

Bougainville

MODERN CUISINE • ELEGANT Warm materials and luxurious designs give Res taurant Bougainville an intimate atmosphere, and its splendour is emphasized b the stunning view of the Dam. Let your taste buds travel from west to east er joying dishes prepared by the highly technical chef, who has a creative, refine and intuitive style of cooking. The sommelier's selection is just as impressive a the cuisine.

Specialities: Pairing of beef and pulpo with yellow curry, papaya and kimch Lamb with bulgur wheat, peas and harissa jus. Creation of white chocolate, cham pagne and calamansi.

Menu 80/105€ - Carte 100/130€

PLAN: 2-G2 - *TwentySeven, Dam 27 - ✆ 020 218 2180 - www.restaurantbougainville.com - Closed 6-19 January, Sunday, lunch Monday-Saturday*

The Duchess

MEDITERRANEAN CUISINE • CHIC The grandeur of this former ticket office i impressive. This is a magnificent venue, where the use of dark marble and th Belle Époque atmosphere lend The Duchess real flair. The beautiful Molter kitchen turns out generous, classic dishes. Where else would you find such a de licious, traditional beef Wellington?

Specialities: Lobster and King crab with avocado and tomato. Tenderloin of Beef Wellington. Apple & Calvados.

Carte 65/90€

PLAN: 2-F1 – *Spuistraat 172 – ✆ 020 811 3322 – www.the-duchess.com*

✿ Graphite by Peter Gast

CREATIVE • INTIMATE Take the QR code you are given when you make your reservation, go to Paardenstraat and look for the door with a scanner, which leads to this mysterious speakeasy restaurant. After a drink in the cocktail bar, head for the intimate and discreet dining room, where Peter Gast combines traditional techniques with inventive ideas, applying his technical ability and know-how with plenty of feeling. Intriguing!

Specialities: Vegetables, herbs and flowers. Lobster with caramelised onions, codium and mussels with curry foam. Star of citrus and white chocolate, mascarpone, pink grapefruit juice and black tea.

Menu 100/150€ – Carte 67/75€

PLAN: 2-G2 – *Paardenstraat 15 – ✆ 06 18829580 – www.graphite.amsterdam – Closed Sunday, Monday, lunch Tuesday-Saturday*

✿ Lastage (Rogier van Dam)

CREATIVE • FRIENDLY Lastage is an appealing little restaurant which will immediately make you feel welcome. Chef Van Dam delights the taste buds with dishes that are full of personality. Nothing on the plate is unnecessary – every ingredient adds interest and is there to enhance the dish. For the quality, the prices are more than reasonable. This is a little establishment with big flavours!

Specialities: Oxtail bouillon with crunchy mustard seed and gruyère. Quail stuffed with duck liver and sage, chard and pepper sauce. Epoisses in brioche with quince, foie gras, muscovado and balsamic vinegar.

Menu 51/93€

PLAN: 2-G1 – *Geldersekade 29 – ✆ 020 737 0811 – www.restaurantlastage.nl – Closed 26-28 April, 3-9 August, lunch Sunday, Monday, lunch Tuesday-Saturday*

✿ MOS (Egon van Hoof)

CREATIVE FRENCH • CONTEMPORARY DÉCOR The interior is relaxed and chic, the large windows offer a fantastic view of the IJ river, and the food is delicious. MOS is sublime. The chef shows how a little creativity conjures up a variety of prominent flavours, producing balanced combinations that are both rich and refined. Guests are advised to ask about parking when reserving.

Specialities: Crispy langoustine with a Riesling vinaigrette, sweet potato compote, sweetcorn and dukkah. Sweetbread with roasted veal tenderloin, grilled palm heart and pepper jus. Combination of coconut, green apple and black sesame.

Menu 40€ (lunch), 60/100€ – Carte 65/81€

PLAN: 1-C1 – *IJdok 185 – ✆ 020 638 0866 – www.mosamsterdam.nl – Closed 26 July-10 August, Sunday, Monday, lunch Saturday*

✿ Restaurant 212 (Richard van Oostenbrugge & Thomas Groot)

CREATIVE • TRENDY The open-plan kitchen has a central place in this modern restaurant where guests enjoy interacting with the chefs from the seats at the counter. Here you can watch Richard van Oostenbrugge and Thomas Groot working with delicate precision, preparing inventive and creative dishes which surprise diners with their unexpectedly striking flavours.

Specialities: Minced veal "os à moelle": smoked herringbone with calf marrow, cockles and caviar. Turbot with sauerkraut, bacon and black truffle, bouillon of vin jaune and black trumpet mushrooms. Green apple, ginger and walnut with salted caramel.

Menu 68€ (lunch), 128/138€ – Carte 78/194€

PLAN: 2-G2 – *Amstel 212 – ✆ 020 334 8685 – www.restaurant-212.com – Closed Sunday, Monday*

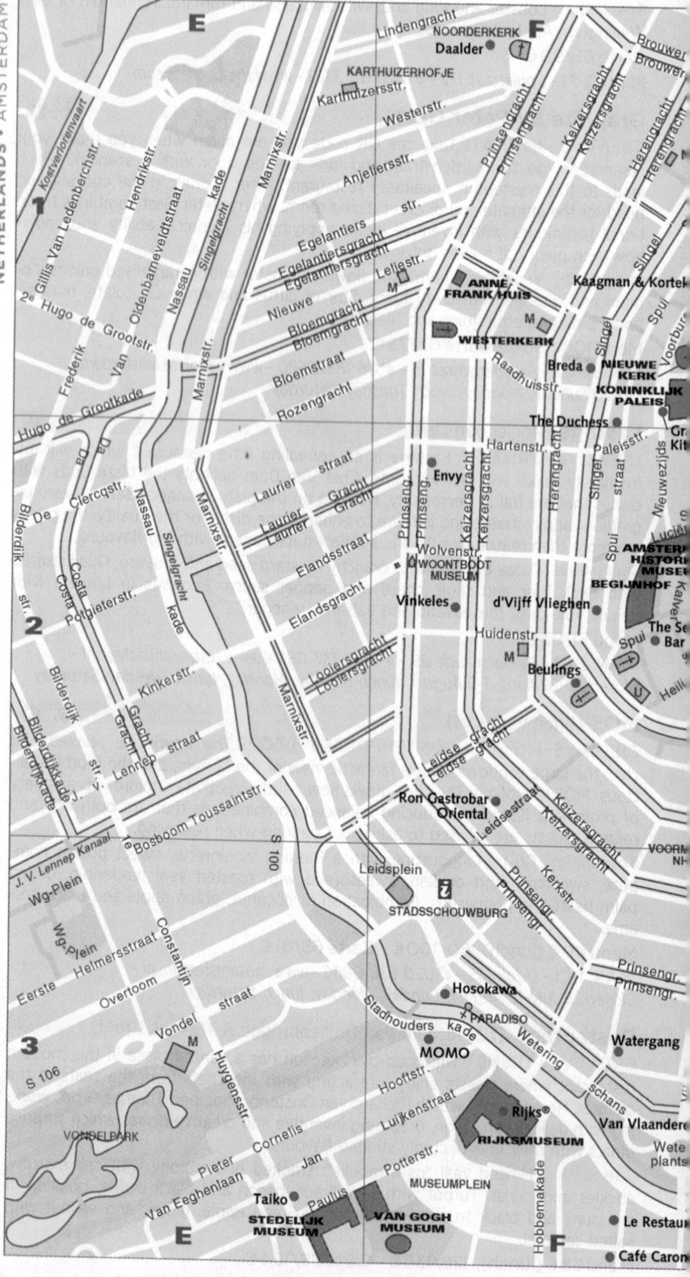
E
F
1
2
3
NOORDERKERK
Daalder
KARTHUIZERHOFJE
Lindengracht
Karthuizersstr.
Westerstr.
Anjeliersstr.
Egelantiers str.
Egelantiersgracht
Leliestr.
ANNE FRANK HUIS
WESTERKERK
Nieuwe Bloemgracht
Bloemstraat
Rozengracht
Raadhuisstr.
Breda
NIEUWE KERK
KONINKLIJK PALEIS
The Duchess
Kaagman & Kortek
Hartenstr.
Paleisstr.
Envy
Laurier straat
Laurier Gracht
Elandsstraat
Elandsgracht
Wolvenstr.
WOONTBOOT MUSEUM
Vinkeles
d'Vijff Vlieghen
BEGIJNHOF
Huidenstr.
Beulings
Spui
Looiersgracht
Leidse gracht
Ron Gastrobar Oriental
Leidsestraat
Keizersgracht
Prinsengracht
Herengracht
Singel
Kerkstr.
Leidsplein
STADSSCHOUWBURG
Hosokawa
PARADISO
Stadhouders kade
MOMO
Wetering schans
Watergang
Rijks
RIJKSMUSEUM
Van Vlaandere
MUSEUMPLEIN
VAN GOGH MUSEUM
STEDELIJK MUSEUM
Taiko
Le Restau
Café Caron
Hobbemakade
Potterstr.
Paulus
Jan Luijkenstraat
Pieter Cornelis Hooftstr.
Van Eeghenlaan
VONDELPARK
Vondel straat
Overtoom
Eerste Helmersstraat
Constantijn Huygensstr.
Wg-Plein
J. V. Lennep Kanaal
1e Bosboom Toussaintstr.
J. v. Lennep straat
Bilderdijkkade
Bilderdijk str.
Kinkerstr.
Costa Potgieterstr.
Da Costa
De Clercqstr.
Hugo de Grootkade
2e Hugo de Grootstr.
Frederik Hendrikstr.
Van Oldenbarneveldtstraat
Gillis Van Ledenberchstr.
Kostverlorenvaart
Nassau kade
Singelgracht
Marnixstr.
S 100
S 106
Brouwer
Voorbu
Nieuwezijds
Kalver
The Se Bar
Heili
Wete plants
VOORM

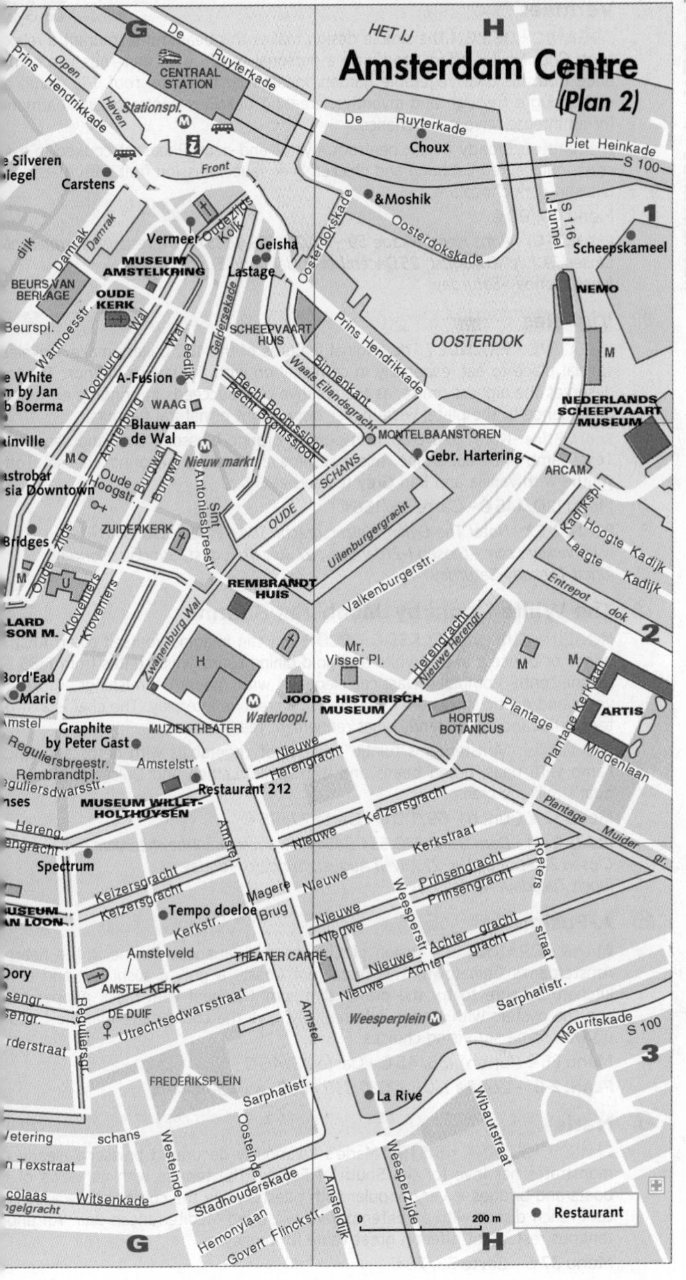
Amsterdam Centre
(Plan 2)
Restaurant
0
200 m
G
H
1
2
3
HET IJ
CENTRAAL STATION
Stationspl.
De Ruyterkade
Prins Hendrikkade
Open Haven
Front
Choux
Piet Heinkade
S 100
&Moshik
Oosterdokskade
IJ-tunnel
S 116
Scheepskameel
NEMO
OOSTERDOK
Carstens
Vermeer
Geisha
Lastage
MUSEUM AMSTELKRING
BEURS VAN BERLAGE
OUDE KERK
Damrak
Warmoesstr.
Beurspl.
Oudezijds Kolk
Geldersekade
SCHEEPVAART HUIS
Zeedijk
A-Fusion
WAAG
Blauw aan de Wal
Nieuw markt
Recht Boomssloot
Binnenkant
Waals Eilandsgracht
MONTELBAANSTOREN
Gebr. Hartering
ARCAM
NEDERLANDS SCHEEPVAART MUSEUM
OUDE SCHANS
Uilenburgergracht
Sint Antoniesbreestr.
ZUIDERKERK
Oude Hoogstr.
Kloveniers
Bridges
REMBRANDT HUIS
Valkenburgerstr.
Kadijkspl.
Hoogte Kadijk
Laagte Kadijk
Entrepot dok
Mr. Visser Pl.
Herengracht
Nieuwe Herengr.
Zwanenburg Wal
JOODS HISTORISCH MUSEUM
Waterloopl.
MUZIEKTHEATER
HORTUS BOTANICUS
Plantage Kerklaan
ARTIS
Plantage Middenlaan
Plantage Muider gr.
Bord'Eau
Marie
Graphite by Peter Gast
Amstelstr.
Reguliersbreestr.
Rembrandtpl.
Restaurant 212
MUSEUM WILLET-HOLTHUYSEN
Spectrum
Keizersgracht
Tempo doeloe
Magere Brug
Kerkstraat
Prinsengracht
Nieuwe Achter gracht
Weesperstr.
Roeters straat
THEATER CARRÉ
Amstelveld
AMSTEL KERK
DE DUIF
Utrechtsedwarsstraat
Weesperplein
Sarphatistr.
Mauritskade
FREDERIKSPLEIN
La Rive
Wibautstraat
Oosteinde
Westeinde
schans
Stadhouderskade
Witsenkade
Hemonylaan
Govert Flinckstr.
Amsteldijk
Weesperzijde
Amstel

Vermeer

ORGANIC • DESIGN The simple design makes this beautiful restaurant a relax spot. Chef Naylor offers food with a personal touch, with generous use of pr duce from his own vegetable garden, located on the hotel roof. His dishes a well thought through and inventive, creating delicious contrasts and harmon for an intense flavour experience.

Specialities: Bloody Peary: beetroot, oyster and pear. Pheasant cooked in a s crust, quince, red cabbage and chicken liver sauce. Passion fruit with macadam nut and dark chocolate.

Menu 70/90€

PLAN: 2-G1 – *Prins Hendrikkade 59 – ✆ 020 556 4885 – www.restaurantvermeer.nl Closed 19 July-10 August, 25 December-10 January, Sunday, lunch Monday-Saturday*

Vinkeles

CREATIVE • FRIENDLY The original features of this 18C bakery make Vinkeles special place to eat, especially in combination with the stylish interior. The foo deserves the highest praise, as the creative chef succeeds in bringing exciteme and nuance to the plate, while never losing sight of natural flavours.

Specialities: North Sea crab with potato, orange blossom, lime and sea urch. Texel lamb with aubergine, miso, sesame and young pecorino cheese. Toffe soufflé with vanilla and Earl Grey tea sorbet.

Menu 120/145€ – Carte 85/166€

PLAN: 2-F2 – *Hotel The Dylan, Keizersgracht 384 – ✆ 020 530 2010 – www.vinkeles.com – Closed 1-21 January, 27 July-11 August, Sunday, Monday, lunch Tuesday-Saturday*

The White Room by Jacob Jan Boerma

MODERN CUISINE • CLASSIC DÉCOR You can imagine yourself as an Austria prince or princess in this white and gold dining room, which dates from 1885 ar magnificently combines classical elegance with modern furnishings. Citrus fla vours and exotic spices are combined in a creative interplay. The chef is a stron technician and understands what refinement really means.

Specialities: "Amsterdams tuintje": platter of vegetables with herbs and spice Lamb with peas, broad beans and wild garlic. Lemon and Dulce de leche wi goat's milk ice cream.

Menu 32€ (lunch), 69/119€ – Carte 77/96€

PLAN: 2-G1 – *Dam 9 – ✆ 020 554 9454 – www.restaurantthewhiteroom.com – Closed 28 April-5 May, 21 July-11 August, Sunday, Monday, lunch Tuesday-Wednesday*

A-Fusion

ASIAN • BRASSERIE A fusion of Chinese and Japanese cuisine in the heart c Amsterdam's Chinatown. This restaurant boasts a grill, a sushi bar and a wo kitchen. Be sure to try the prawn dim sum, the beef with black pepper sauc and the oysters with ginger. Alternatively, give the cooks carte blanche to com up with some surprising choices.

Menu 25€ (lunch), 35/45€ – Carte 23/40€

PLAN: 2-G1 – *Zeedijk 130 – ✆ 020 330 4068 – www.a-fusion.nl*

Marie

CLASSIC CUISINE • BISTRO Marie's luxuriously decorated brasserie clearly de monstrates her love for the South of France. The terrace with its views of th boats and bridges is very popular with guests, while the cuisine showcases typi cal French dishes with a contemporary twist and Mediterranean flair. An unpre tentious restaurant offering great value for money.

Menu 37€ – Carte 38/78€

PLAN: 2-G2 – *Hotel de l'Europe, Nieuwe Doelenstraat 2 – ✆ 020 531 1619 – www.marieamsterdam.com*

Ron Gastrobar Indonesia Downtown

INDONESIAN • COLOURFUL If you're looking for somewhere with a real buzz, immerse yourself in the captivating ambience of this hip and colourful restaurant, where you can order an exotic cocktail before discovering the Indonesian delicacies on offer. The various satés are definitely worth trying, or how about a generous rijsttafel to share? All with Ron Blaauw's characteristic playful touch.

Menu 39/57€ – Carte 40/70€

PLAN: 2-G2 – *Rokin 49 – ✆ 020 790 0322 – www.rongastrobarindonesia.nl – Closed 31 December-1 January, Monday*

Scheepskameel

TRADITIONAL CUISINE • BRASSERIE Scheepskameel is a lively, relaxed establishment, providing honest, straightforward food. Everything here starts with top-quality ingredients, prepared without fuss and beautifully seasoned. The wine list is comprised entirely of German wines and accompanies the food perfectly.

Menu 37/65€ – Carte 31/65€

PLAN: 2-H1 – *Kattenburgerstraat 7 – ✆ 020 337 9680 – www.scheepskameel.nl – Closed 27 April, 24 December-1 January, Sunday, Monday, lunch Tuesday-Saturday*

Tempo doeloe

INDONESIAN • TRADITIONAL Regular diners at Tempo doeloe or 'Times Gone By' find it difficult to hide their enthusiasm when they visit this restaurant. They know that an Indonesian feast like no other in Amsterdam awaits them. The food here is authentically Indonesian, with no concessions to Western tastes. Selamat makan!

Menu 24/38€ – Carte 35/65€

PLAN: 2-G3 – *Utrechtsestraat 75 – ✆ 020 625 6718 – www.tempodoeloerestaurant.nl – Closed Sunday, lunch Monday-Thursday*

Van Vlaanderen

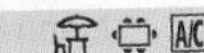

MODERN CUISINE • CLASSIC DÉCOR Van Vlaanderen has long been recognised as the place to go for the good things in life. The restaurant's success lies in its pleasant location right in the centre of Amsterdam with its own jetty on the patio, and attentive service of a young, spirited team whose enthusiasm is evident in the modern, original versions of the classic dishes served here. A heart-warming experience.

Menu 33€ (lunch), 37/80€

PLAN: 2-F3 – *Weteringschans 175 – ✆ 020 622 8292 – www.restaurant-vanvlaanderen.nl – Closed 1-15 January, Sunday, Monday, lunch Tuesday-Thursday, lunch Saturday*

BAK

VEGETARIAN • VINTAGE Take the stairs to the third floor of this unobtrusive warehouse (you'll need to ring the bell in the evening) to discover the industrial-style BAK restaurant with its lovely view over the IJ river. The focus here is on original, vegetarian dishes made from sustainably produced ingredients which are full of surprising and delicious flavours.

Menu 34€ (lunch)/65€

PLAN: 1-C1 – *Van Diemenstraat 408 – ✆ 020 737 2553 – www.bakrestaurant.nl – Closed 20 July-2 August, Monday, Tuesday, lunch Wednesday-Friday*

Beulings

CONTEMPORARY • INTIMATE Beulings is a little gem full of atmosphere. Lisja offers guests a warm welcome, and is also in charge of the excellent wines, while Bas and his team create delicious meals in the open kitchen. They put a lot of effort into the preparation of their dishes, which are full of versatile textures and carefully thought-out flavours. A delightful experience!

Menu 45/82€

PLAN: 2-F2 – *Beulingstraat 9 – ✆ 020 320 6100 – www.beulings.nl – Closed lunch Sunday-Monday, Tuesday, Wednesday, lunch Thursday-Saturday*

Bistrot Neuf

CLASSIC CUISINE • COSY With its clean, modern design, this relaxed bistro ideally located in a lively area of Amsterdam. Traditional French dishes exhi original Amsterdam flair and are impeccably cooked to bring out the true f vours of the ingredients. Efficient service.

Menu 24€ (lunch), 37/45€ – Carte 38/73€

PLAN: 2-G1 – *Haarlemmerstraat 9 – ✆ 020 400 3210 – www.bistrotneuf.nl*

Blauw aan de Wal

MARKET CUISINE • RUSTIC A popular restaurant at the end of a cul-de-sac the lively red light district. Discreet décor, simple and tasty modern cuisi good wine selection and a shady terrace.

Menu 62/82€

PLAN: 2-G2 – *O.Z. Achterburgwal 99 – ✆ 020 330 2257 – www.blauwaandewal.co Closed Sunday, lunch Monday-Saturday*

Breda

MODERN CUISINE • BRASSERIE Welcome to Breda: dazzling, a touch ret and luxurious too, but above all a place for delicious food. Choose from surpr menus featuring a range of inventive dishes created by the chef. Internatior varied and tasty.

Menu 33€ (lunch), 63/87€

PLAN: 2-F1 – *Singel 210 – ✆ 020 622 5233 – www.breda-amsterdam.com*

Bridges

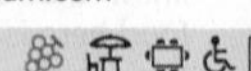

SEAFOOD • ELEGANT Fish reigns supreme at this sleek restaurant, which a offers a beautiful view of the canals. Salted delicacies take centre stage in dish that are distinctly contemporary in style. The chef combines classic sauces w the occasional Asian twist to showcase the fresh flavours of his ingredients.

Menu 42€ (lunch), 69/89€ – Carte 75/143€

PLAN: 2-G2 – *Hotel Sofitel The Grand, O.Z. Voorburgwal 197 – ✆ 020 555 3560 www.bridgesrestaurant.nl – Closed lunch Monday-Tuesday*

Carstens

EUROPEAN CONTEMPORARY • BRASSERIE This large and colourful brasse is situated in a side street in the city centre. Here, the experienced kitchen te focuses on promoting ingredients from the soil and waters of the Netherlands a flexible menu featuring classic and contemporary dishes with something everyone.

Carte 32/52€

PLAN: 2-G1 – *Hasselaerssteeg – ✆ 020 524 0649 – www.carstensbrasserie.nl – Closed lunch Sunday-Saturday*

Choux

MODERN FRENCH • TRENDY Giving prominence to vegetables may not alw be the obvious choice, but at this trendy restaurant it works beautifully. The c tinually surprising ingredients, creative preparations and intense flavours ens complete fulfilment, taking diners on a wonderful voyage of discovery.

Menu 40/72€

PLAN: 2-H1 – *De Ruyterkade 128 – ✆ 020 210 3090 – www.choux.nl – Closed 2-10 August, Sunday, Monday, lunch Saturday*

Daalder

CREATIVE • BISTRO A former local pub has been successfully transformed i this must-visit venue for foodies. Here, the talented Dennis Huwaë expresses personal style, creating carefully considered and interesting dishes marked by constant search for variation and surprise. Excellent value for money.

Menu 38€ (lunch), 69/89€

PLAN: 2-F1 – *Lindengracht 90 – ✆ +31 (0) 20 624 8864 – www.daalderamsterdam.nl – Closed 21 January-4 February, 21 July-11 August, Tuesday, Wednesday, lunch Thursday*

Envy

MEDITERRANEAN CUISINE • TRENDY Looking for a place to eat in trendy surroundings? Then head for this stylish trattoria, where the menu offers a beautiful range of creative recipes in tapas-style portions and the combination of subtle and pronounced flavours adds overall depth to the dishes. Note that the number of tables available for advance booking is very limited.

Menu 23 € (lunch), 49/69 € – Carte 30/60 €

PLAN: 2-F2 – *Prinsengracht 381 – ✆ 020 344 6407 – www.envy.nl – Closed lunch Monday-Thursday*

Gebr. Hartering

FRENCH • BISTRO Niek and Paul Hartering share a love of ingredients. This cheerful venue proposes a short menu, which changes regularly, as the fusion cuisine depends on the ingredients at their best on the day. Flavours don't lie.

Menu 55/80 € – Carte 50/79 €

PLAN: 2-H2 – *Peperstraat 10hs – ✆ 020 421 0699 – www.gebr-hartering.nl – Closed lunch Sunday-Saturday*

Geisha

ASIAN • EXOTIC DÉCOR This trendy Geisha spoils guests with the delicacies of Southeast Asia. The traditional precision and freshness are certainly part of the deal, and are supplemented with more innovative dishes. You can also enjoy hors-d'oeuvres-style options at the bar, accompanied by a choice of delicious cocktails.

Menu 34/55 € – Carte 30/85 €

PLAN: 2-G1 – *Prins Hendrikkade 106a – ✆ 020 626 2410 – www.restaurantgeisha.nl – Closed 27 April, Sunday, lunch Monday-Saturday*

Hosokawa

TEPPANYAKI • TRENDY Experienced chef Hiromichi Hosokawa has mastered Japanese cuisine down to the fine details. In 1992 he opened this smart restaurant, where he continues to prepare traditional teppanyaki, robatayaki and sushi dishes. Characteristic Japanese precision, finesse and full flavours are part and parcel of the experience.

Menu 60/98 € – Carte 31/110 €

PLAN: 2-F3 – *Max Euweplein 22 – ✆ 020 638 8086 – www.hosokawa.nl – Closed lunch Sunday-Saturday*

John Dory

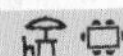

SEAFOOD • FRIENDLY The charm and character of this 1680s warehouse is fantastic. The seats around the open kitchen are in demand for those wishing to discover what 'vistronomie' is. The quality of the fish, which comes directly from the North Sea, shines through here, and comes with all kinds of creative garnishes. The refinement of the 4-10 course menu will surprise you!

Menu 47/87 €

PLAN: 2-G3 – *Prinsengracht 999 – ✆ 020 622 9044 – www.johndory.nl – Closed Sunday, Monday, lunch Tuesday-Saturday*

Kaagman & Kortekaas

MARKET CUISINE • FRIENDLY Giel Kaagman and Bram Kortekaas focus on quality in their informal bistro. The chef likes to work with game and poultry, making his own charcuterie and terrines. Seasonal produce is cleverly worked into a monthly changing menu that presents an up-to-date take on traditional flavours.

Menu 52/67 €

PLAN: 2-F1 – *Sint Nicolaasstraat 43 – ✆ 020 233 6544 – www.kaagmanenkortekaas.nl – Closed 2-24 August, lunch Sunday, Monday, lunch Tuesday-Saturday*

La Rive

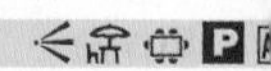

MODERN FRENCH • CHIC On entering this refined establishment, guests immediately sense its rich history, although it is the Amstel that really steals the show here, thanks to the wonderful location on the riverbank. This is a clas restaurant, where the chef also works with the latest trends, taking inspirati from Asia and playing with the acidity balance of his food.

Menu 100/135 € - Carte 130/145 €

PLAN: 2-H3 - *Hotel Amstel, Prof. Tulpplein 1 - ✆ 020 520 3264 - www.restaurantlarive.com - Closed lunch Sunday-Saturday*

Ron Gastrobar Oriental

CHINESE • ORIENTAL Subtle lighting, Asian decor and natural materials set t mood at this stylish restaurant, while a renowned bartender shakes cocktails the extensive bar. Full of flavour, the delicious dishes offer a contemporary ta on traditional Chinese cuisine.

Carte 53/170 €

PLAN: 2-F2 - *Kerkstraat 23 - ✆ 020 223 5352 - www.rongastrobaroriental.nl - Closed lunch Sunday-Saturday*

The Seafood Bar

SEAFOOD • BRASSERIE You will not be surprised to find that this trendy est lishment is a mecca for lovers of seafood. The delicacies glisten on the disp counters and look mouthwatering on the plate, prepared with the minimum fuss. The extensive array of fresh ingredients guarantees a superb meal.

Carte 31/125 €

PLAN: 2-F2 - *Spui 15 - ✆ 020 233 7452 - www.theseafoodbar.com*

Senses

MODERN CUISINE • INTIMATE Lars Bertelsen is a chef bursting with creativ as guests will notice in the presentation, diverse textures and sometimes surp ing flavour combinations in his food. He is also highly talented, as proven by entire experience at Senses. The restyling of the cosy, colourful room emphasi his ambition.

Menu 54/81 €

PLAN: 2-G2 - *Hotel The Albus, Vijzelstraat 45 - ✆ 020 530 6266 - www.sensesrestaurant.nl*

De Silveren Spiegel

CREATIVE FRENCH • HISTORIC The authentic interior of these two buildi with stepped gables, dating back to 1614, has stood the test of time, retain features such as a warm open hearth with matching tiles. In stark contrast w the decor, the food is modern down to the last detail. The young chef wo mainly with Dutch ingredients and has a well-deserved reputation.

Menu 55/96 € - Carte 68/75 €

PLAN: 2-G1 - *Kattengat 4 - ✆ 020 624 6589 - www.desilverenspiegel.com - Closed 27 July-9 August, Sunday, lunch Monday-Saturday*

d'Vijff Vlieghen

TRADITIONAL CUISINE • HISTORIC The classic dishes on offer at these char ing 17C premises are all prepared with typical Dutch products. Various attracti country-style dining rooms where original Rembrandt sketches decorate the wa

Menu 48/58 € - Carte 40/55 €

PLAN: 2-F2 - *Spuistraat 294 - ✆ 020 530 4060 - www.vijffvlieghen.nl - Closed 27 April, lunch Sunday-Saturday*

Watergang

EUROPEAN CONTEMPORARY • BISTRO This lovely little restaurant with space for just 30 guests boasts a genuine warmth and intimacy. The chefs here create a surprise five-course menu that changes each month and is particularly inspired by French and Italian cuisine. The classic comfort food on offer here, featuring the occasional original twist, is highly satisfying!

Menu 46€

PLAN: 2-F3 - *Weteringstraat 41 - ✆ 020 786 6246 - www.restaurantwatergang.nl - Closed Monday, Tuesday, lunch Wednesday-Saturday*

Wolf Atelier

MODERN FRENCH • CONTEMPORARY DÉCOR Michael Wolf plays with flavours and modern combinations, offering diners the opportunity to test them out (as well as a choice of regular dishes), then refines them to retain their best features. The name Atelier is therefore particularly appropriate in this trendy, industrial-style restaurant, which is located on an old railway bridge with a beautiful view of the IJ.

Menu 46/79€ - Carte 51/63€

PLAN: 1-C1 - *Westerdoksplein 20 - ✆ 020 344 6428 - www.wolfatelier.nl - Closed 17-30 August, Sunday*

Museumplein

RIJKS®

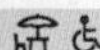

CREATIVE • CONTEMPORARY DÉCOR This lively luxurious brasserie is the culinary pearl of the Rijksmuseum, where guests can enjoy watching the chefs preparing dishes at the kitchen islands. Chef Bijdendijk is full of ideas and seeks to refine typical Dutch produce, with his delicious creativity reflecting exotic influences and an eye for refinement.

Specialities: Scallop with radish, codium and seaweed vinaigrette. Dry-aged duck: breast, drumstick, heart and egg. Roasted beetroot in a salt crust with almond macaroon and hibiscus.

Menu 42€ (lunch)/79€ - Carte 40/65€

PLAN: 2-F3 - *Museumstraat 2 - ✆ 020 674 7555 - www.rijksrestaurant.nl - Closed 27 April, 3-16 August, 31 December-1 January, dinner Sunday*

Brasserie van Baerle

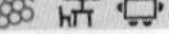

CLASSIC CUISINE • VINTAGE This retro brasserie attracts regular customers, mainly from the local area because of its appealing menu, tasty steak tartare and well-matched wines. Courtyard terrace.

Menu 37/49€ - Carte 49/55€

PLAN: 1-B2 - *Van Baerlestraat 158 - ✆ 020 679 1532 - www.brasserievanbaerle.nl - Closed 31 December-1 January, lunch Monday, lunch Saturday*

Oud-Zuid

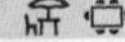

TRADITIONAL CUISINE • BRASSERIE This restaurant, which is full of character, features a trendy brasserie-style decor and a pleasant pavement terrace where you can sit and enjoy the vibe of this neighbourhood. Here, the chef gives tradition a modern twist through an attractive, no-nonsense and mouthwatering menu which mainly focuses on organic produce. Oud-Zuid is less than a 10min walk from the renowned Concertgebouw.

Menu 30€ (lunch), 37/75€ - Carte 43/67€

PLAN: 1-B2 - *Johannes Verhulststraat 64 - ✆ 020 676 6058 - www.restaurantoudzuid.nl - Closed 25-26 December, 31 December-1 January*

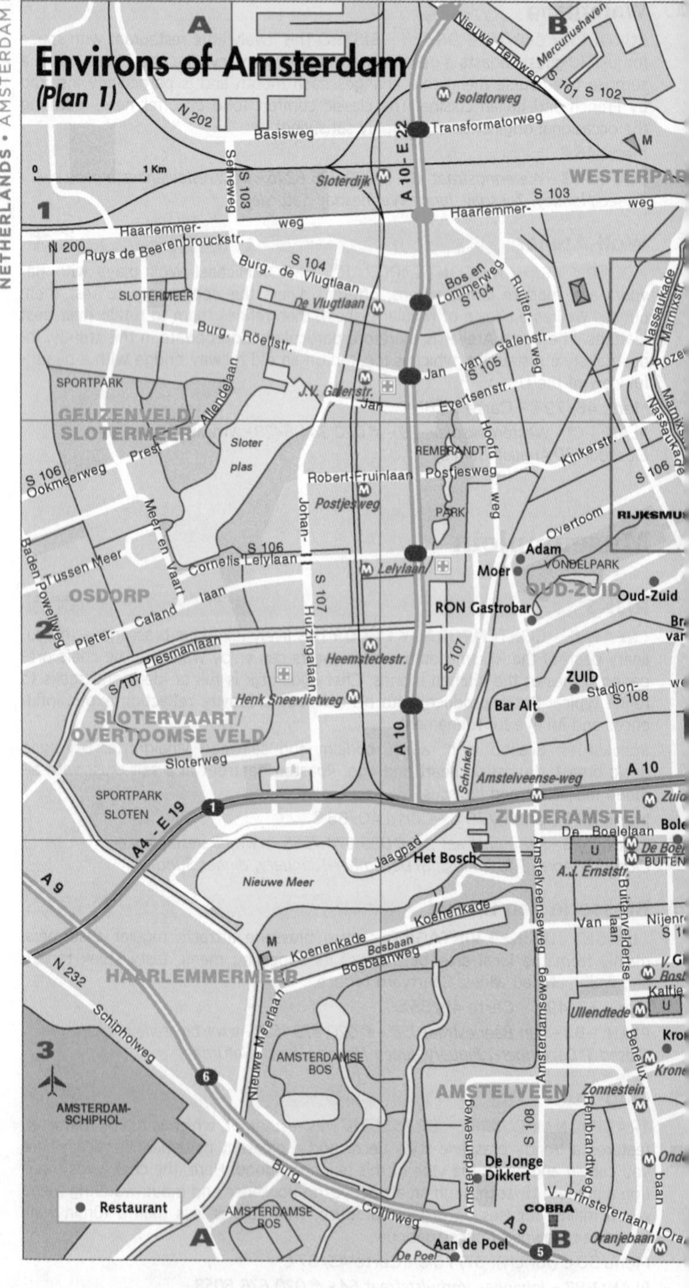
Environs of Amsterdam
(Plan 1)
0
1 Km
Restaurant
A
B
1
2
3
Sloterdijk
Isolatorweg
De Vlugtlaan
J.V. Galenstr.
Postjesweg
Lelylaan
Heemstedestr.
Henk Sneevlietweg
Amstelveense-weg
A.J. Ernststr.
Ullendtede
Zonnestein
GEUZENVELD/
SLOTERMEER
OSDORP
SLOTERVAART/
OVERTOOMSE VELD
HAARLEMMERMEER
AMSTELVEEN
ZUIDERAMSTEL
OUD-ZUID
WESTERPA
SPORTPARK
SPORTPARK
SLOTEN
Sloter
plas
Nieuwe Meer
AMSTERDAMSE
BOS
AMSTERDAM-
SCHIPHOL
Adam
Moer
Oud-Zuid
RON Gastrobar
Bar Alt
Het Bosch
De Jonge
Dikkert
Aan de Poel
COBRA
RIJKSMU
VONDELPARK
REMBRANDT
PARK
ZUID
A 10 - E 22
A 10
A4 - E 19
A 9
N 200
N 202
N 232
S 101
S 102
S 103
S 104
S 105
S 106
S 107
S 108
Transformatorweg
Basisweg
Haarlemmer-
weg
Ruys de Beerenbrouckstr.
Burg. de Vlugtlaan
Bos en Lommerweg
Burg. Röellstr.
Jan van Galenstr.
Jan Evertsenstr.
Kinkerstr.
Robert-Fruinlaan
Postjesweg
Overtoom
Cornelis Lelylaan
Pieter-Calandlaan
Plesmanlaan
Sloterweg
Jaagpad
Koenenkade
Bosbaan
Bosbaanweg
Nieuwe Meerlaan
Schipholweg
Burg. Colijnweg
Amstelveenseweg
Amsterdamseweg
Rembrandtweg
V. Prinstererlaan
Oranjebaan
Buitenveldertse laan
Benelux baan
De Boelelaan
Stadion-
Huizingalaan
Johan-
Baden Powellweg
Tussen Meer
Ookmeerweg
Meer en Vaart
Allendelaan
Hoofdweg
Ruijter-weg
Nieuwe Hemweg
Mercuriushaven
Seineweg
Schinkel
Nassaukade
Marnixstr
Van Nijenr
De Poel

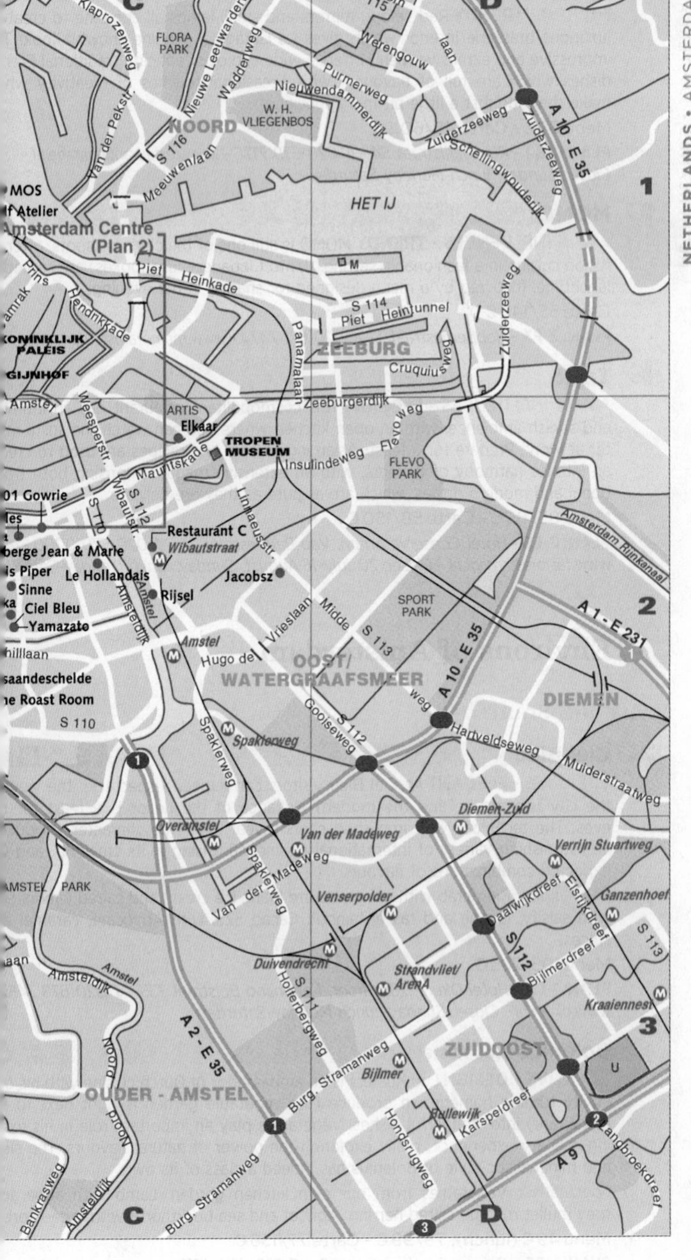
C
D
Klaprozenweg
FLORA PARK
Nieuwe Leeuwarderweg
Wadderweg
Ijdoorn
S 115
Werengouw
laan
Purmerweg
Nieuwendammerdijk
W. H. VLIEGENBOS
NOORD
Van der Pekstr.
S 116
Meeuwenlaan
Zuiderzeeweg
Schellingwouderdijk
A 10 - E 35
1
HET IJ
MOS
Amsterdam Centre (Plan 2)
Piet Heinkade
Prins Hendrikkade
S 114
Piet Heintunnel
Panamalaan
ZEEBURG
Cruquiusweg
KONINKLIJK PALEIS
Amstel
Zeeburgerdijk
Weesperstr.
ARTIS
Elkaar
TROPEN MUSEUM
Mauritskade
Insulindeweg
Flevoweg
FLEVO PARK
Gowrie
S 112
Wibautstr.
S 110
Linnaeusstr.
Amsterdam Rijnkanaal
Restaurant C
Wibautstraat
Jacobsz
Le Hollandais
Amsteldijk
Amstel
Rijsel
Ciel Bleu
Yamazato
Sinne
SPORT PARK
Middenweg
S 113
2
A 1 - E 231
Hugo de Vrieslaan
OOST/ WATERGRAAFSMEER
DIEMEN
The Roast Room
S 110
Gooiseweg
S 112
Spaklerweg
Hartveldseweg
Muiderstraatweg
Overamstel
Van der Madeweg
Diemen-Zuid
Verrijn Stuartweg
AMSTEL PARK
Spaklerweg
Van der Madeweg
Venserpolder
Daalwijkdreef
Elsrijkdreef
Ganzenhoef
S 113
S 112
Duivendrecht
Strandvliet/ ArenA
Bijlmerdreef
Amstel
Amsteldijk
S 111
Holterbergweg
Kraaiennest
3
A 2 - E 35
ZUIDOOST
U
Burg. Stramanweg
Bijlmer
Noord
OUDER - AMSTEL
Bullewijk
Karspeldreef
Hondsrugweg
Landbroekdreef
A 9
Bankrasweg
Amsteldijk
Burg. Stramanweg
C
D

Le Garage

FRENCH • TRENDY Red velour, mirrors and small lamps all combine to creat luxurious brasserie interior which gives Le Garage a genuine showbiz look! T impressive and extensive menu offers a wide choice of enticing traditional Fre dishes which are full of flavour – with occasional touches of creativity wh make the food just a little bit more special.

Menu 37 € - Carte 45/60 €

PLAN: 1-B2 – *Ruysdaelstraat 54 – ✆ 020 679 7176 – www.restaurantlegarage.nl – Closed Sunday, lunch Monday-Saturday*

MOMO

ASIAN INFLUENCES • TRENDY MOMO is still one of the city's hotspots, offe fusion cuisine in a fashionable setting. Bento (Japanese lunchboxes) are servec lunchtime, followed by a menu designed for sharing in the evening.

Carte 55/145 €

PLAN: 2-F3 – *Hobbemastraat 1 – ✆ 020 671 7474 – www.momo-amsterdam.com*

Taiko

ASIAN INFLUENCES • ELEGANT This cosmopolitan restaurant has an intim and stylish ambience, with an open kitchen where you can watch the sushi m ter at work. Prepare for a feast! Asian ingredients and recipes are used to cre an intense harmony of flavours, with an extensive menu comprising both tra tional and modern dishes, which are as pure as they are delicate.

Menu 85/115 € - Carte 58/150 €

PLAN: 2-E3 – *Hotel Conservatorium, Van Baerlestraat 27 – ✆ 020 570 0000 – www.taikorestaurant.nl – Closed 20 July-16 August, Sunday, lunch Monday-Saturo*

Environs of Amsterdam

West and South

Ciel Bleu

CREATIVE • ELEGANT At Ciel Bleu visitors can expect a spectacle: the view the city is fantastic and the modern elegance of the decor is a feast for eyes. The technically accomplished chefs reveal their true character, produc an astonishing variety of international cuisine, surprising in its creativity and expected combinations of flavours.

Specialities: King crab with caviar, beurre blanc ice cream and salted lemon. S with salsify, lovage and ras el hanout. Cacao 52% with Advocaat, caramel spices.

Menu 195/225 €

PLAN: 1-C2 – *Hotel Okura, 23rd floor, Ferdinand Bolstraat 333 – ✆ 020 678 745 www.okura.nl – Closed Sunday, lunch Monday-Saturday*

Bolenius (Luc Kusters)

CREATIVE • DESIGN Luc Kusters is an ambassador of Dutch cuisine with his c ativity turning homegrown produce (the vegetable garden is right next to restaurant) into wonderful dishes. Vegetables play an important role in his ex ing culinary experience, really exploring the power of natural flavours. The sl and minimalistic style of Bolenius has indeed a class of its own.

Specialities: Vegetables from our own kitchen garden. Lamb with auberg grey mullet roe and salted herring. Apricot and sea buckthorns with cacao sor

Menu 49 € (lunch), 79/99 € - Carte 77/136 €

PLAN: 1-B2 – *George Gershwinlaan 30 – ✆ 020 404 4411 – www.bolenius-restaurant.nl – Closed 1-17 August, 26 December-4 January, Sunday*

✿ Le Restaurant (Jan de Wit)

MARKET CUISINE • BISTRO Le Restaurant is as diverse and lively as its surrounding De Pijp neighbourhood. Don't let the somewhat anonymous façade fool you as inside you will find a cosy restaurant with an informal bistro feel. Jan de Wit's formula for success remains the same: a simple but spectacular menu. The best of market produce is prepared without too much fuss and plated up in its authentic form to convince diners with its powerful flavours. The price-pleasure ratio is spot on.

Specialities: Scallops with celeriac and vadouvan sabayon. Roasted veal tenderloin with asparagus, broad beans and gravy. Warm chocolate mousse with liquorice parfait and meringue.

Menu 40/85€

PLAN: 2-F3 – *Frans Halsstraat 26H – ✆ 020 379 2207 – www.lerestaurant.nl – Closed 28 April-7 May, 14 July-5 August, 24 December-6 January, Sunday, Monday, lunch Tuesday-Saturday*

✿ RON Gastrobar (Ron Blaauw)

CREATIVE FRENCH • TRENDY Ron Blaauw returns to basics here, creating cuisine that is pure and prepared with quality ingredients. This urban gastro-bar combines a hip, lively ambience with top class cuisine without the frills. It also means little formality but original, delicious food and sensational flavours. Phenomenal value for money, which is also reflected in the wine list.

Specialities: Omelette of peas with King crab and chorizo. Barbecue spare ribs with home-made sambal. Surprise egg.

Menu 44€ (lunch)/70€ – Carte 62/190€

PLAN: 1-B2 – *Sophialaan 55 – ✆ 020 496 1943 – www.rongastrobar.nl*

✿ Sinne (Alexander Ioannou)

MODERN CUISINE • TRENDY The open-plan kitchen at the back of this warm and friendly restaurant is reminiscent of a theatre scene. Chef Ioannou adds the finishing touch to dishes where French, Mediterranean and Oriental influences meet. The result is remarkable – dishes full of wonderful and complex flavours at affordable prices.

Specialities: Brioche with BBQ chicken, porcini mushrooms and mayonnaise with green herbs. Crispy fried sweetbread, pointed cabbage with kencur, enoki and veal jus with star anise. Poached peach with white chocolate, raspberries, vanilla crumble and sea buckthorn sorbet.

Menu 39/89€

PLAN: 1-C2 – *Ceintuurbaan 342 – ✆ 020 682 7290 – www.restaurantsinne.nl – Closed 22 July-13 August, Monday, Tuesday, lunch Wednesday-Saturday*

✿ Yamazato

JAPANESE • MINIMALIST The intimate, spartan interior and view of the Japanese garden produce a Zen feel. Ladies in kimonos bring authentic kaiseki dishes to the table, showcasing the subtlety and technical accomplishment of Japanese cuisine. This place honours tradition, as visitors will also discover when ordering a simple bento box lunch.

Specialities: Omakase and nigiri sushi. Lobster tempura. Japanese green tea ice cream with red beans and sake.

Menu 50€ (lunch), 105/135€ – Carte 40/160€

PLAN: 1-C2 – *Hotel Okura, 23rd floor, Ferdinand Bolstraat 333 – ✆ 020 678 7450 – www.okura.nl – Closed lunch Monday-Friday*

Arles

MODERN FRENCH • BISTRO This attractive bistro brings a touch of Provence Amsterdam, with framed photos of the chef's native city Arles adorning the wal The chef, a fan of jazz music, creates neo-bistro-style dishes which offer a fre reinterpretation of familiar French flavours. The fixed-price menu, which chang every month, is a real winner!

Menu 37/50 €

PLAN: 1-C2 – *Govert Flinckstraat 251 – ✆ 020 679 8240 – www.arles-amsterdam.nl Closed lunch Sunday-Saturday*

Auberge Jean & Marie

FRENCH • INN Whether you choose to go to the back of the restaurant to sele your own bottle from the wine cellar or you ask Jan and Marije for their exce tional advice, you'll be spoilt for choice in this delightfully informal restaura which is perfect for wine lovers. Rich and tasty traditional French cuisine wi the occasional contemporary twist accompanies these fine wines.

Menu 37/46 € – Carte 37/100 €

PLAN: 1-C2 – *Albert Cuypstraat 58 – ✆ 020 845 2005 – www.aubergeamsterdam.nl – Closed Monday*

Café Caron

CLASSIC FRENCH • BISTRO This cosy bistro is run by Alain Caron (a we known TV personality and chef) and his family. The ambience here is typical French, as is the menu which features traditional, generous bistro-style dish which are a work of art in their own right. Trying out the set menu here is a re joy.

Menu 37 € – Carte 39/49 €

PLAN: 2-F3 – *Frans Halsstraat 28 – ✆ 020 675 8668 – www.cafecaron.nl – Closed lunch Sunday-Saturday*

Serre

MODERN CUISINE • BRASSERIE Like Okura's other restaurants, quality is th focus of this chic brasserie, with its magnificent canal-side terrace. Exceller ingredients go into the international cuisine served here. The chef select techniques from diverse cuisines, unifying them in straightforwardly deliciou dishes.

Menu 37/70 € – Carte 45/70 €

PLAN: 1-C2 – *Hotel Okura, 23rd floor, Ferdinand Bolstraat 333 – ✆ 020 678 7450 www.okura.nl*

101 Gowrie

CREATIVE • SIMPLE Dutch cuisine seen through the eyes of an Australian che with Japanese and German roots is a certain recipe for success. In this restauran with the feel of a private living room, Alex Haupt gives full range to his creativit using Dutch products and traditional recipes to create exciting spicy, sweet an sour dishes. Make sure you try his natural wines!

Menu 55/79 €

PLAN: 1-C2 – *Govert Flinckstraat 326 – ✆ 020 334 6418 – www.101gowrie.com – Closed 6-20 January, 3-31 August, Sunday, Monday, lunch Tuesday-Saturday*

Adam

MODERN CUISINE • FRIENDLY Don't be afraid to put your faith in the hands o the talented Arne Russchen. His surprise menu shows that he enjoys playing wit contrasts and creating bold combinations, without losing control. His contempo rary approach and his relationship with small suppliers result in dishes which ar pleasing to the eye and the palate.

Menu 39/62 € – Carte 42/72 €

PLAN: 1-B2 – *Overtoom 515a – ✆ 020 233 9852 – www.restaurantadam.nl – Closed Sunday, Monday, lunch Tuesday-Saturday*

Bar Alt

CONTEMPORARY • BRASSERIE Bar Alt is the combined story of a talented chef and enthusiastic beer brewers. In this relaxed restaurant featuring an industrial design and decor, discover the full pleasures of beer as you explore its extremely elaborate menu. The highly contemporary cuisine is internationally inspired, playful and creative.

Menu 30€ (lunch), 70/90€

PLAN: 1-B2 – *Stadionplein 103 – ✆ 06 30941899 – www.bar-alt.com – Closed Sunday, Monday, lunch Tuesday-Wednesday*

Het Bosch

MODERN FRENCH • TRENDY From this contemporary restaurant diners enjoy a breathtaking view of the Nieuwe Meer marina. In this dream location the chef entertains diners with lavish, up-to-date dishes prepared with real know-how.

Menu 42€ (lunch), 49/64€ – Carte 50/65€

PLAN: 1-B3 – *Jollenpad 10 – ✆ 020 644 5800 – www.hetbosch.com – Closed Sunday, lunch Saturday*

Gijsbrecht

MODERN CUISINE • CONTEMPORARY DÉCOR Every now and then you'll wonder if you are still in Amsterdam in this restaurant, which is situated in the tranquil haven of Gijsbrecht van Aemstelpark. Here, a light-filled interior brightened with vintage colours acts as the backdrop for a variety of modern, local dishes which are complemented by an interesting wine list.

Carte 38/47€

PLAN: 1-B3 – *Van Leijenberghlaan 320 – ✆ 020 225 9124 – www.restaurantgijsbrecht.com*

Graham's Kitchen

MODERN BRITISH • FRIENDLY Graham Mee's cuisine not only reflects his English origins, but also demonstrates his creative flair and his ability to prepare strong dishes, thanks to his experience in top-class establishments. The restaurant's cosy interior is equally attractive, with an eye-catching mural forming part of the decor.

Menu 39/69€

PLAN: 2-F1 – *Hemonystraat 38 – ✆ 020 364 2560 – www.grahamskitchen.amsterdam – Closed Sunday, Monday, lunch Tuesday-Saturday*

Le Hollandais

CLASSIC CUISINE • VINTAGE Feeling a little nostalgic? Then this is the place for you, as Le Hollandais really turns the clock back. The dining hall is reminiscent of the 1970s and the chef still serves up generous dishes with rich flavours, just like the old days. You will experience classic French cuisine the way it is meant to taste.

Menu 37/55€ – Carte 45/65€

PLAN: 1-C2 – *Amsteldijk 41 – ✆ 020 679 1248 – www.lehollandais.nl – Closed 5-26 August, 24 December-4 January, Sunday, Monday, lunch Tuesday-Saturday*

Izakaya

JAPANESE • BRASSERIE Head off on a voyage of discovery in this beautiful brasserie. Enjoy individual flavours influenced by Japanese cuisine. The small servings allow you to carry out an extensive exploration of the menu.

Menu 25€ (lunch)/30€ – Carte 35/95€

PLAN: 1-C2 – *Sir Albert, Albert Cuypstraat 6 – ✆ 020 305 3090 – www.izakaya-amsterdam.com*

Lars Amsterdam

MODERN FRENCH • CONTEMPORARY DÉCOR Combining an industrial v with an intimate living room feel, Lars is situated at the end of the Houthave and boasts stunning views across the water. In the kitchen, the ambitious L Scharp plays with French traditions and fresh Asian flavours to create bold cc temporary dishes that are a world away from traditional cuisine.

Menu 30 € (lunch), 58/98 € – Carte 72/98 €

Off plan – *Danzigerkade 179 – ✆ 020 214 9729 – www.larsamsterdam.nl – Closed Sunday*

Maris Piper

MODERN CUISINE • CONTEMPORARY DÉCOR There is a chic, London-st atmosphere in this large luxurious brasserie. The menu is equally good w dishes which are not unnecessarily complex yet full of strong flavours and p pared by a chef who delights his guests with his internationally influenced dish The Chef's Table (only available in the evening) is a real experience.

Carte 50/94 €

PLAN: 1-C2 – *Frans Halsstraat 76 – ✆ 020 737 2479 – www.maris-piper.com*

Moer

ORGANIC • NEIGHBOURHOOD The wrenches remind you that this trendy, dustrial restaurant was once a garage. Here, the focus is on organic produ both on your plate and in your glass. Although fish and meat feature on menu, the chef dedicates his attention specifically to vegetables, proving ti and time again that vegetarian dishes can be delicate and versatile!

Menu 30 € (lunch), 44/68 € – Carte 33/54 €

PLAN: 1-B2 – *Amstelveenseweg 7 – ✆ 020 820 3330 – www.restaurantmoer.nl – Closed Monday*

The Roast Room

MEATS AND GRILLS • TRENDY An impressive steakhouse. Glass, steel, wc and meat are the dominant features of the Roast Bar (ground floor brasse and the Rotisserie (upstairs restaurant). See the meat hanging ready to co smell it on the grill and taste the results when it has been cooked to perfecti Excellent side dishes complete the picture.

Menu 48/58 € – Carte 50/90 €

PLAN: 1-C2 – *Europaplein 2 – ✆ 020 723 9614 – www.theroastroom.nl – Closed lunch Sunday, lunch Saturday*

Sazanka

TEPPANYAKI • FRIENDLY After being greeted by ladies dressed in kimon you sit down around the teppenyaki grill and the show begins. Seven to ten p ple can be accommodated here to watch the teppan-chef juggle with all kinds produce. It is an entertaining spectacle that results in delicious Japanese dishe

Menu 115/185 € – Carte 60/115 €

PLAN: 1-C2 – *Hotel Okura, 23rd floor, Ferdinand Bolstraat 333 – ✆ 020 678 745 www.okura.nl – Closed lunch Sunday-Saturday*

Visaandeschelde

SEAFOOD • TRADITIONAL The Scheldeplein is the place to come for tasty f The attractive nautical décor and the lively atmosphere contribute to the succ it has achieved since 1999. Guests love to come and enjoy fresh delicac plucked straight from the sea. A creative approach to classic combinations gi the flavours plenty of punch!

Menu 45/65 € – Carte 65/90 €

PLAN: 1-C2 – *Scheldeplein 4 – ✆ 020 675 1583 – www.visaandeschelde.nl – Closed lunch Sunday, lunch Saturday*

ZUID 

MODERN FRENCH • TRENDY Zuid-Amsterdam is booming, as is demonstrated by establishments such as ZUID. This pleasant restaurant is open throughout the day; whether you choose a sandwich or a three-course dinner, you can rest assured it will be delicious. The cuisine is modern, varied and international in flavour. No fuss and plenty of fun!

Menu 28 € (lunch), 35/51 € – Carte 35/46 €

PLAN: 1-B2 – *Stadionweg 320 – ✆ 020 210 3321 – www.restaurantzuid.amsterdam – Closed Monday*

ast

Elkaar 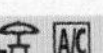

MODERN FRENCH • FAMILY If you are looking for a relaxed meal out together, this friendly establishment with a pleasant summer terrace is a great option. The set menu is a good choice, offering a selection from the à la carte menu. The chef combines quality ingredients in a contemporary manner, creating beautiful flavours without overcomplicating things.

Menu 37/55 € – Carte 45/55 €

PLAN: 1-C2 – *Alexanderplein 6 – ✆ 020 330 7559 – www.etenbijelkaar.nl – Closed 1-14 January, 18-31 August, Sunday, Monday, lunch Tuesday-Saturday*

Rijsel

TRADITIONAL CUISINE • SIMPLE Rijsel's simple interior resembles a classroom, and the restaurant happens to share its entrance with a school. In the open kitchen you can see the master at work preparing his delicious French cuisine. He has an excellent knowledge of ingredients and his traditional dishes also include a nod to Flemish food.

Menu 37/55 €

PLAN: 1-C2 – *Marcusstraat 52b – ✆ 020 463 2142 – www.rijsel.com – Closed 27 April, 1-14 August, Sunday, lunch Monday-Saturday*

Jacobsz 

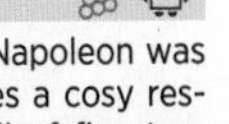

SEASONAL CUISINE • FRIENDLY It was here that 200 years ago Napoleon was given the keys to the city of Amsterdam. Today the building houses a cosy restaurant serving delicious contemporary cuisine, which is varied, full of fine textures and flavoured with exotic touches here and there. A good wine selection completes this delightful picture.

Menu 37/59 €

PLAN: 1-C2 – *Ringdijk 1 – ✆ 06 42454677 – www.jacobsz.amsterdam – Closed 27 April, Sunday, lunch Monday-Saturday*

Restaurant C 

CREATIVE FRENCH • TRENDY The contemporary, chic Restaurant Celsius is a dazzling spot, especially the kitchen bar. The reference to degrees emphasises the precision the chefs strive for, because that is what makes the difference between good food and delicious cuisine. Creativity in the combination of strong flavours and textures makes C a top choice.

Menu 35 € (lunch), 48/78 € – Carte 40/55 €

PLAN: 1-C2 – *Wibautstraat 125 – ✆ 020 210 3011 – www.c.amsterdam – Closed lunch Monday-Thursday*

Amstelveen

✿✿ Aan de Poel (Stefan van Sprang) 

CREATIVE • ELEGANT A successful marriage of technical skill and brilliant produce ensures that every dish is a feast for the senses. Here, contemporary cuisine can be savoured in one of its most beautiful and tasteful forms. What's more, this restaurant benefits from a superb lakeside setting, a chic and sophisticated designer interior and a skilled sommelier.

Specialities: Roasted spicy langoustines with mango, cucumber and peca Grilled succade with goose liver terrine and morel sauce. Sugar-blown carr with Dulce de leche, dragon fruit and passion fruit.

Menu 58 € (lunch), 115/125 € – Carte 88/123 €

PLAN: 1-B3 – *Handweg 1 – ✆ 020 345 1763 – www.aandepoel.nl – Closed 12-27 July, 27-31 December, Sunday, Monday, lunch Saturday*

De Jonge Dikkert

COUNTRY COOKING • ROMANTIC The Jonge Dikkert has given this 17C wir mill a new lease of life with its modern decor, intimate atmosphere and attracti dining room with wooden beams. Here the chef uses predominantly Dutch pr duce (up to 80%!) in his creative, contemporary-style dishes, resulting in a su prisingly refined cuisine.

Menu 35 € (lunch), 38/79 € – Carte 41/61 €

PLAN: 1-B3 – *Amsterdamseweg 104a – ✆ 020 643 3333 – www.jongedikkert.nl – Closed 19 July-16 August, 31 December-5 January, lunch Sunday, lunch Saturday*

Kronenburg

MODERN CUISINE • TRENDY This is a welcome oasis in the Kronenburg bu ness quarter, where you can dine surrounded by lush greenery beside a lake, e joying the beautiful setting through the glass façade of the terrace. The light, a interior is equally stunning. The young chef here creates modest-sized dish with sophisticated, diverse and delicious modern flavours.

Menu 29 € (lunch), 36/49 € – Carte 36/42 €

PLAN: 1-B3 – *Prof. E.M. Meijerslaan 6 – ✆ 020 345 5489 – www.restaurant-kronenburg.nl – Closed 1-6 January, 27 July-10 August, Sunday, lunch Saturday*

ROTTERDAM
ROTTERDAM

DutchScenery/iStock

ROTTERDAM IN...

→ **ONE DAY**
Blaak area including Kijk-Kubus and Boompjestorens, Oude Haven, Museum Boijmans Van Beuningen.

→ **TWO DAYS**
More Museumpark, Delfshaven, take in the view from Euromast, cruise along the Nieuwe Maas.

→ **THREE DAYS**
Kop Van Zuid, a show at the Luxor Theatre.

Rotterdam trades on it earthy appeal, on a roug and ready grittiness that tie in with its status as the larges seaport in the world; it handle 350 million tonnes of goods year, with over half of all th freight that is heading int Europe passing through i Flattened during the Secon World War, Rotterdam wa rebuilt on a grand scale, jet tisoning the idea of streets full of terraced houses in favou of a modern cityscape of concrete and glass, and there ar few places in the world that have such an eclectic range c buildings to keep you entertained (or bewildered): try th Euromast Space Tower, the Groothandelsgebouw (whic

translates as 'wholesale building'), the 'Cube Houses' or the fabulous sounding Boompjestorens for size. The city is located on the Nieuwe Maas but is centred around a maze of other rivers – most importantly the Rhine and the Maas – and is only a few dozen kilometres inland from the North Sea. It spills over both banks, and is linked by tunnels, bridges and the metro; the most stunning connection across the water is the modern Erasmusbridge, whose graceful, angular lines of silver tubing have earned it the nickname 'The Swan', and whose sleek design has come to embody the Rotterdam of the new millennium. It's mirrored on the southern banks by the development of the previously rundown Kop Van Zuid area into a sleek, modern zone.

EATING OUT

otterdam is a hot place for dining, the literal and metaphorical sense. here are lots of places to tuck into ne flavours of Holland's colonial ast, in particular the spicy delicacies f Indonesia and Surinam. The long ast/west stretch of Oude and Nieuwe nnenweg is not only handy for many f the sights, it's also chock-full of good afés, café-bars and restaurants, and ne canal district of Oudehaven has troduced to the city a good selec- on of places to eat while taking in ne relaxed vibe. Along the water- ont, various warehouses have been transformed into mega-restaurants, particularly around the Noordereiland isle in the middle of the river, while in Kop Van Zuid, the Wilhelminapier Quay offers quality restaurants and tasty views too. Many establishments are closed at lunchtime, except business restaurants and those that set a high gastronomic standard and like to show it off in the middle of the day as well as in the evening. The bill includes a service charge, so tipping is optional: round up the total if you're pleased with the service.

✿✿ FG - François Geurds

CREATIVE • TRENDY François Geurds has a clear vision and he brings it to l in this restaurant, which is urban, trendy and original. The chef adopts a st that is very detailed, sometimes even playful, but always keeps his focus on t flavours of his high quality ingredients and sauces. FG could easily stand for Fa tastically Good!

Specialities: Potato with marrow and caviar. Anjou pigeon with cherry sorbet a duck liver. Blend of chocolate and blood orange.

Menu 78 € (lunch), 130/210 € - Carte 108/220 €

PLAN: A1 - *Katshoek 37B - ✆ 010 425 0520 - www.fgrestaurant.nl - Closed Sunday, Monday, lunch Tuesday-Thursday*

✿ **FG Food Labs** - See restaurant listing

✿✿ Fred (Fred Mustert)

CREATIVE FRENCH • CHIC Fred Mustert takes his guests on a culinary adv ture in this stylish restaurant, which boasts decorative highlights such as a leat and 24-carat gold work of art and an impressive lighting installation. Less really more according to chef Mustert, who creates well-balanced culinary masterpie which are exciting, modern and with no unnecessary frills.

Specialities: Baked langoustines with melon, blanched celery and a mild cu vinaigrette. Sweetbread and duck liver with pistachio, beetroot, artichoke a Madeira sauce. Parfait of nougat, compote of banana, vanilla foam and ca glacé.

Menu 50 € (lunch), 110/150 € - Carte 86/106 €

Off plan - *Honingerdijk 263 - ✆ 010 212 0110 - www.restaurantfred.nl - Closed 3-16 August, 25 December-1 January, Sunday, lunch Saturday*

✿✿ Parkheuvel (Erik van Loo)

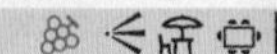

MODERN CUISINE • ELEGANT The elegant Parkheuvel, beautifully situated l side the river Maas, is a big name in Dutch gastronomy. It received its first Mic lin Star in 1990 - and Erik van Loo upholds this tradition with cuisine that's w crafted, meticulously prepared and has a natural generosity. His signature dis are must-tries!

Specialities: Bresse chicken with langoustine ravioli, wild mushrooms and lobs jus. Dutch lamb with artichoke, ratatouille, broad beans and aubergine. Parkh vel-style "Snickers" with peanut, caramel and nougatine.

Menu 62 € (lunch), 110/150 € - Carte 88/125 €

PLAN: A3 - *Heuvellaan 21 - ✆ 010 436 0766 - www.parkheuvel.nl - Closed 26-27 February, 3-25 August, 27 December-5 January dinner Sunday, Monday, Tuesday, lunch Saturday*

✿ Amarone (Jan van Dobben)

MODERN FRENCH • CHIC A cosy open fire and a warm and fashionable in rior... elegance is a quality this restaurant and the wine after which it is nam share. Amarone has a prominent place on the impressive wine list, which be tifully complements the creative dishes from Jan van Dobben. Combinations well-thought-through and, although the flavours can sometimes provide c trasts, they are always in harmony.

Specialities: Terrine of duck liver with yoghurt and matcha. Poached veal t derloin with goose liver ravioli, seasonal vegetables and truffle bouillon. Ch olate ganache with pistachio crumble, orange and cardamom, pistachio cream.

Menu 40 € (lunch), 70/100 € - Carte 74/147 €

PLAN: B1 - *Meent 72a - ✆ 010 414 8487 - www.restaurantamarone.nl - Closed Sunday, lunch Saturday*

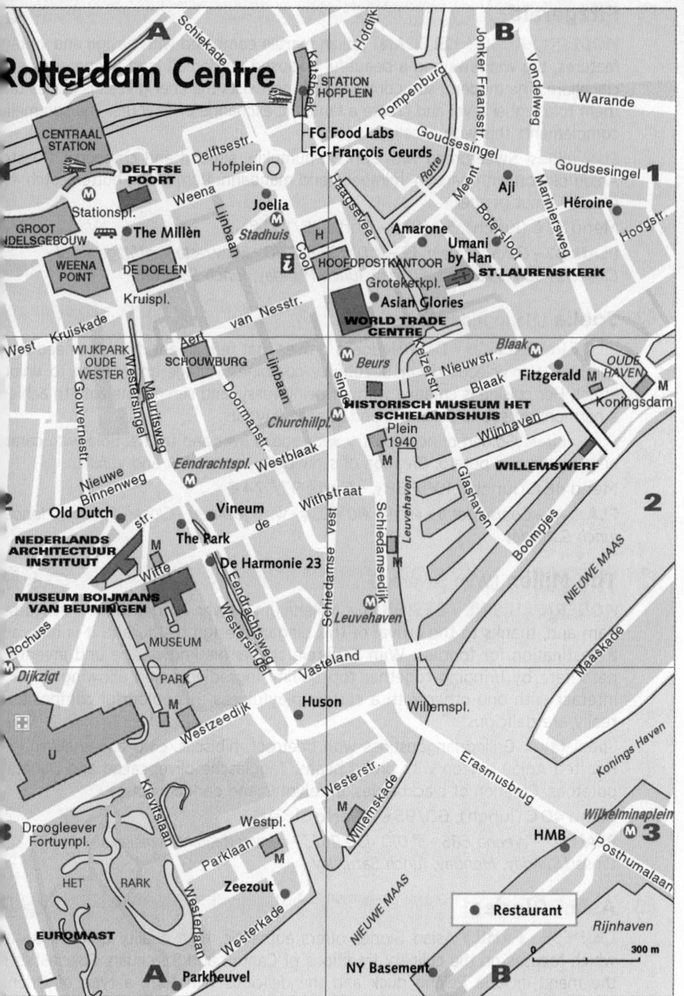

FG Food Labs (François Geurds)

CREATIVE • TRENDY This 'taste laboratory', housed in a trendy version of a train tunnel, is definitely part of the Rotterdam scene. The emphasis is on new flavours and textures and on pushing culinary boundaries. This results in inventive cuisine that is bold and full of character.

Specialities: Nitro "Lab style" in a mortar. Baked cod with oysters, lobster and roasted leek. Chicken-skin, pistachio and popcorn dessert.

Menu 45€ (lunch), 85/125€ - Carte 60/85€

PLAN: A1 - *FG - François Geurds, Katshoek 41 - ✆ 010 425 0520 - www.fgfoodlabs.nl*

✿ Fitzgerald 

MODERN FRENCH • ELEGANT Italian marble combined with design and vintag features, big windows and a beautiful enclosed garden all lend Fitzgerald a sp cial allure. The modern, sometimes surprising twists the chef gives his dishes tal them to a higher level and create a fantastic exchange of flavours. The sommeli complements this with excellent wines.

Specialities: Sweetbread with apricot, pumpkin, almond and cranberry. Roaste Anjou pigeon with parsnip, mirabelle and mandarin. Rum baba, butterscotch, c rus and timut pepper.

Menu 32€ (lunch), 50/91€ - Carte 75/102€

PLAN: B2 - *Gelderseplein 49 - ✆ 010 268 7010 - www.restaurantfitzgerald.nl - Closed 27 July-9 August, Sunday, lunch Monday, lunch Saturday*

✿ Joelia (Mario Ridder)

MODERN FRENCH • DESIGN Joelia proves that refinement does not need to l complex. Her eclectic decor beautifully combines vintage and design to uniq effect. Her cuisine is creative without being fussy, and serves one aim: to achie a harmony of subtle perfumes and intense flavours.

Specialities: Golden brioche pastry with goose liver and truffle. Sole with carab nero prawn and potato. Creation of strawberry, buttermilk and vanilla.

Menu 48€ (lunch), 108/168€ - Carte 97/174€

PLAN: A1 - *Coolsingel 5 - ✆ 010 710 8034 - www.joelia.eu - Closed Sunday, Monda lunch Saturday*

✿ The Millèn (Wim Severein)

MODERN CUISINE • DESIGN The Millennium Tower is a landmark in Rotte dam and, thanks to the arrival of this elegant design restaurant, it is now al a destination for foodies. Wim Severein shows his knowledge and inventiv ness here by bringing together top quality ingredients and allowing them interact with one other with a certain playfulness. His colourful compositio really are delicious!

Specialities: Grilled langoustines with beetroot, hibiscus, curd and shellfish jel Roasted Anjou pigeon with broad beans, Taggiasche olive, cacao and Dauphi potatoes. Creation of blackberries, eucalyptus and dark chocolate.

Menu 40€ (lunch), 60/95€ - Carte 51/81€

PLAN: A1 - *Weena 686 - ✆ 010 430 2333 - www.restaurantthemillen.nl - Closed Sunday, Monday, lunch Saturday*

Asian Glories

CHINESE • FAMILY Asian Glories offers authentic, high quality Chinese cuisir which focuses on the culinary traditions of Canton and Szechuan. Specialities the menu include Peking duck and the delicious dim sum, a type of Orien dumpling that is served either boiled or fried.

Menu 34/54€ - Carte 34/50€

PLAN: B1 - *Leeuwenstraat 15a - ✆ 010 411 7107 - www.asianglories.nl - Closed Wednesday*

Gym & Gin

INTERNATIONAL • VINTAGE The vintage colours and designer furniture in t open-plan restaurant give it a vibrant, funky ambience - the perfect setting chef Kevin Valkhoff's exciting cuisine, which is full of subtle Asian influences a original flavours. The name Gym & Gin is a reference to the balance we all ha to find between pleasure and healthy living - the choice is yours!

Menu 36/54€ - Carte 34/55€

Off plan - *Kralingseweg 224 - ✆ 010 210 4510 - www.gymandgin.nl - Closed 27 December-5 January, Sunday*

Huson

MODERN CUISINE • FRIENDLY Huson is a trendy establishment where a lively industriousness always prevails. Here guests' mouths will water at the marvellous pairing of creativity with international ingredients in small dishes which are as subtle as they are exuberant. The chef is a dab hand at beautifully balancing fullness of flavour with freshness, as his signature dishes show.

Menu 36/80€ – Carte 35/65€

PLAN: A3 – *Scheepstimmermanslaan 14 – ✆ 010 413 0371 – www.huson.nl – Closed lunch Saturday*

In den Rustwat

MODERN CUISINE • INTIMATE In den Rustwat adds an exotic touch to metropolitan Rotterdam with its thatched roof, history dating back to the 16C and an idyllic setting close to an arboretum. The food here is anything but traditional, offering contemporary-style dishes with an abundance of ingredients and cooking methods.

Menu 35€ (lunch), 37/79€ – Carte 52/79€

Off plan – *Honingerdijk 96 – ✆ 010 413 4110 – www.idrw.nl – Closed 20 July-18 August, 29 December-7 January, Sunday, Monday, lunch Saturday*

Kwiezien

MARKET CUISINE • FAMILY Sit back and enjoy the tempting range of dishes which this cosy restaurant has put together. Karin and Remco work exclusively with fresh ingredients and are constantly in search of inspiring combinations. The rich palette of flavours they create is sometimes daring but they always pull it off.

Menu 35/50€

Off plan – *Delistraat 20 – ✆ 010 215 1440 – www.kwiezien.nl – Closed 1 January, 25-26 December, Sunday, Monday, Tuesday, lunch Wednesday-Saturday*

The Park

MODERN CUISINE • TRENDY In this stylish luxury brasserie, brightened with occasional touches of blue, the beautifully presented cuisine is as attractive as the setting. Here, the generous chef prepares creative, inspired and well-composed dishes which are full of fresh Mediterranean flavours, ensuring that guests leave the restaurant feeling completely satisfied.

Menu 33€ (lunch), 37/63€ – Carte 43/64€

PLAN: A2 – *Parkhotel, Westersingel 70 – ✆ 010 440 8165 – www.thepark.nl – Closed 26 July-18 August, Sunday, lunch Saturday*

Umami by Han

ASIAN • TRENDY The trendy, modern interior with bright colours immediately catches the eye, but the trump card of this restaurant is its rock solid concept... a range of Asian dishes with a French twist from which you can choose your heart's desire. A wonderful journey of discovery at amazing prices!

Menu 19€ (lunch), 29/43€

PLAN: B1 – *Binnenrotte 140 – ✆ 010 433 3139 – www.umami-restaurant.com – Closed lunch Monday-Tuesday*

Aji

SOUTH AMERICAN • VINTAGE Aji (a type of chilli pepper) is one of the ingredients that Pelle Swinkels discovered on his travels through Asia and South America – travels which have had a strong influence on his menu. He mixes these influences with basic French techniques to create delicious and intriguing dishes with an adventurous feel which is echoed in the restaurant's bold, vintage lounge-style decor.

Menu 28€ (lunch)/33€ – Carte 37/54€

PLAN: B1 – *Pannekoekstraat 40A – ✆ 010 767 0169 – www.restaurantaji.nl – Closed 22 July-4 August, Sunday, Monday*

C.E.O baas van het vlees

MEATS AND GRILLS • CONTEMPORARY DÉCOR Top-quality meat cooked the American grill is the secret to the success of this lively, urban bistro. The sult is meat that melts in the mouth, accompanied by sophisticated garnish which add both freshness and texture. If you're part of a larger table, make s you order the charcuterie platter and the bigger steaks on the menu.

Carte 41/83€

Off plan – *Sumatraweg 1 – ✆ 010 290 9454 – www.ceobaasvanhetvlees.nl – Closed Sunday, Monday, lunch Tuesday-Saturday*

Gastrobar Ster

MODERN CUISINE • TRENDY The former passion of Terry Priem, aka Ster, clearly evident as soon as you discover the graffiti in the dining room! His co ing style is even more impressive, and sees international flamboyance and d cate acidity combine to create an array of surprising dishes. Make sure you a try a cocktail prepared by the acclaimed barman.

Menu 22€ (lunch), 36/49€ – Carte 36/53€

Off plan – *Jericholaan 82B – ✆ 010 785 2712 – www.gastrobarster.nl – Closed Tuesday, Wednesday*

De Harmonie 23

CREATIVE • ELEGANT The magnificently restored interior of De Harmo 23 adds power to the ambition of chef Somer. His creativity is beautifully pressed here, making the name of his restaurant a reality, with authenticity a honesty combining to exciting effect. The extensive tasting menu allows din to truly discover his cuisine.

Menu 54/110€ – Carte 59/79€

PLAN: A2 – *Westersingel 95 – ✆ 010 436 3610 – www.deharmonierotterdam.nl – Closed 27 July-9 August, Sunday, lunch Saturday*

Héroine

MODERN CUISINE • NEIGHBOURHOOD Every time you enter this industr style building, with its sophisticated retro and designer vibe, it leaves you wa ing more. The diversity of the cooking is tantalising, combining international i piration and a focus on vegetables to create dishes that are trendy, full of s prises and thoroughly modern in feel.

Menu 32€ (lunch), 49/67€

PLAN: B1 – *Kipstraat 12 – ✆ 010 310 0870 – www.restaurantheroine.nl – Closed Sunday, Monday, lunch Tuesday-Wednesday*

HMB

INTERNATIONAL • TRENDY HMB stands for hummingbird, and in keeping w its name, the interior of this restaurant is elegantly playful. The large windo also provide a stunning view of the Rotterdam skyline. The delicious, beautif presented dishes are prepared with care and attention using ingredients from ferent international culinary traditions.

Menu 39€ (lunch), 65/95€ – Carte 63/98€

PLAN: B3 – *Holland-Amerikakade 104 – ✆ 010 760 0620 – www.hmb-restaurant.n Closed 27 April-4 May, 27 July-10 August, Sunday, Monday, lunch Saturday*

NY Basement

MODERN CUISINE • VINTAGE A jazzy vibe reigns supreme in the cellar of New York hotel, which is reminiscent of the Big Apple of the 1920s and 193 After a delicious cocktail at the 11m-long bar, guests can enjoy the modern sine on offer here. Choose from a delicious fish or meat dish, vegetables pared on the charcoal grill and an array of trendy suggestions.

Menu 53/70€ – Carte 48/65€

PLAN: B3 – *New York, Koninginnenhoofd 1 – ✆ 010 439 0525 – www.nybasement. Closed 27 April, lunch Monday-Saturday*

Old Dutch

FRENCH • CLASSIC DÉCOR Old Dutch exudes charm and nostalgia. The serving staff are dressed in suits, the vintage dining room has a distinguished air and the spacious terrace is a must. Here, you can savour classic French cuisine prepared with fitting generosity and finesse. If you enjoy a culinary spectacle, make sure you order the lobster bisque prepared at your table.

Menu 39 € (lunch), 43/63 € - Carte 59/97 €

PLAN: A2 - *Rochussenstraat 20 - ✆ 010 436 0344 - www.olddutch.net - Closed Sunday, Saturday*

Vineum

MODERN FRENCH • FRIENDLY The wine list is the heart and soul of this restaurant with a pleasant city garden at the back. The variety and quality of the wines is truly remarkable, supported by cuisine that showcases excellent ingredients. The experienced chef brings freshness to the plate, using produce at its best.

Menu 36/55 € - Carte 45/75 €

PLAN: A2 - *Eendrachtsweg 23 - ✆ 010 720 0966 - www.vineum.nl - Closed Sunday, lunch Saturday*

Zeezout

SEAFOOD • DESIGN Fish, fish and more fish. In the shipping quarter of one of the most important port cities in the world diners can enjoy the best the water has to offer. Their pure flavours seduce time and again, with dishes such as the salt-crusted sea bream topping the list. The stylishly decorated dining room also offers a view of the River Maas.

Menu 36 € (lunch), 52/72 € - Carte 59/70 €

PLAN: A3 - *Westerkade 11b - ✆ 010 436 5049 - www.restaurantzeezout.nl - Closed Sunday, Monday*

konstantin32/iStock

NORWAY

NORGE

OSLO

OSLO

LeoPatrizi/iStock

OSLO IN…

- **ONE DAY**
  Aker Brygge, Karl Johans Gate, Oslo Opera House.
- **TWO DAYS**
  Akershus, Astrup Fearnley Museum, ferry trip to Bygdøy.
- **THREE DAYS**
  Vigeland Park, Holmenkollen Ski Jump, Grunerlokka, Munch Museum.

Oslo has a lot going fo it – and one slight downsid it's one of the world's mo expensive cities. It also rank high when it comes to i standard of living, howeve and its position at the hea of Oslofjord, surrounded b steep forested hills, is hard t match for drama and beaut It's a charmingly compa place to stroll round, particularly in the summer, when th daylight hours practically abolish the night and, although may lack the urban cool of some other Scandinavian citie it boasts its fair share of trendy clubs and a raft of Michel Stars. There's a real raft, too: Thor Hyerdahl's famous Ko Tiki – one of the star turns in a city that loves its museums

Oslo's uncluttered feel is enhanced by parks and wide streets and, in the winter, there are times when you feel you have the whole place to yourself. Drift into the city by boat and land at the smart harbour of Aker Brygge; to the west lies the charming Bygdøy peninsula, home to museums permeated with the smell of the sea. Northwest is Frogner, with its famous sculpture park, the place where locals hang out on long summer days. The centre of town, the commercial hub, is Karl Johans Gate, bounded at one end by the Royal Palace and at the other by the Cathedral, while further east lie two trendy multi-cultural areas, Grunerlokka and Grønland, the former also home to the Edvard Munch Museum.

EATING OUT

slo has a very vibrant dining scene, beit one that is somewhat expen-ve, particularly if you drink wine. he cooking can be quite classical and efined but there are plenty of restau-ants offering more innovative menus oo. What is in no doubt is the quality f the produce used, whether that's e ever-popular game or the super-tive shellfish, which comes from very old water, giving it a clean, fresh fla-our. Classic Norwegian dishes often clude fruit, such as lingonberries with enison. Lunch is not a major affair; ost prefer just a snack or sandwich at midday while making dinner the main event of the day. You'll find most diners are seated by 7pm and are offered a 6, 7 or 8 course menu which they can reduce at their will, with a paired wine menu alongside. It doesn't have to be expensive, though. Look out for konditoris (bakeries) where you can pick up sandwiches and pastries, and kafeterias which serve substantial meals at reasonable prices. Service is a strength; staff are generally very polite, speak English and are fully versed in the menu.

Galt (Bjørn Svensson)

MODERN CUISINE • RUSTIC The friends who previously ran Fauna and Oscar gate moved on to create this warm, intimate restaurant with an appealingly rus feel. The set menu of 6 courses is nicely balanced, flavour combinations ha been well thought through, and the contrast in textures is a particular strength

Specialities: Langoustine, parsley and spruce. Lamb with rhubarb and cabbag Juniper ice cream, salted caramel and lingonberries.

Menu 995 NOK

PLAN: A2 – *Frognerveien 12B* – *Lille Frogner allé* – *48 51 48 86* – *www.galt.no* *Closed 5 July-4 August, 21 December-5 January, Monday, lunch Tuesday-Saturda Sunday*

Kontrast (Mikael Svensson)

SCANDINAVIAN • DESIGN A modern restaurant with a stark, semi-indust feel created by a concrete floor, exposed pipework and an open kitchen. Se sonal, organic Norwegian produce is used to create refined, original, full-f voured dishes whose apparent simplicity often masks their complex nature. T service is well-paced.

Specialities: Grilled mackerel with charred tomato and rhubarb flavoured with sehip and polypody fern. Lamb with salted unripe plums, ground ivy and turn Bone marrow ice cream with preserved summer berries.

Menu 1350/1850 NOK – Carte 700/960 NOK

PLAN: D1 – *Maridalsveien 15* – *Telthusbakken* – *21 60 01 01* – *www.restaurant-kontrast.no* – *Closed 5-20 April, 22 December-8 January, Monday, lunch Tuesday-Saturday, Sunday*

Omakase by Vladimir Pak

SUSHI • DESIGN Experienced Sushi Master Vladimir welcomes just a handful guests into his intimate restaurant at 7.15pm. The memorable dining experier comprises around 20 servings of Edomae sushi, dextrously crafted from an ar of the world's finest seafood – along with a few added extras, such as reindee

Specialities: Nigiri sushi. Chawanmushi with snow crab. Shellfish miso w smoked haddock.

Menu 1350 NOK

PLAN: B2 – *Ruseløkkveien 3* – *Nationaltheatret* – *456 85 022* – *www.omakaseoslo.no* – *Closed 6-26 July, Monday, lunch Tuesday-Saturday, Sunda*

Statholdergaarden (Bent Stiansen)

CLASSIC CUISINE • INTIMATE A charming 17C house in the city's heart. Th elegant rooms feature an array of antiques and curios, and have wonderfully nate stucco ceilings hung with chandeliers. Expertly rendered classical cook uses seasonal Norwegian ingredients in familiar combinations. Service is w versed and willing.

Specialities: Scallop and Arctic char with cucumber and dill emulsion. Veal che with celeriac, beetroot and shallot sauce. Raspberry, mascarpone, almonds a meringue.

Menu 1245/1950 NOK – Carte 1015/1185 NOK

PLAN: C3 – *Rådhusgate 11* – *Stortinget* – *22 41 88 00* – *www.statholdergaarden.no* – *Closed 6-14 April, 6 July-4 August, 23 December-3 January, Monday, lunch Tuesday-Saturday, Sunday*

Statholderens Mat og Vin Kjeller – See restaurant listing

Smalhans

TRADITIONAL CUISINE • NEIGHBOURHOOD A sweet neighbourhood c with friendly staff and an urban feel. Coffee and homemade cakes are served the morning, with a short selection of dishes including soup and a burger on o between 12pm and 4pm. A daily hot dish is available from 4-6pm, while set n nus and sharing plates are served at dinner.

Menu 175 NOK (lunch), 475/675 NOK

PLAN: C1 – *Ullevålsveien 43* – *St. Hanshaugen* – *22 69 60 00* – *www.smalhans.no* – *Closed lunch Monday-Tuesday*

À L'aise

MODERN CUISINE • INTIMATE This elegant, sophisticated restaurant is run by an engaging and knowledgeable team. The experienced chef is something of a Francophile, so expect refined Gallic dishes which are small of portion but big on flavour. The pressed duck for two has become a house speciality.

Carte 1060/1330 NOK

PLAN: A1 – *Essendrops gate 6 – Ⓜ Majorstuen – ✆ 21 05 57 00 – www.alaise.no – Closed 13 July-6 August, Monday, lunch Tuesday-Saturday, Sunday*

Arakataka

NORWEGIAN • TRENDY A smart glass-fronted restaurant with a central food bar, an open kitchen and a buzzy atmosphere. Choose from a concise menu of seasonal Norwegian small plates – they recommend 3 savoury dishes plus a dessert per person.

Menu 575/655 NOK – Carte 490/590 NOK

PLAN: D2 – *Mariboes gate 7 – Ⓜ Stortinget – ✆ 23 32 83 00 – www.arakataka.no – Closed 8 July-8 August, lunch Monday-Sunday*

Bokbacka

MODERN CUISINE • TRENDY A unique 'food bar' with clean, light styling and fun, idiosyncratic features; most seats are arranged around the open kitchen, with only 4 other tables available. Many of the theatrically presented dishes on the set omakase-style menu have a story.

Menu 690 NOK

PLAN: A2 – *Skovveien 15 – Ⓜ Riddervolds plass – ✆ 41 26 01 44 – www.bokbacka.no – Closed 6-12 April, 15 July-15 August, 23 December-5 January, Monday, lunch Tuesday-Saturday, Sunday*

Bon Lio

SPANISH • NEIGHBOURHOOD Passionate owners Kitty and Cato run this bright neighbourhood restaurant, where you can choose to sit at the bar, a table or the kitchen counter. Numerous courses make up the daily set menu, where Cato brings together elements from both his Majorcan and Norwegian heritage in a playful manner.

Menu 670 NOK

PLAN: D1 – *Sofienberggata 15 – Ⓜ Sofienbergparken – ✆ 47 77 72 12 – www.bonlio.no – Closed Monday, lunch Tuesday-Saturday, Sunday*

Brasserie Blanche

FRENCH • COSY A cosy French restaurant housed in an 18C building which was originally a stable and later spent time as a garage and an interior furnishings store. It has a small front terrace, a bar decorated with wine boxes and a wall made of corks. The chef is a Francophile and creates flavoursome classic French dishes.

Menu 395 NOK – Carte 319/545 NOK

PLAN: B1 – *Josefinesgate 23 – Ⓜ Homansbyen – ✆ 23 20 13 10 – www.blanche.no – Closed 6-27 July, Monday, lunch Tuesday-Sunday*

Brasserie Hansken

MODERN CUISINE • FAMILY A delightfully traditional brasserie, centrally located by the City Hall, with various charming dining areas and a fantastic terrace. Classical cooking follows the seasons and mixes French and Scandic influences; seafood is a speciality.

Carte 465/895 NOK

PLAN: C2 – *Akersgate 2 – Ⓜ Stortinget – ✆ 22 42 60 88 – www.brasseriehansken.no – Closed 23 December-5 January, Sunday*

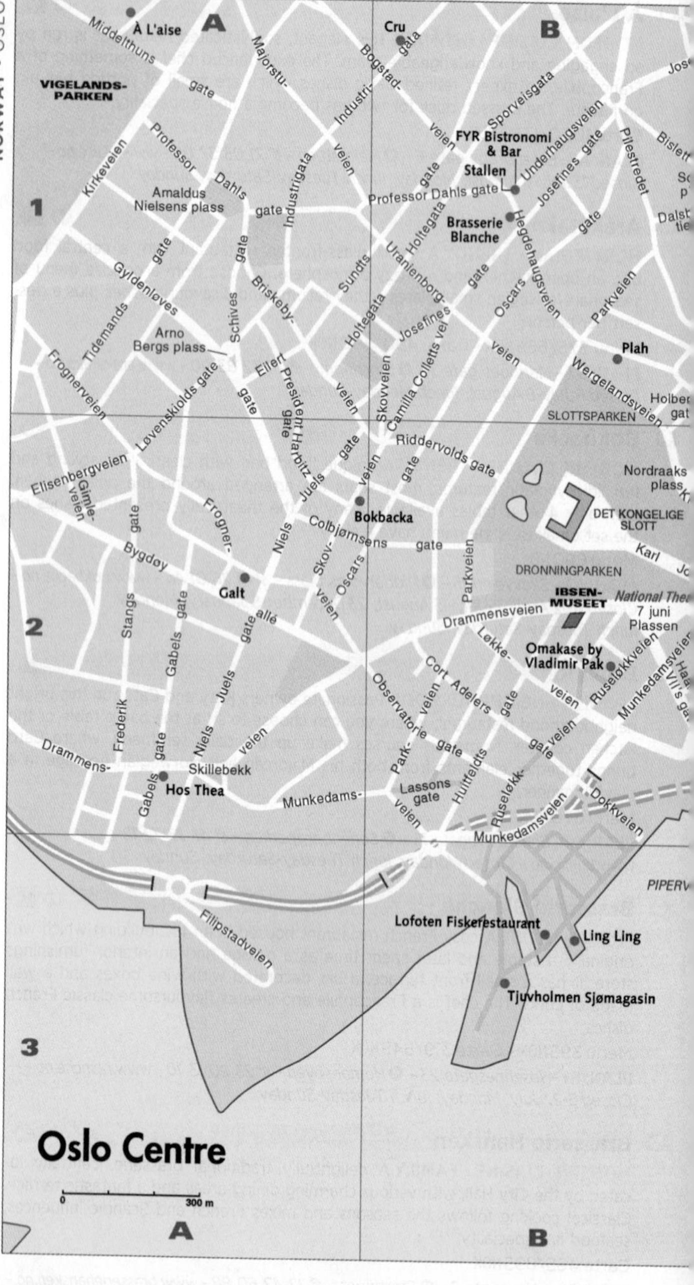
Oslo Centre
0
300 m
A
B
1
2
3
À L'aise
Cru
FYR Bistronomi & Bar
Stallen
Brasserie Blanche
Plah
Bokbacka
Galt
Omakase by Vladimir Pak
Hos Thea
Lofoten Fiskerestaurant
Ling Ling
Tjuvholmen Sjømagasin
VIGELANDS-PARKEN
SLOTTSPARKEN
DET KONGELIGE SLOTT
DRONNINGPARKEN
IBSEN-MUSEET
National Thea
7 juni Plassen
Nordraaks plass
Amaldus Nielsens plass
Arno Bergs plass
PIPERV
Middelthuns gate
Majorstu-veien
Bogstad-veien
Industrigata
Sporveisgata
Underhaugsveien
Josefines gate
Pilestredet
Professor Dahls gate
Kirkeveien
Holtegata
Uranienborg-veien
Hegdehaugsveien
Oscars gate
Parkveien
Wergelandsveien
Gyldenløves gate
Schives gate
Briskeby-veien
Sundts gate
Josefines gate
Camilla Colletts vei
Skovveien
Tidemands gate
Frognerveien
Løvenskiolds gate
Ellert
President Harbitz gate
Riddervolds gate
Elisenbergveien
Gimle-veien
Frogner-
Juels gate
Niels
Colbjørnsens gate
Bygdøy allé
Skov-veien
Oscars
Karl Jo
Drammensveien
Stangs gate
Gabels gate
Frederik
Cort Adelers gate
Løkke-veien
Ruseløkkveien
Munkedamsveien
Observatorie gate
Park-veien
Drammens-
Skillebekk
Niels Juels
Munkedams-
Lassons gate
Huitfeldts
Ruseløkk-veien
Dokkveien
Munkedamsveien
Filipstadveien
Holber gat
Bislett
Dalsb tie
Haa Vil's ga

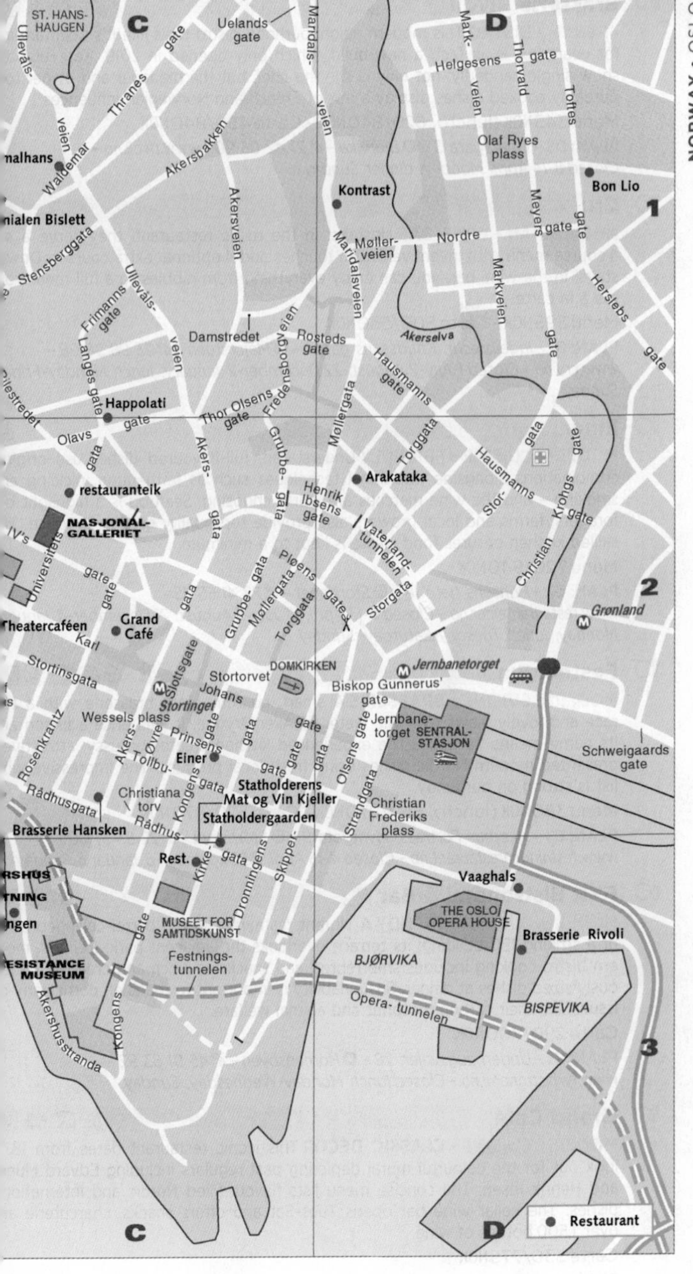
ST. HANS-HAUGEN
C
D
Uelands gate
Maridals-veien
Helgesens gate
Thorvald Meyers gate
Mark-veien
Toftes gate
Olaf Ryes plass
Bon Lio
Kontrast
Thranes gate
Waldemar Thranes gate
Akersbakken
Ullevåls-veien
Akersveien
Stensberggata
Møller-veien
Nordre gate
Markveien
Herslebs gate
Frimanns gate
Langés gate
Damstredet
Fredensborgveien
Rosteds gate
Akerselva
Maridalsveien
Hausmanns gate
Happolati
Pilestredet
Olavs gate
Thor Olsens gate
Akers-gata
Grubbe-gata
Møllergata
Torggata
Arakataka
restauranteik
NASJONAL-GALLERIET
Henrik Ibsens gate
Vaterland-tunnelen
Stor-gata
Christian Krohgs gate
Universitets gata
Grubbe-gata
Møllergata
Pløens gate
Storgata
Grønland
Grand Café
Theatercaféen
Karl Johans gate
Stortingsgata
Slottsgate
Stortorvet
DOMKIRKEN
Jernbanetorget
Biskop Gunnerus' gate
Stortinget
Wessels plass
Jernbane-torget
SENTRAL-STASJON
Schweigaards gate
Rosenkrantz
Akers-gata
Øvre
Prinsens gate
Tollbu-gata
Einer
Statholderens Mat og Vin Kjeller
Olsens gate
Strandgata
Christiana torv
Rådhusgata
Kongens gata
Statholdergaarden
Christian Frederiks plass
Brasserie Hansken
Rest.
Kirke-gata
Dronningens
Skipper-gata
Vaaghals
MUSEET FOR SAMTIDSKUNST
THE OSLO OPERA HOUSE
Brasserie Rivoli
RESISTANCE MUSEUM
Festnings-tunnelen
BJØRVIKA
Opera-tunnelen
BISPEVIKA
Kongens gate
Akershusstranda
1
2
3
Restaurant

Brasserie Rivoli

FRENCH • BISTRO This modern neighbourhood bistro feels like it's been arou[nd] for years but is, in fact, a new-build, which only opened in 2019. Kari runs th[e] show single-handedly: not only is she the chef, but the manager and owner to[o]. Carefully cooked dishes display a mix of French and Norwegian influences.

Menu 345 NOK (lunch), 620/840 NOK – Carte 450/840 NOK

PLAN: D3 – *Operagata 3 – Ⓜ Bjørvika – ✆ 21 42 05 90 – www.rivoli.no – Closed 8-14 April, Monday, dinner Sunday*

Cru

NORWEGIAN • WINE BAR Upstairs, in the rustic restaurant, they serve a se[t] 4 course menu with inventive British touches and 4 optional extra courses. Dow[n]stairs, in the wine bar, you can enjoy everything from nibbles to a full meal fro[m] the à la carte.

Menu 595 NOK – Carte 500/530 NOK

PLAN: B1 – *Ingelbrecht, Knudssøns gate 1 – Ⓜ Majorstuen – ✆ 23 98 98 98 – www.cru.no – Closed 1 July-2 August, 22 December-2 January, lunch Monday-Frida[y], Sunday*

Einer

MODERN CUISINE • FRIENDLY Understated, full-flavoured dishes use origin[al] combinations alongside traditional techniques such as fermenting, pickling an[d] smoking – and the wine matches are worth choosing. Seafood is a highlight bu[t] foragers, farms and local growers also provide top quality organic produce. Th[e] skilled kitchen ensures food waste is kept to a minimum.

Menu 720/940 NOK

PLAN: C2 – *Prinsens gate 18 – Ⓜ Stortinget – ✆ 22 41 55 55 – www.restauranteiner.no – Closed 6-13 April, 13 July-3 August, 21 December-4 Januar[y], Monday, lunch Tuesday-Saturday, Sunday*

Festningen

MODERN CUISINE • BRASSERIE A smart, contemporary brasserie with a ter[r]race and lovely views over the water to Aker Brygge; it was once a prison an[d] its name means 'fortress'. The experienced kitchen creates unfussy, attractivel[y] presented modern Nordic dishes using fresh local produce. The impressive win[e] list is strong on burgundy.

Menu 380 NOK (lunch), 650/870 NOK – Carte 520/870 NOK

PLAN: C3 – *Akerhus Fortress, Myntgata 9 – Ⓜ Stortinget – ✆ 22 83 31 00 – www.festningenrestaurant.no – Closed 4-15 April, 23 December-6 January, Sunday*

FYR Bistronomi & Bar

MODERN CUISINE • TRENDY A vibrant restaurant in the barrel-ceilinged cella[r] of a striking 19C building; its terrace overlooks the adjacent park. Refined, mod[ern] bistro cooking includes smørrebrød and snacks at lunch and creative, gener[o]usly sized dishes at dinner. Sustainability is important to the chef, particularly o[n] issues like their carbon footprint and animal welfare.

Carte 290/700 NOK

PLAN: B1 – *Underhaugsveien 28 – Ⓜ Homansbyen – ✆ 45 91 63 92 – www.fyrbistronomi.no – Closed lunch Monday-Wednesday, Sunday*

Grand Café

MODERN CUISINE • CLASSIC DÉCOR This iconic restaurant dates from 1874, look out for the colourful mural depicting past regulars including Edvard Munch and Henrik Ibsen. The concise menu lists flavour-filled Nordic and internationa[l] dishes. The cellar wine bar opens Tues-Sat and offers snacks, charcuterie and over 1,500 bottles of wine.

Carte 330/775 NOK

PLAN: C2 – *Grand H. Oslo by Scandic, Karl Johans Gate 31 – Ⓜ Stortinget – ✆ 98 18 20 00 – www.grandcafeoslo.no*

Happolati

ASIAN • DESIGN This bright, modish restaurant fuses Asian and Nordic styles; its assured cooking uses good quality ingredients and many dishes are designed for sharing. Tightly packed tables and friendly service add to the vibrant ambience.

Menu 565 NOK – Carte 310/515 NOK

PLAN: C1-2 – *St. Olavs Plass 2 – Ⓜ National Theatret – ✆ 47 97 80 87 – www.happolati.no – Closed 23 December-4 January, Monday, lunch Tuesday-Saturday, Sunday*

Hos Thea

ITALIAN • FAMILY A small, well-established restaurant in a charming residential area. It's decorated in natural hues and hung with beautiful oils. Menus offer a concise selection of Mediterranean dishes; start with the delicious homemade bread.

Menu 575 NOK – Carte 775/940 NOK

PLAN: A2 – *Gabels gate 11 – Ⓜ Skillebekk – ✆ 22 44 68 74 – www.hosthea.no – Closed 9-13 April, 1-31 July, 24-26 December, lunch Monday-Sunday*

Kolonialen Bislett

MODERN CUISINE • BRASSERIE Close to the stadium you'll find this cosy, modern bistro – previously a grocer's shop for nearly 80 years. The concise, keenly priced menu includes oysters, cured meats and wholesome Norwegian classics that have been brought up-to-date.

Carte 500/620 NOK

PLAN: C1 – *Sofies gate 16 – Ⓜ Skillebekk – ✆ 90 11 50 98 – www.kolonialenbislett.no – Closed 1-31 July, lunch Monday-Friday, Sunday*

Ling Ling

CANTONESE • TRENDY This more casual sister to Hakkasan offers an abbreviated menu of its signature Cantonese dishes but made using Norwegian produce. It has a great marina location, a cool lounge and a terrific rooftop bar and terrace come summer.

Carte 502/1060 NOK

PLAN: B3 – *Stranden 30 – Ⓜ Vika Atrium – ✆ 24 13 38 00 – www.linglingoslo.com – Closed 1-7 January, 22-30 December, lunch Monday-Friday, Sunday*

Lofoten Fiskerestaurant

SEAFOOD • BRASSERIE A traditional fjord-side restaurant hung with bright modern artwork and offering lovely views from its large windows and sizeable terrace. Watch as fresh, simply cooked fish and shellfish are prepared in the semi-open kitchen.

Menu 495 NOK (lunch) – Carte 505/785 NOK

PLAN: B3 – *Stranden 75 – Ⓜ Vika Atrium – ✆ 22 83 08 08 – www.lofoten-fiskerestaurant.no*

Plah

THAI • NEIGHBOURHOOD Norwegian ingredients blend with Thai flavours at this well-run restaurant. Choose between the à la carte and 2 tasting menus: 'Journey Through Thailand' or 'Journey Through The Jungle' (vegetarian). Dishes are eye-catching, imaginative and full of flavour. Their neighbouring bar serves Thai street food.

Menu 950/1110 NOK – Carte 610/950 NOK

PLAN: B1 – *Hegdehaugsveien 22 – Ⓜ Frydenlund – ✆ 22 56 43 00 – www.plah.no – Closed 6-12 April, 6-26 July, 21 December-3 January, Monday, lunch Tuesday-Saturday, Sunday*

Rest.

CREATIVE • CONTEMPORARY DÉCOR Three friends have come together to create this pioneering restaurant. Their mantra is 'waste not, want not' and their ethos is based around using imperfect produce and items which would normally be discarded. Ingredients are used in multiple different ways in the skilfully prepared, multi-course menu.

Menu 1450 NOK

PLAN: C3 – *Kirkegata 1-3 – ✆ 922 50 016 – www.restaurantrest.com – Closed 5 April-13 May, 13 July-10 August, 20 December-6 January, Monday, Tuesday, lunch Wednesday-Saturday, Sunday*

restauranteik

MODERN CUISINE • FRIENDLY Colourful abstract screens adorn the walls of this hotel restaurant close to the National Gallery. There's an inventive European element to the cooking, which is also informed by the chef's travels. The wine list offers a good range of older vintages, especially from Burgundy and Bordeaux.

Menu 445 NOK

PLAN: C2 – *Clarion Collection Hotel Savoy, Universitetsgata 11 – Ⓜ National Theatret – ✆ 22 36 07 10 – www.restauranteik.no – Closed 10-17 April, 7 July-7 August, 22 December-1 January, Monday, lunch Tuesday-Saturday, Sunday*

Stallen

NORWEGIAN • RUSTIC Housed in a delightful former stable block is this stylish intimate restaurant fronted by a lovely fire pit. The surprise menu evolves daily and has a playful touch, using the Norwegian larder, their garden and local herbs to full effect. The well-balanced dishes are often served by the chefs themselves.

Menu 1495 NOK

PLAN: B1 – *Underhaugsveien 28 – Ⓜ Homansbyen – ✆ 45 84 17 55 – www.restaurantstallen.no – Closed Monday, Tuesday, lunch Wednesday-Saturday, Sunday*

Statholderens Mat og Vin Kjeller

CLASSIC CUISINE • RUSTIC The informal sister of Statholdergaarden is set over three rooms in the old vaults of the same 17C house. One wall of the large entranceway is filled with wine bottles. Choose from a huge array of small plates or go for the 10 course tasting menu.

Menu 775 NOK – Carte 740/760 NOK

PLAN: C3 – *Rådhusgate 11 – Ⓜ Stortinget – ✆ 22 41 88 00 – www.statholdergaarden.no – Closed 6-14 April, 6 July-4 August, 23 December-3 January, Monday, lunch Tuesday-Saturday, Sunday*

Theatercaféen

TRADITIONAL CUISINE • LUXURY A truly grand café, with tiled flooring, pillars and a vaulted ceiling; it's a lively, informal place that's been a meeting point for the good and the great of the Norwegian cultural scene since 1900. Lunch offers light choices, sandwiches, pastries and cakes; dinner is the time for more classic dishes.

Carte 490/1100 NOK

PLAN: C2 – *Continental Hotel, Stortingsgaten 24-26 – Ⓜ National Theatret – ✆ 22 82 40 50 – www.theatercafeen.no – Closed lunch Sunday*

Tjuvholmen Sjømagasin

SEAFOOD • TRENDY A vast restaurant with three dining rooms, a crab and lobster tank, a superb terrace and a wet fish shop. Its name means 'sea store' and menus are fittingly seafood based. Shellfish is from the nearby dock – the langoustines are fantastic.

Menu 395 NOK (lunch)/795 NOK – Carte 640/900 NOK

PLAN: B3 – *Tjuvholmen Allé 14 – Ⓜ Tjuvholmen – ✆ 23 89 77 77 – www.sjomagasinet.no – Closed Sunday*

Vaaghals

SCANDINAVIAN • BRASSERIE A bright, contemporary restaurant with an open kitchen and a terrace; located on the ground floor of one of the modern 'barcode' buildings. Scandinavian menus feature dry-aged meat; many of the dinner dishes are designed for sharing.

Menu 385 NOK (lunch)/725 NOK – Carte 395/845 NOK

PLAN: D3 – *Dronning Eufemias gate 8 – Ⓜ Jernbanetorget – ✆ 92 07 09 99 – www.vaaghals.com – Closed 6-12 April, 6 July-2 August, 21 December-3 January, lunch Saturday, Sunday*

Velishchuk/iStock

POLAND

POLSKA

WARSAW

WARSZAWA

fotorince/iStock

WARSAW IN...

→ **ONE DAY**
Royal Castle, Warsaw History Museum, National Museum, Lazienki Park.

→ **TWO DAYS**
Monument to the Ghetto Heroes, Saxon Gardens, concert at Grand Theatre or Philharmonic Hall.

→ **THREE DAYS**
The Royal Route, Marshal Street, Solidarity Avenue, Wilanow.

When UNESCO addec Warsaw to its World Heritage list, it was a fitting seal o approval for its inspirec rebuild, after eighty per cent of the city was destroyec during World War II. Using plans of the old city, archi-tects painstakingly rebuilt the shattered capital throughout the 1950s, until it became ar admirable mirror image of its former self. Now grey communist era apartment blocks si beside pretty, pastel-coloured aristocratic buildings, thei architecture ranging from Gothic to baroque, rococo tc secession.

Nestling against the River Vistula, the Old Town was established at the end of the 13C, around what is now the Royal Castle, and a century later the New Town, to the north, began to take shape. To the south of the Old Town runs 'The Royal Route', so named because, from the late middle ages, wealthy citizens built summer residences with lush gardens along these rural thoroughfares. Continue southwards and you're in Lazienki Park with its palaces and pavilions, while to the west lie the more commercial areas of Marshal Street and Solidarity Avenue, once the commercial heart of the city. The north-west of Warsaw was traditionally the Jewish district, until it was destroyed during the war; today it has been redeveloped with housing estates and the sobering Monument to the Ghetto Heroes.

EATING OUT

he centuries-old traditional cuisine of Varsaw was influenced by neighbouing Russia, Ukraine and Germany, vhile Jewish dishes were also added to he mix. Over the years there has been growing sophistication to the cooking nd a lighter, more contemporary style as become evident, with time-honoued classics - such as the ubiquitous ierogi (dumplings with various filngs) and the ever-popular breaded ork dish 'bigos' - having been updated vith flair. These are accompanied, of ourse, by chilled Polish vodka, which overs a bewildering range of styles.

Warsaw also has a more global side, with everything from stalls selling falafel to restaurants serving Vietnamese, and a large Italian business community has ensured there are a good number of Italian restaurants too. Stylised settings are popular, such as a burghers' houses or vaulted cellars; wherever you eat, check that VAT has been included within the prices (it's not always) and add a ten per cent tip. If it's value for money you're after, head for a Milk Bar, a low priced cafeteria selling traditional dairy-based food.

atelier Amaro (Wojciech Modest Amaro)

MODERN CUISINE • DESIGN Owner-chef Wojciech Modest Amaro is a huge a vocate of seasonal Polish ingredients; menus are based on 'Nature's calendar' ar showcase foraged herbs and flowers. Ambitious, innovative dishes are full of co our and use many modern techniques; the Polish spirit matches are a must.

Specialities: Caviar, hazelnuts and elderflower. Lamb with ramsons and nettl Meadowsweet with sorrel and milk.

Menu 149 zł (lunch), 310/420 zł

PLAN: 2-D2 – *Plac Trzech Krzyży 10/14 – Ⓜ Centrum – ✆ 792 222 211 – www.atelieramaro.pl – Closed 3-17 August, 21 December-4 January, Monday, lunch Tuesday, lunch Saturday, Sunday*

Senses (Andrea Camastra)

CONTEMPORARY • ELEGANT It's all in the name: the aim of the chef is to stin ulate your senses with his playful, theatrically presented dishes – many arrange in numerous servings. The 3 tasting menus have a classic Polish heart and Italia and Asian influences; the serving team explain the story behind every dish.

Specialities: Lobster pierogi. Barbecued quail-goulash. Karpatka cake.

Menu 320/550 zł

PLAN: 2-C1 – *ul. Bielanska 12 – Ⓜ Ratusz Arsenał – ✆ 22 331 96 97 – www.sensesrestaurant.pl – Closed 10-31 August, 23 December-7 January, lunch Monday-Saturday, Sunday*

alewino

POLISH • RUSTIC Alewino started life as a wine shop before developing into rustic, modern wine-bar-cum-restaurant divided over 4 cosy rooms. The menu might be concise but portions are generous, with classic Polish recipes reworke in a modern manner. Over 250 great value wines are available by the glass.

Carte 104/139 zł

PLAN: 2-D2 – *ul. Mokotowska 48 – Ⓜ Politechnika – ✆ 22 628 38 30 – www.alewino.pl – Closed 21 December-4 January, Sunday*

Brasserie Warszawska

POLISH • BRASSERIE A smart brasserie with a zinc-topped bar, a black an white tiled floor, and caricatures of its regulars on the walls. Modern Europea dishes are executed with care and passion. Meats come from their own butcher' shop and mature steaks are a feature, with a choice of cuts from Poland, Irelan and Australia.

Carte 38/172 zł

PLAN: 1-B2 – *ul. Górnośląska 24 – Ⓜ Politechnika – ✆ 22 628 94 23 – www.brasseriewarszawska.pl – Closed Sunday*

Butchery & Wine

MEATS AND GRILLS • FRIENDLY The name of this modern bistro says it al staff wear butcher's aprons, there's a diagram of cuts above the pass and glass fronted ageing fridges stand at the back of the room. The emphasis is on steak cooked in the Bertha oven; try a Polish cut with a good value red from the con cise, well-chosen wine list.

Carte 75/235 zł

PLAN: 2-D2 – *ul. Żurawia 22 – Ⓜ Centrum – ✆ 22 502 31 18 – www.butcheryandwine.pl*

Kieliszki na Hożej

MODERN CUISINE • WINE BAR A warm and characterful neighbourhood res taurant serving carefully executed, technically adroit dishes which burst with fla vour. The towering display of Riedel glasses is a clue as to the part wine plays here: over 230 wines – imported directly – are available by the glass.

Menu 49 zł (lunch) – Carte 84/160 zł

PLAN: 2-D2 – *ul. Hoża 41 – Ⓜ Politechnika – ✆ 22 404 21 09 – www.kieliszkinahozej.pl – Closed lunch Saturday, Sunday*

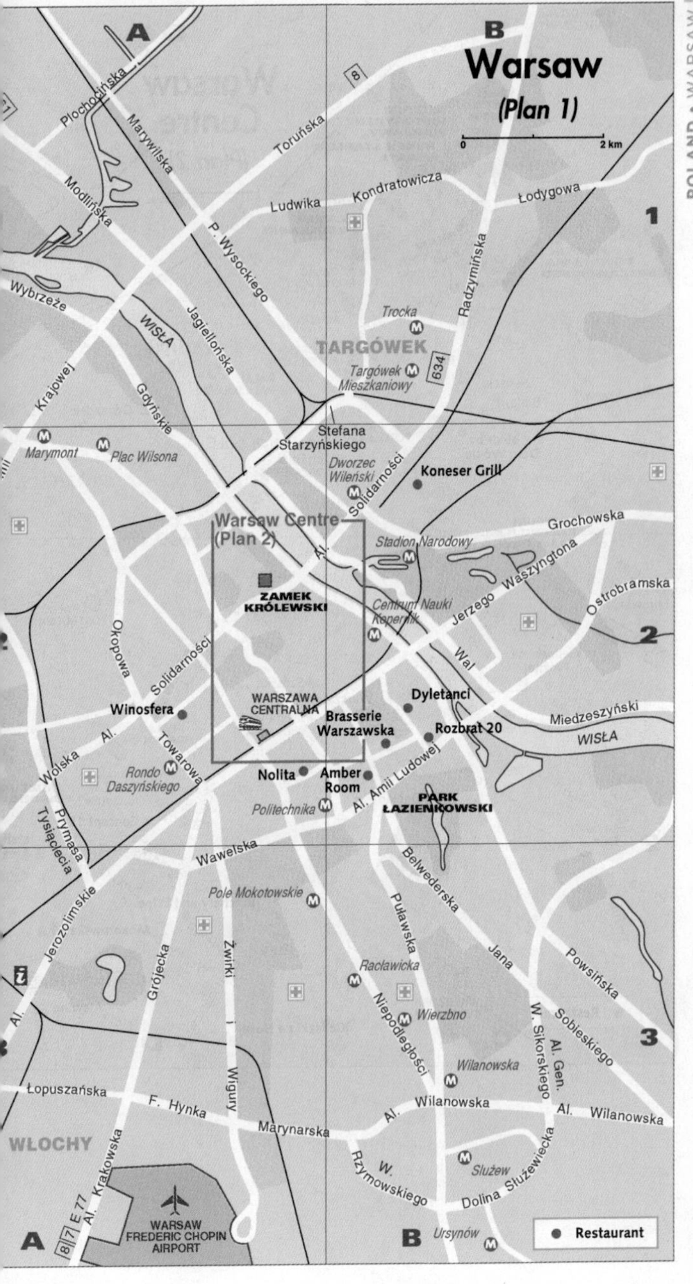
Warsaw
(Plan 1)
0
2 km
A
B
1
2
3
Płochocińska
Marywilska
Modlińska
Toruńska
Ludwika
Kondratowicza
Łodygowa
P. Wysockiego
Radzymińska
Wybrzeże
WISŁA
Jagiellońska
Trocka
TARGÓWEK
Targówek
Mieszkaniowy
634
8
Krajowej
Gdyńskie
Marymont
Plac Wilsona
Stefana
Starzyńskiego
Dworzec
Wileński
Solidarności
Koneser Grill
Warsaw Centre
(Plan 2)
Grochowska
Al.
Stadion Narodowy
ZAMEK
KRÓLEWSKI
Centrum Nauki
Kopernik
Jerzego Waszyngtona
Ostrobramska
Okopowa
Solidarności
Wał
WARSZAWA
CENTRALNA
Dyletanci
Winosfera
Brasserie
Warszawska
Rozbrat 20
Miedzeszyński
WISŁA
Towarowa
Wolska
Al.
Rondo
Daszyńskiego
Nolita
Amber
Room
Al. Armii Ludowej
PARK
ŁAZIENKOWSKI
Politechnika
Prymasa
Tysiąclecia
Wawelska
Belwederska
Pole Mokotowskie
Jerozolimskie
Puławska
Jana
Powsińska
Żwirki
Grójecka
Racławicka
Wierzbno
Niepodległości
Sobieskiego
W. Sikorskiego
Al. Gen.
Wilanowska
Al.
Łopuszańska
F. Hynka
Wigury
Marynarska
Al.
Wilanowska
Al.
Wilanowska
WŁOCHY
Al. Krakowska
E 77
7
8
Rzymowskiego
W.
Służew
Dolina
Służewiecka
WARSAW
FREDERIC CHOPIN
AIRPORT
Ursynów
Restaurant

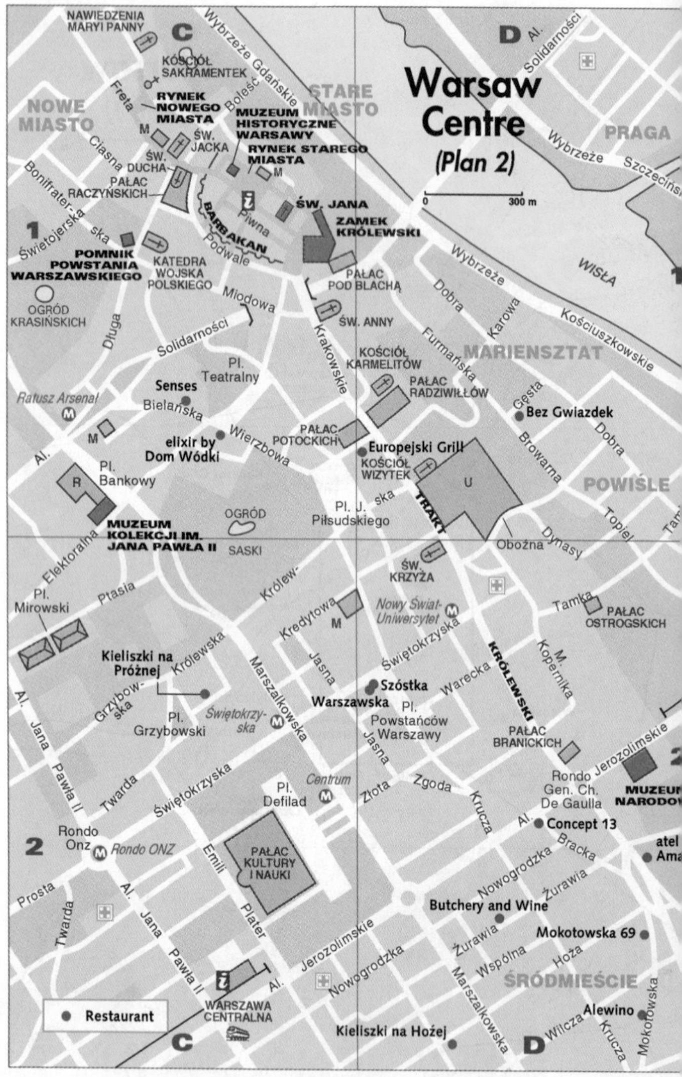
Warsaw Centre
(Plan 2)
0
300 m
Restaurant
NOWE MIASTO
STARE MIASTO
PRAGA
MARIENSZTAT
POWIŚLE
ŚRÓDMIEŚCIE
WISŁA
RYNEK NOWEGO MIASTA
MUZEUM HISTORYCZNE WARSZAWY
RYNEK STAREGO MIASTA
ŚW. JANA
ZAMEK KRÓLEWSKI
BARBAKAN
POMNIK POWSTANIA WARSZAWSKIEGO
KATEDRA WOJSKA POLSKIEGO
PAŁAC POD BLACHĄ
MUZEUM KOLEKCJI IM. JANA PAWŁA II
TRAKT KRÓLEWSKI
MUZEUM NARODOWE
Senses
elixir by Dom Wódki
Europejski Grill
Bez Gwiazdek
Kieliszki na Próżnej
Szóstka
Warszawska
Concept 13
Butchery and Wine
Mokotowska 69
Alewino
Kieliszki na Hożej
PAŁAC KULTURY I NAUKI
WARSZAWA CENTRALNA
Rondo ONZ
Centrum
Świętokrzyska
Nowy Świat-Uniwersytet
Ratusz Arsenał
Pl. Teatralny
Pl. Bankowy
Pl. J. Piłsudskiego
Pl. Mirowski
Pl. Grzybowski
Pl. Powstańców Warszawy
Pl. Defilad
Rondo Gen. Ch. De Gaulla
OGRÓD SASKI
OGRÓD KRASIŃSKICH
Marszałkowska
Al. Jerozolimskie
Al. Jana Pawła II
Krakowskie
Wybrzeże Gdańskie
Wybrzeże Kościuszkowskie
Al. Solidarności

Szóstka

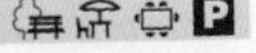

POLISH • DESIGN Take in rooftop views from this appealing glass-walled restaurant and its large terrace, set on the sixth floor of the iconic Prudential building. The small menu offers creative sharing plates which mix Polish and Mediterranean influences and have a vegetable bias. Prices are more than fair.

Carte 100/180 zł

PLAN: 2-D2 – *Warszawa Hotel, Plac Powstańców Warszawy 9* – Ⓜ *Świętokrzyska* – ✆ *22 470 03 42* – *www.warszawa.hotel.com.pl/hotel-warszawa/restaurants/szostka-restaurant* – *Closed Monday, dinner Sunday*

Amber Room

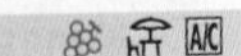

MODERN CUISINE • ELEGANT A grand dining room set within an attractive villa: home to the exclusive 'Round Table of Warsaw'. Top ingredients feature in beautifully presented dishes, which are classically based and come with some original touches. When the sun's shining, the terrace is the place to be.

Menu 79 zł (lunch) – Carte 118/263 zł

PLAN: 1-B2 – *Aleje Ujazdowskie 13* – Ⓜ *Politechnika* – ✆ *600 800 999* – *www.amber-room.pl*

Bez Gwiazdek

POLISH • NEIGHBOURHOOD A cosy neighbourhood restaurant minutes from the castle. Monthly changing menus focus on one of the 16 Polish regions; showcasing ingredients and traditional recipes which have been brought up to date. The team's pride and enthusiasm is clear; wine recommendations add to the experience.

Menu 100/140 zł

PLAN: 2-D1 – *Wiślana 8* – Ⓜ *Nowy Świat-Uniwersytet* – ✆ *22 628 04 45* – *www.bez-gwiazdek.com* – *Closed 4-11 January, 17-24 August, Monday, lunch Tuesday-Saturday, dinner Sunday*

Concept 13

MODERN CUISINE • DESIGN Set atop the chic Vitkac department store, this vast restaurant comes with sleek black furnishings, a glass-walled kitchen and a large terrace; they also own the wine bar and impressive deli on the floor below. Appealing modern dishes are well-presented and have distinct Mediterranean influences.

Menu 69 zł (lunch) – Carte 126/190 zł

PLAN: 2-D2 – *Vitkac, ul. Bracka 9* – Ⓜ *Centrum* – ✆ *22 310 73 73* – *www.likusrestauracje.pl/en/restaurants/concept-13-restaurant/* – *Closed dinner Sunday*

Dyletanci

POLISH • FRIENDLY The brainchild of an experienced chef and a wine importer, Dyletanci has a welcoming modern bistro style and walls laden with wines sourced from across the globe. Seasonal ingredients are prepared in a contemporary manner.

Menu 135 zł – Carte 107/158 zł

PLAN: 1-B2 – *ul. Rozbrat 44A* – Ⓜ *Nowy Świat-Uniwersytet* – ✆ *692 887 234* – *www.dyletanci.pl* – *Closed 25 December, Sunday*

elixir by Dom Wódki

POLISH • WINE BAR A smart, very fashionable bar and restaurant is the setting for this marriage of modern Polish cuisine and top quality vodkas. The likes of local herring, dumplings and beef tartare are paired with over 650 vodkas from around the world.

Menu 39 zł (lunch) – Carte 100/150 zł

PLAN: 2-C1 – *ul. Wierzbowa 9-11* – Ⓜ *Ratusz Arsenal* – ✆ *22 828 22 11* – *www.restauracjaelixir.pl*

Europejski Grill

POLISH • ELEGANT A sophisticated restaurant set in the lovingly restored Europejski Hotel, which overlooks the historic Pilsudski square. Menus feature meat and fish cooked over a charcoal grill alongside modern versions of Polish classics. Try the vodka distilled to celebrate the hotel's reopening.

Carte 160/350 zł

PLAN: 2-D1 – *Raffles Europejski Warsaw Hotel, Krakowskie Przedmieście 13 – Ⓜ Nowy Świat-Uniwersytet – ✆ 22 255 95 90 – www.raffles.com/warsaw*

Kieliszki na Próżnej

POLISH • NEIGHBOURHOOD A huge rack of glasses welcomes you into a parquet-floored room with a striking black and white wildlife mural and zinc ducting. Small growers feature on the wine list, which offers over 250 choices – all available by the glass. Menus feature modern interpretations of Polish classics; lunch is a steal.

Menu 39 zł (lunch) – Carte 72/186 zł

PLAN: 2-C2 – *ul. Próżna 12 – Ⓜ Świętokrzyska – ✆ 501 764 674 – www.kieliszkinaproznej.pl – Closed Sunday*

Koneser Grill

MEATS AND GRILLS • CONTEMPORARY DÉCOR This redeveloped former vodka factory sits to the east of the city and comes with an industrial feel. It's all about steak here, with a focus on Polish beef. Meats are aged in-house and then cooked over a wood-fired grill; choose a sauce and a side for a hearty meal.

Carte 80/195 zł

PLAN: 1-B2 – *Ząbkowska 29 – Ⓜ Dworzec Wileński – ✆ 798 185 692 – www.konesergrill.pl – Closed Monday, dinner Sunday*

Mokotowska 69

MEATS AND GRILLS • TRADITIONAL This unusual circular building has a cosy, romantic atmosphere and the welcoming team make you feel well-looked-after. Menus focus on seafood and regularly changing, prime quality cuts of beef which could include Polish Red, American Black Angus, Scottish Aberdeen Angus and Japanese Kobe.

Carte 94/190 zł

PLAN: 2-D2 – *ul. Mokotowska 69 – Ⓜ Centrum – ✆ 22 628 73 84 – www.mokotowska69.pl*

Nolita

MODERN CUISINE • DESIGN Whitewashed stone and black window blinds are matched inside by a smart monochrome theme, where an open kitchen takes centre stage. Bold, modern dishes feature many flavours and take their influences from across the globe.

Menu 99 zł (lunch) – Carte 190/295 zł

PLAN: 1-A2 – *ul. Wilcza 46 – Ⓜ Politechnika – ✆ 22 292 04 24 – www.nolita.pl – Closed 3-16 August, 24 December-3 January, lunch Saturday, Sunday*

Rozbrat 20

MODERN CUISINE • FRIENDLY What was once a corner bakery and wine shop has become a smart, cosy neighbourhood restaurant; sit in the front room to watch the chefs at work. Modern cooking with pronounced flavours and an emphasis on seasonal Polish ingredients – give the lesser known Polish wines a try.

Carte 69/181 zł

PLAN: 1-B2 – *ul. Rozbrat 20 – Ⓜ Politechnika – ✆ 22 416 62 66 – www.rozbrat20.com.pl – Closed Sunday*

Warszawska

POLISH • RUSTIC The iconic Prudential Insurance building plays host to this cavernous restaurant. The friendly team bring warmth to the room with its raw concrete walls and industrial pillars. Carefully cooked dishes are sure to put a smile on your face, with classic recipes given a refined touch.

Carte 70/144 zł

PLAN: 2-D2 – *Warszawa Hotel, Plac Powstańców Warszawy 9* – Ⓜ *Świętokrzyska* – ✆ *22 470 03 42* – *www.warszawa.hotel.com.pl/hotel-warszawa/restaurants/warszawska-restaurant*

Winosfera

MODERN CUISINE • DESIGN Winosfera sits within an old factory – it retains its industrial feel and, in a nod to the famed cinema which once stood here, comes with a screening room for private events. Modern European menus cover Italy, France and Poland.

Menu 59 zł (lunch) – Carte 112/162 zł

PLAN: 1-A2 – *ul. Chlodna 31* – Ⓜ *Rondo ONZ* – ✆ *22 526 25 00* – *www.winosfera.pl* – *Closed Sunday*

CRACOW

KRAKÓW

martin-dm/iStock

CRACOW IN...

→ **ONE DAY**
St Mary's Church, Cloth Hall, Wawel, main building of National Museum.

→ **TWO DAYS**
Kazimierz, Oskar Schindler's Factory, 'Footsteps of Pope Jean Paul II' tour.

→ **THREE DAYS**
Auschwitz-Birkenau, Wieliczka salt mine.

Cracow was deservedl included in the very firs UNESCO World Heritag List. Unlike much of Polanc this beautiful old city – th country's capital from th 11C to the 17C – was spare Second World War destruc tion because the Germa Governor had his HQ here. S Cracow is still able to boas a hugely imposing market square – the biggest mediev square in Europe – and a hill that's crowned not just wit a castle, but a cathedral too. Not far away there's even glorious chapel made of salt, one hundred metres unde the ground.

Cracow is a city famous for its links with Judaism and its Royal Route, but also for its cultural inheritance. During the Renaissance, it became a centre of new ideas that drew the most outstanding writers, thinkers and musicians of the day. It has thousands of architectural monuments and millions of artefacts displayed in its museums and churches; but it's a modern city too, with an eye on the 21C. The heart and soul of Cracow is its old quarter, which received its charter in 1257. It's dominated by the Market Square and almost completely encircled by the Planty gardens. A short way to the south, briefly interrupted by the curving streets of the Okol neighbourhood, is Wawel Hill, and further south from here is the characterful Jewish quarter of Kazimierz. The smart residential areas of Piasek and Nowy Swiat are to the west.

EATING OUT

ven during the communist era, racow had a reputation as a good lace to eat. In the 1990s, hundreds of ew restaurants opened their doors, ften in pretty locations with medieval r Renaissance interiors or in intimate ellars. Many Poles go misty-eyed at e thought of Bigos on a cold winter's ay; it's a game, sausage and cabbage ew that comes with sauerkraut, nion, potatoes, herbs and spices, and reputed to get better with reheating n successive days. Pierogi is another vourite: crescent-shaped dumplings hich come in either savoury or sweet style. Barszcz is a lemon and garlic flavoured beetroot soup that's invariably good value, while in Kazimierz, specialities include Jewish dumplings - filled with onion, cheese and potatoes - and Berdytchov soup, which imaginatively mixes honey and cinnamon with beef. There are plenty of restaurants specialising in French, Greek, Vietnamese, Middle Eastern, Indian, Italian and Mexican food too. Most restaurants don't close until around midnight and there's no pressure to rush your drinks and leave.

Centre

Fiorentina

CREATIVE • CONTEMPORARY DÉCOR Sit under vaulted, red-brick ceilings enjoy creative modern interpretations of Polish dishes, cooked by an experienc chef using the best of the local larder. Flavours are bold and adventurous a there's a degree of theatre to the service. Go for the speciality 30-day, dry-ag chargrilled Fiorentina steak.

Carte 62/177 zł

PLAN: 2-E3 – *Balthazar Design Hotel, ul. Grodzka 63 – ✆ 12 426 46 08 – www.fiorentina.com.pl*

Albertina

MODERN CUISINE • DESIGN A sophisticated modern restaurant with a bas ment wine bar; 32 wines are available by the glass thanks to the Enomatic wi system. Menus show the chef's passion for hunting and fishing – venison is a sp ciality and they have their own lobster tank. Eye-catching dishes capture the i gredients' true flavours.

Carte 145/229 zł

PLAN: 2-F2 – *ul. Dominikańska 3 – ✆ 12 333 41 10 – www.albertinarestaurant.pl – Closed 24-25 December*

Amarylis

MODERN CUISINE • DESIGN Head down to the hotel's basement and sit in e ther a traditional brick room or a more modern space furnished in black ar white. Cooking mixes Polish and global influences and dishes are well-presente and full of flavour.

Carte 131/154 zł

PLAN: 2-F3 – *Queen Hotel, ul. Józefa Dietla 60 – ✆ 12 433 33 06 – www.queenhotel.pl*

Bianca

ITALIAN • BISTRO Sit on the small terrace opposite St Mary's Basilica and watc the world go by. Classical menus cover all regions of Italy and the pastas and r gus are freshly made; be sure to try the delicious saltimbocca with its sharp, ler ony tang.

Carte 84/168 zł

PLAN: 2-F2 – *Plac Mariacki 2 – ✆ 12 422 18 71 – www.biancaristorante.pl – Closed 24-25 December*

Copernicus

MODERN CUISINE • INTIMATE Set off the atrium of a charming hotel; an inti mate split-level restaurant of less than 10 tables, boasting an ornate hand painted Renaissance ceiling. At dinner, adventurous 5, 7 and 12 course tastin menus offer well-crafted Polish and European dishes. The wine list's strength i its Italian selection.

Menu 220/430 zł – Carte 137/177 zł

PLAN: 2-E3 – *Copernicus Hotel, ul. Kanonicza 16 – ✆ 12 424 34 00 – www.likusrestauracje.pl*

Enoteka Pergamin

POLISH • WINE BAR A modern wine bar situated in the former home of sculp tor Wit Stosz. The menu features sharing boards of cheese and charcuterie a well as tapas, pizza, pasta and some classic Polish dishes. The wine list boast over 400 bottles, with most also available by the glass; finish with a brandy i the cigar room.

Carte 86/162 zł

PLAN: 2-E2 – *ul. Grodzka 39 – ✆ 797 705 515 – www.enotekapergamin.pl*

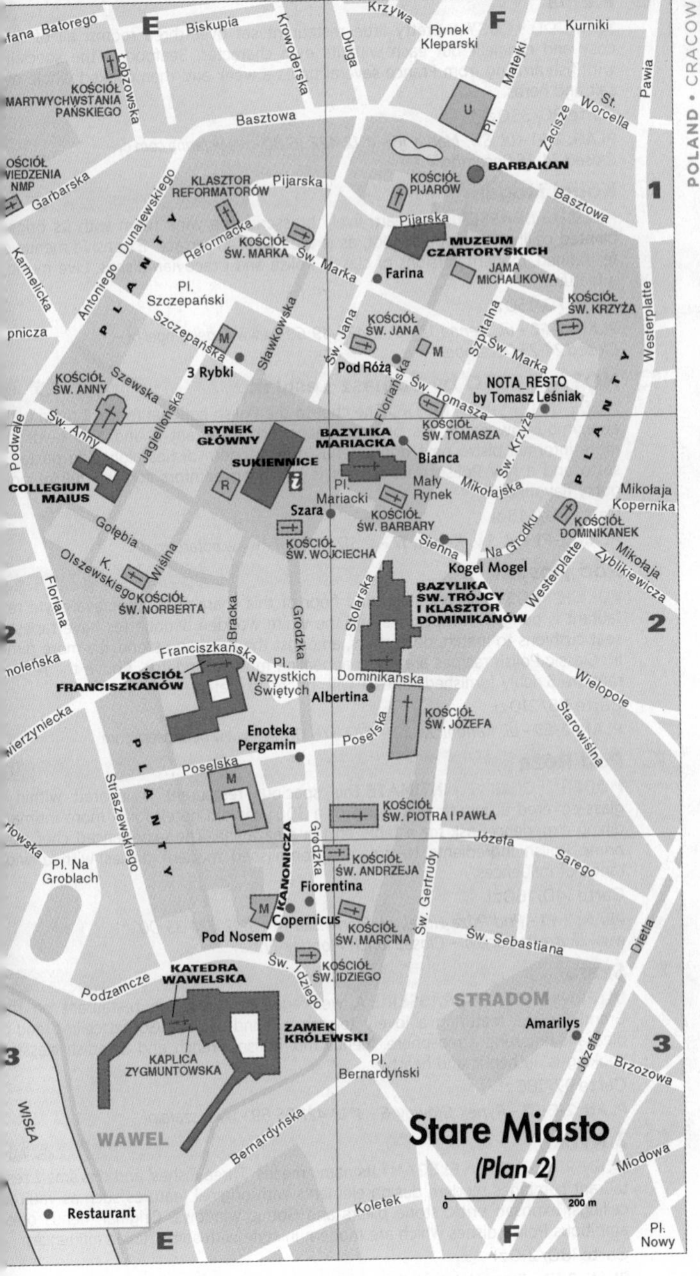
Stare Miasto
(Plan 2)
Restaurant
KOŚCIÓŁ MARTWYCHWSTANIA PAŃSKIEGO
KLASZTOR REFORMATORÓW
KOŚCIÓŁ ŚW. MARKA
KOŚCIÓŁ PIJARÓW
BARBAKAN
MUZEUM CZARTORYSKICH
JAMA MICHALIKOWA
Farina
KOŚCIÓŁ ŚW. KRZYŻA
KOŚCIÓŁ ŚW. JANA
Pod Różą
3 Rybki
KOŚCIÓŁ ŚW. ANNY
NOTA_RESTO by Tomasz Leśniak
KOŚCIÓŁ ŚW. TOMASZA
RYNEK GŁÓWNY
BAZYLIKA MARIACKA
Bianca
SUKIENNICE
COLLEGIUM MAIUS
Pl. Mariacki
Mały Rynek
Szara
KOŚCIÓŁ ŚW. BARBARY
KOŚCIÓŁ DOMINIKANEK
KOŚCIÓŁ ŚW. WOJCIECHA
Kogel Mogel
KOŚCIÓŁ ŚW. NORBERTA
BAZYLIKA ŚW. TRÓJCY I KLASZTOR DOMINIKANÓW
KOŚCIÓŁ FRANCISZKANÓW
Pl. Wszystkich Świętych
Albertina
KOŚCIÓŁ ŚW. JÓZEFA
Enoteka Pergamin
KOŚCIÓŁ ŚW. PIOTRA I PAWŁA
KOŚCIÓŁ ŚW. ANDRZEJA
Fiorentina
Copernicus
Pod Nosem
KOŚCIÓŁ ŚW. MARCINA
KOŚCIÓŁ ŚW. IDZIEGO
KATEDRA WAWELSKA
ZAMEK KRÓLEWSKI
KAPLICA ZYGMUNTOWSKA
WAWEL
STRADOM
Amarylys
Pl. Bernardyński
Pl. Na Groblach
Pl. Nowy
Pl. Szczepański
Rynek Kleparski
PLANTY
WISŁA
Basztowa
Pijarska
Reformacka
Szczepańska
Sławkowska
Floriańska
Szpitalna
Św. Jana
Św. Marka
Św. Tomasza
Św. Krzyża
Mikołajska
Sienna
Na Grodku
Westerplatte
Wielopole
Starowiślna
Stolarska
Grodzka
Bracka
Wiślna
Gołębia
Jagiellońska
Szewska
Św. Anny
Podwale
Karmelicka
Dunajewskiego
Garbarska
Łobzowska
Krowoderska
Długa
Krzywa
Biskupia
Kurniki
Pawia
Matejki
Zacisze
St. Worcella
Franciszkańska
Dominikańska
Poselska
Straszewskiego
Kanonicza
Św. Gertrudy
Józefa
Sarego
Św. Sebastiana
Dietla
Brzozowa
Miodowa
Koletek
Bernardyńska
Podzamcze
Św. Idziego
Mikołaja Kopernika
Zyblikiewicza
200 m

Farina

SEAFOOD • COSY A pretty little restaurant set over three rooms; all of the cosy and candlelit but each with its own character. Seafood is the speciali with fish arriving from France several times a week and then cooked whole ov salt and herbs.

Carte 90/330 zł

PLAN: 2-F1 – *ul. Św. Marka 16 – ✆ 12 422 16 80 – www.farina.com.pl – Closed 24-26 December*

Kogel Mogel

POLISH • BRASSERIE A smart, lively brasserie; the wine room with its origi painted ceiling is a popular spot, as is the enclosed terrace. Extensive menus fer refined, modern versions of classic Polish and Cracovian dishes. Live music a feature.

Carte 70/150 zł

PLAN: 2-F2 – *ul. Sienna 12 – ✆ 12 426 49 68 – www.kogel-mogel.pl – Closed 24-25 December*

NOTA_RESTO by Tomasz Leśniak

MODERN CUISINE • BISTRO The chef to the Polish national football team is t eponymous owner of this brightly decorated restaurant – and also owns t more informal bistro next door. Menus offer modern dishes alongside pasta, sotto and a few Polish classics; this is satisfying comfort cooking full of bo gutsy flavours.

Carte 80/145 zł

PLAN: 2-F1 – *ul. Św. Krzyża 17 – ✆ 517 818 851 – www.notaresto.pl*

Pod Nosem

POLISH • COSY The bright ground floor of this characterful medieval-style re taurant is hung with tapestries and the white wooden banquettes have tapest seat cushions to match; downstairs, amongst the brick and stone, it's more dim lit. Classic Polish recipes are given appealing modern updates. Above the resta rant are 3 richly furnished suites – with prices to match.

Carte 115/210 zł

PLAN: 2-E3 – *ul. Kanonicza 22 – ✆ 12 376 00 14 – www.podnosem.com*

Pod Różą

MODERN CUISINE • INTIMATE This spacious restaurant is located within glass-covered atrium in the centre of a 300 year old hotel; for a more intimat dining experience, ask for a table on the mezzanine. The experienced chef use prime Polish ingredients to create accomplished modern dishes with a wid range of influences.

Carte 140/160 zł

PLAN: 2-F1 – *Pod Różą Hotel, ul. Floriańska 14 – ✆ 12 424 33 00 – www.likusrestauracje.pl – Closed lunch Monday-Friday*

Szara

INTERNATIONAL • BRASSERIE A well-regarded family-run restaurant on th Grand Square, featuring a lovely terrace, a hand-painted Gothic ceiling and pleasant brasserie atmosphere. Menus mix Polish, French and Swedish classic cooking is authentic and hearty.

Carte 97/186 zł

PLAN: 2-E-F2 – *Rynek Główny 6 – ✆ 12 421 66 69 – www.szara.pl*

3 Rybki

MODERN CUISINE • ELEGANT Its name means 'Three Fishes' and this smart res taurant combines modern design elements with original features such as vaulte ceilings, exposed brick, stone pillars and Gothic windows. Original menus offe ambitious Polish dishes which are modern in style with some Italian influences.

Carte 180/210 zł

PLAN: 2-E1 – *Stary Hotel, ul. Szczepańska 5 – ✆ 12 384 08 06 – www.likusrestauracje.pl*

Environs of Cracow

t Kazimierz

Bottiglieria 1881 (Przemysław Klima)

CREATIVE • DESIGN Sit in the century old cellar for an intimate dining experience, or ask for a table opposite the open kitchen to see the talented team at work. The best of the Polish larder is used in creative, well-balanced, modern dishes with a hint of Nordic style. Opt for the carefully chosen wine pairings.

Specialities: Trout with watermelon and juniper. Beef with eggplant and anchovy. Whortleberry with rosemary and sour cream.

Menu 220/280 zł – Carte 125/165 zł

PLAN: C3 – *ul. Bocheńska 5 – ✆ 660 661 756 – www.1881.com.pl – Closed 24-26 December, Monday, lunch Tuesday-Saturday, Sunday*

Zazie

FRENCH • BISTRO You'll find this lively bistro in a corner spot on a pleasant square; ask for a table in the attractive cellar, with its pleasing mix of French memorabilia and brick and stone walls. Gutsy, generously sized, great value Gallic dishes range from quiches and gratins to pork neck and beef Bourguignon.

Menu 31 zł (lunch) – Carte 58/100 zł

PLAN: C3 – *ul. Józefa 34 – ✆ 500 410 829 – www.zaziebistro.pl – Closed lunch Monday*

Hana Sushi

JAPANESE • SIMPLE This simple Japanese-style restaurant has made a real impact in the city. The chef-owner is a Sushi Master who trained in Tokyo and the sushi is prepared with finesse. They also serve some Korean dishes like ramen and bibimbap.

Carte 60/300 zł

PLAN: C3 – *ul. Kupa 12 – ✆ 608 576 255 – www.hanasushikrakow.pl – Closed Monday*

Karakter

MODERN CUISINE • FRIENDLY Karakter is a lively spot, with loud music, cocktails and a minimalist feel. The charming young team serve an extensive menu with a focus on offal; horse meat tartare is one of their signatures. Refined cooking blends many different flavours.

Menu 35 zł (lunch) – Carte 65/105 zł

PLAN: C3 – *Brzozowa 17 – ✆ 795 818 123 – www.facebook.com/karakter.restauracja/ – Closed lunch Monday*

Miodova

POLISH • FRIENDLY In a cobbled square in the busy Jewish district you'll find 'Honey', an ultra-modern restaurant set over 3 floors. It's a comfortable place, with sofa-style banquettes and colourful cushions. Regional specialities are given modern twists.

Menu 39 zł (lunch) – Carte 65/132 zł

PLAN: C3 – *ul. Szeroka 3 – ✆ 12 432 50 83 – www.miodova.pl – Closed 23-25 December*

Szara Kazimierz 

POLISH • BRASSERIE A friendly brasserie with a tiled floor and bold fern wallpaper, situated in the heart of the Jewish Quarter; if the weather's good, ask for a seat on the enclosed rear terrace, or out the front, overlooking the square. Menus reflect the owners' heritage by mixing Polish and Swedish classics.

Menu 38 zł (lunch) – Carte 60/125 zł

PLAN: C3 – *ul. Szeroka 39 – ✆ 12 429 12 19 – www.szarakazimierz.pl*

Environs of Krakow

(Plan 1)

0 400 m

A
B
1
2
3

Kazimierza Wielkiego
Królewska
Leopolda Staffa
Juliusza Lea
Juliusza
Lea
Kijowska
Chocimska
Nowowiejska
Racławicka
Urzędnicza
Kujawska
Konarskiego
Czarnowiejska
Kawiory
Wladyslawa
Stanisława
Reymonta
U
Henryka
Reymana
PARK
JORDANA
3 Maja
BŁONIA
Focha
Oleandry
Mazowiecka
A. Grottgera
Sienkiewicza
Czymsików
ŁOBZÓW
Wrocławska
Lubelska
Prądnicka
Al.
Pl. Nowy Kleparz
KLEPA
Słowackiego
Al. Juliusza
KOŚCIÓŁ ŚW. SZCZEPANA
KOŚCIÓŁ ŚW. JÓZEFA
Łobzowska
Krowoderska
Długa
NOWA WIEŚ
Fryderyka Chopina
PARK KRAKOWSKI
H. Siemiradzkiego
PIASEK
Stare Miasto (Plan 2)
Mickiewicza
Al. Adama
Karmelicka
Garbarska
Rajska
Antoniego Dunajewskiego
Bas
PL
Pl. Szczepańs.
Krupnicza
Szewska
RYI
GŁÓ
Studencka
Garncarska
Wenecja
Podwale
SUKIEN
COLLEGIUM MAIUS
R
Wiślna
Bracka
Jabłonowskich
KOŚCIÓŁ SERCANEK
Piłsudskiego
Al. Zygmunta Krasińskiego
Floriana
NOWY SWIAT
Smoleńska
Franciszkańs
KOŚCI
FRANCISZI
Rotmistrza Zbigniewa Dunin-Wąsowicza
Retoryka
Zwierzyniecka
Straszewskiego
Poselska
PLANTY
Bolesława
Prusa
Salwatorska
Mlaskotów
Włóczków
Powiśle
Emaus
Królowej Jadwigi
Pl. Na Stawach
ZWIERZYNIEC
Podzamcze
Senatorska
Most Dębnicki
Kościuszki
KATEDRA WAWELSKA
ZA
KRÓ
Księcia Józefa
WISŁA
DEBNIKI
Marii Konopnickiej
Tyniecka
Rynek Dębnicki
Barska
KOŚCIÓŁ ŚW. STANISŁAWA KOSTKI
Praska
Konfederacka
Most Grunwaldzki
K
ŚW.
I STA
Zagrody
Rondo Grunwaldzkie
Szwedzka
Dębowa
Cassino
Monte
Twardowskiego
Generala Bohdana Zielinskiego
Kapelanka
Jana
Komandosów
LUDWINÓW
Luc

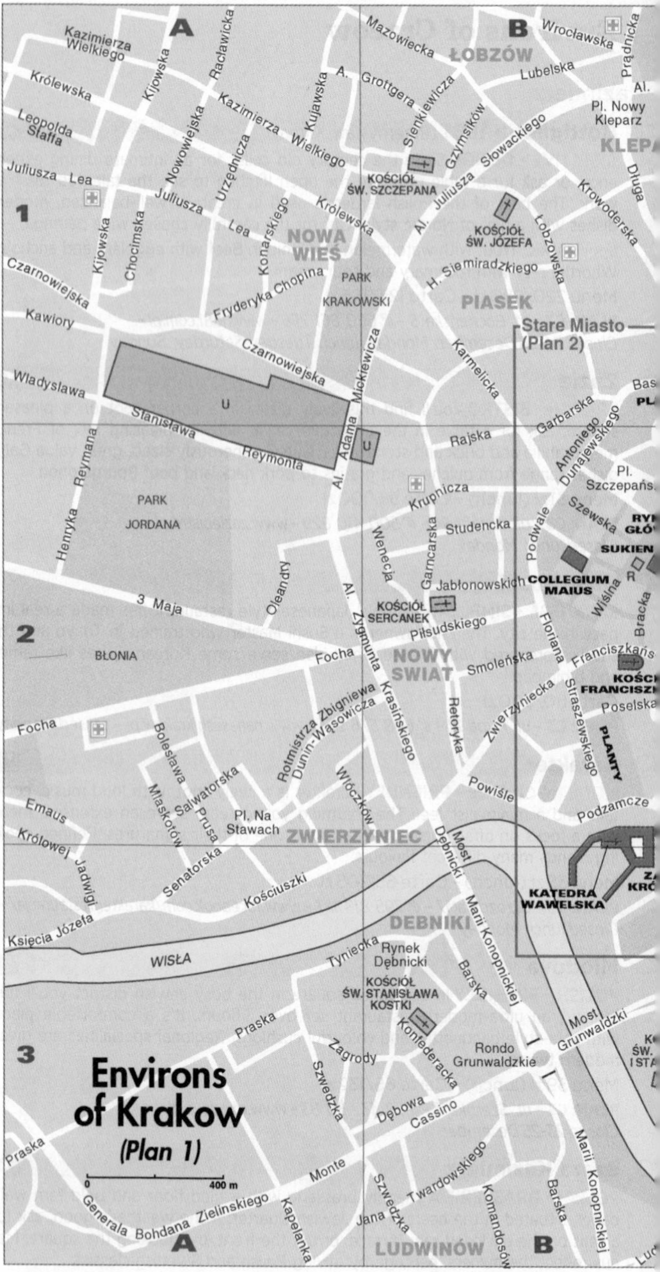

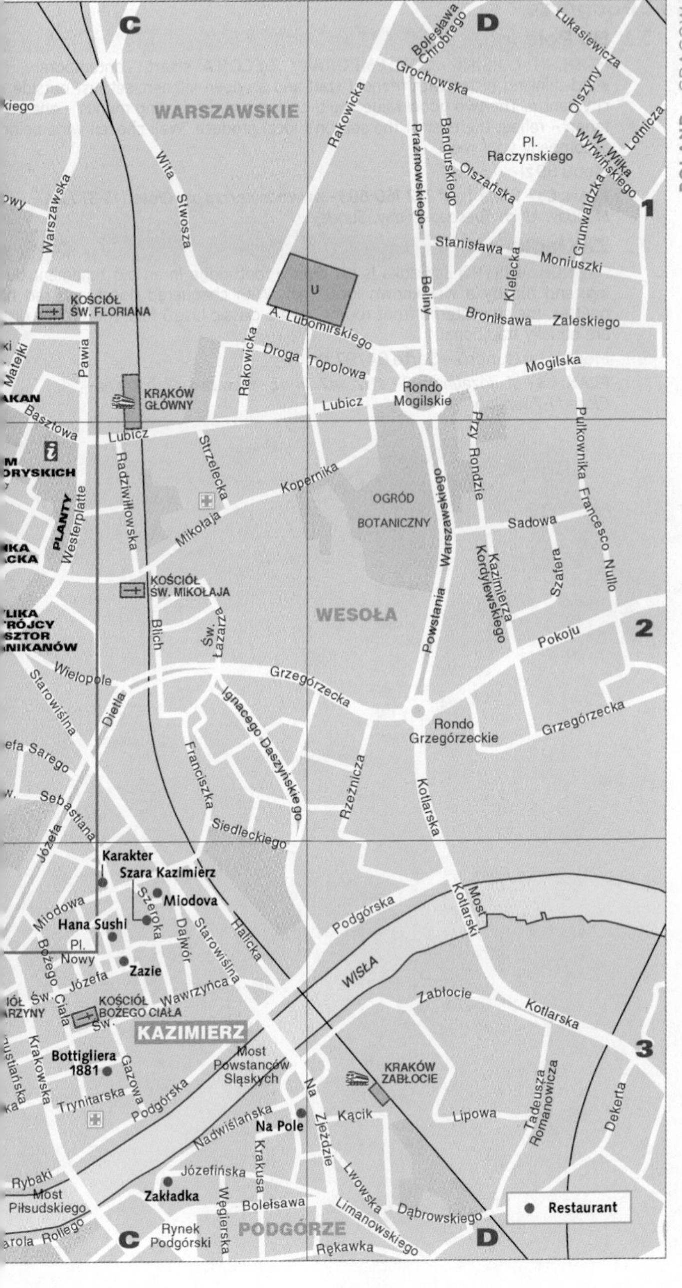
C
D
WARSZAWSKIE
WESOŁA
KAZIMIERZ
PODGÓRZE
KOŚCIÓŁ ŚW. FLORIANA
KRAKÓW GŁÓWNY
KOŚCIÓŁ ŚW. MIKOŁAJA
KOŚCIÓŁ BOŻEGO CIAŁA
KRAKÓW ZABŁOCIE
OGRÓD BOTANICZNY
Rondo Mogilskie
Rondo Grzegórzeckie
Pl. Raczynskiego
WISŁA
Karakter
Szara Kazimierz
Miodowa
Hana Sushi
Zazie
Bottigliera 1881
Na Pole
Zakładka
Restaurant
Grochowska
Rakowicka
Lubicz
Mogilska
Grzegórzecka
Kotlarska
Most Kotlarski
Most Powstańców Śląskich
Most Piłsudskiego
Rynek Podgórski
Podgórska
Zabłocie
Lipowa
Limanowskiego
Dąbrowskiego
Rękawka
1
2
3

at Podgórze

Na Pole

MODERN CUISINE • CONTEMPORARY DÉCOR A smart, contemporary, f ward-thinking bistro with friendly staff and an open kitchen, set just outside t city centre. The two good value, multi-course surprise tasting menus – one ve tarian – reflect the best of the season's local produce. Well-chosen wine pairir accompany your meal.

Menu 89 zł

PLAN: C3 – *Solna 1 – ✆ 722 160 603 – www.napole.com.pl – Closed 13-31 July, Monday, lunch Tuesday-Friday, Sunday*

ZaKładka

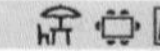

FRENCH • BISTRO ZaKładka is set over a footbridge in an old tenement bui ing, and run by a well-known local chef. With chequered floors and red b quettes, the characterful front rooms have a classic bistro feel; the French dist are equally traditional.

Menu 41 zł (lunch) – Carte 64/97 zł

PLAN: C3 – *ul. Józefińska 2 – ✆ 12 442 74 42 – www.zakladkabistro.pl – Closed 1-7 January*

SeanPavonePhoto/iStock

PORTUGAL

PORTUGAL

LISBON

LISBOA

LeoPatrizi/iStock

LISBON IN...

→ **ONE DAY**
Alfama, Castelo São Jorge, Bairro Alto.

→ **TWO DAYS**
Baixa, Calouste Gulbenkian Museum, Parque das Nações.

→ **THREE DAYS**
Museu Nacional de Arte Antiga, Belém.

Sitting on the north bank the River Tagus, beneath hug open skies and surrounded b seven hills, Lisbon boasts a atmosphere that few citi can match. An enchantir walk around the streets ha an old-time ambience all of i own, matched only by a jau on the trams and funicula that run up and down the steep hills. At first sight Lisbo is all flaky palaces, meandering alleyways and castellate horizon quarried from medieval stone; but there's a 2 element, too. Slinky new developments line the riversid linking the old and new in a glorious jumble which spi down the slopes to the water's edge. The views of the wat from various vantage points all over Lisbon and the vistas the 'Straw Sea' – so named because of the golden reflections of the sun – reach out to visitors, along with the sounds of fado, the city's alluring folk music, which conjures up a melancholic yearning.

The compact heart of the city is the Baixa, a flat, 18C grid of streets flanked by the hills. To the west is the elegant commercial district of Chiado and the funky hilltop Bairro Alto, while immediately to the east is Alfama, a tightly packed former Moorish quarter with kasbah-like qualities. North of here is the working-class neighbourhood of Graça and way out west lies the spacious riverside suburb of Belém, while up the river to the east can be found the ultra-modern Parque das Nações.

EATING OUT

sboetas love their local agricultural roduce and the cuisine of the region an be characterised by its honesty nd simplicity. The city has an aged maritime tradition and there are number of fishing ports nearby, so cean-fresh fish and seafood features in a range of dishes. One thing e locals love in particular is bacalau (cod), and it's said that in Lisbon, ere's a different way to prepare it r every day of the year: it may come ven-baked, slow-cooked or cooked in ilk, and it can be served wrapped in cabbage, with tocino belly pork or in a myriad of other ways. While eating in either a humble tasca, a casa de pasto or a restaurante, other specialities to keep an eye out for are clams cooked with garlic and coriander, traditional beef, chicken and sausage stew with vegetables and rice, bean casserole with tocino belly pork, and lamprey eel with rice. Enjoy them with a vinho verde, the wine of the region. A service charge will be included on your bill but it's customary to leave a tip of about ten per cent.

Old Lisbon

Alma (Henrique Sá Pessoa)

CREATIVE • CONTEMPORARY DÉCOR Located in the heart of the Chiado d trict in an 18C building that was once a warehouse for the famous Bertrand boo shop, the oldest in the world. The interior is one of striking contrasts and p vides the backdrop for seasonal à la carte options and interesting set mer that encompass traditional, international and Mediterranean dishes.

Specialities: Fish and seafood soup with seaweed. Suckling pig, turnip top pur pickled onions, pepper jus. Chocolate "bomb" with salted caramel.

Menu 64/120 € – Carte 70/90 €

PLAN: A2 – *Rua Anchieta 15 – Ⓜ Baixa-Chiado – ✆ 21 347 0650 – www.almalisboa.pt – Closed Monday*

Belcanto (José Avillez)

CREATIVE • COSY Occupying a former convent in the Bairro Alto (Chiado) d trict popular with tourists, the Belcanto offers one of the country's very best di ing experiences. Here, its outstanding chef conjures up serious yet creative c sine, with the option for eight guests to dine at the chef's table in the kitchen.

Specialities: Giant red shrimp with spherified clams xerém. Sea bass with av cado. Cuttlefish, chocolate and cuttlefish ink.

Menu 165/185 € – Carte 106/120 €

PLAN: A2 – *Largo de São Carlos 10 – Ⓜ Baixa-Chiado – ✆ 21 342 0607 – www.belcanto.pt – Closed Monday, Sunday*

EPUR (Vincent Farges)

CREATIVE • TRENDY Haute cuisine and superb views in a restaurant occupyi a renovated building in the Chiado district where the designer look and cuisi come as a pleasant surprise. Here, French chef Vincent Farges has opted for single surprise menu with a creative edge that is highly visual, elegant and r spects the purity of each individual flavour.

Specialities: Bonito, huacatay and cucumber. Rooster fish, oysters, codium ar timur. Strawberries, rhubarb and raspberries.

Menu 35 € (lunch), 65/160 €

PLAN: A2 – *Largo da Academia Nacional De Belas Artes 14 – Ⓜ Baixa-Chiado – ✆ 21 346 0519 – www.epur.pt – Closed 1-20 January, 2-17 August, Monday, Sunday*

O Asiático

ASIAN • TRENDY India, Thailand, China and Japan are all represented by th chef, who has spent time living in Asia. He creates attractive fusion cuisine base around Portuguese ingredients and the dishes are perfect for sharing.

Carte 31/40 €

PLAN: A1 – *Rua da Rosa 317 – ✆ 21 131 9369 – www.oasiatico.com – Closed lunch Monday-Thursday*

A Cevicheria

PERUVIAN • TRENDY Peruvian cooking with a Portuguese edge. The setting tight on space but highly original, including a huge octopus hanging from th ceiling! There's always a queue to get in here.

Carte 20/35 €

PLAN: A1 – *Rua Dom Pedro V-129 – ✆ 21 803 8815*

100 Maneiras

CREATIVE • DESIGN A restaurant that has benefited from a change of locatio and which now boasts a modern look and even a chef's table. The cuisine her is based around several menus with a focus on modern and creative cooking.

Menu 80/110 €

PLAN: A1 – *Rua do Teixeira 39 – ✆ 910 307 575 – www.100maneiras.com – Closed Monday, lunch Tuesday-Sunday*

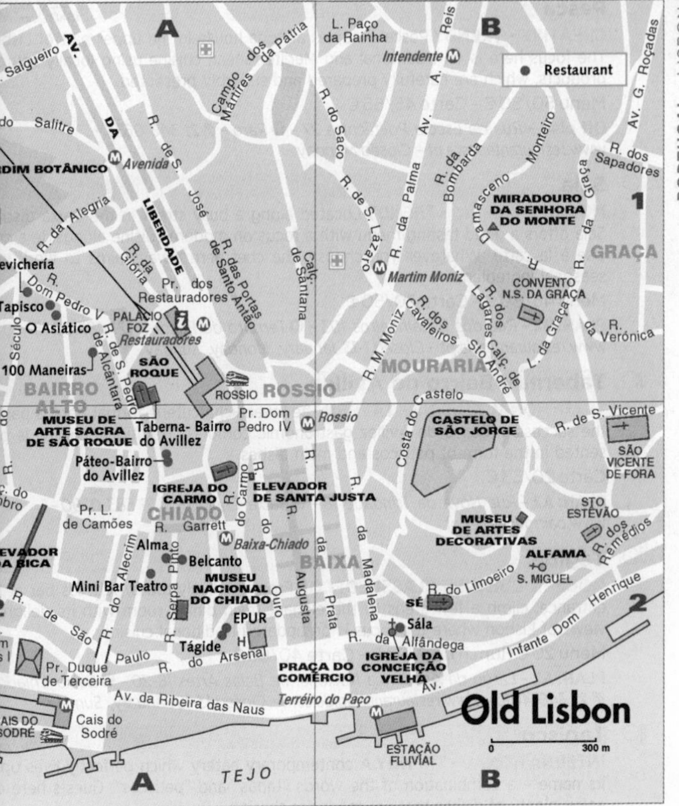

Mini Bar Teatro

CREATIVE • BISTRO An informal, enticing and relaxed eatery in the Bairro Alto theatre district. Diners are in for a pleasant surprise as the dishes on the menu have been created by José Avillez – Michelin-Starred chef at the Belcanto restaurant.

Menu 45/55€ – Carte 39/58€

PLAN: A2 – *Rua António Maria Cardoso 58 – Ⓜ Baixa-Chiado – ✆ 21 130 5393 – www.minibar.pt – Closed lunch Monday-Sunday*

Páteo - Bairro do Avillez

SEAFOOD • MEDITERRANEAN This restaurant occupies the central patio of an attractive gastronomic complex. The focus is on the high quality of the produce used and delicious seafood takes centre stage.

Carte 41/65€

PLAN: A2 – *Rua Nova da Trindade 18 – Ⓜ Baixa-Chiado – ✆ 21 583 0290 – www.bairrodoavillez.pt*

Pesca

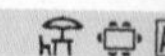

CREATIVE • TRENDY Pesca occupies a stone house in the upper part of Lisbo The focus here is on traditional and Mediterranean cuisine using locally sourc products, which are carefully prepared and superbly presented.

Menu 50/80 € – Carte 45/65 €

Off plan – *Rua da Escola Politécnica 27 – Ⓜ Rato – ✆ 21 346 0633 – www.restaurantepesca.pt – Closed Monday*

Sála

MODERN CUISINE • TRENDY Located along a busy street in the Baixa distri Sála offers a good tasting menu with a focus on modern cuisine alongside a cc cise à la carte. Whatever you choose, the chef here always aims to work wi seasonal ingredients.

Menu 45/80 € – Carte 30/50 €

PLAN: B2 – *Rua dos Bacalhoeiros 103 – Ⓜ Terreiro do Paço – ✆ 21 887 3045 – www.restaurantesala.pt – Closed 1-13 January, Monday, Sunday*

Taberna - Bairro do Avillez

TRADITIONAL CUISINE • TAVERN The tavern-charcuterie format here is part the successful Bairro do Avillez gastronomic complex. Traditional cuisine is pr sented in the form of petiscos and main dishes.

Carte 20/33 €

PLAN: A2 – *Rua Nova da Trindade 18 – Ⓜ Baixa-Chiado – ✆ 21 583 0290 – www.bairrodoavillez.pt*

Tágide

MODERN CUISINE • CLASSIC DÉCOR From the lively tapas/petiscos bar at t entrance, climb a few steps to the elegant main dining room with its delightf views of Lisbon where the focus is on updated traditional cuisine.

Menu 20 € (lunch), 69/88 € – Carte 40/65 €

PLAN: A2 – *Largo da Academia Nacional de Belas Artes 18-20 – Ⓜ Baixa-Chiado – ✆ 21 340 4010 – www.restaurantetagide.com – Closed 13-19 January, Sunday*

Tapisco

INTERNATIONAL • TRENDY A contemporary eatery which perfectly lives up t its name – a combination of the words "tapas" and "petiscos". Guests here ca enjoy plenty of dishes that are made for sharing.

Carte 25/40 €

PLAN: A1 – *Rua Dom Pedro V 81 – ✆ 213 420 681 – www.tapisco.pt*

Environs of Lisbon

At East

Fifty Seconds

CREATIVE • ELEGANT Enjoy a gastronomic experience 120m above ground i this panoramic restaurant in the famous Vasco de Gama tower. Here, Spanis chef Martín Berasategui reveals the true essence of his cuisine, showcased i modern cooking and contemporary techniques which always respect flavours t the full. The incredible views provide the icing on the cake!

Specialities: Oyster with a green olive juice, wasabi emulsion and crunchy sea weed. Pigeon with apple, false white asparagus risotto, toasted butter and vin tage balsamic jus, citrus chutney. Infusion of rice, milk and cardamom, pistachic yuzu and kalamansi.

Menu 130/170 € – Carte 100/130 €

Off plan – *Cais das Naus – Ⓜ Oriente – ✆ 21 152 5380 – www.fiftysecondsexperience.com – Closed 1-23 January, Monday, Sunday*

t West

Eleven (Joachim Koerper)

CREATIVE • ELEGANT Housed in a designer style building above the Amália Rodrigues gardens, this light, airy and modern restaurant boasts splendid views of the Eduardo VII park and the city. Creative gourmet cuisine features on the menu.

Specialities: Duck foie gras, soy, rum and orange. Lobster with sesame, spinach and Madras curry sauce. Cheesecake with avocado and shiso.

Menu 35€ (lunch), 98/185€ – Carte 80/130€

Off plan – *Rua Marquês de Fronteira* – *São Sebastião* – *21 386 2211* – *www.restauranteleven.com* – *Closed Sunday*

Feitoria

MODERN CUISINE • ELEGANT A restaurant of a very high standard, featuring a bar for a pre-dinner drink and a dining room arranged in a contemporary style. The chef offers creative, modern cuisine steeped in tradition, with a focus on high quality products and top-notch presentation.

Specialities: Carabineiro prawns from the Algarve. Fresh fish from Peniche market, bivalves and Carolina rice with burnt samphire. Pastel de nata.

Menu 85/135€ – Carte 75/90€

Off plan – *Hotel Altis Belém, Doca do Bom Sucesso* – *21 040 0208* – *www.restaurantefeitoria.com* – *Closed 1-17 January, Monday, lunch Tuesday-Saturday, Sunday*

Loco (Alexandre Silva)

MODERN CUISINE • TRENDY Located next to the Basílica da Estrela, Loco has just the one dining room with a surprising design and views of the kitchen. Alexandre Silva, famous for winning the first *Top Chef de Portugal* competition, showcases his cuisine via two enticing and creative tasting menus, which make full use of locally sourced ingredients.

Specialities: Carabineiro prawn sashimi. Cured cod with a garlic sauce. Sheep's milk meringue with requeijão cream cheese and ice cream.

Menu 96/112€

Off plan – *Rua dos Navegantes 53 B* – *Rato* – *21 395 1861* – *www.loco.pt* – *Closed 4-19 June, 12-26 November, Monday, lunch Tuesday-Saturday, Sunday*

Saraiva's

INTERNATIONAL • BISTRO A bar-restaurant with lots of character following its renovation, and a good location just a few metres from the Eduardo VII park. It now features a much more informal and relaxed bistro-style look, with an attractive bar at the entrance, bare tables of different heights and a small private room. The attractive contrast between the decor of warm wood and ceramic panels in varying tones of green provides plenty of personality. International and traditional Portuguese cuisine featuring dishes that have been given a modern twist, with the beef tartare, smoked sausage croquettes and confit pork worth a special mention.

Menu 14€ (lunch), 20/35€ – Carte 21/35€

Off plan – *Rua Engenheiro Canto Resende 3* – *São Sebastião* – *21 340 4010* – *www.restaurantetagide.com* – *Closed 13-19 January, Sunday*

Solar dos Nunes

TRADITIONAL CUISINE • RUSTIC One of those restaurants that never disappoints thanks to its combination of friendly and professional service from a dedicated team and the high-quality cooking on offer. The menu here provides the perfect opportunity to discover traditional Portuguese cuisine and, more specifically, that of the Alentejo. It features a bar and two slightly cramped dining rooms with exposed wood beams, azulejo panelling, delightful paved flooring in the style of the city's pavements, and numerous gastronomic awards adorning its walls. You'll find it hard to resist ordering some of the fish in its enticing display cabinet.

Carte 33/42€

Off plan – *Rua dos Lusíadas 68-72* – *21 364 7359* – *www.solardosnunes.pt* – *Closed Sunday*

Go Juu

JAPANESE • DESIGN Enjoy authentic Japanese cooking in this unique, alm minimalist space featuring a profusion of wood and a sushi bar in the din room. There's also an exclusive area for Go Juu's club members.

Menu 15€ (lunch)/23€ – Carte 45/65€

Off plan – *Rua Marquês Sá da Bandeira 46 – Ⓜ S. Sebastião – ✆ 21 828 0704 – www.gojuu.pt – Closed 24-31 August, 21-31 December, Monday, dinner Sunday*

O Talho

MEATS AND GRILLS • TRENDY A highly original restaurant given that access it is via a modern butcher's shop. Not surprisingly, the menu here is cent around meat and its by-products.

Carte 31/48€

Off plan – *Rua Carlos Testa 18 – Ⓜ S. Sebastião – ✆ 21 315 4105 – www.otalho.pt*

Varanda

MODERN CUISINE • ELEGANT The terrace overlooking the Eduardo VII park as impressive as the cuisine here, which includes an extensive buffet at lunchtir and more gastronomic dining in the evening.

Menu 76€ (lunch), 89/105€ – Carte 90/120€

Off plan – *Hotel Four Seasons H. Ritz Lisbon, Rua Rodrigo da Fonseca 88 – Ⓜ Marquês de Pombal – ✆ 21 381 1400 – www.fourseasons.com*

Trifonov_Evgeniy/iStock

SLOVENIA

SLOVENIJA

LJUBLJANA
LJUBLJANA

sonsam/iStock

LJUBLJANA IN...

→ **ONE DAY**
Visit the castle and San Nicola cathedral.

→ **TWO DAYS**
Tivoli Park, Tivoli Mansion – International Centre of Graphic Arts, Dragon Bridge, Triple Bridge (Tromostovje)

→ **THREE DAYS**
Central Market (Centralna Tržnica), Town Square, City Gallery (Mestna galerija), National University Library (NUK), National Museum of Slovenia, Museum of Modern Art

The capital of Sloveni as well as its largest cit Ljubljana boasts larg green spaces thanks t its many parks and ga dens and is also home t a university and open-a cafés lining the banks o the River Ljubljanica whic divides the old town fro the city's commercial ce tre. The symbol of the cit and its main attraction its austere and monume tal castle perched on top of Grajska Planota hill. It is fro the castle's walls and panoramic tower that you can enjo the best views of the city, where each district has retaine

its own distinct historic style – medieval, Baroque or Art Nouveau. Despite this, the signature of Jože Plečnik is everywhere: from the 1920s to the beginning of the Second World War this brilliant architect and town planner was entrusted with the task of redesigning the city, adapting it to his own taste. Art-lovers will find plenty to satisfy their artistic passion in Ljubljana, such as the National Museum of Slovenia and the Museum of Modern Art, the latter exhibiting local works from the 20C, while the city also boasts plenty of pleasant surprises in terms of its good food and relaxed and friendly atmosphere.

EATING OUT

ıfluenced by the gastronomic traditions of its neighbours – Italy, Austria nd Hungary – Slovenia's cuisine is parcularly rich and varied, with a slight mphasis on meat dishes rather than sh and seafood.

mong its highlights, don't miss the cal **kraški pršut**, a cured ham which is avoured with juniper berries and usuly served together with other meats ıch as **divjačinska salama**, a sausage ıade from game. Jota is the queen of ovenia's soups – originally made from hatever frugal ingredients were to and, it has developed into a national elicacy. Made from meat, beans and ıuerkraut, it is served piping hot.

ne country's Mediterranean coastline and the vicinity of the Istrian peninsula have added hints of maritime influence to its cuisine, with grilled or steamed fish flavoured with natural seasonings and accompanied by delicious local produce.

Last but not least, this resolutely hearty cuisine has now found a fitting partner in the country's local wines. Differences in geography, climate and ageing methods in the main wine-producing regions ensure that a wide range of varieties and quality are available, so whether your preference is for red or white, dry or sweet, easy drinking or more robust wines, you'll find that there's something for everyone in Slovenia!

Atelje

CREATIVE • CONTEMPORARY DÉCOR Don't be fooled by appearances – though the cuisine served here may look simple, it is actually elegant and skilf thought out. Fermented products add a touch of acidity to the dishes, while gredients such as kombucha and miso bear witness to the chef's travels arou the world.

Specialities: Confit of butternut squash, homemade x.o., tamarind and pump oil sauce. Venison, quince, whey "brown cheese", bordelaise sauce. Stale bre ice cream, candied black olives, lardo.

Menu 18 € (lunch), 57/90 €

Nazorjeva ulica 2 – ✆ 1 308 19 07 – www.restavracijaatelje.com – Closed 8 Februar 1-2 May, 24-25 December, lunch Saturday, Sunday

Na Gradu

TRADITIONAL CUISINE • HISTORIC Real care and passion go into the prepa tion of the traditional dishes served here, which are influenced by the culin heritage of 24 different regions. To make the most of your dining experien our inspectors recommend that you choose one of the two tasting menus – hi lights of which include the *Kobarid štruklji* (stuffed dumplings). The restaura location in the old castle overlooking the city adds to its appeal.

Menu 20 € (lunch), 35/42 € – Carte 25/50 €

Grajska planota 1 – ✆ 820 51930 – www.nagradu.si

AS

TRADITIONAL CUISINE • TRADITIONAL Serving excellent food for o 20 years, this urban restaurant has a charmingly rustic feel. Classic Mediterran fare features on the menu, with an emphasis on pasta-based first courses a meat cooked over the charcoal grill, as well as fish specialities from the Adria In summer, choose one of the tables on the panoramic terrace with its views the castle in the distance.

Menu 55/65 € – Carte 55/80 €

Čopova ulica 5A – ✆ 1 425 88 22 – www.gostilnaas.si

B-Restaurant

MODERN CUISINE • DESIGN Situated on the panoramic rooftop of the conte porary InterContinental hotel, this large restaurant offers a modern, open spac which the chefs can be seen hard at work on one side, while on the other view extends from the Alps to the old town dominated by its castle. The cuis is both simple and modern, with a particular focus on meat dishes.

Carte 39/58 €

Slovenska Cesta 59 – ✆ 591 28048 – www.brestaurant.si – Closed lunch Saturday-Sunday

CUBO

MEDITERRANEAN CUISINE • CONTEMPORARY DÉCOR This restaurant on edge of the city has a loyal local clientele, although it also welcomes tourists w are drawn here by the delicious Mediterranean-influenced cuisine and occasic Asian-inspired dishes. Generous portions, plus an extensive wine list (with wi also available by the glass) add to the appeal.

Menu 50 € – Carte 45/65 €

Šmartinska cesta 55 – ✆ 1 521 15 15 – www.cubo.si – Closed 1-20 August, Sunday

Harfa

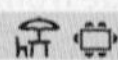

MODERN CUISINE • CONTEMPORARY DÉCOR Thanks to the cheerful serv and modern style at this small place, you will quickly forget the slightly outly location. Mediterranean cuisine with fish given pride of place and Slover wines: just the ticket for a business lunch, a moment of respite from a h day's work or a reunion with friends. It is often a full house: booking advisable

Carte 40/50 €

Koprska Ulica 98 – ✆ 1 423 24 11 – www.harfa-restavracija.si – Closed dinner Monday-Friday, Saturday, Sunday

JB

MODERN CUISINE • **FAMILY** Occupying a Secessionist-style building dating from the 1920s and designed by architect Jože Plečnik, this restaurant is named after its current owner-chef Janez Bratovž. With its high ceilings, marble floors, contemporary artwork adorning the walls and Art Deco-style chandeliers, the restaurant offers the perfect setting for its highly successful cuisine. All the dishes are rooted in classical recipes and yet boast original, intense and cleverly balanced flavours and combinations.

Menu 25 € (lunch), 60/95 € – Carte 45/88 €

Miklošičeva cesta 17 – ☎ 1 430 70 70 – www.jb-slo.com – Closed 8 February, 1-2 May, 24-26 December, lunch Saturday, Sunday

Maxim

MEDITERRANEAN CUISINE • **CLASSIC DÉCOR** Served in a stylish and elegant setting, the cuisine here draws from French culinary traditions. It also showcases influences from the Mediterranean, resulting in dishes that are original and attractive. Attentive, professional service completes the picture.

Menu 25 € (lunch), 50/80 € – Carte 25/80 €

Trg Republike 1 – ☎ 51 285 335 – www.maxi.si/sl/restavracija-maxim – Closed 3-17 August, Saturday, Sunday

Monstera Bistro

MARKET CUISINE • **BISTRO** A classic bistro situated in a quiet, secluded street in the city centre. Market-fresh cuisine (mainly meat) with a few vegetarian dishes, as well as a good wine list that includes organic choices. A young, lively ambience, plus prices which are pleasantly restrained!

Menu 20 € (lunch), 48/58 €

Gosposka Ulica 9 – ☎ 40 431 123 – www.monsterabistro.si – Closed dinner Monday-Wednesday, Sunday

Separé

MARKET CUISINE • **CONTEMPORARY DÉCOR** Situated off the beaten track, this modern restaurant serves cuisine which changes daily according to market availability. For this reason, don't expect a menu or a wine list – dishes are announced at your table and created using excellent ingredients carefully prepared to showcase their superb quality.

Carte 32/45 €

Koprska cesta 92 – ☎ 40 551 155 – www.separe.si – Closed 25 December, dinner Saturday, Sunday

Shambala

ASIAN • **ORIENTAL** A small part of Asia comes to life in the centre of Ljubljana. Guests can dine either in the main dining room with its glass ceiling or in the more intimate room with a vaulted ceiling. The exotic ambience is highlighted by bamboo plants and Asian decor, while the menu features seafood dishes, vegetarian options and grilled specialities. The marinades and sauces are excellent, as are the red and green Thai curries.

Menu 22/47 € – Carte 16 €

Križevniška ulica 12 – ☎ 31 843 833 – www.shambala.si – Closed Sunday

Strelec

MODERN CUISINE • **HISTORIC** This stylish restaurant boasts a charming, historic setting in the picturesque Archers' Tower of Ljubljana castle. Enjoy top-quality Slovenian cuisine which showcases the best of the country's traditional recipes alongside more contemporary fare.

Menu 32 € (lunch), 57/87 € – Carte 46/114 €

Grajska planota 1 – ☎ 31 687 648 – www.kaval-group.si – Closed Sunday

Sushisama

JAPANESE • CONTEMPORARY DÉCOR As soon as you cross the threshold this restaurant situated in an attractive pedestrianised area of the city cen you feel as though you've left Ljubljana and arrived somewhere in Japan, tha to the large sushi counter offering a tempting selection of different cuts of r fish. The service here manages to combine professionalism with informality.

Menu 35/70 € – Carte 25/90 €

Wolfova Ulica 12 – ✆ 40 702 070 – www.sushimama.si – Closed Sunday

Valvas'or

MEDITERRANEAN CUISINE • CLASSIC DÉCOR A stylish restaurant, with a f tables outside in summer and a classic yet romantic atmosphere inside. T hugely varied menu gives a hint of the hard work that goes into the preparati here, with scallops, sea bass and other fish dishes featuring alongside meat c tions and numerous barbecued specialities.

Menu 20 € (lunch), 40/70 € – Carte 25/100 €

Stari Trg 7 – ✆ 1 425 04 55 – www.valvasor.net – Closed 25 December-2 January, Sunday

Vander

MEDITERRANEAN CUISINE • BISTRO Delicious Mediterranean cuisine prepar using carefully selected, fresh ingredients is to the fore in this charming resta rant on the ground floor of a hotel. The personalised interior includes wine bo tles stacked on the walls and wooden tables, while in summer the outdoor dini area offers pleasant views of the river.

Menu 16 € (lunch), 39/89 € – Carte 28/46 €

Krojaska Ulica 6 – ✆ 1 200 90 00 – www.vanderhotel.com

GRATIA PLENA
CIVITAS

RudyBalasko/iStock

SPAIN

ESPAÑA

MADRID
MADRID

benedek/iStock

MADRID IN...

→ **ONE DAY**
Puerta del Sol, Plaza Mayor, Palacio Real, Museo del Prado.

→ **TWO DAYS**
Museo Thyssen-Bornemisza, Retiro, Gran Vía, tapas at a traditional taberna.

→ **THREE DAYS**
Chueca, Malasaña, Centro de Arte Reina Sofía.

The renaissance of Madrid has seen it develop as a big player on the world cultural stage, attracting more international music, theatre and dance than it would have dreamed of a few decades ago. The nightlife in Spain's proud capital is second to none and the superb art museums which make up the city's 'golden triangle' have all undergone thrilling reinvention in recent years. This is a city that might think it has some catching up to do: it was only made the capital in 1561 on the whim of ruler, Felipe II. But its position was crucial: slap bang in the middle of the Iberian Peninsula. Ruled by Habsburgs and Bourbons, it soon made a mark in Europe,

and the contemporary big wigs of Madrid are now having the same effect – this time with a 21C twist.

The central heart of Madrid is compact, defined by the teeming Habsburg hubs of Puerta del Sol and Plaza Mayor, and the mighty Palacio Real – the biggest official royal residence in the world, with a bewildering three thousand rooms. East of here are the grand squares, fountains and fine museums of the Bourbon District, with its easterly boundary, the Retiro park. West of the historical centre are the capacious green acres of Casa de Campo, while the affluent, regimented grid streets of Salamanca are to the east. Modern Madrid is just to the north, embodied in the grand north-south boulevard Paseo de la Castellana.

EATING OUT

Madrileños know how to pace themselves. Breakfast is around 8am, lunch 2pm or 3pm, the afternoon begins at 5pm and dinner won't be until 10pm or 11pm. Madrid is the European capital which has best managed to absorb the regional cuisine of the country, largely due to massive internal migration to the city, and it claims to have highest number of bars and restaurants per capita than anywhere else in the world. If you want to tuck into local specialities, you'll find them everywhere around the city. Callos a la Madrileña is Madrid-style tripe, dating back to 1559, while sopas de ajo (garlic soup) is a favourite on cold winter days. Another popular soup (also a main course) is cocido Madrileño, hearty and aromatic and comprised of chickpeas, meat, tocino belly pork, potatoes and vegetables, slowly cooked in a rich broth. To experience the real Madrid dining ambience, get to a traditional taberna in the heart of the old neighbourhood: these are distinguished by a large clock, a carved wooden bar with a zinc counter, wine flasks, marble-topped tables and ceramic tiles.

Centre - Moncloa

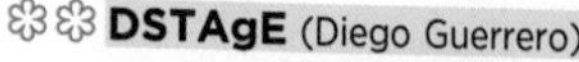

✿✿ DSTAgE (Diego Guerrero)

CREATIVE • TRENDY This restaurant has an urban and industrial look and a laxed feel that reflects the personality of the chef. The name is an acronym of core philosophy: 'Days to Smell Taste Amaze Grow & Enjoy'. Discover cuisine th brings disparate cultures, ingredients and flavours together from Spain, Mexi and Japan.

Specialities: Cured egg yolk tartlet and tear peas. Lamb, kombu, cogollo lettu and piparra chilli peppers. Corn.

Menu 145/170 €

PLAN: 1-C1 – *Regueros 8 – Ⓜ Alonso Martínez – ✆ 917 02 15 86 – www.dstageconcept.com – Closed 1-23 August, 22 December-7 January, Saturday, Sunday*

✿✿ Paco Roncero (Paco Roncero)

CREATIVE • ELEGANT This unique restaurant is accessed via an impressive 1 staircase leading to a cutting-edge space on the top floor. Chef Paco Ronce welcomes guests on a gastronomic journey which offers guests a more visu and interactive dining experience.

Specialities: Grilled razor clams with a vegetable curry. Hake with crab and B bao-style pil-pil. Circus cake.

Menu 148/185 €

PLAN: 1-C2 – *Alcalá 15 – Ⓜ Sevilla – ✆ 915 32 12 75 – www.pacoroncero.com – Closed 1-31 August, Monday, Sunday*

✿ Cebo

CREATIVE • DESIGN A meticulously appointed modern space with a hint of d signer decor, and a splendid bar where dishes are completed in front of guest The creative cuisine is a statement of intent for a culinary experience that is bu around a unique fusion of regional cooking from around Spain.

Specialities: Anchovy 2016. Costa Brava rice with influences from its surroundir area. Bergamot cruni.

Menu 85/130 €

PLAN: 1-C2 – *Hotel Urban, Carrera San Jerónimo 34 – Ⓜ Sevilla – ✆ 917 87 77 70 – www.cebomadrid.com – Closed 1-31 August, Monday, Sunday*

✿ El Club Allard

CREATIVE • CLASSIC DÉCOR This unique restaurant occupies a listed Modernis building dating back to 1908, although you won't find any trace of this on the out side. In the elegant interior, with its mix of classic and contemporary decor, th creative cuisine showcases the personal and oriental influence of the chef. If you'r looking for an even more exclusive experience, make sure you book "La Pecera".

Specialities: Octopus and carrot textures. Turbot on a bed of samphire and spin ach, with a fish bone and toasted corn reduction. Torrija Allard 2. 0 with carro and mandarin.

Menu 80/130 € – Carte 85/115 €

PLAN: 1-A1 – *Ferraz 2 – Ⓜ Plaza España – ✆ 915 59 09 39 – www.elcluballard.com – Closed 4-21 August, Monday, Sunday*

✿ Corral de la Morería Gastronómico

MODERN CUISINE • CONTEMPORARY DÉCOR A unique restaurant thanks to the two completely different dining spaces within it: Tablao, from where you ca watch the show; and the separate gastronomic restaurant with just four tables where the modern cooking is built around seasonality. An impressive array of ta pas, set menus and à la carte choices.

Specialities: Lightly spicy squid noodles with a baby squid broth. Roast pigeon, aniseed-flavoured tomato and spinach leaves. Intxaursaltsa.

Menu 49/65€

PLAN: 1-A3 – *Morería 17 – Ⓜ La Latina – ✆ 913 65 84 46 – www.corraldelamoreria.com – Closed 1 July-31 August, Monday, lunch Tuesday-Saturday, Sunday*

Gofio (Safe Cruz)

A/C

REGIONAL CUISINE • BISTRO A superb homage to the cuisine of the Canary Islands in this contemporary bistro which recreates the flavours of the archipelago from a modern, creative and informal viewpoint. Its tasting menus provide an incredible journey of culinary discovery, offering a perfect insight into the products and personality of these islands.

Specialities: Bocadillo of roast pork cooked in a cast-iron pot and served with its own jus. Millet broth, Iberian pork rib and papa negra potatoes. Roast suckling goat, gofio ice cream and sweet guava.

Menu 50/80€

PLAN: 1-C3 – *Lope de Vega 9 – Ⓜ Antón Martin – ✆ 915 99 44 04 – www.gofiobycicero.com – Closed 6-12 April, 10-25 August, 23 December-7 January, Monday, Tuesday*

Yugo (Julián Mármol)

A/C

JAPANESE • EXOTIC DÉCOR A Japanese restaurant that transports guests to the atmosphere of the country's traditional pubs (izakayas) with its decor of wood, masks and flags. The cuisine here, a fusion of Japanese and Mediterranean cooking, has been adapted to European tastes. The room in the basement, available for the exclusive use of club members, is known as "The Bunker".

Specialities: Moriawase sashimi. Red prawn with chicken comb. Strawberry flan and green tea bonbons.

Menu 90€ (lunch), 110/155€ – Carte 75/110€

PLAN: 1-C3 – *San Blas 4 – Ⓜ Atocha – ✆ 914 44 90 34 – www.yugothebunker.com – Closed lunch Monday, Sunday*

Atlantik Corner

A/C

MARKET CUISINE • TRENDY Located in the popular Las Letras district of the city, Atlantik Corner has a simple, bistro ambience where the unique culinary concept is more of a relaxed global philosophy than a style of cooking. Here, the flavours of the Atlantic are presented as if it were a region, encompassing influences from Portugal and Galicia and much further afield, including Morocco, Mexico and even Brazil. We highly recommend the diced Russian salad with pickles and octopus, the chargrilled Carabinero prawns, and any of its cod dishes.

Menu 15€ (lunch)/45€ – Carte 31/45€

PLAN: 1-C2 – *Ventura de la Vega 11 – Ⓜ Sevilla – ✆ 910 71 72 45 – www.atlantikcorner.com*

Triciclo

A/C

CREATIVE • BISTRO The name fits this restaurant like a glove as the "tricycle" acts as a very accurate metaphor for the three young chefs running the show here. In tandem with this, the simple decor combines the height of rusticity with an endearing bistro charm. However, Triciclo's highlight is its contemporary cuisine which is centred on daily suggestions and highly personal à la carte recipes that are creative and exotic in equal measure. Dishes on the menu can also be ordered as half portions ("medias raciones") and tapas.

Menu 55/80€ – Carte 35/55€

PLAN: 1-C3 – *Santa María 28 – Ⓜ Antón Martin – ✆ 910 24 47 98 – www.eltriciclo.es – Closed 7-14 January, Sunday*

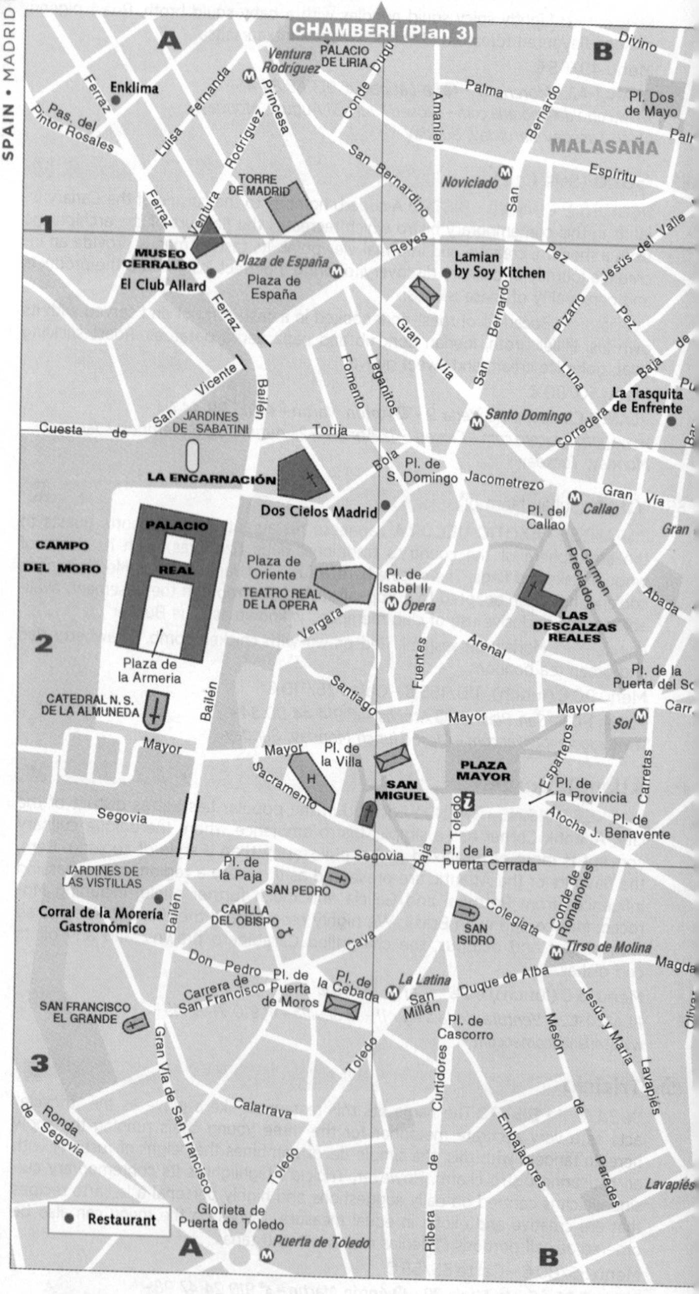
CHAMBERÍ (Plan 3)
A
B
Enklima
Restaurant
Lamian by Soy Kitchen
La Tasquita de Enfrente
El Club Allard
Dos Cielos Madrid
Corral de la Morería Gastronómico
MUSEO CERRALBO
TORRE DE MADRID
PALACIO DE LIRIA
MALASAÑA
LA ENCARNACIÓN
PALACIO REAL
CAMPO DEL MORO
TEATRO REAL DE LA OPERA
LAS DESCALZAS REALES
PLAZA MAYOR
SAN MIGUEL
CATEDRAL N. S. DE LA ALMUNEDA
JARDINES DE SABATINI
JARDINES DE LAS VISTILLAS
SAN PEDRO
CAPILLA DEL OBISPO
SAN ISIDRO
SAN FRANCISCO EL GRANDE
Plaza de España
Plaza de Oriente
Plaza de la Armeria
Pl. Dos de Mayo
Pl. de S. Domingo
Pl. del Callao
Pl. de Isabel II
Pl. de la Puerta del Sol
Pl. de la Villa
Pl. de la Provincia
Pl. de J. Benavente
Pl. de la Puerta Cerrada
Pl. de la Paja
Pl. de Puerta de Moros
Pl. de la Cebada
Pl. de Cascorro
Glorieta de Puerta de Toledo
Ventura Rodríguez
Noviciado
Plaza de España
Santo Domingo
Callao
Ópera
Sol
Tirso de Molina
La Latina
Puerta de Toledo
Lavapiés
Ferraz
Pas. del Pintor Rosales
Luisa Fernanda
Rodríguez
Princesa
Conde Duque
Amaniel
Palma
San Bernardo
Espíritu
San Bernardino
Reyes
Pez
Jesús del Valle
Pizarro
Luna
Gran Vía
Fomento
Leganitos
San Vicente
Cuesta de San Vicente
Bailén
Torija
Bola
Jacometrezo
Corredera Baja de San Pablo
Carmen
Preciados
Abada
Arenal
Vergara
Fuentes
Santiago
Mayor
Sacramento
Esparteros
Carretas
Atocha
Segovia
Toledo
Baja
Colegiata
Conde de Romanones
Cava
Don Pedro
Carrera de San Francisco
Duque de Alba
San Millán
Magdalena
Jesús y María
Mesón de Paredes
Lavapiés
Embajadores
Ribera de Curtidores
Calatrava
Gran Vía de San Francisco
Ronda de Segovia
1
2
3

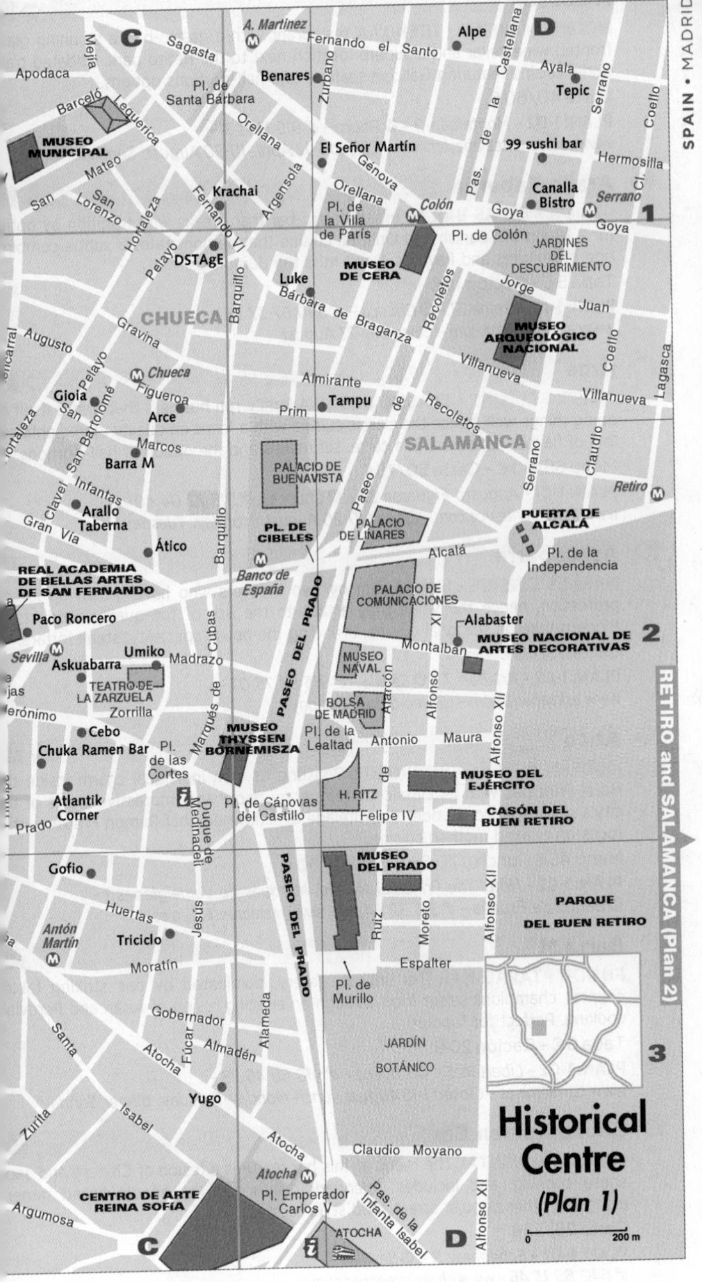

Historical Centre
(Plan 1)
RETIRO and SALAMANCA (Plan 2)
MUSEO MUNICIPAL
CHUECA
SALAMANCA
MUSEO DE CERA
MUSEO ARQUEOLÓGICO NACIONAL
PALACIO DE BUENAVISTA
PL. DE CIBELES
PALACIO DE LINARES
PUERTA DE ALCALÁ
PALACIO DE COMUNICACIONES
REAL ACADEMIA DE BELLAS ARTES DE SAN FERNANDO
MUSEO NACIONAL DE ARTES DECORATIVAS
MUSEO NAVAL
TEATRO DE LA ZARZUELA
BOLSA DE MADRID
MUSEO THYSSEN BORNEMISZA
MUSEO DEL EJÉRCITO
H. RITZ
CASÓN DEL BUEN RETIRO
MUSEO DEL PRADO
PARQUE DEL BUEN RETIRO
JARDÍN BOTÁNICO
CENTRO DE ARTE REINA SOFÍA
ATOCHA
JARDINES DEL DESCUBRIMIENTO
Alpe
Benares
Tepic
El Señor Martín
99 sushi bar
Krachai
Canalla Bistro
DSTAgE
Luke
Gioia
Tampu
Arce
Barra M
Arallo Taberna
Ático
Alabaster
Paco Roncero
Umiko
Askuabarra
Cebo
Chuka Ramen Bar
Atlantik Corner
Gofio
Triciclo
Yugo
A. Martínez
Colón
Serrano
Chueca
Retiro
Banco de España
Sevilla
Antón Martín
Atocha
Pl. de Santa Bárbara
Pl. de la Villa de París
Pl. de Colón
Pl. de la Independencia
Pl. de la Lealtad
Pl. de las Cortes
Pl. de Cánovas del Castillo
Pl. de Murillo
Pl. Emperador Carlos V
PASEO DEL PRADO
Paseo de Recoletos
Pas. de la Castellana
Pas. de la Infanta Isabel
Sagasta
Fernando el Santo
Génova
Orellana
Goya
Villanueva
Alcalá
Gran Vía
Montalbán
Alfonso XII
Felipe IV
Huertas
Moratín
Atocha
Claudio Moyano
Argumosa
0
200 m
C
D
1
2
3

Alabaster

MODERN CUISINE • TRENDY A restaurant with a gastro-bar, a stunning gla fronted wine cellar and a superb location next to the Retiro park. Updated tra tional cuisine featuring Galician seafood and half-portions options.

Carte 40/60€

PLAN: 1-D2 – *Montalbán 9 – Ⓜ Retiro – ✆ 915 12 11 31 – www.restaurantealabaster.com – Closed 5-12 April, 10-30 August, Sunday*

Arallo Taberna

FUSION • TAPAS BAR An urban gastro-bar that breaks with tradition by opti for a fusion of Spanish and Oriental cuisine that demonstrates a subtle combin tion of textures and flavours. Don't miss the dumplings!

Tapa 5€ – Ración 15€

PLAN: 1-C2 – *Reina 31 – Ⓜ Chueca – ✆ 690 67 37 96 – www.arallotaberna.com – Closed 10-23 August*

Arce

CLASSIC CUISINE • CLASSIC DÉCOR A family-run business that prides itself doing things well, hence the classic cuisine with a focus on quality ingredients a lots of flavour. Extensive à la carte, set menus and the option of half-portions.

Menu 65/80€ – Carte 50/75€

PLAN: 1-C1 – *Augusto Figueroa 32 – Ⓜ Chueca – ✆ 915 22 04 40 – www.restaurantearce.com – Closed 10-20 August, Monday, Tuesday*

Askuabarra

MARKET CUISINE • SIMPLE Run by two brothers who have grown up in th profession, hence the value they attach to the use of top-quality products. modern take on seasonal cuisine, including the house speciality: steak tartare.

Carte 35/60€

PLAN: 1-C2 – *Arlabán 7 – Ⓜ Sevilla – ✆ 915 93 75 07 – www.askuabarra.com – Closed dinner Sunday*

Ático

MODERN CUISINE • BOURGEOIS Boasting its own individual charm inside th Hotel Principal, with its classic-contemporary decor and impressive views of th city's skyline. Ático is under the tutelage of renowned chef Ramón Freixa, with focus on relaxed modern cuisine.

Menu 45€ (lunch)/70€ – Carte 40/60€

PLAN: 1-C2 – *Hotel The Principal Madrid, Marqués de Valdeiglesias 1 – Ⓜ Banco de España – ✆ 915 32 94 96 – www.restauranteatico.es*

Barra M

FUSION • TAPAS BAR This unusual eatery, dominated by one striking table counter, champions street food through an enticing fusion of Asian and Peruvia cooking. Perfect for foodies!

Tapa 6€ – Ración 20€

PLAN: 1-C2 – *Libertad 5 – Ⓜ Chueca – ✆ 916 68 46 78 – www.barraeme.es – Closed 1-15 August, lunch Monday-Tuesday, dinner Sunday*

Chuka Ramen Bar

FUSION • ORIENTAL The menu at this bar features a fusion of Chinese and Jap anese cooking, and includes legendary dishes such as noodle based ramen alongside other popular street food style recipes.

Carte 26/37€

PLAN: 1-C2 – *Echegaray 9 – Ⓜ Sevilla – ✆ 640 65 13 46 – www.chukaramenbar.com – Closed 2-25 August, Monday, lunch Tuesday, Sunday*

Dos Cielos Madrid

MODERN CUISINE • DESIGN The Madrid outpost of the famous Torres twins, occupying the stables of a luxurious palace. Tasting menu plus a contemporary à la carte based around seasonal ingredients.

Menu 55 € (lunch)/120 € – Carte 60/90 €

PLAN: 1-B2 – *Hotel Gran Meliá Palacio de los Duques, Cuesta de Santo Domingo 5 – Ⓜ Ópera – ✆ 915 41 67 00 – www.melia.com – Closed 1-31 August, Monday, Sunday*

Enklima

FUSION • SIMPLE A compact and intimate eatery run by an enterprising couple. The menu here features highly personal fusion cuisine with lots of exotic combinations that will please contemporary tastes.

Menu 60/85 €

PLAN: 1-A1 – *Ferraz 36 – Ⓜ Ventura Rodríguez – ✆ 911 16 69 91 – www.enklima.com – Closed Monday, lunch Tuesday-Friday, Sunday*

Gioia

ITALIAN • ROMANTIC An attractive restaurant on two levels run by a couple from Piedmont. Classic Italian cooking complemented by more contemporary dishes. Try the "L'uovo morbido" with poached eggs and truffles and the unusual "Riso e oro" risotto.

Menu 30/45 € – Carte 36/56 €

PLAN: 1-C2 – *San Bartolomé 23 – Ⓜ Chueca – ✆ 915 21 55 47 – www.gioiamadrid.es – Closed 10-23 August, Monday, dinner Tuesday*

Krachai

THAI • ORIENTAL The Krachai is split between two dining rooms, each with attractive lighting and a contemporary feel. The Thai cuisine on offer is listed on the menu according to the way it is prepared.

Menu 35 € – Carte 30/55 €

PLAN: 1-C1 – *Fernando VI-11 – Ⓜ Alonso Martínez – ✆ 918 33 65 56 – www.krachai.es – Closed 9-31 August, dinner Sunday*

Lamian by Soy Kitchen

FUSION • SIMPLE Named after a type of Chinese noodle, this restaurant is the perfect place to try ramen. Its menu features an interesting fusion of Spanish and Oriental cuisine.

Carte 25/50 €

PLAN: 1-B1 – *Plaza Mostenses 4 – Ⓜ Plaza de España – ✆ 910 39 22 31 – www.lamianconcept.com – Closed 12-25 August, Monday*

Luke

CREATIVE • COSY An Asian-inspired restaurant that will definitely impress your palate! Here, South Korean chef Luke Jang prepares fusion cuisine that successfully combines Spanish and Korean ingredients, techniques and flavours.

Menu 65 € – Carte 25/45 €

PLAN: 1-C1 – *Bárbara de Braganza 2 – Ⓜ Alonso Martinez – ✆ 913 19 94 57 – www.lukerestaurante.com – Closed Sunday*

El Señor Martín

TRADITIONAL CUISINE • TRENDY A restaurant with a modern industrial feel where everything revolves around the sea, with dishes prepared with visually impressive products of the very highest quality. The main focus here is on dishes cooked on the grill.

Carte 50/90 €

PLAN: 1-D1 – *General Castaños 13 – Ⓜ Alonso Martínez – ✆ 917 95 71 70 – www.srmartin.es – Closed 9-25 August, Sunday*

Tampu

PERUVIAN • DESIGN A mix of slate, wood and wicker, plus a Quechua nam that is in reference to old lodgings built along the Inca Trail. Classic Peruvian cu sine, including ceviches, raw fish tiraditos, and potato based causas.

Menu 16 € (lunch), 45/65 € – Carte 30/60 €

PLAN: 1-D1 – *Prim 13* – Ⓜ *Chueca* – ✆ *915 64 19 13* – *www.tampurestaurante.com* – *Closed Monday, dinner Sunday*

La Tasquita de Enfrente

INTERNATIONAL • FAMILY An eatery with a very loyal clientele close to th Gran Vía. Pleasantly updated French-inspired cuisine that changes every day ac cording to seasonal availability.

Menu 85/120 € – Carte 50/75 €

PLAN: 1-B1 – *Ballesta 6* – Ⓜ *Gran Vía* – ✆ *915 32 54 49* – *www.latasquitadeenfrente.com* – *Closed 3-30 August, Sunday*

Tori-Key

JAPANESE • FRIENDLY A Japanese restaurant with a difference where th standard cold sushi is abandoned in favour of Yakitori-style cuisine, with a partic ular focus on grilled chicken kebabs.

Menu 15 € (lunch), 30/55 € – Carte 30/50 €

PLAN: 3-H2 – *Plaza del Descubridor Diego de Ordás 2* – Ⓜ *Ríos Rosas* – ✆ *914 38 86 70* – *Closed 18-22 April, 5-30 August, Sunday*

Umiko

JAPANESE • MINIMALIST A fun and different Asian restaurant whose aim is t combine traditional Japanese cuisine with the more traditional cooking of Madric The finishing touches to most of the dishes are added at the bar.

Carte 45/60 €

PLAN: 1-C2 – *Los Madrazo 18* – Ⓜ *Sevilla* – ✆ *914 93 87 06* – *www.umiko.es* – *Closed 5-13 April, 9-24 August, Monday, Sunday*

Retiro - Salamanca

Ramón Freixa Madrid

CREATIVE • DESIGN A magical contradiction between traditional and cutting edge cuisine is the culinary philosophy of Ramón Freixa, a Catalan chef who showcases flavours and classic combinations alongside plenty of creativity. His el egant dining room is connected to a glass-fronted terrace and an open-air space perfect for a pre- or post-dinner drink.

Specialities: The study of the tomato 2020. Micro menu of lobster from ou coasts. Honey, flowers and peppers.

Menu 110/180 € – Carte 100/175 €

PLAN: 2-E1 – *Hotel Único Madrid, Claudio Coello 67* – Ⓜ *Serrano* – ✆ *917 81 82 62* – *www.ramonfreixamadrid.com* – *Closed 5-13 April, 1-31 August, Monday, Sunday*

Álbora

MODERN CUISINE • CONTEMPORARY DÉCOR An attractive modern setting with two distinct sections: the gastro-bar on the ground floor and the gas tronomic restaurant upstairs. Enjoy high level cuisine that makes full use of sea sonal ingredients, with some dishes available in smaller half portions.

Specialities: Crayfish, sauce of their heads and spicy touches. Grilled sole, tomato sauce and basil. Caramelised French toast with cinnamon ice cream.

Menu 65/95 € – Carte 55/85 €

PLAN: 2-E2 – *Jorge Juan 33* – Ⓜ *Velázquez* – ✆ *917 81 61 97* – *www.restaurantealbora.com* – *Closed 10-16 August, dinner Sunday*

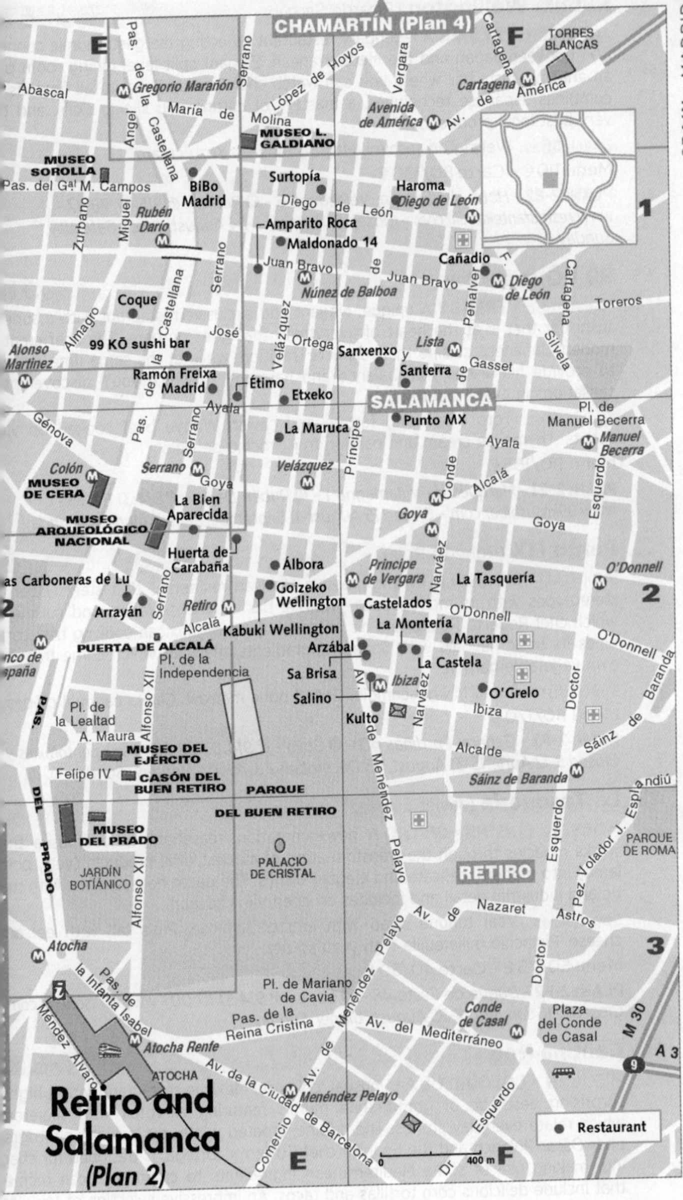
CHAMARTÍN (Plan 4)
E
F
TORRES BLANCAS
Abascal
Gregorio Marañón
Pas. de la Castellana
Serrano
López de Hoyos
Vergara
Cartagena
Cartagena
Av. de América
María de Molina
Avenida de América
Ángel
MUSEO L. GALDIANO
MUSEO SOROLLA
Pas. del Gal M. Campos
BiBo Madrid
Surtopía
Haroma
Diego de León
Diego de León
1
Zurbano
Miguel
Rubén Darío
Amparito Roca
Maldonado 14
Juan Bravo
Juan Bravo
Núñez de Balboa
Cañadio
Diego de León
Peñalver
F.
Coque
Almagro
Toreros
José
Ortega
Velázquez
Sanxenxo
y
Gasset
Lista
Silvela
Alonso Martínez
99 KŌ sushi bar
Santerra
Ramón Freixa Madrid
Étimo
Etxeko
Ayala
SALAMANCA
Punto MX
Pl. de Manuel Becerra
Génova
La Maruca
Ayala
Manuel Becerra
Colón
Serrano
Velázquez
Príncipe
Conde
MUSEO DE CERA
Serrano
Goya
Alcalá
Esquerdo
La Bien Aparecida
Goya
Goya
MUSEO ARQUEOLÓGICO NACIONAL
Huerta de Carabaña
Narváez
Álbora
Príncipe de Vergara
La Tasquería
O'Donnell
Las Carboneras de Lu
Goizeko Wellington
2
Arrayán
Retiro
Castelados
O'Donnell
Alcalá
Kabuki Wellington
La Montería
Marcano
O'Donnell
PUERTA DE ALCALÁ
Arzábal
La Castela
Banco de España
Pl. de la Independencia
Sa Brisa
Ibiza
Alfonso XII
Salino
O'Grelo
Doctor
PAS.
Pl. de la Lealtad
Kulto
Ibiza
A. Maura
MUSEO DEL EJÉRCITO
Alcalde
Sáinz de Baranda
Felipe IV
CASÓN DEL BUEN RETIRO
PARQUE
Sáinz de Baranda
DEL
DEL BUEN RETIRO
Av. de Menéndez Pelayo
Pez Volador
J. Esplandiú
MUSEO DEL PRADO
Esquerdo
PARQUE DE ROMA
PRADO
JARDÍN BOTÁNICO
Alfonso XII
PALACIO DE CRISTAL
RETIRO
Av. de Nazaret
Astros
Atocha
3
Pas. de la Infanta Isabel
Doctor
Pl. de Mariano de Cavia
Méndez Álvaro
Pas. de la Reina Cristina
Av. de Menéndez Pelayo
Conde de Casal
Av. del Mediterráneo
Plaza del Conde de Casal
M 30
Atocha Renfe
A 3
ATOCHA
Av. de la Ciudad de Barcelona
9
Menéndez Pelayo
Esquerdo
Comercio
Dr
Restaurant
E
0
400 m
F
Retiro and Salamanca (Plan 2)

Kabuki Wellington (Ricardo Sanz)

JAPANESE • DESIGN A legendary restaurant reflecting the gastronomic conn tion between Japan and the Mediterranean. Elegant split-level dining room p an enticing sushi bar where you can watch chef Ricardo Sanz in full flow, as combines Japanese techniques, a mastery of cutting and slicing skills, and very best local products.

Specialities: Wellington sashimi. Maguro teriyaki. Yuzu cream.

Menu 110 € – Carte 80/130 €

PLAN: 2-E2 – *Hotel Wellington, Velázquez 6 – Ⓜ Retiro – ✆ 915 77 78 77 – www.restaurantekabuki.com – Closed 6-12 April, 3-24 August, lunch Saturday, Sunday*

99 KŌ sushi bar

JAPANESE • TRENDY A unique, elegant and exclusive restaurant with a supe sushi bar that is at the heart of everything that goes on here. The chef creat modern Japanese cuisine that respects tradition, while at the same time strivi to provide his dishes with balance and harmony, in which you'll discover n sensations in every mouthful!

Specialities: Toro (red tuna) tartare and caviar. Wagyu beef cooked on vi shoots. Thyme ice cream and passion fruit "tocino de cielo".

Menu 110/165 €

PLAN: 2-E1 – *Marqués de Villamagna 1 – Ⓜ Rubén Darío – ✆ 914 31 38 78 – www.99kosushibar.com – Closed 15 August-11 September, lunch Monday, Sunday*

Punto MX (Roberto Ruiz)

MEXICAN • MINIMALIST An impressive Mexican restaurant that steers clear stereotypes with its modern look, "mezcal bar" at the entrance, and cuisine which chef Roberto Ruiz offers his personal vision of Mexican cooking that cor bines its basic flavours with Spanish ingredients, many of which come from own vegetable garden.

Specialities: Punto MX guacamole. Grilled bone marrow. Cajeta caramel crêpes

Menu 110/170 €

PLAN: 2-F2 – *General Pardiñas 40 – Ⓜ Goya – ✆ 914 02 22 26 – www.puntomx.es – Closed 5-12 April, 15-31 August, 23 December-7 January, Monday, Sunday*

La Tasquería (Javier Estévez)

MODERN CUISINE • BISTRO A new-generation, reasonably priced *tasca* th works miracles through the transformation of modest offal products (veal, po lamb) into modern, delicate and elegant dishes. The decor here is urban with ru tic and industrial detail and includes an open-view kitchen.

Specialities: Veal tongue salad with lobster salpicón. Pig's tail with eel an cheese. Pistachio millefeuille with yuzu sorbet.

Menu 50/75 € – Carte 40/50 €

PLAN: 2-F2 – *Duque de Sesto 48 – Ⓜ Goya – ✆ 914 51 10 00 – www.latasqueria.com Closed 7-16 January, 3-25 August, dinner Sunday*

Cantina Roo

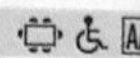

MEXICAN • COLOURFUL An unusual, colourful Mexican restaurant with a high surprising aesthetic of graffiti-style murals featuring ex-votos with skeletor which relate everyday stories. The cuisine, created jointly by Mexican photogra pher Óscar Polanco and the Spanish chef Guillermo Ortega, is designed for sha ing, making use of some Mediterranean ingredients to create Mexican recipe that include delicious corn tortillas and tacos. An impressive selection of tequila mezcals and Mexican beers is also on offer, including the spicy and refreshing M chelada beer!

Menu 15 € (lunch)/25 € – Carte 28/40 €

PLAN: 4-I3 – *López de Hoyos 13 – Ⓜ Gregorio Marañón – ✆ 918 05 20 59 – www.cantinaroo.es – Closed 1-26 August, Monday, dinner Sunday*

La Castela

TRADITIONAL CUISINE • TRADITIONAL A modern, unpretentious yet classic address which perpetuates the tradition of Madrid's historic "tabernas", where the decor of mirrors, stucco and the typical metal bar counter takes guests on a journey back in time. Behind the bar at the entrance is a pleasantly appointed dining room where the owner takes the orders from a traditional menu featuring excellent daily suggestions and dishes prepared with the freshest of ingredients. We recommend any of the fish dishes, the baby squid with onions, and the mille-feuille of ventresca tuna, which Michelle Obama tried when she ate here.

Carte 33/45€

PLAN: 2-F2 – *Doctor Castelo 22 – Ⓜ Ibiza – ✆ 915 74 00 15 – www.lacastela.com – Closed dinner Sunday*

Castelados

TRADITIONAL CUISINE • TRADITIONAL Located just a few metres from the Retiro park, Castelados seems to have found the secret to success by following in the footsteps of its older sibling, the La Castela restaurant, located in the nearby Calle Doctor Castelo. Here, you can choose between the lively tapas bar and the classic-functional dining room offering a high-quality traditional menu with a particularly impressive choice of the freshest fish and an array of daily specials. These include the millefeuille of ventresca tuna, the sautéed chickpeas and prawns, and the delicious oxtail.

Carte 32/45€

PLAN: 2-F2 – *Antonio Acuña 18 – Ⓜ Príncipe de Vergara – ✆ 910 51 56 25 – www.castelados.com – Closed dinner Sunday*

La Maruca

TRADITIONAL CUISINE • FRIENDLY A restaurant that exudes a fresh, optimistic approach through two iconic themes, namely Santander and Cantabria, which are re-presented here in cuisine that is full of characteristic colours, flavours and aromas. This welcoming setting features a multi-purpose bar and contemporary dining spaces embellished with the occasional designer detail. Its menu reflects cuisine that is 100% traditional, with a predominance of Cantabrian dishes with an equal focus on preparation and high-quality products. We can particularly recommend the famous anchovies from Santoña, the fried squid, the Russian salad and the hake with a creamy sauce.

Carte 30/42€

PLAN: 2-E2 – *Velázquez 54 – Ⓜ Velázquez – ✆ 917 81 49 69 – www.restaurantelamaruca.com*

La Montería

TRADITIONAL CUISINE • CLASSIC DÉCOR With its location just a few steps from the Retiro, this restaurant is well worth considering if you're visiting this superb park. With a history dating back over a half a century, this family-run business has had a complete makeover following the passing of the baton from father to son. Today, it features an attractive tapas bar, plus a small, modern dining room with bare walls and a white-inspired decor. Updated traditional cuisine always includes one or two game dishes. The prawns in batter and the "monterías" (stuffed mussels) are hugely popular.

Menu 36/48€ – Carte 35/45€

PLAN: 2-F2 – *Lope de Rueda 35 – Ⓜ Ibiza – ✆ 915 74 18 12 – www.lamonteria.es – Closed dinner Sunday*

Tepic

MEXICAN • RUSTIC This Mexican restaurant steers clear of the more typical and colourful ambience of Mariachi bands and traditional guitars, instead opting for a rustic-contemporary space with wood flooring, white tones and subtle lighting. Named after the capital of the Mexican state of Nayarit, it offers reasonably authentic cuisine from the homeland with a good selection of starters, known as "antojitos", an extensive choice of tacos, plus a few other traditional specialities. Rather than ordering wine, why not choose from the impressive selection of beers, tequilas and mezcals!

Menu 22/31€ – Carte 30/45€

PLAN: 1-D1 – *Ayala 14 – Ⓜ Goya – ✆ 915 22 08 50 – www.tepic.es – Closed dinner Sunday*

Amparito Roca

TRADITIONAL CUISINE • COSY A restaurant that takes its name from a famo pasodoble, where the focus is on honest cuisine that flies the flag for the ve best ingredients. A classic-contemporary dining room with some surprising dec rative details.

Carte 50/75€

PLAN: 2-E1 – *Juan Bravo 12* – Ⓜ *Núñez de Balboa* – ✆ *913 48 33 04* – *www.restauranteamparitoroca.com* – *Closed 11-25 August, Sunday*

Arrayán

CONTEMPORARY • CONTEMPORARY DÉCOR A welcoming and well-a pointed restaurant with a classic-contemporary feel. Its dishes are a modern nc to traditional cuisine and are only available on three surprise menus.

Menu 45€ (lunch), 75/100€

PLAN: 2-E2 – *Villalar 6* – Ⓜ *Retiro* – ✆ *914 35 46 63* – *www.arrayanrestaurante.com* – *Closed 1-31 August, Monday, dinner Sunday*

Arzábal

TRADITIONAL CUISINE • CONTEMPORARY DÉCOR Arzábal features a tapa space looking out on to the Retiro park, with a modern split-level dining roo inside offering elaborate traditional cuisine. Extensive choice of wines an champagnes.

Carte 40/55€

PLAN: 2-F2 – *Menéndez Pelayo 13* – Ⓜ *Ibiza* – ✆ *914 09 56 61* – *www.arzabal.com* – *Closed Sunday*

BiBo Madrid

MODERN CUISINE • BISTRO Inspired by the Málaga Fair, the contemporar menu here bears the seal of award-winning chef Dani García, who takes us on round-the-world gastronomic voyage. A New York-style brunch is available ever weekend.

Carte 45/65€

PLAN: 2-E1 – *Paseo de la Castellana 52* – Ⓜ *Gregorio Marañón* – ✆ *918 05 25 56* – *www.grupodanigarcia.com*

La Bien Aparecida

TRADITIONAL CUISINE • TRENDY Named after the patron saint of Cantabria this restaurant is laid out on two floors with different atmospheres. Updated tra ditional cuisine featuring fine textures and strong flavours.

Menu 75/125€ – Carte 43/75€

PLAN: 2-E2 – *Jorge Juan 8* – Ⓜ *Serrano* – ✆ *911 59 39 39* – *www.restaurantelabienaparecida.com*

Canalla Bistro

MODERN CUISINE • CONTEMPORARY DÉCOR At this bistro, discover the in formal cuisine of Valencian chef Ricard Camarena who is keen to leave his stam on the city via his highly urban cooking. His dishes are perfect for sharing.

Carte 35/45€

PLAN: 1-D1 – *Goya 5 (Platea Madrid)* – Ⓜ *Serrano* – ✆ *915 77 00 25* – *www.plateamadrid.com* – *Closed 1-31 August, Monday, Tuesday*

Cañadío

TRADITIONAL CUISINE • FRIENDLY The name will ring a bell with those famil iar with Santander, given the location of this, the original Cañadio restaurant, or one of the city's most famous squares. Café-bar for tapas, two contemporary din ing rooms, and well prepared traditional cuisine.

Carte 40/55€

PLAN: 2-F1 – *Conde de Peñalver 86* – Ⓜ *Diego de León* – ✆ *912 81 91 92* – *www.restaurantecanadio.com*

Las Carboneras de Lu

TRADITIONAL CUISINE • COSY A welcoming restaurant with a contemporary feel, occupying an old coal bunker. Classic French-inspired cuisine with a particular focus on presentation.

Carte 45/60€

PLAN: 2-E2 – *Villalar 7* – *Retiro* – *910 57 70 03* – *www.lascarbonerasdelu.com* – *Closed 4-26 August, Monday, Sunday*

Étimo

CREATIVE • TRENDY Étimo's interior design comes as a pleasant surprise, combining the past and present and providing the backdrop for consistent, highly technical and delicately prepared contemporary cuisine. A chef's table is also available.

Menu 70/120€

PLAN: 2-E1 – *Ayala 27* – *Goya* – *913 75 98 83* – *www.etimo.es* – *Closed 5-26 August, Monday, Sunday*

Etxeko

CONTEMPORARY • TRENDY With a name that means "home-made" in Basque, Etxeko is the Madrid venture of Martín Berasategui, a chef who takes us on a journey back to his roots.

Carte 50/65€

PLAN: 2-E1 – *Hotel Bless, Velázquez 62* – *Velázquez* – *910 86 13 78* – *www.blesscollectionhotels.com*

Goizeko Wellington

TRADITIONAL CUISINE • CLASSIC DÉCOR The contemporary-classic dining room and the two private rooms have been exquisitely designed. The cuisine on offer is a fusion of traditional, international and creative cooking, and is enriched with a few Japanese dishes.

Menu 85/120€ – Carte 55/75€

PLAN: 2-E2 – *Hotel Wellington, Villanueva 34* – *Retiro* – *915 77 01 38* – *www.goizekogaztelupe.com* – *Closed lunch Saturday, Sunday*

O grelo

GALICIAN • CLASSIC DÉCOR Experience the excellence of traditional Galician cuisine at this restaurant serving a huge variety of seafood. Having undergone gradual renovation, O grelo has a more modern look, which includes a reasonably popular gastro-bar, a main dining room and three private sections.

Carte 55/70€

PLAN: 2-F2 – *Menorca 39* – *Ibiza* – *914 09 72 04* – *www.restauranteogrelo.com* – *Closed dinner Sunday*

Haroma

CONTEMPORARY • ELEGANT Haroma's unusual spelling comes from "H", which stands for Heritage and the word Aroma. An elegant ambience for contemporary cuisine bearing the signature of Mario Sandoval.

Menu 40/78€ – Carte 65/85€

PLAN: 2-F1 – *Hotel Heritage, Diego de León 43* – *Diego de León* – *910 88 70 70* – *www.heritagemadridhotel.com*

Huerta de Carabaña

A/C

TRADITIONAL CUISINE • CONTEMPORARY DÉCOR A traditional culinary dominion where the very best fresh vegetables from Carabaña, 50km outside of Madrid, reign supreme. Choose between the bistro style dining room and a second room offering more gastronomic fare.

Carte 45/75€

PLAN: 2-E2 – *Lagasca 32 – Ⓜ Serrano – ✆ 910 83 00 07 – www.huertadecarabana.es – Closed 1-31 August, dinner Monday, dinner Sunday*

Kulto

A/C

MODERN CUISINE • FRIENDLY This restaurant is pleasant, modern and bright and just a stone's throw from the Retiro park. Contemporary cuisine that showcases seasonal ingredients and a fusion of international flavours and influences.

Carte 45/60€

PLAN: 2-F2 – *Ibiza 4 – Ⓜ Ibiza – ✆ 911 73 30 53 – www.kulto.es – Closed Monday, Tuesday*

Maldonado 14

A/C

TRADITIONAL CUISINE • CLASSIC DÉCOR A single dining room on two levels both featuring classic decor, quality furnishings and wood floors. The à la carte menu has a traditional feel and includes delicious homely desserts, such as the outstanding apple tart.

Menu 42€ – Carte 40/60€

PLAN: 2-E1 – *Maldonado 14 – Ⓜ Núñez de Balboa – ✆ 914 35 50 45 – www.maldonado14.com – Closed 5-25 August, Sunday*

Marcano

A/C

INTERNATIONAL • TRENDY Marcano boasts a contemporary look with bare tables where you can enjoy cooking with well-defined flavours alongside soups, stews and a few international dishes.

Carte 55/70€

PLAN: 2-F2 – *Doctor Castelo 31 – Ⓜ Ibiza – ✆ 914 09 36 42 – www.restaurantemarcano.com – Closed Monday, dinner Sunday*

99 sushi bar

A/C

JAPANESE • MINIMALIST A good restaurant in which to discover the flavours and textures of Japanese cuisine. There is a small bar where sushi is prepared in front of diners, an attractive glass fronted wine cellar, and a modern dining room featuring typical Japanese decor and furnishings.

Menu 90€ – Carte 45/65€

PLAN: 1-D1 – *Hermosilla 4 – Ⓜ Serrano – ✆ 914 31 27 15 – www.99sushibar.com – Closed 1-27 August, Sunday*

Sa Brisa

A/C

FUSION • CONTEMPORARY DÉCOR A pleasant, well-located and modern restaurant offering tapas and à la carte menus on which the majority of dishes use Iberian products which combine with recipes from other cultures.

Menu 29€ (lunch), 48/70€ – Carte 45/65€

PLAN: 2-F2 – *Menéndez Pelayo 15 – Ⓜ Ibiza – ✆ 910 22 45 40 – www.sabrisarestaurante.com – Closed Monday, lunch Tuesday*

Salino

A/C

TRADITIONAL CUISINE • CONTEMPORARY DÉCOR Impressively prepared traditional cuisine that includes the famous bacon "Torreznos de La Raquetista", Russian salad, rice with prawns and a "salmoretta" sauce, and 45-day-aged Finnish beef loin.

Carte 45/55€

PLAN: 2-F1 – *Menorca 4 – Ⓜ Ibiza – ✆ 912 14 16 82 – www.salino.es – Closed dinner Sunday*

Santerra

TRADITIONAL CUISINE • CONTEMPORARY DÉCOR A restaurant with lots of personality that showcases daily the traditional cooking of La Mancha through delicious game dishes and stews. Make sure you order the croquettes!

Carte 40/65€

PLAN: 2-F1 – *General Pardiñas 56 – Ⓜ Núñez de Balboa – ✆ 914 01 35 80 – www.santerra.es – Closed 6-13 April, 10-24 August, Monday, dinner Sunday*

Sanxenxo

SEAFOOD • CLASSIC DÉCOR A classic address for authentic Galician cooking in the Spanish capital in a renovated classic-contemporary space with an enticing fish and seafood display in the front window.

Carte 50/75€

PLAN: 2-F1 – *José Ortega y Gasset 40 – Ⓜ Núñez de Balboa – ✆ 915 77 82 72 – www.sanxenxo.es – Closed 5-20 August, dinner Sunday*

Surtopía

ANDALUSIAN • CONTEMPORARY DÉCOR A restaurant with a modern ambience that translates to its cuisine, which features the aromas and flavours of Andalucia, and Cádiz in particular, and showcases contemporary techniques and an innovative touch. A good place to discover the wines of Sanlúcar.

Menu 50/65€ – Carte 40/60€

PLAN: 2-E1 – *Núñez de Balboa 106 – Ⓜ Núñez de Balboa – ✆ 915 63 03 64 – www.surtopia.es – Closed 5-12 May, 10-30 August, Monday, Sunday*

Chamberí

Coque (Mario Sandoval)

CREATIVE • DESIGN The cuisine proposed by the Sandoval brothers (Mario, Diego and Rafael) goes much further than what you see on the plate, dissecting the culinary experience into several distinct areas (cocktail bar, wine cellar, kitchen, dining room etc), each of which is designed to surprise and elicit different emotions. Superb wine cellar!

Specialities: Frozen pistachio flower with an olive gazpachuelo, caviar and beer foam. Loin of pickled red mullet with a peanut romesco sauce. Spiced chocolate with lavender ice cream.

Menu 195/310€

PLAN: 2-E1 – *Marqués de Riscal 11 – Ⓜ Rubén Darío – ✆ 916 04 02 02 – www.restaurantecoque.com – Closed 4-26 August, 22-31 December, Monday, Sunday*

Santceloni

CREATIVE • ELEGANT Elegance, comfort and good service are the perfect cocktail for a culinary experience that you won't forget in a hurry. In the completely glass-fronted kitchen chef Óscar Velasco creates traditional and international dishes that showcase plenty of creativity. Extensive wine cellar.

Specialities: Grilled prawns in lettuce leaves. Duck lasagne, pistachios, cardamom and Idiazabal cheese whey. Daikon radish, corn, liquorice and passion fruit.

Menu 90€ (lunch), 185/363€ – Carte 126/211€

PLAN: 3-H2 – *Hotel Hyatt Regency Hesperia Madrid, Paseo de la Castellana 57 – Ⓜ Gregorio Marañón – ✆ 912 10 88 40 – www.restaurantesantceloni.com – Closed 1-8 January, 5-12 April, 1-31 August, lunch Saturday, Sunday*

Clos Madrid

MODERN CUISINE • CONTEMPORARY DÉCOR The Madrid outpost of Marcos Granda, the owner of the award Skina in Marbella. In the contemporary-style dining room, the creative cuisine is up to date and based around the most select ingredients. The name Clos is a French word for a high-quality wine estate surrounded by a wall.

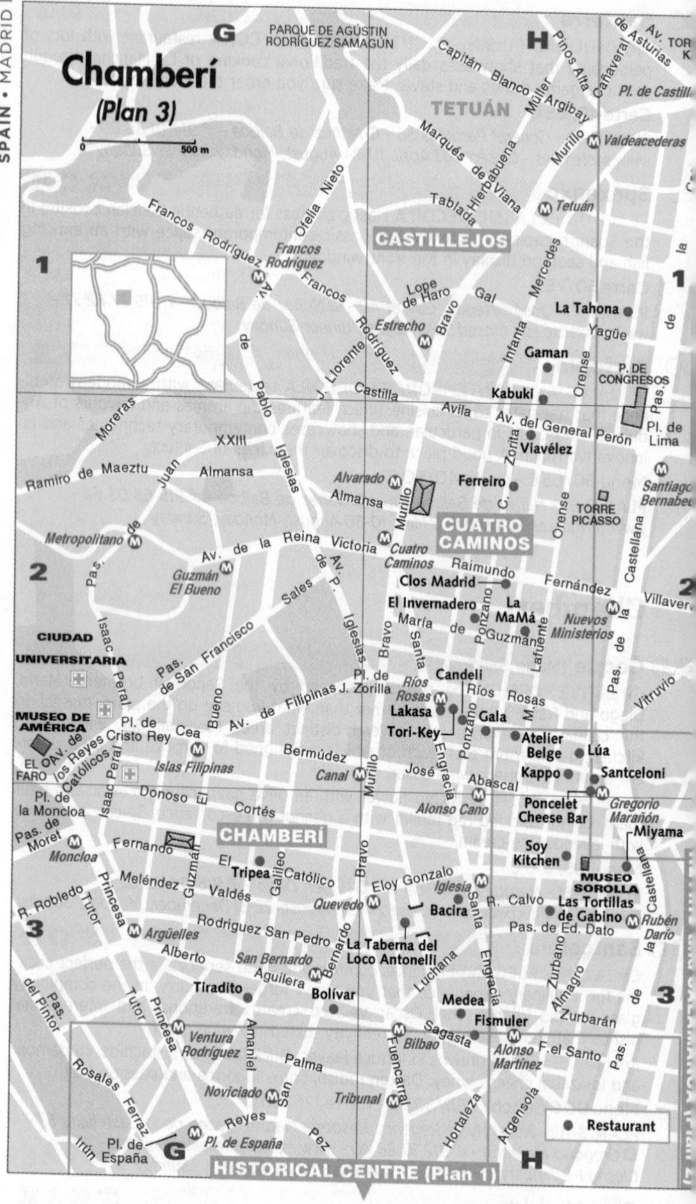
Chamberí
(Plan 3)
0
500 m
G
H
1
2
3
PARQUE DE AGÚSTIN RODRÍGUEZ SAMAGÚN
TETUÁN
CASTILLEJOS
CUATRO CAMINOS
CHAMBERÍ
CIUDAD UNIVERSITARIA
MUSEO DE AMÉRICA
EL FARO
P. DE CONGRESOS
TORRE PICASSO
MUSEO SOROLLA
HISTORICAL CENTRE (Plan 1)
Restaurant
La Tahona
Gaman
Kabuki
Viavélez
Ferreiro
Clos Madrid
El Invernadero
La MaMá
Candeli
Lakasa
Tori-Key
Gala
Atelier Belge
Lúa
Kappo
Santceloni
Poncelet Cheese Bar
Miyama
Soy Kitchen
Las Tortillas de Gabino
Bacira
La Taberna del Loco Antonelli
Tripea
Tiradito
Bolívar
Medea
Fismuler
Valdeacederas
Tetuán
Francos Rodríguez
Estrecho
Alvarado
Cuatro Caminos
Metropolitano
Guzmán El Bueno
Nuevos Ministerios
Santiago Bernabeu
Ríos Rosas
Islas Filipinas
Canal
Alonso Cano
Gregorio Marañón
Moncloa
Argüelles
Quevedo
Iglesia
Rubén Darío
San Bernardo
Ventura Rodríguez
Bilbao
Alonso Martínez
Noviciado
Tribunal
Pl. de España
Capitán Blanco Argibay
Pinos Alta
Müller
Av. de Asturias
Cañaveral
Pl. de Castilla
Marqués de Viana
Hierbabuena
Murillo
Tablada
Ofelia Nieto
Francos Rodríguez
Av. de Pablo Iglesias
J. Llorente
Lope de Haro
Bravo
Gal
Infanta Mercedes
Yagüe
Orense
Castilla
Avila
Av. del General Perón
Pl. de Lima
C. Zorita
Pas. de la Castellana
Moreras
XXIII
Ramiro de Maeztu
Juan
Almansa
Av. de la Reina Victoria
Raimundo Fernández Villaverde
Av. de P. Iglesias
Pas. de Isaac Peral
Sales
Pas. de San Francisco
Bravo Murillo
Santa Engracia
María de Guzmán
Ponzano
Lafuente
Pl. de J. Zorilla
Ríos Rosas
M.
Vitruvio
Av. de Filipinas
Bueno
Pl. de Cristo Rey
Cea Bermúdez
Av. de los Reyes Católicos
Isaac Peral
José Abascal
Pl. de la Moncloa
Donoso Cortés
El
Pas. de Moret
Fernando El Católico
Guzmán
Galileo
Meléndez Valdés
Eloy Gonzalo
R. Robledo
Tutor
Princesa
Rodriguez San Pedro
Alberto Aguilera
Bernardo
Luchana
R. Calvo
Pas. de Ed. Dato
Zurbano
Almagro
Zurbarán
Pas. del Pintor
Sagasta
F. el Santo
Pas.
Amaniel
Palma
Fuencarral
Rosales
Ferraz
Irún
San
Reyes
Pez
Hortaleza
Argensola
Pl. de España

Specialities: Rice with pigeon. Loin of hake, fish bone pil-pil and spinach glass. Natillas a la madrileña.

Menu 60€ (lunch), 70/85€ – Carte 55/70€

PLAN: 3-H2 – *Raimundo Fernández Villaverde 24 – Ⓜ Cuatro Caminos – ✆ 910 64 88 05 – www.restauranteclosmadrid.es – Closed 8-12 April, 10-23 August, lunch Saturday, Sunday*

El Invernadero (Rodrigo de la Calle)

MODERN CUISINE • COSY Chef Rodrigo de la Calle is back in the Spanish capital! In the natural-contemporary dining room, discover the "green revolution" that has broken down borders and where vegetables are the key to his unique menu. Flavour, fantasy and a delicate touch are to the fore here, with the option of always being able to order a fish or meat dish.

Specialities: Essence of beetroot. Rice with desert vegetables. Jerusalem artichoke tiramisu.

Menu 95/135€

PLAN: 3-H2 – *Ponzano 85 – Ⓜ Rios Rosas – ✆ 628 93 93 67 – www.elinvernaderorestaurante.com – Closed 6-13 April, 10-24 August, 23-31 December, Monday, Sunday*

Lúa (Manuel Domínguez)

MODERN CUISINE • COSY Lúa has two completely different ambiences. One a gastrobar at the entrance serving an à la carte of half and full *raciones*, the other a more gastronomic setting on the lower level. Here, guests can enjoy contemporary cuisine with a strong Galician influence focused around an impressive tasting menu.

Specialities: Octopus "á feira". Smoked salmon with miso. Santiago tart.

Menu 72/98€

PLAN: 3-H2 – *Eduardo Dato 5 – Ⓜ Rubén Darío – ✆ 913 95 28 53 – www.restaurantelua.com – Closed Sunday*

Bacira

FUSION • VINTAGE A successful business that extols the virtues of friendship, hard work and, above all, a love for cooking. These three pillars underpin this restaurant run with great dedication by the three owner-chefs, Carlos Langreo, Vicente de la Red and Gabriel Zapata, each of whom specialises in a different type of cuisine (traditional Mediterranean, Japanese and Nikkei) but who are receptive to new trends and inclined towards fusion cooking. The atmosphere here is both welcoming and informal with a vintage decor that includes striking wrought-iron columns that extend from the floor to the ceiling.

Menu 15€ (lunch)/68€ – Carte 30/45€

PLAN: 3-H3 – *Castillo 16 – Ⓜ Iglesia – ✆ 918 66 40 30 – www.bacira.es*

Bolívar

TRADITIONAL CUISINE • FAMILY Despite its somewhat small size, this is one of the most interesting eating options in the popular and traditional Malasaña district in the centre of Madrid. This efficient family-run restaurant, which has half a century of experience cooking well-prepared and seasonally inspired traditional dishes, has adapted aesthetically to modern tastes. Although the à la carte is extensive, we highly recommend one of Bolívar's set menus which showcase the nuances of each dish and include a wine pairing option for each course. The homemade prawn croquettes are a particular speciality.

Menu 20/40€ – Carte 33/45€

PLAN: 3-G3 – *Manuela Malasaña 28 – Ⓜ San Bernardo – ✆ 914 45 12 74 – www.restaurantebolivar.com – Closed 4-30 August, Sunday*

Gala

SPANISH CONTEMPORARY • INTIMATE Located closed to the Nuevos Ministerios district, Gala can already be considered a classic address in the Spanish capital given that few restaurants manage to celebrate over 25 years of nonstop business. It boasts an attractive dining room plus a private dining space both contemporary in style, where guests can enjoy updated traditional cuisine inspired by seasonal market produce on a choice of menus. It also organises interesting gastronomic events with different themes, including wild mushrooms. The most popular specialities requested by its customers are the steak tartar and dishes featuring red tuna.

Menu 35/60 € – Carte 35/49 €

PLAN: 3-H2 – *Espronceda 14 – Ⓜ Alonso Cano – ✆ 914 42 22 44 – www.restaurantegala.com – Closed 3-25 August, dinner Monday, dinner Sunday*

La MaMá

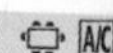

TRADITIONAL CUISINE • FRIENDLY Tasteful simplicity, evident as soon as you enter, is to the fore in this restaurant, where the couple in charge (María and Marcos) have opted unapologetically for a "low cost" decor that reflects their own personality, which is clear in every detail. The chef's training at El Ermitaño, in Benavente, manifests itself to the full, with its roots in the traditional cooking of days gone by, to which he adds his own imprint and the occasional innovative touch. It's possible to try lots of dishes here as many of those on the menu are available in half-portions.

Menu 25 € – Carte 30/43 €

PLAN: 3-H2 – *María Panes 6 – Ⓜ Nuevos Ministerios – ✆ 910 61 97 64 – www.lamamarestaurante.com – Closed 10-23 August, 24 December-1 January, Monday, dinner Tuesday-Wednesday, dinner Sunday*

La Taberna del Loco Antonelli

FUSION • BISTRO Named after the Italian engineer Juan Bautista Antonelli who, in the second half of the 16C began a project to convert Madrid into a sea port by connecting the Manzanares river with the Atlantic, this "taberna" definitely breaks the culinary mould. In its relaxed, bistro-style interior head chef Sergio Menge creates what he refers to as "port" cooking that is fun, international and based around fish and seafood from Spain's coasts, spiced up with culinary elements from his native Mexico, fusion cooking and other cuisines from around the world.

Carte 30/40 €

PLAN: 3-H3 – *Olid 15 – Ⓜ Bilbao – ✆ 912 77 74 89 – www.locoantonelli.com – Closed 19-29 August, Monday, dinner Sunday*

Las Tortillas de Gabino

TRADITIONAL CUISINE • COSY Impressively run by two siblings, this restaurant adopted its name in homage to the chef at La Ancha, a popular restaurant in Madrid that was founded by his grandfather in the 1930s. Las Tortillas de Gabino is located in the heart of the city's Chamberí district, where it features a cosy entrance hall, a private section, a glass-fronted wine cellar, and two contemporary dining rooms which interconnect via a corridor that leads to the kitchen, which is always visible to diners. The updated traditional menu is complemented by a superb choice of omelettes (tortillas), the most popular of which are the traditional potato-based Velazqueña, and the Trufada.

Carte 33/45 €

PLAN: 3-H3 – *Rafael Calvo 20 – Ⓜ Rubén Darío – ✆ 913 19 75 05 – www.lastortillasdegabino.com – Closed 5-12 April, 9-23 August, Sunday*

Tripea

FUSION • FRIENDLY The re-establishment of markets as culinary focal points is a trend that has seen the creation of restaurants such as Tripea, occupying three adjoining stalls at the Vallehermoso market. Visually striking, with its hugely colourful urban mural, a front-on open kitchen and a single long table, this is a place designed for sharing in a space that almost juts out into the market's alleyway. The cooking here is a fusion of Asian and Peruvian, more commonly known nowadays as Nikkei, with specialities such as spicy chicken curry and the delicious shitake mushrooms.

Menu 35 € – Carte 30/43 €

PLAN: 3-G3 – *Vallehermoso 36 (Mercado de Vallehermoso, puesto 44) – Ⓜ Quevedo – ✆ 918 28 69 47 – www.tripea.es – Closed 17-23 August, Monday, Sunday*

Alpe

EUROPEAN CONTEMPORARY • CLASSIC DÉCOR The name is a nod to the years that the chef spent working in leading restaurants in Switzerland. The classic-contemporary decor provides the setting for Swiss-inspired cuisine with influences from Central Europe and the Iberian Peninsula.

Menu 36/59 € – Carte 35/50 €

PLAN: 1-D1 – *Fernando el Santo 25 – Ⓜ Colón – ✆ 917 52 36 25 – www.alperestaurante.es – Closed 1-31 August, Monday, Sunday*

Atelier Belge

BELGIAN • CLASSIC DÉCOR Authentic Belgian cuisine showcasing interesting creative touches. Its mussel specialities and the skate with capers and black butter are particularly worth trying. Superb beer menu.

Menu 14 € (lunch), 28/45 € – Carte 40/64 €

PLAN: 3-H2 – *Bretón de los Herreros 39 – Ⓜ Alonso Cano – ✆ 915 45 84 48 – www.atelierbelge.es – Closed Monday, dinner Sunday*

Benares

INDIAN • CLASSIC DÉCOR Following in the footsteps of its London namesake, Benares' major selling points are its modern take on classic Indian cuisine and its pleasant terrace-garden with a soothing patio pool.

Menu 19 € (lunch)/55 € – Carte 45/65 €

PLAN: 1-D1 – *Zurbano 5 – Ⓜ Alonso Martínez – ✆ 913 19 87 16 – www.benaresmadrid.com – Closed 6-22 August, Sunday*

Candeli

GRILLS • CONTEMPORARY DÉCOR Run by two brothers who put their full faith in dishes prepared with high-quality, additive-free ingredients including the freshest possible fish and matured meats. Grilled dishes are the undoubted stars of the show here.

Carte 35/50 €

PLAN: 3-H2 – *Ponzano 47 – Ⓜ Ríos Rosas – ✆ 917 37 70 86 – www.candelirestaurante.com – Closed dinner Sunday*

Fismuler

TRADITIONAL CUISINE • TRENDY Gastronomy meets interior design in this restaurant with an austere retro-industrial feel. Despite this, the service and ambience is relaxed, with a menu that features pleasantly updated traditional cuisine.

Carte 35/65 €

PLAN: 3-H3 – *Sagasta 29 – Ⓜ Alonso Martínez – ✆ 918 27 75 81 – www.fismuler.com – Closed 1-7 January, 9-23 August, Sunday*

Kappo

JAPANESE • TRENDY An intimate, contemporary address with an enticing sushi bar as its main focus. Diners order from a single yet extensive menu of modern Japanese cuisine.

Menu 58/72 €

PLAN: 3-H2 – *Bretón de los Herreros 54 – Ⓜ Gregorio Marañón – ✆ 910 42 00 66 – www.kappo.es – Closed 5-26 August, Monday, Sunday*

Lakasa

SEASONAL CUISINE • TRENDY A restaurant enjoying lots of popularity to t point where you might need to book a table in the gastro-bar. Market-inspir cuisine with an à la carte that is constantly being updated and the option half-portions.

Carte 42/70€

PLAN: 3-H2 – *Plaza del Descubridor Diego de Ordás 1 – Ⓜ Rios Rosas – ✆ 915 33 87 15 – www.lakasa.es – Closed Saturday, Sunday*

Medea

CREATIVE • MINIMALIST A restrained decor, an underground vibe and ind music characterise this restaurant, where the menus reflect cooking that con bines in-vogue trends and flavours with influences from the Mediterranean, As and South America.

Menu 55/80€

PLAN: 3-H3 – *Nicasio Gallego 14 – Ⓜ Alonso Martinez – ✆ 910 81 97 71 – www.medearestaurante.com – Closed 15-26 March, 3-23 August, Monday, Sunday*

Miyama

JAPANESE • CONTEMPORARY DÉCOR This restaurant is hugely popular in th city. An extensive sushi bar and simply laid tables share space in the single dinin area. The high quality, traditional Japanese cuisine is a hit, including with Japa nese visitors.

Carte 45/70€

PLAN: 3-H3 – *Paseo de la Castellana 45 – Ⓜ Gregorio Marañón – ✆ 913 91 00 26 – www.restaurantemiyama.com – Closed 10-31 August, Sunday*

Poncelet Cheese Bar

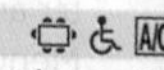

CHEESE, FONDUE AND RACLETTE • CONTEMPORARY DÉCOR An innovativ designer space where cheese is king, with a menu featuring 150 options if you in clude the cheese plates, fondues and raclettes. However, dishes without chees are still available!

Menu 28/58€ – Carte 30/46€

PLAN: 3-H2 – *José Abascal 61 – Ⓜ Gregorio Marañon – ✆ 913 99 25 50 – www.ponceletcheesebar.es – Closed Monday, dinner Sunday*

Soy Kitchen

FUSION • TRENDY The chef here, who hails from Beijing, creates unique dishe that combine Asian (Chinese, Korean, Japanese...) and Spanish and Peruvian in fluences. Dishes are full of colour and flavour.

Menu 65€

PLAN: 3-H3 – *Zurbano 59 – Ⓜ Gregorio Marañón – ✆ 913 19 25 51 – www.soykitchen.es – Closed dinner Sunday*

Tiradito

PERUVIAN • TRENDY A young and easy-going restaurant serving 100% tradi tional Peruvian cuisine. Dishes on the menu include ceviches, tiraditos, picoteos and tapas criollas.

Carte 40/58€

PLAN: 3-G3 – *Conde Duque 13 – Ⓜ San Bernardo – ✆ 915 41 78 76 – www.tiradito.es – Closed Monday, lunch Tuesday, dinner Sunday*

Chamartín

✿✿✿ DiverXO (Dabiz Muñoz)

CREATIVE • DESIGN Forget all your preconceived ideas about food and open up your tastebuds as you discover the highly personal world of Dabiz Muñoz, a celebrity chef with a surprising and ground-breaking approach to cooking. To a backdrop of stunning modern design, enjoy world cuisine that is exciting, irreverent and certain to provoke a reaction. Pure hedonism!

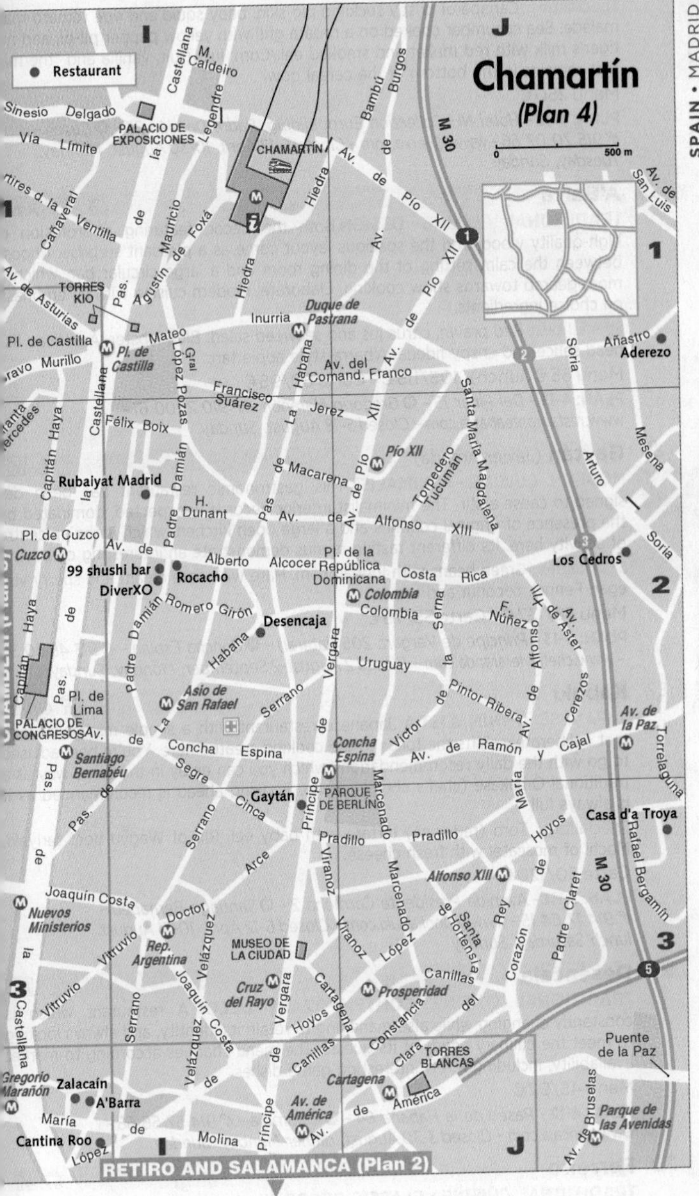
Chamartín
(Plan 4)
0
500 m
Restaurant
Aderezo
Los Cedros
Rubaiyat Madrid
99 shushi bar
Rocacho
DiverXO
Desencaja
Gaytán
Casa d'a Troya
Zalacaín
A'Barra
Cantina Roo
PALACIO DE EXPOSICIONES
CHAMARTÍN
TORRES KIO
PALACIO DE CONGRESOS
MUSEO DE LA CIUDAD
TORRES BLANCAS
PARQUE DE BERLÍN
Puente de la Paz
Duque de Pastrana
Pl. de Castilla
Pío XII
Cuzco
Colombia
Asio de San Rafael
Santiago Bernabéu
Concha Espina
Av. de la Paz
Alfonso XIII
Nuevos Ministerios
Rep. Argentina
Cruz del Rayo
Prosperidad
Cartagena
Av. de América
Gregorio Marañón
Parque de las Avenidas
M 30
Av. de Pío XII
Av. de Alfonso XIII
Av. de Concha Espina
Av. de Ramón y Cajal
Av. de América
Av. de Burgos
Pl. de la República Dominicana
Pl. de Lima
Pl. de Cuzco
RETIRO AND SALAMANCA (Plan 2)

Specialities: Canapé of crispy suckling pig skin, baby squid and ripe tomato marmalade. Sea cucumber cooked on a robata grill with yellow pepper pil-pil and h tiger's milk with red mullet and smoked eel. Corn, lulo fruit, vanilla and "the mi that remains in the bottom of the cereal bowl".

Menu 250 €

PLAN: 4-12 – *Hotel NH Collection Eurobuilding, Padre Damián 23 – Ⓜ Cuzco – ✆ 915 70 07 66 – www.diverxo.com – Closed 5-12 April, 10-30 August, Monday, Tuesday, Sunday*

✿ A'Barra

TRADITIONAL CUISINE • DESIGN Both the decor, featuring a profusion c high-quality wood, and the spacious layout come as a pleasant surprise. Choos between the calm setting of the dining room and a large circular bar, which more geared towards show cooking. Elaborate, modern cuisine with an emphas on choice ingredients.

Specialities: Red prawn, citrus jus and seaweed salad. Blue lobster, American fis head sauce and crispy fideuá. A'barra-style apple tart.

Menu 65 € (lunch), 105/115 € – Carte 60/95 €

PLAN: 4-13 – *Del Pinar 15 – Ⓜ Gregorio Marañón – ✆ 910 21 00 61 – www.restauranteabarra.com – Closed 5-18 August, Sunday*

✿ Gaytán (Javier Aranda)

MODERN CUISINE • MINIMALIST This gastronomic restaurant has been designed to cause a stir. The minimalist interior decor is unexpected, dominated by the presence of original columns and a large open kitchen, which is the epicentre of activity here. Its different tasting menus demonstrate an interesting creativity.

Specialities: Green beans with Iberian ham. Hare with date cream and sherry vinegar. Fennel, coconut and lemon.

Menu 88/137 € – Carte 55/75 €

PLAN: 4-13 – *Príncipe de Vergara 205 (lateral) – Ⓜ Concha Espina – ✆ 913 48 50 30 – www.chefjavieraranda.com – Closed 2 August-2 September, Monday, Sunday*

✿ Kabuki

JAPANESE • MINIMALIST A Japanese restaurant with a simple minimalist look that deliberately shifts the focus to the cooking created here. You're best advised to go with the daily recommendations which you can enjoy in the same way as a traditional Omakase (chef's choice) menu. Booking ahead is recommended as it is always full.

Specialities: Toro (red tuna) tartare with baby eel. Rib of Wagyu beef teriyaki. Mochi of moscatel with fresh cheese.

Carte 60/120 €

PLAN: 3-H1 – *Avenida Presidente Carmona 2 – Ⓜ Santiago Bernabeu – ✆ 914 17 64 15 – www.grupokabuki.com – Closed 6-12 April, 10-31 August, lunch Saturday, Sunday*

Desencaja

TRADITIONAL CUISINE • CONTEMPORARY DÉCOR A restaurant which is constantly changing while also managing to retain its identity, and always looking to meet the culinary needs of its guests. The menu changes according to market availability, including a few interesting game dishes.

Menu 45/92 €

PLAN: 4-12 – *Paseo de la Habana 84 – Ⓜ Colombia – ✆ 914 57 56 68 – www.dsncaja.com – Closed 3-30 August, dinner Monday, Sunday*

Ferreiro

TRADITIONAL CUISINE • CLASSIC DÉCOR Classic-contemporary dining rooms act as a backdrop for traditional cuisine with strong Asturian roots in this restaurant. The extensive menu is supplemented by a good choice of specials.

Menu 32/54 € – Carte 40/60 €

PLAN: 3-H2 – *Comandante Zorita 32 – Ⓜ Alvarado – ✆ 915 53 93 42 – www.restauranteferreiro.com*

Gaman

PERUVIAN • FRIENDLY Gaman is a Japanese word meaning "perseverance"; a quality reflected in chef Luis Arévalo's Peruvian-Nikkei style of cooking, which also features more common Japanese concepts such as the "omakase" menu.

Menu 69€ – Carte 40/70€

PLAN: 3-H1 – *Plaza de San Amaro 8 – Ⓜ Estrecho – ✆ 914 63 36 23 – www.gaman.com – Closed Sunday*

99 sushi bar

JAPANESE • DESIGN A highly successful restaurant, thanks to its traditional Japanese cuisine served alongside fusion dishes combining Spanish and Japanese influences. Make sure you try the wild boar gyoza dumplings.

Menu 90€ – Carte 60/80€

PLAN: 4-I2 – *Hotel NH Collection Eurobuilding, Padre Damián 23 – Ⓜ Cuzco – ✆ 913 59 38 01 – www.99sushibar.com – Closed Sunday*

Rocacho

TRADITIONAL CUISINE • CONTEMPORARY DÉCOR A restaurant with a modern look where top-quality products take centre stage. Seasonal dishes, wild fish, grilled beef and exquisite rice dishes all feature prominently on the menu here.

Carte 45/65€

PLAN: 4-I2 – *Padre Damián 38 – Ⓜ Cuzco – ✆ 914 21 97 70 – www.rocacho.com – Closed lunch Monday, dinner Tuesday*

Rubaiyat Madrid

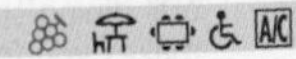

MEATS AND GRILLS • BRASSERIE Discover the flavours of São Paulo in this restaurant, which offers a full menu of meat from its own ranch (including Brangus and Tropical Kobe Beef) and typical Brazilian dishes such as "feijoada" (from November to March).

Carte 60/75€

PLAN: 4-I2 – *Juan Ramón Jiménez 37 – Ⓜ Cuzco – ✆ 913 59 10 00 – www.gruporubaiyat.com – Closed dinner Sunday*

La Tahona

MEATS AND GRILLS • CLASSIC DÉCOR Part of the El Asador de Aranda chain. La Tahona's dining rooms have a medieval Castillian ambience with a wood fire at the entrance taking pride of place. The suckling lamb (lechazo) is the star dish here!

Menu 36/55€ – Carte 38/50€

PLAN: 3-H1 – *Capitán Haya 21 (lateral) – Ⓜ Cuzco – ✆ 915 55 04 41 – www.asadordearanda.com – Closed 4-30 August, dinner Sunday*

Viavélez

CREATIVE • TRENDY Viavélez boasts a stylish tapas bar plus a modern dining room in the basement where you can enjoy creative dishes that remain faithful to Asturian cuisine. The taberna does not close for holidays.

Menu 18€ (lunch)/30€ – Carte 35/55€

PLAN: 3-H2 – *Avenida General Perón 10 – Ⓜ Santiago Bernabeu – ✆ 915 79 95 39 – www.restauranteviavelez.com – Closed Monday, dinner Sunday*

Zalacaín

CLASSIC CUISINE • ELEGANT A legendary address with a new renovated look. Here, the classic-contemporary setting provides the backdrop for cuisine that combines past and present, including an impressive tasting menu and half-portions options.

Menu 98€ – Carte 80/110€

PLAN: 4-I3 – *Álvarez de Baena 4 – Ⓜ Gregorio Marañón – ✆ 915 61 48 40 – www.restaurantezalacain.com – Closed 6-12 April, 1-31 August, lunch Saturday, Sunday*

Environs of Madrid

At East

Aderezo

TRADITIONAL CUISINE • CLASSIC DÉCOR This pleasant restaurant has a cla sic yet contemporary ambience, a bar for a pre-lunch or pre-dinner drink, and superb fish display cabinet. Impressive cooking based around high quality ingr dients and traditional recipes.

Menu 25/60 € – Carte 40/60 €

PLAN: 4-J1 – *Añastro 48 – ✆ 917 67 01 58 – www.aderezorestaurante.es – Closed 1-31 August, Sunday*

Casa d'a Troya

GALICIAN • CONTEMPORARY DÉCOR A long-established family restaura which has recently been updated by the latest generation at the helm. Simpl modestly presented Galician cuisine and generous portions.

Menu 38/48 € – Carte 35/65 €

PLAN: 4-J3 – *Emiliano Barral 14 – Ⓜ Avenida de la Paz – ✆ 914 16 44 55 – www.casadatroya.es – Closed 1-31 August, Monday, dinner Tuesday-Thursday, dinner Sunday*

Los Cedros

TRADITIONAL CUISINE • CLASSIC DÉCOR Although this restaurant has sev eral dining spaces, the highlight is the garden, where the sound of running wate makes you forget you're in Madrid. Updated classic cuisine with a strong empha sis on the best-quality products.

Menu 39/195 € – Carte 43/62 €

PLAN: 4-J2 – *Hotel Quinta de los Cedros, Allendesalazar 4 – Ⓜ Arturo Soria – ✆ 915 15 22 00 – www.restaurantelos cedros.es – Closed 9-12 April, 3-23 August, Sunday*

Jaizkibel

BASQUE • REGIONAL A small Basque "asador" featuring an enticing food dis play cabinet and a large cider barrel ("kupela"). Extensive menu of classic Basqu recipes, including a choice of stews, as well as rice and cod dishes.

Menu 55/70 € – Carte 45/65 €

Off plan – *Albasanz 67 – Ⓜ Suanzes – ✆ 913 04 16 41 – www.jaizkibelartesanoscocineros.com – Closed Sunday*

At North

Filandón

TRADITIONAL CUISINE • CONTEMPORARY DÉCOR This rustic yet moder restaurant is situated in the middle of the countryside. It specialises in rotisserie-style cuisine with a focus on high quality ingredients and grilled fish dishes. The Lenguado Evaristo (grilled sole) is particularly mouthwatering.

Carte 50/70 €

Off plan – *Carretera Fuencarral-El Pardo, km 1,9 (M 612) – ✆ 917 34 38 26 – www.filandon.es – Closed 25 July-20 August, Monday, dinner Sunday*

El Oso

ASTURIAN • REGIONAL A small, two-floored house featuring several contemporary dining rooms, which are spacious and bright – and adorned with a typically Asturian decor. Cooking from the same region is based around fresh produce.

Carte 40/60 €

Off plan – *Avenida de Burgos 214 (vía de servicio La Moraleja, dirección Burgos) – ✆ 917 66 60 60 – www.restauranteeloso.com – Closed dinner Sunday*

BARCELONA

BARCELONA

MasterLu/iStock

BARCELONA IN...

→ **ONE DAY**
Catedral de Santa Eulalia, Las Ramblas, La Pedrera, Museu Picasso, Sagrada Familia.

→ **TWO DAYS**
Montjuïc, Parc Güell, Nou Camp Stadium, Barceloneta Waterfront, Tibidabo.

→ **THREE DAYS**
Barri Gotic and Palau de la Musica Catalana, Via Laietana, Sitges.

It can't be overestimated ho important Catalonia is to th locals of Barcelona: pride i their region of Spain runs dee in the blood. Barcelona love to mix the traditional with th avant-garde, and this exuber ant opening of arms has see it grow into a pulsating city fo visitors. Its rash of theatres museums and concert hall is unmatched by most othe European cities, and many art ists and architects, including Picasso, Miró, Dalí, Gaudí an Subirachs, have chosen to live here.

The 19C was a golden period in the city's artistic devel opment, with the growth of the great Catalan Modernisr

movement, but it was knocked back on its heels after the Spanish Civil War and the rise to power of the dictator Franco, who destroyed hopes for an independent Catalonia. After his death, democracy came to Spain and since then, Barcelona has relished its position as the capital of a restored autonomous region. Go up on the Montjuïc to get a great overview of the city below. Barcelona's atmospheric old town is near the harbour and reaches into the teeming streets of the Gothic Quarter, while the newer area is north of this; its elegant avenues in grid formation making up Eixample. The coastal quarter of Barça has been transformed with the development of trendy Barceloneta. For many, though, the epicentre of this bubbling city is Las Ramblas, scything through the centre of town.

EATING OUT

arcelona has long had a good gastro-omic tradition, and geographically it's een more influenced by France and aly than other Spanish regions. But ıese days the sensual enjoyment of ›od has become something of a main-tream religion here. The city has hun-reds of tapas bars; a type of cuisine hich is very refreshing knocked back ith a draught beer. The city's location rings together produce from the land nd the sea, with a firm emphasis on easonality and quality produce. This xplains why there are myriad mar-ets in the city, all in great locations.

Specialities to look out for include Pantumaca: slices of toasted bread with tomato and olive oil; Escalibada, which is made with roasted vegetables; Esqueixada, a typically Catalan salad, and Crema Catalana, a light custard. One little known facet of Barcelona life is its exquisite chocolate and sweet shops. Two stand out: Fargas, in the Barri Gothic, is the city's most famous chocolate shop, while Cacao Sampaka is the most elegant chocolate store you could ever wish to find.

Old Town - Gothic Quarter

Caelis (Romain Fornell)

CREATIVE • ELEGANT Elegant, contemporary and with an open kitchen su rounded by a bar where guests can also enjoy the cuisine on offer here. Th award-winning French chef showcases his creative talents via several menu from which you can also choose single, individually priced dishes.

Specialities: White asparagus cream with cured egg yolk and caviar. Macaro stuffed with squid and prawns with coconut cream and coriander. Crystal lemo

Menu 42€ (lunch), 92/135€ - Carte 106€

PLAN: 2-F1 - *Hotel Ohla Barcelona, Via Laietana 49 - Ⓜ Urquinaona - ✆ 935 10 12 05 - www.caelis.com - Closed Monday, lunch Tuesday, Sunday*

Dos Palillos

ASIAN • TAPAS BAR A highly original dining option both for its unique "sho cooking" concept and its culinary philosophy. This is centred on the fusion of or ental cuisine and typically Spanish products. There are two counters for dinin one at the entrance (no reservations taken and only for à la carte dining), and an other further inside, which has a more gastronomic focus with its tasting menus

Specialities: Yin yang lobster wonton soup. Octopus aemono. Thai coconut.

Tapa 10€ - Menu 110€ - Carte 45/55€

PLAN: 2-E2 - *Elisabets 9 - Ⓜ Catalunya - ✆ 933 04 05 13 - www.dospalillos.com - Closed 2-24 August, 22 December-6 January, Monday, lunch Tuesday-Wednesday Sunday*

Koy Shunka (Hideki Matsuhisa)

JAPANESE • CONTEMPORARY DÉCOR In this restaurant, the name of whic translates as "intense seasonal aromas", our senses are opened to the flavour emotions and unique world of Japanese cuisine. The head chef, a master of hi art who relies on a team of young chefs, combines the classic flavours and tex tures of Japan with Mediterranean ingredients.

Specialities: Shiokara squid 1987. Ikejime lobster. Mango mousse with mochi.

Menu 89/132€ - Carte 60/90€

PLAN: 2-F1 - *De Copons 7 - Ⓜ Urquinaona - ✆ 934 12 79 39 - www.koyshunka.com - Closed 8-28 August, 24 December-4 January, Monday, Sunday*

Senyor Parellada

REGIONAL CUISINE • COSY A restaurant with undisputed charm thanks to it classic-colonial atmosphere and a variety of rooms where time seems to have stood still. Sitting down to eat here is both a homage to authentic Catalan cuisine and to history, as this property was once an inn with a constant flow of travellers Its current success is for the most part due to its affable service, reasonable prices and its à la carte featuring highly appetising suggestions, including midweek rice specials, the "Surf and Turf" salad and its popular "Traveller's Lunch Menu".

Menu 38€ - Carte 30/43€

PLAN: 2-G2 - *L'Argenteria 37 - Ⓜ Jaume I - ✆ 933 10 50 94 - www.senyorparellada.com*

Ají

PERUVIAN • BISTRO The name, which translates as "chilli pepper" in Peruvian Spanish and "taste" in Japanese, gives us a good insight into the culinary inten- tions of this restaurant. Japanese cuisine with a focus on well defined textures and flavours.

Menu 21€ (lunch), 35/58€ - Carte 30/50€

PLAN: 1-C2 - *Marina 19 - Ⓜ Ciutadella-Vila Olímpica - ✆ 935 11 97 67 - www.restaurantaji.com - Closed 1-19 January, Monday, Sunday*

La Barra de Carles Abellan

TRADITIONAL CUISINE • TRENDY This restaurant will win over guests with its own vision of Mediterranean cuisine that features grilled fish and meats, dishes prepared on the spot and a decor that is particularly striking. The terrace is superb!

Menu 76 € - Carte 60/95 €

PLAN: 1-C3 - *Hotel W Barcelona, Plaza de la Rosa dels Vents 1 (Moll De Llevant) - ☎ 932 95 26 36 - www.carlesabellan.com - Closed 6 January-4 February, Monday, lunch Tuesday, dinner Sunday*

Bodega Sant Antoni Gloriós

TRADITIONAL CUISINE • TAPAS BAR An informal "bodega" with a menu designed for sharing which combines traditional and modern cooking and also includes gourmet tinned products and top-quality cured meats. The "patatas bravas" here are legendary!

Tapa 6 € - Ración 10 €

PLAN: 3-K3 - *Manso 42 - ☎ 934 24 06 28 - Closed 27 January-3 February, 24 August-7 September*

El Cercle

CLASSIC CUISINE • CLASSIC DÉCOR This restaurant, housed in the Reial Cercle Artístic, offers different types of cuisine ranging from Japanese specialities to modern Catalan fare in several different settings (terrace, library and Japanese bar).

Menu 45/65 € - Carte 31/47 €

PLAN: 2-F2 - *Dels Arcs 5-1º - Ⓜ Plaça Catalunya - ☎ 936 24 48 10 - www.elcerclerestaurant.com*

Direkte Boqueria

CONTEMPORARY • TAVERN A tiny and unusual eatery beneath the arcades of the famous Boquería market, offering a fusion of Catalan recipes, Mediterranean ingredients and Chinese and Japanese cuisine.

Menu 45/58 €

PLAN: 2-F2 - *Les Cabres 13 - Ⓜ Liceu - ☎ 931 14 69 39 - www.direkte.cat - Closed 3-11 March, 12-27 August, 24 November-10 December, Monday, dinner Tuesday-Thursday, Sunday*

Dos Pebrots

MEDITERRANEAN CUISINE • NEIGHBOURHOOD Dos Pebrots combines its informal character with a unique concept which focuses on minutely researched cooking that narrates the evolution of Mediterranean gastronomy.

Menu 50/70 € - Carte 30/70 €

PLAN: 2-E2 - *Doctor Dou 19 - Ⓜ Catalunya - ☎ 938 53 95 98 - www.dospebrots.com - Closed 12-27 August, 23 December-7 January, Monday, Tuesday, lunch Wednesday-Thursday*

Estimar

SEAFOOD • MEDITERRANEAN An intimate restaurant that is somewhat tucked away but which has received many plaudits thanks to the passion for the sea shown by the Gotanegra family and chef Rafa Zafra. Grilled dishes and high-quality products are to the fore here.

Carte 70/120 €

PLAN: 2-G2 - *Sant Antoni dels Sombrerers 3 - Ⓜ Jaume I - ☎ 932 68 91 97 - www.restaurantestimar.com - Closed 8-15 April, 5-25 August, 23 December-8 January, lunch Monday, Sunday*

Fonda España

TRADITIONAL CUISINE • COSY An icon of Modernism serving updated traditional cuisine bearing the hallmark of chef Martín Berasategui. Enticing dining options include its "Journey through Modernism" menu.

Menu 79/118 € - Carte 35/60 €

PLAN: 2-F2 - *Hotel España, Sant Pau 9 - Ⓜ Liceu - ☎ 935 50 00 10 - www.hotelespanya.com - Closed 3-23 August, dinner Sunday*

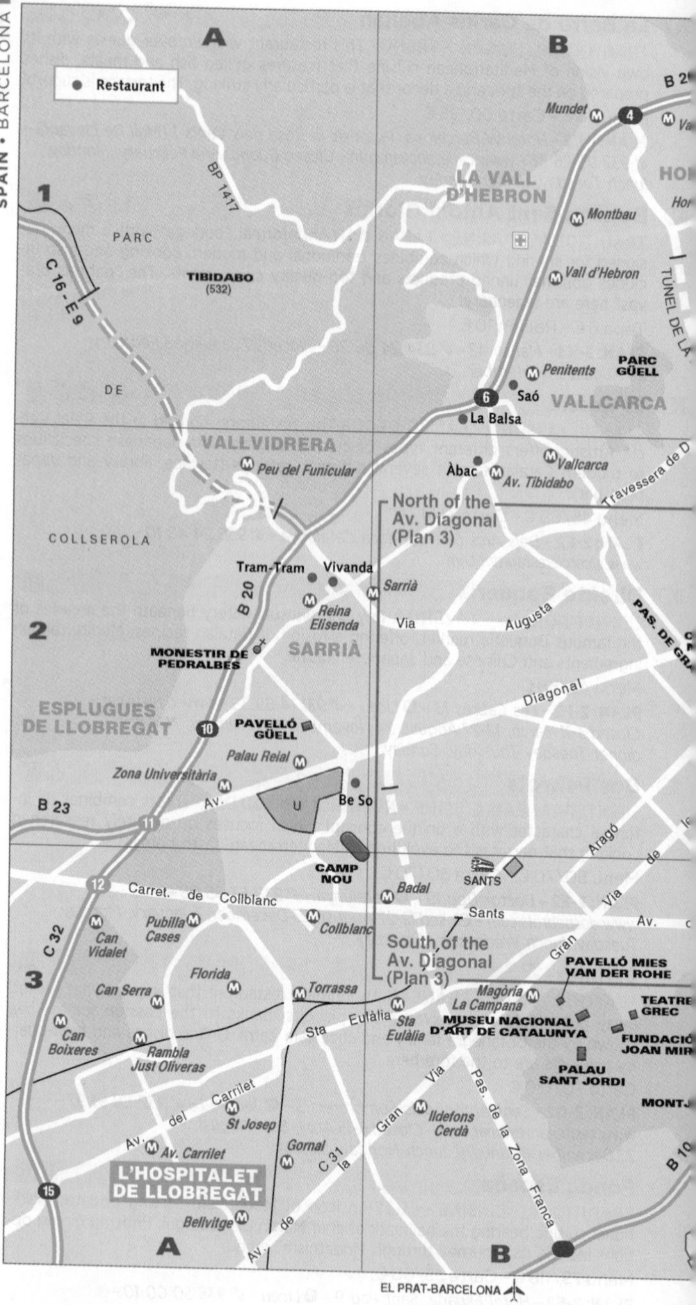
A
B
Restaurant
B 2
Mundet
4
LA VALL D'HEBRON
Montbau
Vall d'Hebron
TÚNEL DE LA
PARC GÜELL
Penitents
Saó
VALLCARCA
6
La Balsa
1
PARC
TIBIDABO
(532)
BP 1417
C 16 - E 9
DE
VALLVIDRERA
Peu del Funicular
Àbac
Vallcarca
Av. Tibidabo
Travessera de D
North of the Av. Diagonal (Plan 3)
COLLSEROLA
Tram-Tram
Vivanda
Sarrià
Reina Elisenda
B 20
2
Via Augusta
PAS. DE GR
MONESTIR DE PEDRALBES
SARRIÀ
Diagonal
ESPLUGUES DE LLOBREGAT
10
PAVELLÓ GÜELL
Palau Reial
Zona Universitària
B 23
Av.
U
Be So
11
CAMP NOU
SANTS
Aragó
Gran Via de
12
Carret. de Collblanc
Badal
Sants
Av.
Pubilla Cases
Can Vidalet
Collblanc
C 32
South of the Av. Diagonal (Plan 3)
3
Florida
Torrassa
PAVELLÓ MIES VAN DER ROHE
Can Serra
Magòria La Campana
TEATRE GREC
Can Boixeres
Sta Eulàlia
Sta Eulàlia
MUSEU NACIONAL D'ART DE CATALUNYA
FUNDACIÓ JOAN MIR
Rambla Just Oliveras
PALAU SANT JORDI
Av. del Carrilet
St Josep
Gran Via
Ildefons Cerdà
Pas. de la Zona Franca
MONTJ
Av. Carrilet
Gornal
C 31
la
B 10
L'HOSPITALET DE LLOBREGAT
15
Bellvitge
Av. de
A
B
EL PRAT-BARCELONA

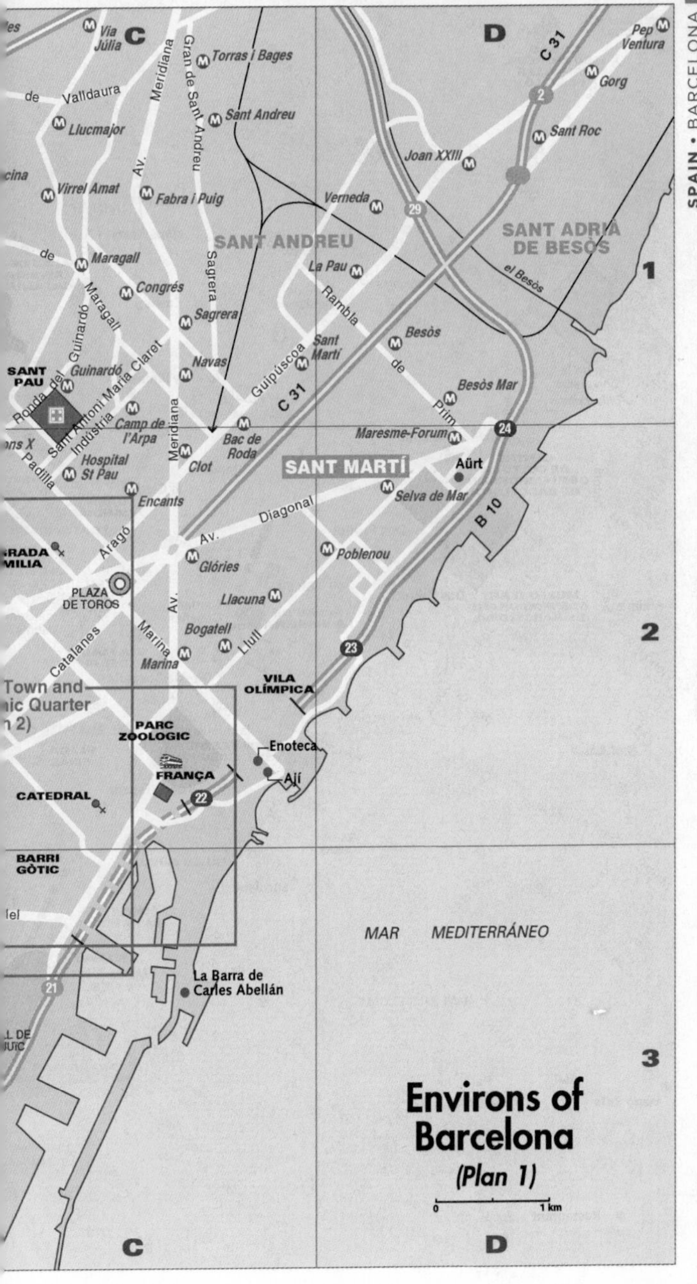
C
D
Via Júlia
Torras i Bages
Pep Ventura
Gorg
Valldaura
Meridiana
Gran de Sant Andreu
Sant Andreu
Llucmajor
Sant Roc
Joan XXIII
Virrel Amat
Fabra i Puig
Verneda
SANT ANDREU
SANT ADRIÀ DE BESÒS
Maragall
La Pau
el Besòs
Congrés
Sagrera
Rambla de Prim
Sagrera
Besòs
Navas
Sant Martí
Guinardó
SANT PAU
Ronda del Guinardó
Sant Antoni Maria Claret
Guipúscoa
C 31
Besòs Mar
Camp de l'Arpa
Indústria
Maresme-Forum
Bac de Roda
Hospital St Pau
Clot
SANT MARTÍ
Aûrt
Padilla
Selva de Mar
Encants
Diagonal
B 10
Av.
Aragó
Glòries
Poblenou
PLAZA DE TOROS
Llacuna
Catalanes
Marina
Bogatell
Llull
Marina
VILA OLÍMPICA
PARC ZOOLOGIC
Enoteca
FRANÇA
Ají
CATEDRAL
BARRI GÒTIC
MAR MEDITERRÁNEO
La Barra de Carles Abellán
1
2
3
Environs of Barcelona
(Plan 1)
0
1 km

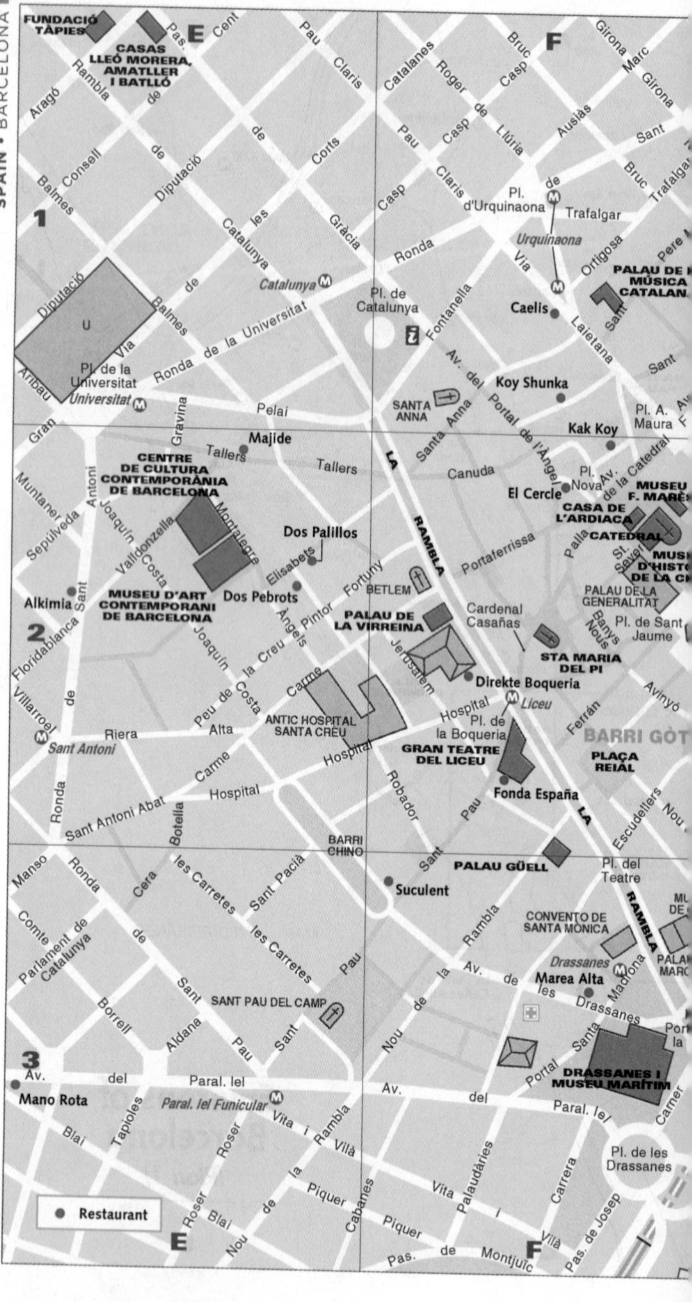
FUNDACIÓ TÀPIES
CASAS LLEÓ MORERA, AMATLLER I BATLLÓ
CENTRE DE CULTURA CONTEMPORÀNIA DE BARCELONA
MUSEU D'ART CONTEMPORANI DE BARCELONA
PALAU DE LA VIRREINA
ANTIC HOSPITAL SANTA CREU
GRAN TEATRE DEL LICEU
PALAU GÜELL
CONVENTO DE SANTA MÒNICA
SANT PAU DEL CAMP
DRASSANES I MUSEU MARÍTIM
STA MARIA DEL PI
CASA DE L'ARDIACA
CATEDRAL
PALAU DE LA GENERALITAT
PLAÇA REIAL
BARRI CHINO
SANTA ANNA
BETLEM
Majide
Dos Palillos
Dos Pebrots
Alkimia
Caelis
Koy Shunka
Kak Koy
El Cercle
Direkte Boqueria
Fonda España
Suculent
Marea Alta
Mano Rota
Catalunya
Urquinaona
Universitat
Liceu
Sant Antoni
Drassanes
Paral. lel Funicular
Pl. de Catalunya
Pl. de la Universitat
Pl. d'Urquinaona
Pl. de la Boqueria
Pl. de Sant Jaume
Pl. del Teatre
Pl. de les Drassanes
LA RAMBLA
● Restaurant

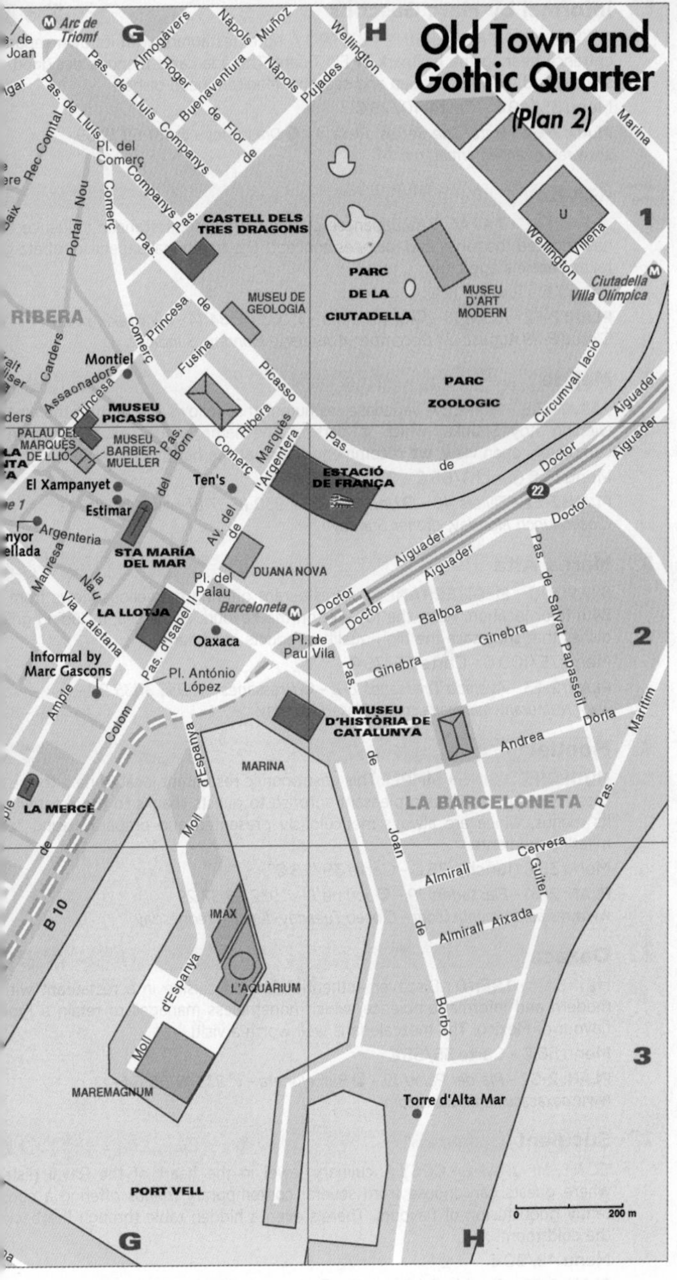

Old Town and Gothic Quarter
(Plan 2)
G
H
1
2
3
Arc de Triomf
CASTELL DELS TRES DRAGONS
MUSEU DE GEOLOGIA
PARC DE LA CIUTADELLA
MUSEU D'ART MODERN
PARC ZOOLOGIC
Ciutadella Villa Olímpica
RIBERA
Montiel
MUSEU PICASSO
PALAU DEL MARQUÈS DE LLIÓ
MUSEU BARBIER-MUELLER
El Xampanyet
Estimar
Ten's
STA MARÍA DEL MAR
ESTACIÓ DE FRANÇA
DUANA NOVA
Pl. del Palau
Barceloneta
LA LLOTJA
Oaxaca
Pl. de Pau Vila
Informal by Marc Gascons
Pl. António López
MUSEU D'HISTÒRIA DE CATALUNYA
MARINA
LA BARCELONETA
LA MERCÈ
IMAX
L'AQUÀRIUM
MAREMAGNUM
Torre d'Alta Mar
PORT VELL
B 10
Almogàvers
Nàpols
Muñoz
Wellington
Pujades
Roger de Flor
Buenaventura
Pas. de Lluís Companys
Pl. del Comerç
Rec Comtal
Portal Nou
Comerç
Pas. Picasso
Princesa
Fusina
Marina
Villena
Circumval. lació
Carders
Assaonadors
Argenteria
Manresa
Via Laietana
Pas. d'Isabel II
Av. del Marquès de l'Argentera
Pas. de Born
Ribera
Pas. de Circumval. lació
Doctor Aiguader
Balboa
Ginebra
Pas. de Salvat Papasseit
Dòria
Andrea
Pas. Marítim
Pas. de Joan de Borbó
Cervera
Guiter
Almirall
Almirall Aixada
Moll d'Espanya
Ample
Colom
0
200 m

Informal by Marc Gascons

MEDITERRANEAN CUISINE • BISTRO A hotel restaurant with its own separa entrance bearing the hallmark of Els Tinars. The à la carte menu is designed f sharing and includes Catalan and seasonal Mediterranean dishes.

Menu 35/49€ - Carte 40/75€

PLAN: 2-G2 - *Hotel The Serras, Plata 4* - *Drassanes* - *931 69 18 69* - *www.restauranteinformal.com*

Kak Koy

JAPANESE • TAPAS BAR Japanese cuisine with a Mediterranean influence th has adopted the tapas and *raciones* concept. The traditional Japanese robata g takes centre stage here.

Tapa 7€ - Ración 12€

PLAN: 2-F2 - *Ripoll 16* - *Urquinaona* - *933 02 84 14* - *www.kakkoy.com* - *Closed 8-28 August, 24 December-4 January, Monday, Sunday*

Majide

JAPANESE • SIMPLE A Japanese restaurant that follows the path of the awar winning Koy Shunka, which is part of the same group. As the kitchen completely open view, we recommend a seat at the bar.

Menu 16€ (lunch)/65€ - Carte 30/55€

PLAN: 2-E2 - *Tallers 48* - *Universitat* - *930 16 37 81* - *www.majide.es* - *Closed lunch Monday, dinner Sunday*

Marea Alta

SEAFOOD • MEDITERRANEAN A restaurant offering marvellous views from i 24th floor location. Here, the focus is on the flavours of the sea, including grille dishes that showcase the high-quality products used here.

Menu 75/100€ - Carte 55/75€

PLAN: 2-F3 - *Avenida Drassanes 6-8* - *Drassanes* - *936 31 35 90* - *www.restaurantemareaalta.com* - *Closed Monday*

Montiel

MODERN CUISINE • SIMPLE This gastronomic restaurant located next to the P casso Museum provides a pleasant surprise to guests thanks to the creativity c its menus, which are always meticulously presented and prepared using "zer miles" ingredients.

Menu 35€ (lunch)/75€ - Carte 39/76€

PLAN: 2-G1 - *Flassaders 19* - *Jaume I* - *932 68 37 29* - *www.restaurantmontiel.com* - *Closed Tuesday, lunch Wednesday*

Oaxaca

MEXICAN • TRENDY Discover authentic Mexican cuisine in a restaurant with modern and informal ambience, which nonetheless manages to retain a typica flavour of Mexico. The mezcalería is well worth a visit!

Menu 56€ - Carte 35/55€

PLAN: 2-G2 - *Pla del Palau 19* - *Barceloneta* - *933 19 00 64* - *www.oaxacacuinamexicana.com*

Suculent

CONTEMPORARY • COSY A culinary jewel in the heart of the Raval district where guests can choose from several contemporary menus offering a consistently good fusion of flavours. There's even a hidden table through the back o the cold room!

Menu 48/80€

PLAN: 2-F3 - *Rambla del Raval 45* - *Liceu* - *934 43 65 79* - *www.suculent.com* - *Closed Monday, Tuesday*

Ten's

MODERN CUISINE • TRENDY A modern gastro-bar overseen by Jordi Cruz. The focus is on tapas, though full portions and superb oysters also feature. Menus take centre stage here at weekends.

Menu 48/62 € – Carte 25/40 €

PLAN: 2-G2 – *Avenida Marqués de l'Argentera 11 – Ⓜ Barceloneta – ✆ 933 19 22 22 – www.tensbarcelona.com*

Torre d'Alta Mar

MODERN CUISINE • CONTEMPORARY DÉCOR A restaurant whose outstanding feature is its location on top of a 75m high metal tower. Highly contemporary glass-fronted circular dining room with superb views of the sea, port and city. Traditional à la carte menu featuring contemporary touches.

Menu 82/98 € – Carte 65/95 €

PLAN: 2-H3 – *Paseo Joan de Borbó 88 – Ⓜ Barceloneta – ✆ 932 21 00 07 – www.torredealtamar.com – Closed 5-23 August, 24-29 December, lunch Monday, lunch Sunday*

El Xampanyet

TRADITIONAL CUISINE • TAPAS BAR This old tavern with a long-standing family tradition boasts a typical atmosphere with its azulejo tiles, wineskin bottles and barrels. Varied selection of tapas with an emphasis on cured meats and high-quality canned products.

Tapa 6 € – Ración 12 €

PLAN: 2-G2 – *Montcada 22 – Ⓜ Jaume I – ✆ 933 19 70 03 – Closed 13-30 January, 1 August-3 September, Monday, Sunday*

On the Avenue Diagonal

South of Av. Diagonal

✿✿ Lasarte

CREATIVE • DESIGN This impeccable contemporary-style restaurant is constantly changing and has the personal stamp of Martín Berasategui and his team. The original and imaginative cuisine bears the innovative hallmark of the chef, whose creativity is evident in the à la carte options and tasting menus alike.

Specialities: Wagyu ravioli and glazed eel, iodised cream, horseradish and caviar. Roasted virrey fish with clam pil-pil, velvet crab, champagne and a delicate hazelnut cream. Cardamom, apple and yoghurt spheres.

Menu 215/245 € – Carte 130/175 €

PLAN: 3-K2 – *Hotel Monument H., Mallorca 259 – Ⓜ Passeig de Gràcia – ✆ 934 45 32 42 – www.restaurantlasarte.com – Closed 1-14 January, 5-13 April, 16 August-8 September, Monday, Sunday*

✿✿ Angle

MODERN CUISINE • MINIMALIST Located on the first floor of the Hotel Cram, Angle has a minimalist look dominated by the presence of large white curtains. The creative cooking here demonstrates a high level of technical skill and is influenced by the very best seasonal products. This is in keeping with the philosophy of chef Jordi Cruz who brings inspiration to every dish.

Specialities: Leek with charcoal bread and spicy romesco. Veal "cap i pota" rice with oysters. Raspberry meringues with beetroot.

Menu 90/115 €

PLAN: 3-K2 – *Aragó 214 – Ⓜ Universitat – ✆ 932 16 77 77 – www.anglebarcelona.com*

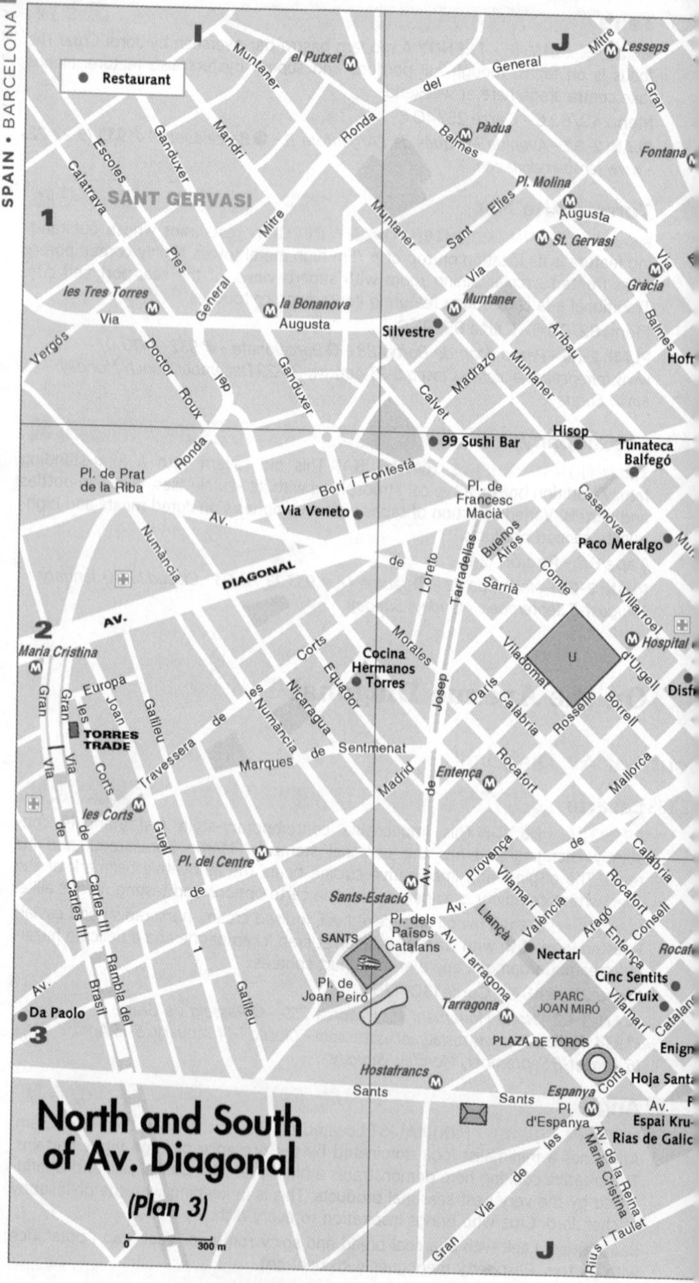

North and South of Av. Diagonal

(Plan 3)

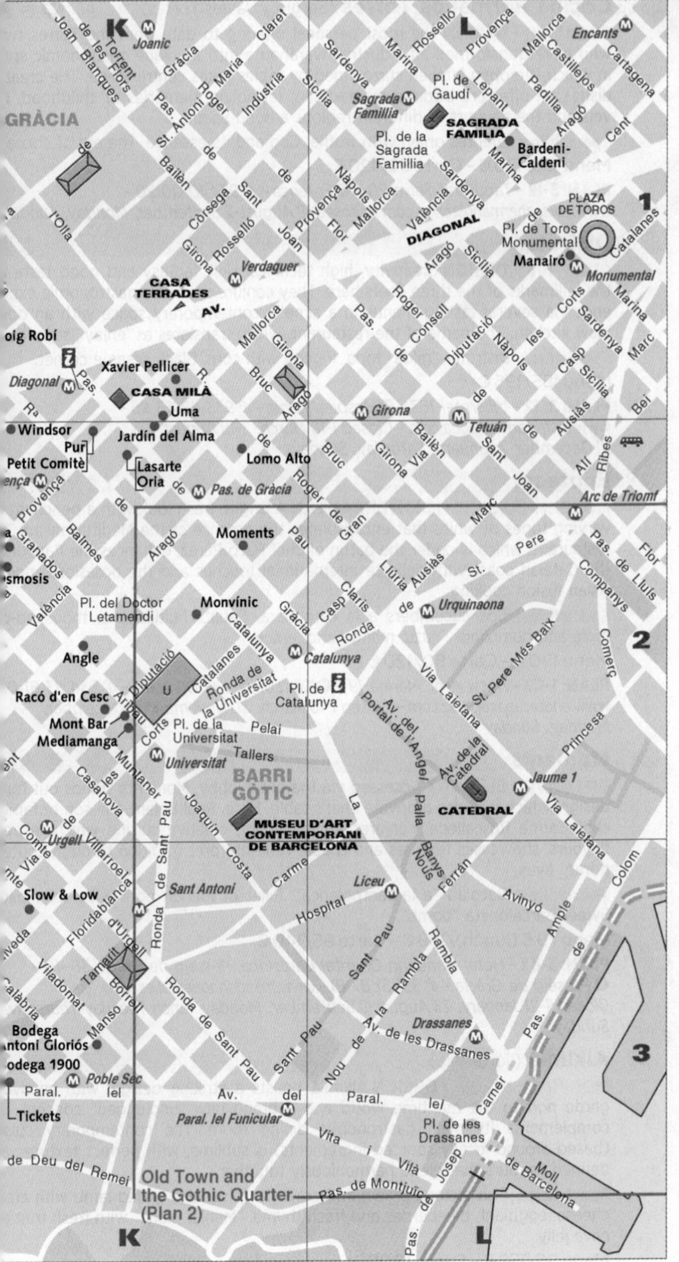
GRÀCIA
Joanic
Sagrada Família
SAGRADA FAMILIA
Pl. de Gaudí
Pl. de la Sagrada Família
Bardeni-Caldeni
Encants
PLAZA DE TOROS
Pl. de Toros Monumental
Manairó
Monumental
DIAGONAL
Verdaguer
CASA TERRADES
Xavier Pellicer
CASA MILÀ
Diagonal
Uma
Windsor
Pur
Petit Comitè
Jardín del Alma
Lasarte
Oria
Lomo Alto
Pas. de Gràcia
Girona
Tetuán
Arc de Triomf
Moments
Monvínic
Pl. del Doctor Letamendi
Angle
Racó d'en Cesc
Mont Bar
Mediamanga
Urquinaona
Catalunya
Pl. de Catalunya
Pl. de la Universitat
Universitat
BARRI GÒTIC
MUSEU D'ART CONTEMPORANI DE BARCELONA
CATEDRAL
Jaume 1
Urgell
Slow & Low
Sant Antoni
Liceu
Drassanes
Bodega Antoni Gloriós
Bodega 1900
Poble Sec
Tickets
Paral. lel Funicular
Pl. de les Drassanes
Old Town and the Gothic Quarter (Plan 2)
K
L
1
2
3

✿✿ Cocina Hermanos Torres (Sergio y Javier Torres)

CREATIVE • DESIGN The most personal offering to date from the Torres tw who have transformed an industrial warehouse into a unique gastronomic spa in which the open kitchen surrounded by tables takes centre stage. The creat dishes on offer are inspired by tradition, rekindling memories of childhood, t vels and the flavours of different regions around Spain.

Specialities: Fuentes onion with truffle. Cod and its essence. The era of cocoa.

Menu 155/170€ – Carte 90/120€

PLAN: 3-I2 – *Taquígraf Serra 20 – Ⓜ Entença – ✆ 934 10 00 20 – www.cocinahermanostorres.com – Closed 18 August-2 September, Monday, Sunday*

✿✿ Disfrutar

CREATIVE • DESIGN Creativity, high technical skill, fantasy and good taste a the hallmarks of the three chefs here. They conjure up a true gastronomic expe ence via several tasting menus in a simple, contemporary space with an ope view kitchen. The name of the restaurant, which translates as 'enjoy', says it all

Specialities: Disfrutar "gilda" tapa. Pigeon with corn. Black sesame cornet.

Menu 155/195€

PLAN: 3-J2 – *Villarroel 163 – Ⓜ Hospital Clinic – ✆ 933 48 68 96 – www.disfrutarbarcelona.com – Closed 1-10 March, 2-18 August, 21 December-7 January, Saturday, Sunday*

✿✿ Enoteca

MODERN CUISINE • MEDITERRANEAN A bright, fresh look with a penchant f varying tones of white that encapsulates the essence of the Mediterranean. Th restaurant, which is under the baton of chef Paco Pérez, enhances the flavours the Catalan coast with delicate international touches and the occasional nod Asian fusion cooking.

Specialities: Sea cucumbers a la carbonara. Squab, huitlacoche, thousand-d mole and dumplings. Yuzu, mango and lemon.

Menu 190€ – Carte 90/120€

PLAN: 1-C2 – *Hotel Arts, Marina 19 – Ⓜ Ciutadella-Vila Olímpica – ✆ 934 83 81 08 www.enotecapacoperez.com – Closed 1-16 March, 30 November-15 December, Monday, Sunday*

✿✿ Moments

CREATIVE • ELEGANT Accessed via the hotel lobby, Moments stands out for it design, which includes a private chef's table. Here, Raül Balam, the son of famou chef Carme Ruscalleda, conjures up intelligent, creative cuisine which respect flavours, showcases textures and is able to reinterpret tradition through contem porary eyes.

Specialities: Bacalao "a la santpolenca". Fillet of Iberian pork with anko paste Sweet Barceloneta "bomb".

Menu 79€ (lunch)/189€ – Carte 95/140€

PLAN: 3-K2 – *Hotel Mandarin Oriental Barcelona, Passeig de Gràcia 38-40 – Ⓜ Passeig de Gràcia – ✆ 931 51 87 81 – www.mandarinoriental.es – Closed 5-21 January, 23 August-9 September, Monday, lunch Tuesday-Thursday, Sunday*

✿ Alkimia (Jordi Vilà)

MODERN CUISINE • DESIGN Alkimia boasts a striking design, with an avant garde nod to the maritime world and a brand new "unplugged" concept tha complements its main gastronomic dining room. The contemporary cuisine (based around locally sourced ingredients) is sublime, with perfect textures and defined flavours that blend harmoniously together.

Specialities: Fish tartare, prawn and crayfish. "Xisqueta" grilled lamb with crean cheese, eggplant, blueberries and fresh thyme. "Menjar blanc" with fresh fruit and cava jelly.

Menu 98/158€ – Carte 72/100€

PLAN: 2-E2 – *Ronda San Antoni 41 – Ⓜ Universitat – ✆ 932 07 61 15 – www.alkimia.cat – Closed 15-30 August, Saturday, Sunday*

✿ **Aürt** (Artur Martínez)

MODERN CUISINE • TRENDY A restaurant with a surprising location in the lobby of the Hilton Diagonal Mar Barcelona hotel. The unusual layout features two bars where you can eat while watching the chefs preparing dishes in front of you, reinterpreting culinary concepts and traditional ingredients through modern techniques and locally sourced products.

Specialities: Red prawn salmorejo. Pluma Iberian pork with green pepper. Sweet potato with coffee.

Menu 70/95€

PLAN: 1-D2 – *Paseo del Taulat 262-264 – Ⓜ El Maresme Fòrum – ✆ 935 07 08 60 – www.aurtrestaurant.com – Closed 1-15 January, 1-25 August, Monday, lunch Tuesday, Sunday*

✿ **Cinc Sentits** (Jordi Artal)

CREATIVE • MINIMALIST Under the baton of chef Jordi Artal, prepare yourself for a culinary and sensory experience to awaken all five senses. Modern and highly personal Catalan cuisine is created with produce from small local suppliers, served in three different spaces: the main dining room, at the chef's table, and in a private room.

Specialities: Grilled oyster with emulsioned water, toasted butter and lemon peel purée. Pork belly, creamy apple rice, pistachio and mustard. Smoked milk, yoghurt and white chocolate stones, dulce de leche with vanilla and crème de cassis.

Menu 99/139€

PLAN: 3-J3 – *Entença 60 – Ⓜ Rocafort – ✆ 933 23 94 90 – www.cincsentits.com – Closed 14-18 January, 11-22 August, Monday, Sunday*

✿ **Enigma**

CREATIVE • DESIGN A truly incomparable restaurant with an unusual modular layout and ground breaking design that, under the helm of Albert Adrià, is aiming to become the gastronomic standard-bearer for the El Barri group. The dining experience takes place in seven different "zones", culminating in the "41º" bar at the end of the meal. Online bookings only.

Specialities: Crystal bread. Cured lobster. Soya, soya, soya.

Menu 220€

PLAN: 3-J3 – *Sepúlveda 38-40 – Ⓜ Plaza España – www.enigmaconcept.es – Closed 6-13 April, 10-24 August, 21 December-13 January, Monday, lunch Tuesday, Wednesday, lunch Thursday-Friday, Sunday*

✿ **Hoja Santa** (Paco Méndez)

MEXICAN • FRIENDLY A small corner of Mexico in Barcelona which takes its name from an indigenous bush and which has now taken over the premises of the former Niño Viejo taco bar. Enjoy top-quality botanas, antojitos, tacos, stews and moles, all adapted to European tastes, in a relaxed contemporary setting.

Specialities: Guacamole with quelites. Suckling pig with white recado. Pan de muerto and churros with chocolate.

Menu 90/150€ – Carte 70/90€

PLAN: 3-J3 – *Avenida Mistral 54 – Ⓜ Espanya – ✆ 933 48 21 94 – www.hojasanta.es – Closed 20 December-1 January, Monday, lunch Tuesday-Friday, Sunday*

✿ **Oria**

MODERN CUISINE • TRENDY The spacious, modern and elegant Oria restaurant opens onto the lobby of the hotel. Here, the cuisine is overseen by chef Martín Berasategui, which translates into dishes that are exquisitely prepared and full of interesting flavours. The à la carte is complemented by a 40 euros "Menú Ejecutivo" and a "Menú a medida", which can be tailored to your specific budget from the same amount upwards.

Specialities: Langoustine in a crunchy bread crust with artichokes, celeriac and a tender sprout salad. Glazed suckling lamb with cream of cabbage. Almond coulant with honey ice cream.

Menu 40€ (lunch), 50/150€ – Carte 67/82€

PLAN: 3-K2 – *Hotel Monument H., Passeig de Gràcia 75 – Ⓜ Passeig de Gràcia – ✆ 935 48 20 33 – www.monumenthotel.com*

Pakta

FUSION • DESIGN A change in decor and cuisine has seen this restaurant mo away from Japanese-Peruvian cuisine to explore the secrets of more Mediterr nean-style Japanese cooking. The restaurant is embellished with striking and co ourful fabric frames and features a large dining counter. You can also admire t impressive sight of Gyotaku prints featuring images of the fish of the day!

Specialities: Cod skin soba. Kombu and squid with rice cooked in ink. Chocola kakigori with green tea borracho biscuit.

Menu 120/150 €

PLAN: 3-J3 – *Lleida 5 – Ⓜ Espanya – ✆ 936 24 01 77 – www.pakta.es – Closed 12-26 August, 21 December-13 January, Monday, lunch Tuesday-Thursday, Sunday*

Tickets

CREATIVE • TAPAS BAR A unique and highly enjoyable restaurant with lots colour and several cutting-edge bar counters. The innovative cuisine on offe prepared in front of diners, plays homage to the legendary dishes that we once created at El Bulli. Don't miss the desserts here, which showcase an ove whelming abundance of imagination.

Specialities: Las oliva-s. Wellington quail from Bresse. Tickets cheesecake.

Ración 15 € – Menu 100/130 € – Carte 30/60 €

PLAN: 3-K3 – *Avenida del Paral.lel 164 – Ⓜ Espanya – www.ticketsbar.es – Closed 4-14 April, 8-25 August, 21 December-7 January, Monday, lunch Tuesday-Friday, Sunday*

Xerta

CREATIVE • DESIGN This elegant, contemporary restaurant oozes personalit thanks to its striking skylights, vertical garden and large open-view kitcher Choose from a concise à la carte with a contemporary Mediterranean focus an several set menus. Everything is centred around the very best products from th Ebro Delta and fantastic fish sourced from the daily fish market.

Specialities: Kabayaki eel. Rice with sea anemones and sea cucumber. Floral textures.

Menu 38 € (lunch), 55/120 € – Carte 60/95 €

PLAN: 3-K1-2 – *Hotel Ohla Eixample, Còrsega 289 – Ⓜ Diagonal – ✆ 937 37 90 80 – www.xertarestaurant.com – Closed Monday, Sunday*

Cruix

CONTEMPORARY • BRASSERIE A modest restaurant close to the Parc de Joa Miró with an informal contemporary look, exposed brick walls and unusua square-shaped designer lamps hanging from the ceiling. The two friends i charge, Miquel and Carlos, were keen to work together on a project once the had graduated hotel school and this is the result of their shared dream, an adventure they are embracing with a friendly approach, excitement and no little professionalism. The excellent menu features tapas and small modern dishes, althoug the most popular choices here are the rice dishes and the Cruix tasting menu (10 courses). Don't miss the cod churros!

Menu 28/34 € – Carte 28/35 €

PLAN: 3-J3 – *Entença 57 – Ⓜ Rocafort – ✆ 935 25 23 18 – www.cruixrestaurant.com – Closed Monday, Sunday*

Be So

TRADITIONAL CUISINE • CONTEMPORARY DÉCOR A restaurant with lots o personality that stands out thanks to its elegant decor, dominated by golder tones, and its updated traditional cuisine. Meticulous presentation.

Menu 49 € (lunch), 80/120 € – Carte 68/99 €

PLAN: 1-A2 – *Hotel Sofía, Plaza de Pius XII-4 – Ⓜ Maria Cristina – ✆ 935 08 10 20 – www.sofiabarcelona.com – Closed 1-31 August, Monday, Sunday*

Bodega 1900

TRADITIONAL CUISINE • TAPAS BAR This restaurant has all the charm of an old fashioned grocery store. The small menu features grilled dishes, Iberian specialities and homemade preserves, all of excellent quality.

Tapa 10 € – Ración 16 €

PLAN: 3-K3 – *Tamarit 91 – Ⓜ Poble Sec – ✆ 933 25 26 59 – Closed 5-13 April, 9-24 August, 22 December-13 January, Monday, Sunday*

Espai Kru

INTERNATIONAL • TRENDY Located on the first floor, Espai Kru has an impressive appearance, enhanced by an open-view kitchen, a private dining room and a cocktail bar. The extensive international fusion menu features both raw and cooked ingredients.

Menu 110 € – Carte 50/80 €

PLAN: 3-J3 – *Lleida 7 – Ⓜ Espanya – ✆ 934 23 45 70 – www.espaikru.com – Closed 8-15 August, Monday, dinner Sunday*

Gresca

MODERN CUISINE • MINIMALIST A good option for those keen to try contemporary dishes that showcase seasonal ingredients. Its top-quality cooking has extended to the bar next door (Gresca Bar), which is more focused on the world of wine.

Menu 70 € – Carte 40/70 €

PLAN: 3-K2 – *Provença 230 – Ⓜ Diagonal – ✆ 934 51 61 93 – www.gresca.net – Closed 12-31 August, Saturday, Sunday*

Jardín del Alma

TRADITIONAL CUISINE • CONTEMPORARY DÉCOR The tree-shaded terrace is a highlight here, giving the impression of being in the countryside. The chef focuses on traditional, seasonal cooking and even comes out of the kitchen to greet every table.

Carte 55/65 €

PLAN: 3-K2 – *Hotel Alma Barcelona, Mallorca 271 – Ⓜ Passeig de Gracia – ✆ 932 16 44 78 – www.almahotels.com – Closed 13-19 January*

Lomo Alto

MEATS AND GRILLS • FRIENDLY A mecca for meat lovers laid out on two floors (Lomo Bajo and Lomo Alto) with impressive vaulted windows. The mature beef is sourced from old Iberian breeds and cooked on the grill.

Menu 95/125 € – Carte 45/80 €

PLAN: 3-K2 – *Aragó 283-285 – Ⓜ Passeig de Gràcia – ✆ 935 19 30 00 – www.lomoalto.barcelona*

Manairó

CREATIVE • CONTEMPORARY DÉCOR A unique restaurant, both in terms of its modern decor and intimate lighting. Contemporary, meticulously presented cuisine with its roots in Catalan cooking.

Menu 25 € (lunch), 55/75 € – Carte 60/80 €

PLAN: 3-L1 – *Diputació 424 – Ⓜ Monumental – ✆ 932 31 00 57 – www.manairo.com – Closed 1-7 January, Sunday*

Mano Rota

MODERN CUISINE • NEIGHBOURHOOD Mano Rota boasts an industrial feel and champions a specific concept: a restaurant with a bar. Its interesting menu includes traditional and contemporary recipes, as well as international dishes from Peru and Japan.

Menu 18 € (lunch)/65 € – Carte 35/55 €

PLAN: 2-E3 – *Creus dels Molers 4 – Ⓜ Poble Sec – ✆ 931 64 80 41 – www.manorota.com – Closed lunch Monday, Sunday*

Mediamanga

MODERN CUISINE • TAPAS BAR A gastro-bar with an eclectic ambience fe turing elements of Modernist and Art Deco. The contemporary cuisine here high on detail and is perfect for sharing.

Tapa 5€ – Ración 17€

PLAN: 3-K2 – *Aribau 13* – Ⓜ *Universitat* – ✆ *938 32 56 94* – *www.mediamanga.es – Closed 27 January-2 February, 24-30 August*

Mont Bar

TRADITIONAL CUISINE • TAPAS BAR This charming and unusual gastro-b serves traditional cuisine prepared using top quality ingredients. Friendly a professional service.

Tapa 7€ – Ración 18€

PLAN: 3-K2 – *Diputació 220* – Ⓜ *Universitat* – ✆ *933 23 95 90* – *www.montbar.com – Closed 13-22 January, 17-25 August, Tuesday*

Monvínic

MODERN CUISINE • WINE BAR This restaurant impresses through its conte porary design and philosophy, with everything revolving around the world wine. A modern take on traditional cuisine, as well as a splendid wine cellar.

Menu 35€ (lunch), 65/75€ – Carte 55/70€

PLAN: 3-K2 – *Diputació 249* – Ⓜ *Catalunya* – ✆ *932 72 61 87* – *www.monvinic.com – Closed 3-31 August, lunch Monday, lunch Saturday, Sunday*

Nectari

MODERN CUISINE • CLASSIC DÉCOR Nectari has just two small contempora style dining rooms and one private area where the Mediterranean-inspired me features a variety of creative and innovative touches.

Menu 35€ (lunch), 75/110€ – Carte 55/75€

PLAN: 3-J3 – *València 28* – Ⓜ *Tarragona* – ✆ *932 26 87 18* – *www.nectari.es – Closed 22 February-5 March, 20 August-15 September, dinner Tuesday, Sunday*

Osmosis

MODERN CUISINE • CONTEMPORARY DÉCOR A restaurant with a pleasa modern ambience arranged over two floors. The contemporary tasting me available in both long and short formats, is created using seasonal, market-fr ingredients.

Menu 28€ (lunch), 45/140€

PLAN: 3-K2 – *Aribau 100* – Ⓜ *Diagonal* – ✆ *934 54 52 01* – *www.restauranteosmosis.com – Closed 24-30 December, Sunday*

Paco Meralgo

TRADITIONAL CUISINE • TAPAS BAR The Paco Meralgo has two bars and t separate entrances, although its most impressive feature is its display cabin filled with fresh, varied, top quality seafood. A private room is also available.

Tapa 4€ – Ración 15€

PLAN: 3-J2 – *Muntaner 171* – Ⓜ *Hospital Clínic* – ✆ *934 30 90 27* – *www.restaurantpacomeralgo.com*

Da Paolo

ITALIAN • CLASSIC DÉCOR Italian restaurant located near the Nou Camp s dium. Both simple and well presented, it has a large pleasant dining room a an elaborate menu.

Menu 16/19€ – Carte 23/35€

PLAN: 3-I3 – *Avenida de Madrid 63* – Ⓜ *Badal* – ✆ *934 90 48 91* – *www.dapaolo.es – Closed 4-21 August, Monday, dinner Sunday*

Petit Comitè

REGIONAL CUISINE • DESIGN This contemporary restaurant is decorated with lots of plates. The focus is on local cuisine prepared using Spanish ingredients, including enticing themed daily specials.

Menu 65 € – Carte 45/80 €

PLAN: 3-K2 – *Pasaje de la Concepció 13* – Ⓜ *Diagonal* – ✆ *936 33 76 27* – *www.petitcomite.cat*

Pur

MARKET CUISINE • DESIGN Pur bears the hallmark of chef Nandu Jubany, with his emphasis on dishes that focus on top-quality ingredients "in their purest form", without sauces or unnecessary embellishment, and presented either grilled, cooked on the barbecue or baked in salt.

Menu 92 € – Carte 65/95 €

PLAN: 3-K2 – *Pasaje de la Concepció 11* – Ⓜ *Diagonal* – ✆ *931 70 17 70* – *www.purbarcelona.com*

Racó d'en Cesc

MODERN CUISINE • CLASSIC DÉCOR A restaurant with a small terrace, a bistro-style section and a classic dining room, with a different creative Catalan menu in each. A wide choice of craft beers is also available.

Menu 42/68 € – Carte 38/54 €

PLAN: 3-K2 – *Diputació 201* – Ⓜ *Universitat* – ✆ *934 51 60 02* – *www.elracodencesc.com* – *Closed 1-31 August, Sunday*

Rías de Galicia

SEAFOOD • CLASSIC DÉCOR Goose barnacles, lamprey, oysters and tuna are among the many culinary treasures from the Atlantic and Mediterranean on offer here. The wine cellar is home to some impressive labels and vintages.

Menu 100 € – Carte 70/100 €

PLAN: 3-J3 – *Lleida 7* – Ⓜ *Espanya* – ✆ *934 24 81 52* – *www.riasdegalicia.com*

Slow & Low

FUSION • TRENDY A restaurant that exudes excitement, a young approach and a desire to please, through modern fusion cuisine with a creative touch, clear Mexican influences and interesting surprise menus.

Menu 30 € (lunch), 42/58 €

PLAN: 3-K3 – *Comte Borrell 119* – Ⓜ *Urgell* – ✆ *936 25 45 12* – *www.slowandlowbcn.com* – *Closed 8-24 January, 9-25 August, Monday, Sunday*

Tunateca Balfegó

MODERN CUISINE • CONTEMPORARY DÉCOR If you're interested in different cuts of tuna and ways of preparing it, you won't want to miss this restaurant decorated in varying tones of blue and featuring attractive decorative details alluding to this magnificent fish.

Menu 83/120 € – Carte 35/55 €

PLAN: 3-J2 – *Avenida Diagonal 439* – ✆ *937 97 64 60* – *www.tunatecabalfego.com* – *Closed Sunday*

Uma

CREATIVE • CONTEMPORARY DÉCOR Taking its name from the Swahili word for "fork", Uma offers a great gastronomic experience. Make sure you're on time as all guests start their surprise menu at the same time!

Menu 96 €

PLAN: 3-K1 – *Mallorca 275* – Ⓜ *Diagonal* – ✆ *656 99 09 30* – *www.espaciouma.com* – *Closed 8-29 January, 10-23 August, Tuesday, Wednesday, lunch Thursday, lunch Sunday*

Windsor

MODERN CUISINE • CLASSIC DÉCOR This restaurant, with its updated clas decor, is enhanced by an exquisite terrace and several dining rooms that all for different configurations. Contemporary Catalan cuisine.

Menu 32€ (lunch), 52/75€ – Carte 55/75€

PLAN: 3-K2 – *Còrsega 286 – Ⓜ Diagonal – ✆ 932 37 75 88 – www.restaurantwindsor.com – Closed 1-31 August, Sunday*

Xavier Pellicer

MARKET CUISINE • CONTEMPORARY DÉCOR The chef here continues champion healthy cuisine with his focus on organic vegetables. Choose betwe a more informal dining section and the more gastronomically focused El Men dor (reservation required) offering a choice of tasting menus.

Menu 28€ (lunch), 54/65€ – Carte 35/60€

PLAN: 3-K1 – *Provença 310 – Ⓜ Diagonal – ✆ 935 25 90 02 – www.xavierpellicer.com – Closed 7-13 January, 3-25 August, Monday, Sunday*

North of Av. Diagonal

ABaC

CREATIVE • DESIGN Discover the unique culinary vision of the bold, medi friendly chef Jordi Cruz who has raised technical skill, creativity and gastronom perfection to even higher levels. His dishes tell stories that are complex yet the same time intelligent and understandable, and which evolve in line with se sonal products.

Specialities: Bloody Mary on the rocks. Grilled ventresca tuna with a garlic cor pote cream, almond milk, dates and olive oil. Fragile chocolate "crate".

Menu 190/210€

PLAN: 1-B2 – *Hotel ABaC, Avenida del Tibidabo 1 – Ⓜ Av. Tibidabo – ✆ 933 19 66 00 – www.abacrestaurant.com*

Hisop (Oriol Ivern)

CREATIVE • MINIMALIST Because of its size, this restaurant named after an a omatic medicinal plant offers guests an intimate and modern dining experienc In its minimalist dining room, enjoy fresh and creative dishes based around trad tional recipes, always prepared using local and seasonal products. Interestir wine pairing options.

Specialities: Palamós prawns with Béarnaise sauce. Red mullet with a mollus mayonnaise. Pineapple with foie gras and brioche ice cream.

Menu 67/95€ – Carte 58/65€

PLAN: 3-J2 – *Pasaje de Marimon 9 – Ⓜ Hospital Clínic – ✆ 932 41 32 33 – www.hisop.com – Closed 1-7 January, lunch Saturday, Sunday*

Hofmann

MODERN CUISINE • CLASSIC DÉCOR The word "gastronomy" reflects th great passion of Mey Hofmann, the founder-chef who created the guideline that are followed in one of the country's most influential restaurant schools. He daughter Silvia and her teaching staff perpetuate her work here, producing cu sine that is full of creativity.

Specialities: Mey Hofmann's classic sardine tartine. Chef's fish of the day. Crur chy vanilla tuile with raisins.

Menu 39/95€ – Carte 60/80€

PLAN: 3-J1 – *La Granada del Penedès 14-16 – Ⓜ Diagonal – ✆ 932 18 71 65 – www.hofmann-bcn.com – Closed 5-12 April, 1-31 August, 24 December-6 January, lunch Saturday, Sunday*

Via Veneto

CLASSIC CUISINE • CLASSIC DÉCOR A famous property in attractive Bell Époque style with a dining room laid out on several levels and a number of pri vate dining areas. Impressively updated classic menu with game in season an interesting tasting menus. Guests can visit the superb wine cellar here, featurin an outstanding collection of Spanish and French wines.

Specialities: Cannelloni stuffed with chicken, truffle sauce. Grilled turbot with saffron rice. Caramelised apple from Girona filled with cinnamon compote, yoghurt ice cream.

Menu 80/240 € – Carte 85/105 €

PLAN: 3-I2 – *Ganduxer 10 – Ⓜ Hospital Clínic – ✆ 932 00 72 44 – www.viavenetorestaurant.com – Closed 1 August-11 September, dinner Saturday, Sunday*

Saó

TRADITIONAL CUISINE • CLASSIC DÉCOR Located in the upper part of the city, Saó boasts an evocative name (which translates as "ripeness" in English) that describes the "perfect maturity" of ingredients used here. Valencia-born chef Juanen Benavent develops his menus based on locally sourced seasonal produce, creating traditional dishes with a strong French influence, which comes from four years working at the Goust restaurant in Paris. Choose from three menus (Llavor, Guerminat and Arrels), which vary in terms of the number of dishes they each offer.

Menu 19 € (lunch), 32/45 €

PLAN: 1-B1 – *Cesare Cantù 2 – Ⓜ Penitents – ✆ 935 66 39 68 – www.saobcn.com – Closed 13-26 January, 17-30 August, Monday, Tuesday, dinner Sunday*

Vivanda

TRADITIONAL CUISINE • COSY Occupying a renovated house in the Sarriá district of the city, Vivanda is mainly popular with a local clientele. Here, the contemporary interior features high tables for tapas, restaurant-style dining tables, plus a tree-shaded patio-terrace (with a retractable roof) that is understandably very popular during the summer months. Traditional Catalan cooking is to the fore here, making full use of market-fresh ingredients and modern techniques in its "platillos" (small dishes) and "dishes of the month" that revive the flavours of the past. Make sure you order its legendary ham croquettes!

Carte 28/35 €

PLAN: 1-A2 – *Major de Sarrià 134 – Ⓜ Reina Elisenda – ✆ 932 03 19 18 – www.vivanda.cat – Closed Monday, dinner Sunday*

La Balsa

MEDITERRANEAN CUISINE • COSY A classic address whose renovation has transformed it into a small architectural jewel nestled amid a haven of peace and quiet. Good Mediterranean cooking with a focus on quality produce, which you can also enjoy on La Balsa's charming outdoor terraces.

Menu 50/70 € – Carte 35/62 €

PLAN: 1-B1 – *Infanta Isabel 4 – ✆ 932 11 50 48 – www.labalsarestaurant.com – Closed 1-31 August, dinner Sunday*

Bardeni-Caldeni

MEATS AND GRILLS • TAPAS BAR A restaurant in which meat is very much centre stage. The ambience is that of an old butcher's shop, with a bar to the rear where guests can also eat.

Ración 12 €

PLAN: 3-L1 – *Valencia 454 – Ⓜ Sagrada Familia – ✆ 932 32 58 11 – www.bardeni.es – Closed 9-30 August, Monday, Sunday*

99 sushi bar

JAPANESE • DESIGN High-quality Japanese cuisine in keeping with other restaurants in the chain. Eat at the bar if there's space so you can enjoy the preparation of the attractive cuisine here at close quarters.

Menu 90 € – Carte 55/75 €

PLAN: 3-J2 – *Tenor Viñas 4 – Ⓜ Muntaner – ✆ 936 39 62 17 – www.99sushibar.com – Closed 1 August-1 September, dinner Sunday*

Roig Robí

REGIONAL CUISINE • CLASSIC DÉCOR A pleasant restaurant in a classic s ting that includes a winter garden style dining room laid out around a patio-g den. Catalan cuisine with a choice of different menus.

Menu 40/66 € – Carte 40/65 €

PLAN: 3-K1 – *Sèneca 20* – *Ⓜ Diagonal* – *✆ 932 18 92 22* – *www.roigrobi.com* – *Closed 1-6 January, 3-23 August, lunch Saturday, Sunday*

Silvestre

TRADITIONAL CUISINE • COSY Cosy and welcoming with various private d ing areas that add an intimate feel. Traditional and international cuisine, includi appealing fixed menus and the option of half-portions.

Menu 27 € (lunch), 45/55 € – Carte 35/55 €

PLAN: 3-J1 – *Santaló 101* – *Ⓜ Muntaner* – *✆ 932 41 40 31* – *www.restaurante-silvestre.com* – *Closed 3-25 August, lunch Saturday, Sunday*

Tram-Tram

MODERN CUISINE • FAMILY A classically furnished restaurant, the name which pays homage to this old form of transport. Updated traditional cuisi with the occasional international influence, and the option of ordering one of t set menus.

Menu 90 € – Carte 45/65 €

PLAN: 1-A2 – *Major de Sarrià 121* – *Ⓜ Reina Elisenda* – *✆ 932 04 85 18* – *www.tram-tram.com* – *Closed 30 March-6 April, 3-31 August, Monday, dinner Tuesday, dinner Sunday*

mikdam/iStock

SWEDEN

SVERIGE

STOCKHOLM
STOCKHOLM

adisa/iStock

STOCKHOLM IN...

- **ONE DAY**
  Gamla Stan, City Hall, Vasa or Skansen museums, an evening in Södermalm.
- **TWO DAYS**
  Coffee in Kungsholmen, museums in Skeppsholmen, a stroll around Djurgården.
- **THREE DAYS**
  Shopping in Norrmalm, boat trip round the archipelago.

Stockholm is the place to go for clean air, big skies and handsome architecture. And water. One of the great beauties of the city is the amount of water that runs through and around it; it's built on 14 islands, and looks out on 24,000 of them. An astounding two-thirds of the area within the city limits is made up of water, parks and woodland, and there are dozens of little bridges to cross to get from one part of town to another. It's little wonder Swedes appear so calm and relaxed.

It's in Stockholm that the salty waters of the Baltic meet head-on the fresh waters of Lake Mälaren, reflecting the

broad boulevards and elegant buildings that shimmer along their edge. Domes, spires and turrets dot a skyline that in the summertime never truly darkens. The heart of the city is the Old Town, Gamla Stan, full of alleyways and lanes little changed from their medieval origins. Just to the north is the modern centre, Norrmalm: a buzzing quarter of shopping malls, restaurants and bars. East of Gamla Stan you reach the small island of Skeppsholmen, which boasts fine views of the waterfront; directly north from here is Östermalm, an area full of grand residences, while southeast you'll find the lovely park island of Djurgården. South and west of Gamla Stan are the two areas where Stockholmers particularly like to hang out, the trendy (and hilly) Södermalm, and Kungsholmen.

EATING OUT

'eryone thinks that eating out in ockholm is invariably expensive, ıt with a little forward planning it ›esn't have to be. In the middle of e day, most restaurants and cafés fer very good value set menus. ›ep in mind that, unlike in Southern ırope, the Swedes like to eat quite ırly, so lunch can often begin at ›ound 11am and dinner may start from ›m. Picking wild food is a birthright Swedes, and there's no law to stop u going into forest or field to pick blueberries, cloudberries, cranberries, strawberries, mushrooms and the like. This love of outdoor, natural fare means that Stockholmers have a special bond with menus which relate to the seasons: keep your eyes open for restaurants that feature husmanskost (traditional Swedish dishes), along with huge buffet-style smörgåsbords. These days, however, you might find that your classic meatball, dumpling, herring or gravlax dish comes with a modern twist.

Centre

✿✿✿ Frantzén (Björn Frantzén)

MODERN CUISINE • DESIGN A unique restaurant set over 3 floors of a property; ring the doorbell, enjoy an aperitif in the living room and have the day's luxurious ingredients explained. A beautiful wood counter borders the sl kitchen and the chefs present, finish and explain the flavour-packed dishes p sonally. Cooking is modern and creative but also uses classic techniques.

Specialities: French toast 'Grand Tradition 2008'. Guinea fowl with pine nuts, olles and pepper jus. Salted carrot, "tea, tea, tea".

Menu 3500 SEK

PLAN: B2 – *Klara Norra Kyrkogata 26 – Ⓜ T-Centralen – ✆ 08-20 85 80 – www.restaurantfrantzen.com – Closed 15 June-17 July, 25 December-13 January, Monday, Tuesday, Sunday*

✿✿ Gastrologik (Jacob Holmström and Anton Bjuhr)

CREATIVE • MINIMALIST The two chef-owners met as apprentices; one is fr the north, one the south – so both bring something different. The day's produ decides the surprise menu of beautiful dishes that are creative in their contra of flavour and texture. Sustainability is a core value here; they nurture relatic ships with local farmers, use renewable energy and minimise food waste.

Specialities: Grilled langoustine with seasonal herbs and langoustine cream. Qu with grilled corn, chanterelles and black garlic. Spruce shoot ice cream with pi cones and crispy lichen.

Menu 1800 SEK

PLAN: C2 – *Artillerigatan 14 – Ⓜ Östermalmstorg – ✆ 08-662 30 60 – www.gastrologik.com – Closed 1-21 July, 17 December-7 January, Monday, lunch Tuesday-Saturday, Sunday*

✿ Agrikultur (Filip Fastén)

MODERN CUISINE • COSY The open kitchen, with its aga and wood-burni oven, is the focus of this homely restaurant, where the passionate chefs give contemporary twist to classic Swedish dishes. Flavours are intense, contrasts a original and ingredients, top quality; they raise their own pigs (which eat the fo waste) and also hunt, forage, pickle and ferment.

Specialities: Smoked heart with white moss and chanterelle mayonnaise. Turb with hay-infused potato purée, anchovy-fried corn and vinegar-marinated carr Tartlet of celeriac, cloudberries and meadowsweet.

Menu 1195 SEK

Off plan – *Roslagsgatan 43 – Ⓜ Odenplan – ✆ 08-15 02 02 – www.agrikultur.se – Closed 18 June-7 July, 20 December-7 January, Monday, lunch Tuesday-Saturday, Sunday*

✿ Ekstedt (Niklas Ekstedt)

MODERN CUISINE • BISTRO It's all about fire at this cosy, pared-back restau rant, so expect smoky flavours and caramelisation – reserve a seat at the count to experience the heat of the wood-burning oven, fire pit and chargrill. Diners ar invited to tour the kitchen; the cooking of their signature 'oyster with apple' quite a sight to behold!

Specialities: Blackened langoustine, squid and sea lettuce. Hay-flamed lamb wit Jerusalem artichoke and beetroot. Roasted oats with raspberries and sorrel.

Menu 980/1260 SEK

PLAN: C1 – *Humlegårdsgatan 17 – Ⓜ Östermalmstorg – ✆ 08-611 12 10 – www.ekstedt.nu – Closed 1-7 January, Monday, lunch Tuesday-Saturday, Sunday*

✿ Etoile (Danny Falkeman and Jonas Lagerström)

CREATIVE • INTIMATE After travelling the world, two young friends returned t their homeland to open Etoile: the lengthy tasting menu draws on influences en countered on their journey. Dishes are intensely flavoured and visually impres sive. They hope to build a sustainable legacy to inspire the next generation c restaurateurs.

Specialities: 'Bagel': pumpkin, carrot and foie gras. 'Forest': mushroom, consommé and toast. 'Tom kha gai': ice cream.

Carte 1500 SEK

Off plan - *Norra Stationsgatan 51 - Ⓜ Odenplan - ✆ 08-10 10 70 - www.restaurantetoile.se - Closed 1-31 July, Monday, lunch Tuesday-Saturday, Sunday*

Operakällaren

CLASSIC CUISINE • **LUXURY** Sweden's most opulent restaurant sits within the historic Opera House, and the stunning, high-ceilinged room boasts chandeliers and original gilt panelling decorated with frescoes and carvings. Carefully constructed traditional French dishes come with a contemporary touch. The impressive wine list offers a notable French selection.

Specialities: King crab with crispy sourdough and carrot sauce. Fillet of lamb with Beluga lentils, ramsons and hazelnuts. Rhubarb semifreddo with almond cake.

Menu 1150/1650 SEK

PLAN: C2 - *Operahuset, Karl XII's Torg - Ⓜ Kungsträdgården - ✆ 08-676 58 01 - www.operakallaren.se - Closed 1-31 July, 1 December-15 January, Monday, lunch Tuesday-Saturday, Sunday*

Sushi Sho (Carl Ishizaki)

JAPANESE • **NEIGHBOURHOOD** With its white tiled walls and compact counter seating, the room couldn't be simpler; the food, by contrast, is sublime. Meals are served omakase-style, with the chef deciding what's best each day and dishes arriving as they're ready. Top quality seafood from local waters features alongside some great egg recipes. Go for the remarkable sake tasting menu.

Specialities: Soy-cured egg yolk with char, okra and roasted rice. Mackerel sababozushi. Herring sujime nigiri with akazu shari.

Menu 785 SEK

PLAN: A1 - *Upplandsgatan 45 - Ⓜ Odenplan - ✆ 08-30 30 30 - www.sushisho.se - Closed 1-31 July, Monday, lunch Tuesday-Friday, Sunday*

Allegrine

FRENCH • **CHIC** Set off the busy Sveavägen thoroughfare, this brasserie provides a hidden oasis. Sit on the attractive front terrace or in the chic dining room, where seats at the kitchen counter are in demand. Variously sized dishes are richly flavoured, with a French base, Scandinavian influences and subtle contrasts.

Carte 280/500 SEK

PLAN: B1 - *Kammakargatan 22 - Ⓜ Rådmansgatan - ✆ 08-410 059 09 - www.allegrine.se - Closed 23-28 December, Monday, lunch Tuesday-Saturday, Sunday*

Brasserie Bobonne

FRENCH • **COSY** This sweet neighbourhood restaurant has a warm, homely feel, and the owners proudly welcome their guests from the open kitchen. Modern artwork hangs on the walls and contrasts with traditional features such as mosaic tiling. Classic cooking has a French core and dishes show obvious care in their preparation.

Menu 515 SEK - Carte 185/630 SEK

PLAN: C1 - *Storgatan 12 - Ⓜ Östermalmstorg - ✆ 08-660 03 18 - www.bobonne.se - Closed 1-31 July, lunch Saturday, Sunday*

Lilla Ego

MODERN CUISINE • **BISTRO** Still one of the hottest tickets in town, Lilla Ego comes with a pared-down look and a buzzy vibe; if you haven't booked, try for a counter seat. The two modest chef-owners have created an appealingly priced menu of robust seasonal dishes. The 'wrestling' sausage will challenge even the biggest of appetites.

Carte 465/675 SEK

PLAN: A1 - *Västmannag 69 - Ⓜ Odenplan - ✆ 08-27 44 55 - www.lillaego.com - Closed 1-31 July, Monday, Sunday*

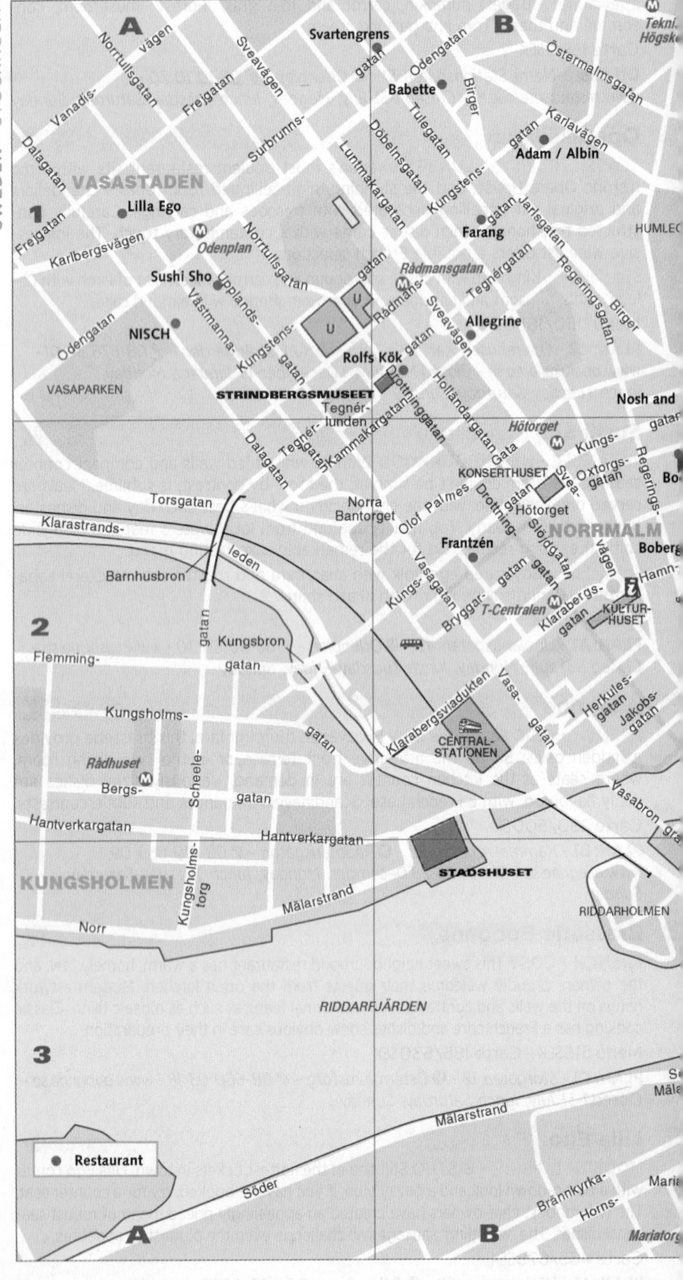
A
B
1
2
3
Svartengrens
Babette
Adam / Albin
Lilla Ego
Farang
Sushi Sho
NISCH
Allegrine
Rolfs Kök
Nosh and
Frantzén
VASASTADEN
NORRMALM
KUNGSHOLMEN
VASAPARKEN
STRINDBERGSMUSEET
KONSERTHUSET
CENTRAL-STATIONEN
STADSHUSET
KULTUR-HUSET
RIDDARHOLMEN
RIDDARFJÄRDEN
HUMLEG
Odenplan
Rådmansgatan
Hötorget
T-Centralen
Rådhuset
Tekni. Högsk
Norrtullsgatan
Vanadisvägen
Sveavägen
Freijgatan
Surbrunnsgatan
Dalagatan
Karlbergsvägen
Odengatan
Västmannagatan
Upplandsgatan
Kungstensgatan
Tulegatan
Döbelnsgatan
Luntmakargatan
Birger Jarl
Östermalmsgatan
Karlavägen
Jarlsgatan
Regeringsgatan
Tegnérgatan
Drottninggatan
Holländargatan
Tegnérlunden
Kammakargatan
Kungsgatan
Olof Palmes Gata
Oxtorgsgatan
Sveavägen
Slöjdgatan
Torsgatan
Norra Bantorget
Klarastrandsleden
Barnhusbron
Vasagatan
Bryggargatan
Klarabergsgatan
Hamngatan
Kungsbron
Flemminggatan
Kungsholmsgatan
Klarabergsviadukten
Herkulesgatan
Jakobsgatan
Scheelegatan
Bergsgatan
Hantverkargatan
Kungsholmstorg
Mälarstrand
Norr Mälarstrand
Vasabron
Söder Mälarstrand
Brännkyrkagatan
Hornsgatan
Mariatorg
Boberg
Restaurant

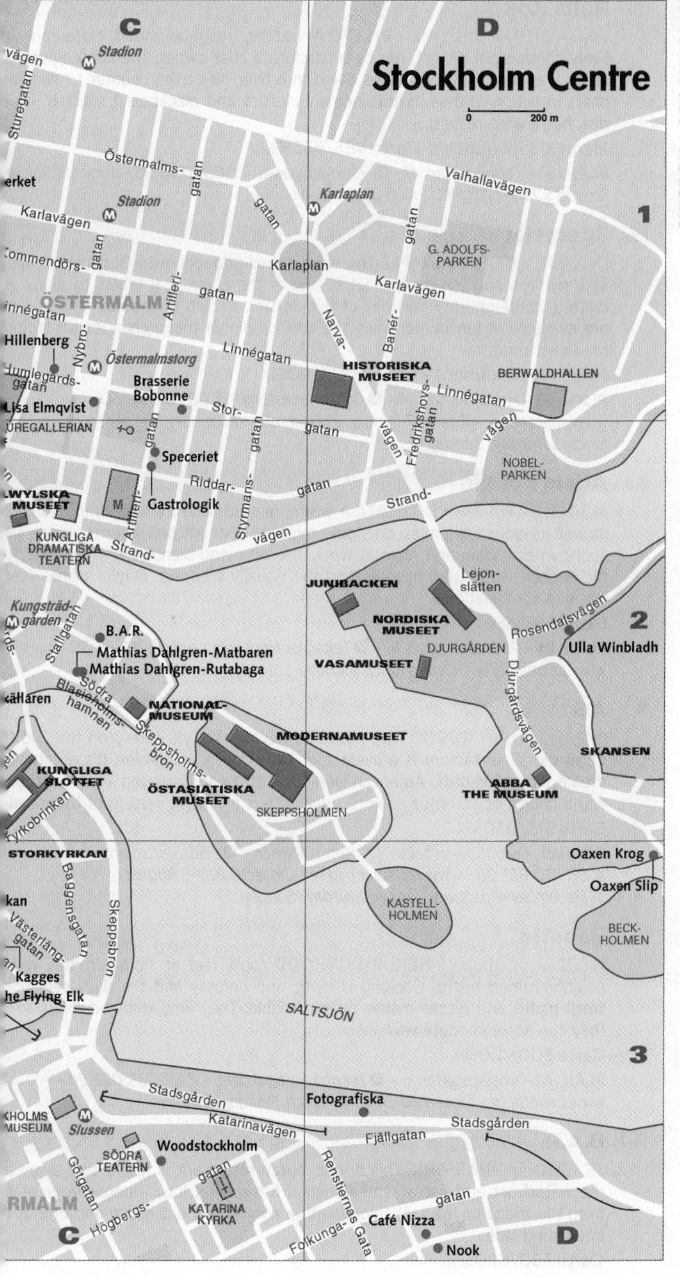
Stockholm Centre
0
200 m
C
D
1
2
3
Stadion
Karlaplan
Stadion
Östermalmstorg
Kungsträdgården
Slussen
Sturegatan
Östermalmsgatan
Valhallavägen
Karlavägen
Karlaplan
Kommendörsgatan
Artillerigatan
ÖSTERMALM
Linnégatan
Narvavägen
Banérgatan
Nybrogatan
Humlegårdsgatan
Storgatan
Riddargatan
Styrmansgatan
Strandvägen
Fredrikshovsgatan
Hillenberg
Brasserie Bobonne
Lisa Elmqvist
Speceriet
Gastrologik
G. ADOLFS-PARKEN
HISTORISKA MUSEET
BERWALDHALLEN
NOBELPARKEN
KUNGLIGA DRAMATISKA TEATERN
Lejonslätten
JUNIBACKEN
NORDISKA MUSEET
DJURGÅRDEN
Rosendalsvägen
Ulla Winbladh
VASAMUSEET
Djurgårdsvägen
B.A.R.
Mathias Dahlgren-Matbaren
Mathias Dahlgren-Rutabaga
Stallgatan
Södra Blasieholmshamnen
NATIONALMUSEUM
Skeppsholmsbron
MODERNAMUSEET
SKANSEN
KUNGLIGA SLOTTET
ÖSTASIATISKA MUSEET
ABBA THE MUSEUM
SKEPPSHOLMEN
STORKYRKAN
Oaxen Krog
Oaxen Slip
Baggensgatan
Skeppsbron
KASTELLHOLMEN
BECKHOLMEN
Västerlånggatan
Kagges
The Flying Elk
SALTSJÖN
Stadsgården
Fotografiska
Katarinavägen
Stadsgården
Fjällgatan
Woodstockholm
SÖDRA TEATERN
Götgatan
Renstiernas Gata
Högbergsgatan
KATARINA KYRKA
Folkungagatan
Café Nizza
Nook

Rolfs Kök

TRADITIONAL CUISINE • **BISTRO** A buzzing neighbourhood restaurant in lively commercial district, run by a passionate chef-owner. The contemporary terior was designed by famous Swedish artists; sit at the counter to watch chefs in action. Dishes include homely classics and blackboard specials – ev dish has a wine match.

Menu 165 SEK (lunch) – Carte 485/635 SEK

PLAN: B1 – *Tegnérgatan 41 – Ⓜ Rådmansgatan – ✆ 08-10 16 96 – www.rolfskok.se Closed 5 July-2 August, lunch Saturday-Sunday*

Speceriet

CLASSIC CUISINE • **SIMPLE** The more casual addendum to Gastrologik will you in the mood for sharing. Sit at one of the communal tables to enjoy w crafted, contemporary versions of the classics; a 'dish of the day' and a des are available at lunchtime, while the concise dinner menu changes according the latest produce.

Menu 195 SEK (lunch) – Carte 420/490 SEK

PLAN: C2 – *Artillerigatan 14 – Ⓜ Östermalmstorg – ✆ 08-662 30 60 – www.speceriet.se – Closed 7-31 July, 21 December-7 January, dinner Monday, lunch Saturday, Sunday*

Adam / Albin

MODERN CUISINE • **INTIMATE** A warm, relaxed restaurant featuring comm as well as individual tables; one looks over the open kitchen where you can wa chef-owners Adam and Albin at work. The set menu blends the ethos of a Sc dic kitchen with Asian flavours and the visually pleasing, playful dishes feat creative combinations.

Menu 1495 SEK

PLAN: B1 – *Rådmansgatan 16 – Ⓜ Tekniska Högskolan – ✆ 08-411 55 35 – www.adamalbin.se – Closed lunch Monday-Saturday, Sunday*

AG

STEAKHOUSE • **RUSTIC** This industrial, New York style eatery on the 2nd f of an old silver factory is a lively spot with closely set tables. It's a carnivo dream, with Swedish, American and Scottish beef displayed in huge cabi and a choice of accompaniments. Lunch offers a simpler version of the menu.

Carte 315/930 SEK

Off plan – *Kronobergsgatan 37, Kungsholmen – Ⓜ Fridshemsplan – ✆ 08-410 681 00 – www.restaurangag.se – Closed 6 July-5 August, 31 December-6 January, lunch Saturday, Sunday*

Babette

MODERN CUISINE • **NEIGHBOURHOOD** You'll feel at home in this moc neighbourhood bistro. Cooking is rustic and unfussy and the daily selectior small plates and pizzas makes dining flexible. They limit their bookings so they can accommodate walk-ins.

Carte 300/410 SEK

PLAN: B1 – *Roslagsgatan 6 – Ⓜ Tekniska Högskolan – ✆ 08-509 022 24 – www.babette.se – Closed 20-26 June, lunch Monday-Sunday*

B.A.R.

SEAFOOD • **BRASSERIE** This bright, buzzy restaurant is just a cast away f the waterfront and has a semi-industrial fish-market look. Choose your seaf from the fridge or the tank, along with a cooking style, a sauce and one of t interesting sides.

Carte 390/620 SEK

PLAN: C2 – *Blasieholmsgatan 4a – Ⓜ Kungsträdgården – ✆ 08-611 53 35 – www.restaurangbar.se – Closed lunch Saturday, Sunday*

Bobergs

MODERN CUISINE • ELEGANT Head past the canteen in this historic department store to the elegant birch-panelled dining room, which dates back to 1915 and features paintings and even some chairs from the period. Choose the set business lunch or from the seasonal à la carte; classic cooking mixes French and Swedish influences.

Menu 395 SEK – Carte 395/645 SEK

PLAN: B2 – *NK Department Store, Hamngatan 18-20 – Ⓜ Kungsträdgården – ✆ 08-762 81 61 – www.bobergsmatsal.se – Closed 16 July-13 August, dinner Monday-Saturday, Sunday*

Boqueria

SPANISH • TAPAS BAR A vibrant, bustling tapas restaurant with high-level seating, located in a smart mall. Appealing menus offer a range of carefully prepared, authentic dishes with a vast selection of jamón ibérico de bellota, grilled meat and tapas. Sangria and pintxos can be enjoyed in their nearby bar.

Carte 300/450 SEK

PLAN: B2 – *Jakobsbergsgatan 17 – Ⓜ Hötorget – ✆ 08-30 74 00 – www.boqueria.se*

Farang

SOUTH EAST ASIAN • MINIMALIST The unusual front door harks back to its Stockholm Electric Company days, and behind it lies a stylish restaurant and bar – the former sits in the old machine hall. Zingy, aromatic dishes focus on South-east Asia and are full of colour.

Menu 285 SEK (lunch)/575 SEK – Carte 410/640 SEK

PLAN: B1 – *Tulegatan 7 – Ⓜ Rådmansgatan – ✆ 08-673 74 00 – www.farang.se – Closed lunch Monday, Sunday*

Hantverket

MODERN CUISINE • RUSTIC Exposed ducting contrasts with chunky tables and leafy plants at this buzzy restaurant. It has a cool lounge-bar, counter seats and a mix of raised and regular tables. Cooking has an artisanal Swedish heart and service is bright and breezy.

Menu 310 SEK (lunch) – Carte 330/400 SEK

PLAN: C1 – *Sturegatan 15 – Ⓜ Stadion – ✆ 08-121 321 60 – www.restauranghantverket.se – Closed 6-31 July, 23 December-4 January, lunch Saturday, Sunday*

Hillenberg

MODERN CUISINE • DESIGN Perfectly pitched for busy Humlegårdsgatan is this stylish take on a classic brasserie. It has a smart, elegant feel and a hugely impressive wine cellar. Appealing Swedish classics are immensely satisfying yet exhibit a subtle modern touch and sense of finesse.

Carte 425/800 SEK

PLAN: C1 – *Humlegårdsgatan 14 – Ⓜ Östermalmstorg – ✆ 08-519 421 53 – www.hillenberg.se – Closed lunch Saturday, Sunday*

Lisa Elmqvist

SEAFOOD • FAMILY While the original 19C market hall is being restored, this established family-run restaurant is operating from the temporary marketplace next door. Top quality seafood from the day's catch features in unfussy, satisfying combinations.

Carte 425/1220 SEK

PLAN: C1 – *Östermalms Saluhall, Östermalmstorg – Ⓜ Östermalmstorg – ✆ 08-553 404 10 – www.lisaelmqvist.se – Closed Sunday*

Mathias Dahlgren-Matbaren

MODERN CUISINE • CHIC A stylish hotel restaurant providing personable, professional service; sit at the zinc-topped bar to watch the chefs at work in the open kitchen. The menu is divided into the headings 'From our country', 'From other countries' and 'From the plant world' and offers tasty, carefully prepared small plates.

Menu 495 SEK (lunch)/1095 SEK – Carte 685/900 SEK

PLAN: C2 – *Grand Hotel, Södra Blasieholmshamnen 6 – Ⓜ Kungsträdgården – ✆ 08-679 35 84 – www.mdghs.se – Closed 10 July-3 August, 23 December-7 January, lunch Saturday, Sunday*

Mathias Dahlgren-Rutabaga

VEGETARIAN • SIMPLE A light, bright restaurant offering something one doe: usually find in grand hotels – vegetarian cuisine. The two set menus come with flavc from across the globe; choose the chef's table for a more personal experience.

Menu 595/895 SEK

PLAN: C2 – *Grand Hotel, Södra Blasieholmshamnen 6 – Ⓜ Kungsträdgården – ✆ 08-679 35 84 – www.mdghs.se – Closed 10 July-3 August, 23 December-7 Janu Monday, lunch Tuesday-Saturday, Sunday*

NISCH

MODERN CUISINE • INTIMATE The walls of this pleasantly relaxed little nei bourhood restaurant are clad with reclaimed timber, the lights are made of spray cans and it also has good eco-credentials in the kitchen. The modern N dic set menu changes every few weeks and the interesting wine list is mainly ganic and biodynamic.

Menu 755 SEK

PLAN: A1 – *Dalagatan 42 – Ⓜ Odenplan – ✆ 08-94 91 13 – www.nischrestaurant.co Closed Monday, lunch Tuesday-Saturday, Sunday*

Nosh and Chow

INTERNATIONAL • BRASSERIE This former bank has been transformed int glitzy cocktail bar and brasserie which displays a smart mix of New York New England styling; head to the rear dining room to watch the young, ambiti chef prepare internationally inspired dishes in the open kitchen.

Menu 315 SEK (lunch) – Carte 300/725 SEK

PLAN: B2 – *Norrlandsgatan 24 – Ⓜ Hötorget – ✆ 08-503 389 60 – www.noshandchow.se – Closed lunch Saturday, Sunday*

Sturehof

SEAFOOD • BRASSERIE This bustling city institution dates back over a cent and is a wonderful mix of the traditional and the modern. It boasts a buzzing race, several marble-topped bars and a superb food court. Classic menus fc on seafood.

Menu 650 SEK – Carte 345/875 SEK

PLAN: C2 – *Stureplan 2 – Ⓜ Östermalmstorg – ✆ 08-440 57 30 – www.sturehof.cc*

Svartengrens

STEAKHOUSE • FRIENDLY The eponymous chef-owner has created a moc bistro specialising in sustainable meat and veg from producers in the archipel Along with smoking and pickling, the dry-aging is done in-house, and the change daily.

Menu 725 SEK – Carte 425/790 SEK

PLAN: B1 – *Tulegatan 24 – Ⓜ Tekniska Högskolan – ✆ 08-612 65 50 – www.svartengrens.se – Closed 14 July-7 August, lunch Monday-Sunday*

Djurgården

✿✿ Oaxen Krog (Magnus Ek)

CREATIVE • DESIGN A rebuilt boat shed in a delightful waterside spot – a c in Oaxen Slip leads into this oak-furnished room with a subtle nautical feel. C tive dishes are allied to nature and the seasons – they're delicate and balar but also offer depth of flavour. The owners also consider the restaurant's im on the environment. The boat opposite provides accommodation.

Specialities: Scallop with fermented pear, gooseberries, horseradish and gı juniper. Pike perch with celeriac and langoustine head sauce. Peach and clc berry compote with lovage, caramelised parsnip and buttermilk parfait.

Menu 2300 SEK

PLAN: D3 – *Beckholmsvägen 26 – Ⓜ Kungsträdgården – ✆ 08-551 531 05 – www.oaxen.com – Closed Monday, lunch Tuesday-Saturday, Sunday*

Oaxen Slip

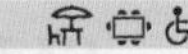

TRADITIONAL CUISINE • BISTRO A bright, bustling bistro next to the old slipway; try for a spot on the delightful terrace. Light floods the room and boats hang from the girders in a nod to the local shipbuilding industry. The food is wholesome and heartening and features plenty of seafood – whole fish dishes are a speciality.

Carte 355/575SEK

PLAN: D3 – *Beckholmsvägen 26 – Ⓜ Kungsträdgården – ✆ 08-551 531 05 – www.oaxen.com*

Ulla Winbladh

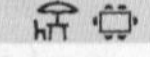

SWEDISH • CLASSIC DÉCOR Ulla Winbladh was originally built as a steam bakery for the 1897 Stockholm World Fair and is set in charming parkland beside the Skansen open-air museum. Sit on the terrace or in the older, more characterful part of the building. Typical Swedish dishes include the likes of fish roe and sweet and sour herring.

Carte 315/730SEK

PLAN: D2 – *Rosendalsvägen 8 – Ⓜ Kungsträdgården – ✆ 08-534 897 01 – www.ullawinbladh.se*

Gamla Stan (Old Town)

Kagges

SWEDISH • TRENDY This cosy restaurant with a lively buzz is run by two enthusiastic friends. Ask for a seat at the counter to watch the team prepare constantly evolving seasonal small plates with plenty of colour and a Swedish heart. 4 plates per person is about right – or go for the 4 course 'Chef's Choice of the Day' menu.

Menu 545SEK – Carte 400/600SEK

PLAN: C3 – *Lilla Nygatan 21 – Ⓜ Gamla Stan – ✆ 08-796 81 02 – www.kagges.com – Closed 15-29 July, 20 December-18 January, Monday, Tuesday, lunch Wednesday-Sunday*

Djuret

MEATS AND GRILLS • RUSTIC Various rooms make up this atmospheric restaurant, including one part-built into the city walls and looking into the impressive wine cellar. Monthly set menus are formed around 3 key ingredients, and the masculine cooking has big, bold flavours.

Menu 495/750SEK

PLAN: C3 – *Lilla Nygatan 5 – Ⓜ Gamla Stan – ✆ 08-506 400 84 – www.djuret.se – Closed 1-31 July, Monday, lunch Tuesday-Saturday, Sunday*

Flickan

MODERN CUISINE • TRENDY Pass through the busy bar to this small 16-seater restaurant, where you'll be greeted by a welcoming team. The 13 course set menu keeps Swedish produce to the fore, and modern dishes have the occasional Asian or South American twist.

Menu 795/990SEK

PLAN: C3 – *Yxsmedsgränd 12 – Ⓜ Gamla Stan – ✆ 08-506 400 80 – www.restaurangflickan.se – Closed 1-31 July, Monday, Tuesday, Wednesday, lunch Thursday-Saturday, Sunday*

The Flying Elk

MODERN CUISINE • INN A good night out is guaranteed at this lively corner spot, which is modelled on a British pub and has several different bars. Choose from bar snacks, pub dishes with a twist or a popular tasting menu of refined modern classics.

Menu 545/725SEK – Carte 445/680SEK

PLAN: C3 – *Mälartorget 15 – Ⓜ Gamla Stan – ✆ 08-20 85 83 – www.theflyingelk.se – Closed lunch Monday-Sunday*

Södermalm

Bar Agrikultur

SWEDISH • COSY The trendy Södermalm district is home to this intimate w bar, whose menu lists fresh, tasty small plates which showcase the region's p duce. The three stainless steel tanks contain home-distilled gin – flavours changed regularly using various herbs, oils or fruits. Bookings are only taken early tables.

Carte 275/435SEK

Off plan – *Skånegatan 79 – Ⓜ Medborgarplatsen – ✆ 070-880 12 00 – www.baragrikultur.se – Closed 19-21 June, 23-25 December, lunch Monday-Sunday*

Nook

MODERN CUISINE • INTIMATE This modern restaurant offers great value. D into the bar for Asian-influenced snacks or head to the intimately lit dining ro for one of two set menus. Creative cooking blends Swedish ingredients with rean influences; order 3 days ahead for the suckling pig feast.

Menu 485/545SEK

PLAN: D3 – *Åsögatan 176 – Ⓜ Medborgarplatsen – ✆ 08-702 12 22 – www.nookrestaurang.se – Closed 1-31 July, Monday, lunch Tuesday-Saturday, Sun*

Café Nizza

SWEDISH • BISTRO Drop in for a drink and some bar snacks or a 4 course menu of unfussy, flavoursome dishes with a mix of Swedish and French in ences. The small room has chequerboard flooring, a granite-topped bar an bustling Parisian feel.

Menu 595SEK – Carte 465/600SEK

PLAN: D3 – *Åsögatan 171 – Ⓜ Medborgarplatsen – ✆ 08-640 99 50 – www.cafenizza.se – Closed 15-21 June, lunch Monday-Friday*

Fotografiska

COUNTRY COOKING • RUSTIC Take in water and city views from the top floo this former warehouse; now a well-known photography museum. The straight ward, largely plant-based menu is supplemented in the evening by fish from aquaponics farm in the basement, which is fed by their on-site composting syst

Menu 250SEK (lunch), 400/680SEK

PLAN: D3 – *Stadsgårdshamnen 22 – Ⓜ Slussen – ✆ 08-509 005 30 – www.fotografiska.com – Closed Sunday*

ICHI

CREATIVE • INTIMATE The chef-owner of this intimate little restaurant ta the best Swedish ingredients and showcases them in creative modern dis which are underpinned by Japanese techniques. Sit at the counter or in fron the open kitchen to make the most of the experience. A good range of sake companies.

Menu 765SEK

Off plan – *Timmermansgatan 38b – Ⓜ Mariatorget – ✆ 08-88 91 30 – www.ichisthlm.se – Closed 24-31 December, Monday, Tuesday, lunch Wednesday-Saturday, Sunday*

Symbios

MODERN CUISINE • CONTEMPORARY DÉCOR A relaxed, friendly restau perfectly suited to the trendy suburb of Södermalm; watch the world go by you relax with an aperitif on the pavement terrace. The experienced team c classic Swedish and French dishes, which are simple, fresh and full of flavour.

Menu 265SEK (lunch) – Carte 510/540SEK

Off plan – *Skånegatan 80 – Ⓜ Medborgarplatsen – www.symbiossthlm.se – Closed Monday, Sunday*

Woodstockholm

MODERN CUISINE • BISTRO A chef-turned-furniture-maker owns this neighbourhood restaurant overlooking the park. Cooking follows a theme which changes every 2 months and dishes are simple yet full of flavour. In summer, the private room opens as a wine bar.

Menu 610 SEK – Carte 550/910 SEK

PLAN: C3 – *Mosebacke Torg 9 – Ⓜ Slussen – ✆ 08-36 93 99 – www.woodstockholm.com – Closed Monday, lunch Tuesday-Saturday, Sunday*

Environs of Stockholm

Älvsjö Southwest: 11 km by Hornsgaten and E20/E4

Aloë (Niclas Jönsson and Daniel Höglander)

CREATIVE • CONTEMPORARY DÉCOR Two talented chefs run this warm, welcoming restaurant, which is located in a former shop in the city suburbs. Enjoy snacks in the lounge before taking your seat at one of the communal tables. The surprise menu sees globally influenced dishes stimulate the senses with their intense flavours and original combinations.

Specialities: Otoro with smoked egg yolk and caviar. Guinea fowl with Tasmanian truffle and parsley. White peach, rose and ras el hanout.

Menu 2100 SEK

Off plan – *Svartlösavägen 52 – Ⓜ Älvsjö – ✆ 073-154 41 51 – www.aloerestaurant.se – Closed 23 December-29 January, Monday, Tuesday, lunch Wednesday-Saturday, Sunday*

Bockholmen Island Northwest: 7 km by Sveavägen and E18

Bockholmen

SWEDISH • TRADITIONAL With charming terraces leading down to the water, and an outside bar, this 19C summer house is the perfect place to relax on a summer's day. It's set on a tiny island, so opening times vary. Wide-ranging menus include weekend brunch.

Menu 475/995 SEK

Off plan – *Bockholmsvägen – Ⓜ Bergshamra – ✆ 08-624 22 00 – www.bockholmen.com – Closed Monday*

Edsvicken Northwest: 8 km by Sveavägen and E 18 towards Norrtälje

Ulriksdals Wärdshus

TRADITIONAL CUISINE • INN A charming 19C wood-built inn located on the edge of a woodland; start with drinks on the terrace overlooking the lake. Every table in the traditional room has an outlook over the attractive gardens and there's a characterful wine cellar. Classic Swedish dishes are supplemented by a smörgåsbord at lunch.

Carte 455/615 SEK

Off plan – *Ulriksdals Slottspark – Ⓜ Bergshamra – ✆ 08-85 08 15 – www.ulriksdalswardshus.se – Closed 1-31 January, Monday*

Lilla Essingen West: 5. 5 km by Norr Mälarstrand

Lux Dag för Dag

MODERN CUISINE • BRASSERIE A bright, modern, brasserie-style restaurant in an old waterside Electrolux factory dating back to 1916. Generously proportioned dishes might look modern but they have a traditional base; sourcing Swedish ingredients is paramount.

Carte 385/640 SEK

Off plan – *Primusgatan 116 – ✆ 08-619 01 90 – www.luxdagfordag.se – Closed 13 July-10 August, 23 December-8 January, Monday, Sunday*

GOTHENBURG
GÖTEBORG

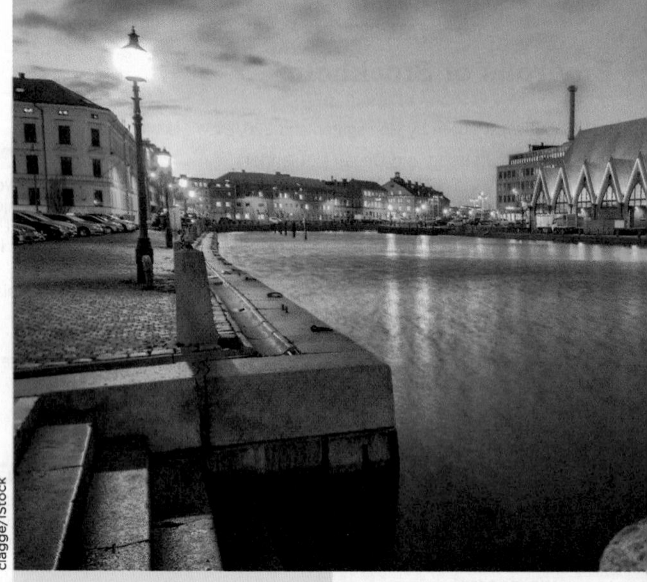

clagge/iStock

GOTHENBURG IN...

→ **ONE DAY**
The Old Town, Stadsmuseum, The Museum of World Culture.

→ **TWO DAYS**
Liseberg amusement park, The Maritiman, Art Museum, a stroll around Linné.

→ **THREE DAYS**
A trip on a Paddan boat, a visit to the Opera House.

Gothenburg is considere
to be one of Sweden's frienc
liest towns, a throwback to i
days as a leading trading ce
tre. This is a compact, prett
city whose roots go bac
four hundred years. It ha
trams, broad avenues an
canals and its centre is bois
terous but never feels tou
ist heavy or overcrowde
Gothenburgers take life at a more leisurely pace than the
Stockholm cousins over on the east coast. The might
shipyards that once dominated the shoreline are now quie
go to the centre, though, and you find the good-time amb
ence of Avenyn, a vivacious thoroughfare full of places

which to shop, eat and drink. But for those still itching for a feel of the heavy industry that once defined the place, there's a Volvo museum sparkling with chrome and shiny steel.

The Old Town is the historic heart of the city: its tight grid of streets has grand façades and a fascinating waterfront. Just west is the Vasastan quarter, full of fine National Romantic buildings. Further west again is Haga, an old working-class district which has been gentrified, its cobbled streets sprawling with trendy cafes and boutiques. Adjacent to Haga is the district of Linné, a vibrant area with its elegantly tall 19th century Dutch-inspired buildings. As this is a maritime town, down along the quayside is as good a place to get your bearings as any.

EATING OUT

othenburg's oldest food market is lled Feskekörka or 'Fish Church'. It es indeed look like a place of wors- but its pews are stalls of oysters, awns and salmon, and where you ight expect to find an organ loft, u'll find a restaurant instead. Food – d in particular the piscine variety – is ig reason for visiting Gothenburg. Its staurants have earned a plethora of chelin stars, which are dotted all over e compact city. If you're after something a little simpler, head for one of e typical Swedish Konditoris (cafés) – two of the best are Brogyllen and Ahlströms. If you're visiting between December and April, try the traditional cardamom-spiced buns known as 'semla'. The 19C covered food markets, Stora Saluhallen at Kungstorget and Saluhallen Briggen at Nordhemsgatan in Linnestaden, are worth a visit. Also in Kungstorget is the city's most traditional beer hall, Ölhallen 7:an; there are only 6 others in town. Gothenburgers also like the traditional food pairing 'SOS', where herring and cheese are washed down with schnapps.

bhoga (Gustav Knutsson)

CREATIVE • DESIGN The knowledgeable team here know both the menu a the wine list inside out. Ultra-seasonal ingredients from small farms feature imaginatively presented dishes which are complex in make-up yet subtle in vour – and these are paired with some interesting wines. The flowers are gro on their urban farm.

Specialities: Baked cod with lemon verbena, peas and sea herbs. Duck, Rosc onions and blackcurrants. Blueberries with marigold sorbet and sour cream.

Menu 650/900 SEK

PLAN: B2 – *Norra Hamngatan 10 – ✆ 031-13 80 18 – www.bhoga.se – Closed 3-20 August, Monday, lunch Tuesday-Saturday, Sunday*

Koka

MODERN CUISINE • DESIGN An understatedly elegant wood-panelled ro with bespoke furnishings that exude Scandic cool. Choose 3, 5 or 7 courses fr the daily set menu. Dishes are light and refreshingly original in their appro and feature some lesser-known ingredients. Well-chosen wines and smooth s vice complete the picture.

Specialities: Langoustine, agretti and roasted tomato. Cod, yellow pea miso a mushrooms. Fermented blueberries with flowers and herbs.

Menu 545/945 SEK

PLAN: B3 – *Viktoriagatan 12 – ✆ 031-701 79 79 – www.restaurangkoka.se – Closed lunch Monday-Saturday, Sunday*

SK Mat & Människor (Stefan Karlsson)

MODERN CUISINE • DESIGN Not only can you watch the chefs at work h they also deliver your food. Cooking is a model of self-restraint, with w thought-through combinations showing a beautiful balance of richness and a ity. The room exudes a cool, modern style and is relaxed and intimate in ec measure.

Specialities: Langoustine with preserved pine spruce and shellfish sauce. S with cabbage, dill and pickled fennel. Raspberry curd with marigold ice cre and dark chocolate.

Menu 650/900 SEK – Carte 580/610 SEK

PLAN: C3 – *Johannebergsgatan 24 – ✆ 031-81 25 80 – www.skmat.se – Closed 20 June-28 July, 21 December-4 January, lunch Monday-Saturday, Sunda*

Thörnströms Kök (Håkan Thörnström)

CLASSIC CUISINE • NEIGHBOURHOOD An elegant, long-standing restau with a stunning wine cave; set in a quiet residential area and run by a welcom knowledgeable team. There's a good choice of menus – they can even creat bespoke option to match your wine choices. Classically based cooking uses produce to create pronounced flavours.

Specialities: Langoustine with fennel and dill. Hake, cabbage and mushroo Blueberries with almond and lavender.

Menu 680/1200 SEK – Carte 700/820 SEK

PLAN: C3 – *Teknologgatan 3 – ✆ 031-16 20 66 – www.thornstromskok.com – Closed 13 July-10 August, lunch Monday-Saturday, Sunday*

28+

MODERN CUISINE • ROMANTIC This passionately run basement restaurant been a Gothenburg institution for over 30 years. Modern cooking showca prime seasonal ingredients, skilfully blending French and Swedish influences create intricate, flavourful dishes. There's an exceptional cheese selection anc outstanding wine list.

Specialities: Mackerel with cucumber, elderflower and caviar. Fillet of brill v asparagus and chervil. Gateau Marcel with white chocolate and rhubarb.

Menu 895/1095 SEK – Carte 685/765 SEK

PLAN: C3 – *Götabergsgatan 28 – ✆ 031-20 21 61 – www.28plus.se – Closed 1 July-20 August, Monday, lunch Tuesday-Saturday, Sunday*

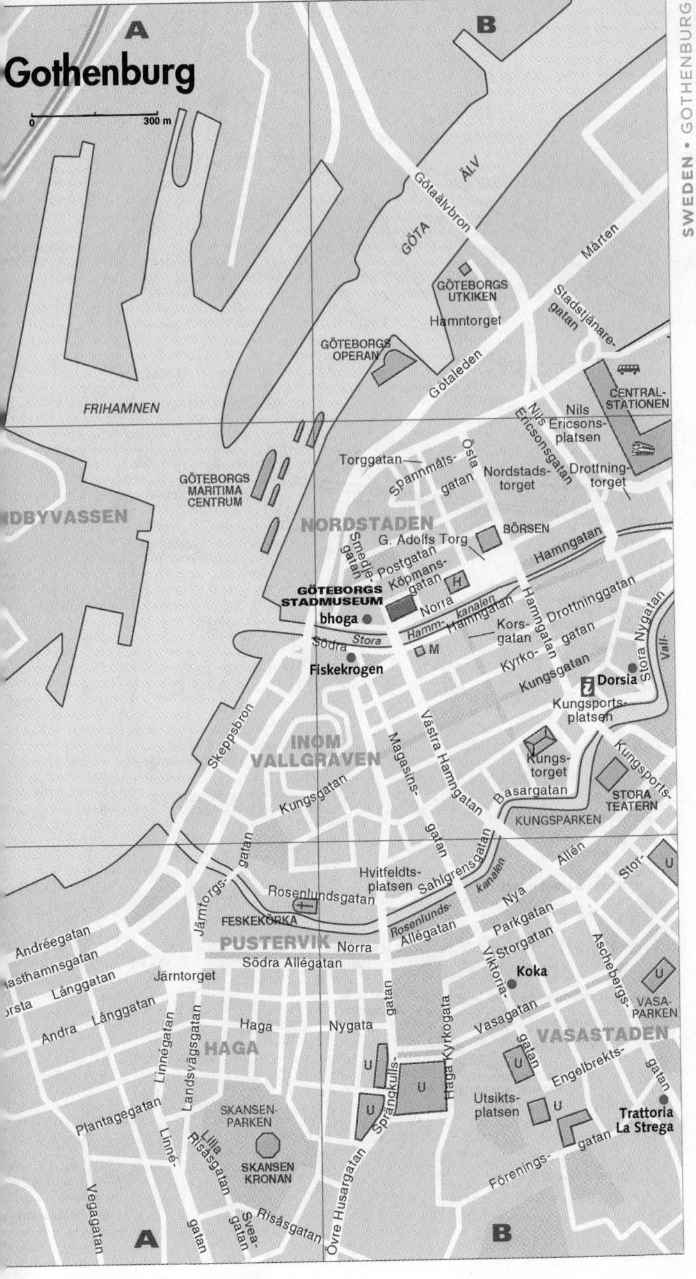
Gothenburg
0
300 m
A
B
GÖTA ÄLV
Götaälvbron
GÖTEBORGS UTKIKEN
Hamntorget
GÖTEBORGS OPERAN
Götaleden
Mårten
Stadstjänare-gatan
CENTRAL-STATIONEN
Nils Ericsons-platsen
Nils Ericsonsgatan
FRIHAMNEN
GÖTEBORGS MARITIMA CENTRUM
Torggatan
Spannmåls-gatan
Östa
Nordstads-torget
Drottning-torget
NORDSTADEN
Smedje-gatan
G. Adolfs Torg
BÖRSEN
Hamngatan
Postgatan
Köpmans-gatan
GÖTEBORGS STADMUSEUM
bhoga
Norra Hamngatan
Hamm-kanalen
Stora
Södra
Fiskekrogen
M
Kors-gatan
Drottninggatan
Kyrko-gatan
Kungsgatan
Stora Nygatan
Vall-
Dorsia
Kungsports-platsen
Skeppsbron
INOM VALLGRAVEN
Magasins-gatan
Västra Hamngatan
Kungs-torget
Kungsports-
STORA TEATERN
Basargatan
KUNGSPARKEN
Kungsgatan
Allén
Stor-
Hvitfeldts-platsen
Sahlgrensgatan
kanalen
Rosenlundsgatan
Nya
Järntorgs-gatan
FESKEKÖRKA
Rosenlunds-
Allégatan
Parkgatan
Andréegatan
PUSTERVIK
Norra
Storgatan
Aschebergs-gatan
Södra Allégatan
Viktoria-gatan
Koka
Järntorget
Långgatan
Andra Långgatan
Haga
Nygata
Vasagatan
VASA-PARKEN
HAGA
VASASTADEN
Linnégatan
Landsvägsgatan
Haga Kyrkogata
Engelbrekts-gatan
U
Plantagegatan
SKANSEN-PARKEN
Sprängkulls-gatan
Utsikts-platsen
Trattoria La Strega
Linné-gatan
Lilla Risåsgatan
SKANSEN KRONAN
Övre Husargatan
Förenings-gatan
Vegagatan
Svea-gatan
Risåsgatan

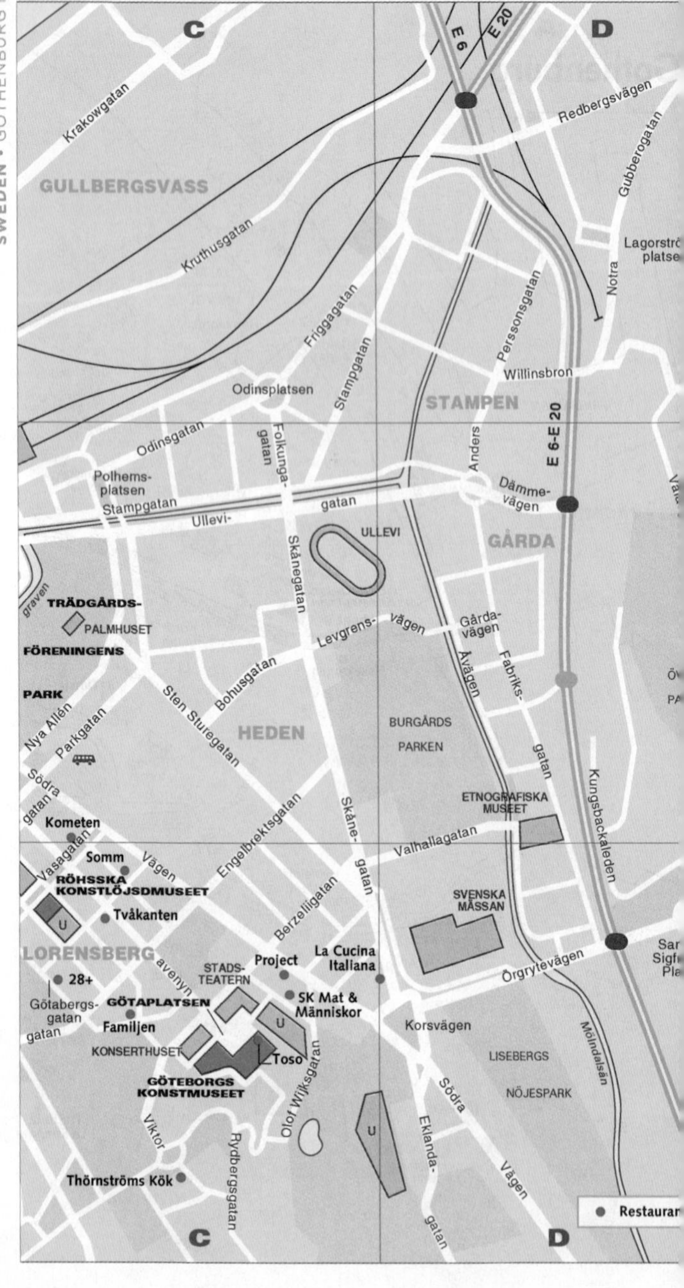
C
D
Krakowgatan
GULLBERGSVASS
Kruthusgatan
Redbergsvägen
Gubberogatan
Lagorströ platse
Notra
Friggagatan
Stampgatan
Perssonsgatan
Willinsbron
Odinsplatsen
STAMPEN
E 6-E 20
Odinsgatan
Folkunga-gatan
Anders
Polhems-platsen
Stampgatan
Ullevi-
gatan
Dämme-vägen
ULLEVI
Skånegatan
GÅRDA
TRÄDGÅRDS-
PALMHUSET
FÖRENINGENS
PARK
Levgrens-
vägen
Gårda-vägen
Bohusgatan
Sten Sturegatan
Åvägen
Fabriks-
gatan
Nya Allén
Parkgatan
HEDEN
BURGÅRDS
PARKEN
Södra
gatan
Kometen
Engelbrektsgatan
Skåne-
gatan
ETNOGRAFISKA
MUSEET
Kungsbackaleden
Valhallagatan
Vasagatan
Somm
Vägen
RÖHSSKA
KONSTLÖJSDMUSEET
Tvåkanten
Berzeliigatan
SVENSKA
MÄSSAN
LORENSBERG
avenyn
Project
La Cucina
Italiana
STADS-
TEATERN
28+
Götabergs-
gatan
GÖTAPLATSEN
SK Mat &
Människor
Örgrytevägen
Familjen
Korsvägen
KONSERTHUSET
Toso
LISEBERGS
NÖJESPARK
Mölndalsån
GÖTEBORGS
KONSTMUSEET
Olof Wijksgatan
Södra
Viktor
Rydbergsgatan
Eklanda-
gatan
Vägen
Thörnströms Kök
Restaurar

Familjen

SCANDINAVIAN • DESIGN A lively, friendly eatery divided into three parts: a bar with bench seating and an open kitchen; a bright red room with a characterful cellar and a glass wine cave; and a superb wrap-around terrace. Cooking is good value and portions are generous. There's an appealing wine, beer and cocktail list too.

Menu 395/495SEK – Carte 385/685SEK

PLAN: C3 – *Arkivgatan 7 – ✆ 031-20 79 79 – www.restaurangfamiljen.se – Closed lunch Monday-Saturday, Sunday*

Project

MODERN CUISINE • NEIGHBOURHOOD A young couple and their charming service team run this cosy little bistro just outside the city centre. The modern, creative, full-flavoured dishes are Swedish at heart with some global influences; the delicious bread takes 5 days to make and the homemade butter takes 2 days.

Menu 425SEK – Carte 535/650SEK

PLAN: C3 – *Södra vägen 45 – ✆ 031-18 18 58 – www.projectgbg.com – Closed 1 January-5 February, Monday, Tuesday, lunch Wednesday-Saturday, Sunday*

Somm

MODERN CUISINE • RUSTIC A simply but warmly decorated neighbourhood bistro with contemporary artwork and a cosy, friendly feel. Quality seasonal ingredients are used to create tasty modern dishes which feature on an à la carte and various tasting menus. The wine list offers great choice and the service is charming and professional.

Menu 395SEK – Carte 550/625SEK

PLAN: C3 – *Lorensbergsgatan 8 – ✆ 031-28 28 40 – www.somm.se – Closed 1-31 July, lunch Monday-Saturday, Sunday*

La Cucina Italiana

ITALIAN • INTIMATE An enthusiastically run restaurant consisting of just a handful of tables. Choose between the à la carte, a daily fixed price menu and a 6 course surprise tasting 'journey'. The chef-owner regularly travels to Italy to buy cheeses, meats and wines.

Menu 460SEK – Carte 545/635SEK

PLAN: C-D3 – *Skånegatan 33 – ✆ 031-16 63 07 – www.lacucinaitaliana.nu – Closed Monday, lunch Tuesday-Saturday, Sunday*

Dorsia

MODERN CUISINE • EXOTIC DÉCOR A dramatic hotel dining room with a sumptuous interior that has a touch of the burlesque about it. Vibrant modern dishes have both Swedish and Mediterranean touches; lunch includes creative smørrebrød and desserts are a highlight. The impressive wine list features some terrific 'verticals' of iconic wines.

Menu 425SEK (lunch) – Carte 405/515SEK

PLAN: B2 – *Dorsia Hotel, Trädgårdsgatan 6 – ✆ 031-790 10 00 – www.dorsia.se – Closed lunch Sunday*

Fiskekrogen

SEAFOOD • ELEGANT This charming restaurant sits within a 1920s grand café and showcases top quality seafood in classical dishes; for the ultimate feast order the shellfish platter de luxe. The seafood buffet on Friday and Saturday is impressive and the wine list comprises an enticing selection of top growers and producers.

Menu 745/895SEK – Carte 490/1200SEK

PLAN: B2 – *Lilla Torget 1 – ✆ 031-10 10 05 – www.fiskekrogen.se – Closed 5 July-6 August, 20 December-7 January, lunch Monday-Thursday, Sunday*

Kometen

SWEDISH • TRADITIONAL The oldest restaurant in town has a classic faça and a homely, traditional feel. It opened in 1934 and retains a loyal cliente with some guests returning over several decades. Sweden's culinary traditic are kept alive in well-executed, generously proportioned dishes; don't miss meatballs.

Carte 335/790SEK

PLAN: C2 – *Vasagatan 58 – ✆ 031-13 79 88 – www.restaurangkometen.se*

Sjömagasinet

SWEDISH • RUSTIC A charming split-level restaurant in an old 1775 East In Company warehouse; sit on the upper floor to take in the lovely harbour vie Cooking offers a pleasing mix of classic and modern dishes; summer lunches s a buffet on the terrace. The wine list offers a good selection of top burgundies

Menu 595SEK (lunch)/925SEK – Carte 685/1195SEK

Off plan – *Klippans Kulturreservat, Adolf Edelsvärds gata 5 – ✆ 031-775 59 20 – www.sjomagasinet.se – Closed 24 December-15 January, Monday, lunch Saturday, Sunday*

Syster Marmelad

VEGETARIAN • SIMPLE The city suburbs play host to this cosy, laid-back re taurant. The concise, daily changing menu of small plates is mainly plant-base with just the occasional meat or fish dish, and modern techniques deliver dep to the seemingly simple combinations. They also offer a 6 course herbal-bas surprise menu.

Menu 495/545SEK – Carte 425/685SEK

Off plan – *Mariagatan 16 – ✆ 031-14 11 60 – www.systermarmelad.se – Closed Monday, lunch Tuesday-Saturday, Sunday*

Toso

ASIAN • CONTEMPORARY DÉCOR There's something for everyone at th modern Asian restaurant, where terracotta warriors stand guard and loud mus pumps through the air. Dishes mix Chinese and Japanese influences; start wi some of the tempting small plates.

Carte 450/620SEK

PLAN: C3 – *Götaplatsen – ✆ 031-787 98 00 – www.toso.nu – Closed lunch Monday-Friday, lunch Sunday*

Trattoria La Strega

ITALIAN • FRIENDLY A lively little trattoria in a quiet residential area; run by charming owner. Sit at a candlelit table to enjoy authentic, boldly flavoured Ita ian cooking and well-chosen wines. Signature dishes include pasta with kin crab ragout.

Menu 480SEK – Carte 280/430SEK

PLAN: B3 – *Aschebergsgatan 23B – ✆ 031-18 15 01 – www.trattorialastrega.se – Closed 1 July-7 August, 31 December-7 January, Monday, lunch Tuesday-Sunday*

Tvåkanten

TRADITIONAL CUISINE • BRASSERIE With its welcoming hum and friend team, it's no wonder this long-standing family-run restaurant is always busy. Th dimly-lit, brick-walled dining room is pleasingly traditional and the covered te race is a popular spot. Homely lunches are served on Friday and Saturday; dir ners are more ambitious.

Menu 485/745SEK – Carte 385/785SEK

PLAN: C3 – *Kungsportsavenyn 27 – ✆ 031-18 21 15 – www.tvakanten.se – Closed lunch Monday-Thursday, lunch Sunday*

MALMÖ

MALMÖ

Allard1/iStock

MALMÖ IN...

- **ONE DAY**
  Lilla Torg and the Form/Design Centre, Western Harbour.
- **TWO DAYS**
  Modern Museum, Contemporary Art Exhibition at the Konsthall.
- **THREE DAYS**
  Skt Petri Church, an evening at the Malmö Opera.

Malmö was founded in th 13C under Danish rule an it wasn't until 1658 that entered Swedish possessic and subsequently estak lished itself as one of th world's biggest shipyard The building of the 8km lon Oresund Bridge in 200 reconnected the city wit Denmark and a year later, th Turning Torso apartment block was built in the old ship yard district, opening up the city to the waterfront. Onc an industrial hub, this 'city of knowledge' has impressive green credentials: buses run on natural gas and there a 400km of bike lanes. There's plenty of green space to you can picnic in Kungsparken or Slottsparken, sit by th

lakes in Pildammsparken or pet the farm animals in 'Folkets'.

At the heart of this vibrant city lie three squares: Gustav Adolfs Torg, Stortorget and Lilla Torg, connected by a pedestrianised shopping street. You'll find some of Malmö's oldest buildings in Lilla Torg, along with bustling open-air brasseries; to the west is Scandinavia's oldest surviving Renaissance castle and its beautiful gardens – and beyond that, the 2km Ribersborg Beach with its open-air baths. North is Gamla Väster with its charming houses and galleries, while south is Davidshall, filled with designer boutiques and chic eateries. Further south is Möllevångstorget, home to a throng of reasonably priced Asian and Middle Eastern shops.

EATING OUT

e gloriously fertile region of Skane ts a wealth of top quality produce on almö's doorstep. Dishes rich in dairy d meat – perhaps a little meatier an expected given its waterside pro-mity – are staple fare and wild herbs d foraged ingredients are the order the day; wild garlic, asparagus, pota-es and rhubarb are all celebrated ere. The locals eat early, so don't be rprised if you're one of just a handful diners at 1pm or 8pm. The popular cial phenomenon 'fika' is a tradition served by most, preferably several nes a day, and involves the drinking of coffee accompanied by something sweet; usually cake or cinnamon buns. Hot meals are popular midday – look out for the great value dagens lunch, which often offers the dish of the day plus salad, bread and water for under 100kr – or for lunch on the run, grab a tunnbrödsrull (sausage and mashed potato in a wrap) from a Korv kiosk. Local delicacies include äggakaka (thick pancakes and bacon), wallenbergare (minced veal patties with mashed potato and peas), marinated herring, eel and goose.

✿✿ Vollmers (Mats Vollmer)

CREATIVE • ELEGANT An elegant, intimate restaurant with charming, professio service, set in a pretty 19C townhouse. The cooking is creative and modern, wit high level of complexity, and the set tasting menu comes with numerous extra cours all inspired and informed by the local region and the chef-owners' childhood memor Carefully chosen wine flights feature wines from around the globe.

Specialities: Chanterelles with crown dill and Jerusalem artichoke. Beetroot w sweetbread and fennel. Yoghurt, pear and lemon verbena.

Menu 1600 SEK

PLAN: E2 – *Tegelgårdsgatan 5 – ✆ 040-57 97 50 – www.vollmers.nu – Closed Monday, lunch Tuesday-Saturday, Sunday*

✿ SAV (Sven Jensen and Alexander Fohlin)

CREATIVE • COSY Firepits and flickering candles provide a warm welcome this four-table destination restaurant set on a farm outside the city. Skilfu crafted, multi-faceted dishes are creative and full of flavour. The preserving, pic ling and fermenting of home-grown and foraged produce is a big part of th ethos and enhances the ultra-fresh, seasonal Skåne ingredients.

Specialities: King crab with almond and rosehip. Pork with mushrooms, tar syr and pepper. Fermented gooseberry tart with hay ice cream and lavender.

Menu 1195 SEK

Off plan – *Vindåkravägen 3, Tygelsjö – ✆ 072-022 85 20 – www.savrestaurang.nu – Closed 19-22 February, 8-11 April, 19 June-5 August, 19 December-6 January, Monday, Tuesday, lunch Wednesday-Saturday, Sunday*

Bastard

CONTEMPORARY • SIMPLE Popular with the locals, this is a bustling venue wi an edgy, urban vibe. Style-wise, schoolroom meets old-fashioned butcher's, wi vintage wood furniture, tiled walls, moody lighting and an open kitchen. Sm plates offer nose-to-tail eating with bold, earthy flavours; start with a 'Basta Plank' to share.

Carte 315/525 SEK

PLAN: E1 – *Mäster Johansgatan 11 – ✆ 040-12 13 18 – www.bastardrestaurant.se – Closed Monday, lunch Tuesday-Saturday, Sunday*

Namu

KOREAN • FRIENDLY Colourful, zingy food from a past Swedish MasterCh winner blends authentic Korean flavours with a modern Scandinavian touc Dishes are satisfying – particularly the fortifying ramen – and desserts are mo than an afterthought. Cookbooks line the shelves and friendly service adds t the lively atmosphere.

Menu 345 SEK (lunch) – Carte 140/570 SEK

PLAN: E1-2 – *Landbygatan 5 – ✆ 040-12 14 90 – www.namu.nu – Closed 24-26 December, Monday, lunch Saturday, Sunday*

Atmosfär

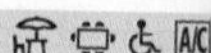

SWEDISH • NEIGHBOURHOOD A formal yet relaxed eatery on the main roa dine at the bar, in the restaurant or on the pavement terrace. The menu consist of small plates, of which three or four should suffice. Fresh Skåne cooking is de livered with a light touch.

Menu 395 SEK – Carte 320/545 SEK

Off plan – *Fersens väg 4 – ✆ 040-12 50 77 – www.atmosfar.com – Closed lunch Monday-Wednesday, lunch Saturday, Sunday*

Bloom in the Park

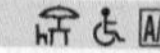

CREATIVE • DESIGN Have an aperitif on the terrace of this charming lakesid lodge before heading inside to enjoy visually appealing, creative modern dishes The menu and matching wines are a complete surprise; what you've eaten is onl confirmed at the end of your meal, when you are given a QR code to scan.

Menu 500/700 SEK

Off plan – *Pildammsvägen 17 – ✆ 040-793 63 – www.bloominthepark.se – Closed lunch Monday-Saturday, Sunday*

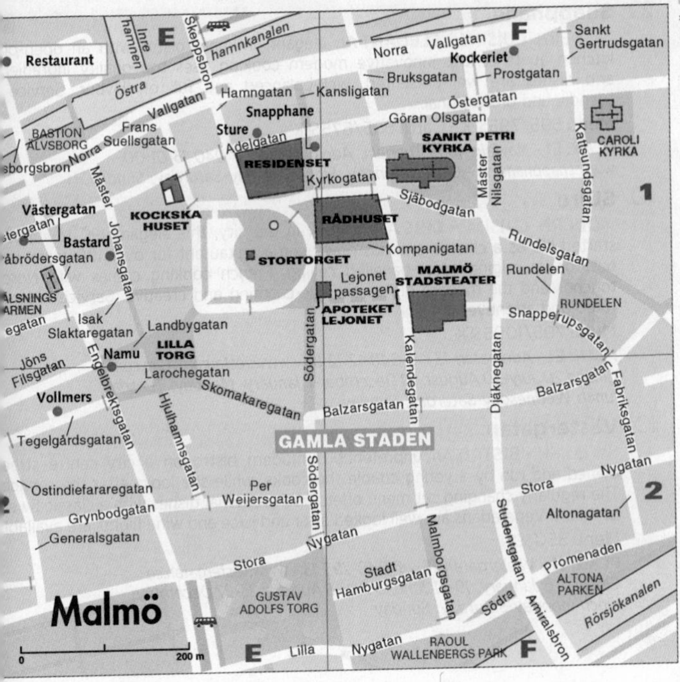

Malmö

Kockeriet

MODERN CUISINE • RUSTIC Well-known TV chef Tareq Taylor uses this characterful timbered 17C grain warehouse to deliver his own brand of modern cuisine, founded on ingredients from his kitchen garden and his extensive travels. Menus take on a tasting format. The beef from the on-view ageing cabinets is particularly good.

Menu 700/850 SEK

PLAN: F1 – *Norra Vallgatan 28 – ✆ 040-796 06 – www.kockeriet.se – Closed 1 July-13 August, lunch Monday-Saturday, Sunday*

Lyran

MODERN CUISINE • NEIGHBOURHOOD A small, simply styled restaurant run by a friendly team; sit at the ground floor counter for the best atmosphere. Set tasting menus are created daily from the best available seasonal and local produce and dishes are carefully prepared and well-balanced, with a classic Swedish heart and a modern style.

Menu 550/600 SEK

Off plan – *Simrishamnsgatan 36a – ✆ 076-324 52 28 – www.lyranmatbar.se – Closed Monday, lunch Tuesday-Saturday, Sunday*

Mutantur

MODERN CUISINE • NEIGHBOURHOOD Semi-industrial styling means concrete floors, brick-faced walls and exposed ducting; there's also an open kitchen and counter dining. The extensive menu offers snacks and small plates with a Nordic style and some Asian influences; they recommend between 3 and 5 per person.

Carte 350/550 SEK

Off plan – *Erik Dahlbergsgatan 12-14 – ✆ 076-101 72 05 – www.restaurantmutantur.se – Closed 13 July-4 August, lunch Monday-Friday, Saturday, Sunday*

Snapphane

MODERN CUISINE • ELEGANT An elegant, intimate bistro with an open-pl kitchen at its centre. Innovative modern cooking uses top quality ingredier and dishes are well-presented, well-balanced and full of flavour. Service friendly and professional.

Menu 595/795 SEK – Carte 555/675 SEK

PLAN: E1 – *Mayfair Hotel Tunneln, Adelgatan 4 – ✆ 040-15 01 00 – www.snapphane.nu – Closed Monday, lunch Tuesday-Saturday, Sunday*

Sture

MODERN CUISINE • CHIC A landmark in the city, this elegant 19C townhou started life as a cinema and has now been a restaurant for over 100 years; lo out for its original glass-panelled ceiling. French cooking comes with Norc touches and the modern dishes are eye-catching and creative. Service is stru tured and attentive.

Menu 795/1095 SEK

PLAN: E1 – *Adelgatan 13 – ✆ 040-12 12 53 – www.restaurantsture.com – Closed 20 July-20 August, 21 December-1 January, Monday, Tuesday, lunch Wednesday-Saturday, Sunday*

Västergatan

SWEDISH • BISTRO An unpretentious modern bistro on a city centre stree owned and run by a young couple (he cooks, while she looks after the service The regularly changing set menu offers fresh seasonal dishes with a classic Swec ish heart. Vegetarians are well looked after and juice and wine flights are availabl

Menu 550 SEK

PLAN: E1 – *Västergatan 16 – ✆ 040-793 13 – www.vastergatan.se – Closed 1-6 January, 19-21 June, 5 July-5 August, 23-27 December, lunch Monday-Saturday, Sunday*

AleksandarGeorgiev/iStock

SWITZERLAND

UISSE, SCHWEIZ, VIZZERA

BERN
BERNE

LeeYiuTung/iStock

BERN IN...

- **ONE DAY**
  River walk, Old Town (cathedral, clock Tower, arcades), Museum of Fine Arts, cellar fringe theatre.
- **TWO DAYS**
  Zentrum Paul Klee, Einstein's house, Stadttheater.
- **THREE DAYS**
  Bern Museum of History, Swiss Alpine Museum, Rose Garden.

To look at Bern, you'd neve believe it to be a capital cit Small and beautifully prc portioned, it sits sedately c a spur at a point where th River Aare curves gracefull back on itself. The little city the best preserved mediev centre north of the Alps – fact recognised by UNESC when it awarded Bern Worl Heritage status – and the la out of the streets has barely changed since the Duke c Zahringen chose the superbly defended site to found th city over 800 years ago. Most of the buildings date fro between the 14 and 16C – when Bern was at the height c its power – and the cluster of cobbled lanes, surrounde

by ornate sandstone arcaded buildings and numerous fountains and wells, give it the feel of a delightfully overgrown village. (Albert Einstein felt so secure here that while ostensibly employed as a clerk in the Bern patent office he managed to find the time to work out his Theory of Relativity.)

The Old Town stretches eastwards over a narrow peninsula, and is surrounded by the arcing River Aare. The eastern limit of the Old Town is the Nydeggbrücke bridge, while the western end is marked out by the Käfigturm tower, once a city gate and prison. On the southern side of the Aare lies the small Kirchenfeld quarter, which houses some impressive museums, while the capital's famous brown bears are back over the river via the Nydeggbrücke.

EATING OUT

ern is a great place to sit and enjoy meal. Pride of place must go to the ood range of alfresco venues in the quares of the old town – popular spots enjoy coffee and cake. Hiding away the arcades are many delightful ning choices; some of the best for cation alone are in vaulted cellars at breathe historic ambience. If you ant to feel what a real Swiss restaurant is like, head for a traditional stic eatery complete with cow-bells nd sample the local dishes like the erner Platte – a heaving plate of hot and cold meats, served with beans and sauerkraut – or treberwurst, a sausage poached with fermented grape skins. There's no shortage of international restaurants either, and along with Germany, France and Italy also have their country's cuisine well represented here – it's not difficult to go from rösti to risotto. And, of course, there's always cheese – this is the birthplace of raclette - and tempting chocolates waiting in the wings. A fifteen percent service charge is always added but it's customary to round the bill up.

Steinhalle (Markus Arnold)

CREATIVE • FRIENDLY This undisputedly cool restaurant offers a fine old inter complete with high ceilings, a gallery and large arched windows and trendy, no-fri decor in which the front cooking station and counter – where you can also eat – tak centre stage. Creative set menu in the evening, simple "Easy Lunch" at midday.

Specialities: Scottish salmon, avocado, soy sauce. Chargrilled sea bass with ri espuma. Coconut sorbet with yoghurt foam, mango and passion fruit.

Menu 102/132 CHF

PLAN: B2 – *Helvetiaplatz 5 – ✆ 031 351 51 00 – www.steinhalle.ch – Closed Monday, Tuesday, Sunday, lunch Wednesday-Saturday*

Zum Äusseren Stand

CONTEMPORARY • COSY This restaurant is housed in a building steeped in his tory (the Swiss Federal Constitution was signed here in 1848). The magnifice dining room is a beautiful place to enjoy modern, produce-oriented cuisine. Re duced menu at lunchtime, plus drinks and light meals served in the Hof-Café.

Specialities: Hamachi, pickled vegetables, Ponzu vinaigrette. Turbot, spinac kohlrabi, black garlic, dill beurre blanc. Pear, chocolate "Grand Cru", elderberry.

Menu 48 CHF (lunch), 58/135 CHF – Carte 68/108 CHF

PLAN: 1-B1 – *Zeughausgasse 17 – ✆ 031 329 50 50 – www.aeussererstand.ch – Closed 27 July-10 August, 23-30 December, Monday, Sunday*

Kirchenfeld

TRADITIONAL CUISINE • BRASSERIE Eating in this loud and lively restaurant great fun! Try the flavoursome zander fish served on Mediterranean couscous an one of the sweets, which include lemon tart and chocolate cake, displayed on th dessert trolley. At lunchtimes the restaurant is full of business people who swea by the daily set menu.

Menu 75 CHF – Carte 44/91 CHF

PLAN: C2 – *Thunstrasse 5 – ✆ 031 351 02 78 – www.kirchenfeld.ch – Closed Monday, Sunday*

Schöngrün

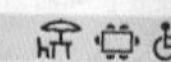

CREATIVE • TRENDY The food on offer here at Schöngrün, a period villa nex to the Zentrum Paul Klee, is now a little more down to earth but has lost non of its flavour. High quality ingredients feature in delicious dishes such as breas of poularde with risini, spring onions, summer truffle and parmesan. The table in the modern glazed pavilion-style annexe are lovely and there's also a prett garden terrace.

Menu 46 CHF (lunch)/51 CHF – Carte 58/80 CHF

Off plan – *Monument im Fruchtland 1 – ✆ 031 359 02 90 – www.restaurants-schoengruen.ch – Closed Monday, Tuesday*

Brasserie Obstberg

CLASSIC CUISINE • BRASSERIE Diners have been coming to Brasserie Obstberg for over 100 years. Today they eat in the lovely, 1930s-style brasserie with its won derful terrace shaded by mature sweet chestnut trees. The food is classically French with Swiss influences and ranges from braised lamb shank to sautéed zander.

Menu 59/89 CHF – Carte 55/88 CHF

PLAN: D2 – *Bantigerstrasse 18 – ✆ 031 352 04 40 – www.brasserie-obstberg.ch – Closed Sunday*

Casa Novo

MEDITERRANEAN CUISINE • FRIENDLY The great location on the River Aare means that the terrace is a real highlight here. The seasonal Mediterranean food on offer includes meagre with crustacean emulsion, beluga lentils and ratatouille as well Swiss classics such as hand-chopped steak tartare. There is also a wine shop and you'll find the Klösterli car park just over the river.

Menu 31 CHF (lunch)/84 CHF – Carte 62/104 CHF

PLAN: D1 – *Läuferplatz 6 – ✆ 031 992 44 44 – www.casa-novo.ch – Closed 1-6 January, 25-31 December, Monday, Sunday, lunch Saturday*

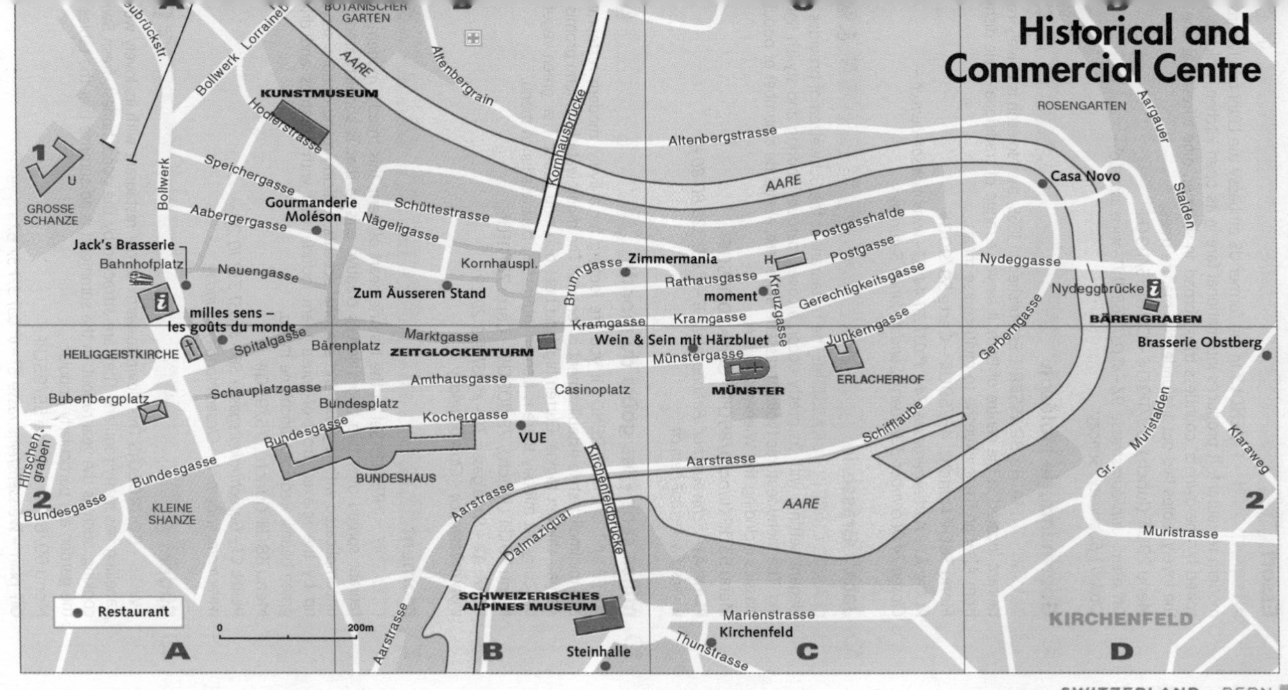
Historical and Commercial Centre
ROSENGARTEN
Aargauer
Stalden
BOTANISCHER GARTEN
AARE
Altenbergrain
Altenbergstrasse
Kornhausbrücke
KUNSTMUSEUM
Hodlerstrasse
Bollwerk
Lorraine
Speichergasse
Schüttestrasse
Gourmanderie Moléson
Aabergergasse
Nägeligasse
GROSSE SCHANZE
Jack's Brasserie
Bahnhofplatz
Neuengasse
Kornhauspl.
Zum Äusseren Stand
milles sens – les goûts du monde
Spitalgasse
HEILIGGEISTKIRCHE
Bärenplatz
Marktgasse
ZEITGLOCKENTURM
Brunngasse
Zimmermania
Postgasshalde
Postgasse
Rathausgasse
moment
Kreuzgasse
Gerechtigkeitsgasse
Kramgasse
Wein & Sein mit Härzbluet
Münstergasse
MÜNSTER
Junkerngasse
ERLACHERHOF
Casa Novo
Nydeggasse
Nydeggbrücke
BÄRENGRABEN
Gerberngasse
Brasserie Obstberg
Bubenbergplatz
Schauplatzgasse
Amthausgasse
Bundesplatz
Casinoplatz
Kochergasse
VUE
Bundesgasse
BUNDESHAUS
Hirschengraben
KLEINE SHANZE
Aarstrasse
Kirchenfeldbrücke
Schifflaube
Gr. Muristalden
Klaraweg
Muristrasse
Dalmaziquai
SCHWEIZERISCHES ALPINES MUSEUM
Steinhalle
Marienstrasse
Kirchenfeld
Thunstrasse
KIRCHENFELD
Restaurant
0
200m
A
B
C
D
1
2
2
U

Essort

INTERNATIONAL • **FRIENDLY** In the former US embassy the Lüthi family runs modern restaurant. It produces international fare in its open kitchen, which is i spired by the owners' countless trips abroad. In summer, dine alfresco at one the lovely tables laid outside under the mature trees.

Menu 29 CHF (lunch), 69/119 CHF – Carte 55/119 CHF

Off plan – *Jubiläumstrasse 97 – ✆ 031 368 11 11 – www.essort.ch – Closed 1-5 January, Sunday*

Gourmanderie Moléson

CLASSIC FRENCH • **BRASSERIE** Established in 1865, the Moléson is a lively re taurant located in the centre of Bern. It serves a range of traditional-style dish from Alsatian flammekueche to multi-course meals.

Menu 38 CHF (lunch), 46/59 CHF – Carte 59/90 CHF

PLAN: A1 – *Aarbergergasse 24 – ✆ 031 311 44 63 – www.moleson-bern.ch – Closed 24 December-3 January, Sunday, lunch Saturday*

Jack's Brasserie

CLASSIC CUISINE • **BRASSERIE** The restaurant at the Schweizerhof provides a elegant setting, with its pretty decor, alcoves, parquet flooring and stylish ligh ing. The menu features typical brasserie-style fare, alongside a number of popula classics including the Wiener schnitzel.

Menu 53 CHF (lunch)/85 CHF – Carte 70/125 CHF

PLAN: A1 – *Schweizerhof, Bahnhofplatz 11 – ✆ 031 326 80 80 – www.schweizerhof-bern.ch*

milles sens - les goûts du monde

INTERNATIONAL • **TRENDY** If you are looking for a lively, modern restauran this minimalist-style establishment is for you. The mouthwatering menu promise Aargau chicken tagine, Gurten highland beef duo, and exotic Thai green vegeta ble curry. At midday there is also an interesting business lunch menu.

Menu 59 CHF (lunch), 78/108 CHF – Carte 73/111 CHF

PLAN: A2 – *Spitalgasse 38 – ✆ 031 329 29 29 – www.millesens.ch – Closed Sunday*

moment

CREATIVE • **TRENDY** Set in the historic heart of Bern, this trendy, modern res taurant spread over two floors serves creative cuisine that is sophisticated ye uncomplicated with regional and seasonal accents. Enticing menu options servec up by the relaxed front-of-house team include veal with potatoes and driec green beans. Reduced lunchtime menu.

Menu 38 CHF (lunch), 75/95 CHF

PLAN: C1 – *Gerechtigkeitsgasse 56 – ✆ 031 332 10 20 – www.moment-bern.ch – Closed Monday, Sunday*

Süder

SWISS • **BOURGEOIS** This down-to-earth corner restaurant with its lovely wood panelling has many regulars. They are attracted by the good, honest, fresh Swiss cooking, such as the veal ragout. In the summer it is no surprise that the tables in the garden are particularly popular.

Menu 69/89 CHF – Carte 55/95 CHF

Off plan – *Weissensteinstrasse 61 – ✆ 031 371 57 67 – www.restaurant-sueder.ch – Closed 1-7 January, 12 July-3 August, 22-30 September, Monday, Sunday, lunch Saturday*

VUE 

MODERN CUISINE • CLASSIC DÉCOR At VUE, meals are served either in the restaurant with its stylish Belle-Époque flair, in the legendary Bellevue Bar or on the terrace with its wonderful views. The cuisine is classic yet modern and the menu features specialities such as flat iron beef tartare and Irish lamb entrecôte with smoked aubergine and yoghurt.

Menu 64 CHF (lunch) – Carte 50/105 CHF

PLAN: B2 – *Bellevue Palace, Kochergasse 3 – ✆ 031 320 45 45 – www.bellevue-palace.ch/vue*

Waldheim 

TRADITIONAL CUISINE • NEIGHBOURHOOD This pretty restaurant is panelled in light wood and located in a quiet residential area. It boasts a healthy number of regulars thanks to the fresh Swiss cuisine (try the marinated leg of lamb, spit-roasted to a perfect pink) and the friendly service.

Menu 34/98 CHF – Carte 48/94 CHF

Off plan – *Waldheimstrasse 40 – ✆ 031 305 24 24 – www.waldheim-bern.ch – Closed Monday, Sunday, lunch Saturday*

Wein & Sein mit Härzbluet

MODERN CUISINE • FRIENDLY A set of steep steps lead down to this congenial restaurant in a vaulted cellar serving modern, seasonal fare preceded by aperitifs and nibbles. The name says it all here, the dedicated owner advising diners on menu and wine choices with "heart and soul".

Menu 78/128 CHF

PLAN: C2 – *Münstergasse 50 – ✆ 031 311 98 44 – www.weinundsein.ch – Closed Monday, Sunday, lunch Tuesday-Saturday*

Zimmermania

CLASSIC FRENCH • TRADITIONAL A restaurant as far back as the 19C, today this charming, picture-postcard bistro caters for fans of traditional cuisine. It offers classics such as calf's head vinaigrette, entrecôte Café de Paris and slow cooked stews.

Carte 40/95 CHF

PLAN: B1 – *Brunngasse 19 – ✆ 031 311 15 42 – www.zimmermania.ch – Closed Monday, Sunday*

GENEVA
GENEVE

Onfokus/iStock

GENEVA IN...

- **ONE DAY**
  St Peter's Cathedral, Maison Tavel, Jet d'Eau, Reformation Wall.
- **TWO DAYS**
  MAMCO (or Art & History Museum), a lakeside stroll, a trip to Carouge.
- **THREE DAYS**
  A day in Paquis, including time relaxing at the Bains des Paquis.

In just about every deta
except efficiency, Genev
exudes a distinctly Lati
feel. It boasts a proud co
mopolitanism, courtesy o
a whole swathe of interna
tional organisations (dealir
with just about every huma
concern), and of the fact th
roughly one in three residen
is non-Swiss. Its renowne
savoir-vivre challenges th
of swishy Zurich, and along with its manicured city parks,
boasts the world's tallest fountain and the world's longe
bench. It enjoys cultural ties with Paris and is often calle
'the twenty-first arrondissement' – it's also almost entire
surrounded by France.

The River Rhône snakes through the centre, dividing the city into the southern left bank - the old town – and the northern right bank – the 'international quarter' (home to the largest UN office outside New York). The east is strung around the sparkling shores of Europe's largest alpine lake, while the Jura Mountains dominate the right bank, and the Alps form a backdrop to the left bank. Geneva is renowned for its orderliness: the Reformation was born here under the austere preachings of Calvin, and the city has provided sanctuary for religious dissidents, revolutionaries and elopers for at least five centuries. Nowadays, new arrivals tend to be of a more conservative persuasion, as they go their elegant way balancing international affairs alongside la belle vie.

EATING OUT

'ith the number of international orga-sations that have set up camp here, is is a place that takes a lot of feeding,) you'll find over 1,000 dining esta-ishments in and around the city. If ›u're looking for elegance, head to a staurant overlooking the lake; if your stes are for home-cooked Sardinian re, make tracks for the charming alianate suburb of Carouge; and if you ncy something with an international :cent, trendy Paquis has it all at a fair ice and on a truly global scale, from exican to Moroccan and Jordanian to Japanese. The old town, packed with delightful brasseries and alpine-style chalets, is the place for Swiss staples: you can't go wrong here if you're after a fondue, rustic longeole (pork sausage with cumin and fennel) or a hearty papet vaudois (cream and leek casserole); for a bit of extra atmosphere, head downstairs to a candlelit, vaulted cellar. Although restaurants include a fifteen per cent service charge, it's customary to either round up the bill or give the waiter a five to ten per cent tip.

Right bank

L'Aparté

MODERN FRENCH • ELEGANT Located in the Hôtel Royal, with just a hand of tables but a focus on the very best products (Swiss veal and beef, fish fr Brittany, Bresse chickens, etc) used to create ambitious cuisine with plenty character. It's best to book ahead, particularly in the evening.

Specialities: Spider crab, cauliflower, black melanosporum truffle. Slow-cook aiguillette of John Dory from Brittany, buckwheat tuile. Genoese sponge cake b cuit, almonds, raspberries.

Menu 54 CHF (lunch)/85 CHF – Carte 93/119 CHF

PLAN: 2-E2 – *Rue de Lausanne 41 – ✆ 022 906 14 40 – www.hotelroyalgeneva.com – Closed 1-5 January, 9-19 April, 18 July-23 August, 19-31 December, Saturday, Sunday*

Bayview

MODERN FRENCH • DESIGN With its chic, carefully designed decor and lar bay windows facing the lake, this restaurant provides the ideal setting to enj some elegant cuisine. French classics are reinterpreted with creativity and su tlety, and the carefully produced dishes are chic and contemporary.

Specialities: Lake fish, floral vegetables, broth infused with wild herbs. Fillet ar rib of matured Swiss beef, confit boulangère, caper leaf. Soufflé tart with 70 Guanaja chocolate.

Menu 60 CHF (lunch), 130/170 CHF – Carte 116/200 CHF

PLAN: 2-F2 – *Président Wilson, Quai Wilson 47 – ✆ 022 906 65 52 – www.hotelpresidentwilson.com – Closed 1-13 January, 26 July-26 August, Monday, Sunday*

Le Chat-Botté

MODERN FRENCH • ELEGANT This appealingly named restaurant ('Puss Boots') serves contemporary-style cuisine with traditional roots, using culina techniques that create harmonious flavours. The food is complemented by th expert work of the sommelier, who skilfully guides guests through the impres sive wine list.

Specialities: Langoustine soufflé and Tibetan caviar. Gyozas of Jussy pork cara melised in honey from our hives and ginger. Soufflé with flambéed green Cha treuse.

Menu 45 CHF (lunch), 120/220 CHF – Carte 115/185 CHF

PLAN: 2-F3 – *Beau-Rivage, Quai du Mont-Blanc 13 – ✆ 022 716 69 20 – www.beau-rivage.ch – Closed 1-5 January, 4-19 April, 13 June-6 September, Saturda Sunday*

Fiskebar

MODERN CUISINE • TRENDY Young and talented chef Benjamin Breton ha brought a breath of fresh air to the city's restaurant scene and is definitely on to watch! His Nordic-inspired cuisine respects local provenance and celebrates lo cal products, which he transforms with his palette of refined technical skills, i particular fermentation. Impressive wine list.

Specialities: Crab, carrots, citrus fruit. Monkfish, mushrooms, coffee, smoked ee Honey, milk, kumquat.

Menu 45 CHF (lunch), 95/125 CHF – Carte 96/150 CHF

PLAN: 3-G2 – *The Ritz Carlton Hôtel De la Paix, Quai du Mont-Blanc 11 – ✆ 022 909 60 71 – Closed 1-6 January, 15 August-7 September, Monday, Sunday, lunch Saturday*

Il Lago

ITALIAN • CLASSIC DÉCOR Offering a taste of Italy on Lake Geneva, this res taurant combines decorative features such as pilasters and paintings with elegan Italian cuisine which is light, subtle and fragant. A delightful dining experience!

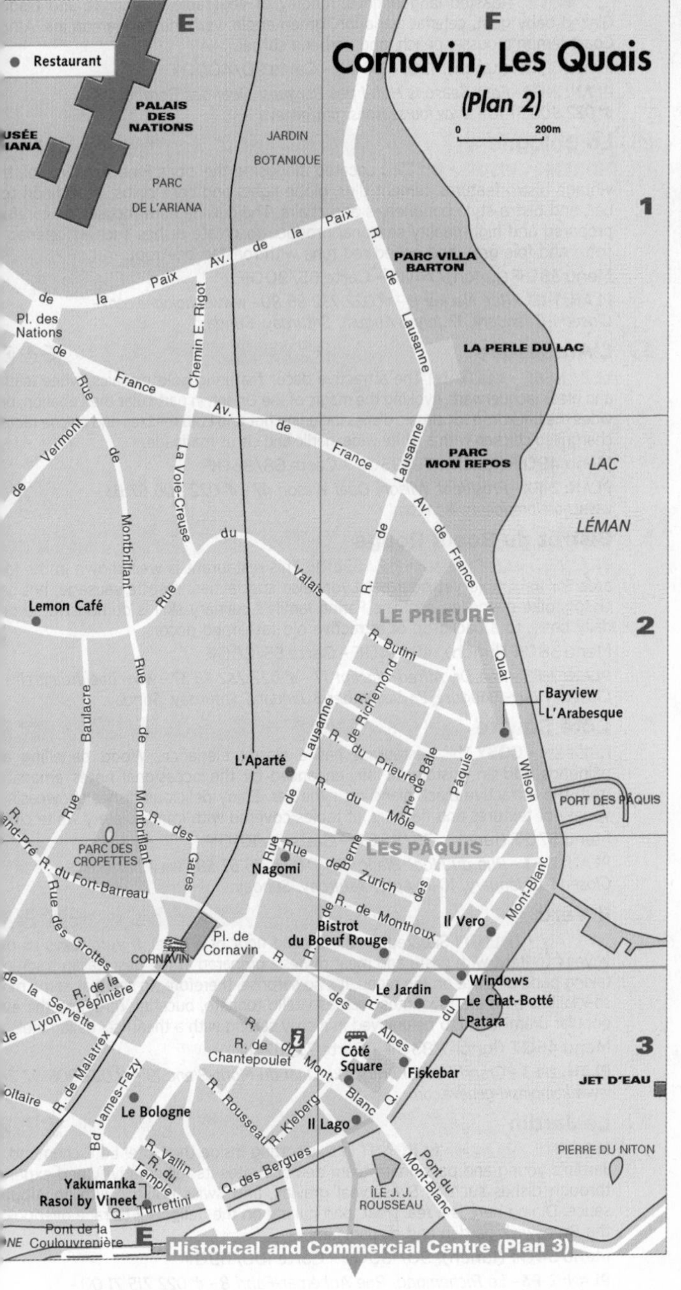
Cornavin, Les Quais
(Plan 2)
0
200m
E
F
1
2
3
Restaurant
PALAIS DES NATIONS
JARDIN BOTANIQUE
PARC DE L'ARIANA
PARC VILLA BARTON
LA PERLE DU LAC
PARC MON REPOS
LAC LÉMAN
LE PRIEURÉ
LES PÂQUIS
PORT DES PÂQUIS
JET D'EAU
PIERRE DU NITON
ÎLE J. J. ROUSSEAU
PARC DES CROPETTES
Pl. des Nations
Av. de la Paix
Av. de France
Chemin E. Rigot
R. de Lausanne
Rue de Vermont
Rue de Montbrillant
La Voie-Creuse
Rue du Valais
Rue Baulacre
R. Butini
R. de Richemond
R. du Prieuré
Rte de Bâle
R. du Môle
Rue de Berne
Rue de Zurich
R. de Monthoux
R. des Pâquis
Quai Wilson
Q. du Mont-Blanc
R. des Gares
R. du Fort-Barreau
Rue des Grottes
R. de la Pépinière
Pl. de Cornavin
CORNAVIN
R. de Chantepoulet
R. du Mont-Blanc
R. des Alpes
R. de la Servette
R. de Lyon
R. de Malatrex
Bd James-Fazy
R. Rousseau
R. Kleberg
Q. des Bergues
Pont du Mont-Blanc
R. Vallin
R. du Temple
Q. Turrettini
Pont de la Coulouvrenière
Lemon Café
L'Aparté
Nagomi
Bistrot du Boeuf Rouge
Il Vero
Windows
Le Jardin
Le Chat-Botté
Patara
Côté Square
Fiskebar
Il Lago
Le Bologne
Yakumanka
Rasoi by Vineet
Bayview
L'Arabesque
Historical and Commercial Centre (Plan 3)

Specialities: Roasted langoustines, medley of vegetables, samphire and bisq Glazed baby goat, celeriac variation, green apple, verbena and lemon jus. Ama Coast lemon mousse, peach, and verbena sorbet.

Menu 65 CHF (lunch), 120/400 CHF – Carte 90/400 CHF

PLAN: 2-F3 – *Four Seasons Hôtel des Bergues, Quai des Bergues 33 – ✆ 022 908 71 10 – www.fourseasons.com/geneva*

Le Bologne

MODERN CUISINE • BISTRO Located alongside the city's Fine Arts School, th vintage bistro features cement tiles, globe lights and bare bulbs, in addition to bar, and bistro-style banquettes and chairs. The cuisine here focuses on carefu prepared and high-quality seasonal produce to create dishes such as celeriac sotto and foie gras, and grilled red tuna with roasted beetroot.

Menu 38 CHF (lunch)/74 CHF – Carte 65/90 CHF

PLAN: 1-C3 – *Rue Necker 9 – ✆ 022 732 86 80 – www.lebologne.com – Closed 1-6 January, 17 July-8 August, Saturday, Sunday*

L'Arabesque

LEBANESE • ELEGANT The attractive decor featuring gold mosaics, white leath and black lacquerware, evoking the magic of the Orient, in particular the Lebanon, pr vides the backdrop for classic dishes including hot and cold mezzes and *chiche taouk* chargrilled chicken with a white wine, garlic and citrus marinade.

Menu 49 CHF (lunch), 79/95 CHF – Carte 68/86 CHF

PLAN: 2-F2 – *Président Wilson, Quai Wilson 47 – ✆ 022 906 67 63 – www.hotelpresidentwilson.com*

Bistrot du Boeuf Rouge

TRADITIONAL CUISINE • BRASSERIE This restaurant is well known in the loc area for its simple yet gourmet Lyonnaise specialities: rosette sausage, hot sau cisson, pike quenelles, etc. The Farina family's culinary skill is demonstrated on daily basis, to a backdrop of attractive old-fashioned decor.

Menu 38 CHF (lunch), 49/54 CHF – Carte 55/88 CHF

PLAN: 2-F3 – *Rue Dr. Alfred-Vincent 17 – ✆ 022 732 75 37 – www.boeufrouge.ch – Closed 11 July-9 August, 24 December-3 January, Saturday, Sunday*

Côté Square

FRENCH • COSY This restaurant has a classic elegance. Wood panelling an paintings add an aristocratic air, enhanced by the occasional notes emanatin from the attractive black piano near the bar. Enjoy delicious dishes showcasing variety of textures and flavours, at tables covered with immaculately white cloth

Menu 57 CHF (lunch), 76/115 CHF – Carte 81/101 CHF

PLAN: 2-F3 – *Rue du Mont-Blanc 10 – ✆ 022 716 57 58 – www.bristol.ch – Closed 1-12 January, 10-19 April, Saturday, Sunday*

Il Vero

ITALIAN • TRENDY Situated on the second floor of a hotel, Il Vero takes us on voyage to Italy, with pasta and meat dishes - prepared in the best Italian tradition taking pride of place on the menu. It's no surprise, therefore, to see that some of th specialities here are favourites such as vitello tonnato, bucatini Verdi and the ever popular tiramisu. All to be enjoyed in a cosy setting with a theatrical Italian feel.

Menu 45 CHF (lunch)/83 CHF – Carte 72/112 CHF

PLAN: 2-F3 – *Grand Hôtel Kempinski, Quai du Mont-Blanc 19 – ✆ 022 908 92 24 – www.kempinski-geneva.com*

Le Jardin

MODERN FRENCH • ELEGANT In this setting inside the Hôtel Le Richemond, Le Jardin's young and passionate team demonstrates its full creativity and expertise through dishes such as Swiss veal gravlax, and Swiss poultry with an Albufera sauce. Dining here is a real treat, particularly on the delightful terrace overlooking the Brunswick garden and mausoleum.

Menu 54 CHF (lunch), 90/130 CHF – Carte 100/119 CHF

PLAN: 2-F3 – *Le Richemond, Rue Adhémar-Fabri 8 – ✆ 022 715 71 00 – www.lerichemond.com – Closed 1-5 January*

Lemon Café

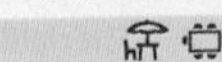

MODERN CUISINE • BISTRO In this quiet residential district above Cornavin station, the chef regales locals with his inspiring, travel-influenced recipes. Options include cod ceviche with a Peruvian flavour, pork spare ribs cooked for 12 hours and served with Maxim's potatoes, and fillet of perch from Lake Geneva.

Carte 34/84 CHF

PLAN: 2-E2 – *Rue du Vidollet 4 – ✆ 022 733 60 24 – www.lemon-cafe.ch – Closed 1-3 January, 20 July-7 August, 21-31 December, Saturday, Sunday*

Nagomi

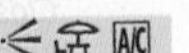

JAPANESE • SIMPLE Two distinct restaurants in the city's Le Paquis district, run by the same family: one dedicated to sushi, prepared by the father; the other to tempura dishes cooked by the son! In both places, the atmosphere is authentic and the service unfussy, ensuring a feast for the senses, with a focus on simplicity.

Menu 60/130 CHF – Carte 60/130 CHF

PLAN: 2-E3 – *Rue de Zurich 47 – ✆ 022 732 38 28 – www.restaurant-nagomi.ch – Closed 1-6 January, 26 July-3 August, 20-31 December, Monday, Sunday*

Patara

THAI • EXOTIC DÉCOR Thai specialities served in one of the most beautiful luxury hotels in Geneva. Stylised gold motifs on the walls evoke the exotic ambience of Thailand, while the delicious specialities on the menu add to the sense of discovery.

Menu 42 CHF (lunch), 95/125 CHF – Carte 62/105 CHF

PLAN: 2-F3 – *Beau-Rivage, Quai du Mont-Blanc 13 – ✆ 022 731 55 66 – www.patara-geneva.ch*

Rasoi by Vineet

INDIAN • ELEGANT All the fragrances and colours of Indian cuisine are interpreted here with incredible refinement. Enjoy the cuisine of the sub-continent at its best in this chic and elegant restaurant where you can imagine yourself as a 21C maharaja!

Menu 59 CHF (lunch), 85/115 CHF – Carte 47/104 CHF

PLAN: 2-E3 – *Mandarin Oriental, Quai Turrettini 1 – ✆ 022 909 00 00 – www.mandarinoriental.fr/geneva – Closed Monday, Sunday*

Windows

CREATIVE FRENCH • ELEGANT Housed in the Hôtel D'Angleterre, this restaurant offers superb views of Lake Geneva, the Jet d'Eau and the mountains in the distance. The menu features delicacies such as scallop carpaccio with lime, avocado tartare and fleur de sel, and half a baked lobster with little gem lettuce and potatoes.

Menu 59 CHF (lunch) – Carte 82/210 CHF

PLAN: 2-F3 – *D'Angleterre, Quai du Mont-Blanc 17 – ✆ 022 906 55 14 – www.hoteldangleterre.ch*

Yakumanka

PERUVIAN • COLOURFUL Nothing stops Gaston Acurio, a chef who has expanded his empire to Switzerland with this delightfully exotic restaurant at the Mandarin Oriental. On the menu you'll find refined, delicious Peruvian specialities (*tiraditos*, *ceviche*, and *anticuchos*) to be savoured in a relaxed setting.

Carte 59/142 CHF

PLAN: 2-F3 – *Mandarin Oriental, Quai Turrettini 1 – ✆ 022 909 00 00 – www.yakumanka.ch*

Left bank

La Bottega (Francesco Gasbarro)

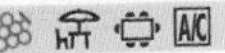

ITALIAN • FRIENDLY In the very heart of Geneva, La Bottega continues its quest to celebrate the best of Italian cuisine. Here, the chef delights guests with authentic dishes teeming with freshness, such as *eliche*, courgette flowers and baby squid, and "Al Capone" pigeon with aubergines, cherries and fresh almonds. A pleasurable dining experience is guaranteed!

Specialities: Tropea Pie. Ravioli with traditional pesto. Fico e Malaga.

Menu 58 CHF (lunch), 110/150 CHF – Carte 60/140 CHF

PLAN: 3-G2 – *Rue de La Corraterie 21 – ☎ 022 736 10 00 – www.labottegatrattoria.com – Closed 1-5 January, 10-13 April, 26 July-6 August, Sunday*

Tosca

TUSCAN • CHIC You'll be immediately won over by Tosca's atmosphere a decor, which is romantically Florentine in feel, a sensation enhanced by t delicious and refined Italian cuisine, with its strong Tuscan influence, and supporting cast of the finest ingredients. A fine selection of Tuscan win and friendly, professional service complete the picture.

Specialities: Beef tartare, hazelnuts and mushrooms. Ravioli de Plin, parmes cream and salmis sauce. Il Latte.

Menu 80 CHF (lunch), 120/180 CHF – Carte 107/132 CHF

PLAN: 1-C3 – *Rue de la Mairie 8 – ☎ 022 707 14 44 – www.tosca-geneva.ch – Closed 1-6 January, 10-15 April, 26 July-30 August, Monday, Sunday, lunch Saturday*

Puccini Café – See restaurant listing

Café des Banques

MODERN FRENCH • BISTRO Having spent 16 years at Windows, where he tablished a solid reputation, Philippe Audonnet has taken over the reins at this egant bistro in the city's old banking district. Here, he expresses his full creativ in a vibrant and convivial atmosphere, creating "bistronomic" cuisine devoid any unnecessary frills.

Carte 49/91 CHF

PLAN: 2-E3 – *Rue de Hesse 6 – ☎ 022 311 44 98 – www.cafedesbanques.com – Closed 27 July-9 August, 21-31 December, lunch Saturday, Sunday*

Chez Philippe

MEATS AND GRILLS • CONTEMPORARY DÉCOR Philippe Chevrier from Domaine de Châteauvieux is the brains behind this huge restaurant inspired New York-style steakhouses. Relaxed atmosphere, meats sourced from the nowned Boucherie du Molard, fish caught by small-scale fishermen, dis cooked over a wood fire, a truly authentic cheesecake and an expansive w list. A real favourite!

Menu 39 CHF (lunch) – Carte 59/129 CHF

PLAN: 3-G1 – *Rue du Rhône 8 – ☎ 022 316 16 16 – www.chezphilippe.ch*

Puccini Café

ITALIAN • FRIENDLY Run with the same passion by the Tosca restaurant tea Puccini's winning formula is also the result of its simplicity and its friendly Tusc *osteria*-style ambience. You'll never tire of the menu here, featuring homema pasta and classic Italian dishes such as *fusilli cacio & pepe* (fusilli pasta w cheese and black pepper), and ricotta and spinach *gnudi* (a type of dumplir all at reasonable prices.

Carte 52/80 CHF

PLAN: 3-G2 – *Tosca, Rue de la Mairie 4 – ☎ 022 707 14 44 – www.tosca-geneva.c Closed 1-6 January, 10-15 April, 26 July-3 August, Monday, lunch Saturday, Sund*

La Cantine des Commerçants

MODERN FRENCH • DESIGN A neo-bistro in the old abattoir district of the c characterised by white and bright green walls, retro decor and a large cour where you can sit and eat. The varied menu is very much in keeping with times: risotto with prawns and wild herbs, grilled fish and pan-fried fillet of be

Menu 25 CHF (lunch), 48/65 CHF – Carte 55/72 CHF

PLAN: 3-G2 – *Boulevard Carl-Vogt 29 – ☎ 022 328 16 70 – www.lacantine.ch – Closed 1-5 January, dinner Monday, lunch Saturday, Sunday*

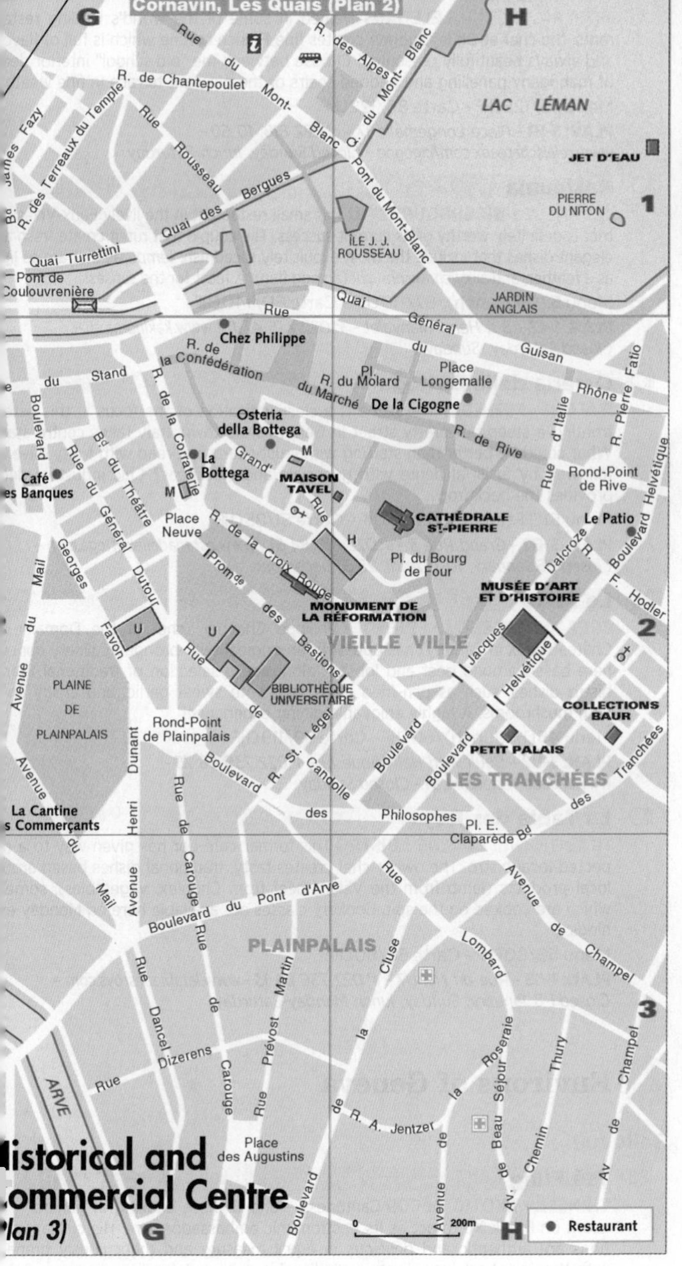

Cornavin, Les Quais (Plan 2)
G
H
Rue du Mont-Blanc
R. des Alpes
Q. du Mont-Blanc
R. de Chantepoulet
LAC LÉMAN
JET D'EAU
R. des Terreaux du Temple
Rue Rousseau
Quai des Bergues
Pont du Mont-Blanc
PIERRE DU NITON
1
ÎLE J. J. ROUSSEAU
Quai Turrettini
Pont de Coulouvrenière
Quai Général Guisan
Rue du Rhône
JARDIN ANGLAIS
Chez Philippe
R. de la Confédération
Bd du Stand
Pl. du Molard
Place Longemalle
R. du Marché
De la Cigogne
R. Pierre Fatio
Osteria della Bottega
R. de la Corraterie
R. de Rive
Rue d'Italie
Boulevard Georges Favon
Rue du Général Dufour
Bd du Théâtre
La Bottega
Grand' Rue
MAISON TAVEL
Rond-Point de Rive
Café des Banques
M
Place Neuve
CATHÉDRALE ST-PIERRE
Le Patio
Boulevard Helvétique
R. de la Croix Rouge
H
Pl. du Bourg de Four
R. Dalcroze
Promde des Bastions
Bd du Mail
MONUMENT DE LA RÉFORMATION
MUSÉE D'ART ET D'HISTOIRE
R. F. Hodler
2
U
VIEILLE VILLE
Jacques
Avenue du Mail
Rue de Candolle
BIBLIOTHÈQUE UNIVERSITAIRE
PLAINE DE PLAINPALAIS
Rond-Point de Plainpalais
COLLECTIONS BAUR
Avenue Henri Dunant
R. St. Léger
Boulevard Helvétique
PETIT PALAIS
Rue des Tranchées
LES TRANCHÉES
Boulevard des Philosophes
La Cantine des Commerçants
Rue de Carouge
Pl. E. Claparède
Boulevard du Pont d'Arve
Rue Lombard
Avenue de Champel
PLAINPALAIS
Rue Prévost Martin
Rue de la Cluse
3
Rue Dancet
Rue Dizerens
Chemin de la Roseraie
Chemin Thury
Av. de Champel
ARVE
Avenue de Beau Séjour
R. A. Jentzer
Place des Augustins
Boulevard de la Cluse
istorical and
ommercial Centre
lan 3)
0 200m
Restaurant

De la Cigogne

MODERN FRENCH • ELEGANT Trained in some of the world's leading resta rants, the chef at De la Cigogne creates fine French cuisine which is full of flavo and always beautifully presented. Choose between the "old school" interior dec of mahogany panelling and padded chairs or the pleasant terrace in fine weath

Menu 65/125 CHF – Carte 86/122 CHF

PLAN: 3-H1 – *Place Longemalle 17 – ☎ 022 818 40 60 – www.relaischateaux.com/cigogne – Closed Sunday, lunch Saturday*

Kakinuma

JAPANESE • NEIGHBOURHOOD This small restaurant in the lively Eaux-Vives d trict is definitely worthy of its current success. The couple that run it create fresh a elegant dishes that include the most exquisitely sliced fish, *tempuras* that are as li as a feather, and silky *chawanmushi* (an egg flan). A feast for the senses!

Menu 52 CHF (lunch), 87/110 CHF – Carte 60/140 CHF

PLAN: 1-C3 – *3 r. Henri-Blanvalet – ☎ 022 735 47 11 – www.kakinuma.ch – Closed Saturday, Sunday*

Osteria della Bottega

ITALIAN • FRIENDLY The name is a clear indication of the focus in this oste fronting a steep but pretty street in Geneva's old town. Italy takes centre sta What could be better than starting with crusty carasau bread with fruity olive followed by fusilli al dente with guanciale and chickpeas? Chic industrial dé provides the backdrop.

Menu 51 CHF (lunch), 62/85 CHF – Carte 51/85 CHF

PLAN: 3-G2 – *Grand Rue 3 – ☎ 022 810 84 51 – www.osteriadellabottega.com – Closed 1-5 January, 10-13 April, 25-31 December*

Le Patio

CREATIVE FRENCH • FRIENDLY Philippe Chevrier (chef at the Domaine Châteauvieux in Satigny) has opted for an original twin-pronged culinary conc here based around beef and lobster, alongside a selection of traditional Fre bistro dishes, such as pan-fried frogs' legs with sweet garlic, and crispy sn with mushrooms. A highly enjoyable dining experience!

Menu 45 CHF (lunch)/60 CHF – Carte 59/119 CHF

PLAN: 3-H2 – *Boulevard Helvétique 19 – ☎ 022 736 66 75 – www.lepatio-restaurant.ch – Closed Sunday*

La Table des Roys

TRADITIONAL CUISINE • BISTRO This former café-bar has given way to a r pected local bistro. The owner-chef creates tasty, traditional dishes based arou local products (lamb from the Valais, beef from Choulex, vegetables), some which are cooked on the spit. Cookery classes are available here on Monday e nings.

Menu 56/80 CHF – Carte 56/80 CHF

PLAN: 1-C3 – *Rue du Nant 7 – ☎ 022 736 64 13 – www.latabledesroys.com – Closed 1-8 January, Sunday, lunch Monday-Saturday*

Environs of Geneva

Bellevue

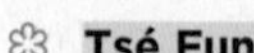

Tsé Fung

CHINESE • EXOTIC DÉCOR Cantonese - and Chinese cooking in general - count on Frank Xu to act as its gastronomic ambassador here. His culinary cr tions are authentic and delicious in equal measure and meticulously prepa with the very best ingredients, including his quite outstanding dim sum, Pek duck and Szechuan eggplant. Exquisite and exotic red and black decor.

Specialities: Red rice rolls with shrimp. Fillet of turbot sautéed with mushrooms, black bean sauce. Mango soup with pomelo and Sago pearls.

Menu 78 CHF (lunch)/188 CHF – Carte 73/284 CHF

PLAN: 1-C1 – *La Réserve, Route de Lausanne 301 – ✆ 022 959 59 59 – www.tsefung.ch*

arouge

❀ Le Flacon

MODERN CUISINE • CONTEMPORARY DÉCOR An enchanting restaurant where the young chef, only just in his 30s, creates delicious cuisine from his open-view kitchen. He demonstrates a fine command of flavour and ingredient combinations, as well as a real eye for detail in his beautifully presented dishes.

Specialities: Marinated sea bass with nectarine and almonds. Beer stein pork, black truffle, Swiss chard and sweet onion. Lemon tart with basil and Timut pepper.

Menu 38 CHF (lunch), 85/115 CHF – Carte 70/107 CHF

PLAN: 1-C3 – *Rue Vautier 45 – ✆ 022 342 15 20 – www.leflacon.ch – Closed 28 July-8 August, 24 December-4 January, Monday, Sunday, lunch Saturday*

Le Bistrot Le Lion d'Or

CLASSIC FRENCH • BISTRO The team from Bistrot Laz Nillo has taken over the restaurant in this hotel dating from 1750. In a light, relaxed atmosphere, they create delicious French dishes full of flavour, such as the chicken salad with lime, rice vinegar and bird's eye chilli pepper. Pleasant terrace in a tranquil setting.

Menu 40 CHF (lunch), 54/86 CHF – Carte 56/82 CHF

PLAN: 1-C3 – *Rue Ancienne 53 – ✆ 022 342 18 13 – www.lebistrot.ch – Closed 1-7 January, 19 December-5 January, Monday, Sunday*

L'Écorce

FRENCH CONTEMPORARY • COSY In this convivial, tastefully furnished restaurant in Carouge's old town the chef conjures up fresh, aromatic cuisine that combines classic and modern dishes such as *mi-cuit* tuna with a beetroot and watermelon bouillon and raw and cooked vegetables. Charming service, plus a small summer terrace.

Menu 34 CHF (lunch), 65/86 CHF

PLAN: 1-C3 – *Rue du Collège 8 – ✆ 022 300 20 98 – www.lecorce-restaurant.ch – Closed 19 July-3 August, 20-31 December, Monday, Sunday*

llonge-Bellerive

Collonge Café

MODERN CUISINE • CONTEMPORARY DÉCOR This reasonably priced auberge is the fiefdom of Angelo and Viviana Citiulo. In this resolutely modern setting of glass, wood and concrete, the cuisine continues to have a foot in Italian cuisine but also has a more global feel thanks to dishes such as soft-shelled crab with a cauliflower and yuzu couscous, and confit of suckling pig with raspberries, spring onions and peppers.

Menu 22 CHF (lunch)/38 CHF – Carte 65/98 CHF

PLAN: 1-D1 – *Chemin du Château-de-Bellerive 3 – ✆ 022 777 12 45 – www.collonge-cafe.ch – Closed 1-8 January, 10-15 April, 27-31 July, 28-31 December, Monday, lunch Tuesday, dinner Sunday*

tigny

❀ Domaine de Châteauvieux (Philippe Chevrier)

CREATIVE • ELEGANT Off the beaten track, standing above the Geneva countryside and its vineyards, this large traditional house teeming with cachet and individual charm cultivates a true sense of excellence! A culinary technician as much as he is an artist, Philippe Chevrier follows a unique path to unearth truly natural flavours that reconnect with the basics. Delightful rooms for those wishing to stay the night.

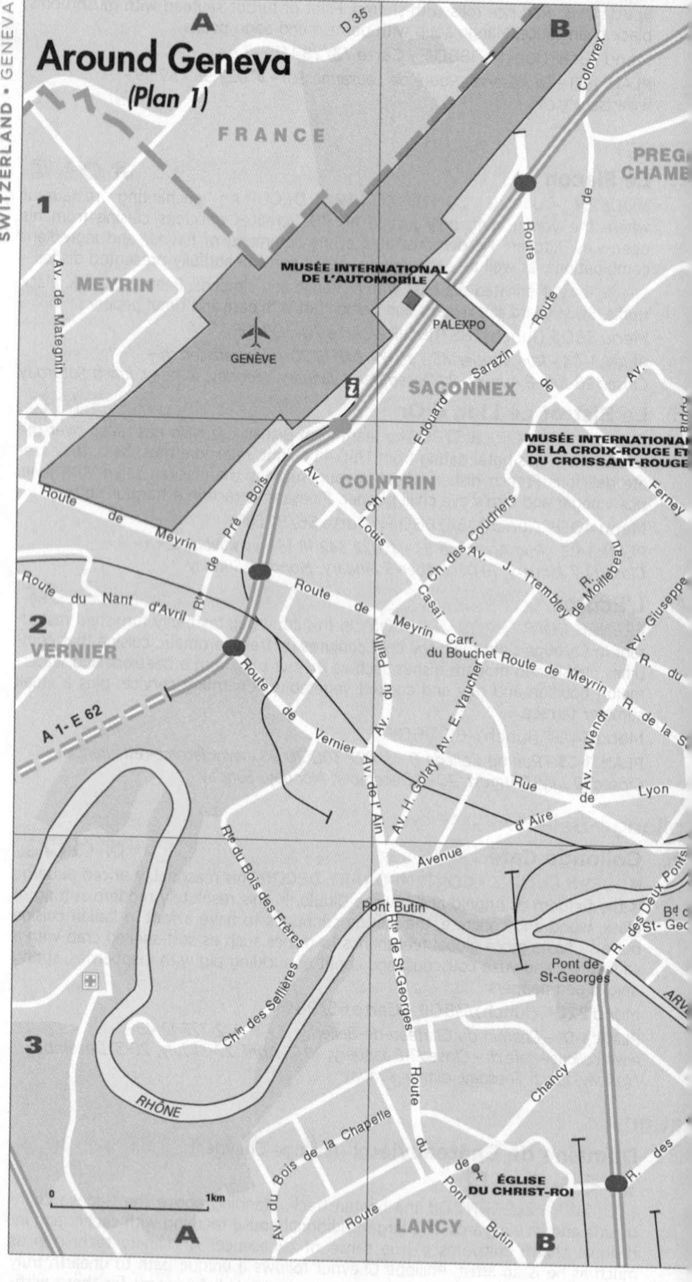
Around Geneva
(Plan 1)
A
B
1
2
3
FRANCE
MEYRIN
VERNIER
SACONNEX
COINTRIN
LANCY
MUSÉE INTERNATIONAL DE L'AUTOMOBILE
PALEXPO
GENÈVE
MUSÉE INTERNATIONAL DE LA CROIX-ROUGE ET DU CROISSANT-ROUGE
ÉGLISE DU CHRIST-ROI
Route de Meyrin
Route du Nant d'Avril
Route de Vernier
Rue de Lyon
Avenue d'Aire
Pont Butin
Pont de St-Georges
Rte de St-Georges
Route du Pont Butin
Route de Chancy
Av. de Mategnin
Route de Colovrex
Route de Ferney
Av. Louis Casaï
Ch. des Coudriers
Av. J. Trembley
R. de Moillebeau
Carr. du Bouchet
Av. du Pailly
Av. E. Vaucher
Av. H. Golay
Av. de l'Ain
Av. Wendt
Av. Giuseppe
Ch. Edouard Sarazin
Av. de Pré Bois
Rte de Pré Bois
Rte du Bois des Frères
Chin des Sellières
Av. du Bois de la Chapelle
R. des Deux Ponts
RHÔNE
A 1- E 62
D 35
0
1km

Tsé-Fung
C
D
Collonge Café
Route d'Hermance
Route de Lausanne
1
LAC LÉMAN
LAIS
ATIONS
ornavin, Les Quais
(Plan 2)
Route de la Capite
Route de Cologny
Paix
France
2
COLOGNY
Route de Vandœuvres
Quai Gustave-Ador
PARC DES
EAUX-VIVES
PARC
DE LA
GRANGE
JET D'EAU
Quai
Route de Frontenex
Ch. de la Gradelle
La Table
des Roys
Kakinuma
Puccini
Café
ST-PIERRE
Route de Chêne
MUSÉE
D'HISTOIRE
NATURELLE
CHÊNE
BOUGERIES
Route de Malagnou
Route du Vallon
3
Ch. Rieu
Ch. du Velours
Route de Florissant
Av. de la Roseraie
Av. Peschier
Av. Louis Aubert
Champel
Ch. Naville
Seymaz
nt des
acias
orical and
mercial Centre
n 3)
de Carouge
Av. de la
Pont de
Fontenette
ROUGE
L'Écorce
Rte de Veyrier
Le Flacon
C
Pont du
Val d'Arve
Rte de Vessy
D
Restaurant

Specialities: Jambonnettes of sautéed frogs' legs, mousseline of potatoes w black garlic and dried tomatoes. Miéral Bresse chicken roasted on the spit serv "en deux services", cardamom gratin with black truffle. Seasonal fruits flambé at your table by maître d' Esteban Valle.

Menu 98 CHF (lunch), 240/310 CHF – Carte 204/282 CHF

Off plan – *Chemin de Châteauvieux 16 – ✆ 022 753 15 11 – www.chateauvieux.ch – Closed 12-21 April, 26 July-11 August, 24-31 December, Monday, Sunday*

Thônex

✿ Le Cigalon (Jean-Marc Bessire)

SEAFOOD • ELEGANT Judging by the fresh fish on the menu, you would be f given for thinking that the Breton coast lies just outside the doors of this rest rant. Le Cigalon has specialised in seafood for over 20 years, with delicacies s as fish soup, scallops and monkfish from Roscoff all featuring on the menu. Ta d'hôte meals for five guests are also available.

Specialities: Ceviche of marinated fish "à la minute". Duo of grilled red mu and squid. Verbena bavaroise, yellow peach cream, white peach sorbet.

Menu 54 CHF (lunch), 70/160 CHF – Carte 90/120 CHF

Off plan – *Route d'Ambilly 39 – ✆ 022 349 97 33 – www.le-cigalon.ch – Closed 1-7 January, 18 July-10 August, Monday, Sunday*

Troinex

✿ La Chaumière by Serge Labrosse

MODERN FRENCH • COSY Serge Labrosse's restaurant is all the enticem you'll need to head out of the city. In its bright interior, savour fine cuisine p pared using the very best ingredients, featuring traditional dishes as well more contemporary creations. A brasserie menu is available for guests in a hu

Specialities: Calamaretti "aller-retour" with artichoke, chorizo and Troinex pe per. Supreme of farm chicken, chanterelles, vin jaune and Anna apple. Ho and lemon millefeuille, lemon sorbet.

Menu 38 CHF (lunch), 75/165 CHF – Carte 68/101 CHF

PLAN: 1-C3 – *Chemin de la Fondelle 16 – ✆ 079 820 56 49 – www.lachaumiere.ch Closed 1-7 January, Monday, Sunday*

ZURICH
ZÜRICH

Juergen Sack/iStock

ZURICH IN...

→ **ONE DAY**
Old Town, Bahnhofstrasse, Zurich West, Grossmünster.

→ **TWO DAYS**
Watch chessplayers on Lindenhof, see Chagall's windows at Fraumünster, Kunsthaus, Cabaret Voltaire, Café Odeon.

→ **THREE DAYS**
Utoquai, Zürichhorn Park, night at the Opera House.

Zurich has a lot of thing going for it. A lot of histor (2,000 years' worth), a lot c water (two rivers and a hug lake), a lot of beauty and, let face it, a lot of wealth. It an important financial an commercial centre, and ha a well-earned reputation fc good living and a rich cultur life. The place strikes a nic balance – it's large enoug to boast some world-class facilities but small enough t hold onto its charm and old-world ambience. The wir dow-shopping here sets it apart from many other Europea cities – from tiny boutiques and specialist emporiums t a shopping boulevard that's famed across the glob

Although it's not Switzerland's political capital, it's the spiritual one because of its pulsing arts scene: for those who might think the Swiss a bit staid, think again – this is where the nihilistic, anti-art Dada movement began. The attractive Lake Zurich flows northwards into the city, which forms a pleasingly symmetrical arc around it. From the lake, the river Limmat bisects Zurich: on its west bank lies the Old Town, the medieval hub, where the stylishly vibrant Bahnhofstrasse shopping street follows the line of the old city walls. Across the Limmat on the east side is the magnificent twin-towered Grossmünster, while just beyond is the charmingly historic district of Niederdorf and way down south, is the city's largest green space, the Zürichhorn Park.

EATING OUT

urich stands out in Switzerland long with Geneva) for its top-class staurants serving international cuine. Zurich, though, takes the prize hen it comes to trendy, cutting-edge aces to dine, whether restaurant or ar, whether along the lakeside or in e converted loft of an old factory. the middle of the day, most locals for the cheaper daily lunchtime enus, saving themselves for the ories of the evening. The city is host many traditional, longstanding alian restaurants, but if you want to try something 'totally Zurcher', you can't do any better than tackle geschnetzeltes with rösti: sliced veal fried in butter, simmered with onions and mushrooms, with a dash of white wine and cream, served with hashed brown potatoes. A good place for simple restaurants and bars is Niederdorf, while Zurich West is coming on strong with its twenty-first century zeitgeist diners. It's custo-mary to round up a small bill or leave up to ten percent on a larger one.

Right bank of the river Limmat

✿✿ The Restaurant

CREATIVE • LUXURY For years now, this stylish restaurant above the roofto of Zürich has been the home of elaborate, creative cuisine full of contrasts ma using only the finest ingredients. Charming service and an excellent wine sel tion. If you fancy trying a little of everything, go for the 5-course amuse-bou menu at lunchtime.

Specialities: Galician crayfish, melon, bronze fennel, coriander and green curry. Bal Brittany turbot in a French dressing. Iced chocolate cake, raspberries, beetroot, ros

Menu 112 CHF (lunch), 198/298 CHF – Carte 163/298 CHF

PLAN: 1-B3 – *The Dolder Grand, Kurhausstrasse 65 – ✆ 044 456 60 00 – www.thedoldergrand.com – Closed 16 February-2 March, 19 July-10 August, Monda Sunday, lunch Tuesday and Saturday*

✿ mesa

MODERN CUISINE • MINIMALIST Tasteful and pleasantly unpretentious, m boasts a friendly atmosphere, great service and excellent, produce-based f that is tasty and full of contrast. Wine lovers will be pleased to hear that e the rare wines on offer here are available by the glass.

Specialities: Kagoshima Wagyu, sea buckthorn, pearl onion. Berglamm, Freg sarda, herbs, black garlic. Rhubarb, wood sorrel, redcurrants.

Menu 55 CHF (lunch), 110/180 CHF

PLAN: 1-A2 – *Weinbergstrasse 75 – ✆ 043 321 75 75 – www.mesa-restaurant.ch – Closed 20 July-13 August, 23-31 December, Monday, Sunday, lunch Tuesday and Saturday*

✿ Ornellaia

ITALIAN • MEDITERRANEAN This gem of a restaurant with its upmarket mod Tuscan interior and professional front-of-house team occupies a building that o housed a bank. Staff in the show kitchen prepare authentic Italian cuisine tha full of imagination and made using the very best produce. Many of the wines the impressive wine list come from the eponymous winery.

Specialities: Home-made mezzelune stuffed with pumpkin and porcini mu rooms served with a veal consommé. Fillet of sole with olives and tomato c sommé. Orange soufflé, orange granita with Grand Marnier and a chocola honey sorbet.

Menu 49 CHF (lunch), 115/140 CHF – Carte 102/151 CHF

PLAN: 2-C2 – *St. Annagasse 2 – ✆ 044 212 00 22 – www.ristorante-ornellaia.ch – Closed 21 July-17 August, Monday, Sunday*

Bauernschänke

COUNTRY COOKING • INN Set in a small alleyway and over 100 years Bauernschänke offers a cosy, rustic interior, fresh regional cuisine and excell value for money – try the marinated zander with Nostrano cucumber and dill. usually here the menu makes no difference between starters, entremets and m courses. Smaller lunchtime menu.

Carte 58/101 CHF

PLAN: 2-D2 – *Rindermarkt 24 – ✆ 044 262 41 30 – www.bauernschaenke.ch – Closed lunch Saturday, Sunday*

Rigiblick - Bistro

MARKET CUISINE • BISTRO This friendly restaurant offers a relaxed bistro a bience. The kitchen team works with regional and seasonal ingredients to cre dishes such as pickled beef fillet with malted bread salad and Brüggli char w broccoli, hazelnuts and saffron. The plant-filled terrace is a pleasant place to The bistro can be reached by taking tram n° 10 and the Rigiblick funicular.

Menu 65/85 CHF – Carte 58/90 CHF

PLAN: 1-B2 – *Germaniastrasse 99 – ✆ 043 255 15 70 – www.restaurantrigiblick.ch – Closed 20 July-9 August*

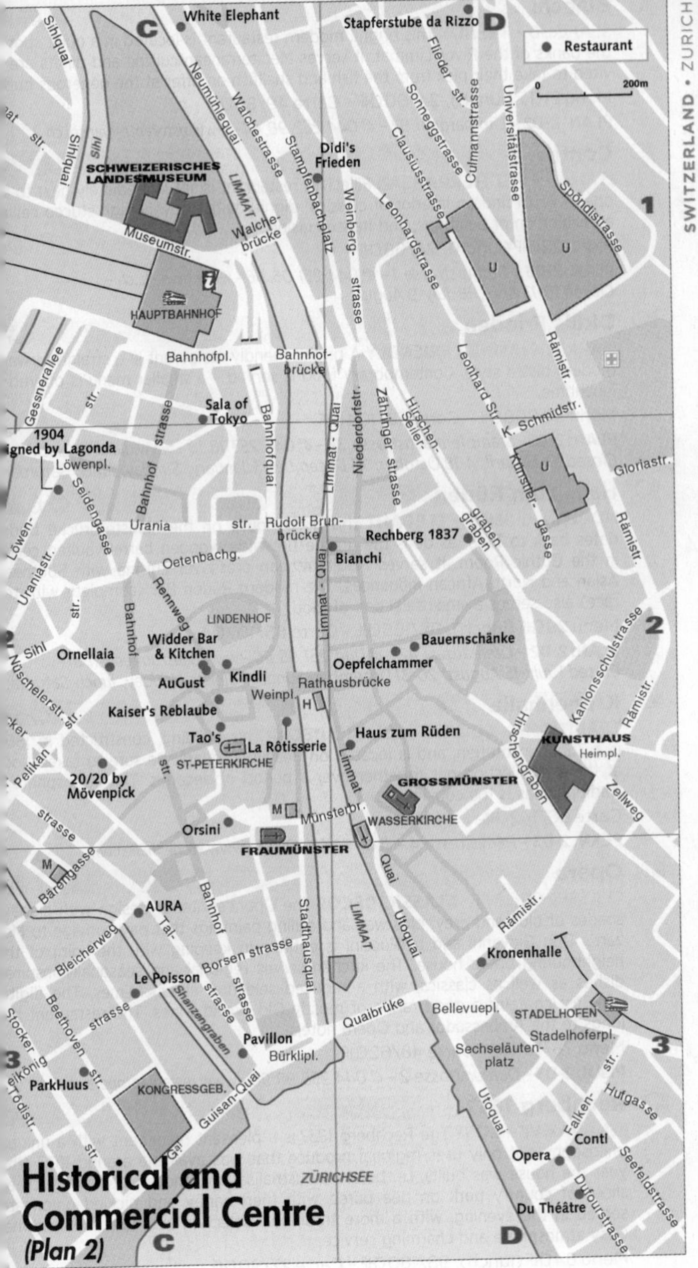
Historical and Commercial Centre
(Plan 2)
Restaurant
0
200m
C
D
1
2
3
White Elephant
Stapferstube da Rizzo
Didi's Frieden
Sala of Tokyo
1904
Rechberg 1837
Bianchi
Bauernschänke
Oepfelchammer
Widder Bar & Kitchen
Ornellaia
AuGust
Kindli
Kaiser's Reblaube
Tao's
La Rôtisserie
Haus zum Rüden
20/20 by Mövenpick
Orsini
AURA
Le Poisson
Pavillon
ParkHuus
Kronenhalle
Conti
Opera
Du Théâtre
SCHWEIZERISCHES LANDESMUSEUM
HAUPTBAHNHOF
LINDENHOF
ST-PETERKIRCHE
GROSSMÜNSTER
WASSERKIRCHE
FRAUMÜNSTER
KUNSTHAUS
STADELHOFEN
KONGRESSGEB.
ZÜRICHSEE
LIMMAT
Sihl
Sihlquai
Neumühlequai
Walchestrasse
Stampfenbachstrasse
Stampfenbachplatz
Weinberg-strasse
Leonhardstrasse
Clausiusstrasse
Sonneggstrasse
Flieder str.
Culmannstrasse
Universitätstrasse
Spöndistrasse
Museumstr.
Walche-brücke
Bahnhofpl.
Bahnhof-brücke
Bahnhofstrasse
Bahnhofquai
Limmat - Quai
Niederdorfstr.
Zähringer strasse
Hirschen-graben
Seiler-graben
Leonhard Str.
K. Schmidstr.
Künstler-gasse
Rämistr.
Gloriastr.
Gessnerallee
Löwenpl.
Seidengasse
Urania str.
Rudolf Brun-brücke
Oetenbachg.
Uraniastr.
Rennweg
Nüschelerstr.
Pelikan strasse
Rathausbrücke
Weinpl.
Münsterbr.
Kantonsschulstrasse
Heimpl.
Zellweg
Hirschengraben
Bärengasse
Tal-strasse
Bleicherweg
Borsen strasse
Stadthausquai
Utoquai
Quai
Shanzengraben
Beethoven str.
Stocker
Quaibrüke
Bellevuepl.
Stadelhoferpl.
Sechseläuten-platz
Bürklipl.
Guisan-Quai
Tödistr.
Falken-str.
Hufgasse
Seefeldstrasse
Dufourstrasse

Bianchi

SEAFOOD • TRENDY This bright, modern restaurant is located in a quiet spot the banks of the River Limmat. It serves Mediterranean cuisine and diners are vited to take their pick from the fish and shellfish on offer at the generous buf

Menu 21CHF (lunch), 24/60CHF – Carte 49/89CHF

PLAN: 2-D2 – *Limmatquai 82 – ✆ 044 262 98 44 – www.ristorante-bianchi.ch*

Conti

ITALIAN • MEDITERRANEAN FilletThis restaurant is set immediately next to opera. You'll find an interior of classical dignity with a lovely high stucco ceili an exhibition of paintings, and Italian cuisine.

Menu 22CHF (lunch), 24/68CHF

PLAN: 2-D3 – *Dufourstrasse 1 – ✆ 044 251 06 66 – www.bindella.ch – Closed 10-13 April, 18 July-9 August*

Didi's Frieden

MARKET CUISINE • FRIENDLY A bright, friendly restaurant in a straightforwa modern bistro style. Contemporary food is served – a smaller menu is offered lunchtime.

Menu 98/108CHF – Carte 63/104CHF

PLAN: 2-C1 – *Stampfenbachstrasse 32 – ✆ 044 253 18 10 – www.didisfrieden.ch – Closed 10-13 April, 4-18 October, 23 December-3 January, Sunday, lunch Saturda*

Haus zum Rüden

MODERN CUISINE • ELEGANT This guild house on the Münsterbrücke brid dates back to 1348, as does the unique 11m-wide wooden barrel-vaulted ceili in the Gothic Room. It serves Mediterranean crossover cuisine with Southe Asian and North African influences. The modern Rüden Bar (complete with te race) also serves a small selection of food.

Menu 29CHF (lunch), 95/165CHF – Carte 65/107CHF

PLAN: 2-D2 – *Limmatquai 42 – ✆ 044 261 95 66 – www.hauszumrueden.ch – Closed 1 July-15 August, 20-31 December, Sunday, dinner Monday, lunch Saturda*

Kronenhalle

TRADITIONAL CUISINE • CLASSIC DÉCOR This building, constructed in 186 is a Zurich institution, and is located on Bellevue Square. Be sure to take a lo at the art collection put together over a period of decades. The atmosphere traditional, as is the cooking.

Carte 66/142CHF

PLAN: 2-D3 – *Rämistrasse 4 – ✆ 044 262 99 00 – www.kronenhalle.com*

Opera

CLASSIC CUISINE • CLASSIC DÉCOR The Opera's interior design with elega shades of blue and grey, plus wall and ceiling paintings that pay homage to M zart's Don Giovanni and to Puccini is entirely in keeping with the spirit of t neighbouring opera house. The kitchen serves regional and seasonally inspire dishes as well as classics, with a reduced selection at lunchtimes. The digi wine list contains a good range of mostly Old World wines. The restaurant b longs to the Ambassador and Opera hotels.

Menu 78/141CHF – Carte 48/62CHF

PLAN: 2-D3 – *Dufourstrasse 2 – ✆ 044 258 98 98 – www.restaurantopera.ch*

Rechberg 1837

INNOVATIVE • COSY The Rechberg 1837 is a pleasant restaurant with a uniqu philosophy – it only uses regional produce that was available around 1837 (th year the house was built), i.e. before industrialisation. Innovative dishes such a slices of country pork on pea puree with fried barley and pickled onion a served in the evening, with a more traditional selection available at lunchtim Cosy atmosphere and charming service.

Menu 64CHF (lunch), 98/160CHF – Carte 27/90CHF

PLAN: 2-D2 – *Chorgasse 20 – ✆ 044 22 18 37 – www.rechberg1837.com – Closed 1-5 January, 27 July-2 August, Sunday, lunch Saturday*

Saltz

INTERNATIONAL • TRENDY The original, modern design takes Switzerland as its theme while the international food concentrates on the essentials. The menu includes burrata with datterini tomatoes, hamachi sashimi, sea bass baked in a salt crust or, if you prefer, a dish of *Zürcher Geschnetzeltes* – veal strips in a cream and white wine sauce.

Menu 54 CHF (lunch), 68/149 CHF – Carte 68/155 CHF

PLAN: 1-B3 – *The Dolder Grand, Kurhausstrasse 65 – ✆ 044 456 60 00 – www.thedoldergrand.com*

Sonnenberg

CLASSIC FRENCH • CHIC The Sonnenberg has been a part of Zurich's gastronomic scene for over 20 years and definitely offers the most beautiful views of the city from both the restaurant and the terrace thanks to its elevated location. Specialities include whole Brüggli trout with nut butter and potato-cucumber salad, as well as classic dishes such as Zurich-style veal and mushroom ragout in a cream sauce, and fillet of pike-perch with saffron and Meaux mustard sauce.

Menu 39 CHF – Carte 44/138 CHF

PLAN: 1-B3 – *Hitzigweg 15 – ✆ 044 266 97 97 – www.dersonnenberg.ch – Closed 10-21 February*

Stapferstube da Rizzo

ITALIAN • RUSTIC Southern Italian Giovanni Rizzo has been calling the shots here at Stapferstube, a well-known Zurich eatery, for some time. As a result, the cooking has a strong Italian feel, as evidenced by the delicious pan-fried squid with garlic, herbs and chilli. The food is served in a friendly, rustic setting and outdoors in summer. Conveniently, the restaurant has its own car park.

Menu 68 CHF (lunch)/79 CHF – Carte 55/111 CHF

PLAN: 2-D1 – *Culmannstrasse 45 – ✆ 044 350 11 00 – www.stapferstube.com – Closed Sunday*

Du Théâtre

TRADITIONAL CUISINE • TRENDY Established in 1890, this fashionable restaurant full of historic charm is located close to the Zurich Opera. It offers traditional and Southeast Asian cuisine ranging from beef tartare to chicken teriyaki with poached egg and mushrooms, as well as 'Sashimi Du Théâtre'. There's a smaller lunchtime menu.

Carte 51/98 CHF

PLAN: 2-D3 – *Dufourstrasse 20 – ✆ 044 251 48 44 – www.du-theatre.ch – Closed 21-31 December, Sunday, lunch Saturday*

White Elephant

THAI • EXOTIC DÉCOR This restaurant in the Marriott Hotel is a must for fans of authentic Thai cuisine. Made with market fresh produce, the food is authentic and authentically spicy! Whatever you do, don't miss the curries.

Carte 60/98 CHF

PLAN: 2-C1 – *Neumühlequai 42 – ✆ 044 360 73 22 – www.whiteelephant.ch*

La Zagra

ITALIAN • COSY A friendly restaurant, La Zagra serves fresh Italian cuisine and delicious pasta that is made on the premises; accompanied by a good selection of Italian wines. Incidentally, *zagra* is the Italian name for the flower of various citrus plants.

Menu 40 CHF (lunch), 60/100 CHF – Carte 58/114 CHF

PLAN: 1-B3 – *Seefeldstrasse 273 – ✆ 044 550 40 00 – www.lazagra.ch – Closed Sunday*

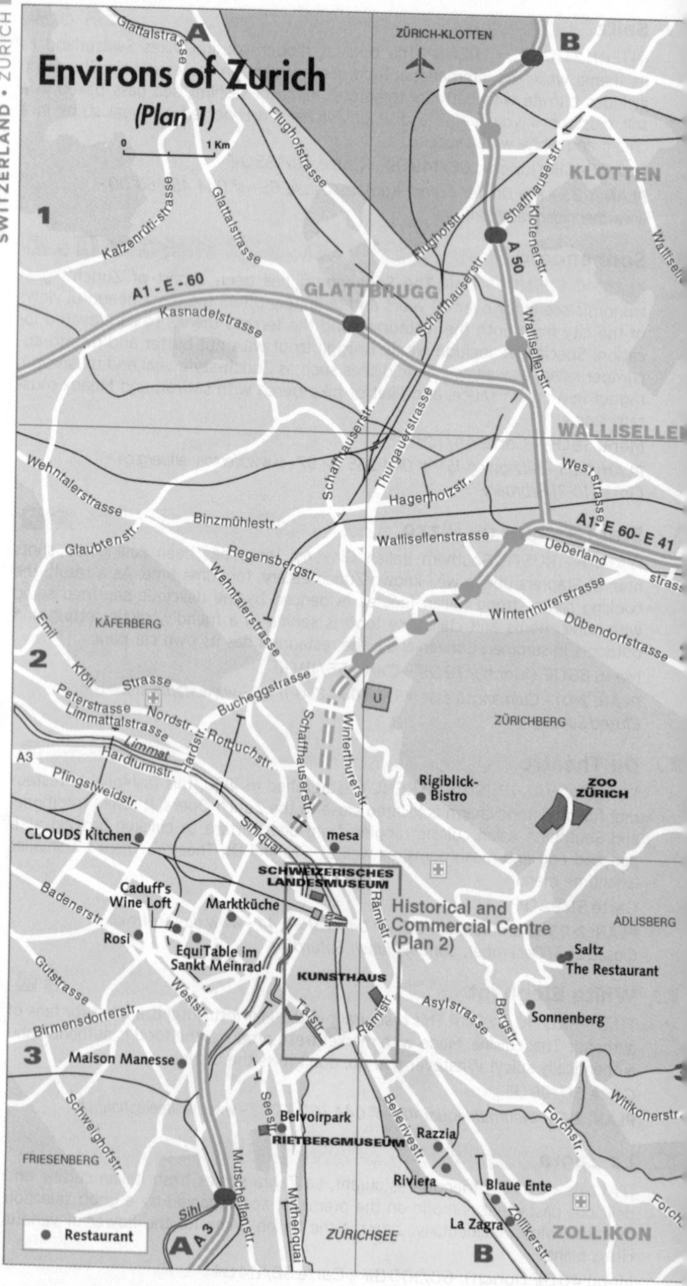

Environs of Zurich
(Plan 1)

0 1 Km

A
B
1
2
3
ZÜRICH-KLOTTEN
KLOTTEN
GLATTBRUGG
WALLISELLEN
KÄFERBERG
ZÜRICHBERG
ZOO ZÜRICH
ADLISBERG
FRIESENBERG
ZOLLIKON
ZÜRICHSEE
Glattalstrasse
Flughofstrasse
Kalzenrüti-strasse
A1 - E - 60
Kasnadelstrasse
Flughofstr.
Shaffhauserstr.
Klotenerstr.
A 50
Schaffhauserstr.
Wallisellerstr.
Thurgauerstrasse
Hagenholzstr.
Weststrasse
A1- E 60- E 41
Wehntalerstrasse
Binzmühlestr.
Glaubtenstr.
Regensbergstr.
Wallisellenstrasse
Ueberlandstrasse
Winterthurerstrasse
Dübendorfstrasse
Emil Klöti Strasse
Bucheggstrasse
Peterstrasse
Nordstr.
Limmattalstrasse
Rotbuchstr.
Hardstr.
Limmat
Hardturmstr.
A3
Pfingstweidstr.
Sihlquai
Winterthurerstr.
U
Rigiblick-Bistro
CLOUDS Kitchen
mesa
SCHWEIZERISCHES LANDESMUSEUM
Historical and Commercial Centre (Plan 2)
Rämistr.
Badenerstr.
Caduff's Wine Loft
Marktküche
Rosi
EquiTable im Sankt Meinrad
KUNSTHAUS
Saltz The Restaurant
Gutstrasse
Weststr.
Talstr.
Asylstrasse
Bergstr.
Sonnenberg
Birmensdorferstr.
Maison Manesse
Witikonerstr.
Forchstr.
Schweighofstr.
Seestr.
Belvoirpark
RIETBERGMUSEUM
Bellerivestr.
Razzia
Riviera
Blaue Ente
Mutschellenstr.
Mythenquai
Sihl
A3
La Zagra
Zollikerstr.
● Restaurant

Left bank of the river Limmat

✿✿ Ecco Zürich

CREATIVE • DESIGN This creative concept is already well known from the Ecco restaurants in Ascona and St. Moritz, but here Stefan Heilemann brings his own personal touch. He cooks innovative food with fine, intelligent contrasts and great depth. The interior is genuinely elegant, while the service is friendly and professional.

Specialities: Alaskan red king crab, carrot, curry, sudachi. Miéral guinea fowl, broccoli, macadamia nut, yuzu. Felchlin Cru Cuba chocolate, sour cherry, cinnamon flower, almond milk.

Menu 160/260 CHF – Carte 85/260 CHF

Off plan – *Atlantis by Giardino, Döltschiweg 234 – ✆ 044 456 55 55 – www.ecco-restaurant.ch – Closed 1-28 January, 20 July-18 August, Monday, Tuesday, lunch Wednesday-Saturday*

✿✿ Pavillon

CLASSIC FRENCH • ELEGANT Star architect Pierre-Yves Rochon designed this elegant Restaurant and the almost 360° glazed rotunda with its country views is wonderful. The exquisite classic cuisine is prepared by Laurent Eperon and includes dishes such as roast sea bass with Périgord truffles.

Specialities: Bouillabaisse. Wild turbot en papillote. Chocolate 1844.

Menu 76 CHF (lunch), 185/205 CHF – Carte 139/246 CHF

PLAN: 2-C3 – *Baur au Lac, Talstrasse 1 – ✆ 044 220 50 22 – www.aupavillon.ch – Closed 15-24 February, 4-19 October, Monday, Sunday, lunch Saturday*

✿ 1904 Designed by Lagonda

MODERN CUISINE • LUXURY The first restaurant in Switzerland to be designed by the British luxury car brand, Lagonda. The distinctive, elegant interior features Carrara marble, wood, leather and steel, plus an eye-catching array of 1904 wooden tubes hanging from the ceiling! The Bar serves breakfast in the mornings, a business lunch at midday and snacks in the afternoons. However, the highlight has to be the dinner menu offering sophisticated, modern and creative cuisine made from the finest ingredients. Excellent wine list.

Specialities: Pea, morel, dashi. Bräggli salmon trout, butterhead lettuce, blueberry. White asparagus, buttermilk, yuzu.

Menu 78 CHF (lunch), 140/220 CHF – Carte 89/98 CHF

PLAN: 2-C2 – *Löwenstrasse 42 – ✆ 071 694 60 50 – www.1904.r-experience.com – Closed Sunday*

✿ EquiTable im Sankt Meinrad

MODERN CUISINE • TRENDY Just as Sankt Meinrad's parent company deals only in fair trade and organic products, so its kitchen team under Fabian Fuchs uses nothing but the best ingredients in its modern cuisine. The whole experience is rounded off by the friendly service and informal atmosphere.

Specialities: Dairy cow, horseradish, apple, radish. Pike perch, onion, Alpine sturgeon caviar. Basil, goat's cream cheese, wild strawberries.

Menu 50 CHF (lunch), 125/190 CHF

PLAN: 1-A3 – *Stauffacherstrasse 163 – ✆ 043 534 82 77 – www.equi-table.ch – Closed 1-9 January, 19 July-15 August, Monday, Sunday, lunch Tuesday-Thursday and Saturday*

✿ Maison Manesse

CREATIVE • RUSTIC If you like relaxed dining, you will enjoy this friendly, informal restaurant and its excellent, creative cuisine prepared using top-quality produce. A must for wine lovers, the 1200 bottles on its wine list include a number of rarities and old vintages. Much reduced lunchtime menu.

Specialities: Jerusalem artichoke truffle terrine with herb salad, macadamia n and Nashi pears. Confit duck leg with semolina dumpling, quince jelly, beetr jus and shiso. Ticino strawberries with hazelnut espuma and malt ice cream.

Menu 120/160 CHF – Carte 75/95 CHF

PLAN: 1-A3 – *Hopfenstrasse 2 – ✆ 444620101 – www.maisonmanesse.ch – Closed Monday, Sunday, lunch Tuesday-Saturday*

20/20 by Mövenpick

MODERN CUISINE • ELEGANT You'll find a casual wine bar on the ground flc here and a gourmet restaurant with elegant, traditional Swiss pine panelling a modern touches on the first. The food is classically based with a certain refir ment and accompanied by some excellent wines, almost all available by t glass. Slightly simpler lunchtime menu.

Specialities: Atlantic black cod with Gillardeau oyster, cucumber, lemon, soy a dill. Scottish Angus entrecôte, house tea, BBQ eel, aubergine and balsamic vin gar. Coconut and passion fruit, pineapple, mango and lemon balm.

Menu 105 CHF (lunch), 135/175 CHF – Carte 125/135 CHF

PLAN: 2-C2 – *Nüschelerstrasse 1 – ✆ 044 211 45 70 – www.20-20.ch – Closed 13 July-18 August, 21-31 December, Monday, Sunday, lunch Saturday*

AuGust

MEATS AND GRILLS • BRASSERIE Diners here enjoy fresh, flavoursome cuisi in a charming, classic brasserie setting. Dishes include some excellent terrin and sausages – try the meatloaf or a dish of venison goulash. Parties of six ar over should book.

Carte 47/122 CHF

PLAN: 2-C2 – *Widder, Rennweg 7 – ✆ 044 224 28 28 – www.au-gust.ch*

Marktküche

VEGETARIAN • TRENDY The name says it all here, where market-fresh veget bles are the order of the day on a menu which is both meat- and fish-free. Moder vegetarian and full of flavour, menu options include artichoke, parsnip, Höngg tru fle, foam and spinach – offered in a lively atmosphere.

Menu 49 CHF (lunch), 70/135 CHF

PLAN: 1-A3 – *Feldstrasse 98 – ✆ 044 211 22 11 – www.marktkueche.ch – Closed 1-6 January, 20 July-10 August, 21-31 December, Monday, Sunday, lunch Tuesday-Thursday and Saturday*

AURA

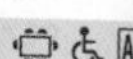

MEATS AND GRILLS • TRENDY A stylishly urban restaurant, a top-flight event venue, a lounge or a club? AURA is a little bit of each, but above all the place t be for lovers of modern crossover cuisine with a weakness for grilled food – jus watch the chefs at work! Located on Paradeplatz in the old stock exchang building.

Carte 64/129 CHF

PLAN: 2-C3 – *Bleicherweg 5 – ✆ 044 448 11 44 – www.aura-zurich.ch – Closed Sunday, lunch Saturday*

Belvoirpark

CLASSIC CUISINE • CLASSIC DÉCOR Belvoirpark is located in a smart, perio villa in the park of the same name and doubles as a teaching facility for Zurich' School of Hotel Management. The interior is elegant, the cuisine predominantl classic. Dishes such as the steak tartare and crêpes Suzette are prepared in th traditional manner at your table.

Menu 119 CHF – Carte 65/119 CHF

PLAN: 1-A3 – *Seestrasse 125 – ✆ 044 286 88 44 – www.belvoirpark.ch – Closed 1-6 January, Monday, Sunday*

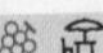

Caduff's Wine Loft

CLASSIC FRENCH • TRENDY This former engineering works serves tasty seasonal cuisine, including pheasant terrine with black chanterelle mushrooms and pistachios, followed perhaps by a raw-milk cheese. The walk-in wine cellar boasts over 2 000 different bottles!

Menu 52 CHF (lunch), 105/135 CHF – Carte 66/118 CHF

PLAN: 1-A3 – *Kanzleistrasse 126 – ✆ 044 240 22 55 – www.wineloft.ch – Closed 1-4 January, Sunday, lunch Saturday*

CLOUDS Kitchen

INTERNATIONAL • CHIC One of Zurich's culinary hotspots, CLOUDS boasts stunning views of the city. But it's not just the spectacle outside that deserves attention. The interesting mix of Mediterranean, Southeast Asian and classic cuisine includes lobster cocktail, slow-cooked pork belly and Japanese sea bass with pak choi. Meanwhile, the Bistro serves simpler fare.

Menu 89/114 CHF – Carte 65/114 CHF

PLAN: 1-A3 – *Maagplatz 5 – ✆ 044 404 30 00 – www.clouds.ch*

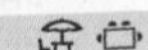

Kaiser's Reblaube

CLASSIC CUISINE • RUSTIC Housed in a building dating from 1260, this restaurant boasts a harmonious setting in a narrow alleyway in the old town. Cosy wine bar on the ground floor, plus a menu featuring classic dishes such as Zurich ragout of veal with a creamy mushroom sauce and rösti potatoes. The Goethe-Stübli on the first floor can be hired for private events.

Menu 58 CHF (lunch), 75/120 CHF – Carte 66/97 CHF

PLAN: 2-C2 – *Glockengasse 7 – ✆ 044 221 21 20 – www.kaisers-reblaube.ch – Closed 20 July-10 August, Monday, Sunday, lunch Saturday*

Kindli

CLASSIC FRENCH • INN The restaurant's charming character comes in part from its wonderful old wood panelling and the bistro-style, communal arrangement of its beautifully laid tables.

Carte 67/116 CHF

PLAN: 2-C2 – *Pfalzgasse 1 – ✆ 043 888 76 76 – www.kindli.ch/restaurant – Closed Sunday*

Orsini

ITALIAN • ELEGANT This elegant restaurant has been serving classic Italian cuisine for over 30 years. The sumptuous poppy design on the carpet, repeated in the filigree motif in the oil paintings on the walls, adds a special touch.

Menu 72 CHF (lunch), 82/160 CHF – Carte 72/160 CHF

PLAN: 2-C2 – *Savoy Baur en Ville, Poststrasse 12 – ✆ 044 215 25 25 – www.orsiniristorante.ch*

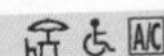

parkhuus

MODERN CUISINE • TRENDY The restaurant here is every bit as contemporary and international as the hotel, and the modern dishes that emerge from the show kitchen are made using good Swiss produce. There is also an impressive glazed wine cellar accessible via a spiral staircase.

Menu 59 CHF (lunch)/69 CHF – Carte 59/121 CHF

PLAN: 2-C3 – *Park Hyatt, Beethoven Strasse 21 – ✆ 043 883 10 75 – www.parkhuus.ch – Closed Sunday, lunch Saturday*

Rosi

COUNTRY COOKING • TRENDY Rosi is friendly, casual, trendy and rustic · popular haunt not just among the locals. This is due not only to its friendly a dedicated staff but also to its ambitious Bavarian and Alpine cuisine, with dis ranging from Obatzter (a savoury cheese spread) to Allgäu Käsepätzle (thim dumplings made with cheese) and pike-perch with Swiss chard, chamomile sc and sea buckthorn oil. Brunch is served at weekends.

Menu 65 CHF – Carte 66/92 CHF

PLAN: 1-A3 – *Sihlfeldstrasse 89 – ✆ 044 291 68 25 – www.rosi.restaurant – Closed lunch Monday-Sunday*

La Rôtisserie

CLASSIC FRENCH • CLASSIC DÉCOR The classically traditional Rôtisse boasts a lovely high-ceilinged dining room with large arched windows and an egant atmosphere and serves French cuisine with Swiss influences. Try the v ravioli with sage foam, the zander Café de Paris or the woodland game. T lovely terrace looks over the River Limmat.

Menu 125/160 CHF – Carte 82/128 CHF

PLAN: 2-C2 – *Storchen, Weinplatz 2 – ✆ 044 227 27 27 – www.storchen.ch*

Sala of Tokyo

JAPANESE • TRENDY Following a move to Zürich's vibrant business and sho ping district, Sala of Tokyo continues to offer authentic Japanese cuisine ma using the very best ingredients. Try the shabu shabu, sushi and sashimi and te pura or the fish and Kobe beef from the robata grill. The designer interior is s ber, modern and upmarket.

Menu 27 CHF (lunch), 100/195 CHF – Carte 32/65 CHF

PLAN: 2-C1 – *Schützengasse 5 – ✆ 044 271 52 90 – www.sala-of-tokyo.ch – Closed 20 July-10 August, 20-31 December, Monday, Sunday*

Tao's

FUSION • EXOTIC DÉCOR Tao's offers a wide range of different dishes from s shi and dim sum to Tao's signature grill and seafood Teppanyaki, as well as Swi favourites such as steak tartare with brioche; all accompanied by an extensive s lection of international wines. The favourably priced lunch menu is also w worth sampling. Stylish, elegant atmosphere with background lounge music, pl an attractive secluded terrace for summer dining.

Menu 48 CHF (lunch)/58 CHF – Carte 62/133 CHF

PLAN: 2-C2 – *Augustinergasse 3 – ✆ 044 448 11 22 – www.taos-zurich.ch – Closed Sunday*

Widder Bar & Kitchen

INTERNATIONAL • COSY The venerable Restaurant Widder is an attractive m of a historic setting and trendy, modern design. Patrons sit in smart dinir rooms or directly opposite the open kitchen. You'll find international dishe such as steamed Asian ravioli with Vietnamese shrimps, seafood sauce and co ander on the menu, plus there's a bar with jazz music and a large selection spirits and whisky.

Menu 38 CHF (lunch), 115/175 CHF – Carte 34/95 CHF

PLAN: 2-C2 – *Widder, Rennweg 7 – ✆ 044 224 24 12 – www.widderhotel.com – Closed 6 July-23 August, Monday, Sunday*

A. Wiewiora/Caiaimages/Photononstop

UNITED KINGDOM

UNITED KINGDOM

LONDON
LONDON

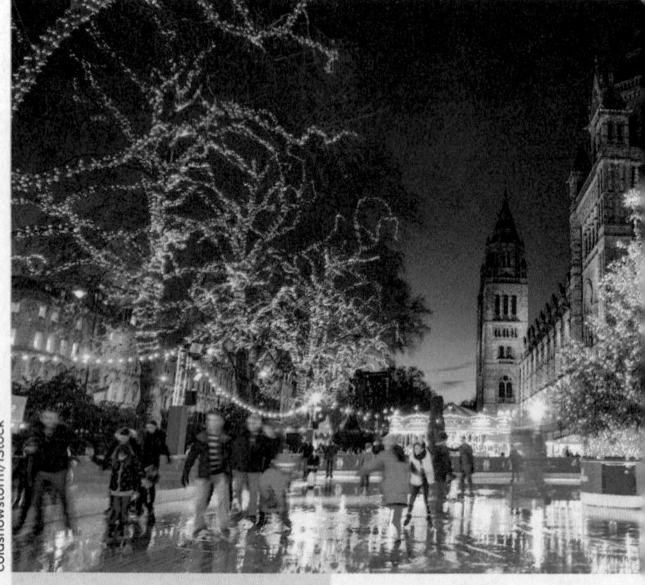
coldsnowstorm/iStock

LONDON IN...

→ **ONE DAY**
British Museum, Tower of London, St Paul's Cathedral, Tate Modern.

→ **TWO / THREE DAYS**
National Gallery, London Eye, Natural History Museum, visit a theatre.

→ **THREE DAYS**
Science Museum, Victoria and Albert Museum, National Portrait Gallery.

The term 'world city' cou have been invented f London. Time zones rac ate from Greenwich, glob finances zap round the Squa Mile and its international re taurants are the equal of an where on earth. A stunnir diversity of population is te tament to the city's famed tc erance; different lifestyles ar languages are as much a pa of the London scene as coc neys and black cabs. London grew over time in a pretty ha hazard way, swallowing up surrounding villages, but retainir an enviable acreage of green 'lungs': a comforting 30 per ce of London's area is made up of open space.

The drama of the city is reflected in its history. From Roman settlement to banking centre to capital of a 19C empire, the city's pulse has never missed a beat; it's no surprise that a dazzling array of theatres, restaurants, museums, markets and art galleries populate its streets. London's piecemeal character has endowed it with distinctly different areas, often breathing down each other's necks. North of Piccadilly lie the playgrounds of Soho and Mayfair, while south is the gentleman's clubland of St James's. On the other side of town are Clerkenwell and Southwark, artisan areas that have been scrubbed down and freshened up. The cool sophistication of Kensington and Knightsbridge is to the west, while a more touristy aesthetic is found in the heaving piazza zone of Covent Garden.

EATING OUT

…ndon is one of the food capitals of …e world, where you can eat everyt…ng from Turkish to Thai and Polish … Peruvian. Those wishing to sample …assic British dishes also have more …oice these days as more and more …efs are rediscovering home-grown …gredients, regional classics and tra…tional recipes. Eating in the capital …n be pricey, so check out good value …e- and post-theatre menus, or try …nch at one of the many eateries that …op their prices, but not their stan…rds, in the middle of the day. "Would …ere in an alehouse in London! I would give all my fame for a pot of ale and safety", says Shakespeare's Henry V. Samuel Johnson agreed, waxing lyrical upon the happiness produced by a good tavern or inn. Pubs are often open these days from 11am to 11pm (and beyond), so this particular love now knows no bounds, and any tourist is welcome to come along and enjoy the romance. It's not just the cooking that has improved in pubs but wine too; woe betide any establishment in this city that can't distinguish its Gamay from its Grenache.

RESTAURANTS FROM A TO Z

A

B

C

D

M

N

O

P

Michelin

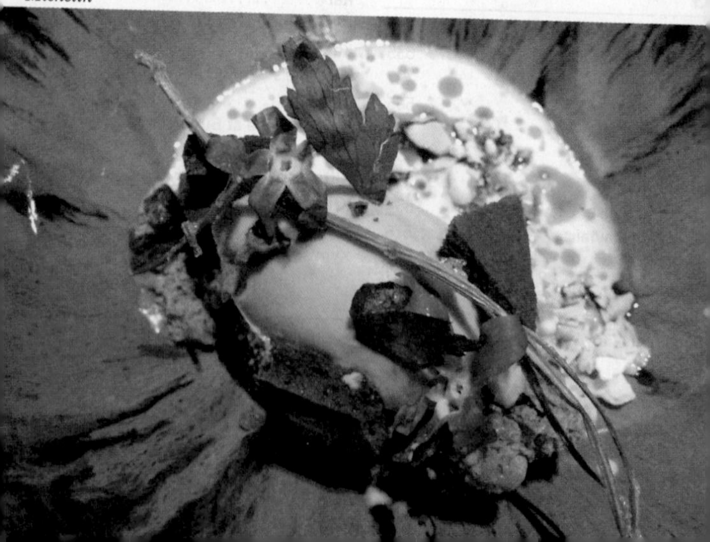

Mayfair

✿✿✿ Alain Ducasse at The Dorchester

FRENCH • ELEGANT Alain Ducasse's elegant London outpost understands th it's all about making the diner feel at ease, so expect service that is as charmi as it is professional. The kitchen uses top-notch British produce to create visua striking dishes with generous flavours. Sauces are a highlight – as is the Rum Bab

Specialities: Dorset crab with celeriac and caviar. Dry-aged beef with artichol and bone marrow. 'Baba like in Monte-Carlo'.

Menu £70 (lunch), £105/185

PLAN: 2-G4 – *Dorchester Hotel, Park Lane – Ⓜ Hyde Park Corner – ✆ 020 7629 8866 – www.alainducasse-dorchester.com – Closed 1-13 January, 10-13 April, 2-25 August, Sunday, Monday, lunch Saturday*

✿✿✿ Sketch (The Lecture Room & Library)

MODERN FRENCH • LUXURY Mourad Mazouz and Pierre Gagnaire's 18C fu house is awash with colour, energy and vim and the luxurious 'Lecture Room Library' provides the ideal setting for the sophisticated French cooking. Rela and enjoy artfully presented, elaborate dishes that provide many varieties of fla vours and textures.

Specialities: 'Perfume of the Earth'. Fricassée of Cornish lobster tail with fres turmeric root. Pierre Gagnaire's 'Grand Dessert'.

Carte £114/126

PLAN: 2-H3 – *9 Conduit Street – Ⓜ Oxford Circus – ✆ 020 7659 4500 – www.sketch.london – Closed Sunday, Monday, lunch Tuesday-Thursday*

✿✿ Le Gavroche (Michel Roux Jnr)

FRENCH • INTIMATE In an age of tedious calorie counting there is somethin exhilarating about Michel Roux and head chef Rachel Humphrey's unapologet cally extravagant French dishes. The ingredients are of the highest order, an the cheese board is one of London's best. A charming service team guide yo through your meal and the hum of satisfaction that pervades the room says all.

Specialities: Soufflé Suissesse. Pigeon d'Anjou. Omelette Rothschild.

Menu £74 (lunch)/178 – Carte £70/180

PLAN: 2-G3 – *43 Upper Brook Street – Ⓜ Marble Arch – ✆ 020 7408 0881 – www.le-gavroche.co.uk – Closed Sunday, Monday, lunch Saturday*

✿✿ Greenhouse

CREATIVE • ELEGANT With its charming setting and elegant appearance, Th Greenhouse is an oasis in the heart of the city. Cooking is underpinned by to quality ingredients and dishes are not only beautifully presented but also tech nically accomplished, with refined, perfectly judged contrasts of texture an flavour.

Specialities: Oeuf noir. Pigeon for two. Seasonal soufflé.

Menu £45 (lunch), £110/155

PLAN: 2-G4 – *27a Hay's Mews – Ⓜ Hyde Park Corner – ✆ 020 7499 3331 – www.greenhouserestaurant.co.uk – Closed 22 December-3 January, Sunday, Monday, lunch Saturday*

✿✿ Hélène Darroze at The Connaught

MODERN CUISINE • LUXURY This historic wood-panelled room was given a contemporary makeover in 2019. Visually appealing dishes are built around one high quality main ingredient and are bold, feminine and full of finesse. The wine list offers an impressive choice and the warm service ensures that the room never feels too formal.

Specialities: Tandoori scallop, carrot, citrus and coriander. Pigeon, foie gras, wild mushroom, turnip and Manuka honey. Signature Baba.

Menu £60 (lunch), £95/185

PLAN: 2-G3 – *Connaught Hotel, Carlos Place* – Ⓜ *Bond Street* – ✆ *020 3147 7200* – *www.the-connaught.co.uk*

✿✿ Umu

JAPANESE • ELEGANT An elegantly dressed restaurant with quiet corners providing intimacy, and the sushi counter, plenty of excitement. The provenance of the ingredients is all-important; choose one of the seasonal kaiseki menus for the full experience. Over 160 different labels of sake.

Specialities: Tuna tartare with yam, myoga and Kaluga caviar. Grade 11 Wagyu beef hoba-yaki with Tokyo leek and miso nut sauce. Charamisu with matcha tea and Ginjo sake.

Menu £50 (lunch)/165 – Carte £100/200

PLAN: 2-H3 – *14-16 Bruton Place* – Ⓜ *Bond Street* – ✆ *020 7499 8881* – *www.umurestaurant.com* – *Closed 22 December-3 January, Sunday*

✿ Gymkhana

INDIAN • INTIMATE If you enjoy Trishna then you'll love Karam Sethi's Gymkhana – that's if you can get a table. Inspired by Colonial India's gymkhana clubs, the interior is full of wonderful detail and plenty of wry touches; ask to sit downstairs. The North Indian dishes have a wonderful richness and depth of flavour.

Specialities: Kid goat methi keema, salli, pao. Wild muntjac biryani with pomegranate and mint raita. Saffron and pistachio kulfi falooda.

Menu £28 (lunch), £85/90 – Carte £35/62

PLAN: 2-H3 – *42 Albemarle Street* – Ⓜ *Green Park* – ✆ *020 3011 5900* – *www.gymkhanalondon.com* – *Closed Sunday*

✿ Hakkasan Mayfair

CHINESE • MINIMALIST If you're coming for lunchtime dim sum then sit on the ground floor; for dinner ask for a table in the moodily lit and altogether sexier basement. All the Hakkasan signature dishes can be found on the extensive menu; cooking is sophisticated, well-balanced and extremely tasty – and cocktails add to the fun.

Specialities: Crispy duck salad with pomelo, peanut and shallot. Stir-fried rib-eye of beef with black pepper. Exotic fruit selection with jasmine syrup.

Menu £32/38 – Carte £38/120

PLAN: 2-H3 – *17 Bruton Street* – Ⓜ *Green Park* – ✆ *020 7907 1888* – *www.hakkasan.com*

✿ Hide

MODERN BRITISH • DESIGN A collaboration between Hedonism Wines and chef Ollie Dabbous; the striking decor is inspired by the park opposite. 'Above' allows you to experience the full repertoire of this talented kitchen, whose immaculately crafted dishes emphasise the natural flavours of ingredients; 'Ground' is a slightly more casual, all-day affair; while 'Below' is a basement cocktail bar.

Specialities: Nest egg. Wagyu with Oscietra caviar and rye in a warm oxtail broth. Sugared almond soufflé with preserved apricots and osmanthus ice cream.

Menu £38 (lunch)/115 – Carte £47/90

PLAN: 2-H4 – *85 Piccadilly* – Ⓜ *Green Park* – ✆ *020 3146 8666* – *www.hide.co.uk*

A

2 MAYFAIR, SOHO AND ST. JAMES'S
3 STRAND & COVENT GARDEN
4 BELGRAVIA AND VICTORIA, HYDE PARK AND KNIGHTSBRIDGE
5 REGENT'S PARK & MARYLEBONE
6 CAMDEN

B

7 BAYSWATER & MAIDA VALE
8 CITY OF LONDON, SOUTHWARK
9 CHELSEA, SOUTH KENSINGTON AND EARL'S COURT
10 KENSINGTON AND NORTH KENSINGTON
11 CLERKENWELL & FINSBURY

1
High Rd
High Road
Church Rd
Manor Park Rd
Willesden Green
Walm Lane
Kilburn
A 5
Willesden Lane
West End Lane
West Hampstead
Finchley Road
Finchley Road
Fitzjohn's Av.
Hampstead
A 502
CAMDEN
Swiss Cottage
Adelaide Rd
St John's Wood
A 41
Prince Albert
Soutine
REGE
PA
Maida Vale
Kilburn Park
Queen's Park
Kensal Green
Harrow Road
A 404
Oak Lane
Willesden Junction
A 219
Scrubs Lane
10
A 404
Harrow Road
Ladbroke Grove
7
East Acton
WORMWOOD SCRUBS
A 40
Westway
A 40
PADDINGTON
Edgware Road
A 5
Marylebo
5
2
EALING
Wood Lane
A 3220
Endo at The Rotunda
The Vale
Uxbridge Road
Bayswater Road
HYDE PARK
Park
Goldhawk Road
A 402
Holland Road
KENSINGTON GARDEN
Kensington Road
4
9
Kensington High St.
VICTORIA AND ALBERT MUSEUM
Turnham Green
Stamford Brook
Hammersmith
Ravenscourt Park
La Trompette
A 4
Great West Rd
Talgarth Road
Warwick Rd
Cromwell Road
HOUNSLOW
Barons Court
West Kensington
Old Brompton Road
HAMMERSMITH AND FULHAM
Fulham Palace Road
Lillie Road
River Café
Castelnau
A 306
Dawes Rd
Road
Fulham Road
King's Road
Chelsea Embankment
BATTERSEA PARK
A 3220
A 304
Fulham
3
RICHMOND UPON THAMES
New King's Road
A 308
Wandsworth Bridge Rd
THAMES
Battersea
Rd
York
WANDSWORTH
Putney Bridge
HURLINGHAM PARK
A 205
Upper Richmond Road
WANDSWORTH PARK
A 3
Battersea Rise
East Putney

● Restaurant

A

B

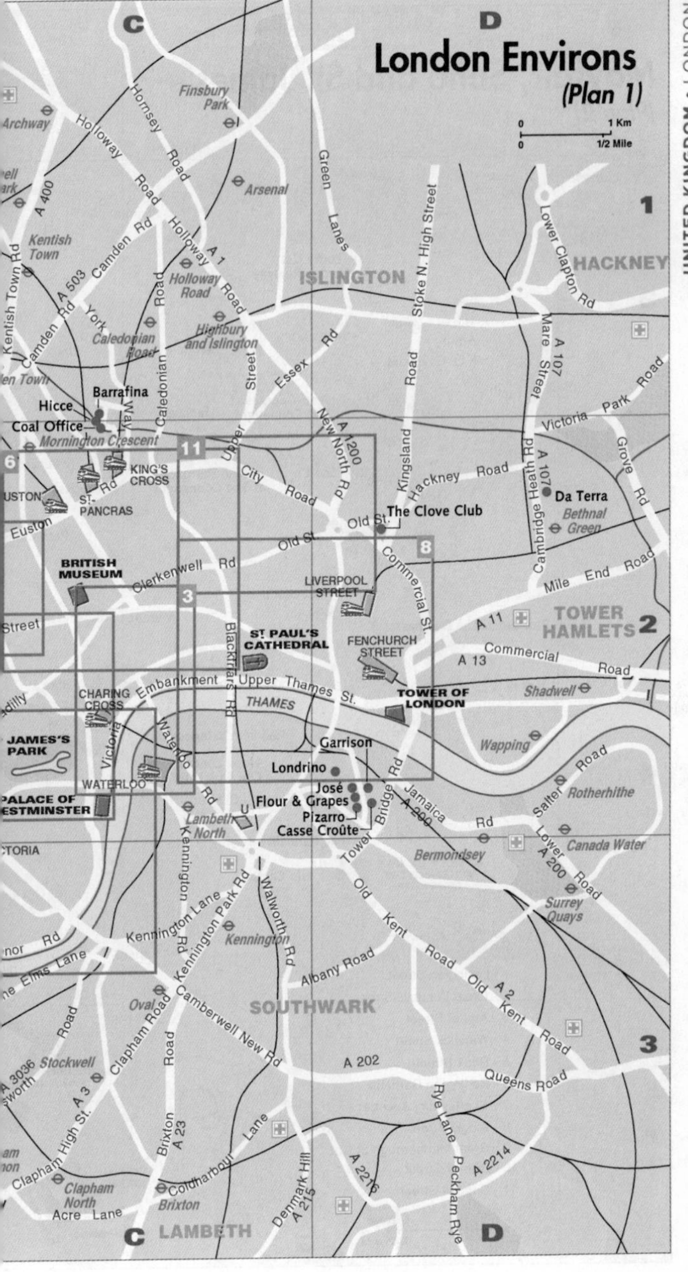
London Environs
(Plan 1)
Barrafina
Hicce
Coal Office
The Clove Club
Da Terra
Garrison
Londrino
José
Flour & Grapes
Pizarro
Casse Croûte
ISLINGTON
HACKNEY
TOWER HAMLETS
SOUTHWARK
LAMBETH
BRITISH MUSEUM
ST. PAUL'S CATHEDRAL
TOWER OF LONDON
KING'S CROSS
ST. PANCRAS
LIVERPOOL STREET
FENCHURCH STREET
CHARING CROSS
WATERLOO
THAMES

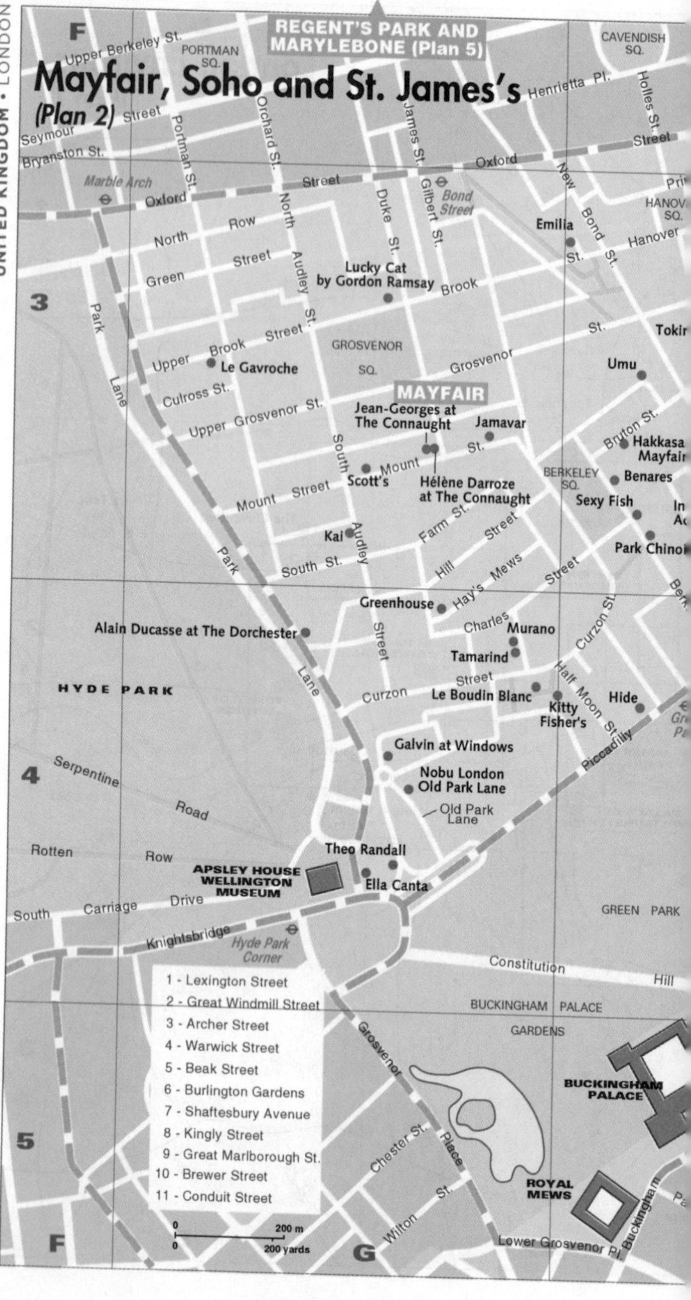
Mayfair, Soho and St. James's
(Plan 2)
REGENT'S PARK AND MARYLEBONE (Plan 5)
MAYFAIR
Lucky Cat by Gordon Ramsay
Le Gavroche
Emilia
Umu
Jean-Georges at The Connaught
Jamavar
Hakkasa Mayfair
Scott's
Hélène Darroze at The Connaught
Benares
Sexy Fish
Kai
Park Chino
Greenhouse
Alain Ducasse at The Dorchester
Murano
Tamarind
Le Boudin Blanc
Kitty Fisher's
Hide
Galvin at Windows
Nobu London Old Park Lane
Theo Randall
Ella Canta
APSLEY HOUSE WELLINGTON MUSEUM
HYDE PARK
GREEN PARK
BUCKINGHAM PALACE GARDENS
BUCKINGHAM PALACE
ROYAL MEWS
1 - Lexington Street
2 - Great Windmill Street
3 - Archer Street
4 - Warwick Street
5 - Beak Street
6 - Burlington Gardens
7 - Shaftesbury Avenue
8 - Kingly Street
9 - Great Marlborough St.
10 - Brewer Street
11 - Conduit Street
0 200 m
0 200 yards

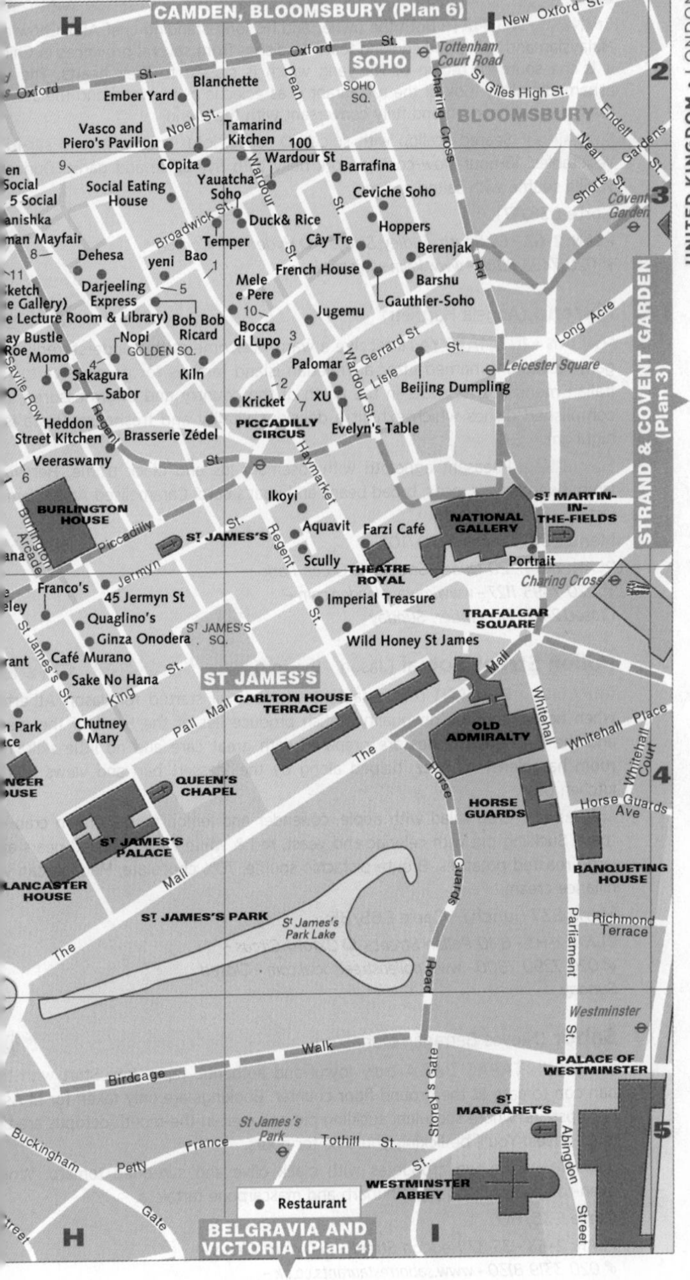

CAMDEN, BLOOMSBURY (Plan 6)
SOHO
BLOOMSBURY
ST JAMES'S
STRAND & COVENT GARDEN (Plan 3)
BELGRAVIA AND VICTORIA (Plan 4)
Blanchette
Ember Yard
Vasco and Piero's Pavilion
Tamarind Kitchen
Copita
Wardour St
Barrafina
Social Eating House
Yauatcha Soho
Ceviche Soho
Duck& Rice
Hoppers
Temper
Cây Tre
Berenjak
Dehesa
yeni
Bao
French House
Barshu
Darjeeling Express
Mele e Pere
Gauthier-Soho
Bob Bob Ricard
Jugemu
Bocca di Lupo
Nopi
Momo
Sakagura
Sabor
Kiln
Palomar
Beijing Dumpling
Kricket
XU
Evelyn's Table
Heddon Street Kitchen
Brasserie Zédel
Veeraswamy
Ikoyi
Aquavit
Farzi Café
Scully
Portrait
Franco's
45 Jermyn St
Imperial Treasure
Quaglino's
Ginza Onodera
Wild Honey St James
Café Murano
Sake No Hana
Chutney Mary
PICCADILLY CIRCUS
BURLINGTON HOUSE
NATIONAL GALLERY
ST MARTIN-IN-THE-FIELDS
THEATRE ROYAL
TRAFALGAR SQUARE
CARLTON HOUSE TERRACE
OLD ADMIRALTY
QUEEN'S CHAPEL
HORSE GUARDS
ST JAMES'S PALACE
LANCASTER HOUSE
BANQUETING HOUSE
ST JAMES'S PARK
St James's Park Lake
PALACE OF WESTMINSTER
ST MARGARET'S
WESTMINSTER ABBEY
Tottenham Court Road
Leicester Square
Charing Cross
Westminster
St James's Park
Restaurant

Kai

CHINESE • INTIMATE Both the owner and his long-standing chef Alex Chow a Malaysian and, while the cooking features dishes from several provinces in Chir it is the southern region of Nanyang which is closest to their hearts. The u ashamedly glitzy look of the restaurant is as eclectic as the food and the servi team are switched on and fully conversant with the menu.

Specialities: Seared scallop with spicy XO sauce, lotus root crisp and stir-fri vegetables. 18-hour slow-cooked pork belly with five spice and garlic. Durian vanilla soufflé with salted caramel.

Carte £38/171

PLAN: 2-G3 – *65 South Audley Street* – *Hyde Park Corner* – *020 7493 8988* – *www.kaimayfair.co.uk*

Murano (Angela Hartnett)

ITALIAN • INTIMATE You'll receive a warm welcome at this understatedly ele gant restaurant, named after a Venetian island famous for its glassware. Th Italian menu has its roots in the north of the country and offers assured, ac complished dishes which exhibit a delicious vitality and freshness. Pasta is highlight.

Specialities: Pheasant agnolotti with rosemary jus and black truffle. Herdwic lamb, sweetbreads, peas, broad beans and goat's curd. Caramelised Amalfi lemo tart.

Menu £32 (lunch), £70/105

PLAN: 2-G4 – *20 Queen Street* – *Green Park* – *020 7495 1127* – *www.muranolondon.com* – *Closed 24-28 December, Sunday*

Pollen Street Social (Jason Atherton)

CREATIVE • ELEGANT The restaurant where it all started for Jason Atherto when he went solo. Top quality British produce lies at the heart of the men and the innovative dishes are prepared with great care and no little skill. Th room has plenty of buzz, helped along by the 'dessert bar' and views of th kitchen pass.

Specialities: Crab salad with apple, coriander and lemon purée, brown crab or toast. Suckling pig with celeriac and yeast, red & white wine poached pears an lardo roasted potatoes. Bronte pistachio soufflé, 70% chocolate, Madagascan va- nilla ice cream.

Menu £37 (lunch) – Carte £65/85

PLAN: 2-H3 – *8-10 Pollen Street* – *Oxford Circus* – *020 7290 7600* – *www.pollenstreetsocial.com* – *Closed Sunday*

Sabor (Nieves Barragán Mohacho)

SPANISH • TAPAS BAR A truly joyful and authentic tapas bar. Start with the pan con tomate at the ground floor counter. Bookings are only taken for El Asa- dor upstairs, where succulent suckling pig and melt-in-the-mouth octopus are the must-haves. You'll be licking your lips for hours.

Specialities: Payoyo croquetas with black olive and sun-dried tomato. Wood oven-roasted suckling pig. Rhubarb and mascarpone tartaleta.

Carte £35/60

PLAN: 2-H3 – *35-37 Heddon Street* – *Oxford Circus* – *020 3319 8130* – *www.saborrestaurants.co.uk* – *Closed 23 December-2 January, dinner Sunday*

✿ Veeraswamy

INDIAN • DESIGN It may have opened in 1926 but this celebrated Indian restaurant keeps producing wonderfully authentic and satisfying dishes from all parts of the country; dishes inspired by royal recipes are worth exploring. The room is awash with colour and is run with charm and obvious pride; ask for a window table.

Specialities: Tandoori green prawns. Lamb rogan josh. Rose kulfi.

Menu £45/65 – Carte £37/75

PLAN: 2-H3 – *Victory House, 99 Regent Street* – Ⓜ *Piccadilly Circus* – ✆ *020 7734 1401* – *www.veeraswamy.com*

Benares

INDIAN • CHIC Set in a commanding location in the heart of Berkeley Square; enjoy Indian street food and cocktails in the lounge, or dine from the à la carte or tasting menus in the lively restaurant. British ingredients like Scottish salmon and New Forest vension feature, as do techniques like pickling and preserving.

Menu £29 (lunch), £50/98 – Carte £70/95

PLAN: 2-H3 – *12a Berkeley Square House, Berkeley Square* – Ⓜ *Green Park* – ✆ *020 7629 8886* – *www.benaresrestaurant.com* – *Closed lunch Sunday*

Black Roe

WORLD CUISINE • BISTRO A dark and moody spot offering appealing, flavoursome dishes with Pacific Rim influences: choose from the likes of sashimi, gyoza and ramen, as well as more substantial dishes cooked on a Kiawe wood grill. Add in a buzzy atmosphere and decent cocktails and you have all the elements for a fun night out.

Menu £60/75 – Carte £25/72

PLAN: 2-H3 – *4 Mill Street* – Ⓜ *Oxford Circus* – ✆ *020 3794 8448* – *www.blackroe.com* – *Closed Sunday*

Bombay Bustle

INDIAN • ELEGANT Tiffin tin carriers on Mumbai's railways inspired Jamavar's second London restaurant. A charming train theme runs through it; the ground floor is the livelier; downstairs is more 'first class'. Before a curry, biryani or dish from the tandoor order some tasting plates, made from family recipes.

Menu £28 (lunch), £55/65 – Carte £31/49

PLAN: 2-H3 – *29 Maddox Street* – Ⓜ *Oxford Circus* – ✆ *020 7290 4470* – *www.bombaybustle.com*

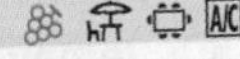

Le Boudin Blanc

FRENCH • RUSTIC Appealing, lively French bistro in Shepherd Market, spread over two floors. Satisfying French classics and country cooking are the draws, along with authentic Gallic service. Good value lunch menu.

Menu £19 (lunch) – Carte £30/66

PLAN: 2-G4 – *5 Trebeck Street* – Ⓜ *Green Park* – ✆ *0207 499 3292* – *www.boudinblanc.co.uk*

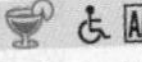

Ella Canta

MEXICAN • DESIGN Martha Ortiz is one of Mexico's most celebrated chefs – and she also has a London outpost at the InterContinental Hotel on Park Lane. Cooking draws on themes of history, philosophy and fantasy to create dishes that are colourful, creative and original. Staff are charming – and there's a great drinks list too.

Menu £25 (lunch) – Carte £34/63

PLAN: 2-G4 – *InterContinental London Park Lane Hotel, 1 Hamilton Place, Park Lane* – Ⓜ *Hyde Park Corner* – ✆ *020 7318 8715* – *www.ellacanta.com* – *Closed dinner Sunday, lunch Monday*

Emilia

ITALIAN • MINIMALIST From the same stable as Portland comes this bright, ha sle-free restaurant adjoining Bonhams auction house. The cooking is influenced the region of Emilia-Romagna – hence the name; the pasta dishes are standou The ground floor wine bar serves an abridged version of the same menu.

Carte £31/70

PLAN: 2-H3 – *7 Haunch of Venison Yard* – Ⓜ *Bond Street* – ✆ *020 7468 5868* – *www.emiliarestaurant.co.uk* – *Closed 23 December-2 January, Sunday*

Galvin at Windows

MODERN CUISINE • FRIENDLY The cleverly laid out room makes the most the spectacular views across London from the 28th floor of the Hilton Hot There's a classical French base to the menu but the Korean chef also incorporat influences from his homeland. Service is relaxed and friendly.

Menu £37 (lunch), £82/119

PLAN: 2-G4 – *London Hilton Hotel, 22 Park Lane* – Ⓜ *Hyde Park Corner* – ✆ *020 7208 4021* – *www.galvinatwindows.com* – *Closed dinner Sunday*

Goodman Mayfair

MEATS AND GRILLS • BRASSERIE A worthy attempt at recreating a New Yo steakhouse; all leather and wood and macho swagger. Beef is dry- or wet-age in-house and comes with a choice of four sauces; rib-eye is the speciality.

Menu £25 (lunch) – Carte £31/107

PLAN: 2-H3 – *26 Maddox Street* – Ⓜ *Oxford Circus* – ✆ *020 7499 3776* – *www.goodmanrestaurants.com* – *Closed Sunday*

Heddon Street Kitchen

MODERN CUISINE • BRASSERIE Gordon Ramsay's follow up to Bread Street spread over two floors and is about all-day dining: breakfast covers all taste there's weekend brunch, and an à la carte offering an appealing range of Euro pean dishes executed with palpable care.

Carte £35/68

PLAN: 2-H3 – *3-9 Heddon Street* – Ⓜ *Oxford Circus* – ✆ *020 7592 1212* – *www.gordonramsayrestaurants.com*

Indian Accent

INDIAN • ELEGANT The third branch, after New Delhi and NYC, is set over tw levels, with a bright, fresh look. The kitchen takes classic dishes from all region of India and blends them with European and Asian notes and techniques. The re sulting dishes are colourful, sophisticated and full of flavour.

Menu £80/85 – Carte £41/56

PLAN: 2-H3 – *16 Albemarle Street* – Ⓜ *Green Park* – ✆ *020 7629 9802* – *www.indianaccent.com*

Jamavar

INDIAN • EXOTIC DÉCOR Leela Palaces & Resorts are behind this smartly dressed Indian restaurant. The menus, including vegetarian, look to all parts of In dia, with a bias towards the north. The 'small plates' section includes Malaba prawns, and kid goat shami kebab; from the tandoor the stone bass tikka is a must; and the biryanis are also good.

Menu £24 (lunch), £60/80 – Carte £34/56

PLAN: 2-G3 – *8 Mount Street* – Ⓜ *Bond Street* – ✆ *020 7499 1800* – *www.jamavarrestaurants.com*

Jean-Georges at The Connaught

MODERN CUISINE • INTIMATE Low-slung bespoke marble-topped tables and comfy sofas make this room at the front of The Connaught hotel somewhere be- tween a salon and a restaurant. It has something for all tastes, from Asian-in- spired dishes to fish and chips. The truffle-infused pizza is a best seller.

Menu £88 – Carte £54/124

PLAN: 2-G3 – *Connaught Hotel, Carlos Place* – Ⓜ *Bond Street* – ✆ *020 7107 8861* – *www.the-connaught.co.uk*

Kanishka

INDIAN • INTIMATE The focus is on north east India at this boldly decorated restaurant from chef Atul Kochhar. Chillies play a prominent role in the cooking; the chicken tikka pie is a speciality; and side dishes like Angoori hing aloo are well worth ordering. The ground floor is more fun than the basement level.

Menu £29/69 – Carte £37/52

PLAN: 2-H3 – *17-19 Maddox Street – Ⓜ Oxford Circus – ✆ 020 3978 0978 – www.kanishkarestaurant.com – Closed lunch Sunday*

Kitty Fisher's

MODERN CUISINE • BISTRO Warm, intimate and unpretentious restaurant – the star of the show is the wood grill which gives the dishes added depth. Named after an 18C courtesan, presumably in honour of the profession for which Shepherd Market was once known.

Carte £38/68

PLAN: 2-H4 – *10 Shepherd Market – Ⓜ Green Park – ✆ 020 3302 1661 – www.kittyfishers.com – Closed Sunday*

Lucky Cat by Gordon Ramsay

ASIAN • CHIC Gordon Ramsay's foray into Asian culture is a moody, masculine space in the former Maze, with a striking bar, a banging soundtrack and a cool, fun feel. Accomplished Japanese and Chinese dishes blend British ingredients and are designed for sharing; the bonito fried duck leg bao is a must-try.

Menu £36 (lunch), £70/125 – Carte £35/75

PLAN: 2-G3 – *10 Grosvenor Square – Ⓜ Marble Arch – ✆ 020 7107 0000 – www.gordonramsayrestaurants.com*

Momo

MOROCCAN • EXOTIC DÉCOR An authentic Moroccan atmosphere comes courtesy of the antiques, berber rugs, gold seating and moucharabieh wooden screens – you'll feel you're eating near the souk. Go for the classic dishes: briouats, pigeon pastilla, mechoui, and tagines with mountains of fluffy couscous.

Menu £25 (lunch), £45/80 – Carte £25/100

PLAN: 2-H3 – *25 Heddon Street – Ⓜ Oxford Circus – ✆ 020 7434 4040 – www.momoresto.com*

No 5 Social

MODERN BRITISH • ELEGANT What was formerly Little Social now sports a smart, stylish look, with on-trend copper, dark wood, and duck egg blue upholstery ensuring it fits in perfectly with its Mayfair surroundings. The seasonal menu name-checks British regions and suppliers, and dishes are modern and creative with plenty of flavour.

Menu £25 – Carte £42/60

PLAN: 2-H3 – *5 Pollen Street – Ⓜ Oxford Circus – ✆ 020 7870 3730 – www.no5social.com – Closed Sunday*

Nobu London Old Park Lane

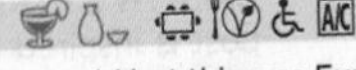

JAPANESE • TRENDY Nobu restaurants are now all over the world but this was Europe's first and opened in 1997. It retains a certain exclusivity and is buzzy and fun. The menu is an innovative blend of Japanese cuisine with South American influences.

Carte £30/95

PLAN: 2-G4 – *Metropolitan by COMO Hotel, 19 Old Park Lane – Ⓜ Hyde Park Corner – ✆ 020 7447 4747 – www.noburestaurants.com*

Park Chinois

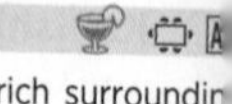

CHINESE • EXOTIC DÉCOR Old fashioned glamour, strikingly rich surroundin and live music combine to great effect at this sumptuously decorated restaura The menu traverses the length of China, with dim sum at lunchtimes and aft noon tea at weekends.

Menu £30 (lunch) – Carte £40/105

PLAN: 2-H3 – *17 Berkeley Street* – Ⓜ *Green Park* – ✆ *020 3327 8888* – *www.parkchinois.com*

Sakagura

JAPANESE • EXOTIC DÉCOR A contemporary styled Japanese restaurant p owned by the Japan Centre and Gekkeikan, a sake manufacturer. Along with impressive drinks list is an extensive menu covering a variety of styles; highligh include the skewers cooked on the robata charcoal grill.

Carte £27/65

PLAN: 2-H3 – *8 Heddon Street* – Ⓜ *Oxford Circus* – ✆ *020 3405 7230* – *www.sakaguralondon.com*

Scott's

SEAFOOD • ELEGANT Scott's is proof that a restaurant can have a long, prou history and still be fashionable, glamorous and relevant. It has a terrific clubb atmosphere and if you're in a two then the counter is a great spot. The choic of prime quality fish and shellfish is impressive.

Carte £36/89

PLAN: 2-G3 – *20 Mount Street* – Ⓜ *Bond Street* – ✆ *020 7495 7309* – *www.scotts-restaurant.com*

Sexy Fish

ASIAN • DESIGN Everyone will have an opinion about the name but what's ir disputable is that this is a very good looking restaurant, with works by Fran Gehry and Damien Hirst, and a stunning ceiling by Michael Roberts. The fis comes with various Asian influences but don't ignore the meat dishes like th beef rib skewers.

Menu £36 (lunch) – Carte £35/60

PLAN: 2-H3 – *4-6 Berkeley Square* – Ⓜ *Green Park* – ✆ *020 3764 2000* – *www.sexyfish.com*

Sketch (The Gallery)

MODERN CUISINE • CHIC The striking 'Gallery' has a smart look from India Mah davi and artwork from David Shrigley. At dinner the room transmogrifies from ar gallery to fashionable restaurant, with a menu that mixes the classic, the moderr and the esoteric.

Menu £59 (lunch) – Carte £38/109

PLAN: 2-H3 – *9 Conduit Street* – Ⓜ *Oxford Circus* – ✆ *020 7659 4500* – *www.sketch.london*

StreetXO

CREATIVE • TRENDY The menu at Madrid chef David Muñoz's London out-post is inspired by European, Asian and even South American cuisines. Dishes are characterised by explosions of colour and a riot of different flavours, tech-niques and textures. The quasi-industrial feel of the basement room adds to the moody, noisy atmosphere.

Menu £30 (lunch)/40 – Carte £45/68

PLAN: 2-H3 – *15 Old Burlington Street* – Ⓜ *Oxford Circus* – ✆ *020 3096 7555* – *www.streetxo.com* – *Closed lunch Monday*

Tamarind

INDIAN • CONTEMPORARY DÉCOR Tamarind now has a light and airy first floor space, as well as its basement where you can watch the chefs working at the tandoor counter. Cooking is lighter than before, with a delicate balance of herbs and spices. Sharing plates are the highlight; choose between a curry and a biryani for your main course.

Menu £30/69 – Carte £30/65

PLAN: 2-G4 – *20 Queen Street* – *Green Park* – *020 7629 3561* – *www.tamarindrestaurant.com*

Theo Randall

ITALIAN • CLASSIC DÉCOR There's an attractive honesty about Theo Randall's Italian food, which is made using the very best of ingredients. The somewhat corporate nature of the hotel in which it is located can sometimes seem a little at odds with the rustic style of food but the room is bright, relaxed and well run.

Menu £29 (lunch) – Carte £35/63

PLAN: 2-G4 – *InterContinental London Park Lane Hotel, 1 Hamilton Place, Park Lane* – *Hyde Park Corner* – *020 7318 8747* – *www.theorandall.com*

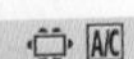

Tokimeitē

JAPANESE • CHIC Yoshihiro Murata, one of Japan's most celebrated chefs, teamed up with the Zen-Noh group to open this good looking, intimate restaurant on two floors. Their aim is to promote Wagyu beef in Europe, so it's understandably the highlight of the menu.

Menu £30 (lunch)/50 – Carte £38/159

PLAN: 2-H3 – *23 Conduit Street* – *Oxford Circus* – *020 3826 4411* – *www.tokimeite.com* – *Closed Sunday*

Soho

Barrafina

SPANISH • TAPAS BAR Expect to queue if you're not here just before opening time – but a seat at the L-shaped counter in the bright and animated room will be well worth the wait. The menu is reassuringly familiar and the dishes burst with flavour, leave a lasting impression and are easy to share.

Specialities: Gamba roja al ajillo. Solomillo de Rubia Gallega. Crema Catalana.

Carte £20/40

PLAN: 2-I3 – *26-27 Dean Street* – *Tottenham Court Road* – *020 7440 1456* – *www.barrafina.co.uk*

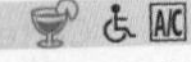

Social Eating House

MODERN CUISINE • BRASSERIE The coolest joint in Jason Atherton's stable comes with distressed walls, moody lighting and a laid-back vibe – it also has a terrific speakeasy-style bar upstairs. The 'Sampler' menu is a good way of experiencing the full breadth of the kitchen's skill at producing dishes with punchy, well-judged flavours.

Specialities: Scallop ceviche with avocado, artichoke, sunflower seeds and horseradish. Corn-fed duck with pickled turnip, puntarelle, salsa verde and lentils. Dark chocolate délice with cocoa nib yoghurt and tarragon ice cream.

Menu £28 – Carte £48/68

PLAN: 2-H3 – *58 Poland Street* – *Oxford Circus* – *020 7993 3251* – *www.socialeatinghouse.com* – *Closed Sunday*

Bao

TAIWANESE • SIMPLE There are some things in life worth queueing for – a
that includes the delicious eponymous buns here at this simple, great va
Taiwanese operation. The classic bao and the confit pork bao are stando
along with 'small eats' like trotter nuggets. There's also another Bao in Wi
mill St.

Carte £15/30

PLAN: 2-H3 – *53 Lexington Street* – *Tottenham Court Road* – *020 3011 1632*
www.baolondon.com – Closed dinner Sunday

Berenjak

PERSIAN • VINTAGE Based on the hole-in-the-wall 'kabab' houses of Teh
with exposed brick and painted plasterwork; the best place to sit is at
open kitchen counter opposite the tandoor, mangal barbecue and vertical ro
serie. Cooking is fresh and tasty; try the coal-cooked aubergine and the g
shoulder kabab.

Menu £30 – Carte £22/26

PLAN: 2-I3 – *27 Romilly Street* – *Leicester Square* – *020 3319 8120* –
www.berenjaklondon.com – Closed Sunday

Brasserie Zédel

FRENCH • BRASSERIE A grand French brasserie, which is all about inclusi
and accessibility, in a bustling subterranean space restored to its original
deco glory. Expect a roll-call of classic French dishes and some very comp
tive prices.

Menu £14/20 – Carte £17/45

PLAN: 2-H3 – *20 Sherwood Street* – *Piccadilly Circus* – *020 7734 4888* –
www.brasseriezedel.com

Hoppers

SOUTH INDIAN • SIMPLE Street food inspired by the flavours of Tamil N
and Sri Lanka features at this fun little spot from the Sethi family (Trishna, G
khana). Hoppers are bowl-shaped pancakes made from fermented rice and co
nut – ideal with a creamy kari. The 'short eats' are great too, as are the prices
expect a queue.

Menu £20 (lunch) – Carte £15/30

PLAN: 2-I3 – *49 Frith Street* – *Tottenham Court Road* – *020 3011 1021* –
www.hopperslondon.com – Closed Sunday

Kiln

THAI • SIMPLE Sit at the far counter to watch chefs prepare fiery Thai food
clay pots, woks and grills. The well-priced menu includes influences from La
Myanmar and Yunnan – all prepared using largely British produce. The cour
is for walk-ins only but parties of four can book a table downstairs.

Carte £10/25

PLAN: 2-H3 – *58 Brewer Street* – *Piccadilly Circus* – *www.kilnsoho.com*

Kricket

INDIAN • SIMPLE A trendy pop-up turned permanent with branches also
White City and Brixton; not many Indian restaurants have a counter, an o
kitchen, sharing plates and cocktails. Well-priced dishes under the headings
'Meat, 'Fish' and 'Veg' are made with home-grown ingredients. Bookings
only taken for groups of 4 or more at dinner.

Carte £20/35

PLAN: 2-I3 – *12 Denman Street* – *Piccadilly Circus* – *020 7734 5612* –
www.kricket.co.uk – Closed Sunday

Palomar

MIDDLE EASTERN • TRENDY A hip slice of modern-day Jerusalem in the heart of theatreland, with a zinc kitchen counter running back to an intimate wood-panelled dining room. Like the atmosphere, the contemporary Middle Eastern cooking is fresh and vibrant.

Carte £20/32

PLAN: 2-I3 – *34 Rupert Street* – Ⓜ *Piccadilly Circus* – ✆ *020 7439 8777* – *www.thepalomar.co.uk*

Barshu

CHINESE • EXOTIC DÉCOR The fiery and authentic flavours of China's Sichuan province are the draw here; help is at hand as the menu has pictures. It's well run and decorated with carved wood and lanterns; downstairs is better for groups.

Carte £20/58

PLAN: 2-I3 – *28 Frith Street* – Ⓜ *Leicester Square* – ✆ *020 7287 8822* – *www.barshurestaurant.co.uk*

Beijing Dumpling

CHINESE • NEIGHBOURHOOD This relaxed little place serves freshly prepared dumplings of both Beijing and Shanghai styles. Although the range is not as comprehensive as the name suggests, they do stand out, especially varieties of the famed xiao long bao.

Menu £25 – Carte £14/38

PLAN: 2-I3 – *23 Lisle Street* – Ⓜ *Leicester Square* – ✆ *020 7287 6888* – *www.beijingdumpling.co.uk*

Blanchette

FRENCH • SIMPLE Run by three frères, Blanchette takes French bistro food and gives it the 'small plates' treatment. It's named after their mother – the ox cheek Bourguignon is her recipe. Tiles and exposed brick add to the rustic look.

Menu £39/45 – Carte £28/50

PLAN: 2-H2 – *9 D'Arblay Street* – Ⓜ *Oxford Circus* – ✆ *020 7439 8100* – *www.blanchettelondon.co.uk*

Bob Bob Ricard

TRADITIONAL BRITISH • VINTAGE Bob Bob Ricard is a small version of a glamorous grand salon; its booth seating and tableside 'Press for Champagne' buttons adding a sense of exclusivity to proceedings. The all-encompassing menu opens with vodka shots at -18° along with caviar – a clue as to the owner's nationality; then moves on to everything from a delicate salmon tartare to beef Wellington for two.

Carte £38/86

PLAN: 2-H3 – *1 Upper James Street* – Ⓜ *Oxford Circus* – ✆ *020 3145 1000* – *www.bobbobricard.com*

Bocca di Lupo

ITALIAN • TAPAS BAR Atmosphere, food and service are all best when sitting at the marble counter, watching the chefs at work. Specialities from across Italy come in large or small sizes and are full of flavour and vitality. Try also their gelato shop opposite.

Carte £25/55

PLAN: 2-I3 – *12 Archer Street* – Ⓜ *Piccadilly Circus* – ✆ *020 7734 2223* – *www.boccadilupo.com*

Cây Tre

VIETNAMESE • MINIMALIST Bustling Vietnamese restaurant offering specialities from all parts of the country. Dishes are generously sized and appealingly priced; their various versions of pho are always popular. Come in a group to compete with the noise.

Menu £13 (lunch)/25 – Carte £14/27

PLAN: 2-I3 – *42-43 Dean Street* – Ⓜ *Tottenham Court Road* – ✆ *020 7317 9118* – *www.caytreyrestaurant.co.uk*

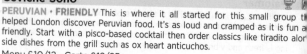

Ceviche Soho

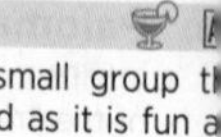

PERUVIAN • FRIENDLY This is where it all started for this small group t helped London discover Peruvian food. It's as loud and cramped as it is fun a friendly. Start with a pisco-based cocktail then order classics like tiradito alor side dishes from the grill such as ox heart anticuchos.

Menu £10/12 – Carte £12/25

PLAN: 2-I3 – *17 Frith Street* – *Ⓜ Tottenham Court Road* – *✆ 020 7292 2040* – *www.cevicherestaurants.com*

Copita

SPANISH • TAPAS BAR This tapas bar – a sister to Barrica – is packed most nigh perch on one of the high stools or stay standing and get stuck into the daily menu small, colourful dishes. Staff add to the lively atmosphere and everything on t thoughtfully compiled Spanish wine list is available by the glass or copita.

Carte £18/40

PLAN: 2-H3 – *27 D'Arblay Street* – *Ⓜ Oxford Circus* – *✆ 020 7287 7797* – *www.copita.co.uk* – *Closed Sunday*

Darjeeling Express

INDIAN • BRASSERIE With Royal Mughlai ancestry and a great love of foc gained from cooking traditional family recipes, the owner couldn't be better qua ified. Her open kitchen is run by a team of housewives; the influences are most Bengali but there are also dishes from Kolkata to Hyderabad. Lively and great fu

Carte £24/29

PLAN: 2-H3 – *Kingly Court, Carnaby Street* – *Ⓜ Oxford Circus* – *✆ 020 7287 2828* *www.darjeeling-express.com* – *Closed Sunday*

Dehesa

MEDITERRANEAN CUISINE • TAPAS BAR Repeats the success of its sist restaurant, Salt Yard, by offering flavoursome and appealingly priced Spanis and Italian tapas. Busy, friendly atmosphere in appealing corner location. Goc drinks list too.

Menu £15 (lunch) – Carte £20/35

PLAN: 2-H3 – *25 Ganton Street* – *Ⓜ Oxford Circus* – *✆ 020 7494 4170* – *www.dehesa.co.uk*

Duck & Rice

CHINESE • INTIMATE Something a little different – a converted pub with a Ch nese kitchen – originally set up by Alan Yau. Beer and snacks are the thing on th ground floor; upstairs, with its booths and fireplaces, is for Chinese favourites an comforting classics.

Carte £21/49

PLAN: 2-I3 – *90 Berwick Street* – *Ⓜ Tottenham Court Road* – *✆ 020 3327 7888* – *www.theduckandrice.com*

Ember Yard

MEDITERRANEAN CUISINE • TAPAS BAR Those familiar with the Salt Yar Group will recognise the Spanish and Italian themed menus – but their 4th fu outlet comes with a focus on cooking over charcoal or wood. There's even a se ductive smokiness to some of the cocktails.

Menu £20 (lunch), £30/45 – Carte £29/48

PLAN: 2-H2 – *60 Berwick Street* – *Ⓜ Oxford Circus* – *✆ 020 7439 8057* – *www.emberyard.co.uk*

Evelyn's Table

MODERN CUISINE • SIMPLE A former beer cellar of a restored 18C inn – muct is made of the whole cramped, underground, speakeasy thing. Watching the chefs behind the counter is all part of the appeal; their modern European dishes are designed for sharing, with fish from Cornwall a highlight.

Carte £39/56

PLAN: 2-I3 – *The Blue Posts, 28 Rupert Street* – *Ⓜ Piccadilly Circus* – *✆ 07921 336010* – *www.theblueposts.co.uk* – *Closed lunch Monday-Tuesday*

French House

TRADITIONAL BRITISH • PUB This historic Soho watering hole, once a favourite haunt of writers and artists such as Dylan Thomas, Brendan Behan and Francis Bacon, has only seven tables in its oxblood and wood-panelled upstairs restaurant. It's run in a bohemian style and offers honest British cooking with integrity and flavour.

Carte £25/50

PLAN: 2-I3 – *49 Dean Street – Ⓜ Leicester Square – ✆ 020 7437 2477 – www.frenchhousesoho.com – Closed Sunday, dinner Monday, dinner Friday, Saturday*

Gauthier - Soho

FRENCH • INTIMATE Detached from the rowdier elements of Soho is this charming Georgian townhouse, with dining spread over three floors. Alex Gauthier offers assorted menus of his classically based cooking, with vegetarians particularly well looked after.

Carte £35/60

PLAN: 2-I3 – *21 Romilly Street – Ⓜ Leicester Square – ✆ 020 7494 3111 – www.gauthiersoho.co.uk – Closed Sunday, Monday*

Jugemu

JAPANESE • SIMPLE Like all the best izakaya, this one is tucked away down a side street and easy to miss. It has three small tables and a 9-seater counter from where you can watch the chef-owner at work. Popular with a homesick Japanese clientele, it keeps things traditional; the sashimi is excellent.

Carte £15/50

PLAN: 2-I3 – *3 Winnett Street – Ⓜ Piccadilly Circus – ✆ 020 7734 0518 – Closed Sunday, lunch Saturday*

Mele e Pere

ITALIAN • FRIENDLY There's a small dining room on the ground floor but all the fun happens downstairs, where you'll find a large vermouth bar with vintage posters and plenty of seating in the buzzy vaulted room. The rustic Italian dishes hit the spot and the pre-theatre menu is great value.

Menu £19 (lunch), £18/20 – Carte £29/48

PLAN: 2-I3 – *46 Brewer Street – Ⓜ Piccadilly Circus – ✆ 020 7096 2096 – www.meleepere.co.uk*

Nopi

MEDITERRANEAN CUISINE • DESIGN The bright, clean look of Yotam Ottolenghi's charmingly run all-day restaurant matches the fresh, invigorating food. The sharing plates take in the Mediterranean, the Middle East and Asia and the veggie dishes stand out.

Carte £31/49

PLAN: 2-H3 – *21-22 Warwick Street – Ⓜ Piccadilly Circus – ✆ 020 7494 9584 – www.ottolenghi.co.uk – Closed dinner Sunday*

100 Wardour St

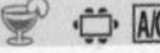

MODERN CUISINE • CONTEMPORARY DÉCOR For a night out with a group of friends, this D&D place is worth considering. At night, head downstairs for cocktails, live music (well, this was once The Marquee Club) and a modern, Med-influenced menu with the odd Asian touch. During the day, the ground floor offers an all-day menu.

Menu £42 – Carte £31/58

PLAN: 2-I3 – *100 Wardour Street – Ⓜ Tottenham Court Road – ✆ 020 7314 4000 – www.100wardourst.com*

Tamarind Kitchen

INDIAN • EXOTIC DÉCOR A more relaxed sister to Tamarind in Mayfair, this Indian restaurant comes with endearingly earnest service and a lively buzz. There's a nominal Northern emphasis to the fairly priced menu, with Awadhi kababs a speciality, but there are also plenty of curries and fish dishes.

Menu £18 (lunch), £24/40 – Carte £20/36

PLAN: 2-I3 – *167-169 Wardour Street – Ⓜ Tottenham Court Road – ✆ 020 7287 4243 – www.tamarindkitchen.co.uk – Closed lunch Monday*

Temper

BARBECUE • CONTEMPORARY DÉCOR A fun, basement restaurant all ab barbecue and meats. The beasts are cooked whole, some are also smoked house and there's a distinct South African flavour to the salsas that accomp them. Kick off with some tacos – they make around 1,200 of them every day.

Carte £20/40

PLAN: 2-H3 – *25 Broadwick Street – Ⓜ Oxford Circus – ✆ 020 3879 3834 – www.temperrestaurant.com – Closed lunch Monday*

Vasco and Piero's Pavilion

ITALIAN • FRIENDLY Regulars and tourists have been flocking to this institut for over 40 years; its longevity is down to a twice daily changing menu of U brian-influenced dishes rather than the matter-of-fact service or simple decorati

Carte £28/40

PLAN: 2-H2 – *15 Poland Street – Ⓜ Oxford Circus – ✆ 020 7437 8774 – www.vascosfood.com – Closed Sunday, lunch Saturday*

XU

TAIWANESE • CHIC They've squeezed a lot into the two floors to create the of 1930s Taipei, including an emerald lacquered tea kiosk and mahjong tab Don't miss the numbing beef tendon and classics like Shou Pa chicken. Tofu made in-house and Chi Shiang rice is flown in from Taiwan.

Carte £24/45

PLAN: 2-I3 – *30 Rupert Street – Ⓜ Piccadilly Circus – ✆ 020 3319 8147 – www.xulondon.com*

Yauatcha Soho

CHINESE • DESIGN The bright ground floor features well-spaced tables and binets full of pastries and chocolates – but ask to sit in the more atmosph basement, with its celestial ceiling lights, tropical fish tanks and glimpses i the kitchen. The menu provides plenty of choice and over-ordering is easy to

Carte £29/72

PLAN: 2-I3 – *15 Broadwick Street – Ⓜ Tottenham Court Road – ✆ 020 7494 888 www.yauatcha.com*

yeni

TURKISH • CONTEMPORARY DÉCOR Anatolian-inspired cooking from exp enced chef-owner Civan Er, who made his name at acclaimed sister restaur Yeni Lokanta in his home city of Istanbul. Daily changing menu of vibrant, gu flavoursome dishes; techniques are rooted in tradition, with dishes cooked c oak in the Josper oven.

Carte £28/57

PLAN: 2-H3 – *55 Beak Street – Ⓜ Piccadilly Circus – ✆ 020 3475 1903 – www.yeni.london – Closed Sunday*

St James's

Aquavit

SCANDINAVIAN • BRASSERIE A younger, more down-to-earth sister to original in NYC, Aquavit is a brasserie with a central bar and a warm, informal mosphere. Cooking delivers as much panache as the Scandinavian styling, v classic Nordic dishes featuring excellent ingredients, natural flavours, and a sul modern touch.

Specialities: Smoked eel with baby gem, tomato and lovage. Beef Rydberg. N wegian omelette with sea buckthorn and vanilla.

Menu £27 (lunch), £22/30 – Carte £32/66

PLAN: 2-I3 – *St. James's Market, 1 Carlton Street – Ⓜ Piccadilly Circus – ✆ 020 7024 9848 – www.aquavitrestaurants.com – Closed 23-27 December, dinner Sunday*

Ikoyi (Jeremy Chan)

CREATIVE • SIMPLE The somewhat colourless development that is St James's Market is the unlikely setting for one of the most innovative and original restaurants to open in the capital in recent times. The two owners, friends since childhood, have put together a kitchen that uses home-grown ingredients enlivened with flavours from West Africa.

Specialities: Plantain & smoked Scotch Bonnet with red mullet velouté, white asparagus and banga. Aged beef & carrot maafe. Wild rice and fonio.

Menu £35 (lunch), £75/100

PLAN: 2-I3 – *1 St. James's Market* – *Piccadilly Circus* – *020 3583 4660* – *www.ikoyilondon.com* – *Closed 24 December-4 January, Sunday*

Ritz Restaurant

MODERN BRITISH • LUXURY Executive Chef John Williams MBE and his team take classic dishes, including some Escoffier recipes, and add their own subtle touches of modernity. Needless to say, the ingredients are luxurious. Thanks to the lavishness of its Louis XVI decoration, there is nowhere grander than The Ritz. The faultless service adds to the experience.

Specialities: Norfolk crab with apple, avocado and caviar. Tournedos of beef with salsify, lovage and smoked bone marrow. Crêpes Suzette.

Menu £59 (lunch), £67/125 – Carte £70/140

PLAN: 2-H4 – *Ritz Hotel, 150 Piccadilly* – *Green Park* – *020 7300 2370* – *www.theritzlondon.com*

Seven Park Place

MODERN CUISINE • CONTEMPORARY DÉCOR William Drabble has been head chef here for over ten years and it's a rare night he's not at the stove. He starts with premier ingredients – most of which he sources himself; using classic flavour combinations and tried-and-tested techniques to create rich, perfectly crafted dishes. Sauces are a highlight.

Specialities: Poached native lobster tail with cauliflower purée and lobster butter sauce. Assiette of Lune Valley lamb with calçot onions and thyme jus. Coffee soaked savarin, gianduja mousse, mascarpone and hazelnuts.

Menu £35 (lunch), £75/95

PLAN: 2-H4 – *St James's Hotel and Club, 7-8 Park Place* – *Green Park* – *020 7316 1621* – *www.stjameshotelandclub.com* – *Closed Sunday, Monday*

Cafe Murano

ITALIAN • CHIC Angela Hartnett and her chef have created an appealing and flexible menu of delicious North Italian delicacies – the lunch menu is very good value. It's certainly no ordinary café and its popularity means pre-booking is essential.

Menu £19/23 – Carte £30/57

PLAN: 2-H4 – *33 St. James's Street* – *Green Park* – *020 3371 5559* – *www.cafemurano.co.uk* – *Closed 24-26 December, dinner Sunday*

Chutney Mary

INDIAN • DESIGN A long-standing and popular Indian restaurant, which is more relaxed and fashionable than its St James's address might suggest. The appealing menu offers lots of choice and the well-judged, flavourful dishes have been subtly updated, whilst still respecting the foundations of Indian cooking.

Menu £46/56 – Carte £50/78

PLAN: 2-H4 – *73 St James's Street* – *Green Park* – *020 7629 6688* – *www.chutneymary.com*

Farzi Café

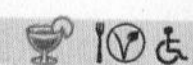

INDIAN • CONTEMPORARY DÉCOR A great spot for a meal before heac next door to the Theatre Royal, this glitzy, buzzy two-floored restaurant ser modern, reinterpreted versions of classic Indian dishes, with some interest global touches. Spicing is clean, distinct and multi-layered – and zodiac-then cocktails add to the fun.

Carte £26/58

PLAN: 2-I3 – *8 Haymarket* – Ⓜ *Piccadilly Circus* – ✆ *020 3981 0090* – *www.farzilondon.com*

45 Jermyn St

TRADITIONAL BRITISH • CHIC Style and comfort go hand in hand at bright, contemporary brasserie. The menu is a mix of European and British cl sics; the beef Wellington and lobster spaghetti are finished off at your table. das, coupes and floats pay tribute to its past as Fortnum's Fountain restauran

Menu £27/39 – Carte £30/77

PLAN: 2-H4 – *45 Jermyn Street* – Ⓜ *Piccadilly Circus* – ✆ *020 7205 4545* – *www.45jermynst.com*

Franco's

ITALIAN • TRADITIONAL Have an aperitivo in the clubby bar before sitti down to eat at one of London's oldest yet rejuvenated Italian restaurants. T kitchen focuses on the classics and they live up to expectations; the regulars, whom there are many, all have their favourites.

Menu £32 – Carte £36/64

PLAN: 2-H4 – *61 Jermyn Street* – Ⓜ *Green Park* – ✆ *020 7499 2211* – *www.francoslondon.com* – *Closed Sunday*

Ginza Onodera

JAPANESE • CHIC A professionally run sister to the Tokyo original, situated the heart of St James; a stylish, elegant basement space featuring a cockt bar and three counters for robata, teppanyaki and sushi. Attractive dishes fe ture excellent ingredients – and are accompanied by one of the best sake lis in London.

Menu £23 (lunch), £35/45 – Carte £29/70

PLAN: 2-H4 – *15 Bury Street* – Ⓜ *Green Park* – ✆ *020 7839 1101* – *www.onodera-group.com*

Imperial Treasure

CHINESE • ELEGANT The first London outpost of this group is housed in an in posing former bank, which provides a luxurious backdrop for the tradition mostly Cantonese cooking. White leather, onyx walls and wood partitions pro vide some intimacy amongst the opulence. The signature Peking duck is wor the expense.

Menu £38 (lunch), £68/128 – Carte £48/130

PLAN: 2-I4 – *9 Waterloo Place* – Ⓜ *Piccadilly Circus* – ✆ *020 3011 1328* – *www.imperialtreasure.com/uk*

Portrait

MODERN CUISINE • CONTEMPORARY DÉCOR Set on the top floor of the Na tional Portrait Gallery with views of local landmarks. Carefully prepared moder European food; dishes are sometimes created in celebration of current exhib tions. Good value pre-theatre and weekend set menus.

Menu £33 – Carte £37/87

PLAN: 2-I3 – *National Portrait Gallery, St Martin's Place* – Ⓜ *Charing Cross* – ✆ *020 7312 2490* – *www.npg.org.uk/portraitrestaurant* – *Closed dinner Sunday-Wednesday*

Quaglino's

MODERN CUISINE • DESIGN This colourful, glamorous restaurant manages to be cavernous and cosy at the same time, with live music and a late night bar adding a certain sultriness to proceedings. The kitchen specialises in contemporary brasserie-style food.

Menu £23/33 – Carte £37/64

PLAN: 2-H4 – *16 Bury Street* – Ⓜ *Green Park* – ✆ *020 7930 6767* – *www.quaglinos-restaurant.co.uk*

Sake No Hana

JAPANESE • MINIMALIST A modern Japanese restaurant within a Grade II listed '60s edifice – and proof that you can occasionally find good food at the end of an escalator. As with the great cocktails, the menu is best enjoyed when shared with a group.

Carte £33/133

PLAN: 2-H4 – *23 St. James's Street* – Ⓜ *Green Park* – ✆ *020 7925 8988* – *www.sakenohana.com – Closed Sunday*

Scully

WORLD CUISINE • FRIENDLY The eponymous chef-owner's travels and family heritage inform his style of food. The small plates feature an array of international influences and the bold, diverse flavours give them an appealing vitality. The kitchen makes good use of the shelves of pickles and spices.

Carte £45/60

PLAN: 2-I3 – *4 St. James's Market* – Ⓜ *Piccadilly Circus* – ✆ *020 3911 6840* – *www.scullyrestaurant.com – Closed dinner Sunday*

Wild Honey St James

MODERN BRITISH • CONTEMPORARY DÉCOR Elegant without being overly formal, this grand brasserie is set in the impressive surrounds of the Sofitel London St James – in what was previously the hall of this Grade II listed former bank. Anthony Demetre's accomplished modern European dishes are the perfect match for the surroundings.

Menu £27 – Carte £45/57

PLAN: 2-I4 – *Sofitel London St James Hotel, 8 Pall Mall* – Ⓜ *Piccadilly Circus* – ✆ *020 7968 2900* – *www.wildhoneystjames.co.uk*

The Wolseley

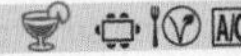

EUROPEAN • ELEGANT Pillars and a high vaulted ceiling give this buzzy restaurant the feel of a grand European café, albeit with the occasional Oriental influence, thanks to a previous incarnation as a Chinese restaurant. It's open from early until late and the appealing menus offer a mix of classic dishes from across Europe.

Carte £33/58

PLAN: 2-H4 – *160 Piccadilly* – Ⓜ *Green Park* – ✆ *020 7499 6996* – *www.thewolseley.com*

Strand and Covent Garden

Bancone

MODERN CUISINE • CONTEMPORARY DÉCOR It's all about freshly made pasta at great prices – and all in the centre of town; the highlight is 'silk handkerchiefs' with walnut butter. Start by sharing some focaccia or panelle with smoked duck. As the name means 'counter' this is where most want to sit, although there are tables available.

Carte £20/30

PLAN: 3-I3 – *39 William IV Street* – Ⓜ *Charing Cross* – ✆ *020 7240 8786* – *www.bancone.co.uk*

Cinnamon Bazaar

INDIAN • EXOTIC DÉCOR Vivek Singh's Covent Garden restaurant provides laxed, all-day contemporary Indian dining in a bright, colourful space wh evokes a marketplace. Menus are influenced by the trade routes of the subco nent, with twists that encompass Afghanistan, the Punjab and the Middle Eas

Menu £17 (lunch), £21/24 – Carte £20/38

PLAN: 3-J3 – *28 Maiden Lane* – Ⓜ *Leicester Square* – ✆ *020 7395 1400* – *www.cinnamon-bazaar.com*

Balthazar

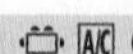

FRENCH • BRASSERIE Those who know the original Balthazar in Manhatt SoHo district will find the London version of this classic brasserie uncannily fa iar in looks, vibe and food. The Franglais menu keeps it simple and the cock are great.

Menu £20/23 – Carte £31/70

PLAN: 3-J3 – *4-6 Russell Street* – Ⓜ *Covent Garden* – ✆ *020 3301 1155* – *www.balthazarlondon.com*

Barrafina

SPANISH • TAPAS BAR The second Barrafina is not just brighter than the S original – it's bigger too, so you can wait inside with a drink for counter seat become available. Try more unusual tapas like ortiguillas, frit Mallorquin or succulent meats.

Carte £27/52

PLAN: 3-I3 – *10 Adelaide Street* – Ⓜ *Charing Cross* – ✆ *020 7440 1456* – *www.barrafina.co.uk*

Barrafina

SPANISH • TAPAS BAR The third of the Barrafinas is tucked away at the far of Covent Garden; arrive early or prepare to queue. Fresh, vibrantly flavoured and shellfish dishes are a real highlight; tortillas y huevos also feature.

Carte £27/52

PLAN: 3-J3 – *43 Drury Lane* – Ⓜ *Covent Garden* – ✆ *020 7440 1456* – *www.barrafina.co.uk*

Clos Maggiore

FRENCH • CLASSIC DÉCOR One of London's most romantic restaurants – be sure to ask for the enchanting conservatory with its retractable roof. The phisticated French cooking is joined by a wine list of great depth. Good value very popular pre/post theatre menus.

Menu £30 (lunch) – Carte £44/64

PLAN: 3-J3 – *33 King Street* – Ⓜ *Leicester Square* – ✆ *020 7379 9696* – *www.closmaggiore.com*

Cora Pearl

MODERN BRITISH • ELEGANT Sister to Kitty Fisher's, and similarly named an infamous courtesan, this elegant restaurant is set in a characterful townh and has a rich, cosy bistro feel, as well as attentive 'old school' service. The cor menu focuses on seasonal British produce in fresh, unfussy boldly flavoured dis

Carte £27/55

PLAN: 3-J3 – *30 Henrietta Street* – Ⓜ *Covent Garden* – ✆ *020 7324 7722* – *www.corapearl.co.uk* – *Closed dinner Sunday*

Delaunay

MODERN CUISINE • ELEGANT The Delaunay was inspired by the grand café Europe but, despite sharing the same buzz and celebrity clientele as its sib The Wolseley, is not just a mere replica. The all-day menu is more mittel-E pean, with great schnitzels and wieners.

Menu £28/75 – Carte £28/75

PLAN: 3-J3 – *55 Aldwych* – Ⓜ *Temple* – ✆ *020 7499 8558* – *www.thedelaunay.co*

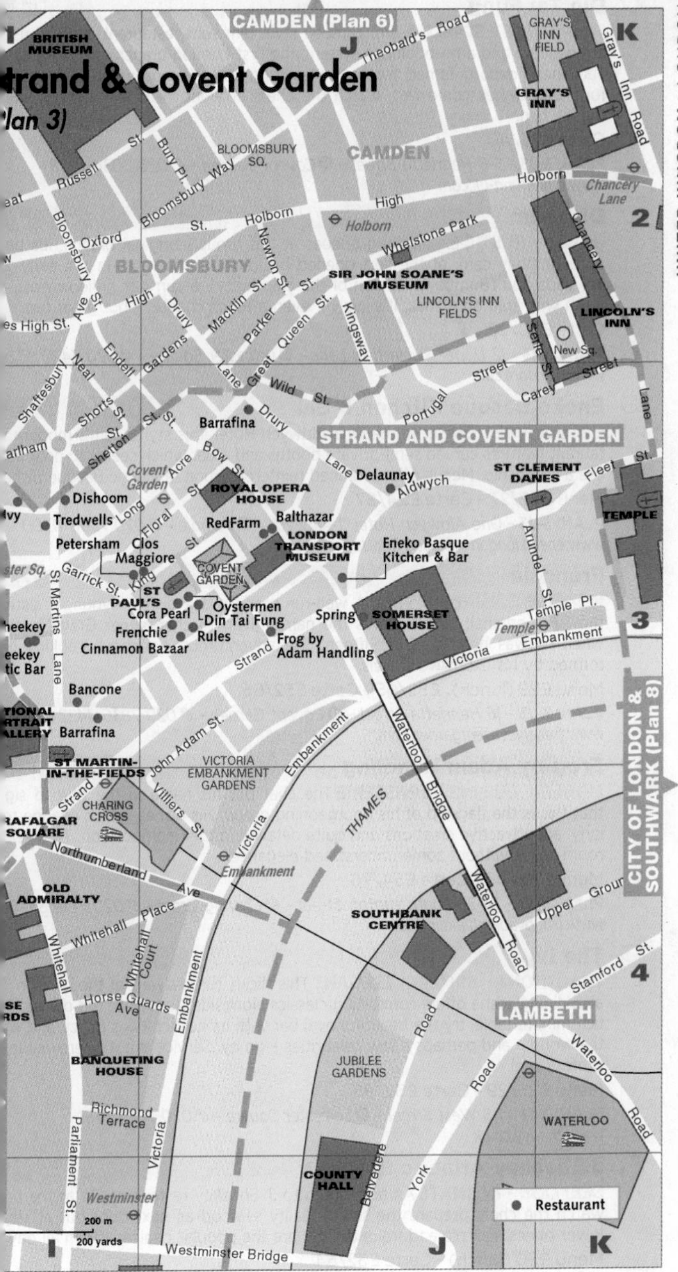
Strand & Covent Garden
(Plan 3)
CAMDEN (Plan 6)
BRITISH MUSEUM
GRAY'S INN FIELD
GRAY'S INN
BLOOMSBURY SQ.
CAMDEN
BLOOMSBURY
SIR JOHN SOANE'S MUSEUM
LINCOLN'S INN FIELDS
LINCOLN'S INN
New Sq.
Holborn
Chancery Lane
STRAND AND COVENT GARDEN
Barrafina
Delaunay
ST CLEMENT DANES
Covent Garden
ROYAL OPERA HOUSE
Dishoom
Tredwells
RedFarm
Balthazar
LONDON TRANSPORT MUSEUM
Eneko Basque Kitchen & Bar
TEMPLE
Petersham
Clos Maggiore
COVENT GARDEN
ST PAUL'S
Oystermen
Cora Pearl
Din Tai Fung
Frenchie
Rules
Cinnamon Bazaar
Spring
SOMERSET HOUSE
Frog by Adam Handling
Temple
Bancone
Barrafina
ST MARTIN-IN-THE-FIELDS
VICTORIA EMBANKMENT GARDENS
CHARING CROSS
THAMES
CITY OF LONDON & SOUTHWARK (Plan 8)
Embankment
OLD ADMIRALTY
SOUTHBANK CENTRE
LAMBETH
BANQUETING HOUSE
JUBILEE GARDENS
WATERLOO
COUNTY HALL
Westminster
Restaurant
200 m
200 yards
Westminster Bridge

Din Tai Fung

TAIWANESE • SIMPLE A fun, canteen-style dim sum restaurant with a bust atmosphere and a no-bookings system; the first London branch of this succes Taiwanese export, famed for their xiao long bao. You order off a pre-prir form and dishes come fast; watch the chefs at work through the glass wal the kitchen.

Carte £25/40

PLAN: 3-J3 – *5-6 Henrietta Street – Ⓜ Covent Garden – ✆ 020 3034 3888 – www.dintaifung-uk.com*

Dishoom

INDIAN • RUSTIC Expect long queues at this group's original branch. It's ba on a Bombay café, of the sort opened by Iranian immigrants in the early 2 Try vada pau (Bombay's version of the chip butty), a curry or grilled meats; a finish with kulfi on a stick. It's lively – even a touch chaotic – but great fun.

Carte £20/28

PLAN: 3-I3 – *12 Upper St Martin's Lane – Ⓜ Leicester Square – ✆ 020 7420 932C www.dishoom.com*

Eneko Basque Kitchen & Bar

BASQUE • DESIGN Set in the One Aldwych Hotel, this stylish, ultra-modern r taurant features curved semi-private booths and a bar which seems to float abc like a spaceship. Menus offer a refined reinterpretation of classic Basque dishe

Menu £22/27 – Carte £24/97

PLAN: 3-J3 – *One Aldwych Hotel, 1 Aldwych – Ⓜ Temple – ✆ 020 7300 0300 – www.eneko.london – Closed Sunday, Monday*

Frenchie

MODERN CUISINE • BISTRO A well-run modern-day bistro – younger sister the Paris original, which shares the name given to chef-owner Greg Marcha when he was head chef at Fifteen. The adventurous, ambitious cooking is formed by his extensive travels.

Menu £29 (lunch), £52/65 – Carte £52/65

PLAN: 3-J3 – *16 Henrietta Street – Ⓜ Covent Garden – ✆ 020 7836 4422 – www.frenchiecoventgarden.com*

Frog by Adam Handling

MODERN CUISINE • BRASSERIE The chef put his name in the title to sign that this is the flagship of his bourgeoning group. His dishes, which change reg larly, are attractive creations and quite detailed in their composition. The well-r room is not without some understated elegance.

Menu £65/96 – Carte £54/76

PLAN: 3-J3 – *34-35 Southampton Street – Ⓜ Charing Cross – ✆ 020 7199 8370 – www.frogbyadamhandling.com*

The Ivy

TRADITIONAL BRITISH • ELEGANT This slickly run stalwart of the London Th atre dining scene offers comforting classics alongside Asian-inspired dishes. For last minute table, try the beautiful oval bar with its no-bookings policy and wat the world – and perhaps a few celebrities – go by. Service is both personable ar professional.

Menu £25/29 – Carte £32/95

PLAN: 3-I3 – *1-5 West Street – Ⓜ Leicester Square – ✆ 020 7836 4751 – www.the-ivy.co.uk*

J.Sheekey Atlantic Bar

SEAFOOD • INTIMATE An addendum to J. Sheekey restaurant. Sit at the bar watch the chefs prepare the same quality seafood as next door but at slight lower prices; fish pie and fruits de mer are the popular choices. Open all day.

Menu £30 (lunch) – Carte £32/54

PLAN: 3-I3 – *33-34 St. Martin's Court – Ⓜ Leicester Square – ✆ 020 7240 2565 – www.jsheekeyatlanticbar.co.uk*

J.Sheekey

SEAFOOD • CHIC Festooned with photographs of actors and linked to the theatrical world since opening in 1890. Wood panels and alcove tables add famed intimacy. Accomplished seafood cooking.

Menu £25/30 – Carte £34/118

PLAN: 3-I3 – *28-32 St. Martin's Court* – *Leicester Square* – *020 7240 2565* – *www.j-sheekey.co.uk*

Little Kolkata

INDIAN • SIMPLE What started as two friends holding pop-up supper clubs has led to this simply styled but delightfully friendly restaurant. Cooking comes from the East of India, particularly Calcutta, with many of the recipes handed down through the generations; dishes are fresh and vibrant with punchy, refreshing flavours.

Carte £20/35

PLAN: 6-J3 – *51-53 Shelton Street* – *Covent Garden* – *020 7240 7084* – *www.littlekolkata.co.uk* – *Closed dinner Sunday*

The Oystermen

SEAFOOD • RUSTIC Covent Garden isn't an area usually associated with independent restaurants but this bustling and modestly decorated little spot is thriving. From its tiny open kitchen come oysters, crabs and expertly cooked fish.

Carte £29/49

PLAN: 3-J3 – *31-32 Henrietta Street* – *Covent Garden* – *020 7240 4417* – *www.oystermen.co.uk*

Petersham

MEDITERRANEAN CUISINE • ELEGANT Along with a deli, shop and florist is this elegant restaurant with contemporary art, Murano glass and an abundance of fresh flowers. The Italian-based menu uses produce from their Richmond nursery and Devon farm. The lovely terrace is shared with La Goccia, their more informal spot for sharing plates.

Menu £30/34 – Carte £43/70

PLAN: 3-I3 – *2 Floral Court* – *Covent Garden* – *020 7305 7676* – *www.petershamnurseries.com*

RedFarm

ASIAN • CHIC The original resides in New York and its buzzy London counterpart shares its rustic, Asia-meets-America vibe. Three floors of fun come with a cocktail bar, communal tables and chatty service; modern Chinese dishes include super crispy shrimp-stuffed chicken and the made-for-Instagram Pac-Man dumplings.

Menu £23 – Carte £30/56

PLAN: 3-J3 – *9 Russell Street* – *Covent Garden* – *020 3883 9093* – *www.redfarmldn.com*

Rules

TRADITIONAL BRITISH • TRADITIONAL London's oldest restaurant boasts a fine collection of antique cartoons, drawings and paintings. Tradition continues in the menu, specialising in game from its own estate.

Carte £39/71

PLAN: 3-J3 – *35 Maiden Lane* – *Leicester Square* – *020 7836 5314* – *www.rules.co.uk*

Spring

ITALIAN • ELEGANT Spring occupies the 'new wing' of Somerset House that for many years was inhabited by the Inland Revenue. It's a bright, feminine space under the aegis of chef Skye Gyngell. Her cooking is Italian-influenced and ingredient-led.

Menu £32 (lunch) – Carte £51/71

PLAN: 3-J3 – *New Wing, Somerset House* – *Temple* – *020 3011 0115* – *www.springrestaurant.co.uk* – *Closed Sunday*

Tredwells

MODERN BRITISH • BRASSERIE Chef-owner Chantelle Nicholson's contemrary cooking makes good use of British ingredients and also displays the ocsional Asian twist. It's set over three floors, with a subtle art deco feel. A gc choice for a Sunday roast.

Menu £29/41 – Carte £30/55

PLAN: 3-13 – *4a Upper St Martin's Lane* – Ⓜ *Leicester Square* – ✆ *020 3764 084*
www.tredwells.com

Belgravia - Knightsbridge - Victoria

Belgravia

Amaya

INDIAN • DESIGN Over 15 years since this ground-breaking restaurant f opened, it remains at the forefront of the Indian scene in London. Your sen: are fired up by the shooting flames and enticing aromas emanating from tawa, tandoor and sigri grills – and the dishes are well presented and wond fully vibrant.

Specialities: Black pepper chicken tikka. Tandoori wild prawns. Lime tart with moncello jelly and spiced blueberry compote.

Menu £45 (lunch), £55/75 – Carte £40/79

PLAN: 4-F5 – *Halkin Arcade, 19 Motcomb Street* – Ⓜ *Knightsbridge* – ✆ *020 7823 1166* – *www.amaya.biz*

Céleste

MODERN FRENCH • ELEGANT With its crystal chandeliers, immaculat dressed tables, Wedgwood blue friezes and fluted columns, this is an unapo getically formal room in which you feel truly cosseted. Menus showcase seaso British ingredients in classically based European dishes with intense flavours a modern touches.

Specialities: Blanched green asparagus , Mimosa egg, Oscietra caviar and crèr fraîche. Morels stuffed with chicken farce and mixed herb-smoked mashed pot toes. Chocolate pudding, roasted cereal, olive oil tuile and malted gelato.

Menu £39 – Carte £72/100

PLAN: 4-G4 – *The Lanesborough Hotel, Hyde Park Corner* – Ⓜ *Hyde Park Corner* ✆ *020 7259 5599* –
www.oetkercollection.com/hotels/the-lanesborough/restaurants-bars/restaurants/celeste/

Marcus

MODERN CUISINE • ELEGANT The MasterChef maestro's eponymous flagsh set within the glamorous Berkeley Hotel, is eminently comfortable with touch of opulence, but the Chef's Table, with its view into the kitchen, provides t best seats in the house. British dishes showcase top quality produce from all co ners of the country.

Specialities: Scallops and beetroot cannelloni. Herdwick lamb with kale flowe and pesto. Coffee, mascarpone and bourbon.

Menu £60 (lunch), £75/135 – Carte £64/106

PLAN: 4-G4 – *Berkeley Hotel, Wilton Place* – Ⓜ *Knightsbridge* – ✆ *020 7235 1200*
www.marcusrestaurant.com – *Closed Sunday*

Pétrus

FRENCH • LUXURY Gordon Ramsay's Belgravia restaurant is a sophisticated ar elegant affair. The service is discreet and professional, and the cooking is roote in classical techniques but isn't afraid of adding its own touches of creativity ar originality. The superb wine list has Château Pétrus going back to 1928.

Specialities: Orkney scallop with kombu, bacon & egg sabayon. Fillet of Dexter beef with Roscoff onion, nasturtium and charcuterie sauce. 'Black Forest' kirsch mousse with Amarena and Morello cherry sorbet.

Menu £45 (lunch), £85/125

PLAN: 4-F5 – *1 Kinnerton Street – Ⓜ Knightsbridge – ✆ 020 7592 1609 – www.gordonramsayrestaurants.com/petrus*

Zafferano

ITALIAN • CLASSIC DÉCOR The immaculately coiffured regulars continue to support this ever-expanding, long-standing and capably run Italian restaurant. They come for the reassuringly familiar, if rather steeply priced dishes from all parts of Italy.

Menu £33 (lunch) – Carte £36/85

PLAN: 4-F5 – *15 Lowndes Street – Ⓜ Knightsbridge – ✆ 020 7235 5800 – www.zafferanorestaurant.com*

Hyde Park and Knightsbridge

Dinner by Heston Blumenthal

TRADITIONAL BRITISH • CLASSIC DÉCOR Heston Blumenthal's menu celebrates British culinary triumphs through the ages, with the date of origin given to each dish along with information about its provenance. An impressively well-manned kitchen works with obvious intelligence, calm efficiency and attention to detail to produce dishes that look deceptively simple but taste sublime.

Specialities: Mandarin, chicken liver parfait and grilled bread (c.1500). Spiced squab pigeon with onions, artichokes, ale and malt (c.1780). Tipsy cake with spit roast pineapple (c.1810).

Menu £45 (lunch) – Carte £90/105

PLAN: 4-F4 – *Mandarin Oriental Hyde Park Hotel, 66 Knightsbridge – Ⓜ Knightsbridge – ✆ 020 7201 3833 – www.dinnerbyheston.com*

Bar Boulud

FRENCH • CHIC Daniel Boulud's London outpost is fashionable, fun and frantic. His hometown is Lyon but he built his considerable reputation in New York, so charcuterie, sausages and burgers are the highlights.

Menu £26 (lunch) – Carte £30/65

PLAN: 4-F4 – *Mandarin Oriental Hyde Park Hotel, 66 Knightsbridge – Ⓜ Knightsbridge – ✆ 020 7201 3899 – www.barboulud.com*

Zuma

JAPANESE • CONTEMPORARY DÉCOR Now a global brand but this was the original. The glamorous clientele come for the striking surroundings, bustling atmosphere and easy-to-share food. Go for the more modern dishes and those cooked on the robata grill.

Carte £40/141

PLAN: 9-F5 – *5 Raphael Street – Ⓜ Knightsbridge – ✆ 020 7584 1010 – www.zumarestaurant.com*

Victoria

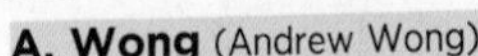

A. Wong (Andrew Wong)

CHINESE • NEIGHBOURHOOD Flavours, traditions and techniques from all across China are celebrated here by Andrew Wong. Inspired by his travels through the provinces, he presents his own interpretations of classic dishes using modern techniques and a creative eye, whilst always respecting their heritage.

Specialities: Shanghai steamed dumplings with ginger infused vinegar. Shaanxi pulled lamb 'burger' with Xinjiang pomegranate salad. 'Postcard from Yunnan' with banana, chocolate and white truffle.

Menu £95 – Carte £24/54

PLAN: 4-H6 – *70 Wilton Road – Ⓜ Victoria – ✆ 020 7828 8931 – www.awong.co.uk – Closed 22 December-6 January, Sunday, lunch Monday*

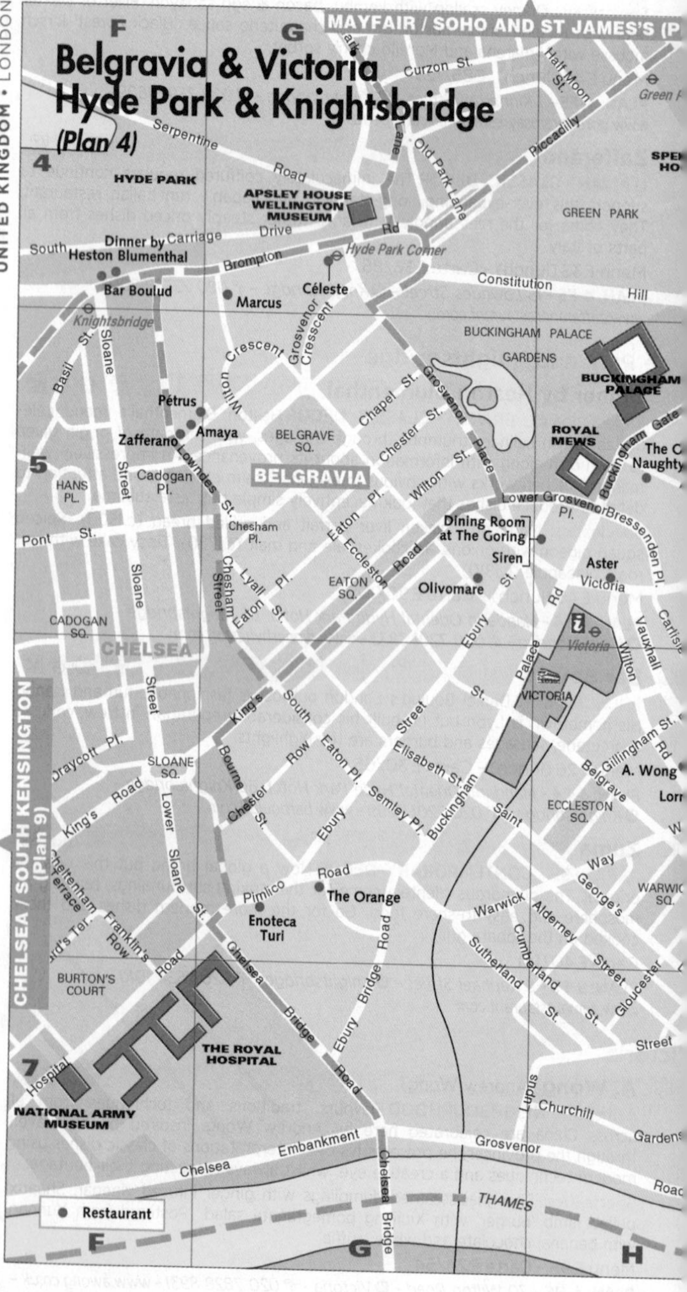
Belgravia & Victoria
Hyde Park & Knightsbridge
(Plan 4)
MAYFAIR / SOHO AND ST JAMES'S (P
CHELSEA / SOUTH KENSINGTON (Plan 9)
HYDE PARK
APSLEY HOUSE WELLINGTON MUSEUM
GREEN PARK
Dinner by Heston Blumenthal
Bar Boulud
Marcus
Céleste
Hyde Park Corner
Knightsbridge
BUCKINGHAM PALACE GARDENS
BUCKINGHAM PALACE
ROYAL MEWS
Pétrus
Amaya
Zafferano
BELGRAVE SQ.
BELGRAVIA
HANS PL.
The C Naughty
Dining Room at The Goring
Siren
Aster
Olivomare
EATON SQ.
CADOGAN SQ.
CHELSEA
VICTORIA
SLOANE SQ.
A. Wong
ECCLESTON SQ.
The Orange
Enoteca Turi
WARWIC SQ.
BURTON'S COURT
THE ROYAL HOSPITAL
NATIONAL ARMY MUSEUM
THAMES
Restaurant

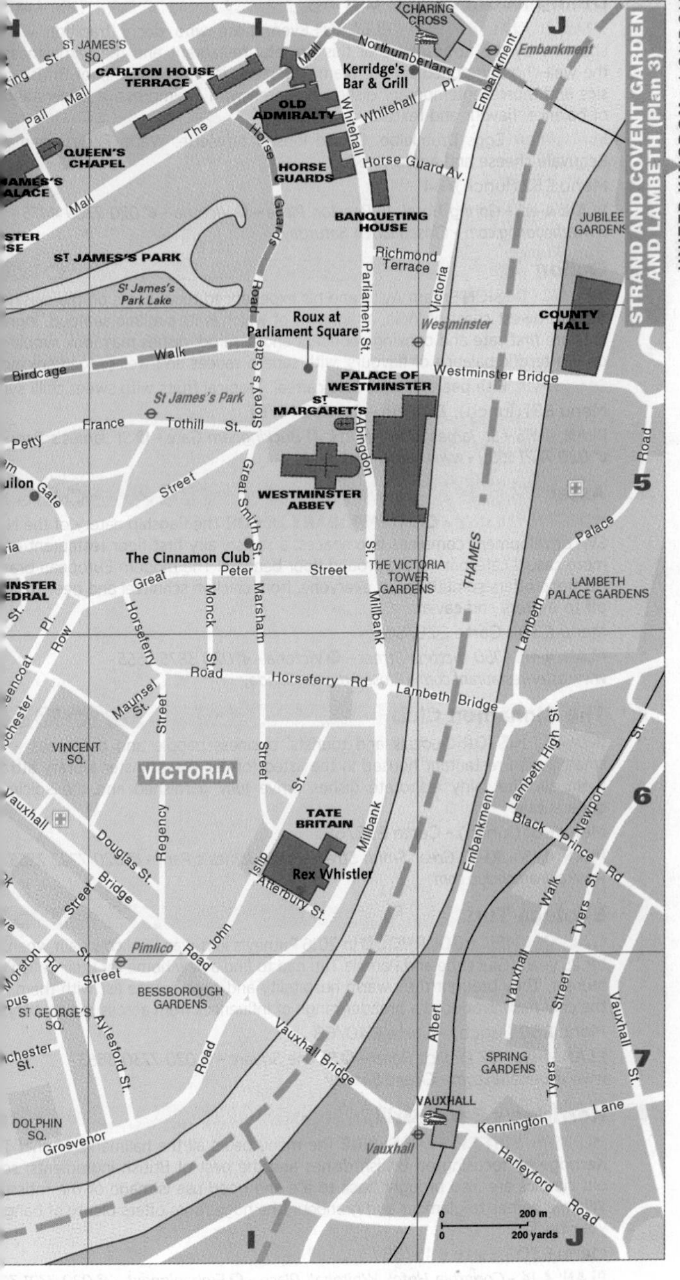
STRAND AND COVENT GARDEN AND LAMBETH (Plan 3)
CHARING CROSS
Embankment
Kerridge's Bar & Grill
CARLTON HOUSE TERRACE
OLD ADMIRALTY
QUEEN'S CHAPEL
HORSE GUARDS
BANQUETING HOUSE
ST JAMES'S PARK
St James's Park Lake
Richmond Terrace
JUBILEE GARDENS
COUNTY HALL
Roux at Parliament Square
Westminster
PALACE OF WESTMINSTER
Westminster Bridge
St James's Park
ST MARGARET'S
WESTMINSTER ABBEY
The Cinnamon Club
THE VICTORIA TOWER GARDENS
THAMES
LAMBETH PALACE GARDENS
VINCENT SQ.
VICTORIA
TATE BRITAIN
Rex Whistler
Pimlico
BESSBOROUGH GARDENS
ST GEORGE'S SQ.
SPRING GARDENS
VAUXHALL
Vauxhall
DOLPHIN SQ.
200 m
200 yards

Dining Room at The Goring

TRADITIONAL BRITISH • ELEGANT Even those who decry tradition will charmed by the atmosphere of this graceful restaurant and the earnestness the well-choreographed service team. The menu is a pleasing mix of British cl sics and more contemporary dishes, prepared with an impressive understand of balance, flavour and texture.

Specialities: Eggs Drumkilbo. Glazed lobster omelette. Warm Eccles cake w Beauvale cheese and apple vinegar.

Menu £52 (lunch)/64

PLAN: 4-H5 – *Goring Hotel, 15 Beeston Place – Ⓜ Victoria – ✆ 020 7769 4475 – www.thegoring.com – Closed lunch Saturday*

Quilon

INDIAN • DESIGN Sriram Aylur and his experienced team focus on the cuisine the southwest coast of India, a highlight of which is its sublime seafood. Ingre ents are first-rate and cooking confident and assured; dishes may look simple offer a terrific balance of flavours, with superb sauces and well-judged spicing

Specialities: Fish peera. Lemon sole cafreal. Tropical fruits with sweet chilli syr

Menu £31 (lunch), £70/85 – Carte £40/61

PLAN: 4-H5 – *St James' Court Hotel, 41 Buckingham Gate – Ⓜ St James's Park – ✆ 020 7821 1899 – www.quilon.co.uk*

Aster

MODERN CUISINE • CONTEMPORARY DÉCOR The flagship eatery of the Nc SW1 development combines two spaces: a stylish, airy first floor restaurant anc more casual café/bar on the ground floor beneath. The modern European brass rie menu offers something for everyone, from chicken schnitzel and beef stroga off to oysters and caviar.

Menu £30 – Carte £28/56

PLAN: 4-H5 – *150 Victoria Street – Ⓜ Victoria – ✆ 020 3875 5555 – www.aster-restaurant.com – Closed dinner Sunday*

The Cinnamon Club

INDIAN • HISTORIC Locals and tourists, business people and politicians – t smart Indian restaurant housed in the listed former Westminster Library attrac them all. The fairly elaborate dishes arrive fully garnished and the spicing quite subtle.

Menu £31 (lunch) – Carte £38/66

PLAN: 4-I5 – *30-32 Great Smith Street – Ⓜ St James's Park – ✆ 020 7222 2555 – www.cinnamonclub.com*

Enoteca Turi

ITALIAN • NEIGHBOURHOOD In 2016 Putney's loss was Pimlico's gain when, a ter 25 years, Giuseppe and Pamela Turi had to find a new home for their Italian re taurant. They brought their warm hospitality and superb wine list with them, ar the chef has introduced a broader range of influences from across the country.

Menu £30 (lunch) – Carte £40/68

PLAN: 4-G6 – *87 Pimlico Road – Ⓜ Sloane Square – ✆ 020 7730 3663 – www.enotecaturi.com – Closed Sunday*

Kerridge's Bar & Grill

MODERN BRITISH • BRASSERIE The menu bears all the hallmarks of chef To Kerridge by focusing on British dishes and the best of British ingredients; som old classics are also brought back to life and good use is made of the rotisseri When it comes to glamour and grandeur, the huge room offers plenty of bang fc your buck.

Menu £30 – Carte £45/68

PLAN: 4-I4 – *Corinthia Hotel, Whitehall Place – Ⓜ Embankment – ✆ 020 7321 324 – www.kerridgesbarandgrill.co.uk*

Lorne

MODERN CUISINE • SIMPLE A small, simply furnished restaurant down a busy side street. The experienced chef understands that less is more and the modern menu is an enticing list of unfussy, well-balanced British and European dishes. Diverse wine list.

Menu £27 (lunch) – Carte £37/50

PLAN: 4-H6 – *76 Wilton Road – Ⓜ Victoria – ✆ 020 3327 0210 – www.lornerestaurant.co.uk – Closed 23 December-2 January, dinner Sunday, lunch Monday*

Olivomare

SEAFOOD • DESIGN A busy, well-run Italian championing the cuisine of Sardinia; the monthly changing menu offers appealingly simple dishes created with high quality produce; much of which is also available in their deli next door. It's dimly lit, with a stark white interior and also boasts a striking feature wall.

Carte £35/49

PLAN: 4-G5 – *10 Lower Belgrave Street – Ⓜ Victoria – ✆ 020 7730 9022 – www.olivorestaurants.com*

The Orange

MODERN CUISINE • PUB The old Orange Brewery is as charming a pub as its stucco-fronted façade suggests. Try the fun bar or book a table in the more sedate upstairs room. Seasonal menus offer modern British dishes, with spelt or wheat-based pizzas a speciality. The upstairs bedrooms are stylish and comfortable.

Menu £25/43 – Carte £31/43

PLAN: 4-G6 – *37 Pimlico Road – Ⓜ Sloane Square – ✆ 020 7881 9844 – www.theorange.co.uk*

The Other Naughty Piglet

MODERN CUISINE • SIMPLE A light, spacious restaurant with friendly staff and a relaxed atmosphere, set on the first floor of The Other Palace theatre. Eclectic modern small plates are designed for sharing and accompanied by an interesting list of natural wines.

Menu £18 (lunch), £27/30 – Carte £26/44

PLAN: 4-H5 – *The Other Palace, 12 Palace Street – Ⓜ Victoria – ✆ 020 7592 0322 – www.theothernaughtypiglet.co.uk – Closed 22 December-2 January, Sunday, lunch Monday*

Rex Whistler

MODERN BRITISH • CLASSIC DÉCOR A hidden gem, tucked away on the lower ground floor of Tate Britain; its most striking element is Whistler's restored mural, 'The Expedition in Pursuit of Rare Meats', which envelops the room. The menu is stoutly British and the remarkably well-priced wine list has an unrivalled 'half bottle' selection.

Menu £35 (lunch)/57

PLAN: 4-I6 – *Tate Britain, Millbank – Ⓜ Pimlico – ✆ 020 7887 8825 – www.tate.org.uk/visit/tate-britain/rex-whistler-restaurant – Closed 24-26 December, dinner Sunday-Saturday*

Roux at Parliament Square

MODERN CUISINE • ELEGANT Light floods through the Georgian windows of this comfortable restaurant within the offices of the Royal Institute of Chartered Surveyors. Carefully crafted, elaborate and sophisticated cuisine, with some interesting flavour combinations.

Menu £42 (lunch), £59/89 – Carte £42/59

PLAN: 4-I5 – *Royal Institution of Chartered Surveyors, 11 Great George Street, Parliament Square – Ⓜ Westminster – ✆ 020 7334 3737 – www.rouxatparliamentsquare.co.uk – Closed 1-5 January, 21-30 December, Sunday, Saturday*

Siren

SEAFOOD • ELEGANT Nathan Outlaw's latest venture – the first new restaur at the Goring Hotel in 109 years – is inspired by the Goring family's ties w Cornwall, and showcases the very best of Cornish seafood, with a focus on wo derfully fresh fish, delivered daily. The elegant, orangery-style dining room ov looks the gardens.

Carte £50/102

PLAN: 4-H5 – *Goring Hotel, 15 Beeston Place – Ⓜ Victoria – ✆ 020 7396 9000 – www.thegoring.com*

Regent's Park and Marylebone

Locanda Locatelli (Giorgio Locatelli)

ITALIAN • CHIC Giorgio Locatelli's Italian restaurant may be well into its seco decade but it still looks as dapper as ever. The service is smooth and the roo was designed with conviviality in mind. The hugely appealing menu covers all r gions; unfussy presentation and superb ingredients allow natural flavours to shi

Specialities: Pappardelle with broad beans and rocket. Rabbit with Parma ha polenta and char-grilled radicchio. Ricotta mousse with pistachio sponge, candi fruit and pistachio ice cream.

Carte £50/100

PLAN: 5-G2 – *8 Seymour Street – Ⓜ Marble Arch – ✆ 020 7935 9088 – www.locandalocatelli.com*

Portland

MODERN CUISINE • INTIMATE The look is just the right side of austere, servi is knowledgeable and wine is given equal billing to the food. One glance at t menu and you know you'll eat well: it changes daily and the combinations ju sound right. The kitchen trusts the quality of the ingredients and lets natural fl vours shine.

Specialities: Isle of Mull scallops with pickled Yorkshire rhubarb and roasted sa sify. Cotswold venison with juniper and hay-baked purple carrots. Baked app terrine with hazelnut ice cream and lemon thyme soft-serve.

Menu £30 (lunch)/69 – Carte £49/60

PLAN: 5-H2 – *113 Great Portland Street – Ⓜ Great Portland Street – ✆ 020 7436 3261 – www.portlandrestaurant.co.uk – Closed 22 December-3 January, Sunday, lunch Monday-Tuesday*

Roganic

MODERN BRITISH • MINIMALIST Simon Rogan's London outpost is certainl not a copy of his L'Enclume restaurant in the Lake District but is intended to de liver elements of it. Much of the produce, however, comes from their farm i Cartmel. The cuisine style – which uses plenty of techniques including picklin and curing – will leave you feeling closer to nature.

Specialities: Chicken with cod's roe and carrot. Monkfish with brassicas. Rhubar with buttermilk and Earl Grey.

Menu £35 (lunch), £65/85

PLAN: 5-G2 – *5-7 Blandford Street – Ⓜ Bond Street – ✆ 020 3370 6260 – www.roganic.uk – Closed 1-6 January, Sunday, Monday*

Texture (Agnar Sverrisson)

CREATIVE • DESIGN Technically skilled but light and invigorating cooking fror an Icelandic chef-owner, who uses ingredients from his homeland. Bright restau rant with high ceiling and popular adjoining champagne bar. Pleasant servic from keen staff, ready with a smile.

Specialities: Scallops with coconut, soup, kaffir lime leaves and lemongrass. Cod with avocado, brandade, tomatoes and chorizo. Icelandic skyr with ice cream, Gariguette strawberries and rye breadcrumbs.

Menu £29 (lunch), £89/99 - Carte £70/116

PLAN: 5-G2 - *34 Portman Street* - *Ⓜ Marble Arch* - *✆ 020 7224 0028* - *www.texture-restaurant.co.uk* - *Closed 5-13 April, 9-24 August, 23 December-6 January, Sunday, Monday, lunch Tuesday-Wednesday*

Trishna (Karam Sethi)

INDIAN • NEIGHBOURHOOD A double-fronted, modern Indian restaurant dressed in an elegant, understated style. The coast of southwest India provides the influences and the food is vibrant, satisfying and executed with care - the tasting menus provide a good all-round experience, and much thought has gone into the matching wines.

Specialities: Aloo tokri chaat. Dorset brown crab with coconut oil, pepper, garlic and curry leaf. Mango and saffron kheer.

Menu £25 (lunch), £60/70 - Carte £34/58

PLAN: 5-G2 - *15-17 Blandford Street* - *Ⓜ Baker Street* - *✆ 020 7935 5624* - *www.trishnalondon.com*

Arros QD

MEDITERRANEAN CUISINE • CONTEMPORARY DÉCOR From celebrated Spanish chef Quique Dacosta comes this huge, strikingly decorated restaurant celebrating rice, and in particular the Valencian dish paella. Ask for a table on the ground floor so you can watch the action in the open kitchen and see the flames from the wood-fired stoves.

Menu £28 (lunch)/85 - Carte £42/76

PLAN: 5-H2 - *64 Eastcastle Street* - *Ⓜ Oxford Circus* - *✆ 020 3883 3525* - *www.arrosqd.com* - *Closed dinner Sunday*

Bonnie Gull

SEAFOOD • SIMPLE Sweet Bonnie Gull calls itself a 'seafood shack' - a reference perhaps to its modest beginnings as a pop-up. Start with something from the raw bar then go for classics like Cullen skink, Devon cock crab or fish and chips. There's another branch in Soho.

Carte £32/50

PLAN: 5-H2 - *21a Foley Street* - *Ⓜ Goodge Street* - *✆ 020 7436 0921* - *www.bonniegull.com*

Carousel

MODERN CUISINE • RUSTIC A unique, fun and well-run dining operation in which international and up-and-coming chefs showcase their talents. The chef changes every fortnight; each one cooking dishes for a set menu which is then eaten at two large communal tables. Advance bookings only for the one sitting per evening.

Menu £45

PLAN: 5-G2 - *71 Blandford Street* - *Ⓜ Baker Street* - *✆ 020 7487 5564* - *www.carousel-london.com* - *Closed Sunday, lunch Monday-Friday, Saturday*

Chiltern Firehouse

WORLD CUISINE • TRENDY How appropriate - one of the hottest tickets in town is a converted fire station. The room positively bursts with energy but what makes this celebrity hangout unusual is that the food is rather good. Nuno Mendes' menu is full of vibrant North and South American dishes that are big on flavour.

Carte £37/63

PLAN: 5-G2 - *Chiltern Firehouse Hotel, 1 Chiltern Street* - *Ⓜ Baker Street* - *✆ 020 7073 7676* - *www.chilternfirehouse.com*

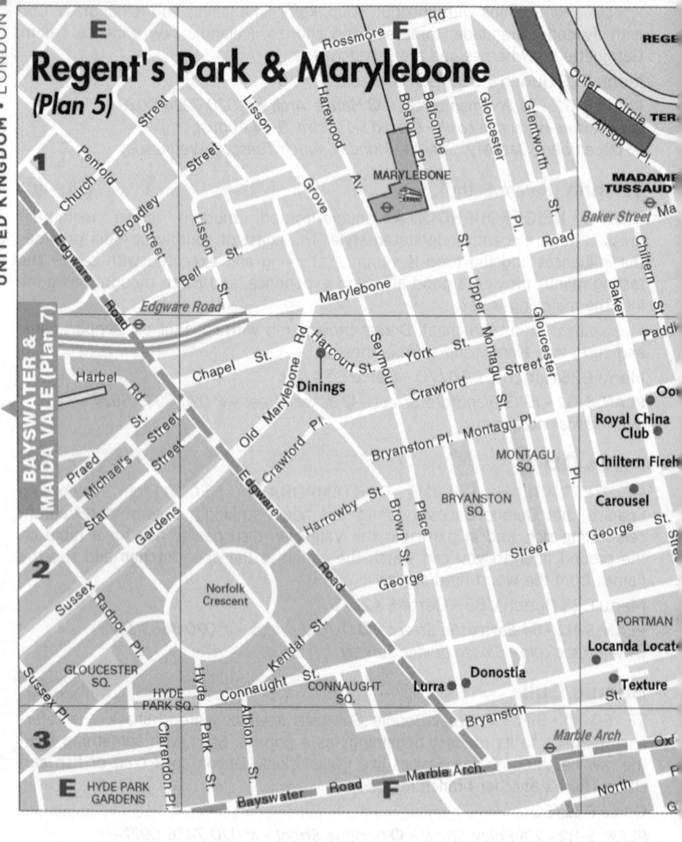

Clipstone

MODERN CUISINE • COSY Sister to Portland, just around the corner, is wonderful neighbourhood spot. Ingredients are good quality and cooking is object lesson in flavour and originality. Add a cleverly conceived wine list, sc cocktails and a relaxed, buzzy atmosphere and you've a recipe for all-round c tentment.

Menu £26 (lunch), £39/48 – Carte £26/48

PLAN: 5-H2 – *5 Clipstone Street* – Ⓜ *Great Portland Street* – ✆ *020 7637 0871* – *www.clipstonerestaurant.co.uk – Closed Sunday*

Dinings

JAPANESE • COSY It's hard not to be charmed by this sweet little Japar place, with its ground floor counter and basement tables. Its strengths lie the more creative, contemporary dishes; sharing is recommended but pr can be steep.

Carte £33/80

PLAN: 5-F2 – *22 Harcourt Street* – Ⓜ *Edgware Road* – ✆ *020 7723 0666* – *www.dinings.co.uk/harcourt – Closed lunch Sunday-Saturday*

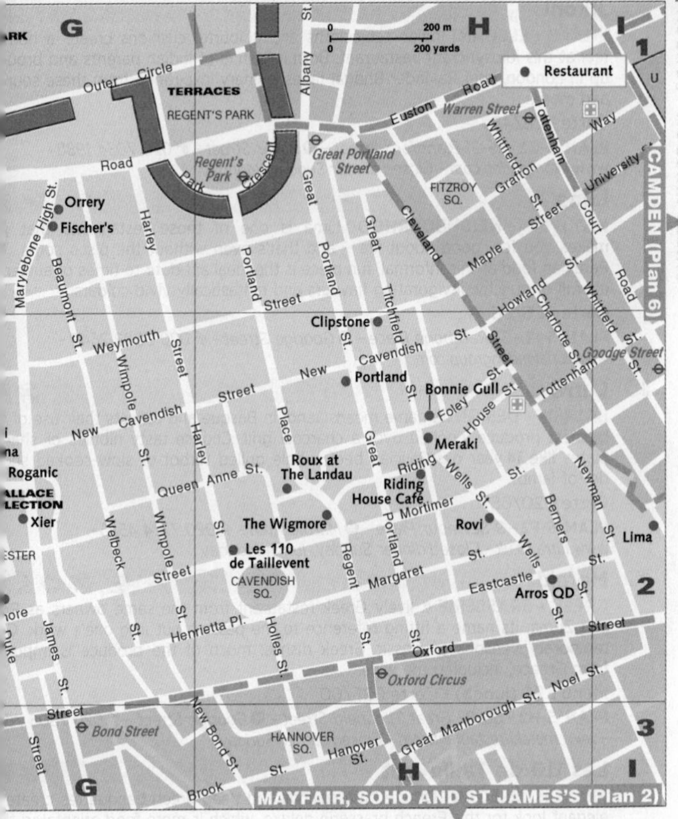

Donostia

BASQUE • TAPAS BAR The two young owners were inspired to open this pintxos and tapas bar by the food of San Sebastián. Sit at the counter for Basque classics like cod with pil-pil sauce, chorizo from the native Kintoa pig and slow-cooked pig's cheeks.

Menu £20 (lunch) – Carte £20/45

PLAN: 5-F2 – *10 Seymour Place* – *Marble Arch* – *020 3620 1845* – *www.donostia.co.uk* – *Closed lunch Sunday-Monday*

Fischer's

AUSTRIAN • BRASSERIE An Austrian café and konditorei that summons the spirit of old Vienna; from the owners of The Wolseley et al. It's open all day and breakfast is a highlight – the viennoiserie are great. The schnitzels are also good; upgrade to a Holstein.

Carte £19/55

PLAN: 5-G1 – *50 Marylebone High Street* – *Baker Street* – *020 7466 5501* – *www.fischers.co.uk*

Jikoni

INDIAN • ELEGANT Indian tablecloths and colourful cushions create a hom feel at this idiosyncratic restaurant. Born in Kenya of Indian parents and brou up in London, chef Ravinder Bhogal takes culinary inspiration from these sour and more.

Carte £28/45

PLAN: 5-G2 – *19-21 Blandford Street – Ⓜ Baker Street – ✆ 020 7034 1988 – www.jikonilondon.com – Closed dinner Sunday, Monday*

Lima

PERUVIAN • NEIGHBOURHOOD Lima is one of those restaurants that j makes you feel good about life – and that's even without the pisco sours. T Peruvian food at this informal, fun place is the ideal antidote to times of auster it's full of punchy, invigorating flavours and fantastically vivid colours.

Carte £26/56

PLAN: 5-I2 – *31 Rathbone Place – Ⓜ Goodge Street – ✆ 020 3002 2640 – www.limalondongroup.com*

Lurra

BASQUE • DESIGN Its name means 'land' in Basque and reflects their use of t freshest produce, cooked over a charcoal grill. Choose tasty nibbles or shari plates like 14 year old Galician beef, whole grilled turbot or slow-cooked sho der of lamb.

Carte £20/65

PLAN: 5-F2 – *9 Seymour Place – Ⓜ Marble Arch – ✆ 020 7724 4545 – www.lurra.co.uk – Closed dinner Sunday, lunch Monday*

Meraki

GREEK • BRASSERIE A lively Greek restaurant from the same owners as Ro and Zuma; its name a fitting reference to the passion put into one's work. Co temporary versions of classic Greek dishes; much of the produce is importe from Greece, including the wines.

Menu £20 (lunch) – Carte £25/60

PLAN: 5-H2 – *80-82 Great Titchfield Street – Ⓜ Goodge Street – ✆ 020 7305 768 – www.meraki-restaurant.com – Closed dinner Sunday*

Les 110 de Taillevent

FRENCH • ELEGANT Ornate high ceilings and deep green banquettes create a elegant look for this French brasserie deluxe, which is more food orientated tha the Paris original. It also offers 110 wines by the glass: 4 different pairings for eac dish, in 4 different price brackets.

Menu £28 (lunch)/32 – Carte £48/65

PLAN: 5-H2 – *16 Cavendish Square – Ⓜ Oxford Circus – ✆ 020 3141 6016 – www.les-110-taillevent-london.com – Closed 17-23 August, Sunday*

Ooty

SOUTH INDIAN • BRASSERIE Named after a hill station in Tamil Nadu, Ooty is roomy, stylish restaurant whose creative kitchen adds contemporary touches t the southern Indian specialities. Service is attentive and sweet-natured. Ooty Sta tion is a more casual all-day space and Ooty Club is the handsome bar downstair

Menu £25 (lunch) – Carte £25/66

PLAN: 5-G2 – *66 Baker Street – Ⓜ Baker Street – ✆ 020 3727 5014 – www.ooty.co.uk – Closed Sunday*

Opso

GREEK • NEIGHBOURHOOD A modern Greek restaurant which has proved a good fit for the neighbourhood – and not just because it's around the corne from the Hellenic Centre. It serves small sharing plates that mix the modern wit the traditional.

Carte £35/51

PLAN: 5-G1 – *10 Paddington Street – Ⓜ Baker Street – ✆ 020 7487 5088 – www.opso.co.uk – Closed 23 December-5 January*

Orrery

MODERN CUISINE • NEIGHBOURHOOD The most recent redecoration left this comfortable restaurant, located in what were converted stables from the 19C, looking lighter and more contemporary; the bar and terrace are also smarter. Expect quite elaborate, modern European cooking, strong on presentation and with the occasional twist.

Menu £27 (lunch), £59/89 – Carte £27/89

PLAN: 5-G1 – *55 Marylebone High Street* – Ⓜ *Regent's Park* – ✆ *020 7616 8000* – *www.orrery-restaurant.co.uk*

Riding House Café

MODERN CUISINE • RUSTIC It's less a café, more a large, quirkily designed, all-day New York style brasserie and cocktail bar. The small plates have more zing than the main courses. The 'unbookable' side of the restaurant is the more fun part.

Carte £17/42

PLAN: 5-H2 – *43-51 Great Titchfield Street* – Ⓜ *Oxford Circus* – ✆ *020 7927 0840* – *www.ridinghousecafe.co.uk*

Roux at The Landau

FRENCH • ELEGANT There's been a change to a more informal style for this restaurant run under the aegis of the Roux organisation – it's now more akin to a modern bistro in looks and atmosphere and is all the better for it. The cooking is classical French and informed by the seasons; shellfish is a highlight.

Menu £35/90 – Carte £39/80

PLAN: 5-H2 – *Langham Hotel, 1c Portland Place, Regent Street* – Ⓜ *Oxford Circus* – ✆ *020 7965 0165* – *www.rouxatthelandau.com* – *Closed Sunday, Monday*

Rovi

WORLD CUISINE • BRASSERIE Yotam Ottolenghi's bright and colourful brasserie uses lots of fermenting and chargrilling. Dishes are designed for sharing, influences come from far and wide and vegetables are given equal billing as meat and fish.

Carte £25/75

PLAN: 5-H2 – *59 Wells Street* – Ⓜ *Oxford Circus* – ✆ *020 3963 8270* – *www.ottolenghi.co.uk/rovi* – *Closed dinner Sunday*

Royal China Club

CHINESE • ORIENTAL Service is fast-paced and to the point, which is understandable considering how busy this restaurant always is. The large menu offers something for everyone and the lunchtime dim sum is very good; at dinner try their more unusual Cantonese dishes.

Carte £35/80

PLAN: 5-G2 – *40-42 Baker Street* – Ⓜ *Baker Street* – ✆ *020 7486 3898* – *www.royalchinagroup.co.uk* – *Closed 25-27 December*

The Wigmore

TRADITIONAL BRITISH • PUB The impressively high ceiling can only mean one thing – this was once a bank. Booths, high tables, a sizeable bar and bold emerald green tones lend a clubby feel to this addendum to The Langham. Classic, hearty British dishes are given an update.

Carte £22/46

PLAN: 5-H2 – *Langham Hotel, 15 Langham Place, Upper Regent Street* – Ⓜ *Oxford Circus* – ✆ *020 7965 0198* – *www.the-wigmore.co.uk* – *Closed Sunday*

Xier

INNOVATIVE • DESIGN A 10 course set menu, along with a vegetarian alternative, is offered upstairs in the formal surroundings of Xier. Here the cooking is ambitious, original and informed by the Italian chef's international travels. XR on the ground floor is a more casual alternative and serves European dishes.

Menu £90

PLAN: 5-G2 – *13-14 Thayer Street* – Ⓜ *Bond Street* – ✆ *020 7486 3222* – *www.xierlondon.com* – *Closed Sunday, Monday, lunch Tuesday-Saturday*

UNITED KINGDOM • LONDON

Zoilo

ARGENTINIAN • FRIENDLY Sharing is the order of the day here, so grab a s at the counter and discover Argentina's regional specialities. Typical dishes clude baked Provolone cheese, crab on toast, and grilled lamb sweetbread and these are accompanied by an appealing all-Argentinian wine list.

Carte £30/60

PLAN: 5-G2 – *9 Duke Street – Ⓜ Bond Street – ✆ 020 7486 9699 – www.zoilo.co.*
Closed Sunday, lunch Monday

Camden

Bloomsbury

Kitchen Table at Bubbledogs (James Knappett)

MODERN CUISINE • CONTEMPORARY DÉCOR Behind a curtain you'll fin counter where chef-owner James Knappett and his team prepare a surp menu of around 14 dishes. The produce is some of the best you can find and small dishes come with a clever creative edge. The chefs interact with their c tomers over the counter and are helped out by James' wife Sandia, who is cha personified.

Specialities: Scallops with charcoal-infused cream, extra virgin olive oil and moor caviar. Cornish glazed duck with damson purée, yoghurt, black garlic turnips. Beetroot marmalade with sour cream ice cream and sweet wood granité.

Menu £150

PLAN: 6-H2 – *70 Charlotte Street – Ⓜ Goodge Street – ✆ 020 7637 7770 – www.kitchentablelondon.co.uk – Closed 1-14 January, 1-15 August, 22-29 December Sunday, Monday, Tuesday, lunch Wednesday-Saturday*

Hakkasan Hanway Place

CHINESE • EXOTIC DÉCOR There are now Hakkasans all over the world but was the original. It has the sensual looks, air of exclusivity and glamorous atr sphere synonymous with the 'brand'. The exquisite Cantonese dishes are prepa with care and consistency by the large kitchen team; lunch dim sum is a highli

Specialities: Smoked beef ribs with jasmine tea. Spicy prawn with lily bulb almond. Jivara bomb.

Menu £38 (lunch) – Carte £35/135

PLAN: 6-I2 – *8 Hanway Place – Ⓜ Tottenham Court Road – ✆ 020 7927 7000 – www.hakkasan.com*

The Ninth (Jun Tanaka)

MEDITERRANEAN CUISINE • BRASSERIE Jun Tanaka's first restaurant – ninth in which he has worked – is this neighbourhood spot with a lively do stairs and more intimate first floor. Cooking uses classical French techniq with a spotlight on the Med; dishes look appealing but the focus is firmly on vour. Vegetables are a highlight.

Specialities: Salted beef cheek with beetroot and horseradish. Chargrilled bream, lemon confit and miso. Pain perdu with vanilla ice cream.

Menu £28 (lunch) – Carte £39/59

PLAN: 6-I2 – *22 Charlotte Street – Ⓜ Goodge Street – ✆ 020 3019 0880 – www.theninthlondon.com – Closed 23 December-2 January, Sunday*

Pied à Terre

CREATIVE • ELEGANT One of the reasons for the impressive longevity of Da Moore's restaurant has been its subtle reinventions: nothing ever too grandios just a little freshening up with some new art or clever lighting to keep the p looking relevant and vibrant. The cooking is still based on classical French tec ques but dishes now display a more muscular edge.

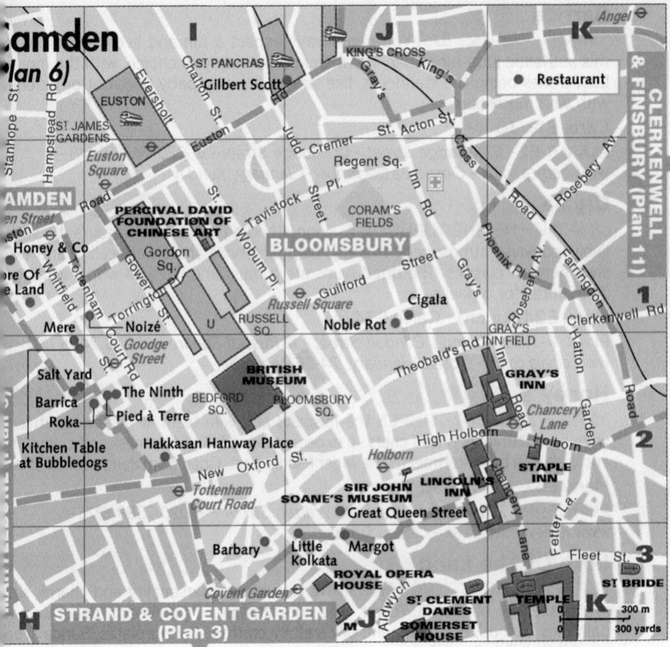

Camden (Plan 6)

Restaurant
I J K
Angel
ST PANCRAS
KING'S CROSS
Gilbert Scott
EUSTON
ST JAMES'S GARDENS
Euston Square
CAMDEN
CLERKENWELL & FINSBURY (Plan 11)
Eversholt
Chalton St.
Euston Rd
Judd St.
Cremer St.
Gray's Inn Rd
King's Cross Rd
St. Acton St.
Regent Sq.
Stanhope St.
Hampstead Rd
PERCIVAL DAVID FOUNDATION OF CHINESE ART
Tavistock Pl.
Woburn Pl.
CORAM'S FIELDS
BLOOMSBURY
Honey & Co
Gordon Sq.
Gower St.
Guilford Street
Russell Square
Cigala
Noble Rot
Tottenham Court Rd
Whitfield St.
Torrington Pl.
Mere
Noizé
RUSSELL SQ.
Goodge Street
Rosebery Av.
Phoenix Pl.
Farringdon Road
Clerkenwell Rd
GRAY'S INN FIELD
Theobald's Rd
Salt Yard
The Ninth
Barrica
Roka
Pied à Terre
BRITISH MUSEUM
BEDFORD SQ.
BLOOMSBURY SQ.
GRAY'S INN
Chancery Lane
Hatton Garden
Kitchen Table at Bubbledogs
Hakkasan Hanway Place
New Oxford St.
High Holborn
Holborn
STAPLE INN
Tottenham Court Road
SIR JOHN SOANE'S MUSEUM
LINCOLN'S INN
Great Queen Street
Fetter La.
Barbary
Little Kolkata
Margot
ROYAL OPERA HOUSE
Fleet St.
ST BRIDE
Covent Garden
Aldwych
ST CLEMENT DANES
SOMERSET HOUSE
TEMPLE
300 m
300 yards
STRAND & COVENT GARDEN (Plan 3)
1 2 3 H

Specialities: Smoked quail with celeriac, truffle and hazelnuts. Honey-glazed lemon sole with asparagus, baby artichokes and morels. Chocolate crémeux with dulce de leche, passion fruit and fennel pollen.

Menu £43/145

PLAN: 6-I2 – *34 Charlotte Street* – Ⓜ *Goodge Street* – ✆ *020 7636 1178* – *www.pied-a-terre.co.uk* – *Closed 23 December-3 January, Sunday, lunch Saturday*

Barbary

MIDDLE EASTERN • TAPAS BAR A sultry, atmospheric restaurant from the team behind Palomar: a tiny place with 24 non-bookable seats squeezed around a horseshoe-shaped, zinc-topped counter. The menu of small sharing plates lists dishes from the former Barbary Coast. Service is keen, as are the prices.

Carte £21/38

PLAN: 6-I3 – *16 Neal's Yard* – Ⓜ *Covent Garden* – *www.thebarbary.co.uk*

Salt Yard

MEDITERRANEAN CUISINE • TAPAS BAR A ground floor bar and buzzy basement restaurant specialising in good value plates of tasty Italian and Spanish dishes, ideal for sharing. Ingredients are top-notch; charcuterie is a speciality. Super wine list and sincere, enthusiastic staff.

Carte £25/40

PLAN: 6-H2 – *54 Goodge Street* – Ⓜ *Goodge Street* – ✆ *020 7637 0657* – *www.saltyard.co.uk*

Barrica

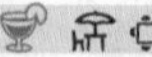

SPANISH • TAPAS BAR You can always expect a fun and lively atmosphere this authentic little tapas bar. The menu offers plenty of choice, with the more bust dishes being the standouts, like lamb neck with baby beetroot or ox chee with wild mushrooms.

Carte £19/30

PLAN: 6-H2 – *62 Goodge Street* – *Goodge Street* – *020 7436 9448* – *www.barrica.co.uk* – *Closed 22 December-1 January, Sunday*

Cigala

SPANISH • NEIGHBOURHOOD A long-standing Spanish restaurant, with lively, convivial atmosphere, friendly, helpful service and an appealing and exte sive menu of classics. The dried hams are a must and it's well worth waiting 30 minutes for a paella.

Menu £24 (lunch) – Carte £34/46

PLAN: 6-J1 – *54 Lamb's Conduit Street* – *Russell Square* – *020 7405 1717* – *www.cigala.co.uk* – *Closed 1 January, 24-26 December*

Honey & Co

MIDDLE EASTERN • SIMPLE The husband and wife team at this sweet little c were both Ottolenghi head chefs so expect cooking full of freshness and colour. Inf ences stretch beyond Israel to the wider Middle East. Open from 8am; packed at nig

Menu £32 – Carte £30/40

PLAN: 6-H1 – *25a Warren Street* – *Warren Street* – *020 7388 6175* – *www.honeyandco.co.uk* – *Closed Sunday*

Lore Of The Land

EUROPEAN CONTEMPORARY • PUB A pub with personality and charm, sitt in the shadow of the BT Tower. The cute upstairs dining room, decorated w paintings of food, offers a menu of carefully crafted sharing plates; Sunday roa are a speciality. Beers from owner Guy Ritchie's Wiltshire brewery also featur

Menu £20 (lunch) – Carte £30/44

PLAN: 6-H1 – *4 Conway Street* – *Great Portland Street* – *020 3927 4480* – *www.gritchiepubs.com* – *Closed dinner Sunday, Monday*

Mere

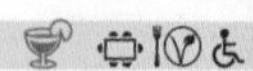

MODERN CUISINE • DESIGN Monica Galetti's first collaboration with her h band, David, is an understatedly elegant basement restaurant flooded with na ral light. Global, ingredient-led cooking features French influences with a nod the South Pacific.

Menu £35 (lunch)/77 – Carte £55/75

PLAN: 6-H2 – *74 Charlotte Street* – *Goodge Street* – *020 7268 6565* – *www.mere-restaurant.com* – *Closed Sunday*

Noble Rot

TRADITIONAL BRITISH • RUSTIC A wine bar and restaurant from the peo behind the wine magazine of the same name. Unfussy cooking comes with bo gutsy flavours; expect fish from the Kent coast as well as classics like terrines, lettes and home-cured meats.

Menu £16 (lunch)/20 – Carte £39/60

PLAN: 6-J1 – *51 Lamb's Conduit Street* – *Russell Square* – *020 7242 8963* – *www.noblerot.co.uk* – *Closed Sunday*

Noizé

MODERN FRENCH • NEIGHBOURHOOD A softly spoken Frenchman, an alum of Pied à Terre, took over the former Dabbous site and created a delightfully rela modern bistro. The unfussy French food is served at fair prices; sauces are a gr strength. The wine list, with plenty of depth and fair mark-ups, is another highlight.

Carte £35/50

PLAN: 6-I1 – *39 Whitfield Street* – *Goodge Street* – *020 7323 1310* – *www.noize-restaurant.co.uk* – *Closed 21 December-2 January, Sunday, Monday, lunch Saturday*

Roka

JAPANESE • MINIMALIST The original Roka, where people come for the lively atmosphere as much as the cooking. The kitchen takes the flavours of Japanese food and adds its own contemporary touches; try specialities from the on-view Robata grill.

Carte £42/75

PLAN: 6-I2 – *37 Charlotte Street* – Ⓜ *Goodge Street* – ✆ *020 7636 5228* – *www.rokarestaurant.com*

Holborn

Margot

ITALIAN • ELEGANT Bucking the trend of casual eateries is this glamorous, elegant Italian, where a doorman greets you, staff sport tuxedos and the surroundings are sleek and stylish. The seasonal, regional Italian cooking has bags of flavour and a rustic edge.

Menu £26/29 – Carte £35/55

PLAN: 6-J3 – *45 Great Queen Street* – Ⓜ *Holborn* – ✆ *020 3409 4777* – *www.margotrestaurant.com*

King's Cross St Pancras

Barrafina

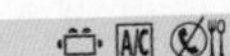

SPANISH • TAPAS BAR This is the fourth and largest Barrafina, occupying a prime spot in the new Coal Drops Yard development. Expect their trademark counter seating and famous pan con tomate; the rest of the menu is inspired by the cuisine of Catalonia and features dishes that blend fish and meat (Mar Y Montana).

Carte £28/46

PLAN: 1-C1 – *27 Coal Drops Yard* – Ⓜ *King's Cross St Pancras* – *www.barrafina.co.uk*

Coal Office

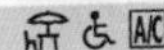

MIDDLE EASTERN • DESIGN A super-stylish collaboration between Israeli chef Assaf Granit and renowned designer Tom Dixon, with a long narrow interior, an open kitchen and striking pendant lights. The menu showcases Assaf's unique style of modern Israeli cuisine, with breads cooked to order in the wood-burning oven.

Carte £30/52

PLAN: 1-C2 – *2 Bagley Walk, Coal Drops Yard* – Ⓜ *King's Cross St Pancras* – ✆ *020 3848 6085* – *www.coaloffice.com*

Gilbert Scott

TRADITIONAL BRITISH • BRASSERIE Named after the architect of this Gothic masterpiece and run under the aegis of Marcus Wareing, this restaurant has the splendour of a Grand Salon but the buzz of a brasserie. The appealing menu showcases the best of British produce, whilst incorporating influences from further afield.

Menu £30/40 – Carte £31/73

PLAN: 6-J0 – *St Pancras Renaissance Hotel, Euston Road* – Ⓜ *King's Cross St Pancras* – ✆ *020 7278 3888* – *www.thegilbertscott.com*

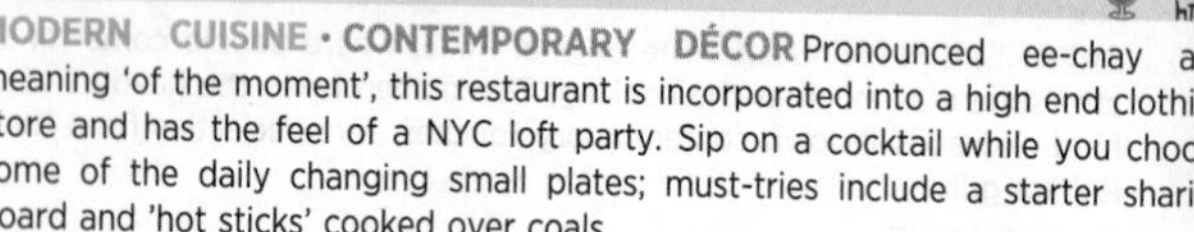

Hicce

MODERN CUISINE • CONTEMPORARY DÉCOR Pronounced ee-chay a meaning 'of the moment', this restaurant is incorporated into a high end clothi store and has the feel of a NYC loft party. Sip on a cocktail while you choc some of the daily changing small plates; must-tries include a starter shari board and 'hot sticks' cooked over coals.

Carte £22/37

PLAN: 1-C1-2 – *102 Stable Street, Coal Drops Yard* – *Kings Cross St Pancras* – *0203 869 8200* – *www.hicce.co.uk*

Bayswater and Maida Vale

Hereford Road

TRADITIONAL BRITISH • NEIGHBOURHOOD A converted Victorian butche shop; now a relaxed and friendly neighbourhood restaurant. It specialises in tas British dishes without frills, made using first-rate seasonal ingredients; offal is highlight. Booths for six people are the prized seats.

Menu £16 (lunch) – Carte £26/34

PLAN: 7-C2 – *3 Hereford Road* – *Bayswater* – *020 7727 1144* – *www.herefordroad.org* – *Closed 29-31 August, 22 December-5 January, lunch Monday-Wednesday*

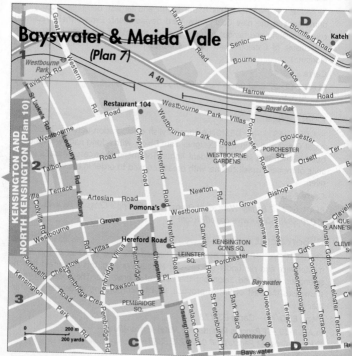

Bayswater & Maida Vale
(Plan 7)

Restaurant 104
Pomona's
Hereford Road
KENSINGTON AND NORTH KENSINGTON (Plan 10)

Kateh

MEDITERRANEAN CUISINE • NEIGHBOURHOOD Booking is imperative if you want to join the locals who have already discovered what a little jewel they have in the form of this buzzy, busy Persian restaurant. Authentic stews, expert chargrilling and lovely pastries and teas.

Carte £23/35

PLAN: 7-D1 – *5 Warwick Place* – *Warwick Avenue* – *020 7289 3393* – *www.katehrestaurant.co.uk* – *Closed 1-3 January, lunch Monday-Friday*

104

MODERN BRITISH • INTIMATE A cosy spot with only six tables; its set four course menu comes with a choice of mains and numerous extras. Classical combinations are finished with a modern style and dishes are delicate, easy to eat and full of flavour. This is confident cooking from a chef who has a real understanding of balance.

Menu £43/110

PLAN: 7-C2 – *104a Chepstow Road* – *Westbourne Park* – *020 3417 4744* – *www.104restaurant.com* – *Closed dinner Sunday, Monday, lunch Tuesday-Thursday*

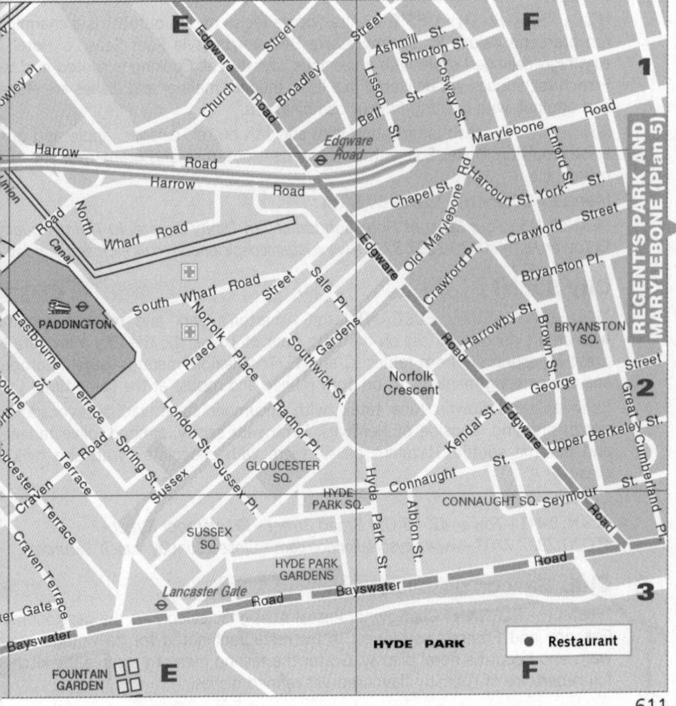

Pomona's

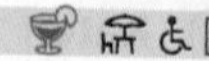

MODERN BRITISH • NEIGHBOURHOOD A large neighbourhood restaurant w... a relaxed atmosphere. The all-day menu offers seasonal British dishes under t... headings 'From the Earth/Land/Sea', while the sharing tasting menu is availab... with matching wine flights – and also comes in a vegetarian version. Start wi... cocktails in the bar or garden.

Carte £25/55

PLAN: 7-C2 – *47 Hereford Road* – Ⓜ *Bayswater* – ✆ *020 7229 1503* – *www.pomonas.co.uk*

Soutine

FRENCH • BRASSERIE It may only have opened mid-2019 but consummate re... taurateurs Corbin and King have created a warm, lively, Parisian-style bistro albeit one with hints of Edwardiana – that feels like it's been here for year... The all-day menu offers a rollcall of French classics, from confit de canard t... sole Véronique.

Carte £24/46

PLAN: 1-B2 – *60 St John's Wood High Street* – Ⓜ *St John's Wood* – ✆ *020 3926 8448* – *www.soutine.co.uk*

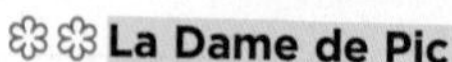

City of London - Southwark

City of London

La Dame de Pic

MODERN FRENCH • DESIGN Anne-Sophie Pic's London outpost is a charmingl... run brasserie deluxe in the impressive Beaux-Arts style Four Seasons Hotel; a... airy, high-ceilinged room with a spacious, stylish feel. Cooking is rooted in classi... French techniques yet delivered in a light, modern manner and dishes are elegar... and original, with exciting flavour combinations.

Specialities: Scottish langoustine with shellfish butter, celeriac, apple and gree... anise emulsion. Dover Sole with smoked beetroot, rose and grapefruit. The whit... millefeuille.

Menu £42 (lunch) – Carte £75/114

PLAN: 8-N3 – *Four Seasons Hotel London at Ten Trinity Square, 10 Trinity Square* – Ⓜ *Tower Hill* – ✆ *020 3297 3799* – *www.ladamedepiclondon.co.uk* – *Closed Sunday*

City Social

MODERN CUISINE • ELEGANT Jason Atherton's dark and moody restauran... with an art deco twist, set on the 24th floor of Tower 42; the City views are im... pressive, especially from tables 10 and 15. The flexible menu is largely Europear... and the cooking manages to be both refined and robust at the same time.

Specialities: Yellowfin tuna tataki with cucumber salad, radish, avocado anc... ponzu dressing. Topside of Herdwick lamb with salsify, almond, olive tapenade... and pomme soufflé. Hazelnut plaisir sucré with chocolate syrup and milk ice... cream.

Carte £45/91

PLAN: 8-M3 – *Tower 42, 25 Old Broad Street* – Ⓜ *Liverpool Street* – ✆ *020 7877 7703* – *www.citysociallondon.com* – *Closed Sunday, lunch Saturday*

Club Gascon (Pascal Aussignac)

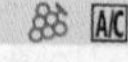

FRENCH • ELEGANT Chef-owner Pascal Aussignac celebrates the gastronomy of Gascony and France's southwest in his restaurant noted for its vintage marble walls and beautiful floral display. Go for the tasting menu to sample the kitchen's full repertoire of robustly flavoured yet refined dishes.

Specialities: Barbecued foie gras with pine, mushroom and razor clams. Monkfish with pork crackling, crosnes and umami consommé. Gianduja with matcha sponge and passion fruit.

Menu £35 (lunch), £85/110 - Carte £46/86

PLAN: 8-L2 - *57 West Smithfield - Ⓜ Barbican - ✆ 020 7600 6144 - www.clubgascon.com - Closed 1-8 January, Sunday, lunch Saturday*

Bob Bob Cité

FRENCH • BRASSERIE Sister to the iconic Soho original is this impressively ostentatious brasserie deluxe, set on the third level of the Cheesegrater building. Ensconce yourself in a booth, find the button and 'Press for Champagne'; the classic French dishes are hearty and full of flavour with some luxury touches.

Carte £45/83

PLAN: 8-M3 - *122 Leadenhall Street - Ⓜ Bank - ✆ 020 3928 6600 - www.bobbobcite.com*

Brigadiers

INDIAN • EXOTIC DÉCOR The army mess clubs of India provide the theme for this large restaurant on the ground floor of the Bloomberg building. BBQ and street food from around India is the focus; with 'Feast' menus for larger parties. Beer and whisky are also a feature. The atmosphere is predictably loud and lively.

Menu £25 (lunch), £60/80 - Carte £22/55

PLAN: 8-M3 - *1-5 Bloomberg Arcade - Ⓜ Mansion House - ✆ 020 3319 8140 - www.brigadierslondon.com*

Cabotte

FRENCH • WINE BAR An appealing bistro de luxe with distressed décor and a rustic charm, offering accomplished French classics which are simple in style and rich in flavour. It is owned by two master sommeliers who share a passion for the wines of Burgundy, and its stunning wine list offers a top-notch selection.

Menu £45 - Carte £35/52

PLAN: 8-M3 - *48 Gresham Street - Ⓜ Bank - ✆ 020 7600 1616 - www.cabotte.co.uk - Closed 21 December-2 January, Sunday, Saturday*

Cigalon

FRENCH • ELEGANT Hidden away among the lawyers' offices on Chancery Lane, this bright, high-ceilinged former auction house pays homage to the food and wine of Provence and Corsica. Fresh, flavoursome French classics like salade niçoise, bouillabaisse and ratatouille remind you of sunny Mediterranean days.

Menu £27 (lunch)/38 - Carte £35/45

PLAN: 8-K3 - *115 Chancery Lane - Ⓜ Chancery Lane - ✆ 020 7242 8373 - www.cigalon.co.uk - Closed 21 December-6 January, Sunday, lunch Saturday*

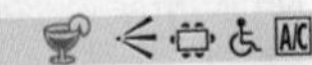

Fenchurch

MODERN CUISINE • DESIGN Arrive at the 'Walkie Talkie' early so you can first wander round the Sky Garden and take in the views. The smartly dressed restaurant is housed in a glass box within the atrium. Dishes are largely British and the accomplished cooking uses modern techniques.

Menu £39 (lunch), £60/85 - Carte £54/85

PLAN: 8-M3 - *Sky Garden, 20 Fenchurch Street - Ⓜ Monument - ✆ 0333 772 0020 - www.skygarden.london*

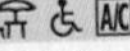

José Pizarro

SPANISH • TAPAS BAR The eponymous chef's third operation is a good fit here: it's well run, flexible and fairly priced - and that includes the wine list. The Spanish menu is nicely balanced, with the seafood dishes being the standouts.

Carte £17/56

PLAN: 8-M2 - *36 Broadgate Circle - Ⓜ Liverpool Street - ✆ 020 7256 5333 - www.josepizarro.com - Closed Sunday*

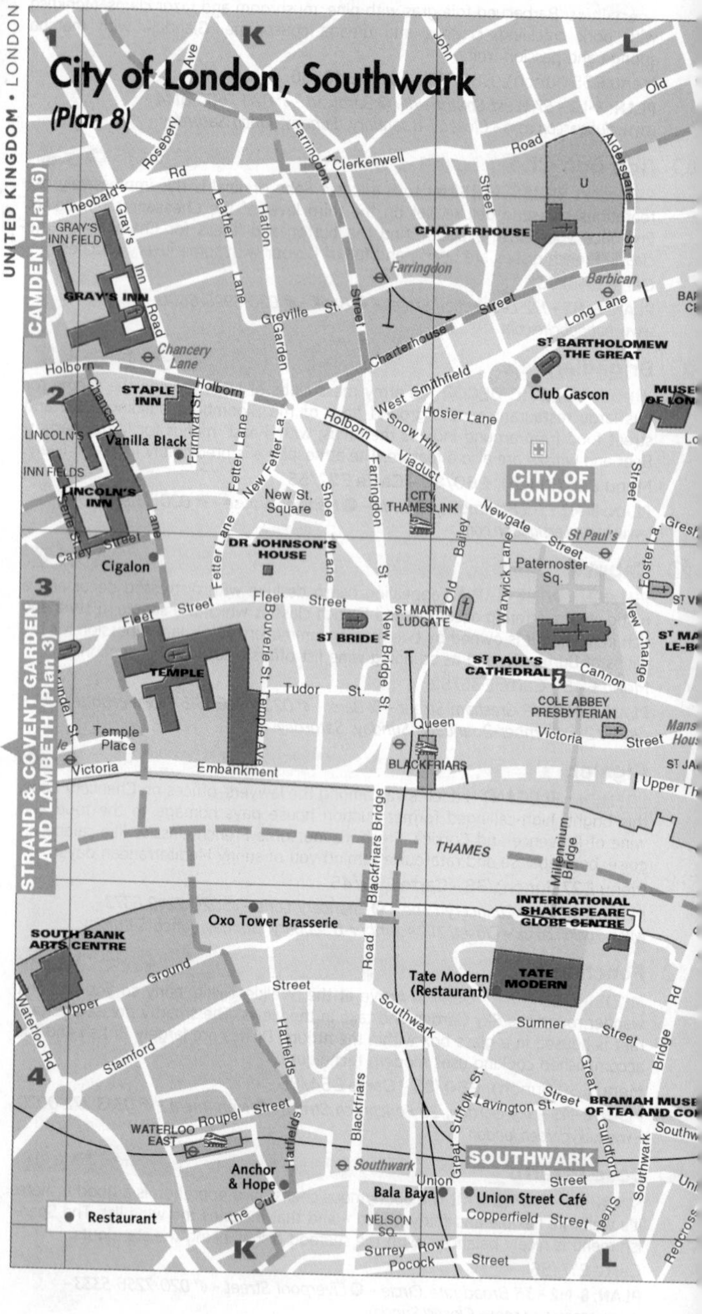

City of London, Southwark

(Plan 8)

CAMDEN (Plan 6)

STRAND & COVENT GARDEN AND LAMBETH (Plan 3)

1
K
L
2
3
4

John
Old
Rosebery Ave
Farringdon Rd
Clerkenwell Road
Aldersgate St.
U
Theobald's Rd
GRAY'S INN FIELD
Gray's Inn Road
Leather Lane
Hatton Garden
Farringdon Street
Street
CHARTERHOUSE
Farringdon
Barbican
GRAY'S INN
Greville St.
Charterhouse Street
Long Lane
Chancery Lane
Holborn
ST BARTHOLOMEW THE GREAT
STAPLE INN
Holborn
West Smithfield
Club Gascon
Chancery
Furnival St.
Hosier Lane
Holborn Viaduct
Snow Hill
LINCOLN'S INN FIELDS
Vanilla Black
Fetter Lane
New Fetter La.
Farringdon St.
CITY THAMESLINK
CITY OF LONDON
Street
LINCOLN'S INN
New St. Square
Shoe Lane
Newgate Street
Serle St.
Lane
Carey Street
DR JOHNSON'S HOUSE
Old Bailey
Warwick Lane
St Paul's
Foster La.
Cigalon
Fetter Lane
Paternoster Sq.
Fleet Street
Fleet Street
New Bridge St.
ST MARTIN LUDGATE
New Change
Bouverie St.
ST BRIDE
TEMPLE
ST PAUL'S CATHEDRAL
Cannon
Arundel St.
Tudor St.
Temple Ave
COLE ABBEY PRESBYTERIAN
Queen Victoria Street
Temple Place
Victoria
Embankment
BLACKFRIARS
Upper Th
Blackfriars Bridge
THAMES
Millennium Bridge
INTERNATIONAL SHAKESPEARE GLOBE CENTRE
Oxo Tower Brasserie
SOUTH BANK ARTS CENTRE
Road
Tate Modern (Restaurant)
TATE MODERN
Upper Ground
Street
Southwark
Rd
Waterloo Rd
Hatfields
Sumner Street
Bridge
Stamford Street
Blackfriars
Great Suffolk St.
Great Guildford
Lavington St.
BRAMAH MUSE OF TEA AND CO
Roupel Street
WATERLOO EAST
Hatfields
Southwark
SOUTHWARK
Anchor & Hope
Union Street
Bala Baya
Union Street Café
The Cut
NELSON SQ.
Copperfield Street
Street
Surrey Row
Pocock Street
Redcross
Restaurant

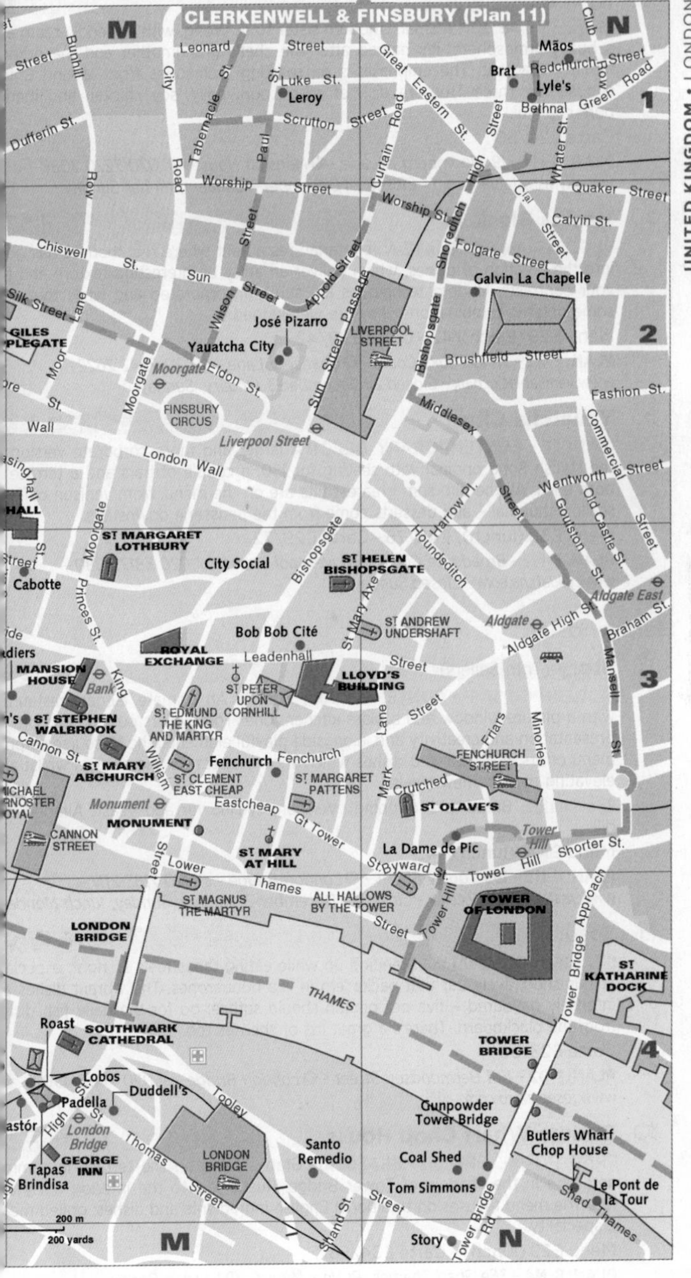
CLERKENWELL & FINSBURY (Plan 11)
M
N
Leonard Street
Bunhill Row
City Road
Tabernacle St.
St. Luke St.
Leroy
Scrutton Street
Paul Street
Curtain Road
Great Eastern St.
Dufferin St.
Worship Street
Worship St.
Chiswell St.
Sun Street
Wilson Street
Appold Street
Sun Street Passage
Club Row
Mãos
Brat
Redchurch Street
Lyle's
Bethnal Green Road
High Street
Shoreditch
Whater St.
Quaker Street
Calvin St.
Folgate Street
Galvin La Chapelle
Bishopsgate
Brushfield Street
Fashion St.
Commercial Street
Silk Street
Moor Lane
José Pizarro
Yauatcha City
LIVERPOOL STREET
Moorgate
Eldon St.
FINSBURY CIRCUS
Liverpool Street
Middlesex Street
Wall
London Wall
Wentworth Street
Old Castle St.
Goulston St.
Harrow Pl.
Houndsditch
HALL
ST MARGARET LOTHBURY
City Social
ST HELEN BISHOPSGATE
Cabotte
Princes St.
St Mary Axe
ST ANDREW UNDERSHAFT
Aldgate East
Aldgate
Aldgate High St.
Braham St.
Bob Bob Cité
ROYAL EXCHANGE
Leadenhall Street
MANSION HOUSE
Bank
King
ST PETER UPON CORNHILL
LLOYD'S BUILDING
Mansell St.
ST STEPHEN WALBROOK
ST EDMUND THE KING AND MARTYR
Lane
Street
Friars
Minories
Cannon St.
ST MARY ABCHURCH
William
Fenchurch
Fenchurch
ST CLEMENT EAST CHEAP
ST MARGARET PATTENS
Mark
Crutched
FENCHURCH STREET
ST OLAVE'S
Monument
Eastcheap
Gt Tower
MONUMENT
CANNON STREET
Street
ST MARY AT HILL
La Dame de Pic
Tower Hill
Shorter St.
Lower Thames
St. Byward St.
Tower Hill
ALL HALLOWS BY THE TOWER
ST MAGNUS THE MARTYR
TOWER OF LONDON
LONDON BRIDGE
Tower Bridge Approach
ST KATHARINE DOCK
THAMES
Roast
SOUTHWARK CATHEDRAL
TOWER BRIDGE
Lobos
Padella
Duddell's
Tooley
Gunpowder Tower Bridge
High St.
London Bridge
Thomas Street
Santo Remedio
Coal Shed
Butlers Wharf Chop House
Tapas Brindisa
GEORGE INN
LONDON BRIDGE
Tom Simmons
Le Pont de la Tour
Shad Thames
Shand St.
Tower Bridge Rd
Story
200 m
200 yards
1
2
3
4

Kym's

CHINESE • DESIGN A smart, modern sister to A. Wong, with a friendly team a a buzzy atmosphere; it's named after the chef's grandmother and the origir family restaurant. The emphasis is on roasting techniques from around Chir choose the Three Treasure dish of crispy pork belly, soy chicken and Iberi pork char sui.

Carte £20/50

PLAN: 8-M3 – *19 Bloomberg Arcade – Mansion House – 020 7220 7088 – www.kymsrestaurant.com – Closed 24 December-4 January, dinner Sunday*

Vanilla Black

VEGETARIAN • INTIMATE A vegetarian restaurant where real thought has go into the creation of dishes, which deliver an array of interesting texture and fl vour contrasts. Modern techniques are subtly incorporated and while there a some original combinations, they are well-judged.

Menu £29 (lunch)/42 – Carte £29/42

PLAN: 8-K2 – *17-18 Tooks Court – Chancery Lane – 020 7242 2622 – www.vanillablack.co.uk – Closed 24 December-3 January, Sunday*

Yauatcha City

CHINESE • CONTEMPORARY DÉCOR A larger and more corporate version the stylish Soho original with seating for 180, a couple of bars and a terrace both ends. All the dim sum greatest hits are on the menu, from venison puffs scallop shui mai – and desserts come from the patisserie downstairs.

Menu £38 (lunch), £48/75 – Carte £29/72

PLAN: 8-M2 – *Broadgate Circle – Liverpool Street – 020 3817 9880 – www.yauatcha.com – Closed Sunday*

Bermondsey

Story (Tom Sellers)

MODERN CUISINE • CONTEMPORARY DÉCOR An intimate, elegant restaurar with a picture window and a glass kitchen. Chef Tom Sellers puts great store o presentation and creativity and, alongside playful elements, the 10 course surpris menu offers well-balanced dishes which show respect for the classics whilst als elevating them to new levels.

Specialities: Bread and 'dripping'. Venison, cauliflower and yeast. Almond an dill.

Menu £100 (lunch)/145

PLAN: 8-N5 – *199 Tooley Street – London Bridge – 020 7183 2117 – www.restaurantstory.co.uk – Closed 22 December-3 January, Sunday, lunch Monday*

José

SPANISH • MINIMALIST Standing up while eating tapas feels so right, especially at this snug, lively bar that packs 'em in like boquerones. The vibrant dishes are intensely flavoured – five per person should suffice; go for the daily fish dishes from the blackboard. There's a great list of sherries too.

Carte £23/30

PLAN: 1-D2 – *104 Bermondsey Street – London Bridge – 020 7403 4902 – www.josepizarro.com*

Butlers Wharf Chop House

TRADITIONAL BRITISH • BRASSERIE Grab a table on the terrace in summer and dine in the shadow of Tower Bridge. Rustic feel to the interior; noisy and fun. The menu focuses on traditional English ingredients and dishes; grilled meats a speciality.

Menu £29 (lunch) – Carte £34/58

PLAN: 8-N4 – *36e Shad Thames, Butlers Wharf – London Bridge – 020 7403 3403 – www.chophouse-restaurant.co.uk*

Casse Croûte

FRENCH • BISTRO Squeeze into this tiny bistro and you'll find yourself transported to rural France. A blackboard menu offers three choices for each course but new dishes are added as others run out. The cooking is rustic, authentic and heartening.

Carte £31/37

PLAN: 1-D2 – *109 Bermondsey Street – Ⓜ London Bridge – ✆ 020 7407 2140 – www.cassecroute.co.uk – Closed dinner Sunday*

Coal Shed

MEATS AND GRILLS • DESIGN Coal Shed was established in Brighton before opening here in this modern development by Tower Bridge. It's set over two floors and specialises in steaks but there's also plenty of seafood on offer. Desserts are good too; try the various 'sweets'.

Menu £15/24 – Carte £30/44

PLAN: 8-N4 – *Unit 3.1, One Tower Bridge, 4 Crown Square – Ⓜ London Bridge – ✆ 020 3384 7272 – www.coalshed-restaurantlondon.co.uk*

Flour & Grape

ITALIAN • SIMPLE The clue's in the name – pasta and wine. A choice of 7 or 8 antipasti are followed by the same number of homemade pasta dishes, with a dessert menu largely centred around gelato. Add in a well-chosen wine list with some pretty low mark-ups and it's no wonder this place is busy.

Carte £15/28

PLAN: 1-D2 – *214 Bermondsey Street – Ⓜ London Bridge – ✆ 020 7407 4682 – www.flourandgrape.com – Closed lunch Monday*

Garrison

TRADITIONAL BRITISH • PUB Known for its charming vintage look, booths and sweet-natured service, The Garrison boasts a warm, relaxed vibe. Open from breakfast until dinner, when a Mediterranean-led menu pulls in the crowds.

Carte £28/50

PLAN: 1-D2 – *99-101 Bermondsey Street – Ⓜ London Bridge. – ✆ 020 7089 9355 – www.thegarrison.co.uk*

Gunpowder Tower Bridge

INDIAN • CONTEMPORARY DÉCOR In contrast to the first Gunpowder, this branch sits within a modern development, is spread over two floors and takes bookings; ask for one of the booths. The well-priced dishes allow for uninhibited ordering; crispy pork ribs, spiced venison doughnuts and soft-shell crab are must-haves.

Menu £25 – Carte £16/40

PLAN: 8-N4 – *One Tower Bridge, 4 Duchess Street – Ⓜ London Bridge – ✆ 020 3598 7946 – www.gunpowderlondon.com – Closed dinner Sunday*

Pizarro

SPANISH • RUSTIC José Pizarro has a refreshingly simple way of naming his establishments: after José, his tapas bar, came Pizarro, a larger restaurant a few doors down. Go for the small plates, like prawns with piquillo peppers and jamón.

Carte £28/50

PLAN: 1-D2 – *194 Bermondsey Street – Ⓜ London Bridge – ✆ 020 7378 9455 – www.josepizarro.com*

Le Pont de la Tour

FRENCH • ELEGANT Few restaurants can beat the setting, especially when you're on the terrace with its breathtaking views of Tower Bridge. For its 25th birthday it got a top-to-toe refurbishment, resulting in a warmer looking room in which to enjoy the French-influenced cooking.

Menu £30 – Carte £35/75

PLAN: 8-N4 – *36d Shad Thames, Butlers Wharf – Ⓜ London Bridge – ✆ 020 7403 8403 – www.lepontdelatour.co.uk*

Santo Remedio

MEXICAN • COLOURFUL The cooking inspiration comes from the owner's tin spent in Mexico City, the Yucatan and Oaxaca. Ingredients are a mix of import – like grasshoppers to liven up the guacamole – and home-grown like Hertfor shire pork. Spread over two floors, the rooms are as colourful as the food.

Menu £15 (lunch) – Carte £24/32

PLAN: 8-M4 – *152 Tooley Street – Ⓜ London Bridge – ✆ 020 7403 3021 – www.santoremedio.co.uk*

Tom Simmons

BRITISH CONTEMPORARY • SIMPLE The eponymous chef went from being contestant on 'MasterChef: The Professionals' to having his name above th door of his own restaurant here in this modern development near Tower Bridg His Welsh heritage comes through on the modern menu, with its use of Wels lamb and beef.

Menu £27 (lunch)/32 – Carte £36/57

PLAN: 8-N4 – *2 Still Walk – Ⓜ London Bridge – ✆ 020 3848 2100 – www.tom-simmons.co.uk – Closed 1-8 January, Sunday, Monday*

Southwark

Padella

ITALIAN • BISTRO This lively little sister to Trullo offers a short, seasonal men where hand-rolled pasta is the star of the show. Sauces and fillings are inspire by the owners' trips to Italy and prices are extremely pleasing to the pocket. S at the ground floor counter overlooking the open kitchen.

Carte £12/22

PLAN: 8-M4 – *6 Southwark Street, Borough Market – Ⓜ London Bridge – www.padella.co*

Anchor & Hope

MODERN BRITISH • PUB As popular as ever thanks to its congenial feel anc lived-in looks but mostly because of the appealingly seasonal menu and the gutsy, bold cooking that delivers on flavour. No reservations so be prepared tc wait at the bar.

Menu £18 (lunch) – Carte £23/44

PLAN: 8-K4 – *36 The Cut – Ⓜ Southwark. – ✆ 020 7928 9898 – www.anchorandhopepub.co.uk – Closed 24 December-2 January, dinner Sunday, lunch Monday*

Bala Baya

MIDDLE EASTERN • DESIGN A friendly, lively restaurant which celebrates the Middle Eastern heritage of its passionate owner. Dishes are fresh, vibrant and designed for sharing and the bright, modern interior is inspired by the Bauhaus architecture of Tel Aviv.

Menu £25 (lunch), £33/53 – Carte £31/60

PLAN: 8-L4 – *Arch 25, Old Union Yard Arches, 229 Union Street – Ⓜ Southwark – ✆ 020 8001 7015 – www.balabaya.co.uk – Closed dinner Sunday*

Elliot's

BRITISH CONTEMPORARY • RUSTIC A lively, unpretentious restaurant which sources its ingredients from Borough Market, in which it stands. The appealing menu is concise and the cooking is earthy, pleasingly uncomplicated and very satisfying. Four plates per person will suffice; try the Isle of Mull cheese puffs. Natural wines are a focus.

Carte £35/56

PLAN: 8-L4 – *12 Stoney Street, Borough Market – Ⓜ London Bridge – ✆ 020 7403 7436 – www.elliotscafe.com – Closed Sunday*

El Pastór

MEXICAN • BISTRO A lively, informal restaurant under the railway arches at London Bridge; inspired by the taquerias of Mexico City. Flavours are beautifully fresh, fragrant and spicy; don't miss the Taco Al Pastór after which the restaurant is named.

Carte £14/32

PLAN: 8-M4 – *7a Stoney St, Borough Market – Ⓜ London Bridge – ☎ 020 7440 1461 – www.tacoselpastor.co.uk – Closed dinner Sunday*

Lobos

SPANISH • TAPAS BAR A dimly lit, decidedly compact tapas bar under the railway arches – sit upstairs to enjoy the theatre of the open kitchen. Go for one of the speciality meat dishes like the leg of slow-roasted milk-fed Castilian lamb. There's another branch in Soho.

Carte £20/48

PLAN: 8-M4 – *14 Borough High Street – Ⓜ London Bridge – ☎ 020 7407 5361 – www.lobostapas.co.uk*

Native

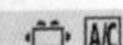

INNOVATIVE • RUSTIC Wild food and foraging underpin this restaurant occupying an ersatz industrial space close to Borough Market; Ivan runs the kitchen and Imogen the service. It also boasts strong eco credentials and seeks to reduce waste; start with the 'snacks' made from what that would otherwise be discarded.

Carte £31/50

PLAN: 8-L2 – *32 Southwark Street – Ⓜ London Bridge – ☎ 07507 861570 – www.eatnative.co.uk – Closed 23 December-4 January, Sunday, Monday*

Oxo Tower Brasserie

MODERN CUISINE • DESIGN Set on the eighth floor of the iconic converted factory and providing stunning views of the Thames and beyond. The open-plan kitchen produces modern, colourful and easy-to-eat dishes with influences from the Med. Great views too from the bar.

Menu £30 (lunch) – Carte £27/49

PLAN: 8-K4 – *Oxo Tower Wharf, Barge House Street – Ⓜ Southwark – ☎ 020 7803 3888 – www.oxotower.co.uk*

Roast

MODERN BRITISH • FRIENDLY Known for its British food and for promoting UK producers – not surprising considering the restaurant's in the heart of Borough Market. They take quite a lot of large tables but the bright room is big enough to cope.

Carte £35/66

PLAN: 8-M4 – *The Floral Hall, Borough Market – Ⓜ London Bridge – ☎ 020 3006 6111 – www.roast-restaurant.com – Closed dinner Sunday*

Tapas Brindisa

SPANISH • TAPAS BAR A blueprint for many of the tapas bars that subsequently sprung up over London. It has an infectious energy and the well-priced, robust dishes include Galician-style octopus and black rice with squid; try the hand-carved Ibérico hams.

Carte £14/38

PLAN: 8-M4 – *18-20 Southwark Street, Borough Market – Ⓜ London Bridge – ☎ 020 7357 8880 – www.brindisatapaskitchens.com*

Tate Modern (Restaurant)

MODERN BRITISH • DESIGN Allow time to get to this bright, open restaurant on the 9th floor of Tate Modern's Blavatnik Building as the lifts are often crowded. The modern menus champion seasonal British ingredients in flavoursome, uncomplicated dishes and the wine list is varied and well-priced.

Menu £29/35

PLAN: 8-L4 – *Blavatnik Building (9th floor), Tate Modern, Bankside – Ⓜ Southwark – ☎ 020 7401 5108 – www.tate.org.uk – Closed dinner Sunday-Thursday*

Union Street Café

ITALIAN • DESIGN Occupying a former warehouse, this Gordon Ramsay restarant has been busy since day one and comes with a New York feel, a faux industrial look and a basement bar. The Italian menu keeps things simple and stays true to the classics.

Menu £19/23 – Carte £30/50

PLAN: 8-L4 – *47-51 Great Suffolk Street* – *London Bridge* – *020 7592 7977* – *www.gordonramsayrestaurants.com* – *Closed dinner Sunday*

Chelsea - South Kensington

Chelsea

✿✿✿ Restaurant Gordon Ramsay

FRENCH • ELEGANT A kitchen redesign in 2018 proved that Gordon Ramsay's flagship restaurant is not one to ever rest on its laurels. The large kitchen team create dishes that are classical in make-up but never backward-looking. Dishes are executed with great confidence and the component parts marry perfectly. Service is polished and professional but also has personality.

Specialities: Ravioli of lobster, langoustine and salmon with sorrel. Herdwick lamb with courgette, romesco, black olive and marjoram. Raspberry soufflé with almond ice cream.

Menu £70 (lunch), £120/185

PLAN: 9-F7 – *68-69 Royal Hospital Road* – *Sloane Square* – *020 7352 4441* – *www.gordonramsayrestaurants.com* – *Closed Sunday, Monday*

✿✿ Claude Bosi at Bibendum

FRENCH • ELEGANT Bibendum – on the first floor of the historic art deco building which was built as Michelin's London HQ in 1911 – sports a clean, contemporary look, and its handsome interior cannot fail to impress. Claude Bosi's cooking shows a man proud of his French heritage and confident of his abilities. His dishes are poised and assured.

Specialities: Duck jelly with smoked sturgeon and special selection caviar. Brittany rabbit with langoustine and artichoke barigoule. Black Forest soufflé with Griottine ice cream.

Menu £65 (lunch), £120/185 – Carte £71/107

PLAN: 9-E6 – *Michelin House, 81 Fulham Road* – *South Kensington* – *020 7581 5817* – *www.bibendum.co.uk* – *Closed 1-7 January, 6-14 April, 30 August-8 September, Monday, Tuesday, lunch Wednesday*

✿ Elystan Street (Philip Howard)

MODERN BRITISH • ELEGANT This elegant, understated restaurant is a joint venture between chef Philip Howard and experienced restaurateur Rebecca Mascarenhas. Cooking has a classical base yet displays a healthy lightness of touch; there's also a vigour and energy to it which suggests that it comes from the heart.

Specialities: Cashew nut hummus with roast vegetables, curry dressing, nut milk and lime. Fillet of Cornish cod with garlic leaf & nettle pesto, creamed potatoes and buttered morels. Lemon tart with yoghurt.

Menu £30 (lunch) – Carte £46/84

PLAN: 9-E6 – *43 Elystan Street* – *South Kensington* – *020 7628 5005* – *www.elystanstreet.com*

✿ Five Fields (Taylor Bonnyman)

MODERN CUISINE • NEIGHBOURHOOD A formally run yet intimate restaurant, with a discreet atmosphere and a warm, comfortable feel. Modern dishes are skilfully conceived, quite elaborate constructions; attractively presented and packed with flavour. Produce is top-notch and often comes from the restaurant's own kitchen garden in East Sussex.

Specialities: Foie gras with pickled shimeji mushrooms, rainbow carrots and beetroot. Venison with salsify, sour cream and rye. Pineapple baba with Chantilly cream and Somerset brandy.

Menu £65 (lunch), £80/95

PLAN: 9-F6 – *8-9 Blacklands Terrace – Ⓜ Sloane Square – ✆ 020 7838 1082 – www.fivefieldsrestaurant.com – Closed 1-12 January, 10-23 August, 21-27 December, Sunday, Monday, lunch Tuesday-Wednesday*

Adam Handling Chelsea

MODERN BRITISH • ELEGANT The eponymous chef's latest opening is in the beautifully restored Cadogan Hotel; to the front there's an elegant cocktail bar; further back, two high-ceilinged dining rooms with ornate plasterwork and a subtle contemporary style. Modern menus showcase the freshest of ingredients in creative British dishes.

Menu £50 – Carte £20/70

PLAN: 9-F5 – *Belmond Cadogan Hotel, 75 Sloane Street – Ⓜ Knightsbridge – ✆ 020 8089 7070 – www.adamhandling.co.uk*

Bandol

FRENCH • COLOURFUL Stylishly dressed restaurant with a 100 year old olive tree evoking memories of sunny days spent on the French Riviera. Sharing plates take centre stage on the Provençal and Niçoise inspired menu; seafood is a highlight.

Menu £20 (lunch) – Carte £30/57

PLAN: 9-D7 – *6 Hollywood Road – Ⓜ Earl's Court – ✆ 020 7351 1322 – www.barbandol.co.uk*

Colbert

FRENCH • BRASSERIE With its posters, chessboard tiles and red leather seats, Colbert bears more than a passing resemblance to a Parisian pavement café. It's an all-day, every day operation with French classics from croque monsieur to steak Diane.

Carte £26/65

PLAN: 9-G6 – *50-52 Sloane Square – Ⓜ Sloane Square – ✆ 020 7730 2804 – www.colbertchelsea.com*

il trillo

ITALIAN • FRIENDLY The Bertuccelli family have been making wine and running a restaurant in the Tuscan Hills for over 30 years. Two of the brothers now run this smart local which showcases the produce and wine from their region. Delightful courtyard.

Carte £36/50

PLAN: 9-D7 – *4 Hollywood Road – Ⓜ Earl's Court – ✆ 020 3602 1759 – www.iltrillo.net – Closed Monday, lunch Tuesday-Friday*

Kahani

INDIAN • ELEGANT Service is charming at this smart, easy-going basement restaurant. It's name means 'Story' in Urdu; the story in question being that of chef-owner Peter Joseph, whose influences include his Indian heritage, the concept of sharing food picked up on his travels in Spain and the best of British produce.

Menu £25/70 – Carte £26/70

PLAN: 9-F6 – *1 Wilbraham Place – Ⓜ Sloane Square – ✆ 020 7730 7634 – www.kahanidining.com – Closed lunch Monday*

Kutir

INDIAN • EXOTIC DÉCOR A pretty end-of-terrace townhouse in an elegant Chelsea street; there's a lively buzz throughout the various smart yet cosy rooms – if you're on a date, ask to sit upstairs. Assorted menus – including a vegetarian tasting menu – offer refined and original cooking from different Indian regions.

Menu £20/65 – Carte £32/45

PLAN: 9-F6 – *10 Lincoln Street – Ⓜ Sloane Square – ✆ 020 7581 1144 – www.kutir.co.uk – Closed Monday*

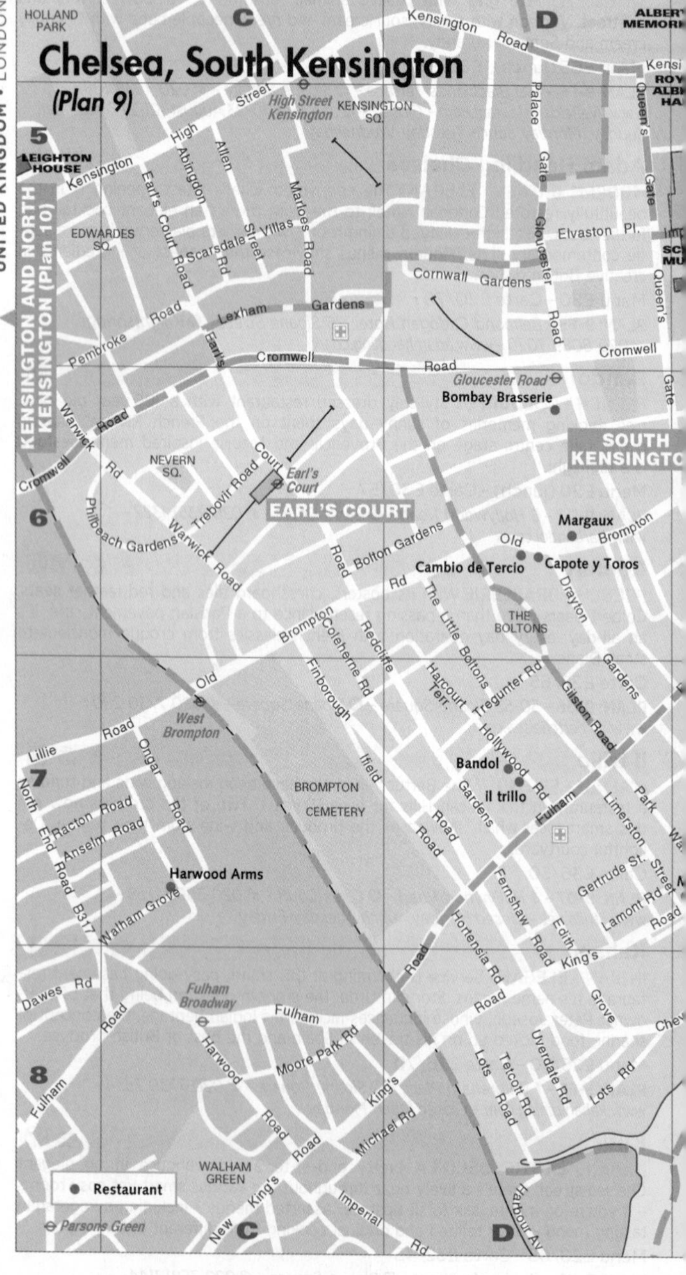
Chelsea, South Kensington
(Plan 9)
HOLLAND PARK
C
D
5
6
7
8
LEIGHTON HOUSE
KENSINGTON AND NORTH KENSINGTON (Plan 10)
Kensington Road
High Street Kensington
KENSINGTON SQ.
Kensington High Street
Abingdon Rd
Allen Street
Earl's Court Road
Marloes Road
EDWARDES SQ.
Scarsdale Villas
Palace Gate
Queen's Gate
Gloucester Road
Elvaston Pl.
Cornwall Gardens
Lexham Gardens
Pembroke Road
Cromwell Road
Gloucester Road
Bombay Brasserie
SOUTH KENSINGTON
Warwick Road
Cromwell Road
NEVERN SQ.
Earl's Court
EARL'S COURT
Trebovir Road
Philbeach Gardens
Warwick Road
Warwick Rd
Bolton Gardens
Margaux
Old Brompton Rd
Cambio de Tercio
Capote y Toros
The Little Boltons
Drayton Gardens
THE BOLTONS
Coleherne Rd
Redcliffe Road
Finborough Road
Harcourt Terr.
Tregunter Rd
Gilston Road
Old Brompton Road
West Brompton
Lillie Road
Ongar Road
Ifield Road
Hollywood Rd
Bandol
il trillo
BROMPTON CEMETERY
Redcliffe Gardens
Fulham Road
Limerston Street
Park Walk
North End Road B317
Racton Road
Anselm Road
Harwood Arms
Walham Grove
Fernshaw Road
Gertrude St.
Lamont Rd
Hortensia Rd
Edith Grove
King's Road
Dawes Rd
Fulham Broadway
Fulham Road
Harwood Road
Moore Park Rd
Uverdate Rd
Tetcott Rd
Lots Road
Lots Rd
King's Road
Michael Rd
WALHAM GREEN
Restaurant
New King's Road
Imperial Rd
Parsons Green
Harbour Av

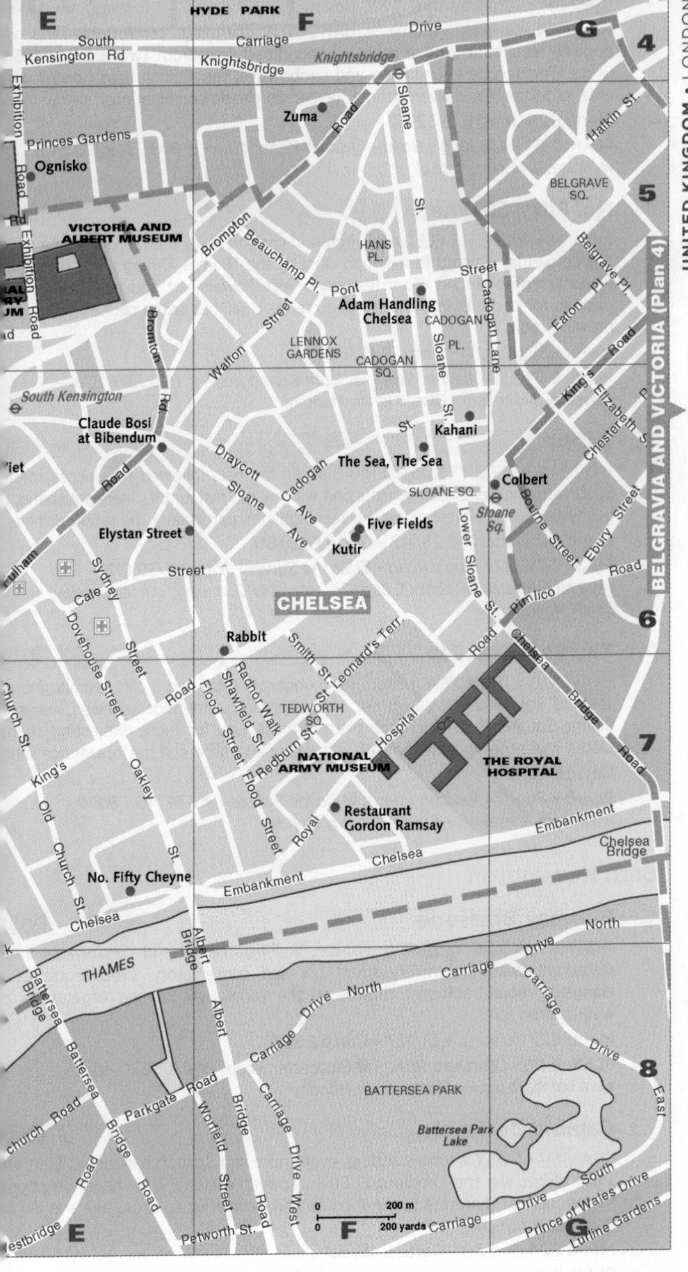
HYDE PARK
E
F
G
4
5
6
7
8
South Kensington Rd
Carriage Drive
Knightsbridge
Knightsbridge
Sloane St.
Zuma
Road
Halkin St.
Exhibition Road
Princes Gardens
Ognisko
BELGRAVE SQ.
VICTORIA AND ALBERT MUSEUM
Brompton
Beauchamp Pl.
HANS PL.
Pont Street
Adam Handling Chelsea
CADOGAN PL.
Cadogan Lane
Belgrave Pl.
Eaton Pl.
Walton Street
LENNOX GARDENS
CADOGAN SQ.
Sloane St.
Brompton Rd.
South Kensington
Kahani
King's Road
Elizabeth St.
Chester
BELGRAVIA AND VICTORIA (Plan 4)
Claude Bosi at Bibendum
The Sea, The Sea
Draycott
Cadogan
SLOANE SQ.
Colbert
Sloane
Ave
Sloane Sq.
Bourne Street
Ebury Street
Road
Five Fields
Kutir
Lower Sloane St.
Elystan Street
Fulham
Sydney Street
Cale Street
Dovehouse Street
CHELSEA
Pimlico Road
Rabbit
Smith St.
St Leonard's Terr.
Chelsea Bridge Road
Church St.
Flood Street
Radnor Walk
Shawfield St.
TEDWORTH SQ.
Redburn St.
Hospital Road
NATIONAL ARMY MUSEUM
THE ROYAL HOSPITAL
King's
Oakley
Old Church St.
Restaurant Gordon Ramsay
Royal
Embankment
Chelsea Bridge
Chelsea
No. Fifty Cheyne
Embankment
Chelsea
Albert Bridge
North
Drive
THAMES
Carriage
Battersea Bridge
North
Carriage Drive
Carriage
Drive
Albert
Carriage
8
East
Battersea Bridge Road
Parkgate Road
Worfield Street
Bridge
Carriage Drive West
BATTERSEA PARK
Battersea Park Lake
church Road
Road
South
Drive
Prince of Wales Drive
0
200 m
200 yards
Carriage
Petworth St.
Lurline Gardens
estbridge

Medlar

MODERN CUISINE • NEIGHBOURHOOD A charming, comfortable and ve popular restaurant with a real neighbourhood feel, from two alumni of Ch Bruce. The service is engaging and unobtrusive; the kitchen uses good ingre ents in dishes that deliver distinct flavours in classic combinations.

Menu £25 (lunch), £32/53

PLAN: 9-E7 – *438 King's Road – Ⓜ South Kensington – ✆ 020 7349 1900 – www.medlarrestaurant.co.uk*

No. Fifty Cheyne

MODERN BRITISH • ELEGANT High-end comfort food is the order of the day this colourfully painted former pub close to the Thames. Dining takes place in elegant, high-ceilinged room festooned with flowers, art and chandeliers; hea upstairs for cocktails in the plush deep red cocktail bar or the country house sty drawing room.

Menu £35 (lunch) – Carte £42/68

PLAN: 9-E7 – *50 Cheyne Walk – Ⓜ South Kensington – ✆ 020 7376 8787 – www.fiftycheyne.com – Closed lunch Monday*

Rabbit

MODERN BRITISH • RUSTIC The Gladwin brothers followed the success of Th Shed with another similarly rustic and warmly run restaurant. Share satisfying, r bustly flavoured plates; game is a real highlight, particularly the rabbit dishes.

Menu £17 (lunch), £25/42 – Carte £20/50

PLAN: 9-F6 – *172 King's Road – Ⓜ Sloane Square – ✆ 020 3750 0172 – www.rabbit-restaurant.com – Closed 23 December-2 January, dinner Sunday, lunch Monday*

The Sea, The Sea

SEAFOOD • TRENDY A modern fishmonger's by day and a chic champagne an seafood bar in the evening; set in a charming semi-pedestrianised mews o Sloane Square. Cold lunchtime platters make way for more interesting sharin plates; must-tries include the crab with seaweed waffle, and the lobster rice sand

Carte £29/60

PLAN: 9-F6 – *174 Pavilion Road – Ⓜ Sloane Square – ✆ 020 7824 8090 – www.theseathesea.net – Closed Sunday, Monday*

South Kensington

Bombay Brasserie

INDIAN • EXOTIC DÉCOR A well-run, well-established and comfortable India restaurant, featuring a very smart bar and conservatory. Creative dishes si alongside more traditional choices on the various menus and vegetarians ar well-catered for.

Menu £27 (lunch), £51/127 – Carte £39/60

PLAN: 9-D6 – *Courtfield Road – Ⓜ Gloucester Road – ✆ 020 7370 4040 – www.bombayb.co.uk – Closed lunch Monday*

Cambio de Tercio

SPANISH • COSY A long-standing, ever-improving Spanish restaurant. Start with small dishes like the excellent El Bulli inspired omelette, then have the popula Pluma Iberica. There are super sherries and a wine list to prove there is life beyond Rioja.

Menu £24 (lunch) – Carte £45/60

PLAN: 9-D6 – *163 Old Brompton Road – Ⓜ Gloucester Road – ✆ 020 7244 8970 – www.cambiodetercio.co.uk – Closed 23 December-2 January*

Capote y Toros

SPANISH • TAPAS BAR Expect to queue at this compact and vividly coloured spot which celebrates sherry, tapas, ham... and bullfighting. Sherry is the star; those as yet unmoved by this most underappreciated of wines will be dazzled by the variety.

Carte £30/60

PLAN: 9-D6 – *157 Old Brompton Road* – Ⓜ *Gloucester Road* – *☎ 020 7373 0567 – www.cambiodetercio.co.uk – Closed 22 December-2 January, Sunday, Monday, lunch Tuesday-Saturday*

gõ

VIETNAMESE • CONTEMPORARY DÉCOR A Vietnamese restaurant from experienced chef Jeff Tan. Lunch concentrates on classics like pho and bun, while dinner provides a more sophisticated experience, offering interesting flavourful dishes with a distinct modern edge.

Carte £27/38

PLAN: 9-E6 – *53 Old Brompton Road* – Ⓜ *South Kensington* – *☎ 020 7589 6432 – www.vietnamfood.co.uk*

Margaux

MEDITERRANEAN CUISINE • NEIGHBOURHOOD An earnestly run modern bistro with an ersatz industrial look. The classically trained kitchen looks to France and Italy for its primary influences and dishes are flavoursome and satisfying. The accompanying wine list has been thoughtfully compiled.

Menu £15 (lunch), £40/55 – Carte £27/56

PLAN: 9-D6 – *152 Old Brompton Road* – Ⓜ *Gloucester Road* – *☎ 020 7373 5753 – www.barmargaux.co.uk*

Ognisko

POLISH • ELEGANT Ognisko Polskie – The Polish Hearth Club – was founded in 1940 in this magnificent townhouse; its elegant restaurant serves traditional dishes from across Eastern Europe and the cooking is without pretence and truly from the heart.

Menu £18/22 – Carte £29/37

PLAN: 9-E5 – *55 Prince's Gate, Exhibition Road* – Ⓜ *South Kensington* – *☎ 020 7589 0101 – www.ogniskorestaurant.co.uk*

Kensington - North Kensington

Kensington

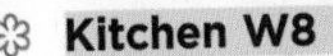

Kitchen W8

MODERN CUISINE • NEIGHBOURHOOD A joint venture between Rebecca Mascarenhas and Philip Howard. Not as informal as the name suggests but still refreshingly free of pomp. The cooking has depth and personality and prices are quite restrained considering the quality of the produce and the kitchen's skill.

Specialities: Grilled Cornish mackerel, smoked eel, sweet mustard and leek. Roast rump of veal, young garlic, white asparagus, Jersey Royals and morels. Yoghurt parfait, with lemon curd, warm vanilla beignets and basil.

Menu £25 (lunch), £30/75 – Carte £36/52

PLAN: 10-C5 – *11-13 Abingdon Road* – Ⓜ *High Street Kensington* – *☎ 020 7937 0120 – www.kitchenw8.com*

Akira

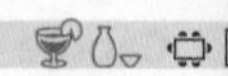

JAPANESE • ELEGANT Japan House promotes all things Japanese so it's a propriate that upstairs there's a stylish restaurant celebrating the country's c sine. The open kitchen is the focal point of the room, which offers both coun and table seating. The best things on the menu are dishes from the rob charcoal grill.

Menu £40 (lunch), £60/72 – Carte £38/50

PLAN: 10-C4 – *Japan House, 101-111 Kensington High Street – High Street Kensington – 020 3971 4646 – www.japanhouselondon.uk/eat/restaurant/ – Closed dinner Sunday*

Clarke's

MODERN CUISINE • NEIGHBOURHOOD Its unhurried atmosphere, enthusi tic service and dedication to its regulars are just a few reasons why Sa Clarke's eponymous restaurant has instilled such unwavering loyalty for ov 30 years. Her kitchen has a light touch and understands the less-is-more pr ciple.

Menu £34 (lunch)/39 – Carte £42/100

PLAN: 10-C4 – *124 Kensington Church Street – Notting Hill Gate – 020 7221 9225 – www.sallyclarke.com – Closed 24-30 August, 24-31 December*

Launceston Place

MODERN CUISINE • NEIGHBOURHOOD A favourite of many thanks to its p pable sense of neighbourhood, pretty façade and its nooks and crannies wh make it ideal for trysts or tête-à-têtes. The menu is fashionably terse and t cooking is quite elaborate, with dishes big on originality and artfully p sented.

Menu £25 (lunch), £55/65 – Carte £42/70

PLAN: 10-D5 – *1a Launceston Place – Gloucester Road – 020 7937 6912 – www.launcestonplace-restaurant.co.uk – Closed Monday, lunch Tuesday*

Mazi

GREEK • FRIENDLY It's all about sharing at this simple, bright Greek restaur where traditional recipes are given a modern twist to create vibrant, colou and fresh tasting dishes. The garden terrace at the back is a charming spot summer.

Menu £20 (lunch) – Carte £30/75

PLAN: 10-C3 – *12-14 Hillgate Street – Notting Hill Gate – 020 7229 3794 – www.mazi.co.uk – Closed lunch Monday*

The Shed

MODERN BRITISH • RUSTIC It's more than just a shed but does have a co feel, a higgledy-piggledy charm and a healthy dose of the outdoors. It's r by three brothers, whose family farm in West Sussex supplies many of the gredients for the earthy, satisfying small plates – as well as some of the wi

Menu £42 – Carte £23/34

PLAN: 10-C3 – *122 Palace Gardens Terrace – Notting Hill Gate – 020 7229 4024 – www.theshed-restaurant.com – Closed Sunday, lunch Monday*

Zaika

INDIAN • CONTEMPORARY DÉCOR The cooking focuses on the North of In and the influences of Mughal and Nawabi, so expect rich and fragrantly spic dishes. The softly-lit room makes good use of its former life as a bank, with wood-panelling and ornate ceiling.

Menu £21/55 – Carte £20/40

PLAN: 10-D4 – *1 Kensington High Street – High Street Kensington – 020 7795 6533 – www.zaikaofkensington.com – Closed lunch Monday*

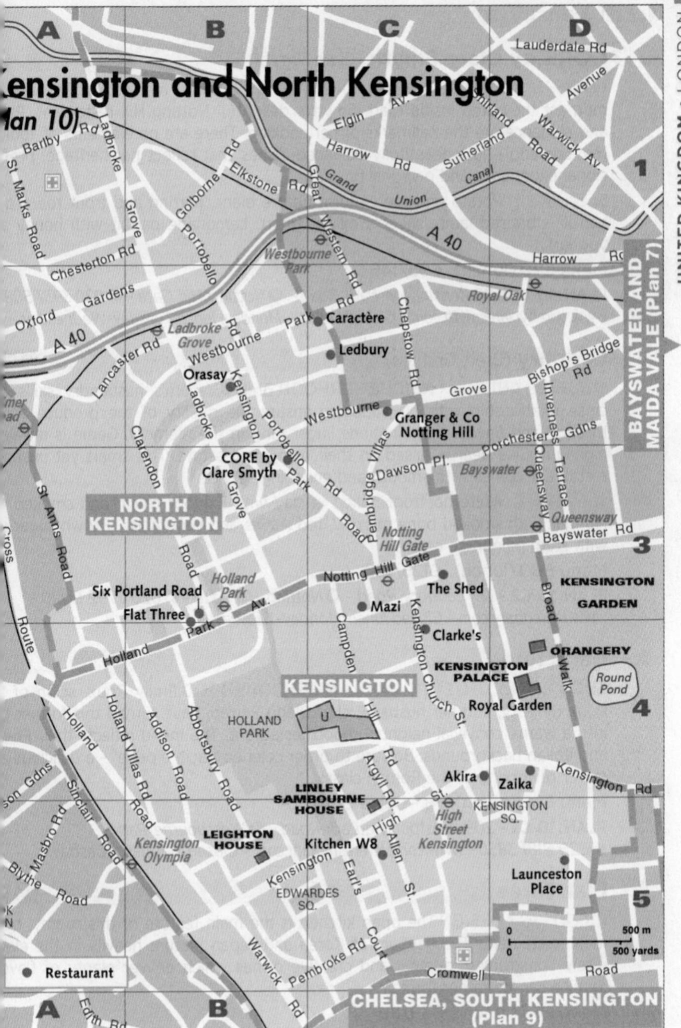
Kensington and North Kensington
(Plan 10)
A
B
C
D
1
3
4
5
Lauderdale Rd
Elgin Av.
Shirland Rd
Avenue
Warwick Road
Warwick Av.
Harrow Rd
Sutherland
Grand Union Canal
Barlby Rd
Ladbroke Grove
St Marks Road
Golborne Rd
Elkstone Rd
Great Western Rd
A 40
Westbourne Park
Harrow Rd
Chesterton Rd
Portobello
Oxford Gardens
Royal Oak
Ladbroke Grove
Westbourne Park Rd
Caractère
Ledbury
Chepstow Rd
Lancaster Rd
Orasay
Kensington Park Rd
Bishop's Bridge Rd
Grove
Westbourne
Granger & Co Notting Hill
Inverness Terrace
Porchester Gdns
Clarendon Road
CORE by Clare Smyth
Pembridge Villas
Dawson Pl.
Bayswater
Queensway
St Anns Road
NORTH KENSINGTON
Portobello Road
Notting Hill Gate
Bayswater Rd
Holland Park
Notting Hill Gate
The Shed
KENSINGTON GARDEN
Six Portland Road
Broad Walk
Flat Three
Mazi
Holland Park Av.
Campden Hill
Kensington Church St.
Clarke's
ORANGERY
Route
KENSINGTON PALACE
Round Pond
KENSINGTON
Royal Garden
Holland Road
Holland Villas Rd
Addison Road
Abbotsbury Road
HOLLAND PARK
Argyll Rd
Akira
Zaika
Kensington Rd
LINLEY SAMBOURNE HOUSE
KENSINGTON SQ.
Sinclair Road
Masbro Rd
High Street Kensington
Kensington Olympia
LEIGHTON HOUSE
Kitchen W8
Allen St.
Blythe Road
Kensington High St.
EDWARDES SQ.
Earl's Court Rd
Launceston Place
500 m
500 yards
Restaurant
Warwick Rd
Pembroke Rd
Cromwell Road
Edith Rd
BAYSWATER AND MAIDA VALE (Plan 7)
CHELSEA, SOUTH KENSINGTON (Plan 9)

North Kensington

✿✿ CORE by Clare Smyth (Clare Smyth)

MODERN BRITISH • CONTEMPORARY DÉCOR Diners feel instantly at ease t moment they step inside Clare Smyth's delightful Notting Hill restaurant. Pur and elegance are the hallmarks of her cooking. There are no elements of 'look me' bravado – just beautifully balanced dishes that reflect her heritage, prof sional experience and personality.

Specialities: 'Potato and roe' - dulse beurre blanc, herring and trout roe. 'Lar carrot' - braised lamb, sheep's milk yoghurt. Lemonade parfait with honey a yoghurt.

Menu £70 (lunch), £95/145

PLAN: 10-B3 – *92 Kensington Park Road – Ⓜ Notting Hill Gate – ✆ 020 3937 5086 www.corebyclaresmyth.com – Closed Sunday, Monday, lunch Tuesday-Wednesday*

✿✿ Ledbury (Brett Graham)

MODERN CUISINE • NEIGHBOURHOOD Brett Graham's husbandry skills a close relationship with his suppliers ensure the quality of the produce shin through and flavour combinations linger long in the memory. Game is always highlight; Sika deer is raised on their own small estate. This smart yet unshov restaurant comes with smooth and engaging service.

Specialities: White beetroot baked in clay with Exmoor caviar and smoked e Muntjac with smoked bone marrow, red leaves and vegetables. Brown sugar ta with stem ginger ice cream.

Menu £80 (lunch), £125/150

PLAN: 10-C2 – *127 Ledbury Road – Ⓜ Notting Hill Gate – ✆ 020 7792 9090 – www.theledbury.com – Closed lunch Monday-Tuesday*

Caractère

EUROPEAN CONTEMPORARY • NEIGHBOURHOOD Emily Roux, scion of th Roux dynasty, and her husband, chef Diego Ferrari, have turned this former pu into a warm, convivial neighbourhood restaurant. The menu reflects their Frenc and Italian backgrounds. Be sure to order celeriac 'cacio e pepe' – a delicious an clever reworking of the Roman classic.

Menu £39 (lunch)/78 – Carte £44/60

PLAN: 10-C2 – *209 Westbourne Park Road – Ⓜ Westbourne Park – ✆ 020 8181 3850 – www.caractererestaurant.com – Closed Monday, Tuesday*

Flat Three

CREATIVE • DESIGN The open kitchen is the main feature of this roomy, base ment restaurant. The flavours of Korea and Japan feature heavily in the elabo rately constructed, original and creative dishes which deliver plenty of flavou Service can be rather formal.

Menu £33 (lunch), £39/59

PLAN: 10-B3-4 – *120-122 Holland Park Avenue – Ⓜ Holland Park – ✆ 020 7792 8987 – www.flatthree.london – Closed Sunday, Monday, lunch Wednesday-Thursday*

Granger & Co. Notting Hill

WORLD CUISINE • FRIENDLY Bill Granger's first London restaurant is a grea fit for this neighbourhood – and its airy, relaxed style a perfect match to his cooking. Food is fun and comes with a riot of flavours; alongside plenty o tasty breakfast dishes are signatures like chicken schnitzel or sticky chilli belly pork.

Carte £23/38

PLAN: 10-C2 – *175 Westbourne Grove – Ⓜ Bayswater – ✆ 020 7229 9111 – www.grangerandco.com*

Orasay

MODERN BRITISH · FRIENDLY A relaxed, contemporary bistro named after the Scottish island where chef-owner Jackson Boxer holidayed as a child. Small plates of modern British food rely on excellent seasonal ingredients, which are expertly cooked to produce clean, natural flavours. Subtle Mediterranean and Asian influences feature.

Menu £20 (lunch) – Carte £32/52

PLAN: 10-B2 – *31 Kensington Park Road – Ⓜ Ladbroke Grove – ✆ 020 7043 1400 – www.orasay.london – Closed dinner Sunday, Monday, lunch Tuesday*

Six Portland Road

FRENCH · NEIGHBOURHOOD A reliably good meal can be found at this intimate and personally run neighbourhood bistro, owned by the hands-on Oli Barker. The seasonal European menu changes frequently; ingredients are good quality and the hearty dishes are reassuringly recognisable, skilfully constructed and full of flavour.

Menu £20 (lunch), £45/65 – Carte £20/65

PLAN: 10-B3 – *6 Portland Road – Ⓜ Holland Park – ✆ 020 7229 3130 – www.sixportlandroad.com – Closed 15-29 August, 24 December-4 January, Sunday, lunch Saturday*

Clerkenwell - Finsbury

lerkenwell

St John

TRADITIONAL BRITISH · SIMPLE A glorious celebration of British fare and a champion of 'nose to tail' eating. Utilitarian surroundings and a refreshing lack of ceremony ensure the food is the focus; it's appealingly simple, full of flavour and very satisfying.

Specialities: Brown shrimps with white cabbage. Lamb sweetbreads with peas and mint. Eccles cake with Lancashire cheese.

Carte £36/50

PLAN: 11-L2 – *26 St. John Street – Ⓜ Farringdon – ✆ 020 7251 0848 – www.stjohnrestaurant.com – Closed dinner Sunday, lunch Saturday*

Comptoir Gascon

FRENCH · BISTRO A friendly, buzzy bistro; sister to Club Gascon. Rustic specialities from the SW of France include wine, bread, cheese and plenty of duck, with cassoulet and duck rillettes perennial favourites and the duck burger popular at lunch. There's also produce on display to take home.

Carte £23/44

PLAN: 11-K2 – *61-63 Charterhouse Street – Ⓜ Farringdon – ✆ 020 7608 0851 – www.comptoirgascon.com – Closed 25 December-1 January, Sunday, Monday, lunch Saturday*

Luca

ITALIAN · DESIGN Owned by the people behind The Clove Club, but less a little sister, more a distant cousin. There's a cheery atmosphere, a bar for small plates and a frequently changing menu of Italian dishes made with quality British ingredients.

Carte £49/67

PLAN: 11-L1 – *88 St John Street – Ⓜ Farringdon – ✆ 020 3859 3000 – www.luca.restaurant – Closed 22 December-6 January, Sunday*

Palatino

ITALIAN · DESIGN Stevie Parle's airy, canteen-like, all-day restaurant has an open kitchen, yellow booths and an industrial feel. The seasonal Italian menu has a strong emphasis on Rome, with dishes like rigatoni with veal pajata.

Menu £16/20 – Carte £16/41

PLAN: 11-L1 – *71 Central Street – Ⓜ Old Street – ✆ 020 3481 5300 – www.palatino.london – Closed 23 December-3 January, Sunday*

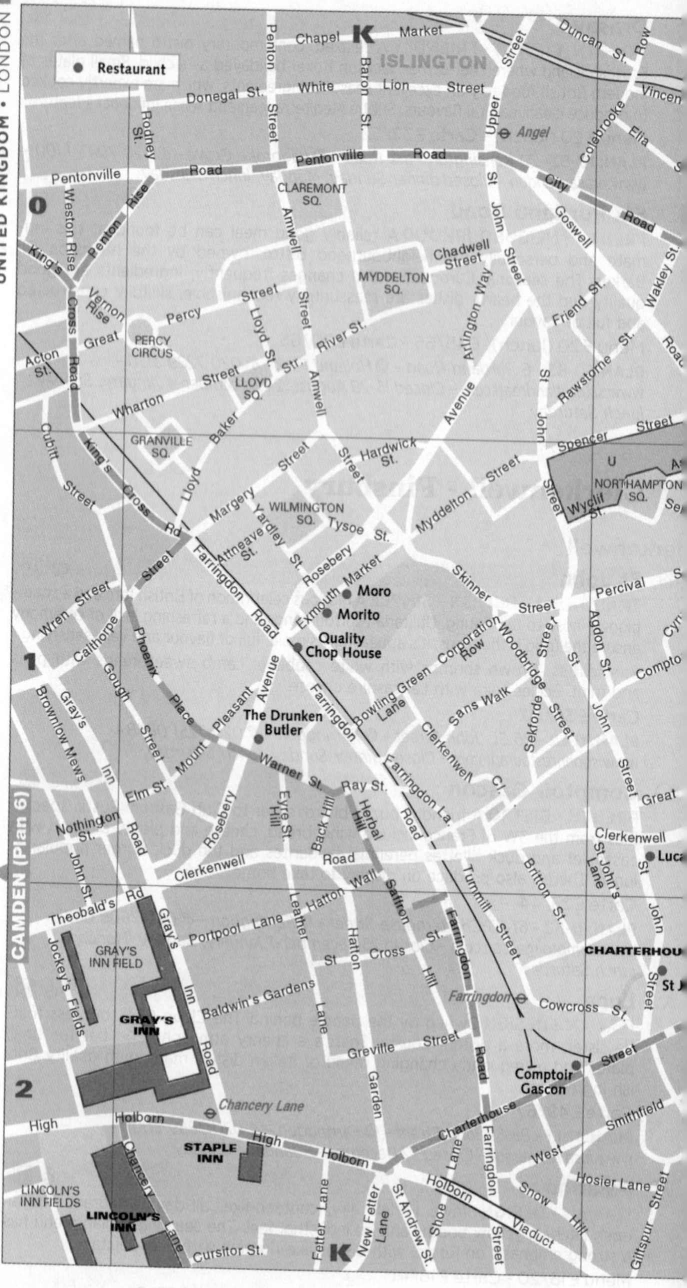

● Restaurant

ISLINGTON

K
O
1
2

Chapel Market
Penton Street
Baron St.
Donegal St.
White Lion Street
Upper Street
Duncan St.
Vincent
Angel
Colebrooke Row
Elia
Rodney St.
Pentonville Road
Pentonville Rise
Penton Rise
King's Cross Road
Weston Rise
CLAREMONT SQ.
Amwell Street
City Road
Goswell
St John Street
Chadwell Street
MYDDELTON SQ.
Arlington Way
Wakley St.
Friend St.
Vernon Rise
Percy Street
PERCY CIRCUS
Great Percy Street
Lloyd St.
River St.
Acton St.
Lloyd Baker Str.
LLOYD SQ.
Rawstorne St.
Wharton Street
Avenue
GRANVILLE SQ.
Cubitt Street
Hardwick St.
Spencer Street
NORTHAMPTON SQ.
Wyclif St.
Margery Street
Myddelton Street
WILMINGTON SQ.
Tysoe St.
Yardley St.
Attneave St.
Rosebery Avenue
Exmouth Market
Skinner Street
Percival Street
Wren Street
Calthorpe
Farringdon Road
Moro
Morito
Quality Chop House
Corporation Row
Woodbridge Street
Agdon St.
Gough Street
Phoenix Place
Bowling Green Lane
Sans Walk
Compton
Gray's Inn Road
Brownlow Mews
Mount Pleasant
The Drunken Butler
Clerkenwell Cl.
Sekforde Street
Warner St.
Ray St.
Farringdon La.
Great
Elm St.
Eyre St. Hill
Back Hill
Herbal Hill
Clerkenwell Road
Nothington St.
John St.
Theobald's Rd
Leather Lane
Hatton Wall
Saffron Hill
Turnmill Street
Britton St.
St John's Lane
Luca
Portpool Lane
Cross St.
Hatton Garden
Farringdon Road
CHARTERHOUSE
GRAY'S INN FIELD
Jockey's Fields
Baldwin's Gardens
Farringdon
Cowcross St.
St J
GRAY'S INN
Greville Street
Comptoir Gascon
Chancery Lane
High Holborn
Charterhouse Street
Smithfield
STAPLE INN
West
Hosier Lane
LINCOLN'S INN FIELDS
LINCOLN'S INN
Fetter Lane
New Fetter Lane
St Andrew St.
Shoe Lane
Holborn Viaduct
Snow Hill
Giltspur Street
Farringdon Street
Cursitor St.

CAMDEN (Plan 6)

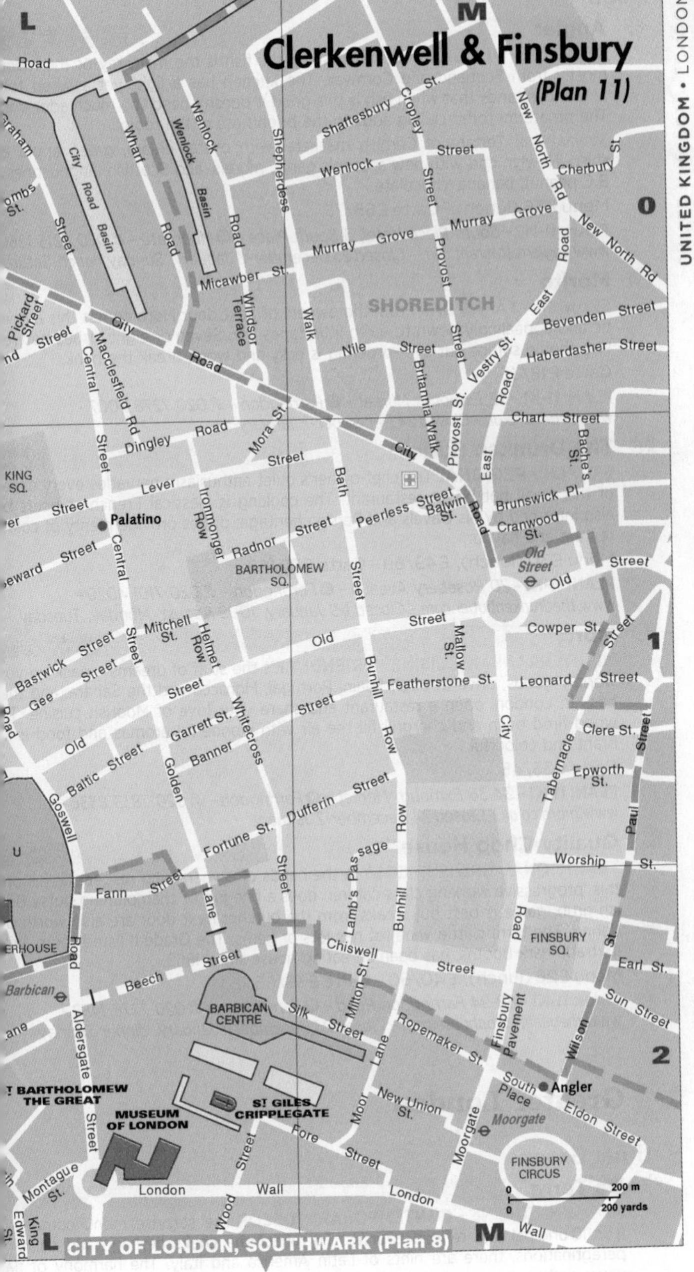
Clerkenwell & Finsbury
(Plan 11)
L
M
O
1
2
SHOREDITCH
City Road
City Road Basin
Wharf Road
Wenlock Basin
Wenlock Road
Shepherdess Walk
Shaftesbury St.
Cropley Street
Wenlock Street
Murray Grove
Provost Street
New North Rd
Cherbury St.
East Road
Micawber St.
Windsor Terrace
Pickard Street
Macclesfield Rd
Central Street
Nile Street
Britannia Walk
Vestry St.
Bevenden Street
Haberdasher Street
Chart Street
Bache's St.
Dingley Road
Mora St.
Lever Street
KING SQ.
Palatino
Ironmonger Row
Bath Street
Peerless Street
Baldwin St.
Brunswick Pl.
Cranwood St.
Old Street
Radnor Street
BARTHOLOMEW SQ.
Seward Street
Mitchell St.
Helmet Row
Mallow St.
Cowper St.
Bastwick Street
Gee Street
Old Street
Featherstone St.
Leonard Street
Garrett St.
Whitecross Street
Bunhill Row
City Road
Tabernacle Street
Clere St.
Baltic Street
Banner Street
Golden Lane
Epworth St.
Goswell Road
Dufferin Street
Fortune St.
Lamb's Passage
Paul Street
Worship St.
Fann Street
FINSBURY SQ.
Chiswell Street
Earl St.
Barbican
Beech Street
Aldersgate Street
BARBICAN CENTRE
Silk Street
Milton St.
Ropemaker St.
Finsbury Pavement
Sun Street
Wilson St.
South Place
Angler
Eldon Street
ST BARTHOLOMEW THE GREAT
MUSEUM OF LONDON
ST GILES CRIPPLEGATE
Moor Lane
New Union St.
Moorgate
Fore Street
Wood Street
FINSBURY CIRCUS
Montague St.
London Wall
King Edward St.
200 m
200 yards
CITY OF LONDON, SOUTHWARK (Plan 8)

Finsbury

Angler

SEAFOOD • DESIGN As the name suggests, fish is the mainstay of the men mostly from Scotland and Cornwall. The kitchen has a light yet assured tou and understands that when fish is this good it doesn't need too much adornme The ornate mirrored ceiling adds to the brightness of the room.

Specialities: Tartare of Cornish mackerel with oyster cream, green apple a shiso. Newlyn cod with new season's garlic, morels, and Scottish langoustines. B.C-peanut, banana, chocolate.

Menu £36 (lunch) – Carte £65/75

PLAN: 11-M2 – *South Place Hotel, 3 South Place – Moorgate – 020 3215 126 www.anglerrestaurant.com – Closed 25 December-3 January, Sunday, lunch Saturd*

Morito

SPANISH • TAPAS BAR From the owners of next door Moro comes this authe tic and appealingly down to earth little tapas bar. Seven or eight dishes betwe two should suffice but over-ordering is easy and won't break the bank.

Carte £18/33

PLAN: 11-K1 – *32 Exmouth Market – Farringdon – 020 7278 7007 – www.morito.co.uk – Closed 24 December-2 January*

The Drunken Butler

FRENCH • REGIONAL The chef-owner's quiet enthusiasm pervades every aspe of this small but bright restaurant. The cooking is classical French at heart b also informed by his travels and Persian heritage; dishes provide plenty of colo texture and flavour.

Menu £30 (lunch), £49/69 – Carte £30/69

PLAN: 11-K1 – *20 Rosebery Avenue – Farringdon – 020 7101 4020 – www.thedrunkenbutler.com – Closed 1-9 January, 10-19 August, Monday, Tuesday*

Moro

MEDITERRANEAN CUISINE • FRIENDLY It's the stuff of dreams – pack up yo worldly goods, drive through Spain, Portugal, Morocco and the Sahara, and the back in London, open a restaurant and share your love of Moorish cuisine. Th wood-fired oven and chargrill fill the air with wonderful aromas and food is v brant and colourful.

Carte £33/45

PLAN: 11-K1 – *34-36 Exmouth Market – Farringdon – 020 7833 8336 – www.moro.co.uk – Closed 24 December-2 January*

Quality Chop House

TRADITIONAL BRITISH • COSY In the hands of owners who respect its histor this 'progressive working class caterer' does a fine job of championing gutsy Bri ish grub; game is best but steaks from the butcher next door are also worth o dering. The terrific little wine list has lots of gems. The Grade II listed room, wit its trademark booths, has been an eating house since 1869.

Menu £26 (lunch), £40/60 – Carte £38/65

PLAN: 11-K1 – *88-94 Farringdon Road – Farringdon – 020 7278 1452 – www.thequalitychophouse.com – Closed 23 December-1 January, dinner Sunday*

Greater London

Bethnal Green

Da Terra

MODERN CUISINE • CONTEMPORARY DÉCOR The surprise menu comprise 8 or 10 original and refined courses. To reflect the chef's heritage and culinar peregrinations, there are hints of Latin America and Italy. The harmony of fla vours and contrast in textures are memorable. The chefs serve the dishes them selves and explain them with zeal.

Specialities: Scallop with fennel and apple. Beef with artichoke and chard. Topinambur with white chocolate.

Menu £73/90

PLAN: 1-D2 – *Town Hall Hotel, 8 Patriot Square* – Ⓜ *Bethnal Green* – ✆ *020 7062 2052* – *www.daterra.co.uk* – *Closed 2-18 August, 23 December-7 January, Sunday, Monday, Tuesday, lunch Wednesday-Friday*

✿ Mãos

INNOVATIVE • CONTEMPORARY DÉCOR A "kitchen, table and wine room" is how Nuno Mendes described the restaurant he set up at the Blue Mountain School – a collaborative space for design and art. Up to 16 guests are served together around a large table and the multi-course surprise menu offers a masterclass in originality, balance and depth.

Specialities: Mushroom and kombu chawanmushi. Grilled hogget, prawn miso and hispi cabbage. Celeriac with white truffle.

Menu £150

PLAN: 8-N1 – *41 Redchurch Street* – Ⓜ *Shoreditch High Street* – ✆ *020 7033 6788* – *www.bluemountain.school* – *Closed Sunday, Monday, Tuesday, lunch Wednesday-Friday*

Chiswick

✿ La Trompette

MODERN BRITISH • NEIGHBOURHOOD A warm, relaxed neighbourhood restaurant with a loyal, local following – a perfect fit for Chiswick. While the influences are varied, its heart is French with occasional nods to the Med. The dishes themselves are free of unnecessary adornment, so the focus remains on the top quality ingredients.

Specialities: Roast veal sweetbread with chestnut mushrooms and ricotta & spring green agnolotti. Grilled turbot with wild garlic spätzle, new season morels and peas. Rhubarb crumble soufflé with vanilla ice cream.

Menu £40 (lunch), £58/75

PLAN: 1-A3 – *3-7 Devonshire Road* – Ⓜ *Turnham Green* – ✆ *020 8747 1836* – *www.latrompette.co.uk*

Clapham Common

✿ Trinity (Adam Byatt)

MODERN CUISINE • CHIC A bright, warmly run neighbourhood restaurant enthusiastically supported by the locals. Adam Byatt's cooking focuses on prime ingredients and classic flavour combinations. Don't miss crispy pig's trotter with sauce Gribiche and it's worth pre-ordering the tarte Tatin with prune and Armagnac ice cream for two.

Specialities: Crispy pig's trotters with sauce gribiche and crackling. Wild turbot 'bonne femme' with morels and creamed ratte potatoes. Tarte Tatin with prune and Armagnac ice cream.

Menu £40 (lunch), £60/70

PLAN: 1-C3 – *4 The Polygon* – Ⓜ *Clapham Common* – ✆ *020 7622 1199* – *www.trinityrestaurant.co.uk*

Fulham

✿ Harwood Arms

MODERN BRITISH • PUB The menu here is British to its core and game season is certainly not to be missed as the owners' shoots produce plenty of bounty for the kitchen – but that skilful kitchen is so resolutely governed by the country's seasonal produce that it's worth calling in at this Fulham pub any time of year.

Specialities: Crab tartlet. Deer Wellington. Marmalade ice cream sandwich.

Menu £33 (lunch)/50

PLAN: 9-C7 – *Walham Grove* – Ⓜ *Fulham Broadway.* – ✆ *020 7386 1847* – *www.harwoodarms.com* – *Closed lunch Monday*

Hammersmith

River Cafe (Ruth Rogers)

ITALIAN • MEDITERRANEAN It's more than 30 years since this iconic restaur opened, and superlative ingredients are still at the centre of everything they Dishes come in hearty portions and are bursting with authentic Italian flavou The on-view kitchen with its wood-fired oven dominates the stylish and buzz riverside room.

Specialities: Chargrilled squid with fresh chilli and rocket. Wood-roasted turb on the bone. Chocolate Nemesis.

Carte £68/95

PLAN: 1-A3 – *Thames Wharf, Rainville Road – Ⓜ Barons Court – ✆ 020 7386 420 www.rivercafe.co.uk – Closed dinner Sunday*

Kew

The Glasshouse

MODERN CUISINE • ROMANTIC 2019 saw the 20th birthday of this very mod of a modern neighbourhood restaurant. The quirkily-shaped room comes w textured walls and vibrant artwork and, as the name implies, it's a bright sp The unfussy, natural style of cooking focuses on seasonal flavours that compl ment one another.

Specialities: Scottish salmon sashimi with pickled rhubarb, ginger and crèn fraîche. Sea bream with king prawn samosa, black rice, chilli, coriander and garl Warm chocolate croustade with milk ice cream and roasted nuts.

Menu £40 (lunch)/58

Off plan – *14 Station Parade – Ⓜ Kew Gardens – ✆ 020 8940 6777 – www.glasshouserestaurant.co.uk – Closed dinner Sunday, Monday*

Richmond

Dysart Petersham

MODERN CUISINE • INTIMATE Overlooking Richmond Park and built in th early 1900s as part of the Arts and Crafts movement, this warm, homely spac successfully blends its period features with more contemporary design element The classic, ingredient-led menu features well-crafted dishes with bold flavou and no unnecessary gimmicks.

Specialities: Charred mullet with radish, ginger and champagne. Longhorn be with kombu braised Swiss chard, Belle de Fontenay potatoes and red wine ju Valrhona chocolate & praline bar with cherries and raspberry sorbet.

Menu £30 – Carte £41/63

Off plan – *135 Petersham Road – ✆ 020 8940 8005 – www.thedysartpetersham.co.uk – Closed dinner Sunday, Monday, Tuesday, Wednesday*

Shepherd's Bush

Endo at The Rotunda

JAPANESE • DESIGN Endo Kazutoshi's stylish space on the top floor of th former BBC TV Centre comes with a beautiful counter fashioned from 200 year-old hinoki wood. He was trained in Edomae techniques but has consider able international experience; his superlative nigiri is interspersed with equall exquisite dishes.

Specialities: Yamadanishiki "kunkou" salmon nigiri. Miyazaki wagyu beef wit Rokko miso. Rice soufflé.

Menu £60 (lunch), £150/180 – Carte £47/98

PLAN: 1-A2 – *The Helios, 101 Wood Lane – Ⓜ Wood Lane – ✆ 020 3972 9000 – www.endoatrotunda.com – Closed Monday, Tuesday*

Shoreditch

Brat (Tomos Parry)

A/C

TRADITIONAL BRITISH • NEIGHBOURHOOD In this room on the first floor of a pub, it's all about cooking over fire – the stove, grill and oven were all hand-built to chef-owner Tomos Parry's own specification. Whole turbot, grilled in a hand-made basket over lump wood charcoal, is a speciality but there are plenty of other dishes to enjoy, some inspired by his Welsh heritage.

Specialities: Soused red mullet. Grilled whole turbot. Burnt cheesecake with rhubarb.

Carte £25/65

PLAN: 8-N1 – *4 Redchurch Street* – *Shoreditch High Street* – *www.bratrestaurant.com* – *Closed dinner Sunday*

The Clove Club (Isaac McHale)

MODERN CUISINE • CLASSIC DÉCOR Set in the ornate and rather glamorous former Shoreditch Town Hall; chefs perform centre stage in the smart, blue-tiled kitchen. Understated dishes use top-notch produce; there is originality, verve and flair but combinations are always expertly judged and complementary. Seafood dishes are a highlight.

Specialities: Tartare of hay-smoked trout with potato and sansho pepper. Slow-roast Lincolnshire chicken with walnut emulsion. Loquat sorbet & mousse with amaranth and popcorn.

Menu £65 (lunch), £95/145

PLAN: 1-D2 – *Shoreditch Town Hall, 380 Old Street* – *Old Street* – *020 7729 6496* – *www.thecloveclub.com* – *Closed 23 December-7 January, Sunday, lunch Monday*

Leroy (Sam Kamienko)

A/C

MODERN BRITISH • NEIGHBOURHOOD How can you not fall for a place where the first thing you see is a couple of shelves of vinyl? Putting all their experience to bear, the owners have created a restaurant with a relaxed, easy vibe and great food. The core ingredient shines through in every unshowy dish; there's little division between starters and main courses – just order a few dishes to share.

Specialities: Cured grey mullet with tomato and lovage. John Dory with spring vegetables and ham broth. Chocolate ganache and boozy prunes.

Menu £22 (lunch) – Carte £37/46

PLAN: 8-M1 – *18 Phipp Street* – *Old Street* – *020 7739 4443* – *www.leroyshoreditch.com* – *Closed 22 December-2 January, Sunday, lunch Monday*

Lyle's (James Lowe)

A/C

MODERN BRITISH • SIMPLE The pared-down, ersatz industrial space gets its warmth from the delightful service team. The cleverly composed and technically accomplished dishes, using superb seasonal British ingredients, are much more sophisticated than their initial appearance suggests.

Specialities: Peas & Ticklemore. Dexter flank, bitter leaves and anchovy. Espresso meringue and caramel.

Menu £59 – Carte £35/45

PLAN: 8-N1 – *Tea Building, 56 Shoreditch High Street* – *Shoreditch High Street* – *020 3011 5911* – *www.lyleslondon.com* – *Closed 23 December-6 January, Sunday*

Spitalfields

Galvin La Chapelle (Jeff Galvin)

A/C

FRENCH • ELEGANT With its vaulted ceiling, arched windows and marble pillars, this restaurant remains as impressive now as when it first opened a decade ago. Service is professional and the atmosphere, relaxed and unstuffy. Cooking is assured, with a classical French foundation and a sophisticated modern edge.

Specialities: Lasagne of Dorset crab with beurre Nantais and pea shoots. Tag of Bresse pigeon, couscous, confit lemon and harissa sauce. Tarte Tatin with N mandy crème fraîche.

Menu £38 – Carte £55/77

PLAN: 8-N2 – *35 Spital Square* – Ⓜ *Liverpool Street* – ✆ *020 7299 0400* – *www.galvinrestaurants.com* – *Closed 1-2 January, 24-27 December*

Wandsworth

Chez Bruce (Bruce Poole)

FRENCH • BRASSERIE The longevity of this neighbourhood restaurant is no ac dent. Cooking techniques are kept unapologetically traditional; the base is larg classical French but with a pronounced Mediterranean influence and the food is about flavour and balance. The atmosphere is clubby and the service sprightly.

Specialities: Fishcake with creamed Cornish mussels, quail eggs and samph Anjou pigeon with spiced pastilla, roast foie gras, bitter leaf stir-fry and pea Apple croustade with vanilla ice cream and butterscotch sauce.

Menu £40 (lunch)/57

Off plan – *2 Bellevue Road* – Ⓜ *Tooting Bec* – ✆ *020 8672 0114* – *www.chezbruce.co.uk*

RUM KITCHEN
LIFT
PLEASE TAKE CARE OF YOUR BAGS AND VALUABLES

EDINBURGH

EDINBURGH

walencienne/iStock

EDINBURGH IN...

→ **ONE DAY**
Calton Hill, Royal Mile, Edinburgh Castle, New Town café, Old Town pub.

→ **TWO DAYS**
Water of Leith, Scottish National Gallery of Modern Art, Leith.

→ **THREE DAYS**
Arthur's Seat, National Museum of Scotland, Holyrood Park, Pentland Hills.

The beautiful Scottish capit is laid out on seven, former volcanic, hills – a contrast t the modern city, which is ele gant, cool and sophisticate It's essentially two cities one: the medieval Old Tow huddled around and beneat the crags and battlemen of the castle, and the sma Georgian terraces of the Ne Town, overseen by the 18 architect Robert Adam. Yo could also say there's now a third element to the equatio the revamped port of Leith, just two miles away.

This is a city that's been attracting tourists since the 19C; ar since 1999 it's been the home of the Scottish Parliamen

adding a new dimension to its worldwide reputation. It accepts its plaudits with the same ease that it accepts an extra half million visitors at the height of summer, and its status as a UNESCO World Heritage site confirms it as a city that knows how to be both ancient and modern. In the middle is the castle, to the south is the Old Town and to the north is the New Town. There's a natural boundary to the north at the Firth of Forth, while to the south lie the rolling Pentland Hills. Unless you've had a few too many drams, it's just about impossible to get lost here, as prominent landmarks like the Castle, Arthur's Seat and Calton Hill access all areas. Bisecting the town is Princes Street, one side of which invites you to shop, the other, to sit and relax in your own space.

EATING OUT

linburgh enjoys a varied and interes-g restaurant culture so, whatever the casion, you should find somewhere at fits the bill. The city is said to have ore restaurants per head than anyw-re in the UK and they vary from lavish tablishments in grand hotels to cosy tle bistros; you can dine with ghosts a basement eatery or admire the city om a rooftop table. Scotland's great der provides much of the produce, d cooking styles range from the novative and contemporary to the nple and traditional. There are also some good pubs to explore in the old town, and drinking dens also abound in Cowgate and Grassmarket. Further away, in West End, you'll find enticing late-night bars, while the stylish variety, serving cocktails, are more in order in the George Street area of the new town. If you'd rather drink something a little more special then try the 19C Cadenhead's on the Royal Mile – it's the place to go for whiskies and it sells a mindboggling range of rare distillations. The peaty flavoured Laphroaig is a highly recommended dram.

Centre

Condita

MODERN CUISINE • DESIGN Origami blackbirds sit on branches protrud from plain white walls at this small, understated restaurant. Two surprise mer list interesting modern dishes which are confidently prepared and skilfully p sented. Flavours are honest yet delicate and the well-crafted dishes are delive with pride.

Specialities: Haddock sandwich with chicken skin biscuit, confit egg yolk a smoked crème fraîche. Venison with kale, broccoli and fermented wild gar Parsnip mousse with cocoa butter, honeycomb and roasted parsnip.

Menu £50/80

PLAN: C2 – *15 Salisbury Place – ✆ 0131 667 5777 – www.condita.co.uk – Closed 6-20 January, Sunday, Monday, lunch Tuesday-Saturday*

Number One

MODERN CUISINE • INTIMATE A stylish, long-standing restaurant with a c cocktail bar, set in the basement of a grand Edwardian hotel. Richly upholster banquettes and red lacquered walls give it a plush, luxurious feel. Cooking is cla sically rooted yet modern and intricate, and prime Scottish ingredients are key

Specialities: Roast langoustines with squash, wakame and shell butter. Highla Wagyu beef, beetroot, smoked bone marrow and bitter leaf. Roast pineap soufflé with coconut and liquorice root.

Menu £90/105

PLAN: C2 – *Balmoral Hotel, 1 Princes Street – ✆ 0131 557 6727 – www.roccofortehotels.com/hotels-and-resorts/the-balmoral-hotel/restaurants-and-bars/number-one/ – Closed 2-17 January, lunch Sunday-Saturday*

Merienda

MEDITERRANEAN CUISINE • BISTRO Merienda is a sweet little place run by passionate owner and is the perfect fit for the neighbourhood of Stockbrid The menu changes daily and is formed of around 20 or so small plates with strong seasonal bent. These are skilfully prepared and mix Scottish and Medite ranean influences.

Carte £20/32

PLAN: B1 – *30 North West Circus Place, Stockbridge – ✆ 0131 220 2020 – www.eat-merienda.com – Closed 13-28 January, 14-29 September, Monday, Tuesda*

The Scran & Scallie

SCOTTISH • PUB A smart, village-like suburb plays host to one of Tom Kitchin more casual ventures. It has a wood-furnished bar and a dining room whic blends rustic and contemporary décor. Extensive menus follow a 'Nature to Plat philosophy and focus on the classical and the local.

Menu £19 (lunch) – Carte £28/47

PLAN: A1 – *1 Comely Bank Road, Stockbridge – ✆ 0131 332 6281 – www.scranandscallie.com*

21212

CREATIVE • ELEGANT A stunningly refurbished Georgian townhouse designe by William Playfair. The glass-fronted kitchen is the focal point of the stylis room. Cooking is innovative and features quirky combinations; '21212' reflect the number of dishes per course. Some of the luxurious bedrooms overlook th Firth of Forth.

Menu £32 (lunch)/70

PLAN: D1 – *3 Royal Terrace – ✆ 0345 222 1212 – www.21212restaurant.co.uk – Closed 5-15 January, 30 August-11 September, Sunday-Tuesday*

Aizle

MODERN CUISINE • SIMPLE Modest little suburban restaurant whose name means 'ember' or 'spark'. Well-balanced, skilfully prepared dishes are, in effect, a surprise, as the set menu is presented as a long list of ingredients – the latest 'harvest'.

Menu £55

PLAN: D3 – *107-109 St Leonard's Street – ✆ 0131 662 9349 – www.aizle.co.uk – Closed 8-18 July, 25 December-21 January, Sunday, Monday, Tuesday, lunch Wednesday-Saturday*

Baba

MIDDLE EASTERN • MEDITERRANEAN Follow a long bar with cosy booths through to the lively dining room decorated in bright colours and hung with kilims. A mix of small and large Middle-Eastern sharing dishes show vibrancy in both their colours and flavours, and can be accompanied by some lesser-known wines from Lebanon and Greece.

Carte £16/30

PLAN: B2 – *Kimpton Charlotte Square Hotel, 38 Charlotte Square – ✆ 0131 527 4999 – www.baba.restaurant*

Castle Terrace

MODERN CUISINE • INTIMATE Set in the shadow of the castle is this bright, contemporary restaurant with hand-painted wallpapers and a mural depicting the Edinburgh skyline. Cooking is ambitious with a playful element and combines many different textures and flavours. The wine list also offers plenty of interest.

Menu £35/75

PLAN: B2 – *33-35 Castle Terrace – ✆ 0131 229 1222 – www.castleterracerestaurant.com – Closed 22 December-13 January, Sunday, Monday*

DINE

SCOTTISH • BISTRO The Usher Hall, with its busy calendar of events and shows, is also home to this buzzy brasserie. It's a spacious place with an unusual octagonal shape and a huge cocktail bar and lounge. Seasonal dishes promote Scottish produce – the set menu is great value and the fishcakes are a must.

Menu £21/27 – Carte £29/46

PLAN: B2 – *10 Cambridge Street – ✆ 0131 218 1818 – www.dineedinburgh.co.uk*

Edinburgh Food Studio

MODERN CUISINE • NEIGHBOURHOOD The Edinburgh Food Studio provides a valuable lesson in the less-is-more approach. You dine communally at two long tables and the skilfully prepared, understated dishes are seasonal, natural and harmonious in their flavours. Produce is sourced from the best – and most ethical – Scottish suppliers.

Menu £60 – Carte £25/50

Off plan – *158 Dalkeith Road – www.edinburghfoodstudio.com – Closed 1-2 January, 27 February-1 March, 31 October-3 November, 25-26 December, dinner Sunday, Monday, Tuesday, lunch Wednesday*

Fhior

CREATIVE • DESIGN A husband and wife team run this appealing Scandic-style restaurant whose name means 'True'. Creative modern cooking showcases Scottish produce, including foraged and home-preserved ingredients. Lunch sees small plates which are ideal for sharing, while dinner offers two surprise tasting menus.

Menu £17 (lunch), £40/65

PLAN: C1 – *36 Broughton Street – ✆ 0131 477 5000 – www.fhior.com – Closed 1-14 January, 25-27 December, Sunday, Monday, Tuesday, lunch Wednesday-Thursday*

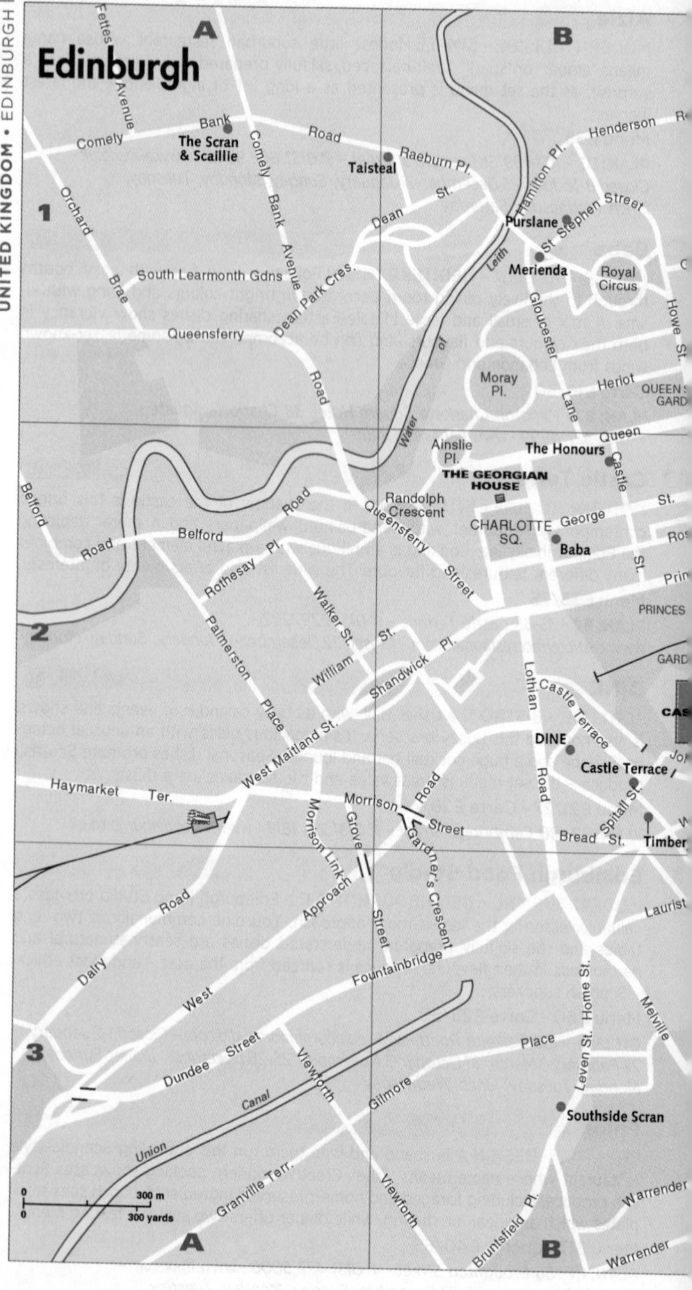
Edinburgh
A
B
1
2
3
Fettes Avenue
Comely Bank Road
The Scran & Scaillie
Comely Bank Avenue
Taisteal
Raeburn Pl.
Henderson
Hamilton Pl.
St. Stephen Street
Purslane
Merienda
Royal Circus
Orchard Brae
South Learmonth Gdns
Dean Park Cres.
Dean St.
Water of Leith
Gloucester Lane
Howe St.
Queensferry Road
Moray Pl.
Heriot
Queen
Ainslie Pl.
The Honours
Castle St.
THE GEORGIAN HOUSE
Randolph Crescent
Queensferry Street
CHARLOTTE SQ.
George St.
Baba
Belford Road
Rothesay Pl.
Walker St.
Palmerston Place
William St.
Shandwick Pl.
West Maitland St.
Lothian Road
Castle Terrace
DINE
Castle Terrace
Haymarket Ter.
Morrison Street
Morrison Link
Grove Street
Gardner's Crescent
Bread St.
Spittall St.
Timber
Dalry Road
West Approach Road
Fountainbridge
Lauriston
Home St.
Leven St.
Melville
Dundee Street
Viewforth
Union Canal
Gilmore Place
Southside Scran
Granville Terr.
Bruntsfield Pl.
Warrender
0
300 m
300 yards

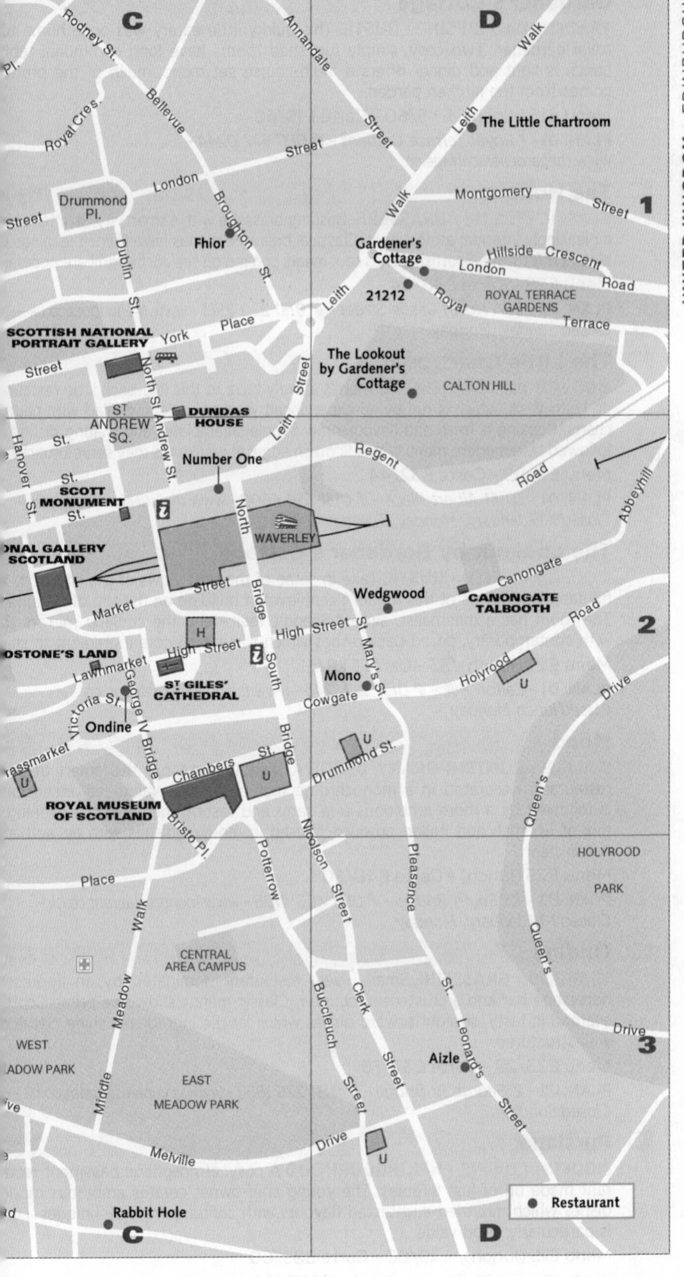
C
D
1
2
3
The Little Chartroom
Fhior
Gardener's Cottage
21212
The Lookout by Gardener's Cottage
Number One
Wedgwood
Mono
Ondine
Aizle
Rabbit Hole
SCOTTISH NATIONAL PORTRAIT GALLERY
DUNDAS HOUSE
SCOTT MONUMENT
WAVERLEY
CANONGATE TALBOOTH
ST GILES' CATHEDRAL
ROYAL MUSEUM OF SCOTLAND
ROYAL TERRACE GARDENS
CALTON HILL
HOLYROOD PARK
CENTRAL AREA CAMPUS
WEST
EAST MEADOW PARK
ST ANDREW SQ.
Drummond Pl.
Rodney St.
Bellevue
Royal Cres.
London Street
Broughton St.
Dublin St.
Annandale Street
Leith Walk
Montgomery Street
Hillside Crescent
London Road
Royal Terrace
York Place
North St Andrew St.
Leith Street
Regent Road
Abbeyhill
Canongate
Hanover St.
North Bridge
Market Street
High Street
Lawnmarket
George IV Bridge
Victoria St.
Cowgate
South Bridge
St Mary's St.
Holyrood Road
Drive
Chambers St.
Drummond St.
Bristo Pl.
Potterrow
Nicolson Street
Pleasence
Queen's Drive
Place
Walk
Meadow Walk
Middle
Buccleuch Street
Clerk Street
St. Leonard's Street
Melville Drive
Restaurant

Gardener's Cottage

TRADITIONAL CUISINE • RUSTIC This quirky little eatery was once home t royal gardener. Two cosy, simply furnished rooms have long communal tab Lunch is light and dinner offers a multi-course set menu; much of the produ comes from the kitchen garden.

Menu £15 (lunch), £45/60 – Carte £19/60

PLAN: D1 – *1 Royal Terrace Gardens – ✆ 0131 677 0244 – www.thegardenerscottage.co*

The Honours

CLASSIC CUISINE • BRASSERIE Bustling brasserie with a smart, stylish interior a pleasingly informal atmosphere. Classical brasserie menus have French leanings always offer some Scottish dishes too; meats cooked on the Josper grill are popula

Menu £26 – Carte £38/64

PLAN: B2 – *58A North Castle Street – ✆ 0131 220 2513 – www.thehonours.co.uk – Closed Sunday, Monday*

The Little Chartroom

MODERN BRITISH • SIMPLE There's a lively buzz to this laid-back little restaur on Leith Walk, which is run by an experienced young couple and filled with naut charts. Cooking is fresh and flavoursome. Simple small plates and sharing dishes followed by a modern menu with a Scottish edge; at weekends they serve brunch.

Menu £16/19 – Carte £32/44

PLAN: D1 – *30-31 Albert Place – ✆ 0131 556 6600 – www.thelittlechartroom.com – Closed 1-15 January, Monday, Tuesday*

The Lookout by Gardener's Cottage

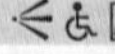

MODERN BRITISH • RUSTIC Take in some of the best views of the city from full-length windows of this modern cantilevered building on the top of Calton H The room has a minimalist, almost Scandic feel – and the cooking mirrors t with contemporary, pared-back dishes which allow each core ingredient to sh

Menu £27 (lunch)/33 – Carte £28/51

PLAN: D1 – *Calton Hill, – ✆ 0131 322 1246 – www.thelookoutedinburgh.co – Closed lunch Monday*

Mono

ITALIAN • CONTEMPORARY DÉCOR A friendly team run this smart desig restaurant, decorated in a monochrome theme. A good value set priced lu is followed by a more ambitious à la carte and tasting menus in the evening mix of Scottish and Italian produce is used in modern dishes with an authe Italian heart.

Menu £25 (lunch) – Carte £40/50

PLAN: D2 – *85 South Bridge – ✆ 0131 466 4726 – www.monorestaurant.co.uk – Closed 1-16 January, Monday*

Ondine

SEAFOOD • BRASSERIE Smart, lively restaurant dominated by an impress horseshoe bar and a crustacean counter. Classic menus showcase prime Scott seafood in tasty, straightforward dishes which let the ingredients shine. Servic well-structured.

Menu £23/29 – Carte £37/78

PLAN: C2 – *2 George IV Bridge – ✆ 0131 226 1888 – www.ondinerestaurant.co.uk – Closed Sunday*

Purslane

MODERN CUISINE • NEIGHBOURHOOD A cosy, atmospheric basement rest rant made up of just 9 tables. The young chef-owner creates ambitious mod dishes which mix tried-and-tested flavours with contemporary techniques. Lu is particularly good value.

Menu £15 (lunch), £29/60 – Carte £29/60

PLAN: B1 – *33a St. Stephen Street – ✆ 0131 226 3500 – www.purslanerestaurant.co.uk – Closed Monday*

Rabbit Hole

TRADITIONAL CUISINE • SIMPLE Hidden away in the suburbs is this appealing neighbourhood restaurant with tightly packed tables and paper place mats displaying the menu. Passion oozes from the knowledgeable owners and the appealing dishes show plenty of personality. The classically based puddings are a real highlight.

Menu £16 (lunch) – Carte £28/38

PLAN: C3 – *11 Roseneath Street – ✆ 0131 229 7953 – www.therabbitholerestaurant.com – Closed Sunday, Monday*

Southside Scran

SCOTTISH • BISTRO The Southside area of the city is home to this smart restaurant. The room has a French bistro feel and a Maestro Rotisserie takes centre stage. Legs of lamb, whole chickens and pineapples turn on the open grill, and sit alongside top ingredients like Isle of Skye scallops and Scottish venison on the menu.

Menu £22 (lunch) – Carte £28/59

PLAN: B3 – *14-17 Bruntsfield Place – ✆ 0131 342 3333 – www.southsidescran.com*

Taisteal

MODERN BRITISH • NEIGHBOURHOOD Taisteal is Irish Gaelic for 'journey' and is the perfect name: photos from the chef's travels line the walls and dishes have global influences, with Asian flavours to the fore. The wine list even has a sake section.

Menu £16 – Carte £26/37

PLAN: B1 – *1-3 Raeburn Place, Stockbridge – ✆ 0131 332 9977 – www.taisteal.co.uk – Closed 1-10 January, 31 August-15 September, Sunday, Monday*

Timberyard

MODERN CUISINE • RUSTIC Trendy warehouse restaurant; its spacious, rustic interior incorporating wood-burning stoves. The Scandic-influenced menu offers 'bites', 'small' and 'large' sizes, with some home-smoked ingredients and an emphasis on distinct, punchy flavours. Cocktails are made with vegetable purées and foraged herbs.

Menu £40 (lunch), £57/79 – Carte £26/31

PLAN: B2 – *10 Lady Lawson Street – ✆ 0131 221 1222 – www.timberyard.co – Closed 1-8 January, 31 March-8 April, 20-28 October, Sunday, Monday*

Leith

Kitchin (Tom Kitchin)

MODERN CUISINE • DESIGN A smartly converted whisky warehouse provides the perfect setting for this patriotic restaurant, where the windswept highlands are brought indoors courtesy of tartan tweed, tree bark, whisky barrels and dry stone walls. Menus mix boldly flavoured classics with fresh modern dishes. Each ingredient has a purpose and is allowed to shine; vegetables are the chef's passion.

Specialities: Boned & rolled pig's head with roasted tail of langoustine and crispy ear salad. Loin of roe deer with braised haunch, root vegetables and red wine sauce. Rhubarb crumble soufflé with vanilla ice cream.

Menu £35 (lunch)/80

Off plan – *78 Commercial Quay – ✆ 0131 555 1755 – www.thekitchin.com – Closed 7-11 April, 21-25 July, 24 December-14 January, Sunday, Monday*

Martin Wishart

MODERN CUISINE • ELEGANT This elegant, modern restaurant has beco something of an Edinburgh institution. Choose between a Classic or Vegetar set menu and a concise à la carte. Top ingredients are used in well-judged, vourful combinations and while dishes are classically based, they exhibit elab rate, original touches.

Specialities: Ceviche of Gigha halibut with mango and passion fruit. John Do with Jerusalem artichoke, confit potato, parsley and lemon. Strawberries w fennel crémeux and strawberry & yoghurt sorbet.

Menu £35 (lunch), £80/120

Off plan *– 54 The Shore – ✆ 0131 553 3557 – www.martin-wishart.co.uk – Closed 28 July-4 August, 13-14 October, 31 December-16 January, Sunday, Monda*

Borough

MODERN CUISINE • NEIGHBOURHOOD A young but experienced couple this smart restaurant, which sits on a cobbled street in a residential area n the port. Well-crafted, keenly priced dishes have a clean, modern style. Seaso Scottish produce is kept to the fore, with usually no more than 4 ingredients f tured on each plate.

Menu £19 (lunch)/35

Off plan *– 50-54 Henderson Street – ✆ 0131 554 7655 – www.boroughrestaurant.com – Closed 1-14 January, dinner Sunday, Monday, Tuesd lunch Wednesday-Thursday*

Tell us what you think about our products.

Give us your opinion

satisfaction.michelin.com

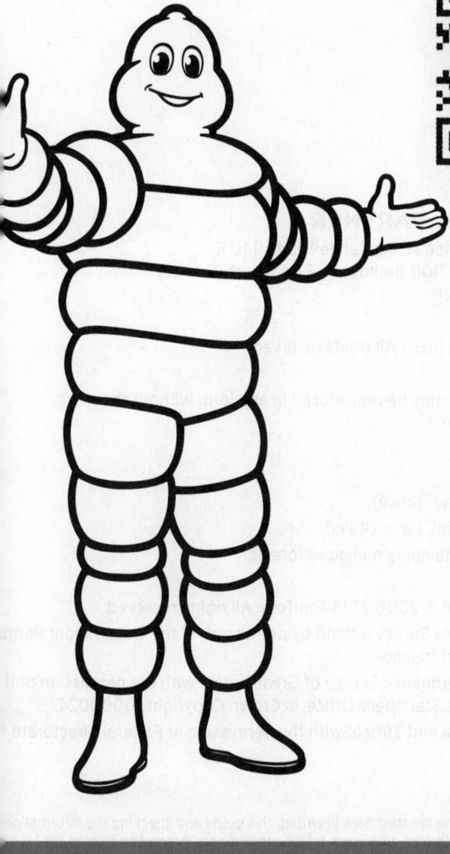

MICHELIN TRAVEL PARTNER
Société par actions simplifiée au capital de 15 044 940 €
27 cours de l'Ile Seguin - 92100 Boulogne - Billancourt (France)
R.C.S. Nanterre 433 677 721

Legal deposit: 02-2020

Printed in Italy: 02-2020

Typesetting: JOUVE, Saran (France)
Printing-binding: LEGO Print, Lavis (Italie)
Printed on paper from sustainably managed forests